Solicitors' Negligence and Liability

Second Edition

Solicitors' Negligence and Liability

Second Edition

by

William Flenley

MA (Oxon), LLM (Cornell), BCL

Barrister, Hailsham Chambers

Tom Leech

MA (Oxon), BCL

Barrister, Maitland Chambers

Chapter 6 on Solicitors' Duties of Confidentiality contributed by

Thomas Grant

BA (Hons), Dip Law, Barrister

Chapter 9 on Conveyancing revised by

Paul Mitchell

MA (Cantab), MA (SOAS), PhD (Cantab), Barrister

Tottel
publishing

Tottel Publishing Ltd, Maxwelton House, 41–43 Boltro Road, Haywards Heath, West Sussex, RH16 1BJ

A CIP Catalogue record for this book is available from the British Library.

ISBN 978 1 84592 060 9

Typeset by Kerrypress Ltd, Luton, Beds

Printed and bound in Great Britain by CPI Antony Rowe, Chippenham, Wiltshire

Preface

Since the last edition of this book eight years ago, the law relating to claims against solicitors has developed prolifically. The result is that the second edition is more than twice the length of the first. Partly, this is because of the addition of two new chapters: chapter 5, on authority, vicarious liability, and undertakings, and chapter 6, on solicitors' duties of confidentiality. We are grateful to Thomas Grant of Maitland Chambers for contributing chapter 6. But to a large degree the increase in length is due to the pace of development in areas that were already discussed in the first edition.

We have found that in some areas the new material, often at House of Lords level, has required not simply the addition of new paragraphs here and there but rather a radical rethink and consequent revision of the structure that we had previously proposed for the subject. The gap of eight years between editions is perhaps long by today's standards, but it has had the benefit of enabling us to do some fundamental rethinking.

We have, however, retained the basic form of the book, whereby Part 1 deals with general principles of law applicable to claims against solicitors, Part 2 with specific areas of solicitors' practice which may give rise to claims, and Part 3 with the procedural issues of costs orders against solicitors and disclosure. We are grateful to Paul Mitchell of Hailsham Chambers for undertaking the major task of revision to incorporate the new material in relation to chapter 9, on conveyancing. We have attempted to state the law as at 1 December 2007.

Lord Neuberger of Abbotsbury has been involved in many of the developments in the law to which we refer: there are more than 50 references to him in the text. We are therefore particularly grateful to him for writing the foreword. We would also like to thank Tim Bullimore, Spike Charlwood, Adrian Neve, and Dan Stacey for commenting on earlier drafts of parts of the text. Finally, we would like to thank everyone at Tottel for their help and forbearance in producing the book.

This book is dedicated to Hilary and Hannah Flenley, and Jane, Rosie, Alicia, Fleur and Nina Leech.

William Flenley   Tom Leech
Hailsham Chambers   Maitland Chambers

January 2008

Foreword

Solicitors' negligence is in some ways a melancholy topic to contemplate, especially for anyone who is or was a practising lawyer. Almost every case involving a justified allegation of solicitors' negligence that I have seen either had me thinking 'there but for the grace of God go I', or made me wonder how on earth the mistake could have occurred. Almost every case involving an unjustified allegation caused me to think that the system had failed, either because the claimant had been badly advised by new lawyers, or because there was a gap in the law. Most cases also engender some sympathy for the solicitor concerned, even if guilty of negligence: unless one is incompetent or shameless, it is both worrying and upsetting to have a claim of negligence over one's head. The truth is that no busy professional person, least of all a solicitor, can get through a full career without committing an act, and probably several acts, of negligence. Both the intricacies of the law and communication between people can be complex, multi-faceted, and prone to misunderstandings, so it is not surprising that mistakes get made. Of course, by no means all mistakes constitute negligence, and, happily, the great majority of incidents of negligence do not result in loss.

Whatever feelings may be engendered by the topic, there can be no denying that solicitors' negligence is a subject which raises wide-ranging legal issues, often of considerable difficulty, and, indeed, sometimes of much wider legal significance. That is partly because claims against solicitors can arise out of their handling of transactions and claims in any area of law. But it is also because the role of solicitors is wide-ranging and multifarious in nature. Recent examples of difficult and important issues raised in solicitors' negligence cases, in the House of Lords alone, within the past 10 years include accessory liability (the subject of the controversial decision in *Twinsectra v Yardley*), conflicts of interest (discussed in *Hilton v Barker Booth Eastwood*), the rule against reflective loss (considered, although, I suspect, not for the last time, in *Johnson v Gore Wood*), and vicarious liability (see *Dubai Aluminium v Salaam*).

Difficult and important points arise from negligence claims against other professionals. Recent examples in the House of Lords include *Gregg v Scott*, concerning the right to damages for a reduction in life expectation (a topic on which, again, I doubt we have heard the last word), and *Law Society v Sephton*, which involved a difficult point as to when time starts to run under the Limitation Act 1980. (It must have been difficult as the House of Lords

vii

held that the conclusion I had reached in the Court of Appeal had been wrong.)

The fact that so many difficult and important issues have been raised in such a short period underlines the challenges facing those involved in advising and acting in relation to claims against solicitors. The breadth and number of the disciplines with which a person practising in the field needs to be familiar has grown almost beyond recognition in the past ten years. It follows from this that it is of enormous value to have a book which covers such challenges as well as providing a complete guide to all aspects of solicitors' negligence, especially if it deals with the topic in a full, reliable, comprehensive, and up-to-date manner. Because of the growth to which I have referred, and also because of the sheer number of decided cases, solicitors' negligence may now only be capable of being fully covered in a book dedicated to the topic.

This second edition of *Flenley and Leech*, which already has the benefit of a solid reputation thanks to the previous edition, satisfies the four requirements identified in the preceding paragraph. The structure of the book is logical, which helps ensure that it is comprehensive and that readers will find it relatively easy to locate the passages relevant to their requirements. The book treats difficult issues fully and thoughtfully, which is important in any serious modern book for practitioners. It is also readable, but the authors have not thereby caused reliability to be damaged. As one would expect, the book also covers very recent decisions.

The amount of work which went into the preparation of this second edition must have been considerable, and, particularly with their busy workloads as barristers and mediators, William Flenley and Tom Leech are to be congratulated on having found the time, and summoned up the application, to produce such a good book on such a difficult and important topic.

The Rt Hon Lord Neuberger of Abbotsbury
January 2008

Foreword to the first edition

Practitioners will agree that a textbook on solicitors' negligence is timely, if not overdue. This is not because solicitors are more prone to be negligent than other professionals. It is rather *because,* when they are, they tend to give rise to a wider range of problems than usual.

Professional negligence, other than medical negligence, is a discrete branch of the law of negligence. It occasions economic loss rather than personal injury, usually (though not always) arises in the course of a contractual relationship, and rarely gives rise to problems of proximity.

The difficulty in finding a sufficient relationship between the parties which has beset the development of the modern law of negligence is generally absent. But there are three problems which, though not peculiar to solicitors, are particularly acute in cases of solicitors' negligence.

The starting point in any case of professional negligence is to ascertain the scope of the defendant's duty. It is easy enough to say that the scope of a solicitor's duty depends on his retainer, but this is rarely in express and precise terms. There is no single or simple answer to the question whether a solicitor is under a general duty to give advice. Even if negligent breach of duty is established, it may give rise to particularly difficult questions of causation. Recent cases have explored the allied issues of causation and measure of damages in the case of valuers' negligence, but much more difficult questions remain to be decided in relation to solicitors. The distinction between the loss of a chance and other cases is better understood than it was, but the last word has certainly not been spoken on this subject.

Other problems arise from the fact that the relationship between a solicitor and his client is a fiduciary one. The solicitor is consequently subject to fiduciary obligations as well as duties in contract and tort. While the common law duties in contract and tort are similar and overlap, the equitable obligations imposed by the fiduciary nature of the solicitor's relationship with his client are distinct and yield different remedies in the event of breach. Moreover, the solicitor is a trustee of the money in his clients' account, so that misapplication of the money, even if merely the result of negligence, may render him liable to an action for breach of trust. Some of the problems to which these interacting relationships give rise have been considered in a spate of cases resulting from the mortgage frauds of the late 1980s. Those which relate to limitation are particularly difficult. Their authoritative resolution may have to await legislation when the Law Commission presents its report. In the meantime, practitioners will welcome all the help they can get.

This is a carefully researched and thoughtful book, which draws on the experience gained in some of the most difficult cases to have come before the courts.

I unreservedly recommend it to practitioners, common law and equity alike.

The Rt Hon The Lord Millett
September 1999

Contents

Contents

Contents

Contents

Contents

Table of statutes

Paragraph references printed in **bold** type indicate where the Act is set out in part or in full.

Table of statutory instruments

Those paragraph numbers in **bold** type indicate where a Statutory Instrument is set out in part or in full.

Table of cases

Table of cases

PARA

Table of cases

Table of cases

PARA

PARA

Part 1

General Principles

Chapter 1

The solicitor's duties in contract and tort

A DUTIES IN CONTRACT

1 Introduction

1.01 The relationship of solicitor and client is primarily a contractual one and, as with any contractual relationship, a solicitor's retainer is governed by the terms of the contract agreed with his or her client.[1] This relationship is also regulated both by statute and by the rules of professional conduct of the profession (formerly the Solicitors Practice Rules 1990 (as amended) and now the Solicitors' Code of Conduct 2007). The Solicitors Act 1974 imposes certain constraints on the freedom of solicitor and client to contract.[2] The rules regulate the conduct of the profession as a whole. They are also the product of statute and enforced by means of a special statutory procedure: s 31 of the Solicitors Act 1974 empowers the Council of the Law Society to make rules governing the professional practice, conduct and discipline of solicitors and s 46 provides for the establishment of a Solicitors Disciplinary Tribunal to hear and determine allegations of misconduct and breaches of the rules.[3] The rules and procedure for the investigation and hearing of professional complaints are governed by public law and administered by an independent regulator.[4] But subject to these constraints, the contract between solicitor and client need take no special form and need contain no specific terms.[5] It may be express or implied and oral or written.[6] In practice this contract is more likely to be a written one and the solicitors to set out in an engagement letter the express terms of their remuneration and the procedure for complaints.[7] The nature and scope of the work which a solicitor undertakes to carry out may also be the subject of detailed written instructions.[8] But it is still relatively uncommon for solicitors to set out precisely the nature and scope of the work to be undertaken. Indeed often it will be impossible to do so. For this reason, claims for professional negligence are mainly concerned with the standard of reasonable care to be expected of a reasonably competent solicitor judged against the backdrop of the practice commonly adopted by the profession. Nevertheless because the relationship between solicitor and client is primarily a contractual one, any consideration of a solicitor's retainer must begin with the express terms agreed between the parties.

1.01 *The solicitor's duties in contract and tort*

1 'A solicitor's duty to his client is primarily contractual and its scope depends on the express and implied terms of his retainer': *Hilton v Barker Booth Eastwood* [2005] UKHL 8, [2005] 1 WLR 567, at [28] (Lord Walker of Gestingthorpe).

2 The Act principally regulates the recovery of remuneration and confers jurisdiction on the court to order a solicitor to deliver a bill: see s 68. It also distinguishes between 'Non-contentious business agreements' (which are regulated by s 57) and 'Contentious business agreements' which are regulated by ss 60–66. Section 57(4) provides that a client may sue on a NCBA as an agreement not relating to the remuneration of a solicitor but only subject to sub-ss (5) and (7). Those subsections give a client the right to challenge the agreement as unfair and unreasonable on an assessment and to challenge the amount of costs. Section 61 contains similar terms which apply to a CBA but sub-s (2) also provides that the court may set aside a CBA if the agreement is unfair or unreasonable. For the position in relation to exclusion clauses more generally see para 1.5, below.

3 The Consumer Complaints Service (formerly the Client Relations Office of the Office for the Supervision of Solicitors) exercises certain of the powers of the Council of the Law Society to discipline solicitors, e g by issuing a reprimand or to impose conditions on a solicitor's practising certificate under ss 12 and 13A of the Solicitors Act 1974. Section 37A of and Sch 1A to the Act were also inserted to provide that the Law Society would have power to direct that a solicitor should pay compensation to a client for inadequate professional service. The maximum compensation that can currently be ordered is £15,000. For a brief description of the procedure: see *R (Thompson) v Law Society* [2004] EWCA Civ 167, [2004] 1 WLR 2522, CA.

4 The Solicitors' Regulation Authority regulates the conduct of solicitors and refers complaints to the Solicitors' Disciplinary Tribunal. The Solicitors' Code of Conduct came into force on 1 July 2007 pursuant to the Solicitors Act 1974, s 9 of the Administration of Justice Act 1985 and Sch 4 to the Courts and Legal Services Act 1990.

5 It is possible to argue that it is an implied term of any contractual retainer that the solicitor must comply with the rules. But we consider that the better view is that no term to this effect should be implied into a solicitor's retainer as a matter of course: see paras 2.14 and 2.15, below. In *Hilton v Barker Booth Eastwood* [2005] UKHL 8, [2005] 1 WLR 567 where a solicitor acted for two parties to a property transaction, the House of Lords held that the solicitor was in breach of a contractual duty by failing to report to one client that the other client had criminal convictions (of which the solicitor was aware). The case was argued on the basis that the solicitor owed a contractual duty of confidence and of loyalty to his or her client that was identical (or, at least, very similar) to his fiduciary duties. One reading of the speech of Lord Walker suggests that the solicitor owed a contractual duty to comply with Practice Rule 6 of the Solicitors' Practice Rules 1990: see [28]–[31]. It is suggested that he was not intending to go that far but only to state that a breach of Practice Rule 6, which was designed to prevent a solicitor from placing himself or herself in a position of conflict, might well involve a breach of the solicitor's contractual duty. It is also suggested that an implied obligation to comply with the Practice Rules or, now, the Solicitors' Code of Conduct 2007 does not satisfy any of the standard tests for an implied term and is not a standardised implied term: see *Equitable Life Assurance Society v Hyman* [2002] 1 AC 408 at 458H where Lord Steyn stated that such terms 'operate as general default rules'. The primary basis for enforcement should therefore be disciplinary proceedings.

6 Section 57(3) of the Solicitors' Act 1974 provides that an NCBA must be in writing. But it has never been suggested that a failure to comply with the subsection renders the contract of no effect or prevents either party from suing on it (including the solicitor suing for his or her remuneration). In *Hilton v Barker Booth Eastwood* (above), for example, there were no written instructions and no documentary evidence of the retainer: see [28].

7 Rule 2.02 of the Code provides:

'(1) You must: (a) identify clearly the client's objectives in relation to the work to be done for the client; (b) give the client a clear explanation of the issues involved and the options available to the client; (c) agree with the client the next steps to be taken; and (d) keep the client informed of progress, unless otherwise agreed. (2) You must, both at the outset and, as necessary, during the course of the matter: (a) agree an appropriate level of service; (b) explain your responsibilities; (c) explain the client's responsibilities; (d) ensure that the client is given, in writing, the name and status of the person dealing with the matter and the name of the person responsible for its overall supervision; and (e) explain any limitations or conditions resulting from your relationship with a third party (for example a funder, fee sharer or introducer) which affect the steps you can take on the client's behalf.'

Rules 2.03 and 2.04 now deal with costs and r 2.05 now deals with complaints handling. The position before 1 July 2007 was governed by Practice Rule 15 which required solicitors to:

'(a) give information about costs and other matters, and (b) to operate a complaints handling procedure in accordance with the Solicitors' Costs Information and Client Care Code'. This code set out the detailed information which was required to be given to each client in relation to both aspects of the rule. Rule 2.03(5) of the Code of Conduct requires that costs information must now be 'clear and confirmed in writing'. The previous code did not as such require that this information should be given in writing but para 1(d) stated that it was 'good practice to record in writing' all of the necessary costs information.

8 See, for example, the CML standard form instructions (intended to give effect to the Solicitors Practice (Conveyancing) Amendment Rules 2005) considered in chapter 10, section A.4. Less commonly, large institutions and commercial clients also have standard instructions to solicitors.

1.02 The terms of the contract may impose a strict obligation on the solicitor and, if it does, he or she may be sued for a breach of that obligation in contract whether or not the court would characterise that breach of contract as a failure to take reasonable care. There is no reason in principle why the client should not instruct the solicitor to undertake more onerous obligations than the common law would normally impose if the client wishes to do so.[1] But by accepting instructions to act in a particular matter, a solicitor does not normally agree to undertake a strict obligation to achieve a particular outcome or give a warranty that this outcome will be achieved.[2] In *Barclays Bank plc v Weeks, Legg & Dean*[3] a solicitor acting for a purchaser gave his client's bank an undertaking to apply the bank's funds solely for the purpose of acquiring a good marketable title to the property which his client was about to purchase. The undertaking was construed by the court as an undertaking to apply those funds for the purpose of acquiring a title which 'a reasonably competent solicitor acting with proper skill and care would accept as a good marketable title'. To construe the undertaking otherwise would impose a greater duty to the bank than the solicitor owed to his client and would require him in effect to guarantee the title to the property. The same approach was adopted in *Midland Bank plc v Cox McQueen*.[4] In that case the solicitor agreed to carry out a bank's instructions to 'act on our behalf by obtaining the signatures of' a husband and wife to a number of documents. The bank's instructions also contained a request to 'explain the implications of our mortgage form'. The wife never signed the documents because the husband had her impersonated by an employee of his. Because of the duty to explain the Court of Appeal held that the obligation to obtain the wife's signature was not absolute but 'better suited to a requirement to exercise a reasonable standard of care'. In reaching this conclusion the court gave the following general guidance for the construction of legal instructions, particularly from commercial clients:[5]

'If commercial institutions such as banks wish to impose an absolute liability on members of a profession they should do so in clear terms so that the solicitors can appreciate the extent of the obligations which they are accepting. Frequently this sort of task is undertaken by small firms of solicitors who are already finding it difficult to remain viable. This is partly because they are heavily burdened by the costs of insurance. If they are to be liable for very substantial sums of damages as a result of the fraud of customers of the bank which they cannot prevent, then either they will have to withdraw from providing those services or they will have to charge for their services at a rate which is very different from that which was charged here. Neither result is in the interests of the banks or their customers or the public. The result is not in the interests of the banks' customers as they will not benefit from the explanation of the transaction from a member of the legal profession who is qualified to give an explanation. It is not in the interests of banks as they will have to pay higher fees which they may or may not seek to recover from their customers. It is not in the interests of the public because it is important that legal services are readily available and this will not be the case if small firms are unable to survive. Unless the language used in a retainer clearly has this consequence, the courts should not be ready to impose obligations on solicitors which even the most careful solicitor may not be able to meet.'

1 See *Bristol and West Building Society v Kramer* (1995) Independent, 26 January and *Zwebner v The Mortgage Corpn Ltd* [1998] PNLR 769, CA.
2 See *Greaves & Co (Contractors) Ltd v Baynham Meikle & Partners* [1975] 1 WLR 1095. CA in which Lord Denning said this at 1110D: 'The surgeon does not warrant that he will cure the patient. Nor does the solicitor warrant that he will win the case.' See also the House of Lords in the same case to the same effect in (1978) 11 BLR 29 at 49–52 and *Thake v Maurice* [1986] QB 644 at 687–8, CA holding that a strict duty will be imposed on a professional only in 'special circumstances'. For an example see *Green v Turner* [1999] PNLR 28 (HHJ Hegarty QC). In that case the allegation that a statement by the vendor's solicitor that the sale of a property would be registered within a specified period was a warranty to the purchaser was not pursued.
3 [1999] QB 309 at 327H–328A, CA.
4 [1999] Lloyd's Rep PN 223.
5 Per Lord Woolf MR. *Zwebner v The Mortgage Corporation Ltd* [1998] PNLR 769, CA was distinguished on a number of specific grounds which are considered at para 10.41, below. On the general question of construction the court considered that it should not be given a wide application. This approach was followed in *Mercantile Credit Co Ltd v Fenwick* [1999] Lloyd's Rep PN 408, CA and *UCB Corporate Services Ltd v Clyde & Co* [2000] PNLR 84, CA.

1.03 In the same way it is also important to recognise that the duty to exercise reasonable care is not a duty to achieve a particular result. This is illustrated by *Matrix Securities Ltd v Theodore Goddard*[1] in which the defendants, a firm of solicitors and a barrister, were instructed by the claimant with the aim of obtaining tax clearance for a particular scheme. Tax clearance was obtained and then successfully challenged by the Inland Revenue on the grounds essentially of non-disclosure. It was argued that 'if reasonable skill and care could have achieved a letter which, if replied to favourably, would stand no risk that the Revenue would revoke that reply, then each defendant was bound to achieve that result and is in breach of duty and liable for the fact that it was not achieved'.[2] The judge rejected this argument stating:[3]

> 'I hold that the duty ... was to exercise such skill and care as a reasonably competent practitioner in the relevant sector of the profession would have done with a view to securing such a clearance. I do not accept that their duties were to secure a clearance which was 100% reliable, or to do so if the exercise of reasonable skill and care could achieve such a thing. That formulation turns the common law position set out in *Saif Ali*[4] by Lord Diplock on its head. Instead of imposing legal liability on the professional only if he does that which no reasonably competent member of the relevant profession or part of the profession would have done in the same situation, he would be rendered liable for breach of duty if he omitted anything which any one of the reasonably competent members of the relevant group or class would have done, even if, as might be the case in an area involving judgment between different choices, the steps that a number of reasonably competent members of the profession would reasonably have taken would be incompatible with each other. That is not the law.'

1 [1998] PNLR 290 (Lloyd J). See also *Turner v Eversheds* [2007] EWHC 401 (QB) (HHJ Wilkinson QC) (solicitors engaged to re-negotiate terms of investment contract) at [24]:

> 'The duty of a solicitor is to act in the manner of a reasonably competent member of that profession. It does not extend to a requirement to achieve a particular result. In this case the result desired by Mr Turner was beyond achievement by the route that he now suggests would have succeeded.'

2 [1998] PNLR 290 at 318O.
3 [1998] PNLR 290 at 321E–G.
4 See para 2.2, below.

1.04 Apart from the express terms agreed between the parties, the principal term implied by the law into the contract of retainer is that the solicitor should take reasonable care in providing legal services. Chapter 2 is devoted to exploring the standard to be expected of a solicitor to comply with this obligation. There is no difference between the content of this obligation which is imposed by the Supply of Goods and Services Act 1982, s 13, and the general tortious duty of care considered below. The only practical difference between the two duties is that caused by the different limitation periods in contract and tort. That difference is considered and explored in Chapter 7.

2 Exclusion or limitation of liability

1.05 Again, it is unusual for a solicitor to seek to exclude liability to his or her client altogether for the consequences of negligence or any other breach of duty.

the Solicitors Act 1974 expressly prohibits a solicitor undertaking contentious business from excluding liability for any breach of duty. Contentious business is defined by the Act as 'business done, whether as solicitor or advocate, in or for the purposes of proceedings begun before a court or before an arbitrator appointed under the Arbitration Act 1950' and it provides that any agreement to exclude liability for negligence or liability for 'any responsibility to which he would otherwise be subject as a solicitor' is void.[1] There is no equivalent prohibition for non-contentious business. However, such a term must satisfy the provisions of the Unfair Contract Terms Act 1977 (UCTA) and the Unfair Contract Terms in Consumer Contracts Regulations 1999 (UCTCCR).[2] *The Guide to the Professional Conduct of Solicitors* has stated for some time that as a matter of principle it is acceptable for a solicitor to limit any liability in excess of his or her insurance cover[3] and the Solicitors' Code of Conduct 2007 now contains a specific rule to this effect.[4] The guidance to the rule states that it is subject to the requirements of the general law.[5] Any exclusion of liability that does not comply with the code is highly unlikely therefore to be enforceable. The enforceability of a contractual term limiting a solicitor's liability to a client to a specified amount has never been tested[6] but the guidance given by both the UCTCCR itself and the Office of Fair Trading suggest that exclusions contained in engagement letters since 1 July 2007 that comply with the code would be enforceable provided that the insurance cover is adequate for the particular engagement.[7] This is also borne out by the guidance in the Code.[8]

1 Solicitors Act 1974, ss 59, 60(5) and 87 and Administration of Justice Act 1985, Sch 2, para 24. The definition of a 'contentious business agreement' quoted in the text expressly excludes non-contentious probate business as defined by Supreme Court Act 1981, s 128.
2 SI 1999/2083. If the exclusion is in a standard form engagement letter, it must satisfy the test of fairness. Regulation 5(1) provides that a contractual term 'which has not been individually negotiated' shall be regarded as unfair 'if, contrary to the requirement of good faith, it causes a significant imbalance in the parties' rights and obligations arising under the contract, to the detriment of the consumer'. Regulation 5(2) provides that a term is always regarded as not individually negotiated where it has been drafted in advance. Even if the exclusion is not in a standard form, reg 7(1) imposes an obligation upon the supplier to satisfy the plain language requirement: 'to ensure that any written term of a contract is expressed in plain intelligible language'. Finally, if there is no face to face meeting between solicitor and client the contract will also have to satisfy the Consumer Protection (Distance Selling) Regulations 2000, SI 2000/2334.
3 See the *Guide to the Professional Conduct of Solicitors* (1999), Principle 12.11: 'Although it is not acceptable for solicitors to attempt to exclude by contract all liability to their clients, there is no objection as a matter of conduct to solicitors seeking to limit their liability provided that such limitation is not below the minimum level of cover required by the Solicitors' Indemnity Rules.' For the original guidance given by the Law Society see the Council's statement at (1987) 84 LSG at 1545.
4 See the Solicitors' Code of Conduct 2007, r 2.07:

   'If you are a principal in a firm you must not exclude or attempt to exclude by contract all liability to your clients. However, you may limit your liability, provided that such limitation: (a) is not below the minimum level of cover required by the Solicitors' Indemnity Insurance Rules for a policy of qualifying insurance; (b) is brought to the client's attention; and (c) is in writing.'

5 See para 68 which states that r 2.07 'is subject to the position at law'. It draws attention to the provisions discussed in this paragraph (and, in particular, to the absolute exclusion in relation to CBAs). It should be noted that the guidance to the Code is expressed to be non-binding.

6 For a consideration of the application of both UCTA and the UCTCCR see Arnull 'Professional advisers and limitations on liability' (2003) 19 PN 494 where it is suggested that there is no difference between the test of reasonableness under UCTA and the fairness requirement under the UCTCCR. The only reported decision on the scope of an exclusion clause in an engagement letter appears to be *University of Keele v Price Waterhouse* [2004] EWCA Civ 583, [2004] PNLR 43 (accountant). The validity of the clause under UCTA or the UCTCCR was not, however, addressed because the clause was held not to cover the relevant loss.

7 See Sch 2 to the UCTCCR which sets out an indicative and non-exhaustive list of terms which may be regarded as unfair. Paragraph 1(b) indicates that terms which have the object or effect of 'inappropriately excluding or limiting the legal rights of the consumer vis-à-vis the seller or supplier or another party in the event of total or partial non-performance or inadequate performance by the seller or supplier of any of the contractual obligations' will be regarded as unfair. It will be therefore for solicitors to satisfy the court that cover for the engagement was adequate. But see also the Unfair Contract Terms Guidance first published in February 2001 by the Office of Fair Trading at 2.3.12–2.3.11 which suggests that any limitation of liability might be considered repugnant. The guidance states: 'If a contract is to be fully and equally binding on both seller and buyer, each party should be entitled to full compensation where the other fails to honour its obligations.' However, note the terms listed by the OFT in Appendix A, Group 2(c) which have been withdrawn or amended. Most are concerned with attempts to limit recovery significantly by purporting to exclude 'consequential' losses. It is suggested, therefore, that the Law Society's view would be accepted by a court.

8 Paragraph 69 of the guidance to r 2.07 provides:

> 'You should also note that if you want to limit your firm's liability to a figure above the minimum level for qualifying insurance but within your firm's top-up insurance cover, you will need to consider whether the top-up insurance will adequately cover a claim arising from the matter in question.'

1.06   The court is therefore likely to enforce terms that limit a firm's liability to the amount of its cover (provided that cover is adequate) or which exclude its liability to third parties. The effect of a provision that purports to exclude liability to third parties is considered separately below in the context of duties to third parties.[1] More difficult is the question whether a solicitor may be permitted to limit the scope of the specific retainer which he or she is prepared to undertake, for example by excluding tax advice or advice on detailed technical matters such as the specification for building works. In *Hurlingham Estates Ltd v Wilde & Partners*[2] Lightman J held, albeit obiter, that a limitation imposed by a solicitor upon his clients at a meeting without their 'fully informed consent' would not be binding upon them. No authority was cited in support of this finding and it remains to be seen whether this obiter dictum will be followed more widely. But in that case the solicitor agreed to act in relation to the purchase of shares, the acquisition of a lease and the grant of a sub-lease. At a meeting with the clients he attempted to limit his duties to drafting the relevant documents for the structure agreed by the clients but to exclude any duty to give advice on the financial and tax consequences of that structure. It is suggested that the decision in *Hurlingham Estates Ltd v Wilde* can be justified on the basis that the solicitor owed a pre-contractual duty of care to the clients or potential clients and that he should have advised them to consider instructing another solicitor with the relevant expertise before agreeing to the proposed limitation. Whether or not the reasoning can be supported on that basis, it is suggested that the court would have struck the limitation down under the UCTCCR. It was unfair for the solicitor to attempt to impose such a limitation without informing the clients that he did not have the necessary expertise and suggesting that they should consider instructing a solicitor who did before agreeing to instruct him.[3]

1 See paras 1.30–1.32.
2 [1997] 1 Lloyd's Rep 525 at 528–9.
3 Regulation 6(2) excludes the fairness requirement where the term relates to the core obligations of the supplier. It provides that 'the assessment of fairness of a term shall not relate …to the definition of the main subject matter of the contract.' It is difficult to distinguish (in terms of language at least) between those cases in which the scope of the retainer is limited and the solicitor agrees to undertake a specific but limited task and those cases in which the solicitor seeks unfairly to cut down the scope of the duty. But it is suggested that reg 6(2) does not apply and the solicitor has to satisfy the fairness requirement where he or she seeks to exclude a standard duty (eg to report on title to the purchaser of a property) or (as in *Hurlingham Estates Ltd v Wilde*) cannot properly accept instructions to act on a limited basis without exposing the client to a risk of loss. Lightman J also criticised the defendant for failing to put the limitation in writing and giving the client an opportunity to take it away and consider it. It should be noted that reg 6(2) only excludes the fairness requirement if the plain language requirement has already been satisfied. The OFT's Unfair Contract Terms Guidance states (at 19.13): 'As such, the "core terms exemption" is seen as conditional upon such terms being expressed and presented in such a way as to ensure that they are, or are at least capable of being, at the forefront of the consumer's mind in deciding whether to enter the contract.' For judicial consideration of the core terms exemption more generally see *Bairstow Eves London Central Ltd v Smith* [2004] EWHC 263 (QB) (Gross J) where the issue was whether the exemption applied to the commission rates contained in an estate agency contract.

3 Formation and duration of the retainer

1.07 A solicitor is normally retained by express agreement. The agreement may be oral or written but the usual way in which the contract is formed or recorded is for the solicitor to send an engagement letter which the client is requested to countersign or the terms of which the client is asked to agree.[1] In order to comply with the Money Laundering Regulations[2] a solicitor must also carry out detailed checks to establish and confirm the identity of a new client[3] and the CML Handbook imposes an express obligation upon a solicitor retained by a mortgage lender to check the borrower's identity.[4] Although a solicitor is required by the money laundering regulations to check the identity of a new client and will usually comply with the practice rules by sending out an engagement letter, the failure to comply with these requirements will not prevent a contract coming into existence and a solicitor may be retained by express agreement in the most casual of circumstances. In *Whelton Sinclair v Hyland*[5] it was held that a telephone call by the claimant to an unidentified person (who might have been a secretary or receptionist) brought a retainer into existence. The recipient of the telephone call did no more than tell the client that she would inform the partner who had acted for the client before and that 'he would get on with it'.[6]

1 The circumstances leading to the formation of the retainer must be capable of being analysed by reference to offer and acceptance in the normal way. For an analysis of this kind see *Masons v WD King Ltd* [2003] EWHC 3124 (TCC) (HHJ Humphrey Lloyd QC) at [15]–[16] and [55]–[57]. For an example of a case in which the client unsuccessfully sought to argue that the terms of the engagement letter were not binding on the basis that the terms were not intended to be enforceable unless the client succeeded in the litigation, see *McFaddens v Chandrasekaran* [2006] EWHC 1357 (QB) (Irwin J).

2 SI 2003/3075. The regulatory position remains as it was before the Law Society's Code of Conduct 2007 came into force on 1 July 2007 and solicitors' duties continue to be governed by these regulations. The Law Society has published detailed guidance to the regulations which is contained in Annex 3B to the *Guide to the Professional Conduct of Solicitors* (1999). It has also published guidance for property lawyers (22 February 2005), guidance for private client lawyers (22 February 2006), specimen terms for client care letters (5 February 2007) and guidance for company and commercial lawyers (4 April 2007). The current regulations themselves came into force on 1 March 2004.

3 See Annex 3B(7) of the *Guide to the Professional Conduct of Solicitors* (1999) at paras 3.84–3.121 in which detailed guidance is set out for all types of client (both individual and corporate). Note, in particular, the relevant sections for disadvantaged or mentally incapacitated clients, asylum seekers and estates and trusts at paras 3.95–3.107 (where the solicitor may be instructed by or through a third party).

4 See para 3 headed 'Safeguards' and Chapter 10, section A.4.

5 [1992] 2 EGLR 158, CA. Contrast *Horsley v Burton* [2003] All ER (D) 413 (David Clarke J) in which an informal letter of advice and a short meeting (for which the solicitor refused to accept payment) did not give rise to a contract of retainer. For a further (and more complex) example in which a client was held to have instructed a solicitor to act and thereby ratified his conduct of arbitration proceedings principally on the basis of a telephone conversation see *SEB Trygg Aktiebolag v Manches* [2005] EWHC 35 (Comm), [2005] 1 Lloyd's Rep 129 (Gloster J) (a point that was not considered in the CA).

6 The question whether the unidentified recipient of the call had authority to bind the firm (whether actual or ostensible) was not argued. Whether the solicitor also owed the client a duty to provide the relevant information required by Practice Rule 15 (which was then in force) or to give advice before taking any steps on the client's behalf were not considered either.

1.08 Equally, a solicitor may be retained by a client under an implied contract. The question whether such a contract should be implied often arises where the solicitor has already been instructed to act by one party and the issue is whether he or she has also been retained by any other party or parties. Common relationships in which this issue arises involve corporate clients and their shareholders or directors, parent companies and subsidiaries, co-owners of property, trustees and beneficiaries and joint venture parties. The circumstances in which a solicitor may be taken to have assumed a duty of care to a related party in tort are examined in section B.2[1] of this chapter and one rationalisation for the range of circumstances in which liability in tort is imposed is that the relationship between the solicitor and the third party is closely analogous or akin to a contract. There may be circumstances, however, in which a genuine contract can be implied between the solicitor and a party who is not the direct source of his instructions. According to Scott LJ in *Groom v Crocker*:[2]

'The relationship is normally started by a retainer but will be presumed if the conduct of the parties shows that the relationship of solicitor and client has in fact been established between them.'

The question is an objective one and a retainer will only be implied where on an objective assessment the solicitor either appreciated or ought to have appreciated that he or she was being instructed by the client or prospective client. In those circumstances a collateral contract may genuinely be implied between the solicitor and persons or bodies other than the individual from whom the solicitor receives instructions, and it is no answer for the solicitor to argue that he has not been instructed by, or on behalf of, the claimant expressly.[3] The appreciation of the solicitor in question will carry great weight where the solicitor is careful and competent[4] and the solicitor's fee note may also be a powerful indication that there is an implied retainer although this is not conclusive.[5] In *Dean v Allin & Watts*[6] the court gave the following guidance:

> '"All the circumstances" include the fact, if such be the case (as it is here), that the party in question is not liable for the solicitor's fees and did not directly instruct the solicitors. These are circumstances to be taken into account but are not conclusive. Other circumstances to be taken into account include whether such a contractual relationship has existed in the past, for where it has, the court may be readier to assume that the parties intended to resume that relationship, and where there has been such a previous relationship the failure of the solicitor to advise the former client to obtain independent advice may be indicative that such advice is not necessary because the solicitor is so acting.'

In a number of cases the court has found the existence of an implied retainer between solicitors or other professionals, usually in circumstances where the claimant is so closely connected with another client that a separate or collateral contract should be implied.[7] In other cases, where the parties are on separate sides of a transaction, the court has refused to imply the existence of a retainer (where, eg, a solicitor is asked to draw up a document on behalf of one party but the other party fails to obtain separate advice).[8] In situations of this kind it is possible that one or more of the parties might take advantage of the Contracts (Rights of Third Parties) Act 1999 even where there is no implied retainer or no duty of care in tort. But under the Act, a party is only entitled to sue on the contract of retainer where the parties intend to confer a benefit on that party and the party is mentioned by name.[9]

1 Paragraphs 1.13–1.29.
2 [1939] 1 KB 194 at 222, CA. This passage was cited by Oliver J in *Midland Bank Trust Co Ltd v Hett, Stubbs and Kemp* [1979] Ch 384 at 396D and by Ipp J in *Pegrum v Fatharly* [1996] WSR 92 (SC of WA) who added this gloss (which was cited by Goldring J in *Munro-Wilson v Olswang* [2003] EWHC 721 (QB) at [6]): 'A contractual retainer of solicitor and client will therefore be presumed if it is proved that the relationship of solicitor and client de facto existed between a solicitor and another person. Upon proof of that kind it would not be necessary to prove when, where, by whom or in what particular words the agreement was made ...the de facto relationship ...has to be a necessary and clear inference from the proved facts before a retainer will be presumed.'

3 See *Searles v Cann & Hallett* [1999] PNLR 494 at 503D (cited by Lightman J in *Dean v Allin & Watts* [2001] EWCA Civ 758, [2001] Lloyd's Rep PN 605 at [22] and Goldring J in *Munro-Wilson v Olswang* [2003] EWHC 721 (QB) at [6]): 'No such retainer should be implied for convenience, but only where an objective consideration of all the circumstances make it so clear an implication that [the solicitor] ought to have appreciated it.' See also *Jewo Ferrous BV v Lewis Moore* [2001] PNLR 328 at 340 (Chadwick LJ): 'In determining the effect of what was said in the course of the conversation on February 2, 1990 it is, in my view, helpful to recall the passage in the Scottish textbook *Gloag on Contract* (2nd edn) p 7 cited by Lord Reid in *McCutcheon v David MacBrayne Ltd* [1964] 1 WLR 125 at 128: "The judicial task is not to discover the actual intentions of each party; it is to decide what each was reasonably entitled to conclude from the attitude of the other." '

4 See *Jewo Ferrous BV v Lewis Moore* [2001] PNLR 328 at 340 (Chadwick LJ).

5 See *Jewo Ferrous BV v Lewis Moore* [2001] PNLR 328 at 341 (Chadwick LJ). In that case the solicitor *had* rendered a fee note to the claimant but the judge accepted his evidence that he was asked to render the fee note to the claimant directly and that this did not make the claimant his client. See also *Midland Bank Trust Co Ltd v Hett, Stubbs and Kemp* [1979] Ch 384 at 396A (Oliver J): 'Who actually paid the bill, however, does not. I think, matter.'

6 [2001] EWCA Civ 758, [2001] Lloyd's Rep PN 605 at [22]. Lightman J gave *Madley v Cousins Combe & Mustoe* [1997] EGCS 63, CA as an example of the kind of case in which a new retainer was presumed from a previous retainer and the failure to advise the former client to take independent advice. For a similar example see *Harris v Nantes & Wylde* [1997] NPC 7, CA.

7 *Midland Bank Trust Co Ltd v Hett, Stubbs and Kemp* [1979] Ch 384 at 395–6 (Oliver J) (retainer implied between a number of family members and family solicitors); *R P Howard Ltd v Woodman Matthews & Co* [1983] BCLC 117 (HHJ Finlay QC) (where Ds were held to owe a contractual duty of care to both a company and its principal shareholder in relation to a lease renewal); *Punjab National Bank v de Boinville* [1992] 3 All ER 104, CA at 114g–116g (implied retainer between bank and insurance brokers); *Christensen v Scott* [1996] 1 NZLR 273 (CA of NZ) (where it was held arguable that accountants owed a duty to directors and shareholders guaranteeing a company's debts although the court's approach to the recoverability of damages was disapproved in *Johnson v Gore Wood & Co* [2002] 2 AC 1 (below)); *Johnson v Gore Wood & Co* [2002] EWHC 776 (Ch) (Hart J) at [74]–[87] (contractual duty of care owed to both company and shareholder in relation to the conduct of litigation); *Ball v Druces & Attlee (No 2)* [2004] EWHC 1402 (QB), [2004] PNLR 745 (Nelson J) (Ds instructed to set up a charitable trust also held to be acting for the promoters individually); and *Hughes v Richards* [2004] EWCA Civ 266, [2004] PNLR 706 at [31] (Jacob LJ) (accountant owed contractual duties to parents and children).

8 *Searles v Cann & Hallett* [1999] PNLR 494 (Philip Mott QC) (no implied retainer between private mortgagee and solicitors instructed by the mortgagor to draw up the charge); *Jewo Ferrous BV v Lewis Moore* [2001] PNLR 328, CA (no implied retainer between supplier and solicitors instructed by purchaser to prepare a debenture); *Dean v Allin & Watts* [2001] EWCA Civ 758, [2001] Lloyd's Rep PN 605, CA (no implied retainer between private lender and solicitors instructed by the borrower to prepare promissory notes); *Munro-Wilson v Olswang* [2003] EWHC 721 (QB) (Goldring J) (no implied retainer between litigation solicitors instructed by company and largest shareholders – on the facts it was held that Ds expressly refused to act unless C agreed to provide money on account which he failed to do); *Masons v WD King Ltd* [2003] EWHC 3124 (TCC) (HHJ Humphrey Lloyd QC) at [15]–[16] and [55]–[57] (Ds who were expressly retained by company A in relation to a development were not retained by company B which was a special purpose vehicle).

9 It is unlikely however that the Act will provide a remedy unless the parties entered into the contract of retainer on the express basis that it would apply. Section 1 provides that: '… a person who is not a party to a contract (a 'third party') may in his own right enforce a term of the contract if- (a) the contract expressly provides that he may, or (b) subject to subsection (2), the term purports to confer a benefit on him. (2) Subsection (1) (b) does not apply if on a proper construction of the contract it appears that the parties did not intend the term to be enforceable by the third party. (3) The third party must be expressly identified in the contract by name, as a member of a class or as answering a particular description but need not be in existence when the

contract is entered into.' It is possible that the parties might wish to do this, e g where a special purpose vehicle is formed for the purpose of a specific transaction. See also the Law Commission Report No 242 (1996) which preceded the Act at paras 7.19–7.27 (dealing, in particular, with the disappointed beneficiary cases).

1.09 If solicitors wish to decline instructions they owe a duty to potential clients to inform them immediately.[1] Once a solicitor agrees to act for a client it is an implied term of the contract that the solicitor may terminate the retainer only on reasonable notice and for good reason.[2] In *Underwood, Son & Piper v Lewis*[3] it was held that the retainer of a solicitor who accepted instructions to act on behalf of a client in litigation gave rise to an entire contract which the solicitor could terminate only on reasonable notice. But the retainer will not continue indefinitely. In the normal case it will be relatively easy to identify the time when the solicitor's retainer is terminated (the date on which he closes his file or renders a final bill), and it is well accepted that there is no such thing as a 'general retainer' in the sense that a solicitor may be obliged to continue to act for a client indefinitely without instructions.[4] It is therefore a question of fact when the retainer was terminated. In the context of limitation it is often argued that a solicitor who accepts instructions to act for a client comes under a continuing duty either to put right a mistake or to inform his client that it has been made. In *Bell v Peter Browne & Co*[5] it was held that a solicitor who had failed to register appropriate entries at the Land Registry on behalf of his client had a continuing duty to his client in contract. According to Mustill LJ:

> 'Certainly, a solicitor may have a continuing retainer from his client and no doubt there are retainers which require the solicitor to be constantly on watch for new sources of potential danger and to take immediate steps to nip them in the bud.'

Whether or not the solicitor's retainer continues in this way will depend on the precise circumstances. But the question whether the retainer continues should be carefully distinguished from the question when the solicitor committed a breach of retainer and the cause of action accrued.

1 *Whelton Sinclair v Hyland* [1992] 2 EGLR 158 at 161B–C, CA.
2 See the Solicitors' Code of Conduct 2007, r 2.01(2): 'You must not cease acting for a client except for good reason and on reasonable notice.' See also the *Guide to the Professional Conduct of Solicitors* (1999), Principle 12.10 (which was the predecessor to Rule 2.01(2)) and *Young v Purdy* [1997] PNLR 130, CA where there was no appeal against the finding of the judge that the summary termination of a retainer by the solicitor was wrongful. Section 65(2) of the Solicitors Act 1974 provides that: 'If a solicitor who has been retained by a client to conduct contentious business requests the client to make a payment of a sum of money, being a reasonable sum on account of the costs incurred or to be incurred in the conduct of that business, and the client refuses or fails within a reasonable time to make that payment, the refusal or failure shall be deemed a good cause whereby the solicitor may, upon giving reasonable notice to the client, withdraw from the retainer.' In *Collyer Bristow v Robichaux* [2001] All ER (D) 288 Crane J held that solicitors gave notice within a reasonable time and were entitled to rely on the section. In *Perotti v Collyer Bristow* [2003] EWHC 25 (Ch) at [138] to [145] Jonathan Parker J held that a firm of solicitors was entitled to terminate its retainer in the conduct of an action because (i) there

was a conflict between the interests of the clients, (ii) there was a breakdown in confidence between the claimant and the defendants and (iii) there was a natural break. He also held that the defendants would have been entitled to terminate on grounds (i) or (ii) alone.

3 [1894] 2 QB 306, CA. It was cited by Tuckey LJ in *Donsland Ltd v Van Hoogstraten* [2002] EWCA Civ 253, [2002] PNLR 603 at 608 and applied by Laddie J in *Young v Robson Rhodes* [1999] Lloyd's Rep PN 641 where forensic accountants were held to be in repudiatory breach of contract for declining to act further when their firm merged with the defendants. See also *Perotti v Collyer Bristow* [2003] EWHC 25 (Ch) at [137] where Jonathan Parker J considered it unnecessary to decide whether *Underwood, Son & Piper v Lewis* was still good law because he held that as a matter of long practice an engagement to act in an administration action does not give rise to an entire contract.

4 *Midland Bank Co Ltd v Hett Stubbs and Kemp* [1979] Ch 384 at 402G–H (Oliver J). See also *Regent Leisuretime Ltd v Skerrett* [2006] EWCA Civ 1184, [2007] PNLR 9 at [34] (Peter Gibson LJ): '[T]here is no such thing as a general retainer imposing a duty to consider all aspects of the client's interests whenever the solicitor is consulted.'

5 [1990] 2 QB 495 at 512G, CA.

4   The rule against reflective loss

1.10   Although a solicitor may be found to have assumed a duty to act for two clients under an express or implied retainer on the basis explained above, it does not follow that both clients will be able to recover damages for a breach of contract if one of those clients is a company. This is because of the rule against reflective loss.[1] In *Johnson v Gore Wood* Lord Millett stated the rule in the following terms:[2]

> '[W]here the company suffers loss caused by the breach of a duty owed both to the company and to the shareholder ......[t]he shareholder's loss, in so far as this is measured by the diminution in value of his shareholding or the loss of dividends, merely reflects the loss suffered by the company in respect of which the company has its own cause of action. If the shareholder is allowed to recover in respect of such loss, then either there will be double recovery at the expense of the defendant or the shareholder will recover at the expense of the company and its creditors and other shareholders. Neither course can be permitted. This is a matter of principle; there is no discretion involved.'

The rule is a powerful one because it prevents a shareholder bringing a claim against a solicitor or other professional who has assumed separate legal duties even if the company resolves not to bring a claim itself. The rule has been considered in a number of recent cases (often in the context of an application to strike out the claim).[3] In *Gardner v Parker*[4] Neuberger LJ summarised the relevant principles for the application of the rule in the following terms:

> '(1) a loss claimed by a shareholder which is merely reflective of a loss suffered by the company – i e a loss which would be made good

if the company had enforced in full its rights against the defendant wrongdoer – is not recoverable by the shareholder *save in a case where, by reason of the wrong done to it, the company is unable to pursue its claim against the wrongdoer*; (2) where there is no reasonable doubt that that is the case, the court can properly act, in advance of trial, to strike out the offending heads of claim; (3) the irrecoverable loss (being merely reflective of the company's loss) is not confined to the individual claimant's loss of dividends on his shares or diminution in the value of his shareholding in the company but extends … to "all other payments which the shareholder might have obtained from the company if it had not been deprived of its funds" and also to other payments which the company would have made if it had had the necessary funds even if the plaintiff would have received them *qua* employee and not qua shareholder save *that this does not apply to the loss of future benefits to which the claimant had an expectation but no contractual entitlement*; (4) the principle is not rooted simply in the avoidance of double recovery in fact; it extends to heads of loss which the company could have claimed but has chosen not to and therefore includes the case where the company has settled for less than it might …; (5) provided the loss claimed by the shareholder is merely reflective of the company's loss and provided the defendant wrongdoer owed duties both to the company and to the shareholder, it is irrelevant that the duties so owed may be different in content.' (emphasis added).'

As this extract indicates the rule applies not only to the diminution in value of a shareholder's shares but also to the dividends that he or she could have expected to receive from the company and to any future remuneration, directors' fees and pension entitlements (to the extent that contributions have been reduced or prevented as a consequence of the company's loss).[5] It also applies to payments that the shareholder could have expected to receive from the company as a creditor.[6] As the extract also indicates, however, there is a general exception to the rule where the wrongdoer's conduct has prevented the company from pursuing its claim.[7] Finally, the rule applies not only where the third parties owe different duties to the company and shareholder (e g in contract and tort) but also where the third parties owes duties in a different capacity. Thus, the rule applies where a beneficiary of a trust has a claim against the trustees for breach of trust but they are also liable to the company which forms the principal for breach of their duties as directors.[8]

1 This was the description given to the rule in *Gardner v Parker* [2004] EWCA Civ 78, [2004] 1 BCLC 417, CA at [23]. But as the court explained, it is derived from the rule in *Foss v Harbottle*: see *Prudential Insurance Co Ltd v Newman Industries Ltd (No 2)* [1982] 1 Ch 204 (esp at 222–3). Indeed, it was described by Peter Gibson LJ in *Shaker v Al-Bedrawi* [2002] EWCA Civ 1452, [2003] Ch 350, CA at [2] as 'the *Prudential* principle'.

2 [2001] 2 AC 1 at 62E. Some formulations of the rule are expressed in terms of causation rather than principle: see, eg, *Gerber Garment Technology Inc v Lectra Systems Ltd* [1997] RPC 443 at

471: 'If the company is able to recover from the third party, the company will be indemnified and the value of the shareholder's shares will not have been reduced. If the company chooses not to exercise the remedy, the loss to the shareholder will have been caused by the decision of the company not to pursue its remedy, not the defendant's fault.'

3   *Johnson v Gore Wood & Co* [2002] 2 AC 1 (C sued Ds, a firm of solicitors, after the company which he controlled had compromised a claim for negligence against them for failing to exercise an option on its behalf, his claim for the diminution in the value of his shares was struck out and also his claim for lost pension entitlements (to the extent that the company contributed to them) and when the remaining claims were tried C recovered principally under one head: see *Johnson v Gore Wood & Co (No 2)* [2002] EWHC 776 (Ch) (Hart J) and [2003] EWCA Civ 1728, CA); *Day v Cook* [2001] EWCA Civ 592, [2002] 1 BCLC 1, CA (C invested in a number of joint venture schemes on the advice of his solicitor, D, in most cases through his operating company and a number of its subsidiaries but apart from a personal claim for £40,000 under a consultancy agreement which was permitted to go to trial the remainder of the claims were struck out); *Humberclyde Finance Group Ltd v Hicks* (Neuberger J, unreported, 14 November 2001) (C's claim for conspiracy resulting in loss of dividends, earnings and diminution in value of his shareholding of a company struck out); *Ellis v Property Leeds (UK) Ltd* [2002] EWCA Civ 32, [2002] 2 BCLC 175, CA (claim by directors of company against valuer for diminution in value of shares in the company held on trust for them struck out); *Shaker v Al-Bedrawi* [2002] EWCA Civ 1452, [2003] Ch 350, CA (claim by C that D1 held shares in a company on trust for him and had misappropriated US $6m from the sale of two subsidiaries permitted to go to trial together with claims for accessory and recipient liability against D2, D1's solicitor); *Giles v Rhind* [2002] EWCA Civ 1428, [2003] Ch 618, CA (C recovered substantial damages against D for breach of shareholders' agreement for misuse of confidential information and breach of restrictive covenants); *Gardner v Parker* [2004] EWCA Civ 78, [2004] 1 BCLC 417 at [33] (claim by C for misappropriation of company assets or transfer at an undervalue against D, a director, struck out because C's shareholding in the company was held through another company and there was no evidence that that company could not have brought a claim); and *Shahar v Tsitsekkos* [2004] All ER (D) 293 (Mann J) (claim to ownership of company and for damages for conspiracy).

4   *Gardner v Parker* [2004] EWCA Civ 78, [2004] 1 BCLC 417 at [33]. The extract is a quotation from the judgment of Blackburne J at first instance in *Giles v Rhind* [2002] EWCA Civ 1428, [2003] Ch 618 at [57] subject to two qualifications made by Chadwick LJ in the Court of Appeal: see [61] and [62]. Those qualifications are reflected in the text in italics which was added by Neuberger LJ to the original extract from Blackburne J's judgment in *Giles v Rhind*.

5   *Johnson v Gore Wood & Co* [2002] 2 AC 1 at 67B-H (Lord Millett), *Humberclyde Finance Group Ltd v Hicks* (Neuberger J, unreported, 14 November 2001) at [29]–[34] and *Gardner v Parker* [2004] EWCA Civ 78, [2004] 1 BCLC 417 at [31]–[32] (Neuberger LJ). It is not clear how far the second qualification extends. In *Giles v Rhind* [2002] EWCA Civ 1428, [2003] Ch 618 at [81] it was held that the benefits which C might have expected to earn following the termination of his employment were not reflective of the company's loss although they flowed from the unlawful conduct of D.

6   *Gardner v Parker* [2004] EWCA Civ 78, [2004] 1 BCLC 417 at [33].

7   The exception was identified and applied in *Giles v Rhind* [2002] EWCA Civ 1428, [2003] Ch 618 at [63]–[80] where the company was placed in administrative receivership following D's breaches of duty and unable to pursue its claims because D applied for security for costs.

8   See *Walker v Stones* [2001] QB 902 and *Shaker v Al-Bedrawi* [2002] EWCA Civ 1452, [2003] Ch 350, CA. Both cases suggest that the rule may be applied more restrictively in the context of claims for breach of trust and there must be complete identity between the two losses. In *Shaker v Al-Bedrawi* (above) at [83] Peter Gibson LJ stated: 'In our judgment the *Prudential* principle does not preclude an action brought by a claimant not as a shareholder but as a beneficiary under a trust against his trustee for a profit unless it can be shown by the defendants that the whole of the claimed profit reflects what the company has lost and which it has a cause of action to recover.' In *Walker v Stones* [2001] QB 902 at 922–3 Sir Christopher Slade suggested that there might be policy reasons why the rule should not always afford a defence but in *Gardner v Parker* the court rejected the argument that it should apply to breaches of fiduciary duty: see [53].

B   DUTY OF CARE IN TORT

1   Duty to the client

1.11   In *Midland Bank Co Ltd v Hett, Stubbs & Kemp*[1] Oliver J held that solicitors owed a concurrent duty of care to their client independently of their contractual obligations and his decision has now been approved by the House of Lords in *Henderson v Merrett Syndicates*.[2] The nature of the solicitor's duty was explained by him as follows:[3]

> 'The extent of his duties depends upon the terms and limits of [the] retainer and any duty of care to be implied must be related to what he is instructed to do. Now no doubt the duties owed by a solicitor to his client are high, in the sense that he holds himself out as practising a highly skilled and exacting profession, but I think that the court must beware of imposing upon solicitors – or upon professional men in other spheres duties – which go beyond the scope of what they are requested or undertake to do. It may be that a particularly meticulous and conscientious practitioner would, in his client's general interests, take it upon himself to pursue a line of inquiry beyond the strict limits comprehended by his instructions. But that is not the test. The test is what the reasonably competent practitioner would do having regard to the standards normally adopted in his profession.'

The point was re-emphasised by Peter Gibson LJ in *National Home Loans Corpn v Giffen, Couch & Archer*[4] where he summarised the relevant authorities as follows:

> 'As Oliver J said in *Midland Bank Trust Co Ltd v Hett, Stubbs and Kemp* [1979] Ch 384, 402, in relation to the duties of a solicitor to a client by whom he has been retained: "The extent of his duties depends upon the terms and limits of that retainer and any duty of care to be implied must be related to what he is instructed to do." Donaldson LJ stated in *Carradine Properties Ltd v D J Freeman & Co* (1982)126 Sol Jo 157; Court of Appeal (Civil Division) Transcript No 60 of 1982[5] in relation to the solicitor's duty of care to his client that:
>
> > "the precise scope of that duty will depend, inter alia, upon the extent to which the client appears to need advice. An inexperienced client will need and will be entitled to expect the solicitor to take a much broader view of the scope of his retainer and of his duties than will be the case with an experienced client."
>
> That statement was cited with approval by this court in *Virgin Management v De Morgan Group plc* [1996] NPC 8, CA.'

1 [1979] Ch 384.
2 [1995] 2 AC 145 at 190B.
3 At 402G–403B, applied in *Searles v Cann* [1999] PNLR 494 (Philip Mott QC) at 504B-F.
4 [1998] 1 WLR 207 at 2136–H, CA, applied in *Searles v Cann* (above) at 504B-F and *Jewo Ferrous BV v Lewis Moore* [2001] PNLR 328, CA at [49]–[51]. The court held that there was no doubt that in an arm's length transaction a solicitor acting for a creditor owed a duty to carry out company searches to enable him or her to advise on the effect and priority of the security. In the instant case, however, the loan was between connected parties and the solicitor's duty was at most to enquire whether the creditor wished searches to be made.
5 Now reported at [2003] Lloyd's Rep PN 483 and [1955–1995] PNLR Key Cas 219. In *John Mowlem Construction plc v Neil F Jones & Co* [2004] EWCA Civ 768, [2004] PNLR 925, CA at [16] Tuckey LJ stated: 'As a decision on its own facts this case is a useful illustration of the extent of solicitors' duties, but I do not think it was intended to lay down principles of general application to cases of this kind. Each case must depend on its own facts.'

1.12 Whilst these authorities suggest that it is generally true to say that the nature and scope of the duty in tort assumed by the solicitor will be determined by the terms of the retainer agreed with the client, it has been held by the Court of Appeal that the duty in contract and duty in tort are not precisely the same. In *Holt v Payne Skillington*[1] it was held that in principle a professional (in this case an agent and valuer) may owe a more extensive duty of care in tort than he or she does under the terms of his or her contractual retainer. And although these authorities suggest that a solicitor's duty of care is limited to carrying out the express instructions of the client, the nature of those instructions may impose a duty upon the solicitor to clarify those instructions:[2]

> 'The retainer when given puts into operation the normal terms of a contractual relationship, including in particular the duty of the solicitor to protect the client's interest and carry out his instructions in the matters to which the retainer relates, by all proper means. It is an incident of that duty that the solicitor shall consult with his client on all questions of doubt which do not fall within the express or implied discretion left to him, and shall keep the client informed to such an extent as may be reasonably necessary according to the same criteria.'

It probably does not matter whether the duty to clarify instructions (depending on the circumstances) is regarded as an implied term of the contractual retainer or an incident of the solicitor's duty of care in tort (or both). The important point is that in appropriate circumstances the client is entitled to rely on the solicitor to take further instructions if the original instructions were either unclear or inadequate to enable the solicitor to protect the client's interests. In *Ball v Druces & Attlee (No 2)*[3] two joint venture partners established a charitable trust to create and then hold the Eden Project in Cornwall. They instructed the defendant solicitors to act for them in forming the trust although it was made clear to the solicitors that they anticipated some kind of profit-sharing arrangement. When the relationship later broke down, one of them claimed damages against the defendants for failing to protect his personal interests as well as the interests of the joint venture. The court held that they owed a duty to take further instructions when the trust was formed and to advise the partners to enter into binding heads of terms which would have entitled the claimant to some element of profit. In *Keith v Davidson Chalmers*[4] the claimant was a director of a property company. He instructed the defendants to form a company for a property venture that he wished to set up with another employee of the company and to advise him whether this amounted to a breach of the restrictive covenants in his contract of employment. The defendants were held liable for failing to go beyond their instructions and warn him of the risk that he might be liable for breach of fiduciary duty.[5]

1 (1996) 77 BLR 51 at 73B–H, CA. It may be that this was no more than a pleading point.
2 *Groom v Crocker* [1939] 1 KB 194, CA at 222 (Scott LJ). See also *Boyce v Rendells* (1983) 268 EG 278, CA at 272 (Lawton LJ): '[I]f in the course of taking instructions, a professional man like a ...solicitor learns of facts which reveal to him as a professional man the existence of obvious risks, then he should do more than merely advise within the strict limits of his retainer. He should call attention to and advise upon the risks'; *Credit Lyonnais v Russell Jones and Walker* [2002] EWHC 1310 (Ch), [2003] PNLR 17 (Laddie J) at [28]: 'He is under no general obligation to expend time and effort on issues outside the retainer. However, if in the course of doing that for which he is retained, he becomes aware of a risk or a potential risk to the client, it is his duty to inform the client. In doing that, he is neither going beyond the scope of his instructions nor is he doing extra work for which he is not to be paid. He is simply reporting back to the client on issues of concern that he learns as a result of and in the course of carrying out his express instructions'; and *Feakins v Burstow* [2005] EWHC 1931 (QB) at [66] to [76] (where the passage from *Midland Bank Co Ltd v Hett, Stubbs & Kemp* set out in para 1.11 above was cited but Jack J held that the solicitor owed a wider duty).
3 [2004] EWHC 1402 (QB), [2004] PNLR 745 (Nelson J). The judge found that it was no defence to advise the client to take separate advice from accountants or from counsel.
4 [2003] PNLR 220 (Lord Macfadyen, Court of Session).
5 There is an obvious overlap between this issue and the standard of care to be expected: see paras 2.32 ff, below.

2 Duty to third parties: general

1.13 Although the liability of solicitors and other professionals is ordinarily governed by contract, a professional may yet be liable to a third party for economic loss suffered as a consequence of a negligent misstatement or negligent advice despite the absence of any contractual relationship between them. In *Hedley Byrne & Co Ltd v Heller & Partners Ltd, Smith v Eric S Bush, Caparo Industries plc v Dickman, Henderson v Merrett Syndicates, White v Jones, Williams v Natural Life Health Foods Ltd, Phelps v Hillingdon LBC* and *Commissioners of Customs & Excise v Barclays Bank plc*[1] the House of Lords has explored the nature and scope of this professional liability. As the nature of liability has been clarified, three approaches to the imposition of a duty of care can be detected: the threefold test (foreseeability, proximity and reasonableness), the incremental test (analogy with decided cases) and the assumption of responsibility test (analogy or equivalence with contract).[2] It is now clear that if the assumption of responsibility test is satisfied, this will be sufficient to impose liability[3] although in many cases the application of the three tests will tend to lead to the same result.[4] The assumption of responsibility test is most useful in cases where the relationship is 'equivalent to contract'[5] but the less applicable the analogy with a contract becomes, the less reliable or suitable a guide the assumption of responsibility test provides.[6] In *Customs & Excise Comrs v Barclays Bank plc*[7] Lord Mance drew attention to the two core areas in which the assumption of responsibility test has led to the imposition of a duty of care: '(1) where there was a fiduciary relationship and (2) where the defendant has voluntarily answered a question or tenders skilled advice or services in circumstances where he knows or ought to know that an identified plaintiff will rely on his answers or advice.' He then stated:[8]

> 'This review of authority confirms that there is no single common denominator, even in cases of economic loss, by which liability may be determined. In my view the threefold test of foreseeability, proximity and fairness, justice and reasonableness provides a convenient general framework although it operates at a high level of abstraction. The concept of assumption of responsibility is particularly useful in the two core categories of case identified by Lord Browne-Wilkinson in *White v Jones*, at p 274F-G, when it may effectively subsume all aspects of the threefold approach. But if all that is meant by voluntary assumption of responsibility is the voluntary assumption of responsibility for a task, rather than of liability towards the defendant, then questions of foreseeability, proximity and fairness, reasonableness and justice may become very relevant. In *White v Jones* itself there was no doubt that the solicitor had voluntarily undertaken responsibility for a task, but it was the very fact that he had done so for the testator, not the disappointed beneficiaries, that gave rise to the stark division of opinion in the House. Incrementalism operates as an important cross-check on any other approach.'

1 [1964] AC 465 (bankers), [1990] 1 AC 831 (valuers), [1990] 2 AC 605 (auditors), [1995] 2 AC 145 (Lloyd's agents), [1995] 2 AC 207 (solicitors), [1998] 1 WLR 830 (company directors), [2001] 2 AC 201 (educational psychologist) and [2006] UKHL 28, [2007] 1 AC 181 (bankers) respectively. See also Gee 'The remedies carried by a freezing injunction' (2006) 122 LQR 535. In *Merrett* the House of Lords clarified the point that liability will be imposed as much for a failure to provide information or advice as for negligent misstatement or for the negligent provision of services: see [1995] 2 AC 145 at 181F.

2 See *Bank of Credit and Commerce International (Overseas) Ltd v Price Waterhouse (No 2)* [1998] PNLR 564, CA at 582E-583B (Sir Brian Neill): 'An examination of the cases discloses that the courts have been searching for a principle or test by which the existence or presence of liability in any particular circumstances can be tested ...It seems that the search has followed three separate but parallel paths.' In the remainder of the passage he identified the three tests referred to in the text. See also *Customs & Excise Comrs v Barclays Bank plc* [2006] UKHL 28, [2007] 1 AC 181 at [4] (Lord Bingham).

> 'The parties were agreed that the authorities disclose three tests which have been used in deciding whether a defendant sued as causing pure economic loss to a claimant owed

him a duty of care in tort. The first is whether the defendant assumed responsibility for what he said and did vis-à-vis the claimant, or is to be treated by the law as having done so. The second is commonly known as the threefold test: whether loss to the claimant was a reasonably foreseeable consequence of what the defendant did or failed to do; whether the relationship between the parties was one of sufficient proximity; and whether in all the circumstances it is fair, just and reasonable to impose a duty of care on the defendant towards the claimant (what Kirby J in *Perre v Apand Pty Ltd* (1999) 198 CLR 180, para 259, succinctly labelled "policy"). Third is the incremental test, based on the observation of Brennan J in *Sutherland Shire Council v Heyman* (1985) 157 CLR 424, 481, approved by Lord Bridge of Harwich in *Caparo Industries plc v Dickman* [1990] 2 AC 605, 618, that: "It is preferable, in my view, that the law should develop novel categories of negligence incrementally and by analogy with established categories, rather than by a massive extension of a prima facie duty of care restrained only by indefinable "considerations which ought to negative, or to reduce or limit the scope of the duty or the class of person to whom it is owed." '

This passage was recently cited by Dyson LJ in *Rowley v Secretary of State for Work and Pensions* [2007] EWCA Civ 598 at [47].

3 *Customs & Excise Comrs v Barclays Bank plc* [2006] UKHL 28, [2007] 1 AC 181 at [4] (Lord Bingham), [33] (Lord Hoffmann), [52] (Lord Rodger), [73] (Lord Walker) and [83] (Lord Mance).

4 See *Bank of Credit and Commerce International (Overseas) Ltd v Price Waterhouse (No 2)* at 586F (proposition (b)): 'If the facts are properly analysed and the policy considerations are correctly evaluated the several approaches will yield the same result' and *Customs & Excise Comrs v Barclays Bank plc* [2006] UKHL 28, [2007] 1 AC 181 at [83] (Lord Mance): 'All three approaches may often (though not inevitably) lead to the same result. Assumption of responsibility is on any view a core area of liability for economic loss. All three tests operate at a high level of abstraction. What matters is how and by reference to what lower-level factors they are interpreted in practice …'

5 See *Customs & Excise Comrs v Barclays Bank plc* (above) at [4] (Lord Bingham):

'First, there are cases in which one party can accurately be said to have assumed responsibility for what is said or done to another, the paradigm situation being a relationship having all the indicia of contract save consideration. *Hedley Byrne* would, but for the express disclaimer, have been such a case. *White v Jones* and *Henderson v Merrett Syndicates Ltd*, although the relationship was more remote, can be seen as analogous.'

See also [85] (Lord Mance):

'The concept of assumption of responsibility derives from the fountain of most modern economic claims, *Hedley Byrne & Co Ltd v Heller & Partners* [1964] AC 465. The concept appears most clearly in the speech of Lord Devlin, who, at pp 528–529, founded himself on the proposition that a duty of care might arise in relationships: "which … are 'equivalent to contract', that is, where there is an assumption of responsibility in circumstances in which, but for the absence of consideration, there would be a contract." Lord Devlin went on to emphasise, at p 529, that, in the light of the bank's disclaimer in that case, the claim failed because: "Responsibility can attach only to the single act, that is, the giving of the reference, and only if the doing of that act implied a voluntary undertaking to assume responsibility." Where there has been an assumption of responsibility in the core sense considered in *Hedley Byrne*, questions of "foreseeability", "proximity" and "fairness, justice and reasonableness" tend to answer themselves (c f *Henderson v Merrett Syndicates Ltd* [1995] 2 AC 145, per Lord Goff of Chieveley, at p 181C).'

6 For a recent example of a case in which the assumption of responsibility test seems inapposite see *Rowley v Secretary of State for Work and Pensions* [2007] EWCA Civ 598 (above) at [51]–[55].

7 [2006] UKHL 28, [2007] 1 AC 181 at [93] citing the speech of Lord Browne-Wilkinson in *White v Jones* [1995] 2 AC 207 at 274B.

8 See also [4] (Lord Bingham):

> 'The problem here is, as I see it, that the further this test is removed from the actions and intentions of the actual defendant, and the more notional the assumption of responsibility becomes, the less difference there is between this test and the threefold test'.

(*a*) *The threefold test*

1.14 In *Smith v Bush* and *Caparo*[1] the threefold test of foreseeability, proximity and reasonableness coupled with reasoning by analogy with decided cases was favoured. According to Lord Bridge in *Caparo*:[2]

> 'What emerges is that, in addition to the foreseeability of damage, necessary ingredients in any situation giving rise to a duty of care are that there should exist between the party owing the duty and the party to whom it is owed a relationship characterised by the law as one of "proximity" or "neighbourhood" and that the situation should be one in which the court considers it fair, just and reasonable that the law should impose a duty of a given scope upon the one party for the benefit of the other. But it is implicit in the passages referred to that the concepts of proximity and fairness embodied in these additional ingredients are not susceptible of any precise definition as would be sufficient to give them utility as practical tests, but amount in effect to little more than convenient labels to attach to the features of different specific situations which, on a detailed examination of all the circumstances, the law recognises pragmatically as giving rise to a duty of care of a given scope. Whilst recognising, of course, the importance of the underlying general principles common to the whole field of negligence, I think that the law has now moved in the direction of attaching greater significance to the more traditional categorisation of distinct and recognisable situations as guides to the existence, the scope and the limits of the varied duties of care which the law imposes.'

1 The majority of the House of Lords also adopted the same formulation in *Marc Rich & Co v Bishop Rock Marine Co Ltd* [1996] AC 211. See also *Goodwill v British Pregnancy Advisory Service* [1996] 2 All ER 161, CA.
2 [1990] 2 AC 605 at 617H–618C.

(*b*) *The incremental test*

1.15 In the passage from *Caparo* set out above Lord Bridge emphasised the importance of an incremental approach of testing any new set of facts against existing categories of liability. In *Reeman v Department of Transport*[1] Phillips LJ described the incremental approach for the imposition of liability in the following terms:

'When confronted with a novel situation the court does not, however, consider these matters in isolation. It does so by comparison with established categories of negligence to see whether the facts amount to no more than a small extension of a situation already covered by authority, or whether a finding of the existence of a duty of care would effect a significant extension to the law of negligence. Only in exceptional cases will the court accept that the interests of justice justify such an extension of the law.'[2]

1 [1997] PNLR 618, CA at 625B.
2 For a good example of the incremental approach see *Gorham v British Telecommunications plc* [2000] 4 All ER 867 at 881a (Schiemann LJ):

'The position of an investor who goes to a financial adviser seeking investment or pensions advice in relation to the provision for his family after his death is analogous to that of a person who goes to a solicitor seeking advice in relation to making provision by will for his family after his death.'

(c) The assumption of responsibility test

1.16 In *Merrett,* however, the House of Lords gave much greater prominence to the concept of assumption of responsibility for giving advice or providing services which was the cornerstone of liability in *Hedley Byrne.* Lord Goff gave a strong indication that this ought to be adopted as the principle underlying the imposition of a duty of care. He stated:[1]

'In subsequent cases concerned with liability under the *Hedley Byrne* principle in respect of negligent misstatements, the question has frequently arisen whether the plaintiff falls within the category of persons to whom the maker of the statement owes a duty of care. In seeking to contain the category of persons within reasonable bounds, there has been some tendency on the part of the courts to criticise the concept of "assumption of responsibility" as being "unlikely to be a helpful or realistic test in most cases" (see *Smith v Eric S Bush* [1990] 1 AC 831, 864–865 per Lord Griffiths; and see also *Caparo Industries v Dickman* [1990] 2 AC 605, 628 per Lord Roskill). However, at least in cases such as the present, in which the same problem does not arise, there seems to be no reason why recourse should not be had to the concept, which appears after all to have been adopted, in one form or another, by all of their Lordships in *Hedley Byrne* [1964] AC 465 ... Furthermore, especially in a context concerned with a liability which may arise under a contract or in a situation "equivalent to contract", it must be expected that an objective test will be applied when asking the question whether, in a particular case, responsibility should be held to have been assumed by the defendant to the plaintiff: see *Caparo Industries v Dickman*

[1990] 2 AC 605, 637, per Lord Oliver of Aylmerton. In addition, the concept provides its own explanation why there is no problem in cases of this kind about liability for economic loss; for if a person assumes responsibility to another in respect of certain services, there is no reason why he should not be liable in damages to that other in respect of economic loss which flows from the negligent perform-ance of those services. It follows that, once the case is identified as falling within the *Hedley Byrne* principle, there should be no need to embark upon any further enquiry whether it is "fair just and reasonable" to impose liability for economic loss–a point which is, I consider, of some importance in the present case. The concept indicates too that in some circumstances, for example where the undertaking to furnish the relevant services is given on an informal occasion, there may be no assumption of responsibility; and likewise that an assumption of responsibility may be negatived by an appro-priate disclaimer.'

1 [1995] 2 AC 145 at 180G–181E.

1.17 A majority of the House of Lords in *White v Jones* also favoured the same test. According to Lord Browne-Wilkinson:[1]

'[T]he special relationship is created by the defendant voluntarily assuming to act in the matter by involving himself in the plaintiff's affairs or by choosing to speak. If he does so assume to act or to speak he is said to have assumed responsibility for carrying through the matter he has entered upon.'

It is also clear from the speeches in *White v Jones,* however, that the term 'assumption of responsibility' and similar expressions were not being used solely to describe situations in which there was direct communication between the claimant and the defendant or the defendant had agreed by words or conduct to act for the claimant (even on a gratuitous basis).[2] Nor is the term being used to describe the state of mind of the defendant who consciously assumes a legal liability to the claimant.[3]

1 [1995] 2 AC 207 at 274G.
2 This is clearest from Lord Nolan's example of the car driver assuming responsibility to other road users at 293H.
3 See per Lord Browne-Wilkinson [1995] 2 AC 207 at 273G–274B. See also the analysis of Lord Mance in *Customs & Excise Comrs v Barclays Bank plc* [2006] UKHL 28, [2007] 1 AC 181 at [84] to [93].

1.18 In *Williams v Natural Life Health Foods Ltd*[1] the House of Lords chose to affirm again the primacy of the assumption of responsibility test. Lord Steyn, with whom the other members of the House of Lords agreed, stated this:[2]

'It is clear, and accepted by counsel on both sides, that the governing principles are stated in the leading speech of Lord Goff of Chieveley in *Henderson v Merrett Syndicates* [1995] 2 AC 145. First, in *Henderson's* case it was settled that the assumption of responsibility principle enunciated in *Hedley Byrne & Co Ltd v Heller & Partners Ltd* [1964] AC 465 is not confined to statements but may apply to any assumption of responsibility for the provision of services. The extended *Hedley Byrne* principle is the rationalisation of a technique adopted by English law to provide a remedy for the recovery of damages in respect of economic loss caused by the negligent performance of services. Secondly, it was established that once a case is identified as falling within the extended *Hedley Byrne* principle, there is no need to embark on any further inquiry whether it is "fair just and reasonable" to impose liability for economic loss: p 181. Thirdly, and applying *Hedley Byrne,* it was made clear that

> "reliance upon [the assumption of responsibility] by the other party will be necessary to establish a cause of action (because otherwise the negligence will have no causative effect) ..." (p 180).

Fourthly it was held that the existence of a contractual duty of care between the parties does not preclude the concurrence of a tort duty in the same respect.'

He also confirmed that the basis of liability is purely objective and not based on any assessment of the state of mind of the defendant:[3]

> 'The touchstone of liability is not the state of mind of the defendant. An objective test means that the primary focus must be on things said or done by the defendant or on his behalf in dealings with the plaintiff. Obviously, the impact of what a defendant says or does must be judged in the light of the relevant contextual scene. Subject to this qualification the primary focus must be on exchanges (in which term I include statements and conduct) which cross the line between the defendant and the plaintiff.'

1 [1998] 1 WLR 830
2 [1998] 1 WLR 830 at 834E–H.
3 [1998] 1 WLR 830 at 835F–G. See also *Customs & Excise Comrs v Barclays Bank plc* [2006] UKHL 28, [2007] 1 AC 181 at [35] (Lord Hoffmann):

> 'In these cases in which the loss has been caused by the claimant's reliance on information provided by the defendant, it is critical to decide whether the defendant (rather than someone else) assumed responsibility for the accuracy of the information to the claimant (rather than to someone else) or for its use by the claimant for one purpose (rather than another). The answer does not depend upon what the defendant intended but, as in the case of contractual liability, upon what would reasonably be inferred from his conduct against the background of all the circumstances of the case.'

1.19   In hindsight *Williams v Natural Life Health Foods Ltd* can be seen as the high water mark for the assumption of responsibility test. In *Phelps v Hilling-*

don LBC[1], however, where it was held that local authorities could be vicariously liable for the negligence of their educational psychologists, the House of Lords appeared to withdraw from the position adopted in *Williams* and, although he recognised the importance of the assumption of responsibility test, Lord Slynn stated[2] that there are some cases in which: 'the phrase means simply that the law recognises that there is a duty of care. It is not so much that responsibility is assumed as that it is recognized or imposed by law.' In *Customs & Excise Comrs v Barclays Bank plc*[3], where a bank mistakenly made payments out of certain bank accounts with notice of a freezing injunction obtained by the claimant, the court had to determine the question whether the bank owed the claimant a duty of care to comply with the order. Because the bank was not acting voluntarily but under the compulsion of a court order, this case raised directly the question whether it is always necessary to establish an assumption of responsibility for the imposition of a duty of care in negligence. In reaching the conclusion that the bank did not owe the claimant a duty of care the House of Lords rejected the argument that an assumption of responsibility was a necessary ingredient of liability in negligence for economic loss in every case.[4] A number of the speeches also stressed that, in order to provide a meaningful test, it was necessary to show that responsibility was assumed voluntarily (whether expressly or impliedly).[5] That the bank had not assumed responsibility to the claimant for compliance with the order was found to be a significant factor in reaching the conclusion that the bank owed no duty of care.[6] Lord Mance concluded:[7]

> 'This brings me back to what is in my opinion the determinative factor in this case, that is the absence of any real voluntary aspect to the involvement of a third party such as the bank in relation to a claimant's freezing order such as the present. Al-Kandari is a quite different case to the present, since the specific task was there voluntarily undertaken. In *White v Jones* and *Dean v Allin & Watts* the solicitors also acted voluntarily on their clients' instructions, although the scope of their resulting duty was extended to third parties for whose benefit they so acted.'

1 [2001] 2 AC 619.
2 [2001] 2 AC 619 at 654C.
3 [2006] UKHL 28, [2007] 1 AC 181.
4 See, in particular, [4] (Lord Bingham), [35] (Lord Hoffmann), [52] (Lord Rodger) and [93] (Lord Mance) (quoted above). Lord Walker did not expressly address the issue although it is clear from [74] to [77] that he would have been prepared to impose a duty of care in the absence of an assumption of responsibility: see [74] to [77].
5 See, in particular, Lord Walker at [73]:

> '[T]here are (at any rate for a lawyer) two threads of meaning in the word 'voluntary': without compulsion and without remuneration ....The old cases show liability being imposed despite the defendant's conduct having been (in one or both senses) voluntary. As the law has developed (and in the field of pure economic loss) liability is imposed because of the voluntary assumption of responsibility. But in the modern context the word "voluntary" is being used, it seems to me, with the connotation of "conscious",

"considered" or "deliberate". That appears, for instance, in *White v Jones* [1995] 2 AC 207, both in the speech of Lord Browne-Wilkinson, at p 274, and in the dissenting speech of Lord Mustill, at pp 286–287. That is particularly important in considering whether the defendant has undertaken responsibility for economic loss towards anyone other than the person or persons with whom he is in an obviously proximate relationship. In such cases the voluntary assumption of responsibility towards others, judged objectively, may provide the necessary proximity.'

See also *Rowley v Secretary of State for Work and Pensions* [2007] EWCA Civ 598 (above) at [51]–[55] (claim that CSA owed a duty of care to mothers struck out). Dyson LJ stated (at [54] and [55]):

'It is true that the 1991 Act gives the Secretary of State certain discretionary powers, for example, the power to make an interim maintenance assessment, to collect maintenance and to seek liability orders for the purposes of enforcement. But in my judgment, if he decides not to exercise one of these statutory powers, he is not, in making that decision, assuming a voluntary responsibility towards those who are foreseeably affected by it. Likewise, if he decides he will exercise one of the powers, it is not apt to describe what he does when he exercises the power as a voluntary assumption of responsibility. He is not doing anything that is "akin to contract". Even if the tasks performed by caseworkers involve the exercise of skill and judgment, that does not of itself mean that, in performing those tasks, they are voluntarily assuming responsibility to those who are foreseeably affected by what they do. To focus on the elements of skill and judgment is to ignore the requirement that the assumption of responsibility be voluntary if it is to found a common law duty of care.'

6 For Lord Rodger and Lord Mance this was decisive: see [65] and [109]. For Lord Bingham and Lord Hoffmann it was an important element of the reasoning: see [14] and [38]. Lord Walker would have been prepared to impose a duty of care on a bank in the absence of an assumption of responsibility had it not been for the potential consequences to other third parties affected with notice of a freezing order: see [74]–[77].
7 See [109].

1.20   The current position may therefore be stated as follows: it is unnecessary for the claimant to establish in every case that the defendant expressly or impliedly assumed responsibility to the claimant for his or her advice or actions. Even if, on an objective analysis, the defendant cannot be said to have assumed responsibility to the claimant for his or her actions, the court may be satisfied that either of the other tests are satisfied and that it is either fair, just and reasonable to impose a duty of care on the defendant or that the imposition of a duty of care would be 'analogous with or incremental to any previous development of the law'.[1] But where the relationship between the claimant and defendant is sufficiently close or proximate to be 'equivalent to contract' or closely analogous to a contractual relationship, the question whether the defendant assumed responsibility to the claimant is likely to be decisive.[2] This is likely to include almost every case apart from the most exceptional[3] in which it is argued that a solicitor owes a duty of care to a third party who is not a client. Both *Al-Kandari v J R Brown & Co*[4] and *Dean v Allin & Watts*[5] (the two authorities referred to in the extract from Lord Mance's speech in *Customs & Excise Comrs v Barclays Bank plc* above) involved the imposition of a duty of care on a solicitor and in both cases there was a clear assumption of responsibility.[6] Indeed, in each case the critical question is likely to be not whether the solicitor undertook or assumed responsibility for the relevant advice or engagement but whether he or she assumed responsibility for that advice or engagement to the claimant (as well as his or her client).[7]

1 *Customs & Excise Comrs v Barclays Bank plc* [2006] UKHL 28, [2007] 1 AC 181 at [113] (Lord Mance).
2 In *Bank of Credit and Commerce International (Overseas) Ltd v Price Waterhouse (No 2)* [1998] PNLR 564, CA at 587E-588B (auditors) Sir Brian Neill gave the following practical guidance for satisfying the threefold test and the assumption of responsibility test:

> 'The threefold test and the assumption of responsibility test indicate the criteria which have to be satisfied if liability is to attach. But the authorities also provide some guidance as to the factors which are to be taken into account in deciding whether these criteria are met. These factors will include: (a) the precise relationship between (to use convenient terms) the adviser and the advisee. This may be a general relationship or a special relationship which has come into existence for the purpose of a particular transaction. But in my opinion ...there may be an important difference between the cases where the adviser and the advisee are acting at arm's length and cases where they are acting "on the same side of the fence". (b) the precise circumstances in which the advice or information or other material came into existence. Any contract or other relationship with a third party will be relevant. (c) the precise circumstances in which the advice or information or other material was communicated to the advisee, and for what purpose or purposes, and whether the communication was made by the adviser or by a third party. It will be necessary to consider the purpose or purposes of the communication both as seen by the adviser and as seen by the advisee, and the degree of reliance which the adviser intended or should reasonably have anticipated would be placed on its accuracy by the advisee, and the reliance in fact placed on it. (d) the presence or absence of other advisers on whom the advisee would or could rely. This factor is analogous to the likelihood of intermediate examination in product liability cases. (e) the opportunity, if any, given to the adviser to issue a disclaimer.'

This guidance was applied by Lightman J in *Dean v Allin & Watts* [2001] EWCA Civ 758, [2001] Lloyd's Rep PN 605 at [33] (although the case was considered to be an assumption of responsibility case in *Customs & Excise Comrs v Barclays Bank plc*: see n 7, below).
3 For a recent example of a case in which the court has continued to apply the assumption of responsibility test as the primary test for the imposition of a duty of care: see *Precis (521) plc v William M Mercer Ltd* [2005] EWCA Civ 114, [2005] PNLR 28 at [17] to [32] (Arden LJ).
4 [1988] QB 665, CA.
5 [2001] EWCA Civ 758, [2001] Lloyd's Rep PN 605, CA.
6 See *Customs & Excise Comrs v Barclays Bank plc* [2006] UKHL 28, [2007] 1 AC 181 at [21] to [22] (Lord Bingham) and [107] to [109] (Lord Mance).
7 See the helpful comments of Lindsay J on the assumption of responsibility test in *Customs & Excise Comrs v Barclays Bank plc* (above) in the Court of Appeal ([2004] EWCA Civ 1555, [2005] 1 Lloyd's Rep 165 at [51]):

> 'It is useful as it draws attention to the subjective facts: has the defendant, in his conduct with the claimant, said or done anything by which, in effect, he says to the claimant "I'll see to it". His saying so is neither conclusive nor necessary in every case but it is always likely to be relevant. The expression is useful, too, in requiring there to be an examination of the objective situation; there will be collocations of facts which can as fairly require the defendant to be treated as if he had said "I'll see to it" as he would have been had he said it. Lastly, the expression draws attention to the possibility of a negative: was there a subjective disavowal of any assumption responsibility?'

1.21 Where a solicitor is the defendant, therefore, it is unlikely that he or she will be able to show that the damage suffered by the claimant was unforeseeable or that there was insufficient proximity between them in the sense either that the defendant was unaware of the claimant's existence or identity or that the action or advice given by the defendant was not causally connected with the loss suffered. In almost all cases the claim will concern either a transaction or a piece of litigation in which the parties affected are finite and their interests known. The difficulty for the court in deciding whether to impose liability will be that the defendant was not retained by the claimant and was in all likelihood acting for someone else. The principal issue between the parties is likely to remain whether the defendant assumed responsibility to the claimant and, in particular, whether it was reasonable for the claimant to rely on the defendant (and the claimant did so) and whether either expressly or by conduct the defendant led the claimant to believe that he or she could do so.

1.22 It will not be easy for a claimant to satisfy the court on this issue. It is not an automatic bar to a claim that the defendant was not retained by the claimant but retained by someone else. In *Henderson v Merrett* itself it was held that managing agents at Lloyd's owed a duty of care in tort not only to those Names who had contracted with them directly (as members' agents) but also to Indirect Names with whom they had no contract. Lord Goff also stated:[1]

'I for my part cannot see why in principle a party should not assume responsibility to more than one person in respect of the same activity.'

But he later and crucially added:[2]

'I wish however to add that I strongly suspect that the situation which arises in the present case is most unusual; and that in many cases in which a contractual chain comparable to that in the present case is constructed it may well prove to be inconsistent with an assumption of responsibility which has the effect of, so to speak, short circuiting the contractual structure so put in place by the parties. It cannot therefore be inferred from the present case that other sub-agents will be held directly liable to the agent's principal in tort. Let me take the analogy of the common case of the ordinary building contract, under which main contractors contract with the building owner for the construction of the relevant building and the main contractor sub-contracts with sub-contractors and suppliers ... [I]f the sub-contracted work or materials do not in the result conform to the required standard, it will not ordinarily be open to the building owner to sue the sub-contractor or supplier direct under the *Hedley Byrne* principle, claiming damages from him on the basis that he has been negligent in the performance of his functions. For there is generally no assumption of responsibility by the sub-contractor or supplier direct to the building owner, the parties having so structured their relationship that it is inconsistent with any such assumption of responsibility.'[3]

In *Riyad Bank v Ahli United Bank (UK) plc*[4] Moore-Bick J held that an arranging bank owed a direct duty of care to an investing bank and its subsidiary for the evaluation of a fund invested in equipment leases despite the absence of any contractual relationship between the parties. The principal reason why the parties had adopted such a contractual structure was to comply with Sharia law. He held that the relationship between the parties was analogous to the relationship between the managing agents and Indirect Names in *Henderson v Merrett* and that the nature and terms of the contracts governing that relationship were not inconsistent with the assumption of responsibility. His decision was upheld by the Court of Appeal.[5] All of the members of the court agreed that the question whether one took a two-stage approach (i e to consider whether the defendant assumed responsibility to the claimant and then to consider whether this duty was displaced by the contractual arrangements between the various parties) or a single-stage approach (i e to consider whether overall the defendant assumed responsibility to the claimant) was largely a semantic issue.[6] Neuberger LJ summarised the reasons for imposing a duty of care in the following passage:[7]

'In the present case, there were a number of factors which together satisfy me that Moore-Bick J was quite right to conclude that UBK assumed responsibility to the Fund in relation to the advice and other assessments it agreed to provide under the TSA, notwithstanding the contractual structure the parties adopted. Those factors are as follows: i) UBK held itself out as experienced and expert in the field in which it was tendering advice, namely the setting up, the marketing, and the administration of, and the assessing and the acquiring of leases for, entities such as the Fund; ii) The original proposal was that RBE should market the UBK Fund, and when that was changed, and what became the actual structure was proposed, it was not "intended to vary or further refine the relationship between UBK and RBE" (judgment para 53); iii) UBK advised Riyad Bank and its subsidiaries (which included RBE) on, and was closely involved, from the inception, with devising the structure, setting up and marketing, of the Fund, as reflected in the Outline Proposal; iv) As UBK knew, the only reason for the structure which was set up and the establishment of the Fund, and for interposing RBE between UBK and the Fund, was because the Fund did not want to appear to be directly run by a Kuwaiti company; v) Neither RBE nor any other company in the Riyad Bank group had, as UBK knew, any experience or expertise in the field in which the advice was being given by UBK, in particular as to the characteristics and values of leases for the purpose of acquisition by a fund; vi) It was "obvious" (judgment, paragraph 53) to UBK that its advice on leases and their values was provided to RBE on the basis that it would be passed on (effectively uncritically) to the Fund, who would be likely to act on it as the sole expert advice that the Fund would be receiving; vii) Mr Weist, the person responsible for the day-to-day operations of the UBK Fund, regularly attended the Board meetings of the Fund "in an advisory capacity" (judgment, paragraph 55), as well as preparing three detailed reviews of the Fund's portfolio of leases in 1998/9; viii) There was nothing in the express or implied terms of the contract between UBK and RBE, the TSA, or of the contract between RBE and the Fund, the IAA, which is inconsistent with UBK assuming responsibility to the Fund in respect of its advice; ix) There is no logical conceptual or commercial conflict between either or both of the contractual duties owed by UBK to RBE, and by RBE to the Fund, and the tortious duty said to be owed by UBK to the Fund. It is fair to say that, factor (i) merely serves to found the basis for a claim in tort as a matter of principle, and that factors (viii) and (ix) are, as it were, defensive. However, it appears to me that factors (ii) to (vii) inclusive, particularly when taken together, make out a formidable case for justifying the notion that UBK owed a tortious duty of care to the Fund. They also show that this case is very different in its factual background (as well as being very different in its nature and in terms of the contractual provisions it involves) from the type of case discussed by Lord Goff at 195G to 196F in the Henderson case.'

The existence of a parallel contract will not by itself, therefore, displace a duty of care.[8] However, the terms of a parallel contract or chain of contracts may prevent a duty of care arising either because the terms are inconsistent with a duty of care or (contrary to the position in *Riyad Bank v Ahli United Bank (UK) plc*) because they demonstrate that the claimant has not placed reliance on the defendant to ensure that the advice is provided or the engagement is carried out or because the terms may demonstrate that it is unreasonable for the claimant to have placed reliance on the defendant and the defendant could not have been expected to anticipate that reliance.[9]

1   [1995] 2 AC 145 at 195C.
2   [1995] 2 AC 145 at 195G–196F, citing *Simaan General Contracting Co v Pilkington Glass Ltd (No 2)* [1988] QB 758 at 781, CA. For a more recent survey of the authorities relating to contractual chains see *BP plc v Aon Ltd* [2006] EWHC 424 (Comm) at [88] to [110] (Colman J).
3   See also the dissenting speech of Lord Mustill in *White v Jones* [1995] 2 AC 207 at 279B-G where this point is particularly strongly articulated.
4   [2005] EWHC 279 (Comm), [2005] 2 Lloyd's Rep 409.
5   [2006] EWCA Civ 780.
6   See Longmore LJ at [21]:

> 'For my part I regard this as only a terminological debate. Whether one poses a single composite question or a twofold question asking first whether there is, apart from contractual considerations, a duty of care as a matter of general law and secondly whether contractual considerations militate against the imposition of such a duty cannot, in my judgment, matter. The conclusion will be the same in each eventuality. I agree with Mr Brindle that Lord Goff did, in the course of expressing his views, approach the matter in two stages. This may have been as much for clarity of exposition as for any other reason. I do not consider the judge can be criticised for adopting the same approach. I am satisfied that if the judge had asked one composite question, he would have answered it in the same way. The question is whether he was right.'

See also Neuberger LJ at [48] and Buxton LJ at [134].
7 See [49] and [50].
8 See also *BP plc v Aon Ltd* [2006] EWHC 424 (Comm) at [166] where Colman J made the point that:

> 'The presence of a contract or of a contract chain has to have a particular impact. If there is a contract binding between the claimant and defendant, it may exclude liability in tort. If there is no contract binding between them, but instead a chain of contracts by which they are indirectly linked, the existence of the chain and the character of the contracts which comprise it may prevent the defendant's conduct being reasonably understood as the kind of representation necessary to found liability in negligence.'

9 Compare *BP plc v Aon Ltd* [2006] EWHC 424 (Comm) above. See, in particular, [168] where Colman J relied on Lord Steyn's speech in *Williams v Natural Life Health Foods Ltd* [1998] 1 WLR 830, HL at 837: 'This reasoning is instructive. The test is not simply reliance in fact. The test is whether the plaintiff could reasonably rely on an assumption of personal responsibility by the individual who performed the services on behalf of the company.'

3 Duty to third parties: solicitors

1.23 In *Gran Gelato Ltd v Richcliff Ltd*[1] Sir Donald Nicholls V-C held that a solicitor acting for a landlord owed no duty of care to a potential tenant in respect of pre-contract inquiries which were inaccurate. Directing himself by the threefold test he held that it would not be reasonable to impose a duty on the solicitor to a potential purchaser in respect of the work he had undertaken to carry out for the vendor. He stated:

> '[C]aution should be exercised before the law takes the step of concluding that, in any particular context, an agent acting within the scope of his authority on behalf of a known principal, himself owes to third parties a duty of care independent of the duty of care he owes to his principal. There will be cases where it is fair, just and reasonable that there should be such a duty. But, in general, in a case where the principal himself owes a duty of care to the third party, the existence of a further duty of care, owed by the agent to the third party, is not necessary for the reasonable protection of the latter. Good reason, therefore, should exist before the law imposes a duty when the agent already owes to his principal a duty which covers the same ground and the principal is responsible to the third party for his agent's shortcomings. I do not think that there is good reason for such a duty in normal conveyancing transactions.'

In *Dean v Allin & Watts*[2] by contrast the Court of Appeal held that a solicitor acting for a mortgagor owed a duty of care to the mortgagee to ensure that the security (a deposit of title deeds) was effective. In that case, however, the loan was a private one and the solicitor knew that the mortgagee did not intend to instruct his own solicitors and that both parties regarded the security as crucial.

1 [1992] Ch 560 at 571D–E. For a detailed examination of the reasoning in *Gran Gelato* see Evans *Lawyers Liabilities* (2nd en, 2002) ch 2 at 31–47. Evans considers that one justification for treating solicitors differently is that legal advice privilege may prevent them from defending themselves. The High Court of Hong Kong followed *Gran Gelato* in *Trend Publishing (H.K.) Ltd v Vivien Chan & Co* [1996] 2 HKLR 227. In *Green v Turner* [1999] PNLR 28 (HHJ Hegarty QC) the court held that a conveyancing solicitor acting for a purchaser who represented that the Land Registry would accept a statutory declaration and that registration would be effected in four to six weeks owed no duty of care to the purchaser. But in that case the purchaser relied on the information in deciding to enter into a sub-sale and it was held that the loss which he suffered was not within the scope of his duty. See also *Masons v WD King Ltd* [2003] EWHC 3124 (TCC) (HHJ Humphrey Lloyd QC) at [61] where the court found that the solicitors owed no duty of care to a special purpose vehicle formed on the instructions of the client:

> 'The client was the entity which would or might suffer the real loss, namely the sponsor or guarantor of the SPV, here WDK. If the SPV is able to claim then it must have the benefit of a contract or there must be special circumstances to take the situation out of the norm and create a duty of care towards it and, if not discharged properly, resulting liability. Here there were no such circumstances.'

2 [2001] EWCA Civ 758, [2001] Lloyd's Rep PN 605 which was approved by Lord Bingham in *Customs & Excise Comrs v Barclays Bank plc* [2006] UKHL 28, [2007] 1 AC 181 at [22]:

> 'An unsophisticated lender running the business of a car mechanic wanted to lend money to borrowers on the security of real property owned by an associate of the borrowers. The borrowers instructed the defendant solicitors to give effect to this transaction. The solicitors knew that the lender had no solicitor of his own, and there was a meeting between the solicitors and the lender. The solicitors' instructions from the borrower were to provide the lender with effective security, which was for his benefit and was fundamental to the transaction …There was, as the solicitors at all times knew, an identity of interest between borrower and lender. In this situation there was, again, a voluntary assumption of responsibility by the solicitors towards the lender and the trial judge's decision that no duty arose was, I respectfully think, rightly reversed.'

1.24 It is not easy to explain why the existence of a liability owed by the vendor (as principal) to the purchaser was held to prevent the solicitor (as agent) from assuming a duty of care.[1] There are three reasons why this explanation now appears unconvincing. First, principal and agent often owe concurrent duties of care and *Henderson v Merrett* is a good example (albeit in different factual circumstances). In *Merrett* the contracts between the parties were regulated by a by-law and there was a continuing relationship between the Names, the members' agents and the managing agents. Secondly, the liability of the principal to the third party is usually a vicarious liability rather than a personal one which makes it conceptually difficult to see how the principal can be liable if the agent is not. In *Gran Gelato* the vendor would have been liable to the purchaser for damages under the Misrepresentation Act 1967 or for rescission because of the misrepresentation of his agent, his solicitor. Thirdly, in *Standard Chartered Bank v Pakistan National Shipping Corp (Nos 2 and 4)*[2] the House of Lords has confirmed that an agent who commits a tort on behalf of his employer or principal is personally liable for his own wrong whether or not the claimant has a remedy against the employer.

1 See, eg, *BP plc v Aon Ltd* [2006] EWHC 424 (Comm) at [166] where Colman J considered that the fact that D had sub-contracted services to X (i e X was acting as his or her agent) did not change the relevant test for the imposition of a duty of care: 'What then is the position where there is indeed no contract between the claimant (C) and the defendant because the defendant has sub-contracted with X to provide services to C? *Henderson v Merrett Syndicates Ltd* [1995] 2 AC 145, *Williams v Natural Life Health Foods Ltd* [1998] 1 WLR 830 and more recently *Riyad Bank v Ahli United Bank (UK) plc* [2005] 2 Lloyd's Rep 409 clearly show that, subject to one qualification, the test is in substance precisely the same: has there been a sufficient assumption of responsibility?'

2 See [2002] UKHL 42, [2003] AC 959 at [38]–[41] (Lord Hoffmann):

> 'My Lords, the maxim culpa tenet suos auctores may not be the end, but is the beginning of wisdom in these matters. Where someone commits a tortious act, he at least will be liable for the consequences; whether others are liable also depends on the circumstances.'

1.25 In *Gran Gelato* the court also rejected the other argument advanced by the solicitors, that to impose a duty of care to a purchaser on a solicitor would expose the solicitor in every case to a potential conflict of interest.[1] Indeed, in *Dean v Allin & Watts* the conflict between the interests of two parties to a commercial transaction did not prevent the imposition of a duty of care.[2] If *Gran Gelato* cannot be justified on the basis that the solicitor was acting purely as an agent or that there was a potential or actual conflict of interest, the decision cannot be justified either on the basis that the defendants were simply passing on information and were not giving any personal assurance or undertaking to the claimant that the answers were accurate. The answer to the pre-contract inquiry was a legal one, the vendor owed to the purchaser a duty of disclosure and both vendor and purchaser were relying in a real sense on the vendor's solicitors. It may be that the simple explanation for the decision is that the relationship between the vendor's solicitor and the purchaser is more closely analogous to a building sub-contractor and employer[3] or to a solicitor acting for one party in litigation[4] and the opposing party so that the court will not impose a duty of care unless the circumstances are so exceptional that the solicitor can be seen to have given a personal assurance to the purchaser.

1 [1992] Ch 560 at 571B–D.
2 [2001] EWCA Civ 758, [2001] Lloyd's Rep PN 605 at [34] where Lightman J stated: '[W]hilst there was a conflict of interest between the Borrowers and Mr Dean in respect of many aspects of the transactions (e g the rate of interest before and after a default) there was an identity of interest in the provision of effective security.' Robert Walker LJ considered at [69] that there was 'a sufficient identity of interest'. In *Young v Clifford Chance* (Popplewell J, 21 December 1995, unreported) it was held that the client and third party had a community of interest but not an identity of interest but this was insufficient to justify the imposition of a duty of care.
3 This was the reasoning of Popplewell J in *Young v Clifford Chance* (21 December 1995, unreported) although this reasoning now seems inconsistent with the authorities discussed in para 1.22, above. If liability on the part of the vendor was not excluded and there was no exclusion of liability to third parties in the contract of retainer, the contractual relationships between the parties would provide no reason why the solicitor could not have assumed a direct duty of care.
4 In *Customs & Excise Comrs v Barclays Bank plc* [2006] UKHL 28, [2007] 1 AC 181 only Lord Bingham considered the fact that no duty of care is owed by opposing parties in litigation to be decisive. He stated (at [18]):

> 'Secondly, it cannot be suggested that the customer owes a duty to the party which obtains an order, since they are opposing parties in litigation and no duty is owed by a litigating party to its opponent:... It would be a strange and anomalous outcome if an action in negligence lay against a notified party who allowed the horse to escape from the stable but not against the owner who rode it out.'

1.26   Although *Gran Gelato* was cited with approval by Lord Goff in *White v Jones*[1] there is a residual doubt whether it would now be upheld by the Court of Appeal. It was the subject of further analysis by Hobhouse LJ in *McCullagh v Lane Fox & Partners Ltd*[2] who suggested that unless it was confined to a special rule applicable to solicitors in conveyancing transactions, it was inconsistent with the decision of the Court of Appeal in *Punjab National Bank v de Boinville*.[3] However, the majority of the court (Sir Christopher Slade and Nourse LJ) found it unnecessary to consider this point. In *First National Commercial Bank plc v Loxleys*[4] the Court of Appeal accepted, at the strike out stage, that there was sufficient uncertainty in the authorities to make it arguable that a solicitor owed a duty of care to a third party purchaser for the accuracy of pre-contract inquiries and that a disclaimer would be ineffective to prevent that duty arising. Finally, in *Dean v Allin & Watts*[5] the decision was cited with approval although the agency point was not considered. The question of when a solicitor is liable to a potential purchaser for the answers to pre-contract enquiries is considered in detail in chapter 9.[6]

1 [1995] 2 AC 207 at 256D.
2 [1996] 1 EGLR 35 at 44G–J, CA.
3 [1992] 1 Lloyd's Rep 7 (Hobhouse J) and [1992] 3 All ER 104, CA. At first instance Hobhouse J had himself held that insurance brokers, whose function was to place marine cargo policies, owed duty of care in respect of an allegedly negligent placing to a bank to which the policies were assigned to secure payment for the cargo. He also held that the two individual brokers, who were both employees of the corporate brokers, personally owed a duty of care to the assignee bank. He said this (at 27):

> 'Similarly, the liability of the actual employee who is himself involved in the commission of a tort when he is aware of all the facts which give rise to the duty of care owed to the relevant client and is himself the individual through whom the brokerage duties are being carried out likewise falls within established principles.'

The Court of Appeal upheld his conclusion. Staughton LJ stated ([1992] 3 All ER 104 at 118–9):

> 'It is not every employee of a firm or company providing professional services that owes a personal duty of care to the client; it depends what he is employed to do ...But here Mr de Boinville and Mr Deere, whether in their employment with Wrights or with Fieldings, were evidently entrusted with the whole or nearly the whole of the task which their employers undertook. Mr Milligan argued that they were more remote from the bank than their employers. On the contrary, I think that in fact their proximity was greater. While they were employed by Wrights I hold that, as professional men, they owed a duty of care to the bank, since the bank was a client or the client of Wrights. While they were employed by Fieldings they owed a duty of care to the bank by justifiable increment of an existing category, until the bank became a client of Fieldings in July when their duty came within an existing category.'

4 [1997] PNLR 211 at 215B–C.

5 [2001] EWCA Civ 758, [2001] Lloyd's Rep PN 605 at [69] (Robert Walker LJ). Lightman J cited the passage from *White v Jones* referred to above: see [36]. The decision was also cited with approval by the Court of Appeal in *J Jarvis & Sons Ltd v Castle Wharf Developments Ltd* [2001] EWCA Civ 19, [2001] Lloyds Rep PN 308 at [51] (Peter Gibson LJ).
6 At para 9.41 ff.

4 'Stepping outside the solicitor's role'

1.27   In *Gran Gelato*[1] the judge recognised that there would be cases in which a duty of care to a third party would be imposed on a solicitor. He characterised those instances as cases in which the solicitor steps outside his or her role as solicitor for the client and assumes 'a direct responsibility' to the third party. This notion appears to offer the most constructive rationalisation of a solicitor's liability to non-clients. In *Al-Kandari v J R Brown & Co*[2] a solicitor in a matrimonial case who had agreed to hold a defendant's passport (which was also the passport of his two children, who were the subjects of a custody dispute) to the order of the court was held liable to the claimant personally for releasing the passport to an official of the Kuwaiti embassy and failing to attend the following day when the defendant himself obtained the passport and abducted his children. The solicitor was held liable on the basis that 'in voluntarily agreeing to hold the passport to the order of the court the solicitors had stepped outside their role as solicitors for the client and accepted responsibilities towards both their client the plaintiff and the children'[3]. This is, therefore, a good example of a situation in which a solicitor voluntarily assumes a personal responsibility to the claimant. The test whether the defendant had 'stepped outside his role' was applied again in *Abrams v Abrams*.[4] But it was held on the facts of that case that a solicitor acting for one party in litigation owed no duty of care in respect of representations made to the other party in that litigation.[5] Finally, in *Dean v Allin & Watts* where the lender had not instructed his own solicitors and the solicitor acting for the borrowers knew that the lender was relying on him to ensure that the security was effective, Robert Walker LJ considered the circumstances to be exceptional.[6]

1 [1992] Ch 560 at 571G–572B.
2 [1988] QB 665, CA, approved by Lord Bingham in *Customs & Excise Comrs v Barclays Bank plc* [2006] UKHL 28, [2007] 1 AC 181 at [21]:

> 'A defendant husband had on a previous occasion kidnapped two children whose custody was the subject of proceedings before the English court. The plaintiff mother was anxious that the same thing should not happen again. To reassure her the husband deposited his passport (on which the children were entered) with his solicitor, who negligently allowed him to regain possession of the passport and again remove the children. The wife sued her husband's solicitor in negligence, and it was held at first instance [1987] QB 514 and on appeal that the solicitor owed the wife a duty of care. The judge (p 523) found that the solicitor had given the wife an implied undertaking. The Court of Appeal held that the solicitor had accepted responsibilities towards the wife [1998] QB 665, 672, 675 and had acted as an independent custodian of the passport

subject to the joint directions of both parties as well as the court: pp 676, 675. There was in that case a very clear and entirely voluntary assumption of responsibility by the solicitor towards the wife.'

3 [1998] QB 665, 672D.
4 [1996] PNLR 129 (Gage J).
5 The decision on this issue was strictly obiter because Gage J found that the representations alleged by the claimant had not been made and that the representations actually made were not false: see [1996] PNLR 129 at 134–6. Compare *ADT Ltd v BDO Binder Hamlyn* [1996] BCC 808 (May J), a claim made against auditors in which the inquiry was virtually identical.
6 [2001] EWCA Civ 758, [2001] Lloyd's Rep PN 605 at [69]: 'I do not see this as an extension of *White v Jones* but as an example of the sort of exceptional case contemplated by the Vice-Chancellor in *Gran Gelato v Richcliff (Group) Ltd.*'

1.28 The clearest indication that a solicitor has stepped outside his original retainer and undertaken a responsibility to the claimant is where there are direct discussions or communications between the solicitor and the third party. Even if a contract cannot be implied the court is likely to impose a duty of care if the third party has informed the solicitor that he or she is relying on the solicitor's advice and the solicitor has expressly or impliedly accepted this.[1] Where there is no contact at all the court is unlikely to impose a duty of care even if the solicitor is fully aware that the third party is relying on his or her actions or advice. In *A & J Fabrication (Batley) Ltd v Grant Thornton*[2] the absence of any direct relationship between the claimant and the solicitor was held to be critical. In that case no duty of care to an individual creditor was imposed on a liquidator's solicitors who permitted the time limit for bringing misfeasance proceedings to expire. No duty was imposed even though the solicitor was aware that the creditor had originally petitioned to wind the company up and that it had agreed with the liquidator to fund the claim. There are exceptional cases, however, in which the absence of direct communication between the claimant and the solicitor may not prevent the solicitor from assuming a duty of care because the proximity of the parties is so close. In *N M Rothschild & Sons Ltd v Berensons*[3] the defendant solicitors, who were acting for a purchaser, were held to owe a duty of care to the claimant (which was one of a syndicate of banks) for the accuracy of a request for funds. The solicitors did not act for the claimant but for the proposed mortgagee, CFL, to whom the claimant was providing finance under a revolving credit facility. The claimant did not see or receive the funds request which was addressed to the lead bank under the credit facility and it had no communication of any kind with the solicitors. Saville LJ held that there was a duty of care on the basis that it should have been 'self-evident to any reasonably competent solicitor that all those lending would be doing so on the basis that the solicitors had provided to Barclays Bank a true and accurate Funds Request'.[4]

1 The nature and context of the discussions would plainly be relevant to any assumption of responsibility but duties of care outside contract have been imposed in the most informal of circumstances. Compare *Whelton Sinclair v Hyland* [1992] 2 EGLR 158, CA, *Holt v Payne-Skillington* (1996) 77 BLR 51, CA, *ADT v BDO Binder Hamlyn* [1996] BCC 808 (May J) and *Dean v Allin & Watts* [2001] EWCA Civ 758, [2001] Lloyd's Rep PN 605 at [10] and [61] to [62].

2 [1999] PNLR 811 at 817B-818A. Astill J relied on *Young v Clifford Chance* (Popplewell J, 21 December 1995, unreported) and *Wells v First National Commercial Bank* [1998] PNLR 552, CA. The decision is fully consistent with the principle that professionals or office holders ordinarily owe no duty of care to individual creditors or guarantors. For recent decisions in an insolvency context: see *Raja v Austin Gray* [2003] Lloyd's Rep PN 126, CA (no duty of care owed by surveyors acting for receivers to the guarantor of the principal debtor) and *Oldham v Kyrris* [2003] EWCA Civ 1506, [2004] PNLR 317 (no duty owed by administrators to creditors where the directors would have owed no duty). In *Welburn v Dibb Lupton Broomhead* [2002] EWCA Civ 1601, [2003] PNLR 547 a debtor's claim against his solicitors was dismissed on the grounds that the benefit of the claim was vested in his supervisor when he entered an IVA and that he himself had suffered no loss.

3 [1995] NPC 107, [1997] NPC 15, CA.

4 See also *Allied Finance and Investments Ltd v Haddow & Co* [1983] NZLR 22 which was very similar on its facts. It was cited by Nicholls V-C in *Gran Gelato* as a 'stepping outside' case: see [1992] Ch 560 at 572A–B. These two cases are considered further paras 9.41 and 9.46, below. These two cases might also be compared with *Peach Publishing Ltd v Slater & Co* [1998] PNLR 364, CA, where an accountant was held not liable to the purchaser of a company for confirming directly to the purchaser the accuracy of certain management accounts where the *purpose* for which the statement was required was to obtain a warranty from the vendor.

1.29   Where there is no direct contact between the solicitor and the third party at all the following are some of the factors which may indicate whether the proximity of the parties is so close that the solicitor may be taken to have stepped outside the retainer and assumed a duty of care:

(a)   the extent to which the solicitor is aware of the existence and identity of the third party and the nature of his or her interests;

(b)   the extent to which the interests of the third party are the same as the interests of the client and the existence of any actual or potential conflict between them;

(c)   whether the third party has instructed his or her own solicitors and, if so, their role and the extent of their participation in the transaction or litigation;

(d)   the nature of the contractual relationship (or potential relationship) between the client and the third party and the extent to which that relationship is consistent or inconsistent with the existence of a direct duty of care;

(e)   the nature of the information and advice provided to the third party or the actions undertaken by the solicitor and relied upon by him;

(f)   the purpose for which the solicitor supplied the information or advice or undertook the work and the purpose for which the third party made use of it; and

(g)   the existence and terms of any disclaimer.

5   Exclusion of liability

1.30   As indicated, one important question in determining whether a solicitor has undertaken a duty of care is whether he or she disclaims any responsibility to the third party for the consequences of the inaccuracy of information provided or advice tendered. In *Smith v Bush*[1] it was held both that UCTA applied to a disclaimer of liability made by a valuer to a potential purchaser, with whom he had no direct contractual relationship, and that the disclaimer could not negative the existence of a duty of care so that the defendant could escape its provisions.[2] In *Henderson v Merrett Syndicates*,[3] however, it was suggested that an appropriately worded disclaimer might be effective to prevent a duty of care arising at all. The point was then considered in *McCullagh v Lane Fox & Partners Ltd*[4] where it was held that a disclaimer given by an estate agent to the purchaser of a property marketed by him was effective to negative the existence of a duty of care. In both that case and in *Omega Trust Co Ltd v Wright Son & Pepper*[5] it was accepted that a disclaimer would be effective to negative the existence of a duty of care but only if it satisfied the test of reasonableness prescribed by UCTA, s 11(3).[6] In *First National Commercial Bank Plc v Loxleys*,[7] a strike-out case in the context of answers to pre-contract inquiries, this issue was considered again. It was argued that it was illogical to permit the court to take into account a disclaimer at the stage of deciding whether a duty of care arose if the disclaimer could be held unreasonable under UCTA. It was nevertheless held arguable that a disclaimer ought to be taken into account when deciding whether the vendor's solicitor owed a duty of care to the claimant for inaccurate answers, and the Court of Appeal made no attempt to resolve the question whether UCTA could be avoided altogether by a suitably worded disclaimer.[8] Although the effect of UCTA on a direct disclaimer still remains to be resolved, there is clear authority that a defendant who assumes a duty of care in tort to the claimant cannot rely on a limitation or disclaimer contained in a contract with a third party.[9]

1 [1990] 1 AC 831, at 848D and 861D.
2 See UCTA, ss 1(1), 2(2), 11(3) and 13(1). It is clear that UCTA was intended to apply the test of reasonableness to a notice purporting to disclaim a common law duty of care although there is little authority on the meaning of the word 'notice'. UCTCCR (discussed in para 1.05, above) is of no application in this context because it applies only to contractual terms.
3 [1995] 2 AC 145 at 181D–E.
4 [1996] 1 EGLR 35, CA. The decision was obiter because a majority held that no duty arose in any event.
5 [1997] 18 EG 120, CA.
6 In *McCullagh v Lane Fox & Partners Ltd* the whole court appeared to accept that UCTA would apply to *any* disclaimer which assisted the defendant to negative the existence of a duty of care.
7 [1997] PNLR 211, CA, decided before *Omega* but after *McCullagh v Lane Fox & Partners Ltd* which was cited to the court.
8 In *Killick v PWC* [2001] PNLR 1 at [14]–[23] Neuberger J also held that it was arguable that a limitation clause was effective to restrict a duty of care. A similar conclusion was reached by Leveson J in *Partco Ltd v Wragg* (25 September 2001, unreported) where the court refused to strike out a claim that directors of a target company owed a duty of care to the takeover bidder and it was held arguable that a disclaimer in a confidentiality agreement did not satisfy UCTA, s 2(2): see [26] and [35]. In both cases it was assumed that UCTA would apply. Interestingly, Leveson J accepted that oral assurances might negative the effect of the disclaimer altogether: see [28]–[32].
9 See *Precis (521) plc v William M Mercer Ltd* [2005] EWCA Civ 114, [2005] PNLR 28 at [25]–[28] (Arden LJ). In *Killick v PWC* [2001] PNLR 1 (Neuberger J) at [36]–[39] this issue

was permitted to go to trial although the court gave a strong indication that the defendant was likely to fail. In *Killick* the court also considered that the question whether the claimant had seen the limitation clause was likely to be significant in determining whether it satisfied the test of reasonableness under UCTA.

1.31 In the absence of clear authority on this point, it is suggested that the two-stage approach adopted by Hobhouse LJ in *McCullagh v Lane Fox & Partners Ltd*[1] ought to be adopted to direct disclaimers. First, if the defendant gives the claimant a disclaimer, that disclaimer is not to be construed as a contractual provision but to be treated 'as one of the facts relevant to answering the question whether there has been an assumption of responsibility' by the defendant for the relevant statement.[2] The court must ask whether a reasonable person would understand that the defendant was assuming responsibility for the statement in the light of both the disclaimer and all other relevant facts. If the court concludes that, as a consequence of the disclaimer, the defendant owed no duty of care to the claimant, the court must nevertheless go on to consider whether the defendant is precluded from relying on the disclaimer by UCTA.

1 [1996] 1 EGLR 35 at 45F–M, CA. In *Killick v PriceWaterhouseCoopers* [2001] PNLR 1 Neuberger J reached the conclusion that auditors owed a duty of care to shareholders notwithstanding the limitation of liability: see [50]–[53].
2 It is suggested that an appropriately worded disclaimer given by the defendant to a third party *of which the claimant is aware* may be relevant to the question whether the defendant has assumed a duty of care notwithstanding the decision in *Precis (521) plc v William M Mercer Ltd* [2005] EWCA Civ 114 (above). Such a clause may demonstrate that it is unreasonable for the claimant to rely on the defendant or that he or she has not done so.

1.32 If UCTA applies, it is an open question whether a disclaimer of liability made to a third party would be held reasonable. The following factors were identified in *Omega Trust Co Ltd v Wright Son & Pepper*[1] as relevant to the reasonableness of a disclaimer:

  (i)   the burden of satisfying the reasonableness of the disclaimer rests upon the defendant;

  (ii) the court should assess the relative bargaining strengths of the parties;

  (iii) whether it would be reasonably practicable for the third party to have obtained the relevant information or advice for himself or herself;

  (iv) whether to provide the information or advice was 'a straightforward, easily duplicated task'; and

  (v)   the practical consequences of the disclaimer.

On this last point, Henry LJ stated:

'At this moment it is necessary to look at the purpose of the disclaimer. The first and obvious purpose of the disclaimer, as obtained by construction of the document, is to limit the assumption of responsibility to Omega and to no one else. It was clearly entered into to assure clarity, to assure transparency and to assure certainty. The valuer was entitled to do all that could be done to prevent himself having to fight a difficult law suit as to whether he owed a duty to an unknown lender. If his disclaimer had been complied with by either Omega or by the bank, that would have been his position. If his document had been complied with and consent from him had been sought, he could, had he wished, have declined to assume the additional responsibility ... Against this the bank submits that this is simply an uncovenanted benefit to the valuer and it would be unreasonable to let him rely on it. Unreasonable because, had in fact they asked permission of him, he would have granted permission. As to whether he would have granted permission or not we will never know because he was never asked. Certain it was that no fee was paid to him and that he would have been entitled to a fee had permission been sought of him.'[2]

On this basis the disclaimer was held lawful. The same reasoning will apply to most disclaimers given by a professional to a party who is not his client but seeks to rely upon his work if that party could have obtained his own advice or instructed his own solicitors. Even if UCTA applies to a disclaimer given by a solicitor to a third party, the disclaimer is likely to be effective unless there are exceptional circumstances.

1 [1997] 18 EG 120, CA.
2 See also *Killick v PriceWaterhouseCoopers* [2001] PNLR 1 at [19] where Neuberger J set out the following list of factors: 'The way in which the term came into being and is used generally; the strength and the bargaining position of the parties relative to each other; whether the client had an opportunity of entering into a similar contract without having to accept a similar term; how far it would have been practical and convenient to go elsewhere; the reality of the consent of the customer to the term; the size of the limit compared with other limits and widely used standard terms; the availability of insurance to the supplier; the possibility of allowing for an option to contract without the limitation clause but with a price increase in lieu.'

6   An exception: White v Jones

1.33   In *Ross v Caunters*[1] it was held at first instance that a solicitor engaged by a testator owed a duty of care to a potential beneficiary in the preparation and execution of a will. In *White v Jones*[2] the House of Lords confirmed by a majority of three to two that a solicitor did indeed owe such a duty to carry out a client testator's wishes promptly and to prepare a new will for execution. Although the members of the majority each drew comfort from the existing law, it appears that the imposition of liability in such a case should be regarded more as an anomalous exception to the principle upon which a duty of care will be imposed rather than as a development or extension of that principle. Lord Goff considered that *Ross v Caunters* could not be justified on existing principles but relying on the European concept of 'transferred loss' was prepared to 'fashion a remedy to fill a lacuna in the law'. Lord Browne-Wilkinson agreed that the case did not fall within the existing categories of relationship to which the law attaches a duty of care but that it was appropriate to develop a novel category of negligence on the basis that there was a close analogy with existing categories of special relationship giving rise to a duty of care.[3] In *Carr-Glynn v Frearsons*[4] the Court of Appeal confirmed that the duty of care owed by a solicitor to a disappointed beneficiary should be regarded as an exceptional one and this has been emphasised in all subsequent cases.

1 [1980] Ch 297 (Sir Robert Megarry V-C).
2 [1995] 2 AC 207.
3 [1995] 2 AC 207 at 267H–268F, 274E–275E and 292F–295D. Lord Nolan, who agreed with Lord Goff, did not address the novel features of the case. It may be that he would not have imposed a duty of care in every case of a disappointed beneficiary and considered that the involvement and reliance of the beneficiaries in the process of drawing up the will was important, if not critical.
4 [1999] Ch 326, CA.

1.34 At this point it is worth noting briefly what was exceptional about the duty of care owed by a solicitor to a disappointed beneficiary. It is exceptional for two principal reasons. First, reasonable reliance is normally central to the imposition of a duty of care and in almost all other cases it will be necessary to show that the claimant relied on the solicitor either directly or indirectly.[1] In *White v Jones*,[2] by contrast, it was held that reliance is not an essential ingredient of liability. If it were necessary for the beneficiary to establish reliance he or she would not be able to do so. The beneficiary may know about the will and its contents and may have an expectation that the testator will not change it. But the testator is free to change the will at any time. Secondly, where a solicitor acts negligently in the preparation or execution of a will there will be no liability to anyone at all unless a duty of care to the disappointed beneficiary is imposed. Because the will takes effect on death the testator suffers no loss during his or her lifetime as a consequence of his solicitor's negligence. The estate suffers no loss either because, however much the testator's wishes have been frustrated, the net assets in the estate remain the same. If the solicitor owes no duty to the disappointed beneficiary and the individual to whom he or she did owe duties and who relied on his expertise has suffered no loss, a solicitor would escape liability for his or her negligence altogether.[3] In *White v Jones* this reason was considered by Lord Goff to be critical to the imposition of a duty of care.[4]

1 See *N M Rothschild & Sons Ltd v Berenson* [1997] NPC 15, CA (referred to in para 1.28) for an example of 'indirect reliance'. In that case no one from the claimant *read* the report on title which was submitted to the lead bank, Barclays. But the claimant would not have permitted CFL to draw down the credit facility without it.
2 See Sir Donald Nicholls V-C in the Court of Appeal [1995] 2 AC 207 at 221H–222B and Lord Browne-Wilkinson at 272D–G. Lord Goff suggested at 262C that it may be a requirement in the normal case. But compare his views in *Henderson v Merrett Syndicates* [1995] 2 AC 145 at 180E–F.

3 See *Ross v Caunters* [1980] 1 Ch 297 (Sir Robert Megarry V-C) at 303A: 'The only person who
  has a valid claim has suffered no loss, and the only person who has suffered a loss has no valid
  claim.'
4 See [1995] 2 AC 207 at 268E and 276D. See also Stapleton 'Duty of Care: Peripheral Parties and
  Alternative Opportunities for Deterrence' (1995) 111 LQR 301 esp at 324–6 and Evans *Lawyers'
  Liabilities* (2nd edn, 2002), ch 1, 1–30.

1.35 In *White v Jones*[1] the House of Lords recognised as a matter of policy the
unique importance of solicitors in the preparation of wills and the nature and
scope of the exception are considered in detail in chapter 11. But the principle of
transferred loss has also been applied outside the context of wills. In *Hughes v
Richards*[2] the Court of Appeal refused to strike out a claim brought by children,
who were the beneficiaries of a life time settlement, and in *Gorham v British
Telecommunications plc*[3] the Court of Appeal found that a pension provider
owed a duty of care to the dependants of a customer who purchased pension and
life cover. Finally, in *Chappell v Somers & Blake*[4] it was held that an executrix
was entitled to bring a claim on behalf of the beneficiaries of an estate on the
basis that the solicitors whom she had instructed to administer the estate owed a
duty of care to her directly. Neuberger J identified two points of policy which
justify the imposition of a duty of care in cases of this kind.[5] 'The first is that it
would be wrong if the solicitors escaped any liability in a case such as this,
merely because they could identify a dichotomy between the person who can
claim against them for a breach of duty, namely the executrix, and the person
who can be said to have suffered the damage, namely the beneficiary.' 'The
second policy principle appears to me to be that, given that any damages would
ultimately come to the beneficiary, irrespective of who has the right to sue, the
question of whether it is the executrix or the beneficiary who can bring the
proceedings is not of great significance. The essential point is to ensure that
there cannot be double recovery (i e the same damages cannot be recovered
twice, once by the beneficiary and once by the executor).'[6]

1 See [1995] 2 AC 207 at 260E–G (Lord Goff) and 276A–C (Lord Browne-Wilkinson).
2 [2004] EWCA Civ 266, [2004] PNLR 706. See also O'Sullivan 'Professional liability to third
  parties for inter vivos transactions' (2004) 21 PN 142. See paras 11.32 and 11.33, below.
3 [2000] 4 All ER 867, CA.
4 [2003] EWHC 1644 (Ch), [2004] Ch 19. For the facts see para 11.19, below. For further
  discussion, see chapter 11.
5 At [16] and [17].
6 In *Dean v Allin & Watts* [2001] EWCA Civ 758, [2001] Lloyd's Rep PN 605 the Court of Appeal
  placed some reliance on *White v Jones* in reaching the conclusion that a solicitor owed a duty of a
  care to a third party but did not go so far as to suggest that it was a case of transferred loss and
  Robert Walker LJ did not consider the case to be an extension of the *White v Jones* principle. In
  Searles v Cann & Hallett [1999] PNLR 494 (Philip Mott QC) the court also relied on *White v
  Jones* in reaching the conclusion that a firm of solicitors acting for a borrower owed a duty of care
  to a lender to perfect an assignment of a security. In *Goodwill v British Pregnancy Advisory
  Service* [1996] 2 All ER 161, CA, *Reeman v Department of Transport* [1997] PNLR 618, CA at
  635C–D (Phillips LJ), *Wells v First National Commercial Bank* [1998] PNLR 552, CA and *Frost
  v James Finlay Bank Ltd* [2002] EWCA Civ 667, [2002] Lloyds Rep PN 473 at [122]–[128]
  (Longmore LJ), however, the court refused to impose a duty of care at all. None of those cases fell

within the exception or offered a sufficiently close analogy. In the last case the claim failed principally because the claimant was unable to make out her case on the facts that the bank had undertaken to give her insurance advice.

7 An employee's duty of care

1.36 In *Merrett v Babb*[1] an employed valuer was held to be personally liable to a borrower for negligently carrying out a building society valuation. The valuer was employed by a firm whose sole principal had been made bankrupt and who had no insurance against the claim and the employee (who had no insurance either) was held to be liable although in carrying out the valuation he was acting on behalf of his employer and not on his own behalf. In *Merrett v Babb* the Court of Appeal reached this conclusion by following the decision of the House of Lords in *Harris v Wyre DC*[2] where a staff valuer employed by a local authority was held to owe a duty of care to the borrower under a local authority mortgage. May LJ considered[3] that the following statement of Lord Griffiths in *Harris v Wyre DC* applied just as much to the employee of a private firm as it did to a local authority staff valuer:[4] 'The essence of the decision is that the professional person who carries out the inspection and makes the valuation is the person on whom the purchaser relies to exercise proper skill and judgment.' Although there was no contract between the borrower and the firm and no contract between the employee and the building society, the employee was held to have assumed personal responsibility to the borrower on the basis that he was providing a professional service. The reasoning in *Merrett v Babb* appears to be of general application and an employed solicitor who takes personal responsibility for carrying out a particular engagement under a retainer with the firm will also assume a duty of care personally to the relevant client.[5] In the normal case the solicitor can expect a client to claim against the firm and if a claim is made against the solicitor personally he or she can expect to be indemnified against it by an express or implied indemnity from the firm's principals. But this will be of little value if the principal is a sole practitioner and uninsured.[6]

1 [2001] EWCA Civ 214, [2001] QB 1174, CA. The decision was applied by HHJ Mutrie (sitting as a judge of the High Court of Hong Kong) to two employed solicitors (who acted directly for the client) in *Yazhou Travel Investment Co Ltd v Bateson Starr* [2005] PNLR 31 at [44]–[66].
2 [1990] 1 AC 831. This was one of the conjoined appeals heard with *Smith v Eric S Bush*. There was no consideration of the position of the employee. But the defendant was the local authority and not the valuer himself. As a matter of logic, however, it is difficult to see how the local authority could be liable under the principle of vicarious liability unless the valuer was himself liable. Compare the discussion in para 1.24 above.
3 See [44]. Wilson J agreed with May LJ. Aldous LJ dissented on the basis that there was no personal assumption of responsibility by the employee.
4 [1990] 1 AC 831 at 865G.
5 It was cited in *Partco Ltd v Wragg* (Leveson J, 25 September 2001, unreported) at [17] and [18] (where the point was the extent to which an employee can be personally liable) and *Lloyds TSB Bank Ltd v Cooke-Arkwright* (Wright J, 10 October 2001, unreported). It was also referred to by Longmore LJ in the Court of Appeal in *Customs & Excise Comrs v Barclays Bank plc* [2004] EWCA Civ 1555, [2005] 1 Lloyd's Rep 165, CA at [44]. However, *Gran Gelato Ltd v*

Richcliff Ltd [1992] Ch 560 (Sir Donald Nicholls V-C) and *Punjab National Bank v de Boinville* [1992] 1 Lloyd's Rep 7 (Hobhouse J) and [1992] 3 All ER 104, CA (referred to in para 1.26 n 3, above) were not cited to the court.

6 The Law Society's Minimum Terms ensure that one or more of the original principals will be insured against the claim even if the employee is no longer employed by the firm and the firm no longer exists. Even if the employee is sued personally (e g because there is some doubt about the name or make up of the firm at the date on which the cause of action accrued), he or she should be expressly or impliedly indemnified against the claim. It is only where the principals are uninsured (and the employee is also uninsured against the claim) that the decision will work hardship because an employed solicitor will face a claim without insurance cover. This is likely to be in cases where the principal of the firm was a sole practitioner and has either gone bankrupt or failed to maintain any run-off insurance.

Chapter 2

Breach of duty

A THE STANDARD OF CARE

1 Introduction

2.01 Rarely is there any need to make a distinction between the standard of care to be expected of a solicitor in complying with his or her contractual obligations and that imposed by the law of tort. Although it is not suggested that the approach should be different, it is as well to remember that the source of the contractual duty is the implication of a term. The term is either a statutory one implied by virtue of s 13 of the Supply of Goods and Services Act 1982 or implied as a matter of law.[1] The standard required of a solicitor does not go beyond that necessary to give effect to the contract in the relevant circumstances. According to Lord Wilberforce in *Liverpool County Council v Irwin*:[2]

> 'My Lords if, as I think, the test of the existence of the term is necessity the standard must not surely exceed what is necessary having regard to the circumstances. To imply an absolute obligation to repair would go beyond what is a necessary legal incident and indeed would be unreasonable. An obligation to take reasonable care to keep in reasonable repair and usability is what fits the requirements of the case. Such a definition involves–and I think rightly– recognition that the tenants themselves have their responsibilities. What it is reasonable to expect of a landlord has a clear relation to what a reasonable set of tenants should do for themselves.'

This statement has equal relevance to the contractual relationship between a solicitor and his or her client. The solicitor's contract of retainer imposes a duty to achieve a standard of reasonable conduct. As stated, the extent of the duty also depends on what reasonable clients should do for themselves.[3]

1 In *Equitable Life Assurance Society v Hyman* [2002] 1 A.C. 408 at 458G to 459A Lord Steyn distinguished between 'a case in which a term can be implied by law in the sense of incidents impliedly annexed to particular forms of contract' of which he said '[s]uch standardised implied terms operate as general default rules' and 'a term implied from the language [of the contract] read its particular commercial setting' of which he said '[s]uch implied terms operate as ad hoc gap fillers'. The implied term in a contract between solicitor and client falls into the former category. Lord Steyn did not suggest that the scope of the term will differ depending on which

category it falls into but he did suggest that 'an individualised' term can be implied to give effect to the reasonable expectations of the parties: see 459H.
2 [1977] AC 239 at 256G dealing with the obligation to repair.
3 See, eg, *Football League Ltd v Edge & Ellison* [2006] EWHC 1462 (Ch), [2007] PNLR 2 at [266] to [270] considered in para 2.38 (below). In that case the fact that a duty could only be implied as a matter of necessity played an important part in Rimer J's reasoning.

2.02 A solicitor will be liable in negligence if he or she fails to achieve the standard of the reasonably competent practitioner. This standard has been defined, variously, as follows:

> '[W]here you get a situation which involves the use of some special skill or competence, then the test as to whether there has been negligence or not is not the test of the man on the top of the Clapham omnibus, because he has not got this special skill. The test is the standard of the ordinary skilled man exercising and professing to have that special skill; it is well established law that it is sufficient if he exercises the ordinary skill of an ordinary competent man exercising that particular art.'[1]

> 'The test is what the reasonably competent practitioner would do having regard to the standards normally adopted in his profession.'[2]

> 'Those who hold themselves out as qualified to practise other professions, although they are not liable for damage caused by what in the event turns out to have been an error of judgment on some matter upon which the opinions of reasonably informed and competent members of the profession might have differed, are nevertheless liable for damage caused by their advice, acts or omissions in the course of their professional work which no member of the profession who was reasonably well-informed and competent would have given or done or omitted to do.'

> 'No matter what profession it may be, the common law does not impose on those who practise it any liability for damage resulting from what in the result turn out to have been errors of judgment, unless the error was such as no reasonably well-informed and competent member of that profession could have made.'[3]

> 'The standard of care to be applied in negligence actions against an advocate is the same as that applicable to any other skilled professional who has to work in an environment where decisions and exercises of judgment have to be made in often difficult and time-constrained circumstances. It requires a plaintiff to show that the error was one which no reasonable competent member of the relevant profession would have made.'[4]

The burden of proof is on the claimant to establish that the solicitor failed to meet the relevant standard. In other professions it is accepted that this burden is a high one.[5] In the case of solicitors (or barristers) the situation is more problematic because the court may be inclined to apply a higher standard than it would apply in relation to other professions.[6] It is suggested that the appropriate way to resolve this difficulty in cases where the standard of care is in issue is to consider the conduct of the solicitor in two stages: first, whether the advice given or action taken was wrong and, secondly, whether the mistake was one which no reasonable member of the profession would have made.[7] In cases of real doubt on the second question it may be appropriate to adduce expert evidence of practice in the profession. It may also be appropriate to consider whether the practice itself was reasonable. Both of these courses are considered in more detail below.

1 *Bolam v Friern Hospital Management Committee* [1957] 1 WLR 582 at 586, McNair J, formally approved in *Greaves & Co (Contractors) Ltd v Baynham Meikle* [1975] 1 WLR 1095, CA at 1101F (Lord Denning MR), *Maynard v West Midlands Regional Health Authority* [1984] 1 WLR 634, HL at 638 (Lord Scarman) and *Eckersley v Binnie* [1988] 18 CLR 1 at 79, CA ('applied and approved time without number', per Bingham LJ). For recent citations see *Chester v Afshar* [2004] UKHL 41, [2005] AC 134 at [51] (Lord Hope): 'the standard of the ordinary skilled man exercising and professing to have that special skill' and *Jemma Trust Co Ltd v Kippax Beaumont Lewis* [2004] EWHC 703 (Ch) (Etherton J) at [67].

2 *Midland Bank Trust Co Ltd v Hett, Stubbs and Kemp* [1979] Ch 384 at 403 (Oliver J), cited with approval in *Martin Boston & Co v Roberts* [1996] PNLR 45 at 50, CA, in *Balamoan v Holden & Co* [1999] All ER (D) 566, CA and in *John Mowlem Construction plc v Neil F Jones & Co* [2004] EWCA Civ 768, [2004] PNLR 925 at [15].

3 *Saif Ali v Sydney Mitchell & Co* [1980] AC 198 at 218D–E and 220D per Lord Diplock. See also *Ridehalgh v Horsefield* [1994] Ch 205 at 233C–D, CA. For recent citations see, eg, *Bark v Hawley & Rodgers* [2004] EWHC 144 (QB), [2005] PNLR 56 at [34] and *Gosfield School Ltd v Birkett Long* [2005] EWHC 2905 (QB) at [94].

4 *Arthur J.S. Hall & Co v Simons* [2002] 1 AC 615 at 737G (Lord Hobhouse) cited by Baroness Hale in *Moy v Pettman Smith* [2005] UKHL 7, [2005] 1 WLR 581 at [25].

5 See *Phelps v Hillingdon LBC* [2001] 2 AC 619 at 672F (cited in *Carty v Croydon LBC* [2005] EWCA Civ 19, [2005] 2 All ER 519 at [36]) (both education cases): 'Any fear of a flood of claims may be countered by the consideration that in order to get off the ground the claimant must be able to demonstrate that the standard of care fell short of that set by the *Bolam* test: *Bolam v Friern Hospital Management Committee* [1957] 1 WLR 582. That is deliberately and properly a high standard in recognition of the difficult nature of some decisions which those to whom the test applies require to make and of the room for genuine differences of view on the propriety of one course of action as against another.'

6 See Hoffmann 'The Reasonableness of Lawyer's Lapses' (1994) 10 PN 6, Evans *Lawyers' Liabilities* (2nd edn, 2002), ch 4 and *Moy v Pettman Smith* [2005] UKHL 7, [2005] 1 WLR 581 at [26] (Baroness Hale): 'In claims against members of other professions, the court will have expert evidence on whether their conduct has fallen short of this standard. In cases against advocates, however, the court assumes that it can rely upon its own knowledge and experience of advocacy to make that judgment. This brings, as Lord Hope has pointed out, an obvious risk that a judge will ask himself what he would have done in the particular circumstances of the case. But that is not the test. The doctor giving expert evidence in a medical negligence claim is not asked what he himself would have done, but what a reasonable doctor might have done.' See the observations of Brooke LJ to similar effect in *Balamoan v Holden & Co* [1999] All ER (D) 566, CA.

7 This was the approach adopted by Jack J in *Hickman v Blake Lapthorn* [2005] EWHC 2714 (QB), [2006] PNLR 20 at [43]: 'It was submitted to me by Mr Graeme McPherson for Mr Fisher that I should first consider whether the advice was 'wrong' in the light of the instructions and information before Mr Fisher, and second whether it was negligent in the sense that no reasonably

competent barrister would have given it. I accept that this two stage approach may often be helpful, provided that the circumstances are such that a distinction readily appears between what is wrong, or in error, and what is negligent.'

2 The standard of reasonable competence

(*a*) *Level of expertise*

2.03 There is obviously no ideal norm of a solicitor with certain qualifications and experience against which the court can measure the conduct of a defendant. In order to practise a solicitor must hold a valid practising certificate.[1] There are also a number of specific functions carried out by a solicitor's firm for which qualification as a solicitor is a statutory requirement.[2] But many, often more mundane tasks, will be carried out by unqualified staff, possibly trainees, legal executives or paralegals provided that they are subject to adequate supervision.[3]

1 Solicitors Act 1974, s 1 and r 20 of the Solicitors' Code of Conduct 2007. The Law Society has discretion to renew a practising certificate subject to certain conditions: see ss 12 and 13. But even if a solicitor fails to renew his or her practising certificate in time he or she will not automatically lose the benefit of the expired certificate: see s 14.
2 See Solicitors Act 1974, ss 20–25. For instance, s 22 makes it an offence for an unqualified person to draw or prepare, inter alia, a contract for sale or a transfer, conveyance, lease or mortgage relating to land in expectation of fee, gain or reward. See also the Solicitors' Code of Conduct 2007, r 20.02 (which incorporates the section as a rule of professional conduct) and para 8 of the guidance notes to r 8: 'You should also be careful, when dealing with unqualified persons, that you are not involved in possible breaches of the Solicitors Act 1974 in terms of the prohibitions relating to reserved work.' For the position before 1 July 2007 see the *Guide to the Professional Conduct of Solicitors* (1999), Principle 17.04 and Annex 25A.
3 See the Solicitors' Code of Conduct 2007, r 5. For the position before 1 July 2007 see r 13(1) of the Solicitors Practice Rules 1990. A new version of the rule was introduced in 1999: see Annex 3C of the *Guide to the Professional Conduct of Solicitors* (1999). All of these rules provide that every office of a solicitor's firm must be attended and supervised by a solicitor of at least three years' experience: see, in particular, the Solicitors' Code of Conduct 2007, r 5.03(2) and the qualifications for supervision.

2.04 In *Freeman v Marshall & Co*[1] Lawton J held that an unqualified surveyor with limited experience had to satisfy the standard of a trained surveyor when carrying out a professional task. Most clients, however, would not expect every aspect of the work which they entrust to their solicitor to be carried out by a fully qualified member of staff[2] provided that it is appropriate to delegate the task and the unqualified member of staff is properly supervised.[3] There is no decision of an English court which requires that where legal work is properly delegated to an unqualified employee (whether a trainee solicitor or a legal executive), that employee must meet the standard of care to be expected of a fully qualified solicitor. Again, there is no decision which requires that a fully qualified solicitor must have a minimum level of experience. The standard of care which the court will require of a firm and its employees in a negligence action should depend, therefore, on the nature of the particular task which is to be performed, whether it is necessary for a fully qualified solicitor to perform it and, if so, whether a minimum level of experience is also required. It the task is carried out by an unqualified employee or a recently qualified solicitor, it will also depend on whether the task was adequately supervised by a partner or principal.

1 (1966) 200 Estates Gazette 777. See also *Baxter v Gapp* [1938] 4 All ER 457 (Goddard LJ at first instance).
2 See *Zwebner v Mortgage Corpn Ltd* [1997] PNLR 504 at 512D–513D (Lloyd J) (affirmed on appeal [1998] ECGS 104, [1998] PNLR 769, CA), for a factual description of the use of unqualified staff. The judge refused to find that in completing a report on title (which required signature by a qualified solicitor) for a commercial lender an unqualified conveyancing assistant committed a breach of fiduciary duty.
3 For the requirements imposed by the Law Society on the supervision by principals of their staff see the Solicitors' Code of Conduct 2007, r 5.03. In particular, r 5.03(3) provides: 'The system for supervision under 5.03(1) and (2) must include appropriate and effective procedures under which the quality of work undertaken for clients and members of the public is checked with reasonable regularity by suitably experienced and competent persons within the firm, law centre or in-house legal department.' For the position before 1 July 2007 see r 13 of the Solicitors Practice Rules 1990, the *Guide to the Professional Conduct of Solicitors* (1999), Principle 3.07 and Annex 3M. Practice Rule 13 was originally updated in October 2004 and Annex 3M was aimed at sole practitioners but also dealt with the situation where the principal of an office was not always present, eg, because he or she was in court or with a client.

2.05 In most cases the difficulty in identifying the standard of care is probably more apparent than real. The standard which the court will require the solicitor to achieve will depend on a number of issues such as the scope of the retainer, the expertise or experience professed by him or her to the client, the nature of the mistake made (whether a point of law or not), the relevance of any advice sought or received from counsel and any relevant body of practice or rules of conduct. But if the client insists on being represented by a fully qualified solicitor, it will be a breach of duty not to ensure that this instruction is carried out. Furthermore, where the level of expertise required is not addressed by the parties, the client is entitled to assume that day-to-day conduct is in the hands of a qualified solicitor. The decision of the Court of Appeal in *Pilbrow v De Rougemont & Co*[1] emphasises the need to adopt a proper procedure when the client gives instructions.[2] In that case the client called the firm and asked for an appointment. The receptionist put him through to an unqualified legal executive. Throughout the retainer he assumed that she was qualified and she did not correct this impression. The court held that this was a breach of contract:[3]

> 'The crucial initial question is whether the contract between Mr Pilbrow and the firm under which the firm was suing for its fees was a contract to provide legal services or a contract to provide legal services by a solicitor. The fact that he was under the impression that Miss Lee-Haswell was a solicitor and that she did not know this, is entirely attributable to the firm, the way in which its receptionist acted and the firm's failure to send an appropriate client care letter. The firm must take responsibility for this. In my judgment, in the

circumstances of the present case the initial contract was one to provide legal services by a solicitor. The firm did not perform that contract at all. No legal services were provided by any solicitor. Not until all the legal services had been performed did Mr Pilbrow know that the provider was not a solicitor.'

The decision was followed in *Adrian Alan Ltd v Fuglers*.[4] These cases are not authority for the proposition that a solicitor may not delegate simple tasks to a legal executive or a trainee (subject to supervision) and there is clear authority that a solicitor may delegate tasks in appropriate circumstances.[5] However, in complex situations it may be negligent to entrust work to an individual who is insufficiently skilled or experienced to undertake it competently, whatever level of expertise the client is prepared to accept.[6]

1 [1999] 3 All ER 355, CA. The claim was not a claim for negligence and the defence that the work was carried out by an unqualified employee was held to be a defence to the claim.

2 See the Solicitors' Code of Conduct 2007, r 2.02(2)(d): which requires that a solicitor must 'ensure that the client is given, in writing, the name and status of the person dealing with the matter and the name of the person responsible for its overall supervision'. It does not go so far as to require in terms that the solicitor should draw the client's attention to the fact that unqualified or trainee staff may be required to carry out fee-earning work on the file but it may be advisable to make this clear. For the position before 1 July 2007 see para 7(a)(ii) of the Solicitors' Costs Information and Client Care Code (last amended in November 2005) which provides that every solicitor in private practice must ensure that the client is given the name and status of the person dealing with the matter and the name of the principal (or director or member) responsible for overall supervision.

3 [1999] 3 All ER 355 at 359h-i (Schiemann LJ).

4 [2002] EWCA Civ 1655, [2003] PNLR 305. It was held that the client was entitled to recover fees of £20,350 incurred between 1994 and 1997 on the grounds that the defendant firm had employed a struck off solicitor who had misled the client into believing that he was a qualified solicitor.

5 See *Arbiter Group plc v Gill Jennings & Every* [2000] Lloyd's Rep PN 669 at [20] (Swinton Thomas LJ): 'A professional man in appropriate circumstances is entitled to delegate tasks. Whether he is entitled to delegate a particular task will depend upon the nature of the task. He is entitled to delegate some tasks to others but is not entitled to delegate others. It all depends on the nature of the task involved. If he does delegate he must delegate to a suitably qualified and experienced person.' This decision was followed in *Sharratt v London Central Bus Co Ltd* [2003] EWCA Civ 718, [2003] 4 All ER 590 at [181] to [185] where the court also referred to r 13 of the Solicitors Practice Rules 1990 and Annex 21G of the *Guide to the Professional Conduct of Solicitors* (1999). The court also received written submissions from the Law Society.

6 See *Richards v Cox* [1943] 1 KB 139, CA (solicitor's clerk) applied in *Balamoan v Holden & Co* [1999] All ER (D) 566, CA (Brooke LJ): 'A one-man firm cannot expect a lower standard of care to be applied to it merely because it delegates the conduct of its client's affairs to an unqualified member of its staff, however experienced. If the conduct of that member of staff falls below the standard appropriate for a solicitor, and he does not seek appropriate advice from counsel or from a solicitor in the firm when need arises, then the firm cannot complain about a finding of negligence against it.' See also *Summit Financial Group Ltd v Slaughter & May* (Times, 2 April 1999) where the judge held that the defendants were negligent because the drafting of a complicated document was split between two departments without one person assuming overall responsibility and the tax lawyer dealing with it was only very recently qualified and inexperienced and *Hicks v Russell Jones & Walker* [2007] EWHC 940 (Ch) where the defendants were held to be negligent in failing to take advice from leading counsel in relation to an appeal and to respond to certain affidavits filed by the opposing party. Henderson J stated this (at [147]):

'In reaching this conclusion, I do not wish to be unduly critical of Mr Samuels. He was a young and still relatively inexperienced lawyer, with many excellent qualities. He was faced with a very difficult assignment, and demanding clients. It is not surprising that, as he frankly admitted, he felt overwhelmed at times. What he needed was effective and supportive supervision, but on the evidence I have heard this seems to have been signally lacking. His supervising partner, Mr Taylor, was not himself a specialist in commercial litigation or insolvency: I was told that his main area of expertise was defamation. Although Mr Samuels consulted him on a number of occasions, I can find no indication that he got a personal grip on the case or that he provided the necessary leadership in the areas of 'strategy, tactics, economics and merits" for which he said he would be responsible in his letter of 6 January 1998 to the clients. Mr Taylor did not give evidence before me. There was no suggestion that he was for any reason unable to do so, and I think it is reasonable for me to infer that it was not considered his evidence would assist RJW's case.'

2.06   It may also be negligent for a firm or a fully qualified individual to undertake work that calls for particular expertise where the individual defendant or firm has insufficient experience in the relevant field. For instance, it may be negligent for a firm to take on the drafting of a deed of trust or settlement if it is unable to give tax advice on the consequences of the deed. In *Hurlingham Estates Ltd v Wilde & Partners*[1] Lightman J held that a solicitor who had 'next to no knowledge of tax law and was quite unqualified to give tax advice' was negligent in failing to appreciate the application of s 34 of the Income and Corporation Taxes Act 1988, to advise the client of the potential exposure to a tax charge and to structure a commercial agreement to avoid it.

1 [1997] 1 Lloyd's Rep 525 followed by Arden J in *Estill v Cowling, Swift & Kitchen* [2000] Lloyd's Rep PN 378 at 394. In *Stanton v Callaghan* [1998] 4 All ER 961 the decision was treated as authority for the proposition that if the solicitor's scope of work is not defined at the outset of the retainer, it is assumed to include all areas where advice is customarily provided. Compare *Silver v Morris* (1995) 139 NSR (2d) 18 where the court reached the opposite conclusion.

2.07   Where the nature of the retainer requires the services of a solicitor, the standard of the reasonably competent practitioner requires a reasonable level of experience and knowledge on the part of the defendant. It is not unreasonable for a client to expect a firm or an individual to meet a standard which is no lower than that of the solicitor with a reasonable period of experience behind him judged at the date on which the cause of action accrued. In *Duchess of Argyll v Beuselinck*[1] Megarry J left open the question whether the standard of care to be expected of a solicitor is that of the solicitor in general practice or whether a higher standard is required if he or she is an expert in a particular field.[2] A number of decisions since then have confirmed that the appropriate yardstick is the level of expertise to be expected of a solicitor practising in the area or areas in which the defendant practises and has held himself out has having expertise. A solicitor with a predominantly commercial practice should be judged by the standard of his or her peers whereas a High Street firm whose practice consists, for the most part, of domestic conveyancing and general litigation, should be judged by the standards of an experienced practitioner of that type. In *Locke v Camberwell Health Authority*[3] at first instance Morland J held that a litigation solicitor in a medical negligence case was not required to have the specialised expertise of a partner in a firm specialising in medical negligence work but rather that of a solicitor, engaged in litigation in general practice'. But if the solicitor holds himself out as having certain expertise which is greater than that normally to be expected of the reasonably competent solicitor and the retainer requires a solicitor with that expertise, the court will usually require him to demonstrate it.[4] This is consistent with the approach adopted by the court to other professions[5] although there may be cases in which it may be negligent for a solicitor in general practice to accept instructions without having or obtaining some knowledge of a specialist area sufficient to enable him to give adequate instructions to counsel or to appreciate that counsel's advice had omitted to deal with a key point.[6] In *Hicks v Russell Jones & Walker*[7] Henderson J summarised the position in relation to a well-known firm with specific litigation expertise but acting for a legally aided client in the following five propositions:

'(1) Mr Hicks must establish that RJW failed to meet the standard of what a reasonably competent solicitor would do having regard to the standards normally adopted in his profession: see *Midland Bank v Hett, Stubbs & Kemp* [1979] Ch 384, especially at 402–3 per Oliver J (2) RJW should not be judged by the standard of a "particularly meticulous and conscientious practitioner" (ibid). Nor are they liable for what may in the result turn out to have been errors of judgment, "unless the error was such as no reasonably well-informed and competent member of that profession could have made": see *Saif Ali v Sidney Mitchell & Co* [1980] AC 198 at 220D, per Lord Diplock. (3) However, the standard to be applied is in my judgment that of a reasonably competent solicitor with experience in the fields of commercial litigation and insolvency, including the conduct of complex appeals. RJW are a well-known City of London firm, and it would be absurd to judge them by the same standard as a small country firm. In my view it was clearly implicit in Mr Taylor's letter of 6 January 1998 to Mr Hicks and Mrs Spence that RJW held themselves out as possessing the necessary specialist expertise in those areas to deal competently with all the technical and procedural issues raised by the appeal. Compare Jackson & Powell on Professional Liability, sixth edition (2007), at paras 11–096 and 11–097. (4) The conduct of RJW must be judged in the light of events as they appeared at the time, and not with the benefit of hindsight. The warning given by Megarry J in *Duchess of Argyll v Beuselinck* [1972] 2 Lloyd's Rep 172 at 185 is apt, and bears repetition.[8] (5) As Mr Hicks and Mrs Spence were legally aided, RJW were bound to act on their behalf as if they were private clients of moderate means. Furthermore, it was an express (or alternatively an implied) term of RJW's retainer that they would not be required to carry out any work for which legal aid was not available. However, I would emphasise that this principle did not in my judgment absolve RJW from taking all reasonable steps to ensure that legal aid was promptly obtained for the work which they considered it appropriate to carry out on the clients' behalf.'

1 [1972] 2 Lloyd's Rep 172 at 185 col 1.
2 The point was also left open in *Martin Boston & Co v Roberts* [1996] PNLR 45 at 50E, CA.
3 [1990] NLJR 205, affd at [1991] 2 Med LR 249.
4 See *Elcano Acceptance Ltd v Richmond, Richmond, Stambler & Mills* (1989) 68 OR (2d) 165 at 177b where the test applied was the 'reasonably competent solicitor engaged in commercial practice'; *Hurlingham Estates Ltd v Wilde & Partners* [1997] Lloyd's Rep 525 at 529 where Lightman J applied the test of 'any reasonably competent solicitor practising in the field of conveyancing or commercial law'; *Matrix-Securities Ltd v Theodore Goddard* [1998] PNLR 290 where Lloyd J used 'such skill and care as a reasonably competent solicitor in the relevant sector of the profession'; *Balamoan v Holden & Co* [1999] All ER (D) 566, CA (in the passage immediately before the one quoted above) Brooke LJ applied 'the standard of care reasonably to be expected of a reasonably careful litigation solicitor who holds himself out as competent to practise in the field of law in which his client has engaged his services'; and *Green v Collyer Bristow* [1999] Lloyd's Rep PN 798 (Douglas Brown J) at 809: 'a reasonably competent practitioner specialising in whatever area of law the Defendant holds himself out as specialising.'
5 See *Henderson v Merrett Syndicates* [1996] PNLR 32 at 37C (Cresswell J) (accountants and Lloyd's managing agents); *Seymour v Caroline Ockwell & Co* [2005] EWHC 1137 (QB), [2005] PNLR 39 (HHJ Havelock-Allen QC) at [91] (financial adviser): 'It is true that whilst in all cases of professional negligence the standard to be applied is that of a reasonably competent professional, the yardstick of competence may vary according to whether the professional has specialist expertise. A solicitor in the specialist tax department of a firm of solicitors will be judged by reference to what firms with specialist tax departments would do, not by reference to what a high street solicitor would do who has little or no experience of tax work (see eg *Matrix Securities Ltd v Theodore Goddard* [1998] PNLR 290)'; and *Earl of Malmesbury v Strutt & Parker* [2007] EWHC 999 (QB), [2007] PNLR 29 (Jack J) at [110] (surveyor):

> 'The standard of professional skill and care to be expected from Strutt and Parker was that to be expected of a major national firm. It was the competence to be expected from such a firm holding itself out as having the competence to act in connection with the development of land adjacent to an airport. It was to be the competence which might be drawn from the whole firm: that is to say that, if Mr Ashworth was not himself fully competent to deal with a situation, he should draw on the resources of the firm. If the firm could not provide the necessary expertise in a particular situation, it might be necessary to go outside it.'

6 See *Estill v Cowling, Swift & Kitchen* [2000] Lloyd's Rep PN 378 in which D's practice consisted of 'acting for private clients in mainly conveyancing and probate matters' and he had been in practice for over 40 years. Arden J held that he was negligent in failing to appreciate that C would be exposed to an IHT liability by transferring shares in to a discretionary trust rather than adopting another alternative. She stated (at [85]):

> 'To carry out what he had undertaken to do, a reasonably competent solicitor would in my view have taken steps to give himself some general knowledge of the subject. In other words, as respects the tax considerations, he would have read some general outline of the tax implications of setting up a trust, and (having discovered IHT applied to all transfers of value subject to exemption) looked to see what exemptions were available. The point was not some obscure point of tax law.'

7 [2007] EWHC 940 (Ch) at [138]
8 The relevant warning is quoted in para 2.27, below.

(*b*) *Level of fees*

2.08 It has been suggested from time to time that if a solicitor charges a low level of fees, eg, to carry out a basic conveyancing service, the standard of care which the law should impose on him or her should be commensurately lower.[1] In *Johnson v Bingley, Dyson & Furey*[2] expert evidence was admitted to show that in 'cut price conveyancing' a solicitor would not necessarily communicate with his or her client in person. The judge found that if true, this was regrettable but it did not affect the liability of the defendants. This case is, therefore, some authority for the proposition that the standard of care to be expected of a professional in relation to a particular engagement should be the same whatever level of fees he or she charges for that piece of work. It is suggested that where the client cannot afford to pay or the solicitor has agreed to accept reduced fees, the standard to be expected to the solicitor is that set out by Henderson J in *Hicks v Russell Jones & Walker*[3] (above); that he or she is bound to act for the client 'as if they were private clients of moderate means'.

1 See *Duchess of Argyll v Beuselinck* [1972] 2 Lloyd's Rep 172 at 183 col 1. No comment was made on this issue in *Boston v Roberts* [1996] PNLR 45, CA.
2 [1997] PNLR 392 at 406G–407C (Mr Benet Hytner QC).
3 [2007] EWHC 940 (Ch) at [138]. See proposition (5) set out in para 2.07, above.

(*c*) *Knowledge of the law*

2.09 According to Bingham LJ in *Eckersley v Binnie:*[1]

'[A] professional man should command the corpus of knowledge which forms part of the professional equipment of the ordinary member of his profession. He should not lag behind other ordinary assiduous and intelligent members of his profession in knowledge of new advances, discoveries and developments in his field. He should have an awareness as an ordinarily competent practitioner would of the deficiencies in his knowledge and the limitations on his skill. He should be alert to the hazards and risks inherent in any professional task he undertakes to the extent that other ordinarily competent members of the profession would be alert. He must bring to any professional task he undertakes no less expertise, skill and care than other ordinarily competent members of his profession would bring, but need bring no more. The law does not require of a professional man that he be a paragon, combining the qualities of polymath and prophet.'

A similar view had also been taken in Canada in *Central Trust Co v Rafuse*[2] where it was stated that:

'[A] solicitor must have sufficient knowledge of the fundamental issues or principles of law applicable to the particular work he has undertaken to enable him to perceive the need to ascertain the law on the relevant points.'

Because the defendant should have realised when it was necessary to research a point or take counsel's advice it will rarely be a defence that the defendant failed to identify a point of law which would have affected the advice which he or she would have given, the document which he or she would have drafted or the course of action which was adopted.

1 (1988) 18 Con LR 1 at 79, CA. See also *Henderson v Merrett Syndicates* [1996] PNLR 32 (managing agent) at 35 (Cresswell J); *Barings plc v Coopers & Lybrand* [2003] EWHC 1319 (Ch), [2003] PNLR 34 (Evans-Lombe J) (accountant) at [578], [579]: 'BFS' contention on this issue would require Mr Mah to be a prophet rather than ordinarily competent'; and *Regent Leisuretime Ltd v Skerrett* [2006] EWCA Civ 1184, [2007] PNLR 9 at [37] (Sir Peter Gibson): 'It is important to bear in mind the limits of what would be expected of a solicitor. A solicitor is not bound to know all the law. His duty is merely to exercise that reasonable degree of care and skill to be expected of competent and reasonably experienced solicitors.'
2 (1986) 31 DLR (4th) 481.

2.10   Where on the other hand the defendant identifies the point but fails to reach the right answer after adequate consideration, the court is far less likely to find negligence.[1] Again if the defendant identifies the point but is unable to provide full advice (either by personal researches or by instructing counsel) because of the urgency to take action, it is unlikely that the court would find that he or she was negligent.

1 See *Ridehalgh v Horsefield* [1994] Ch 205 at 244B–F, CA.

(d) Reliance on counsel's advice

2.11   In general it is a good answer to a claim for negligence that the defendant relied upon the advice of counsel. In *Locke v Camberwell Health Authority*[1] the Court of Appeal laid down the following principles:

'(1) In general, a solicitor is entitled to rely upon the advice of counsel properly instructed.

(2) For a solicitor without specialist experience in a particular field to rely on counsel's advice is to make normal and proper use of the Bar.

(3) However, he must not do so blindly, but must exercise his own independent judgment. If he reasonably thinks counsel's advice is obviously or glaringly wrong, it is his duty to reject it.'

2.11 *Breach of duty*

In *Ridehalgh v Horsefield*[2] the Court of Appeal qualified the guidance which it had set out in *Locke* by adding a fourth proposition:

> 'A solicitor does not abdicate his professional responsibility when he seeks the advice of counsel. He must apply his mind to the advice received. But the more specialist the nature of the advice, the more reasonable it is likely to be for a solicitor to accept it and act on it'

There are a number of reported decisions in which these propositions have been applied.[3] A solicitor will not be liable unless the issue is within the competence of the solicitor and the advice of counsel is obviously wrong[4] or he or she failed to give adequate instructions.[5] In *Matrix-Securities Ltd v Theodore Goddard*[6], for example, the claimants brought an action against both solicitors and counsel for failure to obtain a tax clearance which was itself the subject of proceedings which reached the House of Lords. The judge held that neither defendant was liable. In relation to the solicitors he accepted as a general proposition that a solicitor is required to bring his own expertise to bear on the issue. But he held that there was no distinction in principle between a general practitioner and a specialist (in this case in tax) and applied the guidance in *Locke*. He concluded[7] that:

> '[I]t is only a solicitor's duty to differ from it [counsel's advice] at that time and to give separate advice or to record reservations separately to the client if there was an important point on which the solicitor regarded Counsel's advice as being seriously wrong.'

1 [1991] 2 Med LR 249 at 254.
2 [1994] Ch 205 at 237G. For a recent statement of the principles based on *Locke* and *Ridehalgh* (which Sir Peter Gibson described as 'impeccable'): see *Regent Leisuretime Ltd v Skerrett* [2006] EWCA Civ 1184, [2007] PNLR 9 at [26] and [34].
3 The authorities to date were reviewed by Sir Christopher Bellamy QC in *Bond v Livingstone* [2001] PNLR 30.
4 See *Davy-Chiesman v Davy-Chiesman* [1984] Fam 48, CA (solicitor held negligent for failure to advise that litigation was doomed to fail despite counsel's advice); *Green v Collyer Bristow* [1999] Lloyds Rep PN 798 (Douglas Brown J) (failure by solicitor and counsel to realise that contract for the sale of land was void under section 2 of the Law of Property (Miscellaneous Provisions) Act 1989); and *Green v Hancocks* [2000] Lloyd's Rep PN 813 (Ferris J) (where the failure by the solicitor to appreciate that the cause of action had vested in the claimant's trustee in bankruptcy was held to be 'something which should be within the competence of an ordinary high street solicitor' although counsel had failed to address the point); and *Hickman v Blake Lapthorn* [2005] EWHC 2714 (QB), [2006] PNLR 20 (Jack J) at [51] (solicitor failed to raise the possibility that rehabilitation might not work in a personal injury claim). See also *Isaac Partnership v Umm Al-Jawaby Oil Service Co Ltd* [2003] EWHC 2539 (QB), [2004] PNLR 136 at [44] where a firm of solicitors were held liable for wasted costs for commencing proceedings when they should have known that there was no contract between the parties. In that case there had been no waiver of privilege in counsel's advice but he had not been involved at a vital stage.
5 See *Estill v Cowling, Swift & Kitchen* [2000] Lloyd's Rep PN 378 (Arden J) (solicitor held liable for failure to give counsel adequate instructions or to appreciate that he had failed to advise on IHT, counsel also liable). See also the first principle formulated by Sir Peter Gibson in *Regent Leisuretime Ltd v Skerrett* [2006] EWCA Civ 1184 at [26] and the reference to 'properly instructed counsel'.

6 [1998] PNLR 290 (Lloyd J). The case can be contrasted with *Hickman v Blake Lapthorn* [2005] EWHC 2714 (QB), [2006] PNLR 20 where it was held that a solicitor was negligent in failing to raise an issue in conference. See also *Reaveley v Safeway Stores plc* [1998] PNLR 526, CA (solicitor held not liable for rejecting Calderbank offer on the advice of counsel); *FirstCity Insurance Group Ltd v Orchard* [2003] PNLR 9 (solicitor held not liable for relying on leading counsel in relation to presentation of a case and counsel not liable either); *Luke v Wansbroughs* [2003] EWHC 3151 (QB), [2005 PNLR 2 (Davis J) (advice of solicitors and counsel to settle was reasonable); *Foster v Alfred Truman* [2003] EWHC 95 (QB) (solicitor held not liable for failure to check additional documents to verify counsel's opinion); *Regent Leisuretime Ltd v Skerrett* [2006] EWCA Civ 1184, [2007] PNLR 9 (solicitors held not liable for relying on counsel's advice in relation to a reflective loss claim and for failing to instruct counsel to advise on whether to join a company to a counterclaim before the limitation period for the claim expired).

7 [1998] PNLR 290 at 323A–B.

(e) Failure to obtain counsel's advice

2.12 In *Ridehalgh v Horsefield*[1] the appellant solicitors acted in both the preparation and advocacy of a case which took two days in the county court but proceeded on the wrong basis. The resulting confusion generated a number of further hearings and appeals. Sir Thomas Bingham MR stated:

> 'The solicitors do not appear to have approached the case in a careless way. There is nothing to contradict their statements that the textbooks they consulted did not give a clear answer to their problem. They could not be expected to bring the expertise of specialist counsel to the case. Nor could they reasonably be expected to be remunerated for prolonged research. We do not think their error was one which no reasonably competent solicitor in general practice could have made.'

This dictum offers some support for the converse proposition that a solicitor is not always obliged to consult counsel on points of law, even where the answer to the question is not straightforward. But the case in question was a possession action in the county court which a solicitor in general practice would usually be able to conduct without any specialist advocacy training or a wide experience. It will not take much, however, for a solicitor to come under a duty to offer his client the opportunity of instructing counsel. In *Balamoan v Holden & Co*[2], for example, the claimant was advised that his claim was worth only £3,000 and when he refused to accept this advice his legal aid certificate was discharged. However, acting in person he accepted an offer of £25,000 plus costs in settlement of his claim. His former solicitors were held liable for failing to seek counsel's advice or taking the necessary steps themselves.[3] Further examples of cases concerned with counsel's advice are considered in chapters 12 and 13.[4]

1 [1994] Ch 205 at 244C, CA.
2 [1999] All ER (D) 566.
3 The claim was remitted to the county court for re-hearing. Brooke LJ stated: 'I am nevertheless of the clear opinion that between January 1989 and May 1991 the defendants failed in the duty of

care they owed to Mr Balamoan to take such steps as were reasonable to ensure either that they took him to see counsel promptly (so that counsel could advise on what evidence should be gathered before the trail went cold) or that they gathered such evidence competently of their own initiative, and that he suffered as a consequence of this breach of duty.'

4 See paras 12.19ff and 13.50ff.

3   The relevance of professional standards and practice

2.13   In *Bolam v Friern Hospital Management Committee*[1] McNair J directed the jury that it would not be right to find a professional guilty of negligence where he had acted in accordance with a practice accepted as proper by a responsible body of medical men skilled in a particular art even if another body of opinion took the contrary view. The correctness of the *Bolam* test was not challenged for 30 years until in *Bolitho v City and Hackney Health Authority*[2] the House of Lords was invited to overrule it. The House declined to do so and, whilst recognising that the court is not bound to accept expert evidence unless it is reasonable, Lord Browne-Wilkinson concluded:[3]

> 'I emphasise that, in my view, it will seldom be right for a judge to reach conclusions that views genuinely held by a competent medical expert are unreasonable. The assessment of medical risks and benefits is a matter of clinical judgment which a judge would not normally be able to make without expert evidence. As the quotation from Lord Scarman makes clear,[4] it would be wrong to allow such assessment to deteriorate into seeking to persuade the judge to prefer one of two views both of which are capable of being logically supported. It is only where a judge can be satisfied that the body of expert opinion cannot be logically supported at all that such opinion will not provide the bench mark by reference to which the defendant's conduct falls to be assessed.'

1 [1957] 1 WLR 582 at 587.
2 [1998] AC 232.
3 [1998] AC 232 at 242C–E.
4 In *Maynard v West Midlands Regional Health Authority* [1984] 1 WLR 634 at 639, HL.

(a) *Professional standards*

2.14   For cases which involve conduct prior to 1 July 2007 the benchmark of the solicitors' profession is the Solicitors Practice Rules 1990, which were amended and updated from time to time and published in the *Guide to the Professional Conduct of Solicitors* (the last full edition of which was published in 1999). For cases which involve conduct after 1 July 2007 the benchmark is the Solicitors' Code of Conduct 2007. Both codes have the force of delegated legislation and the Solicitors Act 1974 contains specific provisions for their enforcement.[1] Although a failure to comply with them may in extreme cases render the contract of retainer between the client and solicitor void for illegality on public policy grounds[2] not every breach automatically renders the retainer unenforceable and not every breach of the subordinate rules or guidance promulgated by the Law Society amounts to a breach of either the Practice Rules or the Code of Conduct.[3] The test for professional misconduct applied by the Solicitors Disciplinary Tribunal in deciding on the appropriate sanction against a solicitor who has committed breaches of the relevant rules of professional conduct is not the standard of reasonable care but a failure to act with integrity, probity or trustworthiness.[4] In some cases the breach or failure may be attributable to a lack of care but in others it may not (or it may be attributable to fraud or dishonesty).

1 Section 31(2) of the Solicitors Act 1974 provides the specific remedy of a complaint to the Solicitors Disciplinary Tribunal. Section 37A of, and Sch1 to, the Act provide an alternative remedy under which the Council of the Law Society may limit the amount of costs recoverable by the solicitor and award compensation for inadequate professional service up to a limit of £15,000. The Council's powers are delegated to the Consumer Complaints Service: see para 1.01 above.
2 See *Awwad v Geraghty* [2001] QB 570 (confidential fee agreement).
3 See *Garbutt v Edwards* [2005] EWCA Civ 1206, [2006] 1 All ER 553 at [37] (Arden LJ) in which it was held that a failure to comply with the Introductions and Referrals Code did not automatically amount to a breach of r 15 of the Solicitors Practice Rules 1990 (now r 2.02 of the Solicitors' Code of Conduct 2007) or render the retainer unenforceable unless it was sufficiently serious. It is suggested that a failure to comply with the individual Principles and general guidance contained in the *Guide to the Professional Conduct of Solicitors* (1999) or the guidance notes to the Solicitors' Code of Conduct 2007 (which is expressed to be non-binding) should be approached in the same way.
4 See *Bolton v the Law Society* [1994] 1 WLR 512, CA at 518B-E (Sir Thomas Bingham MR):

> 'Any solicitor who is shown to have discharged his professional duties with anything less than complete integrity, probity and trustworthiness must expect severe sanctions to be imposed upon him by the Solicitors' Disciplinary Tribunal. Lapses from the required high standard may, of course, take different forms and be of varying degrees. The most serious involves proven dishonesty, whether or not leading to criminal proceedings and criminal penalties. In such cases the tribunal has almost invariably, no matter how strong the mitigation advanced for the solicitor, ordered that he be struck off the Roll of Solicitors … If a solicitor is not shown to have acted dishonestly, but is shown to have fallen below the required standards of integrity, probity and trustworthiness, his lapse is less serious but it remains very serious indeed in a member of a profession whose reputation depends upon trust. A striking-off order will not necessarily follow in such a case, but it may well. The decision whether to strike off or to suspend will often involve a fine and difficult exercise of judgment, to be made by the tribunal as an informed and expert body on all the facts of the case. Only in a very unusual and venial case of this kind would the tribunal be likely to regard as appropriate any order less severe than one of suspension.'

2.15   The Practice Rules or the Code of Conduct provide an obvious starting point for establishing what conduct would be regarded as acceptable by a responsible body of the profession. But not every breach of the Practice Rules or the Code of Conduct (or any failure to comply with the provisions of the *Guide* or the guidance notes to the Code) should be treated as a breach of contract or negligence. In *Hilton v Barker Booth & Eastwood*[1] the House of Lords held that the claimant was entitled to recover substantial damages on the basis that Practice Rule 6 was a contractual term of the retainer between solicitor and client. Practice Rule 6 falls into a special category, it is suggested, because it is a reflection of the fiduciary relationship between solicitor and client[2] and *Hilton* should not be treated as authority for the proposition that it is an implied term of the retainer that a solicitor should comply with the Practice Rules or the Code of Conduct. Such an implied term is not necessary for giving effect to the contract of retainer between solicitor and client. Furthermore, it would have the effect of codifying the duties of a solicitor and imposing strict liability for a failure to comply with rules of conduct and, for the reasons explained above, the Solicitors' Disciplinary Tribunal exercises a disciplinary function and professional misconduct does not have the same boundaries as a private action for negligence. But even if there is no implied obligation to comply with the Practice Rules or the Code of Conduct, a serious failure to do so will carry substantial weight in determining whether a solicitor has been negligent. Three authorities illustrate this point. In *Omega Trust Co Ltd v Wright Son & Pepper (No 2)*[3] the judge stated that the Guide was the 'starting point' in considering whether the defendants had been negligent. In *Mortgage Express Ltd v Bowerman*[4] Sir Thomas Bingham MR relied upon Annex 24L of the *Guide to the Professional Conduct of Solicitors* (which was then in force) in rejecting the submission that a solicitor owed no duty to pass on certain information[5] and in *Patel v Daybells*[6] (which is considered in more detail in para 2.17, below) the Court of Appeal placed some weight on Annex 24N of the *Guide* in reaching the conclusion that the practice of the profession in accepting undertakings was logically defensible. Finally, the court will also pay regard to other views expressed or endorsed by the Law Society.[7]

1 [2005] UKHL 8, [2005] 1 WLR 567 at [30] (Lord Walker):

> 'On this issue of liability both sides have been content for the case to be dealt with as a claim for breach of contract. However, the content of BBE's contractual duty, so far as relevant to this case, has roots in the parties' relationship of trust and confidence.'

2 See also *Ratiu v Conway* [2005] EWCA Civ 1302, [2006] 1 All ER 570 at [73] (Auld LJ):

> 'Where there is a contractual retainer and where it provides expressly or by implication obligations of a fiduciary nature, such obligations must clearly prevail, or "mould" or "inform" the fiduciary nature of the contractual relationship.'

3 [1998] PNLR 337 at 347D–E (Douglas Brown J). The decision of the Court of Appeal striking out the valuer's claim shortly before trial is considered in para 1.32. above. See also *Johnson v Bingley, Dyson & Furey* [1997] PNLR 392 (Benet Hytner QC) at 407E–G (where the judge considered that a failure to comply gave rise to a prima facie case which could have been rebutted by demonstrating that the guidance did not apply in the instant case) and *Kenyon-Brown v Banks & Co* (5 June 1998, unreported) (Peter Leaver QC).
4 [1996] 2 All ER 836 at 842a–d.
5 For a further example see also *Nash v Phillips* (1974) 232 Estates Gazette 1219 (Foster J) at 1222 col 2.
6 [2001] EWCA Civ 1229, [2002] PNLR 6, at [55] and [67] (Robert Walker LJ).

7 See the quotation from Millett LJ's judgment in *Bown v Gould & Swayne* set out in para 2.16, below. In *Edward Wong* (below) the Privy Council was heavily influenced by a report of a subcommittee of the Hong Kong Law Society which was critical of Hong Kong style completions: see 306F–307G. In *G & K Ladenbau v Crawley & De Reya* [1978] 1 WLR 266 Mocatta J relied upon a warning in the Law Society's Gazette: see 278H–279D. In *Sharratt v London Central Bus Co Ltd* [2003] EWCA Civ 718, [2003] 4 All ER 590 (a case on costs) at [185] the Court of Appeal relied on the written opinion of the Law Society.

(b) *Professional practice*

2.16 By contrast, however, there are virtually no reported examples of cases in which the court's decision has turned on the practice adopted by a body of the profession, as expressed by an expert solicitor.[1] One reason for this may be that many cases involve specific transactions where the point is usually whether the drafting was adequate or whether specific advice should have been given.[2] Another reason may be that given by Millett LJ in *Bown v Gould & Swayne*[3] (where one party sought to adduce evidence of conveyancing practice):

> 'Two hundred and fifty years later the practice of investigating title has settled down sufficiently to be well established and recorded in the textbooks. If it is necessary to assist the judge to understand the proper machinery for the deduction and investigation of title, the proper way to do it is to cite the textbooks such as Emmett, Farrand, Williams and Dart, if necessary supplemented by Law Society opinions. In fact, this is a straightforward case in which I doubt that even such references would be necessary.'

In many cases standard conveyancing textbooks will provide the Court with the same assistance that any expert would have done.[4] However, textbooks should not be treated as the equivalent of a respectable body of opinion and there is no authority that a solicitor will be found not liable if he or she adopts a practice endorsed by an academic textbook.[5] In relation to litigation and the other specialist heads of practice considered in Part 2 of this book, an analysis of the individual cases shows that there is rarely a difference of opinion as to the proper practice to be adopted.

1 The only reported modern example is *Esterhuizen v Allied Dunbar Assurance plc* [1998] 2 FLR 668 (Longmore J) where the judge held that a lay will-writer was negligent in relying on the practice of solicitors. In *Patel v Daybells* [2001] EWCA Civ 1229, [2002] PNLR 6 the court heard evidence from one expert on the relevant practice but the principal issue for the court was whether it was logically defensible. In *Societe Internationale de Telecommunications Aeronautiques SC v Wyatt Co (UK) Ltd* [2002] All ER (D) 122 (Park J) at [61] the judge recorded that he had heard expert evidence and found it helpful but that his conclusions represented an overall assessment of the case.

2 See *Tain Investments Ltd v Loxleys* [2004] EWHC 2708 (Ch) in which Blackburne J refused to admit expert evidence on whether it was usual conveyancing practice to agree to a chain of positive covenants. He stated (at [10]): 'Whether or not cl 5 was unusual or abnormal, upon which alone, as I follow it, Mr Gilbert's evidence is proposed to be adduced, appears to me somewhat to

miss the point. The point is whether, in the circumstances of this particular transaction, the proposed inclusion of that clause was something which the defendant firm should have brought to the claimant's attention.' [1996] PNLR 130 at 137A, CA. See also *Football League Ltd v Edge Ellison* [2006] EWHC 1462 (Ch) referred to in para 2.24, below.

3   [1996] PNLR 130, CA.

4   See, eg, *Prestige Properties Ltd v Scottish Provident Institution* [2002] EWHC 330 (Ch) [2003] Ch 1 in which Lightman J referred to the relevant edition of Silverman *The Law Society's Conveyancing Handbook* and described *Ruoff & Roper's Law and Practice of Registered Conveyancing* as 'what may almost be regarded as an official publication of the Land Registry': see [46] and [51].

5   See, eg, *Cottingham v Attey, Bower & Jones* [2000] PNLR 557 in which Rimer J was not prepared to accept the standard form enquiry which the *Conveyancing Handbook* recommended. However, the enquiry was not directly in point and the issue was whether a purchaser's solicitors should have attempted to obtain a copy of a building regulation consent when the vendor's solicitor stated that the vendor no longer retained a copy. The case does demonstrate, however, that textbooks will not be accepted uncritically.

2.17   In those rare cases where it is argued that the routine practice or procedure adopted by an individual solicitor is negligent, it ought to be relevant to that issue whether that same practice is also adopted by a substantial body of the profession.[1] Despite the absence of concrete examples from the authorities, we consider that where solicitors adopt a practice that is also adopted by a substantial body of their profession, there should be no finding of negligence unless, in accordance with *Bolitho,* the practice cannot be defended on a logical basis. Having said this, the court will be less reluctant in cases concerning solicitors' or barristers' negligence than in medical cases to make the judgment that a professional practice is negligent and cannot be defended on a logical basis. In *Edward Wong Ltd v Johnson, Stokes & Master*[2] the Privy Council held that a purchaser's solicitor in Hong Kong who paid the purchase price directly to the vendor's solicitor against an undertaking to provide documents of title was negligent when the vendor's solicitor absconded with the money, even though this practice was commonly followed in Hong Kong. Lord Brightman stated in delivering the judgment of the Board:[3]

> 'As already indicated, the prevalence of the Hong Kong style of completion is established beyond a peradventure. It is particularly well adapted to the conditions in Hong Kong. It has obvious advantages to both solicitors and their clients. Their Lordships intend to say nothing to discourage its continuance. However, in assessing whether the respondents fell short of the standard of care which they owed towards the appellants, three questions must be considered: first, does the practice, as operated by the respondents involve a foreseeable risk? If so, could that risk have been avoided? If so, were the respondents negligent in failing to take avoiding action?'

Having answered the first two questions affirmatively, Lord Brightman then said this:[4]

> 'The risk inherent in the Hong Kong style of completion as operated in the instant case being foreseeable, and readily avoidable, there can

only be an affirmative answer to the third question, whether the respondents were negligent in not foreseeing and avoiding that risk. Their Lordships wish to add that they do not themselves attach blame to Miss Leung for the calamity which occurred. In entrusting the vendor's solicitor Mr Danny Liu with the whole of the money she was merely following the normal practice of her firm, and she had never been instructed to act otherwise in such a case or to take any special precautions.'

If therefore a practice is inherently negligent because it involves a risk to the client which is both reasonably foreseeable and easily avoidable, it is no defence for the defendant to rely upon the fact that it has been adopted either by a substantial body of his profession or, indeed, by the whole profession.

1 For one example see *Brenner v Gregory* (1972) 30 DLR (3d) 672 in which the court accepted that a reasonable body of the solicitor's profession would not have advised a purchaser to give general commercial advice before entering into a contract. This is the only recorded example but it is unlikely that an English court would adopt the same course. Evans *Lawyers' Liabilities* (2nd edn, 2002) para 4—04 states that the practice is different in Canada where it is common to call expert lawyers even on questions whether it is reasonable to make mistakes.
2 [1984] AC 296.
3 [1984] AC 296 at 306E–F.
4 [1984] AC 296 at 308G–309A.

2.18 In *Patel v Daybells*[1] the Court of Appeal had to decide the same question in relation to the practice of accepting undertakings on completion in England some 20 years later. In that case the vendor's solicitor gave an undertaking to discharge the existing charge over the property and to provide a Form 53 (which is no longer in use) evidencing the discharge of the charge. Under normal conveyancing practice at the time the defendants, the purchaser's solicitor, would then have submitted it to the Land Registry with their application to be registered and it would have been discharged and the purchaser registered as the proprietor of the property. However, the vendor was unable to discharge the existing charge, the new lender repossessed the property and it was sold at a loss. The purchaser commenced proceedings against his solicitors. The claimant invited the Court of Appeal to follow *Wong* and argued that the Law Society's Code for Completion by Post[2] and the practice of completing on undertakings was not a reasonable one. The Court of Appeal accepted the general principle that to provide a defence the practice of accepting undertakings had to be logically defensible[3] but unlike the Privy Council in *Wong* concluded that it was. Their reasons for doing so were that the alternative (initially put forward in *Wong*) would have significant disadvantages. It would involve additional costs and, possibly, delay and would involve a new risk.[4] The extent to which *Patel v Daybells* provides general guidance and the question whether a solicitor may always complete in reliance on undertakings are examined in chapter 9. What is of note in the general context is that the Court of Appeal accepted that there was a risk of loss to the purchaser and that it was foreseeable but nevertheless concluded that a solicitor was entitled to adopt it.

2.19 *Breach of duty*

1 [2001] EWCA Civ 1229, [2002] PNLR 6. The Law Society has issued specific guidance
following the decision which may be found on the website of the Solicitors Regulation Authority.
2 The judge did not accept that the code had been adopted although this made no difference to the
central issue (because the parties had completed on the basis of undertakings as the code
provided): see [20]–[23] and [48].
3 See [41] (Robert Walker LJ):

> 'We would unhesitatingly accept the general principle in *Wong*, as restated in the context
> of clinical negligence in *Bolitho*, that conformity to a common (or even universal)
> professional practice is not an automatic defence against liability; the practice must be
> demonstrably reasonable and responsible if it is to give protection.'

4 See [64] (Robert Walker LJ):

> '… the profession's failure to adopt an alternative system cannot be ascribed to compla-
> cency, conservatism, inertia or an unreasonable reluctance to contemplate that a fellow
> solicitor might be dishonest. The alternative system would in our judgment have
> significant disadvantages. It would involve the purchaser in matters (that is, the state of
> the account as between the vendor and his mortgagee) which ought not to be his concern.
> It would involve additional expense and, sometimes, delay. It would also create a new
> risk. If a purchaser's solicitor felt himself obliged to address direct inquiries to the
> mortgagee, and to insist on answers to them, it might be argued that the purchaser had
> been relying on those rather than on the vendor's solicitor's undertaking. If doubt were
> cast on the purchaser's reliance on an unconditional undertaking then the cure might be
> worse than the disease.'

2.19 In both *Wong* and *Patel v Daybells* there was no question that the practice
under scrutiny was employed by a large body of the profession. But it is
important to remember that in all cases involving professionals the *Bolam* test is
not satisfied unless there is evidence of an accepted practice. The court must be
satisfied that both experts are giving evidence of an accepted *practice*. In cases
of professional negligence other than those involving solicitors or barristers the
court cannot usually determine whether the *Bolam* test is satisfied unless the
parties call expert evidence. But where there is a conflict of evidence between
experts it is open to the court to resolve this by deciding that there are two
respectable bodies of opinion or separate but equally respectable schools of
thought (in which case the *Bolam* test is satisfied).[1] Where the two experts are
simply expressing their own views about the way in which they would have
acted in the relevant circumstances, the *Bolam* test is not satisfied. In *JD
Williams & Co Ltd v Michael Hyde & Associates Ltd*[2] the Court of Appeal
identified three exceptions or situations in which the *Bolam* test does not apply:
(1) the professional practice cannot withstand logical analysis (which we have
already considered); (2) the expert evidence does not constitute evidence of a
responsible body of opinion accepting that a particular practice should be
adopted or followed; and (3) if the advice involved no special skill. In that case
the judge had rejected the expert evidence of one party but had not found that it
was logically indefensible. The Court of Appeal dismissed the appeal on the
basis that they would have found that the views expressed by the expert were no
more than his own personal views and not evidence of a particular practice. But
it also concluded that the judge had rejected the expert evidence on the basis that
the case involved no special skill. The issue was whether the defendant architect

should have warned against a specific risk and this did not involve a question of professional skill or judgment that required expert evidence.[3] Similarly, in *G & K Ladenbau Ltd v Crawley and de Reya*[4] the judge was not prepared to accept that 'two equally well-established schools of practice' had emerged by the time the act complained of had taken place. Instead he preferred to accept the evidence of the claimant's expert as laying down, so far as possible, 'a general rule of useful guidance'.[5]

1 See *Nye Saunders & Partners v Alan E Bristow* (1987) 37 Build LR 97, CA at 103.
2 [2001] PNLR 8.
3 This reasoning may appear inconsistent with *Bolitho* (as applied in medical negligence cases) because as a matter of law the court still applies the *Bolam* test in deciding whether a surgeon has a duty to warn: see *Chester v Afshar* [2004] UKHL 41, [2005] 1 AC 134 at [15] (Lord Steyn) and Lord Hope at [48] to [59] describing the difference between 'the reasonable doctor standard' applied in the UK and 'the prudent patient standard' applied in the USA. In practice, however, the inconsistency is more apparent than real because the question whether it is the responsibility of a doctor to inform the patient of a significant risk depends on whether the information is needed so that the patient can determine for him or herself as to what course he or she should adopt: see *Pearce v United Bristol Healthcare NHS Trust* (1998) 48 BMLR 118, CA at 124 (Lord Woolf MR).
4 [1978] 1 WLR 266 at 288H (Mocatta J).
5 For further examples see *Elcano Acceptance Ltd v Richmond, Richmond, Stambler & Mills* (1989) 68 OR (2d) 165 where the defendant had drafted a number of promissory notes for the claimant which contained an interest provision, which was defective for a highly technical reason. This came to light when the promisor took the point, although the action was later settled. The defendant's expert witnesses stated that this was a completely novel defence and that no commercial lawyer would have checked or considered the relevant statute in question. O'Leary J accepted the claimant's evidence but stated that 'even if all the solicitors called to testify had given the same opinion as those called by the defendants' he would still have concluded that the defendant had been negligent: see at 177g–178e. See also *Deeny v Gooda Walker* [1994] CLC 1224 in which Phillips J was not prepared to accept that because a significant number of underwriters were prepared to write 'spiral business' in the market, that was evidence of what constituted reasonable skill and care.

4   The admissibility of expert evidence

2.20 If it is rare that a case gives rise to issues about compliance with a particular practice or the competence of a solicitor or barrister who adopts it, there should be little need for expert evidence from a solicitor or a barrister. For it is only in those cases that the practice of a significant body of the profession is genuinely relevant. Until the advent of the Civil Procedure Rules in 1998 there was a tendency for parties to seek to adduce expert evidence to criticise or defend the conduct of the defendant almost as a matter of routine. But the principle that it is desirable to limit the calling of expert evidence is now embodied in the Civil Procedure Rules themselves and it has become more difficult to obtain permission to adduce expert evidence in the field of solicitors' negligence than it is in cases in other fields.

(a) Jurisdiction

2.21 The jurisdiction to call an expert witness is derived from s 3 of the Civil Evidence Act 1972 which provides that where a person is called as a witness in any civil proceedings, his or her opinion on any relevant matter on which he is qualified to give expert evidence shall be admissible in evidence (although prior to the Act there was jurisdiction to call an expert witness at common law). However, the Court will not permit a party unlimited freedom to call an expert and this principle is clearly embodied in CPR 35.1: 'Expert evidence shall be restricted to that which is reasonably required to resolve the proceedings.' CPR 35.4 sets out the specific powers of the Court to restrict expert evidence:

'(1) No party may call an expert or put in evidence an expert's report without the court's permission. (2) When a party applies for permission under this rule he must identify— (a) the field in which he wishes to rely on expert evidence; and (b) where practicable the expert in that field on whose evidence he wishes to rely. (3) If permission is granted under this rule it shall be in relation only to the expert named or the field identified under paragraph (2). (4) The court may limit the amount of the expert's fees and expenses that the party who wishes to rely on the expert may recover from any other party.'

The question whether to permit a party to call an expert witness and, if so, on what terms is usually determined at a case management conference or pre-trial review.[1] In *Mann v Chetty & Patel*[2] the claimant commenced proceedings against his former solicitors in relation to their conduct of ancillary relief proceedings. The claimant proposed to call four expert witnesses. The Court of Appeal refused to overturn the judge's decision to permit the parties to call one joint valuation expert and permitted the claimant to call one other expert on a limited basis (and also exercised the power under CPR 35.4(4) to limit the amount of the expert's recoverable fees). In reaching this conclusion the court took into account three factors: (a) how cogent the evidence would be; (b) how helpful it would be in resolving any of the issues; and (c) how much it would cost and the relationship of that cost to the sums at stake.[3] In cases of real doubt about whether to permit a party to call an expert there also appears to be jurisdiction to leave the issue to the trial judge rather than deal with it at the case management stage.[4]

---

1 Although this may now seem surprising, it involved a significant departure from the position as it was understood for many years. In *Sullivan v West Yorkshire Passenger Transport Executive* [1985] 2 All ER 134 the Court of Appeal held that the Court had no power to exclude an expert's report in advance of trial. In *Bown v Gould & Swayne* [1996] PNLR 130 the Court of Appeal effectively overruled the decision by holding that there was jurisdiction to do so at a pre-trial review and this was affirmed in *Woodford & Ackroyd v Burgess* [1999] Lloyd's Rep PN 231, CA (which was decided shortly before the CPR were introduced).
2 [2000] EWCA Civ 267, [2001] CP Rep 24.

3 At [31] (Hale LJ).
4 See *Phipson on Evidence* (16th edn, 2005) at 33—28. In *Beazer Homes Ltd v Stroude* [2005] EWCA Civ 265 (referred to by *Phipson*) the Court of Appeal was prepared to leave the question of admissibility of documents to the trial judge. There would be stronger practical reasons for dealing with the issue at an earlier stage in the case of expert evidence.

(b) Admissibility

2.22   The relevance of evidence of a particular practice is dealt with above and, although rarely deployed in cases involving solicitors, it has always been admissible in professional negligence cases where genuinely relevant to an issue in the action. But is an expert confined to giving evidence of this nature or can he give his opinion on whether he considers that the defendant was negligent or has made a mistake which no reasonably competent professional would have made? Prior to the passing of the Civil Evidence Act 1972 it was an open question whether a witness could give evidence on the 'ultimate question', i e the issue which the court had itself to decide.[1] Whatever the right answer at common law the Act abolished the rule and in a proper case expert evidence can now be received on the very question which the judge has to decide.[2] What is a proper case? In *United Bank of Kuwait v Prudential Property Services Ltd*[3] it was held that an expert banker was entitled to state his opinion on the question whether the claimant had been guilty of contributory negligence. In reaching this conclusion, the Court of Appeal emphasised that there is no category of expert evidence that is automatically admissible or inadmissible. The 'overriding principle' is whether the evidence is 'helpful in assisting the Court to reach a fully informed decision'. It may be unnecessary to call evidence relating to a professional practice in simple cases and the court may not be able to reach an informed decision on critical issues of fact without the guidance of an expert in others.[4] It is the current practice of the court in commercial disputes to discourage expert evidence unless clearly necessary.[5]

1 See *Phipson on Evidence* (16th ed, 2005) at 33—12 (earlier editions of which supported the view that expert evidence was admissible on the ultimate question where that question was in substance one of science or skill).
2 See *Glaverbel SA v British Coal Corpn* [1995] RPC 255 at 276, lines 15–29, CA and In *Re M and R (minors)* [1996] 4 All ER 239, CA at 253 (Butler-Sloss LJ).
3 [1995] ECGS 190. CA.
4 Evans LJ, transcript at p 7. In *Routestone Ltd v Minories Finance Ltd* [1997] BCC 180 Jacob J adopted the same approach in admitting the evidence of a specialist valuer about marketing a property: see 188E–190F. Contrast *The Hellespont Ardent* [1997] 2 Lloyd's Rep 547 (Mance J) where the judge refused to admit the evidence of a ship broker on the basis that 'it would not derive from any objectively ascertainable standard or consensus within a recognised profession'; *Re Barings plc (No 5)* [2000] 1 BCLC 523, where the Court of Appeal upheld Jonathan Parker J's refusal to admit expert evidence from an investment banker in relation to a director's disqualification ([1998] All ER(D) 669); and *JP Morgan Chase Bank v Springwell Navigation Corp* [2006] EWHC 2755 (Comm), [2007] 1 All ER (Comm) 549 (Aikens J) at [??]:

'It was argued by Mr Hapgood QC, on behalf of Chase, that it is impermissible for an expert in a particular profession or trade to examine the acts and omissions of a party and express an opinion as to what he, the expert, would himself have done in similar factual circumstances. I accept that submission. However, an expert is entitled to examine an assumed set of facts, which can include assumptions as to what a particular person or party has or has not done, and then give an opinion on whether or not the actions (or inactions) of the relevant person fall below the standard of practice in that profession. Such an opinion can, indeed must, be based on the experience of the particular expert. But the expert's opinion must not reflect what he would or would not have done in certain circumstances. Instead it should say what would reflect the proper standard of practice in the profession concerned in the circumstances being considered.'

5 See *JP Morgan Chase Bank v Springwell Navigation Corpn* (above) at [23]:

'There is a natural tendency of parties and their advisors to consider employing experts to assist in digesting this material, particularly if it relates to any area that might be recondite, such as trading in Russian debt in the 1990s. There is a tendency to think that a judge will be assisted by expert evidence in any area of fact that appears to be outside the 'normal' experience of a Commercial Court judge. The result is that, all too often, the judge is submerged in expert reports which are long, complicated and which stray far outside the particular issue that may be relevant to the case. Production of such expert reports is expensive, time-consuming and may ultimately be counter-productive. That is precisely why CPR Pt 35.1 exists. In my view it is the duty of parties, particularly those involved in large scale commercial litigation, to ensure that they adhere to both the letter and spirit of that rule. And it is the duty of the court, even if only for its own protection, to reject firmly all expert evidence that is not reasonably required to resolve the proceedings.'

2.23 *Barings plc v Coopers & Lybrand*[1] (where one party applied to adduce the evidence of a banking expert) was the first case after the introduction of the CPR to consider the principles to be applied to the admissibility of expert evidence in professional negligence claims. Evans-Lombe J reviewed the relevant authorities[2] and held that expert evidence was admissible. He did so on the basis that there was a body of expertise with recognised standards in relation to futures and derivatives trading. He also considered it significant that this was an area of commerce which was highly regulated, practitioners in which were required to be licensed by the regulator and in respect of which the regulator had prescribed standards of required competence. In the course of his judgment he set out the following guidance:[3]

'In my judgment the authorities which I have cited above establish the following propositions: expert evidence is admissible under s 3 of the Civil Evidence Act 1972 in any case where the Court accepts that there exists a recognised expertise governed by recognised standards and rules of conduct capable of influencing the Court's decision on any of the issues which it has to decide and the witness to be called satisfies the Court that he has a sufficient familiarity with and knowledge of the expertise in question to render his opinion potentially of value in resolving any of those issues. Evidence meeting this test can still be excluded by the Court if the Court takes the view that calling it will not be helpful to the Court in resolving any issue in the case justly. Such evidence will not be helpful where the issue to be decided is one of law or is otherwise one on which the Court is able to come to a fully informed decision without hearing such evidence.'

In *Clarke v Marlborough Fine Art (London) Ltd (No 3)*[4] Patten J adopted the approach set out in the judgement of King CJ in the Australian case of *R v Bonython*[5] (referred to by Evans-Lombe in *Barings*) in deciding whether to admit the evidence of a member of the New York Bar:

'Before admitting the opinion of a witness into evidence as expert testimony, the Judge must consider and decide two questions. The first is whether the subject matter of the opinion falls within the class of subjects upon which expert testimony is permissible. This first question may be divided into two parts: (a) whether the subject matter of the opinion is such that a person without instruction or experience in the area of knowledge or human experience would be able to form a sound judgement on the matter without the assistance of witnesses possessing special knowledge or experience in the area and (b) whether the subject matter of the opinion forms part of a body of knowledge or experience which is sufficiently organised or recognised to be accepted as a reliable body of knowledge or experience, a special acquaintance with which of the witness would render his opinion of assistance to the Court. The second question is whether the witness has acquired by study or experience sufficient knowledge of the subject to render his opinion of value in resolving the issue before the Court.'

Both decisions were applied by Aikens J in *JP Morgan Chase Bank v Springwell Navigation Corp*[6] which involved the consideration whether to admit expert evidence both from a solicitor and from a number of experts on banking and financial markets.[7]

1 [2001] Lloyd's Rep PN 379.
2 Including the authorities on the admissibility of solicitor experts considered below in the context of what amounts to a practice.
3 [2001] Lloyd's Rep PN 379 at [45].
4 [2002] 2 All ER (D) 105.
5 [1984] SASR 45 at 46. See *Barings* (above) at [35]. It was also cited by Mance J in *The Ardent* (above).
6 [2006] EWHC 2755 (Comm), [2007] 1 All ER (Comm) 549.
7 See, in particular, [24] to [33] where Aikens J excluded the evidence of a solicitor directed at the question whether certain financial instruments fell within a specific definition. He distinguished those authorities on which expert evidence is admissible to prove a technical financial meaning on the basis that no technical meaning was pleaded: see, eg, *Kingscroft Insurance Co Ltd v Nissan Fire & Marine Insurance Co Ltd* [2000] 1 All ER (Comm) 272 (Moore-Bick J).

(c) *Solicitor experts*

2.24 Although therefore expert opinion evidence can be admissible as a matter of law on the question whether the defendant was negligent (where the expert evidence relates to another profession), English courts have been very reluctant to allow one solicitor to give evidence criticising or defending the conduct of another solicitor. The reasons for this were explained by Oliver J in *Midland Bank Trust Co Ltd v Hett, Stubbs and Kemp*:[1]

> 'I heard the evidence of a number of practising solicitors. Mr Harman modestly contented himself with calling one; but Mr Gatehouse–mindful, no doubt, of what is said to be divine preference for big battalions–called no less than three. I must say that I doubt the value, or even the admissibility of this sort of evidence, which seems to be becoming customary in cases of this type. The extent of the legal duty in any given situation must, I think, be a question of law for the court. Clearly, if there is some practice in a particular profession, some accepted standard of conduct which is laid down by a professional institute or sanctioned by common usage, evidence of that can and ought to be received. But evidence which really amounts to no more than an expression of opinion by a particular practitioner had he been placed hypothetically and without the benefit of hindsight, in the position of the defendants, is of little assistance to the court; whilst evidence of the witnesses' view of what, as a matter of law, the solicitor's duty was in the particular circumstances of the case is, I should have thought, inadmissible, for that is the very question which it is the court's function to decide.'

This approach was expressly approved by the Court of Appeal in *Bown v Gould & Swayne*[2] where Simon Brown LJ said this:

> 'Each of the seven respects in which the appellant's first affidavit sought to contend that expert evidence would assist the court proves, on analysis, to involve either a question of law or a question of fact. None of those matters can sensibly be regarded as inviting a view as to some practice in [the solicitors'] profession, some accepted standard of conduct ... laid down ... or sanctioned by common usage.
>
> I entirely share the view of the judge below that, on the contrary, the evidence here sought to be adduced falls foul of Oliver J's dictum. It would amount to no more than an expression of opinion by the expert, either as to what he himself *would have done*, which could not assist, or as to what he thinks *should have been done*, which would have been the very issue for the judge to determine.'

Before the introduction of the CPR there was a residual doubt whether these cases were correctly decided and whether the court should adopt the wider approach adopted in relation to other kinds of expert and admit evidence which goes directly to the question whether the defendant was negligent.[3] But whether it is to be regarded as a rule of evidence or a rule of practice upon which the court will exercise its case management powers under CPR 35.4, it is now settled that leave to adduce expert evidence will not be given in solicitors' negligence cases unless that evidence goes to a professional practice and that practice is genuinely relevant to an issue in the action. In the recent case *Football League Ltd v Edge & Ellison*[4] Rimer J confirmed this to be the case. He stated that:

> 'The basic principle is that, with one exception, expert evidence on the duties of a solicitor is not admissible: it is a question of law for the court. It is then a question of fact for the court whether the duty, once identified, has been breached. The exception is that expert evidence is admissible to prove some "practice in a particular profession, some accepted standard of conduct which is laid down by a professional institute or sanctioned by common usage …". (*Midland Bank Trust Co Ltd v Hett, Stubbs & Kemp (a firm)* [1979] Ch 384, at 402, per Oliver J, approved in *Bown v Gould & Swayne* [1996] 1 PNLR 130, at 135 (per Simon Brown LJ) and 136/137 (per Millett LJ)).'

1 [1979] Ch 384 at 402B–E.
2 [1996] PNLR 130 at 135B–D.
3 Unfortunately, the effect of the Civil Evidence Act 1972 was not considered either by Oliver J in *Midland Bank Trust Co Ltd v Hett, Stubbs and Kemp* or by the Court of Appeal in *Bown* and neither *United Bank of Kuwait plc v Prudential Property Services* [1995] ECGS 190, CA nor *Routestone Ltd v Minories Finance Ltd* [1997] BCC 180 (Jacob J) were cited to the court. In *Portman Building Society v Bond & Ingram* [1998] CLY 320 it was argued that both decisions were per incuriam because they failed to take into account the fact that Civil Evidence Act 1972, s 3 had made expert evidence on the ultimate question admissible. This argument was 'unhesitatingly rejected' by the judge.
4 [2006] EWHC 1462 (Ch), [2007] PNLR 2 at [278]. In that case the judge heard evidence from a solicitor in relation to the negotiation of sports rights agreement without prejudice to its admissibility. In his final judgment he concluded that the evidence was inadmissible on the basis that there was no special practice or standard of conduct: see [279]–[280]. See also *JP Morgan Chase Bank v Springwell Navigation Corpn* [2006] EWHC 2755 (Comm), [2007] 1 All ER (Comm) 549 (Aikens J) at [24] to [33] (referred to in para 2.23 n 7 (above)).

2.25 Even in cases where expert evidence of a particular practice may be relevant to issues in the action, the court can still exercise its power under CPR 35.4 to refuse to admit it. But there is little or no guidance in the authorities on the circumstances in which the court should admit that evidence or the factors which should be applied. As Patten J stated in *Clarke v Marlborough Fine Art (London) Ltd (No 3)*[1]:

> 'In the context of claims in negligence an issue has often arisen as to whether the expert may legitimately go so far as to express a view as to whether the conduct of the person in question fell below recognised standards of competence or whether such evidence ought to be limited to more generalised guidance on the usual practice and procedures adopted by professionals in a similar situation. There is

authority both at first instance (*Midland Bank Trust Company Ltd v Hett Stubbs and Kemp* [1979] Ch 384, [1978] 3 All ER 571) and in the Court of Appeal (*Bown v Gould and Swain* [1996] PNLR 130) that expert evidence in this field ought to be restricted to the accepted practice and standards of conduct relevant to the type of defendant professional involved. But neither of these decisions throws light on the question of the admissibility of evidence about the customs and practices of a particular type of business where evidence of that kind would assist the judge in reaching a proper understanding of the issues in the case before him.'

In that case he applied the *Bonython* test that is set out above. He was prepared to accept without deciding that there was a practice and that the proposed expert had relevant experience but declined to admit the evidence on the grounds that the expert's evidence would be limited because of confidentiality and also because the issue to which his evidence was directed (whether the terms agreed between the painter, Francis Bacon, and the Marlborough Gallery was manifestly disadvantageous to him) was essentially a factual question.[2] There are a few comments in other recent authorities that suggest that in the context of undertakings and litigation it may be useful for the court to admit expert evidence but the issue was not fully considered in those cases and they do not go so far as to support a trend towards the admission of expert evidence.[3]

1 [2002] 2 All ER (D) 105 at [6].
2 See [9]–[13], esp at [12]: 'I am not persuaded that for the purpose of considering whether Bacon's dealings with Marlborough call for a justification from the gallery I will be much assisted by being told by Mr Silberman that in his opinion Bacon could have obtained (to use his words) a better deal. That is not the question. A practising lawyer's assessment of what he thinks he or someone in his position might have achieved is necessarily subjective. It seems to me that the Court can perfectly adequately assess whether the terms agreed with Bacon were significantly out of line by knowing the rates of commission or profit and the terms commonly obtained by galleries at the relevant time.'
3 See *United Bank of Kuwait v Hammoud* [1988] 1 WLR 1058 at 1063 quoted in para 5.8, below, and *Moy v Pettman Smith* [2005] UKHL 7, [2005] 1 WLR 581 at [19] (Lord Hope):

'Where a claim is brought for professional negligence the court will usually expect to be provided with some evidence to enable it to assess whether the relevant standard of care has been departed from. No such evidence was adduced in this case. Judges, recalling how things were when they were in practice, no doubt feel confident that they can do this for themselves without evidence. But judges need to be careful lest the decision in the case depends on the standard they would set for themselves. If this were to happen, it would vary from judge to judge and become arbitrary.'

And [26] (Baroness Hale):

'In claims against members of other professions, the court will have expert evidence on whether their conduct has fallen short of this standard. In cases against advocates, however, the court assumes that it can rely upon its own knowledge and experience of advocacy to make that judgment. This brings, as Lord Hope has pointed out, an obvious risk that a judge will ask himself what he would have done in the particular circumstances of the case. But that is not the test. The doctor giving expert evidence in a medical negligence claim is not asked what he himself would have done, but what a reasonable doctor might have done.'

5 Errors of judgment and slips

2.26 In many cases a solicitor or barrister is called on to exercise his or her judgment in deciding what advice to give to a client or what action to take. The court will not automatically hold a solicitor liable even if, with the benefit of hindsight, the advice that was given or the action that was taken (or not taken) turns out to be wrong. The court draws a distinction between 'an error that is so blatant as to amount to negligence and an exercise of judgment that, though in the event it turned out to be mistaken, was not outside the range of possible courses of action that in the circumstances reasonably competent members of the profession might take.'[1] This standard was defended by Bingham LJ in *Eckersley v Binnie*[2] on the following basis:

'[I]t is easy and tempting to impose too high a standard in order to see that the innocent victims of the disaster are compensated by the defendants' insurers. Many would wish that the right to recovery in such cases did not depend on proof of negligence. But so long as it does, defendants are not to be held negligent unless they are in truth held to have fallen short of the standards I have mentioned.'

In *Wilsher v Essex Area Health Authority*[3] Mustill LJ made the following statement to the same effect:

'The risks which actions for professional negligence bring to the public as a whole, in the shape of an instinct on the part of the professional man to play for safety, are serious and are now well recognised. Nevertheless, the proper response cannot be to temper the wind to the professional man. If he assumes to perform a task, he must bring to it the appropriate care and skill. What the courts can do, however, is to bear constantly in mind that, in those situations which call for the exercise of judgment, the fact that in retrospect the choice actually made can be shown to have turned out badly is not itself a proof of negligence; and to remember that the duty of care is not a warranty of a perfect result.'

1 *Saif Ali v Sydney Mitchell & Co* [1980] AC 198 at 220H–221A (Lord Diplock). See also 214F–G (Lord Wilberforce), 218D (Lord Diplock) which is quoted in para 2.02 (above) and 231C–D (Lord Salmon); *Martin Boston & Co v Roberts* [1996] PNLR 45, CA at 50E; *McFarlane v Wilkinson* [1997] 2 Lloyds Rep 259, CA at 274–5 (Brooke LJ); *Arthur JS Hall & Co v Simons* [2002] 1 AC 615 at 737H (Lord Hobhouse); and *Griffin v Kingsmill* [2001] EWCA Civ 934, [2001] Lloyd's Rep PN 716 at [61] and [62] (Stuart-Smith LJ).

2   (1988) 18 Con LR 1 at 79. CA, applied in *Barings plc v Coopers & Lybrand* [2003] EWHC 1319
    (Ch), [2003] PNLR 34 at 579 and *Day v High Performance Sports Ltd* [2003] EWHC 197 (QB) in
    which Hunt J emphasised the importance of distinguishing between errors of judgment and
    negligence.
3   [1987] QB 730, CA at 747A–C.

2.27   However difficult the process is, the court must also apply the appropriate standard without the benefit of hindsight. According to Megarry J in
Duchess of Argyll v Beuselinck:[1]

> 'In this world there are few things that could not have been better
> done if done with hindsight. The advantages of hindsight include the
> benefit of having a sufficient indication of which of the many factors
> are important and which are unimportant. But hindsight is not a
> touchstone of negligence.'

1   [1972] 2 Lloyd's Rep 172 at 185 col 1 (Megarry J) applied in *Prestige Properties Ltd v Scottish
    Provident Institution* [2002] EWHC 330 (Ch), [2003] Ch 1 at [45] (reliance on a Land Registry
    search held not to be negligent), *Brinn v Russell Jones & Walker* [2002] EWHC 2727 (QB),
    [2003] Lloyd's Rep PN 70 at [20] (failure to join editor and journalist to a libel action personally
    held not to be negligent) and *Hicks v Russell Jones & Walker* [2007] EWHC 940 (Ch) (Henderson
    J) at [138] quoted in para 2.7, above (failure to take advice from counsel and to respond to
    evidence held to be negligent).

2.28   What will the court characterise, without hindsight, as an error of
judgment that does not amount to negligence? As Lord Fraser stated in *White-
house v* Jordan:[1] 'Merely to describe something as an error of judgment tells us
nothing about whether it is negligent or not. The true position is that an error of
judgment may, or may not be, negligent; it depends on the nature of the error.'
This issue often arises in the context of advice given by solicitors and counsel to
accept or reject settlement offers in litigation. In *Griffin v Kingsmill*[2] Stuart-
Smith identified the sort of factors which would influence the court's decision:

> 'The circumstances in which barristers and solicitors have to exer-
> cise their judgment vary enormously. On the one hand decisions
> have frequently to be made in court with little time for mature
> consideration or discussion. That is a situation familiar to any
> advocate. It is one in which it may be very difficult to categorise the
> advocate's decision as negligent even if later events proved it to have
> been wrong. Or in a complex case it may be that in advising
> settlement too much weight is given to some factors and not enough
> to others. Here again a difficult judgment has to be made; and unless
> the advice was blatantly wrong, i e such as no competent and
> experienced practitioner would give it, it cannot be impugned and
> the prospects of successfully doing so would seem very slight.'[3]

The issue arises less frequently in the context of transactional advice.[4] But the
principle remains the same. If the court considers that the defendant was

justified in advising or permitting the client to take or ignore a risk, he or she will not be found negligent. But if the risk was unjustifiably high the defendant will nevertheless be found negligent even though it may have been consciously considered and discounted. Although it is a case involving litigation *Martin Boston & Co v Roberts*[5] illustrates the kind of commercial risk which it will be negligent for a solicitor to discount or ignore. In that case the defendants acted for a firm of surveyors in a claim brought against them by a former client (a company). They were found negligent for accepting an offer by the claimant to provide security for costs by means of a personal guarantee from an individual without insisting on some form of security to back the guarantee (e g a charge or restriction on property). In correspondence, the claimant's solicitors had indicated that the guarantor owned freehold property in which there was equity of £65,000. The third party later defaulted on the guarantee and by the time of enforcement had recharged the property a number of times. It was argued on appeal that the court had imposed too high a standard of care. A majority of the Court of Appeal rejected this submission on the basis that the risk of the third party charging the property, if free to do so, was both clearly and obviously foreseeable and also avoidable, and in those circumstances the solicitors ought to have protected their client's position by insisting on some form of security or at least obtaining the client's instructions to take this risk.[6]

1 [1981] 1 WLR 246, HL at 263E–F.
2 [2001] EWCA Civ 934, [2001] Lloyd's Rep PN 716 at [63] (Stuart-Smith LJ).
3 Both solicitors and counsel were held liable for advising the claimant to accept a poor offer. In relation to the solicitors the court found that the advice to accept flowed from 'an unjustified rejection or assessment' of one witness's evidence and 'the failure to appreciate the weakness' in the evidence of another and 'to appreciate the alternative line of argument' which it provided: see [63]. Compare *Wilkinson v McFarlane* [1997] 2 Lloyd's Rep 259, CA (failure to plead alternative claim for breach of statutory duty not negligent); *Firstcity Insurance Group Ltd v Orchard* [2002] EWHC 1433 (QB), [2003] PNLR 9 at [81] (failure to take an alternative argument not negligent); *Walker v Chruszcz* [2006] EWHC 64 (QB) 64 at [101] (advice to settle not negligent because the view taken that the reliability of the claimant and his performance in the witness box were central to success on liability was a justified and reasonable one); *David Truex Solicitor v Kitchin* [2007] EWCA Civ 618 (failure to advise promptly to apply for legal aid held negligent); and *Woodfine Leeds Smith v Russell* [2007] EWHC 603 (QB) (failure to advise an interim payment not negligent but failure to advise an application under CPR Part 31.16 held negligent). See also *Vision Golf Ltd v Weightmans* [2005] EWHC 1675 (Ch) (where it was conceded that a failure to apply for relief against forfeiture was negligent).
4 For a conveyancing example of an error of judgment that was not negligent, see *Neighbour v Barker* (1992) 40 EG 140, CA. For a commercial example where solicitors were held not liable for failing to include specific provisions in an employee share scheme, see *SITA v Wyatt Co (UK) Ltd* [2002] EWHC 2025 (Ch) at [91] to [105]. For a further example where counsel was held not to be negligent where he considered but dismissed the possibility of serving a second protective notice under the Leasehold Reform Act 1967, see *Jassi v Gallagher* [2006] EWCA Civ 1065, [2007] PNLR 4.
5 [1996] PNLR 45, CA.
6 See Simon Brown LJ at 52A–G and Henry LJ at 56E–F and 57D. Ward LJ dissented on the basis that this was 'an error of judgment': see 60D–E. He considered that the defendants were justified in taking the view that the application for security might not succeed. Both Simon Brown and Henry LJJ considered it a wholly obvious case: see 54C and 55G.

2.29 The majority of claims for negligence do not involve the exercise of judgment but routine mistakes. A more lenient attitude to such mistakes can be detected in the cases before the development and expansion of the tort of negligence in *Hedley Byrne*.[1] In *Simmons v Pennington*[2] a solicitor's clerk answered a requisition on title in a standard form but because of the circumstances of the case, inadvertently gave the purchaser an opportunity to rescind, which was taken. Denning LJ described this as 'a mistake' and 'one of those misadventures or misfortunes that sometimes happen even in the best conducted businesses'. Where an isolated mistake is made by an otherwise blameless solicitor of unimpeachable reputation and experience, a mistake that any professional is bound to make in the course of his practice, this will nevertheless be characterised as negligence. In *Sykes v Midland Bank Executor and Trustee Co Ltd*[3] the mistake in issue was described thus by Salmon LJ:[4]

> 'Reluctant though I am to find any negligence against a dead man who enjoyed the highest professional reputation I feel driven to the conclusion that Mr Rignall was negligent in overlooking this clause and failing to bring it to his clients' attention. The common law, of course, recognises no degrees of negligence, but I should like to say that, in my view, the degree of blame in the present case was slight. It was the sort of negligence many a competent professional man many have committed on some isolated occasion in the course of his career.'[5]

In an article published in 1996 called 'The Reasonableness of Lawyers' Lapses'[6] Lord Hoffmann identified the increasing, insurance-driven, willingness of the courts to find solicitors in non-contentious work negligent without the attribution of any moral fault and this remains the trend.[7]

1 [1964] AC 465.
2 [1955] 1 WLR 183 at 186–7 and 189, CA. As late as 1955 Hodson LJ was applying the test of 'crassa negligentia' in *Fletcher & Son v Jubb, Booth & Honeywell* [1920] 1 KB 275.
3 [1971] 1 QB 113, CA.
4 [1971] 1 QB 113 at 126E.
5 See also *Creech v Mayorcas* (1966) 198 Estates Gazette 1091 esp col 2, in which Pennycuick J had 'formed a high opinion' of the solicitor and considered the slip 'an understandable one' but nevertheless found the defendants negligent. The same approach was also adopted in Commonwealth jurisdictions. In *Ron Miller Realty Ltd v Wotherspoon and Beedell* (1992) 4 OR (3d) 492, varied (1993) 16 OR (3d) 255 it was expressly argued that the mistake made by the defendants would have been made by most lawyers but, even though the judge accepted this, they were held to be liable.
6 (1994) 10 PN 6. See also Evans *Lawyers' Liabilites* (2nd edn, 2002), ch 4.
7 See, eg, *Fulham Leisure Holdings Ltd v Nicholson Graham & Jones* [2006] EWHC 2017 (Ch), [2006] 4 All ER 1397 in which a solicitor was held negligent for removing words from a draft by mistake. Mann J stated this at [186]: 'It was, as I have said, an accident. However, it was still negligent. The fact that it occurred should in no way be taken to detract from the conscientiousness and thoroughness of Mr Talbot. Such things happen and in some ways are understandable in a fast-moving and complex transaction such as this, but it was negligent nonetheless.'

B THE EXTENT OF THE DUTY TO ADVISE

1 Introduction

2.30 In every case where an allegation of negligence is made against a solicitor, the court may need to have recourse to the materials explored in the previous parts of this chapter in deciding whether he or she fell below the accepted standard. However, whether a finding of negligence is finally made, particularly in those cases where it is said that the advice given on a particular occasion was inadequate, will depend on the circumstances of the particular case. In *Duncan v Cuelenaere, Beaubier, Walters, Kendall & Fisher*[1] the court provided this helpful guidance:

> 'The test to be applied where a solicitor's negligence is alleged will depend on various circumstances: the sophistication of the client; the experience and training of the solicitor; the form and nature of the client's instructions; the specificity of those instructions; the nature of the action or the legal assignment; the precautions one would expect a solicitor, acting prudently and competently, to take; the course of the proceeding or assignment; and the influence of other factors beyond the control of the client and the adviser.'

1 [1987] 2 WWR 379 at 382.

2.31 In Part 2 of this book we attempt to organise and classify the particular duties of a solicitor in common, specific situations. In this section, we address one particular issue of general application, the extent to which a solicitor ought to advise the client and, in particular, the extent to which a solicitor ought to advise the client about the wisdom of the particular transaction which he or she proposes to enter.

2 The nature of the client

2.32 A solicitor's duty is to advise the client in terms that are appropriate to his or her own understanding and experience. According to Lord Scott in *Pickersgill v Riley:*[1]

> 'It is plain that when a solicitor is instructed by a client to act in a transaction, a duty of care arises. But it is also plain that the scope of that duty of care is variable. It will depend, first and foremost, upon the content of the instructions given to the solicitor by the client. It will also depend on the particular circumstances of the case. It is a duty that it is not helpful to try and describe in the abstract. The scope of the duty may vary depending on the characteristics of the

79

client, in so far as they are apparent to the solicitor. A youthful client, unversed in business affairs, might need explanation and advice from his solicitor before entering into a commercial transaction that it would be pointless, or even sometimes an impertinence, for the solicitor to offer to an obviously experienced businessman.'[2]

To take a simple example, if the client is foreign or unable to speak English, the solicitor may have to ensure that any document that he or she is required to sign is translated for him or her and that wider and more basic explanations are given. In *Siasati v Bottoms & Webb*[3] it was held that a solicitor owed a duty to explain the nature and scope of all of the obligations that the client was undertaking to clients whose knowledge of English was so limited that they needed to communicate with the solicitor through an interpreter. Where the client's understanding or experience is limited, the solicitor may also have the duty to clarify the precise extent of his or her retainer and may be found liable for any loss suffered by the client as a consequence of any misunderstanding. In *Gray v Buss Murton*[4] the testator drew up a new will with the intention of leaving his home and chattels to his partner absolutely. He prepared it without the assistance of his solicitors (but based on an earlier one which they had prepared). He then gave it to his partner and one of the executors to take to his solicitor to check. They asked him to confirm that it had been validly executed and about the tax implications but fatally they did not ask him to check that the principal dispositions of the will gave effect to the testator's revised intentions. It was held that the solicitor was negligent because he crucially failed to clarify his instructions.

1 [2004] UKPC 14, [2004] PNLR 31 at [7].
2 See also *Yager v Fishman & Co* [1942] 1 All ER 552, CA at 556F–H (Goddard LJ); *County Personnel (Employment Agency) Ltd v Pulver* [1987] 1 WLR 916, CA at 922D (Bingham LJ): 'It seems obvious that legal advice, like other communication, should be in terms appropriate to the comprehension and experience of the particular recipient'; and *Carradine Properties Ltd v D J Freeman & Co* [1999] Lloyd's Rep PN 483, CA at 486–7 (Lord Denning MR) and 487 (Donaldson LJ).
3 Mr Geoffrey Brice QC [1997] EGCS 22. For clients in similar circumstances see also *Donmez v Barnes* [1996] EGCS 129 and *Peyman v Lanjani* [1985] Ch 457 at 480B, CA.
4 [1999] PNLR 882 (Rougier J) at 892D–893A.

2.33 In *Siasati v Bottoms & Webb* it was held that the solicitor owed a duty to put his advice in writing because of the particular language difficulties of the client. Apart from exceptional cases of this kind, however, there is no duty to give advice in writing or to confirm it by letter. In *Harwood v Taylor Vinters*[1] the court refused to accept that as a matter of law it was ever necessary for a solicitor to give advice in writing as opposed to orally. Whilst this is undoubtedly correct, it also in the interests of a solicitor to keep a written record of the advice and the presence or absence of an attendance note or letter confirming the advice will be strong evidence in the event of a dispute about whether the advice was given or its precise terms:

'One might have expected that in circumstances where the lay client was determined to disregard the advice of the solicitor, the attendance note would, as a matter of protection for the solicitor if nothing more, contain a specific reference to the firm instructions that had been given in disregard of the advice. Furthermore, one might have expected there to have been a letter to the client, recording the advice and the instructions given. Here there was neither.'[2]

1 [2003] EWHC 471 (Ch)
2 *Middleton v Steeds Hudson* [1998] FLR 738 (Johnson J) at 741. In both that case and *Harwood v Taylor Vinters* the court accepted the solicitor's account that he had given advice which the client had decided not to accept. Compare *Hurlingham Estates Ltd v Wilde & Partners* [1997] 1 Lloyd's Rep 525 at 526 Lightman J refused to accept that a solicitor had orally agreed a fundamental limitation on the scope of the retainer without that limitation being recorded in writing. By contrast in *Walker v Medlicott* [1999] PNLR 531, CA the court accepted that a testatrix had not given specific instructions to a solicitor because they were not recorded in his detailed attendance note despite the conflicting oral evidence of the potential beneficiary and even though the solicitor had no independent recollection of the meeting.

2.34 There is no duty either as a matter of law to see and interview the client personally and there is no reported decision in which a solicitor has been held liable for taking instructions from the client in writing or by telephone.[1] Where instructions are communicated by a third party, however, e g a family member or a friend, the Solicitors Code of Conduct 2007, r 2.01(1) provides as follows:

'You are generally free to decide whether or not to take on a particular client. However, you must refuse to act or cease acting for a client in the following circumstances: ...(c) where instructions are given by someone other than the client, or by only one client on behalf of others in a joint matter, you must not proceed without checking that all clients agree with the instructions given; or (d) here you know or have reasonable grounds for believing that the instructions are affected by duress or undue influence, you must not act on those instructions until you have satisfied yourself that they represent the client's wishes.'[2]

In *Johnson v Bingley, Dyson & Furey*[3] a solicitor was held negligent for failing to comply with a predecessor of this provision in a case of doubt. Obviously if a solicitor acts for more than one person and fails to take instructions from each of them, he or she runs the risk that the client's instructions have not been transmitted correctly or that any advice has not been received or properly understood. This may expose the solicitor to a claim from the client that he or she is acting without authority or that one or more of the clients has been inadequately advised. It may also expose the solicitor to a claim for breach of warranty of authority.[4]

1 In *Marplace (Number 512) Ltd v Chaffe Street* [2006] EWHC 1919 (Ch) at [409] Lawrence Collins J stated that: 'Whether a solicitor has a duty to attend any particular meeting depends on

the circumstances. Normally, a corporate lawyer would expect to be asked at short notice to go to lengthy meetings (and sometimes meetings stretching late into the night), and it must be an implied term that a firm of corporate lawyers will have adequate resources to deal with the client's reasonable requirements. But whether there will be a duty to attend any particular meeting, or arrange for someone to be there, will depend on the client's instructions and requirements.' In one Commonwealth decision, *Hallmark Finance Insurance Brokers Ltd v Fraser & Beatty* (1990) 1 OR (3d) 641 at 647 f–g, where the client was an experienced businessman, it was held that there was no obligation to meet the client face to face.

2 For further comment see para 9.10 ff. The *Guide to the Professional Conduct of Solicitors* (1999), Principle 12.04 (which applied before 1 July 2007) provided as follows: 'Where instructions are received from a third party a solicitor should obtain written instructions from the client that he or she wishes the solicitor to act. In any case of doubt the solicitor should see the client or take other appropriate steps to confirm instructions.'

3 [1997] PNLR 392 (Benet Hytner QC). See also *Linaker v Keith Turner & Ashton* Garland J (5 November 1998, unreported).

4 See paras 5.13–5.20. For examples of the kind of case identified in the text see *Penn v Bristol & West BS* [1997] 1 WLR 1356, CA (claim by W that not bound by charge forged by H) or *Mortgage Corn v Shaire* [2001] Ch 743 (Neuberger J) (claim for an order for sale by bank to enforce equitable charge created by H's forgery). In each case the solicitors were joined as third parties.

3 The nature of the advice

(*a*) *Advice generally*

2.35 A solicitor is obliged to give advice, not simply to pass on information. In *Mortgage Express Ltd v Newman*[1] Carnwath J stated:

> 'If the solicitors' duty is to draw attention to matters which might affect the value of the security, it must be their duty to do so in terms which draw attention to the reason for taking that view. It cannot be sufficient simply to pass the information across, perhaps by telephone.'

In *Nationwide Building Society v Balmer Radmore*[2] the judge applied the standard of a solicitor writing a letter of advice to an intelligent layman. He also stated that the solicitor was obliged to give reasons for his advice.

1 [1996] PNLR 603 at 611B–C.
2 [1999] Lloyd's Rep PN 241 at 270 (Blackburne J).

2.36 Where a solicitor is instructed to draw up or give advice on a legal document, however, this does not mean that he or she is bound to read out every clause in the contract or lease to ensure that the client understands it. There must be an exercise of professional judgment in deciding which provisions to draw to the client's attention[1] and it seems obvious that the more unusual the provision, the more important it is to point it out.[2] Further it may not be enough simply to point out unusual or unexpected provisions. It may also be necessary to spell out their legal consequences.[3] For example, a relatively sophisticated client might not understand that a break option which is conditional upon strict compliance with the covenants in a lease makes it very difficult in practical terms to exercise the option because of the covenant to yield up the premises in repair and that the client would be well-advised to negotiate an agreed sum in lieu of compliance with the covenant.[4] There may also be circumstances in which it is not enough for a solicitor simply to express an opinion about the merits. In cases of doubt about the effect of a provision the solicitor may be negligent if he or she fails to point out the risk that the court might form a different view.[5]

1 See *County Personnel (Employment Agency) Ltd v Pulver* [1987] 1 WLR 916, CA at 922D (Bingham LJ):

> 'It is also, I think, clear that in a situation such as this the professional man does not necessarily discharge his duty by spelling out what is obvious. The client is entitled to expect the exercise of a reasonable professional judgment. That is why the client seeks advice from the professional man in the first place. If in the exercise of a reasonable professional judgment a solicitor is or should be alerted to risks which might elude even an intelligent layman, then plainly it is his duty to advise the client of these risks or explore the matter further.'

See also *Reeves v Thrings & Long* [1996] PNLR 265, CA at 275E–F (Sir Thomas Bingham MR) to similar effect.
2 See *Sykes v Midland Bank* [1971] 1 QB 113, CA at 124B and 130F.
3 For an example where the claim failed on the facts because, unusually, the principal witness was not called by either party: see *Accident Assistance Ltd v Hammonds Suddards Edge* [2005] EWHC 202 (Ch), [2005] PNLR 29. The principal allegation was that the defendants had failed to explain the implications of the advice of leading counsel (which it was accepted was correct).
4 The decision of Laddie J in *Credit Lyonnais SA v Russell Jones & Walker* [2002] EWHC 1310 (Ch), [2003] PNLR 17 (considered in para 2.39, below) certainly suggests that compliance with a break clause is a technical area of the law on which most clients will require advice: see [33].
5 See *Queen Elizabeth's Grammar School Blackburn Ltd v Banks Wilson* [2001] EWCA Civ 1360, [2001] Lloyd's Rep PN 840 in which the defendant gave advice on the construction of a restrictive covenant but failed to advise the client of the risk that the court would take a different view. At first instance the judge accepted the defendant's construction of the covenant and dismissed the claim. On appeal, the Court of Appeal did not determine the issue of the construction of the covenant but held the defendant liable on the basis that there was real scope for dispute: see [47] and [48] (Arden LJ). In doing so the court followed *Dixie v Parsons* [1964] 192 EG 197, CA. The decision is criticised by Gee 'The solicitor's duty to warn that a court might take a different view' (2003) 19 PN 362. However, a similar approach was adopted in *Simmons v Overbury Steward & Eaton* (HHJ Bradbury QC, 31 July 2001, unreported).

(b) Advice on commercial matters

2.37 The traditional principle is that a solicitor is not obliged to advise his or her client about the wisdom of the transaction which the client is about to enter.[1] This approach was taken by the Court of Appeal in *Reeves v Thrings & Long*[2] and by the Privy Council in *Clarke Boyce v Mouat*:[3]

'When a client in full command of his faculties and apparently aware of what he is doing seeks the assistance of a solicitor in the carrying out of a particular transaction, that solicitor is under no duty whether before or after accepting instructions to go beyond those instructions by proffering unsought advice on the wisdom of the transaction. To hold otherwise could impose intolerable burdens on solicitors.'

In *Pickersgill v Riley*[4] the claimant sold shares in a company that was the tenant under a lease whose obligations the claimant had guaranteed personally. He sold the shares in the company to a third party and because the landlord was unwilling to release his guarantee he took an indemnity from the third party against his personal liabilities. The tenant became insolvent and rent arrears built up that the claimant discharged under his personal guarantee. When he attempted to enforce the indemnity it became apparent that the purchaser was a shell company with no assets. He then claimed damages for negligence against the solicitor who had acted for him on the sale of the shares claiming that he owed him a duty to investigate the purchaser's financial position. The Privy Council held that he did not. After discussing both *Reeves v Thrings & Long* and *Clarke Boyce v Mouat* Lord Scott analysed the transaction. The claimant was aware of the risks involved in continuing to guarantee the tenant's liability, he had negotiated the share sale himself and although both he and the defendant had assumed that the purchaser was a company of financial substance, the decision to accept the indemnity did not involve any hidden pitfalls and the solicitor had advised the claimant of the potential danger of contracting with a limited company. He therefore found that the defendant owed no further duty to the claimant:[5]

'It was, in their Lordships' view, a matter for the commercial judgment of Mr Riley whether to he was prepared to accept the protection of the contractual undertaking on offer from WEN. He decided to do so, but not in reliance on any advice to do so given by Mr Pickersgill. It was his, Mr Riley's, commercial decision. His decision may, with hindsight, be regarded as imprudent and to have been based on a mistake as to WEN's financial substance at the time of the transaction. But Mr Riley cannot, in their Lordships' opinion, extend Mr Pickersgill's role from that of his solicitor acting on his instructions to that of his commercial adviser, or to that of his insurer against his commercial misjudgement. Mr Pickersgill did not, in their Lordships' judgment, owe the extended duty of care as pleaded or as expressed by the courts below as the basis of their respective findings of liability ...'

1 For a very early example see *Bowdage v Harold Michelmore & Co* (1962) 106 Sol Jo 512 in which Melford Stevenson J held that a solicitor:

'could not be said, in the absence of specific instructions, to undertake the duty of advising the client whether the transaction was from the client's view a prudent one. The defendants were never asked to advise the plaintiff about the value of the land and neither the nature of the transaction nor the lack of experience on her part imposed a duty to do so.'

2 [1996] PNLR 265 at 275E per Bingham LJ, at 279C per Simon Brown LJ and at 285A per Hobhouse LJ, CA. Unusually, the court reached different conclusions about whether the solicitor ought to have advised further, largely according to the differing weight they attached to parts of the evidence and the judge's findings of fact.
3 [1994] 1 AC 428 at 437D–E (Lord Jauncey).
4 [2004] UKPC 14, [2004] PNLR 31.
5 [17] and [18].

2.38 The principle that a solicitor owes no duty to go beyond the scope of his or her express instructions and to give advice on matters of commercial judgment has been applied in a number of recent cases.[1] In *John Mowlem Construction plc v Neil F Jones & Co*[2] the Court of Appeal held that a solicitor acting for a party in a construction arbitration owed no duty to advise the client to disclose a potential counterclaim when renewing its professional indemnity insurance. The solicitors were not retained to give advice about insurance by the client who was perfectly competent to deal with such matters.[3] In *Football League Ltd v Edge & Ellison*[4] Rimer J followed *Pickersgill v Riley* in holding that solicitors owed no duty to advise a commercial client to consider requesting parent company guarantees for the liabilities of the successful bidder for a broadcasting licence. The judge held that there was no implied duty to advise the relevant committee on the solvency of the successful bidder or to prompt them to consider the need for them even though in practice other solicitors might have done so.[5] Finally, in *Marplace (Number 512) Ltd v Chaffe Street*[6] it was held that a firm of solicitors owed no duty to give advice that a party with whom their clients were negotiating amendments to a share purchase agreement was (or might be) in breach of contract where the clients could have asked for advice if they had wanted it, they were represented in the negotiations by financial advisers and the solicitors understood that the issue was itself the subject of negotiation.[7]

1 For some earlier examples see *Haigh v Wright Hassall & Co* [1994] EGCS 54, CA, *Nixon v Stephensons* (3 April 1996, unreported) (Mr John Martin QC) and *Mean v Thomas* [1998] EGCS 2 (Stephen Tomlinson QC) where the claimant bought a property at auction without giving his solicitor an opportunity to examine the title. The defendants were held not liable for failing to advise him against it.
2 [2004] EWCA Civ 768, [2004] PNLR 45. In his judgment Tuckey LJ cited the passage from *Credit Lyonnais SA v Russell Jones & Walker* [2002] EWHC 1310 (Ch), [2003] PNLR 17 at [28] quoted in the text below.
3 See [20].
4 [2006] EWHC 1462 (Ch), [2007] PNLR 2.
5 See [266]–[270]. As stated in para 2.01 (above) it formed an important part of Rimer J's reasoning that it was not necessary to imply a duty to give the relevant advice on the implied terms test.
6 [2006] EWHC 1919 (Ch). The judgment of Lawrence Collins J contains a helpful summary of the law: see [402]–[409].
7 See the principal finding of fact at [420] and the detailed explanation at [421]–[439]. Both the clients and their financial advisers were aware that there was a potential breach but did not seek advice. Although the court did not find it necessary to decide whether the vendor was actually in breach, it was influenced by the fact that the claimant's argument was a very sophisticated one and it was not so clear that it would have imposed a duty to advise pro-actively: see [440]–[442].

2.39 This general approach can only be adopted, however, with important qualifications. First, and most obviously, the defendant may be specifically instructed to give advice on the commercial consequences of the proposed transaction. For instance, it is the function of a solicitor who is retained to advise a spouse or partner being asked to provide a guarantee to provide practical advice spelling out the potential consequences of providing the guarantee even though those consequences will be obvious to many clients.[1] Secondly, as a result of information which comes to light in the course of carrying out the relevant instructions a solicitor may have a duty to give advice to the client and ask for further instructions even if the solicitor was not instructed to give advice in relation to the transaction and it may involve advice which would have been obvious to a sophisticated client. In *Credit Lyonnais SA v Russell Jones & Walker*[2] the defendants were instructed to negotiate with the claimant's landlords to extend the period for exercising a break clause. The claimant then changed its mind and instructed the defendants to serve a notice in accordance with the existing terms. The defendants served the relevant notice but it was ineffective because the claimant had failed to make a payment that was a strict condition of the exercise of the option. Although they were not instructed to give advice on the terms of the lease, the defendants were held liable for failing to point out the conditions for compliance and checking that the claimant understood them. It was (or should have been) apparent from the two letters of instructions that the claimant had overlooked this point or had not fully appreciated it. Laddie J stated:[3]

> '[T]he solicitor only has to expend time and effort in what he has been engaged to do and for which the client has agreed to pay. He is under no general obligation to expend time and effort on issues outside the retainer. However if, in the course of doing that for which he is retained, he becomes aware of a risk or a potential risk to the client, it is his duty to inform the client. In doing that he is neither going beyond the scope of his instructions nor is he doing 'extra' work for which he is not to be paid. He is simply reporting back to the client on issues of concern which he learns as a result of and in the course of carrying out his express instructions. In relation to this I was struck by the analogy drawn by [counsel for the claimant]. If a dentist is asked to treat a patient's tooth and on looking into the latter's mouth he notices that an adjacent tooth is in need of treatment, it is his duty to warn the patient accordingly. So too, if in the course of carrying out instructions within his area of competence a lawyer notices or ought to notice a problem or risk for the client of which it is reasonable to assume that the client may not be aware, the lawyer must warn him.'

Thirdly, and perhaps most importantly, it is not always easy to distinguish between legal and commercial advice, particularly where what is in issue is the implication of a specific clause or provision in a legal document.[4] The solicitor obviously owes a duty to point out and explain terms or provisions that the layman cannot be expected to understand.[5] But it is more difficult where the issue in question does not fall into that category. At one extreme, any changes in a document have the potential to generate a commercial effect and at the other a solicitor cannot be expected to question the fundamental terms which the client has negotiated. The difficulty is the grey area in between. A good example of an issue which fell within that grey area is provided by the recent case of *Stone Heritage Developments Ltd v Davis Blank Furniss*[6]. In that case the claimant obtained a licence over a development site. The licensor was in occupation of another parcel of land that formed part of the site physically but was not included in the development agreement and the licensor had no title to it. The claimant was aware of this but intended to buy in the land from the owner of the paper title after the deal had been completed. However, the licensor bought in the land first and then held the claimant to ransom. The judge at first instance held that the defendants, who were the claimant's solicitors, were negligent in failing to advise the claimant to consider whether the development agreement ought to contain provisions dealing with the land to which the licensor had a possessory title. The Court of Appeal reversed this decision on the basis that the solicitor's instructions were very limited, the individuals with whom he dealt had accountancy and property development experience and the pitfall against which the judge had found that the solicitor had a duty to warn was by no means obvious.[7] Sir Andrew Morritt, the Chancellor, considered that:[8]

'Had the issue been raised by Mr Shalom it would have prompted a host of further questions such as whether the acquisition of part, and if so which part, of the Bolton Clear Title Land would suffice and what time limit should be imposed for the satisfaction of the condition. In the light of his instructions Mr Shalom had no responsibility to explore these matters. Had he done so he would not have been entitled to payment for his time; and it is plain from the matters to which I have already referred that Mr Mortazavi was concerned to keep costs to a minimum.'

Fourthly, and finally, it is suggested that there may be exceptional cases in which it is so obvious that the course of action which the client proposes is so unwise or improvident that the solicitor is required to raise the issue and ask the client to reconsider (if not to give positive advice against it).[8] In summary, a solicitor's duty must be to point out the legal consequences of important clauses or provisions sufficiently forcefully and in layman's terms so that the client can appreciate their full commercial significance and this inevitably requires the adviser to make a judgment about (a) those clauses that are complex or unusual and likely to require explanation to any client and (b) those clauses that are sufficiently important in commercial terms to merit detailed discussion and to require confirmation that they accord with the client's instructions.

2.39 Breach of duty

1 See *Royal Bank of Scotland v Etridge (No 2)* [2001] UKHL 44, [2002] AC 773 at [64] and [65]. This advice was described by Lord Nicholls as a minimum.
2 [2002] EWHC 1310 (Ch), [2003] PNLR 17. See the critical finding at [33]. For an example in the context of litigation see *Feakins v Burstow* [2005] EWHC 1931 (QB), [2006] PNLR 6 at [66]–[76]. In that case Jack J held that a litigation solicitor owed a duty to take instructions on a crucial letter which would have enabled the claimant to raise a defence to a counterclaim which was not taken.
3 [28]. This principle was accepted as correct by Sir Andrew Morritt C in *Stone Heritage Developments Ltd v Davis Blank Furniss* [2007] EWCA Civ 765 at [34].
4 Bingham LJ rejected this crude distinction in *County Personnel (Employment Agency) Ltd v Pulver* [1987] 1 WLR 916 at 924A, CA. In a Commonwealth decision, *Hallmark Finance Insurance Brokers Ltd v Fraser & Beatty and McNairn* (1990) 1 OR (3d) 641, Dunnet J drew what might be a more a helpful distinction between 'business components' of the transaction and 'legal provisions': see 646d–f. (The clause in issue was an overage clause.)
5 In *Pickersgill v Riley* [2004] UKPC 14, [2004] PNLR 31 at [11] Lord Scott described the solicitor's duty as one to point out any hidden pitfalls and in *Marplace (Number 512) Ltd v Chaffe Street* [2006] EWHC 1919 (Ch) at [407] Lawrence Collins J described it as: 'the duty of pointing out to the client any legal obscurities of which the client might have been unaware, or of drawing the attention of the client to any hidden pitfalls.'
6 [2007] EWCA Civ 765.
7 [2007] EWCA Civ 765 at [39]–[43].
8 [2007] EWCA Civ 765 at [44].
8 *Reeves v Thrings & Long* [1996] PNLR 265, CA is concerned with precisely this process but no real ratio decidendi can be extracted from the case. Sir Thomas Bingham MR plainly did not believe that this had been done: see 277. Simon Brown LJ was satisfied that the claimant was aware of the legal position but was not concerned whether he understood the commercial implications: see 280G–281A. Hobhouse LJ did not fully address this issue. He stated at 288D that:

> 'provided that a solicitor uses language which would lead a reasonable person in the position of the solicitor to believe that his advice was being understood, and there is no evidence that the solicitor should reasonably have observed that his advice was not being understood, the solicitor has discharged his duty.'

The point was also dealt with by Lawrence Collins J in *Marplace (Number 512) Ltd v Chaffe Street* [2006] EWHC 1919 (Ch) at [408] where he stated that the solicitor has a duty to understand the relevant document, must be equipped to correct the client's misunderstanding and cannot be heard to say that he or she does not understand terms simply because the client is sophisticated. On the other hand, the solicitor: 'is not under a duty to review the whole range of commercial considerations that underlie a particular deal and to work out to which the client may not have given sufficient thought and to remind the client about them'. Both cases also illustrate the difficulty of providing any clear or neat test.

Chapter 3

Causation and damages at common law

A   INTRODUCTION

3.01   Suppose that, in a claim in contract or tort[1], the claimant has proved that the defendant owed the claimant a duty and has breached it. How does the court assess the claimant's entitlement to damages? Claims against solicitors are usually contractual since generally the claimant retained the defendant as a solicitor. But the standard of the solicitor's duty in contract is normally the same as in tort, namely to take reasonable skill and care. As a result, the principles applied to causation in this area derive principally from cases in tort.[2] As to causation in tort, in *Kuwait Airways Corpn v Iraqi Airways Corpn (Nos 4 and 5)*[3] Lord Nicholls said:

> 'How, then, does one identify a plaintiff's "true loss" in cases of tort? ... I take as my starting point the commonly accepted approach that the extent of a defendant's liability for the plaintiff's loss calls for a two-stage inquiry: whether the wrongful conduct causally contributed to the loss and, if it did, what is the extent of the loss for which the defendant ought to be held liable. The first of these inquiries, widely undertaken as a simple "but for" test, is predominantly a factual inquiry ... The second inquiry, although this is not always openly acknowledged by the courts, involves a value judgment (*"ought* to be held liable".) Written large, the second inquiry concerns the extent of the loss for which the defendant ought fairly or reasonably or justly to be held liable (the epithets are interchangeable). To adapt the language of Jane Stapleton ... the inquiry is whether the plaintiff's harm or loss should be within the scope of the defendant's liability, given the reasons why the law has recognised the cause of action in question.'

Although the first inquiry is 'predominantly' factual, it would be wrong to say that, in every case, the court simply applies the 'but for' test in a way which involves no value judgments and no other legal principles. In his own speech in *Kuwait*, Lord Hoffmann said that legal rules derived from the nature of the tort on which the claim is based will prescribe what the law's requirements as to causation are.[4]

---

1   See chapter 4 for claims in equity.

2 In solicitors' cases the obligation is normally identical or similar in either contract or tort, namely a duty to take reasonable care, and the function of damages is to place the claimant in the position in which he or she would have been had the defendant exercised such care. This 'performance' based approach has been criticised by some commentators: see Stapleton 'The Normal Expectancies Measure in Tort Damages' 113 LQR 257 at 260.
3 [2002] UKHL 19, [2002] 2 AC 883, at [69]–[70].
4 *Kuwait* at [127–8]. Lord Hoffmann returned to this theme writing extra-judicially in 'Causation' (2005) 121 LQR 592. See further para 3.35ff, below. Further, at [72] in *Kuwait* Lord Nicholls said that even in considering the 'but for' test it was necessary to have in mind the purpose of the relevant cause of action.

3.02   In this chapter we consider the issues in accordance with Lord Nicholls's two-stage inquiry: first, factual causation and the 'but for' test, together with the related of issue of how third parties would have acted. The latter concerns principles of damages for the loss of a chance. Secondly, we look at control techniques that the courts use in order to limit the extent of defendants' liability. These include the *SAAMCo* principle ('extent of liability'), the significance of alternative causes, remoteness and mitigation. Thirdly, we consider the date at which damage will be assessed, and fourthly the availability of damages for psychological damage or injured feelings. Finally, we look at the principles governing the recovery of interest. Except where otherwise stated, so far as tort is concerned in this chapter we deal only with negligence rather than other torts.

B   FACTUAL CAUSATION

1   The 'but for' test

(a) *The normal rule*

3.03   The function of damages in negligence is to put the claimant in the position which he or she would have been in if there had been no breach of duty[1]. The 'but for' test follows from this. Lord Nicholls commented on this test in *Kuwait* as follows[2]:

> 'This guideline principle is concerned to identify and exclude losses lacking a causal connection with the wrongful conduct. Expressed in its simplest form, the principle poses the question whether the plaintiff would have suffered the loss without ("but for") the defendant's wrongdoing. If he would not, the wrongful conduct was *a* cause of the loss. If the loss would have arisen even without the defendant's wrongdoing, normally it does not give rise to legal liability … Of course, even if the plaintiff's losses pass this exclusionary threshold test, it by no means follows that the defendant should be legally responsible for the loss.'

So in almost all cases in negligence or breach of the contractual duty to take reasonable skill and care the claimant must show[3] that, but for the defendant's conduct, the claimant would not have suffered the loss which is claimed. If the claimant passes this test in relation to any particular item of loss then the court moves on to consider the further control factors on the recovery of damages that we consider below.

1 In tort the standard answer was given by Lord Blackburn in *Livingstone v Rawyards Coal* (1880) 5 App Cas 25, 39:

> 'I do not think that there is any difference of opinion as to its being a general rule that, where any injury is to be compensated by damages, in settling the sum of money to be given for reparation of damages, you should as nearly as possible get at that sum of money which will put the party who has been injured, or who has suffered, in the same position as he would have been if he had not sustained the wrong for which he is now getting his compensation or reparation.'

2 Above, at [72].
3 As to what must be shown on the balance of probabilities and what must be shown on the loss of a chance basis see para 3.19ff, below.

3.04 The claimant may, however, increase the chances of winning the 'but for' issue by increasing the range of duties which it is alleged that the defendant has breached. A workman falls to his death at work. In breach of duty, the employer had failed to supply a safety harness. But the workman never used safety harnesses even when they were supplied. The workman's estate sues the employer for the death. If the only breach alleged is failure to supply the harness then the estate fails to pass the 'but for' test: had the employer supplied it, the workman would not have used it. If, however, it is proved that the employer also had a duty to ensure that the workman used the harness then the estate passes the 'but for' test and the employer is liable.[1] One might see the recent decision in *Hilton v Barker Booth & Eastwood*[2] as an example of this. The defendant solicitors acted for two clients, A and B, in a deal between A and B. The defendants knew that B was dishonest, but they did not tell A, who proceeded with the deal and lost a lot of money as a result. The trial judge held that the solicitors had acted in breach of duty in that they had continued to act for A, but that this had caused A no loss, because if the defendants had ceased to act A would have gone to other solicitors who would not have known of B's dishonesty, so that A would have suffered the same losses on the transaction as he in fact suffered: A could not pass the 'but for' test. In the House of Lords, Lord Walker said that the solicitors' first duty was to inform A that they could not act for him and that he should seek advice from other solicitors, not relying on any advice he had already received from themselves. But, as the solicitors did not do this, and carried on acting, they then came under a duty to do their best for A, which required them to tell A that B was dishonest even though this would amount of a breach of their duty to B. They failed to tell A this, and so had to pay damages to put A in the position he would have been if he had known that B was dishonest: he would have withdrawn from the transaction and not suffered any losses from it. So by focussing on a different breach of duty the claimant was able to escape the problem that the trial judge had found that he did not pass the 'but for' test.

1 The example is Stapleton's: 'Cause-in-fact and the Scope of Liability for Consequences,' (2003) 119 LQR 388 at 391.
2 [2005] UKHL 8, [2005] 1 WLR 567. For the contractual significance of this decision see para 1.1 and n 5 and para 2.15, above. For discussion of the equitable issues, see para 4.36, below.

3.05 These examples show that, in formulating the duties which it is said that the defendant has breached, the claimant must consider factual causation. Further, in asking 'what would have happened but for the defendant's negligence', there are two possible approaches: (i) what would have happened if this particular defendant would had *not* been involved, or (ii) what would have happened if this defendant *had* been involved but had acted with reasonable skill and care? In many solicitor cases, the two approaches will produce the same result: if this defendant solicitor had not acted, another solicitor would have acted with reasonable skill and care.[1] But the facts of *Hilton* show that this will not necessarily be so. This point has been considered further in the misrepresentation cases: see para 3.08, below.

1 Stapleton (2003) 119 LQR 388 at 414–5.

(b) *Impossible to satisfy 'but for' test*

3.06 In some cases, it is impossible to prove, as between two parties both acting in breach of duty, which one caused the loss that the claimant has suffered. In *Fairchild v Glenhaven Funeral Services Ltd*[1] it was scientifically impossible to prove which wrongful period of exposure to asbestos dust had caused the claimants' mesothelioma. It followed that no claimant could satisfy the 'but for' test. The House of Lords held that each employer who had, in breach of duty, exposed a claimant to asbestos dust was liable to that claimant, even though the 'but for' test could not be satisfied. But this was an exceptional rule, designed to meet the exceptional problem that it was truly impossible to prove that the 'but for' test was satisfied. A later case establishes that the *Fairchild* exception from the need to satisfy the 'but for' rule applies only if the impossibility of proof arises because it is possible that the injury was caused by another factor which operated in substantially the same way as that for which the defendant is liable.[2] So the exception does apply if the claimant's injury must have been caused by asbestos dust and some other kind of dust operating in the same way, but not if the injury may have been caused by a number of different medical factors whose precise influence cannot be proved. Although it is clear that the extent of this exception remains to be worked out in later cases[3], it also appears that, even within the law of personal injury, the courts are reluctant to extend it. It therefore seems unlikely that it will be extended to non-medical professional negligence cases such as claims against solicitors.

Further, however, *Fairchild* can be seen as the court determining the test of causal connection to be applied according to policy or value judgments.[4]

1 [2002] UKHL 22, [2003] 1 AC 32. A similar problem might arise if each of two hunters carelessly fires a bullet and a bullet from one of them kills a person but it cannot be proved whose bullet it was. See *McGregor on Damages* (17th edn, 2003) at [6–016].
2 *Barker v Corus UK Ltd* [2006] UKHL 20, [2006] 2 AC 572, per Lord Hoffmann at [18]–[24].
3 Per Lord Hoffmann in *Barker* at [11].
4 See per Lord Nicholls in *Kuwait* at [74]. In *Kuwait*, the House of Lords decided that inability to prove 'but for' causation was not fatal to a claim in the tort of conversion.

(c) *Chester v Afshar*[1]

3.07 A similar conclusion applies in relation to a different attempt to import authorities dealing with clinical negligence into the area of non-medical professional negligence. In *Chester v Afshar*[1], a surgeon negligently failed to warn the claimant patient of risks associated with an operation she was about to undergo. The surgeon performed the operation non-negligently but one of the unmentioned risks eventuated and the claimant developed cauda equine syndrome as a result. The trial judge held that, if the surgeon had explained the risks to the claimant, she would still have undergone the operation, but later. It followed, at least on an orthodox view[2], that the claimant could not satisfy the 'but for' test. The House of Lords, by a majority of 3 to 2, nevertheless held the surgeon liable. As Lord Hoffmann has written:

> '... the case is another illustration of how the causal requirements which the law prescribes for liability may vary from the standard criteria when the courts think the basis upon which liability is imposed requires such a difference.'[3]

The courts may think that the 'but for' test should be abandoned on the facts of *Chester*, but in *White v Paul Davidson & Taylor*,[4] a solicitors' negligence case alleging failure to advise a tenant that a landlord could not rely on a notice to quit, the Court of Appeal rejected a submission that *Chester* applied so that the claimant need not satisfy the 'but for' test. Arden LJ restricted *Chester* to cases of failure to obtain consent to medical treatment. It seems unlikely that *Chester* would apply in solicitors' negligence cases, except conceivably in the case where a solicitor fails to warn a client of the risks of a course of action, such as applying for a freezing order, before the client gives instructions to undertake it.[5]

1 [2004] UKHL 41, [2005] 1 AC 134.
2 It is submitted that Stapleton's suggestion that the case may be explained on orthodox grounds is unlikely to be accepted in court. See 'Occam's Razor Reveals an Orthodox Basis for *Chester v Afshar*' (2006) 122 LQR 426.
3 (2005) 121 LQR 592 at 602.

4 [2004] EWCA Civ 1511, [2005] PNLR 15, at [33] and [40]. See also *Beary v Pall Mall Investments* [2005] EWCA Civ 415, [2005] PNLR 35 (financial advisor), where the Court of Appeal was considerably more robust in rejecting a similar argument on behalf of the claimant.
5 Levey (2004) 101 Law Society's Gazette 44.

(d) Causation in misrepresentation cases

3.08   Doubt has been cast on the application of the 'but for' test in misrepresentation cases. Where the claimant's claim is for common law deceit, it is sufficient for him or her to show that the defendant's statement induced the course of conduct which caused the loss and it is unnecessary to show that, if properly informed or advised, he or she would have acted differently. According to Hobhouse LJ in *Downs v Chappell*:[1]

'In general, it is irrelevant to inquire what the representee would have done if some different representation had been made to him or what other transactions he might have entered into if he had not entered into the transaction in question.'

If the application of the 'but for' test in deceit cases were more favourable to the claimant than in negligence cases, that would accord with the law's general policy that the rules of causation in relation to deceit are more favourable to the claimant than in relation to negligence.

1 [1997] 1 WLR 426 at 441B–C, CA.

3.09   But, though *Downs v Chappell* was a case in deceit, Millett LJ applied the same approach to claims for negligent misstatement against solicitors in *Bristol and West Building Society v Mothew*. He suggested a distinction between two types of case:[1]

'Where a client sues his solicitor for having negligently failed to give him proper advice, he must show what advice should have been given and (on a balance of probabilities) that if such advice had been given he would not have entered into the relevant transaction or would not have entered into it on the terms he did. The same applies where the client's complaint is that the solicitor failed to give him material information.

Where, however, a client sues his solicitor for having negligently given him incorrect information, the position appears to be different. In such a case it is sufficient for the plaintiff to prove that he relied on the advice or information, that is to say, he would not have acted as he did if he had not been given such advice or information. It is not necessary for him to prove that he would not have acted as he did if he had been given the proper advice or the correct information. This was the position in *Downs v Chappell*.'

1 [1998] Ch 1 at 11B-D, CA.

3.10   In *Downs v Chappell* the vendor of a business and his accountant falsified financial information about a bookshop in selling it to the claimants and the claimants clearly relied on this information in judging whether to buy it. The judge found that the true financial position, whilst worse, would not have influenced the claimants' decision to buy and they would have gone ahead. On this basis he awarded nominal damages. The Court of Appeal reversed his finding and awarded the claimants all the losses flowing from their investment in the business.[1] It hardly lay in the mouths of the defendants (who had deliberately misrepresented the accounts) to argue that their misrepresentations had no significance in law. In *Swindle v Harrison*[2] Hobhouse LJ explained the decision in *Downs:*

'In conclusion, I would add a footnote about the statement in *Bristol and West Building Society v Mothew (t/a Stapley & Co)* [1996] 4 All ER 698 at 705–6, [1997] 2 WLR 436[3] at 443 that *Downs v Chappell* [1996] 3 All ER 344, [1997] 1 WLR 426 was authority for the proposition, and bound to hold, that it was sufficient to succeed in the tort of negligence for a plaintiff to prove that the defendant had made a negligent misrepresentation on which he, the plaintiff, had relied and that it was irrelevant what representation the defendant would have made if he had been careful. That was not in fact the decision in *Downs v Chappell.* In that case, the negligent accountant had purported to verify figures for a business at a time when he had no basis to confirm any figures at all (see [1996] 3 All ER 344 at 349, [1997] 1 WLR 426 at 431). The accurate figures were then unknown and the accountant should have said so. If he had said so, the plaintiff would not have purchased the business. The figures used by the judge were not produced for at least another 16 months, by which time the plaintiff had long since bought the business and become committed to the losses which formed the subject-matter of the action. The court in *Downs v Chappell* reversed the judge on this point because he had based his decision on the later, irrelevant, figure (see [1996] 3 All ER 344 at 35 1–352, [1997] 1 WLR 426 at 433).'

1 [1997] 1 WLR 426 at 443G–444H. Hobhouse LJ introduced a 'qualification' to fraud damages which reflected the concern that damages might compensate the plaintiffs not for the consequences of the tort but for the consequences of market forces and their own misjudgment. On the facts this did not influence the outcome, but the approach was disapproved by Lord Steyn in *Smith New Court Securities Ltd v Scrimgeour Vickers Ltd* [1997] AC 254 at 283B–G.
2 [1997] 4 All ER 705 at 728g–j, CA.
3 Now reported at [1998] Ch 1.

3.11 Elias J had to deal head on with the effect of Millett LJ's dictum in *Mothew* in *Hagen v ICI Chemicals and Polymers Ltd.*[1] He began by observing at [115] that Millett LJ's approach (emphasis added):

'... leads to a distinction between cases where no advice is given and those where bad advice is given. In the former, it is necessary for the claimant to show that he would have acted differently had *the correct advice* been given; in the latter, it is necessary for him merely to show that he acted differently than he would have done had *no advice* been given. It is difficult to see much logic in such an arbitrary distinction ...'

It will be observed that this passage refers to the distinction, as to what the defendant would have done, identified at para 3.05, above. Elias J continued by analysing *Mothew* and concluding that he was not bound by Millett LJ's dictum, because the other two judges in the case had not adopted it;[2] alternatively, it was inconsistent with subsequent House of Lords authority[3]. Having held that he was not bound by Millett LJ's dictum, he proceeded as follows[4]:

'The potential difficulty with negligent misstatement is that the defendant can avoid committing the tort in one of two ways. Either he can give no information at all; or he can give information which is not negligent. Ms Booth submits that one should assess loss by assuming that no information at all would have been given unless there was a specific legal duty to give information ... I do not accept that. It seems to me that at the very least when the claimant is looking to the defendant to provide information and the latter has agreed to do so, it is unrealistic to say that it should be assumed, when assessing loss, that no information would have been given. If a surgeon negligently carries out an operation, the damages are assessed by asking what would have happened had he carried the operation out properly, not by asking what would have befallen the patient he had left to fester. This is so even where there is no specific duty to carry out the operation. Sometimes, as in *Downs v Chappell*, the only proper answer that the defendant could properly give to someone seeking information is that no information can be given, because it is not available, or at least not to the defendant. It is only in those exceptional circumstances that it is appropriate to ask whether the plaintiff would have entered into the transaction even if the information had not been forthcoming at all rather than asking what would have happened if the information had been correct. That would then reflect what the defendant should have done to avoid committing the tort.'

It is submitted that this reflects the correct approach. In *White v Paul Davidson & Taylor*[5], Arden LJ considered that 'every case of giving incorrect advice necessarily involves failing to give proper advice', and doubted whether there was 'any coherent basis' on which the distinction could be drawn, though she said that she was content to apply the *Mothew* distinction. She proceeded to summarise the gist of the complaint made and concluded that it was a case of failing to give proper advice rather than giving incorrect advice, so that the claimant had to satisfy the 'but for' test. It is thought that future courts are likely either to hold that they are not bound by Millett LJ's dicta, as Elias J did, or that, properly analysed, the case is one to which even on Millett LJ's approach the 'but for' test applies, so that difficulties introduced by Millett LJ's distinction are avoided.

1 [2002] Lloyd's Rep PN 288, at [109]–[127].
2 [116]–[117].
3 [121]–[124]
4 [125].
5 [2004] EWCA Civ 1511, [2005] PNLR 15. See also O'Sullivan 'Acts, omissions and negligent professionals: confusion over counterfactuals' (2001) 4 PN 272.

3.12 Similarly, it is thought that a dictum of Stephenson LJ in *JEB Fasteners v Marks & Bloom*[1], to the effect that in misrepresentation cases it is sufficient to show that a misrepresentation need only play 'a real and substantial part' in the claimant's decision in order to count as a cause of the claimant's loss, should not be taken as the test of causation in solicitors' negligence cases. The other two members of the court did not apply this test, and the test normally applied in non-medical professional negligence cases[2] is the 'but for' test.

1 [1983] 1 All ER 583, CA.
2 In personal injury and clinical negligence cases, however, the 'material contribution' test is used. See per Lord Rodger in *Barker v Corus UK Ltd* [2006] UKHL 20, [2006] 2 AC 572 at [84]. He dissented on a different point.

3.13 As already discussed, the 'but for' test calls for comparison of (i) the position the claimant is in fact in and (ii) the position the claimant would have been in if there had been no breach of duty. Stage (ii) requires an assessment of a hypothetical situation. It appears from the passage just cited from *Hagen* that, in considering how the defendant would have acted, it should generally be assumed that the defendant would have acted in accordance with its duty, rather than that the defendant would not have been involved at all. But, in carrying out its hypothetical enquiry, the court must sometimes consider how the claimant would have acted; sometimes how the defendant would have acted; and sometimes how third parties would have acted. We consider the court's approach to these different issues below.

2 How would the claimant have acted?

(a) General test

3.14 Where the defendant's wrongdoing consists of a positive *act* the question of causation is 'one of historical fact': did the defendant's act cause the claimant's loss? This must be decided on the balance of probabilities.[1] Where, on the other hand, the defendant's negligence is an *omission* to perform a particular act, the question is how the claimant would have reacted if there had been no negligence. This is of course a hypothetical question. It has already been suggested above at para 3.11 that, where the defendant gave negligent advice, the question will generally be how the claimant would have acted if the defendant, or perhaps another solicitor, had given non-negligent advice, rather than how the claimant would have reacted if he or she had received no advice at all. In relation to a defendant's omission to perform a particular act, it is again established that the claimant must prove on the balance of probabilities that, if there had been no negligence, he or she would have acted in a way which would have avoided the loss now claimed.[2] In each of these cases, if the claimant succeeds then there is no deduction in damages for the chance that he or she might not have acted as claimed. Note, however, that in the context of claims against solicitors whose negligence has caused the claimant to lose his or her cause of action in litigation altogether, the court is likely to assess some aspects of the claimant's conduct on the loss of a chance basis as opposed to on the balance of probabilities.[3]

1 *Allied Maples Group Ltd v Simmons & Simmons* [1995] 1 WLR 1602 at 1610A, CA. But if the reference to 'past historical fact' is intended to mean that, in this first category of case, there is no need to refer to hypothetical examples, then it is doubtful whether this is correct. In the case of a negligent act, one compares (i) the position the claimant was in fact in with (ii) the position the claimant would have been in if the negligent act had not occurred. Stage (ii) is a hypothetical question as to what would have happened, in the past, if there had been no negligent act, so it still requires one to imagine a hypothetical, and different, world where the negligent act had not occurred.
2 [1995] 1 WLR 1602 at 1610D–E. For (muted) criticism of the distinction between these two categories, see *McGregor on Damages* (17th edn, 2003) at [8–035]. It is doubtful whether the act/omission distinction is helpful in the context of solicitors giving wrong advice: see para 3.11, above.
3 See further para 12.32ff, below.

3.15 In *Sykes v Midland Bank Executor & Trustee Co Ltd*,[1] where the defendant failed to advise the claimants about the terms of an underlease, the claimants' evidence was that they would have executed the underlease in that form even if they had been properly advised. They recovered nominal damages only. Salmon LJ said this:[2]

'Nevertheless Mr Sykes was a remarkably candid witness. He, no doubt disappointingly, would not say that it would have made any difference had the proper advice been given ... At the end of his evidence it certainly appeared that in his view it was as likely as not that the plaintiffs would have acted just as they did even if they had had proper advice about the effect of clause 2(xi) of the underleases.'

In *Sykes* the evidence was particularly, and unusually, unequivocal. In most cases, however, the question whether the advice would have made a difference to the claimant's conduct involves quite a sophisticated inquiry. In *Brown v KMR Services Ltd*,[3] Hobhouse LJ stated:

> 'The question of causation has to be approached on the basis of identifying first what specific advice he ought to have received and then what he has proved, on a balance of probabilities, would have been the consequence of his receiving such advice.'

In most cases this question will depend purely upon the evidence of the claimant, although the court will inevitably wish to be certain that this evidence has not been coloured, whether consciously or unconsciously, with the benefit of hindsight. In *Allied Maples Group Ltd v Simmons & Simmons*[4] Stuart-Smith LJ said:

> 'The plaintiff's own evidence that he would have acted to obtain the benefit or avoid the risk, while important, may not be believed by the judge, especially if there is compelling evidence that he would not. In the ordinary way where the action required of the plaintiff is clearly for his benefit, the court has little difficulty in concluding that he would have taken it. But in many cases the risk is not obvious and the precaution may be tedious or uncomfortable, for example the need to use ear-defenders in noisy surroundings or breathing apparatus in dusty ones ...'

1 [1971] 1 QB 113, esp at 124G–125E and 127B–H, CA.
2 [1971] 1 QB 113 at 127G–H.
3 [1995] 4 All ER 598 at 638d–c, CA, a Lloyd's Name suing a member's agent.
4 [1995] 1 WLR 1602 at 1610D.

3.16   Depending on the facts, the court's analysis of causation may be more complex. In *BBL v Eagle Star*[1] Phillips J found that the claimant had not relied upon the defendant's valuation in deciding whether to make a loan because the main purpose of obtaining the valuation was to satisfy Eagle Star, the claimant's indemnity insurers. The judge indicated, however, that he would have found the defendants liable if Eagle Star had relied upon the valuation (which they had not) because the claimant would not have entered the transaction without Eagle Star's agreement. In *N M Rothschild & Sons v Berensons*,[2] a lenders' claim[3], the defendants were held liable to the claimant even though the claimant had not seen the certificate of title, contained in the Funds Request, which the defendants had negligently completed, because 'all those lending would be doing so on the basis that the solicitors had provided to Barclays Bank a true and accurate Funds Request'.[4]

1 [1995] 2 All ER 769 at 793h–796d.
2 [1997] NPC I5, CA.
3 See further chapter 10.
4 Transcript, p 8 per Saville LJ.

(*b*) Burden of proof

3.17 Despite the occasional suggestion to the contrary[1] it is settled by *Wilsher v Essex Area Health Authority*[2] and *Allied Maples*[3] that the burden of proving the causal link between the defendant's act and the claimant's loss is squarely on the claimant. But this does not necessarily mean that the claimant must call direct oral evidence to show what would have occurred. In *Cavendish Funding Ltd v Henry Spencer & Sons Ltd*[4] it was held that the claimant had relied upon the defendants despite the absence of direct evidence from the claimant as to what it would have done. The judge was able to reach this conclusion by inference from the agreed or unchallenged documents in the claimant's loan file; the Court of Appeal upheld his finding.

1 See *Heywood v Wellers* [1976] QB 446 at 459, CA.
2 [1988] AC 1074.
3 Above, at para 3.15. See *Boateng v Hughmans* [2002] Lloyd's Rep PN 419, CA, for a claim in which the claimant failed to satisfy the burden of proof.
4 [1998] PNLR 122, CA. In so doing the Court of Appeal followed *O'Donnell v Reichard* [1975] VR 916.

3 How would the defendant have acted?

3.18 We have already suggested that, in considering what the defendant would have done if there had been no breach of duty, the court will generally assume that the defendant would non-negligently have performed his or her duty rather than that the defendant would not have been involved at all.[1] Although the principle is not demonstrated in the solicitors' negligence cases, it appears that the defendant may rely on the principle that, as long as the conduct in question was non-negligent, the defendant would have behaved in the way that was most beneficial to the defendant rather than most beneficial to the claimant.[2] Finally, it seems likely that the defendant's conduct must be assessed on the balance of probabilities rather than the loss of a chance basis, which we discuss in the next section. This is because the defendant, like the claimant, is likely to be before the court.

1 See para 3.11, above.
2 See *McGregor on Damages* at [8–060].

4 How would third parties have acted? Damages for the loss of a chance

(*a*) Basic issues

3.19 In *Allied Maples v Simmons & Simmons*,[1] a solicitors' negligence case, Stuart-Smith LJ, with whom Hobhouse LJ agreed, said that where the claimant's loss depends on showing what a third party would have done if the defendant had given the appropriate advice, the claimant will succeed if there is a substantial chance that the third party would have acted so as to avoid the loss. The court will then quantify damages by discounting the total sum claimed to reflect the percentage chance that the loss would have been avoided. So if due to my solicitor's negligence I lost a 30% chance of winning £100,000 then I would be entitled to £30,000 in damages. This notion has led to a substantial body of cases, particularly against solicitors, in which courts have awarded damages for the loss of a chance that a third party would have acted in a way that would have benefited the claimant. These cases may be divided into two categories, depending on whether the solicitor's negligence related to litigation or to non-contentious business. The principles relating to each category are not precisely the same.

1 [1995] 1 WLR 1602 at 1611B and 1618H.

3.20 The cases on damages for the loss of a chance give rise to some basic questions, not all of which have yet received convincing answers. The most obvious are these:

(i) why are damages for the loss of a chance available in claims for economic loss but not in claims for physical damage?

(ii) Are damages for the loss of a chance available in all cases where, due to the defendant's negligence, a claimant has missed the opportunity of a third party conferring an economic benefit on the claimant?

(iii) In considering what would have happened in the same hypothetical situation, why is it appropriate to determine what the claimant would have done on the balance of probabilities and what a third party would have done on a loss of a chance basis?

(iv) Why should there be separate rules, in relation to solicitors' negligence, as between claims for the loss of litigation and other claims?

As to question (i), it is correct to say that, in personal injury cases, once a claimant has proved that the defendant caused him or her physical injury, the court may assess the quantification of damages attributable to that injury by looking at chances of future events happening and discounting them. So the driver who negligently injures a young footballer, on his way to a trial with Manchester United, may have to pay 50% of what the footballer would have earned if he turned out to be the next David Beckham[1]. It is thought, however, that that type of exercise differs from the economic loss cases: in the example, it has already been proved that the driver is liable for having caused some degree of personal injury, which sounds in damages, to the claimant. The loss of a chance approach is used to quantify the additional damages flowing from the injury. In economic loss cases, however, it is clear that the court may award damages purely for the loss of a chance, regardless of whether the defendant has also caused the claimant other loss. So in the economic loss cases damages for the loss of a chance need not be consequential on other types of loss, whereas in personal injury cases they must. Why the distinction?

1 See *McGregor on Damages* at [8–046].

3.21 The House of Lords considered question (i) in *Gregg v Scott*[1]. The claimant contended that, due to his general practitioner's failure to diagnose a lump as being potentially cancerous, his chances of dying from cancer had been increased. Only two members of the committee, Lord Hoffmann and Baroness Hale, considered that there were no circumstances in which damages should be awarded for the loss of a chance in clinical negligence cases.[2] Both of them took the view, however, that damages were properly recoverable for the loss of a chance of economic loss. That led to the question of why there should be such a distinction. Lord Hoffmann said that[3]

'... most of the cases in which there has been recovery for loss of a chance have involved financial loss, where the chance can itself plausibly be characterised as an item of property, like a lottery ticket.'

Further, in *Barker v Corus UK Ltd*,[4] referring to the cases on loss of a(n economic) chance, Lord Hoffmann said:

'Sometimes the law treats the loss of a chance of a favourable outcome as compensatable damage in itself. The likelihood that the favourable outcome would have happened must then be quantified ...'

Barker was a case considering the consequences of *Fairchild*.[5] Three other judges agreed with Lord Hoffmann. The effect of the majority's decision was that, in a case where it is impossible to prove whether the claimant's mesothelioma was caused by the defendant's wrongful exposure of the claimant to asbestos dust or by some other exposure to asbestos dust, the defendant is liable to the claimant for the extent to which the defendant increased the claimant's risk of contracting mesothelioma. Increasing the claimant's risk of contracting a disease is very similar to losing the claimant a chance of avoiding such a disease. So the majority's decision in *Barker* is a decision that, in the exceptional case where it is impossible to prove which asbestos dust caused the claimant's mesothelioma, the claimant can recover damages for what amounts to the loss of a chance to avoid physical injury[6]. Lord Rodger dissented, but he agreed that this was the effect of the majority's decision; that was part of the reason for his dissent.

1 [2005] UKHL 2, [2005] 2 AC 176.
2 Per Lord Hoffmann at [82] and [83] and Baroness Hale at [218] and [220].

3 [2006] UKHL 20, [2006] 2 AC 572, at [36]. He referred also to the theory that the conduct of human beings is not determined by impersonal laws of causality, and that this might explain why their conduct is judged on a 'loss of a chance' basis.
4 At [83].
5 See para 3.06, above.
6 McGregor 'Loss of a chance: where has it come from and where is it going?,' address to the Professional Negligence Bar Association on 14 October 2007. On the other hand the mere presence of pleural plaques, which are associated with a risk of future injury but do not themselves amount to an injury, does not cause recoverable damage: *Rothwell v Chemical and Insulating Co Ltd* [2007] UKHL 39, [2007] 3 WLR 876.

3.22 These dicta suggest that the courts may be moving towards the recognition of a theory primarily put forward by Stapleton that, where the court awards damages purely for the loss of a chance, in other words in cases *other* than those using loss of a chance to quantify losses consequential on a personal injury (referred to in para 3.20, above), the lost chance is the 'gist of the action'.[1] In the tort of negligence, damage is an essential part of the cause of action and when the court awards damages for the loss of a chance, the lost chance is what counts as the damage which the claimant has suffered. Hence, since the lost chance is the damage which the tort compensates, the lost chance is the gist of the action. Stapleton therefore suggests that the claimant must prove on the balance of probabilities that the defendant's negligence lost him or her the chance, whereupon the court assesses the value of the lost chance by asking what was the total potential value of the lost benefit and discounting for the chance that it would not have been obtained. She suggests that, on this approach, at the stage of quantifying the chance both the claimant's conduct and the third party's conduct should be assessed on a loss of a chance basis. One might support Stapleton's theory with the following point. When we look at cases where a solicitor's negligence has caused the claimant to lose the chance of having a trial, by for example causing the claim to be struck out, we find that the courts have in fact taken essentially this approach, of assessing the claimant's conduct in the lost litigation on a loss of a chance rather than a balance of probabilities basis: see the discussion of *Dixon v Clement Jones*[2] at para 12.32ff, below.

1 See Stapleton (2003) 119 LQR at 406–9 and (2005) 68 MLR 996 at 1005. For an alternative theory, also referred to in *Gregg v Scott*, see Reece 'Losses of Chances in the Law' (1996) 59 MLR 188, though we are doubtful whether the suggestions as to the judges' reasoning set out there are correct. See also Evans *Lawyers' Liabilities* (2nd edn, 2002), ch 12; Reid 'The hypothetical outcome in professional negligence claims', parts I, (2001) 17 PN 129, and II, (2001) 17 PN 262; Sir David Neuberger 'Loss of a Chance', notes of a lecture delivered to the Professional Negligence Bar Association on 9 February 2005; and Cannon 'Why Allied Maples is wrong', notes of a paper given to the Professional Negligence Bar Association in October 2005.
2 [2004] EWCA Civ 1005, [2005] PNLR 6.

3.23 This approach also fits well with cases where a defendant's breach of duty has lost the claimant a contractual right to participate in a beauty contest.[1] It might suggest that damages for the loss of a chance are not necessarily available in every case of economic loss, and some cases suggest that this is so.[2] In *Equitable Life Assurance Society v Ernst & Young*[3] Langley J suggested that:

'Those few circumstances in which the law has recognised a claim for the loss of a chance are, I think, ones where the relevant duty has been one the purpose of which was to provide the claimant with a chance or opportunity lost.'

Langley J's decision was appealed. The Court of Appeal did not deal directly with this quotation, but did hold that the loss of a chance approach could apply to lost opportunities to obtain sales, which were the facts of *Equitable Life*.[4] In *Normans Bay Ltd v Coudert Brothers*[5], the defendant solicitors Coudert had negligently failed to ensure that a particular risk that a transaction on which they were advising the claimant client might be void was minimised. Waller LJ, with whom Laws and Carnwath LJJ agreed on this point, said that damages for loss of a chance were available because:

'what Coudert was contractually bound to supply but failed to supply was "the chance" that the transaction would not be defeated, and even that chance is dependant on a second element the hypothetical acts of third parties at the advice stage. It is of course also dependant on the hypothetical acts of third parties at the stage of assessing what the chances were of the transaction actually being safe. It seems to me that one thing ought to be clear, if under their contractual obligations this is a case where the chance should have been provided unless that chance is of no real value at all or totally incapable of being quantified, damages for that loss should be recoverable ... a contract to provide a chance can be enforced, and ... damages can be given for a failure to fulfil that contract if the chance has some real value.'

1   *Chaplin v Hicks* [1911] 2 KB 786, CA. This case is the modern origin of claims for damages for the loss of a chance.
2   See *McGregor on Damages* at [8–037].
3   [2003] EWHC 112 (Comm), [2003] PNLR 23, at [94].
4   [2003] EWCA Civ 1114, [2004] PNLR 16, at [85].
5   [2003] EWCA Civ 215, *The Times*, 24 March 2004, at [34]–[35].

3.24   It is thought that the courts have yet to work out the full nature of the loss of a chance doctrine. It is by no means certain that, as *Allied Maples* might suggest, such damages are available in every case where a claimant's economic loss is dependent on what a third party would have done. But if there is some limit to the recovery of such damages then it has yet to be fully articulated. The scope of this book is claims against solicitors. So far as we are aware, there are no claims against solicitors, post-*Allied Maples*, in which the court has expressly held that, although proving loss depends on what a third party would have done, the loss of a chance approach should not be applied. The Privy Council has recently upheld the loss of a chance approach in cases relating to solicitors' negligence causing litigation to become statute-barred.[1] There can be little if any doubt that the loss of a chance approach is the correct one in that type of case, and it may be that Langley J's explanation is the best one: the solicitors' function is to give the client the chance of winning at trial, so if the chance is lost due to negligence, damages should be awarded for the loss of the chance. This would be consistent with the passage quoted from Waller LJ in *Normans Bay*, which was a lost transaction case as opposed to a lost litigation case. Hence one might say that, if solicitors' function is to give the client the chance of a better outcome in its transaction, then damages for the loss of a chance are available against the solicitors. Perhaps the position is that most of a solicitor's work involves attempting to give the client a better chance of a more favourable outcome, so that the loss of a chance approach is applicable to all or almost all of a solicitor's work.

1 *Phillips & Co v Whatley* [2007] UKPC 28, [2007] PNLR 27.

3.25 As to question (iii) posed at para 3.20, above, the lost litigation cases (chapter 12, below) show that in some circumstances the court will assess the claimant's own conduct on the loss of a chance basis. In *Gregg v Scott*[1], Lord Hoffmann said that the reason why the claimant's conduct was assessed on the balance of probabilities and a third party's on a loss of a chance basis was a matter of policy. But he did not say what the policy was. In *Stone Heritage Developments Ltd v Davis Blank Furniss*[2], HHJ Hodge QC sitting as a deputy High Court judge suggested, obiter, that the policy might be that it was likely to be difficult for a claimant to prove what third parties would have done. In the instant case, however, the third parties had given evidence so that this difficulty did not arise. The judge suggested that, in cases where all potentially relevant material was before the court, the rationale for applying the loss of a chance approach was no longer present and he should apply the standard balance of probabilities test to determining what the third parties would have done. It is thought, however, that this approach could lead to difficulties in determining whether a case is one in which there is enough evidence before the court to allow the balance of probabilities as opposed to the loss of a chance approach to apply in deciding what third parties would have done. Further, McGregor suggests that the policy is that, since a claimant is the party bringing the claim, it ought to be possible for the claimant to prove what he or she would have done, so that the balance of probabilities approach should apply to determining what the claimant would have done.[3] This casts doubt on Judge Hodge QC's suggestion, since Judge Hodge thought that the policy behind the distinction was a different one. Moreover, if the 'loss of an economic asset' theory is the correct explanation of loss of a chance cases, then perhaps the correct approach will ultimately turn out to be that suggested in *Dixon v Clement Jones*[4] in relation to lost litigation cases: in terms of proving that, if the defendant had not acted negligently, the claimant would have followed the defendant's advice, the claimant must as usual prove his or her case on the balance of probabilities. Once this is proved, however, in quantifying the value of the right or asset which the claimant has lost, the conduct of both the claimant and the third party should be assessed on a loss of a chance basis. At the time of writing, however, this is certainly not the law in relation to cases other than those relating to the loss of litigation. But the answer to question (iv) posed at para 3.20 above is not entirely clear: why should there be a distinction between lost litigation and other cases?[5]

1 Above, at [83].
2 Ch D, 1 June 2006 at [330]–[334]. Although the case went to the Court of Appeal, the latter did not deal with the loss of a chance issue: see [2007] EWCA Civ 765 at [47].
3 *McGregor on Damages* at [8–035].
4 [2004] EWCA Civ 1005, [2005] PNLR 6.
5 Further, as Lord Neuberger has pointed out extra-judicially, if the question is whether the claimant would have reached an agreement with a third party, the task of asking on the balance of probabilities whether the claimant would have entered into the deal and on a loss of a chance basis whether the third party would have done so is a difficult exercise for judges to carry out. See his talk to the Professional Negligence Bar Association referred to above. See also *Veitch v Avery* [2007] EWCA Civ 711. Due to the defendant's negligence the claimants lost the chance to defend possession proceedings in relation to the country house hotel which they ran as a business. Auld LJ held that *Dixon v Clement Jones* applied, but then said at [26] that (i) the question of what the claimants would have done should be determined on the balance of probabilities, and (ii) for these purposes, one of the claimants' father should be treated as if he were the claimant, so that the balance of probabilities test should apply to what the father would have done. The correctness of (i) is doubted, in light of the view expressed above as to the effect of *Dixon*; (ii) appears to be novel.

(b) Claims involving the negligent conduct of litigation

3.26 As indicated above, among claims against solicitors those involving the negligent conduct of litigation provide perhaps the most obvious application of the loss of a chance approach. Such cases are, however, fully dealt with in chapter 12[1], and need not be dealt with here, though it is possible that some of the techniques used in those cases may be imported into non-litigation cases: see below. As indicated above, the most striking difference between these cases and the remaining cases awarding damages for the loss of a chance against solicitors is that there are circumstances in which, in the loss of litigation context, the court will use the loss of a chance approach to assess not only what the third party would have done but also what the claimant would have done.

1 At para 12.31ff, below.

(c) Other claims against solicitors

3.27 The first question is whether the claimant can show that there is more than a speculative chance that, in the absence of negligence, he or she would have obtained the benefit, or avoided the detriment, said to be the subject of the chance based on the third party's action.[1] The court then assesses what the claimant would have gained if successful, and discounts for his or her chance of success. In *Allied Maples* itself, this approach was found to be applicable to the question of whether the claimant carpet company would have been able to negotiate a revised contract to purchase shares in another company: would the vendor have agreed to include protection for the claimant against a contingent liability? The loss of a chance approach was held appropriate on the similar facts of *Football League Ltd v Edge Ellison*[2]. The Football League alleged that the defendant solicitors had negligently failed to advise it to procure guarantees from the parent companies of the other party to a commercial contract. The claim failed on the basis that the defendant had no duty to give such advice, but, obiter, Rimer J summarised the principles relating to damages for the loss of a chance which would have applied in the following way:[3]

> 'The [claimant] must prove that, had guarantees been sought on May 10/11, 2000, it had a real or substantial chance of getting them, as opposed to a speculative chance. If it fails to prove this, the claim also fails on causation. But if it can prove it, the evaluation of the chance it has so lost is part of the assessment of the recoverable damages, the available range being between something that just qualifies as real or substantial at one end and near certainty at the other end (see *Allied Maples...*). If the [claimant] crosses the threshold, then if there is a range of possible outcomes, it may be appropriate for the court to assess the likelihood of each outcome in making its overall assessment of the lost chance (see *Ball v Druces & Atlee (A Firm) (No 2)* [2004] PNLR 39). Further, in assessing the loss, and in the circumstances that it is the defendant's negligence which lost the claimant the opportunity of (in this case) obtaining full security for [the third party]'s covenant, it may be appropriate for the court to err on the side of generosity towards the claimant (see *Mount v Barker Austin ...*). I do not interpret this last guidance as meaning that the court should assess the appropriate measure and then give the claimant a bonus. I interpret it rather as meaning that if the court has a doubt as to the percentage within a given bracket that correctly reflects the lost chance, it should be disposed to give the benefit of the doubt to the claimant.'

Three points arise from this passage. First, the approach of erring on the side of generosity towards the claimant originated in claims where due to the defendant's negligence a piece of litigation was struck out for want of prosecution. That was the context of *Mount v Barker Austin*, and, at least originally, the principle was expressed to apply only in such cases. The principle was then extended to cover a wider range of cases of lost litigation. Rimer J does not explain why the principle should also be applied outside the context of lost litigation claims, but presumably the rationale is that if there is doubt in the assessment process, and the reason there is doubt is because the defendant's negligence prevented the matter from being dealt with earlier, then such doubt should redound to the disadvantage of the defendant. This raises the question of whether other principles which have been applied in the lost litigation context should be applied outside that context. See chapter 12 for a detailed discussion of those principles. Secondly, at least in the context of lost litigation cases, it appears that a chance as low as 10% may be sufficient to count as 'substantial' as opposed to 'speculative' or 'negligible': see para.12.37, below.

1 See *Allied Maples Group v Simmons & Simmons* [1995] 1 WLR 1602 at 1611B. In the context of lost litigation cases, in *Mount v Barker Austin* [1998] PNLR 493, Simon Brown LJ preferred the formulation 'more than negligible', but that was because he held that, in such cases, any uncertainty caused by delay due to the loss of the litigation should count against the defendant rather than the claimant. This is not necessarily the case outside that context.
2 [2006] EWHC 1462 (Ch), [2007] PNLR 2.
3 At [286].

3.28 Thirdly, the approach in *Ball*, where the question was whether in the absence of negligence the claimant would have had a share in the profits of the Eden Project, is derived from personal injury cases where the claimant might, if not injured, have achieved varying levels of success in his career. Nelson J said[1]:

'Where there are various possible outcomes to an assessment of quantum the right approach is to evaluate the chance of success of each of the possible outcomes, giving a percentage assessment for each category of lost chance ... double counting must be avoided and the chance of failure evaluated.'

Note, however, that Rimer J said only that the court 'may' adopt this approach. In *Earl of Malmesbury v Strutt & Parker*[2], Jack J found it most helpful and realistic to decide what the most likely figure was, rather than looking at a range of figures. He observed that his was in accord with the Court of Appeal's decision in *Browning v Brachers*.[3] *Browning* was a loss of litigation case, discussed in chapter 12. So again this shows the court drawing on the lost litigation cases in a slightly different context.

1 See [2004] PNLR 39 at [275].
2 [2007] EWHC 999 (QB), [2007] PNLR 29, at [149].
3 [2005] EWCA Civ 753 at [122] and [212]. See para 12.45, below. The case was an appeal from Jack J himself.

3.29 But earlier cases show further differences of approach in assessing the outcome of commercial negotiations. In *Allied Maples* there was a difference of opinion about the inferences which the court could draw about the conduct of the third parties. Hobhouse LJ stated:[1]

'Negotiations may depend on the will of the parties and neither party was under any obligation at that stage to agree anything. But it is unrealistic to treat the outcome of further negotiation between the commercial parties as arbitrary and wholly unpredictable.'

Millett LJ, who dissented, did not consider that the outcome of commercial negotiations could be considered in the same light as, for example, the likelihood that a husband would have changed his will in favour of his wife. He said:[2]

'The outcome would then have depended on Gillow's perception of the relative strengths of the parties' bargaining positions, the extent of the risk which they were being asked to assume and the effect on the deal if they refused. These are all subjective matters; none of them is known and none can be inferred.'

In the event it was unnecessary for the Court of Appeal to evaluate the chance.

1 [1995] 1 WLR 1602 at 1620G.
2 [1995] 1 WLR 1602 at 1624F.

3.30 Further, compare the courts' approaches in the following three cases. In *Inter-Leisure Ltd v Lamberts*[1] where the defendants, who were acting for the landlord claimant, had inserted an upwards downwards rent review clause in a lease when they should have inserted an upwards only provision, the judge had to evaluate two chances: first, whether the tenant would have agreed to an upwards only rent review clause; and, secondly, whether the tenants would have exercised a break option in the lease available for the first three years in the event that the upwards only rent review clause had been inserted.[2] Neither side called the evidence of the tenants on either issue. But the judge was able to find on the available evidence that there was a 75% chance that the tenants would have agreed to an upwards only clause and a one-third chance that they would not have exercised the break option, leaving a 50% chance that the claimant would have had a lease with an upwards only rent review clause after three years. In *Titanic Investments Ltd v MacFarlanes*[3] where the defendants, acting for the claimant vendors, had agreed to a price formula for the exercise of a number of options without instructions, the judge found that, despite the absence of any direct oral evidence from the purchaser, '[t]he parties would have most probably agreed a short extension of time to permit further urgent negotiations to take place' and 'I do not find that there was any substantial chance that [the purchaser] would walk away from the options'. Finally, in *Hartle v Laceys*[4] the defendant solicitors negligently indicated to their client's neighbours that they had failed to register a restrictive covenant with the consequence that their client, the claimant, lost an opportunity to sell the property free of the covenant. The principal question for the Court of Appeal was whether there was a substantial chance that the claimant would have completed a sale before registration and this turned on four different contingencies: when the neighbour would have registered, whether planning permission could have been obtained, whether the claimant would have sold to one interested party or whether he would have sold to anyone else. After a detailed analysis of the evidence on each contingency, Ward LJ found that there was a 60% chance that a sale would have been achieved. It is significant that all of the relevant parties gave evidence: the claimant, the neighbour and the potential purchasers. Unlike the judge in *Inter-Leisure Ltd v Lamberts*, Ward LJ made no attempt to quantify the chance of each contingency.

1 [1997] NPC 49.

3.31 *Causation and damages at common law*

2 On the first review date when the tenants could still have exercised the break clause the rent was reviewed down by approximately £50,000 per annum.

3 [1997] NPC 105, CA. This point was not argued on appeal (3 December 1998, unreported), CA.

4 [1999] Lloyd's Rep PN 315, CA.

3.31 In each of the three cases, there was a range of possible outcomes. In *Inter-Leisure* the judge accepted that, even if the tenants had exercised the break clause after three years, the claimant would have been left with a freehold which was more valuable than the reversion to a defective lease. Whatever the actions of the third parties, the claimant would have been better off to some extent. Because he had found that there was a 50% chance that the claimant would have had a lease with an upwards only rent review clause and a 50% chance that it would have had vacant possession, he awarded the claimant damages to reflect *both* contingencies: first, 50% of the difference between the value of the reversion with a good lease and its value with the lease as granted and, secondly, 50% of the difference between the vacant possession value of the property and the value with the lease as granted.[1] In *Titanic Investments*, by contrast, the judge found that there were, again, two likely outcomes. Instead of calculating damages on each basis and then discounting each by the percentage chance, the judge calculated damages on the following basis:[2]

> 'In this case I have thought it right to examine in some detail what seem to me to be the two most likely outcomes, that is success in resumed negotiations between the parties to arrive at a fixed price and (less probably) reference to an expert. Having done so I must take a broad view and arrive at a figure at some appropriate mean or median point within the range of possibilities, with no further discount because the particular outcome was only a chance; other comparable chances would lie on either side, cancelling each other out.'

In *Hartle v Laceys,* where there was range of possible sales between £350,000 and £410,000, the court also adopted a final figure (after deduction of legal and estate agent's fees) of £360,000. Ward LJ stated:[3]

> 'We have found that Mr Hartle lost the chance of selling his property before the market slumped. We have decided that he had a real chance of selling for £375,000, that being our valuation of the price which would have been agreed between a willing vendor – Mr Hartle – and a willing purchaser in the market conditions of the day. Had such a sale taken place, only the net proceeds would have enured for his benefit and so the estate agent's and solicitor's costs fall to be deducted. Making some estimate of those and perhaps rounding down, I assess the net proceeds of the lost sale to be £360,000. That is my starting point. The parties are at liberty to calculate a more precise figure but I do not encourage it.'

It is suggested that neither approach is necessarily wrong. Some cases may lend themselves to one form of analysis rather than the other. Where there are one or two potential outcomes each of which places the claimant in a better position, the former approach will lead to more accurate compensation. Where, however, there are a number of contingencies and a number of outcomes, it seems more suitable to assess the chances globally.

1 A similar approach was adopted on one particular element of damages in *Blue Circle Industries plc v Ministry of Defence* [1999] Ch 289, CA. See per Simon Brown LJ at 414d–415b.
2 Transcript, pp 32–3.
3 [1999] Lloyd's Rep PN 315 at 329, col 2.

3.32 Finally, in *Hartle v Laceys* the Court of Appeal also considered whether the amount which the claimant actually achieved from the sale of the property should be deducted from the amount which he would, or might have achieved, before the 40% reduction was made or after the discount. The court concluded that this amount should be deducted *before* any discount was applied, thereby increasing the amount of damages. This conclusion was reached on the basis that what the court was being called upon to value was the chance that the claimant might achieve a better price than he actually did:

> 'Look at it another way. When Miss Chaplin lost the opportunity to participate in Mr Hicks' beauty contest, there was nothing left for her. She had lost the only chance she would ever have had of winning the prize. Having lost the chance, she was left with nothing. Mr Hartle did not lose everything when he lost this sale. He lost the chance of the sale but he did not lose the property itself. He retained the chance to sell it at some indeterminate time for some indeterminate price. He lost the chance of getting the excess of a over b but his chance of getting a–b was only 60% and so he should only recover 60% of it'.[1]

1 Per Ward LJ, [1999] Lloyd's Rep PN 315 at 330, col 1.

3.33 In *Stovold v Barlows*[1] the defendants acted for a vendor. On 13 September 1989 a secretary failed to check whether the purchaser's solicitors were on the DX and sent the title deeds to the wrong firm altogether. As a consequence the purchaser withdrew and bought another property. The purchaser first looked at the other property which he ultimately bought on 15 September 1999, which was the day he was told that the deeds for the first property had not arrived. In evidence he said that he would probably not have gone to see it otherwise. The claimant vendor claimed the difference between the price agreed with this first purchaser and the price for which the property was ultimately sold. The question of damage turned, therefore, on two questions: first, whether, if posted, the deeds would have arrived on 15 September 1989 and, secondly, whether the purchaser would still have gone to look at the second property in any event. The Court of Appeal held that there was a 50% chance that the purchase would have gone ahead and the claimant recovered 50% of the price reduction.[2] In *First Interstate Bank of California v Cohen Arnold & Co*[3] it was found that, but for the defendants' negligence, the claimant bank would have begun to market its security two months earlier than it did. The market was falling. The judge found that 'his best estimate' was that the property would have been sold for £3m. He awarded damages without evaluating the chance that this price would not be achieved and discounting it. The Court of Appeal ruled that there was a two-thirds chance that this price would be achieved and discounted damages accordingly. The critical factor was the uncertainty of the market at the time and the speed at which it was falling.[4] This is an odd case, as Sedley J recognised.[5] In the normal case the court will be able to make reliable findings about market values. But in this case, market conditions were so volatile that the judge felt unable to do so.

1 [1996] PNLR 91, CA.
2 The trial took place before *Allied Maples* had been decided and there had been no expert evidence about the probabilities of a postal delivery on 15 September 1989.
3 [1996] PNLR 17, accountant's negligence.
4 See [1996] PNLR 17 at 25D, 30F–31C and 3112.
5 [1996] PNLR 17 at 31D–E.

3.34 Also concerning property and planning permission, in *Motor Crown Petroleum Ltd v SJ Berwin*[1] the claimant was awarded damages for the chance that a challenge to a local authority's local plan would have been successful and that an appeal against a refusal of planning permission would therefore have succeeded. This is similar to negligence in the conduct of litigation. In *Finley v Connell Associates*[2] the court awarded damages for the loss of the chance that, in the absence of negligence, the claimant would have been able to negotiate a change to a development agreement without having to pay a premium for consent for the change.

1 [2000] Lloyd's Rep PN 438, CA.
2 [2002] Lloyd's Rep PN 62, Ouseley J.

C THE *SAAMCO* PRINCIPLE: EXTENT OF THE DEFENDANT'S LIABILITY

1 General approach to extent of liability

3.35 In para 3.01 we suggested, following the passage quoted there from Lord Nicholls, that there should be a two-stage approach to the question of causation and damages.[1] The first stage was the predominantly factual enquiry which, we have argued, in solicitors' negligence cases will generally amount to asking whether, but for the claimant's breach of duty, the defendant would have suffered the loss claimed. If the claimant fails at that stage the claim fails.

Assuming, however, that the claimant passes the 'but for' test, the law imposes further tests to determine the extent of the defendant's liability. The tests applied at this second stage depend on value judgments as to (i) the kind and (ii) the extent of damage for which it is fair to hold the claimant liable. Lord Nicholls said that those questions are answered by reference to 'the reasons why the law has recognised the cause of action in question'. In many cases it was easy to determine which of the causal factors leading to the claimant's loss should be treated as the factor which the law regarded as bearing responsibility for it. But, in the cases where this was difficult:

> 'it is of crucial importance to identify the purpose of the relevant cause of action and the nature and scope of the defendant's obliga-tion in the particular circumstances. What was the ambit of the defendant's duty? In respect of what risks or damage does the law seek to afford protection by means of the particular tort?'[2]

In modern times, the principal author of this approach is Lord Hoffmann. He originally described it as asking what the scope of the legal duty imposed was, but in a more recent article has stated that the question is more accurately described as concerning the extent of the liability.[3] We therefore use the latter term here. In the case commonly known as *SAAMCo*[4], he said that in tort the extent of the duty depended on the purpose of the rule imposing the duty, and in contract it depended on construing the agreement as a whole in its commercial setting; the extent of the liability, in the sense of the consequences for which a contracting party would be responsible if in breach of contract, depended on what the law regarded as giving best effect to the express obligations assumed by that party. In a subsequent lecture given in 1999, Lord Hoffmann said that the argument in difficult cases over causation was:[5]

> '... almost always an argument over the law. It is an argument over the true scope of the rule which imposes liability. In particular, there are two kinds of questions about the rule which have to be answered before you can properly formulate the question of fact about causa-tion. The first is to identify the grounds upon which the rule imposes liability. The second is to identify the kind of loss for which it provides compensation. Once those questions have been answered, the question of causation does indeed become a question of fact and usually a pretty obvious one at that.'

This approach is derived from Hart & Honoré. They give a simple example, in relation to statutes[6]:

> 'A bus company admits passengers in excess of the maximum imposed for the safety of the vehicle, and a pickpocket, taking advantage of the crush, steals a passenger's property. The reason why in such cases there is no liability [sc: of the bus company] is to be found by asking what the purpose or scope of the statute is.'

The purpose of the statute is not to protect passengers from thieves, so the bus company is not liable for the theft, even though it would not have occurred if the bus company had not breached the statute.

1 *Kuwait Airways Corpn v Iraqi Airways Co (Nos 4 and 5)* [2002] UKHL 19, [2002] 2 AC 883, at [70].
2 [2002] UKHL 19, [2002] 2 AC 883 at [71].
3 (2005) 121 LQR 592 at 596.
4 But reported sub nom *Banque Bruxelles SA v Eagle Star* [1997] AC 191, HL, 212D–F.
5 'Common Sense and Causing Loss', lecture to the Chancery Bar Association given on 15 June 1999.
6 *Causation in the Law* (2nd edn, 1995) 103.

3.36   If, therefore, the claimant passes the 'but for' test, the court must ask whether the kind of loss that the claimant claims is the kind of loss for which the defendant's breach of duty ought to render the defendant liable, and whether the extent of loss claimed ought to be as much as the claimant contends. This depends on a value judgment to be made by reference both to the purpose of the rule imposing liability and to the detailed facts of the particular case. In *Johnson v Gore Wood*[1] Arden LJ said that

> 'Starting with *Caparo v Dickman,* the courts have moved away from characterising questions as to the measure of damages for the tort of negligence as questions of causation and remoteness. The path that once led in that direction now leads in a new direction. The courts now analyse such questions by enquiring whether the duty which the tortfeasor owed was a duty in respect of the kind of loss of which the victim complains. Duty is no longer determined in abstraction from the consequences or vice-versa. The same test applies whether the duty of care is contractual or tortious. To determine the scope of the duty the court must examine carefully the purpose for which advice was being given and generally the surrounding circumstances. The determination of the scope of the duty thus involves an intensely fact-sensitive exercise. The final result turns on the facts, and it is likely to be only the general principles rather than the solution in any individual case that are of assistance in later cases.'

The net effect of the passages quoted is that, in cases where the extent of the claimant's liability is not obvious, such as those where there are plausible alternative causes for the loss which the claimant has suffered, the correct approach is to ask whether the kind and extent of the loss which the claimant claims is properly to be regarded as within the scope of the duty which the defendant has breached. It is thought that this approach is generally preferable to asking whether, as a matter of common sense, the defendant caused the loss claimed: the latter question obscures rather than reveals the court's reasoning[2]. The *SAAMCo* approach is intended to clarify it. But, if this approach is adopted, that is not to say that it will necessarily make it easy to decide such difficult cases. As Arden LJ pointed out, precedent may be of limited value in deciding cases, and there may be no substitute for mastery of the facts. It is thought, however, that this is not a fault of the theory; it is simply the position that deciding difficult cases requires a lot of careful work. What it suggests, though, is that the value of precedent in determining such cases may be limited to indicating the general approach to be adopted.

1 [2003] EWCA Civ 1728, at [90]–[91].
2 For a contrary view, see Kinsky '*SAAMCo* 10 years on: causation and scope of duty in professional negligence cases' (2006) PN 86.

3.37 It would, however, be wrong to conclude that the effect of the *SAAMCo* approach is simply to provide general guidance as to the assessment of damages at a very abstract level. In the context of lenders' claims, the cases show a very specific application of SAAMCo: see para 10.79ff, below. But, at a more general level, in addition to the principles we have already discussed, Lord Hoffmann has indicated a more specific approach to be applied in cases of negligent failure to provide information, which will often encompass solicitors' negligence claims, and as to what might be termed the standard problem cases in causation, those where the acts of the claimant or of third parties, or natural events, are plausible alternative candidates for being treated as the cause of the loss. We consider these below.

2   Extent of liability: negligently providing information; information/advice distinction

3.38 In *SAAMCo*, Lord Hoffmann said that where a party was in breach of a duty to take reasonable care in providing information on the basis of which someone else (the claimant) would decide upon a course of action, the defendant[1]

'is not generally regarded as responsible for all the consequences of that course of action. He is responsible only for the consequences of the information being wrong.'

He illustrated this principle by reference to an example[2]:

'A mountaineer about to undertake a difficult climb is concerned about the fitness of his knee. He goes to a doctor who negligently makes a superficial examination and pronounces the knee fit. The climber goes on the expedition, which he would not have undertaken if the doctor had told him the true state of his knee. He suffers an injury which is an entirely foreseeable consequence of mountaineering but has nothing to do with his knee ... On what I have suggested

115

is the more usual principle, the doctor is not liable. The injury has not been caused by the doctor's bad advice because it would have occurred even if the advice had been correct.'

The effect of this principle is that, in cases where the defendant has breached a duty to take reasonable care to provide information on the basis of which the claimant will decide what to do, even if the claimant passes the 'but for' test, in assessing damages the court should compare (i) the position the claimant is in fact in with (ii) the position the claimant would have been in if the information had been correct. If this test shows no loss then, unless there is some reason why Lord Hoffmann's principle should not apply[3], the claimant should be awarded only nominal damages. The point of the principle is to limit damage recoverable from the defendant to that which is truly caused by the defendant's breach of duty and not by some other factor. So if the defendant is a valuer whose duty is limited to estimating the current value of a property, and does not extend to predicting later falls in the residential property market, then the defendant's liability will be limited to the amount of any negligent over-valuation, assessed as at the date of the valuation. It will not include losses caused by later falls in the property market which it was not part of the defendant's duty to predict.[4] If an actuary negligently advises a client that pensions with company A will attract statutory protection if A becomes insolvent, when they will not, and the client takes a pension with A only because he thought the pension would attract statutory protection, the client will recover nothing if his pension with A performs badly but A does not become insolvent: even if the information had been correct, the client would have been no better off, because the statutory protection for insolvency would not have been triggered.[5]

1 [1997] AC at 214D.
2 [1997] AC at 213D–F.
3 Such as cases of fraudulent misrepresentation, breach of warranty, or possibly misrepresentation inducing a party to enter a contract contrary to Misrepresentation Act 1967, s 2(1). See [1997] AC at 215F-216D.
4 Compare the facts of *SAAMCo* itself.
5 *Andrews v Barnett Waddingham LLP* [2006] EWCA Civ 93, [2006] PNLR 24.

3.39 Lord Hoffmann distinguished the case of the person with a duty to provide information from the case of a person with a duty to advise someone what to do[1]:

'If the duty is to advise whether or not a course of action should be taken, the adviser must take reasonable care to consider all the potential consequences of that course of action. If he is negligent, he will therefore be responsible for all the foreseeable loss which is a consequence of that course of action having been taken.'

It is thought that solicitors will generally be found to have been under duties to provide information, rather than duties to advise what to do.[2] But in *Gerson v*

Haines Watts[3] Rimer J considered the distinction and said that it was possible that the answer to the question of whether a professional bears all the risks of a transaction:

> 'would ultimately be a policy driven one and would not simply depend on whether the case was an information one or an advice one.'

He analysed the facts and concluded that, on the special facts of the case, it was arguable that solicitors who knew that the client depended entirely on their advice and might suffer considerable losses if they were wrong must bear all the client's loss and not just that part which was referable to the information being wrong.

1 [1997] AC at 214E–F.
2 For an example, see *Petersen v Personal Representatives of Rivlin* [2002] Lloyd's Rep PN 386, CA.
3 [2002] Lloyd's Rep PN 493 at 498 col.2.

3 New intervening causes and alternative causes

3.40 Once it has been shown that the defendant's conduct was a 'but for' cause of the loss, the question may arise of whether other causes, such as the conduct of the third party or the claimants themselves, should be treated as the cause of the loss. In *Kuwait Airways*[1], Lord Nicholls said that:

> 'In most cases, how far the responsibility of the defendant ought fairly to extend evokes an immediate intuitive response. This is informed common sense by another name. Usually, there is no difficulty in selecting, from the sequence of events leading to the plaintiff's loss, the happening which should be regarded as the cause of the loss for the purpose of allocating responsibility.'

Pausing there, Stapleton makes a similar point[2]:

> 'Of course, the law is never overburdened by a huge range of historical factors leading to an outcome because the elements of a cause of action that precede this issue in the analysis, such as duty and breach, focus the cause-in-fact inquiry only on the few factors of legal concern.'

Lord Nicholls continued:

> 'In other cases, when the outcome of the second inquiry is not obvious, it is of crucial importance to identify the purpose of the

relevant cause of action and the nature and scope of the defendant's obligation in the particular circumstances. What was the ambit of the defendant's duty? In respect of what risks or damage does the law seek to afford protection by means of the particular tort? Recent decisions of this House have highlighted the point. When evaluating the extent of the losses for which a negligent valuer should be responsible the scope of the valuer's duty must first be identified: see [*SAAMCo*]. In *Reeves v Metropolitan Police Comr* [2000] 1 AC 360 the free, deliberate and informed act of a human being, there committing suicide, did not negative responsibility to his dependants when the defendant's duty was to guard against that very act.'

To paraphrase, in such difficult cases where there are two or more plausible candidates as to the cause of the claimant's loss to which the court should ascribe legal responsibility, the *SAAMCo* approach of asking what is the kind, and extent, of loss from which it is the purpose of the relevant tort to protect the claimant, may help to answer the question of whether it is the defendant's conduct, or the other possible cause, to which liability should be ascribed.

1   Above, [2002] 2 AC 883 at [71].
2   [2003] LQR 388 at 392.

3.41   As Lord Nicholls also said in *Kuwait*[1], principles which are used to limit loss 'assist in promoting some consistency of general approach' but 'these are guidelines, some more helpful than others, but they are never more than this'. So there are no hard and fast rules. One may, however, suggest that, in the context of negligence, where the defendant's negligence is a 'but for' cause of the claimant's loss but there is an alternative candidate for the cause to which legal liability might be attached, there are some general guideline principles which may apply.

1   [2002] 2 AC 883 at [70].

(*a*) *Claimant's conduct*

3.42   Where the claimant's conduct is at fault, there may be a deduction from damages on account of contributory negligence. The defendant may be able to argue that the claimant's conduct invokes the doctrine of *volenti non fit injuria* or *novus actus interveniens* (new intervening cause) so as to excuse the defendant of liability. In *Young v Purdy*[1] the Court of Appeal held that the defendant's conduct was the 'occasion but not the cause' of the claimant's loss. The claimant retained the defendant solicitor to act for her in relation to claims against her former husband for ancillary relief. The law was that, if the claimant remarried before commencing a claim for financial provision for herself from her former husband, she was barred absolutely from making such a claim. The defendant knew that the claimant was living with another man. She instructed the defendant that she had no intention of remarrying. The defendant advised the claimant not to remarry pending the hearing of her proposed application for ancillary relief. The defendant wrongfully terminated her retainer by the claimant. Two days later, the claimant, acting in person, drew up a form seeking ancillary relief and lodged it at court. The claimant knew that she had to lodge the application for financial relief before remarrying, although she did not realise that her application was defective in that it failed to claim financial provision for herself. Three weeks later she remarried. The effect of remarrying, when taken with the defective application, was to bar absolutely any claim she might have had for financial provision for herself from her husband. Leggatt LJ said:[2]

'… the loss of the claimant's right to claim was entirely due to the claimant acting on her own, failing to complete the Form 11 correctly and remarrying before her error had been rectified. These matters the solicitor could not, in my judgment, reasonably have been expected to foresee whether separately or in combination.'

It is submitted that the court ascribed principal responsibility for the loss to the fault of the claimant, and for that reason held that the defendant's breach of duty was not the cause of the loss in law. Similarly, in *Gorham v British Telecommunications plc*,[3] the claimant received negligent pensions advice from the defendant. Later, he learnt the true position. The court held that losses that the claimant suffered after he had learnt the true position were not caused by the defendant's negligence. On the other hand, the 'extrication' cases, where a claimant reasonably attempts to mitigate the effect of the defendant's negligence, are examples of cases where the claimant's conduct is not at fault and so does not negative the causal effect of the defendant's negligence.[4] Further, the former rule that a claimant could not recover loss caused by the claimant's pre-existing 'impecuniosity', or, in non-legal language, lack of money, has been abandoned and is no longer the law.[5] So if it costs a particular claimant more to take remedial action to reduce the effect of the defendant's negligence because the claimant is poor, and has to borrow the money, the defendant must pay the extra cost: the defendant takes his victim as he finds him.[6]

1 [1997] PNLR 130.
2 At 138G.
3 [2000] 1 WLR 2129, CA. See 2143H–2144C. In *Finecard International Ltd v Urquart Dyke Lord* [2005] EWHC 2841 (Ch), [2006] PNLR 16, (patent agents) at [34] Peter Smith J said that the test of whether the claimant's conduct negatived causation by the defendant was not necessarily a question of whether the intervening act was negligent; rather, the question was whether the impact of the intervening act was 'of so powerful a nature' as to prevent the defendant's conduct being a cause of the loss.
4 See per Lord Hoffmann in *SAAMCo* [1997] AC 191 at 219A–B, and para 9.95ff, below. See also per Hobhouse LJ in *County Ltd v Girozentrale Securities* [1996] 3 All ER 834, CA, at 857A-E: claimant not at fault so claimant's conduct did not negative causation by defendant's breach of duty.
5 *Lagden v O'Connor* [2003] UKHL 64, [2004] 1 AC 1067.
6 Compare also the cases on interest at common law discussed below in section H of this chapter.

3.43 Note, however, that where there is deliberate and wrongful conduct of the claimant, which causes the damage, but is also 'the very thing' against which the defendant has a duty to protect the claimant, as where the police have a duty to protect prisoners who are known to be suicide risks from killing themselves, then it is not open to the defendant to argue that the claimant's conduct is so blameworthy as to negative the defendant's legal responsibility for the result, or, in the language of the standard cliché, 'break the chain of causation'. The damage suffered, in the example the claimant killing himself, is the damage against which the defendant has a duty to protect the claimant, so the defendant cannot assert that if the claimant kills himself the defendant is not liable for that kind of loss. The defendant is liable for it, subject to questions of contributory negligence.[1]

1 *Reeves v Comr of Police of the Metropolis* [2000] 1 AC 360, HL. Compare *Stone & Rolls Ltd v Moore Stephens* [2007] EWHC 1826 (Comm) [2008] PNLR 4 (Langley J).

3.44 Although it was decided before *SAAMCo*, it is submitted that the result in the solicitors' case of *British Racing Drivers' Racing Club v Hextall Erskine & Co*[1] may be interpreted in this way. The solicitors were found liable for failure to advise the board of the claimant company that a joint venture agreement for the acquisition of shares had to be approved by the company in meeting because one of the directors was interested in the contract. When the transaction was eventually put to the company at an extraordinary general meeting, the members refused to approve the contract and the company took steps to rescind it. After proceedings were commenced the company settled the litigation by reselling the shares to the interested director for £2.1m less than it had paid for them. It was argued that the loss suffered by the company was caused not by the negligence of the defendants but by the poor commercial judgment of the board. But Carnwath J found that the loss 'was within the reasonable scope of the dangers against which it was the solicitor's duty to provide protection'.[2] This seems right. The defendant should have protected the claimant against the danger that the board would make a contract with a director of substantial personal benefit to the director without the agreement of the company in meeting.

1 [1996] 3 All ER 667, Carnwath J.
2 [1996] 3 All ER 667 at 681f.

(b) Intervening acts of third parties

3.45 A similar principle applies in relation to third parties. If a third party's wrongful conduct was conduct of a kind from which it was the defendant's duty to guard the claimant, then the claimant should be able to contend that the defendant is liable to the claimant even though it might be argued that the loss was caused by the deliberate conduct of the third party. For a recent application of this principle in the context of auditors' liability, see *MAN Nutzfahrzeuge AG* *v Freightliner Ltd*[1]. On the other hand, if the third party's conduct passes the 'but for' test, but is not a risk against which the defendant had a duty to guard the claimant, and the third party's conduct was not at fault, then the court may hold that the third party's conduct does not prevent the defendant's conduct from being counted as the cause of the loss in law. In *Cook v S*,[2] the defendant solicitors acted for the claimant in divorce proceedings and negligently allowed her husband's petition to be heard as an undefended suit. A month after pronouncement of the decree nisi, the defendant approached counsel, who wrongly advised that there was no point in the claimant defending the suit, even if it were possible. The judge considered that counsel's advice, although mistaken, was not negligent. He held that counsel's advice was not a new cause of the claimant's difficulties, so it did not break the chain of causation. Further, the question often has to be addressed where the claimant is faced with litigation brought by a hostile third party as a consequence of, or after, the defendant's negligence. The claimant may have no choice and be faced with an implacable third party. In both *Barnes v Hay*[3] and *Connor & Labrum v Regoczi-Ritzman*[4] the conduct of third parties in pursuing court proceedings, even to an unsuccessful conclusion, did not break the chain of causation because it was the solicitor's duty to protect the client against litigation and within his or her contemplation that a failure to give appropriate advice before a transaction might expose the client to the risk of litigation.

1 [2007] EWCA Civ 910 [2008] PNLR 6. This is a popular theme in claims against auditors: see *Barings plc v Coopers & Lybrand* [2003] PNLR 24 and *Sasea Finance Ltd v KPMG* [2000] 1 All ER 676, CA. In *Sasea*, the difficult case of *Galoo v Bright Grahame Murray* [1994] 1 WLR 1360, CA, was explained on the basis that the defendant auditors had no duty to warn against losses of the types incurred by the claimant, namely losses due to the fraud of employees of the company. This also appears to be Lord Hoffmann's view of *Galoo*: see 'Common Sense and Causing Loss', lecture to the Chancery Bar Association, 15 June 1999 at pp 13–14.
2 [1967] 1 WLR 635, Lawton J.
3 (1988) 12 NSWLR 337, CA.
4 (1995) 70 P & CR D41–3, Robert Walker J.

3.46 What if the third party's conduct was *not* conduct against which the defendant had a duty to guard the claimant, *was* a 'but for' cause of the loss, and the third party was at fault? In *Rahman v Arearose Ltd*[1] Laws LJ, with whom the other judges agreed, considered the submission that B's later negligence always extinguishes the continuing causative effect of the negligence of A, an earlier tortfeasor. He said:

> '… it does not seem to me to be established as a rule of law that later negligence always extinguishes the causative potency of an earlier tort. The law is that every tortfeasor should compensate the injured claimant in respect of that loss and damage for which he should justly be held responsible. To make that principle good, it is important that the elusive concept of causation should not be frozen into constricting rules.'

This suggests that there may be no clear rule as to this situation.[2] In *Webb v Barclays Bank plc & Portsmouth Hospital Trust*[3], the first defendant's negligence caused injury to the claimant, its employee. The claimant's condition was then worsened by negligent treatment by the second defendant hospital. The Court of Appeal did not consider that the second defendant's negligence meant that the first defendant was not liable for all the claimant's injuries. In *Luke v Kingsley Smith*,[4] it had to be assumed that solicitors A had negligently delayed the claimant's claim so as to render it susceptible to be struck out for want of prosecution, but that solicitors B, who had been instructed in place of A, had then negligently under-settled the claim. Davis J considered that it was arguable that, if those assumptions were proved, A and B were both liable for all the damage which the claimant suffered. Further, in *Vision Golf Ltd v Weightmans*,[5] solicitors A had failed to apply for relief from forfeiture of a lease for their client the claimant. The claimant then instructed solicitors B. If B had acted swiftly, they could have applied in time for relief from forfeiture, but they failed to do so. Lewison J rejected the argument that B's errors meant that A was not liable to the claimant for the whole loss.[6] Of course, in such circumstances, A could then seek contribution from B.[7]

1 [2001] QB 351, CA, at [29].
2 In *Horton v Evans* [2006] EWHC 2808 (QB), [2007] PNLR 365, Keith J said at [53] that 'the guiding principle is that there is no guiding principle in this area of the law'. He said, quoting *Clerk & Lindsell*, that four issues needed to be addressed: 'Was the intervening conduct of the third party such as to render the original wrongdoing merely a part of the history of events? Was the third party's conduct either deliberate or wholly unreasonable? Was the intervention foreseeable? Is the conduct of the third party wholly independent of the defendant, i e does the defendant owe the claimant any responsibility for the conduct of the intervening third party?'
3 [2001] EWCA Civ 1141, [2001] Lloyd's Rep Med 500.
4 [2003] EWHC 1559 (QB), [2004] PNLR 12.
5 [2005] EWHC 1675, [2005] All ER (D) 675, Lewison J. See also *Estill v Cowling, Swift & Kitchin* [2000] Lloyd's Rep PN 378, per Arden J at 395–6, where a solicitor's attempt to argue that counsel's negligence broke the chain of causation also failed.
6 A further attempt by negligent defendant solicitors to assert that the true cause of the loss was the acts of others failed in *Redbus LMDS Ltd v Jeffrey Green Russell* [2007] PNLR 12, HHJ Behrens QC.
7 See chapter 8.

(c) Defendant's conduct

3.47 Generally speaking, it will not help a defendant to argue that the true cause of the claimant's loss was not the negligent act of the defendant on which the claimant relies, but rather a different negligent act of the defendant which is not pleaded in the claimant's particulars of claim. This is because, if correct, the answer to this contention would simply be for the claimant to amend the particulars of claim to rely on this further negligent act of the defendant's. What, however, if the claimant's limitation period for suing in respect of the further negligent act has expired so that it is no longer open to the claimant to sue the defendant in respect of the second negligent act? This was the position in *Normans Bay Ltd v Coudert Brothers*[1]. Laws LJ, with whom Carnwath LJ agreed on this point, said:

> '... I have reached the clear conclusion that in principle a defendant should not be allowed to rely on wrong perpetrated by himself in order (in whole or in part) to break the chain of causation put forward by the claimant to establish and quantify the damage sustained by him by reason of the defendant's breach of contract or tort. This may be seen (as Waller LJ expresses it: para 46) as an application of the general rule of the common law that a party may not rely on his own wrong to secure a benefit, and I agree that some support is to be found for that approach in the speech of Lord Browne-Wilkinson in *Bolitho*. But I think it is also consonant with modern ideas of causation now being developed in the cases. Authority supports the proposition that the resolution of causation issues, certainly in the law of tort, is by no means a merely fact-finding exercise; in many instances it is an evaluative judgment, concerned to establish the extent to which a defendant should justly be held responsible for what has befallen the claimant.'

It will be seen that the view expressed in the last sentence of this passage is consistent with the passages quoted above at paras 3.01 and 3.40 from Lord Nicholls as to the nature of causation in tort. As indicated in the quotation from Laws LJ, Waller LJ agreed with the principle which Laws LJ stated, though he supported it by slightly different reasoning. It therefore appears that, once the claimant has proved some negligence that caused him or her some loss, a defendant cannot argue that its own negligence, in relation to which the claimant is barred by limitation from suing, is an independent cause of the loss which the claimant has suffered, at least in loss of a chance cases such as *Normans Bay*.

1 [2003] EWCA Civ 215, *The Times* 24 March 2004. See per Laws LJ at [64]–[65] and Carnwath LJ at [69].

(d) Events

3.48 As to supervening causes that are not related to human agency, it is likely that the rules which apply generally in tort and contract would apply equally in professional negligence cases. If the event was foreseeable then the court is unlikely to hold that it negatived causation by the defendant if it was an event that occurred in the ordinary course of events and could reasonably be anticipated.[1] It if was a wholly unforeseeable event which could not be expected then the court might hold that its consequences fell outside the extent of the defendant's liability to the claimant.

1 *Monarch SS v Karlshamns Oljefabriker* [1949] AC 196, HL.

D   REMOTENESS OF DAMAGE

3.49   As Arden LJ said in the passage quoted at para 3.36, above, it appears that the focus of attention in the search for control factors to limit the recoverability of damages has moved away from the concept of remoteness and towards the *SAAMCo* principle; in other cases, the same conclusion may be expressed by reference to both the *SAAMCo* principle and remoteness. This may be why, in terms of the most recent cases, there are few relating only to remoteness. Further, it used to be the law that loss caused by a claimant's lack of money, and consequent inability to take remedial measures to put right damage caused by the defendant's wrongful act, was too remote to be recoverable. But this rule has now been abandoned and no longer represents the law.[1]

1 *Lagden v O'Connor* [2003] UKHL 64, [2004] 1 AC 1067.

1   Foreseeability of damage

3.50   A defendant solicitor's failure to perform a professional service to his or her client is generally a breach of contract and the classic formulation of the test of remoteness is that stated by Alderson B in *Hadley v Baxendale*:[1]

> 'We think the proper rule in such a case as the present is this: where two parties have made a contract which one of them has broken, the damages which the other party ought to receive in respect of such a breach of contract should be such as may fairly and reasonably be considered either arising naturally, i e according to the usual course of things, from such breach of contract itself, or such as may reasonably be supposed to have been in the contemplation of both parties at the time they made the contract, as the probable result of the breach of it.'

There are clear differences between the test for remoteness of damage in contract and that in the tort of negligence, not least that the question of reasonable foreseeability is tested at the moment of contracting in one and at the moment of damage in the other. Damages, to be recoverable in contract, must either be considered as arising naturally or within the reasonable contemplation of the parties at the date on which the contract was made but, according to Lord Reid in *Koufos v C Czarnikow Ltd*, the position in tort is as follows:[2]

> 'The defendant will be liable for any type of damage which is reasonably foreseeable as liable to happen even in the most unusual case, unless the risk is so small that a reasonable man would in the whole of the circumstances feel justified in neglecting it.'

In professional negligence cases it has usually been unnecessary for the courts to distinguish between the two forms of action and reported cases show that they have tended not to do so.[3] Where a single test has been adopted, it has usually been the test of remoteness in contract.[4] But it should be recognised that the ability to frame an action in both contract and tort does give the claimant the option of the more generous rule of remoteness in tort in that rare case where damage would be too remote in contract. In practical terms the form of action is likely to affect the outcome only where the defendant acquires significant knowledge between the date of instructions and the date of breach.[5]

1 (1854) 9 Exch 341 at 354–5.
2 [1969] 1 AC 350 at 385.
3 See e g *Banque Bruxelles Lambert SA v Eagle Star Insurance Co Ltd* [1995] QB 375, CA, at 450D-E. This passage was unaffected by the appeal to the House of Lords (*SAAMCo*). See also *Brown v KMR Services Ltd* [1995] 4 All ER 598 at 620f–621j and 641j–643f, CA and *McElroy Milne v Commercial Electronics Ltd* [1993] NZLR 39, CA per Cooke J.
4 See e g *Simmons v Pennington* [1955] 1 WLR 183 at 187, CA, *Rumsey v Owen, White and Caitlin* (1977) 245 Estates Gazette 225, CA and *Matlock Green Garages Ltd v Potter Brooke-Taylor & Wildgoose* [2000] Lloyd's Rep PN 935 (Wright J), all considered below.
5 There appears to be no reported decision which has turned on this difference.

2 Type and extent

3.51 The requirement of reasonable foreseeability (whether in contract or tort) does not require the claimant to show that the defendant knew or ought to have known the precise nature or details of the damage or the precise way in which it was suffered, or the full extent of the loss. It is sufficient for the claimant to show that the defendant either did or should have foreseen that the kind or type of loss in question was not unlikely to occur. In *Banque Keyser Ullmann SA v Skandia (UK) Insurance Co Ltd*[1] Slade LJ considered it unnecessary that there should be: '[F]oresight of the manner and means by which the particular loss was caused or the extent of the loss suffered.'[2] Thus in *Brown v KMR Services Ltd,* where Lloyd's Names sued members' agents for failure to advise them about the character of high risk syndicates of which they were members, and those syndicates had made unprecedented losses, it was argued that the defendants should be liable only for the scale of losses which could reasonably have been foreseen for the syndicates in question. This argument was rejected and the defendants were held liable for all losses however unforeseeable their scale or extent.[3] In *Simmons v Pennington*[4] by contrast, where the defendants were found negligent in failing to advise the claimant to mitigate his loss by selling the subject property pending the determination of legal proceedings, the defendants were not liable to compensate the claimant for the loss of his premises through fire. The market value of the premises did not go down and it was not reasonably foreseeable either that the claimant would fail to insure or that the premises would burn down.

3.52   *Causation and damages at common law*

1 [1990] 1 QB 665 at 767E, CA, cited with approval by Staughton LJ in *British & Commonwealth Holdings plc v Quadrex Holdings Inc* (10 April 1995, unreported) CA, transcript 125C.
2 See, to the same effect, *BBL v Eagle Star* [1995] QB 375 at 405D–G, CA.
3 Above. See also *Wroth v Tyler* [1974] Ch 30 (Megarry J) at 60G–61A. Increase in house prices was foreseeable but not the steep increase which took place.
4 [1955] 1 WLR 183, CA.

3.52   It is not always easy to define, or even identify, particular types of losses where, as is usually the case, the claimant's losses are all financial. The loss suffered by the claimant in *Simmons v Pennington* was obviously of a different type from that which could have been reasonably foreseen, i e physical rather than financial damage, but in most cases such a clear cut distinction is not possible. In *British & Commonwealth Holdings plc v Quadrex Holdings Inc,* Staughton LJ stated:[1]

> 'I can find very little guidance as to what constitutes a kind or type; in the nature of things no more precise definition is to be expected. It is up to the judge to determine on the facts whether the requirement is satisfied … Mr Stadlen for British & Commonwealth proposes, as the relevant type or kind in this case, financial loss … Mr Newman for Samuel Montagu proposes, as a type or kind, reduction in the price obtainable for [certain companies] through a general fall in the market level of value for such companies. He defines the type or kind more narrowly, although he still leaves room for some unexpected developments within his framework. Who is right? In my opinion the law does not answer this question. It is a matter for the judge to decide, which test fairly compensates British & Commonwealth for their loss.'

1 Transcript at 124G–125A, 125F–G, 126A (10 April 1995, unreported), CA.

3.53   A good example of the pragmatic approach to different 'types' of financial loss which perhaps Staughton LJ had in mind is provided by *Matlock Green Garages Ltd v Potter Brooke-Taylor & Wildgoose*[1] in which the claimant claimed damages against the defendant for failure to renew a tenancy of a garage and filling station under the Landlord and Tenant Act 1954, Pt II. The claimant recovered damages for losing the garage. But as a consequence of the claimant's loss of this one site, it also had to close two related businesses, a body shop and a vehicle recovery service, both of which were undertaken from different premises. Wright J stated:

> 'While the Defendant firm of solicitors carried on practice in Matlock, and may perhaps be taken to have known that the business of the Plaintiff company was not restricted to the service station and garage located on the Matlock Green sites, there is no evidence before me and I do not consider that I would be justified in assuming that the Defendants had any knowledge, whether at the time of the

contract or at the time of its breach, of the detailed inter-relationship between the various elements of the Plaintiffs' business, still less the extent to which, as it is claimed, the continued commercial viability of any of the elements of the Plaintiffs' business depended upon the continuing existence of other parts thereof.'

As a result, damages were not recoverable in respect of the parts of the business other than the service station and Matlock Green site.

1 [2000] Lloyd's Rep PN 935, per Wright J at 943, col 2, to 944 col 1.

3.54 Given this indication that the court will not bracket or pigeon-hole types of financial loss into fixed categories, only a few types of loss call for special mention. In *Al-Kandari v J R Brown & Co,*[1] the claimant sued the defendant solicitors for damages arising out of her husband's abduction of her two children to Kuwait. The Court of Appeal held that damage of this type was not too remote, because the solicitors had known sufficient facts to put them on notice that there was a risk that, if they acted negligently, the husband would abscond with the children. On the other hand, in *Pilkington v Wood,*[2] the Court of Appeal awarded the claimant damages for the defendant solicitor's failure to ensure that he obtained good title to the house which he had bought in Hampshire. The principal award of damages was the difference between the value of the property with good title and its actual value, with the defective title. By the time he came to sell the property, the claimant had moved employment from Surrey to Lancashire. Harman J considered that his claims for hotel accommodation in Lancashire, travel by car to Lancashire, and telephone calls to his wife while away were not within the reasonable contemplation of the parties at the time when the contract of retainer was entered. Neither party had known at the time that the claimant would find work in Lancashire, so these costs were too remote.

1 [1987] QB 514.
2 [1953] Ch 770.

3 Market changes

3.55 Whether or not they can be attributed to the defendant's breach of duty, increases or decreases in price or cost due to market forces which the claimant is forced to bear as a direct consequence of the defendant's negligence, however unexpected, are ordinarily treated as within the contemplation of the parties.[1] The reason for this was given by Sir Thomas Bingham MR in *BBL v Eagle Star*:[2]

'[I]t has not been argued that L's claim for any part of his loss, including that part attributable to the fall in the property market, is too remote. The reason is obvious. L and V know, as everyone knows, that in any market prices may move upwards or downwards. That is the essence of a market. No one in recent times has expected property prices to remain stable over a prolonged period. It was plainly foreseeable that if, on the strength of an overvaluation by V, L entered into a mortgage transaction he would not otherwise have entertained, his risk of loss would be increased if the market moved downwards or reduced if it moved upwards.'

1 A distinction may be drawn between those situations where the claimant is forced to bear additional loss, such as the higher cost of building materials or the forced resale of property in a falling market, and those where the claimant alleges that the solicitor's negligence has deprived him or her of yet greater profits in a rising market. In the latter situation, the court's principal enquiry is into the nature of the solicitor's duty rather than into questions of remoteness. Cf paras 9.103–9.111, below.
2 [1995] QB 375 at 405F, CA.

3.56 Increases in market prices have been considered in a number of cases. In *Inder Lynch Devoy & Co v Subritzky*[1] it was held that the claimant was not entitled to recover the increased building costs of his new property, which were due to a lack of local builders and a building boom, from the defendants, whose negligence caused a substantial delay in completing the sale of his property. Such losses were held to be too remote notwithstanding that the defendants knew of the claimant's intention; that building costs were a matter of public knowledge; and that a direct causal link was found between the defendants' breach and the claimant's loss. In *King v Hawkins & Co*[2] by contrast, where the claimant also sought to recover increased building costs, these costs were held to be recoverable. And in *Snipper v Enever Freeman & Co*[3] where the defendants failed to serve a notice under the Leasehold Reform Act 1967 within time and the claimant took steps to mitigate her loss by obtaining an extended lease, damages were assessed on the date when she had obtained the lease and was first able to sell her property. Sheen J stated:

'Between 1983 and 1990 the ravages of inflation have reduced the purchasing power of the pound sterling. This is reflected in higher prices. In my judgment it would be wrong in principle and unjust to assess the plaintiff's damages by calculating the loss at July 1983 [when the breach occurred] and then subtracting from that figure the benefit obtained from the steps in mitigation expressed in pounds which have lost much of their value. There should be only one date on which damages are assessed.'

1 [1979] 1 NZLR 87, CA. The correctness of the decision is in doubt: see para 3.57.
2 (1982) Times, 28 January (Mars Jones J).
3 [1991] 2 EGLR 270 at 271J (Sheen J). See also the discussion of the date on which damages are assessed in chapter 9 below.

3.57 Where the effect of a fall in the market is within the scope of the defendant's duty, the court may also have to consider whether such a fall is too remote. In *Rumsey v Owen, White and Caitlin*[1] the Court of Appeal held that it was not. As a consequence of the defendant's negligent advice, the claimant agreed to sell three shops with vacant possession in order to set up a factory. He could not obtain vacant possession because his tenants had security of tenure and he should have been advised to sell the properties subject to the tenancies. Because he could not obtain possession immediately, the claimant entered into an agreement with the purchaser to give vacant possession at a later date or to repurchase the properties. When he was unable to give vacant possession again, he was obliged to repurchase the properties when they were worth only half the original sale price. He could not complete the repurchase and damages were awarded to the purchaser against him. The Court of Appeal awarded the claimant not only the difference between the amount which he could have received for the three shops if he had sold them subject to the tenancies, that is, the diminution in value of the properties, but also the damages that he was obliged to pay to the purchaser and which reflected the unexpected collapse in their value. Again, in *McElroy Milne v Commercial Electronics Ltd*[2] the defendant's negligent failure to obtain a guarantee left the claimant, who was the developer of a custom-built property, with a less saleable asset and delayed its sale until the market had collapsed. The New Zealand Court of Appeal chose to follow *Rumsey* and not their own decision in *Subritzky*.[3] Hardie Boys J stated:[4]

> '[I]t was plainly foreseeable that the failure to obtain the guarantee at the contract stage left the respondent vulnerable to a change of heart by Studio [the proposed guarantor]; and that its absence at the marketing stage was very likely to cause both delay in finding a purchaser and a reduction in the price that could be obtained; and further, that delay at that later stage left the respondent vulnerable to the vagaries of the market itself. Thus on any view of likelihood, the delay in selling, and the fall in market price occurring because of it, were reasonably foreseeable consequences of this contractual breach.'

1 (1977) 245 Estates Gazette 225, CA.
2 [1993] NZLR 39 at 53, line 11 to 56, line 12. See also para 9.172, below.
3 [1979] 1 NZLR 87, CA.
4 [1993] NZLR 39 at 45, lines 28–35.

4 Special contracts

3.58 In the normal case a defendant solicitor will not be liable to a claimant who loses the benefit of a particular contract as a consequence of his or her negligence unless the solicitor either had, or ought to have had, the contract in contemplation: see *Pilkington v Wood*.[1] Thus a defendant will not usually be liable to his client for the loss of a profit on resale of property unless he or she knew that the property had been acquired for resale. In a number of cases damages on this basis have been refused[2] but in *G & K Ladenbau (UK) v de Reya*[3] where there was an express finding that the solicitor should have foreseen that a loss on resale was likely, damages for the delay and increased costs on resale were awarded.

1 [1953] Ch 770 (Harman J). This appears to mirror the development of contracts for the sale of land rather than the sale of goods or commercial contracts: see *Diamond v Campbell-Jones* [1961] Ch 22 (Buckley J).
2 See para 9.87, below.
3 [1978] 1 WLR 266, esp at 289C–F (Mocatta J). See, generally, para 9.88 below where the precise circumstances of the case are considered further.

3.59 That said, it may be that the court will accept that the price under the special contract which the claimant had lost is persuasive evidence of the value of the property at the date of breach. In *Homsy v Murphy*[1] the Court of Appeal held that the court could take into account a special interest purchaser, to whom the claimant proposed to sell the property, in assessing the open market value of a property at the date of breach. In the instant case the claimant had a purchaser not only for the land he had contracted to purchase but also for his own land at a price which reflected the marriage value of the two interests. The defendant would have known of the existence of that interest and could have foreseen that the marriage of the two would increase their value, even if he was unaware of the purchaser's existence. Hobhouse LJ stated:

> 'The question of remoteness has to be determined by reference to the type of loss or damage, not its quantum. Provided that the loss is within the contemplation of the parties, it does not matter that its amount may be greater than expected … Here, as previously explained, the loss was of a type which was within the reasonable contemplation of the parties. That Mr Graf was prepared to pay so much over the odds does not affect the position unless it shows that he was not a commercial purchaser of those premises but some collateral benefactor of Mr Homsy. The evidence was clearly that Mr Graf would have been a bona fide commercial purchaser, albeit a special interest purchaser. Therefore his interest is properly to be taken into account in assessing the value of the freehold in 1988/9.'

1 (1996) 73 P & CR 26, CA. This case is not concerned with negligence but with the breach of a contract for the grant of an option.

E   MITIGATION OF DAMAGE

1   General principles

3.60 A defendant may seek to reduce the amount of damages that he or she must pay by alleging that claimants have failed to act reasonably to reduce, or mitigate, the amount of loss which they have suffered. The classic statement of the mitigation rule is in *British Westinghouse Electric and Manufacturing Co Ltd v Underground Electric Rlys Co of London Ltd*[1]. Speaking of the assessment of damages at common law, Viscount Haldane LC said:

'The fundamental basis is thus compensation for pecuniary loss naturally flowing from the breach; but this first principle is qualified by a second, which imposes on a plaintiff the duty of taking all reasonable steps to mitigate the loss consequent on the breach, and debars him from claiming any part of the damage which is due to his neglect to take such steps. In the words of James LJ in *Dunkirk Colliery Co v Lever* (1878) 9 Ch D 20, at p 25, "The person who has broken the contract is not to be exposed to additional cost by reason of the plaintiffs not doing what they ought to have done as reasonable men, and the plaintiffs not being under an obligation to do anything otherwise than in the ordinary course of business." As James LJ indicates, this second principle does not impose on the plaintiff an obligation to take any steps which a reasonable and prudent man would not ordinarily take in the course of his business. But when in the course of his business he has taken action arising out of the transaction which action has diminished his loss, the effect in actual diminution of the loss he has suffered may be taken into account even though there was no duty on him to act.'

It will be seen that this passage contains at least two principles as to mitigation[2]: first, the defendant need not compensate the claimant for loss which the claimant has in fact suffered, but would not have suffered if he or she had acted reasonably; secondly, the defendant need not compensate the claimant for loss that the claimant has in fact avoided (whether the claimant avoided suffering the loss by acting reasonably or unreasonably). As to the first principle, however, the court tends to take a relatively lenient attitude toward the claimant's behaviour, once it has been shown that the defendant acted in breach of duty. The classic statement of this latter approach is the following[3]:

'Where the sufferer from a breach of contract finds himself in consequence of that breach placed in position of embarrassment the measures which he may be driven to adopt in order to extricate himself ought not to be weighed in nice scales at the instance of the party whose breach of contract has occasioned the difficulty. It is often easy after an emergency has passed to criticise the steps which have been taken to meet it, but such criticism does not come well from those who have themselves created the emergency. The law is satisfied if the party placed in a difficult position by reason of the breach of a duty owed to him has acted reasonably in the adoption of remedial measures and he will not be held disentitled to recover the

131

cost of such measures merely because the party in breach can suggest that other measures less burdensome to him might have been taken.'

So the claimant alleging a failure to mitigate loss tends to face an uphill battle.

1 [1912] AC 673 at 689.
2 For more detailed discussion of principles of mitigation see *McGregor on Damages* (17th edn, 2003), ch 7.
3 *Banco de Portugal v. Waterlow* [1932] AC 452, per Lord Macmillan at 506; cited, for example, by Jonathan Parker LJ in *Williams v Glyn Owen & Co* [2003] EWCA Civ 750, [2004] PNLR 20, at [68].

3.61 The cornerstone of the first mitigation principle is to ask whether the claimant has acted reasonably after the defendant's breach of duty, but the courts sometimes consider that question as going either to causation or to remoteness, rather than simply to mitigation. Further, the same issue can also be a critical factor in determining the date on which damages fall to be assessed,[1] an issue which is considered below. In professional negligence claims the reasonableness of the claimant's conduct tends to be characterised most commonly as a question of mitigation where the point at issue is whether the claimant ought to have commenced or continued proceedings against another party to reduce or recover his or her loss before turning to pursue the defendant. We now consider that question.

1 See e g *Radford v de Froberville* [1977] 1 WLR 1262 at 1258, in which Oliver J stated that the rationale of the rule as to the date for the assessment of damages in sale of goods cases lay 'in the inquiry – at what date could the plaintiff reasonably have been expected to mitigate the damages by seeking an alternative performance of the contractual obligation'.

2 Further litigation

3.62 In *London and South of England Building Society v Stone*,[1] a valuer's case, Stephenson LJ summarised the principles on which the court would act:

'[The defendant] must prove it was unreasonable and when the court has to decide that question of fact, the [claimant's] conduct in not taking steps to reduce the loss will not be weighed in nice scales at the instance of the party who has occasioned the loss: see what Lord Macmillan said of the plaintiff's conduct in taking positive steps to reduce his loss in *Banco de Portugal v Waterlow & Sons* [1932] AC 452, 506... I accept these principles as establishing by authority and applicable to this case: (1) a plaintiff need not take the risk of starting an uncertain litigation against a third party, for which *Pilkington v Wood* [1953] Ch 770 is authority and that includes litigation which may be reasonably certain to result in judgment for the plaintiff but there is no certainty that the judgment will be satisfied; (2) a plaintiff need not take steps to recover compensation for his loss from parties who, in addition to the defendant, are liable to him, for which *The Liverpool (No 2)* [1963] P 64 is authority. There the other party was a tortfeasor, unlike the borrowers in this case; but (3) a plaintiff need not act so as to injure innocent persons, and (4) need not prejudice its commercial reputation.'

The defendant must satisfy the court that the claimant should have commenced and proceeded with litigation against another party, that those proceedings would have succeeded and a judgment could have been enforced. If the claimant has the benefit of advice from counsel, particularly leading counsel, that he or she should not pursue a claim, it is highly unlikely that the court would take a different view. Further, even if the claimant could reasonably have proceeded against another professional, such as a valuer or an accountant, *The Liverpool (No 2)* referred to by Stephenson LJ above remains good authority for the proposition that this is no defence to recovery in full by the claimant who is entitled to choose his or her defendants.

1 [1983] 1 WLR 1242 at 1262–3, CA.

3.63   In *Pilkington v Wood*[1] a purchaser of land brought proceedings against his solicitor when the title turned out to be defective and the defendants contended that the purchaser should have mitigated his loss by suing the vendor on an implied covenant of title. Harman J held[2] that:

> '[T]he so-called duty to mitigate does not get so far as to oblige the injured party, even under an indemnity, to embark on a complicated and difficult piece of litigation against a third party.'

London and South of England Building Society v Stone and *Pilkington v Wood* were both followed in *Segenhoe Ltd v Atkins,* which provides an interesting illustration of the principle.[3]

1 [1953] Ch 770.
2 [1953] Ch 770 at 777. For the facts, see para 9.71 below. It is questionable whether the defect in title would now be found to give rise to a 'complicated and difficult piece of litigation' (even if the issue were to arise again). On the facts, it seems clear that the plaintiff would have been entitled to a declaration and an indemnity against the vendor.
3 [1990] ACSR 691, (1992) 29 NSWLR 569. Claim by company to recover dividends paid to shareholders as a consequence of accountants' negligence held to be too uncertain. P relied on a statement in *Halsbury* (adopted in both *Pennington* and *Palmer*) which Ds contended was wrong. The judge found that support for the position in *Halsbury* was 'far from overwhelming'. Nevertheless he held that P was not obliged to pursue either individual shareholders or the single largest shareholders, whose dividend was A$484,476. It is thought, however, that it is hardly unreasonable to require a claimant to test a proposition in *Halsbury* with a large sum at stake.

3.64   On the other hand these cases were distinguished in *Western Trust & Savings Ltd v Travers & Co Ltd,* where the claimant lender had taken no steps to seek possession of a mortgaged property before turning its attention to the defendants. The litigation in question was 'no more than a possession action with which the plaintiffs in this case were well familiar and which would have been a necessary step whether or not there were defects in the security'.[1] The submission that the court should 'attach significance' to the fact that the defendants would not offer an indemnity or take an assignment of the claimants' rights was also rejected. Phillips LJ stated:[2]

'In my judgment these matters have very little relevance. It is for the court to decide what should or should not reasonably have been done by the plaintiffs in the circumstances of the case not for the defendants or their solicitors.'

In that case it was so clear that the claimants should have taken possession proceedings that the offer of indemnity was unnecessary. It is suggested that there will be cases, especially where the claimant is unable to fund the litigation, where the offer of an indemnity will be highly material. In *Hitchens v Higgens & Bacchus*[3] the claimants were found to have acted unreasonably because they had not commenced proceedings for specific performance of a contract which later fell through. Finally, in *Walker v Geo H Medlicott & Son*[4] it was held that a claimant beneficiary had failed to mitigate his loss in that he had failed to commence proceedings for rectification of a will before commencing proceedings against the solicitor who had drafted it. Although the general principle quoted in para 3.63 was accepted, it was held[5] that, where a claimant claims that a solicitor has failed to record a testator's instructions adequately, a claim for rectification should usually be brought before, or instead of, a claim for negligence. This is because the evidence in both actions will be virtually identical. It therefore cannot be said that it is unduly onerous to require the claimant to seek rectification first: in the rectification action, the claimant must prove no more than what he or she would have to prove in the negligence action against the solicitor.

1 [1997] PNLR 295 at 303G, CA.
2 [1997] PNLR 295 at 304D.
3 NLD 17 July 1997, CA. The short report suggests that the Court of Appeal might have taken a different view of a legal issue to Giles J in *Segenhoe*. The contract specified that P would produce a root of title dating from 1911 when Ps could only do so from 1930. The court found that P could have obtained specific performance despite the contractual provision.
4 [1999] 1 WLR 727, CA. The case is discussed in detail in paras 11.06 and 11.27, below. Compare *Horsfall v Haywards* [1999] Lloyd's Rep PN 332, CA (considered in para 11.28), where it would not have been worth bringing rectification proceedings. *Walker* was also distinguished in *Wiliams v Glyn Owen & Co* [2003] EWCA Civ 750, [2004] PNLR 20, at [70], on the ground that in *Walker* the claimants' activities in suing the negligent solicitors led to 'adventitious benefits' whereas in *Williams* they did not.
5 [1999] 1 WLR 727 at 738H–739H, 741E–742H and 743H–744G.

3 Consequential benefits

3.65 A different problem arises when the claimant *does* receive a benefit as a consequence of the defendant's breach of duty, so that it can be shown that, but for the breach of duty, the claimant would not have received the benefit. Must the claimant give credit for the benefit in the assessment of damages? This issue usually arises where claimants establish that they would not have purchased property or entered the transaction in question if they had been properly advised; instead they would have entered into an alternative transaction which would have yielded some advantage; the claimants claim damages for the loss of that advantage. The court must decide whether the *defendant* can take the benefit of everything which flows from the alternative transaction into which the claimants *in fact* entered, including benefits which the claimants have in fact obtained for themselves, possibly by good fortune or possibly by their own skill and hard work. In *Hussey v Eels*,[1] which was applied in *Gardner v Marsh and Parsons*,[2] *Needler v Taber*[3] and *Primavera v Allied Dunbar Assurance plc*,[4] it was held that the claimant, who had purchased a defective property in reliance on the defendant's misrepresentation, was not obliged to give credit for the profit which he had made by obtaining planning permission and selling to a developer and that the negligence which caused the loss did not cause the profit. In *Gardner*, as a consequence of the claimants' negotiations, the landlord repaired their flat some years after purchase and cured the defect which the defendant surveyor had failed to notice. In each of these two cases the claimant recovered the difference between (i) the price paid for the property and (ii) its market value if its true condition were known at the date of acquisition.

1 [1990] 2 QB 227.
2 [1997] 1 WLR 489, CA (Peter Gibson LJ dissenting).
3 [2001] EWHC Ch 5, [2002] 3 All ER 501, Sir Andrew Morritt V-C.
4 [2002] EWCA Civ 1327, [2003] PNLR 12.

3.66 In each case, statements of principle were avoided. In *Hussey v Eels*[1] Mustill LJ determined the question in this way:

> 'To my mind the reality of the situation is that the plaintiffs bought the house to live in, and did live in it for a substantial period. It was only after two years that the possibility of selling the land and moving elsewhere was explored, and six months later still that this possibility came to fruition. It seems to me that when the plaintiffs unlocked the development value of their land they did so for their own benefit, and not as part of a continuous transaction of which the purchase of land and bungalow was the inception.'

In *Gardner*, Hirst LJ followed this approach finding as follows:[2]

> 'In my judgment, having regard to the intervening events and to the long interval of time, the repairs executed in 1990 were not part of a

continuous transaction of which the purchase of the lease as a result of Mr Dyson's negligence was the inception. Furthermore these repairs undertaken by Guidedale [the landlord] at the plaintiffs' insistence were res inter alios acta and therefore collateral to Mr Dyson's negligence.'

Pill LJ noted that the defendants would not have been entitled to take the benefit of any market increase in the value of the property after acquisition and that, if the claimants had wished to sell it at any time before the repairs were done, they would have suffered a loss. He stated:[3]

> 'In my judgment the present case, on its facts, is on the *Hussey v Eels* side of the line … Years after the defendant's negligence, the freeholders performed their obligation to the plaintiffs under a contract which the plaintiffs had negotiated with them. That had the effect of rectifying the damage resulting from the defendants' negligence. The benefit came by reason of the performance of a contractual obligation by a third party. The plaintiff had to undertake protracted negotiations with that third party and other third parties, the other tenants in the building. Before that obligation was performed by the freeholder, there was considerable lapse of time in the course of which the plaintiffs, because of the structural defect, were unable to sell the property which they wished to do in 1988. In my judgment, the facts relied upon as affecting the measure of damages are too remote to be taken into consideration and, on the facts, the judge was entitled to find for the plaintiffs as he did.'

1 [1990] 2 QB 227 at 2410, cited by both Hirst and Pill LJJ in *Gardner* at 500B and 514A. The decision was also followed in *Blue Circle Industries plc v Ministry of Defence* [1999] Ch 289, CA where the defendant was not entitled to take the benefit of the claimant's decision to wait and sell in a more favourable market.
2 [1997] 1 WLR 489 at 503H.
3 [1997] 1 WLR 489 at 514C–F.

3.67   In *Needler*, due to the defendant's negligence the claimant had changed his pension arrangements. As a result, he had taken a personal pension scheme with Norwich Union. When Norwich Union later demutualised, the claimant received shares in Norwich Union which he sold for £7,815.77. The question was whether, in the assessment of damages, he should give credit for the £7,815.77. Sir Andrew Morritt said that the authorities established two relevant propositions[1]:

> 'First, the relevant question is whether the negligence which caused the loss also caused the profit in the sense that the latter was part of a continuous transaction of which the former was the inception. Second, that question is primarily one of fact.'

In his view, the gain from the demutualisation was not part of a continuous transaction of which the negligence was inception, so the claimant did not have to give credit for its benefits. Further, couching the question in the language of causation, he considered that 'the breach of duty gave rise to the opportunity to receive the profit, but did not cause it'.[2] It is, however, suggested, on the basis of the analysis set out earlier in this chapter, that the question of whether a cause which, as here, passes the 'but for' test, should be treated by the law as the cause of a loss is part of the second of the two-stage assessment which Lord Nicholls set out in the *Kuwait* case, and, following Lord Nicholls[3], should therefore be seen primarily as depending on a value judgment rather than on an assessment of the facts of the case. The question with which we are currently concerned may therefore be formulated as being: does the court consider that the claimant ought fairly to give credit for the benefit which, but for the defendant's negligence, he or she would not have enjoyed? In assessing that question, the court will ask whether the gain of the benefit can fairly be said to be part of a continuous chain of events that began with the defendant's negligence. But in answering this second question the court is, it is submitted, asking whether it considers that the claimant has gained the benefit by his or her own hard work, or that of professional advisers whom the claimant has engaged, or some other factor which renders it unfair that the defendant take advantage of the benefit. In short, this is not simply a question of fact: it is a question of making findings of fact as to what caused the benefit to be gained and then making a value judgment as to whether, in light of the facts, it is fair that the claimant give credit for the benefit. It is submitted that this analysis explains the Court of Appeal's subsequent decision in *Primavera*[4], which again concerned a claimant who, due to the defendant's negligence, had changed his pension arrangements. By the time of trial the claimant's pension fund had increased in value but the court held that this was due to the advice of his subsequent professional advisers, and he therefore did not have to give credit for it[5].

1 [2001] EWHC Ch 5, [2002] 3 All ER 501 at [24].
2 At [26].
3 See the passages cited at paras 3.01 and 3.40, above.
4 [2002] EWCA Civ 1327, [2003] PNLR 12.
5 The same explanation may not apply to the decision in *Needler*, but that decision is controversial: see *McGregor on Damages* at 7–134. For a further application of the *Hussey* principle, see *Devine v Jeffreys* [2001] Lloyd's Rep PN 301, HHJ Raymond Jack QC. Surveyors' negligence caused the claimants' loss when they bought a property in 1988, though they did not discover the problem until 1996. In 1999 they managed to persuade their mortgage lender to enter into a deal the effect of which was that ultimately they suffered no loss. The judge, however, assessed their loss as at 1988, plus interest, so that they received substantial damages, because he held that the events of 1999 were too remote from those of 1988, and came about due to a combination of factors and not simply the defendant's negligence. It is submitted that the result in this case may be analysed in the terms suggested above: the judge considered that the 1999 agreement came about as a result of the claimants' hard work so they did not have to give credit for it.

3.68 One way of giving effect to the conclusion that the claimant should not give credit for benefits acquired later is to assess damages as at the date of the breach of duty and ignore what happens later. None of the cases discussed so far involved solicitors. The courts have shown a greater willingness to depart from assessment of damages as at the date of breach of duty in cases of solicitors' negligence, although in three similar cases it has been applied. In *Westlake v J P Cave & Co*[1] a claim against a solicitor for failure to give adequate advice to a client joining a partnership to develop land, Ebsworth J followed the approach in *Hussey v Eels* and assessed damage at the date on which the claimant advanced money to his partner to purchase the land and, therefore, first suffered loss. She ignored the fact that the claimant later acquired part of the land and obtained planning permission to develop it. The same approach was taken in *Owen v Fielding*[2] in which the defendants had failed to advise the claimants about rights of common. They were awarded the difference between the price paid and the actual value of the land at date of purchase. Steel J ignored the profit made by the claimants when they later divided the land, obtained planning permission for another house and eventually sold both properties. In *Shaw v Fraser Southwell*[3] the facts were similar to, albeit stronger than, *Gardner*, and the principle was applied. It will be seen that these cases all involved transactions concerning land. The authorities on the assessment of damages in this area are discussed in greater detail in chapter 9, to which reference should be made.

1 [1998] NPC 3.
2 [1998] EGCS 110.
3 (25 March 1999, unreported), CA.
4 See para 9.83ff, below.

3.69 Even if the court is satisfied that a benefit formed part of a continuous transaction beginning with the defendant's negligence, the claimant must also show that the benefit goes to the same loss.[1] In *Nadreph Ltd v Willmett & Co*[2] the defendant's negligent advice to the claimant landlord caused the tenant to vacate the holding and claim compensation for disturbance under the Landlord and Tenant Act 1954, Pt II. The claimant did, however, recover possession and was able to make use of the premises. The court held that the defendant was entitled to set off against the compensation the value of having vacant possession of the premises.[3]

1 This was accepted by the whole court in *Gardner* [1997] 1 WLR 489.
2 [1978] 1 All ER 746 (Whitford J).
3 The reasons why Whitford J reached this conclusion are not easy to discern. Two factors were: first, the subsequent occupation arose in the ordinary course of the claimants' business: see [1978] 1 All ER 746 at 751g: and, secondly, the defendant's negligence was the direct cause of the tenant vacating: see 752g.

F DATE OF ASSESSMENT

1 The breach date rule and beyond

(a) *The date of breach*

3.70 The traditional date for assessing damages in contract and tort is the date of the breach of duty in question. This date was and is particularly suited to claims involving the sale of goods where non-delivery or delivery of defective goods will coincide with the claimant's opportunity to accept them or to reject them and look for an alternative means of performance. Although the practice of assessing damages at the date of breach had a long history,[1] in two modern decisions the House of Lords elevated the practice to the status of a rule which was only to be departed from 'if to follow it would give rise to injustice'[2] though the most recent House of Lords authority suggests that the court may not be slow to depart from the rule if necessary in order to give fair compensation.[3]

1 '"[T]he breach-date rule" has a long history, possibly, but I think not clearly, extending back to the Year Books' per Lord Wilberforce in *Miliangos v George Frank (Textiles) Ltd* [1976] AC 443 at 459F.
2 *Miliangos* [1976] AC 443 at 468. The citation is from Lord Wilberforce's speech in *Johnson v Agnew* [1980] AC 367 at 401C. The High Court of Australia took a similar line in *Johnson v Perez* (1988) 82 ALR 587. The case is of particular interest because it was a claim of solicitors' negligence. The plaintiffs' claims for personal injury were struck out for want of prosecution. When the claims against the solicitors were heard 10 years later the effect of inflation would have reduced substantially the awards that they would have received (even taking into account interest). By a majority the court affirmed the traditional rule. Damages were assessed at the date on which the actions were dismissed for want of prosecution. Mason CJ concurred that the appropriate date was the date of breach but thought that the appropriate date was the date on which the actions should have been heard. For the date of assessment in lost litigation cases generally, see chapter 12.
3 *Golden Strait Corpn v Nippon Yusen Kubishika Kaisha* [2007] UKHL 12, [2007] 2 WLR 691.

(b) The date of transaction

3.71 In a claim for the sale of defective goods the date of breach is usually the date of sale, that is when the seller contracts to deliver the goods and transfer property in them to the buyer, the buyer contracts to pay the price and the transfer of risk takes place. In a claim for defective advice against a professional the date of breach does not necessarily coincide with the date on which the claimant acts in reliance on it, suffers damage or has an opportunity either to mitigate the loss or obtain an alternative performance. But the time lapse between the date of a surveyor's report or a solicitor's letter and the date on which the claimant acts on it will in most cases be a matter of days and of little or no significance. In professional negligence cases in the 1980s and early 1990s the breach date rule was generally applied on the basis that the date of breach and the date on which the claimant became committed to the transaction were, for all practical purposes, one and the same. But the fact remains that the court cannot assess damages at the date of breach if the claimant has not entered the transaction at that date, as the facts of *Shaw v Halifax (SW) Ltd*[1] show. The defendant valuer valued the property at £37,000 in June 1988 when it was worth only £32,000. In August 1988 the claimants exchanged contracts to buy it for £42,000. By this time the true value had appreciated by £5,000 and the property was genuinely worth £37,000. It was argued that the claimants had suffered no loss because by the time they bought the property it was worth what the

defendants had said it was worth. This argument was rejected on the grounds
that the claimants had been entitled to rely on the report two months later when
they paid what they believed to be the market price of the property given the rise
in the market between the date of report and the date of purchase. If the breach
date rule had been applied strictly, it would have been impossible to assess loss
because the claimants had not committed themselves to the purchase at that date
or nominal damages would have been awarded because when they later purchased the property it had the higher value.

1 [1996] PNLR 451.

3.72 *Smith New Court Securities Ltd v Scrimgeour Vickers (Asset Management) Ltd*[1] clarified the law. In *SAAMCo* Lord Hoffmann had stated[2] that there
was no general principle that damages were to be assessed at the date of breach
although it represented a prima facie rule in relation to sale of goods. Then in
Smith New Court[3] Lord Browne-Wilkinson said that the old 19th century cases
that had established the breach date rule could no longer be treated as laying
down 'a strict and inflexible rule'. He continued:

> 'In many cases, even in deceit, it will be appropriate to value the
> asset acquired as at the transaction date if that truly reflects the value
> of what the plaintiff has acquired. Thus, if the asset acquired is a
> readily marketable asset and there is no special feature (such as a
> continuing representation or the purchaser being locked into a
> business that he has acquired) the transaction date rule may well
> produce a fair result. The plaintiff has acquired the asset and what he
> does with it thereafter is entirely up to him, freed from any
> continuing adverse impact of the defendant's wrongful act. The
> transaction date has one manifest advantage, namely that it avoids
> any question of causation. One of the difficulties of either valuing
> the asset at a later date or treating the actual receipt on realisation as
> being the value obtained is that difficult questions of causation are
> bound to arise. In the period between the transaction date and the
> date of valuation or resale other factors will have influenced the
> value or resale price of the asset. It was the desire to avoid these
> difficulties of causation which led to the adoption of the transaction
> date rule.'

Lord Steyn agreed that in general the date of transaction 'would be a practical
and just date to adopt'.[4]

1 [1997] AC 254.
2 [1997] AC 191 at 220H.
3 [1997] AC 254 at 266C.
4 [1997] AC 254 at 284B.

(c) The flexible approach

3.73 The citation from Lord Browne-Wilkinson's speech above shows, however, that the date of transaction is not to be elevated into an inflexible rule either. In *Smith New Court* Lord Steyn stressed that it is only prima facie the right date and will usually only be appropriate (if at all) when what he described as 'the valuation method' of assessing damages is adopted. He used this term, which we adopt, to describe what had been commonly known as 'the diminution in value rule'. The new term indicates that it should no longer be accorded rule status but is merely a method of assessing damages that may or may not be appropriate to any particular case.

3.74 In *Golden Strait Corpn v Nippon Yusen Kubishika Kaisha*[1], the majority in the House of Lords was prepared to depart from the date of the transaction as the date for assessing damages in a case of the breach of a commercial contract, namely a charterparty for the charter of a ship. The charterparty was entered into on 10 July 1998 for a term of seven years. Either party could terminate it in the event of war breaking out between certain countries. On 14 December 2001 the charterers repudiated the contract and on 17 December 2001 the shipowners accepted the repudiation. The shipowners were entitled to damages from the charterers for the charterers' breach of contract. But on 20 March 2003 the second Gulf War broke out. This would have entitled the charterers lawfully to terminate the charterparty if they had not already repudiated it. The arbitration took place after 20 March 2003, so the arbitrator knew that the charterers could have terminated the contract on 20 March 2003. The question was whether the shipowners should be awarded damages in relation to the balance of the seven-year period that remained after 20 March 2003, in other words after the period when the charterers would have been entitled to terminate the contract if they had not already wrongfully repudiated it. The majority decided that no damages were payable in respect of this period: the court knew that the charterers would have been entitled to terminate on 20 March 2003, and should compensate on the basis of what it knew had happened after termination of the contract.

1 [2007] UKHL 21, [2007] 2 WLR 691, per Lords Scott of Foscote, Carswell and Brown of Eaton-under-Heywood.

3.75 *Golden Strait* was a contractual case and the basic measure of damages was damages to put the shipowners in the position they would have been in if the contract had been performed, in other words if the charterers had continued to abide by the terms of the charterparty until they were entitled to terminate it. Although claims against solicitors are normally for breach of contract, so far as causation is concerned the position the client would have been in in the absence of breach of duty is normally that a different transaction would have been entered into, a different result in litigation achieved, or something similar[1]. The solicitor almost never warrants a result, so damages are almost never concerned with putting the client in the position he would have been in if what the solicitor stated had been correct. Hence one might consider that the principles discussed in *Golden Strait* are of limited relevance to claims against solicitors. It is thought, however, that what is material is that even the dissenting minority considered that it might often be acceptable to depart from the breach date rule in cases other than those concerning contracts between two commercial parties, such as charterparties. Lord Bingham, with whom Lord Walker agreed, accepted at [13] that the court in contractual or tortious cases would be prepared to depart from the breach date rule 'where it judges it necessary or just to do so in order to give effect to the compensatory principle'. He pointed out in the same paragraph that none of the cases in which this had occurred 'involved the accepted repudiation of a commercial contract such as a charterparty'. In summary, therefore: the majority was prepared to depart from the 'breach date' rule even in a case involving a commercial contract such as a charterparty; but even the minority accepted that the court could depart from the breach date rule in non-commercial cases if it were necessary to do so in order to give fair compensation. For the purposes of this book, therefore, it is thought that, although not directly relevant because claims against solicitors are generally not analogous to claims for the repudiation of a charterparty, *Golden Strait* gives further mild support to the proposition that the court will be prepared to depart from the breach date rule if good reason is shown to suggest that it does not provide fair compensation.

1 Cf para 3.01, above.

2   The valuation method

3.76 What Lord Steyn labelled the valuation method originally became known as the diminution in value rule following the decision of the Court of Appeal in *County Personnel v Alan R Pulver & Co*,[1] although it had been steadily applied before that case. It was explained in these terms by Browne-Wilkinson LJ:

> 'The diminution in value rule is concerned with a case where the client has purchased for a capital sum a property having a capital value. Such client thinks it has certain features which render it more valuable. Due to the shortcomings of his professional adviser he is not aware of the fact that it lacked these features.'

1 [1987] 1 WLR 916 at 927F–G.

3.77 From this description it is clear that the valuation method of assessing damages is particularly suited to cases where the claimant has acquired a capital asset such as land or property and it is in the context of conveyancing and real property that it has been applied most frequently in solicitors' negligence cases. If applied at the date of transaction the method often provides a just and convenient way of assessing damages that avoids the difficulties that Lord Steyn later identified in *Smith New Court*. These cases are considered in detail in chapter 9, to which reference should be made. The discussion need not be repeated here. It will be seen from para 9.99 that, in relation to cases where purchasers sue their former solicitors, our conclusion is that, at least in practice, there appears to be no general rule that damages will be assessed using the valuation method as at the date of the breach of duty. In cases where a solicitor's negligence has led the client to lose the chance of pursuing a claim to trial, the court will adopt a much more sophisticated approach to the assessment of damages: see chapter 12. Further, in cases where the court awards damages for the loss of a chance that a client would have entered into a transaction, the analysis is different from the simple valuation method: see para 3.19ff above. Thirdly, in the context of lenders' claims again a more detailed approach is often taken: see chapter 10. It is therefore doubtful whether it is helpful to think of the valuation method as anything more than an approach that the court may find helpful in achieving the overall compensatory principle, but from which it may easily depart depending on the context of the claim.

3.78   As a footnote to this discussion, the decision of Phillips J in *Deeny v Gooda Walker Ltd*[1] shows that the court has, and may in special cases where future losses are claimed exercise, a discretion not to assess damages at the date of trial but postpone further assessment until the future losses have been suffered and can be quantified.

1 [1995] 1 WLR 1206. See now CPR 3.1(2)(e) and (f).

G   DAMAGES FOR MENTAL DISTRESS AND PSYCHIATRIC ILLNESS

3.79   Damages for these types of loss are not generally recoverable against solicitors. The area in which claimants have had some element of success in claiming is in claims relating to the negligent conduct of litigation. The authorities are therefore considered in chapter 12.[1]

1 See paras 12.73–12.75. See also *Seymour v Ockwell* [2005] EWHC 1127, [2005] PNLR 39 (HHJ Havelock-Allen QC), at [185]: it was not an important object of the defendant financial advisor's contract to give pleasure, relaxation or peace of mind, so damages for stress, anxiety and inconvenience were not recoverable.

H   INTEREST

1   At common law

3.80   Interest *as* damages, including compound interest if the evidence merits it, has frequently been awarded in the context of lenders' claims, for example where lenders claim that in the absence of a solicitor's breach of duty they would not have lent to a borrower and therefore would not have incurred the cost of borrowing the principal sum lent to the borrower, including the interest costs of that borrowing. See further the discussion of the lenders' cases at paras 10.75–10.80, below. The effect of those lenders' cases was approved in the recent *Sempra Metals*[1] decision in the House of Lords. Outside the lenders' context, however, there was formerly a rule in English law to the effect that, at common law, the court would not award damages for a defendant's failure to pay money to the claimant when the defendant should have paid it.[2] It is thought that this rule has not survived the *Sempra Metals* decision. Lord Nicholls said at [95] that the nature of the claimed lost interest would depend on the nature of the evidence:

> 'The loss may be the cost of borrowing money. That cost may include an element of compound interest. Or the loss may be loss of an opportunity to invest the promised money. Here again, where the circumstances require, the investment loss may need to include a compound element if it is to be a fair measure of what the plaintiff lost by the late payment. Or the loss flowing from the late payment may take some other form.'

It therefore appears that there is no longer any rule in contract or tort to the effect that a claimant may not claim interest for the late payment of a debt or damages, nor that a claimant may not claim compound interest as damages[3]. A claimant making such a claim must, however, plead and prove the amount of interest said to have been lost, and show that it passes the normal tests of foreseeability in tort and contract. If the interest claim is not specifically pleaded then a claimant may have to fall back on the statutory jurisdiction to award simple, but not compound, interest on damages.[4] It will not always be the case that a claim for lost interest was foreseeable.[5]

1 *Sempra Metals Ltd v Inland Revenue Comrs* [2007] UKHL 34, [2007] 3 WLR 354. See per Lord Nicholls at [99] and Lord Mance at [217].
2 See para 3.60ff in the first edition of this book.
3 See per Lord Nicholls at [92]–[100], Lord Hope at [16], Lord Scott at [132], Lord Walker at [154] and [165], and Lord Mance at [216]–[217]. Strictly speaking these passages were obiter because the *Sempra* claim itself was for restitution of money paid under a mistake, rather than a claim in tort or contract, but it is thought that they will be followed in future cases in tort and contract. For the position in equity see para 4.63ff, below.
4 See per Lord Nicholls at [96]. The statutory jurisdiction is pursuant to Supreme Court Act 1981, s 35A.
5 See per Lord Mance at [216]–[217]. The effect of the latter paragraph may be that by relying on a solicitor's duty in tort claimants will more easily be able to show that the loss of interest is not too remote to be recoverable.

2 Under statute

3.81 Neuberger J reviewed the principles applicable to the award of statutory interest, pursuant to s 35 of the Supreme Court Act 1981, in *Harrison v Bloom*

Camillin (No 2).[1] As just indicated, under statute the court has power to award simple but not compound interest. Having referred to the Judgment Act rate, which tends to be higher and to be altered very infrequently, and the short term investment account rate, which varies more frequently as bank rates move, Neuberger J said that the relevant principles were:

> 'First, the appropriate rate of interest is a matter of discretion, which obviously must be exercised judiciously and fairly. Secondly, the tendency has been to award the judgment debt rate. Thirdly, in appropriate cases there is much to be said for the judgment debt rate (see per Nicholls LJ in *Pinnock*). Fourthly, use of the judgment debt rate in some cases may not be appropriate, for the reasons given by Bingham LJ in *Watts* and by the editors *Jackson & Powell*.[2] Fifthly, the court has to select a rate which appears to reflect justice between the parties in the particular case.'

The rationale for Nicholls LJ's preference for the judgment debt rate in *Pinnock v Wilkins*[3] appears to have been that the short-term investment account rate would not give the claimant the higher figure which he would have received if the interest were calculated on a compound as opposed to simple basis. Hence it was preferable, if awarding simple interest, to take the higher judgment debt rate. It is possible that this rationale may fall away, given the terms of Lord Nicholls' judgment in *Sempra*: if a claimant is entitled to compound interest, it should now be awarded at common law. The statutory regime of simple interest should now apply only if the claimant is not entitled to compound interest. In that case, as Bingham LJ said in *Watts v Morrow*[4], since the purpose of an award of interest is to compensate the claimant for being kept out of money, the short-term investment account rate seems preferable since it tends to vary in accordance with bank interest rates. This was the rate which Neuberger J applied in *Harrison*, though it appears from *Pinnock* that, unless the decision in *Sempra* has changed the position, a decision to apply the judgment debt rate by a first instance judge will not be overturned on appeal.

1 [2000] Lloyd's Rep PN 404 at 410 col 1.
2 The passage referred to was in the 1997 edition and has been removed from the 5th edition: see para 3–024 of the 5th edition of *Jackson & Powell*.
3 CA, *The Times*, 29 January 1990.
4 [1991] 1 WLR 1421, CA, at 1446A-C.

Chapter 4

Claims in equity

A   THE RELEVANCE OF EQUITY

1   Introduction

4.01   There is a fiduciary relationship between a solicitor and his or her client.[1] For this reason claims against solicitors often involve equitable considerations which go beyond contract and tort. Moreover, cases involving solicitors have supplied a number of leading authorities in relation to the duties of trustees and fiduciaries. Four decisions in particular have altered the landscape in the last decade. Claims for equitable compensation for breach of trust came into vogue after the Court of Appeal's decision in *Target Holdings Ltd v Redferns*[2] as claims by lenders against solicitors increased. The effect of that decision was widely perceived to be that, if the client could show a breach of duty on the part of the solicitor, it could obtain summary judgment for all its losses without the need to comply with common law rules of causation and remoteness and without facing reductions for contributory negligence or failure to mitigate the loss. Understandably, this was attractive to claimants. This perception was corrected by the House of Lords' decision in the same case[3] but by the time it came to be reported, it had fuelled enormous interest in equitable claims. Claimants began routinely to make claims for breach of trust and breach of fiduciary duty against solicitors in addition to claims for negligence. Because of this it became necessary for the Court of Appeal to examine the extent of liability for breach of trust and breach of fiduciary duty in *Bristol and West Building Society v Mothew*.[4] The judgment of Millett LJ in that case provided (and continues to provide) authoritative guidance on the scope of a solicitor's fiduciary duties and the importance of distinguishing between those duties and the solicitor's duties in contract and tort.[5] In *Twinsectra Ltd v Yardley*[6] the House of Lords held that a solicitor's undertaking to hold sums on trust for a third party gave rise to a *Quistclose* trust and also considered the circumstances in which one solicitor would be liable as an accessory in assisting another solicitor to commit a breach of that undertaking (and therefore a breach of trust). Finally, in *Hilton v Barker Booth & Eastwood*[6] the House of Lords had to consider the consequences of a breach of Practice Rule 6 of the Solicitors Practice Rules 1990 (which embodied the double employment rule).[7]

1   See, eg, *Nocton v Lord Ashburton* [1914] AC 932, *Moody v Cox & Hatt* [1917] 2 Ch 71 and *Brown v IRC* [1965] AC 46.
2   [1994] 1 WLR 1089, CA.
3   [1996] AC 421.
4   [1998] Ch 1.
5   See also Millett 'Equity's Place in the Law of Commerce' (1998) 114 LQR 214 at 217:

> '[P]laintiffs and their advisers have discovered the apparent advantages of alleging breach of trust or fiduciary duty, with the result that a statement of claim is considered to be seriously deficient if it does not contain inappropriate references to these concepts which are often scattered throughout the pleadings with complete abandon'.

For a similar sentiment see *Blythe v Northwood* [2005] NSWCA 221 at [210] and [211] (Bryson JA):

> 'Equitable claims arising out of fiduciary relationships are so encrusted with diffuse scholarship as to give colour to claims with little discernible relationship to the deeply underlying basis of jurisdiction in equity, in which the court has power to prevent reliance on legal rights and to remedy consequences of so doing in cases where such reliance is unconscionable. Outside well-worn paths of equitable relief this power is only available for exercise to redress enormities. Idiosyncratic or otherwise excessively ready exercises of the power threaten its existence. Designation of a relationship as fiduciary is not a signal for exercise of judicial bounty. Fiduciaries characteristically have areas of responsibility which have boundaries, and are free to act in their own interests in all matters outside those boundaries.'

6   [2002] UKHL 12, [2002] 2 AC 164.
7   [2005] UKHL 8, [2005] 1 WLR 567. For the contractual significance of this decision see para 1.01 and n 4 and para 2.15, above. For discussion of the equitable issues, see para 4.36, below. For the position since 1 July 2007 see the Solicitors' Code of Conduct 2007, r 3.

4.02   This chapter considers claims against solicitors on the grounds of breach of trust and breach of fiduciary duty. Claims for breach of trust arise where a solicitor, who is entrusted with client monies or other trust property, deals with them in breach of his authority. Claims for breach of fiduciary duty arise where a solicitor fails to comply with his or her obligations as a fiduciary, such as the duty of confidence or the duty to be loyal. These are often difficult and technical areas and it is not possible to provide a full survey of the law of equity in this book. But what can be attempted is a discussion which focuses upon the sort of claim against a solicitor which arises at the same time as a claim for negligence. In section B we consider liability for breach of trust which usually arises out of dealing with client funds held under the Solicitors Accounts Rules 1998. We also consider a solicitor's liability as a constructive trustee (and, in particular, accessory liability). In section C we discuss liability for breach of fiduciary duty where a solicitor acts for more than one client and a conflict of interest and duty or a conflict of duty and duty either exists or arises. Finally, in section D we discuss the principles of equitable compensation. Although that discussion highlights the differences between common law damages and equitable compensation recent developments in both branches of the law suggest that the differences are not so marked as they appeared when the first edition of this book was published and also that an underlying theme in both branches of the law is that the nature and scope of the duty which has been broken will determine the losses for which the solicitor is liable.[1]

1 Compare Millett (1998) 114 LQR 214 at 225:

> 'It is misleading to speak of breach of trust as if it were the equitable counterpart of breach of contract at common law; or to speak of equitable compensation for breach of fiduciary duty as if it were common law damages masquerading under a fancy name.'

We do not suggest that this view is incorrect. But we do suggest that in relation to issues such as causation, remoteness and assessment, where the policy of the law is primarily to compensate, the outcome at common law and in equity ought to be much the same: see paras 4.43ff and 4.57ff, below.

B   BREACH OF TRUST

1   Express, implied and resulting trusts

(*a*) *Express trusts*

4.03   A large part of the traditional work of a solicitor in the nineteenth and early twentieth centuries consisted of acting as a trustee. The terms of the solicitor's authority, powers and duties were –and remain today – governed by the express terms of the solicitor's appointment and the relevant legislation which assists in the construction or amplification of trust powers and duties.[1] A breach of trust:

> 'may be deliberate or inadvertent; it may consist of an actual misappropriation or misapplication of the trust property or merely of any investment or other dealing which is outside the trustees' powers; it may consist of a failure to carry out a positive obligation of the trustees or merely of a want of care on their part in the management of the trust property; it may be injurious to the interests of the beneficiaries or be actually to their benefit.'[2]

Unlike the law of obligations considered in the remainder of this book, the duties of a trustee do not principally depend upon him or her acting in accordance with a general standard set by the court. Whether a particular act, omission or course of dealing will amount to a breach of trust will turn on the terms of the trust deed or other instrument of the trustee's appointment. Some of the obligations of the trustee will be strict and some will require the trustee to exercise reasonable care. But, as a matter of general law, a trustee may owe a beneficiary neither:

> 'I accept the submission made on behalf of [the claimant] that there is an irreducible core of obligations owed by the trustees to the

beneficiaries and enforceable by them which is fundamental to the concept of a trust. If the beneficiaries have no rights enforceable against the trustees there are no trusts. But I do not accept the further submission that these core obligations include the duties of skill and care, prudence and diligence. The duty of the trustees to perform the trusts honestly and in good faith for the benefit of the beneficiaries is the minimum necessary to give substance to the trusts, but in my opinion it is sufficient.'[3]

1 See the Trustee Acts 1925 and 2000 and the Trustee Investment Act 1961.
2 See *Armitage v Nurse* [1998] Ch 241, CA at 251A–B (Millett LJ).
3 [1998] Ch 241 at 253H–254A (Millett LJ).

4.04 It is worth beginning therefore by contrasting the basic duties of a solicitor under his or her contract of retainer and the core duties of a trustee in the classical sense:

- The touchstone of liability in equity is unconscionability[1] not fulfilment of expectations or foreseeability or risk of damage which are the basis for enforcing a solicitor's duties in contract and in tort.

- The position of a trustee is best described as 'an office'. A trustee's duties to the beneficiaries of a trust are not contractual even if they arise out of a contract[2] whereas the core obligation or 'main subject matter'[3] of a solicitor's contractual retainer is the duty to provide legal advice. This has a number of important legal consequences. In providing legal advice a solicitor owes a common law and statutory implied duty to take reasonable care which the solicitor cannot exclude[4] and although a trustee owes a statutory duty to take reasonable care in relation to a number of functions[5] it is possible for a trustee to exclude that duty.[6]

- Except in limited circumstances[7] a trustee in the classical sense owes no duty to advise or consult his beneficiaries before exercising his powers or discretions.[8] Indeed, a trustee has no obligation to give reasons to a beneficiary for exercising a power and an express trust will ordinarily limit a beneficiary's right to information. By contrast the principal duty of a solicitor is to keep his or her client informed and to take instructions at all relevant points.

- The purpose of a remedy awarded by a court of equity is not necessarily to compensate the claimant for a loss which he or she has suffered. Equitable remedies were, and are, necessarily elastic. The claimant in a 'trust' action may be a beneficiary who believes that a trustee is not acting in his or her best interests but it may be the trustee himself.[9] The traditional remedy provided by a court of equity to a beneficiary against a trustee was to order an account to be taken of the way in which trust property had been dealt with. Following the taking of the accounts or inquiries, the beneficiary might be entitled to further relief either individually or on behalf of all of the beneficiaries. The nature of the relief and its relationship with compensation and damages are considered in more detail below.

1 See *Gillett v Holt* [2001] Ch 210 at 225 where this was described as a 'fundamental principle'.
2 See *Air Jamaica Ltd v Charlton* [1999] 1 WLR 1399.
3 This terminology is borrowed from Unfair Contract Terms in Consumer Contracts Regulations 1999 (UCTCCR), reg 6(2): see para 1.06, n. 3, above.
4 For the limited circumstances in which a solicitor may exclude or limit his or her duty of care at common law: see paras 1.05 and 1.06, above.
5 A trustee owes a duty of care in exercising his or her power of investment, power to acquire land, power to delegate, power to insure, power to compound and certain powers contained in s 21 of the Trustee Act 1925: see Sch 1 to the Trustee Act 2000.
6 See, eg, ss 6(1) and 9(1) of the Trustee Act 2000. See also *Baker v JE Clark (Transport) UK Ltd* [2006] EWCA Civ 464 at [17]:

   '[T]rustees undertake obligations and are entitled to limit the extent of the duties they assume other than the core duties of honesty and good faith. If a beneficiary wishes to take advantage of the terms of a settlement of this kind, he must do so on its terms.'

   The court held that a trustee exemption clause in a pension scheme was binding notwithstanding that there was no evidence that the settlor was aware of it. They also held that s 2(1) of the Unfair Contract Terms Act 1977 (UCTA) had no application to such a clause: see [18]–[21].
7 See, eg, the Trusts of Land and Appointment of Trustees Act 1996, s 11.
8 See *Schmidt v Rosewood Trust Ltd* [2003] UKPC 26, [2003] 2 AC 709 at [67] (Lord Walker of Gestingthorpe): 'However, the recent cases also confirm (as had been stated as long ago as *Re Cowin* 33 Ch D 179 in 1886) that no beneficiary (and least of all a discretionary object) has any entitlement as of right to disclosure of anything which can plausibly be described as a trust document. Especially when there are issues as to personal or commercial confidentiality, the court may have to balance the competing interests of different beneficiaries, the trustees themselves, and third parties. Disclosure may have to be limited and safeguards may have to be put in place. Evaluation of the claims of a beneficiary (and especially of a discretionary object) may be an important part of the balancing exercise which the court has to perform on the materials placed before it. In many cases the court may have no difficulty in concluding that an applicant with no more than a theoretical possibility of benefit ought not to be granted any relief.' Contrast the US *Uniform Trust Code*, which imposes a duty to inform the beneficiaries in advance 'of material facts in connection with a non-routine transaction which significantly affects the trust estate'. In *X v A* [2000] 1 All ER 490 at 496b–g Arden J stated that it was 'a good discipline' for a trustee to consult with the beneficiaries in the context of the exercise of proposed investment powers although there was no legal duty to do so.
9 See e g *Finers v Miro* [1991] 1 WLR 35, CA.

(b) Implied or resulting trusts: the client

4.05   Recent decisions have tended to focus on the more informal trust where the solicitor receives and holds money on behalf of his or her client without express appointment or a trust deed and usually pending the completion of a transaction on which the client has embarked. But the same principles should apply. There has never been much doubt that a solicitor holds money or property on trust in these circumstances[1] and, as a matter of professional conduct, the terms on which a solicitor holds a client's money are governed by the Solicitors Accounts Rules 1998[2]. Rule 1 sets out certain general principles and r 22 sets out the detailed rules for the withdrawal of funds from a solicitor's client account (the most important of which is that funds may only be withdrawn on the client's written instructions or on the oral instructions of the client confirmed by the solicitor in writing):

'*Rule 1 Principles*

The following principles must be observed. A solicitor must: (a) comply with the requirements of rule 1 of the Solicitors' Code of Conduct 2007 as to the *solicitor's* integrity, the duty to act in the *client's* best interests, and public trust in the *solicitor* and the *solicitor's* profession; (b) keep other people's money separate from money belonging to the *solicitor* or to the practice; (c) keep other people's money safely in a *bank* or *building society* account identifiable as a *client account* (except when the rules specifically provide otherwise);(d) use each *client's* money for that *client's* matters only ....

Rule 22 Withdrawals from a Client Account

(1) Client money may only be withdrawn from a client account when it is: (a) properly required for a payment to or on behalf of the client (or other person on whose behalf the money is being held); (b) properly required for payment of a disbursement on behalf of the client; (c) properly required in full or partial reimbursement of money spent by the solicitor on behalf of the client; (d) transferred to another client account; (e) withdrawn on the client's instructions, provided the instructions are for the client's convenience and given in writing or are given by other means and confirmed by the solicitor to the client in writing; (f) a refund to the solicitor of an advance no longer required to fund a payment on behalf of the client ...; (g) money which has been paid into the account in breach of the rules (for example, money paid into the wrong separate designated client account)...; (h) money not covered by (a) to (g) above, withdrawn from the account on the written authorisation of the Society ... (7) Money held for a client or controlled trust in a separate designated client account must not be used for payments for another client or controlled trust ...'

Plainly, a payment out of a client account without the authority of the client and in breach of r 22 of the Solicitors Accounts Rules will in almost all circumstances amount to a breach of trust. Furthermore, there is authority at first instance that the Solicitors Accounts Rules are terms of the implied trust on which the client's funds are held.[3] A breach of this trust is strict and it is not necessary to prove negligence or dishonesty. The critical question is whether the solicitor has complied with his or her strict obligations to

151

administer the fund and only to distribute to the correct beneficiary.[4] There is far more difficulty in establishing the other duties of the solicitor trustee under an implied or resulting trust or, perhaps more precisely, breach of which terms of the contractual retainer also amount to a breach of trust. The difficulty is identifying the scope of the solicitor's authority and what breaches of the retainer will bring his or her authority to deal with the client's money to an end.

1 See *Burdick v Garrick* (1870) 5 Ch App 233 at 240 and 243, CA, *Brown v IRC* [1965] AC 244 for client monies and *Target Holdings Ltd v Redferns* [1996] 1 AC 421 at 436. See also *Twinsectra Ltd v Yardley* [2002] UKHL 12, [2002] 2 AC 164 at [12] (Lord Hoffmann): 'Money on a solicitor's client account is held on trust. The only question is the terms of that trust.'

2 Amended most recently on 16 October 2007.

3 See *Bristol & West BS v May, May & Merrimans* [1996] 2 All E.R. 801 at 819b (Chadwick J):

> 'Absent any express trust imposed by the client at the time that the moneys are paid to the solicitor, it seems to me that the trust which attaches to clients' money …is an implied trust imposed to in order to give effect to the Accounts Rules made under S32 of the 1974 Act. The solicitor's obligations under that trust are the obligations imposed by the rules. It follows that a payment made out of clients' money to or to the order of a third party which is not authorised by, or "properly required" on behalf of, the client is a payment made in breach of trust.'

In *Re Ahmed & Co* [2006] EWHC 480 (Ch) at [28] Lawrence Collins J spoke of the Solicitors Accounts Rules underpinning a solicitor's duties:

> 'The solicitor's duties are underpinned by a regulatory regime whereby (a) the Solicitors' Accounts Rules require client money to be held in separate client bank accounts, prescribe the records which must be kept and the circumstances in which the solicitor is permitted to draw on client money and guard against the mixing of client money and office money; (b) clients have the right to apply to court (inter alia) for delivery of a cash account, a list of money held for the client and payment over of that money: CPR, r 67.2.'

4 See *Re Ahmed*, above at [102], where Lawrence Collins J summarised the duties of a private law trustee as follows:

> 'Those duties would include the following: first, a trustee has to ascertain the identity of the beneficiaries, and to ascertain their beneficial entitlement. Second, a trustee is obliged to inform a beneficiary of full age and capacity of his interest in and rights under the trust: *Lewin on Trusts* (17th edn, 2000, Mowbray et al), para 23–03. Third, a trustee is obliged to give beneficiaries a full and accurate record of the stewardship and management of the trust, and is required to keep and render proper, clear and accurate financial accounts: *Lewin on Trusts*, para 23–05. Fourth, a trustee has to distribute to the correct beneficiaries of a trust fund, and that obligation is a strict obligation: *Lewin on Trusts*, para 26–03. This principle is onerous and places a trustee in a demanding position, in terms of correctly distributing to the right beneficiaries of the trust.'

4.06   The law on this issue appears principally in Lord Browne-Wilkinson's speech in *Target*[1] and Millett LJ's judgment in *Bristol and West Building Society v Mothew*.[2] In the former Lord Browne-Wilkinson made clear that, although a solicitor did hold his client's money on trust, the nature of the trust was different from a traditional trust and that not every duty owed by the solicitor was a trust obligation. The solicitor held the lender's money on a bare trust and Lord Browne-Wilkinson said that this was:[3]

'[B]ut one incident of a wider, commercial transaction involving agency. In the case of moneys paid to a solicitor by a client as part of a conveyancing transaction, the purpose of that transaction is to achieve the commercial object of the client, be it the acquisition of property or the lending of money on security. The depositing of money with the solicitor is but one aspect of the arrangements between the parties, such arrangements being for the most part contractual. Thus, the circumstances under which the solicitor can part with money from client account are regulated by the instructions given by the client: they are not part of the trusts on which the property is held. I do not intend to cast any doubt on the fact that moneys held by solicitors on client account are trust moneys, or that the basic equitable principles apply to any breach of such trust by solicitors. But the basic equitable principle applicable to breach of trust is that the beneficiary is entitled to be compensated for any loss he would not have suffered but for the breach.'

1 [1996] AC 421 at 428. Each of the other law lords agreed with him.
2 [1998] Ch 1 at 22D to 24D, CA.
3 [1996] AC 421 at 436B–D.

4.07   This passage suggests that arguments to the effect that the terms of the trust are the same as the terms of the solicitor's contract, so that any breach of contract automatically amounts to a breach of trust, are wrong. In the case of money paid by a purchaser or a lender, the purpose of the arrangement is presumably to be taken as the acquisition of an asset or the lending of money on security. The question which arises is this: if it is wrong to suppose that any breach of contract amounts to a breach of trust, what does amount to a breach of trust? In *Target*, the defendants had admitted breach of trust, and so strictly speaking the House of Lords did not need to deal with that issue. Lord Browne-Wilkinson did, however, set out the basis of the concession, and it looks from his judgment as if he considered that it had been properly made. The facts of *Target* were very briefly as follows. A was selling a property to B for £775,000; B was then to sell it to C for £1.25m; and C was to sell it to D for £2m. The defendant solicitors acted for each of B, C and D, so they knew of the price increase. The lenders, Target, agreed to lend D £1.706m on the understanding that D was purchasing the property for £2m. Of the sum of £1.706m, £1.525m was to be used for the purchase of the property, and the rest for payment of various insurance premiums. Target did not know of the previous contracts. Target instructed Redferns, the defendants, as their solicitors. Target paid the £1.525m to Redferns without giving any express instructions as to its release. Before D had purchased the property or executed charges in favour of Target, Redferns paid £1.525m of Target's money to B. This was the sum which C owed B to purchase the property. There was common ground as to the basis on which Redferns had acted in breach of trust. First, it was agreed that Redferns 'had implied authority to pay the money to or to the order of [D] when the property

153

had been conveyed to [D] and [D] had executed charges in Target's favour'.[1] Further, it was agreed that Redferns acted in breach of trust when they paid away Target's money 'to a stranger who had no contractual relationship with [D] and before completion of the purchase by [D] or the mortgages by [D] to Target'.[2]

1 [1996] 1 AC 421 at 429A.
2 [1996] 1 AC 421 at 429H.

4.08 Strictly speaking anything said as to liability for breach of trust in *Target* is obiter. But we can summarise the basis of the parties' agreement, which the House of Lords appears to have accepted was correctly made, in the following way. The solicitor holds the client's money on a bare trust for the purpose of facilitating the commercial purpose of the transaction, which, in *Target,* was to obtain a valid security over the property which it understood the borrower to be purchasing. The solicitor's trust obligations depend upon the authority which the court will imply into the retainer to part with the client's money. The court is likely to hold that the terms of the solicitor's authority – and his or her duty as trustee – are that he may not part with the client's money except to the payee identified by the client or to whom the client is indebted and, where the solicitor is acting on an acquisition or disposal, only upon receipt of the assets, money or documents of title for which the client has bargained.[1] *Collins v Brebner*[2] provides an example of this analysis, In that case a solicitor was instructed to pay funds to the vendor of 50% of the shares in a Spanish company but in breach of his instructions paid them to another shareholder for reasons which were not adequately explained and then concealed this from his client. Following *Target,* the trial judge found this to be a breach of trust and this finding was not challenged on appeal.[3]

1 In the case of a mortgage this will be that (a) the property has been conveyed to the borrower, and (b) the borrower has executed a valid charge in favour of the lender. If the mortgage is an endowment mortgage, it will probably be a breach of trust to fail to obtain an assignment of the policy: see *Nationwide Building Society v Mian* (12 September 1997, unreported) (Chadwick J).
2 [2000] Lloyds Rep PN 587, CA.
3 The case is considered in the context both of dishonest breach of trust and causation in paras 4.17 n 3, 4.48 and 4.49, below.

4.09 Millett LJ considered the matter further in *Bristol and West Building Society v Mothew*.[1] He said that the solicitors held the lender's money:[2]

> '. . . in trust for the [client] but with the [client]'s authority (and instructions) to apply it in the completion of the transaction of purchase and remortgage of the property. Those instructions were revocable but, unless previously revoked, the defendant was entitled and bound to act in accordance with them.'

In *Mothew* the lender argued that its instructions to the solicitor were to be construed as making the solicitor's authority to complete the transaction conditional upon his having complied with all of his contractual obligations to the lender; thus, as he had failed to comply with all those obligations, it was said that he had no authority to complete; hence, when he did complete, he did so without authority and in breach of trust. Millett LJ rejected this argument. While it was possible that a lender could adopt instructions which would have this effect, the result would be very inconvenient: 'it would in my judgment require very clear wording to produce so inconvenient and impractical a result' because 'no solicitor could safely accept such instructions, for he could never be certain that he was entitled to complete' [3] Millett LJ added that the defendant's authority to apply the mortgage money in completion of the purchase was not vitiated by the misrepresentations for which he was responsible but of which he was unaware'.[4] These dicta were applied in *Nationwide Building Society v Balmer Radmore*[5] in which it was a held that a solicitor who released a mortgage advance before he had complied with his express instructions to confirm the purchase price of the property did not commit a breach of trust. It was also held that he had not committed a breach of trust by agreeing with the vendor's solicitors that payment of the balance of the purchase price could be deferred without taking his lender client's instructions. There was nothing in the latter's instructions to indicate that the advance could only be released if the balance of the price was paid at the same time. The practical effect of these decisions is that a failure to comply with a term of the retainer or the making of a negligent misrepresentation will not determine a solicitor's authority to release funds unless there is an express term to that effect[6], and in the usual case a failure to exercise reasonable care in carrying out the other terms of the retainer, whether it is investigating title or advising the client about the terms of a contract, will not amount to a breach of trust.[7]

1 [1998] Ch 1.
2 [1998] Ch 1 at 22E.
3 [1998] Ch 1 at 22B–C.
4 [1998] Ch 1 at 22D.
5 [1999] Lloyd's Rep PN 235 (Blackburne J).
6 For example, para 10.3.1 the current edition of the CML Lenders' Handbook (which came into force on 1 June 2007) provides:

> 'You are only authorised to release the loan when you hold sufficient funds to complete the purchase of the property and pay all stamp duty land tax and registration fees to perfect the security as a first legal mortgage or, if you do not have them, you accept responsibility to pay them yourself. You must hold the loan on trust for us until completion.'

Paragraph 10.3.4 also provides: 'If completion is delayed, you must return it to us when and how we tell you …' (and Part 2 contains provisions dealing with the return of the advance). It is suggested that these provisions would not vitiate the authority of a solicitor to release the advance if, say, the solicitor failed to complete the certificate of title accurately or failed to carry out adequate searches.

7 For another example of a breach of an incidental term of the retainer which did not amount to a breach of trust see *Nationwide BS v Vanderpump & Sykes* [1999] Lloyds Rep PN 422 (Blackburne J) at 434.

(c) *Implied or resulting trusts: third parties*

4.10   A solicitor may also incur liability to a third party in respect of funds held (usually in the firm's client account), if he or she gives a solicitor's undertaking only to utilise those funds for a specific purpose. This often arises in the context of bridging loans and commercial loans, where a lender requires the solicitor's undertaking as a temporary security pending repayment of the loan or the taking of a long-term security. For instance, where a solicitor gives the standard form undertaking to a bank only to use an advance for the purposes of his or her client's acquisition of a specific property, the undertaking imposes a liability both in contract and trust:

> 'From the bank's point of view, the undertaking is intended to facilitate the completion of a transaction to which its own customer is already committed. Although capable of being included in a general retainer, it is designed to stand alone as the only communication passing between the solicitor and the bank. In such a case the scope of the solicitor's obligations is determined exclusively by the terms of the undertaking.
>
> The undertaking is a contractual undertaking which sounds in damages. It is not a warranty of title. Although positive in form it is negative in substance. The only obligation undertaken by the solicitor is not to part with the money except in the circumstances prescribed. Although it may be provided at any stage of the transaction, it is clearly designed to be provided to the lender on the eve of completion and to become effective only when the completion money is received. The function of the undertaking is to prescribe the terms upon which the solicitor receives the money remitted by the bank. Such money is trust money which belongs in equity to the bank but which the solicitor is authorised to disburse in accordance with the terms of the undertaking but not otherwise. Parting with the money otherwise than in accordance with the undertaking constitutes at one and the same time a breach of a contractual undertaking and a breach of the trust on which the money is held.'[1]

This is an example of the *Quistclose* trust which arises where one person, A, advances money to another, B, on the understanding that B is not to release or part with it except for a limited purpose (usually although not exclusively to pay a creditor). The nature of this trust was explained by the House of Lords in *Twinsectra Ltd v Yardley*[2] in which A made a loan to B for the purpose of completing a purchase of a specific property. A was only prepared to make the advance against a solicitor's undertaking to use the loan for that purpose and S1, a firm of solicitors, gave an undertaking that: 'The loan monies will be utilised solely for the acquisition of property on behalf of our client and for no other purpose.'[3] S1 then transferred the sum into the client account of S2, a second firm of solicitors, who paid it away to the client in breach of S1's undertaking. The House of Lords held that the money was held by S1 in their client account on trust for A subject to a power to use it for the specified purpose.[4] Until S1 exercised the power they held it on trust for A (and not B who was the intended recipient[5]) and they were liable to A for breach of trust by failing to comply with the undertaking. Although the facts of *Twinsectra Ltd v Yardley* are unusual[6] it is of general application to undertakings given by solicitors to hold funds for third parties which solicitors are often obliged to give to enable a wide range of commercial transactions to take place. The most obvious examples apart from the standard form undertaking given by a solicitor to a lender discussed above are the undertakings given by both the vendor's solicitors and the purchaser's solicitors on the sale of land. The purchaser's solicitor gives an undertaking to the mortgagee funding the purchase to use it for that purpose and the vendor's solicitor gives an undertaking to use the purchase monies to discharge the existing charges over the land.[7]

1 *Barclays Bank plc v Weeks, Legg & Dean* [1999] QB 309 at 323G–324A (Millett LJ).
2 [2002] UKHL 12, [2002] 2 AC 164 at [99] (Lord Millett). Lords Slynn and Steyn agreed with Lord Hoffmann: see [3] and [9]. At [25] Lord Hutton agreed with Lord Hoffmann and Lord Millett who delivered a concurring speech on this issue. The critical issue for decision was whether S2 was liable as an accessory for assisting S1 to commit a breach of trust and on this point Lord Millett dissented.
3 The terms of the undertaking are set out in Lord Hoffmann's speech at [9].
4 See Lord Hoffmann at [13] and Lord Millett at [100]:

> 'The lender pays the money to the borrower by way of loan, but he does not part with the entire beneficial interest in the money, and in so far as he does not it is held on a resulting trust for the lender from the outset. Contrary to the opinion of the Court of Appeal, it is the borrower who has a very limited use of the money, being obliged to apply it for the stated purpose or return it. He has no beneficial interest in the money, which remains throughout in the lender subject only to the borrower's power or duty to apply the money in accordance with the lender's instructions. When the purpose fails, the money is returnable to the lender, not under some new trust in his favour which only comes into being on the failure of the purpose, but because the resulting trust in his favour is no longer subject to any power on the part of the borrower to make use of the money.'

5 For a case in which the contest was between the original payor and the intended recipient see *Freeman v HM Commissioners and Excise* [2005] EWHC 582 (Ch) (Michael Crystal QC).
6 Lord Hoffmann recognised the unusual nature of the transaction at [15]. The lender did not require security over the property. The loan was unsecured but the lender wanted the security of a solicitor's undertaking to ensure that it was applied solely for that purpose.
7 See Lord Millett at [99]:

> 'There is clearly a wide range of situations in which the parties enter into a commercial arrangement which permits one party to have a limited use of the other's money for a stated purpose, is not free to apply it for any other purpose, and must return it if for any reason the purpose cannot be carried out. The arrangement between the purchaser's solicitor and the purchaser's mortgagee is an example of just such an arrangement. All such arrangements should if possible be susceptible to the same analysis.'

See also para 5.34 n 6, below.

4.11 This book is not the place for a detailed discussion of the trust law principles considered by the House of Lords in *Twinsectra* but there are a number of practical consequences of the decision which are worth noting or remain to be worked out. First, Lord Millett indicated that in principle a *Quistclose* trust could still arise even if the solicitor owed a duty to use the money for the specified purpose and even though the payor, A, could not withdraw the instructions.[1] In those circumstances, it remains to be determined whether the fund is held on trust for the intended recipient, B, or whether B has a sufficient interest in the fund to enforce its terms.[2] Secondly, Lord Millett also dealt with the question of certainty. Provided that the power is stated with sufficient clarity to enable the court to determine whether it could still be carried out or whether the fund has been misapplied the court can enforce the trust. But if the trust is too uncertain to be enforced then the solicitor has no authority to deal with the fund and must return it to A under the resulting trust.[3] Moreover, there is a special principle which applies to solicitors' undertakings that an ambiguous undertaking is construed in favour of the recipient which may save the undertaking.[4] Thirdly, Lord Millett made it clear that the trust arises immediately, which may have some significance in the context of insolvency.[5] Fourthly, and finally, the primary remedy is restoration of the fund although where some or all of the funds have been applied for the purpose of the transaction, the principles considered in Part D of this Chapter will apply.[6]

1 [2002] UKHL 12, [2002] 2 AC 164 at [100]:

> 'Whether the borrower is obliged to apply the money for the stated purpose or merely at liberty to do so, and whether the lender can countermand the borrower's mandate while it is still capable of being carried out, must depend on the circumstances of the particular case.'

2 In *Freeman v HM Commissioners and Excise* [2005] EWHC 582 (Ch) at [24] Michael Crystal QC considered the circumstances in which B under a *Quistclose* trust obtains a beneficial interest in the fund.

3 See [101].

4 See *Reddy v Lachlan* [2000] Lloyd's Rep PN 858, CA cited by Lewison J in *Templeton Insurance Ltd v Penningtons Solicitors LLP* [2006] EWHC 685 (Ch) at [8]. For further discussion of both cases see para 5.29, below.

5 See [102].

6 In *Templeton Insurance Ltd v Penningtons Solicitors LLP* [2006] EWHC 685 (Ch) (Lewison J) S, a firm of solicitors, had given an undertaking to apply £500,000 for the 'express purpose' of acquiring a property. £240,000 was applied towards the purchase and paying stamp duty, £175,000 was paid to third parties and S retained the balance in their client account. They were ordered to repay the latter two sums at a summary stage because the latter sums had not been applied for the purpose of acquiring the property. In *Freeman v HM Commissioners and Excise* [2005] EWHC 582 (Ch) (Michael Crystal QC) a property was sold for a fixed price plus VAT (if payable). The purchaser was unwilling to pay over the VAT to the vendor and it was paid to the purchaser's solicitors to be held on the terms of an undertaking. In breach of the undertaking S paid it to the purchaser's accountants. Either they misappropriated it or it was stolen from them. The purchaser went into liquidation and the liquidators succeeded in recovering some of the money from the accountants. It was held that the liquidators could now reconstitute the fund and use it as officers of the court to ensure that it was applied for the original purpose.

(d) *Fraudulent or dishonest breach of trust*

4.12   In *Mothew* it was a term of the defendant solicitor's instructions that he should report any proposal that the purchaser might arrange a second mortgage. The report on title also required him to confirm that the balance of the purchase price was being provided by the purchaser personally without resort to further borrowing. He was told that the borrower intended to leave a sum of £3,350 outstanding to another lender after completion and that it would be secured by a second charge. He failed to report this to the plaintiff and gave the confirmation requested. It was accepted that this failure was in breach of contract but there was no allegation of dishonesty or bad faith, and Millett LJ said that 'on the [lender]'s pleaded case the defendant must be taken to have known the facts at one time but to have forgotten or overlooked them so that they were not present in his mind when he came to complete his report to the society'.[1] In the context of the breach of trust he said this:

> 'The defendant knew that he was a trustee of the money for the [lender]; but he did not realise that he had misled the [lender] and could not know that his authority to complete had determined (if indeed it had). He could not be bound to repay the money to the [lender] so long as he was ignorant of the facts which had brought his authority to an end, for those are the facts which are alleged to affect his conscience and subject him to an obligation to return the money to the [lender].'[2]

It was unnecessary, therefore, for the court to consider what the position would have been if a fraudulent, dishonest or deliberate breach of trust had been alleged.

1 [1998] Ch 1 at 15G.
2 [1998] Ch 1 at 23G–H.

4.13   If the defendant had known that the report on title was misleading when he completed it, the plaintiff could have recovered damages for deceit at common law. But this would also have been a fraudulent breach of trust, which Millett LJ himself defined in *Armitage v Nurse*:[1]

> 'The expression "actual fraud" in clause 15 is not used to describe the common law tort of deceit. As the judge appreciated it simply means dishonesty. I accept the formulation put forward by Mr Hill on behalf of the respondents which (as I have slightly modified it) is that it
>
> > "connotes at the minimum an intention on the part of the trustee to pursue a particular course of action, either knowing that it is contrary to the interests of the beneficiary or being recklessly indifferent whether it is contrary to their interests or not".

It is the duty of the trustee to manage the trust property and deal with it in the interests of the beneficiaries. If he acts in a way which he does not honestly believe is in their interests then he is acting dishonestly. It does not matter whether he stands or thinks he stands to gain personally from his actions. A trustee who acts with the intention of benefiting persons who are not the objects of the trust is not the less dishonest because he does not intend to benefit himself.'

1 [1998] Ch 241 at 251D–G. The judge was defining 'actual fraud' for the purpose of a trustee exemption clause.

4.14 It is hard to think of a stronger example of a trustee intentionally or recklessly disregarding his or her beneficiary's interests than a fraudulent misrepresentation. But, as Millett LJ was at pains to point out, the notion of a fraudulent or dishonest breach of trust is not co-terminous with a common law action for deceit. In *Alliance & Leicester Building Society v Edgestop*[1] it was held that a solicitor who knew that his borrower client had made fraudulent misrepresentations to his lender client but concealed this fact from his client was liable for breach of trust. This knowledge made it apparent to the solicitor that the transaction was wholly different from the transaction which the lender client had intended to authorise and, accordingly, vitiated the solicitor's authority to release the money. The judge stated:[2]

'The case against them is put in various ways but the principal cause of action relied upon is misapplication of the society's funds. It is said that upon receipt of the money from the society, the solicitors held it in trust to apply it in accordance with the society's instructions and subject thereto in trust for the society. The society's instructions authorised the money to be advanced for the purposes of the purchases set out in the instructions and not for some materially different transactions. It also required that the society should, before completion, be notified of matters which ought reasonably to have been brought to its attention. The solicitors knew or ought to have known that the true nature of the transactions had been concealed from the society and I think that there can be no doubt that if the facts known to the solicitors had been brought to the attention of the society before completion it would not have made any of the advances.'

1 [1999] Lloyd's Rep (PN) 868 (Hoffmann J). The decision was approved but distinguished by the House of Lords in *Target* [1996] AC 421 at 439B–D.
2 [1999] Lloyd's Rep (PN) 868 at 870 col 1.

4.15 *Edgestop* was a strong case. There was no doubt that the borrower was fraudulent or that the solicitor was aware of this and party to a criminal conspiracy.[1] But in other cases the position may be less clear cut. The test for dishonesty in the context of fiduciary relationships was the subject of detailed consideration in *Twinsectra Ltd v Yardley*[2], a claim of dishonest assistance against a solicitor. As discussed, the House of Lords held that the undertaking given by the first solicitor gave rise to a trust but that the second solicitor did not act dishonestly when he assisted the first solicitor to commit a breach of the undertaking by accepting the funds and paying them over to his client. In *Royal Brunei Airlines v Tan*[3] Lord Nicholls had appeared to adopt a test based on an objective standard of honesty although informed by the knowledge of the relevant wrongdoer. In *Twinsectra* this test was interpreted by the majority as laying down a 'combined'[4] test 'which requires that before there can be a finding of dishonesty it must be established that the defendant's conduct was dishonest by the ordinary standards of reasonable and honest people and that he himself realised that by those standards his conduct was dishonest.'[5] Indeed, Lord Hoffmann distinguished between a solicitor who was dishonest and one who took 'a blinkered approach to his professional duties' (which was not dishonest).[6] This test was criticised by commentators[7] both because the majority had misunderstood *Tan* (and the dissenting speech of Lord Millett[8]) and because it introduced a test which was too complex to apply.

1 The judge's use of the phrase 'knew or ought to have known' should not be taken as authority for the proposition that a solicitor who *ought* to have known that his or her client was fraudulent but did not was in breach of trust. But if this is what he intended, it appears to have been obiter dictum in the light of his findings of fact and will not stand with the comments made by Millett LJ in *Mothew* discussed below.
2 [2002] UKHL 12, [2002] 2 AC 164.
3 [1995] 2 AC 375 at 390–1. See also the analysis of Sir Anthony Clarke MR in 'Claims against professionals: negligence, dishonesty and fraud' [2006] 22 PN 70 at 73–5.
4 It was described as a combined test by Mummery LJ in *Gwembe Valley Development Co Ltd v Koshy* [2003] EWCA Civ 1048, [2004] 1 BCLC 131 at [132].
5 Lord Hutton at [2002] UKHL 12, [2002] 2 AC 164. In *Walker v Stones* [2001] QB 902 at 939E Sir Christopher Slade considered that the penniless thief 'who picks the pocket of the multi-millionaire is dishonest even though he genuinely considers that the theft is morally justified as a fair distribution of wealth and that he is not therefore being dishonest'.
6 Lord Hoffmann at [22]. This distinction has been consistently applied in professional misconduct cases: see, eg, *Baxendale-Walker v the Law Society* [2006] EWHC 643 (Admin), [2006] 3 All ER 675 at [40]: 'The tribunal must have considered that, in the absence of dishonesty, the appellant took 'a blinkered approach to his professional duties as a solicitor''. That, as Lord Hoffmann pointed out in *Twinsectra Ltd v Yardley* [2002] UKHL 12 at [22], [2002] 2 AC 164 (not cited to the tribunal or to the court), is not dishonest.' See also *Constantinides v the Law Society* [2006] EWHC 725 (Admin) at [35].
7 See, eg, Tjio and Yeo 'Knowing what is Dishonesty' (2002) 118 LQR 502, McIlroy 'What has happened to Accessory Liability is Criminal' (2004) 7 JIBFL 266. See also the criticisms of two members of the New Zealand Court of Appeal (Anderson J and Glazebrook J) in *US International Marketing Ltd v National Bank of New Zealand* [2004] 1 NZLR 589.
8 See, in particular, the passages at [118]–[125].

4.16 In *Barlow Clowes International Ltd v Eurotrust International Ltd*[1] the Privy Council considered the question of dishonesty again. In that case the judge found that a director of a company was liable for dishonestly assisting in the misappropriation of funds from investors in Barlow Clowes by two individuals who used the money for their own purposes. She found that by the time of the relevant payments the defendant strongly suspected that the money passing through his hands had been received from members of the public who thought they were subscribing to a scheme for investment in gilt-edged securities.[1] The test to be applied was set out in the following passage from the judgment delivered by Lord Hoffmann:[2]

> 'The judge stated the law in terms largely derived from the advice of the Board given by Lord Nicholls of Birkenhead in *Royal Brunei Airlines Sdn Bhd v Tan* [1995] 2 AC 378. In summary, she said that liability for dishonest assistance requires a dishonest state of mind on the part of the person who assists in a breach of trust. Such a state of mind may consist in knowledge that the transaction is one in which he cannot honestly participate (for example, a misappropriation of other people's money), or it may consist in suspicion combined with a conscious decision not to make inquiries which might result in knowledge: see *Manifest Shipping Co Ltd v Uni-Polaris Insurance Co Ltd* [2001] UKHL 1, [2003] 1 AC 469. Although a dishonest state of mind is a subjective mental state, the standard by which the law determines whether it is dishonest is objective. If by ordinary standards a defendant's mental state would be characterised as dishonest, it is irrelevant that the defendant judges by different standards. The Court of Appeal held this to be a correct statement of the law and their Lordships agree.'

The judge found that the unsuccessful defendant had been dishonest because he had an 'exaggerated notion of dutiful service to clients, which produced a warped moral approach'. His argument on appeal was that he was not dishonest unless he had appreciated that he was acting dishonestly and that the judge had made no finding to this effect. The Privy Council rejected this argument although it was based on statements made by Lord Hutton and Lord Hoffmann in Twinsectra. Lord Hoffmann acknowledged that there was some ambiguity in those statements but ultimately concluded that there was no difference between the reasoning of the majority in *Twinsectra* and in the judgment of Lord Nicholls in Tan.[3] *Twinsectra* continues to represent the law in England but it is highly unlikely that an English court would refuse to follow the gloss placed on the decision by the Privy Council in *Barlow Clowes* and at first instance this has been the approach which the court adopted.[4] It can be stated with reasonable confidence[5] therefore that the test of dishonesty for breach of trust or breach of fiduciary is an objective one, in the sense that the wrongdoer's state of mind is judged against an objective standard of honesty but only after taking into account: 'subjective considerations such as the defendant's experience and intelligence and his actual state of knowledge at the relevant time'.[6]

1 [2005] UKPC 37, [2006] 1 WLR 1476. The judgment of the judge at first instance was delivered after the appeal had been heard in *Twinsectra* but before it had been decided.
2 [10]. Lord Hoffmann was a member of the majority in *Twinsectra*. Significantly, Lord Nicholls who delivered the judgment *Tan* was also a member of the Board.

3 See [11]–[18].
4 See *Abou-Rahmah v Abacha* [2005] EWHC (QB) 2662 (Treacy J) at [34]–[52], *Barnes v Tomlinson* [2006] EWHC 3115 (Ch) (Kitchin J) at [78] and *A-G of Zambia v Meer, Care & Desai* [2007] EWHC 952 (Ch) (Peter Smith J). In *Abou-Rahmah v Abacha* [2006] EWCA Civ 1492, [2007] 1 Lloyds Rep 115 the Court of Appeal refused to disturb the findings of the trial judge, Treacy J, without attempting an authoritative reconciliation of *Twinsectra* and *Barlow Clowes*. The defendant was not represented and although the Court heard full argument Rix LJ (with whom Pill LJ agreed) was not prepared to determine the issue and put his decision on the basis that it would not be appropriate to interfere with the judge's findings: see [40]. Arden LJ did address the question and held that this was an exceptional case in which the Court of Appeal should follow the Privy Council rather than the House of Lords: see [66]–[71]. In *Zambia* Peter Smith J discussed the Court of Appeal's decision and applied *Barlow Clowes*.
5 See Clarke 'Claims against professionals: negligence, dishonesty and fraud' [2006] 22 PN 70 at 84–5. See also Yeo 'Dishonest Assistance: A Restatement from the Privy Council' [2006] 122 LQR and Conaglen and Goymour 'Dishonesty in the context of assistance – again' [2006] 65 CLJ 18.
6 Lord Millett in *Twinsectra* at [121]. See also Clarke (supra):

> '[I]t is a test which requires a court to assess an individual's conduct according to an objective standard of dishonesty. In doing so, the court has to take account as to what the individual knew; his experience, intelligence and reasons for acting as he did. Whether the individual was aware that his conduct fell below the objective standard is not part of the test.'

Etherton J also provided the following summary in *Mortgage Express v Newman* [2000] Lloyd's Rep PN 745 at 753 and although delivered before the decision in the House of Lords in *Twinsectra* it may now be particularly helpful in solicitors' cases: 'In cases where dishonesty is in issue, the mind of the person responsible, the understanding and practice of solicitors at the relevant time and the events which took place are all relevant. Once the facts have been found, the judge has to decide, according to the standards of right thinking members of society, whether the act or omission was due merely to incompetence or to dishonesty. That, as Millett J pointed out in *Agip*, is essentially a jury question.'

(e) Deliberate Breach of trust

4.17   In a passage in *Bristol and West Building Society v Mothew*[1] Millett LJ drew a distinction between a dishonest and an intentional breach of fiduciary duty The deliberate but innocent breach of trust is familiar to trust lawyers and in *Armitage v Nurse*[2] Millett LJ said this immediately before setting out the test quoted in para 4.13, above:

> 'By consciously acting beyond their powers (as, for example, by making an investment which they know to be unauthorised), the trustees may deliberately commit a breach of trust; but if they do so in the interest of the beneficiaries their conduct is not fraudulent. So a deliberate breach of trust is not necessarily fraudulent. Hence the remark famously attributed to Selwyn LJ by Sir Nathaniel Lindley MR in the course of argument in *Perrins v Bellamy* [1899] 1 Ch 797,798: "My old master, the late Selwyn LJ used to say 'The main duty of a trustee is to commit *judicious* breaches of trust'".'

In that case the distinction was relevant to the terms of an exemption clause in a trust deed. The distinction may also be relevant to the measure of compensation or to the court's decision to relieve a trustee from the consequences of his or her breach of trust.[3] But a conscious, if innocent, breach of duty by a solicitor will not automatically elevate a claim for negligence or breach of contract into a claim for breach of trust. This turns on the terms of the solicitor's authority to release the money or property. Where it is necessary to imply a term, the court might well distinguish between the release of funds after an inadvertent breach of duty and the release of funds by a solicitor after a conscious or deliberate breach of duty.[4] But it will depend on the precise wording of the instructions and the nature of the breach.

1 [1998] Ch 1, CA at 19E.
2 See *Armitage v Nurse* [1998] Ch 241 at 251D, CA.
3 In *Collins v Brebner (No 2)* [2000] Lloyds Rep PN 587 at [54] the Court of Appeal held that the principles to be applied in *Target Holdings Ltd v Redferns* [1996] 1 AC 421 applied equally to a fraudulent breach of trust, i e the claimant had to show that the breach of trust caused the loss. It is also hard to believe that the court would excuse a 'judicious' breach of trust nowadays where the trustee had time to apply to the court for directions. See *Phipps v Boardman* [1965] Ch 992 per Lord Denning MR, CA.
4 The terms of the retainer will make it clear what steps the solicitor has to take prior to completion. Although the parties will not be taken to have intended that the solicitor's authority will be determined by an inadvertent failure to carry all of them out, it is clearly arguable that the parties cannot sensibly intend that the solicitor may complete when he knows that he has failed to comply with his instructions. This was not, however, the view of Millett in 'Equity's Place in the Law of Commerce' (1998) 114 LQR 214.

2 Constructive trusts

4.18 The liability of a solicitor to his or her client as constructive trustee was considered by the Court of Appeal in *Paragon Finance plc v DB Thakerar & Co*,[1] where the facts were similar to *Target* and *Edgestop* and the defendant solicitors had been involved in a series of fraudulent transactions. Each of them involved a sub-sale in which there was a substantial price rise on the second transaction; in each case the amount of the mortgage advance which the borrower was obtaining from the plaintiff lender was substantially in excess of the price payable by the sub-vendor to the original vendor. The defendant solicitors failed to report these matters. The claimant lender had pleaded breach of contract, negligence, and breach of fiduciary duty, although no intentional breach had been alleged. It then sought leave to amend to allege that the defendant was liable to the claimant as a constructive trustee of the advance monies outside the normal six year limitation period for breach of trust. The question for the court was whether this claim was statute-barred. Millett LJ, with whom the other judges in the Court of Appeal agreed, analysed the different types of constructive trust in a passage which merits quoting at length:[2]

'Regrettably, however, the expressions "constructive trust" and "constructive trustee" have been used by equity lawyers to describe two entirely different situations. The first covers those cases already mentioned, where the defendant, though not expressly appointed as trustee, has assumed the duties of a trustee by a lawful transaction which was independent of and preceded the breach of trust and is not impeached by the plaintiff. The second covers those cases where the trust obligation arises as a direct consequence of the unlawful transaction which is impeached by the plaintiff.

A constructive trust arises by operation of law whenever the circumstances are such that it would be unconscionable for the owner of property (usually but not necessarily the legal estate) to assert his own beneficial interest in the property and deny the beneficial interest of another. In the first class of case, however, the constructive trustee really is a trustee. He does not receive the trust property in his own right but by a transaction by which both parties intend to create a trust from the outset and which is not impugned by the plaintiff. His possession of the property is coloured from the first by the trust and confidence by means of which he obtained it, and his subsequent appropriation of the property to his own use is a breach of that trust. Well known examples of such a constructive trust are *McCormick v Grogan* (1869) 4 App Cas 82 (a case of a secret trust) and *Rochefoucauld v Boustead* [1897] 1 Ch 196 (where the defendant agreed to buy property for the plaintiff but the trust was imperfectly recorded). *Pallant v Morgan* [1953] Ch 43 (where the defendant sought to keep for himself property which the plaintiff trusted him to buy for both parties) is another. In these cases the plaintiff does not impugn the transaction by which the defendant obtained control of the property. He alleges that the circumstances in which the defendant obtained control make it unconscionable for him thereafter to assert a beneficial interest in the property.

The second class of case is different. It arises when the defendant is implicated in a fraud. Equity has always given relief against fraud by making any person sufficiently implicated in the fraud accountable in equity. In such a case he is traditionally though I think unfortunately described as a constructive trustee and said to be "liable to account as constructive trustee". Such a person is not in fact a trustee at all, even though he may be liable to account as if he were. He never assumes the position of a trustee, and if he receives the trust property at all it is adversely to the plaintiff by an unlawful transaction which is impugned by the plaintiff. In such a case the expression "constructive trust" and "constructive trustee" are misleading, for there is no trust and usually no possibility of a proprietary remedy; they are "nothing more than a formula for equitable relief": *Selangor United Rubber Estates v Cradock* [1968] 1 WLR 1555 at p 1582, per Ungoed-Thomas J.

The constructive trust on which the plaintiffs seek to rely is of the second kind. The defendants were fiduciaries, and held the plaintiffs' money on a resulting trust for them pending completion of the sub-purchase. But the plaintiffs cannot establish and do not rely upon a breach of this trust. They allege that the money which was obtained from them and which otherwise would have been subject to it was obtained by fraud and they seek to raise a constructive trust in their own favour in its place.'

1 [1999] 1 All ER 400, CA.
2 [1999] 1 All ER 400 at 408–409. This passage was the subject of detailed discussion in *Gwembe Valley Development Co Ltd (in receivership) and another v Koshy (No 3)* [2003] EWCA 1048, [2004] 1 BCLC 131 at [86]–[88]. For further discussion of the decision see para 7.83, below See also *Abbey National plc v John Perry & Co* [2001] EWCA Civ 1630 where the claimant had also applied to amend pleading that a solicitor held a mortgage advance on 'constructive' trust. The Court of Appeal accepted that this was a mistake and that what was really meant was an implied trust and gave permission to amend on the basis that this involved no new cause of action: see [13]–[27].

4.19   The reasons why the claimants in *Paragon* sought to amend to plead a constructive trust of the second kind rather than a breach of the implied or resulting trust of the *Target* or *Edgestop* kind are obscure.[1] The relevance of the distinction drawn between the two types of constructive trust is considered in relation to limitation periods elsewhere in this work.[2] For present purposes, however, the question is whether the solicitor's liability to account as a constructive trustee will arise in circumstances any different from those which give rise to a claim of deceit at common law or a claim of dishonest or fraudulent breach of trust of the kind discussed above. This is unlikely. Millett LJ said that the claimant's amendments were:[3]

'[B]ased on the same factual allegations as the common law claims for fraud and conspiracy to defraud. The equitable jurisdiction which the plaintiffs invoke is thus the concurrent jurisdiction. The new claims are not different causes of action (which is historically a common law concept) but merely equitable counterparts of the claims at common law.'

If this second type of constructive trust arises simply as equity's response to the same facts which, at common law, would amount to deceit or conspiracy to defraud[4], then the only obvious advantage in pleading them would appear to arise in relation to matters such as limitation. But in fact, as we explain elsewhere[5], there is generally no advantage in advancing the claim in this alternative way because the limitation period for deceit will in most cases apply by analogy. Indeed it may be that there is a distinct disadvantage in alleging a constructive trust against a solicitor in these circumstances.[6]

1 The amendment is not quoted in full in the text of the judgment although it is summarised by Millett LJ: see [1999] 1 All ER 400 at 407. The application was heard by Chadwick J at first

instance on 4 June 1997 and after both *Target* and *Mothew* had been fully reported. In *Nationwide Building Society v Thimbleby & Co* (16 December 1998, unreported), the Court of Appeal allowed an amendment outside the six year period to plead a fraudulent breach of trust of the *Edgestop* kind.

2 See para 7.79ff, below.

3 [1999] 1 All ER 400 at 406.

4 In *Gwembe Valley Development Co Ltd v Koshy (No 3)* [2003] EWCA 1048, [2004] 1 BCLC 131 at [88] Mummery LJ described the second class of constructive trust in the following way: 'The constructive trust is the response of equity in supplying a remedial formula for dealing with the consequences of fraud. It is different from the response of equity to the consequences of a breach of a pre-existing trust obligation. It is used to prevent the legal owner of property, which he has received in his own right, from asserting a beneficial interest in it.'

5 See para 7.82, below.

6 If the claimant alleges the existence of a constructive trust of this kind, it will be necessary for him or her to establish that the acts which go to establish the liability were performed by the solicitor in the course of his employment (if an employee or salaried partner) or in the ordinary course of business of the firm (if a partner): see *Lister v Hesley Hall Ltd* [2001] UKHL 22, [2001] 2 AC 215 at [69] (Lord Millett) and *Majrowski v Guy's and St Thomas's NHS Trust* [2006] UKHL 34, [2007] 1 AC 224 at [10] (Lord Nicholls of Birkenhead) for employees and *Dubai Aluminium Co Ltd v Salaam* [2002] UKHL 12, [2002] 2 AC 366 for partners. Vicarious liability is considered in para 5.21ff, below, but a wrong is committed in the course of employment only if the conduct is so closely connected with acts the employee is authorised to do that, for the purposes of the liability of the employer to third parties, the wrongful conduct may fairly and properly be regarded as done by the employee while acting in the course of his or her employment. The House of Lords held that the partners of a solicitor were (on assumed facts) liable for his dishonest assistance to an agent misappropriating assets because he drafted the relevant agreements and this was within the ordinary course of the firm's business: see Lord Nicholls of Birkenhead at [36].

4.20 It follows that claims against solicitors involving a constructive trust are likely to be limited to the established categories of dishonest assistance in a breach of trust and knowing or unconscionable receipt of trust property. The state of mind necessary to establish dishonesty in cases of breach of trust has been considered in paras 4.15 and 4.16, above. In *Abou-Rahmah v Abacha*[1] Treacy J helpfully set out the following necessary ingredients of a claim for dishonest assistance (including the element of dishonesty after *Twinsectra* and *Barlow Clowes*):

'(i) A dishonest state of mind on the part of the person assisting is required in the sense that that person's knowledge of the relevant transaction had to be such as to render his participation contrary to normally acceptable standards of honest conduct. (ii) Such a state of mind may involve knowledge that the transaction is one in which he cannot honestly participate, (e g a misappropriation of other people's money), or it may involve suspicions combined with a conscious decision not to make enquiries which might result in knowledge. (iii) It is not necessary for the claimants to show that the person assisting knew of the existence of a trust or fiduciary relationship between the claimants and the first to third defendants and/or that the transfer of the claimants' moneys to Trusty International via the defendant involved a breach of that trust or fiduciary relationship. (iv) As

167

Lord Hoffmann put it in the *Barlow Clowes* case [2006] 1 All ER 333 at [28]: "It was not necessary ... that Mr [H] should have concluded that the disposals were of moneys held in trust. It was sufficient that he should have entertained a clear suspicion that this was the case. Secondly, it is quite unreal to suppose that Mr [H] needed to know all the details ... before he had grounds to suspect that [X] and [Y] were misappropriating their investors' money." He later continued: "Someone can know, and can certainly suspect, that he is assisting in a misappropriation of money without knowing that the money is held on trust or what a trust means: see *Twinsectra Ltd v Yardley* [2002] UKHL 12 at [19], [2002] 2 AC 164 (Lord Hoffmann) and [135] (Lord Millett)."[2]

In the case of a solicitor the assistance may often take the form of chanelling the proceeds of fraud through the solicitor's client account on the instructions of the client (as in *Twinsectra*) or it may take the form advising on, preparing, drafting and negotiating documents which facilitate the breach of duty.[3] The assistance of the accessory must be of more than minimal importance. It may be given in the context of assisting the fiduciary to commit the relevant breach of duty. But assistance may also be given after the breach of duty has been committed, e g by assisting the trustee to put the assets out of reach of the claimant or to launder the money.[4] Apart from equitable compensation, detailed consideration of the remedies available for dishonest assistance are outside the scope of this book. However, an accessory may be liable not only for losses suffered by the trust. He or she may also be liable to account for any profits which he or she has made out of exploiting trust property.[5] There are limits, however, on the availability of relief. The beneficiaries of the trust will have no proprietary interest in the proceeds of any liability for dishonest assistance and will be unable to trace into the proceeds of the breach of duty by the accessory.[6]

1 [2005] EWHC 2662 (QB)
2 Ingredients (i)–(iii) were cited by Rix LJ in the CA ([2006] EWCA Civ 1492, [2007] 1 Lloyd's Rep 115 at [14]). He continued (at [16]): 'Without intending or attempting myself to restate the authorities, I would merely hazard this analysis. It would seem that a claimant in this area needs to show three things: first, that a defendant has the requisite knowledge; secondly, that, given that knowledge, the defendant acts in a way which is contrary to normally acceptable standards of honest conduct (the objective test of honesty or dishonesty); and thirdly, possibly, that the defendant must in some sense be dishonest himself (a subjective test of dishonesty which might, on analysis, add little or nothing to knowledge of the facts which, objectively, would make his conduct dishonest).'
3 See, eg, *Dubai Aluminium Co Ltd v Salaam* [2002] UKHL 12, [2002] 2 AC 366 at [15] for acts of assistance and *Balfron Trustees Ltd v Peterson* [2002] Lloyd's Rep (PN) 1 (Laddie J).
4 See *Balfron Trustees Ltd v Peterson*, above at [17]: 'The accessory is liable not because he carried out all, or even the majority, of the acts which constitute the primary breach of trust. His liability arises from the fact of assistance to the primary wrongdoers. If he has assisted, then equity imposes a liability on him. It is no answer that he only participated in a part of a chain of events all of which led to the breach of trust, or to assert that the breach of trust would probably have occurred without his assistance.' See also *Gruppo Torras SA v Al-Sabah* [1999] CLC 1469 where Mance J held that it is not necessary to prove a specific causal connection between the assistance and the loss.

5 See *Ultraframe (UK) Ltd v Fielding* [2005] EWHC 1638 (Ch) (Lewison J) at [1589]–[1601] followed by Rimer J in *Sinclair Investment Holdings SA v Versailles Trade Finance Ltd* [2007] EWHC 915 (Ch) at [130].
6 See *Sinclair, above* at [128]:

> 'More generally (and cases involving fiduciaries apart), the only type of case in which it will ordinarily be open to a claimant to claim an account of profits from the defendant will be those cases in which the wrong sued on can be said to be property based, and in which the profits can be said to have derived from the use of the claimant's property. Typical examples are intellectual property cases, for example copyright infringement claims, in which the claimant has an option to elect for damages or an account of profits. He cannot, however, have both; and if he elects for an account, that will merely give him a personal claim against the defendant. An election for an account will not turn the profits into property in which the claimant can assert a proprietary right. He has no proprietary right in respect of such profits and never did.'

4.21   As Lord Hoffmann stated in *Barlow Clowes* and Treacy J emphasised in *Abou-Rahmah v Abacha*, it is no answer for third parties who have real grounds to suspect that they are assisting in a breach of trust or the misappropriation of funds by a director or agent to assert that they were not aware of the terms of the trust. The Law Society has given clear guidance in relation to banking instrument fraud[1] and property fraud.[2] Failure to comply with that guidance is not direct evidence of dishonesty but in strong cases may justify the conclusion that the solicitor suspected fraud but turned a blind eye to it.[3] In cases of real doubt a solicitor may be placed in a very difficult position. If the solicitor harbours real doubts that funds that he or she has received from the client are the proceeds of fraud, he or she may be required to make disclosure under the Proceeds of Crime Act 2002[4] or at the very least should cease to act.[5] What of any funds the solicitor holds for the client? If he or she releases them on the instructions of the client, the solicitor may subject himself or herself to a liability as an accessory to any third party who is entitled to the fund. If he or she refuses to release them, the solicitor may be liable to his client for failure to comply with his instructions. The Law Society has now provided detailed guidance to the solicitor who is placed in this position.[6] If the factual situation remains unclear, the solicitor has the ultimate option of resolving this dilemma by applying to Court for directions (if he or she is a trustee) or for an interim declaration under CPR Part 25.1(1)(b).[7] If there is a sufficient prima facie case of fraud, the solicitor's obligations of confidentiality to the former client will be overridden and the solicitor will be at liberty to notify the third party with the adverse claim that he or she is holding the funds and to give that party an opportunity to apply to be joined.[8] If there is insufficient evidence to give rise to a prima facie case of fraud, the court can direct the solicitor to release the money and grant an interim declaration that the money is not the subject of any equitable claim.

1 See the 'Yellow Card' warning on banking instrument fraud (first published in September 1997 at Annex 12B of the *Guide to the Professional Conduct of Solicitors* as the Banking Instrument Fraud Warning Card) revised in July 2001 and replaced by Annex 3B, section 14 of the *Guide to the Professional Conduct of Solicitors* (1999 ed) and headed 'Money Laundering Guidance ("Pilot Guidance")'. The current regulations came into force on 1 March 2004 and the regulatory position remains as it was before the Law Society's Code of Conduct 2007 came into force on

1 July 2007. The Law Society has also published guidance for private client lawyers dated 22 February 2006, specimen terms for client care letters dated 5 February 2007 and guidance for company and commercial lawyers dated 4 April 2007.

2 See the Property Fraud Warning Card II at Annex 15 of the Pilot Guidance published in July 2002. The Law Society has also published further guidance for property lawyers dated 22 February 2005.

3 A useful yardstick is the decision of Etherton J in *Mortgage Express v Newman* [2001] Lloyd's Rep PN 669. Matters which the judge relied on as demonstrating that Mrs. Newman was not dishonest, although in breach of duty of care, were: (a) knowledge of mortgage fraud within the profession at the relevant time; (b) the fact that Mrs. Newman was in breach of her duties to her borrower client; (c) the fact that she approached the Law Society for guidance; and (d) lack of motive. His finding was that 'she was trying to do her best to deal with the various obstacles that presented themselves to her and that, by completion she genuinely considered that she had overcome them all to the advantage both of her client and providing a good title with vacant possession, to Mortgage Express': see 685. For an example on the other side of the line see *Attorney General of Zambia* v *Meer Care & Desai* [2007] EWHC 1540 (Ch). See, in particular, [585] where Peter Smith J said this: 'I remind myself of what Mance J said in *Grupo Torras*: "… no honest lawyer would have implemented the instructions which Mr Folchi recounts in this transaction unquestioningly and uncomprehendingly in the manner in which Mr Folchi did. There can be no question about Mr Folchi's competence. An honest lawyer in his position would, to safeguard himself and his clients, have insisted on obtaining a proper understanding and assurances regarding the situation (quite possibly in writing despite the supposed confidentiality of what was occurring). If his clients would not give him this, he would have refused to become involved … . I conclude that Mr Folchi received and complied with instructions which conflicted, on their face and in the most obvious way, with the most fundamental of fiduciary duties, to keep private and corporate affairs and money separate." ' For a recent case on strong facts see also *Pulvers v Chan* [2007] EWHC 2406 (Ch) (Morgan J).

4 Sections 327–329 create offences of money laundering. There is a defence to these offences if an 'authorised disclosure' was made under section 338. 'Appropriate consent' is required where a disclosure made before the acts prohibited by sections 327 to 329 takes place. Following the decision in *Bowman v Fels* [2005] EWCA Civ 226, [2005] 4 All ER 609 funds changing hands in the course of litigation are largely excluded from the operation of the sections but they are directly relevant to transactional work.

5 Where there is no duty to make disclosure, this appears to be the appropriate response: see the guidance issued by the Law Society on *Bowman v Fels* at Annex 3 to the Pilot Guidance, para 6.4. The solicitor is placed in a position where his or her personal interest (in avoiding the commission of a criminal offence) and his or her duty to the client conflict. The Act also contains offences of tipping off: see ss 333 and 342 which may prevent the solicitor from giving advice to the client.

6 See section 7 and the Appendix of Annex 3 to the Pilot Guidance.

7 See *Bank of Scotland v A Ltd* [2001] 3 All ER 58 at 74 (Lord Woolf MR):

'The use of the court's power to grant interim declarations in proceedings involving the SFO will protect a bank from criminal proceedings but it will not automatically provide protection against actions by customers or third parties. However, it seems almost inconceivable that a bank which takes the initiative in seeking the court's guidance should subsequently be held to have acted dishonestly so as to incur accessory liability. The involvement of the court should, however, enable, in the great majority of cases, a practical solution to be determined which protects the interests of the public but allows the interests of a bank to be safeguarded.'

8 *Finers v Miro* [1991] 1 WLR 35. The solicitor will need to take care about whether to join the client (or former client) to avoid committing any tipping off offences.

C   BREACH OF FIDUCIARY DUTY

1   Introduction

4.22   The blurring of the distinction between a breach of fiduciary duty and a breach by a fiduciary of a duty of care is largely historical. In *Nocton v Lord Ashburton*[1] the House of Lords awarded compensation in equity for a solicitor's failure to advise his client at a time when the common law gave no remedy for negligent misstatement causing economic loss. The decision of the House of Lords in *Hedley Byrne & Co Ltd v Heller & Partners Ltd*[2] overtook this development and since then the problem addressed in *Nocton v Lord Ashburton* has largely become the province of the common law. In some jurisdictions, most notably New Zealand[3] and Canada[4], the analytical difficulty of distinguishing between a solicitor's duties at common law and his or her fiduciary duties has been resolved by expanding the scope of the fiduciary principle and of equitable obligations and awarding equitable compensation on much the same basis as at common law. In England, however, this approach has not been adopted. In *Henderson v Merrett Syndicates Ltd*[5] Lord Browne-Wilkinson drew a distinction between the breach by a fiduciary of his or her obligations of skill and care and a breach of the fiduciary's fiduciary obligations. The point was taken up and applied by the Court of Appeal in *Bristol and West Building Society v Mothew*,[6] in which Millett LJ pointed out that:

> '[T]he expression "breach of fiduciary duty" is properly confined to those duties which are peculiar to fiduciaries and the breach of which attracts legal consequences differing from those consequent upon the breach of other duties.'

Thus, not every breach of duty by a fiduciary should be described as a breach of fiduciary duty and, although fiduciaries owe contractual duties and duties to act with reasonable skill and care, these duties are not peculiar to fiduciaries.[7] This section is, therefore, concerned with the special fiduciary duties (and, in particular, the duty of loyalty) owed by a solicitor to his or her client and enforced in equity.[8]

1 [1914] AC 932.
2 [1964] AC 465.
3 See *Day v Mead* [1987] 2 NZLR 443 (followed in *Russell McVeagh Mckenzie Bartleet & Co v Tower Corpn* [1998] 2 NZLR 641 at 668). See also the survey of the law of New Zealand by Blackburne J in *Nationwide Building Society v Balmer Radmore* [1999] Lloyd's Rep PN 241 at 279–282. But compare now *Bank of New Zealand v New Zealand Guardian Trust Co Ltd* [1999] 1 NZLR 664, 687–8 (Tipping J) set out in para 4.40 nn 3 and 6, below, where a more conventional hierarchy of duties was adopted. For a recent decision see *Ilion Technology Corpn v Johannink* [2006] NZHC 27 (adopting Tipping J's taxonomy).
4 See *Hodgkinson v Simms* [1994] 3 SCR 377, (1994) 117 DLR (4th) 161 (investment adviser and accountant held liable for breach of fiduciary obligations to his client), *R v Neill*, [2002] SCC 70 [2002] 3 SCR 631 and *Strother v 3464920 Canada Inc* [2007] SCC 24 (solicitor held liable for

failure to offer a tax scheme to one client and taking a personal interest in a second client). Binnie J (delivering the judgment of the majority) stated at [56] under the heading 'The duty of loyalty is concerned with client representation':

> 'While the duty of loyalty is focussed on the lawyer's ability to provide proper client representation, it is not fully exhausted by the obligation to avoid conflicts of interest with other concurrent clients. A "conflict of interest" was defined in *Neil* as an interest that gives rise to a substantial risk that the lawyer's representation of the client would be materially and adversely affected by the lawyer's own interests or by the lawyer's duties to another current client, a former client, or a third person.'

5 [1995] 2 AC 145 at 204D–206G.
6 [1998] Ch 1 at 16C, CA.
7 See *Hilton v Barker Booth & Eastwood* [2005] UKHL 8, [2005] 1 WLR 567 at [29]:

> 'The relationship between a solicitor and his client is one in which the client reposes trust and confidence in the solicitor. It is a fiduciary relationship. But not every breach of duty by a fiduciary is a breach of fiduciary duty: see the observations of Millett LJ in *Bristol and West Building Society v Mothew* (*t/a Stapley & Co*) [1998] Ch 1 at 16–17. If a solicitor is careless in investigating a title or drafting a lease, he may be liable to pay damages for breach of his professional duty, but that is not a breach of a fiduciary duty of loyalty; it is simply the breach of a duty of care. This may have practical consequences, for instance in relation to causation, as in the *Mothew* case.'

Note also the influential statement by Sopinka J in *Norberg v Wynrib* (1992) 92 DLR (4th) 449 at 481: 'Fiduciary duties should not be superimposed on those common law duties simply to improve the nature or extent of the remedy.'
8 A solicitor also owes his client a duty of confidentiality. Unlike the duty of care this duty arises out of the relationship of trust and confidence rather than the provision of skilled services. Nevertheless it is protected as much by implied terms in the contract as it is by the intervention of equity. It is not considered further in this chapter although various aspects of the duty are considered elsewhere: see chapter 6.

4.23 A solicitor is a fiduciary in the same way as an agent or a company director because of the relationship of trust and confidence between solicitor and client. 'The distinguishing obligation of a fiduciary is the obligation of loyalty. The principal is entitled to the single-minded loyalty of his fiduciary.'[1] It is because the relationship of solicitor and client requires the solicitor to act in the client's interests at all times (to the exclusion of his or her own and other interests) that the relationship is a fiduciary one.[2] As with many fiduciary relationships the fiduciary obligations of the solicitor normally arise out of contract (although the existence of a contract is not always necessary to give rise to a fiduciary relationship[3] and in the case of the fiduciary obligations of solicitors the court will approach the question of the identity of the client flexibly[4]). The terms of the contract between fiduciary and principal normally govern or 'mould' the scope of the fiduciary obligations.[5] But in this respect the scope of a solicitor's fiduciary duty is unlikely to vary very much from case to case because the core obligations (as opposed to the subject matter) of the contract of retainer between solicitor and client are uniform and usually impossible to exclude. Indeed, in *Hilton v Barker Booth & Eastwood*[6] the House of Lords held that in the absence of any express terms a solicitor owed an implied contractual duty not to place himself in a position where his duty to one client conflicted with his duty to another. Although, however, the fiduciary relationship arises out of the contract of retainer, the fiduciary relationship does not necessarily come to an end when the retainer is terminated. If the relationship of trust and confidence continues, the solicitor may remain a fiduciary.[7] The consequences of the existence of a fiduciary relationship or its continuation are that the solicitor is bound by the principles of equity from acting in a way which is inconsistent with the interests of the client. For this reason, it is often said that fiduciary duties are 'proscriptive' rather than 'prescriptive'. Proscriptive duties are disabilities rather than positive requirements to act.[8]

1 *Bristol & West BS v Mothew* [1998] Ch 1 at 18. Millett LJ's judgment was described by Mummery LJ in *Johnson v EBS Pensioner Trustees Ltd* [2002] EWCA Civ 164, [2002] Lloyd's Rep PN 309 at [37] as: 'a judgment widely regarded as a masterly survey of the modern law of fiduciary duties'.

2 Note the famous statement of Frankfurter J in *Securities Commission v Chenery Corpn* (1943) 318 US 80 at 85–6: 'But to say that a man is a fiduciary only begins the analysis; it gives direction to further inquiry. To whom is he a fiduciary? What obligations does he owe as a fiduciary? In what respect has he failed to discharge these obligations? And what are the consequences of his deviation from duty?' The basis for the imposition of fiduciary duties remains a matter of keen debate: see, eg, Millett 'Equity's Place in the Law of Commerce' (1998) 114 LQR 215, esp at 222; Mason 'The Place of Equity and Equitable Remedies in the Contemporary Common Law World' [1994] 110 LQR 238 at 246 (where the fiduciary principle was said to be based on the 'legitimate expectation that the other party will act in the interests of the first party or at least in the joint interests of the parties and not solely self-interestedly'); and the dissenting judgment of Kirby J in *Pilmer v Duke Group Ltd* [2001] 2 BCLC 773 (High Court of Australia) at [136] (where Kirby J effectively adopted the Sir Antony Mason's view). Contrast Birks 'The content of fiduciary obligation' [2000] 34 IsLR 3 (where Professor Birks took the view that: 'the word "fiduciary" is manifestly unstable').

3 See, eg, *Sinclair Investment Holdings SA v Versailles Trade Finance Ltd* [2007] EWHC 915 (Ch) at [77]–[94] where Rimer J discussed the imposition of a fiduciary duty to third parties by a trader (and, in particular, the necessity for reliance).

4 See *Conway v Ratiu* [2005] EWCA Civ 1302, [2006] 1 All ER 571 where the Court of Appeal was prepared to lift the corporate veil. At [78] Auld LJ stated:

> 'There is, it seems to me, a powerful argument of principle, in this intensely personal context of considerations of trust, confidence and loyalty, for lifting the corporate veil where the facts require it to include those in or behind the company who are in reality the persons whose trust in and reliance upon the fiduciary may be confounded.'

5 See *Hospital Products Ltd v United States Surgical Corpn* (1984) 156 CLR 41 at 97 (Mason J) cited by Lord Browne-Wilkinson in *Kelly v Cooper* [1993] AC 205 at 215:

> 'The fiduciary relationship, if it is to exist at all, must accommodate itself to the terms of the contract so that it is consistent with, and conforms to them. The fiduciary relationship cannot be superimposed upon the contract in such a way as to alter the operation which the contract was intended to have according to its true construction.' See also *Strother v 3464920 Canada Inc* [2007] SCC 24 at [135] (MacLachlin CJ dissenting in part): 'The duty of loyalty is not a duty in the air. It is attached to the obligations the lawyer has undertaken pursuant to the retainer.'

6 [2005] UKHL 8, [2005] 1 WLR 567 at [30] (Lord Walker):

> 'A solicitor's duty of single-minded loyalty to his client's interest, and his duty to respect his client's confidences, do have their roots in the fiduciary nature of the solicitor-client relationship. But they may have to be moulded and informed by the terms of the

contractual relationship: see the well-known observations of Mason J in *Hospital Products Ltd v United States Surgical Corpn* (1984) 156 CLR 41 at 97, cited by Lord Browne-Wilkinson in giving the judgment of the Privy Council in *Kelly v Cooper* [1993] AC 205 at 215. In the present case no such moulding is necessary since there were no express terms agreed as to Mr. Hilton's retainer of BBE.'

For further consideration of what *Hilton* decided see para 4.36, below.
7 See *Longstaff v Birtles* [2001] EWCA Civ 1219, [2002] 1 WLR 470 where S, a solicitor, had acted for Cs in relation to the abortive purchase of a public house but then entered into a partnership with them to buy and run a hotel (which failed). Cs did not take independent legal advice or appreciate the risks of the venture. The Court of Appeal held that the fiduciary relationship continued after the termination of the retainer, that the business opportunity originally arose whilst S was acting as Cs' solicitor and that this placed him in a position where his duty conflicted with his own interests and that he acted in breach of fiduciary duty by continuing to deal with Cs without ensuring that they obtained independent advice. This decision is not an example of the wider principle that a fiduciary may not resign his office to exploit a business opportunity but a case in which the client continues to treat as his own solicitor and for this reason failed to take independent advice. Compare *Official Assignee of Collier v Creighton* [1993] 2 NZLR 534 (New Zealand Court of Appeal) where a similar claim failed.
8 See *Snell's Equity* (31st edn, 2005) citing *A-G v Blake* [1998] Ch 439 at 455: 'fiduciary doctrine "tells the fiduciary what he must not do. It does not tell him what he ought to do." ' See also the majority in *Pilmer v Duke Group Ltd* [2001] 2 BCLC 773 at [74] citing Gaudron and McHugh JJ in *Breen v Williams* (1996) 186 CLR 71 at 113: '[E]quity imposes on the fiduciary proscriptive obligations – not to obtain any unauthorised benefit from the relationship and not to be in a position of conflict. If these obligations are breached, the fiduciary must account for any profits and make good any losses arising from the breach. But the law of this country does not otherwise impose positive legal duties on the fiduciary to act in the interests of the person to whom the duty is owed.'

2   Conflict of interest and duty

4.24   Any consideration of the fiduciary duties owed by a solicitor to his client must begin with *Nocton v Lord Ashburton*[1] (a case involving a conflict of interest and duty). The claimant, Lord Ashburton, sued his solicitor, Nocton, to recover the amount of a mortgage advance which he had made to two developers, Douglas and Holloway, to develop a property in Church Street, Kensington. Nocton had originally owned the property with Lord Ashburton's brother, Alexander Baring, and they had sold it on to the developers. The agreement was conditional on the developers obtaining a loan for £60,000 and the vendors themselves making a further loan of £20,000 on the security of a second charge. Nocton wrote to Lord Ashburton asking whether he would be prepared to make a loan to Douglas and Holloway. Despite Nocton's partners warning him of the risk that the security might be inadequate and reminding him of Nocton's interest in the property, Lord Ashburton lent them £65,000. A year later, Nocton wrote to him again asking him to release part of the security to enable the developers to obtain further finance. He failed to inform Lord Ashburton that the effect of the release was to advance the second charge of Nocton and Baring to a first charge and benefit Nocton personally to the tune of £15,000. When the developers defaulted, the remaining security was wholly inadequate and Lord Ashburton commenced proceedings against Nocton. He sought a declaration that Nocton had improperly advised him in relation to making the advance for his own ends. He also sought a declaration that in relation to the release Nocton 'allowed [him] to believe that he was advising the plaintiff independently and in good faith and in [his] interests'.[2]

1 [1914] AC 932. For the background to the case and some explanation for what may have been a surprising result see Gummow 'Compensation for Breach of Fiduciary Duty' in Youdan (ed) *Equity Fiduciaries and Trusts* (1989) at 57–91.
2 [1914] AC 932 at 939.

4.25 Neville J treated the claim as an action in deceit and dismissed it. The Court of Appeal dismissed the appeal in relation to the taking of the original mortgage (because of the warnings given by Nocton's partners) but found that Nocton had been guilty of fraud in relation to the release of the first mortgage. They ordered an inquiry as to damages and an interim payment of £3,789. The House of Lords affirmed the Court of Appeal's order but on different grounds. Viscount Haldane LC stated as follows:[1]

'I have read the evidence of the appellant and, although it is obviously unreliable evidence, it leaves on my mind the same impression that it left on that of the learned judge who heard it, that the solicitor did not consciously intend to defraud his client, but largely owing to a confused state of mind, believed that he was properly joining with him and guiding him in a good faith.

I cannot, therefore, treat the case, so far as it is based on intention to deceive, as made out. But where I differ from the learned judges in the Courts below is as to their view that, if they did not regard deceit as proved, the only alternative was to treat the action as one of mere negligence at law unconnected with misconduct. This alternative they thought was precluded by the way the case had been conducted. I am not sure that, on the pleadings and on the facts proved, they were right even in this ... There is a third form of procedure to which the statement of claim approximated very closely, and that is the old bill in Chancery to enforce compensation for breach of a fiduciary obligation ...

My Lords, it is known that in cases of actual fraud the Courts of Chancery and of Common Law exercised a concurrent jurisdiction from the earliest times. For some of these cases the greater freedom which, in early days, the Court of Chancery exercised in admitting the testimony of parties to the proceedings made it a more suitable tribunal. Moreover, its remedies were more elastic. Operating in personam as a Court of conscience it could order the defendant, not indeed in those days, to pay damages as such, but to make restitution, or to compensate the plaintiff by putting him in as good a position pecuniarily as that in which he was before the injury.

175

But in addition to this concurrent jurisdiction, the Court of Chancery exercised an exclusive jurisdiction in cases which, although classified in that Court as cases of fraud, yet did not necessarily import the element of dolus malus. The Court took it upon itself to prevent a man from acting against the dictates of conscience as defined by the Court to grant injunctions in anticipation of injury, as well as relief where injury had been done ...

My Lords, I have dealt thus fully with this distinction because I think that confusion has arisen from overlooking it. It must now be taken as settled that nothing short of proof of a fraudulent intention in the strict sense will suffice for an action of deceit. This is so whether a Court of Law or a Court of Equity, in the exercise of concurrent jurisdiction, is dealing with the claim ... But when fraud is referred to in the wider sense in which the books are full of the expression used in Chancery in describing cases which were within its exclusive jurisdiction, it is a mistake to suppose that an actual intention to cheat must always be proved. A man may misconceive the extent of the obligation which a Court of Equity imposes on him. His fault is that he has violated, however innocently because of his ignorance, an obligation which he must be taken by the Court to have known, and his conduct has in that sense always been called fraudulent, even in such a case as a technical fraud on a power. It was thus that the expression "constructive fraud" came into existence. The trustee who purchases the trust estate, the solicitor who makes a bargain with his client that cannot stand, have all for several centuries run the risk of the word fraudulent being applied to them. What it really means in this connection is not moral fraud in the ordinary sense, but breach of the sort of obligation which is enforced by a Court that from the beginning regarded itself as a Court of conscience.

When, as in the case before us, a solicitor has had financial transactions with his client, and has handled his money to the extent of using it to pay off a mortgage made to himself, or of getting the client to release from his mortgage a property over which the solicitor by such release has obtained further security for a mortgage of his own, a Court of Equity has always assumed jurisdiction to scrutinise his action. It did not matter that the client would have had a remedy in damages for breach of contract.'

1   [1914] AC 932 at 945–6, 952 and 958.

4.26   The speech of Lord Dunedin also makes it clear that the jurisdiction to give relief in equity was derived from the relationship between the claimant and the defendant and the potential or actual conflict between their interests which made it fraudulent or unconscionable for the defendant not to act or speak out despite the finding made by Neville J:[1]

'If then we turn to the solicitor's position, we may look at it in two aspects, which is not to look at two different things but to look at the same thing from two different points of view. He has contracted to be diligent; he is negligent. Law will give a remedy. It may well be that if a bill had been filed with a bald statement to the effect above, there might have been a demurrer for want of equity ... But from the other point of view he may have put himself in a fiduciary position, and that fiduciary position imposes on him the duty of making a full and not a misleading disclosure of facts known to him when advising his client. He fails to do so. Equity will give a remedy to the client. This it does quite apart from the doctrine of *Derry v Peek* for in that case there was no fiduciary relationship and the action had to be based on the representation alone.'

1 [1914] AC 932 at 964–5.

4.27 In *Swindle v Harrison*, Mummery LJ considered the propositions of law which can be derived from the decision of the House of Lords:[1]

'The decision of the House of Lords in *Nocton v Ashburton* is the seminal case, although, as Lord Devlin observed in *Hedley Byrne & Co Ltd v Heller & Partners Ltd* [1963] 2 All ER 575 at 604, [1964] AC 465 at 520, "it is not easy to determine exactly what it decided." That is a common characteristic of pathbreaking cases: it may take a generation or more to work out the ramifications of broad statements of legal principle. It is possible to extract from the speeches the following principles relevant to this appeal. (1) A solicitor stands in a fiduciary relationship with his client. (2) A solicitor who enters into a financial transaction with his client is under a fiduciary duty, when advising his client, to make full disclosure of all relevant facts known to him. (3) Liability for breach of fiduciary duty is not dependent on proof of deceit or negligence. Equity imposes duties in special relationships above and beyond the minimum legal duties to be honest and to be careful. Fiduciary duties rest on the idea of trust and of conduct offensive to conscience. (4) The equitable remedies available for breach of fiduciary duty are "more elastic" than the sanction of damages attached to common law fraud and negligence.'[2]

The facts of the case itself show that the duty of a solicitor is strict when he or she proposes to enter into a transaction with a client. The claimants were a firm of solicitors who sought to enforce a charge against their client, the second defendant. Her son, the first defendant, persuaded her to purchase a restaurant and she had agreed to put up her house as security for a loan from the bank. A further loan from the brewery was also required. Once contracts had been exchanged and a deposit of £44,000 had been paid, the brewery refused to lend the defendants the balance required to complete. The claimants lent it to them themselves by drawing on a loan facility which they had with their own bank. The venture was disastrous and mother and son lost everything which they had put into the restaurant. The judge found that the claimants were acting in breach of fiduciary duty because they failed to disclose that they were making a profit of 2.5% and £1,000 on the loan and in failing to disclose that they knew that the brewery needed satisfactory references before lending the balance. The judge's conclusion when he asked himself what advice other solicitors would have given was as follows:[3]

> 'I can only imagine that they would have been astounded at the offer being made by the plaintiffs in the circumstances and that with full knowledge of the circumstances they would have said "Grab it". It was, after all, a lifeline for them. There is no evidence that a better offer could have been obtained elsewhere. The alternative was to forfeit the deposit.'

A solicitor's duty is strict, therefore, and an actionable breach of the duty does not depend on showing either that the client has suffered loss or that he or she would have acted differently. The client is entitled to have the relevant transaction set aside.

1 [1997] 4 All ER 705, CA at 731h–732a.
2 It is important to stress that the facts giving rise to the conflict of interest and duty must be known to the solicitor: compare para 4.12, above. For an example of limits to the fiduciary principle see *Blythe v Northwood* [2005] NSWCA 221. In that case the solicitor acted for a borrower in relation to the mortgage of property. The borrower used the loan to repay an existing loan to a company in which the solicitor was interested. Although the facts have a superficial resemblance to *Nocton v Ashburton* the claim failed. The judge rejected the claimant's evidence that the solicitor was aware of the purpose of the loan and the Court of Appeal of NSW held that there was no breach of duty unless the solicitor was aware of the facts giving rise to the conflict.
3 Set out by Evans LJ at 711e–f.

4.28 The contrasting facts of *Spector v Ageda*[1] demonstrate why there is a need for such a strict standard. In that case the claimant, a solicitor, sought to enforce a mortgage against the defendant, who was her client and to whom she had lent money. The claim failed both because the transaction was tainted with illegality and because the claimant had failed to advise the defendant properly. The money was lent by the claimant to repay a loan made by the claimant's sister who was an unlicensed moneylender and the rate of interest in the original loan agreement had also been tampered with by the claimant herself, who was then acting for her sister. The claimant knew that this agreement was unenforceable but she lent the money to the defendant to pay it off. The judge found that the earlier illegalities tainted the later agreement between the parties despite the fact that it was valid in point of form. He also found that the claimant was in breach of her duty to the defendant. He said this:[2]

'[T]he solicitor must be remarkable indeed if he can feel assured of holding the scales evenly between himself and his client. Even if in fact he can and does, to demonstrate to conviction that he has done so will usually be beyond possibility in a case where anything to his client's detriment has occurred. Not only must his duty be discharged but it must manifestly and undoubtedly be seen to have been discharged. I abstain from any categorical negative: the circumstances of life are of such infinite variety. But I can at least say that in all ordinary circumstances a solicitor ought to refuse to act for a person in a transaction to which the solicitor is himself a party with an adverse interest; and even if he is pressed to act after his refusal, he should persist in that refusal. Nobody can insist on an unwilling solicitor acting for him, at all events when there is a conflict of interest.'

It is not entirely clear whether these cases are specific examples of the doctrine of abuse of confidence (otherwise known as the 'fair dealing rule') or whether they should be treated as a separate line of authority dealing with the duty of a solicitor when personally interested in a transaction. Likewise, it is not clear whether a solicitor is disabled from acting in circumstances where he or she makes full disclosure of all material facts to the client but does not decline to act and insist that the client take independent advice.[3] In *Johnson v EBS Pensioner Trustees Ltd*[4] a firm of solicitors arranged a private loan from clients of theirs to the claimant's company (for which he provided a guarantee) but failed to disclose that they had charged their other clients a 1.5% 'service charge'. It was held that the solicitors had committed a breach of fiduciary duty but the Court of Appeal refused to set aside the guarantee (and a number of related transactions). The court approached the issue on the basis that the doctrine of abuse of confidence applied to determine whether the transaction should be set aside.[5] The explanation for the different formulations of the solicitor's duty may lie in the nature of the transaction and reliance placed upon the solicitor. If the client is relying on the solicitor to give disinterested advice, it may not be enough to give full disclosure of the solicitor's interest in the transaction and he or she may be required to go further and insist that the client is separately advised.[6] This position is reflected in the Solicitors' Code of Conduct 2007, Rules 3.01(2)(b) and 3.04.[7]

1 [1973] Ch 30 (Megarry J).
2 [1973] Ch 30 at 47E–F.
3 Compare Mummery LJ's statement of principle in *Swindle v Harrison* with his statement in *Longstaff v Birtles* [2001] EWCA Civ 1219, [2002] 1 WLR 470 which is, if anything, more consistent with the duty as explained in *Spector v Ageda*: 'A solicitor proposing to buy property from, or sell property to, a client is under a duty to cause the client to obtain independent advice.'

4 [2002] EWCA Civ 164, [2002] Lloyd's Rep PN 309. The majority (Dyson LJ and Douglas Brown LJ) held there was a breach of duty because the service charge was material to the claimant's decision and he was entitled to know about it before taking it. Mummery LJ dissented on the basis that it was not material. The decision is important because it establishes that the fair dealing rule applies not only to a transaction under which property passes (usually a sale by the principal to the fiduciary) but also to other transactions.
5 See Mummery LJ at [43]–[51] and Dyson LJ at [66]–[67].
6 The relationship between solicitor and client is, of course, a relationship which automatically gives rise to a presumption of undue influence: see *Snell's Equity* (31st edn, 2005) at 8—25. But the doctrines of undue influence and abuse of confidence may not cover all of the relevant ground. In *Longstaff v Birtles*, above there was no suggestion that the former solicitor had exerted undue influence on the former client or had obtained an undisclosed benefit. The complaint was that the former clients had not properly appreciated the wisdom of the transaction.
7 '3.01(1) You must not act if there is a conflict of interests … (2) There is a conflict of interest if …(b) your duty to act in the best interests of any client in relation to a matter conflicts, or there is a significant risk that it may conflict, with your own interests in relation to that or a related matter …3.04 Where a client proposes to make a lifetime gift or a gift on death to, or for the benefit of: (a) you; (b) any principal, owner or employee of your firm; (c) a family member of any of the above, and the gift is of a significant amount, either in itself or having regard to the size of the client's estate and the reasonable expectations of the prospective beneficiaries, you must advise the client to take independent advice about the gift, unless the client is a member of the beneficiary's family. If the client refuses, you must stop acting for the client in relation to the gift.' For the position before 1 July 2007 see Practice Rule 16D(2)(b)(ii), (2)(c) and (3) of the Practice Rules 1990 (incorporated by the Solicitors' Practice (Conflict) Amendment Rule 2004).

3   Conflict of duty and duty

4.29   The position becomes more complex where the solicitor has no personal interest in the transaction but undertakes to act for more than one client whose interests may potentially conflict with each other and, consequently, the solicitor's duties to each of them. In *Bristol and West Building Society v Mothew*[1] where the Court of Appeal was asked to consider the position of a solicitor acting for two clients, lender and borrower, Millett LJ set out the relevant duties of the solicitor:

> 'The principal is entitled to the single-minded loyalty of his fiduciary. This core liability has several facets. A fiduciary must act in good faith; he must not make a profit out of his trust; he must not place himself in a position where his duty and his interest may conflict; he may not act for his own benefit or the benefit of a third person without the informed consent of his principal. This is not intended to be an exhaustive list but it is sufficient to indicate the nature of fiduciary obligations. As Dr Finn pointed out in his classic work *Fiduciary Obligations* (1977) p 2, he is not subject to fiduciary obligations because he is a fiduciary; it is because he is subject to them that he is a fiduciary.'

He then analysed the fiduciary obligations owed by a solicitor to each of his clients and we adopt the terms which he used in his judgment: the 'double employment rule', the 'duty of good faith', the 'no inhibition principle' and the 'actual conflict' rule.[2]

1 [1998] Ch 1 at 18A–C, CA.
2 [1998] Ch 1 at 18I to 20G.

(a) The double employment rule

4.30 The double employment rule usually comes into play at the outset of the retainer when a solicitor is contemplating taking instructions from a client whose interests may conflict with the interests of another of his or her clients (ie where there is a potential conflict between the interests of each of each client).[1] The rule requires that the solicitor may not act for two principals whose interests may come into conflict with each other unless he or she obtains the informed consent of each client and a failure to comply with the rule also constitutes a breach of fiduciary duty without proof of fault or bad faith.[2] In *Clark Boyce v Mouat*[3] Lord Jauncey set out the rule in the following terms:

> 'There is no general rule of law to the effect that a solicitor should never act for both parties in a transaction where their interests may conflict. Rather is the position that he may act provided that he has obtained the informed consent of both to his acting. Informed consent means consent given in the knowledge that there is a conflict between the parties and that as a result the solicitor may be disabled from disclosing to each party the full knowledge which he possesses as to the transaction or may be disabled from giving advice to one party which conflicts with the interest of the other. If the parties are content to proceed upon this basis the solicitor may properly act.'

In that case the defendant acted for both the claimant and her son in relation to a mortgage granted by the plaintiff to secure the son's borrowings. The defendant advised her that her position as guarantor was substantially different to that of her son as the recipient of the loan. He also advised her to take independent advice and told her that he could arrange it with a local solicitor. On three occasions in total he raised the question of independent advice.[4] It was held that the defendant was not in breach of fiduciary duty by continuing to act for the claimant and without revealing that her son's own solicitor had refused to act.[5]

1 Rule 3.01(1)(a) of the Solicitors' Code of Conduct 2007 now defines a potential conflict of duties in terms of a significant risk: 'There is a conflict of interests if: (a) you owe, or your firm owes, separate duties to act in the best interests of two or more clients in relation to the same or related matters, and those duties conflict, or there is a significant risk that those duties may conflict' The definition of a potential conflict of interest and duty is in the same terms: see r 3.01(1)(b) quoted

in para 4.28 n 7, above. Practice Rule 16D(2)(b) (which governs the position before 1 July 2007) is in almost identical terms: 'There is a conflict of interests if: (i) you owe, or your practice owes, separate duties to act in the best interests of two or more clients in relation to the same or related matters, and those duties conflict, or there is a significant risk that those duties may conflict.' The application of both rules beyond 'same matter transactions' reflects existing authority on the double employment rule: see *Marks & Spencer plc v Freshfields Bruckhaus Deringer* [2004] EWHC 1337 (Ch), [2004] 1 WLR 2331 (Lawrence Collins J) and [2004] EWCA Civ 741, [2005] PNLR 4 (CA) and also *Denekamp v Denekamp* [2004] EWHC 2016 (Ch) at [79]–[81] where Peter Leaver QC said this:

> 'However, the courts take a pragmatic approach to potential conflicts. There must be a reasonable apprehension (as opposed to a mere theoretical possibility) of potential conflict. Thus, in *Boulting v Association of Cinematograph, Television and Allied Technicians* [1963] 2 QB 606 the Court of Appeal stated that the conflict rule "must be applied realistically to a state of affairs which discloses a real conflict of duty and interest and not to some theoretical or rhetorical conflict".'

For further discussion see chapter 6, section D.1.

2 See *Mothew* [1998] Ch 1 at 19A: 'A fiduciary who acts for two principals with potentially conflicting interests without the informed consent of both is in breach of the obligation of undivided loyalty; he puts himself in a position where his duty to one principal *may* conflict with his duty to the other: see *Clark Boyce v Mouat* [1994] 1 AC 428 and the cases there cited. This is sometimes described as "the double employment rule". Breach of the rule automatically constitutes a breach of fiduciary duty.' See also the formulation of the rule by Lewison J in *Ultraframe (UK) Ltd v Fielding* [2005] EWHC 1638 (Ch) at [1315]–[1317].

3 [1994] 1 AC 428 at 43SF–H.

4 See [1994] 1 AC 428 at 433A–C and 433G.

5 See also *Spikins v Wickham & Fine* (18 November 1998, unreported) (Peter Leaver QC) for another example where the court held that informed consent had been given.

4.31 Obviously, the precise nature of the information which it is necessary for the solicitor to disclose will depend on the circumstances of the case but the following is a useful rule of thumb:

> For the client to make an informed decision, the lawyer must reveal the existence of the multiple representation. The lawyer must disclose whether there is a regular and continuing relationship with any of the clients, and in these circumstances, the lawyer must recommend that the client obtain independent representation ... The lawyer must disclose the implications of a joint retainer to the confidentiality of information passing between a lawyer and a client. The lawyer must also discuss the consequences of any unresolvable conflict of interest developing during the retainer.'[1]

The double employment rule is plainly relevant when a solicitor agrees to act for lender and borrower or vendor and purchaser and the disclosure requirements in each of those cases are considered elsewhere in this work.[2]

1 See Perell *Conflicts of Interest in the Legal Profession* (1995) 90–1. Compare r 3.02(4) of the Solicitors' Code of Conduct 2007:

'If you are relying on the exceptions in 3.02(1) or, (2) you must: (a) draw all the relevant issues to the attention of the clients before agreeing to act or, where already acting, when the conflict arises or as soon as reasonably practicable, and in such a way that the clients concerned can understand the issues and the risks involved; (b) have a reasonable belief that the clients understand the relevant issues; and (c) be reasonably satisfied that those clients are of full capacity.'

2 See paras 6.38–6.40 and paras 9.2– 9.8, below.

4.32　The rule is not, however, mechanistically applied. Even if the solicitor fails to give any sort of warning, consent may be implied. In *Kelly v Cooper*[1] the claimant, who was selling his house in an exclusive neighbourhood of Bermuda, sued the defendant, his estate agent, for failing to reveal to him that she was also acting for the vendor of the next door property and that the purchaser wanted them both to create a 'family compound'. The Privy Council found that this information would have been directly relevant to the price negotiations. However the action failed. Lord Browne-Wilkinson stated:[2]

'In a case where a principal instructs as selling agent for his property or goods a person who to his knowledge acts and intends to act for other principals selling property or goods of the same description, the terms to be implied into such agency contract must differ from those to be implied where an agent is not carrying on such general agency business. In the case of estate agents, it is their business to act for numerous principals; where properties are of a similar description, there will be a conflict of interest between the principals each of whom will be concerned to attract potential purchasers to their property rather than that of another. Yet, despite this conflict of interest, estate agents must be free to act for several competing principals otherwise they will be unable to perform their function. Yet it is normally said that it is a breach of an agent's duty to act for competing principals. In the course of acting for each of their principals, estate agents will acquire information confidential to that principal. It cannot sensibly be suggested that an estate agent is contractually bound to disclose to any one of his principals information which is confidential to another of his principals. The position as to confidentiality is even clearer in the case of stockbrokers who cannot be contractually bound to disclose to their private clients inside information disclosed to the brokers in confidence by a company for which they also act. Accordingly, in such cases there must be an implied term of the contract with such an agent that he is entitled to act for other principals selling competing properties and to keep confidential the information obtained from each of his principals.'

In *Mothew* itself informed consent was implied. There was no formal invitation by the solicitor to the lender to consider whether it wished to

instruct the solicitor to act for both the lender and borrower.[3] However, there
are limits to the application of this principle and the consent of both principals
will not be implied automatically from existence of dual engagements unless
that consent is truly informed.[4]

1 [1993] AC 205, PC. For further discussion see para 6.36, below (where we suggest that although
the principle is clear the decision of limited value in relation to implied consent by solicitors).
2 [1993] AC 205 at 214B–D.
3 [1998] Ch 1 at 19B and C:

> 'It [the society] knew the defendant was acting for the purchasers when it instructed him.
> Indeed that was the very reason why it chose the defendant to act for it.' 'Its decision to
> forward the cheque for the mortgage advance to the defendant and to instruct him to
> proceed was based on false information but its earlier decision to employ the defendant
> despite the potentially conflicting interest of his other client was a fully informed
> decision.'

See also *Nationwide Building Society v Balmer Radmore* [1999] Lloyd's Rep PN 241 at
260–264.
4 Compare *Wrexham Association Football Club Ltd v Crucialmove Ltd* [2006] EWCA Civ 237
at [39] where Sir Peter Gibson stated:

> 'The fiduciary cannot act for his own benefit without the informed consent of his
> principal. It would not be enough, in my view, to disclose the existence of his interest in a
> transaction without disclosing the nature and extent of that interest.'

See also *J D Wetherspoon plc v Van De Berg & Co Ltd* [2007] EWHC 1044 (Ch) (Lewison J)
at [22]. Both are conflict of interest and duty cases but emphasise the informed nature of the
consent required.

4.33 By contrast, there may be circumstances in which it is impossible for the
solicitor to act for both parties even with the informed consent of both parties.
Such circumstances will be extreme and there is no reported instance in English
law.[1] In Canada, however, in *Davey v Woolley*,[2] it was held that a firm of
solicitors, which acted for three different parties (including a company in which
a partner in the firm was personally interested) on the sale of a business, had
committed a breach of fiduciary duty by accepting instructions from all three
parties and no answer that each of the clients had signed a release acknowledging the joint retainer and the partner's personal interest. It is suggested that a
solicitor could not accept instructions to act with the informed consent of both
clients (or all of the clients) if this would impose such significant constraints on
the solicitor or limit the retainer in such a way that he or she could not properly
protect the interests of one or more of the clients. This was effectively the
position in *Davey v Woolley*.

1 Rule 3.02(2) of the Solicitors' Code of Conduct 2007 permits a solicitor to act exceptionally in
situations of conflict or possible conflict where clients have a substantially common interest or
they are competing for the same asset (subject to certain conditions including written consent).
However, these exceptions are made subject to an important qualification. Rule 3.02(3) provides:
'When acting in accordance with 3.01(1) or (2) above, it must be reasonable in all the circumstances for you or your practice to act for all those clients.' The explanatory notes to r 3 provide
important guidance on when it is likely to be unreasonable to act: see, in particular, paras 8 and 9.

For the position before 1 July 2007 see Practice Rule 16D(3)(a), (b) and(c) (which are in the same form) and 'Conflict Guidance' (the explanatory notes to the rule published in April 2006), paras 8–17.
2 (1982) 35 OR (2d) 599 (Ontario Court of Appeal). The leading judgment was delivered by Wilson JA.

(b) The duty of good faith

4.34   A solicitor must act at all times in good faith and in the interests of each client and must not prefer the interests of one client over the interests of the other.[1] As stated in para 4.29, when once a solicitor accepts instructions from two clients with competing interests, each one is entitled to single–minded loyalty. But it does not follow from this that because a solicitor is retained by two clients, any breach of retainer or negligence is a breach of fiduciary duty. Although the passage from Viscount Haldane's speech in *Nocton v Lord Ashburton* quoted above demonstrates that equity has historically extended the description of fraud or bad faith to conduct which the court considered 'against the dictates of conscience', something genuinely amounting to bad faith must be shown. As Millett LJ put it in *Mothew*:[1]

'The various obligations of a fiduciary merely reflect different aspects of his core duties of loyalty and fidelity. Breach of fiduciary obligation, therefore, connotes disloyalty or infidelity. Mere incompetence is not enough. A servant who loyally does his incompetent duty is not unfaithful and is not guilty of a breach of fiduciary duty.'

Because it is essentially a jury question, it is hard to define exactly what amounts to a breach of this duty and it is best demonstrated by example. S acts for two clients, C1 and C2, and obtains the informed consent of each of them. C1 gives S information which S considers relevant to his retainer from C2 and which he feels obliged to report. He asks C1 whether he may reveal this information and C1 refuses. S is obliged to withdraw and should cease to act for both parties.[2] Because C1 is an established client, S does not do so but chooses to remain silent and not to reveal the information to C2.[3] In this example, S is guilty of a breach of fiduciary duty to C2. The critical ingredient of C2's claim is that S recognises the conflict of interest and his duty to C2 but chooses to put C1's interests first. As Millett LJ put it in *Mothew*[4] (emphasis added):

'Even if a fiduciary is properly acting for two principals with potentially conflicting interests he must act in good faith in the interests of each and must not act *with the intention* of furthering the interests of one principal to the prejudice of those of the other ... I shall call this "the duty of good faith". He must not allow the performance of his obligations to one principal to be influenced by his relationship with the other. He must serve each as faithfully and loyally as if he were his only principal. Conduct which is in breach of this duty *need not be dishonest but it must be intentional. An unconscious omission which happens to benefit one principal at the expense of the other does not constitute a breach of fiduciary duty,* though it may constitute a breach of the duty of skill and care. This is because the principle which is in play is that the fiduciary must not be inhibited by the existence of his other employment from serving the interests of his principal as faithfully and effectively as if he were the only employer. I shall call this the "no inhibition principle".'

The significance, therefore, of the no inhibition principle is that a solicitor may be guilty of a breach of fiduciary duty even though this involves no dishonesty or corrupt motive on his or her part. Circumstances may often place solicitors in a position where they are forced to choose between the interests of one client and the interests of another client (or, for that matter, their own interests) and this may inhibit the solicitor from protecting or promoting the interests of the first client. If a solicitor does not withdraw at this point and cease to act for both parties, he or she will inevitably end up by acting in the interests of one client and against the interests of the other. But (as explained below) this is no defence to a claim for breach of fiduciary duty because the solicitor must take the consequences of having agreed to accept conflicting or potential conflicting engagements.[5]

1 [1998] Ch 1 at 18F.
2 Rule 3.03 of the Solicitors Code of Conduct 2007 expressly provides that a solicitor may only continue to act for more than one client provided that the duty of confidentiality to the other client or clients is not put at risk:

> 'If you act, or your firm acts, for more than one client in a matter and, during the course of the conduct of that matter, a conflict arises between the interests of two or more of those clients, you, or your firm, may only continue to act for one of the clients (or a group of clients between whom there is no conflict) provided that the duty of confidentiality to the other client(s) is not put at risk.'

The position before 1 July 2007 (which was set out in Practice Rule 16D(4)) was the same. If, therefore, the solicitor has obtained the informed consent of both parties and, particularly, obtained express instructions to withdraw in the eventuality of an actual conflict, this should not present a problem. If the solicitor has not obtained that consent, it may amount to a breach of the contract of retainer to withdraw at this stage. This provides no defence to a claim for breach of fiduciary duty if the solicitor continues to act (see para 4.36, below) but seems infinitely preferable to exposure to such a claim.
3 The information need not be confidential: see Scrutton LJ's example of the flaw in title quoted below. Indeed, in *Hilton v Barker Booth & Eastwood* [2005] UKHL 8, [2005] 1 WLR 567 the information which S did not disclose to C1 was information which was available publicly (but which would have had a material effect on his decision). See Lord Walker's speech at [33]:

'These facts were known to any journalist or member of the public who had been present in the Crown Court at Preston when Mr Bromage pleaded guilty and was sentenced. They were also probably reported in the local newspapers.'

4 [1998] Ch 1 at 19D–G.
5 See para 4.36, below.

(c) *The actual conflict rule*

4.35   Even if, therefore, a solicitor obtains the informed consent of both clients to act where there is a potential conflict of interest, it is clear that he or she cannot continue to act once a direct or actual conflict of interest has arisen. This Millett LJ described as 'the actual conflict rule':[1]

'Finally, the fiduciary must take care not to find himself in a position where there is an *actual* conflict of duty so that he cannot fulfil his obligations to one principal without failing in his obligations to the other … If he does, he may have no alternative but to cease to act for at least one and preferably both. The fact that he cannot fulfil his obligations to one principal without being in breach of his obligations to the other will not absolve him from liability. I shall call this "the actual conflict rule".'

In *Moody v Cox and Hatt*[2] the claimant bought a public house and some cottages from the defendants, who were trustees of an estate. They were also solicitors and acted for both the claimant and as solicitors of the trust. The first defendant who conducted the negotiations on behalf of the trust failed to reveal the existence of certain valuations which would affect the price. Although this was in certain respects a conflict of interest and duty case, the Court of Appeal treated it as a conflict of duties case.[3] At first instance, Younger J found that the failure to reveal the valuations was a breach of fiduciary duty. He made no finding that the defendants were in breach of contract or that Cox made misrepresentations to the claimant.[4] The Court of Appeal upheld his judgment. Scrutton LJ said this:[5]

'It seems to me the full duty to disclose was on Hatt.[6] How did he perform it? Again I take Cox's own evidence. Part of the subject-matter of the contract was some cottages. Cox had had a valuation made within a month or two of valuing those cottages at £160 a cottage. He sold them to Moody at £225 a cottage. He did not tell Moody of the valuation; and in his evidence, moreover, he stated as follows: "I did say the cottages were worth £225; I knew that they were not worth it because I had been advised they were worth a good deal less. I knew the value of the Marquis of Granby had depreciated since the probate valuation; I did not tell him the amount of the

187

probate valuation". A man who says this admits in the plainest terms that he is not fulfilling the duty which lies upon him as a solicitor acting for a client. But it is said that he could not disclose that information consistently with his duty to his other clients, the cestuis que trust. It may be that a solicitor who tries to act for both parties puts himself in such a position that he must be liable to one or the other, whatever he does. The case has been put of a solicitor acting for vendor and purchaser who knows of a flaw in the title by reason of his acting for the vendor, and who, if he discloses that flaw in the title which he knows as acting for the vendor, may be liable to an action by his vendor, and who, if he does not disclose the flaw in title, may be liable to an action by the purchaser for not doing his duty as solicitor to him. It will be his fault for mixing himself up in a transaction in which he has two entirely inconsistent interests, and solicitors who try to act for both vendors and purchasers must appreciate that they run a very serious risk of liability to one or the other owing to the duties and obligations which such curious relation puts upon them.'

1 [1998] Ch 1 at 19G–H. The formulation of the double employment rule by Lewison J in *Ultraframe (UK) Ltd v Fielding* [2005] EWHC 1638 (Ch) (Lewison J) at [1317] makes it clear that the fiduciary can continue to act for both principals only whilst there is a potential but not actual conflict of interest.
2 [1917] 2 Ch 71, CA.
3 See Lord Cozens-Hardy MR at 81 and Warrington LJ at 84–5.
4 See the findings at first instance at 74–5. The Court of Appeal might have made different findings on the evidence quoted above: see Lord Cozens-Hardy MR at 80: 'This being what I can call nothing else but a lie uttered', It is, therefore, a strong case. But liability was based purely on non-disclosure: see *Hilton v Barker Booth & Eastwood* [2005] UKHL 8, [2005] 1 WLR 567 at [5] (Lord Scott): 'The reasoning in *Moody v Cox* did not depend on the circumstance that actual misrepresentations might have been made by the solicitors to their client. It depended on the failure by the solicitors to disclose to their client information that it was their contractual duty to him to disclose'. See also the comments of Lord Walker at [43].
5 [1917] 2 Ch 71 at 91.
6 As Cox's principal. Although both were trustees, Cox was not a qualified solicitor and Hatt was the sole principal of the firm.

4.36 *Moody v Cox & Hatt* was applied by the House of Lords in *Hilton v Barker Booth & Eastwood*.[1] In that case a firm of solicitors had acted for a client, B, in criminal proceedings in which he was imprisoned for various bankruptcy offences. B introduced the claimant (C) to a development opportunity and he agreed to purchase a site and to sell it on to B (who had also agreed to sell it on to a sub-purchaser at a profit without C's knowledge). The solicitors acted for both B and C (and also lent B the deposit, again without C's knowledge). The trial judge found that the C would not have entered into the transaction if he had known about B's history. But he also found that if C had instructed an independent firm of solicitors the transaction would have proceeded and that C had suffered no loss. The Court of Appeal dismissed C's appeal on the basis that it was implicit in the retainer that there was no duty to disclose information which would have involved a breach of duty to B and the solicitors' only duty to the claimant was to advise him that they could not act. The House of Lords allowed C's appeal unanimously on the basis that it was no defence to the claim that the solicitors owed a conflicting duty to B. Lord Walker stated:[2]

> 'The thrust of this passage, and of all three judgments in *Moody v Cox*, is that if a solicitor puts himself in a position of having two irreconcilable duties (in that case, to his beneficiaries and to his client, Moody) it is his own fault. If he has a personal financial interest which conflicts with his duty, he is even more obviously at fault. In this case BBE were in the position (through their own fault) of having two irreconcilable duties, to Mr Bromage and to Mr Hilton, and of also having a personal interest (because of the undisclosed £25,000 loan, which was likely to be recoverable only if Mr Bromage did well in his transaction with Mr Hilton). On the face of it their position was significantly worse than that of the solicitor in *Moody v Cox*.'

One of the difficulties in interpreting and applying *Hilton* is that there was no finding by the judge that the solicitors committed a deliberate breach of duty and that it was treated at all levels as a breach of contract case. This is because no breach of fiduciary duty was alleged and it appears to have been accepted that the outcome would have been the same whether C relied on a breach of fiduciary duty or a breach of the solicitors' contract of retainer.[3] It was also common ground between the parties that the solicitors could not act for both B and C because there was a direct conflict of interest and that they should have advised C to take independent advice.[4] The point which caused difficulty was whether they also owed a duty to disclose what they knew about B's bankruptcy and criminal record (despite their conflicting duty to B not to reveal this information) and whether they could be liable for that separate breach of duty having continued to act and having failed to advise C to take independent advice. The House of Lords held that they did owe such a duty and that they could also be liable for a breach of that duty (and the consequences which flowed from that breach of duty) despite the fact that they should have withdrawn at an earlier stage. For this reason C was entitled to substantial damages. Nevertheless, in the course of his judgment Lord Walker also confirmed the actual conflict rule:[5]

> 'Mr Gibson submitted that a solicitor who has conflicting duties to two clients may not prefer one to another. That is, I think, correct as a general rule, and it distinguishes the case of two irreconcilable duties from a conflict of duty and personal interest (where the solicitor is bound to prefer his duty to his own interest). Since he may not prefer one duty to another, he must perform both as best he can. This may involve performing one duty to the letter of the

obligation, and paying compensation for his failure to perform the other. But in any case the fact that he has chosen to put himself in an impossible position does not exonerate him from liability.'[6]

1 [2005] UKHL 8, [2005] 1 WLR 567.
2 [41].
3 See Lord Walker's speech at [30]: 'Mr Hilton did not expressly plead that BBE was in breach of any fiduciary duty. He did not need to, since at trial he was not seeking to take the sort of causation point that was raised in the *Mothew* case (in this House the appellant's printed case did seek to take points based on a fiduciary relationship but the House did not find it necessary to decide whether to consider those points). On this issue of liability both sides have been content for the case to be dealt with as a claim for breach of contract. However, the content of BBE's contractual duty, so far as relevant to this case, has roots in the parties' relationship of trust and confidence.'
4 See [31] and [32]. These are difficult paragraphs because is not clear whether Lord Walker considered that the solicitors owed a strict contractual duty not to place themselves in a position of conflict or whether he was simply recording a concession of negligence. In *Strother v 3464920 Canada Inc* [2007] SCC 24 Binnie J considered that it was the former (at 57): 'In *Hilton*, relied on by Davis, failure to disclose to one client prejudicial (but not confidential) information about the other client in a case where the defendant law firm acted for both clients in a joint venture was held to be actionable in contract although the quality of the legal work, as such, was not the subject of criticism.' If this is correct, then it leaves open the possibility that a breach of the actual conflict rule may give rise to a strict contractual liability even in the absence of findings of an intentional breach of duty or negligence.
5 [44].
6 For a more difficult case on the existence of irreconcilable duties see *Strother,* above. In that case a specialist tax solicitor provided advice to a client in setting up and operating tax shelter investments for a number of years. The firm also entered into an 'exclusivity' agreement. Revenue Canada then closed the loophole, the client wound down its business and the nature of the retainer changed (although the client remained a client of the firm). Some time after (and despite enquiries from his first client about potential new schemes), the solicitor gave advice to a competitor about a new scheme and was instrumental in setting it up. He also acquired an interest in the client company. The Supreme Court of Canada held by a majority that he was in breach of his fiduciary duty to the first client. There was a sharp divergence of views about whether the solicitor owed contractual and fiduciary duties to disclose the new scheme to the first client or his interest in the new company. McLachlin CJ (on behalf of the minority) stressed the importance of the limited terms of the new retainer. She pointed out that the first client had ceased to be in the tax shelter business and stated (at [144]): 'There was no duty to provide continuing advice on developments of interest, and no provision for remuneration for being available to provide such advice. There was no contractual requirement for Strother to act exclusively for Monarch, and Strother was free to take on competing clients.' The majority, however, took the view that he was acting in breach of the terms of the retainer and in breach of fiduciary duty: see [49]–[73].

4.37 In a number of cases (principally involving lenders' claims) the principles in *Mothew* have been applied. In *Nationwide Building Society v Richard Grosse & Co* and *Nationwide Building Society v Goodwin Harte*,[1] where twelve sample cases were heard at the same time, the judge was prepared to conclude that two solicitors consciously put their borrower client's interests before those of their lender client. In the first case, the critical factor from which the judge was prepared to draw this conclusion was that the solicitor had submitted an unqualified report on title at a time when he had taken no steps to investigate title at all. In that case the solicitor elected to give evidence.[2] In the second case, where the solicitor elected not to give evidence, the judge was also prepared to make a finding of breach of fiduciary duty.[3] In that case, the judge found that on the basis of his admitted knowledge the solicitor must have known that his borrower client was defrauding his lender client and, in the absence of evidence from the solicitor, the judge felt entitled to conclude that his failure to disclose the relevant information to the plaintiff was 'conscious, deliberate and in bad faith'. Both these and *Moody v Cox and Hatt* were strong cases.[4] In *Bristol and West Building Society v Fancy and Jackson*[5] by contrast the judge was not willing to infer, in the absence of evidence, that the solicitor's conduct had been deliberate. More recently, however, *Ball v Druces & Attlee*[6] provides an example of a failure to observe the actual conflict rule (in a context very different from the lenders' cases). In that case a firm of solicitors who acted both for the founders of the Eden Project and the charitable trust which was formed to administer it were held to be in breach of fiduciary duty by continuing to act for one client after an actual conflict arose.[7]

1   [1999] Lloyd's Rep PN 348 and [1999] Lloyd's Rep PN 338 (Blackburne J).
2   [1999] Lloyd's Rep PN 348 at 355–6:

   'The clear picture which emerged from [his] evidence was of someone who paid little regard to the Society's interests. He returned an unqualified report on title without caring whether what he was saying in it was true or not.'

3   [1999] Lloyd's Rep PN 338 at 345.
4   The evidence quoted by Scrutton LJ in the passage from *Moody v Cox and Hatt* [1917] 2 Ch 71 at 91, CA quoted above indicates the sort of evidence from which the court will draw the inference of deliberate breach. See also *Goose v Wilson Sandford* [2001] Lloyd's Rep PN 189, CA where an accountant was held to be in breach of fiduciary duty in failing to make disclosure to his client (although the claim failed because the duty was not causative of loss).
5   [1997] 4 All ER 582 at 613g and 614d–e (Chadwick J): 'I should not draw an inference of dishonesty against a solicitor without cogent evidence; evidence which, in effect, compels me to reach that conclusion.' For other cases in which the court did not find a breach of fiduciary duty made out see *Maes Finance Ltd v Sharp* (HHJ Bowsher QC, 27 July 1999, unreported), *Birmingham Midshires BS v Infields* [1999] Lloyd's Rep PN 874 (HHJ Bowsher QC) and *Leeds & Holbeck BS v Arthur & Cole* [2002] PNLR 23 (Morland J) (all lenders' cases).
6   [2004] EWHC 1402 (QB), [2004] PNLR 39 (Nelson J) at [315]–[340]. There was no separate award of equitable compensation because the claimant recovered damages for negligence.
7   The breaches of duty consisted of revealing the claimant's weak bargaining position to their other client whilst he was still a client of the firm ([322]–[326]) and exploiting confidential information when he had ceased to be a client ([330] and [336]–[337]). The judge also rejected the argument that there was transparency of information between the two clients ([333]–[335]). The judge also pointed out that a different test would apply at trial in relation to a breach of the fiduciary duty of confidentiality than would apply at the interim stage where a client or former client was seeking to restrain a solicitor from acting: see [322].

4.38   Finally, it is important to bear in mind that a failure by a solicitor to disclose information received from one client to the other does not give rise automatically to a breach of the actual conflict rule. If the solicitor has obtained the informed consent of both clients, each accepts that the solicitor must be permitted to carry out the instructions of the other. One client may agree that the solicitor is entitled to reveal confidential information to the other client or, as in *Kelly v Cooper,* that the solicitor's duty of disclosure should be circumscribed by the duty of confidentiality to the other client. Terms to this effect will usually be the subject of express agreement between the solicitor and the clients (as part of the process of obtaining informed consent). But they can also be implied. In *Mothew* there was no conflict of duties when they were properly analysed:

> 'In the present case the judge evidently thought that the defendant was in breach of both the duty of good faith and the actual conflict rule. In *Bristol and West Building Society v May, May & Merrimans*[1] he said:
>
>> "There can be no doubt that the requirement of unconscionable conduct is present where a solicitor who is acting for both borrower and lender misrepresents to the lender some fact *which he knows, or must be taken to know*, will or may affect the lender's decision to proceed with the loan. In those circumstances, the solicitor *is abusing his fiduciary relationship with one client, the lender, to obtain an advantage for his other client, the borrower.* It is as much 'against the dictates of conscience' for a solicitor *knowingly to prefer the interests of one client over those of another client* as it is for him to prefer his own interests over those of his client." (My emphasis.)
>
> I respectfully agree: but no such allegation is made in this case.'

When it came to the actual conflict rule, the judge held at first instance that the solicitor put himself in a position of conflict. In the Court of Appeal Millett LJ rejected this argument because he considered that the solicitor had the implied authority of the borrower to disclose the information necessary to complete the report on title:[2]

> 'By instructing him to act for them, the purchasers must be taken to have authorised the defendants to complete the report without which the mortgage advance would not have been forthcoming; and to complete it truthfully. The defendant was required by the society to report on the purchaser's title as well as to confirm the absence of any further borrowing. The two stood in exactly the same case. The defendant would not have been in breach of his duty to the purchasers if he had disclosed the facts to the society any more than if he had reported a defect in their title. This proposition can be tested by considering what the defendant's position would have been if he had acted for the purchasers and another solicitor had been instructed to act for the society. He would have been required to deduce the purchaser's title to the satisfaction of the society's solicitor, and to confirm to him that no further borrowing or second charge was in contemplation. His duty to the purchasers would have required him to ascertain the facts from them and to report them to the society. Unless they told him the facts and instructed him to lie to the society, instructions which he would have been bound to refuse, his duty to

the purchasers would not inhibit him in providing full and truthful information to the solicitor acting for the society.'[3]

The nature of the information which a solicitor acting for both borrower and lender is free to disclose to each of his clients is considered further at paras 10.14ff, 10.23ff and 10.44ff, below. For present purposes the important point is that before it can be said that an irreconcilable conflict of duties arises, the solicitor's implied authority to disclose information must be considered. If the solicitor has no express or implied authority to disclose or withhold information, it is necessary to consider whether the solicitor owes a duty to disclose the relevant information. In *Hilton* Lord Walker rejected the analogy with the lenders' cases[4] and it was held that the solicitors owed a duty to disclose relevant information about their other client. Because of the nature of the information and the striking similarity between the facts of the case and *Cox v Moody & Hatt* little discussion was needed of the test to be applied in deciding whether there is a duty of disclosure and the actual conflict rule comes into play. In *Strother v 3464920 Canada Inc*[5] the majority held that there was a duty of disclosure if the information would have had a materially adverse effect on the client's interests. This seems consistent with the decision in *Hilton* where the trial judge found that the claimant would not have proceeded with the transaction if he had been aware of B's bankruptcy and conviction.

1 [1996] 2 All ER 801 at 817–818.
2 [1996] 2 All ER 801 at 832.
3 [1998] Ch 1 at 20A–G.
4 See [45] and [46]. The point which Lord Walker made was that these cases often turn on the standard form instructions issued by the lender. Although there was no discussion about the express terms of the solicitor's retainer from the lender in the passage in *Mothew* referred to above, it is clear from it that Millett LJ considered that the informed consent of the lender could be implied from the instructions given by the lender to report on title (which would contain detailed to instructions to provide all of the information which the lender considered material). It is unlikely, however, that there will be many cases in which it is possible to imply fully informed consent to make or withhold disclosure outside the context of a solicitor acting for both borrower and lender where the CML Lenders' Handbook contains detailed and specific instructions which are fully familiar both to lenders and solicitors. In commercial loans where there are no standard form instructions, it may be more difficult to imply informed consent (although this will inevitably turn on the nature of the transaction itself and the extent to which it raises unusual issues).
5 [2007] SCC 24 at [61]: 'Strother is dismissive of the impact his breach had on Monarch's interest (i e in obtaining proper legal advice). He is correct that the test requires that the impact must be "material and adverse" (as set out in the definition of conflict adopted in *Neil*, previously cited). While it is sufficient to show a possibility (rather than a probability) of adverse impact, the possibility must be more than speculation (see *de Guzman v de la Cruz*, 2004 BCSC 36 (CanLII), [2004] B.C.J. No. 72 (QL), 2004 BCSC 36, at para 27).' They also held that once the solicitor's personal interest in the transaction was established the burden was on him to satisfy the court that the failure to disclose was material. This is consistent with the 'fair dealing' rule but it is more questionable whether the burden of proof should be reversed in a conflict of duty and duty case.

(*d*) *Conclusion*

4.39   Apart from the duty of good faith, fiduciary duties are strict. In order to show a breach of the fiduciary duty of good faith, the claimant must establish a conflict of interest and duty or a conflict of duties. If there has been adequate disclosure at the outset and no breach of the double employment rule, the existence of any conflict of duties will turn on the express or implied terms of the solicitor's retainer from each client. If the terms of the consent are to be implied from the nature of the transaction and the relationship between the two clients, this is best tested by considering what the defendant would have been impliedly authorised by C1 to reveal to another solicitor acting for C2. If, properly analysed, there is a genuine conflict of duties, the claimant will also have to show that the defendant was aware of this and preferred the interests of C1 to the interests of C2. Finally, if such a claim is to be advanced at all a breach of the duty of good faith must be clearly pleaded. It is not enough to allege a breach of fiduciary duty. The claimant must plead and prove that the solicitor committed a deliberate or intentional breach of duty amounting to bad faith.[1] If a solicitor lies to a client, the remedy is a claim in deceit. If he or she assists one client to defraud another without making fraudulent misrepresentations, the solicitor may be liable for conspiracy to defraud at common law or for dishonest assistance as an accessory. If he or she is trusted with the money and property of one client and transfers it to another, the solicitor will be liable for breach of trust if the circumstances of the transfer are outside his authority or if he acts dishonestly. It is only if he fails to carry out the instructions of one client on the instructions of the other or in the knowledge that he cannot comply with the instructions of both, that a separate breach of fiduciary duty is properly made out.

1 See *Paragon Finance v D B Thakerar & Co* [1999] 1 All ER 400 at 404–6.

D   COMPENSATION IN EQUITY

1   Introduction

4.40   This part of this chapter is concerned with equitable compensation, i e an award by the court of money under its equitable jurisdiction for losses suffered as a consequence of a breach of duty by a fiduciary. The jurisdiction differs in a number of significant respects from damages at common law partly because of its historical origins[1] and partly because of the underlying policy basis for an award.[2] In *Bank of New Zealand v New Zealand Guardian Trust Co Ltd*[3] the Court of Appeal of New Zealand recognised that the principles for assessing an award of compensation will differ depending on the nature of the duty broken. There will be circumstances in which equitable compensation will resemble damages at common law (and the rules of causation, remoteness and mitigation will be the same). The reason for this is that fiduciaries usually owe a range of duties including duties of care and the nature of the duty broken will determine the basis of the relevant award. As a matter of history, the duty of care owed by a solicitor is a common law development whereas the duty of care of, say, a receiver has taken hold as an equitable duty rather than a contractual or tortious duty.[4] But it is also important to recognise that equitable duties of this kind are not fiduciary duties although the remedy of equitable compensation is available for their breach. In this chapter we are concerned with the fiduciary duties of solicitors (as contrasted with their duties at common law) and in this section compensation for breaches of those duties (as contrasted with common law damages). The fiduciary duties of a solicitor fall into two categories: first, custodial duties (i e to look after assets or money either as an express or implied trustee) and, secondly duties of fidelity or confidence. The rationale for awarding compensation for breaches of these duties and the rules of causation or remoteness differ from damages at common law. In *Bank of New Zealand v New Zealand Guardian Trust Co Ltd*[5] Tipping J said this:

'It is inherent in what I have already written that the existence of the same relationship between the parties i e trustee and beneficiary, does not mandate that the same approach to causation and remoteness should be taken in all cases irrespective of the nature of the breach. In the first kind of case the allegation is that a breach of duty by a trustee has directly caused loss of or damage to the trust property. The relief sought by the beneficiary is usually in such circumstances of the restitutionary kind. The trustee is asked to restore the trust estate, either in specie or by value. The policy of the law in these circumstances is generally to hold the trustee responsible if, but for the breach, the loss or damage would not have occurred. This approach is designed to encourage trustees to observe to the full their duties in relation to the trust property by imposing upon them a stringent concept of causation. Questions of foreseeability and remoteness do not come into such an assessment. In the second kind of case, the trustee or other fiduciary has committed a breach of duty which involves an element of infidelity or disloyalty engaging the fiduciary's conscience – what might be called a true breach of fiduciary duty …In short, in such a case once the plaintiff has shown a loss arising out of a transaction to which the breach was material, the plaintiff is entitled to recover unless the defendant fiduciary, upon whom is the onus, shows that the loss or damage would have occurred in any event, i e without any breach on the fiduciary's part. Questions of foreseeability and remoteness do not arise in this kind of case either. Policy dictates that fiduciaries be allowed only a narrow escape route from liability based on proof that the loss and damage would not have occurred even if there had been no breach. In the third kind of case, the relationship of trustee (or fiduciary) and beneficiary is, in a sense, incidental. It provides the setting in which the breach of duty occurs, and with it such tortious proximity or contractual privity as may be necessary. The duty to take care is one which arises as an incident of the relationship, but for the purpose of determining the proper approach to causation and remoteness, it is the failure to take care which is the material dimension, not the facts that the relationship also creates duties of a fiduciary kind. Those duties are not relevantly engaged.'

It is suggested that the same approach would be adopted under English law. In a passage in *Bristol & West BS v Mothew*[6] Millett LJ adopted a similar analysis. The general principle is, therefore, that the nature of the duty broken determines the approach which the court will adopt to compensation. The mere existence of a fiduciary relationship does not entitle a claimant to a more generous measure of compensation.

1 See para 4.41, below.
2 See para 4.42, below.
3 See [1999] 1 NZLR 664, 687 (Tipping J):

> 'Breaches of duty by trustees and other fiduciaries may broadly be of three different kinds. First, there are breaches leading directly to damage to or loss of the trust property; second, there are breaches involving an element of infidelity or disloyalty which engages the conscience of the fiduciary; third, there are breaches involving a lack of appropriate care. It is implicit in this analysis that breaches of the second kind do not involve loss or damage to the trust property, and breaches of the third kind involve neither loss to the trust property, nor infidelity or disloyalty.'

4 See, eg, *Silven Properties Ltd and another v Royal Bank of Scotland plc* [2003] EWCA Civ 1409, [2004] 4 All E.R. 484 at [22].
5 Above at 697–8. See also Rickett 'Equitable Compensation: Towards a Blueprint' [2003] Sydney Law Review 3. See, in particular, section 2 and his thesis for understanding the role of equitable compensation.
6 [1998] Ch 1, CA at 17G-H:

> 'In my judgment this is not just a question of semantics. It goes to the very heart of the concept of breach of fiduciary duty and the availability of equitable remedies. Although the remedies which equity makes available for breach of the equitable duty of skill and care is equitable compensation rather than damages, this is merely the product of history and in this context is in my opinion a distinction without a difference. Equitable compensation for breach of the duty of skill and care resembles common law damages in that it is awarded by way of compensation to the plaintiff for his loss. There is no reason in principle why the common law rules of causation, remoteness and damage and measure of damages should not be applied by analogy in such a case. It should not be confused with equitable compensation for breach of fiduciary duty, which may be awarded in lieu of rescission or specific restitution.'

See also *Youyang Pty Ltd v Minter Ellison Morris Fletcher* [2003] HCA 15 at [36]–[37] and the comments of McLachlin CJ in *Strother v 3464920 Canada Inc* [2007] SCC 24 at [157].

(a) Historical basis

4.41 It is difficult to appreciate these distinctions or to understand the relationship between an award of compensation for losses caused by a fiduciary and other remedies (such as an account of profits) without some reference to the historical background. Courts of equity had their own jurisdiction to order a party to pay money and one element of that jurisdiction was the power to make a monetary award against an accounting party.[1] The paradigm example of an accounting party was, of course, a trustee. But the duty to account could (and can) arise as a matter of express or implied contract and any agency relationship will usually involve some accounting obligations.[2] Where a trustee failed to be ready with his or her accounts, the beneficiary was entitled to apply to court for an account to be taken. The basis of the jurisdiction was the failure by the trustee to comply with the obligation to account and the remedy was the equivalent of a judicial 'audit' of the trust accounts. On the taking of the account the trustee might satisfy the court that the accounts were accurate and involved no further wrongdoing at all. However, as part of the judicial process the beneficiary was entitled to 'surcharge and falsify' the trust accounts, i e the beneficiary could require the trustee to make up any deficiencies in the books ('surcharge') or disallow trust expenses ('falsify').[3] Once the account was taken the beneficiary could require the trustee to avoid any transactions made between the trustee and the trust for his or her own account and require the trustee to restore the relevant trust property or to reject trust investments made in breach of trust and compel the trustee to make good the loss. If on the taking of the account rescission or specific restitution was impossible, the court could order the trustee to compensate the trust fund in lieu of those remedies. The liability to compensate the fund was principally a personal remedy against the defaulting trustee. It enabled the beneficiaries to obtain an order requiring the trustee to restore trust property in his possession but if the trustee was unable to do so to obtain an order requiring the trustee to provide the money equivalent.[4] In cases of this kind, the court ordered an account because the trustee was in default of the obligation to account. But a beneficiary or principal was also entitled to obtain an order for an account where it could be shown that a trustee was guilty of a specific breach of duty. This form of account was known as an 'account on the basis of wilful default' as compared with a 'common account'. Although both accounts would have taken a similar form the burden of proof on a trustee was higher for an account on the basis of willful default and the power to order the trustee to make good deficiencies was wider. The beneficiary was entitled to insist that the trustee made good actual losses suffered as a consequence of the breach of duty.[5] Finally, on the taking of either form of account, a trustee could also be required to disgorge any profit which he or she had made.[6]

1 For a brief overview of the jurisdiction to make awards of money in equity see *Snell's Equity* (31st edn, 2005), Chapter 18. For general discussion of the remedy of account see Millet 'Equity's Place in the Law of Commerce' (1998) 114 LQR 214.
2 See *Ultraframe (UK) Ltd v Fielding* [2005] EWHC 1638 (Ch) at [1516] (Lewison J) for examples of other relationships which give rise to a duty to account.
3 See *Ultraframe (UK) Ltd v Fielding* [2005] EWHC 1638 (Ch) at [1513]:

'The taking of an account is the means by which a beneficiary requires a trustee to justify his stewardship of trust property. The trustee must show what he has done with that

197

property. If the beneficiary is dissatisfied with the way that a trustee has dealt with trust assets he may surcharge or falsify the account. He surcharges the account when he alleges that the trustee has not obtained for the benefit of the trust all that he might have done, if he had exercised due care and diligence. If the allegation is proved, then the account is taken as if the trustee had received, for the benefit of the trust, what he would have received if he had exercised due care and diligence. The beneficiary falsifies the account when he alleges that the trustee has applied trust property in a way that he should not have done (e g by making an unauthorised investment). If the allegation is proved, then the account will be taken as if the expenditure had not been made: and as if the unauthorised investment had not formed part of the assets of the trust. Of course, if the unauthorised investment has appreciated in value, the beneficiary may choose not to falsify the account: in which case the asset will remain a trust asset and the expenditure on it will be allowed in taking the account.'

See also *Glazier Holdings v Australian Men's Health* (NSW Supreme Court, 22 January 2001) at 37–8 (cited by Rickett in Equitable Compensation: Towards a Blueprint [2003] Sydney Law Review 3 (see 4.40, note 6 above)) at [37] and [38].

4 After the taking of the account, however, the beneficiaries might in certain circumstances be entitled to further proprietary relief: see *Ultraframe (UK) Ltd v Fielding* [2005] EWHC 1638 (Ch) at [1514].

5 See *Armitage v Nurse* [1998] Ch 241 at 252 (Millett LJ):

'A trustee is said to be accountable on the footing of wilful default when he is accountable not only for money which he has in fact received but also for money which he could with reasonable diligence have received. It is sufficient that the trustee has been guilt of a want of ordinary prudence.'

See also *Glazier*, above at [39]–[42].

6 For detailed discussion of the differences between the various forms of account and the underlying principles see Rickett 'Equitable Compensation: Towards a Blueprint' [2003] Sydney Law Review 3.

(b) Modern Rationale

4.42 The benefit of this historical analysis is that it demonstrates that equitable compensation was a remedy developed in the context of the duty of a custodial trustee to account for the assets in his custody where it was an alternative to rescission or specific restitution. Even some of the more modern authorities which are considered below[1] need to be understood in that context. The modern rationale for equitable compensation was put in its historical context in *Canson Enterprises Ltd v Broughton & Co*[2] by McLachlin J in the following passage:

'What is the ambit of compensation as an equitable remedy? Proceeding in trust, we start from the traditional obligation of a defaulting trustee, which is to effect restitution to the estate. But restitution in specie may not always be possible. So equity awards compensation in place of restitution in specie, by analogy for breach of fiduciary duty with the ideal of restoring to the estate that which was lost through the breach.

The restitutionary basis of compensation for breach of trust was described in *Ex p Adamson* (1878) 8 Ch D 807 at 819:

> "The Court of Chancery never entertained a suit for damages occasioned by fraudulent conduct or for breach of trust. The suit was always for an equitable debt or liability in the nature of a debt. It was a suit for the restitution of the actual money or thing, or value of the thing, of which the cheated party had been cheated."

It has been widely accepted ever since. As Professor Davidson states in his very useful article "The Equitable Remedy of Compensation"[3] "the method of calculation [of compensation] will be that which makes restitution for the value of the loss suffered from the breach ..."

In summary, compensation is an equitable monetary remedy which is available when the equitable remedies of restitution and account[4] are not appropriate. By analogy with restitution, it attempts to restore to the plaintiff what has been lost as a result of the breach, ie the plaintiff's loss of opportunity. The plaintiff's actual loss as a consequence of the breach is to be assessed with the full benefit of hindsight. Foreseeability is not a concern in assessing compensation, but it is essential that the losses made good are only those which, on a common sense view of causation, were caused by the breach. The plaintiff will not be required to mitigate, as the term is used in law, but losses resulting from clearly unreasonable behaviour on the part of the plaintiff will be adjudged to flow from that behaviour, and not from the breach. Where the trustee's breach permits the wrongful or negligent acts of third parties, thus establishing a direct link between the breach and the loss, the resulting loss will be recoverable. Where there is no such link, the loss must be recovered from the third parties.'

This statement emphasises that the purpose of an award of equitable compensation for breach of trust or breach of fiduciary duty is a form of restitution and not damages. It is to restore to the principal or beneficiary the asset or assets of which they have been deprived and in the absence of the specific asset to substitute their value on the assumption that the trustee had continued to hold them and exploit them for the benefit of the principal or beneficiaries. This remedy is to be distinguished from damages recoverable at common law. It is also to be contrasted with an account of profits where the basis for ordering the trustee to disgorge the profits which he or she had made is prophylactic (and in keeping with the proscriptive nature of fiduciary obligations).[5] In cases of this kind, the premise on which the court orders an account of profits is that the principal or beneficiaries have suffered no loss (e g because they would not have taken advantage of a corporate opportunity) but the fiduciary is required to disgorge the profit which he or she has made either in breach of the no conflict rule or in breach of the no profit rule.

1 Notably *Re Dawson* [1966] 2 NSWLR 211 (Street J) at 214–6.
2 (1991) 85 DLR (4th) 129 at 157e–h and 163e–h. The seven judges concurred in the result. McLachlin J, with whom L'Heureux-Dube J concurred, wrote the minority opinion. The speech was, however, expressly approved by Lord Browne-Wilkinson in *Target Holdings Ltd v Redferns* [1996] AC 421 at 428D–439B.
3 (1982) 13 Melbourne ULR 349 at 351.
4 It is clear that McLachlin J was using the term 'account' as shorthand for an account of profits: see *Strother v 3464920 Canada Inc* [2007] SCC 24 at [158].
5 See *Murad v Al-Saraj* [2005] EWCA Civ 959, [2005] WTLR 1573 at [108] (Jonathan Parker LJ): 'It is thus clear on authority, in my judgment, that the "no conflict" rule is neither compensatory nor restitutionary: rather, it is designed to strip the fiduciary of the unauthorised profits he has made whilst he is in a position of conflict.' See also *Strother v 3464920 Canada Inc* [2007] SCC 24 at 74 to 77 (Binnie J delivering the judgment of the majority). For a recent detailed discussion of the principles to be applied on an account of profits see *Ultraframe (UK) Ltd v Fielding* [2005] EWHC 1638 (Ch) (Lewison J) at [1307] et seq. For an interesting discussion on the personal and proprietary consequences see *Sinclair Investment Holdings SA v Versailles Trade Finance Ltd* [2007] EWHC 915 (Ch) (Rimer J) at [105].

2   Causation

4.43   In *Target Holdings Ltd v Redferns*[1] the House of Lords affirmed that it was necessary for a beneficiary seeking equitable compensation to establish a causal connection between the breach of trust and the loss suffered.[2] In fact, the appeal to the House of Lords did not involve an issue of causation because it was accepted that the solicitors had an arguable case that the claimant would have made the relevant investment even if the full facts were known. The precise issue for the House of Lords was whether the claimant could avoid the trial of that issue by taking advantage of the traditional remedy of specific restitution, and, in particular, whether it was open for a solicitor trustee, who had paid away a lender's funds prematurely and without the client's authority, to argue that he had made good the loss since the date of breach by getting in the security or whether the lender, who with the benefit of hindsight did not want the security, was entitled to restitution of the mortgage advance in full despite the solicitor trustee's subsequent actions. The Court of Appeal[3] had held that the lender beneficiary was entitled to an order for restitution of the mortgage advance despite the solicitor's later conduct. The House of Lords reached the opposite conclusion and held, first, that a beneficiary was not automatically entitled to restitution of the trust fund for a breach of trust and, secondly, that compensation in equity falls to be determined at the date of trial in the light of all the circumstances then known. The solicitor had belatedly got in the security and, because he had done so, it was arguable that the lender had suffered no loss as a consequence of the breach and was not therefore entitled to equitable compensation.[4]

1 [1996] AC 421.

2 There was existing authority to this effect: see *Nestle v National Westminster Bank plc (No 2)* [1993] 1 WLR 1260 and *Re Miller's Deed Trusts* (1978) 75 LSG 454 (Oliver J).
3 [1994] 1 WLR 1089, CA.
4 The issue arose on the claimant's application for summary judgment and an interim payment. In fact the House of Lords restored the order of Warner J for conditional leave to defend and an interim payment on the grounds that there was a 'high probability' that the claimant would establish that the transaction would not have gone ahead if the money had not been released early.

4.44 Nevertheless, Lord Browne-Wilkinson, with whom the other members of the House agreed, did make the following general observation:[1]

'Equitable compensation for breach of trust is designed to achieve exactly what the word compensation suggests: to make good a loss in fact suffered by the beneficiaries and which, using hindsight and common sense, can be seen to have been caused by the breach.'

Target is, therefore, clear authority for the proposition that causation must be established in a claim for equitable compensation for losses suffered as a consequence of a breach of trust (unlike a claim for an account of profits).[2] One difficulty with the decision, however is not so much whether this principle should be applied but whether a beneficiary under an implied purpose trust (of the kind on which solicitors hold most client funds) can still obtain traditional trust remedies such as specific restitution when the underlying commercial transaction has been completed. This point was identified in a number of authorities which came after *Target*.[3] But in *Templeton Insurance Ltd v Penningtons Solicitors LLP*[4] Lewison J held that a beneficiary was still entitled to recover client funds which were paid away in breach of trust despite the completion of the underlying transaction provided that the necessary causative element had been established. In that case the solicitors had paid away significant part of the relevant client funds but not for an authorised purpose (unlike *Target* where the solicitors obtained the relevant security). In *Harris v Kent*[5] Briggs J considered that Lord Brown-Wilkinson's 'basic principle' (which is set out in the extract above) was applicable to all trusts unless there was some specific reason for reconstituting the fund:

'The first question is whether the basic equitable principle applies in preference to the traditional trust obligation to reconstitute the fund. Lord Browne Wilkinson's speech makes clear that the basic equitable principle is not a special rule applicable only to business trusts, or even to bare trusts, but to all trusts, unless there is good reason to require the reconstitution of the fund, rather than the simple short-cut of compensating the beneficiary: see pp 433 to 435. At p 435B he leaves open the possibility that even in a case where the reconstitution of the fund is not necessary, it may still be appropriate ... In the present case it is not only unnecessary to reconstitute the trust fund. It is the last thing which the litigants would want, since it would force them back into a fiduciary relationship of which they are all no doubt heartily sick.'

1 [1996] AC 421 at 439B.
2 See *Murad v Al Saraj* [2005] EWCA Civ 959, [2005] WTLR 1573 at [59](2) (Arden LJ) and
[165] (Clarke LJ) where the Court of Appeal confirmed that causation was required for equitable
compensation but that causation in equity was different from common law. The case was,
however, concerned with disgorgement of a profit rather than compensation for loss as in *Strother
v 3464920 Canada Inc* [2007] SCC 24 where Binnie J stated at [77]: 'Where, as here, disgorgement is imposed to serve a prophylactic purpose, the relevant causation is the breach of a
fiduciary duty and the defendant's gain (not the plaintiff's loss).'
3 See the discussion in *Bairstow v Queen's Moat Houses plc* [2001] EWCA Civ 712, [2001]
2 BCLC 531 at [49]–[54] (where Robert Walker LJ considered whether a distinction should be
made between directors and express trustees on the basis of *Target*) and *Knight v Duffel, Kentish
& Co* [2003] EWCA Civ 223 at [37]–[39] (where the Court of Appeal distinguished *Target* on the
basis that the transaction had not been completed). See also *Youyang Pty Ltd v Minter Ellison
Morris Fletcher* [2003] HCA 15, (2003) 212 CLR 484 at [48] (where the High Court of Australia
distinguished *Target* on the same basis). The court also stated this at [49]:

> 'Nevertheless, the creation of the trust in favour of Youyang was not an end in itself; the
> terms of the trust which bound Minters were concerned with the application of the trust
> moneys in completion of a larger commercial transaction with Youyang and Minters'
> client, ECCCL, as the principal actors. To acknowledge that situation is not necessarily
> to embrace any theory of reductionism whereby, notwithstanding the rigour of the rule
> requiring observance of the terms of the trust, in certain events 'commercial' trusts do
> not provide for their beneficiaries the full panoply of personal and proprietary rights and
> remedies designed by equity. Rather, it emphasises that, in the administration of the
> pecuniary remedy Youyang seeks for misapplication of its funds by Minters, regard
> should be had to the scope and purpose of the trust which bound Minters.'

Finally, for academic consideration of this point see Rickett 'Equitable Compensation:
Towards a Blueprint' [2003] Sydney Law Review 3.
4 [2006] EWHC 685 (Ch) (Lewison J) at [22]. After citing *Target* Lewison J stated:

> 'That, however, as I see it, is really going to the nature of the remedy and as
> Lord Browne-Wilkinson pointed out earlier, the measure of compensation is likely to be
> the same in many cases as the amount which ought to be restored to the trust fund. The
> essential breach of trust in the present case was the paying out of money for purposes
> other than completion of the purchase of the captioned property. It may be that, so far as
> the money which was paid for the purchase of that property is concerned, Templeton will
> succeed in recovering it or, at any rate, in acquiring some sort of security. But that does
> not apply to the other items of expenditure. I do not see that any real questions of
> causation arise in relation to those monies.'

5 [2007] EWHC 463 (Ch) at [127] and [127]–[131]. See also *Law Debenture Trust Corpn plc v
Elektrim Finance SA* [2006] EWHC 1305 (Ch) (HH Judge Pelling QC) where the rule in
Saunders v Vautier was applied to a trust which had features of both Lord Browne-Wilkinson's
category of trusts.

(a) *The conduct of the claimant*

4.45 In chapter 3[1] we considered the position of a claimant seeking damages
at common law. In an article[2] published shortly after the Court of Appeal had
delivered judgment in *Target,* Mr J D Heydon QC suggested that the decision
might be justified on the basis of the principle expressed by Lord Thankerton in
Brickenden v London Loan & Savings Co,[3] where he said this:

'When a party holding a fiduciary relationship, commits a breach of his duty by non-disclosure of material facts, which his constituent is entitled to know in connection with the transaction, he cannot be heard to maintain that disclosure would not have altered the decision to proceed with the transaction because the constituent's action would be solely determined by some other factor, such as the valuation by another party of the property proposed to be mortgaged. Once the court has determined that the non-disclosed facts were material, speculation as to what course the constituent, on disclosure, would have taken is not relevant.'

This statement suggested that there was a marked difference between equity and the common law, at least in relation to claims based on the tort of negligence. This was because there was a presumption of loss in favour of a beneficiary claiming in equity and it was unnecessary for him to establish that he would have acted differently if the fiduciary had fulfilled his duty.

1 See paras 3.3ff and 3.144, above. In factual terms, this argument is not dissimilar to the argument which arose in *Bristol & West BS v Mothew* [1998] Ch 1, CA about the different way to approach the issue of causation in a case where there is an allegation of a negligent misstatement as well as allegations of breach of a duty of care.
2 Causal Relationships Between a Fiduciary's Default and a Principal's Loss (1994) 110 LQR 328.
3 [1934] 3 DLR 465 at 469, PC.

4.46   *Brickenden* was a case of conflict of interest and duty.[1] A solicitor acted for both borrower and lender but failed to disclose to the lender, which was a company, that its loan was to be used (in part) to repay the solicitor personally. When the borrower defaulted, the claimant sought to recover the loan from the solicitor himself. By the time of trial the relevant officer of the claimant company was dead and the defendant refused to give evidence, placing the claimant in some difficulty. Given the facts of the case it was in some doubt whether Lord Thankerton's dictum should be treated as having the status of principle. Moreover, the decision was not cited to the Court of Appeal in *Target* and because of the way the argument developed, it was unnecessary for the House of Lords to look at the case or consider the point.[2] Nevertheless, in both *Bristol and West Building Society v May, May & Merrimans*[3] and *Swindle v Harrison*[4] *Brickenden* was relied upon in support of the general proposition that it was unnecessary for a principal to establish that he or she would have avoided the loss if the trustee or fiduciary had not committed the breach of duty. In neither case was the dictum accepted without qualification and after both decisions it still remained unclear whether the principle, if principle there was, had survived *Target*; and, if so, whether it applied beyond cases where the trustee or fiduciary was guilty of fraud or bad faith; and whether it made a difference that the fiduciary was guilty of a positive misrepresentation rather than non-disclosure.

1 See [1933] 3 DLR 168 cited by Blackburne J in *Nationwide Building Society v Balmer Radmore* [1999] Lloyd's Rep PN 241 at 273–4. *Brickenden* has been accepted as good authority in cases

where the claimant seeks rescission or an account of profits: see, eg, *Johnson v EBS Pensioner Trustees Ltd* [2002] EWCA Civ 164, [2002] Lloyds Rep PN 309 at [55] (where Mummery LJ considered that there was no duty of disclosure because the information was not material) and *Murad v Al-Saraj* [2005] EWCA Civ 959, [2005] WTLR 1573 at [105].

2   The case was cited in the claimant's printed case but not the subject of oral argument in the House of Lords.
3   [1996] 2 All ER 801 (Chadwick J).
4   [1997] 4 All ER 705, CA.

4.47   The question whether *Brickenden* should be applied to a claim for equitable compensation for loss caused by a fiduciary was considered at first instance by Blackburne J in *Nationwide Building Society v Balmer Radmore*,[1] where, after a comprehensive review of all the authorities, the judge said this:

> 'I take the view that, except where the fiduciary has acted dishon-
> estly or in bad faith (or its equivalent), the correct approach to
> equitable compensation for breach of fiduciary duty is to assess what
> actual loss, applying common sense and fairness, has resulted from
> the breach having regard to the scope of the duty which was broken.
> I am also of the view that nothing in the authorities compels me to
> disregard any inference which, on the evidence, can properly be
> drawn as to what would have happened if the fiduciary had per-
> formed his duty. Failing any such evidence, however, the beneficiary
> is entitled to be put in the position he was in before the breach
> occurred. This assumes that he can show that the breach was causally
> relevant to the course of action which has given rise to his loss in the
> sense that, but for the breach of duty, the beneficiary would not have
> acted in the way which has caused his loss.'

There is now clear authority that the *Brickenden* principle is not applicable to a claim of this kind. In *Gwembe Valley Development Co Ltd v Koshy and others (No 3)*[2] the Court of Appeal held that the consequences of disclosure were irrelevant in a claim to set aside a transaction or for an account of profits. The court accepted that *Brickenden* was authority for the proposition that it is not necessary to establish that the principal or beneficiary would not have entered into the transaction in order to obtain rescission or an account of profits[3] but that as with a claim for damages for tort or breach of contract:[4]

> '[W]hen determining whether any compensation, and, if so, how
> much compensation, should be paid for loss claimed to have been
> caused by actionable non-disclosure, the court is not precluded by
> authority or by principle from considering what would have hap-
> pened if the material facts had been disclosed. If the commission of
> the wrong has not caused loss to the company, why should the
> company be entitled to elect to recover compensation, as distinct
> from rescinding the transaction and stripping the director of the
> unauthorised profits made by him?'

1 [1999] Lloyd's Rep PN 241 at 278. The relevant passages in each of the earlier decisions and in *Target* are set out and analysed in full at 272–279. For this reason the passages in question are not cited here. The judge also relied on *Rama v Millar* [1996] 1 NZLR 257, PC and *Ata v American Express Bank Ltd* (26 June 1998, unreported), CA (referred to in paras 4.49 to 4.51, below).
2 [2003] EWCA Civ 1048 [2004] 1 BCLC 131.
3 See [145]–[146]: 'In considering whether the transaction should be rescinded for non-disclosure or whether the director should account for unauthorised profits, what would have happened, if the required disclosure had been made, is irrelevant.'
4 See [147]. The case involved a director's duty to disclose his interest in a pipeline contract. The Court of Appeal upheld the decision of Rimer J at [2002] 1 BCLC 478 at [277] that the claimant would still have entered into the tranasaction despite the fact that the defendant's failure to disclose his interest was dishonest and deliberate: see [150]. See also *Halton International Inc (Holdings) Ltd v Guernroy Ltd* [2005] EWHC 1968, [2006] 1 BCLC 78 (Patten J) at [155] and Harris v Kent [2007] EWHC 463 (Ch) (Briggs J) at [132].

4.48 *Swindle v Harrison*[1] (which also involved a conflict of interest and duty) provides one example in which a claim for equitable compensation against a solicitor has failed on this ground. There was no challenge to the judge's finding that Mrs Harrison would have accepted the loan from the claimant firm of solicitors even if full disclosure of the benefits which the firm was taking had been made to her.[2] Evans LJ concluded as follows:[3]

> '[T]he prima facie measure of [her] loss is the amount by which she is worse off now than she would have been if those breaches had not occurred. The failure to disclose cannot be said to have led to the making of the loan, even on a "but for" basis, precisely because disclosure of the true facts would not have affected her decision to accept it. Since she would have accepted the loan and completed the purchase, even if full disclosure had been made to her, she would have lost the value of the equity in her home in any event. She cannot recover damages or compensation for that loss, in my judgment, except on proof either that the plaintiffs acted fraudulently or in a manner equivalent to fraud or that she would not have completed the purchase if full disclosure had been made i e if the breach of duty had not occurred. She cannot do either, and in my judgment her claim for damages must fail.'

This passage appears to leave some doubt whether it is necessary to establish causation in cases of fraudulent breach of trust or fraudulent breach of fiduciary duty or whether the *Brickenden* principle should continue to apply in cases of this kind. In *Collins v Brebner (No 2)*[4] however, the Court of Appeal confirmed that causation is a necessary ingredient of the cause of action although the test of causation to be applied is analogous to that in the case of fraud, i e it is for the claimant to establish that the breach of duty induced the transaction and that the loss complained of must have flowed directly from the transaction.[5]

1 [1997] 4 All ER 705, CA. For the facts see para 4.27, above.

4.49 *Claims in equity*

2 See Evans LJ [1997] 4 All ER 705 at 713d–f.
3 [1997] 4 All ER 705 at 718f–j. The precise extent of the fraud exception (which was only mentioned by Evans LJ) has not been explored and it is not clear whether it applies to all breaches of fiduciary duty by a solicitor or only in conflict of interest and duty cases. Blackburne J considered that the approach was 'consistent with the views' of all of the members of the Court of Appeal: see *Nationwide Building Society v Balmer Radmore* [1999] Lloyd's Rep PN 241 at 278.
4 [2000] Lloyds Rep PN 587 at [49]–[63] (Tuckey LJ).
5 In *Youyang Pty Ltd v Minter Ellison Morris Fletcher* [2003] HCA 15 at [42] (the facts of which are considered in para 4.51, below) the High Court of Australia distinguished altogether between cases involving a solicitor's conflict of interest and duty and cases involving conflict of duty and duty: 'In particular, the present is not an instance, of which the decisions of the House of Lords and Privy Council respectively in *Nocton v Lord Ashburton* and *Brickenden v London Loan and Savings Co* are the most celebrated examples, of a solicitor who has had financial transactions with a client, getting the client to prefer the personal interests of the solicitor. Thus, in *Nocton*, one transaction involved the solicitor getting the client to release from his mortgage a property over which, by that release, the solicitor obtained further security for a mortgage of his own. In these cases, as Viscount Haldane put it, a court of equity may order the solicitor to replace the property improperly acquired from a client or to make compensation if that property has been lost.'

4.49 *Collins v Brebner* (*No 2*) involved the misapplication of client funds which were to be used for the purchase of 50% of the shares in a Spanish company. For reasons which were never fully explained the solicitor paid the funds in breach of trust to a related third party whom he knew had no entitlement to the money. The transaction was nevertheless completed and the claimant received the shares for which he had bargained. The Court of Appeal, applying *Target*, held that the claimant had suffered no loss as a consequence of the breach of trust and could not recover the amount of his investment (although they awarded him damages for certain consequential losses).[1] The facts of *Rama v Millar*,[2] which provides another example, were more complex. The case involved a conflict of interest and duty arising out of a partnership to trade in swaps. The claimant and defendant were partners and in order to provide partnership capital, the defendant took out a loan facility from the Bank of New Zealand on which he alone was personally liable. When the parties faced a major loss, the defendant settled his liability to the bank by assigning certain partnership claims to it without the consent of the claimant and against his known wishes. The claimant commenced proceedings for breach of fiduciary duty. The Privy Council found that in a position of deadlock, it was a term of the partnership that the defendant was entitled to 'proceed to settle the matter without further delay unless Mr Millar was able and willing to provide a financial indemnity to Mr Rama'.[3] Because Mr Millar was unable to show that he would have been able to do so, his claim also failed.[4] The conclusion, therefore, to be drawn from these cases is that the test for causation is broadly the same at common law and in equity at least so far as the conduct of the claimant is concerned.

1 [2001] Lloyd's Rep PN 587 at [65]–[72].
2 [1996] 1 NZLR 257.
3 [1996] 1 NZLR 257 at 261 lines 25–35, per Lord Nicholls.

4 It was common ground that he was entitled to recover a commitment fee of NZ$70,000. which the Privy Council did not disturb, although it is hard to see why, in the light of the above finding, Rama was entitled to recover anything at all: see 260 and 262, lines 3–8.

(b) The conduct of third parties

4.50   In chapter 3[1] we considered the cases in which the court has approached the conduct of third parties at common law by valuing the claimant's chance of achieving a different outcome. In *Rama v Millar* the New Zealand Court of Appeal had awarded judgment on the basis that the partnership could have achieved a much better settlement if the defendant had acted in good faith. Lord Nicholls said this:[2]

'There is another difficulty with the conclusion of the Court of Appeal. The partners were in a strong bargaining position against the BNZ but in a weak position against IHD and PB Finance. The terms of settlement which the Court of Appeal regarded as realistic involved no contribution from the BNZ but a significant contribution from IHD or PB Finance, or both of them. Despite the terms of the letter of 17 August and with all respect to the Court of Appeal, it must be highly questionable whether in practice a speedy settlement could have been effected on these terms.'

In the light of the finding that Mr Rama was entitled to settle the claims in a position of deadlock, it was unnecessary for the Board to consider how best to evaluate the prospect that settlement might have been achieved on more advantageous terms and, if so, whether the basis of assessment should be the same as the evaluation of a chance at common law. It is unlikely that the court is *bound* to adopt this approach in the light of the authorities discussed above. We consider that loss of a chance principles should apply just as much to a claim for breach of fiduciary duty as a claim for damages at common law. However, and what little judicial sentiment there is suggests that it is more likely that the court will simply assess loss on the basis of a balance of probabilities but with the benefit of hindsight. As Rix J put it at first instance in *Ata v American Express Bank Ltd*:[3]

'In the first place the element of causation and the need for a plaintiff to prove his loss are emphasised. Secondly, the element of hindsight is used not to enable a plaintiff to demand favourable assumptions in his favour, but to enable the court to evaluate in the round what has happened and what, if anything, the plaintiff has in fact lost by the breach of trust complained of. Thirdly, the need for common-sense is underlined.'

1 See para 3. 19ff, above.

207

4.51   *Claims in equity*

2 [1996] 1 NZLR 257 at 261, lines 46–53.

3 (26 June 1998, unreported), CA. But see now *Take Ltd* v *BSM Marketing Ltd*, HHJ Toulmin QC (unreported, 31 July 2007) at [10]–[16] in which it was agreed that loss of a chance principles applied to a breach of fiduciary duty.

(c) Causation in fact

4.51   There also appears to be a difference between the position at common law and in equity in relation to causation in fact. At common law, it is not enough for the claimant to show that the defendant's breach of duty was the occasion for his loss. He or she must also establish that it was an effective or dominant cause. According to McLachlin J in *Canson Enterprises Ltd v Broughton & Co*,[1] the position in equity is as follows:

> 'The requirement that loss flow from the breach also assists in determining responsibility for the acts of strangers or third parties. If the breach permits a third party to take an unlawful advantage causing loss to the plaintiff, the fiduciary will be liable because there is a causal link between the breach and the loss. This was the case in *Caffrey v Darby*, where a trustee whose neglect permitted another to abscond with trust property was held liable for that loss. Where, on the other hand, the plaintiff suffers loss as a result of the act of a third party after the fiduciary's obligation has terminated and the plaintiff has taken control of the property, the result will be otherwise.'

Youyang Pty Ltd v Minter Ellison Morris Fletcher[2] provides a modern example of a case in which the defendant's breach of duty might not be regarded at common law as the effective cause of the claimant's loss or where the loss might be treated as too remote. The claimant was an investor who subscribed for preference shares in an investment vehicle. A firm of solicitors were instructed to receive funds from the investors and to use part of the subscription moneys to buy a bearer deposit certificate issued by a prime bank in Australia which undertook to pay the bearer an amount equivalent to the amount of the subscription moneys after 10 years (and provided security in the event of insolvency). The balance of the subscription moneys were to be used in speculation by the investment company. At the investment company's direction the defendant firm paid part of the subscription moneys to the prime bank and received in return a letter acknowledging the deposit which was addressed to the investment company. The balance of the subscription moneys were then paid over to the investment company. The prime bank's letter of acknowledgment was not a bearer certificate. It provided the claimant with no security in respect of its investment. About a year after the investment, and at the request of the investment company, the claimant executed a deed poll authorising the withdrawal of the funds on deposit with the prime bank and the deposit of those funds with an overseas bank. No deposit certificate was obtained this time either. The funds were withdrawn and lent to an associate of the investment company. Two and a half years later, a provisional liquidator was appointed to the investment company. It was later wound up, and the claimant lost the whole of its investment. A claim for breach of trust failed at first instance and in the Court of Appeal of New South Wales because the court was not satisfied that the claimant would have refused to go ahead if he had known that the deposit certificate had not been issued, he had agreed to the substitution of one investment for the other and also because the ultimate loss of the fund was wholly unrelated to the original breach of trust. The High Court of Australia reversed this decision because it was the duty of the solicitors not to release the funds without obtaining a deposit certificate.[3] Some of the statements made in the case suggest that the court to a stricter view of causation than the House of Lords in *Target*.[4] However, the facts are very similar to the early English decision in *Caffrey v Darby*[5] (referred to in the extract set out above) where trustees failed to get in certain trust property which was left in the hands of a beneficiary. The beneficiary committed the property to a third party who went bankrupt and the assets were seized. The trustees were held liable for breach of trust.

1 (1991) 85 DLR (4th) 129 at 163c–e.
2 [2003] HCA 15, (2003) CLR 484. The decision was followed by the Supreme Court of Queensland in *Jessup v Lawyers Private Mortgage Pty Ltd* [2006] QCA 432 where solicitors (who were used to hold funds of investors in a contributory mortgage scheme but dispersed it without authority) were also held to be in breach of trust.
3 See the judgment of the Court at [63]:

> 'The execution of the Deed Poll and the implementation of these steps thereunder could be of significance on questions of causation if what had been brought about was the release of an existing bearer certificate of deposit and its replacement by a 'non-bearer' instrument. But that was not the order of events that transpired. Youyang was not provided at any stage with the security for which it had bargained. It is not to the point that, in addition to the breaches of trust by Minters, there may also have been dishonest and discreditable subsequent acts by third parties which led to the loss of the funds. To present the case by fixing upon those subsequent acts, to adopt the remarks of Bowen LJ in *Magnus v Queensland National Bank*, would be "an ocular illusion", because the loss of the trust funds occurred as soon as the trustee wrongly disbursed them, at the completion on 24 September 1993.'

4 See, in particular, [69]:

> 'The trust moneys were lost when paid out in breach of trust. That is the *iniuria* with which equity is concerned, not the failure of the investment transaction. By analogy with common law terms, the damage was then suffered; subsequent events went to quantification.'

5 (1801) 6 Ves 488, 31 ER 1159 Sir William Grant MR said:

> '[I]f they have been guilty of negligence, they must be responsible for any loss in any way to the property: for whatever may be the immediate cause, the property would not have been in a situation to sustain that loss, if it had not been for their negligence. If they

had taken possession of the property, it would not have been in his possession. If the loss had happened by fire, lightning or any other accident, that would not be an excuse to them, if guilty of previous negligence.'

The decision was followed by Lord Cottenham in *Clough v Bond* (1801) 6 Ves 488 at 496 and 31 ER 1159 at 1162 (where it is attributed to Lord Eldon). Both were cited with approval by Lord Browne-Wilkinson in *Target* [1996] AC 421 at 434E:

'Even if the immediate cause of the loss is the dishonesty or failure of a third party, the trustee is liable to make good that loss to the trust estate if, but for the breach, the loss would not have occurred.'

4.52 Liability is not unlimited, however. In *Canson*, the defendant solicitors acted for the claimants, two joint venture companies, in relation to their purchase of development land. The proposal was put to them by an agent, to whom they agreed to pay a 15% commission if the deal was completed. The defendant solicitors also acted for the vendor of the property but failed to disclose to the claimants that the vendor was a company formed by the agent solely to purchase the property and 'flip' it to the claimants at an increase in price. It was common ground that if the claimants had known this, they would not have bought the property. Following the purchase the claimants proceeded with their development. It proved to be a disaster because of the negligence of their contractors, against whom they obtained judgment but were unable to recover in full. They then sued the defendants. The Supreme Court of Canada held that the defendants were liable for the amount of the secret profit made by the agent which the defendants had not reported to them but not liable for the failure of the development because of the negligence of the third parties. The solicitor had ceased to act by then and the claimants were themselves responsible for choosing the engineers and pile-drivers whose negligence caused it to fail. Although the members of the court reached their conclusion by very different routes, all were agreed that the losses were not recoverable and both the majority and the minority emphasised the question of control. Where the trustee or fiduciary is in control of the relevant asset, a failure to protect it adequately will lead to liability. Where, however, the trustee and fiduciary has ceased to act in a fiduciary capacity, independent actions of third parties will break the chain of causation.[1] Stevenson J, who delivered a short judgment concurring with the result, put it most succinctly:[2]

'In my view a court of equity, applying principles of fairness, would and should draw the line at calling upon the fiduciary to compensate for losses arising as a result of the unanticipated neglect of the engineers and pile-driving contractor. The fiduciary had nothing to do with their selection, their control, their contractual or bonding obligations. It follows that I agree with the trial judge and the British Columbia Court of Appeal that these losses are too remote, not in the sense of failing the "but for" test but in being so unrelated and independent that they should not, in fairness, be attributed to the defendant's breach of duty.'[3]

Swindle v Harrison[4] can also be explained on the same basis. Mrs. Harrison's losses were caused by her choice to invest in a restaurant scheme proposed by her son which were unrelated to and independent of the claimants' breach of fiduciary duty. Their involvement came to an end when the purchase was completed and their breaches of duty had nothing to do with the purchase itself. *Youyang* can be distinguished from both cases on the basis that the 'but for' test was satisfied. At all times the subscription agreement provided that the investment company was under an obligation to provide substitute security and the solicitors were only authorised to release the relevant funds against receipt of the relevant deposit certificate. Furthermore, there was no evidence that the claimant would have been prepared to give up the first security without insisting on the investment company providing a substitute security (to which it was contractually entitled).[5] *Caffrey v Darby* is also distinguishable because the defendants in that case were under a continuing duty to get in the trust estate which they failed to carry out.

1 See La Forest J (1991) 85 DLR (4th) 129 at 146b-f and McLachlin J at 164b-g,
2 (1991) 85 DLR (4th) 129 at 162e-g, cited with approval by Lord Browne-Wilkinson in *Target Holdings Ltd v Redferns* [19961 AC 421 at 439G and 440A.
3 Again, this language is not dissimilar to the language used by common lawyers in relation to the *SaamCo* principle. It may be that the true analysis is that the scope of fiduciary duties determines the wider measure of recovery in equity.
4 [1997] 4 All ER 705, CA.
5 [2003] HCA 15, (2003) 212 CLR 484 at [61]–[63].

(d) Remoteness of damage

4.53 In chapter 3[1] we considered remoteness of damage at common law. Again, there is clear authority that foreseeability of damage will not restrict recovery in equity in the same way.[2] But in *Guerin v R*[3] the Crown was authorised by a native American band to negotiate a lease of a golf club on its land on specific terms. In breach of its fiduciary duty to them the Office of Indian Affairs negotiated a lease on terms which were less advantageous than those authorised and on which the band would not have been prepared to contract.[4] They commenced proceedings for breach of fiduciary duty. The trial judge awarded damages not by reference to the value of the land subject to the authorised terms (which the golf club itself would not have accepted) but by reference to the increased development value of the land. The value of the land had escalated due to its development potential in a way that was wholly unforeseen at the date of breach and he awarded compensation of $10m. The Supreme Court of Canada upheld the award of damages on the basis that equitable compensation was a substitute for specific restitution and that the Crown was liable to restore its value however unforeseen the cost of replacement would be.[5] Accordingly, the band was awarded the lost opportunity of

4.54 *Claims in equity*

selling the land for residential development. The analogy with specific restitution is less than convincing in this context[6] but the award seems appropriate subject only to the issue of foreseeability. If the Crown had fulfilled its duty, no lease would have been concluded and the band would have been free to develop the land some years later when land values had increased. The development value of the land genuinely represented the band's loss.

1 See para 3.49ff. In chapter 9, we also consider the measure of damages in relation to the purchase of land where changes in the market are likely to have the most significant effect. Recent authorities suggest that there may is less of a difference between the approach to the recoverability at common law and in equity: see paras 9.102–9.124. Again, the critical issue is likely to be the scope of the duty.
2 See *Canson Ltd v Broughton & Co* (1991) 85 DLR (4th) 129 at 162e–g, cited with approval by Lord Browne-Wilkinson in *Target Holdings Ltd v Redferns* [19961 AC 421 at 439G and 440A. For another Canadian example see also *Hodgkinson v Simms* [1994] 3 SCR 377, (1994) DLR 4th 161 (and, in particular, the minority speech of McLachlin J who would have refused relief on the grounds that the damage was too remote). The case is discussed in more detail in para 4.59 n 1, below.
3 (1984) 13 DLR (4th) 321.
4 See Wilson J (1984) 13 DLR (4th) 321 at 355.
5 See Wilson J (1984) 13 DLR (4th) 321 at 365–7 and Dickson J at 334.
6 See Davies 'Causation, Foreseesbility and Remoteness' in Youdan (ed) *Equity, Fiduciaries and Trusts* (1993) 309. See also the analysis of McLachlin J in *Canson* (1991) 85 DLR (4th) 129 at 160d–g.

(e) Contributory negligence and mitigation

4.54 In England the defence of contributory negligence is purely a statutory one and the Law Reform (Contributory Negligence) 1945 does not apply to a claim for breach of trust or breach of fiduciary duty. In *Day v Mead*,[1] however, the New Zealand Court of Appeal held that contributory negligence was available as a defence to a claim for breach of fiduciary duty by analogy with the equivalent statutory defence in New Zealand.[2] A majority of the Supreme Court of Canada in *Canson Enterprises Ltd v Broughton & Co*[3] agreed with the approach although the point did not arise for decision. In *Nationwide Building Society v Balmer Radmore*[4] Blackburne J had to consider whether the same approach should be applied by an English court. In deciding that contributory negligence was not a defence to a claim of breach of fiduciary duty in English law, the judge recognised that English courts take a narrower view of the conduct which amounts to a breach of fiduciary duty than courts in New Zealand and Canada. He said this:[5]

'The kind of fiduciary duty with which I am concerned in these twelve cases is, as Mr Patten pointed out, one in which, following *Mothew*,[6] a breach must be intentional. The fiduciary cannot be unconsciously disloyal. The betrayal of trust inherent in the breach is necessarily a disloyal act. This feature which, following *Mothew*, is how English law regards breach of fiduciary duty, appears to be different from (and more stringent than) what needs to be shown in New Zealand and Canada. In *Day v Mead* Sir Robin Cooke P (at page 447) quoted with approval the trial judge's findings in relation to breach of fiduciary duty including his observation that the defendant solicitor had "acted quite innocently". In his judgment in *Canson Enterprises Ltd v Broughton & Co* La Forest J (at page 150) referred to the fact that the New Zealand Court of Appeal "agreed that Mead, *though he acted quite innocently*, was, having regard to the circumstances, in breach of fiduciary duties ..." (my emphasis). The "measure of duty" is not, therefore, the same.

In English law contributory negligence has never been a defence to an intentional tort: in such cases the 1945 Act has no application. By parity of approach I can see no good reason why equity, concerned as Lord Dunedin remarked in *Nocton v Lord Ashburton* [1914] AC 932 at page 963 "... to keep persons in a fiduciary capacity up to their duty", should adopt a less rigorous approach.

I therefore take the view that where, in order to establish a breach of fiduciary duty, it is necessary to find that the fiduciary was consciously disloyal to the person to whom his duty was owed, the fiduciary is disabled from asserting that the other contributed, by his own want of care for his own interests, to the loss which he suffered flowing from the breach. To do otherwise, as Gummow J pointed out in his article in "Equity, Fiduciaries and Trusts", risks subverting the fundamental principle of undivided and unremitting loyalty which is at the core of the fiduciary's obligations. In his article he pointed to the "unwisdom of entangling the already complex law as to fiduciary duties with notions of contributory negligence".'

The decision was approved by the House of Lords in *Standard Chartered Bank v Pakistan Shipping Corpn (No 2)* and it can now be taken as clear authority for the proposition that contributory negligence is not a defence to a claim for breach of fiduciary duty.[7] The reasoning is that breach of fiduciary duty is analogous to deceit at common law and because both depend on intentional wrongdoing the defence of contributory negligence is not available. The position must be the same for breaches of trust which are deliberate or accessory liability (which depends on dishonesty). It is also suggested that the defence of contributory negligence is not available in answer to claims for breach of trust which are strict (such as the implied trust to hold client funds and not to release them without authority).[8]

1 [1987] 2 NZLR 443.
2 The breach of duty was a failure to advise the claimant to take independent advice before investing in a company of which the defendant was a director and shareholder. The judge found that the defendant was innocent and there were no findings of negligence at common law.

3 (1991) 85 DLR (4th) 129 at 151–2, per La Forest J.
4 [1999] Lloyd's Rep PN 241. See also *Corporacion Nacional del Cobr de Chile v Sogemin Metals Ltd* [1997] 1 WLR 1396 at 1402–1405 where Carnwarth J took the view that the claimant's contributory negligence would not amount to a defence to claims of conspiracy and breach of fiduciary duty unless it was so egregious that he could be said to be the author of his own misfortune.
5 [1999] Lloyd's Rep PN 241 at 281–2.
6 [1998] Ch 1
7 [2002] UKHL 43, [2003] 1 AC 959 at [18] (Lord Hoffmann):

'In the case of fraudulent misrepresentation, however, I agree with Mummery J in *Alliance and Leicester Building Society v Edgestop Ltd* [1993] 1 WLR 1462 that there is no common law defence of contributory negligence. (See also Carnwath J in *Corporacion Nacional del Cobre de Chile v Sogemin Metals Ltd* [1997] 1 WLR 1396 and Blackburne J in *Nationwide Building Society v Thimbleby & Co* [1999] Lloyd's Rep PN 359.) It follows that, in agreement with the majority in the Court of Appeal, I think that no apportionment under the 1945 Act is possible.'

8 See paras 4.5–4.9, above.

4.55 Again, the traditional view is that a principal or beneficiary who is the victim of a breach of fiduciary duty or breach of trust is not in the same position as the victim of a tort or a breach of contract although his or her actions may prevent recovery if they are so unreasonable that they break the chain of causation. This view was expressed by McLachlin J in *Canson*:[1]

'[W]hile a plaintiff will not be required to act in a reasonable and prudent manner as might be required in negligence or contract, losses stemming from the plaintiff's unreasonable actions will be barred. This is also sound policy in the law of fiduciary duty. In negligence and contract the law limits the actions of the parties who are expected to pursue their own best interest. Each is expected to continue to look after their own interests after a breach or tort, and so a duty of mitigation is imposed. In contrast, the hallmark of fiduciary relationship is that the fiduciary, at least within a certain scope, is expected to pursue the best interest of the client. It may not be fair to allow the fiduciary to complain when the client fails forthwith to shoulder the fiduciary's burden. This approach to mitigation accords with the basic rule of equitable compensation that the injured party will be reimbursed for all losses flowing directly from the breach. When a plaintiff, after due notice and opportunity, fails to take the most obvious steps to alleviate his or her losses, then we may rightly say that "the plaintiff has become the author of his own misfortune." At this point, the plaintiff's failure to mitigate may become so egregious that it is no longer sensible to say that the losses which followed were caused by the fiduciary's breach. But until that point, mitigation will not be required.'

In *Nationwide Building Society v Balmer Radmore*[2] Blackburne J adopted the same approach. He held that the duty to mitigate at common law does not apply to the victim of a breach of a fiduciary duty. He nevertheless held that there is a point at which the fiduciary ceases to be liable:

> 'This does not mean that the conduct of the person to whom the fiduciary duty is owed is irrelevant. There comes a point, following breach of fiduciary duty, where the loss is too remote from the breach to be said to be a loss flowing from it (as exemplified in *Canson Enterprises Ltd v Boughton & Co*) or where the claimant's own conduct comes into play as a factor determining the loss which he can recover.

It is not clear, however, whether *Canson* will continue to be followed on this point. In *Standard Chartered Bank v Pakistan National Shipping Corp*[3] Toulson J rejected the claimant's submission that the proper approach to mitigation in a claim for deceit was that taken by McLachlin J in a claim for deceit and held that the same rule on avoidable loss applied for the purpose of assessing damages in an action for deceit or conspiracy as in any claim based on tort or breach of contract. He rejected McLachlin J's analysis for a number of cogent reasons and it may be therefore that this issue will need to be considered authoritatively by the Court of Appeal. The facts of *Nocton v Lord Ashburton* may be worth remembering at this point.[4] Lord Ashburton chose to lend money a second time despite a clear warning from Nocton's partners, yet this conduct did not prevent recovery.

1 (1991) 85 DLR (4th) 129 at 162e–g.
2 [1999] Lloyd's Rep PN 241 at 282. See also *Extrasure Travel Insurances Ltd v Scattergood* [2002] EWHC 3093 (Ch) (Jonathan Crow) at [159] where the judge stated that he was not satisfied that a cestui que trust is necessarily under the same duty to mitigate as a claimant for damages at common law.
3 [1999] 1 All ER (Comm) 417 at 429–35. The case was a strong one because it concerned the actions of the claimant after it had discovered the fraud.
4 [1914] AC 932. See para. 4.24, above.

4.56 In chapter 3[1] we considered the duty of a claimant at common law to mitigate his loss by commencing or pursuing litigation against third parties. Whatever the precise limits of the duty to mitigate a breach of trust or fiduciary duty, it is clear that in equity a claimant 'is not required to engage in hazardous litigation in order to mitigate his loss'.[2]

1 See para 3.62ff, above.
2 *Target Holdings Ltd v Redferns* [1996] AC 421 at 440B per Lord Browne-Wilkinson discussing *Bishopsgate Investment Management Ltd v Maxwell (No 2)* [1994] 1 All ER 261.

3 Measure of compensation

4.57 Although they may often correspond, the measure of compensation in equity is not always the same as an award of damages at common law. The function of damages at common law, even in a claim for fraud, is primarily compensatory. It is to compensate the claimant, so far as it is possible in money terms, for the defendant's breach of duty. Compensation in equity is primarily restitutionary. Its function is usually to compensate the claimant in money terms for the deprivation of a particular asset or the defendant's inability to restore it. In *Target Holdings Ltd v Redferns*[1] Lord Browne-Wilkinson stated that the basis upon which it is to be assessed as follows:

> 'The quantum is fixed at the date of judgment at which date, according to the circumstances then pertaining, the compensation is assessed at the figure then necessary to put the trust estate or the beneficiary back into the position it would have been in had there been no breach.'

1 [1996] AC 421 at 437D.

4.58 In equity, it is the trustee's duty to repay to the fund or the beneficiaries the amount which would be required to buy in the same asset at judgment together with any interest or income lost. If the relevant asset has increased or decreased in price by the date of judgment, this is a risk which the trustee must take. In the well-known case *Re Dawson*[1] the executors of the deceased's estate had funds in both Australia and New Zealand. One of the trustees allowed £4,700 to be paid out of the New Zealand assets for investment in Australia. A third party absconded with the money and the question was whether the defaulting trustee should restore the money by reference to the currency rate at the date of breach (which favoured him), or by reference to the currency rate at the date of judgment (which favoured the beneficiaries). It was held that the rate prevailing at the date of judgment should be applied.[2] Street J stated:[3]

> '[T]he distinction between common law damages and relief against a defaulting trustee is strikingly demonstrated by reference to the actual form of relief granted in equity in respect of breach of trust. The form of relief is couched in terms appropriate to require the defaulting trustee to restore to the estate the assets of which he deprived it. Increases in market values between the date of breach and the date of recoupment are for the trustee's account: the effect of such increases would, at common law, be excluded from the computation of damages: but in equity a defaulting trustee must make good the loss by restoring to the estate the assets of which he deprived it notwithstanding that market values have increased in the meantime. The obligation to restore to the estate the assets of which he deprived it necessarily connotes that, where a monetary compensation is paid in lieu of restoring assets, that compensation is to be assessed by reference to the value of the assets at the date of restoration and not at the date of deprivation. In this sense the obligation is a continuing

one and ordinarily, if the assets are for some reason not restored in specie, it will fall for quantification at the date when recoupment is to be effected, and not before.'

The fund was situated in New Zealand and would have remained there had there been no breach of trust. The beneficiaries were not penalised for the fall in the value of the Australian dollar and the trustee was obliged to purchase sufficient New Zealand pounds and pay sufficient interest to make good the deficiency in the fund.[4]

1 [1966] 2 NSWR 211.
2 At the date of the decision the common law rule was that a creditor of a foreign debt had to convert it at the date on which the debt fell due: *Re United Railways of Havana* [1961] AC 1007. This is not, of course, the position at common law now. It is not clear what the prevailing position was in New South Wales at the time the case was decided.
3 [1966] 2 NSWR 211 at 215 lines 13–27.
4 In chapter 9 we suggest that in practice there is no default rule provided by the valuation method any longer and it may well be that in 2007 damages at common law would be assessed in a similar way to the assessment of compensation in equity in 1966: see paras 9.118–9.124.

4.59 Where a trustee's breach of duty results in the loss or destruction of an asset and the asset is real property or a stable investment, the amount which must be restored to the trust or beneficiaries should be relatively easy to establish, as *Re Dawson* demonstrates. Where, however, equitable compensation is awarded for a breach of duty which does not involve particular assets but, say, non-disclosure of information, or where the assets of the trust can be freely traded and are perpetually fluctuating in value, the amounts which the principal or trustee is obliged to restore may be more difficult to determine (and the analogy with specific restitution is not so helpful). Nevertheless, the recent decision in *Harris v Kent*[1] illustrates the principle that even in cases involving assets of this kind the trustee remains liable to compensate the beneficiaries for the full amount of loss which, with the benefit of hindsight, they can be seen to have suffered. The claimant and defendants were shareholders in a company and in return for a loan to the company the defendants agreed to transfer 50% of the shares to the claimant and this agreement was held to have created a trust of the shares for the benefit of the claimant. The defendants ignored their agreement with the claimant (who went bankrupt) and floated the company. Briggs J found that the defendants held 50% of the shares on trust for the claimant and that the flotation of the company and the subsequent sales of tranches of its shares amounted to a breach of trust. He also found that if the defendants had complied with their fiduciary duty, the claimant could not have objected to the flotation and would not have avoided bankruptcy. But he also reached the conclusion that the claimant's trustee in bankruptcy would have realised the shares in a professional and orderly fashion (after a one year covenant against their sale in the open market had come to an end) and, on the expert evidence, this would have yielded a higher price for the shares than the defendants obtained either on flotation or the subsequent sale of their remaining shares. He held that the defendants were liable to compensate the claimant on this basis. He stated:[2]

> 'It may be that Mr and Mrs Kent will harbour a sense of grievance at this outcome, since the amount so ascertained exceeds that which may be derived from a strict application of the rule against profits by trustees, or even from a strict application of the old pre *Target v Redferns* principle based upon the trustee's obligation to make restitution to the trust fund. It also substantially exceeds the amount which Mr Harris might have realised had he pursued a proprietary claim to the shares presently held by Mr and Mrs Kent in plc, and to the proceeds of the intermediate sales which have occurred. In my judgment however, that sense of grievance is misplaced, for the following reasons. First, the difference between a valuation of £715,756.50 at the end of August 1999, and a valuation of £795,285 as at the end of July 2000 would be substantially eaten into by the accrual of interest on the earlier amount between those two dates. Secondly, a beneficiary is entitled, as Mr Atkins acknowledged, to choose both between compensation and an account of profits, and between compensation and the pursuit of proprietary claims. Mr Atkins did not suggest that there was any rule which prevents a beneficiary from pursing a proprietary claim and seeking compensation for any shortfall. Thirdly, the pursuit of a proprietary claim on its own necessarily binds the beneficiary to the ups and downs, benefits or vicissitudes in the performance of the traceable assets between the date of breach and the date when they are finally returned to the beneficiary's control. As I have said, while the law entitles the beneficiary to take the benefit of the ups, there is no reason in principle while he should be shackled to the detriment of the downs, caused as it will have been by the trustee's refusal in the meantime to restore the traceable assets to the beneficiary. Finally, the law may occasionally operate harshly towards trustees, *pour encourager les autres*.'

1   [2007] EWHC 463 (Ch) at [130]–[157]. Compare *Simms v Hodgkinson* [1994] 3 SCR 377, (1994) DLR 4th 161 where the claimant successfully claimed compensation for breach of fiduciary duty against his accountant and investment adviser who failed to disclose a personal interest in a tax shelter scheme which he recommended to the claimant. The judge at first instance found that this was a no transaction case and a majority of the Supreme Court of Canada awarded compensation on the basis that the claimant recovered the initial investment and his consequential losses. Contractual damages were also awarded on the same basis. McLachlin J (who delivered the opinion of the minority) would have refused relief because the breaches of duty were not causative of loss and were not reasonably foreseeable. It is doubtful whether an English court would have reached the conclusion that the defendant was a fiduciary.

2   [156]–[157].

4.60   In *Harris v Kent* the court found as a fact that the claimant's shares would have been sold by his trustee in bankruptcy at a particular date and it was unnecessary to have resort to any presumptions about their realisation. But in a number of authorities there has been a debate about whether in relation to shares which can be freely traded it should be presumed in favour of the beneficiary and against the trustee that the shares would be realised at the height of the market. In *Robinson v Robinson*[1] the Court of Appeal considered a claim against a trustee where he had an option of investing in different funds. Lord Cranworth stated:[2]

> 'Where a man is bound by covenants to do one of two things, and does neither, in an action by the covenantee, the measure of damage is in general the loss arising by reason of the covenantor having failed to do that which is least not that which is most beneficial to the covenantee: and the same principle may be applied by analogy to the case of a trustee failing to invest in either of two modes equally lawful by the terms of the trust.'

In *Guerin*,[3] however, the Supreme Court of Canada adopted an entirely different approach. Wilson J stated:

> 'Just as it is to be presumed that a beneficiary would have wished to sell his securities at the highest price available during the period they were wrongfully withheld from him by the trustee (see *McNeil v Fultz* (1906) 38 SCR 198), so also it should be presumed that the band would have wished to develop its land in the most advantageous way possible during the period covered by the unauthorized lease. In this respect also the principles applicable to determine damages for breach of trust are to be contrasted with the principles applicable to determine damages for breach of contract. In contract it would have been necessary for the band to prove that it would have developed the land; in equity a presumption is made to that effect.'

Despite the authority of *Robinson v Robinson,* the approach in *Guerin* was initially preferred by English courts and the decision was treated as authority for the proposition that in valuing trust assets or opportunities, all presumptions are to be made against the trustee and in favour of the beneficiary.[4] Accordingly, it was to be presumed that assets would be sold or realised at their highest value and at the most opportune time.

1   (1851) 1 De GM & G 247.
2   (1851) 1 De GM & G 247 at 257.
3   (1984) 13 DLR (4th) 321 at 367.
4   See *Jaffray v Marshall* [1993] 1 WLR 1285 (Nicholas Stewart QC) at 1290E–1293C. The case was disapproved by the House of Lords in *Target Holdings Ltd v Redferns* [1996] AC 421 at 440E–F. See also *Nestle v National Westminster Bank plc* [1993] 1 WLR 1260 at 1268C–1267A, CA per Dillon LJ. *Robinson v Robinson* was not cited in the former. In the latter Dillon LJ

considered the decision 'flawed'. The decision of the House of Lords in *Hilton v Barker Booth & Eastwood* [2005] UKHL 8, [2005] 1 WLR 567 (and, in particular, the statement made by Lord Walker at [44] (quoted in full at the end of para 4.36, above) is also hard to reconcile with *Robinson v Robinson*. In that case the judge found at first instance that the defendants ought to have advised the claimant that they could not act for him and that if they had done so the transaction would still have gone ahead. The House of Lords held, however, that the defendants were liable for the subsequent breach of duty in failing to advise him about the vendor's bankruptcy and criminal conviction. There was, however, no discussion in any of the speeches about causation or measure of compensation (although these issues were addressed in the printed cases).

4.61 The position was made even more confused by uncertainty about the relevant rule to be applied at common law. In *Michael v Hart*[1] the claimant sued the defendant stockbroker for selling shares in breach of contract. Wills J found as follows:

'[I]t seems to me that the plaintiff is entitled to all the advantages that would have been his or that might have been his if the contract had been carried out. Amongst those advantages was the right to sell the shares whenever he chose during the period over which the transactions were to run, and at different times different prices might have been realised. No doubt the plaintiff would in fact never have realised the best prices that ruled during the period. But I think I am right in saying that the Courts have never allowed the improbability of the plaintiff's obtaining the highest prices to be taken into consideration for the purpose of reducing damages. The defendants are wrongdoers, and every presumption is to be made against them. In my opinion the plaintiff is entitled to the highest prices which were obtainable during the period during which he had the option of selling.'

In *Ata v American Express Bank Ltd*[2] the Court of Appeal had to consider both lines of authority and whether presumptions were to be made against a wrongdoer at common law or in equity. The court reached the conclusion that no presumptions were to be made in either jurisdiction, overruled *Michael v Hart* and approved *Robinson v Robinson,* and held as follows:[3]

'Thus in a claim for equitable compensation it is necessary to prove loss and causation. Accordingly, the judgment of Wills J in Michael v Hart cannot be supported even if confined to claims for equitable compensation for breach of trust or fiduciary duty.'

The position can now be stated with greater certainty: the measure of damages at common law and measure of compensation in equity are quantified by the same principles. Although there is no prima facie rule that damages are to be assessed either at the date of breach or by reference to the valuation method, the claimant must establish on the evidence precisely what loss he would have avoided if there had been no breach of trust or fiduciary duty. Where the loss arises because of the failure to buy or sell an asset, the claimant must prove when and at what price the asset would have been bought or sold in order to recover compensation.

1 [1901] 2 KB 867. The common law was not consistent either, however: see *The Playa Larga* [1983] 2 Lloyd's Rep 171.
2 (1998) Times, 26 June, CA.
3 Transcript at 23. Although Nestle was cited, no mention was made of Dillon LJ's criticism of *Robinson v Robinson*.

4   Set off

4.62 A defaulting trustee or fiduciary is not entitled to set off gains on one breach of trust or breach of fiduciary duty against losses suffered by the beneficiaries arising out of another breach of trust or duty.[1] This principle applies to fiduciaries. It does not, however, apply to an accessory liable for dishonest assistance.[2]

1 *Bartlett v Barclays Bank Trust Co Ltd* [1980] Ch 515 and *A-G of Zambia v Meer Care & Desai* [2007] 1540 (Ch) (Peter Smith J) at [25].
2 *A-G of Zambia v Meer Care & Desai*, above at [26].

5   Interest

(a) History of the equitable jurisdiction

4.63 Until recently, it was considered that there was no power to award interest as damages at common law and that the jurisdiction to award interest on damages was statutory only.[1] In contrast, courts of equity have always awarded interest under their inherent jurisdiction. In the nineteenth century when rates of interest were very stable, the court usually awarded interest at a rate of 4%. Where, however, special circumstances existed the court would either award interest at the higher rate of 5% or award compound interest. The special circumstances usually involved the trustee himself making a profit from the trust. At the same time the court had a power to award interest on the return of money or investments when making an order for rescission. Where the contract was induced by a fraud, a higher rate would again be applied.[2] However, in the light of the decision of the House of Lords in *Sempra Metals Ltd v Inland Revenue*[3] the distinction between the power to award interest at common law and in equity may be of less importance than it has been in the past. The jurisdiction to award compound interest may remain of some significance where the claimant is unable to demonstrate a loss (either because the claimant has borrowed money or because he or she has lost the opportunity to invest it)[4] but the defendant is a fiduciary and is liable to pay compound interest for the reasons set out below. For this reason the power to award interest in equity continues to deserve separate but brief treatment.

1 See the Law Commission Report 'Pre-Judgment Interest on Debts and Damages' (Law Com No 287), para 2.3: 'The English courts have long been reluctant to award interest at common law ... interest is largely a matter for either contract or statute. The court's inherent power to award interest is largely confined to a few limited circumstances, such as where interest is claimed as special damages or under the equitable or Admiralty jurisdictions.'
2 See the analysis of Dunn LJ in *O'Sullivan v Management Agency and Music Ltd* [1985] QB 428 at 449E–458B, CA.
3 [2007] UKHL 34, [2007] 3 WLR 354. In that case the House of Lords chose to depart from the decision in *President of India v La Pintada Compania Navigation SA* [1985] AC 104 and held that at common law, subject to the ordinary rules of remoteness, the loss suffered as result of the late payment of money was recoverable as damages: see [16] (Lord Hope), [132] (Lord Scott), [94] and [95] (Lord Nicholls), [165] (Lord Walker) and [216] (Lord Mance). The principal part of the decision, which is concerned with restitutionary relief, is considered below. For further discussion of the position at common law see chapter 3, para 3.80ff.
4 See, in particular, [94] and [95] (Lord Nicholls) and [215] and [216] (Lord Mance). It is clear from Lord Nicholls' judgment that compound interest is recoverable as damages provided that the normal rules of remoteness of damage in tort or contract (as applicable) are satisfied.

4.64   The principle and practice of the nineteenth century, as they applied to a solicitor trustee, were set out in *Burdick v Garrick*[1] where simple interest at 4% was awarded. The award, whether of simple or compound interest and whether at the higher or lower rates, was intended to be compensatory and not punitive, and the basic principle upon which compound rather than simple interest was awarded was that the defendant should not profit personally from the use of the claimant's assets to which he or she had no right. The practice prevailed well into the twentieth century. In the 1970s the practice of awarding fixed rates of interest disappeared. In *Bartlett v Barclays Trust Co Ltd (No 2)*[2] Brightman LJ awarded interest at the court's short term investment rate:

'I turn now to the question of interest. It is common ground that interest can be claimed on the compensation which is found due. Dispute only arises on the rate of interest to be charged. In former days a trustee was as a rule charged only with interest of 4 per cent unless there were special circumstances. The rate seems to have prevailed as the general rule until recent years. The defendant has helpfully supplied the court with a table of bank and minimum lending rates and bank deposit rates. Between 1963, the year in which the Old Bailey scheme began, and the present day there have been nearly 80 changes of bank rate of minimum lending and nearly 70 changes in Barclays Bank deposit rate. The bank or minimum lending rate during this period has varied between 4 per cent and 17 per cent and the deposit rate has varied between two per cent and 15 per cent. In these days of huge and constantly changing interest rates (the movement being usually upwards so far) I think it would be unrealistic for a court of equity to abide by the modest rate of interest which was current in the stable times of our forefathers.

In my judgment, a proper rate of interest to be awarded, in the absence of special circumstances, to compensate the beneficiaries and trust funds for non-receipt from a trustee of money that ought to have been received is that allowed from time to time on the courts' short-term investment account, established under section 6(1) of the Administration of Justice Act 1965.'

In the past the special account rate has been lower than commercial rates although the difference is not now significant.[3] In any event, in *O'Sullivan v Management Agency and Music Ltd*,[4] where there were no special circumstances either, the court awarded interest at a rate of 1% above the bank minimum lending rate. The position, therefore, at common law and in equity, absent special circumstances, became very much the same.

1 (1870) 5 Ch App 233.
2 [1980] Ch 515 at 546G–547B.
3 For historic interest only see *The Supreme Court Practice* (1998) Vol 1 at 6/L/12 (pp. 60–1).
4 [1985] QB 428, CA.

4.65 *Wallersteiner v Moir (No 2)*[1] was a case of special circumstances, where the claimant and defendant to the counterclaim had been guilty of a number of breaches of his fiduciary duties as a director of a public company. The court awarded interest at 1% above the minimum bank lending rate with yearly rests. The basis on which the award was made was as follows:[2]

'Dr Wallersteiner was at all material times engaged in the business of finance. Through a complex structure of companies he conducted financial operations with a view to profit. The quarter million pounds assistance which he obtained from the two companies in order to finance the acquisition of the shares meant that he was in a position to employ the money or its capital equivalent in those operations. Though the truth is unlikely ever to be fully known, shrouded as it is by the elaborate corporate structure within which Dr Wallersteiner chose to operate, one may safely presume that the use of the money (or the capital it enabled him to acquire) was worth to him the equivalent of compound interest at commercial rates with yearly rests, if not more.'

1 [1975] QB 373, 508n.
2 At 406E–G, per Scarman LJ. See also Buckley LJ at 398E–399A. Lord Denning MR would have awarded interest both for this reason and on a wider basis which is not supported by the authorities: see 388B–H.

4.66 In *Westdeutsche Landesbank Girozentrale v Islington London Borough Council*[1] where the House of Lords refused to award compound interest on a

restitutionary claim either at common law or under the court's equitable jurisdiction in aid of the common law, Lord Browne–Wilkinson said this:[2]

> '[I]n the absence of fraud equity only awards compound (as opposed
> to simple) interest against a defendant who is a trustee or otherwise
> in a fiduciary position by way of recouping from such a defendant an
> improper profit made by him. It is unnecessary to decide whether in
> such a case compound interest can only be paid where the defendant
> has used trust moneys in his own trade or (as I tend to think) extends
> to all cases where a fiduciary has improperly profited from his trust.'

The traditional rule was therefore as follows: in the absence of fraud,
compound interest could be awarded only where the defendant was a
fiduciary and had profited personally from the breach of trust or fiduciary
duty and an account of profits was sought. Where fraud was alleged and
proved against a fiduciary or trustee, the court could also award compound
interest. It remained unclear whether there was a third category of cases in
which the court had an equitable jurisdiction to award compound interest.[3]
Moreover, until very recently, it remained the position that there was no
jurisdiction to award compound interest against a defendant under section 35A of the Supreme Court Act 1981 even if he or she is fraudulent or a
party to a fraud but had not committed a breach of trust or breach of fiduciary
duty.[4] In *Sempra Metals Ltd v Inland Revenue*[5], however, the House of Lords
analysed *Westdeutsche* and concluded that it was based on a concession[6]. A
majority held that compound interest was recoverable[7] although in reaching
this conclusion they made no clear decision about the extent of the common
law right to restitution or the equitable jurisdiction to award compound
interest.[8] The effect of the decision will undoubtedly be to extend the
circumstances in which compound interest may be recovered against a
fiduciary or trustee if the claimant can prove a loss and the test for remoteness
of damage for deceit at common law or for breach of fiduciary duty in equity
are satisfied. In other cases, however, it remains an open question whether the
traditional limits of equity will be observed.[9] The immediate issue in *Sempra*
was whether the claimant was entitled to compound interest either as a
restitutionary right or under any discretion to award compound interest in
equity, Two members of the House of Lords held that there was an immediate
common law right to restitution measured by reference to a conventional
compound interest rate, two members held that there was an equitable
jurisdiction to award interest but only one of them was prepared to award
compound interest in the present case (without deciding what the position was
at common law) and the final member of the panel held that there was no right
to restitution or discretionary power to award interest.

1 [1996] AC 669.
2 [1996] AC 669 at 702D–E. The entire House agreed with the traditional limits of the equitable
jurisdiction. A minority, Lords Goff and Woolf, would have extended the jurisdiction to award
compound interest to a claim for money had and received at common law.

3 See the Law Commission's Consultation Paper No. 167 (31 July 2002) (cited by McCombe J in *Black v Davies* [2004] EWHC 1464 (QB) at [16]): 'Outside the trust field, equity will order interest against an agent or receiver who fails to render an account. A constructive trust found to exist because of fraud, or because of profits made from a fiduciary position (whether or not by an actual trustee), may be treated in the same way as an express trust if it is possible to identify the money and ascertain its investment history. Often however a constructive trust differs from an express trust in that there is no trust fund which preserves its identity throughout the history of investment. The existence of such a fund must then be supposed as a kind of fiction, as in the equitable remedy of tracing. In such cases compound interest will be awarded, on the analogy of the earnings that the putative trust fund ought to have made. Traditionally, in these cases as in the express trust cases, compound interest was only awarded when the fiduciary had a trade in which the money could be invested. It has been argued that since the *Westdeutsche* case this condition is no longer essential; but its existence is still assumed in *Clef Aquitaine SARL v Laporte Materials (Barrow) Ltd*. This kind of interest presents no analogy to compensatory interest on debt or damages; it depends on the proprietary character of the claim, and represents the deemed profit of the defendant rather than the deemed loss of the claimant.'

4 See *Clef Aquitaine Sarl v Laporte Materials (Barrow) Ltd* [2000] 3 All ER 493 (where the point was left open) and Black v Davies [2004] EWHC 1464 (QB) (McCombe J) which was followed in *A-G of Zambia v Meer Care & Desai* [2007] EWHC 1540 (Ch) (Peter Smith J) at [10]–[12].

5 [2007] UKHL 34, [2007] 3 WLR 354.

6 See [8] (Lord Hope), [111] (Lord Nicholls) and [184] (Lord Walker).

7 See [50] (Lord Hope), [111] and [112] (Lord Nicholls) and [184]–[188] (Lord Walker).

8 Lord Hope and Lord Nicholls were prepared to recognise a restitutionary right to recover compound interest at common law. Lord Walker left the issue open (at [184] and [188]): 'Lord Nicholls and Lord Hope propose to cut through the thicket of problems by recognizing a restitutionary remedy available as of right at common law, subject to the Court's power to resort to "subjective devaluation" in order to avoid injustice in hard cases. This would be following a course which, in *Westdeutsche*, was not so much rejected as assumed not to be open. I must confess that my own inclination would be to take the course which this House came very close to taking, but ultimately drew back from taking, in *Westdeutsche*: that is to extend the court's equitable jurisdiction to award compound interest. Before your Lordships the law has been much more fully investigated, and in my opinion there are compelling reasons for departing from *Westdeutsche*, and recognising the force of Lord Goff's and Lord Woolf's powerful dissenting speeches in that case …. In this case either the common law route or the equitable route leads to the same conclusion. The appropriate exercise of discretion is to order the Revenue to pay compound interest at a conventional rate calculated by reference to the average cost of government borrowing during the relevant period. I would therefore dismiss the appeal and make the order proposed by Lord Hope.'

9 Lord Scott (who dissented) was not prepared to award compound interest as a restitutionary remedy because there was no evidence that the Government had received a benefit. He would not have been prepared to extend the equitable jurisdiction to award compound interest either: see [151]–[154]. Lord Mance (who also dissented) took a similar approach to Lord Walker and favoured the approach of extending the equitable jurisdiction (at [239]): 'The courts of equity developed the equitable jurisdiction to award interest. There is no sustainable reason in modern conditions for continuing to limit it artificially in a way which may prevent the court doing equity.' However, he also sounded a warning at ([240]): 'I would in these circumstances respond to Sempra's invitation to revisit the *Westdeutsche* case, by adopting the minority approach in preference to that of the majority and also by determining that in appropriate circumstances equity can go further and provide relief in respect of any actual interest benefit received from any principal sum paid by mistake, even though such principal may be recouped before action brought. However, while the basic aim should be to restore any actual benefit received, I emphasise that I regard equity's jurisdiction in these respects as discretionary, as, it is clear, did the minority in the *Westdeutsche* case. At p 698G in that case Lord Goff would have approved Dillon LJ's exercise of discretion in the Court of Appeal, and at pp 722D and 735C-D Lord Woolf carefully spelled out the discretionary nature of the relief which he would have granted and its

advantages. In my view, these advantages are considerable. Using their discretion, courts will be able to keep equitable claims seeking to investigate and recover any actual benefit obtained by the use of money had and received within sensible bounds, and also to avoid detailed arguments about change of position where these would be likely to give rise to disproportionate expense to resolve. The sensible exercise of such a discretion should go some way to meet concerns like those expressed to and recognised by the Law Commission in cases where the sums or periods involved are small. Courts should be able to discourage or refuse expensive demands for discovery by Claimants hoping to investigate precisely what interest benefit a Defendant may have made, in circumstances where that would be disproportionate. While the general basis of any award made should be to recoup any actual benefit, this does not entitle a Claimant to insist either on full investigation or full disgorgement or to compound interest in every case. The court can take a robust and general approach.'

(b) Compound interest

4.67 It remains unclear, therefore, whether *Sempra* has changed the traditional rules and, if so, to what extent. But it is suggested that, in the absence of fraud, a solicitor should not ordinarily be charged with compound interest unless he or she makes a personal profit from the trust.[1] Equitable fraud is, however, wider than deceit at common law:

'[I]n equity the term "fraud" embraces not only actual fraud but certain other conduct which falls below the standards demanded by equity, and is known as constructive fraud, one of the examples of which is a transaction which has been procured by undue influence, or where one party is in breach of a fiduciary duty to another. As Fox LJ said in the course of argument, it is questionable whether it is morally worse to obtain a benefit by making a statement known to be false, or to obtain the same benefit by taking advantage of a confidential or fiduciary relationship.'[2]

The jurisdiction obviously extends to cases where the solicitor has acted dishonestly or in bad faith or taken advantage of the solicitor–client relationship to further his or her own interests. It is not clear whether an English court would extend the principle to breaches of trust or breaches of the duty of good faith which, although deliberate or intentional, are not characterised as fraudulent or dishonest. In *Re Dawson*[3] Street J held that a deliberate breach of trust took it into the category of special circumstances:

'The Court's jurisdiction in selecting the appropriate rate of interest is exercisable solely for compensatory purposes. Although orders for interest may in some cases appear to have the effect of penalising defaulting trustees, the Court does not, in ordering interest and in selecting a rate, attempt in any way to impose a punishment upon the defaulter (*Vyse v Foster* (1872) 8 Ch App 309, at p 333). The practice of imposing a higher rate in the second class of case is based upon a requirement that the defaulter compensate the estate at the mercantile rate. The lesser rate of four per cent applied in the first class of case is a special rate which represents some concession in favour of the trustee: the assessment is made by reference to interest considered to be obtainable on authorized trustee investments rather than on the higher mercantile rate.

There can be little doubt but that the breach of trust committed by Percy Stewart Dawson belongs to the higher category and not to the lower, or four per cent. It was a deliberate and wilful act the purpose of which was to deprive the estate of the moneys in question; and its intended manner of implementation involved illegalities according to the law of the country where this part of the estate was then situated. It does not appear to me to lie in the mouth of Percy Stewart Dawson to seek some more favourable terms of recoupment than would have been imposed had his wrongful purpose in fact been achieved and the money safely reached the hands of the company. It would be taking too lenient a view of the breach to classify it as being amongst those cases in which four per cent is regarded as the proper rate to apply.'

Ultimately the question is always one of discretion but if this also represents the law in England (and it is suggested that it does), then compound interest is available against a solicitor who is guilty of a deliberate or intentional breach of trust or fiduciary duty.[4]

1 See *Guardian Ocean Cargoes Ltd v Banco do Brasil (No 3)* [1992] 2 Lloyd's Rep 193 (Hirst J) at 198 col 2: 'Thus, as shown in *Burdick's* case, compound interest would be inappropriate in the case of a solicitor trustee who was not engaged in an investment business.'
2 *O'Sullivan v Management Agency and Music Ltd* [1985] QB 428 at 455C–D, per Dunn LJ. This statement seems too wide if it suggests that *every* breach of fiduciary duty entitles the principal to claim compound interest.
3 [1966] 2 NSWR 211 at 218–9. See at 212–3 for the precise facts which Street J considered to give rise to a 'clear and deliberate breach', It is clear that the trustee was prepared to evade exchange controls. He was not, however, seeking to further his own interests against those of the trust but the interests of the beneficiaries as a whole. He was dead by the time of the action.
4 Compound interest could also be awarded as a form of special damage where the trustee had failed to comply with his or her duty to invest in particular interest-bearing securities or a specific fund: see *Lewin on Trusts* (17th edn, 2000) at 39—24. The loss suffered by the trust in such cases was the accumulation of capital year on year. Unless the solicitor is charged with a breach of an express trust of this nature, these cases are unlikely to be relevant.

(c) The appropriate rate

4.68 The appropriate rate will turn on what the claimant could have expected to earn and is a matter of evidence. In *Guardian Ocean Cargoes Ltd v Banco do Brasil (No 3)*[1] Hirst J accepted expert evidence of available rates in New York and ordered 1% above the New York prime rate. He declined, however, to follow the prevailing commercial practice in New York where three-monthly rests were usual and preferred 'to adhere strictly to the *Wallersteiner* formula, and award yearly rests'. In *El Ajou v Dollar Land Holdings plc (No 2)*[2] Robert Walker J awarded interest at the base rate from time to time of one of the London clearing banks. He stated that 'the rate of interest should mirror, so far as possible, the income which the plaintiff might have earned had the principal sum been paid to him in March 1988'. He also declined to award rests any more frequently than yearly.

1 [1992] 2 Lloyd's Rep 193 at 199 col 1.
2 [1995] 2 All ER 213 at 224e–j.

(d) Account of profits

4.69   Where the solicitor is the recipient of the funds in question and makes use of them himself, it may be more appropriate for the court to order an inquiry. In *Mathew v T M Sutton Ltd*[1] Chadwick J set out some helpful guidance in identifying the correct rate or rates of interest to be applied where the fiduciary or trustee is the recipient of the trust monies:

'The question in the present case is whether interest should be awarded at a rate which is linked to some independent commercial rate (say, bank rate or the rate allowed on the short term investment account) or whether I should order an inquiry for the purpose of ascertaining what use was made by the defendant of the money which it held as a fiduciary and what return was made by the defendant upon it.

In my view this is an appropriate case for an inquiry. It would have been open to the defendant to place the surplus proceeds of sale upon an interest bearing account–distinct from any account in which it held its own money–to await the outcome of any claim made by the permanent trustee. If that had been done– and, as it seems to me, that is what should have been done–the defendant would have been accountable for the interest earned on that account. No more and no less. If that was not done, then it must (at the least) be likely that the defendant used the surplus in its business. That business includes the lending of money at rates which have been equal to, or in excess of, 3 per cent per month. If the defendant was, in fact, able to and did obtain a return equivalent to 3 per cent per month on what (on this hypothesis) was the plaintiff's money, I can see no reason why the plaintiff should be required to accept a lesser return.'

Accordingly, the claimant is entitled to an inquiry, if appropriate, to establish what profit the trustee or fiduciary made from the use of the money and to recover the profit actually made.[2]

1 [1994] 1 WLR 1455 at 1462E–H.
2 Subject possibly to the defendant's expenses and reasonable remuneration: see *O'Sullivan v Management Agency and Music Ltd* [1985] QB 428 at 458D–F.

Chapter 5

Authority, vicarious liability and undertakings

A   AUTHORITY

1   Sources of authority

(a) Agency

5.01   The principal source of a solicitor's authority is contract and the extent of an agent's authority is governed by the terms of the contract of agency. In *Freeman & Lockyer v Buckhurst Park Properties (Mangal) Ltd*[1] Diplock LJ stated:

> 'An "actual" authority is a legal relationship between principal and agent created by a consensual agreement to which they alone are parties. Its scope is to be ascertained by applying ordinary principles of construction of contracts, including any proper implications from the express words used, the usages of the trade, or the course of business between the parties.'

But an agency relationship may arise in circumstances where there is no contract between principal and agent. Most fiduciary relationships which do not involve a contract involve some form of agency. One example is *Twinsectra Ltd v Yardley*[2]. In that case S (a solicitor) gave an undertaking to hold sums to the order of L (another solicitor). That undertaking gave rise to a purpose trust under which S owed a duty to T (the lender) to apply it in accordance with the undertaking. Another obvious example is sub-agency. Where P contracts with A1 on terms that A1 may delegate authority to a sub-agent, A2, equity may impose direct fiduciary obligations on A2, eg, to apply money in accordance with P's instructions.[3]

---

1 [1964] 2 QB 480 at 502.
2 [2002] UKHL 12, [2002] 2 AC 164. The decision is considered in detail at paras 4.10 and 4.15–4.16.
3 See *Powell & Thomas v Evan Jones & Co* [1905] 1 KB 11 and *Yasuda Fire & Marine Insurance Co of Europe Ltd v Orion Marine Insurance Underwriting Agency Ltd* [1995] QB 174 at 185F (Colman J):

'Although in modern commercial transactions agencies are almost invariably founded upon a contract between principal and agent, there is no necessity for such a contract to exist. It is sufficient if there is consent by the principal to the exercise by the agent of authority and consent by the agent to his exercising such authority on behalf of the principal'.

For a recent example see *Redcliffe Close (Old Brompton) Management v Kamal* [2003] All ER (D) 160.

(b) Partnership

5.02   The other principal source of a solicitor's authority is partnership and the liability of a firm of solicitors for the actions of a partner is principally governed by ss 5, 10, 11 and 13 of the Partnership Act 1890. The combination of these provisions and the doctrine of vicarious liability at common law mean that in all but the most exceptional cases the acts or wrongs of a partner or an employee will bind his or her firm and it will be unnecessary to consider the authority of the solicitor and the firm separately. The general authority of partners to bind their firm is contained in s 5 of the Partnership Act 1890:

'Every partner is an agent of the firm and his other partners for the purposes of the business of the partnership; and the acts of every partner who does any act for carrying on in the usual way business of the kind carried on by the firm of which he is a member bind the firm and his partners, unless the partner so acting has in fact no authority to act for the firm in the particular matter, and the person with whom he is dealing either knows that he has no authority, or does not know or believe him to be a partner.'

The position in relation to limited liability partnerships is similar:[1]

'(1) Every member of a limited liability partnership is the agent of the limited liability partnership.

(2) But a limited liability partnership is not bound by anything done by a member in dealing with a person if –

(a)   the member in fact has no authority to act for the limited liability partnership by doing that thing, and

(b)   the person knows that he has no authority or does not know or believe him to be a member of the limited liability partnership.'

In *Bank of Scotland v Henry Butcher*[2] four partners of a surveyors firm signed a guarantee for a developer that the firm argued was prohibited by the partnership deed. The firm was held to be bound by virtue of s 5 of the 1890 Act. The Court

231

of Appeal upheld the judge's finding that as a matter of construction of the partnership agreement the partners were permitted to enter into the guarantee. But they also held that the firm was bound by s 5 which confers both implied authority and ostensible authority on a partner. Chadwick LJ explained the operation of the section in the following terms:[3]

'It can be seen that the section comprises two distinct limbs. The first limb may be said to define the circumstances in which a partner has implied authority to bind the firm; the second to define the circumstances in which there will be ostensible authority. The inquiry under the first limb of s 5 of the 1890 Act is whether the act of one partner, say partner A, is done for the purpose of the business of the partnership. If it is, then, in doing that act, A is the agent of the firm and the other partners are bound by A's act. There is no need, in such a case, for the person seeking to rely on the act to invoke the second limb. The hypothesis which underlies the second limb of s 5 is that A's act is not, in fact, done for the purpose of the partnership business – so that the first limb is not in point. The inquiry under the second limb – in a case where it is necessary to invoke that limb – is whether A's act is an "act for carrying on in the usual way business of the kind carried on by the firm". That requires consideration of two elements: (i) what business is "business of the kind carried on by the firm"; and (ii) is A's act "an act for carrying on in the usual way" that business. Where those two elements are present, the person with whom A is dealing is entitled to treat the act as done for the purpose of the business of the partnership unless he knows that A has in fact no authority, or does not know or believe A to be a partner. In effect, A has ostensible authority to bind the firm in relation to acts which appear to be for the purpose of the business of the partnership because they are acts which could be done in the carrying on in the usual way of business of the kind carried on by the firm.'

1 Limited Liability Partnerships Act 2000, s 6.
2 [2003] EWCA Civ 67, [2003] 1 BCLC 575.
3 [2003] EWCA Civ 67, [2003] 1 BCLC 575 at [87]–[89]. This extract demonstrates that the statutory test for whether a solicitor has ostensible authority to bind the firm is in principle the same test for whether he or she has ostensible authority to bind the client (which is governed by the general law of agency (below)).

5.03 Section 5 of the Partnership Act 1890 is concerned with liabilities of all kinds (such as trading debts or liabilities) and is not specifically directed to breaches of contract or torts or breaches of fiduciary duty committed by a partner. Where the conduct of a partner amounts to a breach of duty, however, the other partners of the firm may be liable to third parties under the specific statutory liability imposed by s 10 of the Partnership Act 1890. This provides as follows:

'Where, by any wrongful act or omission of any partner acting in the ordinary course of the business of the firm, or with the authority of his co-partners, loss or injury is caused to any person not being a partner in the firm, the firm is liable therefor to the same extent as the partner so acting or omitting to act.'

The section is wide in its operation and in *Dubai Aluminium Co Ltd v Salaam*[1] Lord Millett explained that 'dishonest and deliberate conduct committed by a partner for his own sole benefit is legally capable of being in the ordinary course of business of the firm.' Again, although s 10 provides a statutory basis for attributing liability to partners and the doctrine of vicarious liability is the product of the common law, substantially the same test applies both to the liability of co-partners under either s 5 or s 10 of the Partnership Act 1890 and to the vicarious liability of the firm for the conduct of employees.[2]

1 [2002] UKHL 48, [2003] 2 A.C. 366 at [130]. Peter Smith J applied *Dubai Aluminium* to the dishonest conduct of a solicitor in Attorney-General of Zambia v Meer Care & Desai [2007] EWHC 952 (Ch) at [660] to [679].
2 See paras 5.21–5.24 (below).

5.04 Sections 11 and 13 of the Partnership Act 1890 deal with liability of partners to account for the misappropriation or misapplication of client funds by another partner. Section 11 provides as follows:

'In the following cases; namely—

(a)   Where one partner acting within the scope of his apparent authority receives the money or property of a third person and misapplies it; and

(b)   Where a firm in the course of its business receives money or property of a third person, and the money or property so received is misapplied by one or more of the partners while it is in the custody of the firm;

the firm is liable to make good the loss.'

Section 13 of the 1890 Act deals with the specific situation where a solicitor holds money in the capacity of a trustee. It provides:

'If a partner, being a trustee, improperly employs trust property in the business or on the account of the partnership, no other partner is liable for the trust property to the persons beneficially interested therein. Provided as follows:

(1) This section shall not affect any liability incurred by any partner by reason of his having notice of a breach of trust; and

(2) Nothing in this section shall prevent trust money from being followed and recovered from the firm if still in its possession or under its control.'

The liability to account under both sections is a primary one imposed on the partners of the firm and not a vicarious liability for the breach of duty of the defaulting partner. In *Bass Brewers Ltd v Appleby*[1] Millett LJ explained the different operations of the two sections:

'Section 11 and s 13 are both concerned with third party money received by the firm. Section 11 deals with money which is properly received by the firm (or by one of the partners acting within the scope of his apparent authority) for and on behalf of the third party but which is subsequently misapplied. The firm is liable to make good the loss. Section 13 is concerned with money held by a partner in some other capacity, such as trustee, which is misapplied by him and then improperly and in breach of trust employed by him in the partnership business. His partners can be made liable only in accordance with the ordinary principles of knowing receipt.'

If a firm receives funds in the ordinary course of business and one of the partners then misapplies them, it is no answer to a claim under s 11 on the part of the other partners to say that the partner acted outside the scope of the business or without authority.[2] The critical issue for the purpose of the section is whether the funds received by the firm are received in the course of the firm's business. For this reason it is essential to examine the reason why the funds were paid to the solicitor. It is part of the usual or normal course of business of a solicitor to receive funds from or on behalf of a client in the course of handling a client transaction, but not part of a solicitor's business simply to accept funds from one party and to pay them to another where there is no underlying transaction.[3] In *Antonelli v Allen*[4] Neuberger J held that it was not within the ordinary course of business of a solicitor to accept funds from a party who was not an existing client of the firm and without any further instructions (other than to hold it). In that case Mr and Mrs Antonelli took £100,000 out of a company that they controlled, converted it into a banker's draft and paid it into the client account of a firm of solicitors who had acted for a business contact. The business contact misappropriated the funds by convincing one of the partners that it was his own money. Mr and Mrs Antonelli's claim against the firm failed on the basis that the partner who had accepted the money was not acting in the ordinary course of the business of a solicitor.

1 [1997] BCLC 700 at 711g–j. See also *Walker v Stones* [2001] QB 902 at 948h–949A (Sir Christopher Slade).

2 See *Dubai Aluminium Ltd v Salaam* [2002] UKHL 48, [2003] 2 AC 366 at [110] (Lord Millett):

> 'Section 11 deals with money which is properly received by the firm in the ordinary course of its business and is afterwards misappropriated by one of the partners. The firm is not vicariously liable for the misappropriation; it is liable to account for the money it received, and cannot plead the partner's wrongdoing as an excuse for its failure to do so. Section 13 deals with money which is misappropriated by a trustee who happens to be a partner and who in breach of trust or fiduciary duty afterwards pays it to his firm or otherwise improperly employs it in the partnership business. The innocent partners are not vicariously liable for the misappropriation, which will have occurred outside the ordinary course of the firm's business. But they are liable to restore the money if the requirements of the general law of knowing receipt are satisfied.'

3 See *United Bank of Kuwait Ltd v Hammoud* [1988] 1 WLR 1051, *Hirst v Etherington* [1999] Lloyds Rep PN 938 and *Ruparel v Awan* [2001] Lloyd's Rep PN 258 (all considered in the context of undertakings in para 5.11, below).
4 [2001] Lloyds Rep PN 487 at [58] to [77]. Judgment was handed down before the House of Lords had decided *Dubai Aluminium Co Ltd v Salaam* (above) but it is suggested that both the decision and the reasoning would have been the same.

5.05 In *JJ Coughlan Ltd v Ruparelia*[1] the Court of Appeal considered the limits of one partner's authority to bind his or her partners under ss 5 and 10 of the Partnership Act 1890. The case concerned a prime bank or advanced fee fraud. The principal fraudster, H, told the claimant that, if the claimant lent $500,000 for one month, the claimant would be given a payment of $2.5m, a return of 6000%. The claimant had to give the money to R, a solicitor, who would undertake to return the $500,000 to the claimant if the $2.5m was not paid. The claimant paid the money and R gave the undertaking. The claimant did not receive the $2.5m and sued R for deceit and on the undertaking. The claimant succeeded against R and the question was whether RT, the firm of which R was a partner, was also liable on the undertaking. R's conduct consisted of drawing up two agreements (which contained a number of fraudulent representations) and accompanying his client to a meeting at which he and his client promoted a fraudulent investment scheme. Dyson LJ began by asking the question whether a general description of the conduct fell within the scope of the solicitor's ordinary course of business:[2]

> 'What are the criteria for determining whether an act is of a class or kind which it is the ordinary business of solicitors to carry out? A useful starting point is to ask whether the general description of the act falls within the scope of the ordinary business of solicitors. It is a necessary condition that the act should satisfy this requirement. Thus, for example, if the solicitor enters into a contract for the sale of double-glazing, he cannot bind his firm under s 5, nor will his firm be vicariously liable for any wrongful act in relation to the transaction under s 10. It is not the ordinary business of solicitors to sell double-glazing. The transaction is of a general nature that falls outside the scope of a solicitor's ordinary business. It is unnecessary to examine the transaction further to see that this is so. Whatever the

terms of the contract of sale, it is not made by the solicitor as part of the ordinary business of a solicitor.'

However, he held that the fact that the act is of a general description which falls within the scope of the ordinary course of business is not a sufficient condition. Having accepted that the motive or purpose of the solicitor is irrelevant[3] he concluded that it was also necessary to examine the details of the transaction itself:[4]

'The issue is not how the transaction ought properly to be described, or whether, without distortion of language, it can be given the label of a transaction in which solicitors ordinarily engage. Rather, it is necessary to examine the substance of the transaction to see whether, viewed fairly and properly, it is the kind of transaction which forms part of the ordinary business of a solicitor. This exercise requires the detail of the transaction to be taken into account. Most transactions will obviously fall on one side of the line or the other. There will be a few cases where the answer may not be plain. For the policy reasons that I have mentioned, the court should not be too ready to find that the ordinary business requirement is not satisfied.'

In the instant case the investment scheme that the solicitor was promoting was so abnormal that it could not be regarded as within the ordinary course of business of a solicitor. The judge had found as a fact that there was nothing normal about the transaction and that the claimant's representatives did not believe that the solicitor was acting in the ordinary course of business and viewed objectively they were not. He also arrived at the same conclusion under s 10 of the Partnership Act 1890.

1 [2003] EWCA Civ 1057, [2004] PNLR 4 (decided after *Dubai Aluminium*). For other examples see *Flynn v Thomson & Partners* (26 January 2000, unreported), CA, where an assault by a solicitor on a claimant outside court was held to be outside the firm's ordinary course of business and *Balfron Trustees Ltd v Peterson* [2002] Lloyd's Rep PN 1, though this was decided before *Dubai Aluminium* in the House of Lords and is only a decision that the claimant had an arguable case.

2 [2003] EWCA Civ 1057, [2004] PNLR 4 at [25].

3 This follows from the decision of the House of Lords in *Dubai Aluminium Co Ltd v Salaam* [2002] UKHL 48, [2003] 2 A.C. 366: see *A-G of Zambia v Meer Care & Desai* [2007] EWHC 952 (Ch) (Peter Smith J) at [674].

4 [2003] EWCA Civ 1057, [2004] PNLR 4 at [30]–[36]. See also Longmore LJ at [41]:

'Both sides agree that the question is whether the transactions described in the judge's judgment were within the ordinary course or usual way of business of a firm of solicitors. Once one appreciates that the proposed transaction was that, in return for the transfer of $500,000 and without risk as to that sum, the claimants would within one month receive $2,500,000 (a return of 500% or, if annualised, 6,000%), it can be seen at once that neither that transaction itself nor advising upon it was within the ordinary course of a solicitor's business. The judge called it preposterous. So it is and I would dismiss the appeal.'

2 Types of authority

5.06   In terms of legal doctrine there are only two types of authority: actual and ostensible. Since agency is usually based on contract or some form of consensual arrangement between principal and agent actual authority can only be based on an express or an implied term of the agreement between them. Actual authority can therefore be divided up into express actual authority and implied actual authority. Ostensible authority on the other hand is a form of estoppel.[1] The elements of ostensible authority are set out below. The doctrine is based on a representation by the principal to a third party that the agent has his or her authority. Usual authority is generally used in the modern cases to describe a form of implied actual authority. Those agents (such as solicitors) whose profession or occupation involves them carrying out certain functions or performing certain acts also have the authority usually possessed by members of that profession or occupation. Usual authority is also used sometimes to describe another form of implied actual authority perhaps best termed 'incidental authority'. In *Hopkins v TL Dallas Group Ltd*[2] Lightman J described incidental authority in the following way:

> 'This authority extends to doing "whatever is necessary for, or ordinarily incidental to, the effective execution of his actual authority": *Bowstead* art 27. The authority may in appropriate circumstances extend to raising funds and giving security for borrowings for the purpose of fulfilling the functions and duties assigned to him. Where a board of directors appoint one of the members to an executive position "they impliedly authorise him to do all such things as fall within the usual scope of that office" (*Hely-Hutchinson v Brayhead Ltd* [1968] 1 QB 549 at 583).'

Apparent authority is more usually used as a synonym for ostensible authority in the modern authorities although there can be a significant overlap between usual authority (in the sense of implied actual authority or incidental authority) and apparent authority (in the sense of ostensible authority). The materials upon which the third party relies to demonstrate that the agent had usual authority will often tend to demonstrate that the principal has also held out to the third party that the agent has authority.

1 See *Freeman & Lockyer v Buckhurst Park Properties (Mangal) Ltd* [1964] 2 Q.B. 480 at 503 (Diplock LJ).
2 [2004] EWHC 1379 (Ch), [2005] 1 BCLC 543.

(a) *Actual authority*

5.07   Express actual authority depends on the express terms of the retainer between solicitor and client.[1] In the same way that the existence of a retainer may be implied[2], so may a relationship of agency and the terms of the agent's authority.[3] There are virtually no modern examples in the authorities that genuinely turn on contractual implication. One genuine example, however, is probably *Little v Spreadbury*[4] (where a solicitor read over the terms of a compromise to his client who appeared to assent to them but later repudiated the agreement). One reason for the absence of many cases in which a solicitor can truly be said to have implied actual authority is that a solicitor is under a duty to consult on questions of doubt.[5]

1 For an example of a case in which a solicitor's express authority from his client was scrutinised see *Carr v Cotton* [2002] EWCA Civ 1788 where Chadwick LJ said this at [52]:

'A solicitor's understanding of instructions which he has received cannot, of course, be determinative. If the instructions are contained in a document, the court's task is to construe the document. But, where the document has been signed by the client immediately following a discussion between client and solicitor as to the need for it, the solicitor's contemporary understanding as to the instructions which he has been given in that document is, to my mind, a powerful indication of the meaning which they both intended the words used in that document to bear. And that indication is the more powerful where the client is himself a solicitor and acts in a way which is consistent (and only consistent) with that meaning.'

2 See *Midland Bank Trust Co Ltd v Hett, Stubbs and Kemp* [1979] Ch 384 at 396D and para 1.8, above.
3 See, eg, *SEB Trygg Liv Holding Aktiebolag v Manches* [2005] EWHC 35 (Comm), [2005] 2 Lloyd's Rep 129 (Gloster J) (upheld on appeal at [2005] EWCA Civ 1237, [2006] 1 WLR 2276).
4 [1910] 2 KB 610. The case is often relied on as authority for the proposition that solicitors have *implied* (as opposed to *ostensible*) authority to compromise: see *Bowstead & Reynolds on Agency* (18th edn, 2006) at 3—029 n 4.
5 See *Groom v Crocker* [1939] 1 KB 194 at 222 (Scott LJ) (cited in *Ball v Druces & Attlee* (*No 2*) [2004] EWHC 1402 (QB) (Nelson J), [2004] PNLR 745):

'The retainer when given puts into operation the normal terms of a contractual relation-ship, including in particular the duty of the solicitor to protect the client's interest and carry out his instructions in the matters to which the retainer relates, by all proper means. It is an incident of that duty that the solicitor shall consult with his client on all questions of doubt which do not fall within the express or implied discretion left to him, and shall keep the client informed to such an extent as may be reasonably necessary according to the same criteria.'

(*b*) *Usual or incidental authority*

5.08 A number of old cases suggest that the usual or incidental authority of solicitors is wide.[1] All of the old decisions need to be treated with care. Most of them date from a period when the distinction between actual and ostensible authority had not been properly understood[2] and in *United Bank of Kuwait v Hammoud*[3] Staughton LJ stated that:

'We were referred to some elderly decisions, and to 44 *Halsbury's Laws of England* (4th edn, 1983) pp 109–111, para 140 which is supported by elderly cases in the footnotes, as showing what types of transactions are and are not within the ordinary authority of a solicitor. That material should today be treated with caution, in my judgment; the work that solicitors do can be expected to have changed since 1888; it has changed in recent times and is changing now. I prefer to have regard to the expert evidence of today in deciding what is the ordinary authority of a solicitor'.

It may be that the court would be less receptive to admitting expert evidence[4] on this issue today but the decision does demonstrate that a solicitor's usual or incidental authority depends on current practice and not a body of case law. It is not, therefore, possible to provide an authoritative list of those actions that a solicitor has usual authority to undertake but in principle a solicitor only has authority to carry out any procedural steps that are directly incidental to the transaction or proceedings in which he or she is instructed. Some examples of this are as follows: a solicitor has usual authority to serve replies to preliminary enquiries;[5] a solicitor holding a signed contract for the sale of land with authority to exchange has usual authority to exchange at any time and by telephone;[6] a solicitor who is on the record has incidental authority to accept service of documents on behalf of the client in litigation and has a general authority to carry out procedural steps;[7] and a solicitor has incidental authority to give an undertaking on behalf of his or her firm in transactions where he or she is holding money or documents on behalf of the client and an undertaking is required as part of the relevant transaction.[8] On the other hand, a solicitor has no usual or incidental authority to bind the client in matters of substance that reasonably require the decision of the client and which are not properly incidental to the solicitor's existing instructions. Some examples of this are as follows: a solicitor has no usual authority to accept service of notices on behalf of the client unless expressly authorised;[9] to enter into a contract on behalf of the client;[10] to exchange contracts on behalf of a client; or to receive money unless expressly authorised;[11] or to amend a contract by substituting the name of a new purchaser and then to exchange it[12]. A solicitor does not have authority either to issue proceedings or accept service of them even though instructed to act in relation to the dispute;[13] and a solicitor on the record for a party to litigation has no incidental authority to enter into a compromise without express instructions[14].

1 See *Chitty* on Contracts (29th edn, 2004) vol 2 at 31—016 and *Cordery on Solicitors* (2007) Vol 1 at F-3 et seq. For a survey of the authorities on litigation see *Waugh v HB Clifford & Sons* [1982] Ch 374, CA at 383G–387C (Brightman LJ).

2 See *Waugh v HB Clifford & Sons* [1982] Ch 374, CA (above) at 387C–D (Brightman LJ):

'In none of the cases cited to us has there been any debate on the question whether the implied authority of the advocate or solicitor as between himself and his client is necessarily as extensive as the ostensible authority of the advocate or solicitor vis-à-vis the opposing litigant. The possibility of a difference seems to have been adverted to by Byles J in Prestwich v Poley (see 18 CB (NS) 806 at 80). In my judgment there is every reason to draw a distinction.'

3 [1988] 1 WLR 1058 at 1063. See also *Bank of Scotland v Henry Butcher* [2003] EWCA Civ 67, [2003] 1 BCLC 575 at [22] (Chadwick LJ).
4 For the admissibility and relevance of expert evidence see paras 2.20–2.25, above.
5 *Gran Gelato Ltd v Richcliff* [1992] Ch 560 (Sir Donald Nicholls V-C) at 570G–571A.
6 *Domb v Isoz* [1980] Ch 548.
7 See *Prestwich v Poley* (1865) 18 CB (NS) 806 at 816: 'The attorney is the general agent of the client in all matters which may reasonably be expected to arise for decision in the cause'.
8 See *United Bank of Kuwait v Hammoud* [1988] 1 WLR 1058 (para 5.11, below).
9 See *Re Munro* [1981] 1 WLR 1358 (Walton J) at 1361E:

> 'It is of course a common fallacy to think that solicitors have an implied authority on behalf of their clients to receive notices. They may have express authority so to receive them but in general a solicitor does not have any authority to accept a notice on behalf of his client.'

10 See *Eccles v Bryant* [1948] Ch 93 at 106 (Cohen LJ):

> 'It seems to me to be plain from the cases which were cited to us, including the case of *Lockett v Norman-Wright* [1925] Ch 56 at 62 that the solicitor would have no authority to make any such bargain. In that case Tomlin J as he then was, said "Solicitors are not, in the absence of specific authority, agents of their client to conclude a contract for them ...." '

11 See *Gavaghan v Edwards* [1961] 2 QB 220, CA where solicitors acting for both parties already in agreement were held to have implied authority to make an additional memorandum for the purpose of recording a final term agreed by the parties.
12 See *OPM Property Services Ltd v Venner* [2003] EWHC Ch 427 (Michael Brindle QC).
13 See *Wright v Castle* (1817) 3 Mer 12 and *Re Gray* (1891) 65 LT 743.
14 See *Waugh v HB Clifford & Sons* [1982] Ch 374, CA at 387F–G.

(c) Ostensible authority

5.09 In order to establish that a solicitor had ostensible authority it is necessary for the third party to establish that the client held the solicitor out as having authority and that the third party relied on that representation. The classic statement of the test is set out by Diplock LJ in *Freeman & Lockyer v Buckhurst Park Properties (Mangal) Ltd*:[1]

> 'It must be shown: (1) that a representation that the agent had authority to enter on behalf of the company into a contract of the kind sought to be enforced was made to the contractor; (2) that such representation was made by a person or persons who had "actual" authority to manage the business of the company either generally or in respect of those matters to which the contract relates; (3) that he (the contractor) was induced by such representation to enter into the contract, that is, that he in fact relied upon it; and (4) that under its memorandum and articles of association the company was not deprived of the capacity either to enter into a contract of the kind sought to be enforced or to delegate authority to enter into a contract of that kind to the agent.'

Where a client instructs a firm of solicitors to act on his or her behalf in relation to a particular transaction (e g the sale of land) he or she implicitly authorises the solicitors to hold themselves out as acting on the client's behalf whatever the specific nature of their detailed instructions. Likewise where a firm of solicitors gives a solicitor personal conduct of a transaction, the partners of the firm hold out that solicitor as having the firm's authority to act on its behalf whatever the limits on his or her internal authority.[2] The question whether a specific action falls within the ostensible authority of the solicitor crises in two distinct factual situations: first, whether the client is bound by the solicitor's actions; and, secondly, whether the firm is bound by the individual solicitor. But is in each case the issue is same. It is answered by considering whether that action fell within the ordinary course of business of a solicitor. Thus, where the issue is whether the client is bound by the actions of the firm, the solicitor has ostensible authority if the action of the solicitor was within the range of actions for which a third party would usually expect the solicitor to have authority on behalf of a client. If the actions taken by the solicitor fall within that range, the client will be bound even though the client has placed internal limits on the solicitor's authority.[3] For example, a solicitor who holds a signed contract for the sale or purchase of land has the ostensible authority of his or her client to exchange contracts even if the client has instructed the solicitor not to exchange without further instructions. Likewise, where the issue is whether an individual solicitor has bound the firm, the solicitor has ostensible authority if the action taken was within the range of actions which a third party would usually expect a solicitor to have authority to undertake on behalf of his or her other partners or employers.[4]

1 [1964] 2 QB 480 at 505–6 (Diplock LJ).
2 See *SEB Trygg Liv Holding Aktiebolag v Manches* [2005] EWCA Civ 1237, [2006] 1 WLR 2276 at [32] (Buxton LJ):

> 'As to the facts of this case, Bowstead and Reynolds points out that ostensible authority covers two types of case: where the agent has been permitted to assume a particular position that carries a usual authority; and where a specific representation is made as to the agent's authority. If either type of conduct on the part of the principal gives rise to an estoppel, that is because of the understanding that it creates in the mind of the third party representee. An alteration on the principal's part of the relationship between himself and the agent cannot, once the estoppel has been created, alter or withdraw the representation if the alteration of the relationship is not communicated to the representee.'

3 See *McCarthy v Prison Service* [2005] All ER (D) 145 (Park J):

> 'When solicitors are involved in litigation or a negotiation of some transaction, the solicitors plainly have some authority from their own clients. There are well understood areas of authority within which the other party to the litigation or to the negotiated transaction assumes, because it is the usual thing, that the solicitor is authorised by the client to bind him. If the solicitor does purport to enter into a binding contract on behalf of the client within those areas of usual authority which anyone would normally understand to exist, then the client will be bound to the third party on the basis of ostensible authority. It is no use the client saying to the third party something like this. "Oh, I know that a solicitor would normally have had authority from his client to bind the client in this sort of situation, but in fact I had told my solicitor that he did not have

authority to bind me in this case." That would only help the client if the client had put the other party on notice that there were restrictions on the solicitor's authority which made it narrower than it would normally be assumed to be.'

4 See the test applied by Glidewell LJ in *United Bank of Kuwait v Hammoud* [1988] 1 WLR 1058 set out in para 5.11, below.

5.10 Some recent examples of cases in which a solicitor has been held to have the ostensible authority of the client are as follows: a solicitor who is on the record for a client in litigation has ostensible authority to enter into a compromise;[1] to withdraw a claim;[2] to conduct arbitration proceedings (such as, eg, the service of written submissions or attending a hearing);[3] to make an admission on behalf of his client in criminal proceedings;[4] or to make concessions in civil proceedings[5]. Some recent examples of cases in which a solicitor has not been held to have the ostensible authority of the client are as follows (and all can be explained on the basis that the opposing party would not reasonably expect the relevant act to be within the authority of the solicitor carrying out the underlying transaction): a solicitor has no ostensible authority to enter into a contract for the sale or purchase of land;[6] a solicitor has no ostensible authority bind the Legal Services Commission to a compromise;[7] or to withdraw an enforcement notice on behalf of a local authority[8].

1 See *Waugh v HB Clifford & Sons Ltd* [1982] Ch 374, CA at 387D–E:

'It follows in my view that a solicitor (or counsel) may in a particular case have ostensible authority vis-à-vis the opposing litigant where he has no implied authority vis-à-vis his client. I see no objection to that. All that the opposing litigant need ask himself when testing the ostensible authority of the solicitor or counsel, is the question whether the compromise contains matter "collateral to the suit". The magnitude of the compromise, or the burden which its terms impose on the other party, is irrelevant. But much more than that question may need to be asked by a solicitor when deciding whether he can safely compromise without reference to his client.'

2 See *McCarthy v Prison Service* [2005] All ER (D) 145.
3 See *SEB Trygg Liv Holding Aktiebolag v Manches* [2005] EWHC 35 (Comm), [2005] 2 Lloyd's Rep 129 (Gloster J) at [127] (upheld on appeal at [2005] EWCA Civ 1237, [2006] 1 WLR 2276).
4 See *R v Hayes* [2004] EWCA Crim 2844 at [12].
5 See *Clarke v Securitas UK Ltd* [2002] EWCA Civ 1179 at [12].
6 See *James v Evans* [2000] 3 EGLR 1 at 5C–E: (Wright J):

'Eccles v Bryant and D'Silva v Lister House Development Ltd make it clear that it is not within the ordinary course of a solicitor's authority, when negotiating the sale or purchase of an interest in land that has been conducted on a "subject to contract" basis, to conclude a contract on behalf of his client.'

7 See *McCarthy v Prison Service* [2005] All ER (D) 145 (Park J).
8 See *South Buckinghamshire DC v Flanagan* [2002] EWCA Civ 690.

5.11 The question of a solicitor's ostensible authority to give an undertaking requires separate consideration. In *United Bank of Kuwait v Hammoud*[1] the Court of Appeal held that a solicitor does not have ostensible authority unless the undertaking was referable to the provision of some other legal services for which the solicitor or the firm has been retained. Staughton LJ stated this:[2]

> 'The evidence establishes that two requirements must be fulfilled before an undertaking is held to be within a solicitor's ordinary authority. First, in the case of an undertaking to pay money, a fund to draw on must be in the hands of, or under the control of, the firm; or at any rate there must be a reasonable expectation that it will come into the firm's hands. Solicitors are not in business to pledge their own credit on behalf of clients unless they are fairly confident that money will be available so that they can reimburse themselves. Secondly, the actual or expected fund must come into their hands in the course of some ulterior transaction which is itself the sort of work that solicitors undertake. It is not the ordinary business of solicitors to receive money or a promise from their client, in order that without more they can give an undertaking to a third party. Some other service must be involved.'

The court held that undertakings given by a solicitor to two banks had been given in the ordinary course of business. The test which Glidewell LJ applied in deciding this issue was whether 'a reasonably careful and competent bank [would] have concluded that there was an underlying transaction of a kind which was part of the usual business of a solicitor.'[3] This test was applied in *Hirst v Etherington*.[4] In that case a client was asked to make a short-term loan at a high rate of interest and with a premium and was offered a solicitor's undertaking as security. His own solicitor rang up the solicitor who was to give the undertaking and he assured her that it was binding on his partner (who was unaware of it). Nevertheless, the Court of Appeal held that undertaking was not binding on the innocent partner because it was in effect a guarantee, and distinguished *Hammoud* on the basis that there the underlying transactions appeared to be normal conveyancing transactions.[5] In *Ruparel v Awan*[6] a solicitor had given two undertakings on behalf of a third party that were not related to any other legal services. The court rejected the argument that the claimant was entitled to rely on representations made by the third party to satisfy the test in *Hammoud* on the ground that any belief induced by the third party was irrelevant.[7]

1 [1988] 1 WLR 1058. The case was decided under the Partnership Act 1890, s 5.
2 [1988] 1 WLR 1058 at 1060G–H.
3 [1988] 1 WLR 1058 at 1058H.
4 [1999] Lloyd's Rep PN 938. Although no single test was adopted by the three members of the Court in *Hirst* both Stuart-Smith LJ and Pill LJ adopted Glidewell LJ's test set out in the text above: see 942 and 945.
5 See [1999] Lloyd's Rep PN 93 at [13] and [23] (Stuart-Smith LJ):

> 'It is part of the usual normal course of business of a solicitor to be in possession or receipt of funds of or for a client in the course of handling a substantial transaction for that client. On the other hand it is not part of the usual normal business of a solicitor

either to receive money or a promise from a client in order that without more they can give an undertaking to a third party or to give a guarantee for the debt incurred by the client.'

See also *Twinsectra Ltd v Yardley* [2002] UKHL 12, [2002] 2 AC 164 at [15] (Lord Hoffmann):

'I agree that the terms of the undertaking are very unusual. Solicitors acting for both lender and borrower (for example, a building society and a house buyer) commonly give an undertaking to the lender that they will not part with the money save in exchange for a duly executed charge over the property which the money is being used to purchase. The undertaking protects the lender against finding himself unsecured. But Twinsectra was not asking for any security over the property. Its security was cl 3 of the Sims undertaking. So the purpose of the undertaking was unclear. There was nothing to prevent Mr Yardley, having acquired a property in accordance with the undertaking, from mortgaging it to the hilt and spending the proceeds on something else. So it is hard to see why it should have mattered to Twinsectra whether the immediate use of the money was to acquire property. The judge thought it might have been intended to give some protective colour to a claim against the Solicitors' Indemnity Fund if Sims failed to repay the loan in accordance with the undertaking. A claim against the fund would depend upon showing that the undertaking was given in the context of an underlying transaction within the usual business of a solicitor (see United Bank of Kuwait v Hammoud, City Trust Ltd v Levy [1988] 1 WLR 1051). Nothing is more usual than for solicitors to act on behalf of clients in the acquisition of property. On the other hand, an undertaking to repay a straightforward unsecured loan might be more problematic.'

6   [2001] Lloyd's Rep PN 258 (David Donaldson QC).
7   See [2001] Lloyd's Rep PN 258 at 266:

'Against this legal background Mr Ruparel's argument based on "appearance" fails at the outset. Mrs Dhaliwal did not tell him (nor does Mr Ruparel so suggest) that she or the firm would be acting as solicitor on transactions under which the firm would be receiving monies which it would be authorised to remit to Mr Ruparel. The belief which Mr Ruparel claimed to have had was based on what he said he had been told by Mr Sayed, and therefore, for the reasons explained above, was irrelevant.'

5.12   Finally, in two recent authorities dealing with the authority of directors the court has held that the bad faith of the agent or third party may vitiate his or her authority. In *Criterion Properties plc v Stratford UK Properties LLC*[1] Lord Scott indicated that if it is obvious to the third party that the agent is acting against the interests of his or her principal it may be impossible for the third party to rely on the agent's *ostensible* authority:[2]

'If a person dealing with an agent knows that the agent does not have actual authority to conclude the contract or transaction in question, the person cannot rely on apparent authority. Apparent authority can only be relied on by someone who does not know that the agent has no actual authority. And if a person dealing with an agent knows or has reason to believe that the contract or transaction is contrary to the commercial interests of the agent's principal, it is likely to be very difficult for the person to assert with any credibility that he believed the agent did have actual authority. Lack of such a belief would be fatal to a claim that the agent had apparent authority.'

In *Hopkins v TL Dallas Group Ltd*[3] Lightman J went even further and held that if the agent is acting in bad faith this may vitiate his or her *actual* authority:[4]

> 'The grant of actual authority to an agent will not normally include authority to act for the agent's benefit rather than that of his principal and therefore, without agreement, the scope of actual authority will not include this. The grant of actual authority should be implied as being subject to a condition that it is to be exercised honestly and on behalf of the principal: *Lysaght Bros & Co Ltd v Falk* (1905) 2 CLR 421. It follows that, if an act is carried out by an agent which is not in the interests of his principal, for example signing onerous unconditional undertakings, then the act will not be within the scope of the express or implied grant of actual authority.'

1 [2004] UKHL 28, [2004] 1 WLR 1846 (a poison pill case where the terms on rights attached to the shares in a company were designed to prevent a takeover and one issue was whether the directors were acting within the scope of their authority).
2 [31].
3 [2004] EWHC 1379, [2005] 1 BCLC 543 (undertakings given by a director of a company to a supplier).
4 [2004] EWHC 1379, [2005] 1 BCLC 543 at [88]. The effect is to collapse the traditional distinction between (1) directors acting ultra vires the company in which case their actions do not bind it and (2) directors acting within their powers but for a collateral or improper purpose in which case their actions bind the company but they are liable for breach of fiduciary duty. *Hopkins v TL Dallas Group Ltd* was, however, followed by Peter Smith J in *Parti v Al-Nassir Al Sabah* [2007] EWHC 1869 (Ch) (which did not involve consideration of ostensible authority or the authority of directors to bind the company but the authority of an agent to sell land under a power of attorney).

3 Breach of warranty of authority

5.13 There is no difference between the liability of a solicitor for breach of warranty of authority and any other agent. But such claims against solicitors are common. Proceedings are often brought against solicitors by one party on the basis that the solicitor had no authority to take certain steps and by another party on the basis that the solicitor acted in breach of warranty of authority. Claims of this nature tend to arise in three factual contexts:

- *Litigation*: A solicitor either commences or carries on proceedings on behalf of a client who has died or does not exist. The obvious example here is a solicitor purporting to act on behalf of a company which has been struck off the register.[1]

- *Identity fraud*: A solicitor accepts instructions from someone who provides a fictitious identity or accepts instructions from a person who claims to have the authority of a third party.[2]

5.13 *Authority, vicarious liability and undertakings*

- *Capacity*: A solicitor commences proceedings on behalf of a client who does not have the mental capacity to give instructions.[3]

Much stronger safeguards now exist to prevent identity fraud. Most firms of solicitors insist on sending even established clients a client care letter and in order to comply with the Money Laundering Regulations a solicitor must also carry out detailed checks to establish and confirm the identity of a new client.[4] But identity fraud is still common. One obvious example is where an agent provides a forged power of attorney to a solicitor and executes a transfer in his or her name. Capacity cases may arise very acutely either because the client repudiates the actions of the solicitor (e g settling a claim) or because an opposing party alleges in the proceedings themselves that the claimant has no capacity to give instructions to his or her solicitors. A firm of solicitor owes a duty to its clients to continue to act in their best interests but may expose itself to a claim for breach of warranty of authority if the client does not have legal capacity and the opposing party is unable to enforce an order for costs.

1 See, eg, *SEB Trygg Liv Holding Aktiebolag v Manches* [2005] EWCA Civ 1237, [2006] 1 WLR 2276 (claim by German company that arbitration proceedings commenced in the name of a predecessor company not binding) or *Re Alan Meek Wagstaff Ltd* (Robert Englehart QC, 11 December 2000, unreported) (application under the Companies Act 1985, s 653(2B) by professional indemnity insurer of a company operating a surveyor's business to validate the steps taken by a solicitor on its behalf).

2 See, eg, *Penn v Bristol & West BS* [1997] 1 WLR 1356, CA (claim by W that not bound by charge forged by H) or *Mortgage Corpn v Shaire* [2001] Ch 743 (Neuberger J) (claim for an order for sale by bank to enforce equitable charge created by H's forgery). In each case the solicitor was joined as a third party.

3 See, eg, the famous case of *Yonge v Toynbee* [1910] 1 KB 215 (where the C had become incapable without S's knowledge) and *Masterman-Lister v Brutton & Co* [2003] EWCA Civ 1889, [2003] 1 WLR 1511, a claim for damages for professional negligence where the claimant claimed that he did not have capacity to enter into the settlement of a personal injury claim. There is a presumption that a party has capacity unless otherwise proved. In *Masterman-Lister v Brutton & Co* Kennedy LJ said (at [17]):

> 'It is common ground that all adults must be presumed to be competent to manage their property and affairs until the contrary is proved, and that the burden of proof rests on those asserting incapacity. Mr Langstaff submitted that where, as in the present case, there is evidence that as a result of a head injury sustained in an accident that doctors who have been consulted agree that for a time the Plaintiff was incapable of managing his property and affairs he can rely on the presumption of continuance. That I would not accept. Of course, if there is clear evidence of incapacity for a considerable period then the burden of proof may be more easily discharged, but it remains on whoever asserts incapacity.'

4 See, eg, *the CML Handbook* (updated on 2 July 2007), Part 1, section A3 which imposes a number of express obligations upon a solicitor retained by a mortgage lender to check the borrower's identity. A3.4 provides:

> 'You should check that any document you use to verify a signatory's identity appears to be authentic and current, signed in the relevant place. You should take a copy of it and keep the copy on your file. You should also check that the signatory's signature on any document being used to verify identity matches the signatory's signature on the document we require the signatory to sign and that the address shown on any document used to verify identity is that of the signatory.'

(a) Basis of liability

5.14   Liability for breach of warranty of authority is strict. The origin of the modern doctrine is *Collen v Wright*[1], a decision of the Exchequer Chamber. In that case an agent executed an agreement for lease with a third party. He executed it purporting to act 'as agent to [P]' but he did not in fact have authority to do so. The agent was not liable in deceit because he believed that he had his principal's authority and it could not be said that he had contracted personally because he expressly stated that he was acting as an agent. The Court found that there was an implied or collateral contract between the agent and the third party. Willes J stated:[2]

'I am of opinion that a person, who induces another to contract with him as the agent of a third party by an unqualified assertion of his being authorised to act as such agent, is answerable to the person who so contracts for any damage which he may sustain by reason of the assertion of authority being untrue. This is not the case of a bare misstatement by a person not bound by any duty to give information. The fact that the professed agent honestly thinks that he has authority affects the moral character of his act; but the moral innocence, so far as the person whom he has induced to contract is concerned, in no way aids such person or alleviates the inconvenience and damage which he sustains. The obligation arising in such a case is well expressed by saying that a person professing to contract as agent for another, impliedly, if not expressly, undertakes or promises the persons who enter into such contract, upon the faith of the professed agent being duly authorised, that the authority which he professes to have does in point of fact exist. The fact of entering into the transaction with the professed agent, as such, is good consideration for the promise.'

In *Yonge v Toynbee*[3] a firm of solicitors who defended an action for libel were not aware that his authority had been terminated by the incapacity of the client (who had been certified and detained). The Court of Appeal held (following *Collen v Wright*) that they were liable even though they were unaware of the client's incapacity (and there was no suggestion of negligence). The most recent statement of principle is to be found in *OBG Ltd v Allan*:[4]

'An innocent third party, with whom the agent has purported without authority to make a contract or to reach a settlement of outstanding liabilities under a contract, will be able to hold the agent liable for breach of the warranty of authority which the law decided long ago should be implied to give a remedy in such a situation (see *Collen v Wright* (1857) 8 E & B 647. Liability for breach of warranty of

247

authority is strict. It does not depend on whether the agent has been negligent or not: Chitty on Contracts (29th edn, 2004) vol 2, p 62 (para 31–099).'

1   (1857) 8 E&B 647.
2   (1857) 8 E&B 647 at 657–8.
3   [1910] 1 KB 215.
4   [2005] EWCA Civ 106, [2005] QB 762 at [87] (Peter Gibson LJ) (upheld at [2007] UKHL 21, [2007] 2 WLR 920).

5.15   There is an obvious conceptual difference between a solicitor executing a contract without authority and a solicitor commencing or defending proceedings without authority. In the case of litigation there is no contractual relationship between a claimant and defendant and (in the absence of special circumstances) a solicitor owes no duty of care to an opposing party. A number of attempts have been made to explain what appears to be an anomaly that a solicitor can be strictly liable for breach of warranty of authority in litigation even though there is no contract between the solicitor and the opposing party. In the early cases there was some debate about whether the basis of liability was contractual or quasi-contractual or tortious (and analogous with deceit). It is now authoritatively established that the basis of liability is contractual. In *SEB Trygg Liv Holding Aktiebolag v Manches*[1] Buxton LJ stated this:[2]

'The legal basis for making a solicitor liable was settled by this court in Yonge v Toynbee [1910] 1 KB 215. In that case, unknown to his solicitors, the client was of unsound mind and therefore lacked capacity to instruct the solicitors to defend proceedings on his behalf. The court held that the solicitors were liable to pay the plaintiff's costs on the basis of an implied warranty or contract that they had authority. This contractual theory had been developed in earlier cases involving agents other than solicitors, notably Collen v Wright (1857) 8 E & B 647 at 657–658… In other words he was describing what we would now call a collateral contract. Although this contractual theory presents some conceptual problems in the case of a solicitor conducting litigation, this is nevertheless the established basis for the liability. It is clear, as with any warranty, that liability for its breach is strict. Making the solicitor liable in such circumstances avoids the injustice which would otherwise be caused by the fact that the person for whom the unauthorised solicitor was purporting to act could not himself be made responsible for the opposing party's costs.'

1   [2005] EWCA Civ 1237, [2006] 1 WLR 2276.
2   [2005] EWCA Civ 1237, [2006] 1 WLR 2276 at [60]–[61].

(b) The nature of the warranty

5.16   Because liability is strict and not dependent on negligence or actual knowledge attempts have been made to confine the nature of the warranty to very narrow bounds. Moreover, the nature of the warranty will differ depending on the context in which it is given. Where a solicitor acts for a party in litigation the warranty is that the agent has the authority of his or her principal. The solicitor warrants that he or she has a client, that the client exists and that the client has given the solicitor authority. The solicitor does not warrant that the client is solvent.[1] In *SEB Trygg Liv Holding Aktiebolag v Manches*[2] it was also held that the solicitor did not warrant that he had correctly named his client in legal proceedings. In that case a German company was incorrectly named as a party to arbitration proceedings. It sought to contest jurisdiction on the bases that the solicitors had no authority to act for it in the proceedings; that it was not named as a party to the proceedings; and that those proceedings could not be cured by the application of the misnomer doctrine. Buxton LJ said this:[3]

> '[G]enerally a solicitor conducting proceedings does not warrant what he says or does on behalf of his client. Thus he does not warrant that his client, the named party to the proceedings, has title to sue, is solvent, has a good cause of action or defence or has any other attribute asserted on his behalf. The solicitor relies upon his client's instructions for all these things, as he will normally do for naming his client correctly. As he gives no warranty as to the accuracy of his instructions generally, it is difficult to see why the naming of his client should be treated as an exception. Why should this be any different, for example, from the naming of a client who has no title to sue? There is an obvious distinction between such matters and the solicitor's own authority to act because the solicitor will usually know whether he has such authority or not. The imposition of strict liability on a solicitor for breach of warranty of authority is justified because otherwise the opposing party will be left without remedy against his supposed client. The warranty which a solicitor gives is that he has a client who has instructed him to assert or deny the claims made in the proceedings against the opposing party. We do not think he warrants that the client has the name by which he appears in the proceedings. As a matter of principle it would not be right to impose strict liability upon a solicitor for incorrectly naming his client. Otherwise solicitors could be made liable for any case of misnomer including, for example, typographical errors or change of corporate name without a change of rights.'

1   See *Nelson v Nelson* [1997] 1 WLR 233, CA.
2   [2005] EWCA Civ 1237, [2006] 1 WLR 2276.

3 [2005] EWCA Civ 1237, [2006] 1 WLR 2276 at [66]–[67]. In fact a predecessor company had been named as the party but it was common ground that under the German law of universal succession the party contesting jurisdiction had succeeded to both its rights and liabilities.

5.17 The leading case on identity fraud is *Penn v Bristol & West BS*[1] in which a husband forged his wife's signature on a transfer of property which was owned jointly by them both. The firm of solicitors whom the husband had instructed held themselves out as acting for both husband and wife and it was held that this warranty of authority was given by the solicitors not only to the purchaser but also to the lender who was funding the purchase. It was held that it was not necessary that a transaction between the vendor and the party seeking to enforce the warranty should have been induced. It was also held that the warranty arose simply from the holding out in the course of correspondence. It is a traditional principle that an agent may qualify or exclude an implied warranty of authority with express words[2] and this probably provides the best explanation of the familiar decision in *Midland Bank v Cox McQueen*[3]. In that case a husband deposited the deeds to his wife's house with a bank. The deposit was supported by a letter that the wife had apparently signed in the presence of a solicitor and included a certificate that the contents of the document had been fully explained to her, that she understood it and had signed it voluntarily. In 1987 the husband persuaded the bank to lend on the security of the house and a firm of solicitors recommended by him were instructed by the bank to explain the documents to the wife and to obtain her signature. When the bank attempted to enforce the charge, it discovered that the wife had not signed it and that the husband had passed off an imposter to them as his wife. The bank brought a claim against the solicitors alleging both negligence and breach of warranty of authority (based on the certificate). The Court of Appeal held that the nature of the retainer was to be determined as a matter of construction and that the bank had not intended to ask for, or the solicitors to give, a guarantee against the husband's fraud even if it could not be detected by exercising proper care. They also adopted the same approach to the construction of the certificate containing the warranty of authority.[4] In the lenders' cases, therefore, the implied warranty of authority given by the solicitor on any certificate is likely to be qualified unless it is made clear that the solicitor intends to undertake strict liability.

1 [1997] 1 WLR 1356 (followed in *Bristol & West BS v Fancy & Jackson* [1997] 4 All ER 582). For a detailed description of the facts and the more detailed findings about the scope of the warranty see paras 10.111–10.114.
2 See *Bowstead & Reynolds on Agency* (18th edn, 2006) at 9—67. For a simple example see *Suleman v Shahsavari* [1988] 1 WLR 1181 (Andrew Park QC) at 1184G–1185D.
3 [1999] Lloyd's Rep PN 223, CA (followed in *UCB Corporate Services Ltd v Clyde & Co* [2000] 2 All ER (Comm) 257).
4 See 226 and 229. For a more complex case in which a solicitor acted for both borrower and lender and in which the Court held that the warranty of authority was qualified by the terms of the retainer see *Brookes v Parry* (HHJ Behrens QC, 23 May 2000, unreported).

(c) Damages for breach of warranty of authority

5.18 The purpose of compensation for breach of warranty of authority is to place the claimant in the position in which he or she would have been if the warranty had been true, i e to be put in the position in which he or she would have been if the agent had been authorised to enter into the transaction. Where the principal is in existence and solvent the normal measure of damage is the amount which the third party could have recovered from the principal for breach of contract if the principal had been bound.[1] Thus, where the solicitor enters into a contract for the sale of goods or shares without authority of the client the measure of damage will be the difference between the contract price and the market value of the shares at the date of delivery. Where the solicitor enters into a contract for the sale of land without authority the measure of damage will usually be the difference between the contract price and the market value of the property at the date of sale. The position becomes more complex, however, in cases where the solicitor is acting for the purchaser. In *Suleman v Shahsavari*[2] the court applied *Johnson v Agnew*[3] where the House of Lords had held that damages should be assessed at the date when the principal elected to accept the repudiation of the contract and claim damages. Likewise, where the principal is insolvent or would have had a number of defences to a claim for breach of contract against the third party, the agent is entitled to rely on the same defences in answer to a claim for breach of warranty of authority or to reduce the damages. In *Singh v Sardar Investments Ltd*[4] Patten J stated this:[5]

> 'It is clear that the loss for which the Claimants are seeking to be compensated is that occasioned by the solicitor's lack of authority. Put another way the damages are those required to put the Claimants in the position in which they would have been had the warranty been true. Damages calculated on this basis can of course include damages for loss of bargain including the difference between the contractual purchase price and the value of the property at trial: see Suleman v Shahsavari [1998] 1 WLR 1181. But in such cases the solicitor's lack of authority is the only impediment to the enforceability of the contract. Where, for example, the contract would in any event be unenforceable because it was illegal or failed to comply with the formalities prescribed by statute then no damages would be recoverable: see Fay v Miller, Wilkins & Co [1941] Ch 360. Although I can no find no authority which deals precisely with this point it seems to me that on principle an agent sued for breach of warranty of authority ought to be able to rely upon any defences which would have been available to his principal had the contract in fact been authorised. If this is right then the claim against the Fourth Defendant must fail.'

An example of the application of this principle is *Campden Hill Ltd v Chakrani*[6] in which Hart J held that the defences which would have been available to a party to a loan agreement to avoid enforcement were also available to the agent found liable for breach of warranty of authority. The two defences in question were statutory (Law of Property (Miscellaneous Provisions) Act 1989, s 2 and the Consumer Credit Act 1974, s137) and although neither defence was made out on the facts Hart J found that there was a chance that the second defence would have succeeded and discounted the damages on the loss of a chance basis.[7] He also held that the fact that the warranty was given fraudulently did not affect the measure of loss.[8]

1 See *Habton Farms v Nimmo* [2003] EWCA Civ 68, [2004] QB 1 at [49]–[55] (Clarke LJ), [110]–[113] (Jonathan Parker LJ) and [119]–[120] (Auld LJ). The court will not always apply the contractual measure, however. In *Habton* itself A entered into a contract for the sale of a horse without authority, P refused to honour the contract and the horse died a month after A had entered into it purporting to act on P's behalf. It was argued that the true measure of damage was the difference between the contract price (£70,000) and its actual value (which was the same) and that T was entitled to nominal damages only because its loss had occurred after T had taken the decision to keep the horse. The Court of Appeal held that T was entitled to recover the full contract price on the basis that when P refused to comply with the contract, it was reasonable for T to keep the horse and take proceedings to enforce the contract against both P and A. The majority held that the loss of the horse was the consequence of the breach of warranty of authority: see Clarke LJ at [94] and Auld LJ at [127]–[129].
2 [1988] 1 WLR 1181 (Andrew Park QC).
3 [1980] AC 367.
4 [2002] All ER (D) 243. Patten J also held that the insolvency of the principal was a factor which the court could take into account in assessing damage: see [60] and *Skylight Maritime SA v Ascot Underwriting Ltd* [2005] EWHC 15 (Comm), [2005] PNLR 450 (Colman J) at [20]. He also held that events which occurred after the date on which the breach of warranty occurred were irrelevant in order to determine whether the third party would have obtained an order for specific performance against the principal. The decision was upheld on this point by the Court of Appeal: see [2002] EWCA Civ 1706.
5 [2002] All ER (D) 243 at [58].
6 [2005] EWHC 911 (Ch).
7 See [2005] EWHC 911 at [62]:

> 'Accordingly I am not persuaded that, had there been a genuine transaction, Mr Chakrani would have successfully taken the point. I think however that this case has to be approached on the basis of assessing the chance that he would successfully have taken the point and the chance that the circumstances would then have been such as to persuade the court to exercise its discretion in his favour. I would assess those chances as about 20%. Accordingly I would discount the element of damages attributable to the facility fee by that amount.'

8 [2005] EWHC 911 at [56].

(d) Liability for costs

5.19 Where a solicitor commences or defends proceedings without authority, the usual consequence is that he or she is ordered to pay the costs of the proceedings personally from the point in time at which the solicitor first became involved until the mistake is discovered. In *Skylight Maritime SA v Ascot Underwriting Ltd*[1] Colman J stated:

'It is important not to lose sight of the fact that the relevant breach of warranty is the non-existence of the authority that was warranted. Therefore, the opposite party or promise has lost the benefit of the position he would have been in had the warranty been true. In other words, the court is concerned to quantify what benefit has been lost by reason of the fact that the supposed client is not after all a party to the proceedings. In the ordinary case, the promisee will have lost the ability to recover from the client the costs of the proceedings in the event of a costs order in the promisee's favour. This is usually quantified as the amount of costs thrown away by the promisee in relation to the proceedings from the first participation in them of the solicitor until the promisee is apprised of the solicitor's lack of authority.'

This is not an invariable rule, however. It remains open to the solicitor to demonstrate that the opposing party would not have recovered any of these costs if the warranty had been true. It also remains open to the solicitor to prove (if he or she is able to do so) that the proceedings were in fact authorised. In *Skylight* the solicitors had come off the record and the court struck the proceedings out. In defence of the claim to breach of warranty of authority the solicitors asserted that they had in fact had authority to bring the proceedings. The court ordered this (and the question of loss) to be tried. The court may also make an order for costs against the solicitor in the existing proceedings under its summary jurisdiction without the need for the opposing party to commence separate proceedings.[2] Where there are serious issues to be tried, however, the court may refuse to make a summary order and require the opposing party to commence separate proceedings.[3] Costs are assessed on the usual principles and it does not follow from the fact that the solicitor has been acting without authority that costs will be awarded on an indemnity basis.[4]

1 [2005] EWHC 15 (Comm), [2005] PNLR 450 at [16].
2 See *Yonge v Toynbee* [1910] 1 KB 215. In *Babury Ltd v London Industrial plc* [1989] NLJ 1596, Steyn J stated that the general rule was that:

'our courts have for many years exercised a summary jurisdiction to order solicitors, who acted without authority on behalf of a plaintiff or defendant, to pay the costs needlessly incurred by the opposing party'. But he also acknowledged that 'the general rule may have to yield to special circumstances'.

3 See *Skylight Maritime SA v Ascot Underwriting Ltd* [2005] EWHC 15 (Comm), [2005] PNLR 450 (above) at [13]:

'The result of the authorities and the demands of the twin objectives of making solicitors accountable for their unauthorised conduct of litigation and yet of protecting them against untested allegations of want of authority is that, whereas in clear cases of breach of warranty of authority and consequent recoverable loss, the court can summarily determine the solicitors' liability for damages, in cases where there are real issues of facts or law, the courts should not do so but should leave the opposite party to start proceedings by issuing a claim for breach of warranty of authority.'

4 In *Penn v Bristol & West BS* [1997] 1 WLR 1356, CA the court rejected the argument that the solicitors were obliged to pay indemnity costs as a matter of course because the opposing party would have been entitled to recover those costs by separate action. Waller LJ stated this (at 1366B-C):

> 'I have accordingly concluded that for an order for indemnity costs to be appropriate there should be some additional factor of the nature which normally gives rise to such an order. I am not going to attempt further definition of the ingredients of that additional factor, because as I understand it, no factor other than that the costs would have formed part of the claim to damages was relied on in this case.'

(e) Unauthorised proceedings

5.20 Where a claim form or acknowledgement of service (or subsequent statements of case) have been served without authority, they must be struck out unless the proceedings can be cured.[1] It is open to the client named in the proceedings to ratify and adopt them (even if a limitation period has expired in the meantime).[2] The client may also ratify the proceedings even if they have been brought in the wrong name (provided that it is case of misnomer and they were not intended to be commenced on behalf of a different party).[3] Where the solicitor has commenced or defended proceedings in the name of a company that has been struck off the register, the court may in certain circumstances restore the company to the register purely in order to validate the actions of a solicitor.[4]

1 See *Civil Procedure* (2007 edn) vol 2 at 7C–211. The point should be taken immediately either on an application to strike out or stay the proceedings.
2 See *Presentaciones Musicales SA v Secunda* [1994] Ch 271, CA.
3 See *The Elikon* [2003] EWCA Civ 821, [2003] 2 Lloyd's Rep 430 at [75] and *SEB Trygg Liv Holding Aktiebolag v Manches* [2005] EWCA Civ 1237, [2006] 1 WLR 2276.
4 See, eg, *Re Alan Meek Wagstaff Ltd* (Robert Englehart QC, 11 December 2000, unreported) referred to in para 5.13 n 1, above.

B   VICARIOUS LIABILITY

1   General principles

5.21 Closely related to the issue of a solicitor's authority is the question of the vicarious liability of a firm of solicitors for the acts of solicitor employees. Whereas liability of partners for the acts of other partners turns on the provisions of the Partnership Act 1890 (discussed above[1]) the vicarious liability of employers for employees is determined solely by case law. However, although the wording of the Partnership Act 1890 has to be considered separately from the common law cases on employers' liability, the Court of Appeal has indicated that the principles are 'indistinguishable' in the two classes of case.[2] Until recently, the test generally used to determine employers' liability was that set out in *Salmond on Torts*:

'A master is not responsible for a wrongful act done by his servant unless it is done in the course of his employment. It is deemed to be so done if it is either (a) a wrongful act authorised by the master, or (b) a wrongful and unauthorised *mode* of doing some act authorised by the master.'

In *Lister v Hesley Hall Ltd*[3] the House of Lords held that test (a) 'is not an example of vicarious liability at all'[4] because the employer has directly authorised the wrongful act and so is liable for it personally (and it cannot be said that the employer is being made liable for a wrong for which he or she would otherwise have no liability) and also dispensed with test (b) at least so far as vicarious liability for the intentional acts of employees is concerned. The House took the opportunity to consider the rationale of vicarious liability and Lord Millett pointed out that vicarious liability is a form of strict liability: the employer is liable for the acts of the employee even though the employer is not personally at fault. Since the basis for imposing liability was not the fault of the employer personally, it had to be something else. In Lord Millett's view the rules imposing vicarious liability:[5]

'are based on the more general idea that a person who employs another for his own ends inevitably creates a risk that the employee will commit a legal wrong. If the employer's objectives cannot be achieved without a serious risk of the employee committing the kind of wrong which he has in fact committed, the employer ought to be liable. The fact that his employment gave the employee the opportunity to commit the wrong is not enough to make the employer liable. He is liable only if the risk is one which experience shows is inherent in the nature of the business.'

This rationale underlay Salmond's test (b). Thus, an employer was liable for an unauthorised mode of doing an act authorised by the employer. But the facts of *Lister* showed that test (b) could no longer be correct. The defendant employer owned a school with a boarding house. The employee, a warden of the boarding house, had sexually abused the boys in his care. Lord Millett said that:[6]

'In the present case the warden was employed to look after the boys in his care and secure their welfare. It is stretching language to breaking-point to describe the series of deliberate sexual acts on them on which he embarked as merely a wrongful and unauthorised mode of performing that duty.'

According to test (b), the employer was not liable for the warden's sexual abuse but the House of Lords held that it was vicariously liable for it. Lord Millett, while stating that the precise terminology was not critical, suggested that an alternative test might be that vicarious liability should be imposed:[7]

'where the unauthorised acts of the employee are so closely connected with acts which the employer has authorised that they may properly be regarded as being within the scope of the employment.'

He then referred to experience that showed that in cases of boarding schools, prisons, nursing homes and similar institutions there was an inherent risk that those placed in a position of trust might commit indecent assaults on those in their care. Hence employers of such persons might be liable for indecent assaults committed by their employees.

1 See paras 5.3 and 5.4, above.
2 See *Mattis v Pollock* [2003] 1 WLR 2158, CA at [18] and the discussion of Lord Nicholls in *Dubai Aluminium Co Ltd v Salaam* [2002] UKHL 48, [2003] 2 AC 366 at [19].
3 [2001] UKHL 22, [2002] 1 AC 235.
4 The passage from *Salmond* [2001] UKHL 22, [2002] 1 AC 235 set out in the text was quoted by Lord Millett at [67] and prompted this comment.
5 [2001] UKHL 22, [2002] 1 AC 235 at [65].
6 [2001] UKHL 22, [2002] 1 AC 235 at [68].
7 [2001] UKHL 22, [2002] 1 AC 235 at [69]. In the subsequent case of *Bernard A-G of Jamaica* [2005] IRLR 398 at [18] Lord Steyn, giving the opinion of the Privy Council, summarised the effect of *Lister* in the following way:

'The correct approach is to concentrate on the relative closeness of the connection between the nature of the employment and the particular tort, and to ask whether looking at the matter in the round it is just and reasonable to hold the employers vicariously liable. In deciding this question a relevant factor is the risks to others created by an employer who entrusts duties, tasks and functions to an employee.'

5.22 The House of Lords returned to the general principles of vicarious liability in the solicitors' case of *Dubai Aluminium Co Ltd v Salaam*.[1] That case concerned the vicarious liability of innocent partners in a solicitors' firm for wrongs committed by another partner, rather than employers' liability, but Lord Nicholls, who gave the leading speech, considered that the rationale for imposing vicarious liability was essentially the same as set out in *Lister* in relation to employees. It was based on:[2]

'the recognition that carrying on a business enterprise necessarily involves risks to others. It involves the risk that others will be harmed by wrongful acts committed by the agents through whom the business is carried on. When those risks ripen into loss, it is just that the business should be responsible for compensating the person who has been wronged.'

This led him to suggest that the best general test for the imposition of vicarious liability was:[3]

'that the wrongful conduct must be so closely connected with acts the partner or employee was authorised to do that, for the purpose of the liability of the firm or the employer to third parties, the wrongful conduct *may fairly and properly be regarded* as done by the partner while acting in the ordinary course of the firm's business or the employee's employment.'

Lord Nicholls recognised, however, that this test was imprecise and left the court needing to make a value judgment on the facts of each case. For this reason, authority was likely to prove particularly helpful in this area. Finally, so far as expressions of general principle are concerned, 'vicarious liability is not imposed unless all the acts which are necessary to make the servant personally liable took place within the course of the employment.'[4] It does not matter if the employee did other acts while acting outside the course of the employment. But if an act constituting an essential element of liability was done outside the course of employment then there can be no vicarious liability.

1 [2002] UKHL 48, [2003] 2 AC 366. In *Bernard A-G of Jamaica* [2004] UKPC 47, [2005] IRLR 398 at [21], the Privy Council stressed that, because vicarious liability was a variety of strict liability, it must be kept within clear limits and quoted with approval a passage from the Canadian case of *Bazley v Curry* (1999) 174 DLR (4th) 45 at [62]:

  'The policy purposes underlying the imposition of strict liability on employers are served only where the wrong is so connected with the employment that it can be said that the employer has introduced the risk of the wrong (and is thereby fairly and usefully charged with its management and minimisation).'

2 [2002] UKHL 48, [2003] 2 AC 366 at [21].
3 [2002] UKHL 48, [2003] 2 AC 366 at [23].
4 [2002] UKHL 48, [2003] 2 AC 366 at at [39] (Lord Nicholls), referring to *Credit Lyonnais Bank Nederland NV v Export Credits Guarantee Department* [2000] 1 AC 486.

2   Cases where the claimant is a client

5.23   In many cases it will be clear that a negligent solicitor acted in the course of his or her employment (or, if a partner, in the ordinary course of the business of the firm) and in practice no issue will be taken as to whether the firm or the other partners are liable for the solicitor's acts. Difficult cases, however, tend to arise where the conduct complained of amounted to an intentional wrong, and, in particular, where the employee (or partner) was dishonest. *Lloyd v Grace Smith & Co*[1] established that an employer, there a firm of solicitors, could be liable for the dishonest acts of an employee, as long as the employee was doing acts of a kind that he was authorised by the firm to do. The employee was authorised by the firm to carry out conveyancing work. The claimant widow engaged him in that capacity in relation to conveyancing of two cottages that she owned. The employee effectively stole them from her. The House of Lords held that the firm was liable for the employee's dishonesty. This can be seen as a holding out case. The firm held out the employee as authorised to undertake conveyancing work on its behalf; the widow believed that he was so authorised and in reliance on this entrusted her conveyancing work to him. The firm was liable because it had held him out as qualified to do this kind of work and it did not matter that the employee was acting for his own rather than the firm's benefit. In *Dubai Aluminium*[2] Lord Millett said that the decisive factor in *Lloyd* 'was that the employee who committed the fraud for his own benefit was the person to whom his employer invited the client to entrust her affairs.' The limits of this principle were reached in *JJ Coughlan Ltd v Ruparelia*.[3] The claimant argued that the scheme in question was an investment scheme, and because it was part of the ordinary business of solicitors to act in relation to such schemes, the principle of *Lloyd v Grace, Smith* applied. The Court of Appeal rejected this argument. The scheme was too incredible or unusual for work relating to it to count as being part of the ordinary business of a solicitor.

1 [1912] AC 716, HL. See also *Morris v CW Martin & Sons Ltd* [1966] 1 QB 716, CA.
2 [2002] UKHL 48, [2003] 2 AC 366 at [129].
3 [2003] EWCA Civ 1057, [2004] PNLR 4. The facts are set out in detail in para 5.5, above.

3   Cases where the claimant is not a client

5.24   *Dubai Aluminium*[1] fell into this category. The claimant was induced by fraud to pay $50m pursuant to a bogus consultancy agreement. The proceeds were shared between the fraudsters who included S and T, by a number of bogus sub-agreements. The claimant alleged that A, S's solicitor, had dishonestly assisted S and T in their breaches of trust by drafting the bogus consultancy agreement and the sub-agreements and the issue was whether (on the assumption that A had done this) he had done it in the ordinary course of his firm's business as solicitors so that his innocent partners were vicariously liable for his actions pursuant to the Partnership Act 1890. Lord Nicholls, giving the leading speech, said that A's acts in drafting the dishonest consultancy agreements were sufficiently closely connected with acts which he was authorised to do, namely the drafting of honest consultancy agreements, as to fairly be regarded as having been done in the ordinary course of the firm's business.[2] He and Lord Millett approved a case in which there was held to be vicarious liability for an employee who had dishonestly done acts of a kind which he was authorised to do honestly in circumstances where he acted in order to advance the interests of the employer.[3]

1 [2002] UKHL 48, [2003] 2 AC 366. See also *Attorney General of Zambia v Meer Care & Desai* [2007] EWHC 952 (Ch) (above) at [669].
2 [2002] UKHL 48, [2003] 2 AC 366 at [36].
3 *Hamlyn v John Houston & Co* [1903] 1 KB 81: see [31]–[32] and [124]–[125].

C UNDERTAKINGS

1 The court's summary jurisdiction

5.25 The court has a disciplinary jurisdiction over the conduct of solicitors which is now reflected in s 50 of the Supreme Court Act 1981.[1] This jurisdiction is an extraordinary one and is most commonly invoked to enforce solicitors' undertakings.[2] But the jurisdiction extends much wider than this[3] and in *Myers v Elman*[4] Lord Wright described it as follows:

> 'The underlying principle is that the court has a right and a duty to supervise the conduct of its solicitors, and visit with penalties any conduct of a solicitor which is of such a nature as to tend to defeat justice in the very cause in which he is engaged professionally, as was said by Abinger C.B. in *Stephens v Hill* (1842) 10 M & W 28. The matter complained of need not be criminal. It need not involve peculation or dishonesty. A mere mistake or error of judgment is not generally sufficient, but a gross neglect or inaccuracy in a matter which it is a solicitor's duty to ascertain with accuracy may suffice. Thus, a solicitor may be held bound in certain events to satisfy himself that he has a retainer to act, or as to the accuracy of an affidavit which his client swears. It is impossible to enumerate the various contingencies which may call into operation the exercise of this jurisdiction. It need not involve personal obliquity. The term professional misconduct has often been used to describe the ground on which the court acts. It would perhaps be more accurate to describe it as conduct which involves a failure on the part of a solicitor to fulfil his duty to the court and to realise his duty to aid in promoting in his own sphere the cause of justice. This summary procedure may often be invoked to save the expense of an action. Thus it may in proper cases take the place of an action for negligence, or an action for breach of warranty of authority brought by the person named as defendant in the writ. The jurisdiction is not merely punitive but compensatory. The order is for payment of costs thrown away or lost because of the conduct complained of. It is frequently, as in this case, exercised in order to compensate the opposite party in the action.'

1 Supreme Court Act 1981, s 50 states:

'(1) Any person duly admitted as a solicitor shall be an officer of the Supreme Court; …

(2) Subject to the provisions of this Act, the High Court, the Crown Court and the Court of Appeal respectively, or any division or judge of those courts, may exercise the same jurisdiction in respect of solicitors as any one of the superior courts of law or equity from which the Supreme Court was constituted might have exercised immediately before the passing of the Supreme Court of Judicature Act 1873 in respect of any solicitor, attorney or proctor admitted to practise there.

(3) An appeal shall lie to the Court of Appeal from any order made against a solicitor by the High Court or the Crown Court in the exercise of its jurisdiction in respect of solicitors under subsection (2).'

Section 142 of the County Courts Act 1984 confers specific jurisdiction on the county court in relation to undertakings:

'A county court shall have the same power to enforce an undertaking given by a solicitor in relation to any proceedings in that court as the High Court has to enforce an undertaking so given in relation to any proceedings in the High Court.'

2 See *Fox v Bannister, King & Rigbeys* [1988] QB 925, CA at 931F-G (Sir John Donaldson MR):

'The jurisdiction is indeed "extraordinary", being based upon the right of the court to see that a high standard of conduct is maintained by its officers acting as such … It is, in a sense, a domestic jurisdiction to which solicitors are only amenable because of their special relationship with the court and it is designed to impose higher standards than the law applies generally.'

See also *Gupta v Comer* [1991] 1 QB 629, CA at 632E-F (Sir John Donaldson MR). Both *Myers v Elman* and *Gupta v Comer* were concerned with the jurisdiction to make a costs order against solicitors under the summary jurisdiction in circumstances where an application for a wasted costs order would now be made. For wasted costs orders see chapter 13, below.
3 Another example of the jurisdiction is an order for costs against a solicitor who acts in breach of warranty of authority: see para 5.19, above.
4 [1940] AC 282 at 319. In *Fox v Bannister, King & Rigbeys* [1988] QB 925, CA at 931G-H Sir John Donaldson MR explained the summary nature of the jurisdiction:

'Its summary character lies not in the burden or standard of proof, although it is only exercisable where there has been a serious dereliction of duty, but in the procedure whereby it is invoked. This is normally by originating summons, although it can be by simple application in an action where the conduct complained of occurred in the course of that action, and will not automatically or usually involve pleadings, discovery or oral evidence, although the court can, in appropriate circumstances, require a definition of the issues (by pleadings or otherwise), discovery and oral evidence.'

2 Undertakings

(a) Introduction

5.26 There are three ways in which the recipient of an undertaking may seek to enforce it: first, by a claim for breach of contract if the undertaking has contractual force; secondly, by an application to the court to exercise the summary jurisdiction over solicitors (as explained above); and, thirdly, by a complaint to the Solicitors Regulation Authority.[1] In *Udall v Capri Lighting Ltd*[2] the Court of Appeal held that an undertaking given by a solicitor to procure that the directors of his client would provide security for a claim by creating second charges on their personal properties was enforceable under the court's summary jurisdiction. In the course of his judgment Balcombe LJ set out the following principles on the exercise of the jurisdiction:[3]

'(1) The nature of the summary jurisdiction is explained in the following passage from the speech of Lord Wright in *Myers v*

Elman:[4] (2) Although the jurisdiction is compensatory and not punitive, it still retains a disciplinary slant. It is only available where the conduct of the solicitor is inexcusable and such as to merit reproof:…(3) If the misconduct of the solicitor leads to a person suffering loss, then the court has power to order the solicitor to make good the loss occasioned by his breach of duty …(4) Failure to implement a solicitor's undertaking is prima facie to be regarded as misconduct on his part, and this is so even though he has not been guilty of dishonourable conduct …However, exceptionally, the solicitor may be able to give an explanation for his failure to honour his undertaking which may enable the court to say that there has been no misconduct in the particular case …(5) Neither the fact that the undertaking was that a third party should do an act, nor the fact that the solicitor may have a defence to an action at law (e g the Statute of Frauds), precludes the court from exercising its supervisory jurisdiction:… However, these are factors which the court may take into account in deciding whether or not to exercise its discretion and, if so, in what manner. (6) The summary jurisdiction involves a discretion as to the relief to be granted …. In the case of an undertaking, where there is no evidence that it is impossible to perform, the order will usually be to require the solicitor to do that which he had undertaken to do ……(7) Where it is inappropriate for the court to make an order requiring the solicitor to perform his undertaking, e g on the grounds of impossibility, the court may exercise the power referred to in paragraph (3) above and order the solicitor to compensate a person who has suffered loss in consequence of his failure to implement his undertaking …'

1 See *Udall v Capri Lighting Ltd* [1988] QB 907, CA at 916D-F (Balcombe LJ). The Solicitors Code of Conduct 2007, r 10.05 now provides:

'(1) You must fulfil an undertaking which is given in circumstances where:

(a) you give the undertaking in the course of practice;

(b) you are a principal in a firm, and any person within the firm gives the undertaking in the course of practice;

(c) you give the undertaking outside the course of practice, but as a solicitor; or

(d) you are an REL based at an office in England and Wales, and you give the undertaking within the UK, as a lawyer of an Establishment Directive State but outside your practice as an REL.

(2) You must fulfil an undertaking within a reasonable time.

(3) If you give an undertaking which is dependent upon the happening of a future event, you must notify the recipient immediately if it becomes clear that the event will not occur.

(4) When you give an undertaking to pay another's costs, the undertaking will be discharged if the matter does not proceed unless there is an express agreement that the costs are payable in any event.'

2 [1988] QB 907, CA.
3 [1988] QB 907 at 916H–918B.
4 The passage is set out in para 5.25, above.

5.27 The term 'undertaking' is defined by the Solicitors Code of Conduct 2007 as: 'a statement made by you or your firm to someone who reasonably relies upon it, that you or your firm will do something or cause something to be done, or refrain from doing something.'[1] The definition also makes it clear that it is unnecessary for the solicitor to use the word 'undertake' or 'undertaking'. This definition is consistent with the way in which the court has interpreted solicitors' undertakings in exercising its summary jurisdiction. In *Fox v Bannister, King & Rigbeys*[2] two solicitors had acted for the same client and one of them remained unpaid. The first agreed to hold £18,000 of the proceeds of sale of a property and not to release it without referring to the second solicitor. He provided the second solicitor with a letter on headed notepaper in which he stated that he would hold the funds until the second solicitor and the client had sorted everything else out. Although he did not use the words 'undertakes' or 'undertaking', he was held to have given an undertaking which could be enforced under the summary jurisdiction.[3] An oral undertaking[4] may be enforced under the summary jurisdiction (although the court may decline jurisdiction if there is a contested issue of fact about whether the undertaking was given) and an undertaking may be enforced against a solicitor personally even if the subject matter of the undertaking is the performance of an obligation by a client (provided that it is clear that the solicitor has assumed a personal liability to ensure that the client's obligation is performed). In *Udall v Capri Lighting Ltd*, for instance, the solicitor gave an oral undertaking to procure that the directors of his client provided certain securities which the court enforced.[5]

1 Rule 24 defines undertaking for the purposes of rr 10.05 and 15.10 (which deal with overseas practice).
2 [1988] QB 925, CA.
3 Nicholls LJ explained the form of the undertaking at [1988] QB 927A–B:

> 'I now come to the crucial day, 30 September. According to the undisputed affidavit evidence, on that day Mr Bannister met Mr Fox and gave him a cheque for £11,500. Mr Bannister retained £18,000, representing the balance of the proceeds after deducting Bannisters' own costs. Mr Bannister retained that sum in accordance with instructions given to him by Mr Watts. Mr Bannister told Mr Fox that he would not part with that sum of £18,000 without referring to Mr Fox. When giving Mr Fox the cheque for £11,500 Mr Bannister also handed to Mr Fox a letter on Bannisters' headed paper, the material part of which read: "this leaves a balance in hand of £29,553.10 as I told you [Mr Watts] wanted me to retain the £18,000 and I enclose a cheque for £11,500.00 in your favour. I see your letter of 29 September and no doubt you and [Mr Watts] will sort out as to the £18,000 which is still in my account and which of course I shall retain until you have sorted everything out." '

See also *Hastingwood Property Ltd v Saunders Bearman Anselm* [1991] Ch 114 (Edward Nugee QC) at 126A–B: 'The use of the word 'undertaking' is not essential in order that a solicitor's obligation shall be enforceable summarily: in *John Fox v Bannister, King & Rigbeys*

(Note) [1988] QB 925 the solicitor did not in terms give an undertaking, nor did he in *Re A Solicitor; ex parte Hales* [1907] 2 KB 539, but in both cases the court enforced the obligations of the solicitor as if he had done so.'

4 Paragraph 34 of the guidance notes to r 10.05 of the Solicitors Code of Conduct 2007 states:

> '[I]t is recommended that oral undertakings be confirmed or recorded in writing for evidential purposes.'

> See also *Udall v Capri Lighting Ltd* [1988] QB 907 at 920A: '... most solicitors would no doubt agree that, as a matter of normal good practice, oral undertakings should be confirmed in writing forthwith by the recipient.'

5 [1988] QB 907 at 912A (Balcombe LJ) setting out the form of the undertaking and 919E–F (Kerr LJ):

> '[T]he fact that a solicitor has undertaken that a third party will do or refrain from doing something does not in itself affect the nature of the undertaking. The court has the same powers in relation to a solicitor who is alleged to have given an undertaking of this nature as in the case of any other undertaking. But the manner in which the court will exercise its powers in such cases may well be different from the more straightforward type of case. To give an undertaking that a third party will do or refrain from doing something may obviously be risky and indeed unwise.'

5.28 The court has jurisdiction to enforce any undertaking given by a solicitor (and not only an undertaking given to the court in the course of proceedings) provided that the undertaking was given by the solicitor in his or her capacity as a solicitor. Again, the fact that a solicitor may choose to use the word 'undertaking' or even purport to give the undertaking on behalf of his or her firm is not determinative. The court's jurisdiction can only be invoked where the solicitor gives the undertaking in the capacity of a solicitor acting for a client.[1] In *Geoffrey Silver & Drake v Baines*[2] an assistant asked another firm of solicitors to make a loan to a client of his and gave an undertaking on behalf of his firm to repay it. His principal was unaware of the undertaking. It was held that the undertaking was not given by the assistant in his capacity as a solicitor because it was effectively a guarantee. Widgery LJ stated this:[3]

> 'But the first requirement of the exercise of that jurisdiction, as Lord Denning M.R. has pointed out[4], is that the undertaking in question must have been given by the solicitor in the course of his activities as a solicitor. It must be given by him professionally as a solicitor and not in his personal capacity. The reason for that is clear enough, because a remedy of this kind is intended primarily to discipline the officers of the court, to ensure the honesty of those officers. The court is thus concerned only with their activities as solicitors, and anything done by a solicitor in his private capacity is outside this jurisdiction. What is the position here?... On its face it is simply an undertaking to repay a debt which is being contracted by the solicitor in question. If a solicitor borrows money personally and incurs a personal obligation in that regard, his promise to pay that money is not a promise in his capacity as a solicitor, even though he sits in his office when he receives the money and even though he

acknowledges the debt on his professionally headed notepaper. Another possible view of this particular case is that this was in truth the giving of a guarantee by a solicitor for a debt incurred by his client. But looking at it in that way it seems to me to make no difference. Here again one cannot describe this as an act done in the capacity of a solicitor merely because a client of the partnership was involved in the transaction. The position, of course, would have been wholly different if the sense of the transaction had been that the solicitor was to receive this money and undertake to apply it in a particular way. In those circumstances one would have a conventional type of solicitor's undertaking. It is a commonplace that solicitors obtain possession of money or documents to which they have no direct right and give an undertaking that in consideration of being supplied with the money or documents they will deal with them in a particular way.'

The decision was applied in *Ruparel v Awan*[5] where the court found that in relation to one undertaking, '[t]here was no element of actual or contemplated work or services in the capacity as a solicitor'. The judge also found that the second undertaking was in effect no more than a guarantee. The reason for the first requirement was explained by Sir John Donaldson MR in *John Fox v Bannister, King & Rigbeys*.[6] Because the jurisdiction is a disciplinary one, it can only be invoked where there has been professional misconduct or a serious breach of a professional duty. If the obligation is not a professional one, the jurisdiction is not engaged.

1 If the solicitor does not give the undertaking in this capacity, it is also unlikely that the undertaking will be binding on the solicitor's partners or employers and in practice the same test applies to determine both whether the obligation assumed by the solicitor was an undertaking amenable to the court's supervisory jurisdiction and also whether it is binding on the firm: see para 5.11, above and *Ruparel v Awan* mentioned in the text where both issues were argued. If the obligation is not assumed by the solicitor in his or her capacity as such, any liability is unlikely to be covered by a standard professional indemnity policy: see the Minimum Terms and Conditions 2006, cl 1.1.
2 [1971] 1 QB 376.
3 [1971] 1 QB 376 at 403F–H.
4 See [1971] 1 QB 376 at 402G–403A.
5 [2001] Lloyds Rep PN 258 (David Donaldson QC) at 262–4. For the facts see para 5.11, above.
6 See [1988] QB 925 at 931H–932B.

(b) Construction

5.29 Although the normal rules of contractual construction generally apply to undertakings, there is a special rule that an ambiguous undertaking given by a solicitor will normally be interpreted in favour of the recipient. This rule was originally a principle of professional conduct.[1] But it was applied by the Court of Appeal as a principle of construction in *Reddy v Lachlan*.[2] In that case a solicitor was instructed to send a letter giving an undertaking to pay £26,000 on the sale of shares in a company. The solicitor then wrote a letter stating that he acted on behalf of the company and its principal shareholder and that: 'on completion of the sale of the business of Lacering Limited, which is anticipated to take place next week, I am to remit £26,000 to you. I now confirm those instructions.' The solicitor was never provided with funds to make the payment and he argued that he had not undertaken an absolute obligation to make the payment but a qualified obligation only to make the payment out of the proceeds of sale. The Court of Appeal rejected this argument on the basis that the reasonable recipient would have regarded it as an unqualified promise to pay the money.[3] However, they also found that if the undertaking had been ambiguous, they would have applied principle 18.07 in favour of the recipient.[4] This principle was also applied in *Templeton Insurance Ltd v Penningtons Solicitors LLP*.[5] The tendency of the court is to treat undertakings given by a solicitor (particularly undertakings to pay money) as unqualified and absolute obligations which do not depend on the performance of the client. Where the undertaking is to pay or hold money, this is likely to be the conclusion which a reasonable recipient would reach. A solicitor's undertaking is normally required by a third party as security for performance of the client's obligations and the solicitor has no professional obligation to the client to give the undertaking and is free to refuse.[6] But in other contexts as well a solicitor's undertaking will be construed in favour of the recipient.[7]

1 See Principle 18.07 of the *Guide to the Professional Conduct of Solicitors* (1999) at 355. The same principle is contained in para 10 of the guidance notes to r 10.05 of the Solicitors' Code of Conduct 2007.

2 [2000] Lloyd's Rep PN 858, CA.

3 See [2000] Lloyd's Rep PN 858 at [15] (Simon Brown LJ):

> 'In my judgment the critical question to be asked in a case like this is: how would the solicitor's letter reasonably have been understood by the recipient in the circumstances in which he received it? On the facts of the present case, would it or would it not reasonably have been understood as an unqualified promise to pay £26,000 on completion?'

4 See [2000] Lloyd's Rep PN 858 at [22] (Simon Brown LJ) and [26] (Judge LJ):

> 'I should add that I do not feel that the letters taken together are ambiguous about whether an undertaking was given or not. If there had been any ambiguity in the circumstances of this case, I should have also been inclined to resolve any ambiguity in favour of Mr Reddy, who was a lay person who was sent both letters which purported to show that he could act in reliance on the guarantee (a word I use in a wholly non-technical sense) that Mr Lachlan was giving, in accordance with his written instructions from Mr Gunter.'

5 [2006] EWHC 685 (Ch) (Lewison J) at [8] and [9]:

> 'In interpreting the undertaking, I must have in mind the ordinary principles for the interpretation of contracts but there is also a special principle which applies to the interpretation of solicitors' undertakings discussed by the Court of Appeal in Reddy v Lachlan [2000] Lloyd's Rep PN 858.'

6 In *Citadel Management Inc v Thompson* [1999] 1 FLR 21 the court held that a solicitor's undertaking imposed a primary liability to make payments of in excess of US $17m (despite the client's default). The facts were unusual and the undertaking was expressed to be: 'an irrevocable undertaking' given by the solicitor 'in his capacity as a solicitor for and on behalf of' his client. Further, Buxton LJ considered it to be appropriate to look at the background circumstances including a letter in which the solicitor had stated that he knew that the funds were available and held a mandate. In *Goldman v Abbott* [1989] 2 EGLR 78, CA it was held that on the construction of an undertaking a solicitor acting for a tenant was liable for the landlord's costs of granting licence to assign even though the transaction did not proceed. In *Hole & Pugsley v Sumption* [2001] Lloyds Rep PN 419 Hart J held that an undertaking to make certain specified payments to discharge a second charge and agents' fees imposed a negative obligation on the solicitor not to pay any greater sums to discharge those liabilities: see [15] to [29]. The facts are set out in more detail in para 5.32 (below). See also *Bhanabhai v Inland Revenue Comer* [2007] NZCA 368 at [42] (Young P):

> 'All of the cases we have just cited illustrate something which might be thought to be obvious: solicitors sometimes give undertakings in relation to events which are not within their personal control. The later cases also show that there is no principle of law which requires an unconditional undertaking in relation to such events to be read down so as to be conditional upon fulfilment of the undertaking being possible. That is not to say, of course, that an undertaking should not be read sensibly and in light of the commercial context in which it is given.'

7 In *Bentley v Gaisford* [1997] QB 627 the Court of Appeal construed an undertaking given by one firm of solicitors to another to release their lien over their file 'to hold the documents/our file to our order in respect of outstanding fees/disbursements' as an undertaking not to take copies and send them to the client. In *Hastingwood Property Ltd v Saunders Bearman Anselm* [1991] Ch 114 (Edward Nugee QC), however, the court held that the fact that a firm of solicitors acting as stakeholder had given undertakings did not enlarge their obligations: see below.

(c) Enforcement

5.30 A solicitor's undertaking may be enforced by an order for committal although, before making an application to commit, the recipient of the undertaking must apply for an order for enforcement.[1] It is no answer to an application for such an order that there was no consideration for the undertaking[2] or that the solicitor (or the client on whose behalf the undertaking is given) would have a defence to a contractual claim, e g because it amounts to a guarantee or a contract for sale of an interest in land[3] or that the underlying transaction did not proceed.[4] Nor is there a limitation period for the enforcement of a solicitors undertaking although an application to enforce an undertaking may be struck out as an abuse of process.[5] In *Rooks Rider v Steel*[6] one firm of solicitors applied to enforce an undertaking given by another firm. The issue was whether the fraud of their clients prevented the first firm of solicitors from enforcing it. One company entered into an agreement to make a loan of £35m to a second company. The borrower's solicitors gave an undertaking to pay the legal costs of the lender's solicitors. The proposed loan was a fraudulent device by the lender to obtain a letter of credit and the loan was never made. The borrower's solicitors refused to honour the undertaking but Knox J held that the solicitors were bound by the undertaking and that the dishonest purpose of the lender did not prevent its solicitors (who were innocent) from enforcing it.[7] He relied on the decision in *Spector v Ageda*[8] for the proposition that a third party to an illegal contract is only affected if he or she has notice of the illegality and the parties to the undertaking were two innocent firms of solicitors. The fact that the undertaking was given without the authority of the client will not affect its enforcement either.[9]

1 See *Geoffrey Silver & Drake v Baines* [1971] 1 QB 396 at 402A (Lord Denning MR) and *Fox v Bannister, King & Rigbeys* [1988] QB 925 at 929F–G (Nicholls LJ)
2 See *Fox v Bannister, King & Rigbeys* [1988] QB 925 at 931G (Sir John Donaldson MR).
3 See *Udall v Capri Lighting Ltd* [1988] QB 907 at 919H–920A (Kerr LJ):

> 'In this connection it should also be mentioned that it was rightly not suggested on behalf of Mr Whiting that his inability to rely on the Statute of Frauds or on s 40 of the Law of Property Act 1925 was any reason against the use of the court's summary jurisdiction over solicitors. This is in line with the authorities which show that lawyers must accept responsibility for, and be able to rely on, any oral undertaking given in the course of their profession.'

See also *Hastingwood Property Ltd v Saunders Bearman Anselm* [1991] Ch 114 (Edward Nugee QC) where the court refused to make an order compelling a firm of solicitors to reconstitute a fund consisting of a deposit plus interest on the sale of land which they held as stakeholders. They were held to be enititled to release the funds under the terms on which the stake was held. The court accepted that the defences open to the parties to a contract would not be available to a solicitor in relation to an undertaking but the fact that the solicitors had given an undertaking did not enlarge their obligations and the claim failed. In the course of the judgment the judge stated (at125H–126A):

> 'It is true that the court in certain respects imposes higher standards on a solicitor than the law applies generally, but so far as is material to the present case this appears to be limited to preventing the solicitor from relying on defences such as absence of consideration or the Statute of Frauds 1677 (29 Ch 2, c 3) or delay short of the statutory period. The summary jurisdiction enables the court to compel solicitors to perform their obligations.'

4 See *Goldman v Abbott* [1989] 2 EGLR 78, CA at 83D–E (Lloyd LJ):

> 'I would like to underline the point made by Kerr LJ on para 15.14 of the *Solicitors' Professional Conduct Handbook*. If that paragraph is to be taken as meaning that undertakings given by solicitors "in connection with any matter" are in all cases subject to an implied term that the solicitors are to be discharged if the matter does not proceed, then I would disagree.'

There is no suggestion in the guidance notes to para 10.05 of the Solicitors Code of Conduct 2007 that an undertaking can be treated as discharged on this basis.
5 See *Taylor v Ribby Hall Leisure Ltd* [1998] 1 WLR 400, CA at 407H–408B (Mummery LJ):

> 'The absence of the limitation period for initiating a proceeding does not preclude the power to strike out for abuse of process. There may exist a legal right to initiate proceedings at any time, but the exercise of that right must nevertheless be subject to the overriding power of the court to protect the integrity of its own processes.'

6 [1994] 1 WLR 818.
7 [1994] 1 WLR 818 at 828G–831B.
8 [1973] Ch 30 (Megarry J).
9 See *Fox v Bannister, King & Rigbeys* [1988] QB 925 at 928H–929A. Nicholls LJ did, however, suggest that if the recipient was aware that the solicitor did not have the client's authority to give

the undertaking, this might affect the court's attitude to the exercise of its residual discretion: see 929B-C. It is suggested that this is unlikely to be persuasive in many cases. If a solicitor chooses to give an undertaking without the client's authority, the third party should be entitled to rely on it whether or not the solicitor discloses the lack of authority. Indeed, it may be that a solicitor's undertaking is requested by a third party precisely because the client is unavailable or unwilling to give authority. Compare *The Gertrud* [1927] WN 265. The court may refuse to enforce the undertaking where it was given in ignorance of facts known to the other party: see *Wade v Simeon* (1845) 13 M & W 647; or where it was given by mistake: see *Mullins v Howell* (1879) 11 Ch D 763.

(d) Impossibility

5.31 The inability of the solicitor to perform the undertaking may, however, be a ground for refusing to make an order requiring the solicitor to perform the undertaking and then an order for committal and instead for making an order for compensation.[1] In *Fox v Bannister, King & Rigbeys*[2] where the solicitor had paid away the fund on the instructions of his client, the court did not make an order compelling the solicitor to comply with the undertaking but ordered him to pay compensation instead. In contrast, in *Citadel Management Inc v Thompson*[3] the Court of Appeal refused to discharge an order for compliance with an undertaking and a subsequent order for committal despite the fact that the solicitor was unable to comply with an undertaking to pay US $17m to a third party. The facts were unusual, however. The solicitor had personally assured the third party (and also the court) that he could perform the undertaking. Buxton LJ stated:

> 'The case does not, in my view, raise any issue of impossibility in the sense in which that term was used in *Udall*. The undertaking in this case was based on a representation by a solicitor and repeated by him to the court that made the original order. The alleged "impossibility" does not spring from a state of affairs or turn of events external to the solicitor, but rather is based on a contention that the solicitor now finds that he cannot perform acts which he assured the court he could perform. The alleged impossibility is thus the inability of the solicitor to do what he assured the court who made the order enforcing the undertaking that he could in fact do. I do not think that a solicitor can be heard to assert that as a reason why he should not suffer the penalty for breach of an order that was properly made on the basis of those assurances.'

In *Hole & Pugsley v Sumption*[4] Hart J also rejected the submission that there was a principle of law that a solicitor is discharged from liability to perform the undertaking if he notifies the recipient that he is unable to perform at the earliest opportunity.

---

1 See proposition (7) of the extract from *Udall v Capri Lighting Ltd* [1988] QB 907 set out in para 5.26, above.

2 [1988] QB 925, CA. See the judgment of Nicholls LJ at 929F–930D.
3 [1999] 1 FLR 21, CA.
4 [2001] Lloyd's Rep PN 419 at [23]–[29].

(e) Compensation

5.32 The principles on which compensation is awarded were set out by Mummery LJ in *Taylor v Ribby Hall Leisure Ltd*:[1]

'The supervisory power over solicitors also stands comparison with criminal proceedings. The power is essentially a summary disciplinary one exercised by the court over its own officers to ensure their observance of an honourable standard of conduct and to punish derelictions of duty. The court has the necessary powers of enforcement which extend, unlike the contempt power ...to the payment of compensation for loss suffered in consequence of misconduct of a solicitor in failing to implement an undertaking given to the court. The award of compensation is not, however, dependent on an enforceable civil law right on the part of the person who has suffered loss:... Compensation is only available under this jurisdiction where the conduct of the solicitor is inexcusable and such as to merit reproof:... The discretionary nature of the jurisdiction should be emphasised.. The discretion extends both to procedure and substantive relief. It is flexible and unfettered by any absolute rules and is to be exercised according to the facts of the particular case.'

In *Hole & Pugsley v Sumption*[2] the court awarded compensation on a contractual basis, i e on the basis that the recipient was entitled to be placed in the position in which she would have been if the solicitors had performed their undertaking. In that case solicitors acting in matrimonial proceedings gave an unqualified undertaking to make certain payments out of the proceeds of sale of trust property, including £275,000 to a bank to discharge a second charge and also £25,000 in agents' fees, and pay half of the remaining balance to the wife. In the event both the bank and the agents required substantially more than £275,000 and £25,000 to discharge the second charge and the fees and the solicitors discharged the second charge and the agents' fees out of the balance of the proceeds of sale. The wife made a claim under the summary jurisdiction for compensation on the basis that the solicitors had undertaken to pay the specific sums of £275,000 and £25,000 and that they had broken their undertaking by paying the bank and the agents in full. Hart J held that they had given an unqualified undertaking to pay the specified sums and had acted in breach of the undertaking. He also held that it was appropriate to award damages on the contractual basis.[3]

1 [1998] 1 WLR 400, CA at 408G–409B.

2 [2001] Lloyds Rep PN 419.
3 See [2001] Lloyds Rep PN 419 at [30]–[33]. Compare *Inland Revenue Comr v Bhanabhai* [2006] 1 NZLR 797 (Laurenson J) (affirmed on appeal at [2007] NZCA 368).

5.33 As the above passage indicates, the court has a discretion both in relation to the procedure to be adopted and in relation to substantive relief. It follows that the court has a residual discretion to refuse to award compensation or enforce the undertaking at all.[1] In *Fox v Bannister, King & Rigbeys*[2] Nicholls LJ suggested that one situation in which the court might refuse to enforce an undertaking or award compensation is 'where there was real scope for genuine misunderstanding on what was said or meant by a solicitor on a particular occasion'. In *Hole & Pugsley v Sumption* Hart J referred to this passage but declined to exercise his discretion in the solicitor's favour:[3]

> 'I have considered whether this is a case where that residual discretion ought to be exercised in the claimants' favour, or at least a decision deferred on that question until trial. I have concluded however that the answer to both questions is negative. On my construction of the correspondence there was not, in my judgment, "real scope for genuine misunderstanding". Moreover, although it is possible that enforcement of the undertaking by ordering compensation will swell the assets available for division on divorce above what they would have been had no undertaking ever been given, that is not a consideration which in the end would justify the court in depriving the defendant of the advantage which was negotiated for her by Miss Hallam. It was for the claimants to satisfy themselves that they could safely give the undertaking which was sought.'

1 This would not, of course, prevent the recipient from seeking to enforce the undertaking if it had contractual force. See *Udall v Capri Lighting Ltd* [1988] QB 907 at 924B (Kerr LJ):

> 'Since the purpose of the procedure is disciplinary, being designed to ensure a high standard of conduct on the part of solicitors, an order for enforcement of the undertaking or for compensation for its non-performance will not necessarily follow as a matter of course. Before making such an order the court will have to be satisfied that by failing to perform the undertaking the solicitor had been guilty of professional misconduct or a serious dereliction of professional duty. If it is not satisfied about this, then it seems to me that it must still be open to the court to decline to make any order, and to hold that the matter must proceed by action, if at all, on the ground that the circumstances do not warrant an order of a disciplinary nature against an officer of the court.'

2 [1988] QB 925, CA at 930G.
3 [2001] Lloyds Rep PN 419 at [35].

(f) Procedure

5.34 An application to enforce an undertaking under the summary jurisdiction should be made under CPR Part 8 or by application in the action if there are existing proceedings.[1] If the claimant applies immediately for an order for committal, the court will normally make an order for enforcement.[2] The jurisdiction to make an order for enforcement should be exercised only in clear cases[3] although, as the passage from Mummery LJ's judgment in *Taylor v Ribby Hall Leisure Ltd* (above) indicates, the court has a flexible and unfettered discretion over the procedure which it may adopt. In *Fox v Bannister, King & Rigbeys*[4] Nicholls LJ stated:

> 'Mr Toulson submitted that to succeed with an application such as this the applicant has to show that he has a plain and obvious case, and that where serious or difficult questions are involved, the case is not one appropriate to be dealt with under the court's summary jurisdiction over its officers. I am unable to accept this submission expressed in such wide terms. If this submission were well founded it would mean that if, for example, a dispute arose over whether a solicitor had given an oral undertaking, or had given a written undertaking the only copy of which had been destroyed or lost, the court would be precluded from investigating the matter. That cannot be right. Since the jurisdiction is disciplinary as well as compensatory, the court must be satisfied that there has been misconduct in that there has been a breach of an undertaking given by the solicitor acting professionally. But, in an appropriate case, the court can resolve issues of fact with the assistance of cross-examination of deponents. If necessary, an order for discovery can be made. Again, if there is a dispute about the true construction of a document, the court can resolve that issue having heard argument on it.'

Finally, in *Taylor v Ribby Hall Leisure Ltd*[5] the Court of Appeal went out of its way to give clear guidance that an application to enforce an undertaking should be made promptly once the recipient of the undertaking becomes aware that it has been broken. Indeed, a solicitor may well be negligent if he or she fails to apply promptly to enforce an undertaking. For instance, where the vendor's solicitor gives an undertaking to discharge a charge on the completion of a sale of land, it is the duty of the purchaser's solicitor to take steps to enforce that undertaking immediately if the vendor's solicitor is in breach and fails to produce the relevant DS1 on completion or apply to discharge the charge.[6]

1 See the extract from the judgment of Sir John Donaldson in *Fox v Bannister, King & Rigbeys* [1988] QB 925, CA at 931G–H quoted in para 5.25 n 4 (above). For an example of the various stages in the procedure (where a suspended order for committal was made): see *Citadel Management Inc v Thompson* [1999] 1 FLR 21.
2 See *Re a Solicitor (Lincoln)* [1966] 1 WLR 1604 (Pennycuick J) at 1608E–F:

> 'No case was cited in which the court made an order for committal upon a direct application to commit for breach of the undertaking without having first made an order to perform the undertaking. I do not say that there is no jurisdiction to make such an order, but neither counsel was able to point to a case in which such an order had been made.'

5.34 *Authority, vicarious liability and undertakings*

See also *Geoffrey Silver & Drake v Baines* [1971] 1 QB 396 at 402AD (Lord Denning MR).

3 See *Geoffrey Silver & Drake v Baines* [1971] 1 QB 396 at 403B–D (Lord Denning MR), 404D–F (Widgery LJ) and 405 B–D (Megaw LJ). The issue was whether an undertaking given by an assistant to repay a loan was amenable to the summary jurisdiction but the Court of Appeal held that it was not a clear case and should be brought by action because the scope of the assistant's authority was a live issue. It is also important that the application for enforcement was made against the principal although the assistant was an admitted solicitor. The real issue was, therefore, whether he was bound by the undertaking: see para 5.11, above. See also *Udall v Capri Lighting Ltd* [1988] QB 907, CA at 919F where Kerr LJ considered that if there was a dispute over the terms of an oral undertaking, the court might decline jurisdiction:

> 'When there is a conflict as to whether or not an oral undertaking of the kind was in fact given, then the court may well conclude that the case is insufficiently clear to justify the application of its inherent summary supervisory jurisdiction over solicitors and that the matter should be left to proceed by action.'

In *Udall* itself in fact the judge at first instance ordered statements of case and disclosure: see 919G and 923C. For a recent decision in which the court refused to exercise the supervisory jurisdiction (with full citation of the English authorities) see *McIlraith v Ilkin* [2007] NSWSC 911 (Brereton J, Supreme Court of New South Wales).

4 [1988] QB 925, CA at 930E. This passage was cited by Knox J in *Rooks Rider v Steel* [1994] 1 WLR 818 at 826H–827E. He refused to exercise his discretion to decline jurisdiction on the basis that there was 'no factual difficulty' that had not been resolved in favour of the solicitors or their client and 'no jurisdictional impediment' to deciding the point of law: see 828A. In *Hole & Pugsley v Sumption* [2001] Lloyd's Rep PN 419 Hart J took the same course on the basis that although there were underlying disputes of fact, the only real issues on enforcement were issues of construction: see [16].

5 [1998] 1 WLR 400, CA at 409H–410A:

> 'In our judgment it is, in general, preferable to make submissions on delay, prejudice, potential injustice and other factors relevant to the court's discretion in its contempt and supervisory powers at the substantive hearing rather than by a preliminary pre-emptive move to strike out. That procedure may be open to the objection that it increases the costs and delay that preliminary procedures are intended to avoid. We add for future guidance that proceedings of this kind should, in the absence of a good reason, be initiated within a reasonable time of a party obtaining knowledge of a breach of a court order or undertaking or other misconduct. In most cases the court is dependent on a party bringing a breach or a case of misconduct to its notice so that appropriate action can be taken.'

6 See *Patel v Daybells* [2001] EWCA Civ 1229, [2001] Lloyds Rep PN 738 at [66] (Robert Walker LJ):

> '[W]e would regard it as being normally part of a purchaser's solicitor's duty to his client to take speedy steps to enforce the undertaking of a vendor's solicitor (in relation to the discharge of a mortgage) once he is aware that the solicitor is in breach of his undertaking. It is an unsatisfactory feature of this case that on one of the very rare occasions on which a completion has gone wrong otherwise than through fraud and the matter has come to court, a solicitor's undertaking seems to have failed to provide the necessary protection.'

Chapter 6

Solicitors' duties of confidentiality

A INTRODUCTION

6.01 It is uncontroversial that a solicitor owes an obligation to his or her client to preserve the client's confidences and not reveal to third parties information learnt in the course of the retainer.[1] Indeed, long before the modern law of confidentiality started to develop in the mid-nineteenth century the courts recognised that a lawyer owed to the client a duty not to disclose the client's confidences except with the client's express or implied consent.[2] The new Solicitors' Code of Conduct 2007[3] states the duty as follows: 'You and your firm must keep the affairs of clients and former clients confidential except where disclosure is required or permitted by law or by your client or former client'.[4] It has even been said that, since solicitors are officers of the court, the solicitor's obligations of confidence are stricter than those of other professional confidants; the court 'can fix a higher standard for the behaviour of its officers than it would be practicable to exact from persons in other confidential relations'.[5] It is easy to state in broad terms the obligation of confidentiality, but nonetheless its precise ambit and application can generate difficulties. The purpose of this chapter is to investigate the width of the solicitor's obligation of confidentiality and the circumstances when it is typically tested in the courts. The chapter will be divided as follows: first we consider the relationship between the solicitor's duty of confidentiality and the law of legal professional privilege (section B); at section C we consider the incidents and content of the duty and how the duty may be breached; finally at section D the remedies available to the client or former client to restrain a breach or otherwise obtain financial recompense are discussed.

1 So Gaselee J in *Taylor v Blacklow* (1836) 3 Bing (NC) 235, at 249, said that it was 'the first duty of an attorney ...to keep the secrets of his client. Authority is not wanted to establish that proposition.' In fact this case appears to be the first decision in which a solicitor's duty of confidentiality was recognised in an action at law for damages: see *Hardy v Veasey* (1868) LR 3 Ex 107. The case is of interest in that the court clearly recognised that the claim did not depend upon it being established that the information communicated to the solicitor could have been withheld from a court as privileged: i e a distinction was drawn between the law of privilege and the law of confidence. For early cases decided by courts of equity, which typically involved attempts to prevent a solicitor acting see *Earl of Cholmondeley v Lord Clinton* (1815) 19 Ves 261; *Beer v Ward* (1821) Jac 77; *Bricheno v Thorp* (1821) Jac 300; *Davies v Clough* (1837) 8 Sim 262; *Johnson v Marriott* (1833) 2 C&M 183; *Lewis v Smith* (1849) 1 Mac & G 417.

2 See *General Mediterranean Holdings SA v Patel* [1999] 1 WLR 272, (Toulson J), at 280–281.
   See also the historical survey of the early cases, dating back to the sixteenth century, in *R v Derby
   Magistrates Court, ex p B* [1996] 1 AC 487.
3 Which came into force on 1 July 2007.
4 Rule 4.01. Rule 4 replicates the former r 16E of the Solicitors Practice Rules 1990, which earlier
   Rule was introduced in 2005. Rule 16E was the first time that confidentiality, disclosure and
   information barriers had been dealt with by practice rules.
5 *Rakusen v Ellis, Munday & Clarke* [1912] 1 Ch 831, 840. This case should be treated with care in
   the light of *Bolkiah v KPMG* [1999] 2 AC 222, CA, discussed below at para 6.55ff, below.

B   CONFIDENTIALITY AND LEGAL
PROFESSIONAL PRIVILEGE

6.02   The solicitor's duty of confidentiality is closely interrelated with the law
of legal professional privilege.[1] Legal professional privilege (LPP) is a substantive[2] right[3] which has two manifestations: the first, known as legal advice
privilege, applies, in summary terms, to communications made in confidence
between lawyers and their clients for the purpose of giving or obtaining legal
advice even at a stage when litigation is not in contemplation[4]; the second,
known as litigation privilege, applies to communications between the client or
the client's lawyer on the one hand and third parties on the other hand, or other
documents created by or on behalf of the client or the client's lawyer, which
come into existence once litigation is in contemplation or has commenced, for
the dominant purpose of obtaining information or advice in connection with, or
of conducting or aiding in the conduct of, such litigation.[5] LPP is a right, vesting
in the client, to resist the compulsory disclosure[6] of information or documents
which are subject to its ambit. However the protection of that right also requires
that where confidential documents otherwise subject to LPP have been mistakenly handed over[7] by the client's former solicitor[8] or surreptitiously obtained[9]
then the court will intervene to protect LPP.[10]

1 We consider issues of disclosure and privilege in the procedural context of claims brought against
   solicitors at chapter 14, below.
2 The old view that LPP was a rule of evidence is now dead and buried. It is now clearly established
   that LPP is a substantive right which, unless waived, cannot be overridden or infringed except by
   statute. See generally *R v Derby Magistrates Court, ex p B* [1996] 1 AC 487, at 507–8; *R (Morgan
   Grenfell & Co Ltd) v Special Commissioner of Income Tax* [2002] UKHL 21, [2003] 1 AC 563; *B
   v Auckland District Law Society* [2003] UKPC 38, [2003] 2 AC 736, at [37]ff.
3 But not a duty, in the sense that one talks of tortious, contractual or equitable duties. One does not
   talk of a breach of legal professional privilege as giving rise to a claim for damages etc.
4 See *Three Rivers District Council v Bank of England (No 6)* [2004] UKHL 48, [2005] 1 AC 610,
   at [50] (Lord Rodger). To what communications the privilege applies is the subject of considerable controversy, as is evident from the recent *Three Rivers District Council v Bank of England*
   litigation: see chapter 14 below, and Thanki (ed) *The Law of Privilege* (1st edn, 2006), at chs 2 and
   3.
5 This description has been adapted from the helpful analysis in Thanki (ed) *The Law of Privilege*
   (1st edn, 2006), at para 3.07. The convoluted description gives an indication of the complexities
   that can arise when applying the law of litigation privilege to particular factual situations. See
   generally *Thanki*, at ch 3.

6 Whether in court or arbitral proceedings or otherwise.
7 See for instance *Guinness Peat Properties Ltd* v *Fitzroy Robinson Partnership* [1987] 1 WLR 1027, CA. Mistaken disclosure of privileged documents by a litigant in court proceedings gives rise to special rules because issues of waiver arise: see para 6.73ff, below.
8 Hence in *Goddard v Nationwide Building Society* [1987] 1 QB 670, CA, the claimant sued the defendant in respect of the valuation of a house which he had purchased. In the usual way the purchase and mortgage was handled by a single firm of solicitors acting for both the claimant and the defendant lender. After proceedings had been issued the solicitors disclosed, in breach of their duty of confidence to the claimant, a document which was confidential to the claimant, to the defendant. The defendant sought to rely on the contents of the document in its defence. It was held that the document was privileged and so could not be relied upon by the defendant in its defence. Further the defendant was ordered to deliver up to the claimant all copies of the document.
9 See the leading case of *Lord Ashburton v Pape* [1913] 2 Ch 469, CA, where the claimant's solicitor's clerk was suborned into handing over privileged letters passing between the claimant and his solicitor to the defendant. An injunction was granted preventing the defendant from adducing the documents in evidence or otherwise making use of them.
10 In doing so the court is exercising its equitable jurisdiction to protect confidential information: see *Goddard* at 680, 684–6. 'The injunction is granted in aid of the privilege which, unless and until it is waived, is absolute' (at 686). The jurisdiction was stated as follows in *Nationwide Building Society v Various Solicitors* [1999] PNLR 52 (Blackburne J):

> 'where ...disclosure of a confidential and privileged communication has been made to a third party by someone bound by the confidence but having no authority of any kind from the person entitled to that privilege, then, ordinarily, the court will act on the latter's application to restrain the third party's use of that communication and will do so however innocent the conduct of the third party'.

> There is controversy whether the equitable jurisdiction is a discretionary one, so that relief can in any circumstances be refused, with the result that a privileged document may be capable of being adduced in evidence. See generally *Istil Group Inc v Zahoor* [2003] EWHC 165 (Ch), [2003] 2 All ER 252 (Lawrence Collins J).

6.03 However LPP can only apply to, and protect, communications which are otherwise confidential.[1] This is because at the root of LPP lies the obligation of confidence which a legal adviser owes his or her client in relation to confidential communications passing between them. LPP provides a form of overlay of added protection to the confidentiality of those communications.[2] It is LPP which distinguishes the confidentiality inhering in other communications between professional and client and those between lawyer and client. Whereas the confidentiality of communications between patient and doctor is not a ground, of itself, to resist disclosure of those communications in court or other proceedings (whether by the patient or the doctor)[3], confidential communications between lawyer and client are (in general) privileged from disclosure by LPP. The justification for this distinct status has been the subject of considerable debate. Its most famous exposition is perhaps that of Lord Taylor CJ in *R v Derby Magistrates' Court, ex p B*[4]:

> 'The principle which runs through all these cases, and the many other cases which were cited, is that a man must be able to consult his lawyer in confidence, since otherwise he might hold back half the truth. The client must be sure that what he tells his lawyer in

confidence will never be revealed without his consent. Legal professional privilege is thus much more than an ordinary rule of evidence, limited in its application to the facts of a particular case. It is a fundamental condition on which the administration of justice as a whole rests ... it is not for the sake of the applicant alone that the privilege must be upheld. It is in the wider interests of all those hereafter who might otherwise be deterred from telling the whole truth to their solicitors.'

LPP thus accords the confidentiality of lawyer/client communications, and hence the duty of confidence owed by the lawyer to his or her client, a special status which, as we will see, affects the way the courts act so as to protect the client's confidentiality and so regulate the conduct of solicitors.

1 It is suggested in Thanki (ed) *The Law of Privilege* (1st edn, 2006), at para 2.85, that, for the purpose of asserting privilege, the precondition that the communication should be 'confidential' should be broadly, and liberally, interpreted.
2 See *Paragon Finance plc v Freshfields* [1999] 1 WLR 1183, CA, at 1188.
3 See, famously, *The Duchess of Kingston's Case* (1776) 20 State Tr 355, at 386–91 where the defendant's doctor was compelled by the court to give evidence of communications which he had had with the defendant which were otherwise confidential. Had the witness been a lawyer not only would he not have been obliged to answer questions tending to reveal such communications, but he would have had a positive obligation to refuse to answer such questions.
4 [1996] AC 487, at 507.

6.04 It follows from this that one of the most important aspects of the solicitor's duty of confidentiality, whether or not the retainer is at an end, is that, if faced with a demand for disclosure by a third party, whether or not in the context of court or arbitral proceedings to which the solicitor is a party, or if served with a witness summons to attend to give evidence at a trial, the solicitor must uphold and assert the client's privilege, even if it would otherwise be in the solicitor's interests to make disclosure.[1] However it appears that where the solicitor is a defendant to proceedings and that solicitor inadvertently discloses to the claimant confidential documents to which privilege applies (the privilege belonging to a client who is not party to the litigation), then the solicitor has no locus to subsequently assert that privilege as against the claimant. It was held in *Nationwide Building Society v Various Solicitors*[2] that the fact that a solicitor is subject to a duty to preserve the confidentiality of privileged communications does not mean that, if, for whatever reason, including the solicitor's own inadvertence, the communications come into the possession of a stranger (in that case the claimant building society), the solicitor acquires a locus to assert his or her client's (or former client's) right of confidence. Any claim to restrain use of those documents, based as it would be on the *Ashburton v Pape* jurisdiction[3], would have to be made by the client rather than the solicitor.[4]

1 See *R v Derby Magistrates Court, ex p B* [1996] 1 AC 487, 504–5. So, if a solicitor is asked a question in cross-examination the answer to which would tend to reveal privileged communica-

tions, he is both entitled and obliged to refuse to answer. Indeed it would appear that the court will intervene to prevent him giving such an answer, even if he is otherwise willing. See for instance *Wilson* v *Rastall* (1792) 4 Durn & E 753.

2 [1999] PNLR 52 (Blackburne J).

3 In *Nationwide* the documents disclosed by the solicitors, and which they tried to claw back, relying on their former client's privilege, were plainly detrimental to their defence. But what if A sues solicitor B and B seeks to deploy in support of his defence plainly privileged documents which are confidential to C. B does not inform C of his decision and is clearly acting in breach of C's rights of confidentiality and privilege. The court would surely intervene to prevent B's breach, regardless of C's failure to intervene. C might be wholly unaware of B's conduct. The position would be analogous to the court's own intervention in the case referred to by Buller J in *Wilson* v *Rastall* (1792) 4 Durn & E 753 to prevent the attorney from giving evidence of privileged communications. In another early case, *Beer v Ward* (1821) Jacob 77 Lord Eldon LC said, at 80, that

'It would be the duty of any Court to stop [a lawyer] if he was about to disclose confidential matters ...the Court knows the privilege of the client, and it must be taken for granted that the attorney will act rightly, and claim that privilege; or that if he does not, the Court will make him claim it'.

Similarly in *R v Derby Magistrates Court, ex p B* [1996] AC 487, at 404–5, Lord Taylor CJ referred to

'... the rule that the privilege is that of the client, which he alone can waive, and that the court will not permit, let alone order, the attorney to reveal the confidential communications which have passed between him and his former client.'

4 See at para 6.02 above, at n9.

C   THE DUTY OF CONFIDENTIALITY

1   Sources of the duty

6.05   Solicitors may be engaged by clients on the basis of contracts of retainer which contain express contractual obligations of confidentiality. But even where, more usually, that is not so, the solicitor will, as part of the wider collection of contractual, tortious and fiduciary duties owed to his or her client, owe obligations of confidentiality to the client. So:

(a)   Even where there are no express terms of the retainer, there will be implied into the contract of retainer between solicitor and client a term imposing a duty of confidentiality.[1]

(b)   The usual criteria for the imposition of an equitable duty of confidentiality, by reference to the general law of confidence, will in almost all (if not all) circumstances be met – i e the solicitor will receive the information knowing, or being taken to know, that it is intended that it be kept secret.[2] Such a duty is recognised whether or not the confidant stands in a fiduciary relationship with the confider.[3]

(c)   The fiduciary duties owed by the solicitor to the client, arising out of the relationship of trust and confidence recognised by the law as subsisting

277

between solicitor and client[4], will carry with them an implicit obligation of confidentiality as an aspect of the wider duty of loyalty owed to the client.[5]

(d)   The tortious duty to exercise reasonable skill and care in the performance of the retainer, which is owed by the solicitor to the client, can itself carry with it duties to preserve and protect the client's confidentiality. The solicitor who leaves confidential documents belonging to his or her client on a train or who mistakenly sends a confidential document to a third party may well be guilty of negligence.[6]

(e)   On 25 April 2006 a new Solicitors' Practice Rule, r 16E, came into force dealing with confidentiality and disclosure. This has since become r 4 of the Solicitors' Code of Conduct 2007. This Rule, like the Rules of the Code of Conduct, does not give rise to directly enforceable duties, but a failure to comply will carry substantial weight when considering whether or not a solicitor has acted in breach of duty.[7]

1   See *Parry-Jones v Law Society* [1969] 1 Ch 1, CA, at 7 per Lord Denning MR: 'The law implies a term into the contract whereby a professional man is to keep his client's affairs secret and not to disclose them to anyone without just cause ...This particularly applies in the relationship of solicitor and client. The solicitor is not to disclose his client's affairs to anyone at all except under the most special and exceptional circumstances.'

2   The classic analysis is to be found in *Coco v A N Clarke Engineers Ltd* [1969] RPC 41, at 48–9, where Megarry J stated the elements to be proved in a claim for breach of confidence. The first was that the information 'must be of a confidential nature.' The second, relevant here, was that 'the information must have been communicated in circumstances importing an obligation of confidence. However secret and confidential the information, there can be no binding obligation of confidence if that information is blurted out in public or is communicated in other circumstances which negative any duty of holding it confidential ...if the circumstances are such that any reasonable man standing in the shoes of the recipient of the information would have realised that upon reasonable grounds the information was being given to him in confidence, then this should suffice to impose upon him the equitable obligation of confidence.' Megarry J's third element was unauthorised use of the information to the detriment of the confider. See also *A-G v Guardian Newspapers (No 2)* [1990] 1 AC 109, at 281B, per Lord Goff (the *Spycatcher* case).

3   However, as discussed below at para 6.39, below, a solicitor may be under a special disability in that he or she may be prohibited from publishing information concerning the client even where that information does not strictly fulfil the criterion of confidentiality.

4   In *Re van Laun, ex p Chatterton* [1907] 2 KB 23, CA, at 29 Cozens-Hardy MR referred to the 'relation between the parties of solicitor and client ...[as]... one of the most important fiduciary relations known to our law.' For fiduciary duties generally, see para 4.22ff, above.

5   In *A-G v Blake* [1998] Ch 439, CA at 454, the duty of confidentiality was described as itself a 'fiduciary relationship' which 'arises whenever information is imparted by one person to another in confidence', and which usually subsists within the context of another fiduciary relationship. Whether the duty of confidentiality was properly to be categorised as a fiduciary one was left open by the Privy Council in *Arklow Investments v Maclean* [2000] 1 WLR 594, at 600. In principle, it seems preferable to characterise the obligation of confidence as an equitable, rather than fiduciary, duty except where it arises within the context of a pre-existing and ongoing fiduciary relationship. This accords with the general law of confidence.

6   See for instance *Weld-Blundell v Stephens* [1919] 1 KB 520, CA, and [1920] 1 AC 956, HL, and *Swinney v Chief Constable of Northumbria Police Force* [1997] 1 QB 464, CA.

7   See para 2.14ff, above.

6.06 Although, therefore, the source of the obligation of confidence can be founded upon three separate juridical bases, in practice the obligation is typically analysed as an aspect of the solicitor's fiduciary duties. This is, first, because the fiduciary duties owed by a solicitor may be wider than his or her contractual duties: the source of the fiduciary duties owed by a solicitor to the client is not the retainer itself, but all the circumstances (including, where relevant, the retainer) creating a relationship of trust and confidence, from which relationship flow obligations of loyalty and transparency.[1] Hence such duties may exist irrespective of a retainer and may pre- and post-date the period of the retainer. On the other hand it is usually said that a solicitor's fiduciary duties generally come to an end at the date of termination of the retainer[2] (though this is not always so as the case of *Longstaff v Birtles* demonstrates) and so the basis for the solicitor's continuing duty of confidence post-retainer will generally be founded upon contract or the equitable duty of confidence. Secondly, there is a potential advantage to the client (or former client) in relying on equitable obligations of confidence (whether or not as an aspect of the solicitor's fiduciary duties), most obviously in the choice of remedies available.[3] Whereas a claimant alleging breach of a common law duty will generally be confined to a remedy reflecting loss sustained flowing from the breach, equitable remedies include claims for an account of profits or that property acquired as a result of a breach of duty is held on constructive trust for the claimant.[4]

1 *Longstaff v Birtles* [2001] EWCA Civ 1218, [2002] 1 WLR 470, at [1]. *Ratiu v Conway* [2005] EWCA Civ 1302, [2006] 1 All ER 571, at [71]–[73]. See also para 4.24ff, above.
2 See *A-G v Blake* [1998] Ch 439, CA, at 453: 'We do not recognise the concept of a fiduciary obligation which continues notwithstanding the determination of the particular relationship which gives rise to it'. See also *Bolkiah v KPMG* [1999] 2 AC 222, at 235C, discussed at para 6.55ff, below.
3 Note however the statement by Sopinka J in *LAC Minerals Ltd v International Corona Resources Ltd* (1989) 61 DLR (4th) 14, at 64 that:

> '... the fact that confidential information is obtained and misused cannot itself create a fiduciary obligation. No doubt one of the possible incidents of a fiduciary relationship is the exchange of confidential information and restrictions on its use. Where, however, the essence of the complaint is misuse of confidential information, the appropriate cause of action in favour of the party aggrieved is breach of confidence and not breach of fiduciary duty'.

This dictum was cited with approval in the Court of Appeal case of *Indata Equipment Supplies Ltd v ACL Ltd* [1998] 1 BCLC 412, at 419. Neither of these cases involved professionals, but rather the attempt by claimants to establish a fiduciary relationship between commercial parties.
4 See para 6.55ff, below.

6.07 Notwithstanding that the solicitor's fiduciary duties are founded upon a juridical basis which is distinct from the solicitor's contractual duties, nonetheless, during the currency of the retainer, those fiduciary duties will typically be co-extensive with the contractual duties owed. 'A solicitor's duty of single-minded loyalty to his client's interest, and his duty to respect his client's confidences, do have their roots in the fiduciary nature of the solicitor-client relationship. But they may have to be moulded and informed by the terms of the contractual relationship'.[1] The point is that although fiduciary duties arise independently of contract (and may exist irrespective of the existence of a contractual relationship), nonetheless where a fiduciary relationship does co-exist alongside a contractual one, then the scope and width of those fiduciary duties will be defined by the terms of the contract (whether implied or express): fiduciary duties do not exist in a vacuum and are not immutable in their ambit and content.[2] The classic statement of the position is in Mason J's judgment in the Australian case of *Hospital Products Ltd v United States Surgical Corpn*:[3]

> 'That contractual and fiduciary relationships may co-exist between the same parties has never been doubted. Indeed, the existence of a basic contractual relationship has in many situations provided a foundation for the erection of a fiduciary relationship. In these situations it is the contractual foundation which is all important because it is the contract that regulates the basic rights and liabilities of the parties. The fiduciary relationship, if it is to exist at all, must accommodate itself to the terms of the contract so that it is consistent with, and conforms to, them. The fiduciary relationship cannot be superimposed upon the contract in such a way as to alter the operation which the contract was intended to have according to its true construction.'

1 *Hilton v Barker Booth & Eastwood* [2005] UKHL 8, [2005] 1 WLR 567, at [30]. Discussed at para 1.1 n 5, para 2.15, and para 4.36, above, and para 6.38, below.
2 See per Lord Browne-Wilkinson in *Henderson v Merrett Syndicates Ltd* [1995] 2 AC 145, at 206:

> 'The phrase "fiduciary duties" is a dangerous one, giving rise to a mistaken assumption that all fiduciaries owe the same duties in all circumstances. This is not the case.'

3 (1984) 156 CLR 41, at 97.

2 Incidents of the duty

(a) The duty post-dates the termination of the retainer

6.08 Although during the period of the retainer the obligation of confidentiality is typically analysed as an aspect of the solicitor's fiduciary duties, the obligation clearly survives the termination of the retainer (which usually marks the end of the fiduciary relationship between solicitor and client). So the obligation to preserve the (former) client's confidentiality continues even after the retainer has come to an end, though the solicitor will generally no longer be subject to fiduciary obligations:

> 'Where the court's intervention is sought by a *former* client, however the position is entirely different. The court's jurisdiction cannot be

based on any conflict of interest, real or perceived, for there is none. The fiduciary relationship which subsists between solicitor and client comes to an end with the termination of the retainer. Thereafter the solicitor has no obligation to defend and advance the interests of his former client. The only duty to the former client which survives the termination of the client relationship is a continuing duty to preserve the confidentiality imparted during its subsistence'.[1]

1 *Bolkiah v KPMG* [1999] 2 AC 222, at 235C per Lord Millett. Emphasis added. Note also the view expressed by Lightman J in *Campbell v Frisbee* [2002] EWHC 328 (Ch), [2002] EMLR 31, at [31] that: 'It is plain beyond question that the obligation of confidence of e g a lawyer, doctor or security consultant survives acceptance by the service provider of the repudiation of his contract by the client. Indeed that is surely the premise upon which the relationship between client and service provider is created'. Although the appeal against Lightman J's order of summary judgment in favour of the claimant was allowed (at [2002] EWCA Civ 1394) this statement is surely correct.

6.09 This duty of silence theoretically continues indefinitely, even after the death of the client.[1] As was pointed out in an early case, where an attorney had been prevented from giving evidence which would have involved imparting information learnt by the attorney in the course of the retainer:

> 'I thought that the privilege of not being examined to such points was the privilege of the party, and not of the attorney: and that the privilege never ceased at any period of time. In such a case it is not sufficient to say that the cause is at an end; the mouth of such a person is shut forever.'[2]

The authors of *Confidentiality* suggest that this dictum may overstate the position in that information can lose its quality of confidentiality and so, applying normal principles relating to the general law of confidence, the obligation will be discharged.[3] While it is undoubtedly the case that in normal circumstances, a confidant will be discharged from his or her duty of confidence where the subject matter of the duty itself ceases to be confidential[4], it is suggested that different principles may apply to fiduciaries (and in particular solicitors) such that even where the subject matter of the duty enters the public domain, the solicitor is still, in general, disabled from disclosure. We discuss this issue further at para 6.21, below.

1 When the duty will become owed to, and the right to sue for breach will vest in, the client's personal representatives. See for instance *Fogg v Gaulter and Blane* (1960) 110 LJ 718: accountants were held liable for breach of confidence where, after the client's death, they disclosed information which damaged his estate. See also para 5 of the Guidance Notes to r 4 of the Solicitors' Code of Conduct 2007.
2 Per Buller J in *Wilson v Rastall* (1792) 4, Durn & E 753, at 759, recalling an earlier case decided by him.
3 *Toulson and Phipps* (2nd edn, 2006), at 16–005.
4 See *Mustad & Son v Dosen* [1964] 1 WLR 109, HL.

(b) To whom is the duty owed?

6.10 It has recently been confirmed that a solicitor may owe fiduciary duties not just to his or her immediate client but also to others. Because, as has been noted above, a fiduciary relationship may exist independently of a contractual relationship, there may be circumstances in which fiduciary duties (including a duty of confidentiality) may arise not only between the solicitor and the client but also between the solicitor and a third party who is closely connected with the client. For instance where a solicitor acts for a special purpose vehicle company incorporated in respect of a particular transaction then the solicitor may additionally owe fiduciary duties to the holding company or owners of the company even though the retainer is solely with that company. It seems that equity may recognise a person who is not as a matter of law in a contractual relationship with the solicitor as 'the true client' and hence a person to whom fiduciary duties may be owed.[1] Referring to the decision in *Ratiu v Conway* the Court of Appeal in *Diamantides v JP Morgan Chase Bank* stated:

> 'The importance of this passage[2] lies in the recognition that, in a case where a fiduciary relationship arises out of a contractual relationship, it does not matter whether the person to whom the [fiduciary] duty is owed entered into the contract directly or through an agent or through a nominee company. What matters is whether a relationship of trust and confidence has come into being. As I understand it, Auld LJ was seeking to emphasise in these passages that because a fiduciary relationship does not depend on the existence of contractual relations, there may be circumstances in which a duty of that kind may arise not only between the fiduciary and the client but also between the fiduciary and a third person who is closely connected with the client'.[3]

A similar principle was recognised in the Australian case of *MacQuarrie Bank Ltd* v *Myers*[4] where it was held that a solicitor could come under a duty of confidence to a person who was 'as good as a client', for instance a director of a client company.

1 See, for instance, *Ratiu v Conway* [2005] EWCA Civ 1302, [2006] 1 All ER 571 (discussed in further detail below at para 6.29) and *Diamantides v JP Morgan Chase Bank* [2005] EWCA Civ 1612.
2 Ie [78] of *Ratiu v Conway*.
3 At [35].
4 [1994] 1 VR 350.

6.11 It is suggested that where a client (in the broad sense used above) discloses to his or her solicitor confidential information concerning, say, a family member, or an associated company, then it is likely that that person/company (as well as the client) could directly enforce an obligation of confidentiality against the solicitor, notwithstanding the absence of any solicitor/client relationship existing between them or indeed any fiduciary relationship between them.

(c) *The duty is absolute*

6.12   The duty of confidentiality owed by a solicitor to his or her client arises out of the relationship of trust and confidence which the law recognises as existing between solicitor and client, not as an aspect of the solicitor's duties in respect of the provision of skilled services. Accordingly the duty to preserve confidentiality is 'unqualified. It is a duty to keep the information confidential, not merely a duty to take all reasonable steps to do so'.[1] So, on this analysis, the duty is not an aspect of the solicitor's duty to take reasonable care (whether arising in contract or tort). It is not therefore a negligence-based liability. It is essentially a strict liability obligation.[2]

1 *Bolkiah v KPMG* [1999] 2 AC 222, per Lord Millett at 235G.
2 Though note that in *Weld-Blundell v Stephens* [1919] 1 KB 520, CA, (on appeal to the House of Lords at [1920] AC 956) each member of the Court of Appeal treated the case (involving a claim against an accountant for having accidently revealed the contents of a confidential letter from his client to a third party) as one requiring proof by the claimant of a breach of an obligation to use reasonable care; see [1919] 1 KB 530, at 526, 531 and 538. However the claimant's pleaded case was for breach of an implied term to use reasonable care to keep secret the contents of letters passing between the claimant client and the defendant accountants, so that the judgments may simply reflect the way the case was put.

6.13   An example of the application of this principle, albeit in circumstances which availed the solicitor, is *Marsh v Sofaer*.[1] In that case the defendant solicitor was acting for the claimant, a woman of low intelligence, in relation to civil proceedings under the Inheritance (Provision for Family and Dependants) Act 1975. The claimant was at the same time being prosecuted for certain fraud offences. She retained separate solicitors to represent her in the criminal proceedings. She was convicted. She later brought proceedings against the civil solicitor alleging that (i) he should have realised during the course of the retainer that she lacked capacity; (ii) he should have disclosed that fact to the criminal solicitors; and (iii) had he done so, she would not have been convicted because she would have been found unfit to plead. The claim was struck out. The judge held that:

(a)   the communications between the client and the civil solicitor were confidential; and equally confidential were any conclusions which were or should have been drawn by the civil solicitor as to the claimant's mental condition;[2]

(b)   therefore it would have been a breach of his duty of confidentiality to inform the criminal solicitors of those conclusions.[3]

While the first stage in this reasoning is sound, and properly recognises the all-encompassing nature of the duty, the second stage leads, it is suggested, to an odd result. Although the issue was not canvassed in detail, it seems at least arguable that in those circumstances the civil solicitor had a duty to seek the claimant's permission to disclose his conclusions to the criminal solicitors and was therefore arguably in breach of that duty.

1 [2003] EWHC 3334 (Ch), [2004] PNLR 443 (Sir Andrew Morritt V-C).
2 At [42]–[44]
3 At [44]–[48].

6.14 However it may be an oversimplification to state the duty as in all circumstances an absolute or strict one and indeed it is notable that the leading case on the subject, *Bolkiah v KPMG*[1], was concerned not with actual breach but with the risk of future breach and the proper remedial response of the court to such a risk. A solicitor has a general implied authority to communicate information to a third party during the course of his or her retainer in order to further the interests of the client. It is this implied authority which permits the solicitor to correspond with third parties on the client's behalf.[2] What if, while corresponding with such a third party, the solicitor discloses information which is of a confidential nature? It may be that the disclosure can be properly justified in the circumstances and hence fall within the implied authority. The issue may well be one of judgment on the part of the solicitor. In such a case it is suggested that the question of whether the disclosure is actionable is more properly analysed by reference to the court's negligence jurisdiction so that it is judged by reference to the duty of skill and care.

1 Discussed at para 6.55ff, below.
2 In the 2006 version of *Cordery on Solicitors* (looseleaf) the issue was put as one of implied consent to what would otherwise be a breach of confidence: 'Implicitly the client will have given consent for his affairs to be discussed by the solicitor with the other party's representatives, but only in so far as disclosure is necessary and relevant to the fulfilment of the solicitor's instructions': para F[147]. See for instance *Hirst v Etherington* [1999] Lloyd's Rep PN 938, CA, at [25]:

> 'if X, wishing to borrower money from Y, wants his solicitor to give an undertaking to Y for the benefit of X, X should and impliedly does, give the solicitor authority to disclose sufficient information to Y to enable him to judge safely whether the undertaking is in the ordinary course of business of a solicitor. If it is important that the undertaking is binding on the other partners, and it usually will be, before Y is prepared to lend, then it seems to me he is entitled to ask for the information.'

Similarly in *United Bank of Kuwait v Hammoud* [1988] 1 WLR 1051, CA, at 1066 Lord Donaldson MR had stated that the duty of confidentiality involved solicitors 'keeping to themselves everything about their clients and their clients' business *which it is not necessary for others to know*' (emphasis added).

(*d*) *The type of information protected*

6.15 The duty of confidentiality extends to everything learnt by the solicitor in the course of the retainer. Subject to the solicitor's implied authority to reveal this information (which may or may not exist, depending on the facts), this includes the identity and address of the solicitor's client. It may be a breach of confidence for the solicitor even to state that he or she has been retained by a particular person. The duty extends to both information acquired and documents received from the client.[1] Likewise the duty extends not just to information learnt concerning the client (or persons connected to the client), but also includes other confidential information (which may be unrelated to the client and which may not be information which, using the term broadly, 'belongs' to the client) which the solicitor learns during the course of the retainer, for instance the views of an expert witness or the evidence of a proposed witness of fact. An example of this is the leading case of *Boardman* v *Phipps*[2]. We discuss the issues raised here in further detail at para 6.17ff, below. It follows that the duty of confidentiality also extends to the opinions which the solicitor forms concerning his or her client's veracity or character, or of the merits of the client's case.[3] The 'trivia' exception recognised in the general law of confidence (i e that the equitable duty of confidence will not apply so as to protect trivial or useless information imparted to the confidant)[4] will not, it is suggested, apply, at least in so far as it relates to matters concerning the client's private life.[5]

1 See for instance the famous case of *Lord Ashburton v Pape* [1913] 2 Ch 469, CA, where the claimant's solicitor's clerk wrongfully disclosed to the other side to litigation letters written by the claimant to the solicitor. An injunction was issued restraining any disclosure or use of copies of those letters, or any information contained therein.
2 [1967] 2 AC 46.
3 *Marsh v Sofaer* [2003] EWHC 3334 (Ch), [2004] PNLR 443, (Sir Andrew Morritt V-C), at [43].
4 See *A-G v Guardian Newspapers* (*No 2*) [1990] 1 AC 109, at 282.
5 As opposed to, say, the client informing the solicitor in passing that there remain tickets available to attend a particular football match. The solicitor would be entitled to 'make use' of that information by then proceeding to book tickets without seeking client consent. The information was entirely extraneous to the solicitor-client relationship and the imposition of a duty in relation to that information could accord no benefit to the client. The law would also probably imply consent on the part of the client to the use of the information.

(e) *Source of the information*

6.16   Where the solicitor learns the information directly from his or her client then there is no difficulty. The solicitor is under a duty to keep that information confidential. But what if the solicitor learns the information from a third party? It seems that the proper analysis is that where the solicitor learns the information 'in the character' of solicitor to a client (as where, for instance, he or she receives an unsolicited letter containing allegations against the client which is written to the solicitor *qua* solicitor for the client) then the solicitor is subject to a duty of confidentiality in respect of the information learnt, irrespective of the identity of the source of the information.[1] The editors of *Cordery on Solicitors* go even further and suggest that the information may be learnt quite casually: 'The duty to keep information about a client and his affairs confidential applies irrespective of the source of the information, so that information obtained about a client from a mutual friend is still subject to the duty of confidentiality.'[2]

1 See the landmark case involving bankers' confidentiality, *Tournier v National Provincial and Union Bank of England* [1924] 1 KB 461, CA, where Bankes LJ said, at 471:

'The case of the banker and his customer appears to me to be one in which the confidential relationship between the parties is very marked. The credit of the customer depends very largely upon the strict observance of that confidence. I cannot think that the duty of non-disclosure is confined to information derived from the customer himself or from his account. To take a simple example. A police officer goes to a banker to make an inquiry about a customer of the bank. He goes to the bank, because he knows that the person about whom he wants information is a customer of the bank. The police officer is asked why he wants the information. He replies, because the customer is charged with a series of frauds. Is the banker entitled to publish the information? Surely not? He acquired the information in his character of banker.'

In Gurry *Breach of Confidence* (1st edn 1984), it is suggested, at 150, that 'a solicitor will be bound to keep secret any information directly received from a client ...and in addition, any information acquired from other sources *while acting as* the client's solicitor'. The case of *Carter v Palmer* (1842) 8 Cl & F 657 is cited in support of this proposition.
2 *Cordery on Solicitors* (2006) at F[147]. The Guidance Notes to r 4 of the Solicitors' Code of Conduct 2007 are in similar form: see at para 4.

3 The contents of the duty

6.17 The solicitor's duty of confidentiality is a duty not to *misuse* any information acquired by the solicitor in the course of his or her retainer in any way, that is to say, not without the consent of the client (or former client), which may be express or implied, to make any use of it or to cause any use to be made of it by others other than for the client's benefit.[1] The concept of *misuse* is a broad one. It may involve use of the information for the professional's own benefit or for the benefit of another client or simply the disclosure of that information to a third party, whether or not for the solicitor's or a third party's benefit.

1 Per Lord Millett in *Bolkiah* [1999] 2 AC 222, at 235–6. The phrase 'other than for the client's benefit', while unqualified in Lord Millett's speech in *Bolkiah*, is a reference, it would appear, to the implied authority of the solicitor to make use of confidential information in relation to the furtherance of the client's interests. It cannot mean that the solicitor has a general right to use confidential information for what the solicitor perceives as 'the client's benefit'.

6.18 However in each case the consent of the client or former client to the particular use in question will absolve the solicitor of liability. This is because a breach of confidence is an *unauthorised* disclosure or use of information.[1] In such a case the burden will probably be upon the solicitor to prove the existence of such consent to justify what would otherwise be a breach of duty. As noted earlier consent may be express or implied. The following instances are situations where the law will typically imply consent on the part of the client to the disclosure or use of confidential information by the solicitor.

(a) The solicitor is permitted to disclose such information as is necessary for the proper conduct of the retainer. During the course of most retainers the solicitor will be involved in correspondence and communication with third parties and will be permitted to disclose such facts which the solicitor has learnt as are required to promote the client's interest in the relevant dispute or issue. This is in reality disclosure of confidential information with the implied consent of the client. We have already discussed this issue above in Section 2.

(b) The solicitor is generally entitled to disclose the information to other partners or employees/support staff within his or her firm who are working on the client's case or file.[2] A solicitor is probably entitled to discuss points with colleagues with a view to obtaining their views.[3] Similarly the solicitor will be entitled to out-source photocopying or word-processing of confidential documents. Again this is on the basis of implied consent.[4]

(c) Likewise, in a transaction where the client has both legal and non-legal advisors, then in appropriate circumstances, it be may that disclosure of information by the legal advisors to the non-legal advisors is permitted by the client's implied consent, as an 'implied qualification to the duty of confidence' owed to the client.[5]

1 *Coco v AN Clark (Engineers) Ltd* [1969] RPC 41, 47 (Megarry J). On consent to disclosure by professionals, see generally Pattenden *Law of Professional-Client Confidentiality* (2003), at ch 13.
2 This is of course subject to Chinese Walls limitations where individuals within the firm may hold information confidential to a third party. We discuss this at para 6.55, below.
3 The daily of experience of lawyers is of course that it is beneficial to discuss difficult points with a professional colleague. See for instance *McKaskell v Bensemen* [1989] 3 NZLR 75.
4 See *Slater v Bissett* (1986) 85 FLR 118, at 121. This may well be the subject of express provision in the terms of engagement.
5 *NRG v Bacon & Woodrow* [1995] 1 All ER 976, 984 (Colman J). See paras 14.22ff and 14.30ff, below. This case related to a substantial share purchase transaction under which the claimant client acquired various insurance companies. The judge held that: 'It is no doubt true that as between [the client] and its legal advisers the duty of confidence owed by those advisers to [the client] was qualified to the extent that, if for purpose of giving advice in relation to the …transaction, the legal advisers exercising their professional judgment considered it necessary in the performance of their duties to disclose to any of the non-legal advisers written or oral communications or advice passing between them and [the client], it was open to those advisers to do so. They had a professional discretion in the matter.' This supports the suggestion, made at para 6.8ff, above, that there will be occasions when the question of whether or not a solicitor is in breach of a duty of confidence should be decided by reference to the criteria applicable to standard negligence claims.

6.19   Where confidential information is obtained by the solicitor in the context of a joint retainer, then any disclosure or use of that information by the solicitor must be with the consent of all the clients. On the other hand where the solicitor obtains information in such a context he or she must disclose it to all of the clients.[1] While there is a community of interest between the clients then there will generally be implied consent to the solicitor to disclose information obtained from each client to the other.[2] Joint retainers of solicitors by assured and insurer, which are of course common in the context of professional negligence claims, can give rise to complex issues concerning confidentiality and privilege as between the two clients. Although the clients have a common interest in defending the third party's claim, their interests may diverge in relation to cover questions. An assured may be taken to have impliedly consented to his or her instructions being relayed by the solicitor to the insurer in furtherance of the common interest, but not where their interests diverge. So where a valuer was being sued in negligence by a bank, and solicitors were jointly retained by the valuer and his insurers to conduct the defence of the action, then, at a time when the insurer was considering repudiating cover, and the solicitors sought to elicit information from the valuer to found such a repudiation, it was held that the information provided by the valuer to the solicitors was confidential and privileged and there could be no implied consent on his part to the information being passed to the insurers (and so no implied waiver of his privilege). At that stage a conflict of interest existed between the clients. The insurer could not plead that information in defence of the valuer's subsequent claim for indemnity under the policy of insurance.[3]

1 See para 6 of the Guidance Notes to r 4 of the Solicitors' Code of Conduct 2007 and *Hellenic Mutual War Risks Association (Bermuda) Ltd v Harrison (The Sagheera)* [1997] 1 Lloyd's Rep 160, (Rix J) at 165.
2 *Brown* v *Guardian Royal Exchange Assurance plc* [1994] 2 Lloyd's Rep 325, CA.
3 *TSB Bank plc* v *Robert Irving & Burns* [2000] 2 All ER 826, CA. The court in fact made no finding on whether the solicitors had breached their duty of confidentiality to the assured, and infringed his privilege, but that seems to be necessarily implicit. Despite the particular facts this case is in reality an application of the *Ashburton v Pape* jurisdiction.

6.20   As we have seen, the solicitor's obligations as regards information learnt or obtained during the course of the retainer can be broken down into two separate broad categories:

(a)   an obligation not to *disclose* to a third party any information which the solicitor learns during the course of the solicitor's retainer.

(b)   An obligation not to *make use* of such information for the solicitor's or some third party's own benefit.

We consider each of these categories in turn.[1]

1 Specific instances where confidentiality is required are set out at para 9 of the Guidance Notes to r 4 of the Solicitors' Code of Conduct 2007.

(a) *Wrongful disclosure*

6.21   Essentially, absent compulsion (as to which see below) or consent, the solicitor cannot disclose information learnt during the course of the retainer to a third party.[1] But how wide is this disability and to what information does it extend? This question has already been partially addressed at para 6.8ff, above. In *Mortgage Express Ltd v Bowerman* the duty was expressed very broadly: 'All information supplied by a client to his solicitor is confidential and may be disclosed only with the consent, express or implied, of his client.'[2] This is an interesting passage, because it suggests that the law deems *all* information supplied by the client to be confidential even if it would not otherwise have the normal indicia of confidentiality. Compare this with the standard equitable obligation of confidentiality recently stated by the Privy Council: 'It is common ground that the obligation not to use confidential information attaches only to information which has the necessary element of confidentiality and continues only so long as the information remains confidential.'[3] It certainly seems to be the case that the special nature of the solicitor/client relationship[4] means that the law affords particular protection to the client so that the solicitor is placed under a special disability as regards information learnt in the course of the retainer pertaining to the client (whether or not directly from the client). This makes sense. Assume that a celebrity seeks advice from a solicitor about a threatened disclosure of information concerning his or her private life by a former employee. During the course of the retainer the celebrity imparts information to the solicitor about the state of the celebrity's marriage. In the event the employee makes substantial disclosures via a newspaper about the client's marriage. The solicitor should be prevented from disclosing the same facts. During the currency of the retainer the prohibition on the solicitor can be easily explained by reference to the fiduciary duties of loyalty and good faith. But it would be extraordinary if the position were different after the termination of the retainer: the continuing prohibition upon the solicitor from disclosure of information learnt during the retainer, even though in the 'public domain', can be ascribed to the special relationship of trust and confidence between solicitor and client which means that some aspects of the fiduciary relationship survive even after the formal termination of the retainer, even though transformed into a particularly strict form of duty of confidence.

1 A recent example of a wrongful disclosure by a professional is *Satnam Investments Ltd v Dunlop Heywood* [1999] Lloyd's Rep PN 201, CA. The defendant surveyors were retained by the claimant developer to acquire a series of adjoining properties which had development potential. The claimant went into administration and the surveyors wrote a letter to a rival company disclosing the fact that the claimant owned various interests in the properties, and had options over others, and that the local authority was disposed to giving planning permission. This was held to be a breach of fiduciary duty, albeit the disclosure could have been characterised as a breach of confidence.
2 [1996] 2 All ER 836, CA, at 845. The case is discussed in the context of lenders' claims in chapter 10.
3 *Arklow Investments Ltd v Maclean* [2000] 1 WLR 594, at 600.
4 Referred to in *Rakusen v Ellis, Munday & Clarke* [1912] 1 Ch 831, CA, at 834–5 and 842.

6.22 The correctness of this position was implicitly accepted by the House of Lords in *Hilton v Barker Booth & Eastwood*[1] where it was acknowledged that solicitors would be in breach of their duty to a client if they were to divulge to a third party that the client had been convicted of a criminal offence. Although such a fact is not strictly speaking confidential, because of course the conviction takes place in open court, nonetheless:

> 'It is a solicitor's duty to act in his client's best interests and not to do anything likely to damage his client's interests, so far as this is consistent with the solicitor's professional duty. To disclose discreditable facts about a client, and to do so without the client's informed consent, is likely to be a breach of duty, even if the facts are in the public domain.'[2]

This prohibition would surely continue after the termination of the retainer (i e at a time when the solicitor is no longer subject to fiduciary or contractual duties) so that the solicitors would be in breach of duty were they, say, to disclose to a prospective employer, or a newspaper, that their former client had, years previously, been convicted of a minor offence.[3] It will be recalled that in *Bolkiah v KPMG* Lord Millett had stated that the only duty to a former client which survived the termination of the retainer was 'a continuing duty to preserve the confidentiality of information imparted during its subsistence.'[4] It is suggested that this statement should be given a broad interpretation so as to extend to all information learnt during the course of the retainer.

1 [2005] UKHL 8, [2005] 1 WLR 567, at [30]. Discussed at para 1.1 n 5, para 2.15, and para 4.36, above. The facts are set out at para 6.38, below.
2 At [34], per Lord Walker. See also at [7], per Lord Scott.
3 This is because the solicitors' duty of confidentiality is an aspect of their fiduciary duty. Although the solicitors may technically cease to be fiduciaries when the retainer is terminated there remains a negative obligation upon them not to do anything to damage their client's interests. This obligation generally manifests itself in the continuing duty of confidentiality in respect of objectively confidential facts; but, it is suggested, it must extend to matters which are not technically confidential.
4 [1999] 2 AC 222, at 235C.

6.23 This is because, it is suggested, information imparted to the solicitor or learnt by the solicitor during the course of the retainer should *in general* be deemed, as between solicitor and client, to be confidential, regardless of whether the information was confidential at the time it was received or has ceased to be so at some later period.[1] The underlying point is that although information may technically have lost its confidentiality (in the sense of it having entered 'the public domain'), nonetheless it may well be that that information still has (or has re-acquired) a degree of relative secrecy[2] and that the former client has an interest in ensuring that there is no fresh publication. It is probable that the courts would approach the issue of the solicitor's post-retainer duty without starting from an absolutist position which prohibited forever the disclosure by the solicitor of any information at all learnt by the solicitor during the course of the retainer, regardless of the status of the information and its public notoriety. On the other hand it is suggested that the court should start from a presumption that any such disclosure was wrongful and should require persuasion that (i) the information sought to be disclosed lacked any degree of confidentiality; and (ii) the former client had no legitimate interest in preventing publication. Such an approach would mean that the former client could prevent disclosure by the solicitor of a criminal offence committed by the client some years earlier or even an account by the solicitor of a civil trial where the client's evidence was disbelieved on oath and he was shown in an unfavourable light. On the other hand such an approach might well permit the solicitor to disclose, for instance in publicity material, that he acted for a particular client in relation to a particular matter (for instance a high-profile takeover of another company).[3] This is consonant with the example provided by the Court of Appeal in *A-G v Blake*:

> 'If the Crown's argument represented the law, then a former director of a public company, who had been privy to secret and highly confidential discussions in the course of a takeover bid, would be prevented from including in his memoirs anything of these negotiations, even though the bid had been successful, he himself had long since retired and the information in question was public knowledge.'[4]

1 Certain dicta in *A-G v Blake* [1998] Ch 439, CA, do not fully support this analysis. There it was held by the Court of Appeal that Blake ceased to stand in a fiduciary relationship with the Crown once he ceased to be an employee; and that his continuing fiduciary duty of confidentiality itself continued only so long as the information remained confidential:

> 'Equity does not demand a duty of undivided loyalty from a former employee to his former employer, and it does not impose a duty to maintain confidentiality of information which has ceased to be confidential ...The duty to respect confidence is also a fiduciary duty but it subsists only so long as the information remains confidential.'

See at 453–4. It is suggested that such dicta should be confined to public confidences where there is a public interest in the revelation of information, subject only to issues of national security.

2 To use a phrase adopted in *Franchi v Franchi* [1967] RPC 149.

3 Although it is not in doubt that the fact that a particular solicitor has been retained by a particular client is itself capable of being confidential information.

4 [1998] Ch 439, at 455B.

6.24 Support for this general approach can be found in the case of *Schering* v *Falkman*.[1] This was not a solicitor case but is nonetheless of direct relevance because it involved a claim against a person whom the court treated as equivalent to a professional adviser. The claimant company had manufactured a drug which was alleged to cause birth defects. Much adverse publicity was generated. The claimant retained a public relations company to provide its executives with training in dealing with the media. The PR company in turn hired E, a professional broadcaster, to provide some of the training. Much information was provided by the claimant to E for the purpose of the training course. Some time later E decided to make a documentary about the drug and the allegations which had been made in relation to it. The claimant sought an injunction to prevent its broadcast. E argued that the film utilised information which was in the public domain and that he had not made use of any information learnt by him from the claimant. The Court of Appeal granted an injunction.[2] The majority took the view that the fact that E may have been able to make the documentary without drawing on anything learned directly from the claimant was irrelevant. The terminology used by Templeman LJ in support of the grant of the injunction shows that it was E's position as a confidential adviser which placed him under a special disability:

> 'By agreeing to advise [the claimant] and by accepting information from them to enable him to advise [the claimant], [E] placed himself under a duty, in my judgment, not to make use of that information without the consent of [the claimant] in a manner which [the claimant] reasonably considered to be harmful to their cause. As between [the claimant] and [E], the information which [E] received from [the claimant] was confidential and cannot be published.'[3]

1 [1982] QB 1, CA.
2 Albeit Lord Denning MR dissented.
3 [1982] QB 1, at 38A–B.

6.25   *Schering v Falkman* is a case which has attracted criticism largely because of the inroads it made into media freedom to broadcast material which was of public interest. However the majority's rejection of E's 'public domain' argument was one which is of direct applicability to the situation of the solicitor. As Shaw LJ said:

> '… though facts be widely known, they are not ever-present in the minds of the public. To extend the knowledge or to revive the recollection of matters which may be detrimental or prejudicial to the interests of some person or organisation is not to be condoned because the facts are already known to some and linger in the memories of others.'[1]

It is suggested, by reference to the approach put forward above, that the solicitor who, having been retained in a well-known case in which his or her client was subjected to criticism, sought to publish a book about it, even though the solicitor was scrupulous to draw on 'public' sources (e g the transcript of the trial), would nonetheless be at risk of an injunction at the instance of his or her former client.[2]

1 [1982] QB 1, at 28D–E.
2 See the Canadian case of *Stewart v Canadian Broadcasting Commission* [1997] 150 DLR (4d) 24.

(b) Wrongful use

6.26   Cases of wrongful use of confidential information learnt during the course of the retainer can involve diverse factual scenarios. They also are often treated as breaches of fiduciary duty because they will typically involve abuses by the solicitor of the duty of loyalty and the duty to promote the client's interests and not to act for the solicitor's own benefit. An unusual, but vivid, example is a Canadian case, *Szarfer v Chodos*.[1] A client informed his lawyer during the course of the retainer that he was impotent and his relationship with his wife was failing. The lawyer made use of the information by starting an affair with the wife. He was found liable for breach of fiduciary duty. This was a clear misuse of confidential information for the benefit of the solicitor.

1 (1988) 66 OR (2d) 250.

6.27 But misuse of confidential information need not relate to information which is specific to or related to the client, or which is learnt directly from the client. The rule is wider and means that the solicitor cannot, without consent, make use, for his or her own (or some third party's) benefit, of any information coming into his or her possession as a result of the retainer.[1] The width of the rule was established in the well-known and controversial case of *Boardman v Phipps*.[2] This case has not been traditionally treated as a breach of confidence claim, but nonetheless it can be properly analysed as such. The defendant (B) was solicitor to a trust. The trust held a minority shareholding in an underperforming company. B was tasked to investigate. He attended board meetings and obtained detailed information relating to the company in his capacity as solicitor to the trust. The trustees themselves had neither any interest in acquiring further shares in the company (nor any funds available to do so). Some (but not all) of the trustees agreed with B's proposal that he should himself acquire a shareholding in the company so that a majority block holding was created which would allow the company to be reorganised, with a view to increasing the value of the shareholdings in the company. This would benefit the trustees as well as B personally. B acquired the shares and re-organised the company. The shareholdings subsequently increased substantially in value. In an action brought against B, it was held that he held the shares on constructive trust and he was required to disgorge his profit. He had acquired confidential information[3] during the course of, and as a result of, his retainer and with that information had acquired an asset and made a profit thereby without the informed consent of his principal. The controversial aspect of the decision in *Boardman v Phipps* was that the principal suffered no harm as a result of the solicitor's conduct (quite the reverse). No opportunity was lost. Nonetheless confidential information had been (mis)used and a restitutionary remedy was imposed.

1 See for instance *Palmer v Carter* (1842) 8 Cl & F 657.
2 [1967] 2 AC 46.
3 A phrase used by Lord Hodson at 107 and 109–10. Lord Hodson, who was in the majority, effectively treated the case as a misuse of confidential information.

6.28 It would seem to follow that the 'misuse' which is prohibited, absent consent, is not only of information provided directly by the client, but of any information which is learnt by the solicitor in the course of the retainer, whether that information is of direct value to the client or not; the rationale being that in such a case it is the fact of the retainer which gave the solicitor the opportunity to acquire the information, with the result that the solicitor acquired it in a fiduciary capacity and could not, without consent, make use of it other than for the benefit of the client.

6.29   A recent example of a wrongful use case is *Ratiu v Conway*.[1] A solicitor, Conway, had acted for a company, PB, which had been incorporated as a special purpose vehicle (and was owned by another company, R) for the purchase and subsequent sale of a property (P1) in St John's Wood, London. During the course of that retainer Conway had acquired knowledge about R's business and intentions. R then proposed to buy a nearby property (P2). It made an offer which was accepted, subject to contract. A director of R then telephoned Conway to seek to instruct him to act for R in respect of the contemplated purchase of P2. The director told Conway that R had made an offer in a particular amount for P2 which had been accepted. Having acquired this information, Conway then himself made an offer to purchase P2 which was in an amount higher than the offer made by R. R wrote a letter to the vendor complaining about Conway's conduct. The circumstances in which the issue of the nature of Conway's obligations arose were unusual; in the event the vendor decided to sell P2 to R at the price originally offered so Conway's conduct, whether wrongful or not, did not cause any loss to R. But Conway sued R for libel and in this context the question of whether Conway had breached any obligation owed to R arose. It was held that even though PB was the purchaser of P1 Conway nonetheless owed fiduciary duties to R because PB was simply a vehicle of R, incorporated for the purpose of purchasing P1, and therefore R was Conway's true client and Conway owed R, as well as PB, fiduciary obligations. Therefore in bidding against R in relation to P2, albeit after the termination of the conveyancing retainer by PB in respect of P1, he was arguably in breach of his fiduciary duty to R (the point was not in fact decided). This aspect of the decision is important because it involves a recognition that fiduciary duties (including duties of confidentiality) may be owed by solicitors (and other professionals) not merely to the client but also to others. This issue has been discussed earlier. But it was also held that when the director of R telephoned Conway with a view to R instructing him as its solicitor in relation to the purchase of P2 then the information provided could have been confidential information which Conway misused in making his own bid (this being a matter for the jury), even though Conway did not accept the retainer.

1   [2005] EWCA Civ 1302 (partially reported at [2006] 1 All ER 571).

6.30   Although the facts in *Ratiu v Conway* were complicated and never fully resolved, nonetheless the implications of the decision are clear.

(a)   So, where a person informs his or her solicitor that he or she has agreed to purchase property for a given price, and, say, that the property is in fact worth considerably more, and the solicitor then puts in a higher offer to purchase the same property (or suggests to another client putting in a higher offer), the solicitor will clearly be guilty of a breach of his or her duty of confidentiality (as well as a breach of fiduciary duty). This analysis will be equally applicable to any type of commercial information or opportunity. If a solicitor learnt during the course of his or her retainer that shares in a particular company were substantially undervalued, then if he or she were to acquire such shares without the client's consent then the solicitor would hold them on constructive trust. The decision in *Boardman v Phipps* suggests that the question whether the client had any interest itself in acquiring the shares is irrelevant.

(b) Even if the solicitor has not been formally retained by the (prospective) client (so that no contract is actually formed between them) then it might well be that the information is nonetheless received subject to a duty of confidentiality and so cannot be lawfully used by the solicitor (whether for the solicitor's personal benefit or that of another client) without consent.

(c) Burden of proof

6.31   It was said in the old case of *Erlanger v New Sombrero Phosphate Co*[1] that where a fiduciary relationship exists between two parties which may be the occasion of unfair advantage to one of them, the burden of proof lies on that party to show that he or she has not used that advantage for his or her own benefit. So, where a bank had acquired, in competition with its customer, the shares in a company, and the customer claimed that the bank had misused confidential information, disclosed by the customer to the bank, in acquiring the shares, it was held that, in view of the fiduciary relationship between the bank and the customer, the onus was upon the bank to prove that it had *not* used the confidential information.[2]

1 (1878) LR 3 App Cas 1218.
2 *United Pan-Europe Communications v Deutsche Bank* [2000] 2 BCLC 461, CA at [34].

4   Multiple principals: conflicting duties of confidentiality and disclosure

(a) Introduction

6.32   As well as being subject to a duty of confidentiality solicitors are also subject to a duty to their client to disclose information known to them which may be relevant to the business in which they are retained by the client. This duty was classically stated as follows:

'A solicitor must put at his client's disposal not only his skill but also his knowledge, so far as is relevant; and if he is unwilling to reveal his knowledge to his client, he should not act for him. What he cannot do is act for the client and at the same time withhold from him any relevant knowledge he has.'[1]

This duty is one of the normal incidents of the relationship between agent and principal. However, there is no principle of attribution or imputation of knowledge in relation to this duty. So where partner A in a firm of solicitors knows facts which would be relevant to the client, but partner B is dealing with that client, and partner B does not know the facts known by partner A, the firm will not be liable for breach of duty.[2]

1 *Spector v Ageda* [1973] Ch 30, (Megarry J) at 48.
2 See *Re a Firm of Solicitors* [1992] Ch 959 at 973 and *Bolkiah v KPMG* [1999] 2 AC 222, CA, at 235F. See, recently, *Bowser v Caley* (Leeds Chancery Division, 6 February 2006, Lawtel).

6.33 On the other hand, using the example above, partner B's duty of disclosure to the client is, generally, not limited to knowledge learnt during the course of the retainer by the client. So if partner B has acquired information from one client which is relevant for another client to know, then the fact that B is subject to a duty of confidentiality to the first client will not absolve B of liability for breach of duty to the other. This can place the solicitor in a situation where he or she owes conflicting duties simultaneously to two clients. Such conflicts usually arise where the solicitor is acting for two clients in the same transaction where the clients are on different sides and have potentially conflicting interests.[1] In such a case it is easy to envisage circumstances where information acquired from client A will be highly material to client B but will likewise be confidential to client A and where disclosure could be damaging to client A. In such a situation the solicitor is placed in an impossible situation, a situation which the law has been notably unsympathetic towards: 'It will be his fault for mixing himself up with a transaction in which he has two entirely inconsistent interests'.[2]

1 The classic case is *Moody* v *Cox & Hatt* [1917] 2 Ch 71, CA.
2 *Moody* v *Cox & Hatt* [1917] 2 Ch 71, CA, 91. See to the same effect *Bristol & West Building Society v May May & Merrimans* [1996] 2 All ER 801 (Chadwick J).

6.34 This difficulty is recognized by the new Solicitors' Code of Conduct 2007. We have already referred to para 4.01 which sets out the duty of confidentiality.[1] Paragraph 4.02 sets out the duty of disclosure:

'You must disclose to a client all information of which you are aware which is material to that client's matter regardless of the source of the information, subject to:

(a)   the duty of confidentiality in 4.01 above, which always overrides the duty to disclose; and

(b)   the following where the duty does not apply:

(i)   where such disclosure is prohibited by law;[2]

(ii)   where it is agreed expressly that no duty to disclose arises or a different standard of disclosure applies; or

(iii) where you reasonably believe that serious physical or mental injury will be caused to any person if the information is disclosed to a client.'

Paragraphs 21–26 of the Guidance Notes provide a commentary on this rule. Paragraph 21 states:

'You have a duty to disclose all information material to your client's matter. Your duty is limited to information of which you are aware (and does not extend to information of which others in your firm may be aware) but is not limited to information obtained while acting on the client's matter.[3] You will not be liable, therefore, for failing to disclose material information held by others within your firm of which you are unaware.'

Paragraphs 22–23 recognise that although as a matter of professional conduct a duty of confidentiality overrides a duty of disclosure, it does not excuse in law a failure to disclose material information to a client. However those paragraphs[4] recognise that terms can be expressly agreed between solicitor and client (whether at the inception of the retainer or by way of variation) so as to excuse the solicitor from complying with the duty of disclosure otherwise imposed by law upon him or her. This would be a way of resolving the problem of the solicitor facing potentially inconsistent duties. Otherwise, where the solicitor owes an inconsistent duty of confidentiality to another client, the solicitor should refuse instructions from or cease to act for the client to whom the duty of disclosure would otherwise be owed.

1 See at para 6.1, above.
2 Eg under statutory money laundering provisions or because the solicitor receives privileged documents which have been disclosed by mistake.
3 The duty is more narrowly stated in the judgment of Sir Thomas Bingham MR in *Mortgage Express Ltd v Bowerman & Partners* [1996] 2 All ER 836, CA, at 842. But this is probably confined to mortgage cases.
4 See also para 26.

6.35   Such an express agreement would involve the solicitor, by contract, limiting and modifying the fiduciary duties to which he or she would otherwise be subject.[1] We have already seen[2] how the law recognizes that the fiduciary relationship must accommodate itself to the contractual one existing between client and professional. This may be the case even where the term of the contract which is said to delimit the fiduciary duty is an implied one. The classic example is the estate agency case of *Kelly v Cooper*.[3] The claimant owned a house fronting the sea and retained the defendant estate agent to market it in return for a commission. The defendant was also separately retained as selling agent by the owner of the adjoining house. A purchaser expressed interest in both houses. He made an offer through the defendant on the adjoining house which was accepted. He then made an offer on the claimant's house. The defendant did not inform the claimant of the purchaser's existing interest in the adjoining house. The claimant accepted the purchaser's offer. Only after the sale had completed did the claimant discover the purchaser's interest in both properties. He alleged that the defendant should have informed him of the purchaser's interest in the adjoining property, as a material fact relevant to his decision to sell his property and at what price. It meant that the purchaser had a special interest in the claimant's property and would therefore have been prepared to pay a premium. In the Privy Council it was accepted that the purchaser's interest in buying both properties was a material factor which could have influenced the negotiations for the price at which the claimant's property was sold. It was also accepted that the normal rule is that agents have a duty to disclose to their principal material information which comes into their possession. However the Privy Council held that, given that estate agents have to act for multiple principals in order to function as businesses, there had to be implied into the terms of their retainer that the agent would keep confidential information learnt during the course of their agency with client 1 even though that information might be material to client 2. The defendant had acquired the information about the purchaser's interest in the adjoining property as agent for the adjoining owner and accordingly owed him a duty to keep that information confidential. '[T]he scope of the fiduciary duties owed by the defendants to the [claimant]… are to be defined by the terms of the contract of agency'.[4] Accordingly the fiduciary obligations of the defendant to the claimant (which would ordinarily require disclosure of all material information) had to be modified to take account of the fact that the defendant would learn information of a confidential nature from other principals which, although material to the claimant, could not be disclosed to him.

1 A recent example is *National Home Loans v Giffen Couch & Archer* [1998] 1 WLR 207, CA, where it was held that where the conveyancing solicitors' duties had been closely defined by the claimant lender then they had no duty to pass on to the claimant the fact, discovered by them, that the borrowers (also their clients) were in arrears on their existing mortgage. See further para 10.54ff, below.
2 See at para 6.7, above.
3 [1993] AC 205. See further para 4.32, above.
4 [1993] AC 205, at 215.

6.36 *Kelly v Cooper* was an example of a case where the implied terms of the contract between the professional and the client shaped – and narrowed – the fiduciary obligations of the professional. The existence of duties of confidentiality owed to one client modified duties of disclosure to another so that there was no conflict between them. The approach in *Kelly v Cooper* was followed in the Court of Appeal in *Hilton v Barker Booth & Eastwood*[1] where it was held that there was to be implied into the retainer between the claimant client and the defendant solicitors a term that the solicitors would not disclose to that client material but confidential information learnt in the course of a retainer by another client.[2] However, as we discuss below, this analysis was rejected in emphatic terms by the House of Lords in the same case. Lord Walker was unable to discern any basis on which such a term could be implied.[3] *Kelly v Cooper* is also the subject of penetrating criticism in the leading modern textbook on conflicts of interest.[4] Apart from in the field of solicitors' duties when acting simultaneously for borrowers and lenders, where special rules apply, it may be that *Kelly v Cooper* has a limited status as authority in the field of solicitors' liabilities.[5]

1 [2002] EWCA Civ 723, [2002] Lloyd's Rep PN 500, CA.
2 At [32].
3 [2005] UKHL 8, [2005] 1 WLR 567, at [37]. Discussed at para 6.38, below.
4 Hollander and Salzedo *Conflicts of Interests and Chinese Walls* (2nd edn, 2004) at paras 3–15ff.
5 *Hollander and Salzedo*, at paras 5–42ff.

(b) Acting for borrower and lender

6.37   The conflicting duties difficulty usually arises in circumstances where the solicitor is retained simultaneously by two parties in the same transaction. The typical situation is of course where a solicitor is retained by both borrower and lender in respect of a purchase of property where the purchaser is acquiring the property with the assistance of loan finance, to be secured on the property. The solicitor has accepted two retainers, albeit with the consent of both clients. Although each client has a mutuality of interest in ensuring that the borrower obtains good title to the security, nonetheless apart from that the clients may well have conflicting interests. The problem of disclosure of information and maintaining confidence as between the two clients has given rise to considerable litigation. In *Mortgage Express Ltd v Bowerman & Partners*[1] it was said:

> 'A solicitor who acts both for a purchaser and a mortgage lender faces a potential conflict of duty. A solicitor who acts for more than one party to a transaction owes a duty of confidentiality to each client, but the existence of this duty does not affect his duty to act in the best interests of the other client. All information supplied by a client to his solicitors is confidential and may be disclosed only with the consent, express or implied, of his client. There is therefore, an obvious potentiality for conflict between the solicitor's duty of confidentiality to the buyer and his duty to act in the best interests of the mortgage lender.'[2]

How the law has resolved the problems arising in such situations is the subject of discussion elsewhere in this book.[3] In a series of decisions the courts have been concerned to delimit the disclosure duties of the solicitor very narrowly. In the light of the House of Lords decision in *Hilton v Barker Booth & Eastwood* it seems likely that these authorities will be confined to the mortgage situation.

1 [1996] 2 All ER 836, CA.
2 Per Millett LJ, at 844–845
3 See at para 10.44ff, below.

(c) Acting for purchaser and vendor

6.38 Similar problems can also arise when a solicitor acts simultaneously for both the purchaser and vendor of a property. The retainer gives rise to an obvious potential conflict between the solicitor's duties to each client. This conflict came into acute focus in *Hilton v Barker Booth & Eastwood*.[1] The claimant (H) had agreed with a man called Bromage (B) that H would acquire from a third party a property with development potential which H would develop into flats and then sell to B at an agreed price. B and H were both established client of the solicitors and jointly instructed them. H acquired the property and developed it. B then failed to complete on his own obligation to acquire the site from H, who suffered substantial losses, having borrowed significant sums to complete the development. In fact B had, prior to the contract with H, been made bankrupt and sent to prison for fraud offences, facts known to the solicitors (who had acted for him in the criminal trial), but not disclosed by them to H. It was found by the judge that H would not have gone ahead with the transaction had he been informed of these facts. It was accepted by the solicitors that they could not properly act for both H and B on the transaction and that they had breached their duty to H. But the solicitors argued that the only breach they had committed was the failure to refuse to act for H and to advise him to consult another solicitor: however, it was argued, had they informed H that they could not act then H would still have entered into the transaction and suffered the same losses.[2]

1 [2005] UKHL 8 , [2005] 1 WLR 567. Also discussed at para 1.1 n 5, para 2.15, and para 4.36, above.
2 At [36].

6.39 It was accepted by the House of Lords that it would have been a breach of the solicitors' duty to B to inform H of the facts of B's bankruptcy and conviction. Although those facts were not strictly speaking confidential, the solicitors' duty to protect and promote their client's interests prevented them from disclosing them to a third party.[1] But, nonetheless, it was held by the House of Lords (disagreeing with the lower courts) that the solicitors were in breach of their duty to H *not simply* in continuing to act for H (when they faced a conflict as between their duties to H and B), *but also*, having wrongly continued to act, in then not disclosing to H the facts of B's convictions and bankruptcy.[2]

The solicitors had put themselves in a position where they owed inconsistent and irreconcilable duties to two clients: a duty of confidentiality to B (in a loose sense) and a duty of disclosure to H in respect of the information the subject of the conflicting duty to B. This gives rise to this paradox: the solicitors could not disclose the information concerning the conviction and bankruptcy to H because it would involve a breach of duty to B, but nonetheless the solicitors were in breach of duty to H. The House of Lords dealt with this paradox as follows:

> 'Since [the solicitor] may not prefer one duty to another, he must perform both as best he can. This may involve performing one duty to the letter of the obligation, and paying compensation for his failure to perform the other. But in any case the fact that he has chosen to put himself in an impossible position does not exonerate him from liability'.[3]

So the solicitors could not rely upon a conflicting duty to one client as a defence to a claim for breach of duty to another client.[4]

1   See [34]. The Court of Appeal had left open the question whether H, having jointly instructed the solicitors with B in relation to the property transaction, had impliedly consented to the solicitors disclosing to H the fact of his bankruptcy and conviction and so released them from their duty to B as regards non-disclosure of these facts: this had not been argued by H. See [2002] Lloyd's Rep PN 500.
2   Pursuant to the general obligation on an agent to disclose to the principal all relevant facts and matters known to the agent, referred to in *Spector v Ageda* [1973] Ch 30: see para 6.32, above.
3   At [44].
4   The House of Lords treated this as a straightforward application of *Moody v Cox and Hatt* [1917] 2 Ch 71, CA.

6.40   The Court of Appeal, in deciding that the only breach committed by the solicitors was in failing to decline to act for H (which breach was not causative of any loss), had held that there had to be implied into the retainer between H and the solicitors a term that the solicitors were not obliged to disclose to H any fact which they were legally obliged (to any other client, including B) to treat as confidential. As we have seen, the House of Lords expressly disagreed with that analysis.[1] The result is the potential for the solicitor to be faced with two conflicting duties to different clients which, unless he or she declines to act for at least one of them at any stage, he or she cannot escape from. Such a conflict will generally arise where the solicitor has accepted a joint retainer from two clients with potentially conflicting interests. But even where a solicitor is instructed by client A in relation to a particular matter, and is subsequently instructed by client B on a different matter, the solicitor may find that his or her duty of confidentiality to client A conflicts with his or her duty of disclosure to client B. As we have seen above, as a matter of professional ethics r 4.02 of the Solicitors' Code of Conduct 2007 provides that, although the solicitor must disclose to a client 'all information of which you are aware which is material to the client's matter regardless of the source of the information', that obligation is subject to the duty of confidentiality, 'which always overrides the duty to disclose'. However the advice offered in the Guidance Notes, which clearly seeks to take account of the decision in *Hilton*, is as follows:

> 'You cannot, however, excuse a failure to disclose material informa-
> tion, because to do so would breach a separate duty of confidential-
> ity. Unless the retainer with the client to which the information
> cannot be disclosed can be varied so that the inability to disclose is
> not a breach of duty, you should refuse the instructions, or, if already
> acting, immediately cease to act for that client. Any delay in ceasing
> to act is likely to increase the risk that you are liable for breach of
> duty.'[2]

1 At [37].
2 Para 23 of the Guidance Notes to r 4 of the Solicitors' Code of Conduct 2007.

5   Overriding or releasing the duty

6.41   The duty of confidentiality owed by the solicitor to his or her client may, in exceptional circumstances, be overridden or released. In this section we consider the type of circumstance (apart from express or implied consent, which has been discussed above) which may give rise to such an overriding or release.

(*a*) *Greater duty to client*

6.42   As has been pointed out in a useful recent article[1] the decision in *Marsh v Sofaer* (referred to earlier[2]) is arguably in conflict with an earlier Court of Appeal decision, *Howell-Smith* v *Official Solicitor*[3] which involved relatively similar facts. In that case the solicitor had been retained by an elderly lady who lived in a residential mental hospital under the care of a doctor, Dr P. The claimant invested £73,000 with Dr P on terms which were unclear. The solicitor was concerned that the claimant might be vulnerable, and, without instructions, sought the return of the £73,000 and reported Dr P to his professional body and to the hospital administrator. In an action brought by the claimant for breach of duty and breach of confidence (the claimant asserting that she had not and would not have consented to those steps) the Court of Appeal held that the solicitor had acted correctly: 'He had a duty to protect her position.' The judgment is not particularly closely reasoned but the analysis of the first instance judge was quoted and was broadly adopted:

> '... where what the solicitor is concerned about is improper influ-
> ence being brought to bear on his client which actually affects the
> instructions which the client is giving, there must be an entitlement
> in a solicitor to break any duty of confidence that there may be and

report that matter to the authorities to enable some independent advice to be given to the client and/or to make some check in relation to the activities of the person about whom the solicitor is complaining.'[4]

1 Ian Gatt QC *The Solicitors' Duty of Confidentiality* (2006) 2 PNBA Professional Negligence Law Review 8.
2 At para 6.13, above.
3 [2006] PNLR 21, CA (but decided in 1996).
4 The Court of Appeal commented on this passage: 'That entitlement may be stated too broadly in that passage, but it demonstrates that the judge had in mind a duty owed by Mr Price to the client herself. Whether it is appropriate for a solicitor to make such a report upon a third party will of course depend on the circumstances of the particular case.'

6.43 The general position is that the solicitor is not entitled to make a disclosure, without client consent, simply because the solicitor perceives it to be in the client's best interests.[1] However it is easy to posit other examples of situations where the solicitor will be entitled to break confidence for the greater benefit of the client. Assume that the client informs the solicitor that he intends to harm himself or to commit suicide: it seems unlikely that the solicitor who informed the client's spouse or doctor would be held liable for breach of duty[2], although the result would plainly be different if the solicitor were to inform a national newspaper. Similarly if the client is a child and reveals to his or her solicitor that he or she is the victim of some form of abuse but refuses to allow the solicitor to disclose this fact the solicitor would be entitled to make appropriate disclosure where he or she considers that the threat to the child's life or health, whether mental and physical, is sufficiently serious to justify a breach of the duty of confidentiality.[3]

1 See *Tournier v National Provincial and Union Bank of England* [1924] 1 KB 461, CA at 481.
2 See *Weld-Blundell v Stephens* [1919] 1 KB 520, CA at 527.
3 See para 14 of the Guidance Notes to r 4 of the Solicitors' Code of Conduct 2007.

(b) Public interest/iniquity

6.44 It is clearly established that a duty of confidentiality may be overridden by reference to some greater public interest in disclosure to a particular person or group of persons, or even the world at large. There is a substantial body of authority which has built up over the last 150 years defining the circumstances where the duty of confidentiality may be overridden and the extent of the disclosure that may be permitted.[1] So, in the professional sphere, a doctor who had been consulted by a psychiatric patient with a view to his providing a report to support an application for relaxation of the conditions of his confinement was entitled to disclose that report to the medical officer of the mental hospital where the patient was confined where the doctor concluded that the claimant patient still presented a danger to the public.[2] The public interest in disclosure, albeit to a limited body of recipients, overrode the patient's entitlement to confidentiality.

1 See Toulson and Phipps *Confidentiality* (2nd edn, 2006), at ch 10, for a review of the authorities.
2 *W v Edgell* [1990] 1 Ch 108, CA.

6.45 As we have seen, the confidential relationship between client and solicitor is fortified by the privilege which attaches to all, or almost all, communications between client and solicitor, a privilege which distinguishes solicitors from other professional advisors or confidants. This means that the courts have not recognised the public interest defence, or exception, as applying to solicitors except in narrowly confined circumstances.[1] The policy that wishes to ensure that when a client retains a solicitor the client should be able to make 'a clean breast'[2] of the position requires that where the client discloses behaviour which is criminal or otherwise unlawful, whether or not within the context of seeking legal advice concerning proceedings directed against the client in respect of that conduct, the solicitor should be prohibited from breaching that confidence, for instance by informing the relevant prosecuting authorities.[3] The solicitor's duty of confidentiality can only be overridden by the solicitor him or herself in closely defined circumstances:

(a) Where the solicitor believes disclosure to be necessary to prevent the client or a third party committing a criminal act likely to result in serious bodily harm.[4]

(b) Where the solicitor believes it necessary to prevent continuing or anticipated child abuse. We have mentioned above the case of the child revealing the existence of abuse but refusing disclosure; a similar analysis would apply where it was the client who was the abuser.[5]

(c) Where the solicitor has reasonable grounds to suspect that the retainer is being used as a cloak for fraud, whether civil or criminal.[6] This is because it is clearly established that where a solicitor, whether knowingly or not, has been retained to carry out or promote a fraudulent enterprise or to stifle or cover up a fraud, no privilege attaches to the communications between solicitor and client and nor is the solicitor subject to any duty of confidentiality in respect of such communications.[7] The usual situation where the issue arises is where disclosure of documents held by the solicitor is sought against the solicitor by a third party in the context of civil proceedings. The solicitor may either be a party to the proceedings or the subject of a third party disclosure application. The other party to the litigation may seek disclosure of the relevant documents on the basis that they are not privileged and are otherwise disclosable by reference to the criteria laid down by CPR Part 31. In such a case the solicitor may be placed in a delicate position: on the one hand he or she is, at least on the face of it, subject to a duty of confidence to his or her client, which carries with it a duty to uphold the client's privilege; on the other hand he or she is subject to a request for disclosure, failure to accede to which may carry an adverse costs sanction if the application is successful. In such a situation the solicitor should discuss with his client or former client the fact of the application and seek instructions. The client him or herself may wish to be represented on the application so as to protect his or her privilege. Of course the solicitor has a duty to guard and assert the client's privilege, but if a strong *prima facie* case of fraud is established by the applicant party then the solicitor may not be obliged to defend the application and act only under a court order, but may voluntarily provide disclosure.[8]

(d)   However it may be that the issue arises not in the context of a subsequent request for disclosure but where the solicitor, during the course of the retainer itself, comes to suspect that he or she is being used as an instrument for a fraudulent purpose. In such circumstances the solicitor may terminate the retainer or apply to court for directions.[9] In *Finers v Miro*[10] the claimant solicitors were retained by the defendant to set up a series of overseas companies and trusts to hold assets belonging to the defendant. The solicitor came to suspect that the assets were derived from a wrongful misappropriation perpetrated by the defendant upon a US insurance company. The solicitors, who were holding funds on behalf of their client, sought directions from the court under the old RSC Ord 85 in relation to what to do with those funds.[11]

In each of these cases it is submitted that if the solicitor has a reasonable basis for believing that there exist grounds which permit disclosure of matters otherwise subject to a duty of confidentiality, then, even if it is subsequently proven by the client that in fact the suspected wrongdoing had not occurred, the solicitor should not be liable for breach of his or her duty of confidentiality to the client.[12]

1   The special position of the solicitor is commented on by Scrutton LJ in his dissenting judgment in *Weld-Blundell v Stephens* [1919] 1 KB 520, CA at 545–546. The judge referred to an unreported case, *Mellor v Thompson*, decided in the 1880s. Two traders, M and P, entered into a secret agreement by which P bought out M but it was provided that P and M would continue to trade as if they were separate and competing concerns. T, in his capacity as M's solicitor, acquired knowledge of this arrangement and threatened to make it public. An interlocutory injunction was granted, which was continued as a final injunction at the trial. T's defence that he wished to expose a fraud upon the Revenue was rejected. This is a notably different approach than that in the line of cases starting with *Gartside v Outram* 26 LJ Ch 113.

2   The phrase is used by Jessel MR in *Anderson v British Bank of Columbia* (1876) 2 Ch D 644, 649. A recent restatement of this principle is Sir Thomas Bingham MR's judgment in *Ridehalgh v Horsefield* [1994] Ch 205, CA, at 224:

> 'Parties must be free to unburden themselves to their legal advisers without fearing that what they say may provide ammunition for their opponent. To this end a cloak of confidence is thrown over communications between client and lawyer, usually removable only with the consent of the client.'

For *Ridehalgh*, see further chapter 13, below.

3   In such case, if 'the solicitor in breach of his confidence and privilege announced his intention of informing the prosecution of the contents of his client's communication, I cannot believe that the Court would not restrain him before publication ...': *Weld-Blundell v Stephen* [1919] 1 KB 520, CA at 544–5.

4   Para 13 of the Guidance Notes to r 4 of the Solicitors' Code of Conduct 2007.

5 Special rules apply to proceedings under the Children Act 1989: see para 15 of the Guidance Notes to r 4 of the Solicitors' Code of Conduct 2007 and the discussion in Toulson and Phipps *Confidentiality* (2nd edn, 2006), at paras 16–041ff.

6 The concept of fraud is treated broadly by the courts and extends, for instance, to conduct in fraud of creditors falling within section 423 of the Insolvency Act 1986: see generally *Barclays Bank* v *Eustice* [1995] 1 WLR 1238, CA, discussed in para 14.26ff, below.

7 See *O'Rourke* v *Derbyshire* [1920] AC 581 and *Finers v Miro* [1991] 1 WLR 35, CA . Such a retainer should of course be distinguished from the situation where the client consults his or her solicitor *after* the commission of a crime for the purpose of seeking legal advice as to the legal position and of being defended against a criminal prosecution or even where the client discloses facts to the solicitor which amount to a criminal offence. The line may not always be easy to draw.

8 See generally *Abbey National plc v Clive Travers* [1999] Lloyd's Rep PN 753, CA. The claimant bank sued the defendant solicitors for negligence. The defendants had acted for the vendor, purchaser/borrower and the bank in the same purchase/mortgage transaction. The claimant sought disclosure from the defendants of documents in their possession which recorded communications between the defendants and its vendor client which were *prima facie* subject to privilege. The solicitors asserted the vendor's privilege. It was held that the claimant had established a prima facie of fraud sufficient to override the privilege. It was remarked that usually in such circumstances the solicitors should ask the clients whether they wished to assert the privilege.

9 Or even make disclosure to the relevant authorities. In *R v Pearson* [2005] EWCA Crim 1412 a solicitor attended a police station to act for an arrested person. That person asked the solicitor in a menacing way to go to a particular address to remove money hidden there. The solicitor disclosed this fact to the police. It was held that this was not a breach of confidence: the solicitor was being asked to commit a criminal offence or at least to remove evidence. There could be no confidence or privilege in such instructions.

10 [1991] 1 WLR 35.

11 See also at para 6.50ff, below, in relation to statutory obligations of disclosure.

12 See Toulson & Phipps *Confidentiality* (2nd edn, 2006), at para 16–022. The authors suggest, by reference to *Finers v Miro*, that the proper test is whether a prima facie case resting on solid grounds has been established justifying the disclosure (at para 16–016).

(c) *Proceedings against or by the solicitor*

6.46   Where a solicitor is sued for negligence or other breach of duty by a former client then the privilege inhering in documents and communications passing between the client and solicitor is waived and the solicitor is released from his or her duty of confidentiality to the extent necessary to allow him or her to defend the claim.[1] The client has invited the court to adjudicate on the dispute and thereby has waived privilege and confidence in communications passing between the client and solicitor to the extent necessary to permit the court to do so fully and fairly.

1 See *Lillicrap v Nalder* [1993] 1 WLR 94, CA and *Paragon Finance plc v Freshfields* [1999] 1 WLR 1183, CA where the test was stated more narrowly. The waiver is not necessarily confined to the documents and communications between solicitor and client within the specific retainer forming the subject matter of the proceedings, as the decision in *Lillicrap* demonstrates. On the other hand this principle does not allow a solicitor (or other defendant) who has been sued to open up the privilege otherwise protecting communications between the claimant and other lawyers where that would be evidentially relevant to an issue. So when a claimant brought negligence proceedings against its accountants in relation to advice given concerning a particular transaction, the accountants could not obtain disclosure of communications between the claimant and its

solicitors evidencing advice provided to the claimant in relation to the same transaction: *NRG Holdings NV v Bacon & Woodrow* [1995] 1 All ER 976 (Colman J). These cases are discussed further in para 14.30ff, below.

6.47   Further a solicitor is apparently entitled to rely upon and reveal confidential information concerning a client to the extent that it is reasonably necessary to establish a defence to a criminal charge brought against the solicitor or where the solicitor's conduct is under investigation by the Solicitors Regulation Authority or under consideration by the Solicitors Disciplinary Tribunal.[1]

1 Para 19 of the Guidance Notes to r 4 of the Solicitors' Code of Conduct 2007. Clearly where the complaint has been made by the former client then privilege is impliedly waived, and the *Lillicrap* principle applies. Toulson and Phipps doubt that a solicitor can, absent consent, deploy privileged material in defence of criminal proceedings, by reference to the absolute nature of legal professional privilege, as stated in *R v Derby Magistrates ex p B* [1996] AC 487: see *Confidentiality*, at para 16–033. Similarly, they express doubt as to the proposition that a solicitor can deploy privileged material in defence of disciplinary proceedings, where the complaint is not made by the client. As regards privilege and investigations by the Law Society see the discussion in *Confidentiality*, at paras 16–036 to 16–038.

6.48   On the other hand where a solicitor is the subject of an application for a wasted costs order by the other party to litigation (as opposed to by his or her or her own client[1]) then, absent the consent of the client, the solicitor is not entitled to rely upon documents or communications, or reveal information, protected by legal professional privilege in order to defend him or herself against such an application.[2] So in *General Mediterranean Holdings SA v Patel*[3] solicitors who had acted for the defendants in court proceedings were the subject of a wasted costs application by the claimant. They were prevented from relying upon privileged communications between themselves and their former clients and the provision of the CPR (r 48.7(3)) which purported to permit such reliance was struck down as ultra vires. The same analysis applies where the solicitor is sued by a third party (i e by a non-client). The solicitor cannot, without the consent of the client or former client, deploy privileged material or documents, even if such documents are relevant to his or her or her defence to the proceedings.

1 When the *Lillicrap* principle will apply.
2 *Medcalf v Mardell* [2003] 1 AC 120. The result is that, in such a case the solicitor (or indeed barrister) is hampered in defending him or herself against the application and so the court should make every allowance in his favour: see [23]ff, and para 13.166ff, below.
3 [1999] 1 WLR 272 (Toulson J).

6.49   Finally, where the solicitor brings proceedings against the former client for unpaid fees, then it may be that the solicitor is entitled to deploy otherwise privileged material. In *Hakendorf v Countess of Rosenborg*[1] the claimant solicitor had referred to privileged material in an affidavit in support of an application for a freezing order. This was held, obiter, to be justified on the basis that where a solicitor has cause to sue for fees he or she should be permitted to rely on material which supports that case. Otherwise the solicitor would be hampered in bringing proceedings to vindicate a right.[2]

1 [2004] EWHC 2821 (Tugendhat J).
2 For criticism see para 14.15 n 7, below.

(*d*) Statutory legal compulsion/right

6.50 Professional obligations of confidentiality, including those owed by solicitors, may be overridden by statutory obligations. So it was said in a case involving solicitors that a 'duty of confidence is subject to, and overridden by, the duty of the party to that contract to comply with the law of the land. If it is the duty of such a party to a contract ...to disclose in defined circumstances confidential information, then he must do so, and any express contract to the contrary would be illegal and void'.[1] Clearly a solicitor who complies with a statutory obligation of disclosure commits no breach of confidence actionable by his or her client or former client.

1 *Parry-Jones v Law Society* [1969] 1 Ch 1, CA at 9.

6.51 Statutes overriding confidentiality and privilege may take a number of forms:

(a) They may empower governmental bodies or agencies to require a person to disclose documents and/or information. It may not be clear in such statutory provisions whether privilege is being abrogated. The recent tendency of the courts is to insist on express wording (or necessary implication) in a statue in order to override legal professional privilege.[1] This is important because if the relevant provision does not abrogate privilege then the solicitor, faced with a demand for disclosure, would not merely be under no duty to disclose privileged documents (which are likely to comprise a substantial proportion of documents within his or her control), but would be potentially in breach of duty to his or her client in complying with any disclosure request by providing privileged documents.[2]

(b) They may oblige or permit the solicitor to specifically report matters otherwise subject to duties of confidentiality and protected by legal professional privilege, to a particular agency in the event of certain conditions being met. The most obvious examples are the Proceeds of Crime Act 2002[3] and the Money Laundering Regulations 2003.

(c) They may empower a court to make a court order which requires disclosure. For instance, section 33 of the Family Law Act 1986 provides that 'where in proceedings ...in respect of a child there is not available to the court adequate information as to where the child is, the court may order *any person* who it has reason to believe may have relevant information to disclose it to the court.'

1 *R (Morgan Grenfell) v Special Commissioner of Income Tax* [2002] UKHL 21, [2003] 1 AC 563, concerning s 20 of the Taxes Management Act 1970.
2 Paragraph 10 of the Guidance Notes to r 4 of the Solicitors' Code of Conduct 2007 provides the following advice: 'A number of statutes empower government and other bodies, for example HM Revenue and Customs, to require any person to disclose documents and/or information. In the absence of the client's specific consent, you should ask under which statutory power the information is sought, consider the relevant provisions and consider whether privileged information is protected from disclosure. You should only provide such information as you are strictly required by law to disclose.' Note also the guidance given at paras 16 and 17 of the Guidance Notes in relation to requests made for disclosure of documents by the police.
3 See generally *Bowman v Fels* [2005] EWCA Civ 226, [2005] 1 WLR 3083.

(e) Loss of confidentiality

6.52 Mention has previously been made of the usual rule in confidentiality cases that once the information the subject of the duty has entered the public domain, then the confidant is released from his or her duty of confidentiality to the confider. The subject matter of the duty has disappeared. However whether this is the case in relation to solicitor/client cases is debatable.[1]

1 See para 6.21, above.

D REMEDIES

6.53 We have seen that a solicitor who has misused confidential information may be in breach of a variety of duties, equitable, contractual and fiduciary.[1] There are a variety of remedies available to the client or former client who has been the victim of a misuse of confidential information, including damages, an account or profits, the imposition of a constructive trust, and an order for delivery up or destruction of documents either belonging to the claimant or said to contain confidential information.

1 And even tortious.

6.54 However the client or former client will generally be most concerned to prevent a breach of confidentiality before it has actually occurred. The classic situation where a solicitor's duty of confidentiality (continuing as it does of course post-retainer) to his or her current or former client is called into question, and is the subject of litigation, is where the solicitor accepts, or seeks to accept, a new retainer from a different client where the existing or former client and the new client have potentially conflicting interests. In such a case the existing or former client may wish to obtain an injunction to restrain the solicitor from acting for the new client so as to prevent any perceived risk of a breach of confidentiality by the solicitor. An injunction simply preventing a breach of confidence itself will typically be unnecessary and will not meet the mischief which is apprehended: the solicitor will not be threatening to breach the former or existing client's confidentiality and will no doubt be providing assurances to the former or existing client to that effect.

1   Claim for an injunction by an existing or former client to protect confidential information

6.55   Where the solicitor accepts a retainer from a new client with interests adverse to the former client, the former client may be concerned that a breach of confidentiality may occur, whether inadvertent or not, in the form of the solicitor disclosing to the new client information confidential to the former client. The former client may seek to enjoin the solicitor from accepting or continuing in the new engagement. Although the typical scenario relates to new engagements after the termination of the prior retainer, the problem can arise even where the prior retainer remains on foot. There are also variants of the scenario which engage the same overall principles: for instance where a partner in a firm of solicitors which has acted for or is acting for a particular client leaves that firm to join a different firm which is acting for a client whose interests are in conflict with the first client.[1] In this section we analyse the principles underlying the exercise of the jurisdiction to grant an injunction to a current or former client to prevent a risk of a breach of professional confidentiality.

1   This example in turn breaks down into at least two sub-scenarios: (i) where the departing solicitor had no or limited involvement with the client but wishes to undertake work, via the new firm, for a new client with adverse interests to the old client (see for instance *Re A Firm of Solicitors* [1997] Ch 1 (Lightman J)); (ii) where the departing solicitor was the solicitor undertaking the work for the old client and has moved to a firm where other solicitors (but not the departing solicitor) are acting for a different client with adverse interests to the old client (see for instance *Koch Shipping Inc v Richards Butler* [2002] EWCA Civ 1280, [2003] PNLR 11).

(a) Bolkiah v KPMG

6.56   The leading case is the House of Lords' decision in *Bolkiah v KPMG*.[1] Lord Millett's speech, which was the only reasoned judgment, provides the starting point for any consideration of the jurisdiction. Although this was a claim for an injunction against a firm of accountants (so as to prevent them acting for a particular client) the case was decided on the basis that the principles were the same whether or not the defendants were solicitors or accountants. KPMG had acted for Prince Jefri Bolkiah providing litigation support services in relation to litigation brought in England to which Prince Jefri was a party. In the course of providing those services KPMG had acquired detailed knowledge of Prince Jefri's assets and the corporate structures which held them. The litigation retainer came to an end. Prince Jefri was the chairman of the Brunei Investment Agency (BIA), which held government funds. KPMG had for many years conducted the annual audit of the BIA. Thereafter, Prince Jefri having been dismissed as chairman of the BIA by the government of Brunei, the BIA instituted an investigation into his chairmanship and what had become of various funds held by the BIA. The BIA retained KMPG to carry out that investigation and to assist in the tracing and recovery of those funds. KPMG accepted the retainer about two months after the litigation retainer had come to an end. It became clear that the assignment was at least in part adverse to Prince Jefri's interests and that the investigations might well lead to civil or criminal proceedings against Prince Jefri. Some of the information which KPMG had obtained during the litigation retainer would be relevant to the later BIA retainer. KPMG undertook various steps to create a 'Chinese Wall' between those personnel who acted on the litigation retainer and those acting on the BIA retainer. Nonetheless Prince Jefri sought an injunction preventing KPMG acting for BIA on the assignment. On appeal by Prince Jefri to the House of Lords the injunction was granted.

1 [1999] 2 AC 222. The previous leading authority was *Rakusen v Ellis, Munday & Clarke* [1912] 1 Ch 831, CA. Parts of the reasoning of this case were disapproved in *Bolkiah*. Important pre-*Bolkiah* cases include *David Lee & Co (Lincoln) Ltd v Coward Chance* [1991] Ch 259, (Browne-Wilkinson V-C) *Re A Firm of Solicitors* [1992] QB 959, CA; and *Re A Firm of Solicitors* [1997] Ch 1, (Lightman J).

6.57 What emerge from *Bolkiah* are the following principles:

(a) The jurisdiction to prevent a solicitor or other professional from accepting or continuing in a particular engagement is founded upon the right of a former client ('the old client') to protect his or her confidential information, not on the avoidance of any perception of possible impropriety. There is no absolute rule in English law (unlike in the USA) that a solicitor cannot act for a client with an interest adverse to that of the former client in 'the same or a connected matter'.[1] The position is different where the client seeking to protect its interests is an *existing* client of the solicitor. We consider that situation below.

(b) Therefore the old client must show that the professional is (i) in possession of information which is confidential to it, and to the disclosure of which it has not consented; and (ii) that such information is or might be relevant to the new matter on which the professional is instructed by the new client in which the interest of the other client is or may be adverse to the old client's own interest. It will generally be simple for the former client to establish these facts.[2]

(c) Because the professional's duty of confidentiality is an absolute one[3] the old client is entitled to prevent the professional from exposing the old client to any avoidable risk of misuse of its confidential information, which includes the increased risk of misuse by acceptance of a later instruction by a new client with an adverse interest to the old client in a matter to which the information is or may be relevant.[4] In the case of

311

solicitors, this is so as to protect the policy that it is of overriding importance for the proper administration of justice that a client should be able to have complete confidence that what the client tells his or her lawyer will remain secret.[5]

(d)   Therefore once the old client establishes the matters set out at (b) above, an injunction (to prevent the risk of disclosure or other misuse of confidential information) will be granted against the professional so as to prohibit it acting for the new client unless the professional can satisfy the court that 'there is no risk of disclosure'. The risk must be real as opposed to fanciful; but it need not be substantial.[6] So, once the old client has established the facts referred to at (b) above, then the evidential burden shifts to the professional.[7] The court will restrain the professional from acting for the new client unless satisfied on the basis of clear and convincing evidence that effective measures have been taken to ensure that no disclosure will occur.[8]

(e)   The law in this area does not involve imputation or attribution of the knowledge of one partner in a professional firm to his or her fellow partners.[9] Therefore the issue will often be the consideration of the degree of risk of information known to one defined set of people (who dealt with the old client) in a firm passing to another defined set of people in the same firm (who are to deal with the new client). Of course where the same person or people who dealt with the old client are going to deal with the new client then the professional cannot act and will in any event be prohibited from doing so. There can never be a Chinese Wall 'of the mind'.

(e)   The jurisdiction whether or not to grant an injunction does not involve a 'balancing exercise'. If the professional cannot discharge the heavy burden upon him or her then an injunction will be granted. On the other hand, although the starting point is that, unless special measures are taken, information moves within a firm, there is not rule of law that Chinese walls or similar measures are insufficient to eliminate the risk of misuse.[10]

1 [1999] 2 AC 222 at 234E.
2 At 235E-F.
3 Although see para 6.8ff, above.
4 At 235H-236A.
5 At 236G.
6 At 237A.
7 At 237H.
8 At 237H-238A.
9 At 235F.
10 At 237H.

6.58   The case thus created a very stringent test which was designed to provide high levels of protection for clients who had, during the course of their retainer of solicitors (or other professionals), imparted confidential information to them. In holding that KPMG had failed to meet the test, and so in granting the injunction preventing KPMG from continuing to act for the BIA, the House of Lords was influenced by the facts that the 'Chinese Wall' in that case had been created ad hoc within the same department of KPMG, and that the number of people engaged on each of the retainers by Prince Jefri and BIA was very large and revolving. Indeed, 168 members of KPMG's staff had been engaged on the earlier retainer by Prince Jefri at various times over 18 months. KPMG had charged around £4.6m for the work. On the other hand 50 of its staff were engaged on the new retainer by BIA.

(b) The Bolkiah test

6.59   It follows that where an old client seeks to prohibit the solicitor from acting for a new client, the court will analyse the case by posing the following questions:

(a)   Does the firm of solicitors hold information confidential to the old client to the disclosure of which the old client has not consented? Establishing this should not be hard, indeed it may readily be inferred.[1] However the claimant will need to identify with some degree of precision the confidential information. The information may be held in the minds of members of the firm, or in files or computer databases.

(b)   If the answer to the first question is yes, then the next question is whether that information is or may be relevant to the new matter in which the interest of the new client may be adverse to the old client's. It is clear that this question breaks down into two sub-issues: (i) the materiality of the information to the new matter, a question which will not usually present problems; and (ii) whether the interest of the new client is 'adverse' to the interests of the old client. This latter issue has received surprisingly little analysis in the cases. In the guidance notes to r 4 of the Solicitors' Code of Conduct 2007 it is suggested that 'adversity arises where one party is, or is likely to become, the opposing party on a matter whether in negotiations or some form of dispute resolution.'[2]

(c)   If the answer to the second question is also yes, then, unless the solicitor can show on the basis of clear and convincing evidence that there is no risk that the confidential information will be disclosed or otherwise used, then an injunction will, in general, be granted.

It remains vital to bear in mind though that the *Bolkiah* test for the grant of an injunction should not be treated as synonymous with or exhaustive of the solicitor's obligations of confidentiality to the old client. So, where a solicitor personally has confidential information learnt from an old client which would be material to the new client, then, even though the old and new client's interests are not 'adverse', the solicitor is still disabled from breaching his or her duty to the old client and therefore should decline the instruction by the new client unless the new client has consented to a lesser duty of disclosure than that imposed by the law.[3] *Bolkiah* is only concerned with identifying the circumstances which justify the intervention of the law by injunction to protect the old client against a possible future misuse of its confidential information; the pre-condition of an adverse interest between the old and new client is a way of keeping the jurisdiction within sensible bounds and confining it to those cases where there is a heightened risk of misuse and harm.

1 Although see *Bricheno v Thorp* (1821) Jac 300 and *Re A Firm of Solicitors* [1997] Ch 1 (Lightman J). In the latter case a solicitor left the solicitors' firm acting for the claimant to go to a new firm which subsequently accepted instructions from a client with interests adverse to the claimant. An application for an injunction to prevent the new firm from acting was refused because it was not shown that the departing solicitor actually had any confidential information relating to the claimant. Lightman J said, at 10:

 'it is in general not sufficient for the client to make a general allegation that the solicitor is in possession of relevant confidential information if this is in issue; some particularity as to the confidential information is required.'

2 See at para 28. It is suggested at para 29 that, by contrast, 'action which seeks to improve the new client's commercial position as against others generally within a particular sector would not be "adverse" to the interests of another client which is one such competitor'.
3 This is a point well made at para 30 of the Guidance Notes to rule 4 of the Solicitors' Code of Conduct 2007.

(c) Cases post-Bolkiah: adequacy of information barriers

6.60 Since *Bolkiah* there has been a spate of applications for injunctive relief by former clients to prevent a particular firm of solicitors (or, in some instances, an accountancy firm) accepting a new engagement by a client with a potentially adverse interest.[1] The cases have sought to wrestle with the practical consequences of the principles established in *Bolkiah* in situations rather different from the unusual and extreme facts in *Bolkiah*. The typical battleground has been whether the professional firm has discharged the burden of proof upon it to show no risk of disclosure. What has emerged is what appears to be a rather less stringent application of the principles set out in *Bolkiah* to more 'everyday' situations. So one can deduce the following:

(a) *There is no rule of law that Chinese Walls etc are per se insufficient to eliminate the risk of disclosure.* The steps taken or proposed by the professional, including undertakings offered to the court, will be scrutinised carefully: the case has often turned on the efficacy (or otherwise) of the Chinese Walls which are proposed by the professional in order to protect the old client's information. 'The crucial question is "will the barriers work?" '.[2]

314

(b)   *There is no rule that ad hoc Chinese Walls are per se objectionable.* In the *GUS*[3] case X and Y were engaged in a heavy arbitration. The legal team acting for X moved from Debevoise Plimpton solicitors to LLGM. LLGM had acted some years earlier for Y in relation to some of the underlying transactions which were in issue in the arbitration. An injunction was refused. It was accepted that the Chinese Wall erected, although ad hoc, would be effective to protect Y.[4] However an existing Chinese Wall is likely to be considered more capable of obviating a risk of leakage.

(c)   *The fewer the number of potential disclosers, the less the risk.* One common situation is where a solicitor moves from firm A to firm B in circumstances where those firms are acting in litigation for respective clients against each other. So in the *Koch Shipping*[5] case X and Y were engaged in an arbitration against each other. Y's solicitor (Ms P) was a partner in the firm of Jackson Parton. X's solicitors were Richards Butler. Ms P left Jackson Parton and was given employment as a consultant at Richards Butler. Y sought to prevent Richards Butler from continuing to act for X. They alleged that there was a risk that Ms P would (inadvertently) disclose information confidential to Y to the lawyers at Richards Butler acting for X. The Court of Appeal refused to grant an injunction. There was only one potential source of disclosure and the Chinese Walls put in place were adequate. The *Halewood*[6] case also involved a solicitor moving from the old client's firm to the new client's firm. An injunction was refused subject to an undertaking being given that the solicitor would not work in or enter the building where the team acting for the new client worked from.

1   Those cases include: *Young* v *Robson Rhodes* [1999] Lloyd's Rep PN 641 (Laddie J)*; Davies v Davies* (4 May 1999, unreported), CA; *Halewood International Ltd* v *Addleshaw Booth* [2000] PNLR 788, CA; *Koch Shipping Inc* v *Richards Butler* [2002] EWCA Civ 1280, [2003] PNLR 11; *Bogle v Coutts & Co* [2003] EWHC 1865 (Peter Smith J); *Marks & Spencer* v *Freshfields* [2004] EWHC 1337 (Ch), [2004] 1 WLR 2331 (Lawrence Collins J); and on appeal [2004] EWCA Civ 741, [2005] PNLR 4 (application for permission refused); *GUS* v *Leboeuf Lamb Greene & Macrae* [2006] EWCA Civ 683, [2006] PNLR 32.
2   See *Young* v *Robson Rhodes*, at [42].
3   [2006] EWCA Civ 683, [2006] PNLR 32.
4   See also *Marks & Spencer* v *Freshfields* [2004] EWHC 1337 (Ch), [2004] 1 WLR 2331, at [18].
5   [2002] EWCA Civ 1280, [2003] PNLR 11.
6   [2000] PNLR 788.

6.61   In practice many such cases will turn upon the adequacy of the Chinese Walls, or information barriers, created and any undertakings offered to the court by the professional. The enquiry will be highly fact-sensitive.

'Each case turns on a careful judicial analysis and assessment of the quality of the evidence about the effectiveness of the precautions taken to protect the confidentiality of the former client's information from the risk of disclosure and misuse. If there is clear and convincing evidence that the precautions taken will provide effective protection, there will be no real risk to justify the grant of an injunction.'[1]

1   *GUS v Leboeuf Lamb Greene & Macrae* [2006] EWCA Civ 683, [2006] PNLR 32, at [31].

6.62   The decided cases show that the following can be relied upon or will be relevant to the question of whether or not the burden of showing that there is no risk has been discharged by the firm of solicitors:

(a)   Undertakings (both by the potential discloser(s) and the potential disclosee(s)) not to communicate with each other.

(b)   The extent of physical separation between the potential discloser(s) and disclosee(s).

(c)   Undertakings and evidence relating to non-attendance at social functions or partners' meetings/lunches etc.

(d)   The extent to which files held on the firm's database are unavailable to the potential disclosees.

(e)   The extent to which the potential discloser(s) have any documents in their possession.

(f)   The professional standing of the potential discloser(s)/disclosee(s).

(g)   The extent of the knowledge of the potential discloser(s) of the confidential information, and the period of time which has elapsed since they obtained it.[1]

1   See also paras 42–45 of the Guidance Notes to r 4 of the Solicitors' Code of Conduct 2007.

(d) Interim or final injunction

6.63   In the ordinary way any injunction will be sought swiftly. Usually the underlying facts will be agreed and the application for an injunction will be treated as the trial of the matter. *American Cyanamid* questions relating to the balance of convenience will not arise, although the decision whether or not to grant an injunction remains finally one of discretion.[1] However this may not always be the case. In *Ball v Druces & Attlee*[2] the claimant was bringing proceedings against the defendant for whom the solicitors were acting and also against the solicitors themselves for negligence. An interlocutory injunction was granted preventing the solicitors from further acting in the underlying action against cross-undertakings given both to the underlying defendant (in relation to the additional cost of instructing new solicitors) and the solicitors themselves for the potential loss of profit which they would make in conducting that litigation.

1 *Marks & Spencer* v *Freshfields* [2004] EWHC 1337 (Ch), [2004] 1 WLR 2331, (Lawrence Collins J) at [23].
2 [2002] PNLR 23 (Burton J).

(e) Claim brought by an existing client

6.64   So far we have considered claims brought by claimants who were, but are no longer, clients of the solicitor. In such a case the retainer has ended and the fiduciary relationship has terminated. As noted earlier, in *Bolkiah* the House of Lords ruled that in such a case it was the protection of confidential information which constituted the basis of the jurisdiction to prevent a professional from undertaking a later engagement for a new client. However Lord Millett went on:

> 'It is otherwise where the court's intervention is sought by an *existing* client, for a fiduciary cannot act at the same time both for and against the same client, and his firm is in no better position. A man cannot without the consent of both clients act for one client while his partner is acting for another in the opposite interest. His disqualification has nothing to do with the confidentiality of client information. It is based on the inescapable conflict of interest which is inherent in the situation.[1]

1 At 234H. Of course in such a case the existing client may also found its objection upon the risk of disclosure of confidential information.

6.65   Here Lord Millett is elaborating upon comments he had made, while sitting in the Court of Appeal, in the earlier case of *Bristol & West Building Society v Mothew*[1]:

> 'A fiduciary who acts for two principals with potentially conflicting interests without the informed consent of both is in breach of the obligation of undivided loyalty; he puts himself in a position where his duty to one principal may conflict with his duty to another ...This is sometimes described as "the double employment rule".'

The question which remained unanswered was whether the double employment rule applied only to situations where the employment related to the same matter, or whether it was wider. It plainly could not apply without some form of restriction, for otherwise no solicitor could ever accept instructions for and against the same client at the same time, notwithstanding that the two instructions might be wholly unrelated.'

1 [1998] 1 Ch 1 at 18–19. For the double employment rule, see para 4.30ff, above.

2 See Hollander and Salzedo *Conflicts of Interest & Chinese Walls* (2nd edn, 2004), at para 2–55. This book contains an invaluable discussion of the law relating to solicitor conflicts.

6.66 The first occasion when the *Bolkiah* principles were applied to a claim brought by an existing client, and the width of the double-employment rule considered, was *Marks & Spencer plc v Freshfields*.[1] In 2004 Marks & Spencer sought an injunction to prevent Freshfields from acting for a company controlled by Mr Philip Green which had launched a take-over bid for M&S. Freshfields also acted for M&S on various matters and had charged about £1.5m for work done in recent years. Indeed Freshfields was then currently engaged in existing and ongoing retainers. It was alleged that as a result of those retainers Freshfields had acquired confidential information relating to all aspects of M&S's business. The claim for an injunction was put on the two bases contemplated in *Bolkiah*:

(a)   M&S was an existing client of Freshfields and there was a potential conflict between Freshfields' duty of loyalty to M&S and to its new client. A fiduciary could not at the same time act both for and against the same client.

(b)   Freshfields had acquired confidential information during the course of its retainers which was or might be relevant to the new client and there was a risk that Freshfields would use that information for the benefit of its new client. This second basis involved an application of the principles already considered in this section.

1 [2004] EWHC 1337 (Ch), [2004] 1 WLR 2331 (Lawrence Collins J); and on appeal [2004] EWCA Civ 741, [2005] PNLR 4.

6.67 The court granted an injunction on both grounds. In relation to the first ground the judge held that the conflict did not need to arise out of the same transaction or matter: all that was necessary was that there should be 'some reasonable relationship between the two matters.'[1] Here there was a serious risk of conflict. In relation to the second ground the fact that a very large number of Freshfields solicitors were privy to M&S confidential information in practice made the erection of an effective Chinese Wall impossible. The *Marks & Spencer* case demonstrates that where there is an existing retainer between the professional and the client then the existing client may, in seeking injunctive relief, rely not only upon the risk of disclosure of confidential information but also on the existence of a conflict of interest, a breach of the double employment rule.

1 At [16]. Contrast the decision in *Re Baron Investments (Holdings) Ltd* [2000] 1 BCLC 272 (Pumfrey J).

(f) The Solicitors' Code of Conduct

6.68 Rule 4 of the Solicitors' Code of Conduct 2007 contains provisions relating to the putting of confidentiality at risk by acting for another party:

'4.03 If you hold, or your firm holds, confidential information in relation to a client or former client, you must not risk breaching confidentiality by acting, or continuing to act, for another client on a matter where:

(a)   that information might reasonably be expected to be material;

(b)   that client has an interest adverse to the first-mentioned client or former client,

except where proper arrangements can be made to protect that information in accordance with 4.04 and 4.05 below.'

This is, broadly speaking, a reflection of the law laid down in *Bolkiah* so far as it relates to the threshold test which the claimant has to surmount.[1]

1 At para 6.5, above, the view is expressed that the Code of Conduct does not of itself create obligations enforceable by the client against the solicitor.

6.69   Rule 4.04 provides that the solicitor may act in circumstances otherwise prohibited by r 4.03 *with* the informed consent of both the existing or former client and the new client, but only if:

'(a)   the client for whom you act or are proposing to act knows that your firm, or a member of your firm, holds, or might hold, material information …in relation to their matter which you cannot disclose.

(b)   you have a reasonable belief that both clients understand the relevant issues after these have been brought to their attention.

(c)   both clients have agreed to the conditions under which you will be acting or continuing to act; and

(d)   it is reasonable in all the circumstances to do so.'

The effect of this rule is that where a firm holds confidential information that firm may not without informed consent take on new instructions adverse to the interests of the existing or former client.

6.70   By contrast r 4.05 permits the solicitor to act for a client in circumstances otherwise prohibited by r 4.03 *without* the consent of the existing or former client for whom the firm holds confidential information and which is material to the new client, but only where the solicitor is *already* acting for the new client *and* if:

'(a)   it is not possible to obtain informed consent under 4.04 above from the client for whom your firm, or a member of your firm, holds, or might hold, material confidential information[1];

(b)   your client[2] has agreed to your acting in the knowledge that your firm, or a member of your firm, holds, or might hold, information material to their matter which you cannot disclose.

(c)   any safeguards which comply with the standards required by law at the time they are implemented are put in place;

(d)   it is reasonable in all the circumstances to do so.'

1 Ie the existing or former client.
2 Ie the new client.

6.71   The structure of these three rules is essentially this: where the factual circumstances identified at r 4.03 arise the solicitor is prohibited from acting for the new client except in so far as the solicitor is able to satisfy either of the provisos created by r 4.04 or 4.05. It is notable that under these rules there is a duty, as a matter of professional conduct, and where the circumstances set out at r 4.03 arise, for the solicitor to seek (where possible) the consent of the existing or former client to the solicitor acting for the new client. The solicitor cannot simply elect to bypass the existing or former client and put in place adequate information barriers, so as to place him or herself within the proviso set out at r 4.05. Rule 4.05 applies, and potentially permits the solicitor to act for the new client despite the circumstances set out at r 4.03 being applicable, *only* where the solicitor is already acting for the new client and discovers that his or her firm has, or has come to possess, confidential information and *once* the solicitor has sought the consent of the existing or former client.[1] Furthermore the solicitor can only act for the new client where the circumstances set out at r 4.03 apply if the new client is aware of the fact that the solicitor holds confidential information which may be material to that new client and has consented to the arrangements and in particular to the fact that, notwithstanding the general entitlement of a principal to be informed of all material information known to its agent, the solicitor cannot disclose to the new client the existing or former client's confidential information. It follows that the duties imposed on the solicitor as a matter of professional conduct are considerably more onerous than those laid down in *Bolkiah* or by the law generally.

1 Where this is possible; presumably where the client is untraceable then no refusal of consent is required.

6.72   In the Guidance Notes to r 4 there is substantial guidance to solicitors as to the proper interpretation of rr 4.03–4.05 as well as the solicitors' legal and ethical obligations concerning the maintenance of client confidentiality.[1] In particular the notes provide detailed guidance concerning the adequacy of information barriers. It is likely that in future cases the courts will have regard to the extent that that guidance has been complied with when considering whether or not the solicitor's firm has discharged the burden upon it of showing that there is no real risk of disclosure.

1 See para 32ff.

2 Injunctions where confidential information learnt from 'the other side'

(a) Mistaken disclosure to the other side

6.73 The jurisdiction to protect confidentiality by an injunction may be invoked against solicitors where they acquire confidential information from parties on the other side of a transaction or a dispute, with whom they have no retainer, and so to whom they owe, in general, no fiduciary, contractual or tortious obligations.[1] In such cases the claim is based simply on the receipt by the solicitor of confidential information 'belonging' to a third party.[2] It is clear that under the general law of confidentiality mere receipt of information (even if it is involuntary and accidental) which is obviously confidential can be sufficient to impose duties upon the recipient to respect the confidentiality of that information, which duties are enforceable by injunction. The equitable right of the owner of confidential information applies as against a third party solicitor (as opposed to the client's solicitor who has himself voluntarily undertaken a direct duty of confidentiality) where there has been an accidental escape of information to the third party.[3]

1 The exceptional circumstances in which a solicitor may assume a duty to a person not his or her client are discussed above at para 6.10ff.
2 Note that the court has a supervisory jurisdiction over solicitors which permits it, in a proper case, to take steps to ensure that a solicitor does not remain on the record for a party to litigation. That jurisdiction was stated by Pumfrey J in *Re Recover Ltd* [2003] 2 BCLC 186, at 191, to be exercised with caution, as in general parties to litigation are entitled to the advisers they have chosen.
3 See *Goddard v Nationwide Building Society* [1987] QB 670, CA.

6.74 The usual situation will be where, during the course of litigation or dispute, confidential (and generally privileged) papers are mistakenly sent to the opposing party's solicitors. A barrister's clerk may inadvertently return papers to the other side's solicitors. In such a case the solicitor's duty is immediately to return the papers unread.[1] The solicitor has no duty to his or her own client to read the papers to promote the client's interests in the litigation. The consequences if he or she does so can be dramatic and seriously interfere with conduct of the litigation on behalf of the solicitor's client. In *Ablitt v Mills & Reeve*[2], the claimant's counsel's clerk mistakenly returned papers to the defendant's solicitor, containing counsel's advice, draft witness statements and a draft expert report, all of which were of course both confidential to the claimant and privileged. The defendant's solicitors (who in turn became themselves defendants to the confidentiality action brought by the claimant) read those papers, on the express instructions of their client, and so became privy to matters of the utmost confidentiality to the claimant in relation to his claim. The court granted an injunction preventing the solicitors' firm from continuing to act for the defendant in the litigation. This injunction was granted so as to protect the claimant against the misuse of his confidential information.

1 An important distinction should be drawn with the mistaken disclosure of privileged documents. The law on this is complex and different principles apply to those discussed in this section: see generally *Pizzey v Ford Motor Co Ltd* [1994] PIQR P15, CA; *IBM Corpn v Phoenix International (Computers) Ltd* [1995] 1 All ER 414 (Aldous J); and *Al Fayed* v *Metropolitan Police Comr* [2002] EWCA Civ 780. See also CPR 31.20.
2 (1995) Times, 24 October (Blackburne J).

6.75 The appropriate remedy will however generally be less draconian. In the earlier case of *English and American Insurance Co Ltd v Herbert Smith*[1] another careless barrister's clerk again sent counsel's papers (who was instructed for the defendant in Commercial Court proceedings) to the claimant's solicitors who read them on the instructions of their client. The defendant in the Commercial Court proceedings (who was the claimant in the injunction proceedings against the solicitors) sought an order for delivery up of any notes taken of the papers and an injunction preventing the solicitors (or their client) from making any use of the information learnt. No claim was made requiring the solicitors' firm to cease to act or preventing the particular solicitors who had read the papers from ceasing to have further conduct of the claim. It seems that the judge in the *Herbert Smith* case would have been entitled to at least prevent the individual solicitors from acting. On the other hand the wider form of order in *Mills & Reeve* seems to have been made because the defendant solicitors did not propose to the court any workable form of Chinese Wall (and indeed did not even suggest, until an advanced stage in the hearing, that the solicitors who had actually read the privileged documents could cease to have conduct of the case in favour of other solicitors within the firm), so that the information obtained by the individual solicitors who read the other side's papers was isolated.[2]

1 [1988] FSR 232 (Browne-Wilkinson V-C).
2 In *Re a firm of solicitors* [1997] Ch 1, at 13 Lightman J drew a distinction between the situation of solicitors who had previously acted for the old client who was seeking to protect its confidential information (i e a *Bolkiah* situation) and the case 'where without any such previous relationship a party's solicitor illegitimately becomes possessed of confidential information of the other party to the suit or dispute'; in such a case 'in the ordinary course the court will merely grant an injunction restraining the solicitor making use of that information; it will not prohibit him from continuing to act'.

6.76 In such cases the court has jurisdiction to fashion an injunction which is designed to prevent any use or leakage of confidential information. We have seen that this can even extend (albeit in limited cases) to an injunction preventing the firm acting at all. But the injunction can also contain orders that any notes or copies of documents taken be destroyed or delivered up, that the solicitor not disclose any information learnt to the client, and/or that the solicitor or client will not make use of the information learnt.[1]

1 In respect of the situation where the supervising solicitor obtains privileged documents pursuant to a search order see Gee *Commercial Injunctions* (5th edn, 2004), at para 18.010ff.

(b) Mediations

6.77 The growth in confidential mediation as a means of attempting to resolve disputes has created further potential for solicitors to acquire confidential information from parties who are 'on the other side'. All participants to such mediations, whether they are the parties to the dispute themselves or their legal advisors, are subject to obligations of confidentiality concerning information learnt during the mediation.[1] Hence duties of confidentiality will arise which are owed to 'the other side'. Typically the existence of such duties will give rise to no difficulty. But what if the claim which is mediated is one of many being brought against the same defendant arising out of the same or similar facts? In such a case the solicitor who participated in the mediation may acquire valuable information as to the defendant's negotiating tactics, views on the merits of the dispute, and settlement position. That information could be very useful for other claimants also proposing to claim against the same defendant. In the New Zealand case of *Carter Holt Harvey Forests Ltd v Sunnex Logging Ltd*[2] this situation arose. The defendant to the underlying claim obtained an injunction[3] preventing the solicitor who participated in the mediation for the claimant from acting for another claimant who wished to bring claims of a similar nature against the same defendant. It was said:

> 'There is an inherent incompatibility between lawyers' participation in a confidential mediation and their desire to act for other clients in parallel litigation. The dilemma cannot satisfactorily be resolved by means of an undertaking to observe the obligations of confidentiality ...the lawyer cannot screen out what was gleaned from the mediation and what was acquired elsewhere ...Therefore, if the relief sought is not granted, the party at risk may not receive the protection for which it stipulated. A breach, particularly one which is not consciously committed, may go undetected ...'[4]

1 These duties may be expressly undertaken by way of confidentiality agreements signed by the participating lawyers; or they may be implied. See the discussion in Toulson and Phipps *Confidentiality* (2nd edn, 2006), at para 15–013ff.
2 [2001] 3 NZLR 343.
3 From a Court of Appeal consisting of five judges.
4 At [30]–[31]. This decision, which has yet to be considered by any English court, is trenchantly criticised in Hollander and Salzedo *Conflicts of Interest and Chinese Walls* (2nd edn, 2004) at para 7–06ff.

(c) Documents disclosed to the other side pursuant to CPR 31

6.78   The final way in which a solicitor may obtain confidential documents from the side is by the normal disclosure process. Confidentiality is of course not normally a ground for resisting disclosure or inspection, though, when considering an application for specific disclosure, the court will take into account the fact that disclosure might breach the confidentiality of the disclosing party or third parties.[1] The standard protection offered to litigants in relation to documents produced on disclosure is provided by CPR 31.22 which provides that a party to whom a document has been disclosed may use the document only for the purpose of the proceedings in which it is disclosed except in defined circumstances, being:

> '(a)   the document has been read to or by the court, or referred to, at a hearing which has been held in public;
>
> (b)   the court gives permission
>
> (c)   the party who disclosed the document and the person to whom the document belongs agree.'

This is a formalisation of the old principle that a party to litigation gives an implied or collateral undertaking to the court that it will not, without permission of the court, make use of documents disclosed by the other side for any purpose other than the proper conduct of the litigation in which the disclosure was given.[2] This undertaking extends to solicitors engaged in that litigation. In *Crest Homes plc v Marks*[3] Lord Oliver said:

> 'a solicitor who, in the course of discovery in an action, obtains possession of copies of documents belonging to his client's adversary gives an implied undertaking to the court not to use that material nor to allow it to be used for any purpose other than the proper conduct of that action on behalf of his client …It must not be used for any 'collateral or ulterior' purpose.'

1 For the relevant principles see *Science Research Council v Nasse* [1980] AC 1028 and *Wallace Smith Trust v Deloitte Haskins & Sells* [1996] 4 All ER 403, CA. For an exception see *Naylor v Beard* [2001] EWCA Civ 1201.
2 See *Alterskye v Scott* [1948] 1 All ER 469, CA and *Riddick v Thames Board Mills Ltd* [1977] QB 881, CA.
3 [1987] AC 829, at 853.

6.79   However where documents are relevant to the litigation but there are legitimate grounds for the imposition of specific express restrictions on who on behalf of the receiving party can have sight of them, the court can order the production for inspection of those documents subject to conditions as to their dissemination and distribution. Such orders are typically made in intellectual property claims or in litigation between competing businesses, categories of case where it may well be vitally important to the disclosing party for the confidentiality of certain documents to be protected.[1] In such cases the normal rule, now encapsulated in CPR 31.22, is not sufficient protection to the disclosing party. The order may involve restrictions on who can actually see the documents. In *Church of Scientology v DHSS*[2], where there was perceived to be a risk that the claimant would misuse confidential documents disclosed by the defendant for a purpose other than the pursuit of the action, it was ordered that disclosure of certain documents should be made by the defendant on condition that only the claimant's solicitor and counsel could read them, and that they could not pass them on, or disclose their contents, to their client. In such a case the solicitor who breached the order would be liable to contempt proceedings, and any threatened breach would be capable of being restrained by an injunction, but it seems unlikely that he or she could be held civilly liable for breach to the owner of the documents on the basis of having assumed an equitable obligation of confidentiality.[3] Similarly, the remedy for breach of the collateral undertaking imposed by CPR 31.22 is the contempt jurisdiction: this is because the undertaking is deemed to have been given to the court.[4] If, say, a solicitor were to utilise documents obtained on disclosure in an action (which remained subject to the collateral undertaking because none of the exceptions to CPR 31.22 applied) to assist another client (or indeed the same client) in relation to an action it is suggested that the appropriate remedy would be an injunction to prevent further use of the documents[5] but might also extend to preventing the solicitor from acting in the new litigation or even to striking out the new proceedings as an abuse of the process.[6]

1 See *Warner-Lambert v Glaxo Laboratories Ltd* [1975] RPC 354, CA.
2 [1979] 1 WLR 723.
3 *Alterskye v Scott* [1948] 1 All ER 469, CA and *Derby v Weldon (No 2)*, (1988) Times, 20 October (Browne-Wilkinson V-C).
4 See *Bourns Inc v Raychem Corp* [1999] 3 All ER 154, CA, at 170, referring to *Prudential Assurance Co Ltd v Fountain Page Ltd* [1991] 1 WLR 756, at 764, CA (Hobhouse J).
5 So in *Bourns v Raychem Corp* [1999] 3 All ER 154, CA, A and B were engaged in litigation in England and the United States. During a taxation of costs in England (A having been successful in the English proceedings) documents were disclosed by A to B in support of the taxation. B and its American lawyers wished to use the documents in the US proceedings which were between the same parties. A obtained an injunction against both B and its lawyers preventing them doing so, because such use would breach the collateral undertaking, CA.
6 As occurred in *Riddick v Thames Board Mills Ltd* [1977] QB 881, CA. There is a line of authority which has developed in relation to the situation where the petitioning creditor's solicitors subsequently act for the liquidator of the insolvent company or trustee of the bankrupt. These cases typically involve applications by the bankrupt or former directors of the company in liquidation inviting the court to exercise its supervisory jurisdiction so as to prevent the solicitors from acting for the trustee or liquidator on the grounds of a conflict of interest between their duties to the trustee/liquidator and their duties to the petitioning creditor or their own personal interests: see *Re Schuppan* [1996] 2 All ER 664 (Robert Walker J), *Re Baron Investments (Holdings) Ltd* [2000] 1 BCLC 272 (Pumfrey J); *Re Recover Ltd* [2003] EWHC 536 (Ch), [2003] 2 BCLC 186 (Pumfrey J).

(*d*) *Arbitrations*

6.80   Documents disclosed in arbitrations are not subject to the CPR Part 31 regime. No analogous collateral undertaking is given by the parties to the arbitrator. Instead the parties to such arbitrations, and their legal representatives, are subject to implied mutual obligations of confidentiality enforceable as such. The classic statement of those obligations is contained in *Dolling Merritt v Merrett*[1]:

> 'As between parties to an arbitration, although the proceedings are consensual and may thus be regarded as wholly voluntary, their very nature is such that there must ...be some implied obligation on both parties not to disclose or use for any other purpose any documents prepared for and used in the arbitration, or disclosed or produced in the course of the arbitration or the award – and indeed not to disclose in any other way what evidence had been given by any witness in an arbitration – save with the consent of the other party, or pursuant to an order or leave of the court.'

The solicitor must equally be subject to such an implied obligation and accordingly owes the other side a duty of confidentiality which is enforceable as a private law right. In such a case the solicitor who makes use (or threatens to make use) of documents disclosed during the course of the arbitration by the other side will be liable to civil remedies for breach of confidence.[2]

1 [1990] 1 WLR 1205, CA, at 1213.
2 See *Ali Shipping Corpn v Shipyard Trogir* [1998] 2 All ER, CA, 136 where A, the party to an arbitration with B, applied successfully to obtain an injunction preventing B from using documents disclosed by A during the course of that arbitration in a later arbitration with C. This was regardless of the fact that A and C were owned by the same parent.

3   Other remedies

6.81   Claims for a financial remedy against a solicitor alleged to have misused confidential information are rare. Not only is the existing or former client's concern likely to arise in the context of seeking a pre-emptive remedy to prevent any future breach but proving financial loss flowing from a breach of confidence will generally be difficult. Therefore there are few if any reported cases involving claims against solicitors for damages for breach of the implied contractual obligation of confidence. On the other hand a breach of the equitable duty of confidence or a breach of fiduciary duty can be the subject of an award of equitable compensation or of an account of profits. In relation to the first head, these will be assessed broadly in accordance with common law damages: the claimant will have to prove loss flowing from the breach. But in relation to the second, which is an alternative to the first, the claimant may claim disgorgement by the solicitor of the profits made as a result of the misuse of the confidential information. So, in *Ratiu v Conway*[1], if the solicitor had acquired the property and then subsequently sold at a profit, and if it had been proven that he had acquired the property as a result of a misuse of the claimant's confidential information, then the claimant could have sought an account of the profit on the resale. The client might alternatively claim that any asset acquired by the solicitor as a result of a misuse of confidential information (in the broad sense discussed above) is held by the solicitor on constructive trust for the client.[2] As we have seen, such a claim, albeit formulated as a claim for breach of fiduciary duty, succeeded in *Boardman v Phipps*.[3]

1 The facts of which are set out at para 6.29, above.
2 The leading modern authority is the Canadian case of *International Corona Resources Ltd v LAC Minerals Ltd* (1989) 61 DLR (4th) 14. In that case the claimant disclosed to the defendant in confidence information relating to mineral deposits in land belonging to the claimant. The defendant used that information to purchase adjoining land, knowing that that land was likely to be mineral-rich. It was held that the defendant owned the adjoining land subject to a constructive trust in favour of the claimant (provided of course that the claimant discharged the purchase price).
3 [1967] 2 AC 46. For a review of financial remedies for breach of confidence see Toulson and Phipps *Confidence* (2nd edn, 2006), at ch 9 and, in the context of professional relationships, Pattenden *The Law of Professional-Client Confidentiality* (1st edn, 2003), at ch 8.

Chapter 7

Limitation

A INTRODUCTION

7.01 Limitation issues often arise in claims against solicitors. As to the substantive law, it is necessary to distinguish between claims at common law, and those in equity. Sections B and C of this chapter consider claims at common law, including the statutory extensions to limitation periods contained in Limitation Act ('LA') 1980, ss 14A and 32. Section D looks at claims in equity: for breach of trust and breach of fiduciary duty. Section E considers limitation in contribution claims, and section F examines two procedural issues: in particular, the principles which apply if the claimant seeks permission to amend to add a new cause of action after expiry of the limitation period. In July 2002 the then Lord Chancellor announced that the Government had accepted the proposals for the reform of limitation law contained in the Law Commission's Working Paper 270[1], but at the time of writing there is still no date for the implementation of the draft bill, indeed it appears that the government intends to revise the Law Commission's draft bill as part of its policy relating to victims of crime.[2] The Law Commission's central proposal was that time should run for three years from the date when the claimant knew, or ought reasonably to have known, the facts giving rise to the cause of action, the identity of the defendant, and that the loss suffered was significant, with a longstop of 10 years from the date of the negligent act or omission relied upon. Thus, if the Bill is implemented, the existing authorities relating to when the cause of action arose may become obsolete so far as the law of limitation is concerned, and the courts will focus instead on principles which are similar to but not the same as the existing questions of actual and constructive knowledge, considered below in relation to s 14A of the Limitation Act 1980. In this chapter, however, the law is considered at the time of writing in October 2007.

1 Available at www.lawcom.gov.uk.
2 On 9 January 2007, the Parliamentary Under-Secretary of State for Constitutional Affairs, Vera Baird QC, told the House of Commons that the Under-Secretary of State for Constitutional Affairs, Baroness Ashton of Upholland, had that day made the following Ministerial Statement:

'In July 2002, my noble and learned Friend the Lord Chancellor, announced his acceptance in principle of the recommendations in the Law Commission's 2001 report Limitation of Actions (Law Com 270) subject to further consideration of certain aspects 16 July 2002, *Official Report, House of Lords*, WA127. As part of the ongoing preparation of these reforms my department will consult in spring 2007 on the detailed content of a draft Bill to implement the Law Commission's recommendations. This consultation will include consideration of the issue of giving the court powers to allow it to hear certain cases beyond current limitation periods, allowing the victim to sue if the offender later receives a windfall, for example. The Government undertook to consult on this in the July 2006 publication, "Rebalancing the Criminal Justice System in favour of the Law Abiding Majority" '.

By October 2007, however, the Department was still working on the consultation and was unable to say when it might take place.

B CLAIMS AT COMMON LAW

7.02 It is helpful to consider the courts' approaches to the various issues which arise in relation to limitation in general terms before considering specific points. It is now clear that solicitors owe their clients concurrent duties in both contract and the tort of negligence, and that a client may rely upon either cause of action if it provides a more favourable regime as to limitation.[1] Except where the claimant's action includes a claim for damages for personal injuries,[2] the limitation period in both contract and the tort of negligence is six years from the date on which the cause of action accrued, unless an extension applies under the Limitation Act 1980.[3] In contract the cause of action accrues at the date of the breach of duty and in the tort of negligence it accrues when the negligence first causes legally recoverable loss. The loss caused in solicitors' negligence cases is almost always economic rather than physical loss. It may often be the case that the claimant is unaware that he or she has suffered economic loss due to the error of his or her solicitor until more than six years after the solicitor's breach of duty, though to some degree this danger is reduced by the House of Lords' recent decision in *Sephton*.[4] If the causes of action in both contract and negligence accrued at the date of the original breach of duty, this could lead to the potential unfairness that the claimant's action would be statute-barred even though he or she could not reasonably have brought an action within the time limit.[5]

1 *Henderson v Merrett Syndicates Ltd* [1995] 2 AC 145, 185F–H, 191C–D. See para 1.11, above.
2 See para 7.06, below.
3 LA 1980, ss 5 and 2, respectively.
4 *Law Society v Sephton & Co* [2006] UKHL 22, [2006] 2 AC 543. See para 7.16ff, below.
5 Bingham LJ adverted to this problem in *D W Moore & Co Ltd v Ferrier* [1988] 1 WLR 267 at 279.

7.03 Parliament's current answer to this problem is contained in s 14A of the 1980 Act[1], which is headed 'special time limit for negligence actions where facts relevant to cause of action are not known at date of accrual'. In theory at least, the question of when the cause of action accrues is one of principle which depends on the general rules of contract and negligence law, as they apply to solicitors. This must be kept distinct from the questions introduced by s 14A, which were designed by Parliament to deal with the potential unfairness mentioned in the last paragraph. Thus, even if a correct application of the principle determining whether a cause of action has accrued leads to a result which appears unfair to the claimant, it is, at least in negligence, still open to the claimant to rely upon s 14A. There is in theory no need for the court to strain the common law principles stating when a cause of action accrues, in order to deal with this potential injustice to claimants.[2] On the other hand, it might be seen as regrettable that the Government, having in 2002 accepted the Law Commission's considered view that in some areas the existing law is unfair and should be reformed, has not by 2008 made parliamentary time for the necessary reforming bill.

1 See para 7.44ff, below.
2 See the speech of Lord Nicholls of Birkenhead in *Nykredit Mortgage Bank plc v Edward Erdman Group Ltd (No 2)* [1997] 1 WLR 1627, HL, at 1630H–1631A.

7.04 In addition, where the defendant has been guilty of fraud or deliberate concealment, or the claimant has made a mistake, there is a further provision for extension of the limitation period, in s 32 of the Act. This is also discussed below.[1] Section 32 will apply, inter alia, in all cases where the claimant is able to rely upon the tort of deceit.

1 See para 7.66ff.

7.05 The issues which will be considered in this part are, first, cases in which a limitation period of only three years applies; and secondly, the date on which the cause of action accrues in contract and the tort of negligence. In section C we look at the statutory extensions to the limitation period under ss 14A and 32 of the Act.

1 Personal injuries: claims in which a limitation period of only three years applies

7.06 The effect of s 11 of the Limitation Act 1980 is that, in relation to actions in either contract or tort to which s 11 applies, the limitation period is only three years. The three years is measured either from the date on which the cause of action accrued, or from the claimant's 'date of knowledge', as defined in LA 1980, s 14, if that provides a later date. The effect of s 14 is considered below in relation to s 14A, which contains a similar extension to the limitation period. Leaving that aside for the moment, the question arises as to which claims fall within the scope of s 11.

7.07 Limitation Act 1980, s 11(1) provides:

'This section applies to any action for damages for negligence, nuisance or breach of duty (whether the duty exists by virtue of a contract or of provision made by or under a statute or independently

of any contract or any such provision) where the damages claimed
by the plaintiff for the negligence, nuisance or breach of duty consist
of or include damages in respect of personal injuries to the plaintiff
or any other person.'

The Court of Appeal considered this provision in *Bennett v Greenland
Houchen & Co.*[1] The claimant had left his employer and begun work for a
rival employer in 1988. The former employer sought to enforce restrictive
covenants against the claimant, who retained the defendant solicitors to act
for him. The action was compromised. Nearly six years later, the claimant
sued the solicitors alleging that their negligence and breach of contract had
caused him both financial loss and clinical depression. The question was
whether the action came within the scope of s 11, so that the limitation period
was only three years rather than six. The Court of Appeal held that it did.
Depression counted as personal injury for these purposes.[2] Both Otton and
Peter Gibson LJJ emphasised that s 11 applies to claims which 'include'
claims for damages in respect of personal injury. One of the claimant's
pleaded claims was for damages for personal injury, in the form of depression. Thus the action did include a claim for damages for personal injury, and
so it was statute-barred.

1 [1998] PNLR 458, CA.
2 By LA 1980, s 38, personal injury is defined to include 'any disease and impairment of a person's
   physical or mental condition'.

7.08 Thus the effect of pleading a claim for damages for depression was that
the claimant's whole claim was held to be statute-barred, including the claim for
damages for financial loss alone. But if the claimant had simply claimed
financial loss, then s 11 would not have applied and the limitation period would
have been six years so that the claim would not have been statute-barred. In
Shade v the Compton Partnership[1], the Court of Appeal held that, if the claimant
applied to delete the claim for personal injury at a time when a new claim
seeking economic loss only would, if brought, not be statute-barred, then
permission should generally be granted for the amendment. This applied to
cases where the principal claim was for economic loss, and there was only a
relatively small claim for personal injury. It might be different if the claim was
for personal injury which had led to economic loss.[2] In *Pounds v Eckford
Rands*[3], the application to delete the personal injury claim was made at a time
when a new professional negligence claim, seeking only damages for economic
loss, would have been time-barred. Nevertheless, the court exercised its discretion to grant permission to delete the personal injury claim: there was a prima
facie case of negligence against the solicitor defendants, the vast bulk of
damages claimed was for economic loss rather than personal injury, both
parties' lawyers had failed to spot the personal injury limitation point, and the
case which survived the amendment was one with which the defendants were
able to deal. It therefore appears that, even after expiry of the limitation period

for a claim purely for economic loss, it may be possible to save the claim for economic loss by applying for permission to delete a related claim for personal injury, at least if the factors present in *Pounds* can be shown.[4] Further, it is unlikely that s 11 will apply in cases where the claim is based on a failure to advise as to legal entitlement to a category of benefits to which the claimant is entitled only if he suffers injury in the course of his work. This is a claim for damages for economic loss rather than for damages for personal injury, even though the claimant is entitled to damages only if he has suffered personal injury, because the entitlement to benefit would have been dependent upon such injury.[5]

1 [2000] Lloyd's Rep PN 81, CA.
2 See p 86 col 1, and *Walkin v South Manchester Health Authority* [1995] 1 WLR 1543, CA.
3 [2003] Lloyd's Rep PN 195, QBD.
4 It is conceivable that it might be possible to save the personal injury claim by making an application pursuant to Limitation Act 1980, s 33; cf *Kamar v Nightingale* [2007] EWHC 2982 (QB) (Eady J).
5 *Gaud v Leeds Health Authority* (1999) Times, 14 May, CA. Compare *McGahie v Union of Shop Distributive & Allied Workers* [1996] SLT 74, per Lord Fraser at 75, cited with approval by Aldous LJ in a different context in *British & Commonwealth Holdings plc v Barclays Bank plc* [1996] 1 WLR 1 at 8F–9C, CA.

2   Contract

(*a*) *General rule*

7.09   As stated above, in contract, the cause of action accrues on the date when the breach of contract occurred, and the claimant then has six years in which to commence proceedings. In most cases it will not be of great importance that the limitation period in contract has expired, because, as mentioned above, the claimant will be able to sue on a concurrent duty in tort, which may provide a later limitation period, and will also, unlike the claim in contract, allow the claimant a chance to rely upon s 14A.[1]

1 *Société Commerciale de Réassurance v ERAS Ltd* [1992] 2 All ER 82n, CA.

(*b*) *Continuing obligations*

7.10   There is, however, one point of potential interest in relation to the limitation period in contract.[1] This was first raised in cases which arose before s 14A had come into force. The argument is, essentially, that where solicitors have acted negligently, after their negligent act the solicitors are subject to a continuing duty to advise their client that they have acted negligently. This duty continues until the date when the client's claim in respect of the original negligence becomes statute-barred, and breach of this further duty is itself actionable. If this argument were correct, then a solicitor who was negligent in 1980 would have a continuing duty to warn the client of his or her own negligence. That duty would be in force until 1986, whereupon the solicitor could presumably be sued in the following six years, until 1992, for failure to warn that he or she had previously acted negligently. In this way the limitation period would effectively run for 12 rather than six years, and possibly ad infinitum. Thus, it is unlikely that arguments of the type set out in this paragraph are correct in principle. In *Ezekiel v Lehrer*[2], Jonathan Parker LJ approved the following passage from the judgment of Neuberger J in *Gold v Mincoff Science & Gold*:[3]

'[Counsel for the Defendants] rightly warns against the Court being too easily persuaded by the Claimant that he has a fresh cause of action against his solicitor on the basis that the solicitor failed to advise, at some point after his initial negligence, that he had been negligent. If such an argument were too readily accepted, it would have two unsatisfactory consequences. First, it would enable the provisions of the 1980 Act to be evaded in many cases in an artificial way. Secondly, it would effectively impose on a solicitor some sort of implied general retainer. Accordingly, I would accept that it would be a relatively exceptional case where the Court would be prepared to hold that a solicitor's negligence claim that was otherwise statute-barred could, albeit in a slightly different guise, be resurrected on the basis that, at a time within the limitation period and less than six years before the issue of proceedings, the solicitor failed to advise that he had been negligent. Only if the facts clearly warrant such a conclusion should the Court adopt it, in my view.'[4]

A question, as yet unresolved, arises as to the position where, some time after the event but within the limitation period, a solicitor discovers his or her own negligence and fails to report it to the client. Rule 20.07 of the Solicitors' Code of Conduct 2007[5] provides:

'(1) If you are a principal in a firm, a director of a recognised body which is a company, a member of a recognised body which is an LLP or recognised body, and you discover an act or omission which could give rise to a claim, you must inform your client.

(2) If a client makes a claim against you, or notifies an intention to do so, or if you discover an act or omission which could give rise to a claim, you must

(a) inform your client that independent advice should be sought (unless your client's loss, if any, is trivial and you promptly remedy that loss);

(b) consider whether a conflict of interests has arisen, and if so not act further for your client in the matter giving rise to the claim; and

(c) notify the qualifying insurer or the Assigned Risks Pool (ARP) Manager in accordance with the terms of the policy or, if appropriate, the Solicitors Indemnity Fund (SIF)'

It is unclear whether this provision is intended to apply to discoveries made after the termination of the retainer but which show that there is a potential claim. It seems unlikely, since para 38 of the guidance on r 20 issued with the Code states that

'Although there is no general duty for you to keep under review work which has been concluded, if you discover an act or omission which could give rise to a claim relating to a former client, you should notify the qualifying insurer or ARP manager (or, if appropriate, SIF) and seek their advice as to what further steps to take.'

Thus r 20.07 appears to relate to the position concerning continuing retainers, in relation to which a solicitor who discovers conduct potentially giving rise to a claim should report it to the client, while para 38 of the guidance refers to the position after termination of the relevant retainer, in relation to which the authors of the guidance suggest that there is an obligation to tell insurers but not, it seems, the client. This interpretation is consistent with the approach taken to s 32 of the Limitation Act in *Williams v Fanshaw Porter & Hazelhurst.*[6]

1 For further commentary see Evans *Lawyers' Liabilities* (2nd edn, 2002) at 15–09.
2 [2002] Lloyd's Rep PN 260, CA, at 271 col 1.
3 [2001] Lloyd's Rep PN 423, Ch D, at [98].
4 Ward LJ also agreed with Neuberger J's approach, at [24] in *Ezekiel*. See below, however, for the result in *Gold*.
5 It appears that the position prior to 1 July 2007 was similar: see the Law Society's guidance on claims handling dated 26 February 2003.
6 [2004] 1 WLR 3185, discussed in the context of s 32 of the Limitation Act at para 7.72, below.

7.11 The claimant did succeed on the basis of a continuing duty in *Midland Bank Trust Co Ltd v Hett, Stubbs and Kemp.*[1] In 1961 Mr Green's father granted him an option to purchase a farm. Mr Green engaged the defendant solicitors, who negligently failed to register the option. In 1967 Mr Green's father conveyed the farm to his wife. This had the effect of rendering the unregistered option worthless, so its value was lost due to the failure to register it. Mr Green's executors commenced an action against the defendants in 1972. Oliver J held that a solicitor 'who ... has acted negligently [does not come] under a continuing duty to take care to remind himself of the negligence of which, ex hypothesi, he is unaware.'[2] But the action in contract was not statute-barred: as the solicitors kept the option agreement and were consulted about it over the years, they had a continuing obligation to register it, which was terminated only after conveyance of the farm. Applying this case in *Gold*,[3] Neuberger J said that

'... the court must be careful of imposing a duty on a solicitor which involves going beyond his specific instructions. Nonetheless, if the subsequent instruction was also negligently implemented by the solicitor, and this later negligence concealed the earlier negligence then, subject to normal questions such as causation and remoteness, if the earlier negligence only comes to light outside the limitation period, the loss of the right to sue in respect of it can properly be the subject of a claim based on the later negligence.'

Gold was such a case. The defendant solicitors acted for the claimant, negligently, in relation to various mortgages which he entered into prior to 1993. In 1993 they then acted for him in the restructuring of those mortgages. If they had acted non-negligently in 1993 they would have advised the claimant as to their own earlier negligence in drafting the earlier mortgages. Hence there was a fresh breach of duty in 1993. The claimant could sue within six years of 1993 in relation to this 1993 breach. The 1993 breach enabled the claimant to issue a writ in 1999 and obtain damages in respect of the pre-1993 defective mortgages, even though by 1999 claims based purely on the original negligent drafting of mortgages were statute-barred.

1 [1979] Ch 384 (Oliver J).
2 At 403C.
3 Above, at [99].

7.12   The Court of Appeal reached a different result in *Bell v Peter Browne & Co*.[1] In that case, the claimant contacted the defendant solicitors in 1977 following the breakdown of his marriage. Pursuant to the claimant's instructions, the defendants prepared a transfer of the former matrimonial home to the claimant's wife, which he executed in 1978. But the defendants negligently failed to protect the claimant's continuing interest in the house, which was that he should receive one sixth of the proceeds of sale. They should have prepared a trust deed to that effect, and registered a caution. In 1986 the claimant's wife told him that she had sold the former matrimonial home and spent all the proceeds. Thus the effect of the defendants' negligence was that the claimant had lost the one sixth interest in the proceeds of sale which he ought to have had. He issued a writ against the solicitors in August 1987.

1 [1990] 2 QB 495, CA.

7.13   The Court of Appeal held that the cause of action in contract had accrued at the date of the original failure, 1978, and rejected a continuing duty argument. Nicholls LJ accepted that there might be

'... exceptional cases where, on the true construction of the contract, the defaulting party's obligation is a continuing contractual obligation. In such cases the obligation is not breached once and for all, but it is a contractual obligation which arises for performance day after day, so that on each successive day there is a fresh breach. A familiar example of this is the usual form of repairing clause in a tenancy agreement ...'

But he distinguished *Hett, Stubbs and Kemp* on the basis that, there, the solicitors continued to have dealings with their client in respect of the unregistered option, whereas in *Bell* there was no evidence that the defendants had had any further contact with the claimant after the conclusion of his divorce proceedings, so that there was no continuing contractual obligation.[1] Beldam LJ too considered that there was only one breach of contract.[2] Like Nicholls LJ, Mustill LJ considered it possible that a solicitor could have a continuing obligation, as part of his or her retainer, 'to be constantly on watch for new sources of potential danger, and to take immediate steps to nip them in the bud'. But there was no express duty to that effect in *Bell*, and Mustill LJ thought it 'impossible to imply such a strange obligation from the mundane facts of the present case'.[3] Thus there was only one breach of contract.[4]

1 See [1979] Ch 385 at 501D–H.
2 See [1990] 2 QB 495 at 509D–E.
3 See [1990] 2 QB 495 at 512G–513B.
4 See also *Morfoot v WF Smith & Co* [2001] Lloyd's Rep PN 658 at [57], where *Hett, Stubbs & Kemp* was distinguished. The claimant's case was that the defendant had negligently failed to secure a deed of release from a charge held by a bank. The claimant pleaded that the defendant should have obtained the deed of release 'as soon as possible'. The court held that there must have come a time when release was possible, so that there was a once and for all breach at that time, and not a continuing breach.

7.14 To conclude, while it is possible that a solicitor's contract of retainer may contain a continuing obligation to check whether the solicitor has made errors and put them right, unless such a term of the retainer is express, the court is unlikely to hold that there is an implied term to this effect. On the other hand, if solicitors are negligent at time A, and are then later instructed at time B to do work which, if correctly done, would reveal their earlier errors at time A, then they may have a duty at time B to report their own earlier negligence at time A. In those circumstances, a failure at time B to report the earlier negligence may give rise to a new cause of action at time B, which in practice will enable the claimant to recover damages in respect of the negligence at time A.

3 The tort of negligence

7.15 In the tort of negligence, the cause of action accrues when the defendant's negligence first causes the claimant loss which is recoverable in law for the tort. Cases in relation to lenders' claims, the loss of litigation, and the loss of benefits under a will are considered separately below.[1] In general, however, the relevant type of loss for these purposes is the loss for which the claimant claims compensation in his or her particulars of claim[2]. In solicitors' negligence cases the principal type of loss claimed is usually economic loss. In many cases it will be obvious when the economic loss was suffered. If I buy a house at a price assuming no major defects, and my solicitor negligently fails to tell me that there is a right of way running through the ground floor, then I suffer economic loss as soon as I exchange contracts to buy the house[3], since at that stage I become legally obliged to complete the purchase of a house which is worth less than it would have been without the right of way. Problems, however, have arisen in cases where the solicitor's negligence has exposed the claimant to a risk of loss, for example by failing to register an option which would prevent a third party from selling the property to persons other than the claimant, but where the event the subject of the risk does not actually take place for several years. In such a case, there are two principal candidates for the date when the loss is first suffered:

(i) the date of the initial negligence, which gave rise to the risk; or

(ii) the date when the event, of which there was a risk, actually took place: in our example, the date when the property was actually sold. An alternative might be the date when it becomes inevitable that that event will take place, even if it has not yet taken place.

One argument in favour of (ii) is that the event which is the subject of the risk might never occur. For instance, in *Hett, Stubbs and Kemp*[4] Mr Green's father might not have sold the farm to his wife, and so might not have deprived Mr Green of the opportunity to buy the farm. If the risk does not occur, the argument runs, the claimant has suffered no loss; so there is no loss unless and until the event actually occurs. Against this is the argument that, as soon as there is a risk of an untoward event happening, the presence of the risk itself causes the claimant loss, because a risk of something untoward happening is in principle capable of being valued. The value of the risk equates to the likelihood of the event happening multiplied by the amount of damage which will be suffered if it does occur. Thus, at time (i), the claimant has suffered loss in the amount of the value of the risk. As Bingham LJ has observed, attaching a money value to a possible future contingency is something which judges do:[5]

'... every day in awarding claimants damages for the risk of epilepsy, the risk of osteoarthritis, the risk of possible future operations, the risk of losing a job and so on. The valuation exercise is [sc. in limitation cases], of course, different, but the difference is one of subject matter, not of kind.'

1 See sections 4, 5 and 6, at paras 7.30, 7.38 and 7.42, below, respectively.
2 A claimant cannot, however, improve the limitation position by simply neglecting to plead loss which occurred more than 6 years before the issue of the claim form, so as to escape the limitation period which would otherwise apply: see para 7.38, below, though the personal injuries cases referred to at para 7.6ff, above may constitute an exception.
3 See para 7.28, below.
4 See para 7.11, above.
5 *D W Moore & Co Ltd v Ferrier* [1988] 1 WLR 267 at 280B–C, CA.

7.16 When writing the first edition of this book, we concluded that the authorities suggested that, in cases where the claimant's loss was dependent upon a contingency which was not within the control of the claimant, then loss was suffered, and time began to run for the purposes of limitation in negligence, when the claimant became subject to the contingency, rather than when the event of which there was a risk actually occurred, as long as value could be assigned to the risk.[1] Following the House of Lords' 2006 decision in the accountants' case of *Law Society v Sephton & Co*[2], however, it is plain that, whatever the position may once have been[3], this is no longer the law: as Lord Hoffmann put it, 'a contingent liability is not as such damage until the contingency occurs'[4]. Lord Walker of Gestingthorpe considered that, if a professional's negligence caused the claimant to incur a 'purely personal and wholly contingent liability, unsecured by a charge on any of the claimant's assets', then loss would not be suffered.[5] Further, all the previous solicitors' limitation cases on this topic must now be read in light of *Sephton*, which seeks to categorise them, even though it holds that most of them were correctly decided[6]. In this section, therefore, we consider the decided cases as they stand after *Sephton*. In doing so we seek to apply the scheme of categorisation set out in *Sephton*, though this is not straightforward, as there were three reasoned speeches and the categorisations employed were not identical in each. What is proposed here is a categorisation set out in particular in Lord Mance's speech, but it is arguable that the first two categories are so similar that they should be treated as one.

1 One basis for this view was Lord Nicholls of Birkenhead's approval, when giving the leading speech in the House of Lords in *Nykredit Mortgage Bank plc v Edward Erdman Group Ltd (No 2)* [1997] 1 WLR 1627, HL, of a passage in the earlier case of *Forster v Outred & Co* [1982] 1 WLR 86 at 94, CA. In that passage it was said that, for these purposes, damage meant: '... any detriment, liability or loss capable of assessment in money terms and it includes liabilities which may arise on a contingency, particularly a contingency over which the plaintiff has no control; things like loss of earning capacity, loss of a chance or bargain, loss of profit, losses incurred from onerous provisions or covenants in leases.'
2 [2006] UKHL 22, [2006] 2 AC 543.
3 The effect of their Lordships' speeches is that only one previously decided case, *Gordon v JB Wheatley & Co* [2000] Lloyd's Rep PN 605, CA, is strictly inconsistent with their analysis and should be regarded as wrongly decided, though Lord Hoffmann accepted at [14] that *Forster v Outred & Co* (above, note 1), might be interpreted more broadly than he interpreted it.
4 [2006] UKHL 22, [2006] 2 AC 543 at [30].
5 [2006] UKHL 22, [2006] 2 AC 543 at [48]. See also per Lord Mance at [77]. Lords Scott and Rodger agreed with Lords Hoffmann, Walker and Mance.
6 Strictly their Lordships' comments on cases other than pure contingencies may be obiter, but they are likely to be highly persuasive.

(a) Cases where the defendant's negligence causes the claimant to enter into a transaction

7.17 In each of the reasoned speeches in *Sephton*[1] it was accepted that, where the defendant's negligence had caused the claimant to enter into a transaction which he or she otherwise would not have entered, and which left the claimant with both benefits and burdens, the question of when loss was first suffered was to be answered by comparing the value of the benefits and burdens to which the claimant was subject under the transaction. The overall balance of benefits and burdens might at first show no loss to the claimant, but later move to a position where there was a loss. This was in accordance with the House's approach in the *Nykredit*[2] case which we discuss in detail below. But this category of case was to be distinguished from *Sephton*, because in *Sephton* the defendants' negligence did not cause the claimant to enter into a transaction; rather, it exposed the claimant to a risk of having to make compensation payments if claims were later made: see the discussion of the facts of *Sephton* below at para 7.24.

1 See per Lord Hoffmann at [21], Lord Walker at [41]–[46], and Lord Mance at [71]–[73], and [77].
2 Above, and see the discussion of *Nykredit* at para 7.30, below.

7.18 Lord Mance also saw *Forster v Outred & Co*,[1] as a case in which the defendant's negligence had caused the claimant to enter into a transaction which she otherwise would not have entered into.[2] In *Forster,* the court had to proceed on the following assumptions of fact. The claimant's son asked her to sign a mortgage, secured on her farm, to assist him in his business. The claimant believed that the mortgage would provide only temporary security for a bridging loan; that her son would soon obtain a permanent mortgage from elsewhere; and that, when this happened, the mortgage over her farm would be terminated. In fact, the mortgage covered all present and future liabilities of her son and was unlimited in time. The defendant solicitors failed to explain this to the claimant. If they had explained it, she would not have signed the mortgage. The court concluded that the claimant had suffered damage when she entered into the mortgage deed, rather than later when the mortgagee made a demand under the mortgage, because she had encumbered her interest in the farm and subjected it to a liability which might mature according to events wholly outside her control. Lord Mance emphasised that the charge on the claimant's farm meant that the value of her assets was reduced 'in a measurable way' as soon as she entered into the transaction,[3] presumably because a farm subject to a charge is worth less than a house not so subject. The views of Lord Hoffmann[4] and Lord Walker[5] were similar. As indicated above, Lord Walker considered that if the claimant in *Forster* had given a purely personal guarantee, then damage would not have been suffered when it was given: it was the fact that there was a charge secured on the property which reduced its value and constituted the damage. The same analysis must follow from the reasoning of Lords Hoffmann and Mance. Suppose, then, that, due to my solicitor's negligence, I give a purely personal guarantee of my son's debts in circumstances where my son owes £1m, I own a house worth £100,000, and there is every chance that tomorrow my son's debts will be called in. In that case it appears that, applying *Sephton*, I suffer no loss until I am called to make payment, even if an informed observer would say, as soon as I signed the guarantee, that it was obvious that I would be called on to make payment under it. On the other hand, if due to the solicitor's negligence I also execute a charge over a derelict shed worth only £1,000, I immediately suffer loss. This would appear to be the result of the House of

Lords' decision that charging property does amount to incurring loss in these circumstances but merely giving a personal guarantee does not, however obvious it may be that the personal guarantee will be called upon.

1 [1982] 1 WLR 86 at 94.
2 See *Sephton* [2006] UKHL 22, [2006] 2 AC 543 at [70].
3 Ibid.
4 At [14] and [30].
5 At [45] and [48].

(b) Cases where the defendant fails to preserve or procure an asset for the claimant

7.19   Lord Mance categorised many of the authorities as being cases where:

> 'the defendant failed to preserve or procure for the claimant an asset (including a particular chose in action) which could and should have been preserved or protected by the proper performance of the defendant's duty in relation to the transaction affecting the claimant's legal position.'[1]

He contrasted these cases with transaction cases such as *Nykredit*, discussed in the last section. One case in the asset category was *Baker v Ollard and Bentley*.[2] The defendants negligently failed to ensure that, on 12 April 1973, the claimant obtained security of tenure of the first floor of a house. The Court of Appeal held that the claimant suffered loss on 12 April 1973, even though, at that date, the quantum of her damages could be assessed only by considering the attitude of Mr and Mrs B who had the power to seek possession of the first floor, but did not in fact do so until December 1973. The claimant should have had security on 12 April 1973, and she did not. It did not matter that the risk of eviction at that date depended upon a contingency. Lord Mance said that the effect of the negligence was that the claimants acquired a less valuable interest in the house.[3]

1 *Sephton* [2006] UKHL 22, [2006] 2 AC 543 at [70].
2 (1982) 126 Sol Jo 593, CA.
3 *Sephton* [2006] UKHL 22, [2006] 2 AC 543 at [67].

7.20   Another such case was *DW Moore & Co Ltd v Ferrier*.[1] On 1 July 1971 the claimant insurance brokers signed a contract with F, whereby he became a director and shareholder of the first claimant. The contract contained a restrictive covenant relating to F. The defendant solicitors prepared the agreement for the claimants and represented to them that it would prevent F from working as an insurance broker within 15 miles of King's Lynn for three years from the date on which he ceased to be a director of or employed by the first claimant. In fact, however, the restrictive covenant did not take effect when F ceased to be an employee or director. The claimants did not discover this until 1980, when F sought to change employment. The Court of Appeal held that the claimants had suffered loss in 1971 when they signed the agreement, because, at that date, they had a worthless restrictive covenant; thus, at that date, they were subjected to the risk that F would leave and do what the restrictive covenant was supposed to prevent him from doing. Neill LJ pointed out that:[2]

> 'a valid restrictive covenant, if it is not personal solely to the covenantee, can be assigned to the purchaser of the goodwill of a business. To my mind, it does not require evidence to establish that such a covenant has some value, particularly when it is given in the context of a broking business where personal contacts may be of particular importance.'

He added that, as in *Baker*,[3] it did not matter that, prior to the date of F's departure, the assessment of damages would depend on his likely future attitude. Although this went to the assessment of damages, it did not mean that, before F's departure, the claimants had suffered no damage at all.

1 [1988] 1 WLR 267, CA.
2 [1988] 1 WLR 267 at 277A-B.
3 (1982) 126 Sol Jo 593, CA: see para 7.19, above.

7.21 Bingham LJ's approach was similar. On the assumptions which the court had to make, it was:

> 'clear beyond argument that from the moment of executing each agreement the claimants suffered damage because instead of receiving a potentially valuable chose in action they received one that was valueless'.

He dealt with the argument that, at the outset, the loss was minimal, as follows:[1]

> 'If the quantification of the plaintiffs' damage had fallen to be considered shortly after the execution of either agreement, problems of assessment would undoubtedly have arisen. It might have appeared that Mr Fenton was unlikely to leave, taking much of the first plaintiff's business with him, to establish a competing business. If so, the plaintiffs' damage would have been assessed at a modest figure. But the risk of his so doing could not have been eliminated altogether, and so long as there was any risk that one of the first plaintiff's two directors might leave, taking much of the first plaintiff's business with him, to establish a competing business, there must necessarily have been a depressive effect on the value of the first plaintiff's business and on that of the second and third plaintiffs' derivative interests.'

341

Lord Mance emphasised that the result of the solicitors' negligence was that the claimant in *Moore* received less valuable legal rights than it ought to have received.[2] Lord Walker also considered that *Moore* had been rightly decided, though he considered it to be a 'transaction' case.[3]

1 [1988] 1 WLR 267 at 279H–280B, CA.
2 *Sephton* [2006] UKHL 22, [2006] 2 AC 543 at [67].
3 *Sephton* [2006] UKHL 22, [2006] 2 AC 543 at [46].

7.22 Also seen as falling into this category was the insurance brokers' case of *Knapp v Ecclesiastical Insurance Group plc*[1]. Due to the brokers' negligence, the claimant paid a premium for a fire insurance policy which the insurers could avoid at any time on account of non-disclosure of material facts. The Court of Appeal held that loss was suffered when the policy was entered into: at that time, the claimant had received a policy which would not bind the insurers, instead of a policy which would bind them. It did not matter that the actual avoidance did not take place until later. The result was approved in *Sephton*. Lord Hoffmann saw it as a case where the liability was for 'the difference between what the plaintiff got and what he would have got if the defendant had done what he was supposed to have done … namely a policy binding on the insurers.'[2] The claimant was left with fewer legal rights than he should have had.

1 [1998] PNLR 172, CA.
2 *Sephton* [2006] UKHL 22, [2006] 2 AC 543 at [21]. See also per Lord Walker at [45] and
  Lord Mance at [68].

7.23 The last leading solicitors' case which should be considered in this category is *Bell v Peter Browne & Co*, the facts of which were considered above in relation to contract.[1] In 1978 the defendant solicitors negligently failed to ensure that the claimant's interest in his former matrimonial home was protected when he transferred it to his wife. The Court of Appeal held that the claimant suffered loss in 1978 when the transfer took effect without him having the formal protection of his interest in the proceeds of sale which he ought to have had. Nicholls LJ reasoned that if the claimant had sued in 1980, before sale of the house, his damages might have been low, but not nominal: 'he would have been entitled at least to recover from the defendants the cost incurred in going to other solicitors for advice on what should be done and for their assistance in lodging the appropriate caution.'[2] Beldam LJ said that, due to the negligence, the claimant's interest was clearly less valuable in 1978 than it would have been if there had been no negligence.[3] In *Sephton*, Lord Hoffmann said that *Bell* was 'readily explicable' as a case in which it was 'possible to infer that the plaintiff's failure to get what he should have got from a bilateral transaction was quantifiable damage, even though further damage which might result from the flaw was still contingent'[4]. It may be observed, however, that the distinction between the unsecured guarantee given to the son in our example given at para 7.18, above, and this explanation of *Bell*, is thin. In both cases, whether the claimant ultimately lost significant sums would depend on the conduct of third parties beyond his control. Whilst in *Bell* the wife made off with all the proceeds of sale, it might, in the case of a different third party, have been possible to predict with accuracy that the risk of such conduct was minimal, such that it might have been possible to say at the outset that in reality there was a minimal risk of the negligence causing loss. Yet it appears that in the House of Lords' view in this type of case loss is suffered at the outset, whereas it is not suffered at the outset if negligence causes me to give a purely personal guarantee of my son's debts, even if they are very considerable and his creditors have expressly stated that they will call on the guarantee as soon as they can have letters of demand produced. To some degree, an understanding of the reason for these puzzling distinctions may be assisted by considering the wider policy factors, which we do at para 7.26, below.

1 See para 7.12 above.
2 [1990] 2 QB 495 at 503G.
3 [1990] 2 QB 495 at 510F.
4 *Sephton* [2006] UKHL 22, [2006] 2 AC 543 at [22].

(c) *Cases where the claimant's loss is purely dependent upon a contingency*

7.24   We come finally to the category into which their Lordships held that *Sephton* itself fell, and thus to the facts of *Sephton*. Mr Payne was a solicitor practising on his own account. Between 1990 and 1996 he stole around £750,000 from his client account. These thefts exposed the Law Society to the risk that clients whose money had been stolen would apply for reimbursement to the Solicitors' Compensation Fund, of which the Law Society was the trustee. No such claim was actually made until July 1996. Ultimately the Law Society paid out over £1m, including interest, to such claimants. Sephton & Co were a firm of accountants who, between 1989 and 1995, certified to the Law Society that they had examined Mr Payne's accounts and were satisfied that he had complied with the requirements of the Solicitors' Accounts Rules 1991. In 2000 the Court of Appeal held that accountants performing such work owed the Law Society a duty of care in the preparation of such certificates.[1] The Law Society claimed from Sephtons the sums which it had paid out through the Compensation Fund, on the basis that Sephtons had owed the Society a duty of care and had negligently breached it in the completion of the accountants' certificates for the relevant years. The Law Society did not, however, issue proceedings until 16 May 2002. It had threatened Sephtons with a claim in October 1996, so it could not rely upon s14A of the Limitation Act (see below) as its three-year period had expired well before the issue of proceedings. The question was when the Society first suffered loss: was it when it was first exposed to the risk of a claim, in other words when Mr Payne stole the money, or later?

1 *Law Society v KPMG Peat Marwick* [2000] 1 WLR 1921, CA.

7.25   Sephtons' case was that loss had been suffered when the Society was first exposed to the risk of having to make a payment. In the House of Lords' view, this amounted to a claim that a pure contingency, or risk of having to make a payment, could constitute actionable damage. As indicated above, the House rejected that contention. The views of Lords Hoffmann and Walker on this issue have already been quoted above.[1] Lord Mance considered that actionable loss was not suffered until the Society first received a claim on the Solicitors' Compensation Fund. The effect of the making of a claim was that the Society was bound as a matter of public law to make a payment, even if it did not decide to do so until later.[2] Lord Mance gave various reasons for declining to hold that loss had occurred earlier: as a matter of law, the Society was not bound to make a payment until it received a claim; until a claim was made it was not possible to know which clients might suffer what loss; it was not appropriate to speak of the Fund as having a suffered a loss until a claim was made.[3] But one might equally say that the mother in *Forster*[4] was not legally bound to make a payment until someone called on her guarantee: if her son did not default, there would be no payment to make; yet loss was held to have occurred as soon as she entered into the transaction.

1 At para 7.16.
2 *Sephton* [2006] UKHL 22, [2006] 2 AC 543 at [83].
3 *Sephton* [2006] UKHL 22, [2006] 2 AC 543 at [76].
4 At para 7.18, above.

7.26   At this stage it is perhaps helpful to consider the wider picture, as Lord Mance did. There is a basic potential for injustice in the proposition that time may start to run when the claimant has no knowledge that it has started to run. The first two categories of English case, referred to above, tend to advance that date and, if anything, exacerbate the risk of this injustice occurring. Looking at the overall pattern of the English law of limitation in this type of case, its answer to this potential injustice is the extended limitation period provided by s 14A of the Limitation Act (below), and the Law Commission has proposed that that period should altogether replace the common law approach to the start of the running of time which we have considered in this section, though the proposals would also reduce the limitation period from six to three years. Adoption of those measures would mean that limitation law would no longer need to consider the questions raised in this section. For the moment, however, Parliament has not acted on those proposals. Nevertheless, it is clear that at least Lord Mance was not keen to extend the areas in which the law would advance the date at which time starts to run, thereby potentially increasing the areas in which the injustice just referred to would apply.[1] Ironically, on the facts of *Sephton* itself, it is doubtful whether the Law Commission's proposals would have helped the Law Society because it appears that the Society had delayed for at least three years after it knew that it had a claim.

1 See Lord Mance at [78].

7.27   The final case to be considered in this category is *Gordon v JB Wheatley & Co.*[1] As it was doubted in *Sephton*, its importance now lies less in what the Court of Appeal decided than in the reasons which the House of Lords gave in *Sephton* for indicating that it was or may have been wrongly decided. The claimant's solicitor negligently advised him that a collective mortgage scheme did not require authorisation under the Financial Services Act 1986. As a result, he was obliged by the Securities and Investment Board to indemnify investors in the scheme against losses. He ultimately paid them £676,000. The Court of Appeal held that the claimant suffered loss when he took investments after having received the negligent advice, and not when the SIB subsequently required him to indemnify investors. Lord Hoffmann, however, considered that he suffered loss when he was required to indemnify by the SIB, because there was no inevitable connection between taking the investments and the SIB using its powers.[2] In Lord Walker's view the risk of enforcement action was not a fetter on the claimant's assets and so did not constitute loss.[3] Lord Mance's analysis was that there was no liability, and no change in the claimant's legal position, until the SIB intervened and the court ordered payment or the claimant agreed to pay.[4] It followed that there was no loss until that date. Further, the claimant's loss did not arise directly from the transaction which the defendant's negligence caused the claimant to enter, but collaterally from the powers of the SIB. These approaches show the court drawing back from the rigour of the first two categories of case with their tendency to advance the date at which time starts to run.

1 [2000] Lloyd's Rep PN 605, CA. Beatson J applied *Sephton* to a claim against financial advisors, on the basis that the loss was at first only contingent, in *Shore v Sedgwick Financial Services Ltd* [2007] EWHC 2509 (Admin) at [212]–[214].
2 *Sephton* [2006] UKHL 22, [2006] 2 AC 543 at [25].
3 [51].
4 [82].

(d) Purchasers' cases

7.28   In *Byrne v Hall Pain & Foster*,[1] flat-buyers sued their surveyors for professional negligence in the provision of the valuation report on which they had relied to purchase the flat. The question arose as to whether the cause of action had accrued at the date when they exchanged contracts to purchase the flat, or when the transaction completed. The Court of Appeal held that the former was the correct date: on exchange, the claimants became irrevocably committed to purchasing the lease of the flat, which, due to the defendants' negligence, was in a worse condition than they believed it to be. Thus, at the time of exchange of contracts, the claimants had suffered some detriment capable of valuation in money terms, and so the cause of action accrued. Cases where the claimant is a lender, which are considered in the next section, were distinguished: there, as will be seen, the claimant's loss depended in part on the borrower's performance of his covenant, and so different principles applied. It might be added that, in lenders' cases, the lender is not generally irrevocably committed to the transaction until completion, because its standard terms generally permit it to withdraw from the transaction at any time prior to completion.

1 [1999] 1 WLR 1849, CA.

7.29 *Byrne* was applied in *Havenledge Ltd v Graeme John*.[1] The claimant purchased a derelict property in Wales with a view to turning it into a nursing home and running it as a business. It alleged that its solicitor had negligently failed to carry out a mining search, which would have revealed mine workings underneath the property. The claimant had purchased in 1987 but the presence of the mine workings became apparent only in 1990, and caused business disruption and consequent financial losses in 1990. By a majority, the Court of Appeal held that loss was suffered when the claimant purchased the defective nursing home, and declined to apply the analogy of the lenders' cases (see below) to the effect that what was being purchased was an asset with income-producing potential, so that it was only when the business started to show losses on account of the mine that loss was suffered. In terms of the first two categories of case in tort considered above, the argument was in a sense as to whether the case should be seen as a transaction case or as a case where the defendant's negligence caused the claimant to get an asset (the home) worth less than it should have been. The latter view prevailed.[2] One might argue that it could have been seen as falling into either category. This is another somewhat dubious distinction which the Law Commission's proposed reform would do away with.

1 [2001] Lloyd's Rep PN 223, CA.
2 The possible harshness of this might have been alleviated by s 14A of the Limitation Act (below), but the claimant had allowed the period of three years under that section to expire.

4   Lenders' cases: Nykredit

7.30   The leading case in this category is the House of Lords' decision in *Nykredit Mortgage Bank plc v Edward Erdman Group Ltd (No 2)*,[1] which was approved in *Sephton*[2]. This was the House's judgment on interest payable in those cases which remained from the *BBL*[3] decision. Although in *Nykredit* the lenders were suing valuers rather than solicitors, the same principles are likely to apply to lenders' claims against solicitors.[4] The question before the House was what interest should be awarded on damages. As statutory interest could be awarded only from the date when the cause of action arose, this raised the question of when the lenders' cause of action had arisen. The House acknowledged that its decision on this point would be relevant not only to claims for interest, but also to questions of limitation.[5] It is submitted that *Nykredit* should be regarded as authoritative in relation to when the cause of action arises, as well as in relation to interest.

1 [1997] 1 WLR 1627. As Lord Hoffmann observed, at [1997] 1 WLR 1639D, the House of Lords' decision was in accordance with the Court of Appeal's earlier decisions in *UBAF Ltd v European American Banking Corpn* [1984] 1 QB 713 and *First National Commercial Bank plc v Humberts* [1995] 2 All ER 673.
2 See [2006] 2 AC 543 at [20], [43], [73].
3 *Banque Bruxelles Lambert SA v Eagle Star Insurance Co Ltd* [1997] AC 191, HL. See further chapter 10.
4 See para 10.84, below.
5 [1997] 1 WLR 1627, per Lord Nicholls at 1630A–B and Lord Hoffmann at 1638B. Lord Hoffmann said that although for purposes of interest the question under Supreme Court Act 1981, s 35A was when the cause of action 'arose', whereas for limitation under the Limitation Act 1980 it was when the cause of action 'accrued', in his view the two words had the same meaning.

(a) *The basic comparison*

7.31   The principal speech was delivered by Lord Nicholls. He considered the question of when the cause of action accrued in a case where, as a result of negligent advice, property was acquired as security. The question was when the lender first sustained loss. The loss was economic rather than physical in character. At the moment after the lender had made the advance, it was not certain that it would suffer financial loss, because (i) the borrower might not default, and, even if he did, (ii) the security might be sufficient to cover the amount of the borrower's debt.

7.32   In assessing when loss was suffered, the court had to consider the appropriate *measure* of loss. In cases where, had there been no negligence, the lender would not have entered into the transaction:[1]

'... a professional negligence claim calls for a comparison between the plaintiff's position had he not entered into the transaction in question and his position under the transaction. That is the basic comparison. Thus, typically in a case of a negligent valuation of an intended loan security, the basic comparison called for is between (a) the amount of money lent by the plaintiff which he would still have had in the absence of the loan transaction, plus interest at a proper rate, and (b) the value of the rights acquired, namely the borrower's covenant and the true value of the overvalued property.'

In the rest of his speech Lord Nicholls referred to this formula as 'the basic comparison'. In order to determine when the lender first suffered a loss, it was necessary to apply the basic comparison to the facts of the case.

1 [1997] 1 WLR 1631E–F. Lord Nicholls did not deal with the position in cases where, had there been no negligence, the lender *would* still have entered into the transaction. Normally these are cases where, in the absence of negligence, the lender would have lent less. Thus it might be said that the cause of action accrues as at the date of completion, because the lender had, at that date, lent more than it would have done. But the logic of *Nykredit* probably means that this approach is wrong: even if the lender is caused to lend more than it should have done, it may suffer no loss,

because the borrower may repay the loan in full. So, even in this type of case, it is probably necessary to assess the date when the cause of action accrues by reference to the basic comparison.

7.33 How should the basic comparison be applied? Lord Nicholls accepted that this might raise difficulties in obtaining evidence, but these difficulties were not difficulties in principle.[1] In other words, the *type* of evidence required was clear; the problem might be in actually obtaining it. As to this evidence, at any given time, it should be possible to obtain figures for part (a) of the basic comparison, namely, the amount of the advance plus interest at a proper rate. As to the appropriate rate of interest, see the discussion of basic loss in chapter 10.[2] Similarly, it should be possible to obtain a retrospective valuation of the security. It might be more difficult to value the borrower's covenant. On this, Lord Nicholls said:[3]

> 'Ascribing a value to the borrower's covenant should not be unduly troublesome. A comparable exercise regarding lessees' covenants is a routine matter when valuing property. Sometimes the comparison will reveal a loss from the inception of the loan transaction. The borrower may be a company with no other assets, its sole business may comprise redeveloping and reselling the property, and for repayment the lender may be looking solely to his security. In such a case, if the property is worth less than the amount of the loan, relevant and measurable loss will be sustained at once. In other cases the borrower's covenant may have value, and until there is default the lender may presently sustain no loss even though the security is worth less than the amount of the loan. Conversely, in some cases there may be no loss even when the borrower defaults. A borrower may default after a while but when he does so, despite the overvaluation, the security may still be adequate.'

1 [1997] 1 WLR 1627 at 1632B–C.
2 See para 10.73ff, below.
3 [1997] 1 WLR 1627 at 1632C–E.

7.34 Lord Nicholls went on to reject the notion that the cause of action could not arise until the property had been sold. It was wrong to suggest that loss could not be suffered until then:[1]

> '... no accountant or prospective buyer, viewing the loan book of a commercial lender, would say that the shortfall in security against outstanding loans to defaulting borrowers did not represent a loss to the lender merely because the securities had yet to be sold.'

On the facts of *Nykredit*, the borrower defaulted at once and its covenant was worthless. The amount lent always exceeded the value of the security. Thus the cause of action accrued at or about the time of the transaction.[2]

1 [1997] 1 WLR 1627 at 1633B.
2 [1997] 1 WLR 1627 at 1635A–B.

7.35 The effect of this is that, where the borrower defaults and disappears without assets at once and the security was always worth less than the advance, the cause of action accrues almost immediately. On the other hand, where the borrower defaults but the value of the security is sufficient to cover the amount of the advance plus interest and costs of repossession, no loss is suffered and so the cause of action does not accrue, unless perhaps there is a delay in sale during which time the amount of the advance plus interest comes to exceed the value of the security.

(b) Cause of action accruing before the borrower has defaulted

7.36 Lord Nicholls indicated that there may be circumstances in which the cause of action accrues before the borrower has defaulted:[1]

> 'An alternative … possibility is that the cause of action does not arise until the lender becomes entitled to have recourse to the security. I am not attracted by this, as a proposition of law. This suggestion involves the proposition that, until then, as a matter of law, the lender can never suffer loss, and the lender can never issue his writ, whatever the circumstances. That does not seem right to me. This proposition, like the date of realisation submission, loses sight of the starting point: that the lender would not have entered into the transaction had the valuer given proper advice. If the basic comparison shows a loss at an earlier stage, why should the lender have to wait until the borrower defaults before issuing his writ against the negligent valuer?'[2]

Lord Nicholls had already observed that there might be cases where the borrower's covenant had value so that until there was default there would be no loss even though the security was worth less than the amount of the advance. But by rejecting the notion that no cause of action could accrue until the borrower defaulted, he implicitly accepted that there could be circumstances in which, although the borrower had not defaulted, the basic comparison showed a loss.

1 [1997] 1 WLR 1627 at 1633E–G.
2 Compare Mummery LJ's obiter remarks in *UCB Bank plc v Halifax (SW) Ltd* [1999] Lloyd's Rep PN 154 at 158.

7.37 *DnB Mortgages Ltd v Bullock & Lees*[1] is an example of this. Due to the defendant's negligence, the claimant lender entered into a remortgage which was completed in February 1990. The borrowers continued to make mortgage repayments until January 1991. It was nevertheless held that the lender had suffered actionable loss in May 1990. At that time the lender's security was worth £130,000 and the total sum owing pursuant to the mortgage was £140,000. The trial judge held that the borrowers' covenant in May 1990 was worth less than £10,000, so that the lender had suffered loss by that date. Upholding his decision, the Court of Appeal held that the borrowers' covenant had to be valued objectively, on the basis of all evidence available to the court at the date of trial, and not simply by reference to information which might have been available to the market in May 1990.

1 [2000] Lloyd's Rep PN 290, CA.

5 Loss of litigation

7.38 The principal issue of difficulty in relation to lost litigation claims arises when a claim is struck out due to a solicitor's negligence. Does the cause of action in tort accrue only when the claim is actually struck out, or earlier, and, if earlier, when? In *Hopkins v Mackenzie*[1] the Court of Appeal held that the cause of action in tort accrued only when the claim was struck out, and not earlier, but a subsequent line of cases has introduced a different approach. In *Khan v RM Falvey*[2], Chadwick LJ distinguished between two types of loss for which a claimant might seek compensation from a negligent solicitor. Suppose that a claim is worth £100,000. The claimant's solicitor delays the conduct of the action to such an extent that the defendant applies to strike out for want of prosecution. The day before the application is heard, there is a 70% chance that the claim will be struck out. In that case, on that date, the claim is worth only £30,000, since its £100,000 value must be discounted by 70% to reflect the risk of the striking out. That damage, the reduction in value from £100,000 to £30,000, has already occurred before the striking out. On the other hand, suppose then that the application to strike out proceeds and the claim is struck out the next day. In that case, on the date of the striking out the claimant suffers loss of the residual £30,000 value of the claim. On Chadwick LJ's analysis, it is only the £30,000 loss which occurs on the date of the striking out; the £70,000 loss occurs earlier. Hence, on Chadwick LJ's approach, if the claimant seeks compensation only for the £30,000 loss then the damage may be said to occur on the date of the striking out. Generally, however, claimants will seek compensation for both types of loss, so that at least some of the damage claimed will be caused before the date of the striking out. Further, in *Polley v Warner Goodman & Street*[3], Clarke LJ stated that a claimant:

> 'cannot defeat the statute of limitations by claiming only in respect of damage which occurs within the limitation period if he has suffered damage from the same wrongful act outside that period.'

This would suggest that even limiting the claim to Chadwick LJ's second type of loss might not succeed in saving a claim which was otherwise statute-barred.

1 [1995] 6 Med LR 26.
2 [2002] Lloyd's Rep PN 369, and see esp [57].
3 [2003] EWCA Civ 1013, [2003] PNLR 40, at [15].

7.39   *Hatton v Chafes*[1] was another case where the claimant's original claim was struck out for want of prosecution; he sued his solicitors for loss of the original claim. Clarke LJ said that:

> 'It seems to me that there are three possibilities as to when damage is caused by negligence in such a case so that the claimant's cause of action has accrued and time begins to run against him. The first is when the claimant has no arguable basis for avoiding the claim being struck out, the second is when it is more probable than not that the claim will be struck out and the third is when there is a real (as opposed to a minimal or fanciful) risk of the claim being struck out.'

He and the Court of Appeal held that it was unnecessary, on the facts of *Hatton*, to decide which of these three possibilities represented the correct test, because *Hatton* was a case in the first category, and the effect of *Khan* was that in such a case damage was suffered when the first test was satisfied. Similarly, in *Polley v Warner Goodman & Street*[2], Clarke LJ stated that:

> 'In *Hatton v Chafes* it was held that where, in a striking-out for want of prosecution case, a claimant has no arguable basis for avoiding the claim being struck out because of the defendant's solicitors' negligent delay, he has suffered loss as a result of the defendant's negligence and his cause of action has accrued.'

The Court of Appeal held that *Polley* was also a case in which, more than six years before issue of the claim form, an application to strike out was bound to succeed, so that it was unnecessary to decide whether Clarke LJ's second or third categories represented the correct test.

1 [2003] EWCA Civ 341, [2003] PNLR 24, at [17].
2 [2003] EWCA Civ 1013, [2003] PNLR 40, at [20].

7.40   In *Workman v Pannone & Partners*,[1] Davis J read *Khan v Falvey* to hold that 'damage can in this kind of situation occur when the value of an action is appreciably diminishing as its vulnerability to strike out increases.' That interpretation was, however, based on a concession, and appears inconsistent with Clarke LJ's view of the extent to which the authorities go (above). It is doubted whether it is authoritative. In *Cohen v Kingsley Napley*[2] Pill LJ took the test to be whether the action 'would have been struck out had the application been made'. In *Sephton*, Lord Walker[3] took *Hatton* to establish that a solicitor was liable if he carelessly allowed the client's claim to become either statute-barred or '"doomed to failure" because a striking-out application would be bound to succeed'. Lord Mance's formulation[4] was that the cause of action accrued when

351

the claim became time-barred 'or liable to be struck out for want of prosecution.' It seems likely that Lord Mance approved the results and reasoning in *Hatton* and *Polley*, since he cited them, apparently with approval.[5]

1 [2002] EWHC 2366 (QB), at [34]–[35].
2 [2006] EWCA Civ 66, [2006] PNLR 22.
3 Above, at [47].
4 [69].
5 See also *Jessup v Wetherell* [2006] EWHC 2582 (QB), [2007] PNLR 10, where Silber J held that the action was doomed to failure before the order striking out was made.

7.41 The net result of these cases is that the cause of action accrues, at latest, when the underlying action is 'doomed to failure'. It is possible that it runs from an earlier time, as set out in Clarke LJ's second or third classes of case, though this is not yet established. Further, *Cohen* (above) introduced a further hurdle from the defendant's point of view. If a defendant contends that an action was doomed to failure by a particular date on the basis that, at that date, if the negligent solicitor had suddenly reactivated the claim it would nevertheless have been struck out for want of prosecution, the defendant must prove that, if the claim had been reactivated, the defendant to the underlying action would have made an application to strike out. If this cannot be proved, then it cannot be said that the claimant suffered loss on the 'doomed to failure' basis, because if the former defendant would not have applied to strike out then the action would presumably have continued in existence and not been lost until later.

6   Wills and inheritance planning

7.42 In *Bacon v Howard Kennedy*,[1] the defendant solicitors had negligently failed to carry out X's instructions to draft a will by which he would have left his estate to the claimant. The claimant sued the defendants for negligence. The question was whether the claimant's cause of action accrued when the defendants ought to have drafted the will, in which case the claim was statute-barred, or when X died, in which case it was not. The judge opted for the latter date. It was argued that, in accordance with cases such as *Forster v Outred*,[2] the claimant suffered a loss in the sense of a risk that he would receive nothing, as soon as the defendants had negligently failed to draft the will. The judge's rejection of this may be justified on the basis that it is an essential part of the cause of action that the testator has died,[3] because, until that time, the defendant's negligence will not have caused the claimant any loss. This is because, had there been no negligence, the testator could have revoked the part of the will leaving property to the claimant at any time until his death. Thus, until the testator has died, it will always be an open question whether, before death, the testator might have removed the claimant from the will. Further, until the testator has died, if the defect in the will is discovered, it can be remedied.[4] Finally, the decision would appear to be consistent with the approach to claims based on pure contingencies set out in *Sephton* (above).[5]

1 [1999] PNLR 1, HHJ Bromley QC sitting as a Deputy High Court Judge.
2 [1982] 1 WLR 86, CA: see para 7.18, above.
3 Evans *Lawyers' Liabilities* (2nd edn, 2002) at 15–03.
4 The negligent solicitor might be liable for the cost of doing this, but this would be principally liability to the testator not potential beneficiaries under the will.
5 Limitation was also discussed in *Daniels v Thompson* [2004] PNLR 33, though ultimately the case turned on who, if anyone, was the correct claimant. It is considered in chapter 11. The decision in *Cotterell v Leeds Day* (QBD, undreported, 21 December 1999, Buckley J), may be in doubt in light of *Sephton*. Mrs Reece gave a half share in property to Mrs Cotterell but Mrs Reece continued to live there. Due to the defendants' negligence, Mrs Reece did not make an election which, if made, would have meant that no inheritance tax was payable on Mrs Cotterell's share when Mrs Reece died. Later, Mrs Reece sold the property. If Mrs Reece had survived another seven years after that, no inheritance tax would have been payable, on Mrs Reece's death, in respect of Mrs Cotterell's share. But she lived only another two years. Buckley J held that loss was suffered as soon as time to make the election had expired, even though no excess tax might have been payable, depending on for how long Mrs Reece survived. It is submitted that this decision may need reconsideration in light of *Sephton*.

C STATUTORY EXTENSIONS TO THE LIMITATION PERIOD

7.43 Sections 14A and 32 of the Limitation Act 1980 contain statutory extensions of the normal limitation period, in cases to which they apply. These are complicated provisions, and it is not possible to consider every aspect of them.[1] We do, however, attempt to concentrate upon issues which particularly concern solicitors' cases.

1 See McGee *Limitation Periods* (5th edn, 2006) and Oughton, Lowry and Merkin *Limitation of Actions* (1998).

1 Limitation Act 1980, s 14A

7.44 Section 14A was added to the Limitation Act 1980 to deal with cases where the defendant did not know of the facts relevant to the cause of action at the time when it accrued. As mentioned at the start of this chapter, given that loss in solicitors' negligence cases is usually economic, it is quite possible that claimants, through no fault of their own, may not realise that they have suffered loss until more than six years after the accrual of the cause of action. A number of the cases considered above demonstrate this.[1] Under normal principles, such claims would be statute-barred. The purpose of s 14A is to remedy that injustice.[2]

1 See paras 7.15–7.25.
2 See the Twenty-Fourth Report of the Law Reform Committee (Latent Damage) (1984). It appears, however, that the existing provisions of s 14A may have been drafted with inadequate consideration of their impact on solicitors' negligence cases: see O'Sullivan 'Limitation, latent damage and solicitors' negligence' (2004) 20 PN 218.

7.45 The effect of s 14A of the Act is that, in cases to which it applies, if six years have passed since the accrual of the cause of action, the claimant has an alternative possible limitation period in which to sue. The alternative period is three years from the 'starting date', as defined in s 14A, but subject to a longstop of 15 years from the act or omission which is alleged to constitute negligence.[1]

1 Limitation Act 1980, s 14B.

(*a*) *Scope of s 14A*

7.46 Section 14A applies only to claims where the cause of action is the tort of negligence, and not to breaches of contract, even if the breach alleged is a failure to act with reasonable skill or care.[1] This means that, where it is alleged that a solicitor has failed to act with reasonable skill and care, which is actionable in either contract or tort, a claimant wishing to take advantage of s 14A should abandon the claim in contract. Section 14A does not apply to cases to which s 32(1)(b) of the Act applies,[2] that is, cases of fraud, deliberate concealment or mistake. A different extension to the limitation period applies in those cases.[3]

1 Société *Commerciale de Reassurance v ERAS (International) Ltd* [1992] 2 All ER 82n, CA.
2 Limitation Act 1980, s 32(5).
3 See para 7.67ff, below.

(*b*) *The 'starting date'*

7.47 The provisions defining what counts as the starting date, from which the claimant has three years in which to issue a claim form, are complex and require to be quoted in full:

'(5) For the purposes of this section, the starting date for reckoning the period of limitation under subsection (4)(b) above is the earliest date on which the claimant or any person in whom the cause of action was vested before him first had both the knowledge required for bringing an action for damages in respect of the relevant damage and a right to bring such an action.

(6) In subsection (5) above "the knowledge required for bringing an action for damages in respect of the relevant damage" means knowledge both–

(a)   of the material facts about the damage in respect of which damages are claimed; and

(b)   of the other facts relevant to the current action mentioned in subsection (8) below.

(7) For the purposes of subsection (6)(a) above, the material facts about the damage are such facts about the damage as would lead a reasonable person who had suffered such damage to consider it sufficiently serious to justify his instituting proceedings for damages against a defendant who did not dispute liability and was able to satisfy a judgment.

(8) The other facts referred to in subsection (6)(b) are–

(a)   that the damage was attributable in whole or in part to the act or omission which is alleged to constitute negligence; and

(b)   the identity of the defendant; and

(c)   if it is alleged that the act or omission was that of a person other than the defendant, the identity of that person and the additional facts supporting the bringing of an action against the defendant.

(9) Knowledge that any acts or omissions did or did not, as a matter of law, involve negligence is irrelevant for the purposes of subsection (5) above.

(10) For the purposes of this section a person's knowledge includes knowledge which he might reasonably have been expected to acquire–

(a)   from facts observable or ascertainable by him; or

(b)   from facts ascertainable by him with the help of appropriate expert advice which it is reasonable for him to seek;

but a person shall not be taken by virtue of this subsection to have knowledge of a fact ascertainable only with the help of expert advice so long as he has taken all reasonable steps to obtain (and, where appropriate, to act on) that advice.'

Various aspects of this definition of the starting date will be commented upon.

(c) *Burden of proof*

7.48   If the claim form is not issued within six years of the date when the cause of action accrued, the onus is on the claimant to plead and prove that the starting date is a date within the three years preceding issue of the claim form. Pausing there, claimants should take great care in considering the precise nature of the evidence which should be adduced on this issue: in the recent case of *Haward v*

Fawcetts[1], Lords Nicholls and Mance considered that the claimant's case failed simply because he had failed to satisfy the burden of proof; it appeared that his evidence failed even to address the correct issues. As to defendants, if the defendant wishes to allege that the starting date is a date prior to the three years immediately preceding issue of the claim form, then the onus is on the defendant to prove this.[2]

1 [2006] UKHL 9, [2006] 1 WLR 682, at [24] and [138].
2 *Nash v Eli Lilly & Co* [1993] 1 WLR 782 at 796H, CA. That case concerned the provisions of Limitation Act 1980, s 14 but that provision is analogous to s 14A and cases on s 14 are helpful in construing s 14A: see the Court of Appeal's judgment in *Hallam-Eames v Merrett Syndicates Ltd* [1996] 7 Med LR 122. See also *Glaister v Greenwood* [2001] Lloyd's Rep PN 412, Lawrence Collins J.

(d) Degree of certainty required

7.49   Leaving aside the provisions relating to constructive knowledge,[1] what degree of certainty in the claimant's mind counts as (actual) knowledge for the purposes of s 14A(6)? In *Halford v Brookes*[2] Lord Donaldson of Lymington MR said that

> 'The word has to be construed in the context of the purpose of the section, which is to determine a period of time within which a plaintiff can be required to start any proceedings. In this context "knowledge" clearly does not mean "know for certain and beyond possibility of contradiction". It does, however, mean "know with sufficient confidence to justify embarking on the preliminaries to the issue of a writ, such as submitting a claim to the proposed defendant, taking legal and other advice and collecting evidence." Suspicion, particularly if it is vague and unsupported, will indeed not be enough, but reasonable belief will normally suffice. It is probably only in an exceptional case such as *Davis v Ministry of Defence* that it will not, because there is some other countervailing factor.'

Although *Halford* was a personal injury case relating to s 14 Limitation Act, Lord Nicholls approved this passage as applying also to s 14A in *Haward*, which concerned accountants' negligence, and Lord Mance quoted this and similar passages[3]. Lord Mance emphasised that, in relation to sub-s (8)(a), the knowledge in question must be 'of the attributability in whole or in part of the damage suffered to the act or omission alleged to constitute negligence.'

1 See para 7.61, below.
2 [1991] 1 WLR 428, CA, at 443E . He also quoted a passage from *Nash v Eli Lilly & Co* to similar effect.
3 Above. See [9], [112].

(e) Actual knowledge 'that the damage was attributable in whole or in part to the act or omission which is alleged to constitute negligence' (s 14A(8))

7.50 The meaning of this phrase is the most difficult aspect of interpreting s 14A, not least because of the use in sub-s (8) of the word 'attributable'. The basic question is: what facts, or kinds of facts, must the claimant know in order for time to start running under s 14A? Constructive knowledge is dealt with below;[1] for the moment we shall consider only actual knowledge. On one view, to say, as s 14A(8) does, that time will not start running until the claimant knows enough to appreciate that his or her damage was 'attributable' to the defendant's act or omission, tends to suggest that, for time to start running, the claimant needs to know that the defendant's act or omission was responsible in law for the injury caused to him or her. Yet s 14A(9) expressly provides that 'knowledge that any acts or omissions did or did not, as a matter of law, involve negligence, is irrelevant' for the purposes of establishing knowledge for the purposes of s 14A. Problems arise in cases where the defendant argues that the claimant knew all the material *facts* at the time when the cause of action accrued, and that the reason the claimant did not commence proceedings within the limitation period was simply due to ignorance of the law, namely the *law* of negligence showing that there was a cause of action, which has to be ignored. On the face of it this could give rise to the same injustice which the enactment of s 14A was intended to prevent, namely, claimants finding that their claims have become statute-barred before they could reasonably have brought proceedings to enforce them. There is a particular danger of this where, as in many solicitors' negligence cases, the claimant could not have realised that it was worth suing for negligence until he or she realised that the legal advice which the defendant gave at the outset was wrong in law. One might argue that such knowledge is irrelevant, by s 14A(9), so that the claim becomes statute-barred before the claimant is able to sue. It is submitted that the best solution to this problem would be to reform s 14A, but, while the government delays in enacting the Law Commission's proposals, the courts have attempted to mitigate this problem themselves.

1 See para 7.61.

7.51 The Court of Appeal dealt with the issue in *Hallam-Eames v Merrett Syndicates Ltd*.[1] Various Names at Lloyd's sued their active underwriter, managing agents and members' agents on the basis that the writing of various policies had been negligent because the liability to which members of the relevant syndicates were thereby exposed was potentially enormous, and the defendant underwriter did not have the material on which he could have formed any reasonable view of what that liability was likely to be. Delivering the judgment of the court, Hoffmann LJ referred to a previous Court of Appeal decision in relation to s 14, *Dobbie v Medway Health Authority*,[2] which he summarised as follows:[3]

357

'In *Dobbie* the plaintiff was admitted to hospital for the removal of a lump in her breast. The surgeon who excised the lump formed the view that it was cancerous and removed the breast. Afterwards on microscopic examination the lump turned out to be benign. She knew shortly after the operation that the breast had been removed before the microscopic examination but was not advised until 17 years later that it might have been negligent to do so. Again this court held that she knew enough at the earlier stage to satisfy s 14(1)(b).'

In relation to s 14A(8), Hoffmann LJ said that it was not sufficient simply that the claimant knew that there was a causal connection between his damage and an act or omission of the defendant. In addition:[4]

'... the act or omission of which the plaintiff must have knowledge must be that which is causally relevant for the purposes of an allegation of negligence. There may be many acts, omissions or states which can be said to have a causal connection with a given occurrence, but when we make causal statements in ordinary speech, we select on common sense principles the one which is relevant for our purpose. In a different context it could be said that a Name suffered losses because some members' agent took him to lunch and persuaded him to join Lloyd's. But this is not causally relevant in the context of an allegation of negligence.

It is this idea of causal relevance which various judges of this court have tried to express by saying ... that one should

'... look at the way the plaintiff puts his case, distil what he is complaining about and ask whether he had in broad terms knowledge of the facts on which that complaint is based.' (Hoffmann LJ in *Broadley* [1994] 4 All ER 439).

If one asks on common sense principles what Mrs Dobbie was complaining about, the answer is that the surgeon had removed a healthy breast. It would in our view be a seriously incomplete statement of her case to say that it was simply that the surgeon had removed her breast. This is not a matter of elaborating detail by requiring knowledge of precisely how he had come to the act complained of, such as this court rejected in *Broadley*. It was part of the essence of her complaint. Nor is it requiring knowledge of fault or negligence. The court's emphatic rejection of such a requirement is entirely consistent with characterising the act complained of (and of which knowledge was therefore required) as the removal of a healthy breast.

If one asks what is the principle of common sense on which one would identify Mrs Dobbie's complaint as the removal of a healthy breast rather than simply the removal of a breast, it is that the additional fact is necessary to make the act something of which she would prima facie seem entitled to complain. She was suspected of having a cancerous lump and if this had been the case, the removal of her breast would not have been a matter for complaint.

The plaintiff does not have to know that he has a cause of action or that the defendant's acts can be characterised in law as negligent or as falling short of some standard of professional or other behaviour. But, as Hoffmann LJ said in *Broadley,* the words "which is alleged to constitute the negligence" serve to *identify* the facts of which the plaintiff must have knowledge. He must have known the facts which can fairly be described as constituting the negligence of which he complains.'

1 [1996] 7 Med LR 122, CA.
2 [1994] 1 WLR 1234, CA.
3 [1996] 7 Med LR 122 at 125.
4 [1996] 7 Med LR 122 at 126.

7.52 The court went on to consider what, on the facts of *Hallam-Eames,* should be regarded as the facts which fairly constituted the negligence of which the Names complained. Those facts were not simply the writing of the relevant policies or certification of accounts, because:[1]

'these facts in themselves do not amount to acts of which the Names would even *prima facie* be entitled to complain. It is necessary to add the allegation that the run off policies and RTCs exposed the names to potentially huge liabilities and that the certified accounts attributed values to IBNRS, none of which were in fact capable of reasonable quantification.'

1 [1996] 7 Med LR 122 at 126.

7.53 The question of actual knowledge under s 14A reached the House of Lords in *Haward v Fawcetts.*[1] Mr Haward had invested money in a business in reliance upon advice as to the its future profitability from his accountants, Fawcetts. The transaction was disastrous, but Mr Haward kept investing larger and larger sums in the business. Each of their Lordships favoured an approach derived from *Hallam-Eames,* of distilling the essence of what the claimant was complaining about. Each of the five law lords gave a reasoned speech, though they each reached the same result. Lords Nicholls and Mance considered that the claimant had failed to satisfy the burden of proof; Lords Scott, Walker and Brown considered that the claimant had had the requisite knowledge more than three years before issue of the claim form. The case is unusual in that the defendants did not argue in the alternative that the claimant had had constructive knowledge (see below), so that the speeches are almost exclusively concerned with actual as opposed to constructive knowledge. In future cases, defendants will generally wish to assert both actual and constructive knowledge.

1 [2006] UKHL 9, [2006] 1 WLR 682.

7.54 It is clear from *Haward* that the knowledge which the claimant need have in order to start time running is not knowledge of all the facts which may later appear in the particulars of claim: rather, it is knowledge of the broad nature of the claim.[1] After all, the claimant has three years from the starting date in which to make further enquiries and prepare the particulars of claim. As to what the claimant must know, their lordships employed various slightly differing formulations, and it will be necessary to await their application in future cases to see precisely what the test is. Nevertheless, it is submitted that it is in summary whether the claimant knows enough to put him or her on enquiry as to whether he or she might have a claim against the defendant in relation to the matters which ultimately form the subject matter of the claim. This is based on the following quotations from the speeches. Lord Nicholls said that time did not begin to run until the claimant knew that there was a 'a real possibility that his damage was caused by the act or omission in question ...'. He added that:

'... for time to run, something more was needed to put Mr Haward on enquiry. For time to start running there needs to have been something which would reasonably cause Mr Haward to start asking questions about the advice he was given.'[2]

In Lord Scott's view, following *Hallam-Eames*, the requite knowledge was 'knowledge of the facts constituting the essence of the complaint of negligence.'[3] He assessed these, from the particulars of claim, as being:

'... that Fawcetts, their financial advisers, did not give them the advice that the true state of the company's affairs warranted and that, if given, would have warned them against a disastrous investment of their money.'[4]

Lord Walker considered that Mr Haward had to know '"something of which he would prima facie be entitled to complain" '.[5] Applying *Hallam-Eames*, the court was concerned with the identification of the facts which distilled what the complaint was about. Further, Lord Walker emphasised that in areas which called for technical expertise, such as reinsurance at Lloyd's or occupational pensions, 'a claimant may know the basic facts, but not know what, to an expert, they add up to.'[6] In such cases therefore, a claimant might require expert advice before he had the knowledge required to set time running. But *Haward* was not such a case, because it concerned 'a mature businessman's understanding of financial advice on the trading activities of a small company carrying on a fairly straightforward sort of business.'[7] In Lord Brown's view, the claimant had actual knowledge, so as to set time running, when he knew enough:

> 'to realise that there is a real possibility of his damage having been caused by some flaw or inadequacy in his advisers' investment advice, and enough therefore to start an investigation into that possibility, which s 14A gives him 3 years to complete.'[8]

Lord Mance said that, as to actual knowledge, the question was whether the claimant had:

> 'actual knowledge of the material facts about the damage and other facts relevant to the action (including therefore knowledge that the loss was capable of being attributed to an act or omission alleged to constitute negligence)'.

He held that actual knowledge for these purposes:

> 'involves knowing enough to make it reasonable to investigate whether or not there is a claim against a particular potential defendant.'[9]

1 Per Lord Nicholls [2006] UKHL 9, [2006] 1 WLR 682 at [10], Lord Walker at [57], and Lord Mance at [119].
2 [11], [21].
3 [49].
4 [50].
5 [72]. Quoting from Hoffmann LJ in *Hallam-Eames* (referred to at para 7.51, above).
6 [64]. This is discussed further below. A further example in the pensions sphere is *Glaister v Greenwood* [2001] Lloyd's Rep PN 412.
7 [74].
8 [90].
9 [126].

7.55 While these formulations are relatively similar, it is doubtful whether their application to the facts of any given case will necessarily be straightforward. This is because, on the facts of *Haward* itself, three judges, Lords Scott, Walker and Brown, held that the test was satisfied more than three years before issue of the claim form, whereas the remaining two, Lords Nicholls and Mance, decided the case purely on the basis that Mr Haward had failed to satisfy the burden of proof. So even if each judge was applying essentially the same test, they split three to two as to the application of that test.

7.56 There is support in *Haward,* however, for the proposition that, although it is 'facts' which the claimant must know to start time running, these 'facts' may include propositions which are partly judgmental. Lord Nicholls said[1]

> 'Sometimes the essence of a claimant's case cannot easily be described, at least in general terms, without recourse to language

suggestive of fault: for instance, that 'something had gone wrong' in the conduct of the claimant's medical operation, or that the accountant's advice was 'flawed'. Use of such language does not mean the facts thus compendiously described have necessarily stepped outside the scope of s 14A(8)(a). In this context there can be no objection to the use of language of this character so long as this does not lead to any blurring of the boundary between the essential and the irrelevant.'

Lord Walker expressly agreed with this approach.[2] It is doubtful whether a philosopher, or even a linguistic pedant, would describe the proposition that 'something had gone wrong' as a fact. The phrase 'something had gone wrong' implies that something ought to have been done differently, and, on one view, 'ought' statements are not purely factual: they include not merely descriptions of how things are, but also exhortations as to how life ought to be.[3] So why are the courts constrained to say that 'ought' or judgmental statements count as 'facts' within the meaning of s 14A?

1 [2006] UKHL 9, [2006] 1 WLR 682 at [13].
2 At [67].
3 See the philosopher JL Mackie's discussion of 'is' and 'ought' in *Ethics: Inventing Right and Wrong* (1977) at 64.

7.57 It is submitted that the reason may lie in a problem with regard to the drafting of s 14A, and its application to professional and particularly solicitors' negligence cases, to which we drew attention in the first edition of this book. Section 14A(9) provides that 'knowledge that any acts or omissions did or did not, as a matter of law, involve negligence is irrelevant' for the purposes of s 14A. This gives rise to a danger of which *HF Pension Trustees Ltd v Ellison*[1] provides an extreme example. The danger is that it may be said that the solicitors' negligence lay in advice which was negligently given to the claimant because the solicitors made an error of law. The client does not realise that the error of law has been made and therefore does not know that he should bring a claim. More than six years later, the client learns of the error of law and seeks to rely upon s 14A. The defendants respond that s 14A will not assist: the client knew all the facts at the outset; all that he did not know was that the solicitor's advice had been negligent, but that is a matter which s 14A(9) deems irrelevant. The difficulty with such an argument is that, if correct, it means that, in this type of case, s 14A fails to satisfy its purpose of ensuring that time does not expire before claimants could reasonably start proceedings.

1 [1999] Lloyd's Rep PN 489 (Jonathan Parker J). The claimants were successors of the trustees of an occupational pension scheme called the FMC scheme. In May 1989 the FMC trustees sought advice from a solicitor experienced in pension matters as to whether they could transfer a surplus in their scheme to another scheme. The solicitor advised the FMC trustees that they had power to do so and on 17 November 1989, in reliance upon that advice, the FMC trustees made transfers totalling £18.44m. Various pensioners complained about the transfers to the Pensions Ombudsman, who found in a determination dated 11 October 1995 that the transfers were in breach of

trust. On 12 July 1996 Knox J upheld that decision. On 17 October 1997 the claimants issued a writ against the solicitor for negligent advice in 1989, seeking repayment of any sums transferred which could not be recovered, and the costs of dealing with the question of the validity of the transfers. The primary limitation period had expired and the question was whether s 14A could assist the claimants. Jonathan Parker J held that it could not. The material facts for the purposes of s 14A were that the solicitor had advised that the transfers be made, and that they had been made in reliance upon his advice. The claimants had known these facts from the outset. They had not known that the solicitor's advice was negligent, but that was a matter of law which had to be ignored by virtue of s 14A(9).

7.58 One solution to this problem is to hold that it demonstrates a flaw in the drafting of s 14A, which should be reformed.[1] The Law Commission has proposed reform but unfortunately the government has not been able to find parliamentary time in which to introduce it. In the meantime, their Lordships in *Haward* made clear that they considered *HF Pension Trustees* to have been wrongly decided. Lord Walker said that, until the pensions trustees in that case knew that they had received 'seriously incorrect' advice, they did not know that they had suffered any damage at all. 'They knew the bare facts, but were ignorant of their significance'.[2] He considered that, in areas requiring considerable technical expertise such as the law of occupational pensions, it was unlikely that claimants would have the necessary knowledge to start time running until they had technical advice pointing out what had gone wrong.[3]

1 See O'Sullivan 'Limitation, latent damage and solicitors' negligence' (2004) 20 PN 218.
2 [61].
3 Per Lord Walker at [64]. Lord Brown agreed with this analysis, at [88].

7.59 Lord Mance provided the most detailed discussion of this problem[1]. He too disapproved of the result in *HF Pension Trustees*. His solution was to adhere to the distinction, criticised by O'Sullivan[2], between knowledge that a transaction was unsound from the outset, and knowledge that the adviser was negligent at the outset. Regardless of whether one is convinced by this distinction, it is submitted that for practical purposes the message appears to be as follows: the courts appreciate the potential injustice of decisions such as *HF Pension Trustees* and, in the absence of reform by Parliament, are prepared to read s 14A in such a way as to narrow down the scope of s 14A(9), so that knowledge that there may have been an error of law may, in reality, be necessary before time starts to run.[3]

1 [2006] UKHL 9, [2006] 1 WLR 682 at [115]–[117].
2 Above.
3 On this basis, the result in *Gold v Mincoff* [2001] Lloyd's Rep PN 423 might be supported, though the value of referring to pre-*Haward* cases must be in doubt. It is doubtful whether *Fennon v Hodari* [2001] Lloyd's Rep PN 183 and *Bowie v Southorns* [2002] EWHC 1289 (QB), [2002] Lloyd's Rep PN 564 can survive *Haward*. For another solution to the *HF Pensions* problem, see Judge Jack QC's decision in *Perry v Moysey* [1998] PNLR 657. The claimant was considering entering into contracts of employment with two companies. His accountant, the defendant, advised him that it would be acceptable if the contracts provided for him to receive net salaries of £ 1,080 per month, index-linked. In reliance upon that advice, he entered into contracts on that basis in 1989. In September 1994 the companies were advised that the contracts were in breach of

Companies Act 1985, s 311 in that it was unlawful for a director to be paid remuneration net of income tax. The claimant discovered that he was liable to substantial sums in tax. He issued a writ in 1997, after expiry of the primary limitation period. Judge Jack QC held that the claimant was entitled to rely upon s 14A. As to the argument that the only matter of which the claimant had been unaware was a matter of law, namely the effect of s 311, which could not assist him for the purposes of s 14A, he said 'The damage which Mr Perry has suffered is a liability to account for tax either to the revenue or the companies in respect of payments received by him up to September 1994, and the reduction of his payments thereafter. Both situations, namely that relating to the period up to September 1994 and that thereafter, are matters of fact: he owes more money; he is receiving less. They come about by the operation of s 311, which is a matter of law; but the effect of the section's operation is to give rise to factual situations. Subsection (9) is not relevant to these considerations because it relates on the present facts to whether or not Mr Perry knew or did not know that an omission by Mr Moysey to consider s 311 would be negligent.'

(f) Section 14A(7)

7.60 Section 14A(6), which sets out the knowledge required to start time running, has two limbs. The second limb, at s 14A(6)(b), is knowledge of the facts set out in s 14A(8). We have just considered those. The first limb, however, is knowledge 'of the material facts about the damage in respect of which damages are claimed,' and this is defined in s 14A(7) as being

'… such facts about the damage as would lead a reasonable person who had suffered such damage to consider it sufficiently serious to justify his instituting proceedings for damages against a defendant who did not dispute liability and was able to satisfy a judgment.'

This proviso *does* apply to the facts referred to in s 14A(6)(a) and *does not* apply to the facts referred to in s 14A(6)(b). This led Lord Mance to state in *Haward*[1] that:

'To maintain a coherent scheme, the better view therefore appears to be to treat the first aspect of knowledge [sc.: s.14A(6)(a)] as relating solely to matters of quantum and all questions regarding the evaluation or classification of damage as such as falling within the second aspect of the knowledge required [sc s14A(6)(b) and (8)].'

[References in square brackets added].

The Court of Appeal had to consider this passage in *3M United Kingdom plc v Linklaters & Paines*.[2] In 1989 a company owned by the claimant assigned three leases to another company in its group, thereby losing the right, for either company, to terminate the leases under break clauses. The claimant's solicitors, the defendants, negligently failed to spot the problem or advise in relation to it. The question was whether on 30 August 1995 the claimant had sufficient knowledge to start time running under s 14A. At that date, the claimant was aware of the problem but it appeared that the landlord might not take a point on the loss of the right to exercise the break clauses. The Court of Appeal held that this did not prevent the claimant from having the knowledge required by s 14A(7). The claimant knew that the break clauses could not be exercised unless the difficulty could be overcome. A reasonable person, faced with that problem, would have considered it sufficiently serious to justify instituting proceedings against an acquiescent and creditworthy defendant. Moore-Bick LJ said that there was no doubt that the damage had been suffered; the only doubt was as to the possibility that it might be made good. He added that in the commercial context the damage did not have to be very substantial to satisfy the requirements of s 14A(7) in view of the limited cost of issuing proceedings, which was clearly lower than the loss suffered by the claimant.[3]

1   [2006] UKHL 9, [2006] 1 WLR 682 at [107].
2   [2006] EWCA Civ 530, [2006] PNLR 30.
3   See also *Babicki v Rowlands* [2001] EWCA Civ 1720, [2002] Lloyd's Rep PN 121, CA: the judge
    must reach a conclusion as to the reaction of a reasonable person to instituting proceedings.

(g) *Constructive knowledge*

7.61   It is clear from s 14(10) that constructive knowledge of the claimant of the relevant facts will suffice, if he or she does not have actual knowledge. *Haward* indicates which facts are in issue so far as s 14A(8) is concerned. Lord Mance said in *Haward*[1] that constructive knowledge applied where the claimant 'knows sufficient to make it reasonable for him (by himself or with advice) to acquire further knowledge' of the kinds specified by s 14A(8). Bearing in mind that, after *Haward*, even actual knowledge appears to amount to being 'put on enquiry', and therefore to include an element of what might formerly have been considered as constructive knowledge, the precise working out of what amounts to constructive knowledge on the facts of specific cases may be difficult.

1   [2006] UKHL 9, [2006] 1 WLR 682 at [126].

7.62   Although the question of what it was reasonable for the claimant to have done is essentially one which will depend on the facts in each case, *Henderson v Temple Pier Co Ltd*,[1] another case on s 14 rather than s 14A, is a further example of the court taking a fairly firm view to the effect that a claimant ought to have acted earlier to find out the relevant knowledge. The claimant claimed to have slipped and fallen when walking down a gangway leading to a ship which was moored at Temple Pier in London. She was intending to visit a bar on the ship. The accident occurred in January 1993. She instructed solicitors in February 1993 but they did not commence proceedings until April 1997.[2] The Court of Appeal held that it was no defence that the claimant had entrusted her action to solicitors. Insofar as they provided legal advice as to whether the facts in issue constituted negligence, this was irrelevant (s 14A(9)). Insofar as they provided factual advice which assisted the claim, such as helping to identify the owner of the ship on which the claimant had sustained injury, this was information which was ascertainable by the claimant herself without the need for legal expertise. Thus she was unable to rely upon her appointment of solicitors. In the context of s 14A, the effect of this would be that the facts which the solicitors had delayed in finding out were facts which came under s 14A(10)(a): the fact was not one 'ascertainable only with the help of expert advice', so the claimant could not rely on having taken reasonable steps to obtain expert advice, within the meaning of the end of s 14A(10).

1 [1998] 1 WLR 1540, CA.
2 It would therefore appear that the claimant had an action against her solicitors for loss of the litigation: see chapter 12.

7.63　In *Graavgaard v Aldridge & Brownlee*,[1] Arden LJ considered that, in considering the issue of constructive knowledge, the court must in general have regard 'to the characteristics of a person in the position of the claimant, but not to characteristics peculiar to the claimant …' This led her to take into account views which the actual claimant had, to the effect that she should complain to a bank about its behaviour in forcing her to sign a second charge over her property. Further, in Arden LJ's view, if a person in the position of the claimant should reasonably have sought expert advice about a claim against A, and this would have revealed that there was also a claim against B, then time started to run for the purposes of the claimant's claim against B as well as A. The facts of *Webster v Cooper & Burnett*[2] were similar: it involved a claim that solicitors had negligently failed to advise the claimant on the terms of a charge over her home. The mortgage which she signed was an all moneys charge. Her case was that she had thought that it was limited to the £28,000 which she and her husband were borrowing at the time, and that her solicitor had not advised her as to the true effect of what she was signing. Four years after signing the original document, the claimant received from the bank a form of acknowledgement which set out in clear terms that the mortgage secured not only the £28,000 but other sums. The claimant's evidence was that she signed this and returned it to the bank without reading it. The Court of Appeal agreed with the trial judge that the claimant, being a person of normal intelligence, should have read the acknowledgement before signing it; if she had done that, she would have been put on enquiry, so that time ran from the date when she signed the acknowledgement.

1 [2004] EWCA Civ 1529, [2005] PNLR 19, CA. Reference was made in this context to the House of Lords' decision in *Adams v Bracknell Forest BC* [2004] UKHL 29, [2005] 1 AC 76, though it should be noted that (i) that case related to a personal injury claim to which s 14 rather than s 14A of the Limitation Act applied, and (ii) their Lordships were influenced by the existence of the discretion under s 33 of the Limitation Act. That discretion does apply to personal injury cases but does not apply to professional negligence cases to which s14A applies, so the analogy with s 14A is not perfect.
2 [2000] Lloyd's Rep PN 167, CA.

7.64　Turning to lenders' claims, H H J Fox-Andrews QC considered the provisions of s 14A in the context of a claim against solicitors in *Abbey*

National plc v Forsyths.[1] The claimant operated various departments with different functions. In the judge's view:[2]

'… it is unreasonable and therefore unrealistic to consider that in the absence of special circumstances the knowledge of a person in one department can be regarded as the knowledge of a person in another department or that the totality of that knowledge is to be regarded as the knowledge of the society.'

On the facts of the case, however, he went on to hold that, on receipt of a letter which indicated unusual circumstances surrounding the transaction, the claimant should then have acted to gather together all its knowledge, whereupon it would have had the relevant knowledge for the starting date to be reached.[3] See also *Finance for Mortgages Ltd v Farley,*[4] where Kay J considered when the starting date occurred in a claim by a lender against a valuer in relation to a negligent overvaluation. If the lender had acted prudently, it would have repossessed the property by 31 January 1991 and obtained valuations which revealed the overvaluation by March 1991. Thus the lender ought to have known the relevant facts to start time running by the end of March 1991.[5]

1   (11 June 1997, unreported) (Official Referees' Business).
2   At p 26 of the transcript.
3   HHJ Bowsher QC reached a similar conclusion in *Birmingham Midshires Building Society v Infields* [1999] Lloyd's Rep PN 874.
4   [1998] PNLR 145.
5   Further lenders' cases on constructive knowledge, which tend to turn on their facts, are *Abbey National plc v Sayer Moore & Co* [1999] EGCS 114 (lender held to have constructive knowledge of mortgage fraud), *Mortgage Corpn v Lamberts* [2000] Lloyd's Rep PN 624 (defendant had insufficient evidence of how a reasonable lender would have behaved to prove constructive knowledge), *Lloyds Bank plc v Burd Pearse* [2001] EWCA Civ 366, [2001] Lloyd's Rep PN 452 (lender not fixed with knowledge of its solicitors acting on a limited retainer), and *Swansea Building Society v Bradford & Bingley* [2003] PNLR 38 (surveyors).

(h) Knowledge in relation to separate causes of action

7.65   Where a claimant has sufficient knowledge to start time running under s 14A in relation to *one* cause of action against a solicitor, this does not start time running in relation to separate causes of action, even if they arise out of the same defendant's handling of the same transaction on behalf of the same claimant. Thus, in *Birmingham Midshires Building Society v J D Wretham*[1] the claimant, a lender, had known sufficient facts to start time running in relation to a claim that the defendant solicitors had failed to report to it the true purchase price of the property. The claimant also claimed that, in breach of duty, the solicitors had failed to report to the lender that the property was subject to a demolition order. The judge held that this gave rise to a separate cause of action, so that the claimant's knowledge, for s 14A purposes, of the claim in relation to the purchase price did not start time running in relation to the claim concerning the demolition order.

1 [1999] Lloyd's Rep PN 133 (Technology and Construction Court).

2 Limitation Act 1980, s 32

7.66 Section 32 of the Limitation Act 1980 extends the limitation period in cases of fraud, deliberate concealment, or mistake. The relevant parts for present purposes provide:

'(1) Subject to subsections (3) and (4A) below, where in the case of any action for which a period of limitation is prescribed by this Act, either–

(a)   the action is based upon the fraud of the defendant; or

(b)   any fact relevant to the plaintiff's right of action has been deliberately concealed from him by the defendant; or

(c)   the action is for relief from the consequences of a mistake;

the period of limitation shall not begin to run until the plaintiff has discovered the fraud, concealment or mistake (as the case may be) or could with reasonable diligence have discovered it.

References in this subsection to the defendant include references to the defendant's agent and to any person through whom the defendant claims and his agent.

(2) For the purposes of subsection (1) above, deliberate commission of a breach of duty in circumstances in which it is unlikely to be discovered for some time amounts to deliberate concealment of the facts involved in that breach of duty.

(5) Sections 14A and 14B of this Act shall not apply to any action to which subsection (1)(b) above applies (and accordingly the period of limitation referred to in that subsection, in any case to which either of those sections would otherwise apply, is the period applicable under section 2 of this Act).'

7.67 It is submitted that it is helpful to consider the possible bases on which a claimant may show that s 32 applies under four headings: fraud; deliberate concealment (s 32(1)(b); deliberate commission of breach of duty (s 32(2)); and mistake. Finally, the issue of constructive knowledge arises.

(*a*) *Fraud*

7.68 The claimant has to show that the action 'is based upon the fraud of the defendant'. In order to show this, under the previous legislation he had to be relying upon a cause of action which was based upon fraud, such as an action in deceit, or an action claiming the rescission of a transaction brought about by fraud; conversion, for example, was not such an action, because the defendant's fraud was not an essential element of the cause of action.[1] It seems likely that this remains the position under the 1980 Act, though note the House of Lords' warning against the use of authorities decided under the previous legislation, in *Cave v Robinson Jarvis & Rolf.*[2]

1 *Beaman v ARTS Ltd* [1949] 1 KB 550, CA. This case considered identical wording in the Limitation Act 1939. See also *GL Baker Ltd v Medway Building and Supplies Ltd* [1958] 1 WLR 1216.
2 [2002] UKHL 18, [2003] 1 AC 384 per Lord Scott at [58]. Lords Slynn, Mackay and Hobhouse agreed with his speech.

(*b*) *Deliberate concealment (s 32(1)(b))*

7.69 For purposes of exposition, we have distinguished s 32(1)(b) from s 32(2), even though, if a case falls within s 32(2), it is deemed to amount to deliberate concealment within s 32(1)(b). Since the two provisions have different ingredients, it is helpful to consider them separately. It should, however, be noted that the 15-year longstop on bringing claims provided for by s 14B of the Act does not apply to cases in either category.[1]

1 See Limitation Act 1980, s 32(5).

7.70 As to s 32(1)(b), the first point is that 'any fact relevant to the plaintiff's right of action' is to be construed narrowly, as meaning a fact which is essential to the pleading of the cause of action. 'The court therefore has to look for the gist of the cause of action that is asserted, to see if that was available to the claimant without knowledge of the concealed material.'[1] Further, the words refer to 'any fact which the plaintiff has to prove to establish a prima facie case'.[2]

1 *AIC Ltd v ITS Testing Services (UK) Ltd* [2006] EWCA Civ 1601, [2007] 1 Lloyd's Rep 555 per Buxton LJ at [453].
2 Quoted with approval by Rix LJ at [323] of *AIC*, from *Johnson v Chief Constable of Surrey* (unreported, 19 October 1992), CA. See also *C v Mirror Group Newspapers* [1997] 1 WLR 131, CA.

7.71 *Cave v Robinson Jarvis v Rolf*[1] was a case concerning s 32(2), which we consider below, but two judges made comments, obiter, as to the effect of s 32(1)(b). It appears that Lord Millett's view was that s 32(1)(b) applied only where the defendant 'takes active steps to conceal his own breach of duty after he has become aware of it …'[2] Lords Mackay and Hobhouse concurred. Lord Scott, on the other hand, said that:

'A claimant who proposes to invoke s 32(1)(b) in order to defeat a Limitation Act defence must prove the facts necessary to bring his case within the paragraph. He can do so if he can show that some fact relevant to his right of action has been concealed from him either by a positive act of concealment or by a withholding of relevant information, but, in either case, with the intention of concealing the fact or facts in question.'[3]

Lords Slynn, Mackay and Hobhouse agreed with Lord Scott. Thus, whilst Lord Millett appeared to consider that nothing short of active steps to conceal would satisfy the requirements of s 32(1)(b), in Lord Scott's view a withholding of relevant information might be sufficient, albeit that the defendant must also intend to conceal the facts in question.

1 [2002] UKHL 18, [2003] 1 AC 384.
2 [25].
3 [60].

7.72 The Court of Appeal considered this issue in *Williams v Fanshaw Porter & Hazelhurst*.[1] This case demonstrates the potential complexities of s 32(1)(b). The claimant engaged the defendant solicitors to act for her in a medical negligence claim against a Dr Salahuddin. The case was handled by Mr Brown, who was qualifying as a legal executive. Proceedings were commenced against Dr Salahuddin but in August 1994 Mr Brown, without consulting the claimant, consented to an order dismissing the claim against Dr Salahuddin. Mr Brown did not tell the claimant about this. In December 1994, the defendant applied to rejoin Dr Salahuddin to the proceedings but the application was refused on the basis that he had been the only defendant, and he had been removed from the proceedings, so that the action no longer existed. Mr Brown did not tell the claimant about this either. She did not discover the position until July 1995 at earliest; she sued the defendants in December 2000. The question was whether s 32(1)(b) applied so that her claim was not statute-barred. The Court of Appeal held that, as the defendants were the claimant's litigation solicitors, they had a general duty to report to her on the progress of the litigation. This included a duty to report to her that the consent order had been made. That the consent order had been made was a 'fact relevant to the [claimant]'s right of action', pursuant to s 32(1)(b). This was presumably because she had to plead it in any negligence action against the defendants. After the December 1994 hearing, Mr Brown must have chosen not to report the result, or the making of the earlier consent order, to the claimant. He therefore acted deliberately. Further, this amounted to concealment, since it was a failure to report the information even though Mr Brown had a clear professional duty to report it. It did not matter that Mr Brown's motive for not reporting the matter was that he thought it could be remedied later, or that he was embarrassed. The claimant did not have to show that Mr Brown's reason for not reporting the matter to the claimant was to prevent her suing the defendants for negligence.

1 [2004] EWCA Civ 157, [2004] 1 WLR 3185. There were separate judgments, with different emphases, from Park J, Mance LJ and Brooke LJ.

7.73 It seems likely that many solicitors' negligence cases may fall into the same category as *Williams*: the solicitors will have a duty to report to the client matters which go wrong; if they fail to do so, they will be acting in breach of professional duty; and a failure to report such matters, in breach of professional duty, may amount to concealment for the purposes of s 32(1)(b).[1] Whether it is found that the solicitor has deliberately engaged in the concealment will be a question of fact in each case, though the judgments in *Williams* demonstrate that the court may take a robust view of arguments from solicitors that they did not suppress the information, in circumstances where they must have known that they had a duty to report it. *Williams* does not decide the question of whether, in the absence of a duty to report, mere withholding of information, as opposed to active concealment, amounts to deliberate concealment.[2] It also raises various issues as to the mental element, or state of mind of the defendant, required if the subsection is to apply. Mance LJ said[3] that, on a narrow reading of the subsection, the defendant had deliberately to conceal a fact 'in circumstances where the defendant realises that the fact has some relevance to an actual or potential claim against him'. But he added that on a wider reading the subsection would apply to any deliberate concealment, 'even though the defendant did not (and it may be could not) realise that the fact concealed had any relevance to any actual or potential wrongdoing.' Concentrating on the narrower reading, Mance LJ said[4] that recklessness on the part of the defendant would be sufficient to trigger the subsection.[5] Further, it would be sufficient that the defendant realised that the fact was relevant to a potential claim against him; he need not believe that the claim would necessarily succeed.

1 A further issue may arise where a solicitor realises, after the termination of the retainer, that he or she has previously acted in breach of duty. For discussion see para 7.10 above.
2 In *AIC Ltd v ITS Testing Services (UK) Ltd* [2006] EWCA Civ 1601, [2007] 1 Lloyd's Rep 555, Rix LJ observed at [321] that 'there is no decision that anything less than a duty to disclose will suffice in the absence of active concealment.'
3 [37].
4 [38].
5 For a contrary view, prior to *Williams*, see Davidson (2002) Solicitors Journal 430.

7.74 A further important point, which relates also to s 32(2), is that, where the concealment on which the claimant relies occurs after the accrual of the claimant's cause of action, s 32(1)(b) nevertheless applies to that subsequent concealment. The result is that time starts to run only after the claimant has, or could with reasonable diligence have, discovered the deliberate concealment.[1] Thus, if a solicitor acts negligently in 1990, and at that time does not deliberately conceal the negligence from the client, but then re-considers the issue in 1999 and does deliberately conceal it from the client[2], the six year limitation period starts to run from the date when the claimant either does discover, or could with reasonable diligence have discovered, the 1999 concealment. On the other hand, if the claimant was aware of the relevant facts *before* the conceal-ment, s 32(1)(b) will not apply to assist him or her.[3]

1 *Sheldon v R H M Outhwaite (Underwriting Agencies) Ltd* [1996] AC 102, HL. This was a 3–2 decision of the House. See Oughton, Lowry and Merkin at pp 67–9 for criticism.
2 If the solicitor were still acting for the client in 1999 on the same matter then it might be argued that he had a professional duty, in 1999, to reveal the negligence and, by failing to do so, deliberately concealed it. It might be different if the retainer had by then ended: see note 1 to the last paragraph.
3 *Ezekiel v Lehrer* [2002] EWCA Civ 16, [2002] Lloyd's Rep PN 260, CA, at [32].

(c) *Deliberate commission of a breach of duty (s 32(2))*

7.75 Section 32(2) applies to 'deliberate commission of a breach of duty in circumstances in which it is unlikely to be discovered for some time.' This has two elements. The second is whether it is unlikely that the deliberate breach of duty will be discovered 'for some time'. In *JD Wetherspoon Ltd v Van de Berg & Co Ltd*[1] Lewison J said that:

> 'Although the quoted phrase is imprecise, it seems to me that the implicit contrast that it is setting up is one between a breach of duty that would be immediately discovered (e.g. the infliction of a physical injury) and one that would not. If that is right, then the alleged involvement of [the defendants] in transactions in which they had secretly preferred the interests of other clients over those of [the claimant] falls into the latter class. The very secrecy demonstrates that.'

It would appear that, on this test, where solicitors act for lay clients it may often be the case that the consequences of the solicitor's breach of duty may take some time to come to fruition. The first element, 'deliberate commission of a breach of duty', was for a time subject to an extremely broad interpretation which has now been overruled.[2] As to this element, in *Cave* (above), the House of Lords held that s 32(2) would apply only where the defendant 'knew he was committing a breach of duty, or intended to commit a breach of duty'.[3] Lord Millett said that the defendant had to be guilty of 'deliberate wrongdoing,' and that s 32(2) did not apply to a defendant 'if, being unaware of his error or that he has failed to take proper care, there has been nothing for him to disclose.'[4]

1 [2007] EWHC 1044 (Ch), [2007] PNLR 28, Lewison J, at [40].
2 The overruled view appeared in *Brocklesby v Armitage & Guest (Note)* [2002] 1 WLR 598, CA, and *Liverpool Roman Catholic Archdiocese Trustees Inc v Goldberg* [2001] 1 All ER 812.
3 Per Lord Scott at [60]. Lords Slynn, Mackay and Hobhouse concurred.
4 [25]. Lords Mackay and Hobhouse concurred.

(d) Mistake

7.76   Under the previous Limitation Act, the position was that extension of the limitation period on the basis that the action was 'for relief from the consequences of a mistake' would be granted only if the mistake in question was an essential element of the cause of action, in which case it had to be pleaded in the statement of claim.[1] In *Deutsche Morgan Grenfell Group plc v IRC*[2] Lord Walker described this as 'a surprisingly uncertain basis' for applying the same principle in relation to the 1980 Act, but, in light of the Law Commission's proposals and their acceptance by the government, was not prepared to reconsider what he described as the 'now nearly traditional view of the scope of s 32(1)(c).'

1 *Phillips-Higgins v Harper* [1954] 1 QB 411, Pearson J. The case was decided in relation to the equivalent provision of the Limitation Act 1939, but the wording of that provision was identical to s 32(1)(c).
2 [2006] UKHL 49, [2007] 1 AC 558 at [146]–[147].

(e) Constructive knowledge

7.77   In the types of case to which s 32 applies, time begins to run from the date on which the claimant either has actual knowledge of the fraud, deliberate concealment or mistake, or 'could with reasonable diligence have discovered it'. In *Paragon Finance plc v D B Thakerar & Co*,[1] the Court of Appeal considered the meaning of these words. Millett LJ, with whom the other judges agreed, said:[2]

> 'The question is not whether the plaintiffs *should* have discovered the fraud sooner, but whether they could with reasonable diligence have done so. The burden of proof is on them. They must establish that they *could not* have discovered the fraud without exceptional measures which they could not reasonably have been expected to take. In this context the length of the applicable period of limitation is irrelevant. In the course of argument May LJ observed that reasonable diligence must be measured against some standard, but that the six year limitation period did not provide the relevant standard. He suggested that the test was how a person carrying on a business of the relevant kind would act if he had adequate but not unlimited staff and resources and were motivated by a reasonable but not excessive sense of urgency. I respectfully agree.'

In *Biggs v Sotnicks*[3], Robert Walker LJ rejected the suggestion[4] that the word 'exceptional' should be removed from this formulation. The approach of Arden LJ, who gave the principal judgment, was to look at the claimants' particulars of claim, and ask when the claimants knew or should have known the elements of the claim which they later pleaded. A similar point was made in *Imperio v REBX*.[5] Langley J held that, in cases of fraud, the question was when the claimant, with reasonable diligence, could have discovered 'the facts which are necessarily relied upon to justify the allegation of fraud' which was pleaded, as opposed to when the claimant could reasonably have concluded that he or she had been a victim of fraud. Similarly, in relation to deliberate concealment, the question was when the claimant, acting with reasonable diligence, could have discovered 'those facts sufficient to constitute or complete the particular cause of action … the acid test cannot be wider than those facts which were relied upon to support the pleas made in the Points of Claim'. In *JD Wetherspoon Ltd v Van de Berg & Co Ltd*,[6] however, Lewison J pointed out that in *Paragon* the trigger for an investigation by the claimants had occurred at a very early stage. Referring to the passage quoted above, he said:

'It is in that context, where the trigger for an investigation had already occurred, that it made sense to speak of a "reasonable degree of urgency". If there is no relevant trigger for an investigation, then it seems to me that a period of reasonable diligence does not begin.'

1 [1999] 1 All ER 400, CA.
2 [1999] 1 All ER 400 at 418b–d.
3 [2002] EWCA Civ 272, [2002] Lloyd's Rep PN 331, per Robert Walker and Aldous LJJ.
4 Made by Crane J in *UCB Home Loans v Carr* [2000] Lloyd's Rep PN 754.
5 *Companhia de Seguros Imperio v Heath (REBX) Ltd* [1999] Lloyd's Rep PN 571 at 590, col.1. This aspect of the case was not the subject of the appeal reported at [2000] Lloyd's Rep PN 795.
6 [2007] EWHC 1044 (Ch), [2007] PNLR 28, Lewison J, at [42].

7.78 The issues in relation to constructive knowledge under s 32 can be similar to those in relation to constructive knowledge under s 14A, considered above. In particular, a number of authorities deal with fraud-based lenders' claims. They tend to turn on their own particular facts.[1]

1 In addition to *Carr* (above), see *Abbey National Mortgages plc v Leftley Goodwin* (19 April 2000, Silber J), *Halifax plc v Ringrose* [2000] Lloyd's Rep PN 309, and cases cited at [21] in *Carr*.

D   CLAIMS IN EQUITY

1   Breach of trust

7.79 The relevant parts of Limitation Act 1980, s 21 provide as follows:

'21 Time limit for actions in respect of trust property

(1) No period of limitation prescribed by this Act shall apply to an action by a beneficiary under a trust, being an action:–

(a)   in respect of any fraud or fraudulent breach of trust to which the trustee was a party or privy; or

(b)   to recover from the trustee trust property or the proceeds of trust property in the possession of the trustee, or previously received by the trustee and converted to his use.

(3) Subject to the preceding provisions of this section, an action by a beneficiary to recover trust property or in respect of any breach of trust, not being an action for which a period of limitation is prescribed by any other provision of this Act, shall not be brought after the expiration of six years from the date on which the right of action accrued.

For the purposes of this subsection, the right of action shall not be treated as having accrued to any beneficiary entitled to a future interest in the trust property until the interest fell into possession.'

By virtue of s 38 of the Limitation Act, the words 'trust' and 'trustee' have the same meanings as set out in the Trustee Act 1925; by Trustee Act 1925, s 68(17), 'trusts' include implied and constructive trusts.

7.80   In relation to breaches of express trusts, the position is governed by s 21. There is therefore a six year limitation period for claims by beneficiaries unless the claim falls within s 21(1)(a) or (b). By s 21(1)(b), no limitation period applies to an action to recover trust property from a trustee; this is because 'in legal theory [the trust property] has been in [the beneficiary's] possession throughout.'[1] In *Armitage v Nurse*[2], Millett LJ explained that the purpose of the last sentence of sub-s (3) was to ensure that a beneficiary with a future interest should not be compelled to litigate until the beneficiary was sure that he would live to enjoy the interest. Further, in *Cattley v Pollard*[3], the deputy judge held that s 21(3) included, 'at least by analogy, actions brought exclusively on [beneficiaries'] behalf by trustees who do not have any personal interest in the outcome.'

1 *Halton International Inc v Guernroy Ltd* [2006] EWCA Civ 801 per Carnwath LJ at [22].
2 [1998] Ch 241 at 261G–H.
3 [2006] EWHC 3130 (Ch), [2007] 3 WLR 317, per Mr Richard Sheldon QC at [102].

7.81   The position is more complicated in relation to constructive trusts. In *Paragon Finance plc v D B Thakerar & Co*,[1] Millett LJ proposed that these should be considered as falling into two separate categories. His categorisation has been approved by the Court of Appeal in three subsequent cases.[2] The distinction is considered in more detail in chapter 4, but in summary it is between two types of constructive trust:

(i)   cases where the constructive trustee receives the property 'by a transaction which both parties intend to create a trust from the outset and which is not impugned by the [claimant]'. Secret trusts, or cases where a trust is intended but imperfectly recorded, are examples[3]. In Millett LJ's view these cases are correctly called constructive trusts, since the circumstances giving rise to them are close to those in which an express trust would arise.

(ii) Cases in which the defendant is implicated in a fraud, and equity imposes a constructive trust. In Millett LJ's view, the term constructive trust is, in these cases, 'misleading, for there is no trust and usually no possibility of a proprietary remedy; [the words] are 'nothing more than a formula for equitable relief'. In *Cattley v Pollard*[4], the deputy judge held that a claim for dishonest assistance in a fraudulent breach of trust fell within this category.[5]

1 [1999] 1 All ER 400, at 409.
2 *JJ Harrison v Harrison* [2001] EWCA Civ 1467, [2002] BCLC 162, *Gwembe Valley Development Co Ltd v Koshy* [2003] EWCA Civ 1048, [2004] 1 BCLC 131, and *Halton International Inc (Holdings) v Guernroy Ltd* [2006] EWCA Civ 801.
3 *Paragon* itself concerned a lenders' claim which did not fall within category (i), but it is possible that such claims could fall into that category: *UCB Home Loans Corpn Ltd v Carr* [2000] Lloyd's Rep PN 754.
4 Above, at [82].
5 *Halton* (above) was also held to be an example of a category (ii) case.

7.82 The significance of these two categories for limitation purposes is as follows. Section 21 of the Limitation Act does apply to constructive trusts in category (i). It follows that, in such cases, the limitation period is six years unless the claim falls within s 21(1)(a) or (b), in which case there is no limitation period. But s 21 does not apply to constructive trust claims in category (ii). In relation to those claims, however, if it can be argued that they are analogous to common law claims such as deceit or knowingly procuring a breach of contract, then the court will hold that the limitation period should be the same as in relation to the common law claim.[1] Claims for specific performance are not directly analogous to claims at common law, so that the statutory limitation period does not apply by analogy, though such claims may be barred by laches.[2] But since category (ii) cases arise, by definition, where the defendant is implicated in a fraud, it seems likely that in most cases there will be a clear analogy between the equitable claim and deceit at common law, so that in most of these cases the limitation period will, by analogy, be the same as at common law.

1 *Cattley v Pollard*, above, at [92], applying Limitation Act 1980, ss 2 and 36. The latter provisions are discussed below in relation to breach of fiduciary duty.
2 *P & O Nedlloyd BV v Arab Metals Co* [2006] EWCA Civ 1717, [2007] 1 WLR 2288. The case also discusses the circumstances in which a claim may be barred by laches.

2 Breach of fiduciary duty

7.83 The Court of Appeal considered the question of limitation in relation to claims for breach of fiduciary duty in *Gwembe Valley Development Co Ltd v Koshy*[1]. The court summarised the position as follows:[2]

'... in our view, it is possible to simplify the court's task when considering the application of the 1980 Act to claims against fiduciaries. The starting assumption should be that a six-year limitation period will apply – under one or other provision of the Act, applied directly or by analogy – unless it is specifically excluded by the Act or established case law. Personal claims against fiduciaries will normally be subject to limits by analogy with claims in tort or contract (1980 Act, ss 2, 5 – see *Seguros*). By contrast, claims for breach of fiduciary duty, in the special sense explained in *Mothew*, will normally be covered by s 21. The six year time limit under s 21(3) will apply, directly or by analogy, unless excluded by s 21(1)(a) (fraud) or (b) (Class 1 trust).'

The reference to *Seguros* was to the Court of Appeal's earlier decision in *Cia de Seguros Imperio v Heath (REBX) Ltd*.[3] That concerned a claim for equitable compensation for dishonest breach of fiduciary duty which was based on the same facts as claims for breach of contract and breach of duty in tort. The court held that s 36 of the Limitation Act 1980 applied. This provides that the ordinary time limits for claims in, inter alia, contract and tort, shall not apply to claims for equitable relief:

'except in so far as any such time limit may be applied by the court by analogy in like manner as the corresponding time limit under any enactment repealed by the Limitation Act 1939 was applied before 1 July 1940.'

The Court of Appeal was not enthusiastic about having to decide how a court of equity would have treated the claim prior to 1939, but concluded that where, in relation to a claim for equitable compensation against a fiduciary, the claim was based on identical facts as a common law claim, it would apply the common law limitation period by analogy. The reference in *Gwembe* to *Mothew* is to breaches of fiduciary duty in the sense explained in *Bristol & West BS v Mothew*.[4] Claims of this type are considered in chapter 4. It appears that the limitation regime set out in s 21 of the Act, discussed above, will apply to them.

1 [2003] EWCA Civ 1048, [2004] 1 BCLC 131. The court comprised Mummery, Hale and Carnwath LJJ. Applied: *JD Wetherspoon plc v Van de Berg & Co Ltd* [2007] EWHC 1044 (Ch), [2007] PNLR 28, Lewison J.
2 [111].
3 [2001] 1 WLR 112. Applied: *Leeds & Holbeck BS v Arthur & Cole* [2001] Lloyd's Rep PN 649.
4 [1998] Ch 1.

E   CONTRIBUTION CLAIMS

7.84   By s 10 of the Limitation Act, the time limit for bringing a claim for contribution under the Civil Liability (Contribution) Act is two years from the date of settlement, arbitration or judgment. For these purposes, 'judgment' or 'arbitration' means a judgment or arbitral award which ascertains the amount of the damages, and not simply a judgment for damages to be assessed.[1] Where a firm agreement is reached in a settlement which does not require to be embodied in a consent order, time runs from the date of the agreement.[2] In relation to a settlement, what is required is a bona fide settlement of the underlying claim; although s 10(4) speaks of the settlement comprising an agreement to make a 'payment', this may include a payment in kind as long as it is capable of valuation in monetary terms.[3]

1 *Aer Lingus plc v Gildacroft Ltd* [2006] EWCA Civ 4, [2006] 1 WLR 1173.
2 *Knight v Rochdale Healthcare NHS Trust* [2003] EWHC 1831, [2004] 1 WLR 371.
3 *Baker & Davies plc v Leslie Wilks Associates* [2005] EWHC 1179 (TCC), [2006] PNLR 3.

F PROCEDURE

1 Protective claim forms

7.85 These should be issued if time for bringing a claim is about to expire, even if the professional negligence pre-action protocol has not been complied with. The preferable course is to issue the claim form and then seek a stay pending compliance with the protocol.[1] It is possible for the parties validly to agree, in writing, extensions of time for the service of the claim form, as long as the agreement complies with CPR 2.11.[2] Those acting for claimants may, however, prefer to be sure that there is no possible doubt that they have served the claim form in time.

1 See para C7.2 of the protocol.
2 *Thomas v Home Office* [2006] EWCA Civ 1355.

2 Estoppel

7.86 In principle a defendant may give a sufficiently clear representation to the effect that he or she will not take a limitation point that the claimant may rely on the representation, by not issuing proceedings in time, so as to give rise to an estoppel which prevents the defendant from relying upon a limitation defence.[1] In practice however, it may be difficult to prove the representation.[2]

1 *Cotterrell v Leeds Day* (CA, unreported, 13 June 2000).
2 Compare *Law Society v Sephton* [2004] EWHC 544 (Ch), [2004] PNLR 27 (Mr Michael Briggs QC). The appeals did not concern this point.

3 Amendment to add new causes of action after expiry of the limitation period

7.87 The Court of Appeal dealt with this topic, in the context of claims against solicitors under the Rules of the Supreme Court, in *Paragon Finance plc v D B*

Thakerar & Co.[1] It appears that this is not an area in which the Civil Procedure Rules have introduced a change.[2] Where the claimant seeks permission to amend after the expiry of any relevant limitation period, the following questions arise.[3] First, does the proposed amendment add a new cause of action to the statement of case? If it does not, then permission will generally be granted, subject to costs. If it does, then permission should not be granted unless the claimant can show that either:

(i) the defendant does not have a reasonably arguable case on limitation which would be prejudiced by allowing the amendment; or

(ii) the new cause of action arises out of the same, or substantially the same, facts as either a cause of action in respect of which the claimant has already claimed relief or matters which appear in the defence.

These points will be discussed in turn.

1 [1999] 1 All ER 400.
2 See *Civil Procedure 2007* at para 17.4.2, and *Goode v Martin* [2001] 3 All ER 562, reversed on different grounds at [2001] EWCA Civ 1899, [2002] 1 WLR 1828.
3 See Paragon [1999] 1 All ER 400 at 404e–g. *Welsh Development Agency v Redpath Dorman Long Ltd* [1994] 1 WLR 1409, CA, and *Darlington Building Society v O'Rourke James Scourfield & McCarthy* [1999] Lloyd's Rep PN 33, CA.

(a) *What counts as a new cause of action?*

7.88 In *Letang v Cooper*,[1] Diplock LJ said that:

'A cause of action is simply a factual situation the existence of which entitles one person to obtain from the court a remedy against another person.'

Commenting on this passage in *Darlington Building Society v O'Rourke James Scourfield & McCarthy*,[2] Sir Ian Glidewell, with whom the other judges agreed, said:

'Where ... the claim is based on a breach of duty, whether arising from contract or in tort, the question whether an amendment pleads a new cause of action requires comparison of the unamended pleading with the amendment proposed in order to determine:

(a) whether a different duty is pleaded;

(b) whether the breaches pleaded differ substantially; and where appropriate

(c) the nature and extent of the damage of which complaint is made.

379

> ... In my view where an amendment pleads a duty which differs from that pleaded in the original statement of claim it will, or certainly will usually, raise a new cause of action. If there is no allegation of a different duty but different facts are alleged to constitute a breach of the duty it is more difficult to decide whether a new cause of action is pleaded.'

1 [1965] 1 QB 232 at 242–3, CA.
2 [1999] Lloyd's Rep PN 33 at 36, CA.

7.89 An example of the pleading of a different duty appears in *Paragon*.[1] The claimants sought to amend to allege that acts of the defendant solicitors which they had previously contended were merely negligent were, in the alternative, intentional breaches of duty on the part of the solicitors. The Court of Appeal held that this amounted to pleading a new cause of action. Another case in which the court held that two separate causes of action arose out of solicitors' handling of the same transaction was *Birmingham Midshires Building Society v J D Wretham*.[2]

1 [1999] 1 All ER 400. See also *Abbey National plc v Perry* [2001] EWCA Civ 1630 (no new cause of action where new label applied to a trust).
2 [1999] Lloyd's Rep PN 133, Technology and Construction Court, discussed at para 7.65 above.

7.90 As to whether the addition of different facts amounts to a new cause of action, in *Paragon*, Millett LJ said that the selection of the material facts to define a cause of action 'must be made at the highest level of abstraction'.[1] Merely adding particulars will not count as adding a new cause of action.

1 [1999] 1 All ER 400 at 405g.

(b) *Can the claimant show that the defendant does not have a reasonably arguable case on limitation which will be prejudiced by the new claim?*

7.91 The effect of the Limitation Act 1980, s 35(1) and (2) is that, if permission to amend is granted to add or substitute a new cause of action, the new cause of action is treated for limitation purposes as if it had been pleaded in a separate action which had been commenced on the same date as the original proceedings. Thus, if permission to amend is granted to allow a cause of action to be included after expiry of the limitation period in relation to that cause of action, then the defendant will lose the benefit of the accrued limitation defence, and will be unable to rely upon limitation as a defence at all. This would be unfair, unless the claimant can show that the cause of action arises out of the same or substantially the same facts as have already been pleaded. The latter is a ground for permitting the amendment (see below). But leaving that aside for the moment, and assuming that the claimant cannot show that the new cause of action arises out of the same or substantially the same facts, the court's approach is as follows. If the claimant can show that the defendant does not have a *reasonably arguable* defence to the new cause of action, on limitation, then the amendment is allowed. But if the claimant cannot show this, then permission to amend is not granted.[1] The effect of this is that, if the defendant has a reasonably arguable defence to the new cause of action, then, if the claimant wishes to proceed with its new cause of action, it must commence fresh proceedings, in which limitation may be tried as a preliminary issue.

1 *Welsh Development Agency v Redpath Dorman Long Ltd* [1994] 1 WLR 1409, CA, applied in *Goode* (above).

7.92 In judging whether it has been shown that granting permission to amend would deprive the defendant of a reasonably arguable limitation defence, the amendment is treated as being made at the date when the statement of case is amended, which will be not earlier than the date when the application for permission to amend is *granted*, rather than, for example, the date when the summons seeking permission to amend was first issued or served.[1]

1 *Welsh Development Agency v Redpath Dorman Long Ltd* [1994] 1 WLR 1409, CA.

(c) *Does the cause of action arise out of the same or substantially the same facts as those which are already pleaded?*

7.93 The court's power to give permission for an amendment, after expiry of the limitation period, if it arises from the same or substantially the same facts as those already pleaded, derives from Limitation Act 1980, s 35(4) and (5) and, now, CPR 17.4. In borderline cases, the issue of what counts as the same or substantially the same facts is substantially a matter of impression,[1] though in other cases it may be a matter of analysis.[2] In cases where the proposed amendment seeks to introduce a claim of intentional wrongdoing where none was made before, *Paragon*[2] suggests that the amendment should not be said to arise out of the same or substantially the same facts. A claimant may amend to rely on facts which are pleaded in the defence, raising an argument to the effect of 'even if the facts were as you say, you were still in breach of duty'.[3]

1 *Welsh Development Agency v Redpath Dorman Long Ltd* [1994] 1 WLR 1409, CA. For an example of a new cause of action which did arise out of the same or substantially the same facts in a solicitors' case see *Senior & Senior v Pearsons & Ward* (26 January 2001), CA.
2 *Paragon Finance plc v DB Thakerar & Co* [1999] 1 All ER 400, CA. Applied: *Vine-Hall v Hazlems Fenton* [2006] EWHC 2753 (Ch), [2007] PNLR 14 (Pumfrey J).
3 *Goode v Martin* [2001] EWCA Civ 1899, [2002] 1 WLR 1828, CA. Discussed in the solicitors' negligence context in *Coudert Brothers v Normans Bay Ltd* [2003] EWCA Civ 215, per Waller LJ at [47]–[56], though Laws LJ did not apply *Goode* ([65]) and Carnwath LJ agreed with Laws LJ ([69]).

Chapter 8

Contributory negligence and contribution

A CONTRIBUTORY NEGLIGENCE

1 Introduction

8.01 The law as to contributory negligence and claims for contribution are issues of general application. While, in relation to each issue, there are some solicitors' cases which we discuss, to some extent it is necessary to consider cases from other areas of professional negligence in order to see how the principles operate. So we also discuss cases which do not directly concern solicitors.

2 Scope

8.02 Apportionment for contributory negligence on the part of the claimant has becoming increasingly important in solicitors' negligence actions. The statutory basis for reductions on account of contributory negligence is the Law Reform (Contributory Negligence) Act 1945, s 1(1), which provides:

> 'where any person suffers damage as a result partly of his own fault and partly of the fault of any other person or persons a claim in respect of that damage shall not be defeated by reason of the fault of the person suffering the damage but the damages recoverable in respect thereof shall be reduced to such an extent as the court thinks just and equitable having regard to the claimant's share in responsibility for the damage.'

There is no doubt that the defence is available in actions based only upon negligence.[1] The position in relation to other varieties of claim is discussed next.

1 By s 4, fault is defined as 'negligence, breach of statutory duty or other act or omission which gives rise to liability in tort or would, apart from this Act, give rise to the defence of contributory negligence'.

(a) Contract

8.03   Doubt as to whether the Act applied to claims in contract as well as tort was resolved by the Court of Appeal's decision in *Forsikringsaktieselskapet Vesta v Butcher.*[1] The court approved Hobhouse J's analysis, which was that, in considering application of the Act to contractual claims, it was necessary to divide such claims into three categories:[2]

'(1) Where the defendant's liability arises from some contractual provision which does not depend on negligence on the part of the defendant.

(2) Where the defendant's liability arises from a contractual obligation which is expressed in terms of taking care (or its equivalent) but does not correspond to a common law duty to take care which would exist in the given case independently of contract.

(3) Where the defendant's liability in contract is the same as his liability in the tort of negligence independently of the existence of any contract.'

The Court of Appeal held that the Act did apply to category 3 cases, such as *Butcher* itself, but not to category 1 or 2 cases. O'Connor LJ cited with approval the dictum of Prichard J in the New Zealand case of *Rowe v Turner, Hopkins & Partners*[3] that 'the Contributory Negligence Act cannot apply unless the cause of action is founded on some act or omission on the part of the defendant which gives rise to liability in tort' .[4] The rationale for this approach is that, in a case where defendants' liability to the claimant is the same in tort as in contract, as for example in an employer's liability case, defendants may take advantage of arguments as to contributory negligence if they are sued in tort, and it would be unfair if they could not do the same if sued in contract.[5] On the other hand, the terms of the contract may, exceptionally, provide for the exclusion of liability for contributory negligence, in which case the Act will not apply.[6] Further, even in category 1 and 2 cases, it may be possible to argue that there should be a reduction in damages on the ground that the defendant caused only part of the loss.[7] But where the duty which has been broken is solely contractual, that is, would not have existed independently of the contract, or where there is breach of a strict contractual duty, contributory negligence has no application.

1 [1989] AC 852, [1988] 2 All ER 43, approving Hobhouse J's decision at first instance, [1986] All ER 488. The Court of Appeal's decision was affirmed without discussion of the contributory negligence point by the House of Lords, [1989] AC 852. See also *Barclays Bank plc v Fairclough Building Ltd* [1995] QB 214, CA.
2 [1986] 2 All ER 488 at 508f–g.
3 [1980] 2 NZLR 550.
4 [1989] AC 852 at 866C.

5 See [1986] 2 All ER 488 at 509d–e (Hobhouse J) and [1989] AC 852 at 860H–861A (O'Connor LJ).
6 Cf [1986] 2 All ER 488 at 510j.
7 See *Tennant Radiant Heat Ltd v Warrington Development Corpn* [1988] 1 EGLR 41, CA.

8.04   The more negligent a claimant is, the keener he or she will be to show that the case falls into category 1 or category 2 so that there will be no reduction in damages for contributory negligence. The point has arisen in particular in relation to lenders' claims against solicitors and valuers. In *Bristol & West Building Society v Kramer & Co,*[1] the defendant solicitor was in breach of an instruction in the retainer providing that 'any matters which might prejudice the Society's security or which are at variance with the Offer of Advance should be notified to the Society immediately they become known.' The defendant argued that the Society was contributorily negligent in lending on insufficient information as to the value of the security and the status of the borrower. Blackburne J held that any contributory negligence was irrelevant as the claim was for breach of a strict duty, commenting that the:

> 'obligation [in the retainer] is dependent on the knowledge of the matters in question and is not in any way dependent upon negligence on the part of the defendant firm. The fact that [the solicitor] was negligent (as distinct from deliberate) in overlooking his obligation to inform the Society of what he knew does not convert his obligation into one that is *dependent* on negligence.'

But Carnwath J declined to follow this approach, on slightly different wording of the solicitors' instructions, in *Mortgage Express Ltd v Newman*[2] and *Alliance & Leicester v Wheelers.*[3] Further, it is probably inconsistent with Sir Richard Scott V-C's decision in *Maes Finance Ltd v A L Phillips*[4] and Chadwick J's approach in *Bristol and West Building Society v Fancy and Jackson .*[5] The claimant did not seek to rely upon *Kramer,* even though the judge was Blackburne J, in *Nationwide Building Society v Balmer Radmore*[6] , and in a subsequent lenders' claim the Court of Appeal held that the facts fell within category 3 of *Vesta* so that a reduction for contributory negligence could be made.[7] It is doubtful whether *Kramer* would today be followed in any case which was not on all fours with it.

1 (1995) *Times*, 6 February (Blackburne J).
2 [1996] PNLR 603, 612.
3 23 January 1997, unreported.
4 (1997) *Times*, 25 March.
5 [1997] 4 All ER 582.
6 [1999] Lloyd's Rep PN 241.
7 *UCB Bank plc v Hepherd Winstanley & Pugh* [1999] Lloyd's Rep PN 963, CA.

(b) Fraudulent and negligent misrepresentation; breach of warranty of authority

8.05   In *Standard Chartered Bank v Pakistan National Shipping Corpn* (*Nos 2 and 4*)[1] the House of Lords held that damages for fraudulent misrepresentation could not be reduced on account of the claimant's contributory negligence. By contrast, in *Gran Gelato Ltd v Richcliff* (*Group*) *Ltd*[2] it was held that the legislation did apply to claims for *negligent* misrepresentation under the Misrepresentation Act 1967, s 2(1), even though the wording of the section expressly equated liability under the section to that which would result 'had the misrepresentation been made fraudulently'. Thirdly, contributory negligence is not a defence to claims for breach of warranty of authority, because liability for breach of warranty of authority is strict and 'is not dependent on establishing fault'.[3] Hence it does not fall within category 3 defined in *Vesta v Butcher*.[4]

1   [2002] UKHL 43, [2003] 1 AC 959.
2   [1992] Ch 560, CA.
3   *Bristol & West Building Society v Fancy & Jackson*, transcript of 22 July 1997 (Chadwick J), at p 14. This passage was edited out of the report in the All England Law Reports. For breach of warranty of authority generally, see para 5.13ff, above.
4   See para 8.03, above.

(c) Fiduciary duty

8.06   Commonwealth authority has suggested that the common law apportionment regime may be applied by analogy to breach of a fiduciary duty.[1] But this is not the position in England, at least in cases of deliberate breach of fiduciary duty: in *Nationwide Building Society v Balmer Radmore* Blackburne J said:[2]

> 'In English law contributory negligence has never been a defence to an intentional tort: in such cases the 1945 Act has no application. By parity of approach I can see no good reason why equity, concerned as Lord Dunedin remarked in *Nocton v Lord Ashburton* [1914] AC 932 at page 963 "to keep persons in a fiduciary capacity up to their duty" should adopt a less rigorous approach.
>
> I therefore take the view that where, in order to establish a breach of fiduciary duty, it is necessary to find that the fiduciary was consciously disloyal to the person to whom his duty was owed, the fiduciary is disabled from asserting that the other contributed, by his own want of care for his own interests, to the loss which he suffered flowing from the breach.'

Thus the position in relation to deductions for contributory negligence for breaches of fiduciary duty appears to be similar to that in relation to misrepresentation, considered in the last paragraph: if intentional disloyalty is a necessary element of the breach of fiduciary duty then deductions for contributory negligence may not be made, but if mere negligence is sufficient to found the claim then they may be. Thus there is a symmetry between the position at law and in equity.[3]

1 *Day v Mead* [1987] 2 NZLR 443, NZCA; *Canson Enterprises Ltd v Broughton & Co* (1991) 85 DLR (4th) 129, SCC.
2 [1999] Lloyd's Rep PN 241 at 281.
3 Nor are reductions on account of contributory negligence made in claims for breach of trust.

(d) Lenders' claims[1]

8.07 In *Platform Home Loans Ltd v Oyston Shipways Ltd,*[2] the House of Lords had to consider how the 1945 Act applied to a lenders' claim. Although the defendant was a surveyor, it is thought that the same principles apply in solicitors' cases. In order to understand the decision, it is necessary to understand the distinction between basic and attributable loss, which is discussed in chapter 10[3]. In summary, the *basic loss* in a lender's claim is normally the amount of the claimant's loss calculated by taking the amount of the advance, plus the cost, in interest payments, to the lender of funding that advance, but less the amount of any payments made by the borrower and the net proceeds of sale of the property if it has been repossessed and sold.[4] The *attributable loss,* in a valuer's case[5], is normally the difference between the valuation of the property that the valuer in fact gave, and the correct valuation at the time. The notion of attributable loss was introduced by the House of Lords' decision in *SAAMCo.*[6] In a claim by a lender against a valuer, if the basic loss exceeds the attributable loss then damages are limited to the amount of the attributable loss, plus statutory interest; if the basic loss is less than the amount of the attributable loss, then the claimant recovers damages in the amount of the basic loss.

1 For lenders' claims, see further chapter 10, below.
2 [2000] 2 AC 190, HL. See Murdoch [1999] 08 EG 168, Russell and Coffin [1999] 2 PNL Rev 1, Charlwood (1999) 143 Sol Jo 456.
3 See para 10.73ff, below.
4 See *Swingcastle Ltd v Alastair Gibson* [1991] 2 AC 223, HL and *Nykredit Mortgage Bank plc v Edward Erdman (No 2)* [1997] 1 WLR 1627, HL, per Lord Nicholls of Birkenhead at 1631–1632.
5 In a claim against solicitors the attributable loss may be different: see para 10.84ff, below, below.
6 Reported sub nom. *Banque Bruxelles Lambert SA v Eagle Star Insurance Co Ltd* [1997] AC 191, HL.

8.08 In *Platform* the basic loss was £611,000 and the attributable loss £500,000. Thus, leaving aside deductions for contributory negligence, the effect of *SAAMCo* was that damages were limited to £500,000 plus interest. The trial judge assessed contributory negligence at 20%. The first question was whether s 1(1) of the 1945 Act applied at all. This depended on whether the claimant had suffered 'damage partly as a result of its own fault and partly as a result of the fault of the defendant'.[1] The lenders argued that 'damage' for these purposes meant only the attributable loss; only the defendant and not the lender had caused this part of the damage; thus this damage was not suffered 'partly due to the fault of the claimant', and so s 1(1) did not apply at all. The House of Lords rejected this argument. The 'damage' to which s 1(1) referred was the basic loss and not simply the attributable loss. The fault of both parties had contributed to this damage. Thus the Act applied, but on the basis set out in the next paragraph.

1 See the wording of s 1(1) at para 8.02, above.

3 Application

(a) Lenders' claims

8.09 Many of the relatively recent cases in which large deductions on account of contributory negligence have been made were lenders' claims. In chapter 10[1], we consider the types of conduct which may found reductions of damages for contributory negligence in such claims, and the potential size of the reductions. Here, however, we consider an issue of principle relating to reductions of damages for contributory negligence in lenders' claims. The second issue which the House of Lords considered in *Platform Home Loans*[2] was whether the 20% reduction in damages for contributory negligence should be made from the basic or the attributable loss. The basic loss was £611,000 and the attributable loss £500,000. Thus, if the reduction was made from the basic loss it would give a figure of £489,000 in damages and if it was made from the attributable loss it would give £400,000. The House held that the reduction should be made from the basic loss, reversing the Court of Appeal that had deducted it from the attributable loss. Lords Lloyd of Berwick and Hope of Craighead each agreed with the speeches of both Lords Millett and Hobhouse of Woodborough. In Lord Hobhouse's view, in cases where damages were reduced due to the *SAAMCo* measure, the reduction to the amount of the attributable loss was a reduction in damages that was made for reasons similar to those justifying a reduction for contributory negligence.[3] Hence to make a deduction of 20% from the attributable loss on account of contributory negligence:[4]

'... in effect makes the same deduction twice over. The [*SAAMCo*] principle already involves an exercise of attribution in relation to the extent of the defendants' responsibility for the plaintiffs' actual loss.'

1 See para 10.90ff, below.
2 [2000] 2 AC 190, HL. See paras 8.07 and 8.08, above, for the background.
3 [2000] 2 AC 190 at 211F.
4 [2000] 2 AC 190 at 211H–212A.

8.10 Lord Millett reached the same conclusion. He added, obiter, that a different result might be appropriate in cases where the claimant lender's negligence had contributed directly to the overvaluation. In cases of that type, it might be appropriate to apply the reduction for contributory negligence to the attributable loss as well as the basic loss.[1] Lord Hobhouse did not make this distinction. Further, it is not strictly binding, but it must be of considerable persuasive weight.[2]

1 [2000] 2 AC 190 at 215B–C.
2 Lords Lloyd of Berwick and Hope of Craighead both agreed with Lord Millett's speech, but they also agreed with the speech of Lord Hobhouse, who did not make this distinction, so it is unclear whether they supported the existence of the exception to which Lord Millett adverted.

8.11   It is submitted that whether one considers *Platform* to have been correctly decided depends upon whether, like Lord Hobhouse, one considers that the *SAAMCo* reduction in damages performs essentially the same function as reductions on account of contributory negligence. If the two devices perform the same function then plainly it amounts to double counting to make the same reduction twice. It is thought, however, that these two mechanisms in truth perform different roles. The question of whether the court should make a reduction in damages on account of contributory negligence depends principally upon whether the claimant has behaved in a way which was negligent and contributed to the basic loss. It is easy to imagine cases where either there is say a 50% reduction for contributory negligence of the claimant but no reduction on account of *SAAMCo,* or reduction on account of *SAAMCo* but no reduction for contributory negligence. That is because the kinds of facts required to give rise to the two types of reduction are different. Once this proposition is accepted, it is submitted that to make separate reductions on account of both contributory negligence and *SAAMCo* is, in general, the right approach. It does not involve double counting, because the rationales of the two different types of reduction are different. Imagine a case where the basic loss is £200,000, the attributable loss £100,000, there is contributory negligence of 50% and the claimant's negligence did not contribute to the overvaluation. On the House of Lords' principle, the deduction for contributory negligence must be made from the basic and not the attributable loss. Thus damages are £100,000 (50% of £200,000). But this is exactly the same as they would have been, on the *SAAMCo* measure, even if there had been no contributory negligence at all. So the effect of the House of Lords' decision is that there may be cases where a claimant lender recovers the same amount whether its contributory negligence is 0 or 50%. This seems unfair.

8.12   On the other hand, Lord Millett criticised the result of the Court of Appeal's approach in the following terms:[1]

'Instead of awarding the appellant damages of £489,398, representing the 80% of the overall loss of £611,748 which was not attributable to its own fault, as the judge had done, it reduced the award to £400,000, being 80% of the respondents' overvaluation of £500,000.

The remarkable consequence is that, if the award stands, the appellant will bear more than one third of a loss for which it was only 20% to blame.'

It is submitted, however, that what this amounts to is a criticism of the decision in *SAAMCo* itself. If, on the facts of *Platform*, there had been no contributory negligence at all, the effect of *SAAMCo* would have been that the lender would itself have had to bear the difference between the basic and the attributable loss: thus the lender would have borne 18% of the basic loss[2] in a case where it was not to blame at all, or at least not in a way that sounded in contributory negligence. The result to which Lord Millett referred is remarkable only if one considers that a reduction in damages on account of *SAAMCo* is either intended to serve the same purpose as a reduction for contributory negligence, or intrinsically unjustifiable. We have suggested that the former proposition cannot be supported. The latter, a direct attack on the decision in *SAAMCo*, is something which the House of Lords did not openly consider in *Platform*. Yet it appears that what underlies the decision of the majority is a feeling that reductions in damages on the basis set out in *SAAMCo* may be unfair. This nettle was grasped only in the speech of the dissenter, Lord Cooke of Thorndon. In his view, as long as *SAAMCo* stood, deductions for contributory negligence had to be made from the attributable rather than the basic loss, but he added:[3]

'If any anomalies or inequities be thought to arise from approaching the present case in this way, they will be attributable to the limit of a valuer's duty of care, and consequent liability, imposed by your Lordships' House in the [*SAAMCo*] and *Nykredit* decisions, which your Lordships were not asked to reconsider on this occasion.'

On this approach, either *SAAMCo* provides a sound principle, in which case it justifies a reduction in addition to reductions for contributory negligence, or it does not, in which case the House of Lords should have decided not to follow it. For the moment, however, the position is as set out in *SAAMCo* and *Platform*.

1 [2000] 2 AC 190 at 213D–E.
2 £111,000 divided by £611,000.
3 [2000] 2 AC 190 at 199F.

(*b*) *General approach: solicitors' cases*

8.13 Some recent cases contain statements of general principle as to the approach to be taken to issues of contributory negligence in claims against solicitors. In *Football League Ltd v Edge Ellison*[1], Rimer J said, obiter:

'It is only in rare cases that a solicitor is able to advance a plea of contributory negligence with any real prospect of success, and for obvious reasons. This is because his breach of duty will usually be in relation to a matter within his special expertise as a solicitor, being a duty which is not usually one relating to a purely commercial matter of judgment falling squarely within the client's own competence. It will usually relate to a matter upon which the client is depending upon the solicitor's own special expertise.'

He went on to state, however, that on the facts of that case, if he had found the defendants to be liable, he would have reduced damages by 75% on account of contributory negligence. This was because the cause of the claimant's loss was principally its own commercial decision on a matter that fell within its own area of commercial judgment, rather than being a matter of specialist legal expertise on which only the defendant solicitor could usefully comment.

1 [2006] EWHC 1462 (Ch), [2007] PNLR 2, (Rimer J) at [330].

8.14 *Feakins v Burstow*[1] was a claim concerning a solicitor's negligent conduct of litigation. Jack J stated that:

'If a solicitor is acting in litigation, he has control of the proceedings on behalf of his client, and it seems to me that it will be rare that his client will be held in part responsible for any loss-causing failure that may occur in the conduct of the proceedings.'

Thirdly, in *Stone Heritage Developments Ltd v Davis Blank Furniss*,[2] His Honour Judge Hodge QC, obiter, approved the following passages from the judgment of the Hong Kong Court of Appeal in *Hondon Developments Ltd v Power Rise Investments Developments*[3]:

'35. The principle of contributory negligence is well established and is correctly set out by the judge. The second defendant has to establish that the plaintiffs failed to take such care as a reasonable man would have taken in protecting their interests in the transaction and that the failure to take such care was a substantial or material cause leading to the damage they suffered.

36. As a solicitor is remunerated for his services and it is his duty to advise his lay client and protect his interest, public policy requires that such a professional's claim of contributory negligence by the client may only be successfully raised in very limited circumstances: first, where the lay client is particularly well placed to spot or correct the professional's mistake; second, where the lay client has done something quite separate which aggravates the consequence of the professional's breach of duty.'

The second example, where the client does something quite separate which aggravates the situation, might in some circumstances amount to a new intervening cause which has the effect that the defendant is not liable for any of the loss: see chapter 3.[4]

1 [2005] EWHC 1931 (QB), [2006] PNLR 6 (Jack J). See [109].
2 Chancery Division, Lawtel, 31 May 2006 (HHJ Hodge QC sitting as a deputy High Court Judge). See [341]–[342]. This aspect of the case was not considered in the Court of Appeal, [2007] EWCA Civ 765.
3 [2006] PNLR 1.
4 See para 3.42ff, above.

8.15 The first of the two categories in *Hondon* may explain a number of the cases. The lenders' claims in particular demonstrate numerous findings of contributory negligence, in high percentages.[1] It is thought that, in the very specific context of lenders' claims, it cannot be said that findings of contributory negligence are rare. This may be because mortgage lenders, in assessing the borrower's ability to pay, are themselves acting in an almost professional capacity. Whether one describes as professional the activities of those who decide whether and on what terms to lend large sums of money to individuals or businesses does not matter; what does matter is that this is an important activity, carried out by the claimant lenders and for which they are, at least arguably, principally responsible, on which large sums of money turn. The courts have generally found that it is therefore incumbent on mortgage lenders to take considerable care before advancing such sums. In this context, therefore, the solicitor's lender client is, or should be, a sophisticated business, rather than an ingénue. The same applied in the *Football League* case. In cases of this type, therefore, where the client is or should be sophisticated and the loss arises from a cause which the client should have appreciated, there may be scope for large findings of contributory negligence. As to the second type of exception quoted in *Hondon*, where the claimant's own conduct aggravated the consequences of the professional's breach of duty, *Stone Heritage* at first instance[2] is an example.

1 See para 10.90ff, below.
2 Chancery Division, Lawtel, 31 May 2006 (HHJ Hodge QC sitting as a deputy High Court Judge). See [341]–[342]. The Court of Appeal held that there was no breach of duty so that the question of contributory negligence did not arise: [2007] EWCA Civ 765.

8.16 What test determines what counts as 'fault' on the part of the claimant for the purposes of the Act? A tension has emerged, at least in relation to lenders' cases, between two different approaches.[1] In *Banque Bruxelles Lambert SA v Eagle Star Insurance Co Ltd*,[2] Phillips J accepted the submission that the claimant lender's conduct had to be judged against the standard of a reasonably competent merchant bank at the time. Thus, the test was related to how a reasonably competent member of the profession in question would have behaved at the relevant time. The difficulty with this approach is that there may be cases where the court considers that a practice was negligent even though it was one that respected members of a profession did adopt at the time.[3] In

Birmingham Midshires Mortgage Services v David Parry & Co[4] the lender did not require any proof of the existence or level of the borrower's earnings, other than a signed assurance from the borrower himself. Sir John Vinelott explained, obiter, that:[5]

> 'evidence of the way in which other businesses are conducted is not a reliable guide to the question whether a business was conducted prudently – that is whether it took reasonable care to protect itself against the risk of loss. There may be good commercial reasons which lead those engaged in a business enterprise to take risks, pressure of competition or a desire to break into a new market.'

Thus he considered that a standard of prudence was more appropriate. Perhaps the clearest example of cases where this tension may arise concerns 'non-status lending': a lender advances money to a borrower without making any checks on his or her ability to make the repayments required by the loan. This may not be imprudent if the lender has the security of a marketable property and is lending a low percentage of the value of the property, but some lenders are prepared to make such loans even if they are lending a high percentage of the value of the property. In these cases there may be a strong case that making the advance was contributorily negligent even though a number of other lenders behaved in a similar way.

1 For criticism, see the discussion at chapter 8 of Evans *Lawyers' Liabilities* (2nd edn, 2002).
2 [1995] 2 All ER 769 at 821e–f. This point did not arise on appeal.
3 Cf *Lloyds Bank Ltd v EB Savory & Co* [1933] AC 201, HL (as to the practice of bankers) and *Edward Wong Finance Co Ltd v Johnson, Stokes and Master* [1984] AC 296, PC (as to the practice of solicitors). See further para 2.13ff, above
4 [1996] PNLR 494 at 518. Although the case was appealed [1997] NPC 153, CA, this point did not have to be dealt with on appeal.
5 See [1996] PNLR at 516A–B.

(c) General approach: amount of reduction

8.17 The Act empowers the court to reduce the claimant's damages 'to such an extent as the court thinks just and equitable having regard to the claimant's share in responsibility for the damage'. Determining the amount of the reduction is 'essentially an exercise of judgment on matters of fact and degree' and one where an appellate court 'will only interfere if it regards it as plainly wrong or where the judge can be shown to have taken into account some immaterial matter or to have overlooked some material matter'.[1] The relevant factors are generally taken to be the blameworthiness of each party and the causative potency of the relevant conduct.[2] In *UCB Corporate Services Ltd v Clyde & Co*[3], the defendant was unable to obtain any reduction on account of contributory negligence because it could not show that the alleged negligent conduct had caused any of the claimant's loss. A range of percentage reductions, reaching as high as 90%, have been made in relation to awards of damages to lenders to take account of risky lending practices.[4]

1 *Griffin v Mersey Regional Ambulance* [1998] PIQR P34 at 38, CA, per Simon Brown LJ.
2 *Banque Bruxelles Lambert SA v Eagle Star Insurance Co Ltd* [1995] 2 All ER 769 per Phillips J at 821b-c. The appeal did not concern this issue. See also *Sahib Foods Ltd v Paskin Kyriakides Sands* [2003] EWCA Civ 1832, [2004] PNLR 22, at [66] and [76], where the Court of Appeal appeared to proceed on the same basis.
3 [2000] Lloyd's Rep PN 653, CA.
4 See further para 10.93ff, below.

8.18 In *Sahib Foods Ltd v Paskin Kyriakides Sands*[1], the defendant architects worked on the remodelling of the claimants' factory at which ready-made meals were prepared for sale in supermarkets. Subsequently, there was a fire at the factory. The fire was caused by the negligence of the claimants' employees in misusing a deep fat fryer. It was held that the defendants were in breach of duty owed to the claimants, in that they had failed to insist that flame-proof materials be used in the room where the fire had started, and had caused the claimants loss through the fire. The claimants argued that there should be no reduction on account of contributory negligence, because the negligence of the claimants' employees had been the very danger against which the defendants had a duty to guard them. The Court of Appeal rejected this submission, and approved the following passage from the judgment of the majority in the High Court of Australia in *Astley v Austrust Ltd*[2]:

> '29. ... There is no rule that apportionment legislation does not operate in respect of the contributory negligence of a plaintiff where the defendant, in breach of its duty, has failed to protect the plaintiff from damage in respect of the very event which gave rise to the defendant's employment. A plaintiff may be guilty of contributory negligence, therefore, even if the 'very purpose' of the duty owed by the defendant is to protect the plaintiff's property. Thus a plaintiff who carelessly leaves valuables lying about may be guilty of contributory negligence, calling for apportionment of loss, even if the defendant was employed to protect the plaintiff's valuables.
>
> 30. A finding of contributory negligence turns on a factual investigation of whether the plaintiff contributed to his or her own loss by failing to take reasonable care of his or her person or property. What is reasonable care depends on the circumstances of the case. In many cases, it may be reasonable for the plaintiff to rely on the defendant to perform its duty. But there is no absolute rule. The duties and responsibilities of the defendant are a variable factor in determining whether contributory negligence exists and, if so, to what degree. In some cases, the nature of the duty may exculpate the plaintiff from a claim of contributory negligence; in other cases the nature of the duty may reduce the plaintiff's share of responsibility for the damage

suffered; and in yet other cases the nature of the duty may not prevent a finding that the plaintiff failed to take reasonable care for the safety of his or her person or property. Contributory negligence focuses on the conduct of the plaintiff. The duty of the defendant, although relevant, is only one of the many factors that must be weighed in determining whether the plaintiff has so conducted itself that it failed to take reasonable care for the safety of its person or property.'

The Court of Appeal added that another approach was to ask whether the defendants' responsibility was such that the spread of the fire should be treated as wholly their fault. These views are consistent with the House of Lords' decision in *Reeves v Metropolitan Police Comr*[3], which was not cited in *Sahib*. The position therefore appears to be that there is no absolute rule that, if the loss which eventuated was the very thing against which it was the defendants' duty to guard the claimant, there will be no reduction on account of contributory negligence.[4] Each case must be assessed by a careful consideration of the facts, bearing in mind the twin factors of causative potency and blameworthiness of each party's conduct. As the Court of Appeal added in *Sahib*, 'it is never easy to resolve issues of apportionment of this kind.'[5]

1 [2003] EWCA Civ 1832, [2004] PNLR 22.
2 [1999] Lloyd's Rep PN 758.
3 [2000] 1 AC 360, referred to above at para 3.43, above. In *Reeves*, the loss suffered was the very thing against which it was the defendant's duty to guard the claimant, so the defendant was liable for it, but there was still a reduction on account of contributory negligence.
4 This may cast doubt on the result in *British Racing Drivers' Club Ltd v Hextall Erskine & Co* [1996] 3 All ER 667, where Carnwath J refused to impute to the claimant company the negligence of its directors so as to allow the defendant solicitors to plead contributory negligence.
5 At [76].

B CONTRIBUTION[1]

1 Scope

(a) General principles

8.19 Statutory contribution claims are governed by the Civil Liability (Contribution) Act 1978, the key provisions of which are:

'1(1) Subject to the following provisions of this Act, any person liable in respect of any damage suffered by another person may recover contribution from any other person liable in respect of the same damage (whether jointly with him or otherwise).

6(1) A person is liable in respect of any damage for the purposes of this Act if the person who suffered it ... is entitled to recover compensation from him in respect of that damage (whatever the legal basis of his liability, whether tort, breach of contract, breach of trust, or otherwise).'

The provisions of the Act were the subject of detailed consideration in the House of Lords in *Royal Brompton Hospital NHS Trust v Hammond*[2] and *Co-operative Retail Services Ltd v Taylor Young Partnership Ltd*[3]. In *Royal Brompton,* the House of Lords indicated that a relatively restrictive interpretation should be given to the phrase whose application is generally the key question in contribution claims, though more recent authority is less restrictive in relation at least to one aspect of the test[4]. The crucial issue is generally whether B and C are both liable to A, the claimant, for 'the same damage' within the meaning of s 1(1). The effect of a restrictive interpretation of this phrase is to reduce the number of cases in which one party is entitled to claim contribution from another. In order to decide whether a party is entitled to seek contribution, a close analysis of the decision in *Royal Brompton* is necessary. Further, in *Co-Operative Retail Services*, the House considered what counted as 'liability' for the same damage. The issues raised in both cases are considered below.

1 See generally Mitchell *The Law of Contribution and Reimbursement* (2003).
2 [2002] UKHL 14, [2002] 1 WLR 1397.
3 [2002] UKHL 17, [2002] 1 WLR 1419.
4 See para 8.31, below.

8.20 In *Royal Brompton*,[1] Lord Bingham of Cornhill provided a helpful starting point:

'When any claim for contribution falls to be decided the following questions in my opinion arise. (1) What damage has A suffered? (2) Is B liable to A in respect of that damage? (3) Is C also liable to A in respect of that damage or some of it?'

In the example, A is the claimant, and B could be the defendant and C a third party from whom B wishes to seek contribution for A's claim against B. If the answers to questions (2) and (3) are both in the affirmative, then B is entitled to seek contribution from C. It will be seen that, before B may do so, B must show that B and C are both liable to the same party, A. In *Birse Construction Ltd v Haiste Ltd*[2] a water authority appointed a contractor to undertake the design and construction of a storage reservoir and C, one of its own employees, to act as supervising engineer. The contractor appointed B as consulting engineers for the design. When the reservoir proved defective, the contractor settled the claim of the water authority and claimed an indemnity from B who, in turn, claimed contribution from C. The Court of Appeal held that the contribution claim could proceed only if both B and C owed a duty to

395

the contractor. If C owed its duty only to its employer, the water authority, and not to the contractor, the claim must fail as the parties would not have been liable for the same damage.

1 [2002] UKHL 14, [2002] 1 WLR 1397 at [6]. The leading speeches in *Royal Brompton* were those of Lords Steyn and Bingham of Cornhill.
2 [1996] 1 WLR 625, CA. Although this case pre-dates *Royal Brompton* (above), a dictum in it was approved in that case, and the rest of the decision was not disapproved. It was cited and not referred to in *CRS* (above). It is thought that it survives the House of Lords' decisions in those cases and is consistent with them.

8.21 Further, in *Co-Operative Retail Services*[1] the House of Lords held that, subject to statutory exceptions, it was open to parties to enter contracts whose effect would be that a party, C, would not be liable to the main contractor A for matters for which C would normally be liable in breach of contract or negligence. If such a contractual provision was effective then it prevented C from being liable to A for such matters. If A sued another party, B, for the same damage as C had caused, B would not be able to claim contribution from C for such damage because the effect of the parties' contractual arrangements was that C was not liable to A. B could not show that C was liable to A in respect of the same damage, and so B was not entitled to claim contribution from C in respect of A's claim against B. *CRS* was a building case involving many contractors. Under the various contracts, C owed A a duty to restore work damaged by fire, but not at C's expense; the contracts excluded any duty of C to compensate A for A's loss caused by the fire. The House of Lords held that in those circumstances it could not be shown that C was liable to A for the damaged work, and so contribution could not be claimed against C.

1 [2002] UKHL 17, [2002] 1 WLR 1419.

8.22 The central question in many difficult contribution cases is not whether B and C are both liable to A, but whether the damage for which they are both liable to A is 'the same damage' within the meaning of the Act. If it is not, then neither B nor C may claim contribution from the other. The House of Lords considered this issue in detail in *Royal Brompton*.[1] The first point is that the question under the Act is whether B and C are liable in respect of the same damage; the question is not whether B and C are liable in respect of the same 'damages'.[2] Hence the mere fact that A claims the same sum in damages from both B and C is not sufficient to show that contribution is available. Secondly, the Act does not apply to debts, as opposed to claims for damages.[3] It follows that a solicitor sued by a lender cannot claim contribution from the borrower, who is a debtor, though he or she may be able to claim back any overpayment from the lender by reference to principles of restitution and subrogation.[4]

1 [2002] UKHL 14, [2002] 1 WLR 1397.
2 See [27] (Lord Steyn) and [6] (Lord Bingham of Cornhill).

3 See [37] in *Royal Brompton* (Lord Hope); *Howkins & Harrison v Tyler* [2001] Lloyd's Rep PN 1; *Hampton v Minns* [2002] 1 WLR 1 (Mr Kevin Garnett QC sitting as a deputy High Court Judge). This part of the decision in *Howkins* was not disapproved in *Royal Brompton*.
4 *Howkins*, at [20]–[21] (Sir Richard Scott V-C).

8.23 Lord Steyn, who delivered the leading speech, considered the background to the Act and said that:[1]

'The context does not therefore justify an expansive interpretation of the words "the same damage" so as to mean substantially or materially similar damage … no glosses, extensive or restrictive, are warranted. The natural and ordinary meaning of "the *same* damage" is controlling.'

Before their Lordships' decision, the Court of Appeal had suggested a 'mutual discharge' test which was intended to indicate when damage would amount to the same damage for the purposes of the Act.[2] Lord Steyn said that the usefulness of this test might vary according to the circumstances of individual cases and that 'ultimately, the safest course is to apply the statutory test.'[3] It would therefore appear that it is no longer safe to rely on the mutual discharge test. The most helpful course may be to consider the House of Lords' decision on the facts of *Royal Brompton* itself, and the indications that Lord Steyn gave as to the correctness or otherwise of earlier decisions, though one subsequent decision suggests that obiter statements in *Royal Brompton* will not necessarily be followed.[4]

1 [2002] UKHL 14, [2002] 1 WLR 1397 at [27].
2 See *Howkins & Harrison v Tyler* [2001] Lloyd's Rep PN 1, at [17]:

'Suppose that A and B are the two parties who are said each to be liable to C in respect of "the same damage" that has been suffered by C. So C must have a right of action of some sort against A and a right of action of some sort against B. There are two questions that should then be asked. If A pays C a sum of money in satisfaction, or on account, of A's liability to C, will that sum operate to reduce or extinguish, depending upon the amount, B's liability to C? Secondly, if B pays C a sum of money in satisfaction or on account of B's liability to C, would that operate to reduce or extinguish A's liability to C? It seems to me that unless both of those questions can be given an affirmative answer, the case is not one to which the 1978 Act can be applied. If the payment by A or B to C does not *pro tanto* relieve the other of his obligations to C, there cannot, it seems to me, possibly be a case for contending that the non-paying party, whose liability to C remains un-reduced, will also have an obligation under section 1(1) to contribute to the payment made by the paying party.'

Applied, before the House of Lords' decision in *Royal Brompton, in Eastgate Group Ltd v Lindsey Morden Group Inc* [2002] 1 WLR 642, CA, and *Hurstwood Developments Ltd v Motor & General & Andersley & Co Insurance Services Ltd* [2002] Lloyd's Rep PN 195, CA.
3 [2002] UKHL 14, [2002] 1 WLR 1397 at [28].
4 See the discussion of *Charter plc v City Index Ltd* [2006] EWHC 2508 (Ch), [2007] 1 WLR 26 (Sir Andrew Morritt C), at para 8.31, below.

8.24 *Royal Brompton* was a construction law case that concerned a tri-partite relationship between an employer, a contractor and an architect. The parties entered into a standard form JCT contract. Under the contract, the architect could certify that the contractor was entitled to an extension of time for completing the building work. A certificate by the architect had three effects: first, the time at which the employer was entitled to take possession of the works was extended; secondly, the contractor was relieved of the liability to pay liquidated damages in respect of the delay; and thirdly the contractor might be entitled to claim compensation from the employer for extra expense which the delay had caused him. The contract overran by 43 weeks but the architect certified that the contractor was entitled to an extension of 43 weeks. For the purposes of the appeal, it had to be assumed that the contractor was liable to the employer for some or all of the delay, and that the architect was liable to the employer for negligently certifying that the contractor was entitled to an extension. The question was whether, in those circumstances, the contractor was liable to the employer for 'the same damage' as the architect.

8.25 The House of Lords held that the contractor was not liable for the same damage as the architect. The employer's claim against the contractor was simply for 'the late delivery of the building'[1]. In theory there could have been a claim that the architect was also liable for the late delivery of the building, for example if the architect had failed to chivvy the contractor. In that case the architect would have been liable for the same damage as the contractor. But that was not alleged in *Royal Brompton*. Instead, the essence of the contractor's claim against the architect was that the architect's negligent issuing of certificates 'changed the employer's contractual position detrimentally as against the contractor.'[2] It was changed in the three ways set out in the last paragraph. In particular, the employer lost the right under the contract to claim or deduct liquidated damages for the delayed delivery of the building. It was possible for the employer to seek to reverse the position by arbitration proceedings: the arbitrator had power to reverse the effect of the architect's certificate. But the employer had the burden of proof and faced the uncertainties of a potentially complex arbitration. The employer would not have faced these problems if there had been no breach of duty by the architect.

1 [2002] UKHL 14, [2002] 1 WLR 1397 at [22] (Lord Steyn).
2 [23] (Lord Steyn).

8.26 Viewed in this way, the facts are similar to loss of litigation claims against negligent solicitors. A is driving his car when he is hit by B, a negligent driver. A engages solicitors, C, who negligently fail to issue proceedings against B in time. A then sues C for damages for professional negligence, namely, the loss of A's litigation against B. Can C seek contribution from B, the negligent driver? Lord Steyn indicated[1] that he agreed with Canadian authority[2] to the effect that B and C would not be liable for 'the same damage'. B is liable for causing personal injury, while C is liable for professional negligence causing the loss of litigation. Although strictly obiter, this view is likely to be followed in professional negligence claims against barristers and solicitors. On the facts of

Royal Brompton, the analogy is that the contractor caused delay in delivery of the building while the architect weakened the employer's position in the potential arbitration against the contractor.

1 [2002] UKHL 14, [2002] 1 WLR 1397 at [29].
2 *Wallace v Litwiniuk* (2001) 92 Alta LR (3d) 249, Alberta Court of Appeal.

8.27 Lord Steyn went on to deal with the correctness of various previous decisions. In *Hurstwood Developments Ltd v Motor & General & Andersley & Co Insurance Services Ltd*[1] the Court of Appeal had held that a claim by an employer against a contractor for negligent site investigation services and a claim by the employer against an insurance broker for failing to provide insurance cover in respect of the development the subject of the site investigation were claims for the same damage. It followed that the insurance broker could claim compensation from the contractor. Lord Steyn disapproved this decision: the insurance broker had no liability for the remedial work to the site, so it was not responsible for 'the same damage.'[2] Similarly, Lord Steyn indicated that a claim against a builder for defective work was not the 'same damage' as a claim against an insurance company which had provided insurance cover for such a contingency.[3] Lord Steyn's next example concerned accountants[4]. A is buying the shares in a company. A's accountant, B, negligently values the shares at £7.5m. The vendor, C, warrants that the shares are worth £10m. A buys them for £10m but in fact they were worth only £5m. A thus has claims against the accountant B in negligence for £2.5m (extent of the over-valuation, £7.5m – £5m) and against the vendor C for £5m (breach of warranty, £10m – £5m). It appears that Lord Steyn agreed with both counsel that the first £2.5m of the loss was damage for which both B and C were liable, so that there could be contribution in relation to that as they were both liable for the same damage. In relation to the second tranche of £2.5m, however, for which only the vendor C was liable, there could be no contribution because the accountant was not liable at all. Further, in *Co-Operative Retail Services*[5], the House of Lords indicated, obiter, that the liability of an architect for negligently causing a fire would not be liability for causing the same damage as the liability of a contractor for failing adequately to make good the damage caused by the fire. Also in *CRS*, and again obiter, Lords Bingham of Cornhill and Hope of Craighead said that the time at which liability for the same damage had to be shown, in order to claim contribution, was the time at which contribution was claimed, rather than the time at which the damage occurred.[6]

1 [2002] Lloyd's Rep PN 195, CA.
2 *Royal Brompton* [2002] UKHL 14, [2002] 1 WLR 1397 at [33]. Note, however, that the result of *Howkins & Harrison*, above, probably still stands: in a lender's claim against negligent surveyors, there can probably be no contribution between the surveyors and the borrowers.
3 At [34].
4 At [29].
5 [2002] UKHL 17, [2002] 1 WLR 1419. See [8] (Lord Bingham of Cornhill) and [49] (Lord Hope of Craighead).
6 See [9] and [52]–[60] respectively.

8.28 Following *Royal Brompton*, in *Dingles Building (NI) Ltd v Brooks*[1], the Northern Ireland Court of Appeal considered a developer's claim against a clergyman. The developer had signed a contract to buy some land from a charitable trust. The trustees were seven clergymen. Only one of them, the defendant, had signed the contract. The other six trustees declined to sign, so that the deal could not go ahead. The developer sued the clergyman who had signed, for breach of warranty of authority. That clergyman wished to claim contribution from the developers' solicitors. It was held that he was not entitled to do so. The damage caused by the single clergyman was that the developers were left with an unenforceable contract. The damaged caused by the solicitors was that the developer had lost the opportunity to try to persuade the other clergyman trustees to sign. These types of damage were not the same damage for the purposes of the Act.

1 [2003] PNLR 8.

8.29 In *Luke v Kingsley Smith & Co*[1], the claimant, a former soldier, sued the Ministry of Defence for malicious falsehood. He engaged the defendant solicitors to act for him. After some years of delay in the litigation on the part of the defendants, the claimant dismissed the defendants and engaged new solicitors. The claim was for £240,000. The new solicitors, and counsel, settled the claim for £10,000; the low figure in respect of quantum was said to reflect the risk that the claim was likely to be struck out for want of prosecution if there were no settlement. The claimant sued the defendants on the basis that their delay had forced him to settle the claim for such a low sum. The defendants sought contribution from the new solicitors, and counsel, on the basis that they should have advised settlement at a much higher figure than £10,000. The new solicitors, and counsel, applied for summary judgment in the contribution proceedings on the basis that, even if they had been negligent, the damage that they had caused the claimant had not been 'the same damage' as the damage that the defendants had caused him. Davis J rejected the application. It was arguable that the loss suffered would not have occurred but for the negligence of both the defendants and the new solicitors/counsel, in other words that no loss would have been suffered if the new solicitors/counsel had not been negligent. Hence it was arguable that the defendants and new solicitors/counsel were concurrent tortfeasors[2] who could therefore seek contribution from each other. Davis J thought it likely that if one firm of solicitors delayed the conduct of litigation for four years, and then another firm delayed it for a further four years, leading to the action being struck out, each firm would have contributed to the same damage, namely the striking out of the action, and each could claim contribution from the other. Further he referred to *Webb v Barclays Bank plc*[3]. The bank employed the claimant. Due to the claimant's negligence, the claimant tripped over and injured her knee. She was taken to a hospital that treated her negligently. The Court of Appeal held that the hospital's negligence did not break the chain of causation. It followed that the bank was liable for all the claimant's loss, including that caused by the hospital's negligence; hence the bank could

400

claim contribution from the hospital. In other words, the first tortfeasor could claim contribution from the second tortfeasor. Although only a decision declining to give summary judgment, *Luke* suggests that, where different lawyers contribute to the loss of one piece of litigation, each lawyer may be able to claim contribution from the other.[4]

1 [2003] EWHC 1559 (QB), [2004] PNLR 12.
2 See *Rahman v Arearose Ltd* [2001] QB 351, CA.
3 [2001] Lloyd's Rep Med 500, CA.
4 See also *Vision Golf Ltd v Weightmans* [2005] All ER (D) 675, which is to similar effect.

8.30 A final point deriving from *Royal Brompton* is that it appears that B and C may be liable for the same damage even if the damage for which B is liable to A corresponds only in part with the damage for which C is liable to A.[1] Presumably C could seek contribution only in relation to the damage for which liability overlapped.

1 *Royal Brompton* [2002] UKHL 14, [2002] 1 WLR 1397 at [6] (Lord Bingham of Cornhill), and see Lord Steyn's accountants example referred to at para 8.27, above.

(b) *Restitution and knowing assistance in breach of trust*

8.31 Section 6(1) of the Act is quoted above at para 8.19. Referring to the passage in brackets in that sub-section, in *Friends Provident Life Office v Hillier Parker May & Rowden*[1] the Court of Appeal held that if A had a claim in damages against B, negligent surveyors, and a claim for restitution against C, a developer, then C could recover contribution from B, because a claim for restitution could be a claim for the same damage as a claim for damages for negligence. But in *Royal Brompton* Lord Steyn said that the view that a claim for restitution could be a claim for 'damage suffered' was not a correct statement of the law.[2] In *Charter plc v City Index Ltd*,[3] Sir Andrew Morritt C pointed out that, in *Friends Provident*, the Court of Appeal had also decided that a claim for knowing receipt of trust property was a claim 'to recover compensation … in respect of damage' within the meaning of s 6(1) of the Act. Lord Steyn had not disapproved that part of the decision in *Friends Provident*, and in any case Lord Steyn's disapproval of the decision as to restitution in *Friends Provident* was obiter. It followed that a first instance judge remained bound by *Friends Provident* to hold that a claim for knowing receipt of trust property was one to which the Act applied, so that such a claim could form the basis of a contribution claim. In practice, however, it follows from the second part of the Chancellor's decision in *Charter* that in most cases the party liable in knowing receipt will not succeed in claiming contribution.[4]

1 [1997] QB 85, CA.
2 At [33].

3 [2006] EWHC 2508 (Ch), [2007] 1 WLR 26, at [28]. See also *Niru Battery Manufacturing Co v Milestone Trading Ltd (No 2)* [2003] EWCA Civ 487, [2004] 2 Lloyd's Rep 319 per Clarke LJ at [77]–[78]
4 See para 8.40, below.

(c) Settlements

8.32   Where B and C are both liable to A in respect of the same damage, A may sue B and reach a settlement in full and final satisfaction of A's claims with B. A may then sue C. Is C entitled to respond by seeking contribution from B, thereby causing B to have pay out more money, essentially in relation to A's claim, even though B had reached a full and final settlement with A? This may be seen as two questions: (i) may A sue C even though A's settlement with B is said to be in full and final satisfaction of A's claim? (ii) If A is entitled to sue C, may C seek contribution from B? So far as question (ii) is concerned, s 1(3) of the Act provides:

> 'A person shall be liable to make contribution by virtue of subsec-tion (1) above notwithstanding that he has ceased to be liable in respect of the damage in question since the time when the damage occurred, unless he ceased to be liable by virtue of the expiry of a period of limitation or prescription which extinguished the right on which the claim against him in respect of the damage was based.'

As Lord Rodger of Earlsferry pointed out in *Heaton v AXA Equity & Law* [1]:

> '... the key to solving such problems lies not in legal logic but in legal policy ... By enacting s 1(3) of the Civil Liability (Contribu-tion) Act 1978, however, Parliament has resolved the policy issue for English law in cases of tort and breach of contract by coming down in favour of allowing contribution proceedings to be taken against a party who has settled and therefore "ceased to be liable in respect of the damage in question since the time when the damage occurred".'

It follows that the answer to question (ii) is yes: the mere fact that A has settled his or her claim with B does not prevent B being liable to C in contribution proceedings, if C has subsequently been sued by A. That leaves question (i). The answer to question (i) is a matter of construing the settlement agreement between A and B. The court seeks to determine whether the agreement was intended to settle only A's claims against B, in which case A may still proceed against C, or alternatively whether the payment which B made was intended to compensate A fully for all A's losses including those caused by C so that there is no further loss left for A to claim from C. Another possibility is that, in the settlement agreement with B, A undertook not to pursue C. This too might prevent A suing C, and thus prevent B being exposed to a contribution claim from C. Finally, B might seek an indemnity from A against any contribution claims by C. The basis on which the court approaches the task of construction appears in *Heaton* and the House of Lords' further decision, given on the same day, in *Cape & Dalgleish v Fitzgerald*.[2]

1 [2002] UKHL 15, [2002] 2 AC 329 at [85].
2 [2002] UKHL 16.

8.33 The Act provides that, where B has reached a bona fide settlement with A, there is no need for B to prove his own liability in order to claim contribution from C, *provided that* 'he would have been liable assuming that the factual basis of the claim against him could be established'.[1] Thus, in order to obtain contribution from C, B does not need to prove *the facts* which A alleged against him, but does have to show that A's claim against him or her was good *in law*. *Dubai Aluminium Co Ltd v Salaam*,[2] discussed in chapter 5 in relation to vicarious liability, is an example of a case in which, following a settlement, factual assumptions had to be made, and the principal question was one of law as to whether the parties who had settled had in fact been liable to the claimant. The factual assumptions, however, were those that the claimant had pleaded against the party seeking contribution. The question was whether that party, who had settled with the claimant, was in fact liable to the claimant. The claimant's pleaded case against that party was meagre, but the House of Lords declined to look at material that went beyond it.[3] Lord Hobhouse suggested that, in future cases, a party wishing to settle with a claimant and seek contribution against another party might wish to suggest that the claimant first amend his or her case 'so as to make express the basis of claim which justifies the settlement.'[4]

1 Civil Liability (Contribution) Act 1978, s 1(4). Note that s 1(2) also provides that a person who 'has ceased to be liable in respect of the damage in question' may claim a contribution provided he was liable 'immediately before he made or was ordered or agreed to make the payment in respect of which the contribution is sought'. In order to claim under s 1(4), B does, of course, need to show that C is or would have been liable to A.
2 [2002] UKHL 48, [2003] 2 AC 366; see para 5.22ff, above.
3 See [2002] UKHL 48 at [38] (Lord Nicholls) and [16] (Lord Millett). Lords Slynn and Hutton agreed with Lord Nicholls's speech.
4 At [70].

8.34 If B settles with the claimant A, then, in contribution proceedings against C, B must prove that the quantum of the settlement with A was reasonable. Section 1 of the Act:[1]

'... does not affect the right of the person from whom contribution is being sought [C] to assert that the person claiming contribution [B] paid too much or that in assessing contribution the party liable to contribute [C] should not be required to pay compensation for elements of the payment for which that person [C] could never have been held liable had he been sued directly.'

8.35 *Contributory negligence and contribution*

Payments of interest in B's settlement with A do count as damages in respect of which there may be contribution under the Act.[2] It is likely that B may also seek contribution in respect of payments relating to A's costs.[3]

1 *J Sainsbury plc v Broadway Malyan* [1999] PNLR 286, per H H J Humphrey Lloyd QC at 321A–B. Letters in square brackets added.
2 *J Sainsbury plc v Broadway Malyan* [1999] PNLR 286.
3 *BICC Ltd v Cumbrian Industrial Ltd* [2002] Lloyd's Rep PN 526, CA. Entitlement to claim contribution to costs paid under a settlement appears to have been assumed in *Fisk v Brian Thornhill & Son* [2007] EWCA Civ 152, [2007] PNLR 12, at [44]–[45].

8.35 Where a judgment on the merits between C and A has held C not liable, that judgment is conclusive against B, and C is protected from a contribution claim.[1] Where there are joint debtors, if A settles against one (B), without expressly reserving the right to pursue the others (C and D), then A is likely to find that the doctrine of accord and satisfaction prevents him or her from pursuing C and D.[2] In this case, although in general a settlement between A and B provides B with no protection from a claim for contribution from C, A will be prevented from proceeding against *C* and thus there will be no loss in respect of which C can claim contribution from B. Where C has been held not liable or has ceased to be liable to A because of the expiry of the limitation period relating to A's claim, C is not protected against a contribution claim. B may bring a contribution claim against C within two years from the date when B's own liability to A was determined by settlement or judgment.[3]

1 Civil Liability (Contribution) Act 1978, s 1(5).
2 *Morris v Wentworth-Stanley* [1999] QB 1004, CA.
3 Limitation Act 1980, s 10. See further para 7.84ff, above.

8.36 In *Abbey National plc v Gouldman*[1], the claimant ('A') sued, separately, a solicitor ('B') and a firm of valuers ('C'), for losses incurred in consequence of the same lending transaction. The claim against C was discontinued as it was statute-barred. B then joined C as Part 20 defendants to A's claim against B, seeking contribution. B's claim against C was not statute-barred. A then settled its claim against B. The terms of the settlement agreement were that, upon B submitting to final judgment in A's favour in a specified amount, and upon B assigning to A his (B's) rights in the Part 20 claim against C, A would undertake not to execute its judgment against B beyond the sum which A might recover, as B's assignee, in B's Part 20 claim against C. The Part 20 claim was then assigned to A and the court made a consent order that B pay A the specified amount. The court subsequently granted C summary judgment in the Part 20 proceedings. It held that a decision as to what was just and equitable, for the purposes of making an award of contribution, could not be made until it was first known what the quantum of liability in the primary claim of A against B was to be. The essential substance of the agreement between A and B was that B would pay A no more than C was required to pay to B. The court could not determine how much it was just and equitable that C should pay B until it first knew what B was to pay A. But, because of the terms of the settlement agreement between A

404

and B, the amount which, in reality, B was to pay A could not be determined until it had first been determined what C should pay B. The agreement was circular and it was impossible for the court to assess what it was just and equitable that C should pay B, hence no contribution could be awarded.

1 [2003] EWHC 925 (Ch), [2003] 1 WLR 2042 (Mr Simon Berry QC sitting as a deputy High Court judge).

(d) Interrelation with SAAMCo

8.37 In *Ball v Banner*[1], Hart J considered a contribution claim by Scottish solicitors against English surveyors. The solicitors had misrepresented aspects of a tax-saving scheme to the claimant, their client. The solicitors settled with the claimant and sought contribution from the valuers, who were held to have owed the claimant a duty of care and negligently to have breached it. Contribution was available in principle. The question arose as to whether, in assessing contribution, the judge should start from the figure for the total, or basic, loss, and award a percentage of that, or should instead assess the amount of the attributable loss and then consider contribution only as a percentage of that.[2] The judge held, consistently with the position in relation to contributory negligence discussed above, that he should start from the total, or basic, loss figure, rather than the attributable loss figure.

1 [2000] Lloyd's Rep PN 569 (Hart J).
2 For basic and attributable loss, see para 8.07, above, and paras 10.73ff and 10.79ff, below.

2 Application

8.38 The Act provides that the amount of the contribution recoverable shall be 'such as may be found by the court to be just and equitable having regard to the extent of that person's responsibility for the damage in question'.[1] The test involves a consideration not only of the causative potency of a factor, but also of its blameworthiness.[2] In *Downs v Chappell*,[3] the trial judge had indicated that, if he had held the two defendants liable, he would have held them equally responsible for the claimant's damage. The Court of Appeal allowed the claimant's appeal and held that the defendants were liable for the loss. Thus it was necessary to consider the appeal in relation to contribution. The second defendants contended that the trial judge had erred as he had given too little weight to his finding that the first defendants had been fraudulent whereas they, the second defendants, had been only negligent. Hobhouse LJ, with whom the other judges agreed, rejected this. The extent of a person's 'responsibility', within the meaning of the Act, depended upon both causative potency and moral blameworthiness. The judge was entitled to find that, although the first defendants were fraudulent and therefore more blameworthy, the second defendants' conduct had more causative effect, so that each had equal responsibility overall. Further, in *Brian Warwicker Partnership plc v HOK International Ltd⁴*, the Court of Appeal accepted that non-causative factors, such as the blameworthiness of a party's conduct which did not cause damage, could be taken into account, though two judges felt that such material should be given less weight in the exercise of the court's discretion than conduct which was causative of the claimant's loss. A recent example of an apportionment between counsel and solicitors in the negligent conduct of litigation is *Hickman v Blake Lapthorn*.[5]

1 Civil Liability (Contribution) Act 1978, s 2(1).
2 *Madden v Quirk* [1989] 1 WLR 702 at 707.
3 [1997] 1 WLR 426 at 445B–H, CA.
4 [2005] EWCA Civ 962, [2006] PNLR 5.
5 [2005] EWHC 2714 (QB), [2006] PNLR 20, (Jack J), at [60] (two-thirds to counsel, one-third to solicitors).

8.39 Whereas, in relation to contributory negligence, apportionment between claimant and defendant may not be made if the defendant has been guilty of fraudulent misrepresentation,[1] a dishonest defendant may claim contribution from a fellow tortfeasor under the Civil Liability (Contribution) Act 1978.[2] In *K v P*,[3] Ferris J held that, even if its elements were made out, the maxim *ex turpi causa non oritur actio* could be no bar to a claim for contribution. On the other hand, where there is a claim for contribution by parties who are themselves innocent, and liable only vicariously for the wrongs of another, should the court take account of their innocence? In *Dubai Aluminium Co Ltd v Salaam*,[4] the House of Lords held that it could not: the innocent parties stood in the shoes of the other, and had to be judged as if they were the other, thus ignoring their innocence. Further, in assessing the amount of contribution payable by one group of wrongdoers to another, the House was prepared to take into account that, after conclusion of the claimant's action, one group of wrongdoers still held significant proceeds of the fraud the subject of the claim, whereas the other group did not.[5]

1 See para 8.05, above.
2 See for example *Downs v Chappell* [1997] 1 WLR 426, CA.
3 [1993] Ch 140.
4 [2002] UKHL 48, [2003] 2 AC 366. See para 5.22ff, above.
5 See [59] (Lord Nicholls), [76] (Lord Hobhouse) and [163]–[164] (Lord Millett).

8.40 In *Charter plc v City Index Ltd*,[1] Sir Andrew Morritt C indicated that, in the general run of cases, where a party (B) had knowingly received trust money in circumstances where it was inequitable for B to receive it, and B had either retained the money or paid it for his or her own purposes, then it would not be just and equitable to award contribution to B as against other parties who were also liable to the claimant but had not had the use of the money for themselves. Parties such as B would, therefore, generally not be awarded contribution against such other parties.

1 [2006] EWHC 2508 (Ch), [2007] 1 WLR 26 (Sir Andrew Morritt C).

3 Interrelation of contributory negligence and contribution[1]

8.41 Section 2(3) of the Civil Liability (Contribution) Act 1978 provides that where B's liability to A is, or would have been, limited by a reduction for contributory negligence or a limitation of damage clause, that limit caps the amount of the contribution payable by B to C. Thus, in the situation where a solicitor is liable to a lender for the whole of the lender's loss, but a valuer is liable only to the extent of the overvaluation, then if the valuer's liability to the lender was limited by a limitation clause, the valuer's liability to make contribution to the solicitor could not exceed the amount which the lender would have recovered from the valuer after application of the limitation clause. The solicitor might argue that s 2(3) does not refer to limits to the valuer's liability imposed by the House of Lords' decision in *SAAMCo*[2] but it is thought that, if the valuer's liability to the lender were limited in that way, it could not be just and equitable for the court to order the valuer to pay by way of contribution more than he or she would have had to pay to the lender directly.

1 For a comparison of the rules as to contributory negligence and contribution see Charlwood, [2007] 23 PN 82.
2 See para 8.07, above.

Part 2

Specific Claims

Chapter 9

Conveyancing

A   INTRODUCTION

9.1   Claims against solicitors arising from alleged negligence in conveyancing constitute the single largest source of claims against small to medium-size firms of solicitors[1]. Over the period 2000 to 2004, one in every three claims made against firms with up to 10 partners related to conveyancing (29% residential and 6% commercial). That proportion is very similar to the claims experience of the Solicitors' Indemnity Fund over the last ten years of its existence[2]. Analysis by Aon Limited in August 2006 found that most residential conveyancing claims (whether measured by number or by value) arose either from relatively simple procedural failures, such as failing to undertake or understand property searches, or failing to advise the client properly on relevant points of law. The Aon analysis suggested that the increased use of computers might have led to an environment where errors were more easily made and less easily spotted than in former times. Although there are occasions where conveyancing claims involve difficult questions about the existence or breach of a given duty, it is more frequently the case that the most difficult aspect of bringing or defending claims against solicitors arising from conveyancing concerns the assessment of damages[3].

1   Press release from Aon Limited, London 10 August 2006, available at www.aon.com/uk/en/ about/Press_Office/negligence.jsp. Also reported in *Insurance Times* 16 August 2006.
2   'Current and future trends in residential conveyancing', report to the Council of the Law Society, 3 October 2007, para 11, available at http://www.lawsociety.org.uk/secure/meeting /169311/ 169311.pdf. The report records that the Legal Complaints Service received 4,709 complaints regarding conveyancing in the 18 months prior to October 2007.
3   Indeed, Lord Hoffmann, writing extra-judicially, has commented that the courts regard conveyancing as an activity which the client is entitled to expect produces the intended result, such that the risk of failing to achieve that result is more fairly borne by the conveyancer's insurers than by the client: 'The Reasonableness of Lawyers' Lapses' (1994) 10 PN 6.

B   ACTING FOR MORE THAN ONE PARTY

1   Acting for vendor and purchaser

9.2   Joint or multiple retainers may give rise to no conflict of interest, but this is not always the case. It is fundamental to the solicitor's retainer that he or she must exercise his professional judgment solely for the benefit of the client. This can only be achieved if the solicitor is able to give undivided loyalty to that client and is not placed in a position where the interests of two clients may conflict or the loyalty to one client may inhibit or interfere with the loyalty to another. An obvious example of the danger of conflict is where a solicitor is instructed to act for both vendor and purchaser on the sale of land. Solicitors were permitted to act for both under r 6 of the Law Society's Solicitors' Practice Rules 1990, which regulated solicitors' conduct up to 1 July 2007, and remain so permitted under rr 3.07–3.15 of the new Solicitors' Code of Conduct 2007, promulgated by the Solicitors' Regulation Authority. The guidance notes to the Solicitors' Code of Conduct 2007, however, contain the observation that the 'general rule' now is that 'separate representation is required because conveyancing is an area where the risk of a conflict arising between two parties is high and where any conflict may affect a conveyancing chain'[1]. This statement (albeit in non-binding guidance notes) of such a general rule reflects the tighter control exercised over solicitors seeking to act for multiple parties.

1 Rule 3, Guidance Notes, para 72.

9.3 Although rr 3.07–3.15 of the Solicitors' Code of Conduct 2007 are derived from r 6 of the Solicitors Practice Rules 1990, there are significant differences apparently designed to restrict further the number of occasions on which a solicitor will be able to act for both parties[1]. Thus, by r 3.07(1), the rules relating to acting for seller and purchaser apply not only to the particular person acting for one of the parties, but also to any 'associated firm' of that person as defined in r 24. The definition is wide: an associated firm 'means two or more partnerships with at least one partner in common; two or more companies without shares with at least one member in common; two or more LLPs with at least one member in common; two or more companies with shares with at least one owner in common; or any combination of these[2]'. A person to whom the Rules apply 'must not' act for more than one party in conveyancing unless (a) he can bring himself within the exceptions provided for in rr 3.08–3.15 and (b) he acts in accordance with the rules contained in those paragraphs: r 3.07(2). For the purposes of this chapter, the relevant rules are as follows:

'3.08 Conveyancing transactions not at arm's length

Subject to the prohibition in 10.06(3) and (4), you may act for seller and buyer when the transaction between the parties is not at arm's length, provided there is no conflict or significant risk of conflict.

3.09 Conveyancing transactions at arm's length

Subject to the prohibition in 10.06(3) and (4), you may act for seller and buyer if the conditions set out in 3.10 below are satisfied and one of the following applies:

(a)   both parties are established clients;

(b)   the consideration is £10,000 or less and the transaction is not the grant of a lease; or

(c)   seller and buyer are represented by two separate offices in different localities.

3.10 Conditions for acting under 3.09

In order to act for seller and buyer under 3.09 above, the following conditions must be met:

(a)   the written consent of both parties must be obtained;

(b)   no conflict of interests must exist or arise;

(c)   the seller must not be selling or leasing as a builder or developer; and

(d)   when the seller and buyer are represented by two separate offices in different localities:

    (i)   different individuals (either solicitors or RELs qualified to do conveyancing under regulation 12 of the European Communities (Lawyer's Practice) Regulations 2000 (SI 2000/1119)) who normally work at each office, conduct or supervise the transaction for seller and buyer; and

    (ii)   no office of the firm (or an associated firm) referred either client to the office conducting the transactions ....

3.15 Conflict arising when acting for seller and buyer

If a conflict arises during the course of a transaction in which you are acting for more than one party, you may continue to act for one of the parties only if the duty of confidentiality to the other party is not at risk.'[3]

---

1   Note that r 6 of the Solicitors' Practice Rules 1990 was itself amended and added to on various occasions between 1990 and 2007.

2   This enlargement of jurisdiction reflects the recent trend in the law relating to breach of fiduciary duty towards ignoring formal legal distinctions between persons in favour of recognising substantial similarities, as for example by lifting the corporate veil. Cf *Ratiu & Ors v Conway* [2005] EWCA Civ 1302, [2006] 1 All ER 571.

3   Rule 10.06 (referred to in rr 3.08 and 3.09) concerns acting in contract races, discussed in para 9.156, below.

9.4   These parts of r 3 reflect the 'double employment' rule,[1] which provides that a fiduciary may not act for two clients with potentially conflicting interests

413

without the informed consent of each client (which consent need not be recorded in writing as long as it has been given). A failure to comply with these parts of r 3, therefore, is likely to involve the solicitor in breach of an equitable duty to one or more clients, although it should be noted that r 3 impose higher duties on the solicitor than that imposed on fiduciaries more generally. For it is only in certain limited circumstances *and* with the written consent of each client that the solicitor is permitted to act for both of them.

1 Discussed in paras 4.30–4.33, above.

9.5 The fact that a solicitor has committed a breach either of the relevant parts of r 3 or the double employment rule will not of itself make him liable to a claim for compensation in equity. In order to recover, the claimant will have to show that the breach of duty was truly causative of loss[1]. If a solicitor does obtain clear and informed consent from each client in circumstances where he would still be in breach of r 3 (eg, because neither is an established client), or if he obtains the consent of neither in circumstances where that consent would undoubtedly have been forthcoming, it is likely that there will be no actionable breach of fiduciary duty.[2]

1 Since *Swindle v Harrison* [1997] 4 All ER 705, *Ata v American Express Bank* (1998) Times, 26 June, CA (p 25 of the transcript, per Hirst LJ) and *Rama v Miller* [1996] 1 NZLR 257, PC (per Lord Nicholls at 260), it has been generally accepted that causation needs to be proved in a claim for alleged breach of fiduciary duty, contrary to the suggestion in *Brickenden v London Loan & Savings Co* [1934] 3 DLR 465, PC (per Lord Thankerton at 469): see paras 4.43–4.53, above. Cf *Bristol & West Building Society v Daniels* [1997] PNLR 323, where a solicitor was found to be in breach of the double employment rule but no damages were awarded to the claimant because it could not establish a causal connection between breach of the rule and the loss suffered.
2 Cf *Clarke Boyce v Mouat* [1994] 1 AC 428.

9.6 A breach of r 3 in itself does not give the party affected by the breach a cause of action. The Solicitors Code of Conduct 2007, like the Solicitors Practice Rules 1990 before it, was made pursuant to authority delegated to the Council of the Law Society and the Master of the Rolls by s 31 of the Solicitors' Act 1974 and s 9 of the Administration of Justice Act 1985.[1] In *Jenmain Builders Ltd v Steed & Steed*[2], the Court of Appeal expressly left open the question whether a breach of r 6A of the Solicitors Practice Rules 1990 could found a cause of action in tort[3], and in *Thames Trains v Adams*[4], Nelson J held that breach of the Solicitors Practice Rules 1990 generally would not found a cause of action. Indeed, s 31(2) of the Solicitors Act 1974 provides only that any person affected by a solicitor's failure to comply with the Solicitors Code of Conduct 2007 'may make a complaint in respect of that failure' to the Solicitors' Disciplinary Tribunal. It seems therefore that the legislative intention behind s 31 was expressly not to create a civil remedy for breach of the Solicitors Code of Conduct 2007.

1 See *Mohamed v Alaga & Co* [2000] 1 WLR 815, CA, per Lord Bingham MR at 1823–4, and *Awwad v Geraghty* [2001] QB 570, CA, per May LJ at 598, both basing their observations on *Swain v Law Society* [1983] 1 AC 598.

2 [2000] Lloyd's Rep PN 549, CA.
3 [2000] Lloyd's Rep PN 549 at [21] and [37].
4 [2006] EWHC 3291 (Nelson J) at [41].

9.7 On the other hand, the fact that a solicitor may have committed a technical breach of the double employment rule in acting for both vendor and purchaser (or by the same token a breach of r 3) may well be evidence of, or may give rise to, a breach of the common law duty of care to one or even both clients. In *Hilton v Barker Booth & Eastwood*[1], the House of Lords held that a solicitor who acted for both parties but failed to tell the vendor, a property developer, of the purchaser's criminal antecedents (which were such that the vendor would not have proceeded with the transaction) was in breach of the absolute prohibitions contained in r 6 of the Solicitors Practice Rules 1990 against acting for both sides where a conflict of interests arose and where one of the parties was a developer. Since it was professionally improper for the solicitor to act for both sides, he came under a duty (whether by virtue of a term implied into his retainer or at common law) to inform the vendor that he should seek fresh legal advice elsewhere and not rely on any advice already received. Breach of that duty, which arose from the solicitor's professional conduct obligations, was causative of the vendor's losses. The solicitor, however, continued to act, and thus came under a further duty to the vendor to pass on the information in his possession about the purchaser's criminal antecedents. The solicitor had thus put himself into a position where he owed conflicting duties to his two clients, with the result that he was bound to be in breach of duty to one or other of them in continuing to act. The solicitor sought to argue that being in an impossible position should excuse him from liability, but the House of Lords rightly rejected that contention on the ground that it was entirely the solicitor's fault that he found himself in the situation he did. *Hilton* is a further illustration of the difficulty faced by a solicitor seeking to act for both clients where there is a genuine conflict between the interests of the two. Such a conflict is bound to affect the way in which the solicitor discharges the duties to both clients. If a solicitor is unconsciously inhibited in the performance of his duty, he is more likely than not to commit a breach of the common law duty of care.[2] A good example of such a case is *Goody v Baring*[3] in which a solicitor who acted for both vendor and purchaser was held liable to the purchaser for accepting what his vendor client told him and for failing to make adequate further inquiries before exchange of contracts.[4] As Danckwerts J stated:

> 'It is plain that the standard of skill and care required of a solicitor who acts for both parties on a sale and purchase is at least as great as that which would be required of a solicitor who acts for a purchaser alone.'

The fact that the defendant acted for both parties inhibited him in fulfilling this duty to the purchaser. Again, in *Nash v Phillips*[5] a solicitor was held liable in negligence for failing to inform his purchaser client that his vendor client had accepted a cash offer and was about to exchange contracts with a third party (for whom the solicitor was also acting).[6]

1 [2005] UKHL 8, [2005] 1 WLR 567. For further discussion of the contractual significance of this decision see paras 1.1 and 2.14, n 4, above. For further discussion of the equitable issues, see paras 4.3.4–4.36, above.
2 See *Bristol & West BS v Mothew* [1998] Ch 1, CA at 19E-G (Millett LJ) which is quoted in para 4.34, above.
3 [1956] 1 WLR 448.
4 He failed to make adequate inquiries about the rents receivable from the property and, in particular, to satisfy himself that they would not go down as a consequence of rents being registered under the Rent Restriction Acts.
5 (1974) 232 Estates Gazette 1219 (Foster J). It is noteworthy that the judge found that there was an actual conflict of interest and a breach of what is now practice rule 6 because 'one [client] wished an early sale and the other wished to sell his house before he signed a contract', a common occurrence.
6 See also *Lake v Bushby* [1949] 2 All ER 964 (Pritchard J); *Smith v Mansi* [1963] 1 WLR 26 at 30, CA; and *Attard v* Samson (1966) 110 Sol Jo 249 (Phillimore J). For an example of a case where a breach of the double employment rule did not lead to liability at common law, see *Kenyon-Brown v Banks & Co* (5 June 1998, unreported) (Peter Leaver QC).

9.8   If the solicitor is one of the parties to the conveyancing transaction, the duty of the solicitor is all but absolute:[1]

> '[I]n all ordinary circumstances a solicitor ought to refuse to act for a person in a transaction to which the solicitor is himself a party with an adverse interest; and even if he is pressed to act after his refusal, he should persist in that refusal. Nobody can insist upon an unwilling solicitor acting for him, at all events when there is a conflict of interest.'

1 *Spector v Ageda* [1973] Ch 30 (Megarry J) at 47G and *Moody v Cox and Hatt* [1917] 2 Ch 71, CA, considered in para 4.35, above. In the latter, the defendant solicitors were parties to the transaction, although it was treated as a case of conflict of duties.

9.9   In this section we have been considering the situation where the solicitor has acted for both parties innocently either without realising that there is a conflict of interest or without addressing and dealing with that conflict properly. Where the solicitor is consciously aware that there is a conflict and chooses to prefer the interests of one client over the other or chooses to exploit his client by putting his own interests first, he commits a breach of fiduciary duty.[1]

1 This is considered in paras 4.34–4.39, above.

2   Obtaining the authority of the client or clients

9.10   A solicitor who acts only for one client must obtain that client's authority to act. If the solicitor is instructed on behalf of a client by a third party, then the solicitor must ensure that the third party has the client's authority to instruct him. Similarly, if a solicitor is instructed by a number of clients jointly, he must take care to ensure that he checks that all of his clients agree with any step he is about to take regardless of the fact that one or more client has expressed agreement[1]. Rule 2.01(c) of the Solicitors' Code of Conduct 2007 provides:

'You are generally free to decide whether to take on a particular client. However, you must refuse to act or cease acting for a client in the following circumstances:

(a)   When to act would involve you in a breach of the law or a breach of the rules of professional conduct;

(b)   Where you have insufficient resources or lack the competence to deal with the matter;

(c)   Where instructions are given by someone other than the client, or by only one client on behalf of others in a joint matter, you must not proceed without checking that all clients agree with the instructions given.[2]'

It may be helpful to distinguish between those cases where the solicitor has been led to believe that the instructions come from two or more clients jointly when in fact they do not, and cases where the solicitor has been duly instructed by a number of clients jointly, and then failed in his or her duty to some of them to check their instructions as the transaction progressed. In the former type of case, the solicitor has assumed a responsibility to the person thought to be the client (by taking steps which affected that person's interests) and then, in failing to confirm their instructions, has breached the duty that he or she assumed. In the latter type of case, the solicitor has been retained by the clients who are now suing him, but he has breached the retainer by taking steps without their authority. The following two paragraphs consider the two types of case.

1   If the client who has expressed agreement is (to the solicitor's knowledge) a duly appointed agent for the other clients, this is likely to satisfy the requirement that the solicitor check that all of the clients approve of the steps he proposes to take.
2   A similar provision appeared in the *Guide to the Professional Conduct of Solicitors* (1999) as Principle 12.04. Although not having the same legislative force as the Practice Rules 1990 themselves (or now the Solicitors Code of Conduct 2007), the Law Society have always treated a breach of the principles expressed in the guide as capable of amounting to professional misconduct.

9.11   In *Linaker v Keith Turner & Ashton*,[1] the claimant's wife instructed the defendant solicitors to act on behalf of the claimant and the lender in a transaction to remortgage the family home, legal title to which was registered only in the claimant's name. The defendants purported to act for the claimant in the transaction but the judge found that he had never authorised them to do so.

He held that taking instructions from the claimant's wife was not sufficient to give the defendants ostensible or apparent authority to act. The defendants had not complied with Principle 12.04 (the predecessor of r 2.01(c)) because, although they had taken his wife's instructions, they had neither obtained the claimant's written instructions to act nor seen him in person to do so. Further, they had failed to comply with the lender's instructions to explain the mortgage deed to the claimant. The judge held that, for these reasons, the defendants had acted negligently and breached their duty of care to the claimant.[2] A similar decision was reached in *Al-Sabah v Ali*.[3] In that case, it was held that the defendants were negligent in relying on instructions from the claimant's agent and a power of attorney forged by him where the agent himself not only had an interest in the transaction but was a party to it. The judge also relied on Principle 12.04 in deciding that the defendants had a duty to satisfy themselves that they had received proper instructions.[4] Given the case law and the mandatory form of wording used now in r 2.01(c), solicitors in domestic conveyancing transactions who receive instructions from a third party on behalf of a separate client must confirm their instructions with the ultimate client. Having obtained authority to act, similar principles are likely to apply at all stages of the transaction at which the solicitor requires the client's further instructions.[5]

1 (5 November 1998, unreported) (Garland J). See also *Umeweni v J B Wheatley & Co* [1990] EGCS 57, CA (Bar Library Transcript 1990/272).
2 He held that, as the claimant had never given the defendants authority to act, there was no retainer, so the defendants could not owe the claimant any contractual duty. Instead, they owed the claimant a duty of care on the basis that he was plainly within their reasonable contemplation as being a person who would be affected by their actions. See *White v Jones* [1995] 2 AC 207, HL, discussed in paras 1.32–1.34, above, and *Penn v Bristol and West Building Society* [1995] 2 FLR 938 (HHJ Kolbert) at 947H–949G. (This point did not arise on the appeal in *Penn:* see [1997] 1 WLR 1356 at 1360F–G, CA.)
3 [1999] EGCS 11 (Ferris J).
4 The judge also held that the defendants were not entitled to rely on the ostensible authority of the agent.
5 See *Farrer v Copley Singletons* [1998] PNLR 22, CA considered in para 9.12, below.

9.12 Where a solicitor acts for a number of clients in the same transaction, the solicitor's:

> '... contract of retainer is with each and every client; the duties of the solicitor are owed and must be discharged to each of them. It must follow that a solicitor is entitled to communicate with and take instructions from only one of several clients only if he has the authority of the other clients so to do ... From the point of view of [the solicitor] the authority might be actual, whether express or implied, or apparent; but in each case the authority must emanate from the alleged principals, not the alleged agent ...'[1]

Where the solicitor is instructed to act for a number of clients jointly, therefore, he must now ensure that he has the authority of each client to act.

Failure to do so may well amount to a breach of duty owed to the client whose authority was not obtained. It will not be sufficient to rely solely upon a statement from one client that he has the authority of the others to give instructions.[2] Where a solicitor acts for a commercial partnership that consists of a substantial number of partners, the solicitor is not normally required to take the instructions of anyone but the partner who directly instructed him, because a partner in such a firm will normally have his partners' actual or ostensible authority to give instructions.[3] There may, however, be circumstances (particularly where instructions come from a small partnership) in which a solicitor must check that all of the partners are content for him to act in the way proposed.[4] On the other hand, where a solicitor has been instructed to act by the employee of a limited company, no matter how small, he ordinarily will owe no duty to check that the instructions he has received are approved by the company's board of directors[5].

1 *Farrer v Copley Singletons* [1998] PNLR 22, per Brooke LJ at 32G–33B, CA.
2 This is because a purported agent's statement as to his own authority is of no effect: *Armagas v Mundogas SA* (*The Ocean Frost*) [1986] AC 717.
3 See *Sykes v Midland Bank Executor and Trustee Co Ltd* [1971] 1 QB 113 at 1 24B–D, 1 26D–E and 130F–G, CA.
4 See *Madley v Cousins Coombe* [1997] EGCS 63, where the claimant was one of two partners in a firm which had instructed the defendant solicitors from time to time. The two partners had agreed to mortgage certain property to a limited extent, but the mortgagee proposed that the mortgage be by way of an 'all monies' charge (something which benefited the claimant's partner, but not the claimant himself). The solicitors, accustomed to dealing with the claimant's partner, simply sent the mortgagee's charge to be signed by both partners, and offered no advice in relation to it. They were found to have assumed and then broken a duty towards the claimant by allowing him to obtain the impression that the charge was not a detriment to him.
5 Third parties are entitled to assume that directors of a company are duly authorised to act: see the Companies Act 2006, s 40.

9.13 The consequences of a breach of duty by a solicitor who acts without the authority of one or more of the clients may depend on whether the solicitor's actions or words are binding on them. A solicitor who acts on the instructions of one co-owner without the authority of the others warrants to third parties such as a purchaser or a lender that he or she has authority to act on behalf of all of the co-owners. The solicitor may thus become liable to the third parties for breach of that warranty in the event that his or her actions are not genuinely authorised: see *Penn v Bristol and West Building Society*.[1] But he or she does not usually have actual or ostensible authority to bind the clients themselves. In many cases, therefore, a breach of this duty will not yield substantial damages, because the solicitor's actions will not divest the client of his or her interest in the property.[2] In *Al-Sabah v Ali*,[3] however, two properties were transferred under a forged power of attorney and charged to third party mortgagees. The judge held that, although he had the power to rectify the register, he would not do so against the innocent mortgagees. Accordingly, even though the defendants' acts did not bind the claimant as a matter of law, he had lost the properties as a consequence.[4]

1 [1997] 1 WLR 1356, CA. For further discussion see para 5.17, above, and paras 10.111–10.114, below.
2 See para 5.6ff, above. See also *Penn v Bristol and West Building Society* [1995] 2 FLR 938 (HHJ Kolbert) at first instance at 947H–949G and 965A–C. There may be consequential losses. Mrs Penn was unable to obtain payment of her mortgage interest by the DSS because of the transaction which was at the centre of the dispute. It was held that she could recover such losses in principle and an inquiry was ordered.
3 [1999] EGCS 11 (Ferris J).
4 The judge awarded the difference between the values of the two properties in question and the amount required to discharge the mortgages. He also held that right of indemnity under the Land Registration Act 1925 could not be prayed in aid by the defendants. The Land Registry, as an insurer of last resort, was only obliged to indemnify the claimant *after* taking into account his right to damages from the defendants.

9.14 It is the solicitor's duty to convey the property into joint names where he or she acts for joint purchasers.[1] It also the solicitor's duty to explain the consequences of the different forms of ownership to the clients and take their instructions on which form is suitable or appropriate (after taking into account their long term wishes)[2]. A problem that frequently arises in cases of marital or other relationship breakdown is that former co-habitees are unable to prove the extent of their interest in jointly-owned property, too often as the result of a default on the part of their original conveyancer. As Ward LJ observed in *Carlton v* Goodman (original emphasis):[3]

> 'I ask in despair how often this court has to remind conveyancers that they would save their clients a great deal of later difficulty if only they would sit the purchasers down, explain the difference between a joint tenancy and a tenancy in common, ascertain what they want and then expressly declare in the conveyance or transfer how the beneficial interest is to be held because that will be conclusive and save all argument. When are conveyancers going to do this as a matter of invariable standard practice? The court has urged that time after time. Perhaps conveyancers do not read the law reports. I will try one more time: ALWAYS TRY TO AGREE ON AND THEN RECORD HOW THE BENEFICIAL INTEREST IS TO BE HELD. It is not very difficult to do.'

1 See the facts of *Webber v Gasquet, Metcalfe and Watson* (1982) 132 NLJ 665 (HHJ Judge Finlay QC).
2 Cf *Walker v Hall* (1983) SJ 550, CA, where Dillon LJ observed that a solicitor acting for co-purchasers was likely to be under a duty to ask them how they wished to hold the property.
3 [2002] EWCA Civ 545, [2002] 2 FLR 259, at [44].

9.15 A problem encountered relatively frequently in claims against solicitors arises from the situation where joint tenants have, some years after entering their joint tenancy, decided to sever the tenancy and discovered that, regardless of the relative contributions each made to the original purchase price, on severance each is entitled to a full 50% of the value of the property in question[1]. It is submitted that, in giving advice regarding the difference between a joint tenancy and tenancy in common, the reasonably competent solicitor should explain to the prospective tenants what happens in the event of a later severance, in addition to explaining the right of survivorship. In particular, where the two purchasers' contributions are unequal, it is submitted that the solicitor should explain that, in choosing joint tenancy over tenancy in common, the party making the greater contribution is in effect giving away the difference between his or her partner's contribution and 50% of the value of the property. It has been held that, since at least 1993, solicitors have been under a duty to their clients accurately to record in the transfer document the clients' intention to hold the property in question as beneficial joint tenants.[2]

1 For a comprehensive review of the law relating to the nature of joint ownership of property, and to assessing the relative contributions made by co-habitees in the event of relationship breakdown, see the recent House of Lords decision in *Stack v Dowden* [2007] UKHL 17, [2007] 2 WLR 831.
2 *Tee-Hillman v Heppenstalls* (26 June 2001, unreported, HHJ Bradbury sitting as a deputy judge in the QBD), transcript p 31. See also *Taylor v Warners* (21 July 1987, unreported) discussed by Jackson in *Conveyancing for Common Lawyers* delivered to the PNBA and *Walker v Hall* [1984] FLR 126 at 129E–F, CA.

3 Acting for mortgagors, mortgagees and sureties

9.16 Claims can arise from the activities of solicitors in acting in relation to the execution of mortgages or charges over real property if one of those who executed the charge later claims that he or she did not understand the charge which he or she signed, or that he or she signed it only after the application of undue influence. Assume that a lender (L) is proposing to make a a loan to a borrower (B1). L seeks security for its loan by, for example, taking a charge over a property which is owned jointly by B1 and another (B2) (and usually insisting that B2 be party to the loan agreement, in the form of a joint mortgage loan), or a charge over property owned by B2 given by her in support of a guarantee of B1's liabilities. B2 will often but not always be B1's spouse[1]. In due course, B1 is unable to maintain repayments to L and L brings proceedings seeking possession of the charged property. B2 defends the possession proceedings on the basis that he or she signed the charge only after B1 had either misrepresented to him or her the nature of the transaction and the effect of the document which he or she was signing, or exercised undue influence over him or her. On that basis, B2 claims that L cannot enforce the charge against him or her. L will ordinarily have instructed a solicitor (S) to advise B2 in relation to the effect of the charge before he or she signed it. It may have been the same solicitor as was acting for L on the transaction, or it may have been a different solicitor chosen by B2. In either case, L is likely to reply to B2's defence by saying that it had no notice of the alleged undue influence, because it was entitled to assume that, given he or she had had the benefit of independent legal advice, B2 must have willingly entered the transaction. If L establishes that it had no knowledge of any undue influence, B2's defence against L's claim will fail and possession will be granted. B2 might therefore sue S, who witnessed his or her signature to the transaction, for failing to carry out the duties owed to him or her[2]. If, on the other hand, B2 makes out her defence of undue influence, then L might sue S, who advised B2, for its failure to give adequate advice such that B2 entered a transaction which, had L known of the undue influence, should not have taken place.

1 Following the Civil Partnership Act 2004, cases may be expected in which B2 is B1's civil partner as defined in s 1 of the Act.
2 B2 may also sue B1 for undue influence, but B1 has often lost all assets and, for practical purposes, is not worth pursuing.

9.17   These various claims are likely to overlap as, for example, B2's claim against S will not proceed if he or she defeats L's claim to possession; and, the other side of the same coin, any claim by L against S will probably not proceed if L succeeds against B2. In these circumstances, it will often be desirable for the actions to be consolidated and tried together. In order to consider the solicitor's position, it is first necessary to consider the action between L and B2.

(a) *Mortgagors' and guarantors' claims to set aside charges*

(i)   *Non est factum*

9.18   Two types of claim are often made by guarantors or mortgagors who seek to escape the effect of the documents they have signed. The first is that the deed should be set aside on the basis of non est factum. Full discussion of this doctrine is outside the scope of this book.[1] In summary, however, the basis of the claim will be that B2 made a fundamental mistake as to the nature of the document which he or she was signing, so that he or she had no idea that it was a mortgage. The difficulty with a claim of this type for B2 is likely to be that the doctrine will not assist a party who was negligent in signing a document.[2] Normally L will have required that B2 sign in the presence of a solicitor whose duty it was to advise B2 of the effect of the deed. It is thought that, assuming a solicitor is present, then it will normally be negligent for B2 to sign without first asking the solicitor for at least some indication of the nature of the document which he or she is being asked to sign[3]. If the solicitor does provide at least some explanation to the effect that it is a mortgage and of the nature of a mortgage, then it will be hard for B2 to show that his or her mistake as to the nature of the document was sufficiently fundamental to make good a plea of non est factum.

1 See *Chitty on Contracts* (29th edn, 2004) at 5–086 ff.
2 *Barclays Bank plc v Schwartz* [1995] CLY 2492, CA per Millett LJ, and *Hambros Bank Ltd v British Historic Buildings Trust and Din* [1995] NPC 179, CA.
3 Cf *Saunders v Anglia Building Society, on appeal from Gallie v Lee* [1971] AC 1004, at 1016 and 1027.

(ii)   *Undue influence*

9.19   The second type of claim commonly made is that the deed is unenforceable (at least against B2) by L because it was executed due to the undue influence of B1. Two broad issues arise: first, B2 must show that he or she signed the document due to the undue influence of B1; secondly, B2 must show that L had notice of that undue influence, so that its mortgage is unenforceable pursuant to the *O'Brien* principle[1]. The law in relation to undue influence, and the role of solicitors, in cases of this kind was explained and redefined by Lord Nicholls in *Royal Bank of Scotland v Etridge (No 2)*.[2] What follows is not a substitute for reading that case.

1 *Barclays Bank v O'Brien* [1994] 1 AC 180
2 [2001] UKHL 44, [2002] 2 AC 773. *Etridge (No 2)* comprised the hearing of eight appeals. There were five speeches, of which those of Lords Nicholls, Hobhouse and Scott are the longest. Lords Bingham, Clyde, Hobhouse and Scott all expressly agreed with Lord Nicholls, who did not refer to any of the other speeches save insofar as they concerned the individual cases. Lord Nicholls's is accepted here as the leading speech.

9.20   As to the first issue, Lord Nicholls identified two forms of unacceptable conduct: overt acts of improper pressure or coercion (conduct which overlaps with the principle of duress) and conduct which 'arises out of a relationship between two persons where one has acquired over another a measure of influence, or ascendancy, of which the ascendant person then takes advantage'[1]. What matters is not the classification of the relationship, but rather whether one party has reposed sufficient trust and confidence in the other[2]. L's interests (and thus, frequently, S's interests too) lie in B2's failing to show that he or she entered into the transaction as the result of undue influence rather than by the exercise of his or her own free will[3]. One of the principal matters that the court takes into account when assessing whether B2 entered a transaction as the result of undue influence is evidence as to whether he or she received advice from a qualified independent person beforehand and, if so, whether that advice emancipated him or her from any undue influence under which he or she had hitherto been acting[4]. The obvious candidate for giving such advice is a solicitor. Thus, it was in this context that the House of Lords in *Etridge (No 2)* considered the duties of a solicitor retained to advise B2. These are considered further below.[5]

1 *Etridge (No 2)* [2001] UKHL 44, [2002] 2 AC 773 at [8].
2 The words 'trust and confidence' are mere facets of a general principle, and undue influence may arise in circumstances where the influenced party is vulnerable and has been exploited: see [11].
3 The burden of proof is on B2 to show that she was unduly influenced by B1: see [13]. That burden will usually be discharged if B2 can show (a) that she reposed trust and confidence in B1 (or was otherwise vulnerable) and (b) that the transaction in question calls for explanation. When B2 has proved those two facts, a rebuttable evidential presumption arises that he or she entered the transaction in question as the result of B1's undue influence. In practice, B1's interests do not lie in seeking to rebut the evidential presumption once B2 has made out the two matters just described; it is, however, open to any other party to proceedings not merely to challenge B2's evidence but also to seek to rebut the presumption if her evidence has established it. In particular, it is open to L or S to show that B1 exerted permissible pressure on B2, such that there is an acceptable explanation for the transaction in question ([31]). For an example of a case (decided before the House of Lords decision in *Etridge (No 2)*), see *Butigan v Negus-Fancey* [2000] EGCS 67, QBD.
4 [2001] UKHL 44, [2002] 2 AC 773 at [20].
5 At para 9.27ff, below.

9.21 If B2 succeeds in establishing undue influence, the second issue is whether L had notice of it, such that the *O'Brien* principle comes into play. As mentioned above, this is likely to be central to the assessment of damages in any claim against solicitors. If L had no notice, then its charge will be enforceable against B2 even if undue influence is proved. In this case, even if S acted in breach of duty to L,[1] L's damages against S are likely to be low or minimal. But B2 may have a claim against a solicitor who advised him or her in relation to the transaction. On the other hand, if L's claim to possession fails in whole or in part[2] then B2 is unlikely to have such a claim against solicitors, but L may have a claim for failure either to ensure that B2 fully understood what she was signing, or, possibly, for failure to report unusual features of the transaction to L. Each of these possibilities is considered below.

1 See para 9.29, below.
2 See para 9.33, below.

9.22 L may have notice of undue influence in two ways: it may have actual knowledge of facts from which the evidential presumption of undue influence arises, or it may become fixed with constructive knowledge when it is put on enquiry that the transaction might involve undue influence and then fails to take steps to satisfy itself that B2 is entering the obligation freely and with knowledge of the relevant facts[1].

1 It was once thought arguable that, where S is acting for it as well as for B2, L might be fixed with the knowledge of S, such that L had 'imputed' knowledge of the facts giving rise to undue influence (including the fact that S has given B2 inadequate advice). Lord Nicholls held that, since S is acting for B2 and not for L, L cannot be fixed with S's knowledge: see [77]. In the ordinary case, therefore, any deficiencies in the advice given by S are a matter between S and B2, and are not relevant to the assessment of L's knowledge regarding the undue influence.

(1)   Actual knowledge

9.23 Cases where L has actual knowledge are likely to be relatively rare. An example of actual knowledge on the part of L appears to be where L knows of, but does not disclose to B2, unusual features of the proposed transaction in support of which B2 is being asked to provide security, as in *Bank of Scotland v Bennet* (one of the cases decided in *Etridge (No 2)*). The failure to disclose is not a point going to constructive notice;[1] rather, L must make disclosure in order to be satisfied that the wife entered the transaction freely and in possession of the true facts.[2] It seems therefore that where L actually knows that there were features of the loan transaction that would be likely to have a significant impact on B2's decision-making, its failure to disclose those features to her amounts to proof of L's actual knowledge that B2 entered the transaction not of her own free will. Similarly, in *Credit Lyonnais Bank Nederland NV v Burch*[3], where B2 guaranteed a large liability for B1, of whom she was merely a junior employee, the Court of Appeal (while setting the transaction aside on other grounds) commented that the nature of the charge that B2 had entered was so onerous that this by itself was sufficient to set it aside; and the fact of L's knowledge about B1's borrowings, taken with the nature of the charge, meant that L knew full well that B2 was not sufficiently informed about the transaction to be able to enter it of her own free will. If S shared B2's ignorance when advising him or her, L will be unlikely to have any recourse against S. If, on the other hand, S has been made aware by L of the factors which should be brought to B2's attention if he or she is to make a fully-informed decision, L is likely to claim against S for breach of his or her retainer to it by failing to explain the transaction fully to B2.

1 See Lord Scott [2001] UKHL 44, [2002] 2 AC 773 at [345].
2 See Lord Nicholls [2001] UKHL 44, [2002] 2 AC 773 at [114].
3 [1997] 1 All ER 144, CA.

(2) *Constructive knowledge*

9.24 In *all* cases where the relationship between B2 and B1 is 'non-commercial', the bank is taken to have been put on enquiry that B2's involvement in the transaction might have been procured by B1's undue influence[1]. As a result of this very low threshold, L must take various steps to reassure itself that B2 has been independently advised. The steps that L must take to avoid being fixed with constructive notice were set out by Lord Nicholls in *Etridge* (*No 2*), and must be set out in full:[2]

'I now return to the steps a bank should take when it has been put on inquiry and for its protection is looking to the fact that the wife has been advised independently by a solicitor.

(1) One of the unsatisfactory features in some of the cases is the late stage at which the wife first became involved in the transaction. In practice she had no opportunity to express a view on the identity of the solicitor who advised her. She did not even know that the purpose for which the solicitor was giving her advice was to enable him to send, on her behalf, the protective confirmation sought by the bank. Usually the solicitor acted for both husband and wife.

Since the bank is looking for its protection to legal advice given to the wife by a solicitor who, in this respect, is acting solely for her, I consider the bank should take steps to check *directly with the wife* the name of the solicitor she wishes to act for her. To this end, in future the bank should communicate directly with the wife, informing her that for its own protection it will require written confirmation from a solicitor, acting for her, to the effect that the solicitor has fully explained to her the nature of the documents and the practical implications they will have for her. She should be told that the purpose of this requirement is that thereafter she should not be able to dispute she is legally bound by the documents once she has signed them. She should be asked to nominate a solicitor whom she is willing to instruct to advise her, separately from her husband, and act for her in giving the necessary confirmation to the bank. She should be told that, if she wishes, the solicitor may be the same solicitor as is acting for her husband in the transaction. If a solicitor is already acting for the husband and the wife, she should be asked whether she would prefer that a different solicitor should act for her regarding the bank's requirement for confirmation from a solicitor.

The bank should not proceed with the transaction until it has received an appropriate response directly from the wife.

(2) Representatives of the bank are likely to have a much better picture of the husband's financial affairs than the solicitor. If the bank is not willing to undertake the task of explanation itself, the bank must provide the solicitor with the financial information he needs for this purpose. Accordingly it should become routine practice for banks, if relying on confirmation from a solicitor for their protection, to send to the solicitor the necessary financial information. What is required must depend on the facts of the case. Ordinarily this will include information on the purpose for which the proposed new facility has been requested, the current amount of the husband's indebtedness, the amount of his current overdraft facility, and the amount and terms of any new facility. If the bank's request for security arose from a written application by the husband for a facility, a copy of the application should be sent to the solicitor. The bank will, of course, need first to obtain the consent of its customer to this circulation of confidential information. If this consent is not forthcoming the transaction will not be able to proceed.

(3) Exceptionally there may be a case where the bank believes or suspects that the wife has been misled by her husband or is not entering into the transaction of her own free will. If such a case occurs the bank must inform the wife's solicitors of the facts giving rise to its belief or suspicion.

(4) The bank should in every case obtain from the wife's solicitor a written confirmation to the effect mentioned above.'

If L fails to take these steps[3], it will be fixed with constructive knowledge of the fact that the transaction in question might have been procured by undue influence. In most circumstances, if L complies with the guidance given by Lord Nicholls, then even if B2 is able to make out undue influence, L will not be fixed with notice of it. The result will be that, in most cases, if undue influence is made out, L will still obtain possession, and is unlikely to bring (or have any grounds for bringing) any claim against S. The other side of the coin, however, is that if, despite receiving independent legal advice from S, B2 has nevertheless succeeded in making out undue influence, B2 *is* likely to claim against S, because the fact that L can rely on S's involvement will result in B2's losing the property.

1 *Etridge (No 2)* [2001] UKHL 44, [2002] 2 AC 773 at [87]. The circumstances in which L is put on enquiry were thus substantially expanded from Lord Browne-Wilkinson's formulation in *Barclays Bank v O'Brien* [1994] 1 AC 180, at 196.
2 [2001] UKHL 44, [2002] 2 AC 773 at [79].
3 For the steps that needed to be taken by a bank in relation to pre-*Etridge (No 2)* cases to avoid being fixed with undue influence: see [2001] UKHL 44, [2002] 2 AC 773 at [80].

(b) Acting for the mortgagor or guarantor (B2)

9.25 B2 may be a co-habitee who has both legal and beneficial interests in the property to be charged; a co-habitee who has only a beneficial interest in the property; or B2 might have been asked to guarantee B1's liabilities, supporting the guarantee with a charge over property owned by B2 alone. In the first situation, B2 will be asked to become a party to the mortgage; in the second situation, he or she will probably be asked to sign a form consenting to the mortgage and agreeing that any interest of his or hers be postponed, i e will take effect subject to the mortgage.[1] Given the risk now said to be present in all non-commercial transactions of this nature[2] that B1, at whose instance L's money is being borrowed, has applied undue influence to B2, and following the guidance given by Lord Nicholls at para 79 of *Etridge (No 2)*, L will contact B2 to ask her to nominate a solicitor to advise her in relation to what she is being asked to do. S may then be instructed directly by B2, or, more usually, is instructed, and paid by L to give independent legal advice to B2 in person. Failures by S in advising B2 are capable of giving rise to claims against him or her by both B2 and L, as follows.

1 The purpose of this type of form is to prevent L being bound by an overriding interest of B2's in the property. See *Williams and Glyn's Bank Ltd v Boland* [1981] AC 487, HL.
2 See para 9.24, above.

(i) Liability to B2

9.26 Where S is instructed and paid by L, S owes the same duty to B2 that he would owe to any client who had instructed him or her directly and paid his or her fees. The essential feature of S's role is to *advise* B2, not to *approve* of the transaction, a distinction drawn with particular clarity by Fletcher Moulton LJ in *Coomber v Coomber*[1]:

'All that is necessary is that some independent person, free from any taint of the relationship, or of the consideration of interest which would affect the act, should put clearly before the person what are the nature and the consequences of the act. It is for adult persons of competent mind to decide whether they will do an act, and I do not think that independent and competent advice means independent and competent approval. It simply means that the advice shall be removed entirely from the suspected atmosphere; and that from the clear language of an independent mind, they should know precisely what they are doing.'

1 [1911] 1 Ch 723 at 730, cited with approval by Lord Nicholls [2001] UKHL 44, [2002] 2 AC 773 at [60].

9.27 The particular nature of that duty owed by S when instructed to advise B2 (at least with effect from the final appeal in *Etridge* (*No 2*), 11 October 2001) was analysed by Lord Nicholls. His summary must be set out in full:[1]

'I turn to consider the scope of the responsibilities of a solicitor who is advising the wife. In identifying what are the solicitor's responsibilities the starting point must always be the solicitor's retainer. What has he been retained to do? As a general proposition, the scope of a solicitor's duties is dictated by the terms, whether express or implied, of his retainer. In the type of case now under consideration the relevant retainer stems from the bank's concern to receive confirmation from the solicitor that, in short, the solicitor has brought home to the wife the risks involved in the proposed transaction. As a first step the solicitor will need to explain to the wife the purpose for which he has become involved at all. He should explain that, should it ever become necessary, the bank will rely upon his involvement to counter any suggestion that the wife was overborne by her husband or that she did not properly understand the implications of the transaction. The solicitor will need to obtain confirmation from the wife that she wishes him to act for her in the matter and to advise her on the legal and practical implications of the proposed transaction.

When an instruction to this effect is forthcoming, the content of the advice required from a solicitor before giving the confirmation sought by the bank will, inevitably, depend upon the circumstances of the case. Typically, the advice a solicitor can be expected to give should cover the following matters as the core minimum. (1) He will need to explain the nature of the documents and the practical consequences these will have for the wife if she signs them. She could lose her home if her husband's business does not prosper. Her home may be her only substantial asset, as well as the family's home. She could be made bankrupt. (2) He will need to point out the seriousness of the risks involved. The wife should be told the purpose of the proposed new facility, the amount and principal terms of the new facility, and that the bank might increase the amount of the facility, or change its terms, or grant a new facility, without reference to her. She should be told the amount of her liability under her guarantee. The solicitor should discuss the wife's financial means, including her understanding of the value of the property being charged. The solicitor should discuss whether the wife or her husband has any other assets out of which repayment could be made if the husband's business should fail. These matters are relevant to the seriousness of the risks involved. (3) The solicitor will need to state clearly that the wife has a choice. The decision is hers and hers alone. Explanation of the choice facing the wife will call for some discussion of the present financial position, including the amount of the husband's present indebtedness, and the amount of his current overdraft facility. (4) The solicitor should check whether the wife wishes to proceed. She should be asked whether she is content that the solicitor should write to the bank confirming he has explained to her the nature of the documents and the practical implications they may have for her, or whether, for instance, she would prefer him to negotiate with the bank on the terms of the transaction. Matters for negotiation could include the sequence in which the various securities will be called upon or a specific or lower limit to her liabilities. The solicitor should not give any confirmation to the bank without the wife's authority.

The solicitor's discussion with the wife should take place at a face-to-face meeting, in the absence of the husband. It goes without saying that the solicitor's explanations should be couched in suitably non-technical language. It also goes without saying that the solicitor's task is an important one. It is not a formality. The solicitor should obtain from the bank any information he needs. If the bank fails for any reason to provide information requested by the solicitor, the solicitor should decline to provide the confirmation sought by the bank.'

The Law Society has issued additional guidance to solicitors, derived from Lord Nicholls' analysis cited above, and has provided a draft standard form of letter for solicitors to send to B2 after advising him or her. [2]

1 [2001] UKHL 44, [2002] 2 AC 773 at [64]–[67].
2 'Undue Influence – solicitors' duties post *Etridge*', issued by the Law Society's Conveyancing and Land Law Committee in May 2002, reproduced at App V.17 of the *Conveyancing Handbook* (14th edn, 2007). For the model letter, see App VI.9.

9.28 If S fails to comply with these requirements but nevertheless reports to L that B2 has received independent legal advice, B2 is exposed for two reasons:

first, he or she is not given the advice and information required to break free of the undue influence which is in reality motivating his or her decision; and, secondly, the fact that S has reported, wrongly, to L that B2 has been appropriately advised is likely to mean that the charge in question will nevertheless be enforceable against B2 by L[1].

1 Arguably, if L is aware that the independent legal advice given by S is likely to have been of little practical effect, then B2 might yet be able to persuade the court that, notwithstanding the certificate from S, L could not reasonably have assumed that B2 entered the transaction of her own free will. Cf *National Westminster Bank plc v Rashida Bibi Amin* [2002] UKHL 9, [2002] 1 FLR 735, where S, who did not speak Urdu, advised B2, who did not speak English, which gave rise to the doubt that B2 could reasonably have been perceived as having received independent legal advice; *National Westminster Bank plc v Breeds* [2001] Lloyd's Rep Bank 98 (Lawrence Collins J), where L knew or ought to have known that S was conflicted out of advising B2 as a result of S's relationship to B1 and thus could not rely on the fact that S had advised B2; and *Lloyds TSB Bank plc v Gravell* (1 February 2000, unreported), where the Court of Appeal declined to strike out B2's defence that L must have entertained real doubts regarding the adequacy of the legal advice received by B2.

(ii)   *Liability to L*

9.29   If S has been paid by L to advise B2 and fails to ensure that B2 fully understands the nature of the document and consents to the transaction, it is arguable that S may be in breach not only of a duty to B2 but also of the terms of the retainer from L, alternatively of a duty of care arising from the fact that S knew that one of the principal purposes of giving advice to B2 was precisely in order to protect L's interests. S, in advising B2 at L's behest (and expense) in the manner envisaged by Lord Nicholls[1], can only do so if he or she is satisfied that to do so will not place him or her in a situation of having conflicting interests between L and B2[2]. If B2 is subject to undue influence, it is in the interests of both B2 and L that B2 not enter the charge, as the shadow of the potential undue influence defence to any possession action by L has an adverse effect on the quality of L's security. There seems no reason, therefore, why S, instructed by L to advise B2, should not owe both of those parties the same basic duty, namely to take reasonable care to advise B2 in the required manner. In *Connell v Odlum*[3] a husband engaged a solicitor to advise his wife on a pre-nuptial agreement whilst he himself was advised by other solicitors. His wife was later successful in having the prenuptial agreement set aside for undue influence. It was held that the solicitor owed a duty to the husband to ensure that he gave adequate advice to the wife. Even if S owes no duty to L arising out of the fact that he or she has accepted instructions to advise B2, in the event that S certifies (usually on the charge itself) that he or she has fully explained the nature of the document to B2 or given independent advice or advised B2 to seek independent advice when that is not true, S may be open to a claim of misrepresentation by L.

1 See *Etridge* (*No 2*) [2001] UKHL 44, [2002] 2 AC 773 at [64]–[67].
2 See [2001] UKHL 44, [2002] 2 AC 773 at [74] and rr 3.16(2)(a) and 3.17(6)(a) of the Solicitors' Code of Conduct 2007.

3 [1993] 2 NZLR 257.
4 In the light of the views expressed by Lord Nicholls, it would seem that (whatever duty of care S might owe to L in connection with the advice given to B2) S owes L no duty to communicate to L any information which might cause L to reconsider its decision to lend. Contrast *Halifax Building Society v Stepsky* [1996] Ch 1 and 207 (Edward Nugee QC reversed by CA on different grounds). The judge held that S owed L a duty to report that B1 intended to use L's advance to discharge a previous mortgage and repay his business debts whereas L had been told that the advance was required to acquire shares in a family business. Although it was a remortgage, S was instructed to act on behalf of both L and B2 and submitted a report on title.

9.30   Similarly, if S fails to obtain a consent form from B2 in circumstances where B2 has an overriding interest, it is likely that S will have breached the terms of his or her retainer by L.

(iii)   Damages in claims by B2

9.31   As indicated above, if L is fixed with notice of undue influence (which in reality is likely to happen only where L has instructed no solicitor to advise B2, but might also happen if L instructed a solicitor who is known to be incompetent to advise B2), B2's interest in the charged property may be unaffected despite S's breach of duty and B2 will probably have no claim against S. But in most cases L will not be fixed with notice of undue influence and B2's undue influence defence will fail, leaving him or her with a claim for damages against S. Where S has been joined to proceedings, he or she will wish to show that B2's allegation of undue influence is false; furthermore, on the alternative hypothesis that S might be found in breach of duty, S will seek to show that even if S had acted with reasonable care B2 would still have signed the documents in question, so that B2 cannot prove causation of loss against S[1]. If B2 is able to satisfy the court that he or she acted under undue influence and that this was referable to S's breach of duty, however, then B2 may have a claim to recover damages equal to the value of his or her interest in the charged property (plus any recoverable consequential losses).

1 Thus in *Etridge v Pritchard Englefield* [1999] PNLR 839, CA, Mrs Etridge's claim against her solicitors was dismissed despite her having failed in her defence against the Royal Bank of Scotland. The judge held that she would have executed the charge in any event and this was upheld by the Court of Appeal. The decision seems to depend on dicta in *Etridge (No 2)* in the Court of Appeal (reported at [1998] 4 All ER 705) which no longer appear to represent the law. The principal difficulty with this causation argument is that if S had acted with reasonable care, it would have discovered that B2 was acting under B1's undue influence. Even if S could prove that, regardless of its advice, B2 would have insisted on granting the charge, what S should have done in that situation would have been to amend the certificate to L so that it was perfectly clear that B2 was acting under the undue influence of B1 (c f *Bank of Credit & Commerce International v Aboody* [1990] 1 QB 923, CA at 951F to 952E. Note that *Aboody* was effectively overruled in *O'Brien*, but not in relation to this point). Although not determinative of the argument, it is also worth noting that it seems anomalous that S should be entitled to say that B2 would have signed the charge anyway when, as against B1, B2 is entitled to set aside the charge as of right, such that questions of causation do not arise: *UCB Corporate Services v Williams* [2002] EWCA Civ 555, [2002] 19 EG 149 (CS), [85]–[91].

9.32 Difficulties will arise if the subject property was charged prior to the loan by L to B1 or to B1 and B2 and the proceeds of the loan from L have been used to discharge that prior charge. In those circumstances, and if B2 has obtained the benefit of the discharge of the prior charge, then notwithstanding any undue influence in connection with the later charge, L may be subrogated to the rights of the prior chargee.[1] B2 will thus seek damages based upon a comparison between the position he or she is actually in and the position he or she would have been in if he or she had not agreed to the new charge over the property[2]. S may be able to argue that the mere acceptance of a loan by B2 cannot amount to damage.[3] Where B2 has no legal interest in the property, but relies upon an interest under a constructive trust which arises by reason of, for example, contributions to the purchase price or mortgage instalments in respect of the property, valuation of B2's interest may be more complex.

1 See *Boscawen v Bajwa* [1996] 1 WLR 328, CA and *Halifax v Omar* [2002] EWCA Civ 121, [2002] 16 EG 180 (CS).
2 See, e g *Harris v Nantes and Wilde* [1997] NPC 7 where substantial damages were awarded at first instance. In related proceedings B2 appears to have obtained both a declaration that a transfer forged by B1 was not binding on him *and* an order that B1 account to him for the proceeds of sale. The loss alleged against the defendants appears to have been based on the fact that B2 could not recover this sum from B1.
3 See *Saddington v Colleys Professional Services* [1999] Lloyd's Rep PN 140, CA.

(iv) Damages in claims by L

9.33 If L is not fixed with notice of undue influence then any claim which it may have against S for damages is likely to be restricted to consequential damages caused by the delay in obtaining possession and any additional legal costs. If L is fixed with notice of undue influence as a consequence of a breach of duty by S, if it is right that S owes L a relevant duty in relation to the advice given to B2, then S would be liable to L for the net value of B2's interest[1] in the security at the date on which it would have been sold together with any consequential costs. These may, however, be substantial, depending on the length of time B2 remains in the property until an order for sale is made (assuming that such an order is made, as it usually should be[2]).

1 Although the charge signed by B1 will not be legally effective per se, where B1 is guilty of unduly influencing B2, B1's own signature of the charge (if such there is) will be taken as evidence of severance by B1 of any joint tenancy, and B1's beneficial interest in the subject property will be charged in equity to L (c f *First National Bank plc v Achampong* [2003] EWCA Civ 487, [2003] All ER (D) 08 at [54]).
2 See *Achampong* (above) at [61]–[65].

(c) *Acting for both mortgagors*

9.34 S may also be instructed by B1 to act on behalf of both B1 and B2 and this often happens where B1 asks his or her solicitor to witness B2's execution of the charge. In *Etridge* (*No 2*), the House of Lords indicated that they considered the practice of acting for both B1 and B2 to be permissible, provided that there was no conflict between the interests of each client.[1] It will not always be easy for S to decide whether he can continue to represent both where B2 is being asked to charge his or her interest in the family home to secure the business debts of B1. Lord Nicholls gave the following guidance[2]:

> 'The advantages attendant upon the employment of a solicitor acting solely for the wife do not justify the additional expense this would involve for the husband. When accepting instructions to advise the wife the solicitor assumes responsibilities directly to her, both at law and professionally. These duties, and this is central to the reasoning on this point, are owed to the wife alone. In advising the wife the solicitor is acting for the wife alone. He is concerned only with her interests. I emphasise, therefore, that in every case the solicitor must consider carefully whether there is any conflict of duty or interest and, more widely, whether it would be in the best interests of the wife for him to accept instructions from her. If he decides to accept instructions, his assumption of legal and professional responsibilities to her ought, in the ordinary course of things, to provide sufficient assurance that he will give the requisite advice fully, carefully and conscientiously. Especially so, now that the nature of the advice called for has been clarified. If at any stage the solicitor becomes concerned that there is a real risk that other interests or duties may inhibit his advice to the wife he must cease to act for her.'

1 See the facts of *Credit Lyonnais Bank Nederland NV v Burch* [1997] 1 All ER 144, CA and *Mercantile Credit Co Ltd v Fenwick* [1997] NPC 120 (Carnwath J) (upheld in CA, [1999] Lloyds Rep PN 408) for good examples of the circumstances in which the conflict is soluble only by S declining to act for B2. In *Fenwick* S's advice to B2 was plainly inadequate. However, in that case B2 took the initiative and instructed her own solicitors whom she found through the Yellow Pages. This alone saved S from liability.
2 [2001] UKHL 44, [2002] 2 AC 773 at [74].

9.35 As noted by Lord Nicholls, where S reaches the conclusion that he or she cannot safely act for both clients, he or she must advise B2 of the potential conflict and tell him or her to obtain independent advice.[1] In the event that S continues to act for both B1 and B2 in those circumstances, he or she is likely to be in breach of duty to B2 for failing to explain fully the nature of the transaction.[2] As to damages in a claim by B2, the principles which apply are likely to be the same as set out at para 9.31, above.

1 S must also give clear and unequivocal advice: see *Mahoney v Purnell* [1996] 3 All ER 61 at 93g–94f. If S continues to act, having given an inadequate warning, he will be liable in negligence to B2.
2 See, eg, *Atkins v Atkins* [1993] EGCS 54. Solicitors failed to explain to the claimant that the true purpose of the transaction was that she should provide security for the debts of her son.

(*d*) *Acting for the lender alone*

9.36 In the normal course, L owes no duty of care to the persons to whom it lends money secured by way of a mortgage. In *Etridge* cases too, L itself owes no duty of care to either B1 or B2 and correspondingly, if S acts only for L and not for either B1 or B2, S owes B1 and B2 no duty of care either[1]. Before the final judgment in *Etridge* (*No 2*), it had been held that in discharging his duty to L, S is usually entitled to assume that B2 has received independent advice and is under no obligation to obtain written confirmation from B1's solicitor that he is acting for both B1 and B2 or, if not, that B2 has been independently advised.[2] Given that L is now put on notice of potential undue influence in every non-commercial transaction of the type under discussion in this section, it is submitted that S comes under a duty to check with L that it has obtained evidence to satisfy itself that B2 is not acting under the undue influence of B1[3]. Where both B1 and B2 are represented by separate solicitors it makes it extremely unlikely that any pressure placed on B2 will be 'undue'.[4]

1 Save that where B1 or B2 are unrepresented, S must take care (a) not to act in a way which might be characterised as taking unfair advantage of them and (b) not inadvertently to bring a duty of care into existence by volunteering any advice. See r 10.01 of the Solicitors' Code of Conduct 2007 and paras 2 and 3 of the guidance notes to that rule.
2 See *Mercantile Credit Co Ltd v Fenwick* [1999] Lloyd's Rep PN 408, CA. See also the facts of *Bank of Baroda v Shah* [1988] 3 All ER 24.
3 Cf *UCB Corporate Services Ltd v Williams* [2002] EWCA Civ 555, [2002] 19 EG 149 (CS) where the Court of Appeal noted with approval L's concession that, following *Etridge* (*No 2*) in the House of Lords, it could not establish that it did not have constructive knowledge merely by proving that it knew B2 was represented by an independent solicitor, ie, it could not assume that she had been advised regarding the charge.
4 *Fenwick* above is just such an example. B2 only received legal advice at all rather belatedly and on her own initiative.

(*e*) *Acting for the lender and the mortgagor*

9.37 Since most property is purchased with the assistance of mortgage finance, the purchaser's solicitor is almost invariably asked by the lender to act for it in connection with the mortgage. The solicitor may do this provided the terms of his or her retainer by the lender are defined and limited in the ways provided for in rr 3.16–3.22 of the Solicitors' Code of Conduct 2007[1]. The rules are designed to avoid the possibility of conflicts of interest arising and to provide reasonable limitations on the extent of the solicitor's duty to the lender. In the event that a solicitor accepted[2] instructions from a lender which went beyond these 'maximum terms'[3], Rule 3.21 of the Code purports to make the provisions of rr 3.16–3.20 prevail. It remains to be seen how effective that attempt to default to the 'maximum terms' will be.

1 Prior to the Solicitors' Code of Conduct 2007, the solicitor could act for lender and borrower provided that no conflict of interest arose and provided that the lender's instructions did not

exceed the limitations imposed by r 6 of the Solicitors Practice Rules 1990. The Law Society published a useful series of questions and answers relating to these rules when they first appeared in 1999, which is reproduced in App V.10 of the *Conveyancing Handbook* (14th edn, 2007) ('Questions and Answers on Practice Rule 6(3)'), reproduced from the *Gazette* dated 29 September 1999. For detailed discussion of the effect of rr 3.16–3.22 of the Solicitors' Code of Conduct (which are incorporated as contractual terms by member so the Council of Mortgage Lenders): see para 10.14ff and 10.23ff, below.

2 It should not, in theory, be possible for a solicitor to accept instructions that do not comply with Solicitors' Code of Conduct 2007 or its predecessors, because, in the event that a solicitor notices that a lender's instructions do not comply with the relevant rules, he or she should write to the lender expressly offering to vary the terms of the instructions so that the rules are complied with or declining to act altogether: see the standard form letters provided by the Law Society for this purpose, at Apps VI.6 and VI.7 of the *Conveyancing Handbook* (14th edn, 2007). The reality, however, is that lenders have asked solicitors to sign certificates of title that would put solicitors in breach of the relevant rules (see the article published in the *Gazette* dated 22 August 2002, reproduced at App V.19 of the *Conveyancing Handbook*), and it might be that some solicitors have accepted such instructions.

3 The expression is ours, not one used by the Law Society.

9.38 Rule 3.19 specifies what kinds of instruction may be accepted from a lender by a solicitor acting for a borrower, and includes express provision for the solicitor to accept instructions from the lender to advise any third party required to sign any document on the terms of that document (r 3.19(q)). Using again the terminology employed above, pursuant to that rule, S, retained by B1 and L, could accept instructions from L to advise B2 (subject always to the overriding principle that no instructions could be accepted which gave rise to a conflict of interest between the various clients). It may in practice be difficult for S to accept such instructions, as the possibilities for conflict are various. For example (and without limitation): first, S might receive information from B2 which is inconsistent with what, to S's knowledge, B1 had told S or L; second, S might receive information from B2 or make observations from which a reasonable solicitor would conclude that B2 had been coerced or prevailed upon to execute the charge or transfer; and, third, S might fail to advise B2 in sufficiently clear or strong terms, with the consequence that B2 executed a document without fully informed consent. Where S is in possession of information confidential to B1 when instructed by L, it is S's duty either to obtain B1's consent to reporting that information to L or to decline to act. If S continues to act he or she might be forced to choose between his duties to L or B1. If S has been instructed to report all material matters to L but fails to do so, S may be in breach of the terms of the retainer from L.[1] If S reports the information to L, he or she is in breach of duty to B1.

1 See e g the facts of *Halifax Building Society v Stepsky* [1996] Ch 1 and 207 (Edward Nugee QC reversed on other grounds by the Court of Appeal).

9.39 Before September 1999 (when the Law Society introduced r 6(3) of the Solicitors' Practice Rules 1990 and the *CML Handbook* came into existence), lenders occasionally asked solicitors acting to accept very limited instructions in connection with mortgages, e g to witness the borrower's signature on the charge and to undertake to use the loan moneys for the purpose of obtaining 'good marketable title' to the subject property. The limited nature of the instructions meant that the extent of the solicitor's obligations to the lender was restricted. A solicitor who had given such an undertaking was under no obligation to advise on matters which went to the value of the title, rather than to the question of whether the purchaser's title was marketable[1]. Since September 1999, simple forms of undertaking of that nature appear to be less frequent, with lenders preferring to retain the borrower's solicitor to give a more comprehensive advisory service[2].

1 *Barclays Bank plc v Weeks Legg & Dean* [1999] QB 309, CA. For more detailed discussion see paras 10.66 and 10.67, below.
2 See *CML Lenders' Handbook*, Section 5, addressing the 'surrounding circumstances' of the title upon which lenders require solicitors to report.

4 Duties to third parties

9.40 As discussed in chapter 1,[1] a solicitor ordinarily owes no duty to any party to a transaction for whom he or she does not act unless he or she 'steps outside' the terms of the retainer and may be said to have assumed responsibility to that third party. In the context of conveyancing, this issue has generally arisen in two situations: first, in the context of replies given by a vendor's solicitor to pre-contract inquiries; and, second, in the context of certificates of title where these are provided by the purchaser's solicitors to a third party (eg, an insurer) at the purchaser's direction.

1 See paras 1.23ff and 1.27ff, above.

(a) Pre-contract inquiries

9.41 When a vendor's solicitor answers pre-contract enquiries, he or she does so as agent for the client. If the client has given the solicitor misleading information, such that the answers he or she gives to pre-contract enquiries are false, the client may be liable to the purchaser, but the solicitor, as the disclosed agent of his or her principal, has no liability to the third party. If the client has given the solicitor the correct, or no, information, and the solicitor gives a false answer to pre-contract enquiries, then the client may be liable to the purchaser and (if so) the solicitor is likely to be liable to the client for having exposed him to that loss.[1] A question which might arise (if, for example, the vendor is unable to meet any liability to the purchaser) is whether the vendor's solicitor has any direct liability to the purchaser. There are two cases in which it has been held at first instance that a vendor's solicitor will not be held liable to a purchaser for errors made in answering pre-contract inquiries: *Gran Gelato Ltd v Richcliff (Group) Ltd*[2] and *Cemp Properties (UK) Ltd v Dentsply Research and Development Corpn Ltd*.[3] For reasons which are explored in chapter 1[4], it is doubtful whether a court at first instance or the Court of Appeal would be bound to follow them and in two cases it has been held arguable that a solicitor might be liable to third parties for errors in inquiries: *Wilson v Bloomfield*[5] and *First National Commercial Bank plc v Loxleys.*[6] Given the current developing state of the law regarding the imposition of liability in circumstances where a party may be said to have assumed responsibility[7], it is suggested that a duty of care might indeed be recognised in circumstances where (a) the answer given by the solicitor concerned matters regarding which the purchaser had no other means of acquiring knowledge, such that reasonable reliance was placed on the answer received,[8] (b) the context in which the solicitor gave the answer was such that he or she knew or ought to have known that the answer he or she was giving might not be accurate,[9] and (c) the solicitor had not lawfully excluded any liability he or she might otherwise incur by means of an appropriate disclaimer.

1 Cf the analysis of Hobhouse LJ in *McCullagh v Lane Fox* [1996] PNLR 205, CA.
2 [1992] Ch 560 (Sir Donald Nicholls V-C).
3 [1989] 2 EGLR 205, esp at 207 col 1 (Morritt J).
4 See paras 1.23–1.26, above.
5 (1979) 123 Sol Jo 860, CA.
6 [1997] PNLR 211, CA.
7 Cf *Precis (521) plc v William M Mercer Ltd* [2005] EWCA Civ 114, [2005] PNLR 28 at [24] (Arden LJ).
8 Cf the suggestion made by Hobhouse LJ in *McCullagh v Lane Fox* that a duty of care would be more likely to be imposed on an estate agent where the representation concerned matters not included in the particulars of sale or not expected to be included in them.
9 Cf *Williams v Natural Life Health Foods* [1998] 1 WLR 830, HL, per Lord Steyn at 836:

> 'The touchstone of liability is not the state of mind of the defendant. An objective test means that the primary focus must be things said or done by the defendant or on his behalf in dealings with the plaintiff. Obviously the impact of what a defendant says or does must be judged in the light of the relevant contextual scene. Subject to this qualification, the primary focus must be on exchanges (in which term I include statements and conduct) which cross the line between the defendant and the plaintiff'.

9.42 In the event that a solicitor is held to have owed a duty of care in respect of a statement of fact contained in the reply to an inquiry, the nature and effect of any representation contained in the reply will normally turn on the question and answer in issue. It is quite usual, however, for a vendor to answer questions about the existence of adverse rights and incumbrances 'not so far as the vendor is aware', leaving the purchaser to make his own inquiries of third parties or to rely upon the documents of title with which he has been provided. It has been held that this reply:

> '[R]epresents not merely that the vendor and his solicitor had no actual knowledge of a defect but also that they have made such investigations as could reasonably be expected to be made by or under the guidance of a prudent conveyancer.'[1]

1 *William Sindall plc v Cambridgeshire County Council* [1994] 3 All ER 932, CA at 942e (Hoffmann LJ).

9.43 Since the introduction of the Seller's Property Information Form (and, in respect of leasehold property, the Seller's Leasehold Information Form), the nature of the solicitor's exposure to liability for false answers given in pre-contract enquiries (at least in residential conveyancing) has changed. Prior to the introduction of the SPIF and the SLIF, the purchaser's solicitor made enquiries of the vendor's solicitor, to which the vendor's solicitor replied. The replies given were made on a standard form which contained a disclaimer to the effect that they were given on behalf of the vendor and without any responsibility on the part of the solicitors[1]. The SPIF and the SLIF, however, are intended to be completed by the vendor personally[2], and they thus contain no form of disclaimer of the solicitor's liability. Both forms, however, come in two parts, of which the second is to be completed by the vendor's solicitor. In Part II, the vendor's solicitor is required to answer various questions after checking the information given by the vendor in Part I against information in the solicitor's possession. Among the questions the solicitor is required to answer are 'Is the information provided by the seller in this form consistent with the information in your possession?' and 'Do you have any information in your possession to supplement the information provided by the seller?'. The two standard forms thus require the vendor's solicitor to make a direct representation to the purchaser regarding the information provided by the vendor, putting the solicitor under an undoubted duty to the vendor to take care in giving the answers. Perhaps for that reason, a practice took hold among certain solicitors of simply failing to answer Part II of the forms.

1 In *First National Commercial Bank v Loxleys* [1997] PNLR 211, CA, it was held arguable that this disclaimer negatived the existence of a duty of care (subject to the effect of the Unfair Contract Terms Act 1977) although the issue was not finally resolved.
2 See para 9.131, below.

9.44 The Law Society has issued guidance in this regard.[1] The guidance focuses on the fact that failing to complete Part II of the forms might amount to a breach of duty by the solicitor to his or her vendor client, and only briefly discusses the question of duties owed to the purchaser. Of particular interest in that latter discussion is the suggestion that failure by the vendor's solicitor to answer Part II 'would mean that the buyer's solicitor had failed to carry out all usual enquiries', such that he or she could not give a clear certificate of title to the lender, and thus threatening the entire transaction. It would seem arguable in such a situation (particularly if it arose after the Law Society guidance published in October 2004) that the vendor's solicitor could be liable to the purchaser for losses caused arising out of the collapse of the sale, as well as liable to his or her own client. Furthermore, and in any event, if the vendor's solicitor fails to answer Part II but does in fact have the means of discovering that the vendor's answers are inaccurate, the mere fact of not answering Part II is hardly likely to defeat any claim by the purchaser complaining that the answers given on the form were misleading.

1 See para 9.131 and n 4, below. The guidance was originally issued in two parts, one in the *Gazette* of 16 October 2003 and the other in the *Gazette* of 28 October 2004: both are reproduced in the *Conveyancing Handbook* (14th edn, 2007) at App V.24.

9.45 It is not unusual to see contracts of sale containing clauses seeking to exclude the duty to make reasonable investigations as in the following example:

'In the light of the decision in *William Sindall plc v Cambridgeshire County Council* it is hereby agreed and declared that the replies to Enquiries before Contract or information supplied in any Property Information Form are given to the best knowledge, information and belief of the Seller but neither the Seller nor his or her solicitors have made any further enquiries into such matters and the replies are therefore given on this basis.'

A clause such as this thus purports to exclude not only the duty to make reasonable investigations before giving the answer 'not so far as the vendor is aware', but also the solicitor's duty to make reasonable investigations in order to answer the questions quoted above from Part II of the SPIF. We doubt that such a clause would negative any duty of care owed by the vendor's solicitor to the purchaser, because it purports to render valueless the very thing which the solicitor appears (in answering Part II) expressly to have accepted an obligation to do.

(b) Certificates of title

9.46 In *Allied Finance v Haddow & Co*[1] the solicitors of the purchaser of a yacht provided a certificate to a third party insurance company that the proposed mortgage of the yacht would be binding on the purchaser and that there were no other charges over the vessel. In fact, a limited company was acquiring the yacht and the vendor had a lien over it for a part of the purchase price. The solicitor was held to owe a duty of care to the finance company. Cooke J stated:[2]

'That is a classic duty of care situation … The proximity is almost as close as it could be, short of contract. Nor are there any sufficient negativing considerations. Far from disclaiming responsibility, the solicitor has virtually in terms accepted it. It would be strange if the law failed to impose a duty.'

Although *Haddow* was not cited in the judgments[3] the Court of Appeal reached a similar result in *N M Rothschild & Sons Ltd v Berensons*.[4] In that case, the solicitor's client was borrowing money from a syndicate of banks, of which only the lead bank gave any instructions to the solicitor. It is of note that the defendant firm was found liable not to the lead bank Barclays Bank plc, to whom the funds request (which contained the certificate) was addressed, but also to an individual bank in the syndicate, Rothschild, which had agreed to provide the funds. In sophisticated transactions a firm of solicitors may be asked to provide certificates of title both to a purchaser or to a lender or to a syndicate of lenders. Both of these authorities suggest that an English court would impose a duty of care upon the solicitor who failed to exercise reasonable care in providing such certificates.

1 [1983] NZLR 22, which was cited with approval by Sir Donald Nicholls V-C in *Gran Gelato Ltd v Richcliff (Group) Ltd* [1992] Ch 560.
2 [1983] NZLR 22 at p 24, line 45 to p 25, line 2. See Richardson J to similar effect at p 30, lines 1–21.
3 Although it was relied upon by Knox J at first instance [1995] NPC 107. It should also be noted that *Anns v Merton LBC* [1978] AC 728 and *Scott Group Ltd v McFarlane* [1978] 1 NZLR 553 were both relied upon. Neither is now regarded as good law in this country.
4 [1997] NPC 15, CA. The facts are set out in para 1.28, above.

9.47 There appears to be no reported authority on the question whether a disclaimer given by a solicitor to a third party would either negative the existence of a duty of care or, if it were necessary to do so, satisfy the test of reasonableness provided by s 11(3) of the Unfair Contract Terms Act 1977. In the context of certificates of title, it is suggested that the determination of these issues might be of some significance, as it is unlikely that in circumstances where a solicitor had been personally requested to verify legal issues for a potential purchaser or lender, a blanket disclaimer of liability for negligence would he held to be reasonable. That being said, a sufficiently clearly worded disclaimer submitted to a purchaser who had the benefit of legal advice might very well negative any assumption of responsibility. For the present, at least, it would be prudent for a solicitor to assume that any disclaimer might be held unreasonable.

9.48 It is more likely that the court would uphold as reasonable a more limited disclaimer. For instance, if the certificate is a 'for your eyes only' certificate limited to named or identified parties, the court would be likely to follow *Omega Trust Co Ltd v Wright Son & Pepper*[1] (where the disclaimer was of this kind) and limit the solicitor's liability to those parties so named unless express consent had been sought from the solicitor to circulate the certificate to other recipients.

1 [1997] 18 EG 120 (considered further in para 1.32, above).

(c) *Miscellaneous cases*

9.49 In very few cases apart from those discussed above has an English court been prepared to find that a solicitor who acts in relation to a conveyancing transaction owes a duty to anybody other than his client.[1] If a solicitor provides a reference in relation to the financial standing or honesty of his client either to a lender or another party, then it is suggested that he would come under a duty of care for the accuracy of the reference or the financial information provided in the same way as an accountant.[2] Apart from this example, most of the cases in which a duty of care has been extended to a third party are cases in which the third party is intimately connected with the client or the client's personal or corporate alter ego.[3] *Woodward v Wolferstans*[4] is a good example. The claimant's father instructed the defendant firm to act in relation to the acquisition and mortgage of a property on behalf of the claimant who was 22 years old. There was no contact between the claimant and the defendants and she did not rely upon them at all. It was held that they owed a duty of care to her because of the close relationship of proximity, but following *White v Jones*[5] the duty only extended to carrying out her father's instructions and not to advising her personally about the nature of the obligations which she had undertaken. It is not entirely clear why no contractual retainer came into existence. Even if the claimant gave no formal instructions to the defendants, she must have tacitly agreed for them to act on her behalf when she signed the documents and permitted them to be returned to the defendants.[6] A more controversial example (although probably correct on its facts) is *Dean v Allin & Watts*[7], where the defendant solicitor was found liable to his client's mortgage lender (with whom he had no contractual relationship) for failing to obtain good title to the mortgaged property. The court held that, since the solicitor knew the lender had not obtained any legal advice but was relying on him for that, and since there was no conflict of interest in the solicitors acting for the purchaser and the lender, the solicitor came under a duty to take reasonable steps to ensure that the lender obtained a valuable security. Finally, note that in *Jenmain Builders v Steel & Steel*[8], the solicitor defendants, who acted for the vendors of property, had been found liable to disappointed purchasers for breach of duty in failing to inform the purchasers that they were in a contract race with other potential purchasers.

1 The Commonwealth authorities are digested in Jackson and Powell *Professional Negligence* (6th edn, 2007) at11—061.
2 See *Midland Bank v Cameron, Thom, Peterkin & Duncans* [1988] SLT 611. On the facts the solicitor was not held to have assumed responsibility for the accuracy of the statements.
3 For further discussion of cases in which the court has either implied a retainer or held that the solicitor has assumed a duty of care see paras 1.8 and para 1.23,. above. See, for instance, *Johnson v Gore Wood* [2002] EWHC 776 (Ch) (Hart J). The decision on damages was the subject matter of an appeal at [2003] EWCA Civ 1728.
4 [1997] NPC 51 (Martin Mann QC).
5 [1995] 2 AC 207.
6 Compare *Hughes v Richards* [2004] EWCA Civ 266, [2004] PNLR 706 and other cases which consider whether *White v Jones* applies to inter vivos transactions considered in paras 1.33–1.35, above.
7 [2001] Lloyd's Rep PN 605, CA (considered in paras 1.23 and 1.25, above).
8 [2000] Lloyd's Rep PN 549, CA. The decision as to liability is controversial following the remarks made by Chadwick LJ at [21].

(*d*)   *Damages*

9.50   In *Haddow* the lender recovered from the borrower's solicitors the balance of the loan outstanding after the boat had been sold and apart from the question of interest, no issue was raised about damages in the appeal. No guidance can be derived from the cases about the quantum of damages to be recovered from a solicitor in the event that he is found liable to a third party. In lenders' cases where reliance is laid on a certificate of title to a security it seems only right that damages should be restricted to the amount by which the value would have been affected at the date of the certificate by analogy with valuers' cases. In other cases, the valuation method[1] is likely to be applied.

1 For the *SAAMCo* principle see para 3.35ff, above and paras 10.73ff and 10.79ff, below. For the valuation method see paras 9.106–9.116, below.

C   ACTING FOR THE PURCHASER

1   Duties before contract

(a) *Introduction*

9.51   The duty of a solicitor to give his or her client commercial advice is considered in para 2.35ff, above. As discussed there, a solicitor has in general terms no duty to inform his client that the purchase of property he is about to make will be unwise or prove to be commercially imprudent. However, because the purchase of land is complex, involving a number of professionals and a number of stages, a solicitor may well be obliged to give some advice with commercial implications. The nature of that type of advice is now considered. Whilst an attempt is made to generalise as much as possible, it should be noted that the advice which is required by the client will to some extent depend on that individual. Even in the context of relatively straightforward residential convey-ancing, the advice which will be required by a first-time buyer with no legal experience whatsoever may differ substantially from that required by a client who is moving house for the second or third time. As Donaldson LJ put it, in *Carradine Properties Ltd v DJ Freeman*[1]:

> 'A solicitor's duty to his client is to exercise all reasonable skill and care in and about his client's business. In deciding what he should do and what advice he should tender the scope of his retainer is undoubtedly important, but it is not decisive. If a solicitor is instructed to prepare all of the documentation needed for the sale or purchase of a house, it is no part of his duty to pursue a claim by the client for unfair dismissal. But if he finds unusual covenants or planning restrictions, it may indeed be his duty to warn of the risks and dangers of buying the house at all, notwithstanding that the client has made up his mind and is not seeking advice about that ... the precise scope of the duty will depend inter alia upon the extent to which the client appears to need advice.'

1 18 February 1982, CA now reported at [1999] Lloyd's Rep PN 483.

9.52 Regardless of a client's particular degree of experience or expertise, however, it is frequently likely to be unattractive for a solicitor who has omitted[1] to give certain relevant advice to argue that his client's degree of experience meant that it was outside the ambit of his duty to give that advice. Such an argument amounts to a submission by the solicitor that he or she was entitled to assume that the client would know what to do. In *Shelley v Phillips & Co*[2], Rimer J observed, in the context of an allegation of contributory negligence, but in our view equally applicable to the question of whether a solicitor can say that he or she does not owe a duty to advise simply because of the experience of the client[3]:

'... the matter of which complaint is levelled at the solicitor is peculiarly within the area of professional expertise for which the client consulted the solicitor in the first place. In those cases it will generally come ill from a solicitor to assert that his client should have been able to look after himself ...'[4]

1 If the solicitor has volunteered advice which is incorrect, he will of course be liable if that advice turns out to be incorrect.
2 (26 July 2000, unreported).
3 [126].
4 See also, to similar effect, Laddie J's remarks in *Credit Lyonnais SA v Russell Jones & Walker* [2002] EWHC 1310 (Ch), [2003] PNLR 2 at [21]. There are nevertheless occasions on which the court will accept that the claimant was perfectly well able to appreciate for himself the very point which he complains his solicitor should have advised him about. See *Aslan v Clintons* (1983) 134 NLJ 584 (businessman well aware that if he failed to comply with his obligations under a contract he might be sued by the other party); *Haigh v Wright Hassall & Co* [1994] EGCS 54, CA (solicitor owed no duty to advise clients not to exchange contracts until they had raised the funds for the deposit as the clients understood the legally binding nature of an exchange of contracts); and *Stone Heritage Developments Ltd v Davis Blank Furniss* [2007] EWCA Civ 765 (solicitors' retainer limited by the nature of the instructions given, such that no duty arose to give commercial advice as to the wisdom of entering the agreement which the solicitors had been instructed to draft). A number of these cases are considered in detail in para 2.39, above.

9.53 In the converse situation, where the client possesses expert knowledge and the solicitor does not, the solicitor nevertheless comes under a duty to understand the contract of sale and its likely effect to the extent necessary to give that advice which a solicitor might reasonably be expected to give[1].

1 Cf *Clarke v Iliffes Booth Bennett* [2004] EWHC 1731 (Ch) (vendor's solicitors failed to equip themselves with sufficient knowledge to correct the claimant vendor's misunderstanding regarding the trigger for a purchaser to exercise an option to purchase granted by the vendor; the trigger involved a complex question of planning law).

(b) *General advice to be given by the solicitor*

9.54 The Law Society's *Conveyancing Handbook*[1] contains a useful checklist of questions for the solicitor acting for a purchaser[2]. From the checklist, it appears that the Law Society would ordinarily expect practitioners to advise purchasers in relation to: the amount of stamp duty land tax payable given the purchase price; the effect of the timing of completion on the timing of the first mortgage payment; any VAT considerations relating to the transaction; possible sources of finance, including bridging finance; relevant insurance[3]; the ways in which the property might be held by co-owners; and even the affordability of the transaction.[4]

1 (14th edn, 2007) at 1.8. Although it does not have the force of law, the reality is that departure from the guidance given in the *Handbook* is very likely to amount to evidence of breach of duty. Mere compliance with the *Handbook* will not of itself necessarily mean that the solicitor has fulfilled his duty, however, if the court considers that the *Handbook* is in some respect deficient: see *Cottingham v Attey Bower & Jones* [2000] Lloyd's Rep PN 591 (Rimer J) at 600, col 1.

2 Note that solicitors acting in residential conveyancing may use the National Conveyancing Protocol (introduced in March 1990, and now in its 5th edition). A copy can be found at App III.1 of the *Conveyancing Handbook.* That Protocol, albeit not intended to expand the solicitor's common law duties (see the Council of the Law Society's 1990 Statement regarding the National Protocol for domestic freehold and leasehold property, para 4) nevertheless provides a useful checklist of the usual steps to be followed by purchasers' and vendors' solicitors.

3 Cf *Knight v Tuberville Woodbridge* (18 March 1999, unreported), where the defendant solicitors were found in breach of duty in failing to confirm that life insurance was in place before exchange of contracts.

4 Checklist, para (w). Although at first glance surprising, this is arguably consistent with the solicitor's duty under r 1.04 of the Solicitors' Code of Conduct 2007 ('You must act in the best interests of each client').

9.55   The conveyancing solicitor should also ensure that before exchange of contracts the purchaser has been advised to commission a survey and to have considered the results:

> 'since once exchange has taken place the client will no longer have the right to withdraw from the transaction on the grounds of a physical defect in the property. The results of the survey may reveal matters which will require further investigation by the buyer's solicitor, or even give grounds for the negotiation of a reduction in the purchase price, both of which must, where appropriate, be conducted before a binding contract is entered into'[1].

The conveyancing solicitor should also be aware of any potential liability on the part of the client to a future capital gains tax liability and advise the client accordingly[2]. It is suggested that for all practical purposes, the following paragraph of the Final Report of the Royal Commission on Legal Services 1979[3] (the Benson Commission) has now been given legal effect and represents the law:

> 'It is at this point that the solicitor should discuss with his client all matters which the client should consider carefully before deciding whether to enter a binding contract, for example, the means of financing the transaction, the type of mortgage required, the neces-

sity for mortgage protection, the names in which the property will be taken, matters relating to capital gains and capital transfer tax and the date required for completion. In general the solicitor will discuss whether the client is satisfied with the survey, has taken account of any proposed development in the neighbourhood and, in general, whether the property suits his requirements.'

1 See the *Conveyancing Handbook* (14th edn, 2007) at 13.3.2. As we suggested in the first edition of this work, it would seem that general practice has moved on considerably since *Buckland v Mackesy* (1968) Estates Gazette 968, CA, a decision which now seems unlikely to be followed.
2 See the *Conveyancing Handbook* (14th edn, 2007) at 15.1.1. Unless he or she has expressly negatived it by agreeing with the client that taxation advice should be the responsibility of an accountant, it is always the solicitor's duty to point out any tax 'traps for the unwary' arising from the proposed transaction: *Hurlingham Estates Ltd v Wilde* [1997] 1 Lloyd's Rep 525, where Lightman J also remarked that the practice of conveyancing and commercial law 'must necessarily involve time and again tax implications of proposed transactions and decisions' and the reasonably competent practitioner must be aware of such implications. The decision is considered in greater detail in para 1.6, above.
3 Cmnd 7648, Vol 1, para 21.15 cited in *Emmet on Title* (2007) Vol 1 at 1.014.

9.56 Where the client is proposing to acquire a special property (eg, a newly constructed property[1]; a leasehold[2]; part only of the vendor's property[3]; property subject to a draft local development plan[4]; a freehold subject to a statutory tenancy; the lease of a public house; the right to manage leasehold property; the right to collective enfranchisement under the Commonhold and Leasehold Reform Act 2002; or the residue of a long lease in the hope of exercising the right to enfranchise under the Leasehold Reform Act 1967 (as amended) or the Leasehold Reform, Housing and Urban Development Act 1993) there will probably be additional matters on which the client is likely to be entitled to receive advice. In particular, where the client is seeking to exercise a statutory right of enfranchisement and a highly complex valuation exercise must be undertaken, the solicitor is likely to have to advise the client to obtain specialist valuation advice.

1 A solicitor has been held to have been in breach of duty in not confirming that a builder-vendor was duly registered with the National Housebuilders' Council (NHBC), and thus not appreciating that the NHBC certificate offered by the builder was valueless: *Rickards v Jones* [2002] EWCA Civ 1344, [2003] PNLR 13.
2 See paras 9.65–9.68, below.
3 See the *Conveyancing Handbook* (14th edn, 2007), Part J.
4 Cf *Motor Crown Petroleum Ltd v SJ Berwin*, CA (10 March 2000, unreported), where the solicitors were held to have been in breach of duty in failing to advise the claimant developer that a local development plan could be challenged.

9.57 Finally, there may be other reasons why the solicitor should advise his client about the legal effect and consequence of entering a binding contract. In *Attard v Samson*[1] the client assumed possession of the property and carried out extensive repairs in the expectation that a contract would be made. It never was.

The defendant was negligent in failing to advise him of the risk which he was running in carrying out repairs before contract and in ensuring that a binding contract was made immediately.

1   (1966) 110 Sol Jo 249 (Phillimore J). The defendant acted for both parties and negligence was admitted.

(c) Searches and inquiries

9.58   Given that (subject to any duty of the vendor to make disclosure) it is for the purchaser to be sure of what he is purchasing, the purchaser's solicitor's duty arises from the purchaser's need to find out as much as possible about the property before becoming committed to the transaction. Thus the purchaser's solicitor is bound to satisfy himself or herself that the property being sold corresponds with that which the purchaser believes he or she is acquiring; that the vendor has good title to the property to be sold; and to make all necessary inquiries of the vendor to be satisfied that the property which the client wishes to acquire is free from any charges, encumbrances or adverse interests (other than those disclosed by the vendor and agreed to by the purchaser)[1]. The solicitor does not guarantee the title of the property but it is clear that the duty is not discharged simply by submitting standard form preliminary enquiries to the vendor (or, in the case of residential conveyancing) reading the vendor's answers to the Seller's Property Information Form. The solicitor is bound to ask additional inquiries where they are necessary.[2] If those replies turn out to be inconsistent with the information supplied already either by the vendor, his solicitors, the client or estate agents, or they raise doubts about the accuracy of information provided or give rise to additional concerns, the solicitor has a duty to follow them up with the vendor's solicitors and inform his client of any inconsistency.[3] Even if the vendor has (unknown to the purchaser's solicitor) misrepresented the position, it may nevertheless be necessary to make further investigations with third parties, in particular the local authority. [4] On occasion, English solicitors become involved in assisting clients to acquire property abroad. In those circumstances, even where a local lawyer is handling the actual conveyancing, unless their retainer is carefully worded and limited, the English solicitors are likely to owe the client a duty to take care to ensure that the searches that have been carried out by the foreign lawyer have been satisfactorily completed.[5]

1   For an example of solicitors being found in breach of duty for failing to advise their client that it would be taking the property subject to three prior charges, see *Greymalkin v Copleys* [2004] EWCA Civ 1754, [2004] PNLR 44.
2   *Goody v Baring* [1956] 1 WLR 448 esp at 453–48, CA.
3   *Computastaff Ltd v Ingledew Brown Bennison and Garrett* (1983) 268 Estates Gazette 906 (McNeill J), esp at 911, col 1. The duty to pass on to the client such information is discussed in *Mortgage Express Ltd v Bowerman* [1996] 2 All ER 836, CA, in Lord Bingham MR's judgment. It was held there that the solicitor who came into possession of information which suggested that

his client might be over-paying for the property was obliged to communicate this to the client so that the latter could decide what, if anything, to do. See also *Roiter Zucker v Khadijeh Minai* [2005] EWHC 2672 (QB) (Field J) at [69]–[72] where it was held that a solicitor was negligent in failing to point out an inconsistency (although the breach of duty did not result in loss).

4 *Cottingham v Attey Bower & Jones* [2000] Lloyd's Rep PN 591, where Rimer J held that the purchaser's solicitor, having asked for a copy of building regulation consent from the vendors, should have ensured that he obtained a copy (from the vendors or from the local authority) and (when no such copy could be obtained, consent never having been granted) advised the purchasers of the potential ramifications of part of the property being unlawfully built.

5 *Gregory v Shepherds* [2000] PNLR 769, CA.

(i) Boundaries and dimensions

9.59 The responsibility for identifying the precise line of boundaries and the ownership of boundary markers usually lies with the vendor under the terms of the standard form contracts of sale[1]. The vendor's solicitor usually therefore comes under a duty to his client to check the boundaries shown on the title deeds against those shown on any estate agent's particulars. If there are no estate agent's particulars or there is any doubt about the precise extent of the land being acquired, the purchaser's solicitor is likely to be in breach of duty to his client if he or she does not draw the uncertainty regarding boundaries to the client's attention and recommend that a surveyor be instructed or the client otherwise satisfy himself (including by requiring the vendor to enter specific agreements with his or her neighbour(s) regarding the boundaries in question) as to the extent of the property being acquired[2]. Examples of cases where solicitors have been found in breach of duty in this area include the following: *Mercantile Building Society v J W Mitchell Dodds & Co*: part of house not included in registered title, solicitors found liable for failure to check filed plan against agent's plan; *Wapshott v Davies Donovan & Co*: extension built over land owned by neighbour, solicitors found liable for failure to investigate title; *McManus Developments Ltd v Barbridge Properties Ltd*: fence three feet north of the boundary shown on the filed plan, solicitors found liable for failing to identify and point out the discrepancy after the neighbouring owner moved the fence; *Barclay-White v Guillaume & Sons*: solicitors found liable for failure to notice a discrepancy between estate agent's particulars and the filed plan of the property; *Nielsen v Watson*: driveway and garage excluded from property shown on the plan prepared by client's surveyor, solicitor found liable for failing to take instructions from client about the discrepancy; *Hondon Developments Ltd v Powerise Investments Ltd*: solicitor liable for failing to spot discrepancy between plan attached to draft and final agreements.[3]

1 See Standard Conditions of Sale (4th edn) cl 4.4.1 and Standard Commercial Property Conditions of Sale (2nd edn) cl 6.4.1.

2 See the *Conveyancing Handbook* (14th edn, 2007), B26.1.2 and B26.2.2. Note also that the purchaser's solicitor may also owe the purchaser's mortgagee a duty to ensure that the boundaries of the security are properly defined: see para 6.2 of Part 1 of the *Council of Mortgage Lenders Handbook* (2nd edn), 2 July 2007.

3 [1993] NPC 99: [1996] PNLR 361; [1996] PNLR 431: [1996] EGCS 123; (1981) 125 DLR (3d) 326; [2006] PNLR 1. In *Scarfe v Adams* [1981] 1 All ER 843 the Court of Appeal gave general guidance about the scale and dimensions of plans. It is suggested that if a solicitor failed to appreciate that plans to be attached to a contract had been prepared without taking heed of this guidance, or failed to make further inquiries where plans were not sufficiently detailed, this would be a breach of duty.

(ii) Local authority searches

9.60 The solicitor should ordinarily make enquiries of the local authority using the standard form CON 29, which comes in two parts, the first part dealing with standard enquiries, the second with optional enquiries[1]. Local authorities do not, however, accept liability for the answers given to the questions raised on form CON 29 save in cases of negligence[2], and the solicitor must therefore consider the answers given carefully. Where local authority searches give rise to doubts or additional concerns, the solicitor has a duty to follow them up.[3] Given that penalties for breach of planning and building regulations continue to affect the land, a solicitor who fails to discover a breach by the vendors of planning law is likely to be in breach of duty to his or her client. In addition to checking whether the property as built complies with planning requirements, the solicitor should also discover whether his or her client's intended use of the property might involve any alteration of the property which might be prohibited by local planning regulations (eg, property situated in Green Belt land).[4] A solicitor is not always bound to make a commons search in a densely built-up area but should do so if it is vacant land or land which has not been built on.[5] If his or her inquiries reveal the existence of potential encumbrances, restrictions or adverse interests, the solicitor is bound to communicate that information to the client.[6]

1 A copy of the current (2002) edition of form CON 29 may be found in the *Conveyancing Handbook* (14th edn, 2007), App VI.10 and a copy of the guidance notes for solicitors at Appendix V.18.
2 For an example of a case involving a local authority's alleged negligence in giving responses to standard form enquiries, see *Sydney Gooden v Northamptonshire County Council* [2001] EWCA Civ 1744, [2002] PNLR 18.
3 See *Faragher v Gerber* [19941 EGCS 122 (HHJ Lachs). In *GP & P Ltd v Bulcraig and Davies* [1986] 2 EGLR 148 (John Gorman QC) (appeal on damages at [1988] 1 EGLR 138), the judge held at 151A that a surveyor who made an oral inquiry as to the contents of the register might be obliged to follow it up depending on the answer. (The search was negative but as it happened the reply to the solicitor's search in writing revealed the existence of planning consent which turned out to be restrictive of user.) See *Emmet on Title* (2007) Vol 1 at 1.031 et seq for the subject matter of local authority searches.
4 Cf the *Conveyancing Handbook* (14th edn, 2007), B24.3.1–B24.3.3. See also *Raintree v Holmes* (1984) 134 NLJ 522, per Hobhouse J:

'just as any solicitor would check and consider the effect and significance of an easement or restrictive covenant, so also he should clearly check and consider any planning permission'.

5 *G & K Ladenbau Ltd v Crawley v de Reya* [1978] 1 WLR 266 at 278F–H and 289A–C.

6 *Strover v Harrington* [1988] Ch 390 at 409H–410A (Sir Nicolas Browne-Wilkinson V-C). The solicitor has authority to receive all relevant information on the client's behalf and a positive duty to pass it on.

9.61 Cases illustrating solicitors' breaches of duty in this regard include the following: *Lake v Bushby:* solicitor liable for failure to advise that no planning permission had been granted; *G & K Ladenbau Ltd v Crawley & de Reya:* solicitor liable for failure to make commons search; *GP & P Ltd v Bulcraig and Davies:* solicitor liable for failure to notice planning restrictions; *Raintree Ltd v Homes:* solicitor liable for failure to check currency of planning permission (which was due to expire between exchange and completion); *Oates v Pittman & Co:* solicitor liable for failure to find out that there was no planning permission for use as holiday-lets and of building regulation and fire prevention requirements if an application for a retrospective permission was to be made; *Faragher v Gerber:* solicitor liable for failure to follow up a reply to a local authority search which suggested that the purchaser should consult the LDDC; *Owen v Fielding:* solicitor liable for failure to make adequate commons search; *Cygnet Health Care v Elletson & Co*: solicitor liable for failing to obtain full planning history of property being purchased with a view to development; *Fashion Brokers v Clarke Hayes*: solicitor unreasonably relied on information given to him orally by local authority regarding planning permission for proposed user of property because the conversation was short and informal; *Foreman v O'Driscoll*: solicitor in breach of duty in failing to discover that property was subject to a public right of way (but no loss caused); *Gerrard v Read Hind Stewart*: solicitor in breach of duty in not discovering presence of planning restriction (but no loss caused); *Dent v Davis Blank Furniss*: solicitors liable for failing to discover that much of the property was registered as common land; *Harwood v Taylor Vintners*: solicitor in breach of duty in failing to assess local search results and advise claimants of lack of formal grant of rights to use a drain (but no loss caused); *Grosvenor 52 International Ltd v Holy*: solicitor liable for failing to advise generally on the planning position affecting property being purchased by a developer; *Asiansky Television plc v Bayer Rosin*: solicitor failed to appreciate the effect of implementation of compulsory purchase orders which affected land to be acquired by his developer client.[1]

1 [1949] 2 All ER 964; [1978] 1 WLR 266; [1986] 2 EGLR 148 (appeal on damages at [1988] 1 EGLR 138); (1984) 134 NLJ 453, CA; (1998)76 P & CR 490, CA; [1994] EGCS 122; [1998] EGCS 110; (18 May 1999, unreported); [2000] PNLR 473, CA; [2000] Lloyd's Rep PN 720; (CA, 29 November 2000, unreported); [2001] Lloyd's Rep PN 534; [2003] EWHC 471 (Ch), (2003) Times, 1 April; [2003] EWHC 2413 (Ch); [2004] EWHC 1362 (QB).

(iii) Rates and tenancies

9.62 Where the property to be acquired is the reversion to a lease, the vendor's statement of the rent receivable should be checked by the solicitor. Thus in

Goody v Baring, the solicitor was held liable for failure to establish whether rents of the property were liable to be reduced on certification under the Rent Acts. Similarly, where statements have been made regarding the rateable value of a property, the solicitor should take care to check the accuracy of such statements: c f *Computastaff Ltd v Ingledew, Brown Bennison and Garrett.*[1]

1 [1956] 1 WLR 448 and (1983) 268 Estates Gazette 906. The facts of *Goody v Baring* are not likely to arise again in practice, but it remains critical for purchasing landlord's solicitors to satisfy themselves about tenancies because of the Landlord & Tenant Act 1987.

(iv) Easements and restrictive covenants

9.63 The standard form contracts of sale in both residential and commercial conveyancing provide that the purchaser will take the property subject to all encumbrances including those which would have been discoverable by inspection of the property[1]. The purchaser's solicitor's duty to his or her client thus ordinarily includes a duty to check not only that the purchaser will have the benefit of such easements as are necessary for the enjoyment of the property, but also that the property is not subject to easements or restrictive covenants that might adversely affect the enjoyment of the property. The following cases illustrate various ways in which purchasers' solicitors have or have not been in breach of duty in connection with easements and restrictive covenants: *Ford v White:* solicitor liable for failure to advise on terms of restrictive covenant against building; *Piper v Daybell Court-Cooper & Co:* solicitor liable for failure to establish and advise on the existence of a right of way; *King v Hawkins & Co:* solicitor liable for failure to discover public highway; *Strover v Harrington:* solicitor should have advised that he had been told (contrary to the replies to inquiries) that the property had no mains drainage; *Walker v Giffen Couch & Archer:* solicitor liable for failure to discover existence of public footpath; *Hayes v Dodd:* solicitor liable for failing to establish that a workshop and maisonette had a right of way for two way traffic; *Reeves v Thrings & Long:* solicitor not liable for failing to explain that there was no secure right of way to a hotel car park; *Bittlestone* v *Keegan:* solicitor liable for failure to point out a covenant which prevented the owner from carrying out alterations; *Carvin v Dunham Brindley & Linn:* solicitor not liable for failure to advise purchaser that he should not be satisfied with a licence of drainage through an unadopted drain but acquire the freehold (or an easement); *Carter* v *TG Baynes & Sons:* solicitor liable for failure to notice covenant restrictive of development; *Tucker v MB Allen & Co*: solicitors liable for failing to advise claimants that their right of way from one part of the property to the other was not the subject of documentary title and would have to be established by evidence; *Queen Elizabeth's Grammar School Blackburn v Banks Wilson*: solicitor liable for failing to advise claimant that the interpretation of a restrictive covenant was open to dispute.[2]

1 See Standard Conditions of Sale (4th edn) cl 3.1.2(b) and Standard Commercial Property Conditions of Sale (2nd edn) cl 3.1.2(b).

2 [1964] 1 WLR 885; (1969) 210 Estates Gazette 1047; (1982) Times, 28 January; [1988] Ch 390; [1988] EGCS 64; [1990] 2 All ER 815; [1996] PNLR 265; [1997] EGCS 8; [1997] EGCS 90, CA; [1998] EGCS 109; [2001] PNLR 37; [2001] EWCA Civ 1360, [2002] PNLR 14. In *Bittlestone v Keegan* [1997] EGCS 8, Sir John Vinelott stated that it was the solicitor's duty to point out the nature and effect of every restrictive covenant unless unenforceable.

(e) Advice on the terms

9.64   It goes without saying that the solicitor must advise his client fully about the terms of the contract which he is about to enter. In *Walker v Boyle*[1] Dillon J gave the following guidance:

> 'It is, of course, the duty of a solicitor to advise his client about any abnormal or unusual term in a contract, but I think it is perfectly normal and proper for a solicitor to use standard forms of conditions of sale such as the National Conditions of Sale. I do not think he is called on to go through the small print of those somewhat lengthy conditions with a toothcomb every time he is advising a purchaser to draw to the purchaser's attention every problem which on a careful reading of the conditions might in some circumstance or other conceivably arise. I cannot believe that purchasers of house property throughout the land would be overjoyed at having some lengthy explanations of the National Conditions of Sale ritually foisted upon them.'

In *Stinchcombe and Cooper Ltd v Addison, Cooper, Jesson & Co*[2] Brightman J held that it was a solicitor's duty to inform the client 'of what was needed to obtain a conveyance of the land' in relation to a conditional contract which provided for completion 14 days after a building had been completed.

1 [1982] 1 WLR 495 at 507F–H.
2 (1971) 115 Sol Jo 368, a rather extreme example, because the solicitor failed to understand or point out that contracts had been exchanged at all. For a more recent example of a solicitor's failing to understand and then draw to his client's attention the terms of a contract of sale, see *Boateng v Hughmans* [2002] EWCA Civ 593, [2002] PNLR 40, CA.

(f) Leasehold purchasers

9.65   When the client proposes to take the grant or assignment of a lease, one of the key functions of the solicitor will be to explain to the client the terms of the lease which the landlord proposes to grant or the assignor to assign. The solicitor will not be required to recite and explain mechanically every term of the lease, and those which should be mentioned and which ignored will inevitably be a question of judgment. Similar guidance to that quoted above was given by Bingham LJ in *County Personnel Ltd v Alan R Pulver & Co*[1] in the context of leases. Again, without attempting to identify exhaustively the clauses upon which a solicitor should concentrate, solicitors have been found liable or escaped liability in the following cases concerned with the terms of leases.[2]

1 [1987] 1 WLR 916, CA at 923, quoted in para 2.32, above, where further consideration is given to this point.
2 It is noteworthy that a number of these cases are concerned with the terms of the headlease (which the new tenant's solicitors had failed to inspect) and their operation on a sub-lease.

(i)   User clauses

9.66   *Hill v Harris*: solicitor liable for failure to establish that a headlease prohibited the use permitted by the underlease without the head landlord's consent; *Sykes v Midland Bank Executor and Trustee Co Ltd*: solicitor liable for failure to advise that user clause contained a prohibition qualified not only by the lessor's consent (such consent not to be unreasonably withheld) but also by the head landlord's consent and to discover that the headlease contained an absolute prohibition on change of use; *Transportation Agency Ltd v Jenkins*: solicitor liable for failure to advise an investor in a snack bar business that cooking was prohibited by the user clause; *Simple Simon Catering Ltd v Binstock Miller & Co*: solicitor liable for failure to advise a client who was proposing to use premises as a restaurant that there was a covenant to permit the landlord to share use of the kitchen; *Carter v Gamlens*: solicitor not liable (on the evidence) for failing to advise on meaning of a particular definition used in a lease; *Citibase plc v Memery Crystal*: solicitor in breach of duty in failing to draw adverse redevelopment clause to claimant's attention (but no loss caused).[1]

1 [1965] 2 QB 601 at 618B–C; [1971] 1 QB 113; (1972) 223 Estates Gazette 1101; (1973) 228 Estates Gazette 527; CA (19 April 2000, unreported); [2003] EWHC 2673 (Ch) (Sir Donald Rattee).

(ii)   Rent review and break clauses

9.67   *County Personnel Ltd v Alan R Pulver & Co*: solicitor liable for failure to advise about a clause which required a subtenant of part to pay a rent increased by the same percentage differential as under the headlease; *Forbouys v Gadhavi*: rent review due between exchange and completion, solicitor advised as to timing of the review but not liable for failing to advise against a sub-sale until the review had been determined; *Sonardyne Ltd v Firth & Co*: solicitor liable for failure to point out that the new rent would take into account improvements carried out by the tenant; *Halifax Building Society v Grosse*: solicitor liable for failure to advise that rent review was linked to the headlease and that he could not obtain a copy of that lease; *Inter-leisure Ltd v Lamberts* and *Theodore*

Goddard v Fletcher King Services Ltd: solicitors liable for failure to ensure that there was an upwards only rent review clause; *Secretary of State for the Environment Transport and the Regions v Unicorn Consultancy Services*: solicitor jointly liable with managing agent for failing to remind claimant to make payment upon which exercise of break clause was conditional by due date (claimant found 50% contributorily negligent).[1]

1 [1987] 1 WLR 916 (in *Pulver* it was accepted that the client was advised that the original rent would be increased in step with increases in the headlease, but this was held to be inadequate); [1993] NPC 122; [1997] EGCS 84; [1997] EGCS Ill; [1997] NPC 49; [1997] 32 EG 90 (the latter two involving the purchase of the reversion and not the lease); (Rimer J, 19 October 2000, unreported).

(*iii*) Alienation clauses

9.68 *Murray v Lloyd*: solicitor liable for failure to advise that the consequence of a covenant against assignment in a residential lease was that, if the assignment in a residential lease was taken in the name of the company, the landlord could refuse consent to assign to an individual and prevent enfranchisement; *Kennedy v Van Emden*: solicitor liable for failure to advise that it was illegal to charge a premium on assignment; *Siasati v Bottoms & Webb*: solicitor liable for failure to advise that a full repairing lease of a shop and residential premises (which were in poor condition) contained a covenant to charge the residential premises to the landlord and not to create any other mortgage or charge without the landlord's consent; *Shaw v Fraser Southwell*: solicitor liable for failure to advise that the alienation clause in the lease of a flat restricted assignment, transfer, subletting and parting with possession except to a limited company only for the purposes of use as a high class residence for the occupation of one family only; *Grosvenor 52 International Ltd v Secretary of State for Local Government, Transport and the Regions*: solicitor liable for failing to advise developer client in relation to the restricted freedom to assign lease; *Lloyds Bank plc v Parker Bullen*: solicitor liable to lender for failing to report that a lease contained a covenant against alienation; and *Powell v Whitman Breed Abbott & Morgan*, where the defendant solicitors negligently advised the claimant that she should take an assignment of a lease in the name of a limited company without appreciating the impact that this would have on any future re-assignment of the lease.[1]

1 [1989] 1 WLR 1060, [1996] PNLR 409, [1997] EGCS 22, [1999] Lloyd's Rep PN 633; [2000] Lloyd's Rep PN 51; [2003] EWHC 1169 (QB) and [2003] EWHC 1279 (QB) (Tugendhat J) (the judgment is in two parts).

2 Duties on exchange of contracts

9.69 When the solicitor has received instructions to enter a contract it follows that he or she is then under an obligation to do so in a binding form[1] with a person of full capacity[2] containing the terms agreed by the client[3] and within the time limit agreed with the vendor[4] and, if possible, simultaneously with the client's own sale.[5] In practice most difficulties with the form and execution of the contract will be generated by s 2 of the Law of Property (Miscellaneous Provisions) Act 1989 and the requirement that contracts of sale be signed by both parties and contain all of the terms which have been agreed. This section has generated a body of case law which is outside the scope of this book.[6] However, mistakes such as that made in *Harrison v Bauye,*[7] where the contracts signed by each party were not in identical terms and the vendor's solicitor returned the purchaser's signed part rather than his own client's,[8] are not untypical. There are a number of consequences to the exchange of contracts which are also likely to give rise to a duty to advise on the part of the solicitor. Thus, where the purchase is proceeding with the assistance of a mortgage loan, the solicitor must not permit contracts to be exchanged without ensuring that any mortgage conditions that must be met before completion can indeed be satisfied[9]. Furthermore, given the passing of beneficial interest from the vendor to the purchaser at the moment of exchange, it is submitted that the solicitor should remind the client of the need to ensure that buildings insurance is in place effective from the moment of exchange.

1 *Parker v Rolls* (1854) 14 CB 691 (Jervis CJ). In *Summit Property Ltd v Pitmans* (2 October 2000, unreported), Ch D, the defendant solicitors were held to have been in breach of duty in effectively refusing to exchange contracts on behalf of their client, the claimant, but instead accepting instructions from a third party (albeit one very closely connected to their client) to exchange contracts in the name of a new special purpose vehicle. In effect, the third party obtained the transfer of the property into the name of a company of his choosing rather into the name of the claimant. Despite this, the claimant was found to have suffered no loss.
2 *Clarke v Milford* (1987) 38 DLR (4th) 139.
3 *Costa v Georghiou* (1983) 1 PN 201, solicitor failing to insert rent review clause in lease.
4 *Simpson v Grove Tompkins & Co* (1982) 126 Sol Jo 347, CA.
5 *Buckley v Lone Herdman* & Co [1977] CLY 3143 (HHJ Faye).
6 See *Emmet on Title* (2007) at 2.036 et seq.
7 [1975] 1 WLR 58, CA. A checklist of matters to which solicitors should have regard before exchanging contracts is to be found in the *Conveyancing Handbook* (14th edn, 2007), Part C.
8 The first mistake was held to be fatal to a binding contract but not the second. In the absence of estoppel, both would be held to be fatal now.
9 *Bates v Mishcon de Reya* [2006] EWCA Civ 597.

9.70 The Law Society has provided formulae for exchanging contracts by telephone, fax, telex and post.[1] Each formula provides for undertakings to be given by solicitors to each other (and on behalf of their firms). A failure to abide by the terms of the formulae would in all probability be a breach of duty where that breach of duty involved the client in loss. There are also risks inherent in the use of the formulae to exchange contracts by telephone arising from the fact that the contract comes into existence by virtue of the telephone conversation, leaving it open to one party to dispute the contents of the conversation and thus the contract itself. The parties must trust each other to make what may be critical and complicated amendments to contracts, they are at the mercy of the post, and where deposit monies are to fund a deposit further down a chain the risks are obvious. A solicitor may have to draw a client account cheque for his client's deposit before he has received the money himself.[2] In the rare circumstances where the solicitor acts for both parties, no exchange of contracts is necessary if both parties sign the same document.[3]

1 See the *Conveyancing Handbook* (14th edn, 2007), C4 and Apps III.2 and III.3 for copies of the formula and discussion of their application.
2 See Castle 'Exchange of contracts by Formula B: some horror stories' (1986) LS Gaz 18 November. See also Colby 'Rates of Exchange' (1998) 46 EG 180 for pitfalls in the electronic age.
3 *Smith v Mansi* [1963] 1 WLR 26, CA.

3 Duties post-contract

(a) *Searches and investigation of title*

9.71 Traditionally the purchaser's solicitor investigated and considered the adequacy of title after exchange of contracts, but today it would be rare (and almost certainly in breach of duty) not to do this before exchange[1]. In the event that a client were caused loss as a result of decision not to deduce and investigate title before exchange, the decision would be likely to amount to a breach of duty[2]. In registered conveyancing, the only post-exchange search which is usually made by a solicitor is a Land Registry search affording priority to his or her client pending completion. It is not usual to repeat inquiries or searches that have been carried out prior to exchange. However, in *Goody v Baring*[3] Danckwerts J stated that it was still necessary for a solicitor to repeat the inquiries (if only in the form of requesting the vendor to confirm that the replies to inquiries remain correct) after contract and prior to completion.[4] Where searches are out of date, particularly a local land charges registry search, it may be that a solicitor should make a further search before completion. Where the solicitor is instructed after exchange, e g where the property is purchased at auction, it is likely that it would be negligent not to carry out the standard searches, especially if they gave grounds for rescission of the contract. Unregistered conveyancing is now extremely rare but a solicitor may still be called upon to check title to land which is unregistered and then to make an application for first registration. This process traditionally took place after exchange but it suggested that in the modern age a solicitor should require the vendor to deduce title in advance of exchange. *Pilkington v Wood*[5] provides an example of a case in which a solicitor was negligent in examining the vendor's title to unregistered land. In that case (where negligence was admitted) the defendant failed to notice that the vendor had acquired part of the subject property from the trustees of his father's will of whom he was one. It was argued that this was a technical breach of duty only but Harman J held that because the class of beneficiaries who could claim under the will was not closed, the purchaser obtained a defective title only and could be dispossessed.[6]

1 The editors of the *Conveyancing Handbook* (14th edn, 2007) observe (in section D1) that deduction of title should be delayed until after contracts have been exchanged 'only in exceptional circumstances'. The National Conveyancing Protocol, if followed, requires the vendor to provide evidence of his title at the draft contract stage.
2 The contract of sale frequently contains a provision effectively preventing requisitions on title after exchange.
3 [1956] 1 WLR 448 at 456.
4 The words used by the judge were 'requisitions and inquiries'. It is unlikely that he had in mind repeating local authority searches: compare *Kotowich v Petursson* [1994] 3 WWR 669, solicitor not liable for failure to establish the planning position *after* exchange.
5 [1953] Ch 770.
6 [1953] Ch 770 at 775. It is doubtful whether this would constitute a blot on the title to registered land because the purchaser would have no notice of the trusts.

(b) *Encumbrances*

9.72   One important duty of the solicitor after exchange is to ensure that any encumbrances to which the sale is not intended to be subject are discharged and no further encumbrances are registered pending completion. In *Holmes v H Kennard & Sons*[1] the defendants were found liable for a failure to ensure that notice of a charge registered under the Matrimonial Homes Act 1967 was removed from the register of the subject property prior to completion. They had received a form 71 from the wife's solicitors but the Land Registry refused to accept this. It was in the wrong form and the wife's solicitors had no actual or ostensible authority to agree to the discharge of the charge. In the case of the simple residential house purchase, it is usual for the client's interest to be protected between exchange and completion solely by a priority search. In more complex cases (as for example where there is a relatively long period between exchange and completion[2]), it will be negligent if the solicitor fails to protect his client's priority either by registering a unilateral notice or insisting that it is a term of the contract that a notice or restriction be entered in the proprietorship register of the relevant title.[3]

1 (1984) 49 P & CR 202.
2 See the *Conveyancing Handbook* (14th edn, 2007) at C5.3.5 where it is suggested that a period of two months between exchange and completion would make registration advisable. That paragraph also gives other examples of situations where registration would be advisable: where there is reason to doubt the vendor's good faith; where a dispute arises between purchaser and vendor; where the vendor delays completion beyond the agreed completion date; where the purchase price is to be paid by instalments; and where the transaction is a (lawful) sub-sale.
3 See, eg, *Bell v Peter Browne & Co* [1990] 2 QB 495, CA (failure to register caution to protect agreement to receive part of the proceeds of sale).

(c) *Conditions*

9.73   It is axiomatic that the solicitor must satisfy himself or herself that any conditions which require to be satisfied before the purchase is completed are satisfied before completing. In *Creech v Mayorcas*[1] the defendant's clerk failed to ensure that the landlord's licence to assign was obtained before completing the assignment.

1 (1966) 198 EG 1091 (Pennycuick J).

(d) Occupiers

9.74 Until the Land Registration Act 2002 came into force on 13 October 2003, s 70(1)(g) of the Land Registration Act 1925 provided a scheme of protection for the rights of every person in actual occupation of land regardless of whether such rights were noted on the land register or not. These unregistered but nonetheless protected rights were known as overriding interests and were binding on a purchaser except where inquiry had been made of such persons and the rights had not been disclosed. Moreover, any right or interest of a person who went into occupation prior to completion of the purchase was binding as an overriding interest.[1] Finally, a purchaser was fixed with constructive notice of those rights that he could reasonably have discovered from an inspection of the property and inquiries of the occupier.[2] The Land Registration Act 2002 has made significant changes to that scheme of protection with the aim of registering all overriding interests so that they cease to be overriding and are instead registered interests. In pursuit of this aim, the 2002 Act contains various mechanisms including a requirement that on any disposition of registered land, disclosure be made to the Land Registry of the interests of persons in occupation which are within the knowledge of the purchaser.[3] The standard form inquiries before contract ask about occupiers and under both the Land Registration Acts 1925 and 2002 a solicitor is at risk of a claim for negligence if he or she does not advise the purchaser to make further inquiries of the occupiers personally as to their rights in the property if replies disclose the existence of occupiers with potential rights. Furthermore, it not infrequently occurs that a purchaser will agree to purchase a property, which is currently occupied, with vacant possession but on the vendor's assurance that the occupation will be, or is capable easily of being, determined[4]. Again, a solicitor would be at risk of a claim for negligence if he or she failed to advise the purchaser that there could be no guarantee that the tenant would quit and that the tenancy would continue to be binding.[5]

1 *Abbey National Building Society v Cann* [1991] 1 AC 56.
2 See *Kingsnorth Trust Ltd v Tizard* [1986] 1 WLR 783
3 Unlike the scheme which it replaced, the 2002 Act does not provide protection to persons occupying land if, on a reasonably careful inspection of the land, it was not obvious that the person claiming protection was in occupation and the purchaser did not have actual knowledge of such occupation.
4 See *Pankhania v Hackney London Borough Council* (Rex Tedd QC, 31 July 2002, unreported), where the purchaser was misled into buying property at auction by the auctioneer's representations that the property was occupied pursuant to a licence terminable on three months' notice, when in fact the occupation amounted to a business tenancy protected under Part II of the Landlord and Tenant Act 1954.

5 Short of making the contract conditional on the production by the vendor of a deed of surrender executed by the tenant, there appears to be no way of ensuring that vacant possession can be obtained on completion. The solicitor must, therefore, give appropriate advice.

9.75 In unregistered conveyancing, the purchaser is bound by any rights belonging to a person in actual occupation, regardless of any enquiries he may have made about the property and the persons in occupation of it.[1] Again, a solicitor is at risk of a claim for negligence if he or she does not advise the purchaser to make inquiries about individuals in occupation of unregistered land and to follow those enquiries by making enquiries of the occupiers personally.

1 This is the effect of ss 11(4) and 12(4) of (together with para 2 of Sch 1 to) the Land Registration Act 2002.

(e) Advice

9.76 A solicitor has no duty to repeat advice given prior to exchange of contracts once the client is bound.[1] *Neighbour v Barker*[2] illustrates the way in which the solicitor's duties may differ before contract and after. In that case the defendants advised the claimants to have a survey before contract. This advice was not taken but after exchange of contracts the claimants engaged a surveyor who reported that the property suffered from substantial defects. The defendants advised the claimants to complete because they were bound. It later transpired that the claimants had grounds for rescinding the contract. The defendants were found not to be liable for failing to advise the claimants to explore ways of escaping from their obligations. However, in *Peyman v Lanjani*[3] a solicitor was found liable for failure to advise a purchaser that he had grounds for rescinding a contract. Where for instance time is of the essence it is incumbent on the solicitor to remind the client.[4]

1 See *Elland Developments Ltd v Smith* [1995] EGCS 141 (Rattee J). Solicitors are generally obliged to give their advice once and not to revisit it unless information comes to their attention which suggests their earlier advice might need to be revisited: see *Bell v Peter Brown & Co* [1990] 2 QB 495, CA and *New Islington HA v Pollard Thomas* [2001] Lloyd's Rep PN 243, per Dyson J at 247.
2 (1992) 40 EG 140, CA.
3 [1985] Ch 457, CA at 478D–G.
4 See, eg, *Stinchcombe and Cooper Ltd v Addison, Cooper, Jesson & Co* (1971) 115 Sol Jo 368 (Brightman J).

4   Duties on completion

9.77 It is the solicitor's duty to complete the purchase on behalf of his client and this obligation involves ensuring that the client obtains title to the property.[1] In the case of the purchaser's solicitor this usually involves a tender of the purchase price (usually by telegraphic transfer[2]) in return for the documents of title and a statutory receipt and discharge of any mortgage or legal charge.

1 See *Dogma Properties Ltd v Gale* (1984) 136 NLJ 453 (Kilner Brown J) where the purchaser's solicitors purported to complete and released the purchase price but failed to obtain a good title.
2 It is also possible for the completion money to be transmitted by banker's draft, although that is extremely rare now. Cf (1969) 66 LSG 406 and 761.

9.78 Traditionally, completion took place by means of a personal attendance by the purchaser's solicitor on the vendor's solicitor, and it still open to solicitors to use this method of completion (in, for example, very complex or high value transactions where physical inspection of documentation may be considered prudent, or where both sets of solicitors are located in close proximity to each other). In many – perhaps most – cases, however, completion takes place by post, using the Law Society's Code for Completion by Post[1]. Under this system, the vendor's solicitor acts as the purchaser's solicitor's agent, performing those actions which the latter would do if he or she were physically present at the vendor's solicitor's offices. In *Wong (Edward) Finance Ltd v Johnson, Stokes and Master*[2] Lord Brightman suggested that it would be advisable either to make the mortgagee a party to the conveyance or for the purchaser's solicitor to make two separate payments, one directly to the vendor's mortgagee and the other directly to the vendor's solicitor. Despite these remarks, solicitors have in practice in England and Wales have continued to make extensive use of solicitors' undertakings[3]. Thus, at the stage of requisitions on title, the parties' solicitors will usually agree that the proceeds of sale may be used to redeem the vendor's existing mortgage and that on completion the vendor's solicitor will give an undertaking to the purchaser's solicitor to use the proceeds of sale in that way and provide proof that the existing mortgage has been discharged[4]. The vendor's solicitor's undertaking is personal and may be enforced directly against him or her. Since all solicitors must have professional indemnity insurance, the vendor's solicitor's undertaking to discharge his client's existing mortgage is usually sufficient reassurance that the purchaser will in due course obtain good title.[5]

1 See the *Conveyancing Handbook* (14th edn, 2007) at App III.3.
2 [1984] AC 296, PC at 303 and 307–8. See para 2.17, above. It is not clear how accurate the Privy Council's description of conveyancing in England and Wales was even at the time: see *Patel v Daybells* [2001] EWCA Civ 1229, [2001] Lloyd's Rep PN 738 at [45] and [58] (Robert Walker LJ).
3 See paras 5.25–5.34, above.
4 The traditional method of providing such proof, whereby the vendor's solicitor sends the purchaser's solicitor a Land Registry form (currently known as the DS1, previously Form 53), is gradually being replaced with alternative forms as part of the slow move towards e-conveyancing. Thus, where the Electronic Notification of Discharge (END) scheme has been used, the lender may send the purchaser's solicitor notification that it has received a request from the vendor's solicitor to discharge the mortgage; or where the Electronic Discharge (ED) scheme has been used, the lender will send the purchaser's solicitor notification that the charge has been discharged. See Land Registry Practice Guide 31 (contained in *Emmet on Title* (2007) Vol 3 or http://www.landregistry.gov.uk/assets/library/documents/lrpg031.pdf).

5 Where the vendor's solicitor dishonestly appropriates the purchase moneys, compensation may, as a last resort, be available to the purchaser from the Law Society's Compensation Fund.

9.79 In *Patel v Daybells*[1], the Court of Appeal considered for the first time whether the widespread use of undertakings might, in view of the remarks made in *Wong v Johnson Stokes and Master*, amount to an unreasonable practice. After some reluctance the court reached the view that the system of a purchaser's solicitor relying on undertakings given by the vendor's solicitors to discharge subsisting charges is acceptable.[2] A solicitor should not, however, accept an undertaking from an unqualified person given the difficulties of enforcement. Following the judgment in *Patel v Daybells*, the Law Society issued a guidance note to conveyancers highlighting two possible exceptions to the general rule that it is not a breach of duty for a solicitor to accept a vendor's solicitor's undertaking regarding the removal of existing mortgages or charges.[3] First, in situations where the purchase price of the property exceeds the minimum amount of professional indemnity insurance required to be carried by solicitors (currently in most cases £2m) the purchaser's solicitor is either advised to take steps to ensure either that the amount of money secured by the mortgage is less than the £2m minimum level of cover or that the vendor's solicitor's insurance cover exceeds the sum secured by the mortgage or to make other arrangements to ensure that the mortgage will be discharged, as for example by insisting on sending the redemption money direct to the lender. Secondly, the purchaser's solicitor is advised against accepting undertakings where the lender is not a member of the Council of Mortgage Lenders. This is because the CML's members have agreed to discharge a borrower's mortgage even where insufficient funds are remitted if the reason that insufficient funds were remitted was an error on the lender's part in preparing the redemption statement. It is suggested that a solicitor who failed to follow this guidance in the first situation would clearly be negligent. It is not so clear that a solicitor would be negligent to accept an undertaking from a solicitor whose client's lender is not a member of the CML (provided that the vendor's solicitor had adequate insurance cover). Ultimately, the vendor's solicitor's undertaking is enforceable against him or her personally, and any dispute between the lender and the vendor would be no defence to the purchaser's claim arising from any breach of the undertaking.

1 [2001] EWCA Civ 1229, [2001] Lloyd's Rep PN 738. For discussion of the question whether it is negligent to adopt a widespread practice: see paras 2.17–2.20, above.
2 See [64] and [65] (Robert Walker LJ). Although the judgment refers only to undertakings given by solicitors, it seems to have been implicitly accepted that there was no difference between an undertaking given by a solicitor and one given by a licensed conveyancer: see [61]. The Law Society also draws no distinction between solicitors and licensed conveyancers in this connection: see the *Conveyancing Handbook* (14th edn, 2007) at 4.2.14.
3 'Accepting Undertakings on Completion following the Court of Appeal Decision in *Patel v Daybells*' issued by the Conveyancing and Land Law Committee in May 2002.

9.80 The guidance note also points out that there may be other potential exceptions to the general rule that undertakings may be accepted without giving rise to a breach of duty, arising on the particular facts of any given case. The most obvious example is where the vendor's solicitor is a sole practitioner who dishonestly misappropriates the purchase moneys. As a result of the dishonesty, there is unlikely to be professional indemnity insurance available[1]. Although the Law Society's Compensation Fund (which compensates those who have sustained loss arising out of a solicitor's dishonesty) should provide compensation to the purchaser, the process of obtaining compensation can be slow and there is no guarantee that full recovery will be made. A purchaser may find that even after applying to the Compensation Fund, he or she still has still made losses for which it is not possible to obtain compensation. It is suggested that it is not reasonable for a purchaser's solicitor to accept an undertaking from the vendor's solicitor if he or she is a sole practitioner and that the purchaser's solicitor should insist on the vendor providing other safeguards on completion such as direct confirmation from the lender that the vendor's solicitor is its duly appointed agent for the receipt of the redemption money (so that the risk of any default by the vendor's solicitor is borne by the lender). The risk of misappropriation by the vendor's solicitor is an obvious one. It is also obvious that in those circumstances insurance cover will not be available.[2] Finally, it is not too difficult or expensive to provide the necessary protection for the purchaser.

1 Cover for losses caused by dishonest or fraudulent acts or omissions is excluded under the Minimum Terms and Conditions governing all solicitors' professional indemnity insurance.
2 See cll 1.1 and 6.6(c) of the Minimum Terms and Conditions for 2007 at http://www.sra.org.uk/documents/rules/Indemnity-TCs-07.pdf.

9.81 Where there is more than one charge on a property, the purchaser's solicitor should take care to ensure that he or she has obtained an undertaking from the vendor's solicitor in relation to each and every charge. Failure to do so will amount to breach of duty[1]. Where a vendor delays completion beyond the agreed date, the solicitor is also under a duty to advise the purchaser as to his or her legal options and, if necessary, to enforce the undertakings given by the vendor's solicitor promptly.[2] In standard residential and commercial conveyancing, the purchaser facing delayed completion will also be entitled to damages (calculated as interest on the purchase price). The purchaser will not be entitled to rescind the contract, however, unless the vendor has failed to comply with a notice to complete.[3] In *Douglas Williams v Glyn Owen & Co*[4], however, the purchaser's solicitor failed to advise his client that the contract of sale for the farm he had bought at auction permitted him to discharge the contract in the event that the vendor was late in completing. If the purchaser had been aware of this he would have served a completion notice and re-negotiated the purchase price. He would also have obtained possession of the farm in time to make a profit from the lambing season.[5]

1 See *Dogma Properties Ltd v Gale* (1984) 136 NLJ 453 (Kilner Brown J). Cf also *Gregory v Shepherd* [2000] PNLR 769, CA (vendor's charge not discharged) and *Greymalkin v Copleys* [2004] EWHC 1155, [2004] PNLR 44 (vendor purchased in ignorance of three subsisting charges).

2 See *Patel v Daybells* [2001] EWCA Civ 1229, [2001] Lloyd's Rep PN 738 at [66] (Robert Walker LJ).
3 See Standard Conditions of Sale (4th edn) cl 7.3 and Standard Commercial Property Conditions of Sale (2nd edn) cl 9.3. Unless time is expressly made of the essence in the contract, the common law rule is that the innocent party to the breach of contract is not entitled to terminate the contract: *Raineri v Miles* [1981] AC 1050.
4 [2003] EWCA Civ 750, [2004] PNLR 20.
5 Damages were awarded for the loss of the purchaser's chance to earn a profit from the lambing season if he had served a notice to complete on the vendor.

9.82   A solicitor is at risk of a claim for negligence if he or she fails to have the relevant transfer or instrument stamped[1] and he or she has a duty to retain and preserve the relevant documents of title prior to registration. Section 27 of the Land Registration Act 2002[2] provides that a disposition of a registered estate is required to be completed by registration and the disposition does not operate at law until the registration requirements are met. A solicitor who fails to apply to register his client's purchase (or his lender client's charge) will be in breach of duty and exposes his client to the risk that another person will register another disposition which will then take priority.[3] In *Hartle v Laceys*[4] the defendants were found to be negligent for failing to take advantage of this kind of error. They acted for the claimant purchaser and were found liable for informing the vendor after completion that a restrictive covenant given by their own client had not been registered. The vendor's solicitors had failed to realise that the covenant would be void against a subsequent purchaser and as a consequence the purchaser lost the opportunity to sell on before the covenant was registered.

1 Compare *Parker v Rolls* (1854) 14 CB 691 (Jervis CJ).
2 With effect from 13 October 2003 this section replaced the scheme provided in the Land Registration Act 1925, ss 123 and 123A, which had been in force since 1 April 1998. Under the scheme in force between 1998 and 2003 failure to register a disposition within two months (or such longer period as might have been granted by the Land Registry) led to the disposition becoming void.
3 The consequence of a failure to do so may be that the Land Registry will cancel the application and, even if a fresh application is made, the purchaser may lose priority.
4 [1999] Lloyd's Rep PN 315, CA.

5   Damages

(*a*) *Introductory*

9.83   There are three basic questions to be answered in arriving at the quantum of damages in purchaser claims:

(1)   What type or types of loss should the solicitor have prevented the claimant from suffering (the extent of liability question)? [1]

(2)   For each type of loss for which the solicitor is responsible, until what point in time may the effect of the solicitor's breach of duty be said to

continue? Put another way, at what point (if any) may some other factor (such as the fact that the claimant has an opportunity to mitigate his loss) be said to be the cause of the loss (the mitigation question)?[2]

(3) What sum of money will put the claimant in the position he would have been in had the solicitor not been in breach of duty (the measure of damages question)?[3]

The first and second questions involve both fact and law but the third question is purely a matter of fact. It can often be difficult, therefore, to determine which parts of reported cases relating to purchaser claims represent binding authority and which represent mere illustrations of the application of broad principles to specific facts. We discuss this problem in more detail below.

1 See paras 9.85–9.94, below.
2 See paras 9.95–9.96, below.
3 See paras 9.97–9.124, below.

9.84 As for the first question (extent of liability), it is frequently difficult to assess what position the claimant purchaser would have been in but for the solicitor's breach of duty, particularly where the claimant's overall financial position has been negatively affected over a period of time beginning with the negligent act or omission of the solicitor. Which of the claimant's losses are attributable to something done or not done by the defendant and which to other factors? As discussed below[1] the first stage of the answer to that causation question involves the exercise of judgment in accordance with legal principles, albeit it is a highly fact-sensitive exercise. Once the difficult issue of deciding precisely which heads of loss the defendant has caused or was responsible for preventing[2] has been answered, it is necessary to determine how much of the damage caused under each head of loss for which the defendant is responsible may be attributed to his breach of duty and how much is more properly the responsibility of the claimant. As with the first question, that determination is reached by the application to the particular facts of the legal rules relating to mitigation.[3] Finally, having decided, (a) what types of loss the solicitor is responsible for causing or permitting and (b) the moment in time (if such there is) after which further loss of that type may be said no longer to be the solicitor's responsibility, it is slightly easier to tell what position the claimant would have been in but for the defendant's breach of duty. In theory, one can compare the claimant's actual factual situation with the hypothetical alternative he would have experienced if the solicitor had fulfilled his or her duty. Ultimately, this *measure* of damages (i e the amount to be paid) is, as described in *Livingstone v Raywards Coal Co*[4]:

'that sum of money which will put the party who has been injured, or who has suffered, in the same position as he would have been in if he had not sustained the wrong for which he is now getting his compensation or reparation'.

463

9.85   *Conveyancing*

1 See para 9.87, below. For further discussion, see para 3.35ff, above.
2 See *British Racing Drivers Association v Hextall Erskine* [1996] 3 All ER 667 (Carnwath J) at
   681 and *Environment Agency v Empress Car Co (Abertillery) Ltd* [1999] 2 AC 22 at 31C-H
   (Lord Hoffmann).
3 See paras 9.95–9.96, below, and para 3.60ff, above.
4 (1880) 5 App Cas 25, per Lord Blackburn at 39.

(*b*) *Extent of liability*

9.85   Arden LJ's observation in *Johnson v Gore Wood & Co*[1] is a helpful
summary of the current approach of the courts towards resolving the question of
attribution of responsibility for particular damage to a particular breach of a
particular, well-defined, duty:

> 'Starting with *Caparo v Dickman*, the courts have moved away from
> characterising questions as to the measure of damages for the tort of
> negligence as questions of causation and remoteness. The path that
> once led in that direction now leads in a new direction. The courts
> now analyse such questions by enquiring whether the duty which the
> tortfeasor owed was a duty in respect of the kind of loss of which the
> victim complains. Duty is no longer determined in abstraction from
> the consequences or vice versa. The same test applies whether the
> duty of care is contractual or tortious. To determine the scope of the
> duty the court must examine carefully the purpose for which advice
> was being given and generally the surrounding circumstances. The
> determination of the scope of the duty thus involves an intensely
> fact-sensitive exercise. The final result turns on the facts, and it is
> likely to be only the general principles rather than the solution in any
> individual case that are of assistance in later cases.'

1 [2003] EWCA Civ 1728 at [91]. For detailed discussion of the *SAAMCo* principle see para 3.35ff,
   above.

9.86   *Cottingham v Attey Bower & Jones*[1] provides a good illustration of this
principle. In that case, the solicitors were held to be negligent for failing to
inform the claimants that the vendors of the property that they were buying
might not have received building regulation consent for certain works undertaken at the property. The claimants (who had also obtained a surveyor's report
on the property and knew that it suffered from certain defects) sought damages
from the solicitors calculated by reference to the cost of curing *all* of the defects
discovered at the property and this sum was said to represent the difference in
value between the price they paid and the true value of the property. Given the
nature of the duty owed by the solicitors, Rimer J held that the claimants were
entitled to compensation only for the foreseeable damage that flowed from the
absence of building regulation consent. This was the cost of remedying those
defects which would have been identified but for the solicitor's negligence.[2]

1 [2000] Lloyd's Rep PN 591.
2 For a further example of a purchaser claim failing, or only partially succeeding, because of the limited scope of the solicitor's duty see *Hinc v Warren Rees & Co* [2002] EWCA Civ 764.

(*i*) Losses referable to a rise or fall in the property market

9.87 (1) *Profits which would have been achieved on resale* Normally, the claimant cannot recover the loss of potential profit on the resale of the property.[1] This is for three reasons. First, in cases where the claimant is alleging that but for the solicitor's negligence, he would not have bought the property at all, the claimant is seeking to be restored to the position he would have been in (i e not owning the property). A claim for lost profits on resale is inconsistent with the assertion that the claimant should never have owned the property in the first place. In *County Personnel (Employment Agency) Ltd v Alan R Pulver*[2] Bingham LJ stated[3]:

> 'It must, however, be accepted on the findings of the deputy judge that if they had not been negligently advised the plaintiffs would not have entered into this underlease at all. This being so, damage cannot be assessed with reference to a specific gain which the plaintiffs could only have made if they had entered into this underlease, unless it be proper on the facts to conclude that properly advised, the plaintiffs would probably have been able to negotiate the grant of this underlease but without the offending clause.'

Second, the duty breached by the solicitor is the duty to give non-negligent advice and information regarding the property so that the claimants can decide whether or not to proceed with the purchase.[4] It is not a duty to guarantee the outcome of a transaction on the assumption that the advice given is correct. Nor does the solicitor warrant that the information he is providing is true.[5] Third, any claim for loss of profits necessarily involves selecting the date at which those profits would have been realised. This may pose considerable practical difficulties for claimants, who must prove on the balance of probabilities when they would have resold the property.[6]

1 For examples of cases in which the purchaser has not been able to recover an anticipated profit on resale see *Pilkington v Wood* [1953] Ch 770 (Harman J), *Nash v Phillips* (1974) 232 Estates Gazette 1219 (Foster J), *Wapshott v Davies Donovan & Co* [1996] PNLR 361, CA and *Connor & Labrum v Regoczi-Ritzman* (1995) 70 P & CR D41–3 (Robert Walker J).
2 [1987] 1 WLR 916, CA.
3 [1987] 1 WLR 916, at 926E. Note that in *Connor v Regoczi-Ritzman* (1995) P&CR D41, the profit on resale was also refused because it was a 'no transaction' case. The same was also the case in *Stanley K Oates v Anthony Pitman* [1998] PNLR 683, CA.
4 In the context of domestic conveyancing, there is frequently little to be gained by seeking to draw a distinction between whether the solicitor has provided advice or merely given information (i e the *SAAMCo* distinction). See *Cottingham v Attey Bower & Jones* [2000] Lloyd's Rep PN 591 at [46]–[48] where Rimer J's approach suggests that that distinction is only likely to be of

relevance if the solicitor has volunteered advice on the wisdom of entering the transaction. See also *Dent v Davis Blank Furniss* [2001] Lloyd's Rep PN 534 at p 544 col 1 where the approach of Blackburne J was similar.

5 See *Hayes v James & Charles Dodd* [1990] 2 All ER 815, CA, per Staughton LJ at 817.

6 See *Aylwen v Taylor Joynson Garrett* [2001] EWCA Civ 1171, [2001] Lloyd's Rep PN 687, CA at [38] (Arden LJ).

9.88　Where, however, the defendant knew or ought to have known that the claimant was intending to resell for profit, the court is likely to find that this profit was within the reasonable contemplation of the parties (or, put another way, was loss of a type that it was the defendant's duty to prevent the claimant from suffering). In *G & K Ladenbau v de Reya*[1] where resale of the property was delayed by the defendant's failure to identify rights of common over it, the claimant was awarded the additional interest payable on the purchase price and also interest on the purchase price which would have been obtained. Mocatta J stated:

> 'The evidence of Mr Smith, a director of the plaintiff company, who went to see Mr Kaufmann of the defendants when the latter were originally instructed during Mr Franklyn's absence on holiday, was that Mr Kaufmann was told that the plaintiff's intention was to build a factory for shop fittings that would occupy an acre and develop the rest of the area and sell or let off the rest. In the light of these instructions, and in the state of the property market as it was then, the defendants should in my judgment have reasonably contemplated that if they failed to secure an unencumbered title for the plaintiffs without warning them of the defect, the damages the plaintiff would suffer were 'not unlikely' to be the loss of a handsome profit on resale.'

1 [1978] 1 WLR 266 at 289C–F.

9.89　Similarly, in *Carter v TG Baynes & Sons*[1], the defendants failed to advise the claimant developer of a density covenant, with the result that the claimant was unable to sell land which he had developed before discovering the restrictive covenant. The claimant spent some five years having the restrictive covenant removed. Once the covenant was removed, the developed land was sold; but in the five years between 1991 (when the developed land would have been sold had the restrictive covenant not existed) and 1996, when it was finally sold, the property market had collapsed and the claimant's profits were much less than they would otherwise have been. Since the defendant knew of the claimant's plans to develop, the court awarded the claimant damages calculated by reference to the position the claimant would have been in had the properties been sold in 1991 and his actual financial position, including (apparently) the costs of obtaining the release of the covenant and the costs of increased borrowings as a consequence of the delay.

1 [1998] EGCS 109 (HHJ Prosser QC).

9.90 (2) *Profits which could have been made on an alternative transaction* In a period of sharp increases in property prices over a short period of time, as has been experienced in the years since the first edition of this book, claimants may be expected to argue that they are entitled to bring into account the fact that, but for their solicitor's negligence, they would have purchased another, non-defective, property, such that their return on investment would have been higher. In *Keydon Estates Ltd v Eversheds*[1] damages have been awarded on this basis. In that case, the defendants had acted for the claimant in a number of acquisitions of commercial property. From 2000 onwards, the claimant was looking to make an investment and finally found an appropriate property in early 2002. The property was let but the issue arose whether a subsequent underlease by the tenant to its (financially weak) subsidiary had taken effect as an assignment of the lease (because the term of the lease was identical). If the lease had been assigned, the assignee's covenant was too weak to make the investment advisable. The defendants negligently advised the claimant that the underlease has not operated as an assignment. The claimant acquired the property but in due course the sub-tenant went into administration and the tenant successfully argued that its lease had been assigned to the sub-tenant. The claimant was left with an empty property which remained unlet at the date of trial. Evans-Lombe J held that the claimant would not have bought the property but for the defendant's negligent advice and would instead have bought comparable investment property with similar yields. His approach was to come to a factual conclusion as to what use the claimant would have put the investment funds and compare that with what had in fact transpired by the date of the trial. He then awarded damages for (hypothetical) lost past and future rent, the cut-off point in the future being determined by reference to the time it would reasonably take the claimant to let the property which it had instead acquired.

1 [2005] EWHC 972 (Ch), [2005] PNLR 40.

9.91 In the context of residential transactions, it is suggested that the court is likely to be less ready to award damages assessed by reference to hypothetical profits which the claimant would have made on an alternative transaction. This is because, first, any profit made on the purchase and resale of residential property is collateral to the main purpose of the transaction, which is to provide a home for the buyer (and hence no capital gains tax is payable on that profit). Secondly, where the claimant has sold the defective property and purchased another property, he or she is still able to benefit from any rise in the market. Where the claimant retains the property, that property will continue to fluctuate in value as the market changes, and, to the extent that the claimant has made 'less' profit on the defective property than he might have made on the hypothetical alternative, he is compensated for this by the award of damages on the valuation method[1] together with interest[2] (except where the property has no resale value whatsoever). Claimants might therefore find that arguments relating to the appropriate rate of interest on damages are more likely to produce a satisfactory result than a claim for lost potential profits.[3]

9.92 *Conveyancing*

1 The term is Lord Steyn's in *Smith New Court v Citibank* [1997] AC 254. Also sometimes referred to as the 'diminution in value' method. See para 3.70ff, above.
2 See *Wapshott v Davis Donovan & Co* [1996] PNLR 361, where the claimants' claim for lost profits on resale was rejected because their principal case was that but for their solicitor's negligence, they would not have purchased the property in question at all. The court awarded interest at a relatively high rate designed to reflect the increase in property prices over the period.
3 Note that the principles on which interest is ordinarily awarded in a purchaser's claim were reviewed by HHJ Grenfell in *Griffiths v Last Cawthra Feather* [2002] PNLR 27 at [46].

9.92 The position of claimants who have purchased defective property on a 'buy to let' basis is likely to turn on (a) the clarity of their investment strategy and (b) what their solicitor knew of that strategy. A claimant whose known intention was to hold on to particular property indefinitely in a time of high rentals and low interest rates is likely to be awarded damages by reference to the lost value of the rents he or she reasonably could have expected to receive. A claimant whose known intention in buying was with a view to speculative capital gain might succeed in having his or her damages assessed by reference to the market value of the property without the defect at the first opportunity he or she would (having regard to her general investment strategy) have sold it (plus interest but less the actual value received for the defective property when it was sold). A claimant whose known intention in buying was relatively unfocussed (i e who hoped that he or she would receive a good return on investment and make a reasonable capital gain at some point) would be likely to find that the lack of clarity in his or her investment strategy resulted in an award of the mere difference in value between what he or she paid and what the defective property was actually worth with no account taken of his or her hopes of high rentals and capital gains.

(ii)   Damages for inconvenience

9.93 Where a claimant has been physically inconvenienced, the courts have tended to be willing to recognise that physical discomfort with a modest award of damages on the ground that such losses can be characterised as physical consequences of the breach of duty.[1] In *Wapshott*[2], for example, damages of £3,000 were awarded to the claimants for the inconvenience and physical discomfort of living in a cramped and unsuitable flat between 1986 and 1992; in *Faragher v Gerber*[3], the claimant was awarded £6,000 for the physical inconvenience of a new highway development adjacent to the property, and in *Patel v Hooper & Jackson*[4] two claimants were each awarded £2,000 for discomfort.

1 See *Perry v Sidney Phillips & Son (a firm)* [1982] 1 WLR 1297, CA, per Kerr LJ at 1307, cited with approval in *Hayes v James & Charles Dodd* [1990] 2 All ER 815, CA, per Balcombe LJ at 822.
2 [1996] PNLR 361, CA, at 377D–379A.
3 [1994] EGCS 122.
4 [1999] Lloyd's Rep PN 1, CA.

9.94 The courts have, however, been reluctant to acknowledge by a specific monetary award a claimant's distress, worry, or other emotional or mental

trouble arising from a solicitor's breach of duty. Thus, in *Hayes v James &
Charles Dodd*[1] the Court of Appeal set aside the trial judge's modest award of
damages for mental distress suffered as a consequence of the defendant's
breaches of duty despite the claimant's being locked into a disastrous and nearly
ruinous lease for a period of six years. The reluctance to recognise that such
matters sound in damages is purely a matter of policy, as acknowledged in
Verderame v Commercial Union Assurance Co[2]. In that case (a claim against
insurance brokers), it was said that the reason public policy should deny
recovery of damages for such a type of loss was apparently that the rule which
applied in tort should be the same as the rule generally applicable in contract.
Now, after *Farley v Skinner*[3], if a claimant can establish that one of the objects of
his retaining the solicitor was to provide peace of mind, he can recover damages
for distress occasioned by the solicitor's breach of duty.[4] In the context of
residential conveyancing, it may well be possible for a claimant to demonstrate
that one of the reasons he or she retained his or her solicitor was precisely to
provide peace of mind by ensuring that the stressful process of buying her
property was competently managed.

1 [1990] 2 All ER 815, CA.
2 [2000] Lloyd's Rep PN 557, CA, per Balcombe LJ at 563 col 2.
3 [2002] 2 AC 732, HL.
4 See *Hamilton-Jones v David & Snape* [2003] EWHC 3147 (Ch), [2004] 1 WLR 924. See also the
discussion in para 12.73f, below.

(c) Mitigation

9.95 Claimants are required to take responsibility for themselves as soon as
possible after suffering loss, so that it is likely that the effect of a solicitor's
negligence will be 'spent' with the passage of time; or put another way, there is a
tendency to search for the earliest moment at which the claimant may be said to
have control over the relevant asset or transaction and absolve the defendant
from responsibility for further losses of that type after that date[1].

1 See *British Westinghouse Electric and Manufacturing Co Ltd v Underground Electric Railways Co of London Ltd* [1912] AC 673, per Viscount Haldane LC at 688–9; *Payzu v Saunders*
[1919] 2 KB 581, per Scrutton LJ at 589; *Radford v De Froberville* [1977] 1 WLR 1262, per
Oliver J at 1285; and *Dodd Properties (Kent) Ltd v Canterbury City Council* [1980] 1 WLR
433, CA, per Megaw LJ at 453.

9.96 The effect of a court's finding that a claimant has acted reasonably in not
taking steps to mitigate his loss is to extend the period of time during which the
solicitor's negligence may be said to have caused that loss. Thus, in *County
Personnel (Employment Agency) Ltd v Alan R Pulver*[1] the claimant did not seek
to extricate itself from the disadvantageous lease which it had entered as a result
of the defendant's negligence but rather continued to pay rent under that lease
for five years until the onerous rent review clause in the lease became operative.

At that point, it bought itself out of the lease. The claimant sought the cost of buying itself out of the lease as damages. In its guidance to the Master on how to assess damages, the Court of Appeal suggested that this would represent a fair measure of damages unless it could be shown that the payment of this sum was in itself unreasonable. It might therefore be said that the solicitor's breach of duty in that case continued to have effect until the time that the claimant bought itself out of the lease, that apparently being the first opportunity that the claimant could take any sensible step to minimise its loss. Similarly, in *Hayes v James & Charles Dodd*[2] the claimants were locked into the disastrous lease and were thus unable to take any step to mitigate their losses. They were awarded damages which took account of all of the expenditure they had incurred, not merely in acquiring the lease but also in living with it for five years, such as rent, rates and insurance. Again, it might be said therefore that the damage caused by the solicitor's breach of duty continued to have effect until the claimants could finally free themselves of the obligations into which they had become bound.

1 [1987] 1 WLR 916, CA.
2 [1990] 2 All ER 815, CA.

(d) Assessing the measure of damages

9.97 Difficulties can arise in assessing the *measure* of damages (as opposed to the entitlement to damages) if the person seeking to make the assessment treats earlier authorities as laying down rules of general application. As a matter of historical fact, many purchaser claims follow broadly similar paths (as one would expect given the relatively standardised procedure of modern conveyancing). A body of cases has thus built up which can be categorised and those categories are examined below. But the fact that on many occasions a purchaser's loss amounts to no more than that identified by the 'valuation method'[1], for example, does not by itself mean that there is a general rule that every purchaser's losses should be identified by the valuation method unless there are exceptional circumstances. As Oliver J put it in *Radford v De Froberville*[2] (in the context of damages for breach of contract) there is a 'danger in elevating into general principles what are in truth mere applications to particular facts or situations of the overriding general principle as enunciated by Parke B[3]'. The authorities might be thought to suggest that there is a hierarchy for the assessment of damages with the valuation method constituting the usual rule.[4] The suggestion that the valuation method should be used in preference as a general rule derives in part from what is sometimes said to be the general rule that damages should be assessed, in tort as well as in contract, at the date of breach.[5] It is also sometimes said that there may be occasions when the general rule has to give way to assessment at a later date, to reflect the overriding compensatory principle in *Livingstone v Rawyards Coal*.[6]

1 See para 3.70ff, above.

2 [1977] 1 WLR 1262 at 1270F.
3 In *Robinson v Harman* (1848) 1 Exch. 850 at 855.
4 See, eg, *County Personnel (Employment Agency) Ltd v Alan R Pulver* [1987] 1 WLR 916, CA, at 925F; *Griffiths v Last Cawthra Feather* [2002] PNLR 27, at [36]; *Greymalkin v Copleys* [2004] EWHC 1155 (Ch), [2004] PNLR 44 at [86] (although the case went to the Court of Appeal on a different point: see [2004] EWCA Civ 1754); *Keydon Estates Ltd v Eversheds* [2005] EWHC 972 (Ch), [2005] PNLR 40 at [15]; *Green v Alexander Johnson* [2005] EWCA Civ 775, [2005] PNLR 45 at [19].
5 See *Miliangos George Frank (Textiles) Ltd* [1976] AC 443 per Lord Wilberforce at 468; *County Personnel (Employment Agency) Ltd v Alan R Pulver & Co* [1987] 1 WLR 916 at 925H (Bingham LJ); *Smith New Court Securities Ltd v Citibank* [1997] AC 254 at 265H – 266E (Lord Browne-Wilkinson).
6 See the review of the authorities in *Golden Strait Corpn v Nippon Yusen Kubishka Kaisha (The Golden Victory)* [2007] UKHL 12, [2007] 2 WLR 691 at [13] (Lord Bingham), [32]–[35] (Lord Scott) and [79]–[80] (Lord Brown).

9.98 It is more helpful when considering the reported cases to note that on many (if not most) occasions the loss suffered will be likely to be no more than that ascertained by the valuation method. But there is nothing to preclude other losses being recoverable if they can be shown to have been caused by the solicitor's breach of duty. As Lord Steyn put it in *Smith New Court Securities Ltd v Citibank SA* discussing the principles to be applied to the assessment of damages for deceit[1]:

'… the valuation method is only a means of trying to give effect to the overriding compensatory rule …Moreover, and more importantly, the date of transaction rule is simply a second order rule applicable only where the valuation method is employed. If that method is inapposite, the court is entitled simply to assess the loss flowing directly from the transaction without any reference to the date of transaction or indeed any particular date. Such a course will be appropriate whenever the overriding compensatory rule requires it. An example of such a case is to be found in *Cemp Properties (U.K.) Ltd v Dentsply Research & Development Corpn* [1991] 2 EGLR 197, 201, per Bingham LJ. There is in truth only one legal measure of assessing damages in an action for deceit: the plaintiff is entitled to recover as damages a sum representing the financial loss flowing directly from his alteration of position under the inducement of the fraudulent representations of the defendants. The analogy of the assessment of damages in a contractual claim on the basis of cost of cure or difference in value springs to mind. In *Ruxley Electronics and Construction Ltd v Forsyth* [1996] A.C. 344, 360G, Lord Mustill said: 'There are not two alternative measures of damages, as opposite poles, but only one; namely, the loss truly suffered by the promisee.' In an action for deceit the price paid less the valuation at the transaction date is simply a method of measuring loss which will satisfactorily solve many cases. It is not a substitute for the single legal measure: it is an application of it.'

1 [1997] AC 254, at 284B.

9.99 In the context of claims made by purchasers against their former solicitors, any general rule regarding the application of the valuation method or the date of assessment of damages might be said to be a rule more honoured in the breach than in the observance. Of the authorities in this area, damages appear to have been assessed at a time other than the moment when loss first began to be suffered by the claimant at least as often as they have been assessed at that moment. The relevant authorities can be analysed as follows:

(1)   cases where damages were assessed at the moment loss was first sustained, using the valuation method;[1]

(2)   damages assessed three months after loss began to be suffered;[2]

(3)   damages assessed 18 months after loss began to be suffered;[3]

(4)   damages assessed three years after loss began to be suffered;[4]

(5)   damages assessed five years after loss began to be suffered;[5] and

(6)   damages assessed as at date of trial.[6]

It is suggested therefore that there is no prima facie rule of law that damages in this type of case fall to be assessed at the date of breach. It is, however, probably correct to say that the likely starting point will be that some damage was caused at the date of breach, and thus that is where the enquiry as to damage begins. In many cases, the enquiry will also end there because the claimant will have suffered no other loss as a result of the solicitor's breach of duty. But if the claimant has suffered other loss referable to the solicitor's breach of duty, then he or she is entitled to full compensation for that loss.[7] Despite Mustill LJ's observation in *Hussey v Eels*[8] that 'in the field of damages ... broad statements of principle tend to be unreliable' we suggest the following principles on which damages will be assessed in claims by purchasers.

1   *Pilkington v Wood* [1953] Ch 770; *Ford v White* [1964] 1 WLR 885; *Piper v Daybell, Court-Cooper & Co* (1969) 210 Estates Gazette 1047; *Collard v Saunders* (1972) Estates Gazette 795; *Faragher v Gerber* [1994] EGCS 122; *Wapshott v Davis Donovan & Co* [1996] PNLR 361; *Owen v Fielding* [1998] EGCS 110; *Stanley K Oates v Anthony Pitman & Co* [1998] PNLR 685; *Shaw v Fraser Southwell* [1999] Lloyd's Rep PN 633, CA; *Greymalkin Ltd v Copleys* [2004] EWHC 1155, [2004] PNLR 44.
2   *Simpson v Grove Tompkins* (1982) Times, 17 May.
3   *GP & P Ltd v Bulcraig & Davis* [1986] EGLR 148 and [1988] 1 EGLR 138, CA.
4   *Cygnet Health Care plc v Elletson & Co* (10 May 1999, unreported).
5   *County Personnel (Employment Agency) Ltd v Alan R Pulver* [1987] 1 WLR 916, CA; *Hayes v James & Charles Dodd* [1990] 2 All ER 815, CA; *Patel v Hooper & Jackson* [1999] Lloyd's Rep PN 1, CA; *Dent v Davis Blank Furniss* [2001] Lloyd's Rep PN 534 (Blackburne J).

6 *Jarvis v Richards* (1980) 124 SJ 793; *Connor & Labrum v Regoczi-Ritzman* (1995) P & CR D41; *Dodd Properties v Canterbury City Council* [1980] 1 WLR 433, CA; *Smith v South Gloucestershire* Council [2002] EWCA Civ 1131, [2002] 38 EG 206, CA; *Keydon Estates Ltd v Eversheds* [2005] EWHC 972 (Ch), [2005] PNLR 40.
7 See *Watts v Morrow* [1991] 1 WLR 1421, CA at 1444D–F (Ralph Gibson LJ).
8 [1990] 2 QB 227, CA at 233.

(e) General principles

9.100 First, damages are awarded so that *at the date of judgment* the claimant is in the position he would have been in but for the solicitor's negligence. As Schiemann LJ put it in *Kennedy v Van Emden* (original emphasis):[1]

> '... the task of the judge *on the date of judgment* was to award to each plaintiff that sum of money which would *on that date* put him in as near as a money award could do so into the position he would have been in *on that date* had there been no negligence on the part of his solicitor'.

Thus, whatever date is identified as the moment by reference to which damages are to be assessed in respect of each type of loss, if that date is before the time of the trial, the claimant will usually be entitled to interest on the sum assessed, to run between the date by reference to which damages are assessed and the date on which the assessment was made. The fact that the court is awarding damages on this basis means that it can and will look at the realities of what has happened to the claimant since the time of the transaction complained of (sometimes known as the *Bwllfa* principle[2]). In *Kennedy v Van Emden*, for example, the claimant had, as a result of her solicitor's negligence, paid a premium to take an assignment of the lease of a rent-controlled flat in 1983. As the law stood at the time of the assignment, such a premium was unlawful. The law was changed in 1989 and it became no longer unlawful to pay premiums to acquire the leases of such flats. In 1990 the claimant discovered that she had paid an unlawful premium and sued her solicitor for (among other heads of loss) damages assessed by reference to the premium she had paid in 1983. The Court of Appeal upheld the trial judge in denying her claim to this type of loss. Ward LJ stated that:[3]

> '... fairness and justice demand that we approach this case with an eye to reality, judging by reference to what is and not what might have been. As the plaintiffs have got what they wanted, however fortuitously, they have suffered no loss and they are entitled to no damages.'

1 [1996] PNLR 409, CA.
2 After *Bwllfa and Merthyr Dare Steam Collieries (1891) Ltd v Pontypridd Waterworks Co* [1903] AC 426, HL. See also *Golden Strait Corpn v Nippon Yusen Kubishka Kaisha* (*The Golden Victory*) [2007] UKHL 12, [2007] 2 WLR 691.

3 [1996] PNLR 409 at 418G. For further examples of the application of the *Bwllfa* principle see *Charles v Hugh James Jones & Jenkins* [2000] Lloyd's Rep PN 207, CA at 214, col 2 (although the court there does not appear to have expressly considered *Bwllfa*) and *McKinnon v E-Surv Ltd* [2003] EWHC 475 (Ch), [2003] Lloyd's Rep PN (Jonathan Gaunt QC) at [22]. See also *Barclay-White* v *Guillaume* [1996] EGCS 123 (HHJ Crawford QC) where the claimant was awarded his out-of-pocket expenses but no sum assessed by the valuation method because the property had later been sold for its current (defect-free) market value.

9.101   Second, if a particular rule appears to preclude a claimant who, but for that rule, would obviously be entitled to damages in relation to a particular head of loss, then the overriding principle in *Livingstone v Raywards Coal* will operate to displace the particular rule. In *Dodd Properties v Canterbury City Council*[1] Megaw LJ observed:

> 'In any case of doubt, it is desirable that the judge, having decided provisionally as to the amount of damages, should, before finally deciding, consider whether the amount conforms with the requirement of Lord Blackburn's fundamental principle. If it appears not to conform, the judge should examine the question again to see whether the particular case falls within one of the exceptions of which Lord Blackburn gave examples, or whether he is obliged by some binding authority to arrive at a result which is inconsistent with the fundamental principle.'

In *Reeves v Things & Long*[2], Sir Thomas Bingham MR went slightly further:

> 'The assessment of damages is ultimately a factual exercise, designed to compensate but not over-compensate the plaintiff for a civil wrong he has suffered. While this is not an area free from legal rules, it is an area in which legal rules have to bow to the peculiar facts of the case.'

In *McElroy Milne v Commercial Electronics Ltd*[3] Cooke P went yet further. He stated that (emphasis added):

> 'in the end assessment of damages is a question of fact … there is no such thing as a rule, applicable to all cases … the ultimate question as to compensatory damages is whether the particular damage claimed is sufficiently linked to the breach of the particular duty *to merit recovery* in all the circumstances'.

1 [1980] 1 WLR 433, CA at 451.
2 [1996] 1 PNLR 265, CA at 278.
3 [1993] 1 NZLR 39, New Zealand Court of Appeal at 41.

(*f*) *Classification of the authorities by types of loss*

(*i*) *Loss of opportunity to purchase*

9.102   If, as a consequence of the negligence of his or her solicitor, a purchaser of residential property loses the chance to buy a particular property, the appropriate measure of damages is likely to be the difference between the purchase price at which he or she would have acquired the property and its value at the date of contract. In *Nash v Phillips* [1] damages for the cost of acquiring a more expensive substitute property were refused and this measure of damage was adopted subject to a 10% deduction for the risk that contracts would not have been exchanged and the costs which would have been incurred. This case is perhaps best regarded as the application or modification of the usual principle on which loss of bargain damages are awarded for a breach of contract for the sale of land.[2] In *Stinchcombe and Cooper Ltd v Addison, Cooper, Jesson & Co*[3], where contracts had been exchanged but as a consequence of the solicitor's negligence the vendor was able to rescind the contract, the claimant was awarded the difference between the purchase price and the value of the land at the date of rescission.

1 (1974) 232 Estates Gazette 1219.
2 See *Emmet on Title* (2007) Vol 1 at 7.020.
3 (1971) 115 Sol Jo 368.

9.103 Where the disappointed purchaser is a property developer who is seeking to purchase with a view to development, the decision in *Jenmain Builders v Steed & Steed*[1] suggests that in many cases the developer's loss is likely to be minimal. This is because, although it has lost the opportunity to purchase one particular property, it retains the money it would otherwise have used to purchase that property and can thus return to the marketplace to find another development opportunity[2]. If, on the other hand, the developer can prove that the price at which it would have obtained the property but for the solicitor's negligence was less than the true value of the property, then it seems that the measure of damages would be the difference between the price and its actual value.[3] There may be other actual situations which permit a developer to attribute the loss of a development opportunity to its solicitor's breach of duty, e g a preferred bidder for a large project is rejected by the vendor at the last minute as the result of some default on the part of the solicitor leaving it with no comparably profitable development. In such a case, damages would be assessed on the loss of a chance basis to take account of the various contingencies dependent on the behaviour of third parties (such as whether the development would have been built to budget or whether the profits have been as projected).[4]

1 [2000] Lloyd's Rep PN 549, CA.
2 See [31] and [35] (Chadwick LJ).
3 See [31]. This is consistent with the decision in *Stinchcombe and Cooper Ltd v Addison, Cooper, Jesson & Co* (above). In *Bates v Mishcon de Reya* [2006] EWCA Civ 597 the Court of Appeal seems again to have accepted that in principle the claimants might have been able to recover damages assessed by reference to the loss of a bargain, i e the purchase of a property at a significant undervalue. In the Scottish case of *Watts v Bell & Scott* [2007] PNLR 30 (CJ Macaulay QC sitting as a temporary judge of the Court of Session), the claimant developer was awarded damages against the solicitors who had deprived him of development property he would otherwise have acquired on the basis of the profits he would have made on developing the property. The evidence showed that the developer could not use the funds set aside for the

purchase to acquire any comparable property; and the forgone profits were considered to be recoverable in contract as being within the reasonable contemplation of the developer and the solicitor when the solicitor agreed to act.

4 See also *Motor Crown Petroleum Ltd v SJ Berwin* (10 March 2000, unreported), CA, where the solicitors failed to advise the claimant developer that it could challenge a local development plan which adversely affected the proposed development. The chances of the challenge succeeding were put at 40%, and damages were assessed as being 40% of the value of the land as if the lost challenge to the local development plan had succeeded.

(*ii*)   *Delayed purchase*

9.104   Where the solicitor's negligence causes a delay in the purchase rather than the purchase to fall through, the claimant ought to recover any consequential expenditure incurred. This would normally include the cost of additional accommodation, interest paid to the vendor under the terms of the contract and (possibly) general damages for inconvenience[1]. The claimant may also incur additional finance costs which are in principle recoverable provided that avoiding such losses can be shown to have been within the ambit of the duty breached by the solicitor. Where the negligent conduct causes the claimant to lose a purchase at the original price but it is later acquired at a higher price, he or she ought to recover the difference between the price originally agreed and the market price of the property when finally acquired, usually the ultimate purchase price: see *Simpson v Grove, Tompkins & Co*[2]. However the market must be genuinely rising.

1 See, by analogy, *Bailey v Bullock* [1950] 2 All ER 1167, CA (solicitor's failure to obtain possession on behalf of landlord client) and *Raineri v Miles* [1981] AC 1050 at 1094H.
2 (1982) Times, 17 May, CA. In most cases, the market price at the later date will be the price in fact paid by the claimant. In this case, the claimant had in fact paid over the market price in order to ensure that he acquired the property, a decision which was not attributable to his solicitor's breach of duty. Hence his damages were assessed as the difference between the originally agreed price and the true market price.

(*iii*)   *Defective purchase*

9.105   In many cases a claimant's loss on acquiring a defective property is simply that he or she has paid too much. The measure of damages in such circumstances is normally established by comparing the actual price paid with the price which would have been paid on the same date had the purchaser and the vendor both known of the defect. This is the valuation method. Where the claimant's losses go beyond merely having acquired a property at an overvalue in ignorance of a defect, and encompass further losses, such further losses sub-divide into three broad categories. First, there are cases in which the claimant has been effectively locked in to the consequences of the solicitor's negligence until such time as he or she has been able to extricate himself or herself from that position and dispose of the property. Second, there are cases in which the claimant has acted reasonably in expending money on curing the defect blighting his property, or where the defect could be effectively 'cured' by the award of damages. Third, there is a small group of cases in which either the claimant's impecuniosity or the particular characteristics of the property he or she sought to acquire (or both of those factors) have resulted in the court awarding the claimant the sum of money required *at the date of trial* to purchase a property equivalent to the defective property but without the defect. The damages awarded in the first type of case are frequently referred to as being the 'costs of extrication' and those awarded in the second type as 'the cost of cure'. We suggest that the damages awarded in the third type of case should be termed 'the cost of replacement'. In all three types of case, the facts (if made out) will clearly show that the loss suffered is something other than can be assessed using the valuation method.

9.106   (*1*) *Defective purchase: losses assessed by valuation method* There have been many cases in which the measure of damages has been calculated using the valuation method as applied at the date of purchase. The first two (considered in this paragraph) represent the point of departure for the valuation method and are the two cases in which its utility was first recognised. In *Pilkington v Wood*[1] the claimant was awarded the difference between the market value of the property with a good title and its value subject to a defect in title but no damages for improvements which he had carried out to the property. The purchase price was treated as the market value at the date of breach. In *Ford v White*[2] Pennycuick J rejected the submission that damages should be awarded on a warranty basis, i e the difference between the actual value of the property and the value which it would have had without the defect, and awarded as damages the difference between the purchase price and the market value of the property. Given that the vendor had offered it for sale subject to the restrictions and at a market price (albeit the defendants had failed to notice this) damages were nominal. It was accepted by the judge that if the claimant had attempted to sell the property after he became aware of the defect, he might have recovered damages for his wasted expenditure. To the sum arrived at by this calculation will be added interest and any consequential losses.

1 [1953] Ch 770.
2 [1964] 1 WLR 885.

9.107   It will normally be assumed that the price which the claimant would have paid for the property is the fair market price and expert evidence is usually adduced to establish the value of the property as at the date of purchase but on the assumption that any purchaser in the market would have been aware of the defect which is the subject matter of the claim. On occasion, however, the court has assessed a claimant's damages by reference to evidence of what reduction in the purchase price would probably have been achieved by the claimant by means of negotiation with the vendor, as in *Asiansky Television plc v Bayer Rosin*[1]. The cost of repairing the defect may also be helpful evidence as to the difference in value of the property with and without the defect except where the cost of repairing the defect will put the purchaser in a better position than he or she would have been but for the solicitor's negligence.[2] Where the claimant has paid above the open market price which the property would have realised if it had been free of the relevant defect, it appears that he or she will ordinarily be awarded damages calculated by reference to the open market value and not the actual price paid.[3]

1 [2004] EWHC 1362 (QB) at [181] to [184] (Creswell J). See also *Owen v Fielding* [1998] EGCS 110.
2 See *Smith & Smith v Peter North & Partners* [2001] EWCA Civ 1553, [2002] Lloyd's Rep PN 111, CA at [49]–[53] (Jonathan Parker LJ).
3 See *County Personnel v Alan R Pulver* [1987] 1 WLR 916, CA at 925B (Bingham LJ).

9.108   In *Piper v Daybell, Court-Cooper & Co*[1] the claimant recovered the difference between the price paid for the property and its market value at the date of purchase subject to a right of way. In *Collard v Saunders,*[2] the claimant was awarded the difference between the purchase price (representing market value of the property as it was assumed to be) and its value out of repair. In *Faragher v Gerber*[3] the claimant was awarded the difference between the price paid for a property and its value in the light of a proposed highway development to which the defendant ought to have drawn her attention[4].

1 (1969) 210 EG 1047.
2 (1972) 222 EG 795.
3 [1994] EGCS 122.
4 See also *Mercantile Building Society v J W Mitchell Dodds & Co* [1993] NPC 99, CA.

9.109   In *Wapshott v Davies Donovan & Co*[1], the claimants were awarded the difference between the purchase price of the properties and their actual value at the date of breach despite the fact that they were locked into the properties by the defendant's negligence and lost a purchaser at a higher price when the defect came to light. It was common ground that the claimants would not have purchased the property. The award placed them in the position they would have been in if they had never bought and a generous award of interest compensated them for locking up their capital[2]. In *Connor & Labrum v Regoczi-Ritzman*[3] Robert Walker J held that the claimants were entitled to their expenditure on acquiring and improving the property (including mortgage interest) less its value at the date of trial because it remained unsold.

1 [1996] PNLR 361, CA.
2 [1996] PNLR 361, CA at 375E.
3 (1995) 70 P & CR D41–3.

9.110   In *Owen v Fielding*[1] the claimants were awarded the difference between the price paid for the property and its value subject to the rights of common which the defendant had failed to identify. The judge found this to be 80% of the purchase price on the basis that the claimants would have obtained a 20%

discount at the date of purchase if they had known of the defect. The defendant's submission that the claimants' profits on resale should be taken into account was rejected[2]. Damages for inconvenience were also refused. In *Stanley K Oates v Anthony Pitman*[3], the claimants purchased property converted into 13 letting units in January 1988. After the purchase the claimants undertook a programme of improvements and spent around £50,000. The claimants also changed the use made of the letting units. After 18 months of successful trading the claimants discovered that they did not have planning permission for the new use. They obtained retrospective permission, but that brought with it certain large expenses. The claimants therefore sold the property without undertaking the expenses necessary to obtain retrospective planning permission, and sued the defendant for not advising them adequately about the nature and effect of the existing planning permission on their proposed use. The defendant admitted liability. The Court of Appeal assessed damages by reference to the true value of the property at date of acquisition. To make this assessment the court subtracted from the price actually paid in 1988 the costs of the extra works which would have had to be incurred to comply with the retrospective planning permission.

1 [1998] EGCS 110 (David Steel J).
2 The profit was due to the claimants' decision to apply for planning permission, subdivide the property and resell.
3 [1998] PNLR 683, CA.

9.111 In *Patel v Hooper & Jackson*[1] the defendant surveyors negligently failed to tell the claimants that the property which they proposed to purchase was effectively uninhabitable and worth only £65,000. In reliance on the report the claimants paid £95,000 for the property in 1988 but then discovered that they were unable to move in. They were unable to sell the property for some years and were obliged to live in rented accommodation. Although the claimants could have sold the property in 1993, they did not in fact do so. The Court of Appeal was not persuaded that the whole of the claimants' financial outlay over the period for which they claimed could be characterised as loss caused by the defendant's breach of duty and considered it fairer to award them damages assessed using the valuation method together with the costs of alternative accommodation between the date they bought the property and the date that they could have sold it in 1993.

1 [1999] Lloyd's Rep PN 1, CA.

9.112 In *Shaw v Fraser Southwell*[1] the claimant was awarded the difference between the purchase price and the value of the property subject to an onerous alienation covenant. The small profit realised by the claimant eight years after the purchase after he had taken a number of steps to extricate himself was considered not to arise from the defendant's breach of duty and was thus ignored.

1 [1999] Lloyd's Rep PN 633, CA.

9.113 In *Cygnet Health Care plc v Elletson & Co*[1] the claimant bought an estate from Manchester University for less than the open-market value. The estate included three cottages which the claimant intended to develop and sell. The cottages were subject to a planning restriction permitting them to be occupied only by agricultural workers. The claimant would have bought the estate regardless of the planning restriction but would have taken steps to remove the restriction much earlier but did not know about the planning restriction until some time after it had purchased the estate. The claimant was awarded damages from its former solicitors on the valuation method (which were assessed at the date of sale) together with the additional cost to it of capital borrowed from a third party. The latter claim was also successful and damages were awarded on the basis that the claimant would have developed and sold the cottages nearly three years earlier than it in fact managed to do so.

1 (10 May 1999, unreported, HHJ Steel).

9.114 In *Greymalkin Ltd v Copleys*[1] the claimants had purchased a hotel for £240,000 in June 1993 and its solicitors knew that it intended to convert it into flats and bedsits. The solicitors failed to inform the claimant that it would take hotel subject to three existing charges and the claimant started work converting the hotel. In February 1994 the solicitors informed the claimant about the three charges and by 1996 the solicitor's insurers had achieved the release of all three of them. The claimant issued proceedings against the solicitors in 1998 claiming all of the moneys it had spent on acquiring, improving, and later preserving the hotel until it eventually managed to sell the hotel in 2000. Lawrence Collins J awarded damages using the valuation method applied at the date the claimant acquired the hotel, on the grounds that the defect was remedied at no expense to the claimant and the other losses were not caused by the solicitor's negligence. He found that the claimant's actions remained the same both before and after the defect was discovered and that its expenditure could not be attributed to the solicitor's breach of duty. The decision also contains a helpful review of many of the authorities in this area.[2]

1 [2004] EWHC 1155, [2004] PNLR 44 (upheld on appeal at [2004] EWCA Civ 1754). It should be noted that at the trial there was no evidence to show how much the claimant had spent on improvements.
2 See [2004] EWHC 1155, [2004] PNLR 44 at [74]–[84].

9.115 In *Powell v Whitman Breed Abbott & Morgan*[1] the claimant purchased a short lease of property belonging to the Grosvenor Estate in 1997 with a view to developing the property and re-selling it. She asked the defendant solicitors to advise her on the way in which she should hold the lease: as a private individual (in which case she would be liable to pay capital gains tax on any profits she made) or via a company (which would pay less tax on a capital gain). The claimant was concerned that if she held in the name of a company she would only be able to assign the lease to another company once the property had been developed. The defendants negligently advised her to hold the lease through a company. Having developed the property and extended the lease from 30 to 98 years she put it on the market. Although there was no difference between the value of a long lease of the property held in the name of a company or held in the name of a private individual the fact that the lease was held in the name of a company meant that it was likely to take far longer to sell. Since the claimant had only acquired a short lease originally, the defendant argued that the effect of any negligence had been cured by the acquisition of the new long lease in 1998 because the value of the long lease was not affected by the fact that the tenant was a company. Tugendhat J rejected this argument and held that the claimant had sustained a loss as a result of the defendant's breach of duty because she had acquired an asset which took longer to sell than it would otherwise have taken. To assess the value of that loss, the judge employed a fiction. He took the value of a notional long lease granted to an individual in 1997 (when of course no such lease existed) and then discounted that value by a percentage which seemed fair (6%) to reflect the fact that what the claimant eventually acquired in 1998 was a long lease granted to a company. Thus the valuation method was employed as at the date of sale but using two entirely notional comparators.

1 [2003] EWHC 1169 (QB) and supplemental judgment at [2003] EWHC 1279 (QB). Note that the neutral citation number is mistyped on both judgments as [2003] EWCA 1169 and [2003] EWCA 1279.

9.116 On occasion damages have also been assessed by comparing the value of the property on the assumption that it did not have the relevant defect and its actual value at a date other than the date of purchase. In *Dent v Davis Blank Furniss*[1] the claimants purchased a bungalow with outbuildings and a paddock at auction for £94,000 in July 1991. (The actual market value was £60,000 but the claimants bought the property at auction knowing this to be the case.) The claimants then spent £381,000 building a new house on the property and turning the paddock into a garden. In December 1994, the claimants discovered that nearly all of the land they had acquired was registered as common land. They attempted to remove the registration and succeeded in part in August 1995 and October 1996 at a total cost of £20,000. The trial took place in January 1999, and the claimants sought to recover the difference between the total sum they had expended, i e some £495,000, and the current value of property (which they still lived in and had no apparent intention of leaving). Blackburne J held that the solicitor's duty was to provide accurate information about the commons registration position but not to advise the claimants whether to proceed with the purchase. He held that the solicitor was only liable for those losses which flowed from the information being incorrect and that the damages within the scope of the solicitor's duty were the costs expended on improving the property in ignorance of the commons registration position. Against those costs had to be set the value of the property. The judge therefore compared the value of the improved property as at the date when the claimants were able to remove the registration of part of the land (October 1996) with the value of the improved property at that date *as if none of it were registered as common land.* He therefore compensated the claimants for the fact that the asset they had acquired and improved was worth relatively less than it should have been worth on the first occasion on which when they could have realised it (or part of it) and it was fair to make the assessment.[2]

1 [2001] Lloyd's Rep PN 534.
2 See Sir Thomas Bingham MR's remarks on damages in *Reeves v Thrings & Long* [1996] PNLR 265, at 278E, with which Hobhouse LJ agreed, at 281D. The judge in *Connor & Labrum v Regoczi-Ritzman* (1995)70 P & CR D41–3 took a similar approach.

9.117 *(2) Defective purchase: the extrication cases* In *County Personnel Ltd v Alan R Pulver & Co*[1], for example, the claimant was awarded the cost of surrendering a lease with an onerous rent review clause as the primary head of loss. Two slightly different reasons were given by the court for holding that the loss caused was other than could be assessed using the valuation method. Bingham LJ considered that using the valuation method would involve 'a somewhat speculative and unreal valuation exercise intended to reflect the substantive negative value of this underlease'. Sir Nicolas Browne-Wilkinson considered that assessing damages by this method would be 'wholly artificial' for a lease at a rack rent which had no capital value and would have had no capital value even if the rent review clause had not been defective.[2]

1 [1987] 1 WLR 916 at 926C and 928A, CA. This figure also included arrears of rent due as a consequence of a rent review.
2 [1987] 1 WLR 916 at 926B and 927G–928A.

9.118 In *GP & P Ltd v Bulcraig and Davies*[1] the claimant entered a lease unaware that the property was subject to a planning restriction. The claimant would not have taken the lease if properly advised; nor would it have expended the money that it did on refurbishing the demised premises. The claimant was found to be entitled to recover all of its expenditure less a sum it had received on surrender of lease. An unusual feature of the case (which illustrates well the court's concern not to award damages that amount in all the circumstances to a windfall for the claimant) arises from the fact that the claimant had, after improving the premises, occupied them for 18 months at a rent which was below market rent for the improved premises. It was common ground that the claimant had to give credit for the benefit of occupying the premises and the question was whether it had to give credit at a rate equal to the rent it actually paid or at the (higher) market value. It was held that the claimant would not have been able to pay below market rent if it had not entered the transaction as a result of its solicitor's negligence. The lower than market rent was thus found to be a benefit that flowed from the negligence. The correct sum to use to value the benefit to the claimant of occupying the premises was the market rate.

1 [1986] 2 EGLR 148 (John Gorman QC) and [1988] 1 EGLR 138, CA.

9.119 In *Hayes v James & Charles Dodd*[1] the claimants were awarded all of the costs incurred by them in the acquisition, operation and resale of a workshop and maisonette with defective rights of access over a six-year period. The heads of loss included the cost of the lease of the workshop, the freehold of the maisonette, the goodwill of the business and the plant, rates, insurance, bank interest, travel costs and other costs. The reasons given by Staughton LJ for not using the valuation method were that the claimants would not have bought if they had been properly advised; the case was not 'concerned with a readily saleable commodity'; and the claimants (who were only able to trade for one year) did not act unreasonably in taking nearly six years from the date of purchase to dispose of their interest[2]. The claimants were, however, required to give credit for the profit which they realised on resale of the maisonette[3]. The reasoning behind *Hayes v Dodd* was directly applied in *Siasati v Bottoms & Webb*[4].

1 [1990] 2 All ER 815, CA.
2 See also *Bridgegrove v Smith* [1997] 2 EGLR 40, CA, a claim for misrepresentation in which it was held that although the term of a tenancy came to an end after six months, it was reasonable for the claimant to remain in occupation on a monthly tenancy in an attempt to improve the business. Wasted expenditure was also awarded as the primary head of loss in *Transportation Agency Ltd v Jenkins* (1972) 223 Estates Gazette 1101 (Kerr J) where the judge drew up 'a balance of what the plaintiffs had in fact lost and gained'.
3 [1990] 2 All ER 815 at 819g–820b and 822d–h. On the facts, the claimants were only required to give credit for 80% of the profit on resale.
4 [1997] EGCS 22 (Geoffrey Brice QC).

9.120 *(3) Defective purchase: cost of cure* As noted above, the cost of cure measure is most likely to be appropriate either where the claimant has mitigated his loss by curing the defect in question after the breach or where the defect can effectively be cured by the payment of damages. Examples of the first type of 'cost of cure' case include the following. In *Creech v Mayorcas*[1], where the claimant had as a result of the defendant's breach of duty taken an assignment of a lease without the consent of the landlord, he was awarded the cost of obtaining the relevant licence (a relatively modest sum) together with some consequential expenses. In *Nielsen v Watson*[2] the claimant was awarded the cost of buying a missing strip of land together with out-of-pocket expenses. More recently, in *Gregory v Shepherds*[3] the claimant had acquired property in Spain in 1989 which, as a result of the defendant's breach of duty, remained charged to a third party even after the date of transfer to the claimant. In 1999 the charge was vacated at relatively little cost to the claimant. But the fact that it took 10 years to vacate that charge (which should have been vacated in 1989) was not the fault of the claimant. Moreover at a relatively early point during this period the claimant decided to sell the property but found that he was unable to do so. The Court of Appeal awarded the claimant the costs he had spent on curing the defect and damages for being kept out of the capital that was tied up in the property between 1991 and January 2000, when it was eventually sold (apparently as consequential loss[4]). This measure of loss was represented by interest on the sum that would have been realised in the event that the property had been sold in 1991 and the calculation was also ordered to take account (if necessary) of exchange rate fluctuations over the period.

1 (1966) 198 EG 1091.
2 (1981) 125 DLR (3d) 326.
3 [2000] PNLR 769, CA.
4 The court said at [2000] PNLR 769 at 785E that:

> 'the appropriate measure of damages for a removable defect which has been removed
> should be compensation for its existence from the time when it should have been
> removed to the time it was in fact removed.'

9.121   Examples of the second type of 'cost of cure' case are as follows. In *Computastaff Ltd v Ingledew Brown Bennison and Garrett*[1] where the claimant would not have taken a tenancy of the premises in question on the terms offered if it had been advised of their true rateable value, it was awarded the difference between the rates it expected to pay over the term and the rates which it actually had to pay. The judge chose this measure purely for simplicity's sake but took comfort from the fact that the amount was close to that calculated by comparing the expenditure which the claimant had actually incurred with that which it would have incurred had it found cheaper premises. A similar approach was also taken in *Sonardyne Ltd v Firth & Co*[2], where the claimant recovered the difference between the rent it would have paid if the rent review clause had disregarded tenant's improvements and the higher rent it was obliged to pay on review under the terms of the lease (which did not contain this disregard). Curtis J found that the landlord would have agreed to disregard tenant's improvements on review if the point had been raised.

1 (1983) 268 EG 906.
2 [1997] EGCS 84.

9.122   *(4) Defective purchase: cost of replacement* In *Murray v Lloyd*[1] the claimant was advised by her solicitors to take the assignment of a lease for 15 years in the name of a company. In so doing, she lost the opportunity to become a statutory tenant. She was awarded as damages the amount which it would cost to acquire a similar tenancy which would carry such rights on termination. Mr John Mummery (sitting as a deputy) held[2]:

> '... if the plaintiff had not been given negligent advice, the assign-
> ment would have been in her name and she could have become a
> statutory tenant on the expiration of the lease in 1991. She would
> then have enjoyed security of tenure of the property at a relatively
> low rent. As matters have turned out, however, she cannot now
> acquire those benefits which would have been of value to her ... The
> fact that if she had become a statutory tenant the landlord would
> have neither sold her the freehold at a discount nor paid her a sum to
> give up vacant possession does not alter the position that she has
> irretrievably lost the opportunity of becoming a statutory tenant of
> the property and will have to move from where she would otherwise
> have been entitled to remain ... In my judgment, damages are to be
> assessed by reference to what it would cost the plaintiff to acquire

what she has lost, ie, the cost of acquiring similar rights of occupation on similar terms in similar alternative accommodation.'

The reason why the valuation method could not be applied was that the rights in question were personal and non-assignable and, while unquestionably valuable, could not be bought and sold on the open market[3].

1 [1989] 1 WLR 1060.
2 [1989] 1 WLR 1060 at 1065.
3 See [1989] 1 WLR 1060 at 1064D. Compare *Radford v DeFroberville* [1977] 1 WLR 1262, where Oliver J suggested that the lack of an open market would be likely to make assessing damages by the valuation method inappropriate.

9.123 To similar effect is *Layzell v Smith Morton & Long*[1] where the solicitors failed to serve a notice claiming a right to succession of a tenancy under the Agricultural Holdings Act 1986. The claimant was awarded the cost of acquiring the freehold of a similar farm less the amount he would realise on a sale and leaseback of the farm on the terms of the original tenancy. In *Jarvis v Richards*[2] the solicitor failed to complete the transfer to the claimant of her husband's interest in the matrimonial home. The former matrimonial home was then repossessed by the mortgagee and the claimant was unable to buy another property because she was impecunious (something that was itself held to be the solicitor's fault). She was thus awarded such sum as would permit her to get what, but for the solicitor's negligence, she should have acquired in the first place, a house equivalent to the former matrimonial home. Since the property market had risen the claimant's damages were assessed at date of trial.

1 [1992] 1 EGLR 169.
2 (1980) 124 SJ 793.

9.124 Finally, in *Smith v South Gloucestershire Council*[1] the claimants bought land and a farmhouse in March 2005 for £150,000, intending to develop the farmhouse. They then spent £225,000 on that project. In 1998 the claimants learned that the farmhouse was subject to an agricultural tie which had not been revealed by the official search as a result of the defendant's negligence. The claimants tried but failed to get the agricultural tie lifted, and then sued the defendant. The Court of Appeal found that the claimants could not sell the farmhouse because they could not afford to buy a comparable and suitable property until such time as they received damages from the council. Because of the agricultural tie the claimants were unable to sell and this was attributable to the defendant's negligence (and not caused to any failure to mitigate by the claimants). The court awarded damages by reference to the amount which the claimants required to acquire a similar farmhouse *without* the agricultural tie.

1 [2002] EWCA Civ 1131, [2002] 3 EGLR 1, CA. This was a case involving damages under the Local Land Charges Act 1975 to which the valuation method was held to apply: see [13].

D ACTING FOR THE VENDOR

1 Liability

(a) Contract races

9.125   Rule 10.06 of the Solicitors' Code of Conduct 2007[1] provides that where a solicitor is instructed by a vendor client to deal[2] with more than one prospective buyer, or discovers that the client is dealing directly with another purchaser or has instructed another conveyancer to deal with another purchaser, then he or she must disclose the fact that the vendor is treating with more than one purchaser to the solicitor acting for each prospective purchaser (or the purchaser himself if acting in person). If the vendor refuses to authorise such disclosure the solicitor must immediately cease to act. The purpose of this rule was considered by Chadwick LJ in *Jenmain Builders Ltd v Steed & Steed*: [3]

> 'The purpose, as it seems to me, is to avoid the risk that a prospective purchaser, who has agreed a price subject to contract, will take steps, and incur expense, in the course of proceeding towards exchange of contracts in the false belief that there is no other prospective purchaser in competition with him with whom the vendor is dealing. He needs to know that there is another prospective purchaser in competition with him so that he can take decisions as to his own actions in the light of that knowledge. He is then able to make a more informed assessment of the risk that his agreement subject to contract may not lead to an exchange of contracts. The obligation on the vendor's solicitor is an obligation to disclose information so that the person to whom the information is disclosed can take an informed decision as to the course of action which he will adopt.'

It is suggested that it would be an implied term of the solicitor's retainer that he or she could terminate the retainer if the vendor gave instructions which required the solicitor to act in contravention of the rule. It is not easy to discern in the wording of the rule (which appears in a part of the Solicitors' Code of Conduct 2007 devoted to relations with third parties) what, if any, duty the solicitor might owe to the vendor[4] because in nearly all cases it is likely to be in the vendor's financial interests to have the fact that he or she is dealing with more than one purchaser known to all prospective purchasers.

1   Rule 10.06 replaces the former r 6A of the Solicitors' Practice Rules 1990.
2   'Dealing' with in this context means 'having communication with any of the relevant parties intended to progress the matter': see para 42 of the notes to r 10 in the Solicitors' Code of Conduct 2007.
3   [2000] Lloyd's Rep PN 549, CA, per Chadwick LJ at para 27 (553 col 2). The rule under consideration in *Jenmain* was r 6A of the Solicitors' Practice Rules 1990.
4   The vendor's solicitor might owe duties to prospective purchasers as a result of the rule: see para 9.49, above.

(b) Commercial advice

9.126   As with purchasers, unless the facts give rise to a duty to give advice on a particular matter, a solicitor owes no general duty to give commercial advice to a client who is selling property.[1] That said, it is suggested that a solicitor owes a duty to give advice to prospective vendors in relation to at least the following matters.

1 The duty to volunteer advice tends to arise where some relevant information has come to the solicitor's attention such that he comes under a duty to warn (see *Credit Lyonnais v Russell Jones & Walker* [2002] EWHC 1310 (Ch); [2003] PNLR 2 Laddie J) at [21] and [28]) or where the client is not in full command of his faculties or appears to be unaware generally of what he is doing (see *Clarke Boyce v Mouat* [1993] 3 WLR 1021, PC at 1028F (Lord Jauncey). See paras 9.52–9.54, above and para 2.32ff, above.

(i)   The sale price

9.127   In the context of sales of land this issue usually arises where the client has agreed to sell at an undervalue. In *Bowdage v Harold Michelmore & Co*[1] it was held that it was not the solicitor's duty to advise his client that the price at which she had granted an option over her land was unreasonable and to advise her to consult a valuer. In *Johnson v Bingley, Dyson & Furey*[2] the judge also agreed that this was the general rule. However, he found the defendants negligent for failing to advise the client to take fresh valuation advice because (a) the solicitor had a concern about the capacity of the client and the fact that she was taking instructions through her son (who was a wages clerk) and (b) the son had agreed a price reduction which appeared to make no commercial sense.[3]

1 (1962) 106 Sol Jo 512 (Melford Stevenson J).
2 [1997] PNLR 392 (Benet Hytner QC).
3 See [1997] PNLR 392 at 408A–G.

(ii)   The deposit

9.128   Although there is no rule of law that a contract for the disposition of real property must provide for the payment by the purchaser of a non-refundable deposit, it is so common for a deposit to be taken that the *Conveyancing Handbook* states that: 'only in exceptional circumstances should a transaction proceed without a deposit being taken'.[1] The amount of deposit is usually 10% (although it is relatively common for the purchaser to accept an obligation to pay a 10% deposit in the event that the sale falls through after exchange of contracts but only to pay a smaller percentage on exchange[2]). The solicitor should not agree to take a deposit less than 10% without advising his client of the implications of this. Nor should the solicitor agree to accept a lower deposit without his or her client's express instructions[3]. In the event that the vendor is invited by the purchaser to enter a lock-out agreement (i e an agreement not to negotiate with other parties for a certain period) secured by payment of a sum which will either go towards the deposit in the event a deal is struck or be forfeited by the potential purchaser if he or she cannot fulfil the conditions of the lock-out agreement, then the vendor's solicitor should take care to ensure that the lock-out agreement is enforceable against the prospective purchaser.[4]

1 (14th edn, 2007) at B17.2.7. This reflects what was said by Sir John Pennycuick VC in *Potters v Loppert* [1973] Ch 399 at 405.
2 See the *Conveyancing Handbook* (above) at B17.2.3.
3 See *Morris v Duke-Cohan & Co* (1975) 119 SJ 826.
4 See *Gribbon v Lutton* [2001] EWCA Civ 1596, [2002] QB 902, CA, a case that also usefully reviews the authorities analysing the nature of deposits.

(*iii*) Overage clauses

9.129 It appears that a solicitor acting for a vendor is under no general duty to advise his client to seek to secure a share in any enhanced value of land sold.[1] It is suggested that this proposition is correct and that any potential development value of property being sold should have been taken account of in the sale price. Where, however, the purchaser has agreed to grant the vendor an overage entitlement following the decision in *Akasuc Enterprise Ltd v Choudhury*[2] the vendor's solicitor should advise the vendor how to protect that entitlement against the possibility that the obligation to pay overage may be circumscribed by the purchaser re-selling the property and the development being undertaken by that subsequent purchaser .

1 *Montlake v Lambert Smith Hampton Group Ltd* [2004] EWHC 938 (Comm), [2004] 20 EG 167 (CS) (Langley J) at [237].
2 [2003] EWHC 1275 (Ch). See the analysis of the ways in which mechanisms could be inserted into an agreement for sale to protect the vendor's entitlement to overage (which, in the absence of such safeguards, is likely to be a covenant personal to the purchaser and thus not enforceable against any subsequent purchaser who realises the development potential of the property).

(*iv*) The incidence of taxation

9.130 The vendor's solicitor should discover sufficient information from his client to determine whether the sale might attract capital gains tax.[1] Where a transaction is particularly complex, to avoid breach of duty a solicitor should (at the very least) take the step of warning the vendor that there might be taxation consequences arising from the sale and that the vendor should consider taking specialist advice in that regard. Certain commercial property transactions (freehold sales of new commercial buildings within three years of completion) attract VAT and the vendor's solicitor in such transactions will probably be in breach of duty if he or she fails to ensure that the client is either advised or made aware of the need to take advice regarding the implications of the sale.[2]

Similarly, a solicitor acting for a commercial landlord granting a lease to a tenant is under a duty to take instructions from his client as to whether the landlord has opted to pay VAT in relation to the building so that (if the landlord has opted to pay VAT) the lease can be appropriately drafted so as to ensure that the tenant pays VAT on the rent reserved. Failure to deal expressly in the lease with the tenant's liability to pay VAT on rent will result in the rent received by the landlord being treated for VAT purposes as if it were inclusive of VAT, thus reducing the value of the rent to the landlord by seven forty-sevenths.[3]

1 See the *Conveyancing Handbook* (14th edn, 2007) at A1.7.1(gg). See also *Hurlingham Estates Ltd v Wilde* [1997] 1 Lloyd's Rep 525 considered in para 1.8 and para 9.57, above.
2 See the *Conveyancing Handbook* at A16.1.1.
3 See the *Conveyancing Handbook* at A16.7.1 to A16.7.6

(c) Searches and inquiries

9.131   A solicitor owes a duty to his vendor client to answer inquiries and requisitions carefully and accurately. It seems that a careless failure to disclose the existence of adverse rights or encumbrances to the purchaser which exposes the client to an action by the purchaser for rescission of the contract or for damages for misrepresentation will also subject the solicitor to a liability in negligence.[1] In modern residential conveyancing, many of the matters that were once addressed by preliminary enquiries are now covered in the Seller's Property Information Form (SPIF) or Seller's Leasehold Information Form (SLIF), Part I of both of which contains numerous questions required to be answered by the vendor personally, and upon which the purchaser is entitled to rely[2]. Part II of the SPIF contains two questions to be completed by the vendor's solicitor designed to ensure that he or she has no information which contradicts or supplements the answers given by the vendor in Part I of the form. Vendors' solicitors have been reluctant to answer the questions in Part II of the form for fear of incurring liability directly to the purchaser[3] but such reluctance is misplaced and a failure to complete Part II of the form is likely to amount to a breach of duty to the vendor.[4] Whether that breach of duty sounds in damages will depend on whether the solicitor did indeed have information which was materially inconsistent with the representations made by the vendor in Part I of the form. The fact, however, that the vendor would be suing his or her solicitor for failing to prevent him from making what are likely to have been fraudulent misrepresentations[5] might well amount to an abuse of process.

1 See *Cemp Properties (UK) Ltd v Dentsply Research and Development Corpn* [1989] 2 EGLR 205 (Morritt J) where the solicitors admitted liability for failure to disclose to the purchaser deeds which contained rights of light and air.
2 See *McMeekin v Long* [2003] 29 EG 120, where Astill J considered the effect of misrepresenta-tions by vendors on Part I of the SPIF.
3 See paras 9.41–9.45, above, for duties to third parties.
4 See the Law Society's Conveyancing and Land Law Committee's guidance on completing Part II of the SPIF, at appendix H of the National Conveyancing Protocol.

5 The wording of Part 1 of the SPIF 'could not be expressed in clearer language. It is not a lawyer's form but one which has been designed for everyone to understand' (per Astill J in *McMeekin*). There might not be many circumstances in which false answers to any of the questions could be anything other than fraudulent or reckless.

9.132 Of greater difficulty is the case in which the solicitor has obtained information which suggests the existence of an adverse right but is far from conclusive. One example of this sort of information is evidence of the use of a track across the land by neighbours and the occasional member of the public which the client may tolerate without taking action. The definitive map is unlikely to be up to date and show a public right of way and local authority searches are unlikely to be of real assistance. Should the solicitor disclose this information? If it is disclosed the transaction might not proceed, because the client cannot make a clear or satisfactory title to the land, or the purchaser may seek a price reduction. If the evidence is not disclosed and a contract is made the purchaser may later have a claim for rescission for non-disclosure of a latent defect in title. If, on the other hand, the solicitor elects to disclose the information provided and the transaction is adversely affected, the client might legitimately complain that the disclosure was negligent. *Simmons v Pennington*[1] offers some support for the argument that a solicitor should not be held liable to his client in those circumstances. In that case a solicitor was not liable to his vendor client for disclosing to a purchaser that there had been breaches of a restrictive covenant as to user although no attempt had been made to enforce them.[2] It appears that the solicitor had not contemplated that his answer would entitle the purchaser to withdraw and it was held that he could not have been expected to anticipate the purchaser's withdrawal because he gave a standard answer to a standard requisition. If this is the true basis for the decision it is difficult to defend. But we suggest nevertheless that the decision is right. The law encourages the vendor of land to make full disclosure of his title (including disclosure of latent defects[3]) and a solicitor must give adequate disclosure to protect his client. If the consequence is that a purchaser withdraws the solicitor should not be held liable. In *Simmons v Pennington* the solicitor introduced a clause into the contract making the sale subject to any restrictions and he could not have answered the requisition truthfully in any other way. If he could have answered the question fully and truthfully without exposing his client to a liability the decision might have been different.[4]

1 [1955] 1 WLR 183, CA.
2 The inquiry about breaches of covenant was made at the requisition stage rather than before contract, because the property had been acquired at auction. The vendor was asked whether there were any restrictive covenants and whether they had been observed; the defendant's clerk answered truthfully; and, because the answer to the requisitions amounted to evidence that the vendor could not make good title to the property such that it answered the description by which it was sold, this entitled the purchaser to withdraw for repudiatory breach.
3 See *Emmet on Title* (2007) Vol 1 at 4.021.
4 See Parker LJ [1955] 1 WLR 183 at 191 rejecting the claim that the solicitor might have used some more negative words. But if this would have had the effect of keeping the contract alive, it is suggested that the solicitor was negligent in failing to do so.

(d) Leases

9.133 In the same way that the solicitor must advise a potential tenant about the terms of the proposed lease, so must he or she advise a potential landlord. In *Inter-Leisure Ltd v Lamberts*[1] the defendants inserted an 'upwards downwards' rent review clause in the draft lease by mistake and failed to negotiate for an 'upwards only' clause or advise the client that the lease had been executed in this form. In *Theodore Goddard v Fletcher King Services Ltd*[2] the solicitors failed to notice that the part of a rent review clause which ensured that any rent review was upwards only had been removed by mistake. Interestingly they recovered a contribution against the client's agents and surveyors for failing to notice the mistake as well. If the client is proposing to grant a lease to a limited company the solicitor would not usually (unless the client had no commercial experience)[3] be required to advise the taking of a guarantee from the directors of the company or from a parent company but in the event that a guarantee is required, the solicitor will be required to ensure that a binding guarantee in proper form is taken.[4] Where the guarantee is taken from a limited company, although the solicitor should warn the landlord of the risk that the guarantor could become insolvent (so that the landlord can consider whether it is prepared to accept the guarantee), the solicitor will not ordinarily come under any duty positively to advise the landlord to investigate the guarantor's financial standing[5]. Where the client is an original tenant who has negotiated a sale of the lease the solicitor would be obliged to advise him or her of the continuing liabilities.[6]

1 [1997] NPC 49 (Michael Harvey QC). The cases summarised in para 9.69 are equally applicable to landlords.
2 [1997] 32 EG 90 (HHJ Previte QC).
3 See *Allied Maples Group Ltd v Simmons & Simmons* [1995] 1 WLR 1602 at 1616G, CA where Stuart-Smith LJ stated that solicitors for an assignor would probably be negligent if they did not ask for a guarantee by a parent company of a subsidiary which was 'only marginally solvent'.
4 See *McElroy Milne v Commercial Electronics Ltd* [1993] NZLR 39.
5 See *Pickersgill v Riley* [2004] UKPC 14, [2004] PNLR 31, and *Football League Ltd v Edge Ellison* [2006] EWHC 1462, [2006] PNLR 2. In both of these cases, solicitors were found not liable for failing to advise their former clients to take steps to establish a third party's solvency.
6 See *Allied Maples* [1995] 1 WLR 1602 at 1608A–B, CA. The finding of negligence was not challenged on appeal. In fact the claimant in this case was a purchaser, but a purchaser of shares in a number of companies which had sold on a number of leases. The defendants were found liable for failure to advise the claimant of the subject companies' potential first tenant liabilities.

(e) Making title

9.134 Prior to the introduction of registered land the principal task of the vendor's solicitor was to make title to the subject property. This rarely presents a problem in the modern era and this is borne out by a comparison between the relatively large number of cases in which disappointed purchasers claim against their solicitors as against the very small number of cases concerned with claims by disappointed vendors.[1] Nevertheless, the vendor's solicitor should be careful to ensure that his or her client does indeed have good title to the property before exchanging contracts because, in exchanging contracts, the vendor is representing to the purchaser that he or she has title to the property in question and may become liable to compensate the purchaser in the event that he or she has misrepresented the position[2].

1 For a case concerned with a vendor's licensed conveyancer failing to make title to an unregistered development site, see *Hitchens v Higgens & Bacchus* [1997] NPC 115, CA.
2 For an example see *Sharneyford Supplies Ltd v Edge* [1986] 1 Ch 128.

2 Damages

(a) Sale of freehold property

9.135 The valuation method was applied in *Johnson v Bingley Dyson & Furey*[1] where the claimant would not have sold a freehold property ripe for development if she had been properly advised. She was awarded the difference between the market value at the date of breach (the date of sale) and the sale price. Deducted from the sale price was the amount which was required to pay compensation to a business tenant to obtain vacant possession. The valuation method is likely to provide the appropriate measure of damage where the property is freehold and where the claimant would not have sold it on the terms agreed.

1 [1997] PNLR 392 (Benet Hytner QC).

(b) Sale of a leasehold interest

9.136 Where the claimant is a landlord and the property in question a lease, the position is more complicated. Two types of damage are likely to be sustained by a landlord: either the lease which he or she has in fact granted is defective in some way (for example, it contains no upwards only rent review clause) and the landlord has lost a portion of the rent he or she could otherwise have expected to receive. Alternatively, the landlord may have lost a willing and able tenant as the result of some default on the part of the solicitor and thus has lost all of the rent he or she could otherwise have expected to receive. In the first situation, in simple terms the damage sustained by the landlord is that he or she is likely to receive less rent over the term of the lease than would otherwise have been the case. There are, theoretically, two ways of compensating the landlord for this reduced expectation of rent: first, by awarding damages calculated as the discounted value of the 'lost' rent over the term; and, secondly, by comparing the value of the landlord's reversionary interest subject to the hypothetical lease (i e the lease which would have been granted but for the solicitor's negligence) and subject to the actual lease. The calculation of damages in this first situation is made a great deal more complex by (a) the need to reflect various contingencies (e g the chance that the tenant would not have agreed to the form of lease which the landlord would have proposed or the chance that the tenant would exercise any break clause) and (b) the considerable scope for dispute over the date by reference to which damages should be assessed. In the second situation, the landlord might expect to recover from the solicitor lost rent (for a reasonable period until such time as the landlord found, or should have found, a replacement tenant) together with consequential losses such as, for example, the costs of remarketing the property to find a replacement tenant.

9.137 Thus, in *Inter-Leisure Ltd v Lamberts*[1] the judge found that there was a 75% chance that the tenants would in 1989 have taken a lease with an upwards-only rent review. He also found that there was only a 33% chance that the tenants would not have exercised a break clause if they had been faced with an upwards-only rent review in 1992. Finally, he found that the defect in the drafting of the rent review clause did not come to light until the negotiations for the rent review took place in 1992. In those circumstances he assessed damages as 25% (i e 33% of 75%) of the difference between the value of a lease with an upwards-only rent review and the lease as granted at the date of the first review, i e 1992. He also accepted the landlord's argument that, even if the tenants had exercised the break clause on the occasion of the first rent review in 1992, then that in turn would have produced a separate benefit of which the landlord had been deprived, because, had the tenants exercised the break clause, the value of the landlord's reversion would have been higher. The judge calculated the value of this loss as the lost chance of the landlord's obtaining the difference between the value of the freehold with vacant possession in 1992 and the value of the reversion at the same date but subject to the lease. The judge rejected the defendant's argument that damages should be assessed at the date of breach because it required the court to undertake an unacceptably artificial valuation exercise. The valuation of the freehold involved the expert valuers picking investment yields appropriate for the property some five years before trial. Given that these yields would involve assumptions or predictions about the behaviour of the market when this behaviour was now known, an assessment of the actual losses suffered since the date of the transaction was more appropriate.[2] He also considered that damages should be quantified at the first review date because, first, an upwards only rent review clause is designed to protect the landlord against subsequent falls in the market; second, the claimant did not learn of the defect until the first review; and, third, the solicitors had continued to act for the claimant in the meantime.

1 [1997] NPC 49 (Michael Harvey QC): see paras 3.17–3.20, above.
2 For helpful observations about the way in which the court should approach valuation evidence concerned with investment property, see *BBL v Eagle Star* at first instance [1995] 2 All ER 769 at 789 et seq (Phillips J).

9.138 *Roker House Investments Ltd v Saunders*[1] also involved a lease of investment property. The solicitors failed to advise the claimant at the time it was purchasing the freehold and leasing it back that a guarantee signed by the French parent of the tenant company was neither valid nor enforceable. After three years of receiving rents at above market values, the claimant sought to sell the property subject to the lease in a falling market at an asking price £120,000 less than it had originally paid. When a sale had been agreed, the defective guarantee came to light and the sale fell through. The claimant then took a surrender of the lease for a reverse premium of £450,000 and sold the freehold with vacant possession. The net sum recovered by the claimant amounted to only £50,000 less than the price at which it had agreed to sell the property subject to the lease. The claimant argued that damages should be assessed by the valuation method applied *as at the date of purchase* three years earlier. Alliott J directed himself that he had to ensure that the claimant was put in the same position it would have been in as if the resale had not fallen through and thus awarded damages assessed as the loss on resale. Three points are, however, worthy of mention: first, it was the defendants, not the claimant, who submitted that this was the appropriate measure of damage, and thus, it was not argued that such a loss was too remote. Second, this was an investment property and not a residential property. Third, and most important, the judge found that if the invalidity of the guarantee had come to light at the time of the original transaction the parent company would have rectified the situation and the transaction would have gone ahead.

1 Alliott J, 22 October 1997. The case is briefly reported in [1997] EGCS 137.

9.139   In *McElroy Milne v Commercial Electronics Ltd*[1] the claimant developer had developed a warehouse and office complex and granted a lease of the whole to a single tenant with the intention of selling the development subject to the lease. The claimant then found that it was unable to sell the tenanted development because the tenant's covenant was effectively worthless without a guarantee. The claimant recovered the difference between the price which it would have obtained if it had sold the development with the benefit of the guarantee at the time that it intended to sell it (when the market was buoyant) and the price which it actually realised for the property some years later after a market collapse. Damages were awarded on this basis because the solicitor's negligence had deprived the claimant of the ability to market the development as planned, such that the defendant's lost expectation of profits was not too remote.[2] The fact that the market had collapsed by the time that the claimant was able to sell the development was treated as evidence pointing to the defendant's liability (the purpose of the guarantee of the tenant's covenant being precisely to guard against the possible ill-effects of falls in the market).

1 [1993] NZLR 39, esp at 41, lines 48–9.
2 Or, put another way, the solicitor's duty was broad enough to encompass protecting the defendant's ability to make a profit by reselling the development.

9.140   Finally, the valuation method seems particularly inappropriate where the claimant sells a property for more than it was truly worth because of the defendant's breach of duty. In *Cemp Properties (UK) Ltd v Dentsply Research and Development Corpn Ltd*[1] the judge held that the defendant vendor was not entitled to recover from the third party solicitors that part of the sum which the vendor had paid the purchaser which 'represented the difference between the price Cemp paid and the true market value'. But since the purchaser recovered from the vendor the wasted expenditure it had incurred to extricate itself from the lease rather than any loss of value, the solicitors were ordered to indemnify their client against these damages.

1 [1989] 2 EGLR 205 at 207A (Morritt J).

E PARTICULAR KINDS OF PROPERTY

1 Lease renewals

9.141 A fertile source of negligence claims against solicitors has been the procedural requirements of the Landlord and Tenant Act 1954, Pt II, which provides a measure of protection for qualifying business tenancies. Following the amendment of that Act in 2004[1] the number of claims arising from solicitors' failings to follow the procedure for renewing a protected lease is likely to fall substantially. Under the Act before it was amended, there were strict time limits for taking various procedural steps and failure to comply with those steps could result in the tenant's losing the protection of the Act altogether. Tenants who had lost the protection of the Act could suffer two basic types of loss: either they were unable to renegotiate a new lease with their landlords, in which case they had to seek new premises elsewhere (with consequent loss of any goodwill referable to the location of the tenant's business) or they were able to negotiate a new lease, but outside the protection of the Act.

1 By the Regulatory Reform (Business Tenancies) (England and Wales) Order 2003, SI 2003/3096, which made the operation of the procedure contained in the Act more 'tenant-friendly'.

(a) Acting for tenants

9.142 Solicitors have been held liable when acting for tenants for failure to serve a counter-notice under s 25 of the Landlord and Tenant Act 1954 and to make an application to court;[1] failure to advise a client or potential client to take these steps;[2] advising the client wrongly with regard to the time limits for taking these steps[3]; failure to make an application to court;[4] and delay in the conduct of the application with the result that the rent ordered by the court was substantially higher than it should have been.[5] As noted above, many of these breaches of duty would not be possible now that the Act has been amended. Of greater complexity than breach of duty has been the assessment of damages. The

495

principles for assessing the loss of the value of a lease which have emerged in the authorities are of general application where the value of a lease has been lost (as for example in *Vision Golf v Weightmans*[6], where the solicitors failed to apply for relief from forfeiture leading to the otherwise avoidable loss of their client's lease).

1 *Ricci v Masons* [1993] 2 EGLR 159 (Lionel Swift QC).
2 *Whelton Sinclair v Hyland* [1992] 2 EGLR 158, CA.
3 *Fairbrother v Gabb & Co* [2002] EWCA Civ 803, [2002] 23 EG 119 (CS).
4 *R P Howard Ltd v Woodman Matthews & Co* [1983] BCLC 117 (Staughton J) and *Hodge v Clifford Cowling & Co* [1990] 2 EGLR 89, CA.
5 *Teasdale v Williams & Co* (1983) 269 Estates Gazette 1040, CA.
6 [2006] EWHC 1766 (Ch), [2005] PNLR 45 (Christopher Nugee QC).

(i) Cases where the tenant has obtained a new, less advantageous, lease

9.143   The rent payable under most business tenancies protected by the Landlord and Tenant Act 1954 is a market or rack rent but this does not mean that a new lease, when ordered by the court, has no capital value. In most such cases the capital value will be due to the goodwill of the business or the trading location of the premises, and the security offered by the Act will enable a tenant who wishes to sell to maximise that value. Where the new lease would have had a premium value but the tenant has lost security of tenure by taking a contracted-out tenancy or had to negotiate new and unattractive terms because he has lost the protection of the Act, the lease which he is obliged to accept is likely to have no premium value or to have a value that is substantially lower than could have been expected. In these cases the difference between the value of the business with the lease which would have been ordered and the business with the actual lease negotiated is the most obvious loss. In *Clark v Kirby-Smith*[1] the tenant was unable to prove that the new lease would have had any capital value and recovered nominal damages only. But in *Ricci v Masons*[2] the tenant had a restaurant with a rising turnover and substantial goodwill. Once the protection of the Act was lost he was only able to negotiate a five-year contracted-out lease with his landlord. The judge found that if his application for a new lease had been heard, the court would have ordered a ten-year lease subject to a redevelopment break clause at a lower rent which could be sold for £100,000 on the open market. A similar result was achieved in *Aran Caterers v Stephen Lake Gilbert & Paling*[3], where the claimant was awarded the difference in the value of the subject premises with a protected lease and the value with the unprotected lease which had in fact been granted, the value being assessed by reference to the profits of the claimant's business. In a number of other cases a difference in premium value has also been proved despite the fact that the rent payable under the new lease would have been a market or rack rent.[4]

1 [1964] Ch 506 (Plowman J). The tenant gave up possession and also claimed damages for the terminal repairs liability. This was dismissed on the ground that it was caused by the tenant's own

breach of covenant. There was no claim for loss of goodwill or disruption of business. The tenant had allowed options to renew to lapse and had not sought to negotiate.

2 [1993] 2 EGLR 159 (Lionel Swift QC).

3 [2002] 1 EG 76. Although the claimant obtained a new lease, it considered the terms so disadvantageous that it took the commercial decision to relocate early, before the landlord exercised a break clause in order to redevelop. The damages awarded recognised the value of the lost lease but nothing was awarded in relation to the claimant's costs of relocation, which would have been incurred in any event when the landlord exercised a break clause.

4 In *Whelton Sinclair v Hyland* [1992] 2 EGLR 158 (above) the claimant vacated and was awarded £5,000 loss of premium value. In *Jolliffe v Charles Coleman* & Co (1971) 219 Estates Gazette 1608 (Browne J) the claimant was awarded £250 to reflect the difference in capital values.

9.144 In both *Hodge v Clifford Cowling* & Co[1] and *Ricci v Masons*[2] it was held that the appropriate date for assessment of the tenant's capital loss was the date of breach. In the former, the defendants (seeking to have various matters taken into account which would have reduced the damages payable) argued that loss should be assessed at a date later than the date of breach, alternatively that events after the date of breach should be taken into account. The Court of Appeal agreed with the trial judge that in all the circumstances the loss suffered by the claimants was the diminution in value of the goodwill of their business assessed at the date of breach, and that subsequent events were irrelevant. In the latter case it was found that the tenant did intend to realise both the tenancy and his business at a later date; but because the tenant would have had a saleable asset at the date of breach, his present or future intentions were not considered relevant to the date of assessment.

1 [1990] 2 EGLR 89, CA.
2 [1993] 2 EGLR 159.

9.145 Even where the claimant can prove no loss of capital value, the consequence of the solicitor's negligence may be that the tenant is required to pay a higher rent than would have been ordered under the Act. The court may simply assess what the claimant would have paid over the length of the term if his or her rights had been preserved and compare that with the passing rent: see *Teasdale v Williams & Co,*[1] in which the claimant took a seven-year lease at a higher rent instead of the five-year lease at a lower rent which would have been ordered under the Act. He paid less than he would in years 1 and 2, more than he would in years 3–5 and would have applied to court for a new tenancy at the end of year 5. He was awarded the increase in years 3–5 less the gain in years 1 and 2. No damages were awarded for years 6 and 7 because the need to apply to court for a new tenancy two years earlier would have cancelled out any increased rent.

1 (1983) 269 Estates Gazette 1040, CA.

9.146 Until or unless the landlord applies for an interim rent the tenant is entitled to pay rent at the old rate until the determination of his or her application for a new tenancy. If, however, his or her solicitor fails to serve a counter-notice or apply to court for a new tenancy in time, the tenancy will come to an end at the expiry of the section 25 notice. In many cases, therefore, the tenant will begin to pay rent at a higher rate much earlier. In *Jolliffe v Charles Coleman & Co*,[1] the judge awarded the claimant the increased rent payable during the course of the proceedings as well as his capital loss.

1 (1971) 219 Estates Gazette 1608 (Browne J).

(ii)   Cases where the tenant is obliged to vacate

9.147   Where the tenant is obliged to give up possession of the premises but carries on trading, assessing damages reference to the value attributable to the lost lease can be complex. In *Matlock Green Garages Ltd v Potter Brooke-Taylor & Wildgoose*[1], for example, where the tenant company was deprived of the opportunity to obtain a new 10-year lease of a petrol filling station, the tenant was only able to negotiate a short three-year lease terminable on three months' notice. That lease was terminated and the company not only closed down the petrol filling station business but also sold off a number of related businesses and assets which were carried out on different sites. The judge awarded damages by calculating the annual net maintainable profits of the company as a whole, making certain adjustments to the profit figures, splitting out the profits attributable to the other businesses and multiplying the figure by the period of occupation which the claimant had lost. Two additional points are worthy of note: first, the judge rejected an assessment based on the diminution in value of the business at the date of breach as unreal; secondly, he refused to award damages for the sale of the other businesses on the basis that these losses were too remote.

1 [2000] Lloyd's Rep PN 935. The judgment was handed down on 13 November 1996.

9.148   A tenant's loss after being required to vacate premises may not always involve a calculation of lost profits, however. In *Abraxas Computer Services Ltd v Rabin Leacock Lipman*[1], for example, the claimant occupied two buildings, the lease of one of which it wished to have the option to renew as part of a strategy to consolidate its operations either into that building or another building altogether. As a result of the solicitor's negligence, the claimant lost the ability to keep its options open as it had intended, and had to undertake what was accepted as a 'frantic' search for a new building. It was accepted that by the time the claimant discovered the solicitor's negligence, it had already decided that it would have to consolidate into another building (i e it would not have taken up a renewed lease of the old building in any event). The claimant nevertheless successfully sued for damages caused by its being forced to move into a new building under pressure, which had adversely affected its ability to negotiate the terms of its occupation of that building. Damages were assessed as the lost chance to have gone into the market place under less time pressure and thus to negotiate a better deal on a building into which to consolidate.

1 [2000] EG 70 (CS).

9.149 Where the business carried on by the tenant is effectively destroyed by its inability to renew its lease, the measure of loss is likely to be assessed as the value of the lost business itself. Although not a case involving the time limits for renewal of leases under the Act, *Vision Golf v Weightmans*[1] is one illustration of the court's approach to this task. In that case, the solicitors had failed to apply for relief from forfeiture in circumstances where, had such an application been made, relief would have been granted. In the result, the tenant had lost the lease of land which formed part of a golf course being developed by the claimant. The expert evidence was that leases of golf courses were to be valued by reference to the profitability of the business actually operated on the demised premises. An unusual feature of the case was that there was apparently no good evidence available regarding the claimant's trading position at the material times; in the absence of such evidence, the court assessed the value of the lost lease by reference to comparable leases of other (profitable) golf courses[2].

1 [2006] EWHC 1766 (Ch), [2005] PNLR 45. This is the judgment on damages; for the judgment on scope of duty, see [2005] EWHC 1675 (Ch), [2005] 32 EG 66 (Lewison J).
2 Cf the situation where the loss is of an entirely new business (for which profits are hypothetical), when the court is likely to assess the value of the business at what that business might fetch on the open market as at the date it was lost: *UYB Ltd v British Railways Board* (2000) Times, 15 November 2000, CA; see also *Crehan v Inntrepreneur Pub Co CPC* [2004] EWCA Civ 637, [2004] 23 EG 120 (CS), at paras 173–180.

(b) Acting for landlords

9.150 In *Nadreph Ltd v Willmett & Co*[1] the defendant solicitors served a section 25 notice opposing the grant of a new tenancy on a ground under which the tenant could claim statutory compensation when the claimant landlord wished only to recover a part of the premises and would not have served a notice opposing the grant of a new tenancy. The tenant vacated and claimed compensation and the claimant claimed against the defendants for the additional amount payable. Damages were agreed as the amount of compensation subject to one point, namely, whether the claimant had to give credit for its own use of the premises not only against the loss of rent but also against the compensation.[2] In *Talisman Property Co (UK) Ltd v Norton Rose*[3] the claimant was the successor in title of a landlord who had served a notice opposing the grant of a new tenancy on the tenant of premises which were in fact occupied by another company which had acquired the tenant. When the claimant became landlord, it wished to grant a lease to the company which was in actual occupation of the premises, i e it wished to withdraw the previous landlord's notice (which had entitled the tenant to statutory compensation) and conclude a new lease. The claimant's solicitors, in seeking to give effect to the claimant's instructions, negligently served a notice on the occupants (i e not on the lawful tenant) and the notice also stated that the claimant opposing the grant of a new tenancy on the grounds that it wished to redevelop. The claimant's negotiations with the party in actual occupation fell through and it vacated enabling the tenant to claim statutory compensation from the claimant. The claimant sought damages for the lost opportunity of avoiding the payment of statutory compensation and of entering a lease with the party in actual occupation. The Court of Appeal accepted that there was a chance that it could have done so and awarded as damages the amount of statutory compensation paid to the tenant multiplied by the percentage lost chance of avoiding that payment, together with a figure to represent the claimant's lost chance of obtaining rent from the party in actual occupation under a new lease.

1 [1978] 1 All ER 746 (Whitford J).
2 Although the report is not explicit, it appears that the claimant obtained a benefit from the tenant vacating which exceeded the amount of the rent which the tenant would have paid.
3 [2006] EWCA Civ 1104, [2006] 45 EG 192.

2 Options

9.151 Option agreements themselves, whether for the sale or purchase of land or for the grant or termination of a lease, require no separate treatment.[1] It goes without saying that it is the solicitor's duty to make sure that the client fully understands the terms of, and time for, the exercise of the option when the agreement is made.

1 It is now settled that the requirement for signed writing prescribed by s 2 of the Law of Property (Miscellaneous Provisions) Act 1989 is satisfied in the case of options by the original contract: see *Spiro v Glencrown Properties Ltd* [1991] Ch 537 (Hoffmann J). Formalities, therefore, present no special difficulties.

(a) Reminders

9.152 Ordinarily a solicitor owes no duty to repeat advice once given. But this issue often arises where the advice was about the timing of the exercise of an option. In *Yager v Fishman & Co*[1] the defendants were held not liable for failing to remind their client to exercise a break option in a lease or for failing to exercise it themselves. The case has often been taken as authority for the proposition that a solicitor is under no duty to remind. It is clear, however, that the Court of Appeal were not laying down any particular rule in relation to the exercise of options or the issuing of reminders. This was not a case in which the client had forgotten the date. His complaint was that the solicitors should have advised him to take a different course: the client had guaranteed the tenant company's liabilities, the tenant had gone into liquidation, the liquidator had sublet the premises for a time, and the client was negotiating to take an assignment. He could not decide whether to break the lease or to continue to exploit the premises. He claimed that, in response to a letter which he had written, the defendants ought to have advised him to break the lease. This was held to be a matter of commercial judgment. In *Donmez v Barnes & Partners*[2], by contrast, a solicitor who acted for the grantee of a lease which contained an option to purchase the freehold within two years of the commencement of the term was held liable in negligence for failing to ask the claimant to come and see him as the time drew near for the exercise of the option.[3] It cannot be said, therefore, that as a general rule a solicitor owes no duty to remind his client about the need to consider exercising an option. Whether the solicitor will owe a duty is likely to depend on (a) the terms of the option and, in particular, how soon and how often the right to exercise it arises, (b) the nature of the original advice and whether it was given in writing, (c) the existence of a continuing retainer and (d) the knowledge and experience of the client.[4]

1 [1944] 1 All ER 552, esp at 558D, CA.
2 [1996] EGCS 129 (HHJ Prosser QC).
3 See also *West London Observer v Parsons* (1955) 166 Estates Gazette 749 (Gorman J): advice given in 1950 (in writing) and 1951 (orally); opportunity to break lost in 1953.
4 For an example of a case in which the solicitor came under a positive duty to give advice about the exercise of an option see *Credit Lyonnais v Russell Jones & Walker* [2002] EWHC 1310 (Ch); [2003] PNLR 2 Laddie J discussed in para 2.32ff and paras 9.53 and 9.128, above.

(b) Exercise of the option

9.153 In juridical terms an option is a privilege not a right. It is well established that the conditions for the exercise of an option both as to time and manner must be satisfied strictly.[1] If the task of exercising the option is entrusted to a solicitor, it is almost inevitable that he or she will be negligent if the exercise of the option is invalid because the conditions are not satisfied. In *Tonitto v Bassal*[2] the defendant was held liable for a failure to deliver a signed contract for sale with the notice of exercise and a payment, all of which were required by the option agreement. It was contended that the agreement was uncertain and that the solicitor should not be liable for misconstruing it but this argument was rejected. In *Roberts v J W Ward & Son*[3] the defendants failed to specify the price in the notice and also to serve one of the parties. It was likewise held that despite the uncertainty in the conditions required by the option agreement, the defendants were liable not only for failing to serve a party but also for serving an invalid notice. In *Titanic Investments Ltd v MacFarlanes*[4] the vendor's solicitors this time were held liable for agreeing to a formula for the determination of the price without advising their clients fully of the terms proposed and obtaining their agreement to them.

1 See *Emmet on Title* (2007) Vol 1 at 2.079.
2 (1992) 28 NSWLR 564.
3 (1981) 126 Sol Jo 120, CA.
4 [1997] NPC 105 (Robert Walker J) and (3 December 1998, unreported), CA.

(c) Damages (1): grant of the option

9.154 Where the solicitor's breach of duty leads to his client either granting or taking an option on terms which he would not have accepted if properly advised, the appropriate measure of damage is likely to depend on what the outcome would have been if the client had received the proper advice. In *Titanic Investments v MacFarlanes* the court found that agreement would have been reached on some terms and approached the assessment of damages by considering the potential outcomes and evaluating the chances of each occurring. This decision is considered in more detail in Chapter 3.[1]

1 See paras 3.30–3.31, above.

9.155   In *Amerena v Barling*[1] the defendants granted an option over shares in a company without the authority of the claimant. The judge at first instance found that the claimant would not have authorised the grant of the option and the Court of Appeal considered the question of damages on the basis that no option would have been granted at all. They applied the valuation method at the date of breach and assessed damages as the difference between the value of the shares subject to the option and their unfettered value at the date of the option agreement. It was argued that the appropriate date for assessment was the date for the exercise of the option by which time the claimant had spent £1.75m to buy in the rights under the option agreement and to free the shares. Although the judgment of Peter Gibson LJ is couched in negative terms so that he could see no reason to depart from the usual rule, there were a number of reasons why the date of breach was the appropriate date: first, the subject matter of the option was shares; second, it was clear that the claimant had made a good bargain and the value of the shares subject to the option at the date of its grant were no less than their unfettered value; third – and perhaps most importantly – there was little or no explanation for the claimant's decision to buy back the rights at what appeared to be an inflated price. On this last point the Court of Appeal held that the re-purchase of the shares was not reasonable mitigation given that the claimant only opened negotiations some 18 months after the option had been granted.

1 (1993) 69 P & CR 252.

9.156   *Amerena v Barling* may be distinguishable where the subject matter of the option is land and the existence of the option locks the claimant in to a sale at a price which he cannot avoid. If the value of the land changes to the claimant's detriment during the option period, it does not seem just that the claimant should be held to the value at the date of breach. Nevertheless, because an option is an inchoate right, much may turn on the efforts of the claimant to negotiate a release from the option or to mitigate his loss in other ways. If the claimant becomes aware at an early stage of the defendant's mistake but takes no steps to mitigate his loss the court may adopt the same approach whether shares or land are in issue.

(d) Damages (2): exercise of the option

9.157   There is little authority on the measure of damages for breach of an option agreement by one of the parties, let alone a solicitor's negligence action arising out of such a claim. In *Homsy v Murphy*[1] the court awarded damages based on the difference between the purchase price and the value of the land at the date of exercise of the option. The calculation of the loss was complicated by the fact that the claimant had a purchaser for both the option land and his own land at a price which reflected the marriage value of the two interests and it was held that the valuation ought to take into account the marriage value. The general principle also holds good for assessing or quantifying damages where the claimant's complaint is that he has lost the opportunity to exercise an option as a consequence of his solicitor's failure to exercise the option.

1 (1996) 73 P & CR 26, CA.

3   Right to buy transactions

9.158   Although there appear to be no directly relevant[1] reported cases arising from a solicitor's breach of duty towards a client seeking to exercise his or her right to buy under the Housing Act 1985[2] anecdotal evidence suggests that claims in this regard are not uncommon. The provisions of HA 1985 dealing with the exercise of the right to buy are complex and contain various (generous) statutory deadlines by which the tenant must complete certain steps, failing which the tenant's application is deemed to be withdrawn. Although a tenant may serve a fresh notice exercising the right to buy for a second time, in a rising market the price payable for the property (even after the statutory discount) might mean that the tenant is no longer able to obtain a mortgage and buy the property.

1 In *White v Paul Davidson Taylor* [2004] EWCA Civ 1511, [2005] PNLR 15, the claimant's allegations against the solicitors arose from possession proceedings brought against him by a housing association in which he had counterclaimed seeking to exercise a right to buy. The claimant sought no damages in relation to any loss of the right to buy discount, and in any event his claim was dismissed.
2 As amended by the Housing Act 2004.
3 Note that the amount of the statutory discount is subject to change: see, for example, the Housing (Right to Buy) (Limits on Discount) (Amendment) Order 2003, SI 2003/498.

9.159   If the tenant's application is deemed withdrawn as the result of breach of duty on the part of his or her solicitor, the tenant remains in occupation of the subject property but, rather than owning the freehold, has a leasehold interest. In order to be in the position he or she would have been in but for the solicitor's breach of duty, the tenant ought to be awarded as damages an amount which would compensate him or her for any additional sums which he or she had to pay both to acquire the property and as additional rent. Damages should therefore be assessed at the date of trial and on the basis that the risk of the market price moving upwards after the loss of the right to buy should be borne by the solicitor.[1]

1 See *McElroy Milne v Commercial Electronics Ltd* [1993] NZLR 39, discussed at para 9.141, above.

Chapter 10

Lenders' claims

A CONTRACT AND THE TORT OF NEGLIGENCE

1 Introduction and summary of key issues

10.01 In the years following the recession and property crash of the early 1990s, residential mortgage lenders such as banks and building societies suffered enormous losses due to the default of borrowers to whom they had lent, usually in cases where the property on which they had taken security was repossessed but sold at a price which was insufficient to pay off the sums owing under the loan agreement. In many cases they sought to recover their losses from solicitors who had acted for them in arranging the mortgages. The ensuing litigation led to a raft of decisions as to the solicitors' liability, which developed a body of principles which apply in the law of contract, tort, fiduciary duty and trusts. In 1999, as a result of a negotiation between the Law Society and the Council of Mortgage Lenders ('CML'), the Law Society introduced its Practice Rule 6(3)[1] which was intended to govern the contractual terms on which solicitors acted for borrowers and lenders in standard mortgage cases. After about 2000, however, there was a dramatic reduction in the volume of lenders' litigation, so that the effect of the new rules is untested in the courts. Since the guidance of authority is not available in interpreting these new rules, we have compared them with the old rules and make some observations as to their effect which are based on the existing case law. As to the volume of cases in this area, at the time of writing in 2007 it appears that lenders' claims are beginning to return.

1 Now replaced by rr 3.16–3.22 of the Solicitors' Code of Conduct 2007.

10.02 In discussing the case law we concentrate in particular on two decisions in the Chancery Division in relation to managed lists of actions. In 1995, the court effectively consolidated a large number of actions brought by the Bristol and West Building Society against solicitor defendants. Chadwick J's final judgment, concerning eight individual actions, is reported as *Bristol and West Building Society v Fancy and Jackson*[1] (hereafter *Fancy and Jackson*). In 1997, a similar practice was adopted in relation to actions brought by the Nationwide Building Society against various solicitor defendants. Blackburne J gave judgment on all issues other than mitigation and assessment of loss in 1999; most of the judgment is reported as *Nationwide Building Society v Balmer Radmore*[2] and thus it is referred to hereafter as *Balmer Radmore.* The consolidation of actions enabled the court to deal with the issues in more detail than might have been possible on hearing only one action, and to produce more wide-ranging judgments. This is why we deal principally with those decisions, together with the leading judgments which they apply, namely those of the Court of Appeal in *Mortgage Express Ltd v Bowerman & Partners,*[3] *Bristol and West Building Society v Mothew*[4] and *National Home Loans Corpn plc v Giffen Couch & Archer*[5] and the House of Lords in *Target Holdings Ltd v Redferns*[6] and *South Australia Asset Management Corpn v York Montague Ltd*[7]. The latter is generally referred to as *SAAMCo*, a practice which we follow here.

1 [1997] 4 All ER 582. The same judge gave judgment on a large number of applications for summary judgment in *Bristol and West Building Society v May, May & Merrimans* [1996] 2 All ER 801, but that decision has to be treated with some care as the Court of Appeal criticised some aspects of it in *Bristol and West Building Society v Mothew* [1998] Ch 1.
2 [1999] Lloyd's Rep PN 241.
3 [1996] 2 All ER 836.
4 [1998] Ch 1.
5 [1998] 1 WLR 207.
6 [1996] AC 421.
7 [1997] AC 191.

Key issues

10.03 Although we comment below on a number of features of *Balmer Radmore,* it is thought that, for practical purposes, the two most important points which arise out of the case are these. First, in cases where the lender proves only breach of contract or negligence against the solicitor, the effect of *Balmer Radmore* was greatly to increase the benchmark for awards of contributory negligence against claimant lenders. This is dealt with below.[1] But secondly, in cases where the lender succeeds in showing deliberate breach of fiduciary duty against the solicitor, there will be no deduction for contributory negligence, no matter how negligent the lender was in making the offer of advance. For this reason, it is in the interests of lenders to show deliberate breach of fiduciary duty, or breach of trust, and in the interests of solicitor defendants to avoid such findings and to emphasise the contributory negligence of the lender. What is required to show breach of fiduciary duty or breach of trust is discussed in chapter 4[2], and in section E of this chapter.[3] Proving mere negligence on the part of the solicitor will not be sufficient: see those passages for more detailed discussion.

1 Para 10.90ff.
2 See para 4.24ff and 4.06ff, above.
3 Para 10.122ff.

10.04 This chapter begins with a brief discussion of the roles of lenders and solicitors in the typical mortgage transaction, and the basic mechanism of a sub-sale fraud. This need be read only by those unfamiliar with this type of claim. We then deal with claims in contract and the tort of negligence: breach of the express terms of the solicitor's retainer, breach of implied terms, breach of undertakings given to banks who are not clients, causation and the application of *SAAMCo*, interest, contributory negligence, mortgage indemnity guarantees, mitigation, contribution, and claims by multiple lenders. Next are considered other claims at common law: those based on fraud, breach of warranty of authority, and actions for money had and received. Finally we refer briefly to equity, which is dealt with fully in chapter 4.

10.05 In order to understand the issues in lenders' claims, some background knowledge is helpful. This concerns the ways in which lenders normally deal with mortgage applications and solicitors normally deal with residential con-veyancing when acting for both lender and borrower, and the nature of sub-sale frauds.

2 Roles of the lender and solicitor[1]

10.06 A typical transaction might proceed as follows. A prospective house-buyer ('the borrower') applies to a mortgage lender ('the lender') for a mort-gage in order to buy a property ('the property'). Normally the borrower will not apply for a mortgage until he or she has agreed a price for the purchase, subject to contract, although this need not necessarily be the case. In deciding whether to lend money to the borrower, the lender considers essentially two issues: first, the value of the property which is to be taken as security for the loan, and secondly, the ability of the borrower to make the repayments required. The latter will be referred to as the value of the borrower's covenant: the borrower covenants with the lender to make the repayments.

1 For a helpful statement of the procedure followed by the Nationwide Building Society in the period 1989 to 1991, which is typical of many, see *Balmer Radmore* [1999] Lloyd's Rep PN 241 at 247–251.

(a) Value of the security

10.07 The lender will take a first legal charge over the property which should enable it to take possession of, and sell, the property in the event of the borrower defaulting. Hence the lender must consider the value of the property, and the proportion of the valuation which the borrower wishes to borrow. In order to determine the value, lenders will normally commission and receive a written valuation report from a competent valuer. Pausing there, this means that in all claims by lenders against solicitors, the solicitors should consider whether the valuer who prepared the valuation report was negligent, and, if so, whether contribution proceedings should be instituted.[1] Once the lender has received the valuation report, it must consider how much the borrower wishes to borrow. This proportion is known as the 'loan to value' or 'LTV'. For instance, if a property is valued at £100,000 and the borrower wishes to borrow £75,000, then the LTV is 75%. The lender will have written lending criteria which are likely to set out the maximum percentage of the valuation, or LTV, which it is prepared to lend. Some lenders lend up to 75% of the value of the property, others 90%, and others may lend 100%. Lending more than 75% LTV in a market where property prices are known to be falling and after little scrutiny of the borrower's finances may well constitute contributory negligence.[2] Much of the discussion of liability below considers the circumstances in which solicitors who discover information which casts doubt on the value which the lender believes the property to have ought to report such information to the lender.

1 See para 10.101, below.
2 See para 10.94, below .

(b) Value of the borrower's covenant

10.08 The second issue is whether the borrower will be able to afford to make the repayments required in order to finance the proposed loan. Questions are generally asked on the mortgage application form relating to this issue. Two broad categories of loan should be considered. First, in the ordinary case the lender will undertake what are known as 'status checks', in other words enquiries as to the borrower's creditworthiness. Various checks are made by different lenders; again, the precise steps which a particular lender takes will depend on the terms of that lender's mortgage criteria. They may include seeking: a banker's reference; a reference from the borrower's landlord, if the borrower is renting his or her accommodation, or from the previous lender, if it is charged; a search with a credit reference agency to determine whether, for instance, there are any unpaid county court judgments in the borrower's name; in the case of an employee, an employer's reference; in the case of a self-employed person, three years' accounts and possibly an accountant's reference; or a search of the electoral roll to see whether the borrower is recorded as living at the address given in the mortgage application form. The lender may also interview the borrower to satisfy itself of the truth of his or her answers. The extent to which a particular claimant lender has undertaken such enquiries is likely to be relevant in determining whether it has been contributorily negligent. As we shall see below, in general it is doubtful whether solicitors have any implied duty to report matters which they discover which are relevant only to the borrower's ability to pay.

10.09 An alternative approach is for a lender to rely almost entirely on the value of the property as security for the loan, and therefore to make no, or limited, investigation of the borrower's finances. Depending on their precise terms, loans made on this basis may be known as 'non-status' loans, if the lender has not investigated the borrower's financial status at all, or 'self-certifying loans', where the lender has relied upon the borrower's own statement as to his or her means. It appears that loans of these two varieties have led to more losses for lenders than other loans. We discuss the circumstances in which lending on such a basis might amount to contributory negligence below.[1]

1   See para.10.97, below .

10.10   Once the lender is satisfied as to both the value of the security and the borrower's ability to pay, it makes an offer of advance, and issues written instructions to solicitors at the same time. Normally the same solicitors act for both lender and borrower. The lender's instructions to the solicitors will often incorporate part 1 of the CML Lenders' Handbook.[1] The written instructions incorporate the express terms of the lender's retainer of the solicitors. The solicitors are normally required to submit to the lender a report on title or certificate of title. In cases to which r 3.20 of the Solicitors' Code of Conduct applies, the certificate of title must be in the form annexed to r 3 of that Code[2]. The certificate of title is generally the principal document in which the solicitors report information to the lender. If the lender receives a certificate of title which raises no concerns about the transaction then it will normally proceed to forward the advance money to the solicitors so that the transaction may be completed. The lender will expect to be provided by the solicitors with an enforceable and valid first legal charge over the property after completion. We consider the nature of the solicitors' duties further below.

1   Discussed at para 10.14ff, below.
2   Discussed at para 10.23, below.

3   Sub-sales, back to back sales and direct payments

10.11   During the 1990s round of lenders' litigation, many cases involved allegations of a particular type. Although many other kinds of fraud may be the subject of lenders' claims, it is helpful to have this particular variety in mind in interpreting the cases. Simplified, it operates as follows. A sells a property to B, and then B sells it on to C. The sales from A to B and from B to C take place on the same day, or within a short space of time. A sells to B for say £100,000, and B sells exactly the same property to C for, say, £150,000. The true value of the property is £100,000. The property market is falling or static at the time, so there is no reason for C's solicitor to suppose that the value of the property has suddenly increased by 50% in a single day. C's mortgage lender is unaware of the sale from A to B, and may lend, say, £120,000 on C's supposed purchase from B for £150,000. If B and C are in league, then the sale from B to C may be a device to deceive C's lender. B and C can use £100,000 of C's lender's money to pay off A, and retain the remaining £20,000; they then disappear with the £20,000. B and C may inform their respective solicitors that there is no need for payment of a deposit, or even of any of the balance of £50,000, because C has paid the £50,000 directly to B. The point is that the price at which B is selling to C (£150,000) is a sham: the true value of the property is the price at which A is selling to B (£100,000), but C's lender must be deceived into believing the true value to be £150,000. This is why, from the lender's point of view, knowledge of the price at which A is selling to B may be very helpful in detecting the fraud and withdrawing from the transaction. It is also why both the lender and the solicitor may also wish to blame C's lender's valuer who has presumably valued the property at £150,000 rather than £100,000. The word sub-sale tends to be used to describe the case where A sells to B and then B sells on to C soon after.

10.12 The cases suggest that, in the early 1990s, frauds of this type occurred on a considerable scale. The extent to which solicitors realised the risk of such fraud is considered below.[1] In particular, the question arises of the extent to which solicitors should have realised that sub-sales with price uplifts were taking place, and should have reported them to lenders. The effect of the judgment in *Balmer Radmore*[2] is that solicitors often should have realised this risk and reported it to lenders. As indicated above, litigation in this area between 2000 and 2006 almost dried up. This does not, however, necessarily mean that such frauds ceased; it may be that the generally rising property market has either concealed their effect or meant that they resulted in no or minimal losses for the lenders. In July 2002 the Law Society issued its 'Warning – Property Fraud 2', whose effect was that solicitors had to continue to be vigilant to spot mortgage fraud. We consider the implications of this warning below.

1 See para.10.29, below.
2 [1999] Lloyd's Rep PN 241.

10.13 One might ask why fraudsters thought it necessary to enter into such an elaborate series of transactions in order to defraud mortgage lenders. Our example assumes that A is honest and the sale from A to B is at the market price of £100,000. It would of course be possible for a fraudster, B, to purchase the property for £100,000 and tell his lender that the price was £150,000. But this would require the involvement of a dishonest solicitor who was willing to tell his lender client a blatant lie as to the price at which the property was being bought. The advantage of the sub-sale mechanism is that C does not require a dishonest solicitor in order to ensure that his or her lender does not find out the full story of the transactions. As long as C's solicitor either fails to find out the price of the sale from A to B, or does not trouble to consider whether it is a matter which should be reported to C's lender, the transaction may proceed without the lender knowing of it. Thus the transaction may proceed without C needing to find a dishonest solicitor. This was perhaps the reason for its apparent popularity as a fraudulent device.

4 The CML Lenders' Handbook

10.14 The enormous wave of lenders' claims that swept over the solicitors' profession during the 1990s led to a negotiation between the Law Society, major lenders and the CML which in turn brought about agreement on the introduction of a new r 6(3) of the Solicitors' Practice Rules. Practice Rule 6(3) was designed to be used in conjunction with the CML Lenders' Handbook, which was introduced at the same time. In cases where it is used, the Lenders' Handbook comprises part of the lender's instructions to the solicitor. Practice Rule 6(3) was the subject of some modifications between 1999 and 2007, and on 1 July 2007 was replaced by rr 3.16–3.22 of the Solicitors' Code of Conduct. In dealing with any particular case, it is important to consider the terms of the relevant practice rule or conduct rule, and version of the Lenders' Handbook, which were current at the material times. In this book, unless otherwise stated we use the versions of the Lenders' Handbook and the Solicitors' Code of Conduct that are current at the time of writing in October 2007.

10.15 There is no authority, and little commentary, on the effect of the new regime that governs the obligations of solicitors acting in most residential lending transactions. In the absence of judicial guidance, the interpretation set out here is necessarily tentative, though where possible the authorities on equivalent provisions in solicitors' instructions prior to 1999 have been considered and compared. According to the Solicitors' Regulation Authority ('SRA'), the effect of the new regime is to:

> 'give certainty to all the parties (lender, borrower and solicitor), help
> to reduce claims on indemnity insurance, and address any loss of
> public confidence in the profession arising from lender claims.'[1]

It therefore appears that, from the perspective of the solicitors' profession, the introduction of the new rules was intended to reduce the scope of solicitors' duties and the amount of successful claims by lenders against solicitors. There has certainly been a dramatic reduction in the number of lenders' claims against solicitors since 1999, but that may have been brought about more by the rising property market than the effect of the rules. Whether the rules have had the effect for which the solicitors hoped remains to be tested in court.

1 Solicitors' Regulation Authority, briefing paper for Rules and Ethics Committee dated 26 March 2007, 'Practice Rule 6(3) and the City of London Law Society's Certificate of Title for Commercial Transactions' para 10.

10.16 The CML claims to represent around 98% of the UK's residential mortgage lending industry. It would therefore appear that in most cases of residential lending the lender will use the Lenders' Handbook[1]. Part 1 of the Lenders' Handbook contains standard form instructions to solicitors acting for both lenders and borrowers in residential mortgage transactions. Part 2 of the

Handbook allows individual lenders to stipulate their own specific instructions to the solicitor. In the current version of the Lenders' Handbook, however, cl 1.5 provides as follows:

> 'The limitations contained in rule 6(3)(c) and (e) of the Solicitors' Practice Rules 1990 (and where applicable the Solicitors' Code of Conduct 2007) apply to the instructions contained in the Lenders' Handbook and any separate instructions.'[2]

This statement is presumably effective in law. If that is correct, then the solicitor's contractual obligations to the lender cannot go beyond the limitations. The limitations now appear in rr 3.19 and 3.21 of the Solicitors' Code of Conduct 2007. Rule 3.21 provides:

> 'The terms of 3.16 to 3.20 above will prevail in the event of any ambiguity in the lender's instructions, or discrepancy between the instructions and 3.19 above or the approved certificate.'

Rules 3.16–3.20 of the Solicitors' Code of Conduct contain restrictions imposed by the Code on the scope of obligations which solicitors acting in lending transactions may accept from lender clients. It therefore appears that, at least in cases where the lender uses the Lenders' Handbook, the lender is likely to have to accept that the limitations contained in rr 3.16–3.20 apply to the scope of the solicitor's duty owed to the lender, whatever the lender's precise instructions say. As indicated above, the purpose of this from the solicitors' point of view is to prevent the imposition of wide-ranging duties on solicitors leading to the risk of extensive liability to lenders.

1 For the position as to incorporation of terms into the contract of retainer in cases where the Lenders' Handbook is not used, see generally Chadwick J's discussion in *Fancy and Jackson* [1997] 4 All ER 582, 603h–605d, and in *Bristol and West Building Society v May, May & Merrimans* [1996] 2 All ER 801 at 809g.
2 There is an exception for licensed conveyancers, with whom we are not concerned in this book.

Rules 3.16 to 3.22[1] of the Solicitors' Code of Conduct 2007

10.17 Rule 3.16(2)(a) provides that a solicitor may not act for both lender and borrower on the grant of a mortgage of land if a conflict of interest 'exists or arises'. Rules 3.01–3.03 deal with when a conflict of interest arises, though this is a difficult area.[2]

1 Contained in the appendix at p 764ff below.
2 See para 4.24ff, above.

10.18 Assuming that there is no conflict of interest, it is necessary to distinguish between 'standard' and 'individual' mortgages for the purposes of the Rules. Rule 3.17.1 provides that a mortgage is a standard mortgage where:

'(a)   it is provided in the normal course of the lender's activities;

(b)   a significant part of the lender's activities consists of lending; and

(c)   the mortgage is on standard terms.'

It adds that an individual mortgage is any other mortgage, though r 3.17(2) adds that a mortgage will not be on standard terms if material terms in any of the documents relating to the mortgage transaction are negotiated between the borrower and lender's lawyers or conveyancers at the time of effecting the mortgage.[1] The definition of standard mortgage is important because of the rules which apply to such a mortgage, discussed below.

1 See r 3.17 in full for the complete definition of standard and individual mortgages.

10.19   Individual mortgages will be the exception rather than the rule. In relation to them, if the lender and borrower are at arms' length then they must be separately represented,[1] but the remainder of the requirements of rr 3.16–3.22 do not apply. If the lender and borrower are not at arms' length then the Code imposes no limits on the solicitor's duty.

1 Rule 3.16(2)(b).

10.20   In the case of standard mortgages, if the property the subject of the loan is to be used only as the borrower's private residence, r 3.16(2)(c) provides that a solicitor may act for both lender and borrower provided that the lender's instructions do not go beyond the matters stipulated in r 3.19, and do permit use of the standard-form certificate of title required by r 3.20. So in the normal case of a residential mortgage transaction the effect of the Code of Conduct is that the solicitor acting, as is normal, for both lender and borrower must ensure that his or her instructions comply with r 3.19 and that the certificate of title used is as provided for in r 3.20. The purpose of this rule is plainly to limit the extent of the solicitor's duties to the lender. If the property is not to be used only as the borrower's private residence then the requirement to use the certificate of title in accordance with r 3.20 falls away, but the instructions must still not go beyond the matters set out in r 3.19. In either case, the solicitor must notify the lender in writing if he or she proposes to act for each of the seller, the buyer and the lender in the transaction, or if the prospective borrower is linked to the solicitor in the ways set out in r 3.18.

10.21   If the solicitor is acting only for the borrower in relation to a standard mortgage then, if the property is to be used solely as the borrower's private residence, the solicitor may not accept instructions that go beyond the matters set out in r 3.19.[1] On the other hand, if the property *is* to be used other than solely as the borrower's private residence, then the solicitor may give a certificate of title in a form approved by the Solicitors' Regulation Authority ('SRA')[2]. In

2007 the SRA approved the latest form of the City of London Law Society's Certificate of Title for this purpose. This is for use in commercial cases where the solicitor acts only for the borrower but is instructed to provide a certificate of title to the lender. The implication is that the matters dealt with in the City of London Law Society's Certificate of Title *may* go beyond the matters set out in r 3.19, but that this does not matter because it is to be used only in commercial rather than residential conveyancing. This is an important exception to the standard rule, which may have significant consequences in cases where it applies. Further, the provisions of rr 3.16–3.22 do not specifically deal with the position where the solicitor acts only for the lender; it is thought that they do not apply in that case.

1 Rule 3.22(1).
2 Rule 3.22(2).

10.22 Strictly speaking, the provisions of the Solicitors' Code of Conduct, and before it the Solicitors' Practice Rules, are/were disciplinary rules governing solicitors' professional conduct, rather than terms of the retainer between and solicitor and a borrower or lender client. In cases, however, where the Lenders' Handbook is used, it appears that the relevant provisions of the Code or Practice Rules will be incorporated into the retainer by virtue of the provision in the Lenders' Handbook quoted above at paragraph 10.16. In cases where the Lenders' Handbook does not apply, the position may not be as clear cut, though solicitors who fail to ensure that their instructions do not go beyond the extent permitted by the Code of Conduct will be in breach of their professional duties. Whether this means that all solicitors will ensure that, as a matter of contract law, their duties are not expressed to go further than set out in the disciplinary rules remains to be seen.[1]

1 See para 1.01 note 5 and para.2.15, above for discussion of *Hilton v Barker Booth & Eastwood* [2005] UKHL 8, [2005] 1 WLR 567, and the extent to which the court will imply the provisions of professional practice rules into a retainer.

5   Express contractual terms

10.23 It will be seen from the foregoing analysis that in some cases, such as where the solicitor acts only for the lender, rr 3.16–3.22 of the Code of Conduct do not impose any obligations on the solicitor, whereas in others, such as where the solicitor acts for both lender and borrower in a standard residential mortgage, the Code requires compliance with both r 3.19 and r 3.20. Rule 3.19 contains provisions as to the extent of duties which a solicitor may accept from a lender, and r 3.20 contains the approved form of certificate of title. The approved form of certificate of title[1] is drafted so as to certify that the solicitors have investigated the issues set out in r 3.19, but that they accept no further liability:

'OUR duties to you are limited to the matters set out in this certificate and we accept no further liability or responsibility whatsoever. The payment by you to us (by whatever means) of the mortgage advance or any part of it constitutes acceptance of this limitation and any assignment to you by the Borrower of any rights of action against us to which the Borrower may be entitled shall take effect subject to this limitation.'

Whether this disclaimer will be effective in preventing solicitors who rely upon it from being held the subject of additional duties remains to be seen, and is discussed further below[2].

1 Which appears in the appendix at p 764.
2 Para.10.49, below.

10.24   In the remainder of this section, we consider some standard issues as to the effect of express terms of the retainer which arose under the pre-1999 law, which may still apply to cases not governed by r 3.19, such as those where the solicitor acts only for the lender. Having set out that context, we then look at the equivalent provisions of r 3.19, which will govern the position in the circumstances set out above.[1]

1 Para 10.18ff, above.

(a) Reporting sub-sales

(i)   Position at common law

10.25   The nature of a sub-sale fraud combined with a direct payment was summarised in paras 10.11–10.13. A large percentage of the cases decided in both *Fancy and Jackson*[1] and *Balmer Radmore*[2] concerned failure to report matters of these kinds. In only one of those cases had the lender incorporated a term in its instructions which expressly required that solicitors report sub-sales to it.[3] In the other cases, the obligation to report sub-sales, as opposed to direct payments, arose from the solicitors' implied rather than express duties.[4]

1 [1997] 4 All ER 582.
2 [1999] Lloyd's Rep PN 241.
3 This was *Colin Bishop*. The lender was the Cheshunt Building Society, which was subsequently taken over by the Bristol and West. The defendant solicitors claimed that the requirement to report sub-sales applied only to sales where there was only one transfer document, executed by each of the various vendors and purchasers. For example, if A was selling to B who was selling to C on the same day, the defendant's case was that this arrangement was a sub-sale only if each of A, B and C executed the same transfer document. If there were two separate transfer documents, one relating to the sale from A to B and the other to the sale from B to C, then this was not a sub-sale. Chadwick J rejected that argument: see [1997] 4 All ER 582 at 609g. Either type of transaction was a sub-sale which had to be reported to the Cheshunt, under its standard terms. Hence the solicitors were held liable.
4 See para 10.44ff, below.

(ii) Position if r 3.19 applies

10.26   Rule 3.19(e) provides that one of the obligations which a solicitor may accept if acting for lender and borrower in a standard mortgage is:

> 'reporting if the seller or borrower (if the property is already owned by the borrower) has not owned or been the registered owner of the property for at least six months.'

This will cover any sub-sale at the time of or within the six months before the purchase. Note that, where such a report is made, this provision does not state that the solicitor has a duty to point out to the lender the significance of such information, namely that the price at which the lender thinks the property is being sold may not represent its true value. It remains to be seen whether the solicitor has an implied duty to point this out, though the terms of the exclusion at the end of the approved certificate of title, quoted above at para 10.23, suggest not. Although r 3.19(w) provides that the solicitor's duties may include

> 'giving legal advice on any matters reported on under 3.19, suggesting courses of action open to the lender, and complying with the lender's instructions on the action to be taken',

it is submitted that this does not impose a duty to point out the significance, from the point of view of the lender's lending decision, of the information that there has been a sub-sale or the relevance of this to the lender's valuation of the property. It is thought that those are commercial matters for the lender rather than legal matters for the solicitor. On the other hand, however, r 3.19(a)(ii) requires the solicitor to comply with the guidance given by the Law Society or the SRA on property fraud[1] and money laundering. Thus it would appear that, if applying that guidance would require the solicitor to report suspicions of fraud to the lender, then he or she must do so.

---

1   Currently the Law Society's 'Warning: Property Fraud 2' of July 2002: see below at para. 10.43, and the appendix at p 761.

(b) Discrepancies as to the purchase price, and direct payments

(i)   Position at common law

10.27   In relation to direct payments, the obligation to report to the lender could arise pursuant to the express terms of the retainer, in the following way. In *Fancy and Jackson,* Bristol and West's solicitors' instructions required that the solicitor report to Bristol and West any discrepancy in the details shown in the offer of advance. Those details included the purchase price. Further, in signing the report on title the solicitor had to confirm that the details of the transaction accorded exactly with the particulars in the offer of advance, including the purchase price. The general nature of the solicitor's obligation, in Chadwick J's analysis, was as follows.[1] First, solicitors who knew that the true purchase price payable by the purchaser/borrower to the vendor was not the purchase price stated in the offer of advance could not properly sign and return the report without qualification. Secondly, solicitors who signed and returned the report and request without qualification were, at the least, warranting to the lender that they had made those enquiries (if any) which competent solicitors, acting reasonably, would make in order to satisfy themselves that the purchase price stated in the offer of advance was the true purchase price to be paid by the purchaser/borrower to the vendor, and that, in light of those enquiries, they knew of no reason why they could not give the unqualified confirmation to which they had put their signature. Thus, solicitors who signed the report on title in circumstances where either they had not made such reasonable enquiries, or they had made them and they suggested that the true purchase price was different from that stated in the offer of advance, would be in breach of duty.

1 [1997] 4 All ER 582 at 605e–f. Blackburne J's approach in *Balmer Radmore* was similar: [1999] Lloyd's Rep PN 241 at 266–268.

10.28 This raises the question as to what circumstances should have caused a reasonably careful solicitor to conclude that the purchase price might not be that stated in the offer of advance. The Law Society's (original) Guidance on Mortgage Fraud, first published as long ago as 30 November 1990, stated:

> 'Solicitors acting contemporaneously for a buyer and a lender should consider their position very carefully if there is any change in the purchase price, or if the solicitors become aware of any other information which they would reasonably expect the lender to consider important in deciding whether, or on what terms, it would make the mortgage advance available. In such circumstances the solicitors' duty to act in the best interests of the lender would require them to pass on such information to the lender … Solicitors must not withhold information relevant to a transaction from any client and for a lender this includes not only straightforward price reductions but may also include other allowances (e g for repairs, payment of costs, the inclusion of chattels in the price and incentives of the kind offered by builders such as free holidays and part-subsidisation of mortgage payments) which amount to a price reduction and which would affect the lender's decision to make the advance. Solicitors should not attempt to arbitrate on whether the price change is material but should notify the lender.'

Thus allowances of the kinds referred to by the Law Society should have been reported to lenders even in 1990. In *Balmer Radmore,* Blackburne J considered that an agreement by the vendor to pay the purchaser's costs and expenses of the purchase would amount to a price reduction which should be reported, though if the vendor supplied the purchaser with a free structural survey it would not.[1] Further, in *National Home Loans Corpn plc v Stevens & Co*,[2] the lender's documents were similar to Bristol and West's and the solicitor did have an express obligation to report changes in the purchase price. The price stated in the contract and the offer of advance was £62,650, but surveyors' reports suggested that the purchaser would have to carry out significant repairs, and for that reason the vendor agreed to an 'allowance' of £3,000 on the purchase price. In other words, although the sum stated in the contract remained £62,650, the sum which the purchaser actually had to pay the vendor was only £59,650. The solicitor considered that the £3,000 would genuinely be spent on repairs, was an 'allowance' rather than a reduction in price, and therefore did not have to be reported. The Deputy Recorder held that there had been a reduction in price, so that the solicitor had acted in breach of duty in failing to report it to the lender. As to causation, however, he held that if the reduction had been reported the lender would simply have reduced the advance by £297.50, so damages were £297.50 plus interest.

1 *Balmer Radmore* [1999] Lloyd's Rep PN 241 at 265.
2 A decision of Mr John Tackaberry QC sitting as a Deputy Recorder on Official Referee's Business (2 June 1997, unreported).

10.29 As to direct payments, the expert evidence in *Fancy and Jackson* showed that in the vast majority of cases the whole of the price payable on the purchase of domestic property passed through the bank account of the purchaser's solicitor.[1] Thus it was unusual for money to pass directly from purchaser to vendor rather than via solicitors. Addressing the issue in *Balmer Radmore*, Blackburne J said this:[2]

'The failure of the solicitor to obtain verification of a direct payment leaves open the possibility that vendor and purchaser/borrower were misrepresenting the position, that, in truth, no payment had been made and that the true price being paid for the property was the contract price less the direct payment; in short, that the assertion of a direct payment was intended to conceal a price reduction. This possibility, if accurate, meant that vendor and purchaser/borrower were together engaged in a fraud on the Society, representing dishonestly that the price to be paid for the property was £x whereas, in truth, it was £x less the amount of the direct payment. The purpose of such dishonesty could only be to induce the Society, supported by a valuation overstating the true value of the property, into making the advance in the belief that the overall price paid was indeed £x.

There arrived a time when the device of the so-called direct payment, where unverified, came to be recognised by solicitors as one of the

517

badges of mortgage fraud. This, together with a recognition of other indications of mortgage fraud, led in March 1991 to the publication by the Law Society of the so-called "Green Card" warning on mortgage fraud. It included, among one of the signs to watch for in cases of mortgage fraud, "a deposit paid direct–a deposit, perhaps exceeding a normal deposit, paid direct or said to be paid direct, to the seller".

In his evidence, Mr Ward[3] accepted that, after the publication of the Green Card warning, there was what he described as a "fairly absolute" requirement on solicitors to report to the lender an unverified claim by the borrower to have made a direct payment.'

Thus, although none of the cases in either *Fancy and Jackson* or *Balmer Radmore* concerned a failure to report an unverified direct payment after receipt of the Law Society's Green Card, it would appear that such a failure would amount to a breach of duty.

1 See [1997] 4 All ER 582 at 605g–h.
2 [1999] Lloyd's Rep 241 PN at 266.
3 The defendants' solicitor expert.

10.30 Cases requiring resolution now are likely to concern events which took place after February 1999. By then, the current version of the Law Society's 'Green Card' warning on mortgage fraud[1] identified, as signs of mortgage fraud:

'Misrepresentation of the purchase price – ensure that the true cash price actually to be paid is stated as the consideration in the contract and transfer and is identical to the price shown in the mortgage instructions and in the report on title to the lender.

A deposit or any part of purchase price paid direct – a deposit, or the difference between the mortgage advance and the price, paid direct, or said to be paid direct, to the seller ...

Changes in the purchase price – adjustments to the purchase price, particularly in high percentage mortgage cases, or allowances off the purchase price, for example, for works to be carried out.'

In cases relating to events after February 1999, therefore, it seems likely that solicitors acting for lenders had an obligation to report to the lender either alleged direct payments or allowances in relation to the purchase price.

1 See the appendix, at p 759 below. The same text appeared in the replacement guidance, 'Property Fraud 2', which the Law Society published in July 2002 and which appears in the appendix at p 761.

(ii) Position if r 3.19 applies

10.31 Rule 3.19(d) provides that the solicitor's instructions may include:

> 'reporting the purchase price stated in the transfer and on how the
> borrower says that the purchase money (other than the mortgage
> advance) is to be provided; and reporting if you will not have control
> over the payment of all the purchase money (other than a deposit
> paid to an estate agent or a reservation fee paid to a builder or
> developer).'

The last clause would appear to encompass a duty to report any alleged direct
payment: a direct payment arises if the completing solicitor will not have
control over all the purchase money. Hence it is likely that solicitors
instructed pursuant to either Practice Rule 6(3), which contained a similar
provision, or r 3.19 will have an obligation to report direct payments to
lenders.

(c) *Resident borrower*

(i) Position at common law

10.32 In *Birmingham Midshires Mortgage Services Ltd v David Parry & Co,*[1]
the Court of Appeal had to consider the following argument. The solicitor's
instructions required him to ensure that the general and special conditions
specified in the offer of advance were 'complied with and brought to the
[borrower]'s attention on or before completion'. General condition 4 provided
that the borrower must 'personally reside in the property within 30 days of
completion'. The lender contended that the solicitor either did know, or ought to
have known, that the borrower did not intend personally to occupy the property
within 30 days of completion, and that the terms quoted required the solicitor to
inform the lender of this, which he had failed to do. The court disagreed. It
construed these terms as requiring the solicitor to bring the terms of general
condition 4 to the borrower's attention, 'and to report to the plaintiffs knowledge on his part that [the borrower] does not intend to comply with the
condition'. Thus the solicitor would be in breach of duty if he had actual
knowledge that the borrower did not intend to reside in the property at all, and
had not reported this to the lender. But:[2]

> 'There is no obligation imposed on [the solicitor] to check with [the
> borrower] that he intends to reside in the property personally or to
> report to the plaintiffs facts relating to [the borrower]'s current or
> past residence. [The solicitor] was entitled to assume, in the absence
> of information to the contrary, that [the borrower] intended to

comply with the terms of the offer of advance which he had accepted ... Without the benefit of hindsight a reasonably competent solicitor would have been entitled to take the view that the available information about the circumstances and actions of [the borrower] was consistent with an intention on his part to use [the property] as a secondary residence; that would constitute "personal residence" within general condition 4. There was no condition in the offer of advance that [the borrower] should reside in [the property] as his only or primary residence.'

1 [1997] EGCS 150, CA.
2 Transcript p 21. Blackburne J applied this on the facts of the case of *Balmer Radmore* itself: see [1999] Lloyd's Rep PN 558.

(*ii*)   *Position if Rule 3.19 applies*

10.33   Rule 3.19(o) provides that the solicitor's instructions may include an obligation to ask 'the borrower for confirmation that the information about occupants given in the mortgage instructions or offer is correct.' Presumably there is an obligation to tell the lender if the borrower's answer is that the information is not correct. The effect of this appears to be similar to the result in *Parry*. The solicitor's obligation does not appear onerous in this respect: it appears that, if the borrower lies to the solicitor, the solicitor will have no obligation to detect the lie unless, perhaps, he or she is by other means in possession of clear information indicating that the borrower has lied.

(*d*) *Redemption of existing mortgages before completion*

(*i*)   *Position at common law*

10.34   A further point arose in *Parry*.[1] The solicitors' instructions contained a term that the borrower's 'existing mortgages must be redeemed on or before completion of this advance'. It was argued that this term required redemption not only of existing mortgages secured over the property which was to be charged to the lender, but also of charges over other properties which the borrower owned. Read literally, the term would have applied to other charges. But the Court of Appeal construed the term in the context that the borrower was not required, by the terms of the offer of advance, to redeem mortgages over other properties, and on the basis that it is not generally part of the solicitor's duty to report matters relating to the borrower's financial position.[2] Thus the lender's argument was rejected.

1 [1997] EGCS 150, CA.
2 See para 10.54ff, below for the solicitor's duties in relation the borrower's financial position.

(ii)   Position if r 3.19 applies

10.35   Rule 3.19(t) provides that the solicitor's duties may include ensuring the redemption or postponement of existing mortgages secured on the property. Rule 3.19(s) adds that those duties may include:

'procuring the redemption of:

(i)   existing mortgages on property the subject of any associated sale of which you are aware; and

(ii)   any other mortgages secured against a property located in England or Wales made by an identified lender where an identified account number or numbers or a property address has been given by the lender.'

Thus, compared with the result in *Parry*, there is scope for lenders to increase slightly the obligations on the solicitor in relation to the redemption of mortgages over other property.

(e) Obligation to report material changes in circumstances

10.36   In *National Home Loans Corpn v Giffen Couch & Archer*,[1] the lender contended that when, after their instruction by the lender, the defendant solicitors learnt that the borrowers were under threat of legal proceedings from their previous lender, this amounted to a material change of circumstances which ought to have been reported to the lender. By paragraph 6 of the lender's report on title the solicitors certified that 'We are not aware of any material change in the applicant's circumstances subsequent to the date of the offer of loan'. Peter Gibson LJ, delivering the only reasoned judgment, said that this would naturally lead the defendant solicitors to believe that, subject only to a clear bankruptcy search being obtained, the lender was satisfied that the borrowers' circumstances at the date of the offer of advance made them suitable borrowers.[2] Peter Gibson LJ rejected the argument that knowledge that the borrowers were under *threat* of legal proceedings constituted a material change in circumstances. It was the existence of the arrears that was material; the additional information that the previous lenders might be proposing to commence possession proceedings on the basis of those arrears was not a material change of circumstances, and the defendants were not obliged to report it.[3] Rule 3.19, by contrast, does not contain a provision requiring the reporting of material changes in the borrower's circumstances, so this issue is unlikely to arise in cases to which it applies.

1   [1998] 1 WLR 207, CA. This case is discussed in more detail in para 10.54ff, below.
2   See [1998] 1 WLR 207 at 214F.
3   See [1998] 1 WLR 207 at 217A–B.

(f) *Failing to obtain proper security on completion*

(i) *Position at common law*

10.37 The primary function of a solicitor acting for a lender in a standard transaction is to ensure that the lender obtains a valid and effective first charge on the property, which requires in particular that the charge is over good and marketable title.[1] Chadwick J elaborated on this in *Bristol and West Building Society v May, May & Merrimans:*[2]

> '... in signing and returning the report on title, the solicitor warrants or represents that his principal obligation under the contract has been performed –"I/We have investigated the title of this property and report that I/We consider the title to be good and marketable and that it may be safely accepted by the society."
>
> It is, I think, beyond argument that a solicitor who had not investigated title at all or who had not investigated the particular matters which the solicitor's instructions require to be investigated – see, in particular, para 4 (searches), para 5 (vacant possession and rights of persons in occupation) and para 7 (leasehold securities) – would be in breach of his contract with the society if he were to sign and return the report on title without qualification. Alternatively, by returning the report on title without qualification, he would be in breach of warranty or guilty of misrepresentation. So, also, the solicitor would be in breach of his contract with the society if he had failed to exercise the required degree of care and skill in carrying out his investigation. Further, the solicitor would be in breach of contract, breach of warranty or guilty of misrepresentation, if he were to sign and return the report on title without qualification in circumstances where, having made a full investigation of the title, he did not consider the title to be good and marketable. Yet further, he would be in breach of contract if, having made a full investigation of title, he were to sign and return the report on title without qualification in circumstances in which a reasonable conveyancing solicitor, exercising the required degree of care and skill, could not have reached the conclusion that the title was good and marketable on the material available.'

1 See *National Home Loans Corpn plc v Giffen, Couch & Archer* [1998] 1 WLR 207 at 214B, CA.
2 [1996] 2 All ER 801 at 809h–810c.

10.38 Further, in the *Fancy and Jackson* case itself, Chadwick J held that solicitors who did not have an official search certificate from the Land Registry at the time of completion acted in breach of duty. They had not investigated title properly before completion. Again, in *Alliance & Leicester Building Society v*

Wheelers,[1] the lender's instructions to the defendant solicitors contained a term which read 'Completing solicitors to be satisfied that all the necessary planning, byelaw and statutory consents are in force and suitable for the use of the property as offices'. The solicitors wrote to the lender saying that there was planning permission for use of the property as B1 office use. This was incorrect. The permitted use was Dl, as a surgery. For that reason summary judgment was granted against the solicitors.[2]

1 (23 January 1997, unreported, Carnwath J).
2 Further, for a discussion of 'shared ownership' schemes, see *Halifax plc v Gould and Swayne* [1999] PNLR 184, CA, although all the court had to do was conclude that the solicitors had an arguable defence to the allegations of negligence.

(ii) *Position if r 3.19 applies*

10.39 Rule 3.19 requires standard searches to be made (r 3.19(b)), together with investigation of and reporting on title (r 3.19(g)). It is likely that the approach taken to solicitors' obligations in these respects will be similar way to that taken in the cases set out above.

(g) *Forged signatures on charges*

(i) *Position at common law*

10.40 Various cases concern the liability of solicitors who agree with a lender to ensure that specific persons sign a charge in favour of the lender, but then find that the signature of one of those persons on the charge has been forged. If it is found that the solicitors failed to act with reasonable care to ensure that the right people signed the charge then they are likely to be found liable in negligence. Further, if the same solicitors act for both lender and borrowers, then the solicitors may be liable to the lender for breach of warranty of authority.[1] But can lenders argue that, even if the solicitor, acting with reasonable skill and care, would not have detected the forgery, the solicitor is still liable to the lender in contract? In other words, can it be said that the solicitor's contractual obligation to the lender is a strict one, to ensure that the correct people sign the charge, so that the solicitor is liable if the wrong people sign, even though he or she took reasonable skill and care?

1 See para 10.110ff, below, and para 5.13ff, above. In the context of a guarantor who claims that her signature has obtained by undue influence, the Court of Appeal has held that solicitors acting only for the lender have a duty to take reasonable steps to ensure that a guarantor is advised by either the borrower's solicitor or an independent solicitor: *Mercantile Credit Co Ltd v Fenwick* [1999] Lloyd's Rep PN 408.

10.41 In *Zwebner v The Mortgage Corpn Ltd,*[1] the report on title which the lender's solicitors signed contained an undertaking that all appropriate documents would be 'properly executed' on completion. Mr Zwebner was borrowing money from the lender on the security of a house which he owned jointly with Mrs Zwebner, so it was necessary for Mrs Zwebner to sign the mortgage. In fact her signature was forged. The Court of Appeal held that the solicitors' contractual obligation to ensure that the wife signed the mortgage deed was a strict one, so that it would have been breached even if the solicitors had acted with reasonable care. But in *Midland Bank plc v Cox McQueen,*[2] Lord Woolf MR. with whom the other judges agreed, distinguished *Zwebner.* The solicitors had agreed to ensure that a wife signed a charge for a lender, but her signature was forged. The points of distinction were that in *Cox* the solicitors merely certified that the wife had signed, rather than undertaking, and merely agreed that she would sign, rather than stating that the charge would be 'properly' executed. But Lord Woolf added a statement of general principle which applies in construing the terms of solicitors' retainers in this type of case. This is quoted in full at para 1.02, above.[3] The Court of Appeal reached a similar conclusion, interpreting a solicitor's obligation to ensure that the lender obtained good marketable title, in *Barclays Bank plc v Weeks Legg & Dean.*[4] Strictly speaking, decisions on construction all turn on the precise documents in issue, so that authorities do not greatly assist in interpreting documents with slightly different words. But the rationale which Lord Woolf set out in the passage quoted is not of such limited application. Further, the Court of Appeal subsequently applied it in *UCB Corporate Services Ltd v Clyde & Co.*[5]

1 [1998] PNLR 769, CA.
2 [1999] Lloyd's Rep PN 223, CA.
3 [1999] Lloyd's Rep PN 223 at 229. See also *Mercantile Credit Co Ltd v Fenwick* [1999] Lloyd's Rep PN 408, CA.
4 [1999] QB 309. See further para 10.66, below and para 4.10, above.
5 [2000] Lloyd's Rep PN 653. In relation to the different question of a solicitor's duty to a party whom the solicitor claimed to represent, see *Al-Sabah v Ali* [1999] EGCS 11, Ferris J.

(ii)   Position if r 3.19 applies

10.42   By r 3.19(a)(i), the solicitor's duties may include:

> 'taking reasonable steps to check the identity of the borrower (and anyone else required to sign the mortgage deed or other document connected with the mortgage) by reference to a document or documents, such as a passport, precisely specified in writing by the lender.'[1]

By r 3.19(o), the solicitor's duties may also include procuring execution of the mortgage deed and guarantee 'by the persons whose identities have been checked in accordance with the requirements of the lender under (a)...' It is submitted that the clear intention of these provisions is that the solicitor does not guarantee that the person signing is the correct party; rather, he or she has an obligation to take reasonable care by reference to documents which the lender must specify. Hence in this respect r 3.19 takes a similar approach to that set out in the later cases just referred to, with more emphasis on the lender to specify the type of identity required.

1 Section 3 of Part 1 of the CML Lenders' Handbook specifies the types of document which must be used.

(h) *Following Law Society or SRA guidance*

10.43   Rule 3.19(a)(ii) provides that, in cases to which r 3.19 applies, solicitors' duties may include the obligation to comply with guidance of the Law Society or SRA in relation to property fraud or money laundering. It is likely that instructions will include such a requirement. The latest warning in relation to property fraud is the Law Society's 'Warning: Property fraud 2', of July 2002, which appears in the appendix at p 761. It is self-explanatory. It is thought that lenders will wish where possible to show that their claim includes failures to report matters set out in the guidance, or the money laundering guidance. If they can show that, they will be able to escape the limiting effect of other parts of r 3.19, and should be able to show breach of duty without any need to rely on implied terms. This may be a major battleground in any litigation relating to the effect of the Lenders' Handbook: can the lender show that the information that the solicitor failed to report was reportable pursuant to the Law Society or SRA's fraud guidance? We now turn to consider implied duties in contract, and negligence.

6   Liability for breach of implied contractual terms and in the tort of negligence

10.44   Section 13 of the Supply of Goods and Services Act 1982 implies into the solicitor's contract of retainer a term that the solicitor must act with reasonable skill and care. This standard is generally treated as imposing the same standard as the duty which the solicitor owes the client in the tort of negligence, to act with reasonable skill and care. The question is the extent to which, in the absence of breach of an express contractual term, the court will hold that a solicitor acting for a lender has failed to act with such skill or care. In this context, it is helpful to consider, first, the pre-1999 law on implied duties of solicitors to lenders, and then whether the terms of the certificate of title approved under the Solicitors' Code of Conduct, and quoted above at para. 10.23, means that a court today would take a different approach. In considering these issues, the information which it is alleged there is an implied duty to report should be separated into two categories: information relating to the value of the property which is to be taken as security for the loan, and information relating to the value of the borrower's covenant.[1] We consider these two categories in turn. We then look at two further possible limitations on the duty to report information.

1 See paras 10.06ff, and *National Home Loans Corpn plc v Giffen Couch & Archer* [1998] 1 WLR 207 at 216E-G, CA.

(a) Matters relevant to the value of the security

(i) The Bowerman duty

10.45 In *Mortgage Express Ltd v Bowerman & Partners*[1] (*'Bowerman'*), the facts were as follows. On 21 November 1990 the claimant lender sent a letter instructing Mr Gilroy of the defendant solicitors to act for the claimant in relation to the proposed purchase by a Mr Hadi of a flat in Queensway, London for £220,000, with a loan of £180,150 from the claimant. The letter included a valuation of the property in the sum of £199,000, and it was apparent that the claimant's loan was based on this valuation. Mr Gilroy then agreed to act on Mr Hadi's behalf and discovered that the proposed vendor was a Mr Arrach. On 26 November 1990 Mr Gilroy learnt that in fact Mr Arrach had not yet purchased the property: he was due to purchase it from a Mr Rasool for £150,000, and simultaneously to sell it on to Mr Hadi for £220,000, an increase of nearly 50% in price. Mr Gilroy was concerned that Mr Hadi might be paying too much, and that the valuation of £199,000 might be incorrect, so he warned Mr Hadi of the price at which Mr Arrach was purchasing. Mr Gilroy also knew that Mr Rasool had purchased the property only a few days earlier on 2 November 1990, that the London property market was not rising at the time, and suspected that Mr Rasool's purchase had been at a sum lower than £150,000. He did not report any of this information to the claimant lender in his report on title or by other means. The transaction completed, Mr Hadi made only one mortgage payment before defaulting, and the claimant repossessed the property and sold it at a loss.

1 [1996] 2 All ER 836, CA.

10.46 The judge found that, in failing to report such matters to the claimant, the defendant had breached its duty to the claimant. The Court of Appeal upheld that conclusion. Sir Thomas Bingham MR said:[1]

'A client cannot expect a solicitor to undertake work he has not asked him to do, and will not wish to pay him for such work. But if in the course of doing the work he is instructed to do the solicitor comes into possession of information which is not confidential and which is clearly of potential significance to the client, I think that the client would reasonably expect the solicitor to pass it on and feel understandably aggrieved if he did not.

I would accordingly reject the submission originally made on behalf of the solicitors as to the narrow ambit of the duty, as the judge did, and accept, as I understand her to have done, the submission of Mortgage Express. That was that *if in the course of investigating title, a solicitor discovers facts which a reasonably competent solicitor would realise might have a material bearing on the valuation of the lender's security or some other ingredient of the lending decision, then it is his duty to point this out.'*

[Emphasis added].

Millett LJ, concurring, said:[2]

'It might be thought ... that the question which the judge should have asked herself was: "Would a solicitor of ordinary competence have regarded the information that Mr Arrach was paying only £150,000 for the flat as throwing doubt on the valuation of £199,000?" That, however, would not, in my opinion, be an accurate formulation of the question. Mr Gilroy was not a valuer and it was not his responsibility to doubt a professional valuation. *The question which the judge had to ask herself was whether a solicitor of ordinary competence would have regarded the information in question as information which might cause the plaintiffs to doubt the correctness of the valuation which they had obtained.'* [Emphasis added.]

Schiemann LJ agreed with both judgments.

1 [1996] 2 All ER 836 at 842d–f, CA.
2 [1996] 2 All ER 836 at 845e–g, CA.

10.47   The relevant information in *Bowerman* was information which a solicitor of ordinary competence would have regarded as information which might cause the lender to doubt the correctness of the valuation which it had obtained. Sir Thomas Bingham MR formulated the implied duty as going further, and relating not only to information of that kind, but also to information which might have a material bearing on 'some other ingredient of the lending decision'. It will be suggested below[1] that, in light of later authority, it is doubtful whether an implied duty extends to this second type of information. For the moment we concentrate on the first type: information which a solicitor of ordinary competence would have regarded as information which might cause the lender to doubt the correctness of the valuation which it had obtained. For brevity we refer to this as the '*Bowerman* duty'.

1 Paras 10.54–10.60, below.

10.48   Considering *Bowerman* in *Balmer Radmore,* Blackburne J said that he accepted the defendants' submission that:[1]

527

10.49   *Lenders' claims*

'... in considering whether a solicitor acting for a lender is subject to a *Bowerman* type duty, the correct approach is to examine the terms of the retainer and then consider what implied obligations, if any, there are to accompany the expressed ones. Having said that, however, I am inclined to think that the *Bowerman* duty is a species of obligation which the court will ordinarily imply, or find present, where a solicitor acts for a lender in a mortgage transaction except to the extent that to do so would be inconsistent with the express terms of the engagement or with the surrounding circumstances of the relationship.'

Blackburne J did not consider that the terms of Nationwide's instructions were inconsistent with the existence of such a duty.

1 [1999] Lloyd's Rep PN 241 at 258.

(ii)   Cases to which rr 3.19 and 3.20 apply

10.49   Pausing there, however, it is necessary to consider the effect, in cases where the CML Lender's Handbook is used, of rr 3.19 and 3.20 of the Solicitors' Code of Conduct 2007[1]. Regrettably there is as yet no judicial authority on this point. But, as indicated above[2], in cases where a solicitor acts for both borrower and lender, in relation to a standard mortgage, and the property the subject of the loan is to be used only as the borrower's private residence, the solicitors' instructions from the lender must comply with both those rules. Further, the Lenders' Handbook, if used as the basis of the solicitor's instructions, provides that if there is any doubt as to the effect of the instructions then rr 3.19 and 3.20 are to prevail. Thirdly, the scheme of r 3.19 is that in cases to which it applies solicitors may accept only instructions which are limited to the matters set out in r 3.19. Rule 3.19 does not specify any obligation along the lines of the *Bowerman* duty. This suggests that the imposition of such a duty by way of implied term would be inconsistent with the terms of r 3.19, and contrary to the intentions of those who drafted it; such persons must have been aware of the content of the *Bowerman* duty, which was well known by 1999, yet presumably expressly chose not to include such a duty. Fourthly, r 3.20 requires that in cases to which it applies the solicitor must use the approved form of certificate of title. That certificate, quoted above at para 10.23, provides that the solicitor's duties are limited to the matters set out in the certificate and 'we accept no further liability or responsibility whatsoever.' The certificate says nothing about the solicitor having complied with any duty along the lines of the *Bowerman* duty. The terms of the certificate were the product of negotiation between the Law Society and the lending industry representative body the CML. Bearing all this in mind, it is submitted that, in cases where rr 3.19 and 3.20 apply, the court should not imply the *Bowerman* duty. For the reasons just stated, it is thought that it is clear that the representatives of both solicitors and lenders who agreed on the drafting of what are now rr 3.19 and 3.20 did not intend the solicitor's duty, in cases to which those rules apply, to include the *Bowerman* duty. It follows that, in such cases, to imply such a duty would be contrary to both the express terms of the retainer and the surrounding circumstances such as the terms of the certificate of title. It follows from this that, even bearing in mind the pre-Lenders' Handbook quotation from Blackburne J in para 10.48, such a term should not be implied in cases to which rr 3.19 and 3.20 apply.

1 Or, in relation to the period 1999–2007, the equivalent provisions in r 6(3) of the Solicitors' Practice Rules.
2 Para 10.20, above.

(iii) Cases to which rr 3.19 and 3.20 do not apply

10.50 In cases to which rr 3.19 and 3.20 do not apply, however, it is necessary to consider the law as it stood before 1999. Blackburne J concluded on this point in *Balmer Radmore* in the following terms:[1]

> '... a solicitor retained by the Society on the terms of its standard printed conditions was obliged to report to it information obtained by him in the course of investigating title or preparing for completion which was not confidential and which a solicitor of ordinary competence would have regarded as information which might cause the Society to doubt either the correctness of the valuation which, as the solicitor would know, it had obtained or the bona fides of the borrower. It is not necessary for me to express any view on whether the duty extended to a requirement to report information discovered by him which might affect some other ingredient of the Society's lending decision.'

Two points should be noted on this formulation. First, it suggests that, even in cases where there is an implied duty to report, it is subject to two further restrictions: it relates only to information which (i) the solicitor obtains in the course of investigating title or preparing for completion, and (ii) the solicitor is not prevented from reporting by obligations of confidentiality owed to the borrower. These limitations also appear in the passage quoted from Sir Thomas Bingham above. We consider them further below.[2] Secondly, as to the scope of the duty, note that it extends beyond information which the solicitor of ordinary competence would have regarded as information which might cause the lender to doubt the correctness of the valuation:[3] on Blackburne J's formulation, it relates also to information which the same solicitor would have regarded as information which might cause the lender to doubt the bona fides of the borrower. Again, we consider this further below.[4]

1 [1999] Lloyd's Rep PN 241 at 259.

2 Para 10.61ff, below.
3 Which we have called the *Bowerman* duty.
4 Para 10.54ff, below.

10.51 Leaving those points aside for the moment, what is the extent of the *Bowerman* duty in cases where it is not excluded by rr 3.19 and 3.20? The effect of *Balmer Radmore* is that, in cases where the property market was falling, the duty is likely to extend to a duty to report sub-sales or back to back transactions in which there was a price uplift that was anything other than minimal. For example, in *ATM Abdullah*, one of the *Balmer Radmore* managed list cases, the defendant solicitor failed to report a back-to-back transaction in autumn 1991 where there was a price increase from £54,000 to £63,000, an uplift of 17%, but the head vendor was a mortgagee in possession. Blackburne J held the solicitor liable. Property prices were falling at the time. Although a reasonably competent solicitor might have thought that the explanation for the price rise was that the head vendor was a mortgagee in possession selling at a discount:[1]

> '... he would have been mindful that whereas he had no particular expertise in matters of valuation, the Society did have access to persons who possessed such expertise. In these circumstances he would surely not have taken upon himself to conclude that the explanation for the uplift in price was indeed because the head sale was by a mortgagee in possession.
>
> In my view, a reasonably competent solicitor would not have speculated on the reasons for the uplift but would have reported the matter to the Society as being information which might cause the Society to doubt the correctness of the £63,000 valuation which it had obtained of which, having received a copy, Mr Abdullah was aware. £54,000 was almost £6,000 less than the amount of the Society's offer of advance.'

It did not, however, follow that the lender recovered the whole of its loss on the transaction. The judge held that, if this information had been reported, it would still have lent to the borrower, but would have lent £2,800 less than it did lend, so damages were £2,800 plus interest. Further, it is unclear whether the solicitor would have had a duty to report the uplift if property prices had been rising at the material time.

1 [1999] Lloyd's Rep PN 616 at 621 col 2.

10.52 It is no excuse that, before completion, the defendant solicitor did not know the amount of the price increase. In investigating title to registered land, he or she ought to find out who the registered owner is. In the case of a sub-sale, it will not be the party from whom the borrower is buying ('the intermediate vendor'), so the solicitor will know that a sub-sale or back to back transaction is involved. Before completing the transaction, the solicitor ought to insist upon seeing a copy of the contract between the registered owner and the intermediate vendor, in order to be sure that the intermediate vendor can make title. It is possible that, before exchange of contracts, the intermediate vendor might supply the borrower with a copy of his or her own contract with the registered owner from which the price had been redacted, so as to prevent the borrower from finding out the amount of the intermediate vendor's profit. But, after exchange and before completion, it would not matter if the borrower found this out, so the intermediate vendor's solicitors could not refuse to make available an unexpurgated copy of his contract. Thus, before completion, the solicitor acting for the lender and borrower ought to know the amount of the price uplift.[1] If exchange of contracts and completion on both transactions were due to take place on the same day, the borrower's solicitor would not know the price at which the intermediate vendor was buying, but the transaction would be so unusual that the solicitor would have an obligation to explain its nature to the lender.[2]

1 See *ATM Abdullah* in the *Balmer Radmore* judgment: [1999] Lloyd's Rep PN 616.
2 *Balmer Radmore* [1999] Lloyd's Rep PN 241 at 269.

10.53 A similar duty may apply in relation to a re-mortgage. If a borrower purchases a property for £120,000 and then obtains an offer of re-mortgage a few days later in the sum of £134,000, the solicitor acting for the lender offering the re-mortgage ought to find out the amount of the earlier purchase and realise that it casts doubt on the second lender's valuation, since the second lender's valuation must state that the property was worth at least the amount of the advance, £134,000, and thus considerably more than the amount at which the property had been purchased a few days earlier.[1]

1 See *Littlestone & Cowan* in the *Balmer Radmore* judgment: [1999] Lloyd's Rep PN 625.

(b) Creditworthiness of the borrower

10.54 Having considered implied duties to report matters relevant to the value of the property, we now consider implied duties to report matters relevant to the creditworthiness of the borrower. It is thought that, in cases to which rr 3.19 and 3.20 apply, there will be no implied duty on solicitors to report to lenders matters which relate only to the creditworthiness of the borrower. This is for reasons set out above[1]: such a duty is not set out in r 3.19 or the approved certificate of title required by r 3.20. On the other hand, as also indicated above[2], in these cases the solicitor will have a duty to report matters which, on considering the Law Society's guidance on property fraud, suggest fraud; it is possible that those might include matters relevant to the creditworthiness of the borrower. In cases to which rr 3.19 and 3.20 do not apply, it is submitted that there will be no general duty on solicitors to report such matters to lenders, though of course there may be an express duty of this kind, and there may be

10.55   *Lenders' claims*

cases where the solicitors' instructions would be construed to include such a term by implication. This emerges from the Court of Appeal's decision, subsequent to *Bowerman,* in *National Home Loans Corpn plc v Giffen, Couch & Archer* (*'Giffen* '),[3] confirmed by the Court of Appeal in *Birmingham Midshires Mortgage Services Ltd v David Parry & Co.*[4]

1 Para 10.49, above.
2 Para 10.43, above.
3 [1998] 1 WLR 207, CA.
4 [1997] ECGS 150, CA.

10.55   In *Giffen,* a Mr Choudhry borrowed from the Halifax Building Society to purchase 224 Buckingham Road, Bletchley ('the property'). On 30 June 1988 Mr Choudhry transferred title to the property into his own and his wife's names, and Mr and Mrs Choudhry ('the borrowers') remortgaged the property to a company known as Western Trust, using part of the advance to pay off the Halifax. In February 1989 the borrowers wished to re-mortgage the property again. They were introduced to the claimant by an intermediary. They applied to the claimant for a remortgage in an application form dated 10 February 1989. In the application form they stated that they had never at any time been in arrears by more than one month with any existing or previous loan and had never had any county court judgment recorded against them. On 5 April 1989 the claimant offered the borrowers an advance, and on the same day instructed the defendants, solicitors, to act for them 'in the preparation of a mortgage with any other appropriate documents in accordance with the Notes for Guidance and the documents provided'. The claimant sent the defendants its Instructions to Solicitors and Licensed Conveyancers, and instructed them to report on title on the claimant's standard form. On 31 May 1989 the defendants submitted a report on title to the claimant. Completion, using the claimant's money, took place on 9 June 1989. The borrowers quickly fell into arrears and the claimant sold the property as mortgagee in possession on 13 April 1992, leaving a shortfall on the borrowers' account.

10.56   The claimant lender's case was as follows. By 17 May 1989, the defendants had discovered that there were arrears of over £4,000 on the borrowers' mortgage with Western Trust, and that there was a danger of Western Trust commencing legal proceedings to repossess the property. The defendants did not report these pieces of information to the claimant. In particular, they did not refer to them in their report on title dated 31 May 1989. The claimant claimed that the defendants ought to have reported such information to it, and that, by failing to do so, the defendants were in breach of their implied contractual duty and duty of care owed to the claimant.

10.57   The Court of Appeal disagreed. Peter Gibson LJ, with whom the other two judges agreed, set out five factors which were relevant to determining the scope of the defendants' duties:[1]

'(1) The instructions from the plaintiff required the defendants to act for the plaintiff "in the preparation of a mortgage ... in accordance with the Notes for Guidance and the documents provided." Any solicitor of ordinary competence and experience would realise that the defendants' primary function was to make sure that the plaintiff received a valid and effective first mortgage on the property, and that required in particular that the plaintiff should receive a good and marketable title. The approval of the title by the defendants was an express condition of the loan.

(2) The plaintiff, an experienced commercial lender, provided its own detailed printed instructions to the solicitors. Those instructions specified the particular matters on which the plaintiff required to be advised. This made clear, for example, that the investigation of title should go beyond ordinary conveyancing matters, but extended to matters which might affect the valuation put upon the property. To give another example, they were required to advise if any information suggested that the property was not to be the principal residence of [the borrowers] for the sole continuing occupation of them and their family. The plaintiff provided its own form of a report on title which stated precisely what the solicitor was required to certify. In these circumstances, whatever the position in other cases with differing circumstances, there is limited room here for treating the scope of the duty of care as extending to require the solicitor to take action which has not been expressly required by the plaintiff in its instructions.

(3) Subject to para 6 of the report on title, the only action which the defendants were instructed to take relating to the financial circumstances of [the borrowers] was twofold: to do a bankruptcy search and to report on any matter revealed by the search.

(4) The plaintiff did not send a copy of the application by [the borrowers] to the defendants, and there is no evidence that they knew any of its contents.'

Pausing there, the relevance of this was that the defendants could not have known that the information which they had as to the arrears demonstrated that the borrowers had lied to the claimant on the application form. Continuing the quotation:

'(5) Further, the report on title, in requiring the defendants to certify that they were not aware of any material change in the circumstances of [the borrowers] subsequent to the date of offer of loan, would naturally lead the defendants to believe that, subject only to a clear bankruptcy search being obtained, the plaintiff was satisfied that the

533

circumstances of [the borrowers] at that date were such that they were appropriate borrowers. The defendants did not know what inquiries, if any, had been made by the plaintiff. Mrs Butler, a legal executive who was employed by the defendants and who ... dealt with the matter for them, presumed that the plaintiff would have sought a reference from Western Trust.'

The presence of the fifth factor is probably not a necessary condition for concluding that there is no implied duty to report matters relevant to creditworthiness.[2]

1 See [1998] 1 WLR 207 at 214A-G.
2 See *Birmingham Midshires Mortgage Services Ltd v David Parry & Co* [1997] ECGS 150, CA.

10.58   Blackburne J distinguished *Giffen* in *Balmer Radmore* on the following bases:[1]

'The question in that case was whether the solicitor should have reported certain information which cast doubt on the borrowers' ability to pay. The information was of a kind which it would be reasonable to suppose the plaintiff would have obtained from other sources. The instructions were held, where matters of creditworthiness were concerned, to be of very limited scope. The decision does not seek to limit the scope of the duty to report where, as here, the information relates to matters going to the value of the property and therefore to the adequacy of the security or where, as here, the information derives from an investigation of title and therefore from matters which it is the business of the solicitor to investigate and not that of the Society or of others on its behalf.'

Following this approach, it is thought that, in cases to which rr 3.19 and 3.20 do not apply, there is a distinction in the nature of the implied duties which the court will ordinarily imply, between, first, matters which a solicitor would normally discover in the course of his or her investigation of title on behalf of the lender, which are relevant to the value of the security, and secondly, matters going to the creditworthiness of the borrowers, which the solicitor could normally expect that the lender would find out itself, and which a solicitor acting only for the lender and not the borrowers would probably not discover. In such cases, there will normally be an implied duty to report information which falls into the first category, but no implied duty to report information which falls into the second category. The approach of limiting solicitors' duties to those within the solicitor's core function is similar to that taken in *Midland Bank plc v Cox Mc Queen*.[2]

1 *Balmer Radmore* [1999] Lloyd's Rep PN 241 at 258.
2 Referred to at para 1.02 and 10.41, above.

10.59 There is a question as to whether *Bowerman* should be interpreted to give rise to a duty which goes beyond what we have called the *Bowerman* duty. We defined the *Bowerman* duty as being an implied duty to report information which a solicitor of ordinary competence would have regarded as information which might cause the lender to doubt the correctness of the valuation. Further, on Blackburne J's formulation of the duty, the obligation is to report information discovered in the course of investigating title or preparing for completion.[1] In cases outside the scope of rr 3.19 and 3.20, will the implied duty which the court will normally imply as a result of *Bowerman* go further, and encompass, as Sir Thomas Bingham suggested in *Bowerman*,[2] a duty to report information which a solicitor of ordinary competence would have regarded as information which might cause the lender to doubt 'some other ingredient of the lending decision'?

1 This is subject to an exception which we consider at para 10.64, below.
2 See the passage quoted at para 10.46, above.

10.60 It is likely that this broader duty would be inconsistent with the subsequent decision in *Giffen*. In *Giffen*, the Court of Appeal distinguished *Bowerman* on five bases. The key points were that information as to creditworthiness did not relate to title or the adequacy of the security, or to any other matter on which the defendant solicitors were instructed to advise. Peter Gibson LJ pointed out that Millett LJ had decided *Bowerman* on a narrower basis than Sir Thomas Bingham MR, stating that the reportable information appeared on the face of the vendor's title, and thus was information which the defendant solicitors would have discovered in the course of investigating title. It is thought that, in order to be consistent with *Giffen*, it is necessary to construe the duty arising out of *Bowerman* as being confined to what we have called the *Bowerman* duty.[1] This may still be a broad duty, since many matters may be relevant to the value of the property, and in particular information suggesting sub-sale frauds generally will be relevant to value. If, however, one were to construe the *Bowerman* duty as extending, for example, to a duty to report all matters suggesting bad faith of the borrowers, then one might have difficulty in explaining why the claimant lost in *Giffen*: the information as to arrears in that case might be seen as being information which suggested that the borrowers were acting in bad faith and knew that they would never be able to repay the lender.

1 Para 10.47, above.

(c) *Implied waiver of confidentiality by the borrower*

10.61 In cases where it applies, the implied duty, arising out of *Bowerman*, is subject to two limitations: first, it is limited to information which is not confidential; secondly, it is generally limited to information which the solicitor discovers in the course of doing the work which he or she is instructed to do on behalf of the lender, which is principally investigating title and preparing for completion.[1] We consider the second limitation below. As to the first, what counts as confidential information for these purposes? Breach of confidence is considered in detail in chapter 6. In relation to lenders' claims, the problem is likely to arise where, as is normally the case, the same solicitor acts for both lender and borrower. But if the suggestion made above proves correct, so that in such cases there is no *Bowerman* duty because of the terms of rr 3.19 and 3.20[2] of the Solicitors' Code of Conduct, then the question of limitations on the *Bowerman* duty falls away altogether.

1 See the formulations of Sir Thomas Bingham MR at para 10.46 and Blackburne J at para 10.48 above.
2 In the case of a non-residential mortgage r 3.20 will not apply but r 3.19 will still apply, so the point remains: there is probably no *Bowerman* duty.

10.62 If, on the other hand, contrary to the suggestion made above the *Bowerman* duty does arise where the same solicitor acts for both lender and purchaser, then in *Balmer Radmore* Blackburne J set out the position, in relation to information which the solicitor has learnt in the course of handling the transaction for which the borrower seeks a loan from the lender, as follows:[1]

'In *Bowerman,* Millett LJ said this (at page 844j):

"A solicitor who acts for more than one party to a transaction owes a duty of confidentiality to each client, but the existence of this duty does not affect his duty to act in the best interests of the other client. All information supplied by a client to his solicitor is confidential and may be disclosed only with the consent, express or implied, of his client. There is, therefore, an obvious potentiality for conflict between the solicitor's duty of confidentiality to the buyer and his duty to act in the best interests of the mortgage lender.

No such conflict, however, arose in the present case. It is the duty of a solicitor acting for a purchaser to investigate the vendor's title on his behalf and to deduce it to the mortgagee's solicitor. He has the implied authority of his client to communicate all documents of title to the mortgagee's solicitor."

In *Mothew,*[2] he said this (at page 20d):

"By instructing him to act for them, the purchasers must be taken to have authorised the defendant to complete the report without which the mortgage advance would not have been forthcoming; and to complete it truthfully. The defendant was required by the society to report on the purchasers' title as well as to confirm the absence of any further borrowing. The two stood in exactly the same case. The defendant would not have been in breach of his duty to the purchasers if he had disclosed the facts to the society any more than if he had reported a defect in their title."

This proposition can be tested by considering what the defendant's position would have been if he had acted for the purchasers and another solicitor had been instructed to act for the society. He would have been required to deduce the purchasers' title to the satisfaction of the society's solicitor, and to confirm to him that no further borrowing or second charge was in contemplation. His duty to the purchasers would have required him to ascertain the facts from them and to report them to the society. Unless they told him the facts and instructed him to lie to the society, instructions which he would be bound to refuse, his duty to the purchasers would not inhibit him in providing full and truthful information to the solicitor acting for the society.

The answer to the first question, therefore, lies in ascertaining what it is that the solicitor is obliged by his instructions to report on to the lender: the implied authority to disclose covers all matters to which the instructions relate. By naming his own solicitor to act also for the society, which occurred in each of the twelve cases before me, the borrower must therefore be taken to have authorised the solicitor to complete the report on title and make whatever disclosures were necessary to enable the solicitor to comply with the society's instructions, without which the mortgage advance would not be forthcoming, and to complete the report on title truthfully.'

1 [1999] Lloyd's Rep PN 241 at 261.
2 *Bristol and West Building Society v Mothew* [1998] Ch 1, CA.

10.63 It is therefore unlikely that confidentiality owed to the borrowers, in relation to the instant transaction, will be a bar to the solicitor reporting to the lender. On Blackburne J's formulation, where borrowers name their own solicitor to act also for the lender, they impliedly authorise the solicitor to disclose to the lender any matters, concerning the instant transaction, which it is necessary to disclose in order to comply with the lender's instructions. Thus, if a piece of information needs to be reported in order to comply with the lender's instructions, the borrower will be taken to have impliedly authorised such disclosure, even if the information is confidential, so confidentiality will be no bar to disclosure.

(d) *Information learnt from other transactions*

10.64 The second limitation on the implied duty to report information, arising out of *Bowerman,* was that the duty generally related only to information which the solicitor discovered in the course of doing the work which he was instructed to do on behalf of the lender. This is principally investigating title and preparing for completion. Thus, under *Bowerman* it has been held that there is generally no implied duty to report information which the solicitor knows from other sources, for instance, from working for the borrower client on other unrelated transactions.[1] That proposition might, however, appear to be in conflict with the House of Lords' subsequent decision in *Hilton v Barker Booth & Eastwood*[2], which is discussed in chapters 2, 4 and 6.[3] In *Hilton,* the House held that solicitors who acted for two parties to an agreement had a duty to one party (A) to reveal what they knew about the dubious character of the other party (B), though they also owed a duty to B not to reveal the same information to A. They did not reveal the information to A, so they complied with their duty to B but breached their duty to A and had to compensate A. But Lord Walker declined the opportunity to review the lenders' cases.[4] As a result, the question of whether *Hilton* requires the overruling of any lenders' claims remains to be determined in later cases. It is possible that, in cases such as the normal lenders' claim where the solicitors' contractual retainer is detailed, written, and clearly intended to exclude any duty on the solicitor to reveal everything which he or she knows about the borrower to the lender, then the solicitor has no general duty to reveal such information to the lender.[5]

1 *Bristol and West Building Society v Baden Barnes Groves & Co (No 1)* (26 November 1996, unreported) (Chadwick J).
2 [2005] UKHL 8, [2005] 1 WLR 567.
3 See paras 2.15, 4.36 and 6.22, above.
4 [2005] UKHL 8, [2005] 1 WLR 567 at 580C–G.
5 See Lord Walker's comments at [29]–[30], and *Kelly v Cooper* [1993] AC 205, PC. See also Hollander, 'Conflicts of Interest and the Duty to Disclose Information' [2004] 23 CJQ 257.

10.65 The position is different where the information that the solicitors know from other sources, taken with the information that they have in relation to the lender's transaction, provides the solicitors with strong evidence of fraud. In that case, any confidentiality of the borrower's is overridden,[1] and the solicitors will have an implied duty to report to the lender both the information, and the reason why they are reporting it, namely, that it leads them to suspect fraud.[2]

1 *Darlington Building Society v O'Rourke James Scourfield & McCarthy* [1999] Lloyd's Rep PN 33, CA.
2 See Blackburne J's decision in *Vanderpump & Sykes,* part of the *Balmer Radmore* judgment: [1999] Lloyd's Rep PN 422.

7 Forms of undertaking agreed between banks and the Law Society

10.66 In *Barclays Bank plc v Weeks Legg & Dean,*[1] the Court of Appeal considered three cases relating to a solicitor's undertaking to a lender that the lender's money would be used only for the purpose of obtaining 'good marketable title' to the property in question. In each case, the solicitor had provided an undertaking in a form agreed between banks and the Law Society.[2] It is important to recognise that these were not standard lenders' cases, because, with one small exception, the bank did not instruct the solicitors to act for it in the transaction; it did not ask the solicitors to provide a report on title or to advise in relation to any aspect of the transaction; and the solicitors were not paid by the bank for their services.[3] Millett LJ, with whom the other judges agreed, said that, as the undertaking was designed to stand alone as the only communication passing between the solicitor and the bank, the scope of the solicitor's obligations was determined exclusively by the terms of the undertaking.[4] It follows that there would be no room for implied contractual obligations, or a duty of care in tort, which went beyond the express terms of the undertaking. This distinguishes cases based on such an undertaking from the standard case which we have just considered.

1 [1999] QB 309, CA.
2 The undertaking read:

> 'Undertaking by Solicitor
>
> To send Deeds/Land Certificate to Bank on completion of a purchase, the Bank and/or the Customer having provided the purchase monies. TO BARCLAYS BANK PLC
>
> If you provide facilities to my/our client ... for the purchase of the Freehold/Leasehold property ... .
>
> I/We undertake: (a) that any sums received from you or your customer for the purpose of this transaction will be applied solely for acquiring a good marketable title to such property and in paying any necessary deposit legal costs and disbursements in connection with such purpose. The purchase price contemplated is £... gross and with apportionments and any necessary disbursements is not expected to exceed £... (b) after the property has been acquired by ... and all necessary stamping and registration completed to send the Title Deeds and/or Land Certificates and documents to you and in the meantime to hold them to your order.'

3 See [1999] QB 309 at 323B–C.
4 [1999] QB 309 at 323G.

10.67 By the express terms of the undertaking, the solicitors agreed that the bank's money would be applied solely for obtaining a 'good marketable title'. Millett LJ said:[1]

> 'The obligation of a vendor is to deduce sufficient title to the property which he has contracted to sell. The expression "good marketable title" describes the quality of the evidence which the purchaser is bound to accept as sufficient to discharge this obligation. It says nothing about the nature or extent of the property contracted to be sold to which title must be deduced. The expression is a compendious one which describes the title and not the property. It is used in contradistinction to "a good holding title", by which is

539

meant a title which a willing purchaser might reasonably be advised to accept, but which the court would not force on a reluctant purchaser.'

In the first case, the land in question was purchased subject to a special condition that it was subject to a right of way in favour of an adjoining owner. The Court of Appeal held that this did not mean that the solicitors were wrong to state that title to the property was good and marketable: an unwilling purchaser could have been forced to buy the land. The fact that the right of way rendered the land less valuable than the lender bank had thought was irrelevant to the question of whether there was good marketable title to it. Although the case turns on construction, one might observe that the effect of the bank's argument was that the solicitors' obligations were similar to those which they would have had if they had supplied a report on title, even though the solicitors had been paid nothing by the bank and had not supplied a report on title. In that context, it is perhaps unsurprising that the bank's contentions were rejected.

1 [1999] QB 309 at 325F-G.

8 Causation

(a) *Extent of duty to report at common law*

10.68 In contract and the tort of negligence, the test of causation applied to lenders' cases turns on whether, if the solicitors had reported the matters which they ought to have reported, the lender would have made the advance which it in fact made. This is a question of fact which turns on the judge's assessment of the particular lending officer in question. The response of the lending officer would depend in part on the terms in which the solicitor made the report of the relevant information. In *Balmer Radmore,* Blackburne J said that the solicitor ought to have reported as if he or she were writing to an intelligent layman.[1] But his decisions in the individual cases suggest that his approach was rather that the solicitor should assume that he was writing to a layman who needed potential difficulties spelt out in the clearest possible way, which is perhaps not unfair, since, in relation to contributory negligence, he found that the lender's employees did not generally think about applications in a careful or critical way. The judge held that the solicitor's duty was not merely to report the bare facts which ought to be passed to the lender, but also the reason why they were being reported. Thus, in a case where the lender was offering to advance £134,000 by remortgage and the solicitor had a duty to report that the property had been purchased a few days earlier for only £120,000, the solicitor's duty was:[2]

'to state in clear terms, preferably in a letter to the Society so that there could be no mistake about the matter, not simply the essential facts of the [borrowers]' earlier purchase (i e that it had occurred only three or so weeks earlier and had been for £120,000) but why he was reporting the matter (i e that the information might cast doubt on the valuation of the property which the Society would have obtained and without which it would not have been willing to advance £134,000). In my view it is not a sufficient discharge of that duty simply to report the bare facts and leave it to the recipient within the Society, whoever he or she might be, to guess what the reason is for the disclosure.'

1 [1999] Lloyd's Rep PN 241 at 270.
2 *Littlestone v Cowan*: see [1999] Lloyd's Rep PN 625 at 629 col.2.

10.69   Again, in *Vanderpump & Sykes,* Blackburne J set out numerous matters which the defendant solicitor ought to have reported to the lender, including doubts as to the honesty of the transaction.[1] In that case, the lender's surveyor had expressed doubts about the honesty of the transaction, but it nevertheless proceeded with the advance. In Blackburne J's view, there was a critical difference in relation to causation between the society's surveyor expressing such doubts, and its solicitor, who also acted for the borrower, expressing the same doubts: even though the former had not caused the lender to withdraw from the transaction, the latter would have done. This shows that Blackburne J's view that, once a solicitor has a duty to report matters, he or she must spell them out in detail, may be crucial to causation: the more the solicitor has a duty to explain why he or she is reporting matters, the more likely it is that, had such a report been made, the lender would have withdrawn, even if, in other respects, its employees were unthinking or even careless.

1 [1999] Lloyd's Rep PN 422 at 440.

(b) Extent of duty to report in cases subject to rr 3.19 and 3.20

10.70   Should the same approach apply in cases to which rr 3.19 and 3.20 of the Solicitors' Code of Conduct 2007, or their predecessors in Practice Rule 6(3), apply? In the absence of judicial authority, it is thought that the following is the correct interpretation. Rule 3.19 provides that one of the obligations that the solicitor may owe the lender is:

'(w) giving legal advice on any matters reported under 3.19, suggesting courses of action open to the lender, and complying with the
lender's instructions on the action to be taken.'

If the interpretation of rr 3.19 and 3.20 contended for above is correct then, with the exception of factors suggestive of fraud, the purpose of those drafting these rules was to reduce the solicitors' obligations as compared with the obligations imposed by the common law as a result of the 1990s lenders' decisions. Taking the terms of r 3.19(e): as to sub-sales, the solicitor's duty is to be limited to:

'reporting if the seller or the borrower (if the property is already owned by the borrower) has not owned or been the registered owner of the property for at least six months'.

It is submitted that, other than in cases suggestive of fraud, it is clear that what the drafters of this rule intended was that the solicitors should have an obligation to report the bare facts of the sub-sale but should not have an obligation to explain the significance of it: otherwise one would expect r 3.19(e) to go on to say, as Blackburne J did in the passage quoted above, that the solicitors could also have a duty to explain the significance of the facts reported. On this interpretation, when r 3.19(w) provides that 'legal' advice on matters reported could be required, it means advice on 'legal' matters in the narrow sense, in other words issues relating to the quality of the title or other conveyancing risks; it does not mean the significance in terms of the value of the property on which the lender is lending. The position may be different in relation to factors suggestive of fraud because 3.19(a)(ii) expressly provides that solicitors may be required to comply with the terms of the Law Society's guidance on property fraud, and the effect of that guidance is that matters suggestive of fraud should be reported.

(c) What would the lender have done absent breach of duty?

10.71 There are essentially three possible answers to the question of what the lender would have done if the solicitor had reported as he or she ought to have done. First, it might have made the same advance in the same amount. In that case, it can recover only nominal damages, and probably not costs.[1] Secondly, it might have lent to the same borrower but on a lower advance. In that case, its loss is the difference between the advance it in fact made, and the advance it would have made if there had been no breach of duty, plus interest.[2] Thirdly, it might not have lent at all. In that case, one moves to consider basic loss and the effect of *SAAMCo*,[3] which we deal with below.

1 Cf *Alltrans Express Ltd v CVA Holdings Ltd* [1984] 1 WLR 394, CA.
2 See the *ATM Abdullah* decision in *Balmer Radmore*: [1999] Lloyd's Rep PN 616.
3 [1997] AC 191, HL.

10.72 There is a final issue on causation. This concerns the correct test for causation in negligent misrepresentation cases. It arises from what Millett LJ said in *Bristol and West Building Society v Mothew*,[1] as to the Court of Appeal's decision in *Downs v Chappell*.[2] This issue is dealt with in chapter 3, to which reference should be made.[3]

1 [1998] Ch 1 at 11B-D, CA.
2 [1997] 1 WLR 426, CA.
3 See para 3.08ff, above.

9   Basic loss

10.73   The decision of the House of Lords in *SAAMCo* introduced a distinction, in cases to which it applies, between two kinds of loss. Although the case
did not provide labels for these two types, we use here the terms basic loss and
attributable loss. Attributable loss is the loss which is recoverable in accordance
with the principles set out in *SAAMCo,* which we consider below.[1] Basic loss
was a term used by Lord Hobhouse in *Platform Home Loans Ltd v Oyston
Shipways Ltd.*[2] He derived it from Lord Nicholls's definition of the 'basic
comparison' which has to be made in a lender's case, and which we discussed in
chapter 7.[3] The basic loss is assessed according to the principles set out in
Swingcastle Ltd v Alastair Gibson.[4] This is a question of comparing the position
which the lender is in fact in, with the position it would have been in if there had
been no advance. Thus, it depends upon the nature of the evidence which the
claimant provides as to what would have happened if the defendant had not been
in breach of duty.

1 At paras 10.80–10.89. We take the term 'attributable' from *SAAMCo.* See also para 3.35ff, above.
2 [2000] 2 AC 190 at 201G, HL.
3 See para 7.30ff, above.
4 [1991] 2 AC 223, HL.

10.74   In *Swingcastle,* the defendant valuer negligently overvalued the borrowers' property. In reliance on the valuation, the claimant lenders advanced
money to the borrowers, secured by a mortgage. Under the terms of the loan, the
borrowers were required to pay interest at the rate of 36.51% per annum, or
45.619% per annum in the event of default. The issue in the appeal was whether
a lender who made a loan at a high rate of interest in reliance on a negligent
valuation could recover, as part of its damages from the negligent valuer,
interest at the contractual rate which the lender was entitled to be paid by the
borrower and which remained outstanding at the termination of the transaction
between the lender and the borrower. The House of Lords held that it could not.
The valuers had not guaranteed that the borrowers would pay the money owing
under the loan. The correct measure of loss was damages to put the lender in the
position it would have been in if there had been no negligence. If there had been
no negligence, the lender would not have entered into the transaction. Thus the
lender was entitled to damages to compensate it for the difference between (i)
the position it was in fact in, and (ii) the position it would have been in if there
had been no transaction. It was up to the lender to provide evidence as to (ii), so
that the court could make the necessary comparison. But what the lender could
not do was claim from the valuer the interest calculated on the rates of 36.51%
and 45.619% which the borrowers had failed to pay.

10.75   The amount claimed in each case will depend on the evidence which the lender provides as to the position it would have been in if there had been no transaction. In part this will depend on whether the money which was advanced was money which the lender already had in its possession, in other words the money of depositors with the lender, or was money it had to borrow, generally on the wholesale money markets. In the former case, the loss would be calculated by reference to what the lender would have done with the money if there had been no transaction. In *Fancy and Jackson,* for example, Chadwick J summarised the lenders' claim as to quantum of loss as follows:[1]

> 'The society quantifies [its] loss by adding to the principal sum lent the interest which would have been earned on an equivalent sum invested in the money market at London Inter-Bank Offered Rates (LIBOR) and deducting from the aggregate the interest and capital repayments (if any) actually made by the borrowers and the net recoveries (if any) from the realisation of the mortgaged property on sale.'

Presumably the lender's evidence was that, if there had been no transaction, it would have lent the money to others at LIBOR rates. On the other hand, the lender's evidence is often that the lender itself had to borrow the money which it advanced to the borrower. Thus part of the claim is for the cost to the lender of borrowing the money which formed the advance, since, if there had been no transaction, the lender would not have borrowed the money. But, in this case too, the evidence tends to be that the cost of funding should be calculated by reference to LIBOR plus or minus a small percentage. The claimant's calculation of its loss in a case of this second kind might look like this:

			£
Advance			100,000
Cost to the lender of borrowing the amount of the advance (interest it has had to pay to borrow the £100,000)			20,000
			120,000
Less			
Borrowers' payments		5,000	
Sale price	80,000		
Less cost of sale (estate agents' and solicitors' fees)	3,000		
Net proceeds of sale	77,000	77,000	
Total deductions		82,000	
			82,000
Total claim			38,000

Where a lender employs in-house solicitors or estate agents who act in the repossession of the property, their costs are recoverable as though they were those of independent professionals charging reasonable and fair fees for the work done[2]. Further, in principle, deductions for items such as solicitors' fees should be made at the date when the claimant paid the fee, so that interest on such a sum runs only from the date when the claimant suffered the loss. It should be emphasised that the calculation set out in the table is merely an example of what might be claimed. In the next few paragraphs we consider the basis on which the court might agree that it was payable.

1 See [1997] 4 All ER 582 at 616e–f.
2 *Portman Building Society v Bevan Ashford* [2000] Lloyd's Rep PN 354, CA.

Interest

10.76 A number of issues arise in relation to interest. First, there is a question as to the rate at which interest should be awarded.[1] This has often been agreed in lenders' cases. In principle, at least where interest is being awarded *as* damages rather than *on* damages (see below), it is thought that the right approach is to consider the rate at which the claimant actually suffered the loss. This will depend on the claimant's evidence. Note, however, that lenders' claims that all the money used to fund the advance had to be borrowed on the money markets may require further scrutiny. The Northern Rock crisis developed because Northern Rock used wholesale money markets to fund a higher percentage of its loan book than any other major UK lender. 28% of its funds were loaned by depositors and 72% raised from the money markets. In the case of other lenders, it appears that up to 60% of their funds are provided by customers' deposits.[2] It is possible that the cost of funding loans from the money markets may be higher than the cost of funding them from depositors. In that case, a lender 60% of whose loans were funded by deposits might be in difficulty in claiming that any given loan had been funded exclusively from the more expensive money markets. On the other hand, the lender might argue that the additional money required to make the particular loan in question had to be funded exclusively from the money markets. The question of whether the cost of funding should be taken as the average of what the lender has to pay, or as the cost of funding additional capacity over and above cheaper sources such as depositors' funds, has yet to be determined.

1 See para 3.80ff, above.
2 *Financial Times*, 15 September 2007.

10.77 Secondly there is the question of whether lenders are entitled to claim interest on a compound rather than merely a simple basis in cases where the evidence shows that they have in fact suffered a loss calculated by reference to compound rather than simple interest. It is necessary to distinguish between interest *on* damages and interest *as* damages. A claim to interest *on* damages arises where the total amount of damages payable has already been calculated, and interest is payable on that total sum from a date prior to trial until trial. A claim to interest *as* damages arises where part of the damages claimed, and set out in the statement of case, is interest. In the example given in para 10.75, the claim to interest ought to be pleaded, and would then count as a claim for interest *as* damages. The power to award interest *on* damages in common law claims arises from Supreme Court Act 1981,s 35A, but that provision permits the award of only simple and not compound interest. For that reason lenders tend to frame their claims to interest in terms of interest *as* damages rather than interest *on* damages.

10.78 As a result of dicta in the House of Lords' recent decision in *Sempra Metals Ltd v Inland Revenue Comrs*,[1] it appears that former arguments[2] to the effect that there was no power to award compound interest where interest as damages is claimed at common law are wrong. The claimant must plead and prove its entitlement to lost interest, including compound interest, as special damages. The evidence must address the issues referred to in para 10.75, above. The lender must also provide evidence as to the incidence of rests in the compounding of interest. But, if it provides the necessary evidence and can surmount standard rules as to remoteness of damage and mitigation of loss then in principle a claimant lender should be entitled to recover compound interest as damages. It is thought that claimant lenders may well be able to deal with remoteness difficulties: as Lord Nicholls observed at the start of his speech in *Sempra*, 'we live in a world where interest payments for the use of money are calculated on a compound basis'.[3] It would be hard to argue that solicitors acting for lenders are unaware of this.

1 [2007] UKHL 34, [2007] 3 WLR 354. See para.3.80, above.
2 Discussed in the first edition of this book. Even under the former law, it was possible to surmount the difficulties in some cases. See *Hartle v Laceys* [1999] Lloyd's Rep PN 315, CA, and *Mortgage Corpn plc v Halifax (SW) Ltd* [1999] Lloyd's Rep PN 159.
3 [2007] UKHL 34, [2007] 3 WLR 354 at [52].

10   Attributable loss

10.79 Once the claimant has proved its case in breach of duty at common law, causation, and established the amount of the basic loss, the question arises of whether it can recover all the basic loss, or whether there should be a reduction on account of the principles in *SAAMCo*.[1] *SAAMCo* concerned three cases brought by lenders against valuers. We consider the effect of the decision first in relation to valuers, then in relation to interest, and finally in relation to solicitors.

1 [1997] AC 191, HL. See also para 3.35, above.

(a) SAAMCo and valuers

10.80 Each of the cases considered in *SAAMCo* concerned the assessment of damages where a valuer had negligently overvalued a property, and a lender had lent on the security of the property in reliance upon the overvaluation. The practical result of the decision in relation to valuers is that, other than in exceptional cases, the lender's damages are limited to the lower of:

(i) the basic loss, calculated as set out in the last section, and thus probably including compound interest as damages; and

(ii) the amount of the overvaluation.

In cases where (ii) is lower than (i), the lender will be entitled to simple interest on the amount of the overvaluation, from the date when the basic loss reaches the amount of the overvaluation.[1] Thus if the true value of the property was £100,000, and the valuer stated the value to be £150,000, then the amount of the overvaluation would be £50,000. The valuer cannot be liable to the lender in damages for more than the amount of the overvaluation. So in our example, the valuer could not be liable for more than £50,000 in damages, though simple interest would be added.

1 See *Nykredit Mortgage Bank plc v Edward Erdman Group Ltd (No 2)* [1997] 1 WLR 1627, HL.

10.81 The practical effect of this rule is to limit the damages which the lender can recover. Lord Hoffmann explained the rationale for the rule by reference to an example:[1]

'A mountaineer about to undertake a difficult climb is concerned about the fitness of his knee. He goes to a doctor who negligently makes a superficial examination and pronounces the knee fit. The climber goes on the expedition, which he would not have undertaken if the doctor had told him the true state of his knee. He suffers an injury which is an entirely foreseeable consequence of mountaineer-ing but has nothing to do with his knee.'

Lord Hoffmann said that the doctor should not be liable for the injury. The reason was set out in the following principle:[2]

'that a person under a duty to take reasonable care to provide information on which someone else will decide upon a course of action is, if negligent, not generally regarded as responsible for all the consequences of that course of action. He is responsible only for the consequences of the information being wrong. A duty of care which imposes upon the informant responsibility for losses which would have occurred even if the information which he gave had been correct is not in my view fair and reasonable as between the parties. It is therefore inappropriate either as an implied term of a contract or as a tortious duty arising from the relationship between them.'

Hence the principle is that in cases where the defendant is sued for breach of a duty to provide information, the defendant is not liable for losses which would have occurred even if the information had been correct. Thus, in Lord Hoffmann's example, the doctor is not liable for the mountaineer's injury, which would have occurred even if the doctor's advice, that the mountaineer's knee was fit, had been correct. On the other hand, if the mountaineer's injury had been caused by his weak knee, so that the injury would *not* have occurred if the doctor's advice had been correct, then the doctor would be liable for the injury.

1 *SAAMCo* [1997] AC 191 at 213D–E.
2 See *SAAMCo* [1997] AC 191 at 214C–E.

10.82 Applying this test to valuers, Lord Hoffmann assessed the difference between the negligent valuation, and the true value of the property, at the date of the valuation. Taking the example above, £150,000 – £100,000 = £50,000. Lord Hoffmann then said that the consequences of the valuation being wrong were that the lender had less security than it thought, by the amount of the overvaluation.[1] So on our example, the lender had £50,000 less security than it thought. Damages were to be limited to that sum, in other words, to the extent of the overvaluation. The principle did not apply in three exceptional types of case. The first two exceptions were cases based on fraud[2] or breach of warranty.[3] The third was cases where the defendant was in breach of a duty to advise the claimant what course of action to take, rather than a duty to provide information. This third category does not normally apply in lenders' cases.

1 [1997] AC 191 at 215E, 216D.
2 See para 10.108, below.
3 For breach of warranty of authority see para 10.110ff, below.

(b) SAAMCo and interest

10.83 How should interest be assessed in cases where the basic loss exceeds the amount of the attributable loss, so that there is a reduction in damages on account of *SAAMCo*? Assuming that the claim for basic loss includes interest as damages, accumulating as loss which the lender has in fact had to pay but would not have done if there had been no breach of duty, the first step is to calculate when the amount of the basic loss reaches the level of the attributable loss. At that date, interest as damages ceases to be awarded, and the claimant is entitled only to simple interest on the amount of the attributable loss, pursuant to s 35A of the Supreme Court Act 1981, generally until trial.[1] Morritt LJ commented on the calculation of these figures in *Platform Home Loans Ltd v Oyston Shipways Ltd*:[2]

'I confess that I am greatly concerned at the time and expense which is likely to be incurred in carrying out these computations. So far as I can see if the interest representing the cost to [the lender] of the money lent to [the borrower] is the same as the interest awarded under s 35A Supreme Court Act 1981 then whatever the answers to these complicated enquiries[3] the same figure will be produced. In these circumstances I consider that the party requiring the full calculation to be made should pay for it unless it can be demonstrated that it made so significant a difference to the result as would justify the costs involved.'

But the calculations will be the same only if (i) there is no claim for compound, as opposed to simple, interest as part of the basic loss, and (ii) as in *Nykredit,* it is agreed that the appropriate rate for the award of interest under section 35A is the same as the rate claimed as part of the basic loss. We have suggested that, in light of the House of Lords' decision in *Sempra Metals,* it is likely that lenders will now be able to claim compound interest as damages in most cases.[4] If that proves correct then it would appear that, in light of that development in the law, the concern set out in the quotation may have been superseded: the lender will claim compound interest, as damages, until the level of loss reaches the level of the attributable loss; after that date, simple statutory interest will be payable on the damages. The calculation will be complex, but for a good reason.

1 See *Nykredit Mortgage Bank plc v Edward Erdman Group Ltd (No 2)* [1997] 1 WLR 1627, HL.
2 [1998] Ch 466. Although the Court of Appeal's decision was overturned by the House of Lords, the House did not need to comment on this passage.
3 Ie as to the date when the cause of action accrued, calculated in the way set out above.
4 Para 10.78, above.

(c) *SAAMCo and solicitors*

10.84 It is clear from *Bristol and West Building Society v Mothew*[1] and *Fancy and Jackson*[2] that the principles in *SAAMCo* apply to lenders' claims brought against solicitors as well as valuers. Their application, however, is more complex. We consider principally Chadwick J's analysis in *Fancy and Jackson,* which Blackburne J applied *in Balmer Radmore.*[3] The Court of Appeal has approved this approach in *Portman Building Society v Bevan Ashford*[4] and *Lloyds Bank plc v Burd Pearse.*[5] It is necessary to consider three separate categories of case – those where:

(i)   the lender's loss is not attributable to the breach of duty, so that only nominal damages flow from the breach;

(ii) the breach of duty was relevant only to the valuation of the property; and

(iii) if there had been no breach of duty, the lender would not have wished to make any advance to the borrower in question.

1 [1998] Ch 1, CA.
2 [1997] 4 All ER 582, Chadwick J.

3 [1999] Lloyd's Rep PN 241 at 271–272.
4 [2000] Lloyd's Rep PN 354.
5 [2001] EWCA Civ 366; [2001] Lloyd's Rep PN 452; [2001] PNLR 830.

(*i*)   *Loss not attributable to breach of duty*

10.85   In considering the facts of the *Fancy and Jackson* case itself, Chadwick J held that none of the basic loss was recoverable:[1]

> 'The defendants ought to have informed the society that they did not have an official search certificate. If they had done so, the society would not have authorised the advance – or, at least, would not have authorised completion on 6 October 1989. But the loss which the society has suffered as a consequence of making the advance on 6 October 1989 is not caused by the absence of an official search certificate on that day. The title to the property taken as security was not, in fact, defective. The society obtained what it intended to obtain when it decided to enter the transaction. The loss which occurred would have occurred in exactly the same way and to exactly the same extent if the defendants had had what, by implication, they represented they did have on 6 October 1989 – namely a clear search certificate showing good title to the property.'

Putting the matter another way, although the solicitor's breach of duty was relevant to the quality of the title to the property which formed the lender's security, in fact the breach of duty did not reduce the value of that security, because there was no defect in the title. Thus, applying Lord Hoffmann's test in *SAAMCo*, the lender would have suffered the same loss even if the information which the solicitor negligently supplied had been correct. For this reason, no loss was recoverable.

1 [1997] 4 All ER 582 at 621j–622a.

10.86   Similarly, in *Mothew*,[1] in breach of contract and negligently the defendant solicitor failed to report to the claimant lender that the borrowers, Mr and Mrs Towers, were not proposing to comply with an express condition of the advance which required that they provide the balance of the purchase money, apart from the lender's advance, without resort to further borrowing. The information which should have been reported was that the borrowers were arranging for an existing bank debt of £3,350 to be secured by a second charge on the property. Millett LJ said:[2]

> 'The society was told that Mr and Mrs Towers had no other indebtedness and that no second charge was contemplated. The existence of the second charge did not affect the society's security.

The absence of any indebtedness to the bank would not have put money in the purchasers' pocket; it would merely have reduced their liabilities. Whether their liability to the bank affected their ability to make mortgage repayments to the society has yet to be established, but given the smallness of the liability its effect on the purchasers' ability to meet their obligations to the society may have been negligible. It may even be, for example, that the purchasers made no payments at all to the bank at the relevant time, and if so it is difficult to see how any part of the loss suffered by the society can be attributable to the inaccuracy of the information supplied to it by the defendant. *It would have occurred even if the information had been correct.*' [Emphasis added.]

Thus, in cases where the lender would have suffered the same loss as it in fact suffered even if the information which the solicitor wrongly supplied had been correct, then only nominal damages should be awarded. Strictly speaking the test of causation which we considered above[3] is separate from the question of applying *SAAMCo*.[4] Thus, on the facts of the *Fancy and Jackson* case Chadwick J found that, if there had been no breach of duty, the transaction would not have proceeded, at least in the way that it did, so that causation was made out; it was the application of *SAAMCo*, rather than principles of causation, which produced the conclusion that only nominal damages should be awarded. In practice, however, it is possible that, where cases fall into this category, the court will first conclude that, had there been no breach of duty, then the lender would in any event have proceeded, and then go on to hold in the alternative that, even if the lender had proceeded, the loss was not attributable to the solicitor's breach of duty.[5]

1 [1998] Ch 1, CA.
2 [1998] Ch 1 at 12H–13A.
3 At para 10.71.
4 See Lord Hoffmann's emphasis of this in *Nykredit:* [1997] 1 WLR 1627 at 1638F–G, HL.
5 Compare the accountants' negligence case of *Bank of Credit and Commerce International (Overseas) Ltd v Price Waterhouse (No 3)* (1998) Times, 2 April (Laddie J).

(ii)   Breach of duty relevant only to valuation

10.87   In *Colin Bishop,* another of the cases decided in *Fancy and Jackson,* the matters which the solicitor ought to have reported included a sub-sale in which the price increased by 33%. Chadwick J held that, had these matters been reported to the lender, they would not have caused it to conclude that the borrowers were people with whom it did not wish to do business,[1] but would have caused it to doubt its valuation. He held that the recoverable loss was 'the loss suffered by the society as a consequence of the [lender] taking a security which was less valuable than it thought', and added that 'the position seems to me indistinguishable from the valuer cases considered in [*SAAMCo*] itself.'[2] On that basis, the measure of damages ought to be the difference between the amount of security which the lender thought it was obtaining, and the amount which it was in fact obtaining: the difference between the true value of the property at the date of the advance, and the value which the lender believed it to have. So if the lender thought it was obtaining security worth £150,000, but the true value was only £100,000, the measure of damages would be £50,000. This measure is not the same as taking the difference between the advance which the lender in fact made, and the advance which it would have made if it had known the true value, unless, in both cases, the lender would have lent 100% of the valuation. If, in our example, the lender was using an LTV ratio of 80%, then, as it believed the property to be worth £150,000, it would in fact have lent £120,000, whereas, if it had known that the true value was £100,000, it would have lent only £80,000, so the measure of loss would be £120,000– £80,000 = £40,000, rather than the £50,000 produced by *SAAMCo*. The measure which produced £40,000 would be the correct measure if the court concluded, in relation to the prior question of causation, that, had there been no negligence, the lender would still have made the advance, but in a lower amount.[3] Strictly speaking, the application of *SAAMCo* is a different question to causation, which explains why the two measures are slightly different.

1 See para 10.89, below.
2 See [1997] 4 All ER 582 at 622j.
3 See para 10.71, above.

10.88   A result similar to *Colin Bishop* was reached in *Alliance & Leicester Building Society v Wheelers*.[1] The defendant solicitors confirmed to the lender that there was planning permission under category B1 for a block to be used as offices. The lender lent on the security of the block. It transpired that the solicitor had been wrong: the planning permission was for D1 use rather than B1 use. Carnwath J held that it was appropriate to apply *SAAMCo*, and that the measure of loss was the difference between what the property would have been worth with the planning permission which the lender believed it to have, and its value with the planning permission which it in fact had.

1 (23 January 1997, unreported), Ch D.

(iii)   *Lender would not have wished to make any advance to the borrower*

10.89   In *Steggles Palmer*, a further case decided in *Fancy and Jackson*, Chadwick J considered various suspicious facts which the solicitors ought to have reported to the lender, but had not (emphasis added):[1]

'I have held that the defendants were in breach of duty in failing to notify the society that the transaction was by way of sub-sale; in failing to notify the society that they could not confirm that the borrower was to pay the balance of the purchase moneys from his own resources; and in breach of duty in failing to tell the society that they were also acting for the vendor. I have also held that if the society had known of those matters it would not have made the advance. But that is not, in my view, because the society would have been unwilling to lend what it did lend on the security of the property. In deciding how much to lend on the security of the property the society was relying on its own valuation; and there is no evidence that that valuation was wrong, or that it would have been affected by knowledge of the sub-sale or the relationship between vendor and purchaser. The reason why the society would not have made the advance is, in my view, because the society would have been unwilling to lend to that borrower in order to fund a purchase from that vendor. If the society had known what it should have known, *it would have decided that Mr Whittaker was a borrower to whom it did not wish to lend.* In those circumstances it seems to me fair, in accordance with Lord Hoffmann's test, that the defendants should be responsible for the consequences of the society not being in the position to take the decision which it would have taken if the defendants had done what they should have done. That is to say, the defendants should be responsible for the loss suffered by the society as a result of lending to Mr Whittaker. That, subject to questions of mitigation and contributory negligence, is the whole loss arising from the advance.' [Emphasis added.]

To summarise, had the solicitors reported the matters which they ought to have reported, the lender would have had such grave doubts as to the character of the borrower that it would not have wished to risk lending to him at all, presumably due to the risk of mortgage fraud. For that reason, the lender's loss could not be restricted to matters going to valuation, as in the previous category of case; instead, all the lender's basic loss on the transaction was attributable to the solicitor, and recoverable. Most of the individual cases decided in *Balmer Radmore*[2] provide further examples of cases which the court considered fell into this category. Lenders will of course wish to claim that most cases fall into this category, so that their damages are not limited by *SAAMCo,* and solicitors will wish claim that most cases do not, so that damages *are* limited by *SAAMCo.* Blackburne J was not slow to hold that cases fell into this category.[3]

1 [1997] 4 All ER 582 at 622c–f.
2 [1999] Lloyd's Rep PN 241.
3 The judge dealt with the issue in relation to 11 of the 12 cases, though in some cases the view he expressed was not part of the ratio as he had already held that there was no breach of duty. He considered that eight of those 11 cases fell into this category.

11 Contributory negligence

10.90 Reductions of damages on account of contributory negligence may be made in claims where the lender's cause of action is negligence or a contractual failure that amounts to failing to take reasonable skill and care[1]. We have already considered, in chapter 8, the general principles which apply to claims that damages be reduced on account of contributory negligence, as well as the House of Lords' decision in *Platform Home Loans Ltd v Oyston Shipways Ltd*[2] that deductions on account of contributory negligence should be made from the basic loss rather than the attributable loss. We now turn to various matters which apply in particular to lenders' claims. It must of course be borne in mind that allegations of contributory negligence in particular cases turn on the facts of the specific case, so that the value of authority is limited. Nevertheless, some trends may be observed.

1 See further para 8.03ff, above.
2 [2000] 2 AC 190. See paras 8.07–8.12, above.

10.91 Allegations of contributory negligence in lenders' claims tend to be of two kinds. In cases where the valuer was an employee of the lender, there may be allegations of negligence on the part of the valuer, for which the lender is liable. Alternatively, there may be allegations that the lender acted negligently in the scrutiny which it applied to the borrower's application for a mortgage or remortgage, before making the offer of advance. We set out the broad nature of the enquiries which lenders generally carry out above at paras 10.08 and 10.09. Parties may seek to adduce expert evidence in relation to either type of negligence, though it is not always necessary to obtain evidence from lending experts.

10.92 Blackburne J dealt in detail with allegations of contributory negligence, both of a generalised kind and in relation to particular cases, in *Balmer Radmore*.[1] His discussion related to the conduct of the Nationwide Building Society in the period 1990–1991. He found that, prior to March 1991, the society had provided inadequate training of its staff, in particular in relation to the dangers of mortgage fraud. Commenting on the performance of members of the society's staff in considering mortgage applications, he said:[2]

> 'With one or two notable exceptions … I had the impression that, in general, the process was one of going through the motions of ticking off the boxes to see that the relevant information had been supplied and that, applying the relevant lending criteria, the valuation and income disclosed justified the loan applied for. There seemed to be very little critical evaluation of the information supplied looked at overall. For example, the fact that in *Richard Grosse & Co* the information available to the Society indicated that the applicant had written cheques which were dishonoured was either not noticed or simply ignored. On occasions procedures were simply ignored.'

In general the society did not interview applicants, but Blackburne J considered that:[3]

'The utility of conducting an interview, at any rate in the case of new borrowers to the Society is, in most cases, obvious. It serves as a means of reducing the risk of fraud. Over and above that, in cases where the loan applied for is to be a high proportion of the value of the property offered by way of security (and the loan applied for is at or near the maximum allowed applying the Society's income criteria) then, unless the applicant's creditworthiness is clearly evident from the information supplied to the Society and there is no reason to doubt the accuracy of that information, the interview serves as a means of assessing whether the applicant is likely to be able to honour his commitments.'

Whether the approach taken by mortgage lenders has improved since 1990 remains to be seen. It is possible that it is now so long since the fall of the housing market in the early 1990s that the lessons of that period have been forgotten.

1 [1999] Lloyd's Rep PN 241 at 282–299 for the general discussion.
2 [1999] Lloyd's Rep PN 241 at 288.
3 [1999] Lloyd's Rep PN 241 at 288.

(a) *Levels of deduction for contributory negligence*

10.93   Writing about contributory negligence in lenders' claims in 1998, Hugh Evans[1] observed that:

'With two exceptions, none of the reported cases have assessed contributory negligence at above 30 per cent. In the two exceptions, the remarks on contributory negligence were obiter, as the defendants were found not to be negligent.'

Subsequently, in relation to the twelve individual cases which Blackburne J had to decide in *Balmer Radmore,* he made reductions for contributory negligence on a percentage basis in ten.[2] In those ten cases, he made reductions for contributory negligence of 90% in one case, 75% in another, 66% in three cases, 50% in two cases, and in the three remaining cases of 40%, 30% and 20% respectively.[3] In no case did he hold that there was no contributory negligence. It will be seen that these levels of reduction are much higher than had been the norm in previous cases. On the other hand, it may be argued that many of those cases were unusual. Although the amount by which damages should be reduced on account of contributory negligence is essentially a question for the discretion of the judge on which authority does not bind, it is thought that, in light of *Balmer Radmore,* the courts are likely to assess contributory negligence on the part of lenders at considerably higher levels than had previously been the case.[4]

10.94 *Lenders' claims*

1 'Contributory Negligence by Lenders' (1998) 14 PN 43 at 47–8.
2 The other two cases were cases where, if there had been no negligence, the lender would still have lent. Here the contributory negligence was expressed by reference solely to the excessive LTV, and was capable of precise calculation rather than expression merely as a percentage. See *Adams Delmar* and *ATM Abdullah,* and para 10.94, below.
3 In two of these ten cases the deduction for contributory negligence was not made because the solicitor was also in breach of fiduciary duty: see para 10.123, below.
4 See also *The Housing Loan Corpn plc v William H Brown* [1999] Lloyd's Rep PN 185, CA: the Court of Appeal refused to overturn a finding of 75% contributory negligence in a lender's action against a surveyor.

(*b*) *Excessive LTVs*

10.94   A number of points arise in relation to allegations that lenders have advanced an excessive LTV,[1] for example, over 75% of the valuation of the property. In *Fancy and Jackson,*[2] Chadwick J set out a calculation on the following bases: interest rates of roughly 10%, no payments of interest by the borrower, a period of roughly two years to repossess and sell the property, sale at the amount of the valuation, and sale costs of 4%. On those figures, if a lender lent 75% of the valuation, then it would recover all its money and break even on repossession; if it lent more than this, it would lose out. He concluded that, to the extent that the lender's losses had been contributed to by its having lent more than 75% of the value of the property, this had been negligent and, to that extent, its losses must be reduced. Blackburne J considered this part of Chadwick J's judgment in *Balmer Radmore*. While he found force in the point he added:[3]

'I accept Mr Patten's submission that the Society was entitled to lend in excess of 75% LTV without additional security provided that the value of the property (i e the security offered) exceeded the amount of the loan.

I also accept Mr Patten's submission that lending over 75% or 80% LTV is not per se negligent. Whether it is in any particular case must depend on the facts of that case. Thus, it would not, I think, be negligent to lend 95%, or even 100%, LTV to a borrower with an impeccable borrowing record and a sufficient and secured source of income or where property values are rising. If, on the other hand, little or no scrutiny has been applied to the borrower's disclosed source of income or to his loan record and other financial commitments, or where property values are static or falling, it is difficult to see how a decision to lend 95% LTV or more can be prudent. It is no answer in such a case to maintain that, viewed overall, a policy of high LTV lending has proved profitable and that the risk of loss on any individual transaction will be more than offset by the profits made elsewhere and by the cushion against default provided by the SMA scheme.

The question therefore is whether, in the particular case, the decision to lend at the particular LTV was a prudent one.'

In 2007, one might add that interest rates are considerably lower than 10%, so that Chadwick J's calculation may have to be re-considered; as Blackburne J indicated, it may also be material if, at the time of the advance, the property market was rising strongly. In a recent surveyors' negligence claim, the judge held that the lender had been negligent in lending more than 80% of the value of the property, but this was only because the valuation report indicated that the property was unusual and might prove difficult to sell.[4]

1 For 'LTVs' see para 10.07, above.
2 See [1997] 4 All ER 582 at 624e–h.
3 [1999] Lloyd's Rep PN 241 at 289–290.
4 *Preferred Mortgages Ltd v Countrywide Surveyors Ltd* [2005] EWHC 2820; [2006] PNLR 9.

10.95 One of the individual cases which Blackburne J had to decide was *ATM Abdullah,* which provides an example of his application of the principles quoted in the last paragraph. Of the lender's decision to lend on a 95% LTV, he said:[1]

'[The borrower] was just over 24. He had no known track record as an owner or tenant of property. Nothing was known of [the borrower]'s ability to handle a large loan or meet his financial obligations. The housing market was in decline. No one could say how long this would last and whether, in particular, property values would start moving up again. In my view the Society should not have advanced more than 75% of valuation.'

Thus, while there is no general rule that to lend on an LTV of over 75% is negligent, in cases where, at the time of the advance, the property market was falling and the borrower's creditworthiness had not been properly investigated, it is likely that it would be held negligent. Further, if the court does find that the LTV was excessive, it should calculate the precise amount by which the advance was too much, and reduce the basic loss by that precise amount.[2]

1 [1999] Lloyd's Rep PN 616 at 623 col.2.
2 See *Platform Home Loans Ltd v Oyston Shipways Ltd* [2000] 2 AC 190, HL, per Lord Hobhouse at 204A-C and Lord Millett at 213B.

10.96 Some lenders supplement their security by taking a mortgage indemnity guarantee ('MIG'). A condition of the offer of advance is that the borrower pays a premium, which is deducted from the advance, to a third party insurance company. Under the terms of the MIG, if the borrower defaults and the lender repossesses the property, the insurance company becomes liable to pay the lender a sum calculated by reference to, but lower than, the amount of the lender's shortfall after taking account of the net proceeds of sale of the property. It is generally not open to defendant solicitors to require that lenders give credit for the proceeds of such policies.[1] On the other hand, in answering a claim of negligence in lending on a LTV ratio that was too high, it is not open to the lender to rely upon the fact that it has required the borrower to take out a MIG: 'the conduct is negligent or imprudent whether or not the [lender] has insured against consequential loss.'[2]

1 *Bristol and West Building Society v May,May & Merrimans (No 2)* [1997] 3 All ER 206,(Chadwick J); *Portman Building Society v Bevan Ashford* [2000] Lloyd's Rep PN 354, CA; *Arab Bank plc v John D Wood (Commercial) Ltd* [2000] 1 WLR 857, CA.
2 *Fancy and Jackson* at 625e–f.

(c) Non-status lending

10.97 In some cases, lenders make no or almost no enquiries as to the status or creditworthiness of the borrower, and instead rely solely on the value of the property as security. This procedure is inherently more risky, unless the lender has adopted a considerably lower LTV than it would have done had it undertaken status checks. The question of whether this procedure was negligent depends, in any given case, on the LTV which was used, but also has to depend on the other facts of the case.[1]

1 See Jacob J's judgment at first instance in *Platform Home Loans Ltd v Oyston Shipways Ltd* [1996] 2 EGLR 110 and *The Mortgage Corpn v Halifax (SW) Ltd* [1999] 1 Lloyd's Rep PN 159 (H H J Lawrie sitting as a deputy High Court judge).

12 Mitigation

10.98 The issues which arise in relation to mitigation in lenders' cases were best summarised by Chadwick J in *Fancy and Jackson:*[1]

> 'The pattern of realisation in cases of this nature requires a number of sequential steps which may be summarised as follows. First, there is the society's decision to initiate the process of realisation following the borrower's default. Second, there is the issue of a summons for possession. Third, there is the order for possession. Fourth, there is the taking of possession. Fifth, there is the contract for sale. Sixth, there is completion of that contract. Delay in taking any of those steps will prolong the period between the borrower's default and the recovery of moneys advanced. Prolongation of that period will increase that element of the society's claim which is said to represent "lost interest" on the principal advanced. It may also have the effect, in a falling market, of reducing the amount for which the mortgaged property is sold; and so reducing the amount to be set against the claim for principal and lost interest. Accordingly, there are two questions to be considered: (i) whether there has been unreasonable

delay by the society in taking any of the steps which had to be taken towards realisation in the particular case and (ii) whether that delay did, in fact, have the effect of reducing the amount for which the mortgaged property was sold.'

1 [1997] 4 All ER 582 at 623g–j.

10.99 Chadwick J then went on to consider those two questions in relation to the cases of *Steggles Palmer* and *Colin Bishop*[1]. In each case, he set out the lender's progress, or lack of progress, in relation to each of the six steps set out in the quotation. The judge considered that there had been unreasonable delay, of, respectively, 42 months' and 30 months.[2] There is insufficient space to set out here the way in which those conclusions were reached, but it can be said that, in reaching them, the judge subjected the lenders' conduct to fairly severe scrutiny. In each case he concluded that the delay would not have altered the price at which the property was ultimately sold. He held in each case that there should be excluded from the claimants' loss (i) lost interest and (ii) periodic outgoings, in relation to the periods which he had identified as being periods in which the lender delayed unreasonably.[3]

1 This was not included in the All England Law Report. It is necessary to consider p 6 of the transcript (22 July 1997).
2 See p 10 of the transcript (22 July 1997).
3 See also *Western Trust & Savings Ltd v Travers & Co* [1997] PNLR 295, CA, discussed at para 3.64, above.

10.100 The question arises whether deductions for failure to mitigate should be made from the basic loss figure or the attributable loss. We have already seen that, in relation to contributory negligence, the House of Lords has decided that the deduction should be made from the basic rather than the attributable loss.[1] It is thought that, for similar reasons, reductions for failure to mitigate should be made from the basic rather than the attributable loss.

1 See the discussion of *Platform Home Loans Ltd v Oyston Shipways Ltd* [2000] 2 AC 190, HL, at para 8.09ff, above.

13 Contribution

10.101 In chapter 8, we considered the principles which govern claims for contribution in general. A solicitor sued in a lenders' claim will generally have no contribution claim against the borrower.[1] On the other hand, solicitors sued by lenders should normally consider whether it is appropriate to seek contribution from valuers or, in cases where they were involved, from financial intermediaries or even accountants who may have provided financial references. The principles on which valuers may be held liable are beyond the scope of this book. Those representing solicitors, however, will wish to consider the likelihood of successfully showing that valuers have acted negligently, and whether the valuer either was insured or is worth suing. Two lenders' cases in which the court had to consider contribution between solicitors and valuers were *Bristol and West Building Society v Christie*[2] and *Chelsea Building Society v Goddard & Smith*.[3] In each case, the court ordered the solicitors and the valuers to pay 50% of the damages each. Reference should be made to the transcripts for the facts. In *St Paul Travelers Insurance Co Ltd v Okporuah*[4] a supposed borrower who allowed himself to become involved in the fraud of a solicitor deceiving a lender was held entitled to claim contribution of 50% from the solicitor.

1 See para. 8.22, above.
2 [1996] EGCS 53 (HHJ Esyr Lewis QC). Official Referees' Business.
3 [1996] EGCS 157 (HHJ Overend sitting as a judge of the Queen's Bench Division).
4 [2006] EWHC 2107 (Ch), (HHJ Hodge QC).

14 Loans made by multiple lenders

10.102 Where large sums are lent in relation to commercial property transactions, the problem may arise that more than one lender has been involved in the transaction. The variety of possible sets of facts is diverse, but reference may be made to a number of types of loan dealt with in the cases. It is helpful to distinguish between claims in contract and in tort.

(a) Contract

10.103 Where there are simply many lenders lending separate amounts, according to separate loan agreements, in relation to one transaction, and the solicitor is instructed by each lender individually, there should be no difficulty in each lender suing the solicitor in contract. If there was only one loan agreement, to which many lenders were parties, and the solicitor's report on title was addressed to all the lenders, then each of the lenders would probably have a cause of action either in contract or in tort on the basis that the solicitor owed each of the lenders a duty of care.[1]

1 Cf *Interallianz Finance AG v Independent Insurance Co Ltd* [1997] EGCS 91, Thomas J.

10.104 At first instance in *Banque Bruxelles Lambert SA v Eagle Star Insurance Co Ltd*,[1] Phillips J had to consider the position where, after completion of the transaction in which the defendant valuers had acted, the claimant lender, BBL, syndicated parts of the loan. In other words, parts of BBL's loan were transferred to third party lenders by novation. The third parties took parts of BBL's rights pursuant to the original transaction, and in return reimbursed BBL for part of the original loan. BBL contended that these subsequent agreements were *res inter alios acta,* which should not be taken into account in assessing

BBL's damages, so that there should be no deduction from BBL's damages on the basis that some of the loss which BBL would otherwise have suffered on the transaction had been transferred to the third party lenders. Phillips J rejected this argument. The doctrine of *res inter alios acta* did not apply to allow BBL to claim loss which in fact had been suffered by the third parties. This conclusion was not challenged on appeal. The moral of this is presumably that in a similar case in future the third parties would have to consider bringing actions themselves. Although *BBL* was a valuers' case, it is likely that the same principles would apply in relation to solicitors.

1   [1995] 2 All ER 769 at 802g–j.

10.105   *BBL* was distinguished in *Interallianz Finance AG v Independent Insurance Co Ltd.*[1] As in *BBL*, when the defendant valuers undertook their valuation there was only one lender, Interallianz, who instructed them. The valuers were unaware of any plans to share the risk of the loan among different financial institutions. After the transaction had completed, Interallianz spread the risk of the loan by means of sub-participation agreements. These were different from the loan novations which had occurred in *BBL*. The effect of the sub-participation agreements was that, unlike in *BBL*, Interallianz remained the only party with a direct contractual relationship with the borrower. Under the sub-participation agreements, the sub-participators had no direct interest in the mortgage, and were not lenders to the borrower. Rather, they had a loan agreement with Interallianz, but the loan did not have to be repaid if the borrower defaulted. All that the sub-participators were entitled to were the amounts which Interallianz actually recovered under its mortgage with the borrowers. In fact, the sub-participation agreements reduced the amount of Interallianz's losses, because Interallianz had received funds from the sub-participators. But Thomas J held that sums received under those agreements were *res inter alios acta* which should be ignored in calculating Interallianz's loss, because:

'... they were not known to or contemplated by Allsop [the valuer], they were entered into before any loss was contemplated although after Allsop's breach of duty was in fact committed (but unknown to Interallianz), they did not arise out of Allsop's breach of duty and had nothing to do with Allsop's valuation.'

He added, however, that if Interallianz had entered into the agreements with knowledge of the alleged negligence, and they had been part of action taken in consequence of it, then benefits received pursuant to those agreements should have been taken into account. Further, in obiter dicta, Thomas J said that, if he were wrong that the proceeds of the sub-participation agreements should not be taken into account, in any event there was an implied term in the agreements that Interallianz should account to the sub-participators for any damages they received, and so, in any event, there should be no deduction from Interallianz's damages on account of the sub-participation agreements.

1 [1997] EGCS 91.

(b) Tort

10.106 If the third party provider of funds does not sue in contract, it may still have a claim in tort, as in *N M Rothschild & Sons Ltd v Berenson.*[1] Barclays Bank instructed the solicitor, and the request for funds was addressed to Barclays, but the funds were being provided by other banks. When the solicitors were instructed, Barclays explained to them in general terms that it and other financial institutions would be providing the funds for the advance. The Court of Appeal held that, because this had been explained, it should have been self-evident to any reasonably competent solicitor that all those lending would be doing so on the basis that the solicitor had provided a true and accurate request for funds. Hence the solicitors owed a duty of care to the other lenders.

1 [1997] NPC 15, CA. See para 1.28, above.

10.107 In *Secured Residential Funding Ltd v Nationwide Building Society,*[1] a valuers' case, the court held that the defendant valuers could not be liable in tort for losses suffered by a third party lender which had relied upon their valuation report. The judge held that the defendants could not be liable in tort to the third party unless they had in fact known that the third party was lending in reliance upon their report, or ought to have known this. He found that the defendants had had neither actual nor constructive knowledge of the third party's involvement, and so the third party had no claim. As to constructive knowledge, he said that the defendants could not be held liable unless there was, at least, a 'high degree of probability' that someone other than the intended recipient of the valuation report would rely upon its contents.

1 A decision of Mr Daniel Brennan QC sitting as a Deputy High Court judge: [1997] NPC 147. See Coates and Evans-Tovey, 'Duty of care of professional advisers' (1998) 142 Sol Jo 60.

B FRAUD

10.108 Fraud is proved when it is shown that a false representation has been made (1) knowingly, or (2) without belief in its truth, or (3) recklessly, careless whether it be true or false.[1] Because of dangers as to the extent of insurance cover for fraud,[2] even in cases where it lurks in the shadows, it is rare for claimants to allege fraud against sole practitioner solicitors, as they might not be insured, and the claimant might find that the solicitor had insufficient assets to meet the claim. There is less danger in the case of honest partners or employees of allegedly dishonest solicitors.[3]

1 *Derry v Peek* (1889) 14 App Cas 337, per Lord Hershell at 374.
2 See cl 6.8 of the Minimum Terms and Conditions of Professional Indemnity Insurance for Solicitors and Registered European Lawyers in England and Wales 2006.
3 Compare *Kumar v AGE Insurance Ltd* [1999] PNLR 269, Thomas J and see generally para. 5.21ff above.

10.109 If fraud is established, the claimant benefits from a more lenient limitation period,[1] a more favourable rule in relation to causation,[2] no risk of reductions in damages in respect of contributory negligence, even if the claimant was negligent,[3] and no reduction in damages on account of *SAAMCo*. Further, it is no answer to a claim in fraud to contend that the claimants could have discovered the truth but failed to do so on account of their own carelessness.[4] On the other hand, an allegation of fraud must be carefully pleaded.[5] In *Paragon Finance plc v Hare*,[6] Moore-Bick J struck out allegations of conspiracy to defraud against defendant solicitors. It was not enough simply to plead the primary facts: the claimant had to go further and set out clearly how those primary facts gave rise to the inference that the defendants were party to a conspiracy. Further, the court will not infer dishonesty or recklessness without cogent evidence which in effect compels such a conclusion.[7] Thus only the most serious of lenders' cases fall within this category.

1 See para 7.66.
2 *Smith New Court Securities Ltd v Scrimgeour Vickers (Asset Management) Ltd* [1997] AC 254 HL.
3 *Alliance and Leicester Building Society v Edgestop Ltd* [1993] 1 WLR 1462, Mummery J, *Nationwide Building Society v Thimbleby & Co* [1999] Lloyd's Rep PN 359, Blackburne J, and *Standard Chartered Bank v Pakistan National Shipping Corpn* [2002] UKHL 43, [2003] 1 AC 959.
4 *Nationwide Building Society v Dunlop Haywards Ltd* [2007] EWHC 1374 (Comm), Simon J, at [75]. This was a claim by a lender against a valuer; the judge granted summary judgment on a fraud allegation.
5 See para 8.2 of the *Practice Direction – Statements of Case*, which supplements CPR Part 16.
6 (1999) Times, 1 April (Moore-Bick J).
7 Per Blackburne J in *Vanderpump & Sykes*, one of the *Balmer Radmore* decisions: see [1999] Lloyd's Rep PN 422 at 430 col.1.

C BREACH OF WARRANTY OF AUTHORITY

1 Liability

10.110 Breach of warranty of authority is dealt with generally in chapter 5.[1] For present purposes, however, in two lenders' cases, claims for breach of warranty of authority have succeeded against solicitors who believed that they acted for both a husband and wife, but where in fact the wife's signature had been forged on various documents, she knew nothing of the transaction, and she had never given her authority to act to the defendant solicitors who assumed that they had such authority. From a claimant lender's point of view, an allegation of breach of warranty of authority may be attractive because liability is strict: it is no defence that the solicitor acted with reasonable care. Further, the liability imposed is said to be pursuant to a variety of collateral contract, which has consequences beneficial to the claimant in the assessment of damages.

1 See para 5.13ff, above.

(a) Solicitor purporting to act for the vendors

10.111   In *Penn v Bristol & West Building Society*[1], Mr and Mrs Penn owned their home, subject to a mortgage to the Bradford & Bingley Building Society. Mr Penn's business ran into debt, and he decided to engage in a mortgage fraud to obtain the money to pay off the debts. The fraud involved a supposed sale of the property to a Mr Wilson, without Mrs Penn's knowledge. Mr Wilson borrowed £75,293 from the Bristol & West Building Society. That sum was paid to Mr Brill, a solicitor, who believed that he acted for both Mr and Mrs Penn. Mr Brill used £31,769.78 of the money to pay off the Bradford & Bingley, and paid the rest, at the direction of Mr Penn, to Barclays Bank. Unbeknown to Mr Brill, the money paid to Barclays was paid without Mrs Penn's knowledge or consent. When Mrs Penn discovered what had happened she brought proceedings against various parties.

1   [1997] 1 WLR 1356, CA.

10.112   On appeal, the only issue of liability was whether Mr Brill, the solicitor who had believed himself to be acting for both Mr and Mrs Penn, was liable to the Bristol and West, the purchaser's lender, for breach of warranty of authority. The Court of Appeal held that he was, on the following basis. First, a solicitor who signed a contract purporting to act for his or her clients was liable for breach of warranty of authority if he or she did not have their authority to sign it.[1] The same applied on the facts of *Penn,* even though in *Penn* the conduct which amounted to a representation that the solicitor had the authority of both Mr and Mrs Penn went short of actually signing the contract. The conduct which the Court of Appeal considered amounted to a representation that Mr Brill had the authority of both clients to complete the transaction was as follows. The transaction proceeded in the usual way, with Mr Brill corresponding with solicitors who acted simultaneously for both the purchaser, Mr Wilson, and the building society, Bristol and West. During the course of that correspondence, Mr Brill believed himself to be acting for both Mr and Mrs Penn, and held himself out as being so authorised in all the pre-contract correspondence, negotiations and at completion.[2] During the course of taking those steps, Mr Brill knew that the solicitors with whom he was dealing were acting for both the purchaser and the building society. Those solicitors were ultimately a firm called Gartons. It was conceded by Mr Brill's counsel that, had Mr Wilson not himself been a party to the fraud, he would have been able to rely upon

Mr Brill's conduct toward Gartons as amounting to a warranty that Mr Brill had authority to act on behalf of both Mr and Mrs Penn.[3] That being the case, Waller LJ stated the principal issue on the appeal as being as follows:[4]

'... whether in circumstances where a solicitor is acting for a vendor, and negotiating on the vendor's behalf with a solicitor whom he knows to be acting on behalf not only of the purchaser but a building society, through whom the purchaser will be borrowing money to complete the purchase, the solicitor's warranty that he is duly authorised on behalf of the vendor is given not only to the purchaser but to the building society.'

1 *Suleman v Shahsavari* [1988] 1 WLR 1181 approved.
2 [1997] 1 WLR 1356 at 1363G–H, CA.
3 [1997] 1 WLR 1356 at 1363F, CA.
4 [1997] 1 WLR 1356 at 1358G, CA.

10.113 The Court of Appeal's answer was that the solicitor's warranty was indeed given not only to the purchaser but also to the lender. Waller LJ, with whom the other two judges agreed, set out the basis of the court's decision in this way:

'During the negotiation, following which a number of documents were to be executed in order to bring the transaction to fruition, and in completing the transaction, Mr Brill knew that Gartons were also acting for the building society. He knew indeed that Gartons would be arranging the completion of the purchase including arranging for Mr Wilson to execute a mortgage so as to obtain from the building society the purchase price and secure the building society's interest in the house. Thus, he knew that Gartons, in their capacity as the solicitors for the building society, would be relying on his having the authority of Mrs Penn to bring the transaction to fruition, just as much as they were relying on the same as the purchaser's solicitor. What is more, Bristol and West through Gartons did rely on Mr Brill having the authority of Mrs Penn to bring the matter to fruition, in that having obtained from Mr Wilson execution of a charge, money was advanced and available for the purpose of completing the transaction. If at any stage Mr Brill had said he did not have the authority of Mrs Penn the result would have been that Bristol and West would have proceeded no further.'

He went on to say that it did not matter whether Mr Brill the solicitor had known the name of the building society in question; it was sufficient that he knew that a specific lender was involved.

1 [1997] 1 WLR 1356 at 1363G–1364A.

10.114 In *Penn* it was conceded in the Court of Appeal that the solicitors had warranted to the purchaser that they had the vendors' authority, so that the Court of Appeal's view that that concession had rightly been made was obiter. There is an element of doubt as to whether, in light of Lord Woolf's statement of policy in the later case of *Midland Bank v Cox McQueen*[1], such a concession should now be made. The latter case suggests that solicitors will not generally be held to have warranted to lenders that they are guaranteeing the identity of a person purporting to be the borrower's wife. But in *Cox* the solicitor was acting for the purchaser and the lender, rather than for the vendor as in *Penn*. It transpired that the borrower's wife's signature had been forged. It might be argued that, in that situation, the lender was in as good a position to check the wife's identity as the solicitor. The *Cox* type of case, however, might be distinguished from claims such as *Penn* where the solicitor who is sued acted for the vendors. Where the solicitor acted for the vendors, the purchaser is in a worse position than the solicitor defendant to check the identity of the vendors, so Lord Woolf's statement of policy in *Cox* may apply with less force. Further, although the extent of warranty made by a litigation solicitor was relatively narrowly construed in *SEB Trygg Liv Holding Aktiebolag v Manches*[2], that decision did not deal with the position as to conveyancing solicitors. Thirdly, the vendor's solicitors were held to have warranted the identity of their clients in *Penn*[3] at first instance. At least at first instance, therefore, it appears that the lower court's decision in *Penn* is persuasive authority that vendors' solicitors do warrant the identity of their vendor clients.

1 [1999] Lloyd's Rep PN 223. See paras 1.02ff and 5.18ff, above.
2 [2005] EWCA Civ 1237, [2006] 1 WLR 2276. See para 5.16ff, above.
3 [1995] 2 FLR 938 (HHJ Kolbert).

(b) *Solicitor purporting to act for the borrower*

10.115 Will the court apply the decision in *Penn* to the following analogous case? A husband and wife jointly own their matrimonial home. They apply to a new lender for a re-mortgage. The husband appoints a solicitor who also acts for the lender on the re-mortgage, but assumes, without checking, that he has the authority of the wife as well as the husband. The husband provides the solicitor with a legal charge apparently signed by both husband and wife. Only after the solicitor has disbursed the lender's advance moneys does it become apparent that the wife knew nothing of the transaction and that her signature has been forged.

10.116 In *Cooke & Borsay,* one of the cases considered in *Fancy and Jackson,*[1] Chadwick J held that *Penn* did apply on these facts. He said that, if the lender and borrower had instructed separate solicitors, the position of the solicitor acting for the *lender* would have been as follows. If the borrowers' solicitor provided a mortgage deed which appeared to have been signed by the borrowers, and witnessed, and there was nothing irregular on the face of the document, then the *lender's solicitor* would be entitled to accept the document without question, and would not act in breach of duty in doing so. But the reason for this, following *Penn,* would be that the *lender's solicitor* would have an implied warranty, provided by the *borrowers' solicitor,* to the effect that the borrowers' solicitor had the authority of both borrowers to complete the mortgage by delivering the mortgage deed. It is implicit in this that the *borrowers' solicitor* would, in those circumstances, be liable to the lender for breach of warranty of authority if he did not have the authority of both borrowers to complete. Chadwick J then said:[2]

> 'I can see no reason why the position should be different in the circumstances that the same solicitor acts for both lender and borrowers. I do not hold that the duty of the solicitor, as solicitor for the lender, is increased by the fact that he acts also for the borrowers; but, equally, I can see no reason why, as solicitor for the borrowers, he should not be taken to warrant to the lender that he is acting for them in the transaction with their authority. That does not, necessarily, mean that he is warranting that the signature on the mortgage deed is authentic; but it has much the same effect. Mr Borsay must be taken to have warranted to the society that the mortgage deed which he delivered on completion as solicitor for the borrowers was delivered with the authority of both Mr and Mrs Barton. If the deed had been delivered with the authority of Mrs Barton as security for the advance which was made by the society, the fact that it did not, in fact, bear her signature would be relatively unimportant. She would clearly be bound by its terms.'

Although *Cooke & Borsay* concerned a re-mortgage, it is hard to see any distinction in principle in the case of an ordinary mortgage to husband and wife as borrowers. So, subject to the points as to developments in the law since *Penn* was decided[3], it would appear that there, too, solicitors purporting to act for the borrowers who failed to ensure that they had the borrower wife's authority would be liable to the lender for breach of warranty of authority if in fact they did not have the wife's authority, and the transaction proceeded but was subsequently challenged by the wife. But the caveat is important: it is possible that the law has moved on so that solicitors' warranties of authority would today be construed more narrowly, especially in a case where the solicitor acted for the lender, and the fraud was as to the identity of the borrower, so that the lender was arguably in just as good a position to check its borrower's identity as the solicitor. The imposition of strict liability in those circumstances seems harsh. In *Midland Bank plc v Cox McQueen*[4] the solicitors acted for the claimant bank in taking security over property owned solely by the borrower's wife. The Court of Appeal construed the defendant solicitors' retainer as requiring only the taking of reasonable care in establishing the identity of the wife; the solicitors did not guarantee that they had correctly identified her. Having held that the applicable standard was reasonable care in relation to the terms of the retainer, the court rejected an argument that the solicitors were subject to a stricter duty by virtue of a collateral warranty. This would suggest that, where the solicitor acts for the lender, if the retainer is construed as containing only a duty to take reasonable care as to the identities of parties signing documents then it may be inappropriate to hold that the solicitor warrants their identity. As we have seen[5], in cases to which r 3.19 of the Solicitors' Code of Conduct applies, the solicitor's obligation is essentially to take reasonable care with regard to identity fraud. This suggests that it may be the case that a solicitor acting for the lender does not give a warranty that he or she also acts for the lender's borrowers.

1 [1997] 4 All ER 582.
2 See [1997] 4 All ER 582 at 613c–e. Compare *Mercantile Credit Co Ltd v Fenwick* [1999] Lloyd's Rep PN 408, CA.
3 See para 10.114, above.
4 [1999] Lloyd's Rep PN 223, CA. See paras 1.02ff and 5.18ff, above.
5 Para 10.42, above.

10.117   If the last point does not represent the law, then the position would be as follows. First, where the borrowers are husband and wife, if the borrowers' solicitors provide the lenders' solicitors with a mortgage deed, apparently signed and witnessed by both borrowers, then, in the absence of exceptional circumstances, the lender's solicitors may proceed on the basis that both husband and wife have signed the deed. If this proves not to be the case, and if the wife had not authorised those who appeared to be solicitors for both borrowers, then the lender has a claim for breach of warranty of authority against the solicitors who appeared to act for both borrowers. But regardless of the point made in para.10.116, the lender may have a remedy against those who appeared to act for vendors who are husband and wife, if they provided a transfer document apparently signed by both vendors, in circumstances where the wife had not authorised them to act or signed the deed.

2   Causation and measure of loss

10.118   As to causation of loss, it is unlikely that a lender which has proved liability for breach of warranty of authority will fail to establish that, but for the breach of duty, it would not have made the advance:[1]

> 'I think it beyond argument that no advances officer would authorise completion if he were told that the solicitor could not himself verify the signature of one of the borrowers for whom he was acting; and could not warrant that he had any instructions from that borrower.'

Similarly, in *Penn* the Court of Appeal rejected an appeal on the basis that the breach of warranty of authority had not caused the loss.

1 *Fancy and Jackson* at [1997] 4 All ER 582 at 617a–b.

10.119   How does *SAAMCo*[1] apply to cases of breach of warranty of authority? In *Cooke & Borsay,* Chadwick J referred to Millett LJ's analysis of *SAAMCo* in *Mothew,*[2] and said that the measure of damage was:[3]

'... the difference between the position which the society would have been in if the authority had been as warranted and the position that it is in in the absence of authority ... The loss in this case is the difference between the value of security over the whole property and the value of security over the husband's share only.'

1 [1997] AC 191, HL.
2 [1998] Ch 1, CA.
3 See [1997] 4 All ER 582 at 623a–b.

3   Contributory negligence and mitigation

10.120   Chadwick J held that contributory negligence was no defence to a claim for breach of warranty of authority.[1] As to mitigation of loss, he set out the facts and said:[2]

'In my view it is for the [lender] to establish that it has taken reasonable steps to recover the one half share in the property to which it is undoubtedly entitled. The [lender] has made no attempt to establish that it has taken any steps to that end. In these circumstances the [lender] should not recover damages in excess of the value of a one half share of the property – such value to be assessed at the date upon which, with reasonable diligence, it could have had proceedings for an order under section 30 of the Law of Property Act 1925 determined in the county court–together with interest on that amount from that date. I put that date at 1 March 1995, being some eight months from the discovery of the alleged forgery.'

Although each case turns on its own facts, this approach to assessing damages and interest is likely to be at the least highly persuasive in later cases.

1 In a passage which was edited out of the All England Law Report of *Fancy & Jackson,* but appears at p14 of the transcript dated 22 July 1997.
2 This passage was edited out of the All England Law Report, although c f the reference at [1997] 4 All ER 582 at 624h. For the full passage, see pp 12–13 of the transcript dated 22 July 1997.

D   ACTIONS FOR MONEY HAD AND RECEIVED

10.121   In *Portman Building Society v Hamlyn Taylor Neck,*[1] the Court of Appeal struck out as hopeless a claim by a lender against solicitors brought as an action for money had and received. The lender sought to rely on this claim as, unlike its other claims, it was not statute-barred. For the purposes of the application, it had to be assumed that the lender's allegation, which was that it had paid the advance money to the solicitors under a mistake of fact caused by the solicitors, was correct. Millett LJ said that an action for money had and received was a claim for restitution for unjust enrichment. The action could not succeed because the solicitors had not been enriched at all: they had paid away the lender's money in accordance with the lender's instructions. Although those instructions were capable of being revoked, they had not been revoked, and continued to bind the solicitors. Thus the solicitors' defence was that they had properly accounted for the lender's money, in accordance with the lender's instructions. No action for money had and received would succeed unless the lender had revoked its instructions before the solicitors paid away the money. Thus, except in cases where the lender does expressly revoke the solicitor's instructions to pay the money to the borrowers, before the solicitor makes the payment, it is unlikely that actions by lenders for money had and received will succeed.

1 [1998] 4 All ER 202, CA.

E   EQUITY AND CONCLUSION

10.122   Equity is discussed in detail in chapter 4. In this section, we merely refer in broad outline to the issues which are most relevant in lenders' cases. Two types of claim in equity must be considered: breach of trust, and breach of fiduciary duty. It is unlikely that claims for breach of trust will figure largely in lenders' claims in the future, for two reasons. First, in *Target Holdings Ltd v Redferns*[1] the House of Lords indicated that, in relation to claims for breach of trust, the court applied a test of causation which was similar to the common law test.[2] Lenders could no longer argue that, once a breach of trust had been shown, they need prove only that a lending officer had read the report on title in order to be granted summary judgment for their entire basic loss, without having to prove what would have happened if the solicitor had acted in breach of duty.[3] Secondly, the discussion of breach of trust in *Mothew*[4] showed that it was harder for lenders to prove breach of trust than had previously been thought. The practical result of these two developments has been that lenders have viewed claims for breach of trust with considerably less enthusiasm than before: it is harder to prove the case, and when it is proved it does not necessarily lead to any benefit in relation to the test of causation which the court will apply, in comparison to a less exotic claim at common law.

1 [1996] AC 421, HL.
2 Per Lord Browne-Wilkinson, giving the only reasoned speech: [1996] AC 421 at 432E–G.
3 See para 4.43ff, above.
4 [1998] Ch 1, CA and see para 4.09, above.

10.123 The position is, however, different in relation to claims for breach of fiduciary duty. *Balmer Radmore* suggests that, depending on the facts, there may be large reductions for contributory negligence in lenders' claims in contract and the tort of negligence,[1] but there will be no such reductions in cases where the claimant is able to establish a breach of fiduciary duty which amounts to conscious disloyalty by the solicitor to the lender client.[2] Thus it will be in the interests of lenders to characterise solicitors' conduct as being in breach of fiduciary duty whenever possible. But references to breach of fiduciary duty should not be 'scattered throughout the pleadings with complete abandon'.[3] Further, in order to show intentional breach of fiduciary duty it is necessary to show a breach which is 'conscious, deliberate and in bad faith',[4] or a solicitor who returns a report on title either reckless, or not caring, whether it is true or false.[5] In most cases, this will be hard.[6]

1 See para 10.93, above.
2 *Balmer Radmore* [1999] Lloyd's Rep PN 241 at 278 and para 4.47ff, above.
3 'Equity's Place in the Law of Commerce', Sir Peter Millett (1998) 114 LQR 214 at 217.
4 See para. 4.37, above.
5 *Nationwide Building Society v Richard Grosse* [1999] Lloyd's Rep PN 348 at 356 (Blackburne J).
6 Pleas of breach of fiduciary duty succeeded in only two out of 11 cases in *Balmer Radmore;* in the 12th case there was a judgment in default for, inter alia, breach of fiduciary duty.

Chapter 11

Wills, estates and trusts

A THE PREPARATION AND EXECUTION OF WILLS

1 Introduction[1]

(a) *The effect of death on claims in contract and tort*

11.01 With a few limited exceptions, a claim in contract or tort survives the death of the victim.[2] There are, therefore, a whole range of cases in which the estate of a deceased victim may bring proceedings (including proceedings against a solicitor for negligence) and these cases involve no special principles. Take, for instance, the case of a solicitor advising a developer on the acquisition of a development site. If the solicitor fails to advise him or her that there is a restrictive covenant preventing the development of the property, the developer may bring a claim against the solicitor. If he or she dies before the claim can be brought, the estate can pursue the claim to judgment and obtain damages. In this case, although the claim is brought on behalf of the beneficiaries of the developer's estate, they have no claim against the solicitor personally. The claim is vested in the estate and the estate only. The estate may enforce the victim's rights in contract and may recover damages in tort for wrongs which he or she has suffered.

1 For discussion on the limitation issues which arise in relation to the claims discussed in this chapter see paras 7.42 and 7.79ff, above.
2 Law Reform (Miscellaneous Provisions) Act 1934, s 1(1).

(b) *Claims involving a client's will or estate*

11.02 In general the personal representatives of the victim of a tort or breach of contract ('T') will have the right to bring *all* claims for breach of contract or negligence of whatever kind and whether those claims involved the victim's will or estate or not. If T retained a solicitor ('S')[1] and had a claim for breach of that retainer, that claim should vest in his or her personal representatives whether or not it related to the preparation of a will (under which the personal representatives were themselves appointed) and whether or not it had any connection with T's estate. Take the following examples:

- *First,* T is domiciled in the UK. She executes a will settling assets on trust for the benefit of her family. The terms of the trust are defectively drawn and, as a consequence, the estate is subject to a substantial liability to capital gains tax that would have been avoided if the terms of the trust had been structured in a different way. The value of the estate is depleted by the amount of the tax and S is liable to the estate for the tax that would have been avoided if the estate had received competent advice. Before distributing the estate the personal representatives bring a claim for damages.[2]

- *Secondly,* T wishes to change her will. She instructs S, the family solicitor, to draw up a new will and to hold it for safekeeping and to notify the executors upon her death. T then dies. S forgets to notify the executors that they have been appointed by T to act as her executors and no action is taken to administer T's estate. As a consequence, the estate incurs additional tax penalties and interest charges. A valuable lease owned by T is also forfeited and the estate has to bring proceedings to obtain relief against forfeiture incurring substantial legal costs. In those circumstances, the estate is obviously entitled to recover these losses from S.[3]

- *Thirdly,* vary the facts of the second example slightly. T instructs S to draw up a new will under which the principal beneficiaries are completely different from the principal beneficiaries under her earlier wills. As a consequence of S's failure to notify T's personal representatives of the new will, they obtain probate of the wrong will and distribute T's estate to the wrong people. When the new will comes to light, the estate is exhausted and the executors are unable to recover the assets.[4] S is liable to the executors for the value of the assets distributed by mistake. The estate has suffered a substantial loss as a consequence of S's negligence. The personal representatives can recover the value of the assets from S and the costs of the unsuccessful proceedings to recover the assets.[5]

In none of these examples is there any reason why the beneficiaries under the new will need to be parties to the proceedings or to bring a claim themselves. Even in the last example the personal representatives should bring any claim against the solicitors for compensation for the assets, which they mistakenly distributed to the wrong beneficiaries, and for the other consequences of the solicitor's failure to notify them of the new will.

1 The abbreviations 'T' and 'S', and 'B' for beneficiary, are used throughout this chapter.
2 See the example given by Neuberger J in *Chappell v Somers & Blake* [2003] EWHC 1644 (Ch), [2004] Ch 19 at [27]:

'An example which was raised during argument was that of a bare trustee who seeks advice from a solicitor as to whether to distribute trust property, where the right advice is that the property should be distributed as soon as possible, because its income would attract a much lower rate of tax in the hands of the beneficiary than in the hands of the trustee, for some reason. If the solicitor delayed giving this advice for five years, it seems to me that it would be the trustee, and not the beneficiary, who would be entitled to sue the solicitor for the extra tax paid during that period. In such a case, it would be the trustee who was the client of the solicitor, and it would be the trustee who had had to pay the extra tax.'

Inheritance tax (as opposed to other forms of tax) causes special difficulties: see *Daniels v Thompson* [2004] EWCA Civ 307, [2004] PNLR 33 (considered below).

3 See *Hawkins v Clayton* (1988) 78 ALR 69 (HCA). Compare also the facts of *Chappell v Somers & Blake* [2003] EWHC 1644 (Ch), [2004] Ch 19 (Neuberger J). In that case it was held that the solicitors owed a duty to the executors of an estate but not to the beneficiaries to apply for probate and administer the estate: see O'Sullivan 'Solicitors, executors and beneficiaries: Who can sue and who can be sued?' (2003) 19 PN 507.

4 See the example given by Deane J in *Hawkins v Clayton* (1988) 78 ALR 69 at 99, lines 27–44.

5 For further specific examples of claims brought by estates: see paras 11.18 and 11.19, below.

2 Claims brought by beneficiaries or intended beneficiaries

(a) The beneficiary principle

11.03 The independent right of a beneficiary (or an intended beneficiary) under a will to bring a claim against a firm of solicitors who had acted for the testator was first recognised in *Ross v Caunters*[1]. This was a landmark case because it was the first occasion on which liability had been imposed on a professional adviser outside the contractual context and the adviser found to be liable to a third party, who had not retained or instructed him. In *White v Jones*[2] the House of Lords confirmed that a solicitor, who negligently failed to give effect to his client's testamentary intentions, would be liable to compensate the intended beneficiaries for the loss of their interests in the estate. The House of Lords chose not to adopt the reasoning in *Ross v Caunters* but, following their earlier decision in *Henderson v Merrett Syndicates Ltd*[3], confirmed that the rationale for the imposition of liability in tort under the '*Hedley Byrne*' principle (whether inside or outside the contractual context) was the assumption of responsibility. They nevertheless held that the law should recognise an exception to the general rule and impose on a solicitor, who failed to give effect to the testamentary intentions of the client, a liability to compensate the beneficiaries who were intended to benefit if those intentions had been carried out. The House of Lords held by a majority of three to two that a solicitor can be liable to a disappointed beneficiary for negligently carrying out the testator's instructions and depriving him or her of an intended legacy. Although all members of the committee delivered speeches, both Lord Browne-Wilkinson and Lord Nolan agreed with Lord Goff.[4] In *Carr-Glynn v Frearsons*[5] Chadwick LJ analysed Lord Goff's speech as follows:

'He recognised the need "to fashion a remedy to fill a lacuna in the law so as to prevent the injustice which would otherwise occur on the facts of cases such as the present" (at 268B); but to achieve that end he found it unnecessary on the facts in *White v Jones* to go beyond holding (at 268D):

"… that the assumption of responsibility by the solicitor towards his client should be held in law to extend to the intended beneficiary who (as the solicitor can reasonably foresee) may, as a result of the solicitor's negligence, be deprived of his intended legacy in circumstances in which neither the testator nor his estate will have a remedy against the solicitor."

Lord Goff went on to say this (at 269C-D):

"Let me emphasise that I can see no injustice in imposing liability on a negligent solicitor in a case such as the present where, in the absence of a remedy in this form, neither the testator's estate nor the disappointed beneficiary will have a claim for loss caused by his negligence. This is the injustice which, in my opinion, the judges of this country should address by recognising that cases such as these call for an appropriate remedy, and the common law is not so sterile as to be incapable of supplying the remedy when it is required."

Both Lord Browne-Wilkinson and Lord Nolan expressed their agreement with the reasons given by Lord Goff. It must, I think, follow that it is the reasoning in Lord Goff's speech–and only that reasoning–that can be said to have received the support of the majority in the House of Lords.'

The dicta of Lord Goff quoted by Chadwick LJ should therefore be treated as the ratio decidendi of *White v Jones* and the duty of care owed by a solicitor to a disappointed beneficiary treated as a limited exception to the general principle that a solicitor owes duties only to his or her client. The extent of the exception is now considered.

1 [1980] Ch 297 (Sir Robert Megarry V-C).
2 [1995] 2 AC 207.
3 [1995] 2 AC 145.
4 [1995] 2 AC 207 at 276F and 295D.
5 [1999] Ch 326, CA at 334H–335E. See also *Worby v Rosser* [2000] PNLR 140, CA at 148B-149B and *Chappell v Somers & Blake* [2003] EWHC 1644 (Ch), [2004] Ch 19 (Neuberger J) at [16]–[17] (quoted below).

(b) Justification for the principle

11.04 In *Ross v Caunters* the solicitor had failed to spot a procedural defect which invalidated the will. (It was witnessed by a spouse of the beneficiary.) In *White v Jones* the solicitor failed to act on the testator's instructions in time and he died before a new will could be executed. In both cases the personal representatives could recover only nominal damages because the estate had suffered no loss. In both cases the only victims were the disappointed beneficiaries, who had lost their interests in the estate that they would have received if the testator's instructions had been carried out. In *White v Jones* it was recognised that to impose liability in these circumstances would be exceptional. But this exceptional liability was justified on the basis that it was required to fill a gap in the law:[1]

> 'In the forefront stands the extraordinary fact that, if such a duty is not recognised, the only persons who might have a valid claim (i e the testator and his estate) have suffered no loss, and the only person who has suffered a loss (i e the disappointed beneficiary) has no claim: see *Ross v Caunters* [1980] Ch 297, 303A, per Sir Robert Megarry V-C It can, therefore be said that, if the solicitor owes no duty to the intended beneficiaries, there is a lacuna in the law which needs to be filled. This I regard as being a point of cardinal importance in the present case.'

1 [1995] 2 AC 207 at 259H (Lord Goff).

(c) Criticisms of the principle

11.05 The principal policy justification for the rule is that unless the beneficiary can sue the solicitor there is no effective remedy and solicitors will be encouraged to be careless (or, at least, not discouraged from being careless).[1] At various times the principle and the justification for it have been criticised, usually on five principal grounds:[2]

- *First*, the appropriate response to this gap in the law is to reform the law relating to wills rather than the law relating to solicitors' negligence by relaxing the formalities required for making a will. The problem that requires solving is that the formalities required for the execution of wills are far too strict.

- *Secondly*, the interest of the intended beneficiary is no more than an expectancy or a chance and the law of torts does not normally recognise interests as nebulous as this.[3]

- *Thirdly*, the principle subverts the doctrine of privity of contract. The solicitor only owes contractual duties to the testator and, if the estate suffers no loss, the solicitor should escape liability. There is no policy reason for relaxing the rule in these circumstances rather than in others.

- *Fourthly*, it is inappropriate to impose liability on a professional adviser to a third party with whom he has no personal or professional relationship and where the third party has placed no reliance upon him.

- *Fifthly*, the limits of the principle are uncertain and may expose the profession to multiple claims.

1 See *Chappell v Somers & Blake* [2003] EWHC 1644 (Ch), [2004] Ch 19 (Neuberger J) at [16]–[17]:

> 'Considering this issue by reference to general policy, as opposed to legal principle, I am of the view that there are two main points. The first is that it would be wrong if the solicitors escaped any liability for damages in a case such as this, merely because they could identify a dichotomy between the person who can claim against them for a breach of duty, namely the executrix, and the person who can be said to have suffered the damage, namely the beneficiary. I believe that this principle, which is there identified as "the impulse to do practical justice", is supported by the speech of Lord Goff of Chieveley in White v Jones [1995] 2 AC 207 at 259–260. In that case, the majority of the House of Lords held that a solicitor who had been negligent in drafting a will could be sued by the disappointed beneficiary, because otherwise the solicitor could escape liability, as the client, the deceased, had suffered no loss. The speech of Lord Goff contains the ratio of the decision of the House of Lords—see Carr-Glynn v Frearsons (a firm) [1999] Ch 326 at 335 per Chadwick LJ (with whom Thorpe and Butler-Sloss LJJ agreed). Indeed, the same policy point was articulated in Chadwick LJ's judgment ([1999] Ch 326 at 334), citing Lord Browne-Wilkinson's observations in White's case [1995] 2 AC 207 at 276, to the effect that it would be "unacceptable" if a solicitor escaped liability in that case. The second policy principle appears to me to be that, given that any damages would ultimately come to the beneficiary, irrespective of who has the right to sue, the question of whether it is the executrix or the beneficiary who can bring the proceedings is not of great significance. The essential point is to ensure that there cannot be double recovery (i e that the same damages cannot be recovered twice, once by the beneficiary and once by the executor).'

2 For a useful summary of the arguments see *Earl v Hickson* [2000] SKCA 1, (2000), 183 DLR (4th) 45, [2001] WTLR 143 (CA of Saskatchewan) at [26]–[42] (Sherstobitoff JA) (following White v Jones).

3 See, eg, *Seale v Perry* [1982] VR 193 (Supreme Court of Victoria).

(d) Defence of the principle

11.06 None of these objections is particularly compelling:

- The *first* objection gives little or no weight to the competing policy objective of promoting the solemnity of testamentary acts. Because it can only speak from the grave, the law usually requires that a will satisfies more stringent formalities than a contract or a property transfer. But there is no inconsistency in the law seeking to ensure that the strictest formalities are observed whilst at the same time recognising the interests of the intended beneficiary, to whom the testator's estate would have passed if the relevant formalities had been properly observed. Furthermore, in order to make out a claim, the intended beneficiary must satisfy the court to a higher than normal standard of proof that the testator intended to confer the relevant benefit on him or her: see *Walker v Medlicott & Sons*[1].

- The *second* objection fails to recognise that the courts routinely award damages for the loss of a chance or expectancy. It also fails to recognise that the law of torts now recognises all manner of economic interests beyond strict property rights.

- The *third* objection has ceased to be relevant altogether in the light of the Contract (Rights of Third Parties Act) 1999. It is now possible under English law to impose a contractual obligation for the benefit of a third party which may be enforced directly by that third party.

- The *fourth* objection is the most difficult to meet. Perhaps the best answer to it is that provided by Lord Browne-Wilkinson in *White v Jones*.[2] Although there is no direct relationship between the solicitor and intended beneficiary and no reliance by the intended beneficiary upon the solicitor, the solicitor does assume a responsibility for protecting his or her interests, like a trustee or fiduciary:

  'The solicitor who accepts instructions to draw a will knows that the future economic welfare of the intended beneficiary is dependent upon his careful execution of the task. It is true that the intended beneficiary (being ignorant of the instructions) may not rely on the particular solicitor's actions. But, as I have sought to demonstrate, in the case of a duty of care flowing from a fiduciary relationship liability is not dependent upon actual reliance by the plaintiff on the defendant's actions but on the fact that, as the fiduciary is well aware, the plaintiff's economic well-being is dependent upon the proper discharge by the fiduciary of his duty. Second, the solicitor by accepting the instructions has entered upon, and therefore assumed responsibility for, the task of procuring the execution of a skilfully drawn will knowing that the beneficiary is wholly dependent upon his carefully carrying out his function.'

- The *fifth* objection has, with the benefit of hindsight, turned out to be misplaced. Although there have been a number of claims by intended beneficiaries, the number of successful claims has been relatively small. In order to succeed, the intended beneficiary must satisfy the court with convincing evidence that the testator or testatrix intended the beneficiary to receive the gift of which he or she claims to have been deprived. Where the complaint is that the solicitor failed to ensure that the will was effective (as in *Ross v Caunters*) or that the solicitor delayed in carrying out his instructions (as in *White v Jones* itself), this is not a difficult evidential hurdle. But where the claim is that the solicitor misunderstood the testator's instructions or failed to give effect to his intentions, this burden is far more difficult to discharge. In *Gibbons v Nelsons*[3], for example, B alleged that S had failed to point out to T that she was entitled to a half share in a trust fund and to consider how to deal with it in her will. B also alleged that if the point had been raised, she would have appointed her share in the fund to B (her sister and nephew). Although there was substantial circumstantial evidence to show that T would have left her share to B if she had thought about it, the court held that this was insufficient to satisfy the necessary standard of proof.

1 [1999] 1 WLR 727, CA at 731H–732A. Sir Christopher Slade used the word 'exacting'.
2 [1995] 2 AC 207 at 275F–H.
3 [2000] PNLR 734 (Blackburne J).

(e) *The scope of the duty to disappointed beneficiaries*

11.07   From the cases which have followed *White v Jones* four limitations on
the extent of the duty of a solicitor to a beneficiary or intended beneficiary can
be identified.[1] First, the terms of the duty owed to the disappointed beneficiary
are determined by the nature and scope of the original instructions given by the
testator. It follows from the nature of the exception as explained by Lord Goff
that the content of the solicitor's duty to the disappointed beneficiary cannot be
wider than that of the duty that he owed to his original client. If, therefore, the
solicitor owed no duty to the testator, the disappointed beneficiary will have no
claim even though he or she may have suffered loss.[2] In *Carr-Glynn v Frearsons*[3] Chadwick LJ stated:

> 'The duty owed by the solicitors to the specific legatee is not a duty
> to take care to ensure that the specific legatee receives his legacy. It
> is a duty to take care to ensure that effect is given to the testator's
> testamentary intentions. The loss from which the specific legatee is
> to be saved harmless is the loss which he will suffer if effect is not
> given to the testator's testamentary intentions. That is the loss of the
> interest which he would have had as a beneficiary in an estate
> comprising the relevant property.'[4]

1 These are not dissimilar from those identified by Balcombe LJ in *Clark v Bruce Lance & Co*
[1988] 1 WLR 881 at 888–9, CA. There is a suggestion in some of the authorities that there is a
fifth limitation, namely that the solicitor must be aware of the identity of the beneficiaries or class
of beneficiaries who were intended to benefit. In *White v Jones* [1995] 2 AC 207 at 292F–295D
Lord Nolan was expressly influenced by the proximity created by the family relationship
between testator and beneficiaries. In *Gibbons v Nelsons* [2000] PNLR 734 Blackburne J also
considered that it was necessary to establish that the solicitor had the following knowledge (at
752G–753A):

> 'While acknowledging that it may not be necessary for the solicitor to be aware of the
> precise identity of the intended beneficiary (he may, for example, be aware that the
> testator intends to make a gift to someone identified only as "my son" or to a defined
> class e g "my children and grandchildren") I am of the view that the law requires, at the
> very least, that the solicitor should know (1) what the benefit is that the testator-client
> wishes to confer and (2) who the person or persons or class of persons are (in each case
> ascertainable if not actually named) on whom the client-testator wishes to confer the
> benefit. I have seen nothing in any of the authorities which justifies an extension of the
> assumption of responsibility to cases where these two elements are not present.'

2 See *Hall v Estate of Bruce Bennett* [2003] WTLR 827 (CA of Ontario) where S declined to act for
T on the grounds that he was not satisfied that T had testamentary capacity. Charron JA said this
at [57]:

> 'Insofar as the potential liability in negligence to a third party is concerned, the existence
> of a duty of care, as stated earlier, will depend on the presence of both foreseeability and

proximity. Again, it is my view that the existence of a retainer is fundamental to the question of duty of care. In the absence of a retainer, the harm that may be occasioned to the third party beneficiary by the failure to make a will may still be foreseeable but, absent exceptional circumstances, it is my view that there would be insufficient proximity between the parties to give rise to a duty of care. It is usually the retainer that creates the necessary proximity not only between the solicitor and the client but between the solicitor and the third party.'

3 [1999] Ch 326, CA at 337E-F. See also *Worby v Rosser* [2000] PNLR 140 (CA) at 147A (Chadwick LJ): 'It is sufficient to note that the source of those duties is the retainer under which the solicitor is engaged. It is the retainer which both imposes those duties and defines their scope'.
4 See also *Punford v Gilberts Accountants* [1998] PNLR 763, CA at 766G (Sir Christopher Slade): 'On no conceivable footing can the duty owed by the draftsman to the intended beneficiary be greater than that owed by him to the testator himself' and *Trusted v Clifford Chance* [2000] WTLR 1219 (Jonathan Parker J) at 1256:

'1. It appears clearly from the passages I have just quoted – and is a consistent theme throughout the judgments in the Court of Appeal and of the majority in the House of Lords – (a) that the duty owed (in tort) by the solicitor to the intended beneficiary and the duty owed (in contract) by the solicitor to the client are for all practical purposes one and the same, and (b) that the nature and extent of the duty is determined by the terms of the contract between the solicitor and the client, ie, the terms of the solicitor's retainer.'

11.08   Secondly, the solicitor only owes the disappointed beneficiary a duty of care in relation to the will-making process. He or she does not owe the beneficiary a duty in relation to any advice that he gave the testator even if it is that advice which causes the beneficiary loss. In *Carr-Glynn v Frearsons*[1] the will-making process was held to extend beyond the preparation and execution of the will to closely associated acts or advice. In that case, the defendants were found liable for failing to advise a testatrix, who owned a property jointly with her nephew but wished to leave her share to her niece, to serve a notice on the nephew immediately severing their joint tenancy. The testatrix, who was 81 years old, came to the defendants wishing to change her will for the purpose of leaving her half share to the niece; if she failed to sever the joint tenancy it was obvious that the gift would fail; and the defendants themselves recognised the potential need to sever the joint tenancy. It was found that the 'need to take care to ensure that the asset fell into the estate was integral to the carrying into effect of the testatrix's intention …'.[2] In *Clarke v Bruce Lance & Co*[3] by contrast it was held that solicitors owed no duty of care to a disappointed beneficiary for failing to advise their client not to grant an option for a fixed price over a petrol filling station simply because they had earlier prepared his will in which the station had been left to the claimant. The testator was free at any time to deal with his assets as he chose. Although the grant of the option on the advice of the defendants had the effect of reducing the value of the asset that he left to the claimant, the advice that the defendants gave about the option was not part of the will-making process. Whether or not the defendants were negligent in advising him about the option, they could owe no duty of care to the claimant simply because the testator had chosen to dispose of or fetter one of his assets.[4] This case is a clear example of the principle that a solicitor's duty does not extend beyond the testamentary process. More difficult, however, are those cases in which the complaint against the solicitor is that he or she failed to give tax advice or gave wrong tax advice to the testator because the tax advice is so closely related to the will-making process. It has been held, however, that a solicitor owes no duty to the beneficiaries of an estate to give advice to enter into a deed of variation to minimise inheritance tax[5] under an earlier will and no duty to the testator's personal representatives to ensure that inheritance tax measures taken by the testator were effective.[6] However, there is no authority in which the court has gone so far as to find that a solicitor owes no duty of care to the residuary beneficiaries of the estate (or the beneficiaries entitled to the assets on which the tax liability is charged) for negligent tax advice.[7]

1 [1999] Ch 326, CA.
2 [1999] Ch 326 at 335H. The solicitor advised the testatrix to obtain the title deeds from her nephew before serving the notice of severance. There was no reason why a notice could not have been served without waiting for the deeds.
3 [1988] 1 WLR 881, CA. The case is an extreme one and was an application by the defendants to strike out. One oddity is that the claim was not brought by the estate.
4 See also *Punford v Gilberts Accountants* [1998] PNLR 763, CA in which the defendants were a firm of accountants.
5 See *Cancer Research Campaign v Ernest Brown* & Co [1998] PNLR 592 (Harman J), in which it was held that solicitors who acted for a testatrix, who died shortly after her brother, owed no duty to the charitable beneficiaries *under her will* to advise her to execute a deed of variation *of her brother's will* renouncing her interest in favour of them.
6 See *Daniels v Thompson* [2004] EWCA Civ 307, [2004] PNLR 33 (criticised by O'Sullivan [2005] CLJ 29) in which S transferred her property to her son to avoid inheritance tax but the transfer failed to have that effect because she retained a benefit in the property. The issue of limitation was tried as a preliminary issue but the Court of Appeal also held that there was no claim for damages: see [46]. The reasoning was that T had suffered no damage since she was not liable for inheritance tax during her lifetime (and the estate could not therefore bring a claim) but the claimant who was her personal representative had suffered no loss either: see [33]–[38] and [48] (Dyson LJ) and [60]–[67] Carnwath LJ. The decision turns to some extent on s 1 of the Law Reform (Miscellaneous Provisions) Act 1934: see Carnwath LJ at [60]:

   'At first sight, I found this way of putting the case paradoxical and unattractive. However on further consideration, I can see no clear answer to it. At common law, Mrs Daniel's right of action in tort would have died with her. That must equally be true of a potential right of action, which has not yet resulted in damage so as to give rise to an actual cause of action …Section 1(1) of the 1934 Act reverses the common law rule in respect of "causes of action …vested in" the testator at death. But, if the cause of action had not vested in the testator by the time of his or her death, s 1(1) has no effect. Section 1(4) extends the effect of the section to a potential cause of action in tort against a tortfeasor who dies before damage is incurred, but there is no similar extension for a potential claimant.'

7 In *Daniels* there was no claim by the beneficiaries who had suffered the loss and the Court of Appeal did not have to consider whether such a claim would have been available to them (although it would seem consistent with the policy justifications considered in para 11.5, above). In *Macaulay v Premium Life Insurance Co Ltd* (Park J, 29 April 1999, unreported) the court refused to strike out a claim in similar circumstances although the decision was not followed in *Daniels*: see [58] (Carnwath LJ).

11.09 Thirdly, the claimant must satisfy the court that the testator or testatrix intended to confer on the disappointed beneficiary a particular testamentary benefit of which he or she has been deprived. Where there is a formal defect in the will or a delay in its execution, this will usually cause no difficulty.[1] Where, however, the negligence consists in failing to advise the testator to adopt a specific testamentary disposition the difficulty is more acute. In cases where the testator did execute a valid will, the court will require convincing evidence both that the will did not represent the testator's wishes and that the testator's instructions to the defendant were not carried into effect. This is a heavy burden and *Walker v Medlicott & Son*[2] provides a good example of the difficulties involved. In that case, the testatrix visited the defendant's office without an appointment to make a will. She brought with her a handwritten note in which she had written: 'House and contents to Bobbie Walker [the claimant]'. The defendant kept this note. He also kept an attendance note of the meeting, which lasted 18 minutes and which demonstrated that she had changed or modified her wishes in certain respects. In particular, the defendant recorded that she wanted the claimant to have a residuary gift of 'all personal chattels' whilst no mention was made of the house. The will was drawn up on the basis of the instructions recorded in the attendance note and the testatrix visited the defendant briefly on a second occasion to sign the will. The claimant gave evidence that the testatrix told him after the meeting: 'Well, Bob, I've signed it. The house is now yours …'; and called nine other witnesses to give evidence that this was her intention. The defendant gave evidence of his usual practice in preparing a will and, although he could not recall the events in question, was convinced that, when the testatrix was in his office, she must have had second thoughts. Although the judge accepted the claimant's evidence about his conversation with the testatrix, he dismissed the claim on the basis of the defendant's evidence. This decision was upheld by the Court of Appeal. Sir Christopher Slade said this:[3]

> 'Once the judge accepted, as he plainly did, Mr Medlicott as an honest witness on whose evidence as to facts, such as his usual practice, he could rely, he was in my judgment fully entitled to attach weight to the inferences drawn by Mr Medlicott as to the probable course of the interview, based on the available documentary evidence and his usual practice, even though he could not actually remember it. Furthermore, having seen Mr Medlicott in the witness box, he was also entitled to take into account his impressions of his professional competence, intelligence and responsibility; and I have no doubt that he did so.
>
> As I have already pointed out, the onus falls on the plaintiff in the present case to prove by convincing evidence that the testatrix instructed Mr Medlicott to include in her will a gift of the house to the plaintiff and that he failed to carry out those instructions in circumstances which constituted negligence. The judge, in the penultimate sentence of his judgment, found that this had not been proved, and I see no sufficient grounds upon which the court would be entitled to interfere with that finding.'

1 See, eg, *Humblestone v Martin Tolhurst Partnership* [2004] EWHC 151 (Ch), [2004] WTLR 343 where Mann J rejected the submission that B had to show that there was positive evidence that T's intention continued down to the execution of the will. He said this (at [33]):

> 'Mr Cooper accepted in argument that in a case such as this, where one starts from a position where the testator does intend a disposition in favour of the given beneficiary, it does not suffice for his purposes to show that a degree of equivocation has crept in. It has to be apparent that there was some actual change of mind, rather than the creation of a generally open one.'

2 [1999] 1 WLR 727, CA. See also *Gibbons v Nelson* [2000] PNLR 734 the facts of which are set out in para 11.6, above. The issue in that case was whether T was aware of her interest under a trust and, if not, what she would have done with it if she had been. Blackburne J rejected the argument (at 748D-F) that the burden of proof was lower:

> 'where the particular intention which is under challenge (in this case Alice's intention, by her gift of residue, to exercise the power of appointment conferred by her father's will trusts) is not one which is at all obvious from a reading of the will, the quality of the extrinsic evidence needed to displace the court's natural inclination to assume that the testator intended what his professionally drawn will provides does not need to be quite so convincing as where (as in *Walker v Medlicott*) the omission from the will is immediately obvious from a reading of it and where therefore a convincing explanation is necessary if the court is to conclude that the testator's intention was altogether different.'

He reached the conclusion that there was insufficient evidence of T's intention and that the claim failed. In *Trusted v Clifford Chance* [2000] WTLR 1219 (Jonathan Parker J) the claimant also failed to satisfy the court that the testator intended him to have the benefit claimed. In contrast, in *Horsfall v Haywards* [1999] Lloyd's Rep PN 332, CA and *Earl v Hickson* [2000] SKCA 1, (2000), 183 DLR (4th) 45, [2001] WTLR 143 (CA of Saskatchewan) at [26]–[42] (Sherstobitoff JA) it was not in issue that the will failed to give effect to T's intentions. In *Earl v Hickson*, for example, T made a number of specific gifts of land in his will to members of his family. Unfortunately, S (who prepared the will) failed to appreciate that the land was owned by T's company and not by him personally. The court found that the gifts failed and because the shares in the company formed part of T's residuary estate the land passed to the residuary beneficiaries. The disappointed beneficiaries then successfully made a claim against S.

3 [1999] 1 WLR 727 at 737H–737B. It was also accepted (at 731H–732A) that the civil standard of proof was appropriate but following Chadwick J in *Re Segelman decd* [1996] Ch 171 at 184 that 'the probability that a will which a testator has executed in circumstances of some formality reflects his intentions is usually of such weight that convincing evidence to the contrary is necessary.'

11.10 In *Walker v Medlicott* the simple question was whether the testatrix intended the claimant to have her house. In other cases, however, both the form of will adopted by the testator or testatrix and the form advanced by the disappointed beneficiary may be consistent with the broad intentions expressed to the solicitor by the client and unless the claimant can satisfy the court that the testator intended him or her to have the precise testamentary benefit for which he or she seeks compensation and instructed the defendant to this effect, the claim will fail.[1]

1 See *White v Jones* above at 225E–G, per Sir Donald Nicholls V-C and *Sutherland v Public Trustee* [1980] 2 NZLR 536 at 547–548. In *Cancer Research Campaign v Ernest Brown & Co* [1998]

PNLR 592 Harman J found that there was no reason to suppose that T actually wished to vary the provisions of her brother's will however beneficial this might have been to the beneficiaries under her will: see 604G–605A.

11.11 Fourthly, the claim will fail if the beneficiary would not have received the legacy or bequest in any event.[1] This will be the case where the defendant is able to show that the testator would have chosen to dispose of it in his or her lifetime or would have revoked the will or that the assets in the estate would have been distributed in such a way that the claimant would have received no additional benefit. In practice this latter situation is unlikely to arise in relation to claims based on failure to prepare or procure execution of the will except where the estate is insolvent or the asset in question is required to meet the debts and expenses of the estate. The remedy 'fashioned' by the House of Lords in *White v Jones* was designed to deal with the situation where the only person who had suffered a loss had no title to sue. If the asset in question would have been applied exclusively for the benefit of the estate's creditors, the disappointed beneficiary would have no claim.

1 There seems to be no reason why *classes* of beneficiaries should not have a claim or individual beneficiaries within a particular class (some of whom might have been better off with the will which was admitted to probate): see *White v Jones* [1995] 2 AC 207 at 226A–B, per Sir Donald Nicholls V-C.

3 Breach of duty

(a) Preparation

11.12 In the reported cases, solicitors have been found liable to disappointed beneficiaries for failure to carry out a testator's instructions to draw up a new will within a reasonable time.[1] Two decisions serve to illustrates the timescale within which the court will expect a solicitor to act. In *X v Woollcombe Yonge*[2] T (who was in hospital) gave instructions to S to change her will on 25 June. S's probate clerk was away that week and drew up the will early the following week intending to finalise it on 3 July. On 1 July T died. Neuberger J held that S was not negligent. In *Hooper v Fynemores*[3], by contrast, the facts were as follows: on 3 September T instructed S to draw up a new will. On the same day a draft was prepared and an appointment made to see T on 6 October. On 8 September T was admitted to hospital. On 7 October D made an appointment to see him in hospital but later cancelled it. On 21 October T died. Pumfrey J held that S was liable. S was under a duty to keep an appointment with an elderly client in hospital unless the client was content for it to be cancelled. S was also under a duty to satisfy himself that the additional delay was not detrimental to the client's interests. But once the solicitor acts promptly in drawing up the will and sending it to the client there is no automatic obligation to follow this up by chasing the client. In *Atkins v Dunn & Baker*[4] S sent a draft to T but when T gave no further instructions he did not chase him. The Court of Appeal held that in the circumstances this was not negligent. Pill LJ stated this:[5]

> 'I am unable to accept that invariably and inevitably there is a duty upon a solicitor, who has carried out instructions to prepare a draft Will and has sent that draft to the client, to follow the matter up. There will often be situations in relation to Wills and other documents where there is a duty to send a reminder or further guidance to the client. An example which arose in argument is the situation where instructions were given to have a Will executed before budget day. It may be negligent for a solicitor, who had sent a draft, to fail to remind the proposed testator that budget day is approaching and that, if action is to be taken, it should be taken promptly. As Mr Kempson stated in evidence, clients do change their minds, for good reason or bad, maybe following consultation with other members of the family or after their own reappraisal of the circumstances in which they find themselves, or for other reasons. This was a case where there was a potential conflict of interest between the claimant and Winifred, especially as Winifred's health was such that the need for expensive care could have arisen as well as the need to have a roof over her head. In the circumstances of this case, the recorder was entitled to hold that "the ball was in the client's court", and that the failure to send a reminder did not constitute such a fall below the standard to be expected of a competent solicitor as to amount to negligence.'

1 See the facts of *White v Jones* [1995] 2 AC 207. See also *Smith v Claremont Haynes & Co* (1991) Times, 3 September (HHJ Barnett QC), *Whittingham v Crease* [1978] 88 DLR (3d) 353 and *Gartside v Sheffield, Young and Ellis* [1983] NZLR 37.
2 [2001] Lloyd's Rep PN 274. Expert evidence was held not to be of assistance on this issue.
3 [2002] Lloyd's Rep PN 18.
4 [2004] EWCA Civ 263, [2004] WTLR 477.
5 [20] and [21].

(b) Execution

11.13   If a will is not executed in the presence of a solicitor, the solicitor owes a duty to check that it has been properly executed. In *Humblestone v Martin Tolhurst Partnership*[1] Mann J stated this:

> 'I have no difficulty in concluding that in principle a solicitor is capable of owing a duty to both testator and beneficiaries, in an appropriate case, to ensure and check that the proper formalities for the execution of a Will have been complied with. The question therefore arises as to how that law applies to the facts of this case. I consider that it is clear on the facts that I have found that the Defendants owed a duty to Mr Fahy, and a consequential duty to his beneficiaries, to check that the document

executed by him was properly executed and that that duty was broken. I say that for at least two reasons. First, the solicitors were instructed to draft the Will and knew that in due course they would be asked to keep it safe custody. In the course of their functions it became apparent that they would not be supervising its execution. I think that the normal fulfilment of such a retainer would require the solicitors when the document was returned to them for safekeeping, to check that, on its face, and on the facts then known to them, its execution was ostensibly valid … The second reason for the duty arising on the facts of this case is that, on the facts as I have found them, the solicitors assumed such a duty by checking the Wills when they were returned. I have found that they were checked and found "in order". In so doing, the solicitors assumed a duty of care and were in breach of it. It makes no difference if, as may have been the case, that pronouncement was by a secretary, and to be fair to him Mr Cooper did not suggest to me that it did.'

Solicitors are also under a duty to ensure that a will has been witnessed properly. In *Ross v Caunters*[2] Sir Robert Megarry V-C found the defendants liable for failure to warn a testator that a will should not be witnessed by a spouse of a beneficiary and to check that it had been attested properly. As a consequence of this failure, the gift to the beneficiary was void under s 15 of the Wills Act 1837. In *Esterhuizen v Allied Dunbar*[3] it was held to be negligent to leave the will with the testator to get it executed and witnessed by himself. The judge stated that 'in ordinary circumstances just to leave written instructions and to do no more would not only be contrary with good practice but also in my view negligent'. He also approved the practice whereby the solicitor must either ensure that the testator comes into the office to execute the will or visits the testator at home with a member of staff to attest the will.

1 [2004] EWHC 151 (Ch), [2004] WTLR 343 at [28]–[30]: See also *Gray v Richards Butler* [2000] WTLR 143 (cited by Mann J in *Humblestone v Martin Tolhurst Partnership* at [29]).
2 [1980] Ch 297. The decision itself was, and remained for a long time, of substantial importance but following *White v Jones* the reasoning can no longer be relied on. See also, to the same effect, *Watts v Public Trustee* [1980] WAR 97. In *Seale v Perry* [1982] VR 193 the Supreme Court of Victoria refused to follow *Ross v Caunters* and held that a solicitor owed no duty of care to ensure that a will was properly attested under s 7 of the Victorian Wills Act 1958. This section (like s 9(d) of the Wills Act 1837 (as amended)) provides that an attesting witness must attest and sign or acknowledge the signature in the presence of the testator. The defendant witnessed his client's signature but failed to sign the will himself in the presence of the testator and the other attesting witness and to ensure that the other witness did the same. This decision is not likely to be followed in this country and, in any event, appears inconsistent with the decision of *Esterhuizen v Allied Dunbar* (below).
3 [1998] 2 FLR 668 (Longmore J). See also Oats in (1998) 11 Sol Jo 1132, 1135.

11.14   In *Hall v Meyrick*,[1] where the defendants were engaged to advise two clients who subsequently married thereby invalidating their wills, Hodson LJ stated:

'A question of great importance and interest to solicitors is whether the judge was right in holding, as he did, that there was any duty at all on a solicitor, in the circumstances to draw the attention of the client to s 18 of the Wills Act 1837.[2] I have said that I do not propose to give any concluded finding on this point but I think it right to say this. I would not for one moment suppose that it was the duty of a solicitor in all cases to draw the attention of persons who come into his office to make wills to the effect of marriage on a will. In such a case I must use the words which are so well known that "each case depends on its own particular facts". This is a very special and unusual case. The parties came into the defendant's office, a man and a woman each known to the defendant to be single, each desiring to benefit the other substantially to the extent of their whole possessions before death by their Wills. They were known to have been living together for fifteen years as housekeeper and boarder ... On those facts the learned judge's decision at any rate is supported by evidence. I leave that matter, having made it clear, I hope, that I am not going to impose an extravagant duty on solicitors who are making wills for their clients.'

1 [1957] 2 All ER 722 at 724F–I. See also Ormerod LJ at 730B–F. Despite the reluctant conclusion quoted in the body of the text, the action was dismissed for failure to plead the retainer properly, the judge having allowed an amendment after the expiry of the limitation period. The decision predates *Hedley Byrne* and would be decided differently for that reason alone. It is submitted that the court would also be more robust on the issue of substance today.
2 Section 18(4)(b) of the Wills Act 1837 (as amended by the Administration of Justice Act 1982) now contains a saving for the case where the testator was 'expecting to be married' at the date of execution.

(c) Taking instructions

11.15 A solicitor owes a duty to his or her client to take adequate instructions from the client, to be satisfied that a testator or testatrix has considered how to deal with all of his or her assets and to ensure that he or she fully understands the legal effect of the dispositions that are contained in the will.[1] A solicitor also owes a duty to clarify the testator's or testatrix's instructions.[2] There are also a number of dicta in cases concerned with the want of knowledge or approval of a testator or testatrix that suggest that it would be negligent for a solicitor to take instructions through a beneficiary[3] and that it is the solicitor's duty to satisfy himself or herself that the will represents the genuine wishes of the testator or testatrix and that the testator or testatrix has mental capacity to execute it.[4] Furthermore, a solicitor should not accept instructions to prepare a will under which he or she is to be a beneficiary.[5] The effect of accepting instructions in these circumstances is to place the burden of proving that the testator and testatrix knew and approved of the contents of the will[6] and where the solicitor fails to discharge that burden[7] he or she will face a claim either from the

587

disappointed beneficiaries under the will which the court has refused to admit to probate or from the beneficiaries who could have expected to benefit if the will had expressed the true intentions of the testator or testatrix.[8] There is no authority under English law that a solicitor who takes instructions from a client but has some reason to doubt whether the client has mental capacity to make a will owes a duty cease to act but Commonwealth authority suggests that the solicitor is required to carry out his or her instructions but take greater care to record the circumstances in which those instructions are given.[9] Where the solicitor declines to act, Commonwealth authority suggests again that the solicitor cannot be liable to any disappointed beneficiaries.[10]

1 In *Gibbons v Nelsons* [2000] PNLR 734 Blackburne J stated (at 742G-743C):

> 'Although the burden of proof rests with the claimant to establish what the scope was of the solicitor's retainer, once the claimant establishes that the solicitor was retained to prepare a will, the burden must, I think, shift to the solicitor to show, if he can, that his responsibility for the preparation of the will did not extend to advising the client on some aspect of the will relevant to the claim. There being nothing to limit the scope of Mr Moffat's duty when acting in 1986, should he have ascertained what her intentions were concerning her half share of the trust fund? In my view, he undoubtedly should have done. As a trustee of the trust fund aware, as he told me, of the terms of the Thomas Gamble will trusts and aware, in particular, of Alice's general power of appointment over her half share in the trust fund, it was his duty, when advising Alice in the preparation of her will, to remind her that she had this power of appointment and to ascertain from her whether she wished to exercise it and if so in whose favour. In so doing it was his duty to remind her that, if she failed to exercise the power, then, under the will trusts, her half share would pass to Elsie. Having ascertained Alice's intentions in this regard, it was his duty to ensure that her will gave effect to them or, if her wish was that the default provision should take effect, that the will did not operate as an exercise of the power.'

2 See *Gray v Buss Murton* [1999] PNLR 882 (Rougier J) (the facts of which are set out in para 2.32) and *Earl v Hickson* [2000] SKCA 1, (2000), 183 DLR (4th) 45, [2001] WTLR 143 (CA of Saskatchewan) (the facts of which are set out in para. 11.9 n 2, above). See also *Kecskemeti v Rubens Rabin & Co* (Times, 31 December 1992) (cited in *Gibbons v Nelsons* [2000] PNLR 734 (above)) in which the facts were similar to *Carr-Glynn v Frearsons* [1999] Ch 326 except that S failed to take adequate instructions to satisfy himself that two properties were held on tenancies in common rather than joint tenancies and then to advise him to sever them. At p 15 of the transcript Macpherson J stated:

> 'Mr Rubens [i e the solicitor who had acted in 1981] should have discovered what the position was, and he should himself have advised the testator, or renewed the advice if Mr Shapiro [i e the solicitor who acted for the testator when the 1970 will was prepared] had already given it in 1970, that severance was necessary.'

The facts of *Carr-Glynn v Frearsons* (which are set out in para 11.21, below) are similar although it was a clear case in which S failed to give effect to T's intentions (as opposed to clarifying them). In that case S gave advice to T that it might be necessary to sever the joint tenancy but that she should obtain the deeds first. This was held to be negligent. Chadwick LJ stated (at 332D–E):

> 'I am unable to accept that Miss Turner could properly take the view that the sensible course was to wait to see what the position was on the deeds. There was nothing to be gained by that course; and a clear risk that the testatrix's intentions might be defeated by the delay to which it would or might give rise. In my view, a competent solicitor, acting

reasonably, would have advised the testatrix that, in order to be sure that her testamentary wishes should have effect, she should serve a notice of severance in conjunction with the execution of the will.'

3 *Aylwin v Aylwin* [1902] P 203 at 204 (Jeune P).
4 *Wintle v Nye* [1959] 1 WLR 284, HL; *Russell v Fraser* (1980) 118 DLR (3d) 733 at 745–6; *Morrell v Morrell* (1882) 7 PD 68 at 72–3; and *Hall v Estate of Bruce Bennett* [2003] WTLR 827 (CA of Ontario) at [22] (Charron JA): 'The law is equally clear that a solicitor who undertakes to prepare a will has a duty to inquire into his or her client's testamentary capacity'. See also the facts of *Worby v Rosser* [2000] PNLR 140, CA (where the claimants succeeded in the original claim). The Solicitors Code of Conduct 2007, r 2.01(1) is set out in para 2.34. Paragraph 6(c) of the guidance also provides: 'It is important to be satisfied that clients give their instructions freely. Some clients, such as the elderly, those with language or learning difficulties and those with disabilities are particularly vulnerable to pressure from others. If you suspect that a client's instructions are the result of undue influence you need to exercise your judgement as to whether you can proceed on the client's behalf. For example, if you suspect that a friend or relative who accompanies the client is exerting undue influence, you should arrange to see the client alone or if appropriate with an independent third party or interpreter. Where there is no actual evidence of undue influence but the client appears to want to act against their best interests, it may be sufficient simply to explain the consequences of the instructions the client has given and confirm that the client wishes to proceed. For evidential purposes, it would be sensible to get this confirmation in writing.'

Paragraph 6(c) of the guidance also provides:

For further discussion about taking instructions through third parties see para 2.34, above.

5 The Solicitors Code of Conduct 2007, r 3.04 provides:

'Where a client proposes to make a lifetime gift or a gift on death to, or for the benefit of: (a) you; (b) any principal, owner or employee of your firm; (c) a family member of any of the above, and the gift is of a significant amount, either in itself or having regard to the size of the client's estate and the reasonable expectations of the prospective beneficiaries, you must advise the client to take independent advice about the gift, unless the client is a member of the beneficiary's family. If the client refuses, you must stop acting for the client in relation to the gift.'

6 See *Franks v Sinclair* [2006] EWHC 3365 (Ch) (David Richards J) at [59]:

'It is accepted for Mr Franks that because he was instrumental in taking the instructions for and preparing the 1994 will under which he is a substantial beneficiary and because Mrs Franks did not receive any independent advice, the circumstances are such as to put on him a burden to establish affirmatively that Mrs Franks knew and approved the contents of the will. It is fairly pointed out on his behalf that, although he is a solicitor, the facts that he was Mrs Franks' son and that the 1994 will provides for an equal division of the residuary estate between his sister and himself mean that the circumstances of the case are not comparable to those in Wintle v Nye [1959] 1 WLR 284.'

7 See, in particular, the findings of David Richards J in *Franks v Sinclair* [2006] EWHC 3365 (Ch) (above) at [81]–[88] (where he placed reliance on principle 15.08 of the *Guide to the Professional Conduct of Solicitors* (1993) which was in force in May 1994 when the relevant will was made).
8 *Hall v Estate of Bruce Bennett* [2003] WTLR 827 (CA of Ontario) at [49] (Charron JA) (where the point was conceded):

'The solicitor's duty of care is, of course, owed primarily to the client. However, the appellant rightly concedes that a solicitor's duty of care may extend to a person other than the client where that other person is injured as a result of the solicitor's negligence in performing the work for which he or she was retained by the client. Hence, a solicitor who is negligent in his or her professional work may be liable not only in contract (and possibly in tort) in respect of the client, but also in tort in respect of others to whom a duty of care can be shown to exist.'

9 See *Hall v Estate of Bruce Bennett* (above) at [21] (Charron JA) citing Cullitty J in *Scott v Cousins* (2001), 37 ETR (2d) 113 (Ont. SCJ) at [71]–[73]:

'The obligations of solicitors when taking instructions for wills have been repeatedly emphasised in cases of this nature. At the very least, the solicitor must make a serious attempt to determine whether the testator or testatrix has capacity and, if there is any possible doubt – or other reason to suspect that the will may be challenged – a memorandum, or note, of the solicitor's observations and conclusions should be retained in the file …Some of the authorities go further and state that the solicitor should not allow a will to be executed unless, after diligent questioning, testing or probing he or she is satisfied that the testator has testamentary capacity. This, I think, may be a counsel of perfection and impose too heavy a responsibility. In my experience, careful solicitors who are in doubt on the question of capacity, will not play God – or even judge – and will supervise the execution of the will while taking, and retaining, comprehensive notes of their observations on the question.'

10 See also *Knox v Till* [2000] PNLR 67 (CA of New Zealand). In 1991 T made a will under which Bs were residuary beneficiaries. In 1992 T instructed S to draw up two new wills which had the effect of varying Bs' interests. Because he was suffering from mental infirmity, T did not have mental capacity when he made these wills. NZ $430,000 was spent on a probate action before Bs were able to establish their entitlement. Bs then sought to recover this sum from S. The action was struck out because S did not have the expertise to gauge whether T had mental capacity and could not reasonably be expected to investigate it and then decline to act. In *Hall v Estate of Bruce Bennett* (above) at [59]–[63] the court held that S had discharged his duty to T by declining instructions. But the court also went on to doubt whether B could ever found liability on the choice of a solicitor to decline instructions to prepare a will (as S was perfectly entitled to do under the rules of his professional body). The decision is consistent with *Knox v Till* (above) where the court held that S owed no duty to Bs to decline instructions from T. A solicitor was obliged to carry out his client's instructions, there was a conflict between the interests of T and the interests of Bs and no duty should be imposed on S in those circumstances.

11.16 Where a claim is brought against the solicitor for failing to take adequate instructions or to give adequate advice, the greatest difficulty for the claimant will be in showing what the testator's or testatrix's intentions were, whether the advice would have made a difference to those intentions and, if so, whether the disappointed beneficiary would have received a benefit as a consequence. This difficulty is well illustrated by *Sutherland v Public Trustee*[1] in which a claim was brought against a solicitor employed by the New Zealand Public Trustee for failing to ensure that the testator, who proposed to leave his whole estate to his wife, should include a gift over in favour of his stepchildren in the event that his wife predeceased him. Although the judge found that the will was 'unwise and inappropriate in its terms' he found that the solicitor had advised the testator of the possibility of an intestacy. He concluded:[2]

'Admittedly what indicators there are suggest that, even pointedly, the testator wished to benefit the Passmore children but *that is not what his will said,* notwithstanding he was given an opportunity to say so. To hold that there was a duty of care to persons the testator deliberately refused to nominate himself would take the law very far beyond its present limits. It would involve speculation, albeit with some degree of probability, involvement in the consequences of the act rather than the act itself and, worst of all, what testators ought to do. Although unusual, I do not think it so far fetched as to exclude its likelihood, that the testator meant to have his estate distributed according to the rules of intestacy should his wife predecease him. There could not be a duty of care which might prevent that possibility.'

The claim therefore failed because it could not be said with certainty what dispositions the testator genuinely intended in the event that his wife predeceased him.

1 [1980] 2 NZLR 536, Supreme Court of New Zealand (Jeffries J). In *Gibbons v Nelsons* [2000] PNLR 734 Blackburne J reached the same conclusion (at 149A–B):

'It is in finding any real evidence, let alone convincing evidence, that Alice intended Elsie to take her half share (or Robin if, contrary to expectation, Elsie should die first) that Elsie's claim runs into difficulties.'

2 At 548 (the judge's emphasis).

(d) Notification of personal representatives

11.17   In *Hawkins v Clayton*[1] a majority of the High Court of Australia held that it was the duty of a solicitor, who had prepared a will for the deceased and with whom the will had been left for safekeeping, to take reasonable steps to locate and notify the executor of her estate. Because the defendants failed to do so they were found liable to the estate for the losses it suffered both as a consequence of the estate property falling into disrepair and also of a fine levied for late payment of estate duty. Deane J[2] considered that there might also be circumstances in which the failure by a firm of solicitors to communicate the existence or contents of a will in its custody to a person named as executor and principal beneficiary might constitute an actionable breach of duty of care owed to that person in his capacity as a beneficiary. He gave as an example the failure of a firm of solicitors to disclose the existence of a will causing the assets of the estate to be irretrievably distributed to the next of kin on an intestacy or persons claiming under an earlier will. In *Cancer Research Campaign v Ernest Brown & Co*[3] by contrast Harman J held that a solicitor (who was also the sole remaining executor) was under no duty to notify the residuary beneficiaries of the death of the testatrix, the terms of the will and the material facts about the estate so that they could apply to court for a tax efficient variation of the will. As a matter of law, there was no duty on the executors to notify the beneficiaries[4] and Harman J held that there was no duty upon S to notify the beneficiaries both because the solicitor was entitled to rely on the instructions of the executors and because there could be no duty upon the solicitors if there was no duty upon the executors themselves.[5]

1   (1988) 78 ALR 69.
2   (1988) 78 ALR 69 at 99, lines 27–44.
3   [1998] PNLR 592.
4   See *Re Lewis* [1904] 2 Ch 656 (and the other authorities cited by Harman J at 610F–613B). In *Chappell v Somers & Blake* [2003] EWHC 1644 (Ch), [2004] Ch 19 Neuberger J also held that there was no duty owed by the executors to the beneficiaries for losses which accrue to the estate before the will is proved: see [12]. As Neuberger J accepted, this outcome appears surprising. This also appears to be the most questionable element of the decision in *Cancer Research*: see O'Sullivan 'Solicitors, executors and beneficiaries: Who can be sue and who can be sued?' (2003) 19 PN 507. S was the executor but if Bs had been able to bring a claim against the executors, the executors would have been compelled to bring a claim against the solicitors.
5   [1998] PNLR 592 at 608G–609C:

> 'Solicitors acting for a client are entitled to take the instructions of that client. If a client acting as executor, even if he be one of their legal executives, instructs them not to write, there can be no obligation upon them to do anything whatever than abide by those instructions. If he gives them no instructions, either to write or not to write to legatees under the will, I cannot see that thereby there arises upon the solicitors a duty in law to write to beneficiaries under the Will from the fact that their legal executive is the executor of an estate. Could solicitors charge their executor clients a fee for writing a letter for which no instructions had been given? It seems to me that obviously no fee could properly be charged. A legal executive may well be the executor of dozens of estates which are being administered in the office but that of itself can, in my judgement, give rise to no obligation to the legatees. It seems to me that the obligation to communicate, if it exists at all, can only be the obligation of the executor, and there is no foundation in law for a separate obligation upon the solicitors. Of course the executors, on behalf of the estate, are entitled to proper advice and conduct by the solicitors acting for them, and executors probably have a duty to sue solicitors, even if the firm employs the executor, for any breach of duty which harms the estate. But that creates no separate duty at law owed by the solicitors to the legatees.'

4   Claims brought by estates

11.18   In a number of miscellaneous cases claims have been brought by estates against firms of solicitors. What distinguishes these cases is that the solicitor's negligence in acting for the deceased deprives the estate of an asset that would only have accrued on death and for this reason they are considered here. In *Otter v Church, Adams, Tatham & Co*[1] the tenant in tail of settled land who would have become absolutely entitled to it by executing a disentailing deed, received negligent advice from his solicitor that he was absolutely entitled to the property and that it was unnecessary for him to do so. He died and the property passed to his uncle. His administratrix sued the solicitors. It was argued that damages should be nominal because, had the mistake been discovered in the lifetime of the deceased, it would have been his duty to mitigate his loss by executing the relevant deed. This argument was rejected. The estate was awarded damages for the deceased's loss of opportunity to execute the deed. In *Jemma Trust Co Ltd v*

Kippax Beaumont Lewis[2] Etherton J found that solicitors acted negligently in advising executors to apply to the Court of Protection for consent to a variation where the receiver of one of the beneficiaries was a patient. He was critical both of the executors themselves and of the solicitors[3] although he found that the executors had suffered no loss as a result of almost all of the negligent acts which were the subject matter of the claim.[4] The decision is an important one because it illustrates the conflict which will arise between the interests of the executors and the interests of individual beneficiaries in relation to tax planning or mitigation issues (to which solicitors must be alive).[5]

1   [1953] Ch 280 (Upjohn J).
2   [2004] EWHC 703 (Ch).
3   [89]–[115]. The principal claim was that if the solicitors had not been negligent, the executors would have been able to negotiate much better terms with the patient's receiver.
4   The decision at first instance was the subject of an appeal: see [2005] EWCA Civ 248, [2005] WTLR 683. The appeal was solely concerned with the question of loss and did not disturb the judge's original findings. The Court of Appeal dismissed the claimant's appeal in relation to the heads of loss on which they had failed at first instance and allowed the defendants' cross-appeal (on the remaining head of loss) and reversed the judge's decision to order an inquiry on the limited basis on which he found in the claimant's favour. In doing so Chadwick LJ quoted the judge's findings with approval: see [85].
5   See [2004] EWHC 703 (Ch) at [89]–[90]:

> 'I agree with the Claimant that the role adopted by the Executors, on the advice of KBL, in formulating and promoting the DOV, and prosecuting the Application, was inappropriate and improper. The role adopted by the executors inevitably placed them in an impossible position of conflict of duties. As executors, and as trustees, they owed fiduciary duties to all those beneficially interested in the HLF. The tax planning arrangements, of which the DOV formed the central plank, involved a variation of the trusts of the HLF under the Will by elimination of the life interest in possession of Lady Hulton and an acceleration of the interest of Mr Butterfield. That variation was itself dependent upon the payment of a capital sum to Lady Hulton out of the HLF. In assuming the pivotal role in promoting the DOV, putting forward a specific capital sum to be paid to Lady Hulton as a precondition of the elimination of her life interest, and in seeking to persuade the CP to make an order for the execution of the DOV, the executors placed themselves in a position in which it was quite impossible to satisfy their fiduciary obligations to both Lady Hulton and to Mr Butterfield.'

11.19   Cases of the kind discussed in the preceding paragraph do not give rise to the lacuna identified by Lord Goff in *White v Jones*. This issue arose, however, in *McLellan v Fletcher*,[1] where Anthony Lincoln J found a solicitor liable to the deceased's estate for failing to ensure that a life policy securing a mortgage loan was in force on completion of the deceased's purchase of the property. Unlike *Otter* the deceased could never have received the proceeds of the policy during his lifetime and they would only have formed part of his estate if the policy had been in force at his death. Phillips J declined to follow *McLellan* in *Lynne v Gordon Doctors and Walton*[2] on the grounds that the deceased himself had suffered no loss for which the estate could claim. Finally, in *Chappell v Somers & Blake*[3] Neuberger J held that an executor of an estate was entitled to bring a claim against solicitors for failing to take any steps to obtain probate and then to get in and administer the assets. The executrix was properly to be regarded as the representative of the owner, the assets did not vest in the beneficiary and the executor was liable to account to the beneficiary for any damages received.[5] If the executrix is properly to be regarded as the owner of the property until the due administration of the assets and the distribution to the beneficiaries (and this is the orthodox position under English law) then there is no logical difficulty in relation to the claim. Unlike the disappointed beneficiary claims or the claims in *McLellan v Fletcher* and *Lynne v Gordon Doctors and Walton*, the executrix had herself suffered a loss because she had lost the income that she would have received if probate had been obtained and the assets administered promptly. Where the beneficiary of the policy is not the deceased or his or her estate but some identified third party, the third party may have a direct claim against the solicitors under *White v Jones* and there seems to be no reason of policy to deprive the beneficiary of such a claim.[4]

1 [1987] NLJ Rep 593 and (1987) 3 PN 202. The finding of negligence was itself surprising since the defendants wrote letters to the deceased advising him to put the policy on risk but may be explained by the fact that both experts agreed that a solicitor should ensure, if only as part of his duty to the building society, that the policy is on risk before completion. The deceased was found 75% liable for contributory negligence. Compare this finding with *Earl v Hickson* [2000] SKCA 1, (2000), 183 DLR (4th) 45, [2001] WTLR 143 (CA of Saskatchewan) referred to in para 11.23, n 1 (below) (where the court held that contributory negligence was not available as a defence).
2 (1991) 135 Sol Jo LB 29. The decision was a preliminary issue on the question whether the claimants could demonstrate any loss. The judge followed the dicta of Kennedy LJ in *Griffiths v Fleming* [1909] 1 KB 805 at 820–1 which was not cited to Anthony Lincoln J. See also *Dunn v Eairs, Blissard, Barnes and Stowe* (1961) 105 Sol Jo 932 (Barry J) in which executors sued the deceased's former solicitors for accepting instructions from her to purchase an annuity at the age of 77 written and sent from the Marie Curie Hospital. The claim was dismissed on the ground that the solicitor had not been negligent.
3 [2003] EWHC 1644 (Ch), [2004] Ch 19 at [21]–[29]. See also the summary given by Laddie J in *Malkins Nominees Ltd v Societe Financiere Mirelis SA* [2004] EWHC 2631 (Ch) at [55]:

'It seems to me that what Neuberger J was saying was this. The executrix owned the properties and the tortious actions of the solicitors resulted in income "attributable to the properties" being lost. Prima facie she was entitled to recover the losses caused to "her" property by the solicitor's tortious acts. On the other hand the properties were devised to the beneficiary and it was the beneficiary to whom the executrix would have to account for rents received (or damages for loss of such rents). Her personal interest in the rents was no greater or smaller than her personal interest in the properties. Just as she could hold the properties for the benefit of a beneficiary, so too she had an equal interest in collecting rents for the benefit of a beneficiary. She had a like interest in recovering losses on behalf of the beneficiary caused by failure to collect such rents.'

The position adopted in *Chappell v Somers & Blake* appears to be consistent with the general position which applies to claims brought by trustees: see para 11.29, below.
4 See paras 11.32 and 11.33, below and compare *Gorham v British Telecommunications plc* [2001] 1 WLR 2129 where the Court of Appeal held that the intended beneficiaries of a life policy had a direct claim against an insurance company for negligent advice because the estate of the insured had no claim.

5 Claims by personal representatives and beneficiaries

(a) Identical claims

11.20 The basic principle is that where the personal representatives and beneficiaries have identical claims against the solicitor, the claim must be brought by the estate and not the beneficiaries. In those circumstances, there is no gap and no need for the court to provide a remedy. In *Worby v Rosser*[1] Bs were beneficiaries under a will made in 1983. In 1989 T instructed S to draw up a new will. He was induced to do so by the undue influence of his accountant, who was one of the new beneficiaries. Bs brought proceedings against the executors and beneficiaries under the 1989 will and, after a 48-day probate action, were successful in setting aside the new will. When they were unable to enforce the orders for costs against the defendants, they commenced proceedings against S on the ground that he had failed to satisfy himself that T had the proper testamentary capacity to make the new will in 1989 and that, if he had done so, the costs of the probate action would have been avoided. The Court of Appeal dismissed the action on the basis that S owed no duty of care to Bs. The estate was potentially liable to pay their costs[2] and if the estate had suffered a loss the personal representatives should bring the claim:[3]

> 'The remedy is provided in circumstances in which it can be seen that there is a breach of duty by the solicitor to the testator in circumstances in which the persons who have suffered a loss from that breach will have no recourse unless they can sue in their own right ...In the present case there is no lacuna to be filled. If the solicitor's breach of duty under his retainer has given rise to the need for expensive probate proceedings, resulting in unrecovered costs, then, prima facie, those costs fall to be borne by the estate for the reasons which I have already sought to explain. If the estate bears the costs thereby and suffers loss then, if there is to be a remedy against the solicitor, it should be the estate's remedy for the loss to the estate. There is no need to fashion an independent remedy for a beneficiary who has been engaged in the probate proceedings. His or her costs, if properly incurred in obtaining probate of the true will, can be provided for out of the estate. If there has been a breach of duty by the solicitor, the estate can recover from the solicitor the additional costs (including the costs to which the beneficiary is entitled out of the estate).'

In *Chappell v Somers & Blake*[4] Neuberger J reached a similar conclusion. Because the executors had a direct claim against the solicitors, there was no reason to invoke the beneficiary principle by finding that there was a duty of care owed to the beneficiary directly although he ordered that the beneficiary be joined as a party to avoid double recovery.

1 [2000] PNLR 140, CA. Compare *Knox v Till* [2000] PNLR 67 (CA of New Zealand) discussed in para 11.15 n 9, above.
2 The difficulty with the claim was that the beneficiaries had not sought a specific order that their costs be paid out of the estate under the principle in *Sutton v Drax* (1815) 2 Phill 323. If they had done so, a claim could have been mounted by the personal representatives.
3 Chadwick LJ at [2000] PNLR 140 149B-G.
4 [2003] EWHC 1644 (Ch), [2004] Ch 19 at [17] and [32].

(b) Complementary claims

11.21 There may, however, be claims that only the intended beneficiary can bring and which are complementary to any claims brought by the personal representatives. If the testator's intentions cannot be given effect by granting a remedy to the estate, then the court will fill the gap by granting a remedy to the beneficiaries directly. In *Carr-Glynn v Frearsons*[1] T instructed S to draw up a new will leaving to B (her niece) her half share in a property that she jointly owned with her nephew, the other principal beneficiary of her estate. The property was held subject to a joint tenancy and S failed to advise her to serve a notice severing the joint tenancy at the same time as she made her will. S waited for the title deeds before preparing the notice and in the meantime T died. Because of the joint tenancy, the nephew succeeded to the whole of the property and B was deprived of her share in the property. The personal representatives had a good claim against S because the estate had itself been deprived of the asset. But the personal representatives had suffered no loss (or no loss which the court could effectively compensate). If they brought the claim, any damages which they recovered would fall into the residue of T's estate and be divided between her residuary beneficiaries rather than go to B (as T had intended). This was not what T had intended nor was it S's duty to achieve. In those circumstances, the Court of Appeal held that S owed an independent duty of care to B and she could bring a claim in her own right:[2]

> 'The duties owed by the solicitors to the testator and to the specific legatee are not inconsistent. They are complementary. To the extent that the duty to the specific legatee is fulfilled, the duty to the testator is cut down. If and to the extent that the relevant property would have been distributed to the specific legatee in the ordinary course of administration, the other persons interested in the estate can suffer no loss. In so far as the relevant property or any part of it would have been applied in the ordinary course of administration to discharge liabilities of the estate, the specific legatee can suffer no loss.'

It is important, however, to appreciate the scope of the duty under consideration. It is a duty to give effect to T's intentions not to ensure that the beneficiary receives the particular asset. It follows that where B would have been entitled to a specific legacy if T's intentions had been carried out, he or she will normally be able to bring a direct claim against S. But if the estate is insolvent or potentially insolvent, B will not have a claim. This is because, *even if T's intentions had been fulfilled*, B would not have received the relevant legacy and the assets would have been used to satisfy T's creditors. Again, if the estate is insolvent or potentially insolvent, the personal representatives will have a claim instead. This is because the asset would have been realised by them for the benefit of the estate. Likewise, if the personal representatives would have been required to realise the asset or assets in order to meet the liabilities of the estate, e g tax or other liabilities, the personal representatives will have a claim against S to recover these sums and B will have a claim against S for the amount which would have been distributed to him or her. Finally, if B would have received the particular asset or fund net of tax or after some deduction to meet the liabilities of the estate, the direct claim ought to be limited to the amount which he or she would have received from the estate.

1 [1999] Ch 326, CA.
2 Chadwick LJ at 337F–G.

(c) *Conflicting or competing claims*

11.22 Finally, the estate and the intended beneficiaries may have two competing or inconsistent claims. Again, the scope of the duty will also determine which of the personal representatives or the beneficiaries are entitled to recover damages. This is demonstrated by *Corbett v Bond Pearce*[1]. In that case T made a will in February 1989 leaving one farm to her nephew and one farm to her niece and the residue of her estate to them in equal shares. In 1991 she decided that she wanted to make a lifetime gift of the two farms to her niece and nephew and to leave the residue of her estate to her great nephews, who were her niece's sons. She instructed her solicitor, S, to draw up a will and two deeds of gift. S drew up the will and sent it to her for execution with instructions about signing and dating it. In September 1991 she signed the will but returned it to S undated. This was because she did not want it to take effect until she executed the deeds of gift. About two months later she executed the deeds of gift. S then dated the will. When the executors of the new will sought to admit it to probate, the nephew contested its validity on the technical ground that T did not have the required testamentary intention when she executed it (i e because she did not intend it to take effect immediately). After a long probate action, this objection was upheld by the Court of Appeal. The residuary estate which was about £275,000 then passed to the nephew. But the Court of Appeal ordered the costs, which amounted to about £150,000, to be paid out of the estate. The disappointed beneficiaries, the two great nephews, then brought proceedings against S and this action was settled on the basis that S paid the intended beneficiaries the amount which they would have received if the new will had been valid, i e the full £275,000. The nephew, who was the executor of the earlier will, then brought his own proceedings against S to recover the costs of the probate action.

597

He argued that because S had failed to carry out his instructions and ensure that T executed a valid will, the estate had suffered a loss, namely the costs of the probate action. If S had acted competently, the estate would not have incurred the loss but would have been £150,000 better off. The judge at first instance accepted this argument. The Court of Appeal allowed the appeal:[2]

> 'Accordingly, in the present case, it is necessary to determine the scope of the duty of care owed by the defendants to the testatrix by reference to the kind of damage from which they had to take care to keep her harmless, having regard to the terms of their retainer. Having such regard, I think that it is clear that this kind of damage was the loss which those who would become interested in the estate, whether as beneficiaries under the September will or as creditors, would suffer if effect were not given to her latest testamentary intentions. It was not the loss which the various classes of beneficiaries named in the February will would suffer in that event, because the testatrix had no wish or intention that the February will should have any effect after she had signed the September will and the two deeds of gift had been perfected.'

The loss suffered by the personal representatives was outside the scope of S's duty to T. Furthermore, if their claim was a good one, this would lead to double recovery. The intended beneficiaries, the great nephews, had already been compensated in full for the interests, which they would have received if the new will had been valid, i.e. the full value of the residuary estate ignoring the costs of the probate action and on the assumption that it had never taken place. They had, therefore, already been compensated for those losses.

1 [2001] EWCA Civ 531, [2001] PNLR 739.
2 At [31] and [32]. The action was remitted to the High Court for further hearing on the question whether the estate was entitled to recover damages: see [2006] EWHC 909 (Ch). As Rimer J stated at [43] damages should only have been recoverable by the estate if it had been insolvent and unable to pay its debts (which would have been a complementary claim). However, the order made by the Court of Appeal went wider than this and the decision is of interest on the heads of loss which may be recoverable (see below).

6   Damages

(a) *General principles*

11.23   Where disappointed beneficiaries are deprived of a benefit through a formal defect in the will, they will recover the benefit under the will to which they would have been entitled if the testator's instructions had been carried out.[1] They will obviously have to give credit for any other benefits from the estate that they would not have received if the intended testamentary dispositions had taken effect. They will also have to give credit for any ex gratia payment made by the beneficiaries who have received unintended benefits as a consequence of the solicitor's negligence. Where the estate makes a claim, the general principles applicable to the assessment of damages should apply (depending on the nature of the assets and losses claimed). A number of claims by personal representatives, however, relate to costs which they have incurred either in probate or trust proceedings. In order to be recoverable, such costs must be the direct and foreseeable consequence of the solicitor's breach of duty and within the scope of the solicitor's duty to T.[2] Further, the normal principles applicable to the recovery of costs as damages will apply. Thus, the solicitors will be entitled to have any costs that the estate has incurred in litigation assessed on a standard basis.[3] But where the personal representatives' costs have been disallowed on assessment, they will not be entitled to recover them from the solicitors.[4] Nor, in general, will they be entitled to costs which they have been ordered to pay to third parties.[5]

1 In *White v Jones* [1995] 2 AC 207 the Court of Appeal awarded the claimants the full amount of their legacies without deduction for any prospect of a last-minute change of heart although there had been some evidence of this: see 228A–E. In *Gibbons v Nelsons* [2000] PNLR 734 (where the claim failed because B could not establish T's intention) Blackburne J would have awarded damages by reference to the share in the relevant fund to which B would have been entitled at T's death. He also accepted that the preparation of a further will between the will that had been negligently drafted and T's death did not break the chain of causation because on that occasion S was instructed to make specific changes and there was no general change of testamentary intention. For an interesting example of the difficulties of attempting to give effect to T's intentions see *Earl v Hickson* [2000] SKCA 1, (2000), 183 DLR (4th) 45, [2001] WTLR 143. The judge at first instance awarded damages by reference to the value of the lost interest at the date of death. This decision was upheld on appeal although the CA of Saskatchewan ordered S to pay compensation for the value of lost income to which the beneficiaries would have become immediately entitled: see [65]–[69]. The court also refused to accept the defence of contributory negligence on the grounds that T could not be treated as the claimant and his estate had suffered no loss: see [47]–[52]. Although the relevant statutory framework is different, these points seem capable of being taken in an English court.
2 See *Corbett v Bond Pearce* [2006] 909 (Ch) (Rimer J) at [68]–[71].
3 See *Yudt v Leonard Ross & Craig* (unreported, 24 July 1998) (Ferris J) following reluctantly the decision of Carnwath J in *BRDC v Hextall Erskine* [1996] 3 All ER 667. The principle now seems to be accepted at first instance, however: see *Mahme Trust Reg v Lloyds TSB Bank plc* [2006] EWHC 1321 (Ch) (Evans-Lombe J) at [65]–[69] and *Rebus LMDS Ltd v Jeffrey Green & Russell* [2006] EWHC 2938 (Ch), [2007] PNLR 12 (HHJ Behrens).
4 In *Ross v Caunters* [1980] Ch 297 at 323F– 324G Megarry V-C rejected a claim for legal expenses on this basis.
5 See *Corbett v Bond Pearce* [2006] 909 (Ch) (above) at [78]:

'There is authority for the proposition that if C obtains an order for costs against D he cannot in the same claim recover under the guise of damages any part of his costs disallowed on a detailed assessment (Cockburn v Edwards (1881) Ch D 449, at 463, and Ross v Caunters [1980] Ch 297 at 324). That being so, it would be particularly odd if C could recover as damages in the same claim costs he is ordered to pay to D.'

In that case Rimer J considered a number of heads of loss including the costs incurred by the executor's own costs and his remuneration (which he disallowed). He did allow the costs incurred by the executor under the second will on the basis that they were to be treated as a pecuniary legacy: see [91] and [92].

11.24   In other cases the solution may not be so simple. In *Gartside v Sheffield, Young and Ellis*[1] Cooke J stated:

> 'There will, no doubt, be difficulties in assessing the damages but such difficulties do not make assessment impossible – *Chaplin v Hicks* [1911] 2 KB 786. The question must be whether the plaintiff has lost some right of value, something which has reality and substance. Although it may be that this value is not easy to determine it is the duty of the court to do the best it can – *Kitchen v Royal Air Forces Association* [1958] 2 All ER 241. In a given case a court may view the actual loss suffered through the negligence of a solicitor failing to prepare a will as much less than the testamentary provision to be made for him. The possibility of other claims being brought to the detriment of the disappointed beneficiary, had the will been executed, must be taken into account; any amount which the disappointed beneficiary may receive in a claim under the Family Protection Act or the Law Reform (Testamentary Promises) Act will be relevant. In the end a value must be placed upon the benefit that has been lost. Although, therefore, there will be undoubted difficulties in the assessment of any damages I do not think that the courts should shrink from allowing a claim because of them.'

In *Whittingham v Crease & Co*[2] the successful claimant succeeded in obtaining the difference between the one third share of residue which he would have obtained had the defendants not been dilatory in taking instructions and the one fifth share to which he became entitled by intestate succession. The damages were then reduced to take account of the potential claim which the testator's other children could have brought under the family provision legislation in Canada.

1 [1983] NZLR 37 at 56 lines 28–42
2 (1978) 88 DLR (3d) 353 at 374.

11.25   In some cases, therefore, where the court is satisfied that the beneficiary has proved negligence, the court will have to assess the chance that the testator or testatrix would have executed the will in time; in others the court will have to assess whether the gift would have vested in the disappointed beneficiaries; and in others the court will have to assess the probability that other potential beneficiaries would have brought claims under the Inheritance (Provision for Family and Dependants) Act 1975 and place a value on those claims.

(b) Rectification

11.26   Solicitors' claims in relation to the preparation of wills also give rise to one specific issue that is not encountered elsewhere. Where a will does not express the true intentions of the testator or testatrix, it is open to the personal representatives to apply to court for rectification of the will pursuant to s 20 of the Administration of Justice Act 1982. That section provides:

'(1) If a court is satisfied that a will is so expressed that it fails to carry out the testator's s intentions, in consequence –

(a)   of a clerical error; or

(b)   of a failure to understand his instructions, it may order that the will shall be rectified so as to carry out his intentions.

(2) An application for an order under this section shall not, except with the permission of the court, be made after the end of the period of six months from the date on which representation with respect to the estate of the deceased is first taken out.'

11.27   Where a claimant seeks damages from a solicitor for failing to record the instructions of a client faithfully in a will, he or she must establish all the necessary ingredients of a successful claim for rectification under this section before a claim against the solicitor will succeed. Indeed, the claimant might well succeed in obtaining rectification of the will where he or she would not succeed in negligence against the solicitor. This is precisely what happened in *Walker v Medlicott,*[1] where the claimant brought forward cogent evidence of the testatrix's intention but the court found that the defendant had not acted negligently. Sir Christopher Slade said this:[2]

'If it be asked how that finding is reconcilable with the evidence as to the testatrix's intention and understanding, I think there is one possible simple answer. On the available evidence, I, for my part, on the balance of probabilities would be disposed to draw the inference that there was a genuine misunderstanding between the testatrix and Mr Medlicott ...

There is no evidence as to what either party actually said at the interview. It may well be that, in the context of ascertaining the testatrix's final wishes and intentions, there was some discussion as to the respective values of the house and the testatrix's other assets. It may well be that the testatrix unwittingly gave Mr Medlicott the reasonable impression of intending one thing, while in truth intending another. In view of the paucity of the evidence as to the course of that crucial meeting and the judge's assessment of Mr Medlicott's evidence and his calibre as a witness, there is not in my judgment available evidence of a sufficiently convincing nature to establish that any misunderstanding or failure to carry out the instructions on the part of Mr Medlicott constituted negligence ...

If, as the plaintiff asserts, the will failed to carry out the testatrix's intentions, this must, I think, have been in consequence of a clerical error by Mr Medlicott in recording her instructions in his attendance note, leading to a corresponding error in the will as drafted or of a failure on his part to understand her instructions. At least, at first sight, it is difficult to understand why the plaintiff chose to begin by instituting proceedings for negligence rather than rectification.'

It was accepted that the burden of proof in a claim for rectification and a claim for damages against the solicitor were the same and, as an alternative ground of their decision, the court held that the claimant had failed to mitigate his loss by commencing proceedings for an order for rectification. The court distinguished the general principle established by *Pilkington v Wood*,[3] that a claimant is not obliged to mitigate his or her loss by embarking on uncertain and expensive litigation, on the ground that the evidence in both actions would be precisely the same.[4] Sir Christopher Slade concluded:[5]

'This is a situation in which, as a general rule, the Courts can reasonably expect the plaintiff to mitigate his damage by bringing proceedings for rectification of the will, if available, and to exhaust that remedy before considering bringing proceedings for negligence against the solicitor, for example, in relation to costs incurred in the rectification proceedings.'

1 [1999] 1 WLR 727.
2 [1999] 1 WLR 727 at 738B–D.
3 [1953] Ch 770 (Harman J).
4 [1999] 1 WLR 727 at 731G–H and 738G–739H (per Sir Christopher Slade), 742E–G (per Mummery LJ) and 742H–744G (per Simon Brown LJ).
5 [1999] 1 WLR 727 at 739F–G.

11.28 In *Horsfall v Haywards*[1] the general application of this proposition was tested for the first time. In that case, the defendants admitted that they had failed to draft the testator's will in accordance with his instructions. The court did not, however, find that the claimant ought to have commenced rectification proceedings, for three principal reasons: first, on the facts, the judge doubted whether a claim for rectification would succeed; secondly, the principal asset of the estate was the testator's house and the principal beneficiary, whose share was increased as a consequence of the defendants' negligence, had moved to Canada and the proceeds of sale were remitted to her there. Rectification proceedings would have been costly and time-consuming and 'would not have resulted in any material recovery of the funds to compensate the plaintiffs for the loss of their interest under the will'; and, thirdly, and perhaps most importantly, the defendants had acted for the claimants in relation to the grant of probate and had not advised them to take rectification proceedings either before the principal beneficiary moved to Canada or before the time limit for bringing the proceedings had expired. *Horsfall v Haywards* should, therefore, be regarded as an exception to the general rule and where a disappointed beneficiary becomes aware that the solicitor has failed to record the testator's instructions before the expiry of the time limit, he or she ought, in the first place, to bring proceedings for rectification. Indeed, even where the beneficiary becomes aware of the error after the six-month period has expired, it would be sensible to make an application for permission under s 20(1)(b) to bring rectification proceedings out of time before contemplating an action against the negligent solicitor.

1 [1999] Lloyd's Rep PN 332, CA. The leading judgment was delivered by Mummery LJ who was a member of the court in *Walker v Medlicott*.

B INTER VIVOS TRUSTS AND DISPOSITIONS

1 Claims by trustees

11.29 As with executors, trustees who hold assets on trust (including nominees holding assets on bare trust) are usually entitled to bring a claim on behalf of the beneficiaries for damage suffered to the assets of the trust.[1] Indeed, it is the normal rule that if trustees do not pursue a claim on behalf of the trust (e g because they obtain clear advice that such a claim should not be made or apply to the court for directions), the beneficiaries cannot pursue such a claim themselves.[2] Ordinarily, a beneficiary has no cause of action against third parties for damage suffered to the trust assets except in special circumstances where the trustees are guilty of a failure (excusable or inexcusable) to perform the duty that they owe to the beneficiaries to protect the trust's assets or the interests of the beneficiary.[3] Where the trustees are shareholders of a company, this may also give rise to a separate question whether the trustees or the company (or both) should make the claim against the solicitors.[4]

1 See *Malkins Nominees Ltd v Societe Financiere Mirelis SA* [2004] EWHC 2631 (Ch) at [43]–[59] where Laddie J applied *Chappell v Somers & Blake* [2003] EWHC 1644 (Ch), [2004] Ch 19 (discussed in para 11.19, above). He also applied the principles contained in *Lloyds v Harper* (1880) Ch D 290, *Woodar Investment Development Ltd v Wimpey Construction (UK) Ltd* [1980] 1 WLR 277 and *Darlington Borough Council v Wiltshier Northern Ltd* [1995] 1 WLR 68, CA.
2 See *Braddock Trustee Services Ltd v Nabarro Nathanson* [1995] 4 All ER 88 (HHJ Paul Baker QC).
3 See *Roberts v Gill & Co* [2007] All ER (D) 89 (Paul Morgan QC).
4 See para 1.10. There is no reported authority on the issue of non-reflective loss arising where the trustee is a claimant. In *Walker v Stones* [2001] QB 902 the Court of Appeal held that the fact that the company might have a claim itself did not prevent the beneficiaries bringing a claim. At [133] Sir Christopher Slade stated that a claim could be brought if the following conditions were met (and this passage was cited with approval by Lord Hutton in *Johnson v Gore Wood & Co* [2002] 2 AC 1 at 51D–F):

> '(a) the claimant can establish that the defendant's conduct has constituted a breach of some legal duty owed to him personally (whether under the law of contract, torts, trusts or any other branch of the law) and (b) on its assessment of the facts, the Court is satisfied that such breach of duty has caused him personal loss, separate and distinct

from any loss that may have been occasioned to any corporate body in which he may be financially interested. I further conclude that, if these two conditions are satisfied, the mere fact that the defendant's conduct may also have given rise to a cause of action at the suit of a company in which the claimant is financially interested (whether directly as a shareholder or indirectly as, for example, a beneficiary under a trust) will not deprive the plaintiff of his cause of action; in such a case, a plea of double jeopardy will not avail the defendant.'

This was a claim by the beneficiaries against trustees who were also directors of the company. But there appears to be no reason why the same principles should apply to a claim by trustees against third parties (e g solicitors). Indeed, *Walker v Stones* originally included such a claim. See further para 1.10 n 8, above.

11.30   Where a solicitor has been instructed by trustees to act on behalf of a trust he or she owes duties in contract and tort to his or her clients, the trustees. Even though the solicitor may be a trustee himself or have acted for the trust for years, there is no such thing as a general retainer[1] and the nature and scope of the retainer should be determined by the terms of the instructions given by the trustees to the solicitor from time to time. In the 19th century it was common for solicitor trustees to have the day-to-day conduct of all trust matters and to take business decisions on behalf of the trust. *Re Partington*[2] provides an example of this traditional role. In that case a solicitor, who was also a trustee, was held liable for negligently investing trust property on inadequate security. Stirling J stated:

'Mr. Allen, by his own bills of costs, appears to have acted as solicitor on behalf of the mortgagees, namely himself and his co-trustee Mrs. Partington and he has charged, as I understand it, in those bills of costs the full scale fees allowed both for negotiating the loan, for deducing title, and for preparing and completing the mortgage. Therefore he appears to me to have taken upon himself to act, in the words of one of the rules, as solicitor engaged in the whole business relating to the mortgage. By undertaking to negotiate the loan he undertook to procure a borrower from the trustees who was able to give a satisfactory security – that is, a security which would not only be sufficient as regards the legal title, but also ample in point of value to secure the fund which was to be advanced by the trustees, and therefore which would be such a security as the trustees could properly accept.'

1 See para 1.9, above. The administration of an estate is not treated as a single retainer: see *Perotti v Colyer-Bristow* [2003] EWHC 25 (Ch) (Lindsay J) at [135]–[137] citing *Re Hall & Barker* (1878) Ch 538, CA.
2 (1887) 57 LT 654 at 661–2.

11.31   In *Bayer v Balkin*,[1] however, it was held that the duty of a solicitor trustee to the trust is no more onerous than that of any other solicitor and, more recently, in *AMP General Insurance Ltd v Macalister Todd Phillips Bodkins*[2] the Court of Appeal of New Zealand has also held that the fact that a solicitor was also a trustee did not affect the scope of his duties to the trust. But that is not to say that *Re Partington* would not be followed where a solicitor (whether trustee or not) acts in the traditional nineteenth century role of a 'man of affairs' and is 'engaged in the whole business' of the trust.

1 (1995) 31 ATR 295 at 305–6 (Cohen J, Supreme Court of New South Wales).
2 [2006] WTLR 189 (overruled on a different point by the Supreme Court of New Zealand [2006] NZSC 105). For an example of a case in which a claim was made by trustees against solicitors see *Bonham v Blake Lapthorn Linnell* [2006] EWHC 2513 (Ch), [2007] WTLR 189 (Kitchen J) at [193] to [214] where it was held that a solicitor was under no duty to advise trustees to make a *Beddoe* application to the court for directions in relation to litigation. A further claim was struck out by Evans-Lombe J ([2007] EWHC 1859 (Ch)).

2 The duty to disappointed beneficiaries

11.32 As stated above, in the normal course the trustees would bring any claims against a solicitor for negligence in acting as solicitor to the trust (after obtaining the leave of the court) whilst the beneficiaries would bring any claims against a solicitor trustee for any breaches of duty as a trustee. There may, however, be cases analogous to *White v Jones* in which the failure by a solicitor to draw up an inter vivos deed of trust or the failure to do so adequately causes the intended beneficiaries a real loss. In *White v Jones*[1] there was some discussion about claims involving inter vivos transactions and Lord Goff expressed the view that the donee of a lifetime gift would not have the right to bring a claim.[2] In *Hemmens v Wilson Browne*[3], however, HHJ Moseley QC took a different view:[4]

'I can well understand that if a settlor, acting on the advice of his solicitor, executes an irrevocable deed of settlement, conferring benefits on X instead of, as intended, Y the solicitor may owe a duty of care not only to the settlor but also to Y. In such circumstances, leaving aside the possibility of rectification, it will be beyond the power of the settlor, though still alive, to put matters right, and Y will be able to prove an identifiable loss. I can also well understand that a duty of care may be owed by a solicitor to an employee for whose benefit that solicitor is retained by the employer to draft an effective tax avoidance scheme. If the scheme is ineffective, the tax will be payable and it will be beyond the ability of the employer, even if still alive, to put matters right. I accept therefore that there may be circumstances in which a solicitor may owe a duty of care in carrying out an inter vivos transaction. That, however, does not lead to the conclusion that a duty of care is owed in the context of all inter vivos transactions.

In that case it was held that no duty of care was owed by the defendant to the beneficiary because the settlor who had promised to settle a sum of money on her, but reneged on that promise after the solicitor had failed to carry out his instructions, could still put matters right and had a remedy against the defendant himself for breach of contract.[5]

1 [1995] AC 207.
2 At 262A-C he said this:

> 'Let me take the example of an inter vivos gift where, as a result of the solicitor's negligence, the instrument in question is for some reason not effective for its purpose. The mistake comes to light some time later during the lifetime of the donor, after the gift to the intended donee should have taken effect. The donor, having by then changed his mind, declines to perfect the imperfect gift in favour of the intended donee. The latter may be unable to obtain rectification of the instrument, because equity will not perfect an imperfect gift, though there is some authority which suggests that exceptionally it may do so if the donor has died or become incapacitated: see *Lister v Hodgson* (1867) LR 4 Eq 30, 34–35, per Romilly MR. I for my part do not think that the intended donee could in these circumstances have any claim against the solicitor.'

At 265H he also stated:

> 'Moreover, had a gift been similarly misdirected during the testator's lifetime, he would either have been able to recover it from the recipient or, if not, he could have recovered the full amount from the negligent solicitor as damages.'

3 [1995] Ch 223. The case was decided after *White v Jones* in the Court of Appeal but before the House of Lords. The passage quoted in the text was also, necessarily, obiter dictum.
4 [1995] Ch 223 at 236C–F.
5 [1995] Ch 223 at 237B–E.

11.33   In *Hughes v Richards*[1] the factual situation envisaged by the judge in *Hemmens v Wilson Browne* arose. In that case H (an accountant) advised Mr and Mrs R, who wished to set up a trust with £100,000 for the benefit of their children, to set up a series of complex offshore trust arrangements in order to avoid tax. These arrangements had the reverse effect and most of the investment was used up in tax and fees. A claim was brought against H in the name of the children as beneficiaries of the trust and H applied to strike it out on the basis that he owed them no duty of care. The Court of Appeal dismissed this application to strike out but reached the conclusion that H: 'has a strongly arguable case that the parents and not the children are owed the duty of care in respect of the investment claim.'[2] After referring to the extracts from Lord Goff's judgment dealing with inter vivos gifts Peter Gibson LJ's analysis of the legal position was as follows:[3]

> 'Further, it is not obvious that they covered an example correspond-
> ing to the circumstances of the present case where the gift was
> neither imperfect nor misdirected nor were the consequences imme-
> diately apparent, but only emerged several years after the scheme,
> which the parents intended to enter into, was implemented; only then
> was the loss of the investment discovered. The views expressed were
> not tested by consideration of what would be the position if the
> donor, the availability of a remedy to whom was the crucial factor in

the views expressed, died or became bankrupt or was denied the remedy by reason of a limitation defence.[4] However, it is right to note that in *Hemmens v Wilson Browne* [1995] Ch 223 decided after this court's decision in *White v Jones* but before the decision of the House of Lords, His Honour Judge Moseley QC, sitting as a High Court judge, held that the intended beneficiary under an inter vivos gift which, through the negligence of the donor's solicitor, gave the beneficiary no enforceable right, was owed no duty of care by the solicitor as the donor had a remedy against the solicitor. This is consistent with Lord Goff's subsequent comments on imperfect gifts. In *Gorham v British Telecommunications plc* [2000] 1 WLR 2129 p 2140 Pill LJ made a passing (but approving) reference to Lord Goff's example of the imperfect gift. In *Gorham* this court appears to have assumed that the death of a customer of an insurance company, which had given him negligent advice in relation to the provision of benefits after his death for his family, resulted in the customer's estate having no claim against the insurance company, and that only the family would have a remedy; accordingly the family was held to be owed a duty of care by the insurance company in respect of the advice to the customer.'

Apart from cases such as *Hemmens v Wilson Browne* where there is an imperfect gift, there seems to be no policy objection to imposing a duty of care on the solicitor to the disappointed beneficiary or beneficiaries. In most cases the objective or purpose of the transaction is to confer a benefit on a third party, there is close proximity between the solicitor and the intended beneficiary and it will be reasonably foreseeable that a failure to give effect to the donor's intentions will cause loss to the intended recipient.[5] Furthermore, if the donor is not a beneficiary of the trust and the gift is irrevocable, the donor may have difficulty in establishing a loss. The only real objection is the possibility of a multiplicity of claims but this can be dealt with by joining the donor as a party (as proposed in *Chappel v Somers & Blake*).[5] For these reasons, it is suggested that a duty of care should be imposed except in cases where there is an imperfect gift because in those cases it is the policy of the law not to enforce imperfect gifts in the absence of material consideration.

1 [2004] EWCA Civ 266, [2004] PNLR 706. See also O'Sullivan (2004) 21 PN 142: 'Professional liability to third parties for inter vivos transactions.' O'Sullivan argues that the existence of a lacuna should not be determinative in inter vivos cases but in cases where the objective of the transaction is to benefit the third party, there should be a duty of care.
2 [2004] EWCA Civ 266, [2004] PNLR 706 at [28].
3 [2004] EWCA Civ 266, [2004] PNLR 706 at [27] and [28].
4 The decision to bring the claim in the name of the children may well have been influenced by the assumption that they enjoyed a more generous limitation period than the parents and if the parents had brought a claim this would have been met with a limitation defence (but see now the discussion in at paras 7.15–7.29, above). In a short concurring judgment at [31] Jacob LJ suggested that there was a contractual retainer between the children and the solicitors. This analysis is consistent with the implied retainer cases considered at para 1.8, above. But some of

these cases are difficult to justify on objective contractual principles and it is unlikely that a court would find that a beneficiary would be entitled to take advantage of the Contracts (Rights of Third Parties) Act 1999: see the Law Commission Report No 242 (1996) which preceded the Act at paras 7.19–7.27, above. For these reasons, it seems more transparent to accept the existence of a duty of care.

5   [2003] EWHC 1644 (Ch), [2004] Ch 19 (Neuberger J) at [32].

Chapter 12

Litigation

12.01 In this chapter we consider first the removal of advocates' immunity from suit, and the revised doctrine of abuse of process by collateral attack on previous decisions of the court. We then examine the standard of care which solicitors owe their clients in conducting litigation. Thirdly, we look at causation and the assessment of damages, including damages for the loss of a chance. Fourthly, we consider the types of damage recoverable and mitigation of loss.

A   ADVOCATES' IMMUNITY AND ABUSE OF PROCESS

1   Advocates' former immunity

12.02   Before the House of Lords' decision in *Arthur JS Hall & Co v Simons*,[1] advocates, including solicitor advocates, enjoyed immunity from suit by their clients in relation to work done in court or intimately related to such work[2]. The House of Lords held in *Hall* that the immunity was no longer appropriate in relation to either civil or criminal cases, and no longer existed.[3] In *Awoyomi v Radford*[4] Lloyd Jones J held that the effect of *Hall v Simons* was retrospective, and that by 1991 the immunity no longer existed.

1 [2002] 1 AC 615.
2 *Rondel v Worsley* [1969] 1 AC 191, HL; *Saif Ali v Sydney Mitchell & Co* [1980] AC 198, HL.
3 The majority was 7–0 as to the immunity in relation to civil cases but only 4–3 as to the immunity in criminal cases. It appears that the immunity as to the work of criminal advocates still exists in Scotland: *Wright v Paton Farrell* [2007] PNLR 7. Since *Hall*, it has been held that the immunity remains in Australia (*D'Orta-Ekenaike v Victoria Legal Aid* [2005] 214 ALR 92), but not in New Zealand (*Chamberlains v Lai & Lai* [2006] NZSC 70).
4 [2007] EWHC 1671 (QB), [2007] PNLR 34.

2   Abuse of process

12.03   Also in *Hall*, the House of Lords considered the doctrine of abusive collateral attack on previous decisions. In *Hunter v Chief Constable of West Midlands Police*[1], Lord Diplock said that:

'The abuse of process which the instant case exemplifies is the initiation of proceedings in a court of justice for the purpose of

609

mounting a collateral attack upon a final decision against the intending [claimant] which has been made by another court of competent jurisdiction in previous proceedings in which the intending [claimant] had a full opportunity of contesting the decision in the court by which it was made.'

Hunter was not a claim that the earlier decision had been wrong on account of the negligence of defendant lawyers, but the principle was applied in subsequent cases where lawyers were sued for negligence in the conduct of the original action. The rule was the subject of various exceptions which we considered in the first edition of this book.[2]

1 [1982] AC 529, HL.
2 See paras 10.13ff of the first edition (1999).

12.04   In *Hall*, Lord Hoffmann's speech had the support of the majority on the issue of abuse of process[1]. He said that the court's power to strike out cases which sought to relitigate issues previously decided should be exercised if such relitigation would be manifestly unfair to a party or would bring the administration of justice into disrepute.[2] In applying those principles, Lord Hoffmann distinguished between the position in criminal and civil cases respectively.

1 Lords Steyn, Browne-Wilkinson, Hutton and Millett.
2 [2002] 1 AC at 702H–703A. Lord Hoffmann was agreeing with what Lord Diplock had said in *Hunter*: [1982] AC 529 at 536B.

(a) Criminal cases

12.05   Lord Hoffmann said that, outside the realms of professional negligence actions, it was easier to challenge decisions said to have been wrong in relation to criminal as opposed to civil cases. The scope for re-examination was greater. Fresh evidence could more easily be admitted. A conviction could be set aside if the accused had been prejudiced by 'flagrantly incompetent advocacy'. After appeal, a case might be referred back to the criminal courts for re-consideration by the Criminal Cases Review Commission. Lord Hoffmann's conclusion as to professional negligence actions alleging that the accused was convicted due to the negligence of the claimant's lawyers was as follows[1]:

'... in my opinion it would ordinarily be an abuse of process for a civil court to be asked to decide that a subsisting conviction was wrong. This applies to a conviction on a plea of guilty as well as after a trial. The resulting conflict of judgments is likely to bring the administration of justice into disrepute ... The proper procedure is to appeal, or if the right of appeal has been exhausted, to apply to the Criminal Cases Review Commission under section 14 of the 1995

Act. I say it will ordinarily be an abuse because there are bound to be exceptional cases in which the issue can be tried without a risk that the conflict of judgments would bring the administration of justice into disrepute. *Walpole v Partridge & Wilson* [1994] QB 106 was such a case.

Once the conviction has been set aside, there can be no public policy objection to an action for negligence against the legal advisors.'

1   [2002] 1 AC at 706D–F.

12.06   Two points arise. First, Lord Hoffmann did not in terms state why *Walpole* was an exceptional case that would not amount to an abuse of process. His discussion of *Walpole* earlier in the judgment explained that the Court of Appeal had held that there was no abuse of process where the claimant had been convicted of an offence relating to preventing a veterinary officer from inspecting his pigs. The claimant had arguable grounds for success on appeal but his solicitors had negligently failed to lodge an appeal in time.[1] Thus, it appears that Lord Hoffmann's point may have been that if a litigant is convicted and, due to his or her lawyers' negligence, loses the opportunity to defend himself or herself by an argument of law that was not put to the convicting court, a professional negligence claim against the lawyers may not be an abuse of process if the claimant has lost all possibility of redress through the criminal law system. In those circumstances, it may be arguable that it is not unfair to allow the convicted defendant to bring a professional negligence claim against his or her lawyers. It might, for example, be the position that the Criminal Cases Review Commission would be unlikely to deal with small cases of injustice such as occurred in *Walpole*. If that was Lord Hoffmann's view, then it would be consistent with a point which he made later in his speech in relation to civil claims.[2] The extent of this exception, however, remains to worked out in future cases.

1   [2002] 1 AC 703F–H.
2   [2002] 1 AC at 705H; quoted at para 12.08, below.

12.07   Secondly, it is clear both from the passage quoted and from later in his speech[1] that Lord Hoffmann considered that a professional negligence action alleging that the claimant had pleaded guilty on account of his or her lawyers' negligence would ordinarily amount to an abuse of process. One commentator has suggested, however, that as a matter of criminal law it is much harder to appeal following a guilty plea than after conviction, so that the rationale, if not the conclusions, of Lord Hoffmann's speech ought to mean that a claim that a party's lawyers negligently induced a guilty plea will not necessarily amount to an abuse of process[2]. This too is yet to be resolved in case law, and may turn on detailed consideration of the means in criminal law whereby a party who has pleaded guilty and been convicted may challenge the conviction on the ground that it was based on his or her lawyers' mistake. It might also require a finding that parts of what Lord Hoffmann said in *Hall*, admittedly obiter, were incorrect.

1 [2002] 1 AC at 705G.
2 Simpson (ed) *Professional Negligence and Liability* paras 15.57–15.58. As noted there, under the preceding law it had been held that such a claim was an abuse of process, in *Somasundaram v Melchior* [1988] 1 WLR 1394, and that case was not overruled in *Hall*.

(b) Civil cases

12.08   In relation to civil cases, in Lord Hoffmann's view there was, unlike in criminal cases, little public interest in ensuring that the correctness of a first judicial decision was not impugned. He said that[1]:

> 'I can see no objection on grounds of public interest to a claim that a civil case was lost because of the negligence of the advocate, merely because the case went to full trial. In such a case the plaintiff accepts that the decision is res judicata and binding upon him. He claims however that if the right arguments had been used or evidence called, it would have been decided differently. This may be extremely hard to prove in terms of both negligence and causation, but I see no reason why, if the plaintiff has a real prospect of success, he should not be allowed the attempt.'

Taken on its own, that argument might be said to apply equally to some professional negligence actions challenging criminal convictions. But Lord Hoffmann added that:[2]

> '… in civil (including matrimonial) cases, it will seldom be possible to say that an action for negligence against a legal adviser or representative would bring the administration of justice into disrepute. Whether the original decision was right or wrong is usually a matter of concern only to the parties and has no wider implications. There is no public interest objection to a subsequent finding that, but for the negligence of his lawyers, the losing party would have won.'

Thus, in relation to civil cases where it was alleged that the result would have been different if the lawyers had not been negligent in the conduct of the litigation, re-litigation would not generally amount to an abuse of process.

1 [2002] 1 AC at 705H-706C. Applied: *Feakins v Burstow* [2005] EWHC 1931 (QB), [2006] PNLR 6 (Jack J) at [95].
2 [2002] 1 AC at 706H.

12.09   Lord Hoffmann added that there might be exceptional cases which did amount to an abuse of process, such as the case of defendants who published a serious defamation, claimed it was true, and lost a claim for defamation in relation to it. It would be unfair to the claimant in the first action, who had won damages for defamation, if the defendants could sue their lawyers and claim that they lost only because of the lawyers' negligence.[1] The same might apply to a claim in fraud.

1 [2002] 1 AC at 706H–707A.

12.10 After *Hall*, the Court of Appeal considered the issue of abuse in civil cases in *Secretary of State for Trade and Industry v Bairstow*.[1] Sir Andrew Morritt V-C gave the only reasoned judgment. Having considered *Hall*, he summarised the position as to abuse of process in the cases where a party sought to relitigate matters which had formerly been the subject of civil proceedings[2]:

'If the parties to the later civil proceedings were not parties to or privies of those who were parties to the earlier proceedings[3] then it will only be an abuse of the process of the court to challenge the factual findings and conclusions of the judge or jury in the earlier action if (i) it would be manifestly unfair to a party to the later proceedings that the same issues should be relitigated or (ii) to permit such relitigation would bring the administration of justice into disrepute.'

1 [2003] EWCA Civ 321, [2004] Ch 1.
2 [38].
3 The relevance of the parties being parties to, or privies of those who were parties to, the earlier proceedings is that if both parties to the later proceedings were also parties, or privies of parties, to the earlier proceedings then the doctrine of *res judicata* is likely to apply to prevent the second action from proceeding. It is only if *res judicata* does not apply that it is necessary to consider abuse of process by collateral attack on the earlier decision.

12.11 On the facts of *Bairstow*, the court rejected the contention that the later civil proceedings were an abuse of process. Mr Bairstow had been a director of Queen's Moat House plc. He sued the company for wrongful dismissal. He lost before Nelson J. The Secretary of State then commenced proceedings against Mr Bairstow under s 8 of the Company Directors Disqualification Act 1986 for a disqualification order on the ground that Mr Bairstow was unfit to be concerned in the management of a company. The Secretary of State relied heavily on findings which Nelson J had made against Mr Bairstow in Mr Bairstow's action against the company. Mr Bairstow wished to contend that he had not acted in the ways which Nelson J had found. The Secretary of State contended that it would be an abuse of process for Mr Bairstow to seek to re-argue issues which he had lost in the earlier action before Nelson J. The Court of Appeal held that it was not an abuse of process. Mr Bairstow, the defendant to the second action, was only requiring the Secretary of State to prove his case against Mr Bairstow. Factors which weighed heavily with the court were that the Secretary of State's allegations were serious, and the application was quasi-regulatory in nature and different from standard civil proceedings.[1]

1 [2003] EWCA Civ 321, [2004] Ch 1 at [41].

12.12 Further, in *Simms v Conlon & Harris,*[1] Simms had gone into partnership as a solicitor with Conlon & Harris. In February 2004 the Solicitors Disciplinary Tribunal ('SDT') held that Simms had acted dishonestly and struck him off the roll of solicitors. In March 2005 the Divisional Court rejected an appeal from the SDT. Although the appeal was by way of rehearing, it merely considered the evidence which was before the SDT. The Divisional Court did not hear any oral evidence. Subsequently, Conlon & Harris sued Simms on the basis that he had induced them to enter into partnership with him by fraudulent misrepresentations. Simms sought to defend himself. Conlon & Harris alleged that to do so amounted to an abuse of process, in that it was a collateral attack on the findings of the Divisional Court. Jonathan Parker LJ cited the passage quoted above from *Bairstow*. He added that there could be no catch-all formula for identifying an abuse of process since every case depended on its own facts.[2] He considered it an important factor that Simms had not initiated either of the two cases[3]:

'… in general the court should be slower in preventing a party from continuing to deny serious charges of which another court has previously found him guilty than in preventing such a party from initiating proceedings for the purpose of relitigating the question of whether he is guilty of those charges.'

In a sense, therefore, all that Simms was doing was requiring Conlon & Harris to prove their case. Further, Jonathan Parker LJ was unimpressed by Conlon & Harris's attempt to introduce all of the SDT's findings, which he considered it unnecessary to do.

1 [2006] EWCA Civ 1749, [2007] 3 All ER 802.
2 [141].
3 [146].

12.13 Ward LJ was concerned that a man facing serious charges of fraud should not be able to defend himself again.[1] In Moore-Bick LJ's view, the court should be particularly cautious before holding that it would be an abuse of process for Simms to challenge findings of fact made in previous proceedings between himself and a person who was not a party to the current litigation. 'Some additional factor' had to be present in order to do so. The most obvious candidate from the authorities was a conclusion that, although the earlier proceedings were between different parties, 'the parties to the current proceedings were both so closely involved in them that they should be required to accept the outcome for better or worse.'[2] That did not apply in *Simms*. Further, although the earlier proceedings were regulatory, they were not formally part of the criminal justice system and did not count as criminal proceedings for the purposes of the rules of abuse of process.[3] All three judges rejected the contention that it was an abuse of process for Simms to defend himself.[4]

1 [2006] EWCA Civ 1749, [2007] 3 All ER 802 at [178].
2 [168], [170].
3 [173].
4 Further, in *Nesbitt v Holt* [2007] EWCA Civ 249, [2007] PNLR 24, the Court of Appeal applied Sir Andrew Morritt V-C's dictum, quoted above, and emphasised that there was a heavy onus on the party who contended that the subsequent action was an abuse of process ([24]). An important issue for the subsequent proceedings had not been determined in the earlier proceedings. There was no abuse of process.

12.14   In *Taylor Walton v Laing*[1], however, the Court of Appeal did strike out a claim against a solicitor as abusive re-litigation. The claimant, L, fought a lengthy trial as to the terms of an oral agreement between himself and B, relying in part on evidence from his former solicitors TW, and lost. TW had acted for L on the transaction with B but not in the later litigation against B. L then sued TW, alleging that the judge had been wrong, that the terms of the oral agreement with B had been as he had contended all along, and that TW's negligence had prevented the agreement from being reduced to writing, so that TW was liable for L having to pay damages to B pursuant to the judgment. Buxton LJ said that the general test to be applied in determining whether there was an abuse of process was that[2]:

> 'The court ... has to consider, by an intense focus on the facts of the particular case, whether in broad terms the proceedings that it is sought to strike out can be characterised as falling under one or other, or both, of the broad rubrics of unfairness or the bringing of the administration of justice into disrepute.'

The court accepted that, if L had relied in the professional negligence action on new material which had not been before the trial judge, and had contended that if the trial judge had had that new material he would have reached a different decision, then there would have been no abusive collateral attack on the trial judge's decision[3]. But that was not the position[4]:

> '... everything said to us ... in criticism of Judge Thornton's judgment could have been said to Judge Thornton (and mainly was so said); and could have been deployed in the appeal from Judge Thornton that was never brought. What is sought to be achieved in the second claim is, therefore, not the addition of matter that, negligently or for whatever reason was omitted from the first case, but rather a relitigation of the first case on the basis of exactly the same material as was or could have been before Judge Thornton ...
>
> I therefore conclude that it would bring the administration of justice into disrepute if Mr Laing were to be permitted in the second claim

to advance exactly the same case as was tried and rejected by Judge Thornton. If Judge Thornton's judgment was to be disturbed, the proper course was to appeal, rather than seek to have it in effect reversed by a court not of superior but of concurrent jurisdiction hearing the second claim ...

... in order to succeed in the new claim Mr Laing has to demonstrate not only that the decision of Judge Thornton was wrong, but also that it was wrong because it wrongly assessed the very matters that are relied on in support of the new claim. That is an abusive relitigation of Judge Thornton's decision not by appeal but in collateral proceedings ...'

It follows that claims against litigation solicitors, to the effect that due to their negligence the court did not have before it the right evidence, or that a claim was struck out due to their negligence, will not amount to an abuse of process. But if the claimant is not alleging that there is new material in the professional negligence action that was not before the earlier court then it may amount to an abuse of process to contend that the earlier court's decision was wrong, at least where the claimant is challenging the central findings of the earlier court, and where the claimant was a party to the earlier decision but chose not to appeal. Further, abuse may arise in the defamation example given by Lord Hoffmann, and similar examples such as relitigating findings as to fraud, or in the examples quoted by Moore-Bick LJ in *Simms*, where there is a close link between all the parties to the earlier and later litigation.

1 [2007] EWCA Civ 1146.
2 [12].
3 [27] (Buckley LJ), [36] (Moses LJ). This is in accordance with the passage from Lord Hoffmann quoted at para 12.08 above, which was referred to at [26].
4 [22], [25], [27] (Buckley LJ).

12.15 Two further points should be made in relation to cases that appear to be abusive under the principles set out above. First, a claimant cannot save the claim by contending that, in bringing the professional negligence action, he or she had no intention to bring the administration of justice into disrepute: this aspect of the claimant's motivation is irrelevant to the application of the abuse of process doctrine.[1] Secondly, in the pre-*Hall* cases it was held that a claim that was otherwise an abuse of process would not be an abuse if it was based on fresh evidence which had not been available to the first court and which 'entirely changed the aspect of the case'.[2] This test may not apply in terms after *Hall*,[3] but in practice the requirement for fresh evidence that was not before the first court but which, if available to the first court, would have caused it to decide differently, may be often be difficult to meet.

1 *Smith v Linskills* [1996] 1 WLR 763 at 771D–E.
2 *Hunter* [1982] AC 529 at 541H–542D.

3 The point was left undecided in *Secretary of State for Trade and Industry v Bairstow* [2003] EWCA Civ 321, [2004] Ch 1, at 17B, but Buckley LJ's judgment in *Taylor Walton v Laing* [2007] EWCA Civ 1146, at [25], suggests that it may remain.

B LIABILITY

12.16 As in other areas of practice, a solicitor is liable for the conduct of litigation which falls below the standard to be expected of a solicitor of ordinary or reasonable competence. The standard of competence is that of the reasonably competent practitioner specialising in whatever area of law the solicitor holds himself out as a specialist.[1] In 1992, the then Sir Leonard Hoffmann suggested that, in reality, it was wrong to suppose that there was a single standard which applied with equal rigour to all areas of a solicitor's work.[2] In particular, he considered that the courts tended to apply lower standards in judging solicitors' conduct in relation to the handling of litigation than they did in relation to conveyancing. In conveyancing cases, almost any error which prevented the client from obtaining good title would be held negligent, whereas in relation to litigation:

> 'I think that the inherently risky and unpredictable nature of litigation is the reason why judges are more generous to solicitors in fixing the standard of care than they are in conveyancing.'

He added that, in the 19th century, the courts had applied lower standards to all aspects of solicitors' conduct. The standard which the law expected of solicitors in conveyancing cases had risen in recent times. Although judges did not express the reason for this, it was because solicitors were compulsorily insured, so that a finding of liability would have less disastrous consequences for the individual solicitor. It may be observed, however, that solicitors are insured for litigation as well as conveyancing work. Perhaps it is unsurprising that courts seem increasingly keen to find liability in this area too.

1 *Green v Collyer-Bristow* [1999] Lloyd's Rep PN 798 per Douglas Brown J at 809 col 2, and see para 2.01ff, above.
2 The talk was published: (1994) 10 PN 6.

12.17 In the eight years since the first edition of this book, there has been a steady flow of reported cases concerning claims for the negligent conduct of litigation. It is possible that the removal of advocates' immunity from suit for negligence in court has encouraged the bringing of claims, or that the Civil Procedure Rules' emphasis on stricter adherence to timetables has caused the courts to raise the standard which they apply in considering whether lawyers have acted in breach of duty. In considering liability issues, there is a distinction between (i) basic issues in relation to which there is generally no defence, such as missing a limitation period in the absence of exceptional circumstances, and (ii) issues of judgment where it is much harder to show breach of duty[1]. Basic errors tend to appear in many cases, and there will often be no difficulty in showing breach of duty. Outside that category of error, decisions as to liability may be more fact-specific, or may turn on practice in a particular area of the law. In those areas, it is doubtful how useful it is simply to rehearse the facts of previously decided cases, since they may turn on their own facts. We have tried, however, to focus on more recent case law with a view to drawing out themes as to the courts' general approach to allegations of negligence in the conduct of litigation.

1 See for example the passage from *Saif Ali v Sydney Mitchell & Co* [1980] AC 198 quoted at para 2.02, above.

12.18 In considering liability issues, reference should also be made to the discussion of the cases on 'negligence' in the context of wasted costs, in chapter 13[1], which are of considerable help in determining the standard of care which applies in an action for professional negligence. It is possible that the principle in *Medcalf v Mardell*,[2] giving a lawyer the benefit of the doubt where privilege is not waived, also applies outside the sphere of wasted costs. It should be noted, however, that a wasted costs order will compensate only lost costs. A client whose case is that, due to a solicitor's negligence, he or she has wrongly been convicted of an offence or settled a case on bad terms as to quantum of damages will still have to sue for professional negligence.

1 See para 13.45ff, below.
2 See para 13.16ff, below.

1   Basic errors

12.19 In the absence of exceptional circumstances, solicitors who fail to issue claims within the relevant limitation period,[1] allow their clients' cases to be struck out for want of prosecution[2], or allow their clients to be prevented from defending the claim for procedural reasons,[3] will be liable in negligence. The same is likely to apply to failing to bring a case before the court between 26 April 1999 and 25 April 2000, if it gives rise to a stay which cannot later be lifted.[4] Exceptional circumstances might include failure of the client to provide funds or instructions, or being instructed by the client to delay even though the client is fully informed of the risks of so doing. A solicitor who is instructed to bring a personal injury claim but fails to appreciate that the limitation period is three years is likely to be held negligent.[5] Further, where the limitation period in a personal injury action has expired, and the defendant's insurer indicates an intention to rely upon limitation, failing to advise the client of the possibility of an application under Limitation Act 1980, s 33 is likely to be held negligent,[6] though advice on whether such an application will succeed may involve an exercise of judgment which is much harder to criticise.[7] It is arguable that a solicitor whose retainer is terminated shortly before expiry of the limitation period has continuing duties to advise the client to issue proceedings in time,[8] though if a client terminates the retainer shortly before expiry of the limitation period, knowing of the expiry date and intending to issue a claim form in time, but then chooses not to do so, the client breaks the chain of causation and the former lawyers are not liable for loss of the claim.[9]

1 Cf *Saif Ali v Sydney Mitchell & Co* [1980] AC 198, HL. Failing to advise as to the correct limitation period under European Community law may also be negligent: *J J Dent v National Farmers' Union* NLD, 17 June 1999 (Evans-Lombe J); c f *Moffat v Burges Salmon* [2002] EWCA Civ 1977, [2003] PNLR 13.
2 *Allen v Sir Alfred McAlpine & Sons Ltd* [1968] 2 QB 229, CA, per Diplock LJ at 256D–E. The same is likely to apply in relation to allowing a claim to be automatically struck out pursuant to the former CCR Ord 17 r 11.
3 *Godefroy v Jay* (1831) 7 Bing 413.
4 See the Practice Direction to CPR Part 51, para 19.
5 *Bond v Livingstone* [2001] Lloyd's Rep PN 771.
6 *Carlton v Fulchers* [1997] PNLR 337, CA.
7 *Bark v Hawley* [2004] EWHC 144 (QB), [2005] PNLR 3.
8 *Ensor v Archer* [2004] EWHC 1541 (QB), [2005] PNLR 5, at [22].
9 *Kaberry v Freethcartwright* [2002] EWCA Civ 1966.

2   Funding

12.20   Costs law in general is now a specialist subject in its own right that is beyond the scope of this book. As to a solicitor's obligations at the outset of a retainer by an individual client, r 2.03 of the Solicitors' Code of Conduct 2007 requires solicitors to discuss with the client how the client will pay, with particular reference to public, insurance, employer or trade union funding. For the position before July 2007, see the Solicitors' Costs Information and Client Care Code. Further, in *Sarwar v Alam*,[1] a test case in relation to costs, Lord Phillips MR delivering the judgment of the Court of Appeal said that:

'In our judgment, proper modern practice dictates that a solicitor should normally invite a client to bring to the first interview any relevant motor insurance policy, any household insurance policy and any stand-alone BTE insurance policy belonging to the client and/or any spouse or partner living in the same household as the client. It would seem desirable for solicitors to develop the practice of sending a standard form letter requesting a sight of these documents to the client in advance of the first interview. At the interview the solicitor will also ask the client … whether his/her liability for costs may be paid by another person, for example an employer or trade union …

The solicitor will then be able to read through the policy … The solicitor's inquiries should be proportionate to the amount at stake.

The solicitor is not obliged to embark on a treasure hunt, seeking to see the insurance policies of every member of the client's family in case by chance they contain relevant BTE cover which the client might use.'

But that was guidance in relation to costs issues. Further, it has to some degree now been superseded[2]. But returning to *Sarwar*, counsel invited the Court of Appeal to hold that solicitors failing to follow this guidance would be found negligent. The court rejected that approach[3]:

'[Counsel] submitted that the test of the adequacy of a solicitor's inquiries and advice should be the same as the test applied when determining whether the solicitor has been professionally negligent ... We deprecate any attempt to equate the question of reasonableness that a costs judge has to decide[4] with the question whether the claimant's solicitor has been in breach of duty to his/her client. If a solicitor gives advice that is unsound, it will not necessarily follow that the advice was negligent.'

It follows that a solicitor who fails to comply with the guidance in *Sarwar*, or other binding guidance as to costs, will not necessarily be found to have acted negligently or in breach of contract, though such a failure may mean that there is no liability to pay the solicitor's costs. Further, in *John Mowlem Construction plc v Neil F Jones & Co*,[5] specialist construction law solicitors were instructed to act in a fee recovery action. Their client's claim was met with a threat of a counterclaim from the defendant. The solicitors did not advise their client that this threat might constitute circumstances which should be notified to insurers pursuant to the client's professional indemnity policy. The client did not notify its insurers at that stage. As a result the insurers were able to escape having to cover the counterclaim when it was pursued. The Court of Appeal held that the solicitors had not acted in breach of duty in failing to advise the client to notify its insurers of the threatened counterclaim, even though the solicitors' new client/matter form contained a box which asked 'is the client insured for the claim or for costs'? A reasonably competent solicitor could have taken the view that it was not necessary to consider insurance cover for the counterclaim when it was first threatened.

1 [2001] EWCA Civ 1401, [2002] 1 WLR 125, at [45] and [46].
2 See the Court of Appeal's comments in *Garrett v Halton BC* [2006] EWCA Civ 1017, [2007] 1 WLR 554, at [69]–[77].
3 [51].
4 In other words, questions of the kind that were in issue in *Sarwar*.
5 [2004] EWCA Civ 768, [2004] PNLR 925.

12.21 As to public funding, solicitors have an obligation to consider at the start of each retainer whether the client might be eligible for such funding[1]. Further, in *Beswarick v JW Ripman*,[2] solicitors who wrongly concluded that the claimant's half interest in a boat would have to be taken into account for the purposes of calculating her assets in assessing eligibility for legal aid were held to have acted negligently. Thirdly, failing to advise a client whose legal aid has been revoked as to the consequences of the revocation and the options open to him or her is also likely to be negligent.[3]

1 *David Truex v Kitchin* [2007] EWCA Civ 618, [2007] PNLR 33, at [22].
2 [2001] Lloyd's Rep PN 698, HHJ (Griffiths Williams QC).
3 *Casey v Hugh James Jones & Jenkins* [1999] Lloyd's Rep PN 115 (Thomas J).

3 Parties and statements of case

12.22 Solicitors who issue proceedings in the name of A and B, when they know that only B is their client, are likely to be found negligent.[1] On the other hand, solicitors may reasonably take the view that it is necessary to sue only one of three possible defendants if they are unaware that the party sued is in financial difficulties.[2] Although solicitors will be liable for errors in pleading if they undertake that task, deciding which causes of action to plead is a matter of judgment, and failing to plead a cause of action which is properly arguable does not necessarily amount to negligence.[3]

1 Cf *Veasy v Millfeed*, at para13.55, below.
2 *Brinn v Russell Jones & Walker* [2002] EWHC 2727, [2003] Lloyd's Rep PN 70.
3 *McFarlane v Wilkinson* [1997] 2 Lloyd's Rep 259, CA, per Brooke LJ at 277, and c f *Moy v Pettman Smith* [2005] UKHL 7, [2005] 1 WLR 581. These cases relate to pleading by barristers, but the principle must be the same in the case of pleading by solicitors.

4 Interlocutory applications

12.23 Failing to apply for an ouster injunction when necessary[1] or to seek committal for contempt of court when an injunction against harassment has been breached,[2] may be negligent, as may releasing a father's passport that allows him to abduct the children of the family.[3] Similarly, failing to renew a registration of children's names with the Passport Agency, which prevented a husband from removing children from the UK, may amount to a breach of duty to a client wife.[4] Although it is not decided, it seems likely that advocates failing to follow the guidance set out in *Memory Corpn plc v Sidhu (No 2)*[5] when applying for freezing orders will be found to have acted in breach of duty to their clients. Finally, in *Martin Boston & Co v Roberts*,[6] the claimant solicitors acted for the first defendant in an action brought against him by a company, F Ltd. They applied for security for costs against F Ltd. They compromised the application by accepting an unsecured guarantee from A, a director of F Ltd, at a time when they had only her own assertion as to her financial worth. The majority in the Court of Appeal considered that the solicitors acted negligently in taking the risk that, as ultimately came to pass, the guarantee would be worthless, without at least receiving the client's instructions to take this risk.

1 *Dickinson v Jones Alexander & Co* [1993] 2 FLR 521 (Douglas Brown J).
2 Found at first instance and not appealed in *Heywood v Wellers* [1976] QB 446, CA.
3 See the discussion of *Al-Kandari v JR Brown & Co* [1988] QB 665, CA, at para 1.27, above.
4 *Hamilton-Jones v David & Snape* [2003] EWHC 3147 (Ch), [2004] 1 WLR 924 (Neuberger J).
5 [2000] 1 WLR 1443, CA.
6 [1996] PNLR 45, CA. See para 2.28, above.

5 Preparation for trial

12.24 Failing to follow advice from counsel to obtain specific varieties of evidence before trial[1] is likely to be regarded as negligent, whereas acting in reliance upon counsel's advice will generally not be so regarded.[2] Solicitors who have received advice from counsel and other lawyers that conflicts may be negligent if they fail to resolve the discrepancy by reference to the same or different counsel.[3] Failing to obtain evidence from a witness whom it is reasonable to suppose would not wish to give evidence is not negligent.[4] In *Balamoan v Holden & Co*[5] the court was prepared to engage in a thorough analysis of the steps which a small firm of solicitors had taken to prepare a personal injury claim for trial, and did not shrink from findings of breach of duty in that preparation. Further, in general terms, solicitors have a duty to prepare litigation for trial by identifying the key issues and seeking evidence in relation to them; failure to do so may well be held negligent.[6] But there may be a distinction between completely failing to grasp a key issue and address it, which is likely to be held negligent[7], and identifying an issue, considering it, but deciding after an exercise of judgment not to argue it; the latter is less likely to be held negligent, even if the point omitted later turns out to be the crucial and ultimately successful point in the litigation[8]. As indicated above, it is submitted that a distinction should be drawn between questions of judgment, where it may be hard to show breach of duty, and basic procedural steps, or work of analysis of the claim, needed to prepare a case for trial, where findings of breach of duty are more likely. Finally, if a litigation solicitor becomes aware of information suggesting that the opposing party is in a difficult financial position, the solicitor may come under a duty to act swiftly to bring the matter to trial in order to avoid the risk of a judgment being unenforceable.[9]

1 *Acton v Graham Pearce & Co* [1997] 3 All ER 909 (Chadwick J).
2 See the discussion of acting in reliance upon counsel's advice in para 2.11ff, above and para 13.58ff, below.
3 *Green v Hancocks* [2001] Lloyd's Rep PN 212, CA.
4 *Roe v McGregor* [1968] 2 All ER 636, CA.
5 (1989) 149 NLJ 898, CA.
6 See for example *Browning v Brachers* [2004] EWHC 16 (QB), [2004] PNLR 28; *Feakins v Burstow* [2005] EWHC 1931 (QB), [2006] PNLR 6; in the commercial context: *Somatra Ltd v Sinclair Roche & Temperley* [2003] EWCA Civ 1474, [2003] 2 Lloyd's Rep 855; in the

matrimonial context: *Channon v Lindley Johnstone* [2002] EWCA Civ 353, [2002] Lloyd's Rep PN 342; in the criminal context: *Acton v Graham Pearce & Co* [1997] 3 All ER 909 (Chadwick J).
7 For example, *Feakins* [2005] EWHC 1931 (QB), [2006] PNLR 6.
8 *Firstcity Insurance Group Ltd v Orchard & Gee* [2002] EWHC 1433 (QB), [2002] Lloyd's Rep PN 534 (Forbes J).
9 *Pearson v Sanders Witherspoon* [2000] Lloyd's Rep PN 151, CA.

6   Advice on settlement

12.25   Settlement of an action without the client's authority and for a sum that is significantly less than he or she would receive at trial is likely to be held negligent.[1] Similarly, in matrimonial proceedings, solicitors acting for a wife who failed to undertake proper investigation of the husband's means, and consequently advised acceptance of a settlement offer which was too low, were conceded to have been negligent.[2] In *Hickman v Blake Lapthorn*[3], settlement discussions took place at the court door immediately before trial. Counsel negligently failed to consider whether, on the basis of the medical reports, the claimant's claim might be for loss of earnings and lifetime care on the ground that he would never work again. Although the solicitors took a secondary role, they were familiar with the medical reports and should have intervened to point out the possible lifetime claim when it became apparent that counsel was valuing the claim without reference to that; as a result they were held negligent too. On the other hand, *Moy v Pettman Smith*[4] also concerned settlement negotiations in a personal injury claim at court just before the start of the trial. Counsel had to take a difficult decision in advising whether it was likely that medical evidence served late would be admitted in evidence, and whether a settlement offer made at court should be accepted. The latter depended on her assessment of the former. Counsel advised rejection of the settlement offer. In fact the medical report was not admitted in evidence and the client had to accept a lower settlement than had been available. The House of Lords, in holding that counsel had not been negligent, emphasised that counsel faced a difficult decision, not of her own making, under time pressure, and that her judgment was within the range of responses that a reasonable barrister could have reached.[5] But in *Griffin v Kingsmill*,[6] a third personal injury claim, there was no great pressure of time. The Court of Appeal was scathing about counsel's analysis of the claim, which it considered had led to a gross under-settlement, and found counsel's instructing solicitor also to have been in breach of duty in failing to advise rejection of the offer. In the matrimonial context, in *Beswarick v Ripman*[7] the defendant solicitors acted for the mother. They advised a clean break settlement even though they knew that there was a prospect of the children returning to live with the mother. The defendants were held negligent in failing to advise that the settlement should contain a nominal order for periodical payments so that, if the children did return, the claimant could seek increased payments from the husband. In *Green v Collyer-Bristow*,[8] solicitors and counsel were found negligent in advising that specific performance of an agreement between husband and wife might be sought when in fact it was unenforceable by virtue of s 2 of the Law Reform (Miscellaneous Provisions) Act 1989.

1 *Amonoo v Grant, Seifert & Grower* (unreported) 18 December 1998 (HHJ Overend sitting as a deputy High Court judge).
2 *Dickinson v Jones Alexander & Co* [1993] 2 FLR 521 (Douglas Brown J).
3 [2005] EWHC 2714 (QB), [2006] PNLR 20 (Jack J).
4 [2005] UKHL 7, [2005] 1 WLR 581.
5 For further decisions emphasising the breadth of the range of reasonable responses in matters of judgment, see *Luke v Wansbroughs* [2003] EWHC 3151 (QB), [2005] PNLR 2 (Davis J), and *Walker v Chruszcz* [2006] EWHC 64 (QB) (Davis J).
6 [2001] EWCA Civ 934, [2001] Lloyd's Rep PN 716.
7 [2001] Lloyd's Rep PN 698 (HHJ Griffiths Williams QC sitting as a deputy High Court judge).
8 [1999] Lloyd's Rep PN 798 (Douglas Brown J).

7   At court, and appeal

12.26   Failing to attend counsel at court when necessary,[1] failing to appear at court for a hearing when instructed to do so,[2] or failing to ensure that witnesses are warned to attend court when required,[3] are likely to amount to negligence. Failing to follow clear advice from counsel to appeal on a point of law is likely to amount to negligence.[4]

1 *Hawkins v Harwood* (1849) 4 Exch 503.
2 *Holden v Holden and Pearson* (1910) 102 LT 398. The solicitor's conduct of the case was hampered by his work as an agent at the general election.
3 *Dunn v Hallen* (1861) 2 F & F 642, an action by attorneys for their fees. In fact, they won, after Bramwell B had directed the jury that they should have the fees unless their services were 'wholly useless and valueless'. Compare the wasted costs cases in para 13.45ff, below.
4 Cf *Walpole v Partridge & Wilson* [1994] QB 106, CA.

C   CAUSATION AND ASSESSMENT OF DAMAGES

1   General principles: loss of civil claims

12.27   The type of loss most commonly claimed in actions for the negligent conduct of civil litigation is loss of the opportunity either (i) to proceed with a claim to trial, (ii) to defend a claim, (iii) to obtain a settlement of a claim, or (iv) to obtain a better outcome than was in fact achieved, whether at trial or by settlement. The types of negligence most likely to give rise to items (i)–(iii) are negligence leading to the striking out of the claim or the defence or allowing the limitation period to expire without issuing a valid claim. Similarly, in relation to negligent handling of criminal litigation, there may be claims for loss of the opportunity either to have the prosecution dropped or to have won an acquittal, or to have received a more lenient sentence. All these varieties of claim require the court trying the professional negligence action to assess what might have happened in the previous litigation if there had been no breach of duty. Although this may often be a complicated exercise, it is similar to what lawyers do every day in advising their clients as to the likely outcome of litigation, which they have to do in order to advise on settlement. Thus the features which the court trying the professional negligence action has to consider are likely to be factors which practitioners in the relevant area of law are considering on a daily basis. The judge trying the action may not be an expert in the particular field of law in question, but that is a different problem, and in principle surmountable by reference to specialist textbooks.[1]

1 Compare *Bown v Gould & Swayne* [1996] PNLR 130, CA, and see para 2.21ff, above.

12.28 The precise nature of the claim will depend on what the parties contend would have happened if there had been no negligence, and, as in other areas of the law of damages, the principal task in every case is a careful analysis of the facts and assessment of what would probably have happened in the absence of breach of duty. But there are general principles that apply to the assessment of loss in claims against lawyers for the negligent conduct of litigation. The starting point is a passage from the judgment of Lord Evershed MR in *Kitchen v Royal Air Forces Association.*[1] The claimant's husband had been electrocuted and killed in his kitchen. She alleged that his death had been caused by faulty wiring in the cooker, which was the responsibility of an electricity company. The defendant solicitors acted for her in relation to her potential claim against the electricity company, but they failed to issue a writ before expiry of the limitation period. This was negligent. Counsel for the defendants contended that, in relation to damages, the claimant had to show, on the balance of probabilities, that, had there been no negligence, she would have won the action, and that, if there was a lower than 51% chance that she would have won the action, she had failed to satisfy that burden and should recover nothing. The Court of Appeal rejected this, as being the wrong approach to assessing damages in this type of case. Lord Evershed MR said:[2]

'If, in this kind of case, it is plain that an action could have been brought, and, that if it had been brought, it must have succeeded, the answer is easy. The damaged plaintiff then would recover the full amount of the damages lost by the failure to bring the action originally. On the other hand, if it be made clear that the plaintiff never had a cause of action, that there was no case which the plaintiff could reasonably ever have formulated, then it is equally plain that she can get nothing save nominal damages for the solicitors' negligence. I would add, as was conceded by counsel for the plaintiff, that in such a case it is not enough for the plaintiff to say: "though I had no claim in law, still, I had a nuisance value which I could have so utilised as to extract something from the other side, and they would have had to pay something to me in order to persuade me to go away."

The present case, however, falls into neither one nor the other of the categories which I have mentioned. There may be cases where it would be quite impossible to try "the action within the action", as counsel for the second defendants asks. It may be that for one reason or another the action for negligence is not brought until, say, twenty years after the event, and in the process of time the material witnesses, or many of them, may have died or become quite out of reach for the purpose of being called to give evidence. In my judgment, assuming that the plaintiff has established negligence, what the court has to do in such a case as the present is to determine what the plaintiff has lost by that negligence. The question is: has the plaintiff lost some right of value, some chose in action of reality and substance? In such a case it may be that its value is not easy to determine, but it is the duty of the court to determine that value as best it can.'

The trial judge had held that the most the claimant could have recovered at trial would have been £3,000, and reduced it to £2,000 because of difficulties in the action. The Court of Appeal agreed with his approach to assessing damages, though it would have awarded less than £2,000 if there had been an appeal as to quantum.

1 [1958] 1 WLR 563, CA.
2 [1958] 1 WLR 563 at 574–575.

12.29 It is submitted that the cases may helpfully be divided into three categories, which we now consider:

(a)   cases where due to the solicitor's negligence the claimant loses any chance of having the claim tried or settled;

(b)   cases where the underlying claim was settled but it is alleged that the solicitor's negligence caused the settlement to be at an undervalue;

(c)   cases where the underlying claim was tried but it is alleged that the solicitor's negligence caused the claimant to achieve a worse result.

(a) Due to solicitor's negligence claimant loses any chance of having claim tried or settled

12.30   Most cases fall into this category, as did *Kitchen*. Due to the solicitor's negligence, either proceedings are not issued within the limitation period, or the claim form is not served within the period of its validity, or the claim is struck out for want of prosecution, or it is struck out or permanently stayed on account of some other procedural default such as failing to serve a statement of claim in time. The result is the same in each case: the claimant loses all chance of having the claim tried or settled.

(1) Loss of a chance approach

12.31 It is now established, below House of Lords level[1], that the correct approach in assessing loss in this type of case is[2] 'not to seek to try the original claim, but to measure its prospects of success and assess damages on a broad percentage basis'. In such cases the ordering of preliminary issues is particularly risky and to be avoided.[3]

The general approach summarised in the quotation is derived from the principles set out in *Allied Maples Group Ltd v Simmons & Simmons*,[4] which is discussed in chapter 3.[5] It is important to note, however, that the method for assessing loss in loss of litigation cases differs in part from that proposed in *Allied Maples*. Before dealing with that, we must first summarise the approach set out in *Allied Maples*. *Allied Maples* was a lost transaction case rather than a lost litigation case: what the claimant had lost due to the negligence was the chance to enter into an alternative and better transaction with a third party, rather than the chance of a trial. The Court of Appeal held that, where the court had to assess the claimant's loss by considering what *a third party* would have done if there had been no negligence, the correct approach was as follows. First, the court had to consider whether the claimant had shown that there was a real or substantial chance that, in the absence of negligence, the third party would have acted in the way that the claimant asserted. If the claimant failed to prove this, he or she recovered only nominal damages; if he or she proved it, the court then assessed the value of the chance that the claimant had proved, assessing the value of what the claimant would have obtained in the absence of breach of duty and then discounting it to represent uncertainties as to whether it would have been obtained. So if, in the absence of breach of duty, the claimant would have had, say, a 40% chance of obtaining an asset worth £100,000, then damages would be £40,000. Note that, in this example, if the normal balance of probabilities test were applied instead, then the claimant would recover nothing: there would be a less than 50% chance that, in the absence of breach of duty, the claimant would have received the £100,000, so the claimant would have failed to prove his or her case on the balance of probabilities. On a loss of a chance approach, however, the claimant recovers £40,000 in our example. If, on the other hand, the claimant had a 60% chance of recovering the asset worth £100,000, then on a loss of a chance approach the claimant would recover £60,000 but on the balance of probabilities approach he or she would recover £100,000: on the balance of probabilities test, if the claimant shows less than a 51% chance he or she gets nothing but if the claimant shows a 51% or more chance then the claimant takes 100%. This demonstrates the difference between the balance of probabilities and loss of a chance approaches.

12.32 *Litigation*

1 In *Phillips* (below), it was submitted that the approach commonly applied in these cases was inconsistent with the House of Lords' decision in the clinical negligence case of *Gregg v Scott* [2005] UKHL 2, [2005] 2 AC 176. The Privy Council in *Phillips* did not give permission for this point to be argued. It is thought, however, that insofar as *Gregg* touches on the line of authority being considered here it tends to support it: see para 3.21ff, above.
2 *Phillips & Co v Whatley* [2007] UKPC 28, [2007] PNLR 27, per Lord Mance delivering the opinion of the Board of the Privy Council at [2]. He relied on *Kitchen, Hanif v Middleweeks* [2000] Lloyd's Rep PN 920, *Dixon v Clement Jones* [2004] EWCA Civ 1005, [2005] PNLR 6, and *Browning v Brachers (Damages)* [2005] EWCA Civ 753, which are discussed below.
3 *Dudarec v Andrews* [2006] EWCA Civ 256, [2006] 1 WLR 3002, per Waller LJ at [26].
4 [1995] 1 WLR 1602, CA.
5 See para 3.19ff, above.

12.32 The difference between the court's approach in lost transaction cases, such as *Allied Maples*, and in lost litigation cases is as follows. *Allied Maples* held that the loss of a chance approach applied to questions of what a third party would have done if there had been no breach of duty, but that the normal balance of probabilities test applied as to what the claimant would have done in the absence of breach of duty. The rationale[1] is presumably that it is easier for a claimant to prove what he or she would have done than to prove what others would have done, so in relation to what the claimant would have done one adopts the normal balance of probabilities test but in relation to what third parties would have done one adopts the loss of a chance approach. In the context of claims against solicitors for the negligent conduct of litigation, it is clear that the same loss of a chance approach should be applied in relation to what *third parties* would have done if there had been no breach of duty. But, in lost litigation cases as opposed to lost transaction cases such as *Allied Maples*, in relation to hypothetical questions as to what *the claimant* would have done it is necessary to distinguish between two different questions.

(a) *Balance of probabilities:* if the question is what the claimant would have done, had there been no negligence, in the context of prosecuting the litigation which due to the defendant's negligence has been lost, then it is submitted that the normal balance of probabilities test applies. So if, for example, the claimant's case is that the defendant solicitors negligently advised the claimant that the prospects of success in the litigation were 60% when in fact they were 40%, then the question as to what the claimant would have done if advised that the prospects of success were only 40% has to be determined on the balance of probabilities.

(b) *Loss of a chance:* if, however, the question is what the claimant would have done if given the correct advice by the party who was a defendant to the original action, that is to say the action which has now been struck out, then the loss of a chance approach applies.

This somewhat complicated distinction was made in *Dixon v Clement Jones*[2], and can perhaps best by explained by reference to the facts of that case. Rix LJ, with whom Carnwath LJ and Lord Slynn agreed, said that:

'... this kind of litigation against a solicitor for negligence arising out of the dismissal of his client's lost litigation is different from the transaction class of claim discussed in *Allied Maples*. Therefore there was no requirement as a matter of law for [the claimant] to prove on the balance of probabilities or else lose her case entirely that she would not have proceeded if she had received the right advice.'

By 'the right advice' he was referring to 'the right advice from the party who had been a defendant to the claim which had been struck out.' The claimant had received negligent advice from her accountants. In reliance on it, she entered into a loss-making transaction. She instructed the defendant solicitors to bring a claim against the accountants. They did but it was struck out for failure to serve a statement of claim. The trial judge in the action against the solicitors held that the likelihood was that, even if the claimant had received the correct advice from the accountants, she would have gone ahead with the loss-making transaction. The Court of Appeal held that that was not fatal to her claim against the defendant solicitors. As against them, the claimant did not have to prove on the balance of probabilities that, but for the accountants' negligence, she would not have gone ahead with the loss-making transaction. The chance as to whether she would have gone ahead with the loss-making transaction was simply one factor to be assessed on a percentage basis in the same way as all the other uncertainties in the case. It fell into category (b) above and should be distinguished from issues of the kind identified in category (a) above. This is the position even though, if the original action had not been struck out and the claimant had proceeded against the accountants, in the accountants' negligence action she would have needed to prove on the balance of probabilities that, if the accountants had given her the right advice, she would not have gone ahead with the transaction.

1 This rationale was suggested by HHJ Hodge QC, sitting as a deputy High Court Judge, in *Stone Heritage Developments Ltd v Davis Blank Furniss* (Ch D, 1 June 2006). The rationale was, however, criticised by Sir David Neuberger in a talk to the Professional Negligence Bar Association on 9 February 2005.
2 [2004] EWCA Civ 1005, [2005] PNLR 6, at [49].

12.33 One rationale for this was to say that, ultimately, whether the claimant obtained a payment for her accountants' negligence claim depended either on the decision of the judge trying the accountants' negligence claim, or on a settlement with the accountants; in either case, it depended in part on the actions of third parties, which were definitely to be considered on a loss of a chance rather than balance of probabilities basis.[1] It is doubtful, however, whether this alone is sufficient to explain the decision. In a lost transaction case, such as *Allied Maples*, the question of what alternative hypothetical transaction would have been entered into in the absence of negligence depends in part on what the claimant would have done and in part on what third parties would have done. But this does not stop the court holding that the question of what the claimant would have done should be assessed on the balance of probabilities rather than on the loss of a chance basis. That the hypothetical outcome would depend partly on the action of a third party does not mean, assuming that *Allied Maples* was correctly decided, that the claimant's hypothetical conduct should be assessed on the loss of a chance basis. So this rationale falls away.

1 See *Dixon* [2004] EWCA Civ 1005, [2005] PNLR 6, at [42].

12.34 A different way of putting the point might be to say that, in a case where the solicitor's negligence has lost the claimant any chance of having the claim tried, what is being valued is the claim itself, rather as, if the claim had not been struck out, lawyers for either the claimant or defendant might have valued it in advising about settlement. This theme, which it is submitted is correct on the authorities, is considered further below. The argument is that, in giving damages for the loss of a claim which has been struck out, the court is not trying the underlying claim. Instead, it is asking, essentially, what the settlement value of the underlying claim would have been if it had not been struck out. If the claim was so weak that any judge would have rejected it, it had no settlement value other than possibly a nuisance value, but nuisance value is to be ignored for these purposes[1]. If on the other hand it was so strong that any judge would have upheld it, it might have a value of even 100% of the sum claimed. Many claims, however, fall into the intermediate category where some judges might have allowed them and others not. In this latter category, the court assesses the value of the claim by looking at the percentage chance of it succeeding. It would be odd if that percentage chance were applied to all issues in the underlying litigation other than what either the notional trial judge, or the original parties at a notional settlement negotiation, would have decided as to what the claimant would have done if the breach of duty alleged in the underlying litigation had not occurred. Hence, the issue of what the claimant would have done in those circumstances must be considered on a loss of a chance, or percentage, basis rather than on the balance of probabilities.[2]

1 See the passage quoted from *Kitchen*, at para 12.28 above.
2 *Dixon* [2004] EWCA Civ 1005, [2005] PNLR 6, at [42] and [45].

(2) Mount principles

12.35 In *Mount v Barker Austin*,[1] two separate firms of solicitors who were acting for the claimant had allowed two successive sets of proceedings to be struck out for want of prosecution. Simon Brown LJ, with whom Ward LJ agreed, set out four principles in relation to assessing loss in cases where negligence had caused an action to be struck out. Since these have been applied in most of the subsequent cases, they must be considered in detail. First, it should be emphasised that in *Mount* these principles were expressly said to relate to the case where the claim had been struck out; hence in principle (1)

Simon Brown LJ describes the context as being 'that of struck-out litigation'. As discussed below, however, this point has sometimes been under-emphasised in subsequent cases. The principles were:[2]

'(1) The legal burden lies on the plaintiff to prove that in losing the opportunity to pursue his claim (or defence to counter-claim) he has lost something of value i e that his claim (or defence) had a real and substantial rather than merely a negligible prospect of success. (I say "negligible" rather than "speculative"– the word used in a somewhat different context in *Allied Maples Group Ltd v Simmons & Simmons* [1995] 1 WLR 1602 – lest "speculative" may be thought to include considerations of uncertainty of outcome, considerations which in my judgment ought not to weigh against the plaintiff in the present context, that of struck-out litigation.)

(2) The evidential burden lies on the defendants to show that despite their having acted for the [claimant] in the litigation and charged for their services, that litigation was of no value to their client, so that he lost nothing by their negligence in causing it to be struck out. Plainly the burden is heavier in a case where the solicitors have failed to advise their client of the hopelessness of his position and heavier still where, as here, two firms of solicitors successively have failed to do so. If, of course, the solicitors have advised their client with regard to the merits of his claim (or defence) such advice is likely to be highly relevant.

(3) If and insofar as the court may now have greater difficulty in discerning the strength of the [claimant]'s original claim (or defence) than it would have had at the time of the original action, such difficulty should not count against him, but rather against his negligent solicitors. It is quite likely that the delay will have caused such difficulty and quite possible, indeed, that that is why the original action was struck out in the first place. That, however, is not inevitable: it will not be the case in particular (a) where the original claim (or defence) turned on questions of law or the interpretation of documents, or (b) where the only possible prejudice from the delay can have been to the other side's case.

(4) If and when the court decides that the [claimant]'s chances in the original action were more than merely negligible it will then have to evaluate them. That requires the court to make a realistic assessment of what would have been the [claimant]'s prospects of success had the original litigation been fought out. Generally speaking one would expect the court to tend towards a generous assessment given that it was the defendants' negligence which lost the [claimant] the opportunity of succeeding in full or fuller measure. To my mind it is at this

12.36 *Litigation*

rather than the earlier stage that the principle established in *Armory v Delamirie* (1722) 1 Str 505 comes into play.'

The Court of Appeal approved these principles in *Sharif v Garrett,*[3] where Simon Brown LJ added that he had indicated in *Mount* that there should be a two-stage approach[4]:

'First, the court has to decide whether the claimant has lost something of value or whether on the contrary his prospects of success in the original action were negligible. Secondly, assuming the claimant surmounts this initial hurdle, the court must then "make a realistic assessment of what would have been the [claimant]'s prospects of success had the original litigation been fought out".

With regard to the first stage, the evidential burden rests on the negligent solicitors: they, after all, in the great majority of cases will have been charging the claimant for their services and failing to advise him that in reality his claim was worthless so that he would be better off simply discontinuing it. The claimant, therefore, should be given the benefit of any doubts as to whether or not his original claim was doomed to inevitable failure. With regard to the second stage, the *Armory v Delamirie* (1722) 1 Str 505 principle comes into play in the sense that the court will tend to assess the claimant's prospects generously given that it was the defendant's negligence which lost him the chance of succeeding in full or fuller measure.'

1 [1998] PNLR 493, CA.
2 [1998] PNLR 493 at 510D–511C.
3 [2001] EWCA Civ 1269, [2002] 1 WLR 3118.
4 [38]–[39].

12.36 The two-stage approach is clearly derived from the same structure used in *Allied Maples.*[1] Note that the reference at the end of the second quotation to the position 'had the original litigation been fought out' was not intended to mean that the judge trying the professional negligence action had to put himself in the position of a notional judge trying the notional underlying litigation. Instead, as discussed further below, the judge trying the professional negligence has to assess the overall value of the lost claim.[2]

1 Above.
2 See per Rix LJ in *Dixon v Clement Jones* [2004] EWCA Civ 1005, [2005] PNLR 6 at [27], and para 12.42ff, below.

12.37 As to *Mount* principle (1), both *Mount* and *Sharif* were cases where the solicitor's negligence had led to the claim being struck out. Generally speaking, in that context, it will be easy for the claimant to succeed at the first stage and show that he or she has lost something of value. The same may not apply in other categories of case, where the solicitor's negligence has not led to the claimant losing any chance of trial or settlement (see below). In *Sharpe v Addison*,[1] Simon Brown LJ quoted Sir Murray Stuart-Smith:[2]

> ' "For example, if a case in which a solicitor has advised that there is a reasonable prospect of success is struck out for want of prosecution, it will be difficult or impossible for the solicitor to contend that there was no substantial chance of success, at least in the absence of evidence which completely alters the complexion of the case and effectively torpedoes the claim." '

As Simon Brown LJ acknowledged, however, *Mount* itself was a case where, although two separate sets of solicitors had allowed claims to be struck out for want of prosecution, the Court of Appeal found that there was a negligible chance of success if the claims had not been struck out due: it was clear from the documents that the claimant's underlying case was hopeless. So not every case which is struck out merits an award of damages against the negligent solicitor and, as Lord Evershed said in the passage quoted above from *Kitchen*, a claimant will not be awarded damages on the basis that the lost claim was worthless in law but had a nuisance value. In *Sharpe v Addison*, the Court of Appeal considered that the claimant had passed the first hurdle of showing that he had a case that had more than a negligible prospect of success, but ultimately assessed its value at 10% of its value on a full liability basis. So it seems that a claim with prospects of success as low as 10% may be considered to have passed Simon Brown LJ's first hurdle. Rix LJ suggested that the test of whether a claim was worthless for loss of a chance purposes was similar to the question of whether it would be struck out under CPR Part 24 as having no real prospect of success; an alternative approach was to ask whether, if the underlying claim had not been struck out, the defendant's insurers would have made more than a nominal payment into court.[3]

1 [2003] EWCA Civ 1189, [2004] PNLR 23, at [57]–[58].
2 In *Hatswell v Goldbergs* [2001] EWCA Civ 2084, [2002] Lloyd's Rep PN 359, at [49].
3 [2003] EWCA Civ 1189, [2004] PNLR 23, at [27]–[28].

12.38   As to *Mount* principle (2), it is possible that solicitors may have advised their client that the claim was hopeless and should be abandoned. In that case, principle (2) might assist the solicitors rather than the claimant. But if they have given no advice as to the merits, but continued to charge their clients for conducting the litigation, the burden on them to show that the case was hopeless will be heavy. It is submitted that whether the application of principle (2) favours the claimant or the defendant solicitors will depend on the facts of the case, though generally it is likely to favour the claimant.

12.39   The effect of *Mount* principle (3) is that, if the defendant solicitors' negligence in allowing the claim to be struck out weakens the claimant's evidence, then that should tell against the defendant solicitors rather than the claimant. But, as Simon Brown LJ made clear in *Mount*, it is again possible that the facts of a particular case might show that the only prejudice suffered due to the delay was to the case for the other party to the original litigation. In that case, principle (3) might not apply.

12.40   It is easy to see the rationale for principles (2) and (3), although, as we have seen, depending on the facts they may not necessarily favour the claimant. What is perhaps more difficult is to identify the rationale for principle (4) being a free-standing principle in addition to principles (2) and (3). Take a case where, on the facts, principles (2) and (3) do not require assumptions to be made which favour the claimant. Why, in that case, should there be a separate principle (4) which requires generosity toward the claimant even in cases to which the rationales of principles (2) and (3) do not apply in the claimant's favour, and do not require a generous approach toward the claimant? Suppose that the underlying claim has been struck out due to the defendant's negligence, but the defendant always advised the claimant that it was a hopeless claim, and the effect of the delay has simply been to make it harder for the defendant solicitors to put forward the evidence which the defendant to the original action would have put forward at the original trial. If, as Simon Brown LJ said, principle (4) is additional to principles (2) and (3), then presumably it requires the court to take a particularly generous view of the claimant's case even though the defendant has not advised that it is a good claim and the delay has not weakened the claimant's position. Why, in such a case, should the court take a generous approach to the claimant's case?

12.41   Simon Brown LJ said that, at the stage of *Mount* principle (4), the principle of *Armory v Delamirie*[1] should come into play. What does this principle provide? In *Browning v Brachers (Damages)*[2], due to the defendant solicitors' negligence the claimants had lost their counterclaim because they had served their evidence late and had not been permitted to rely on it. The counterclaim had been struck out when the claimants offered no evidence to support it. So it was a case within the category that we are currently considering. Jonathan Parker LJ stated that the principle of *Armory v Delamirie* was:

> 'a general principle to the effect that, in a case where the defendant has wrongfully deprived the claimant of property of value (be it an item of physical property or a chose in action), the court will, save to the extent that it is persuaded otherwise by the defendant, assess the value of the missing property on a basis which is generous to the claimant ...
>
> I respectfully agree[3] that the principle in *Armory v Delamirie* is not directed at the legal burden of proof; rather it raises an evidential (i e rebuttable) presumption in favour of the claimant which gives

him the benefit of any relevant doubt. The practical effect of that is to give the claimant a fair wind in establishing the value of what he has lost.'[4]

The court held that the fair wind was to be applied in the context of *Browning* because the claimants had succeeded in showing that they had lost something of value due to the solicitor's negligence, namely their counterclaim. It is respectfully submitted, however, that this passage does not answer the question of why a claimant whose case does not fall within *Mount* principles (2) and (3) should receive the benefit of any doubt. Perhaps it is simply because of the gravity of the solicitor's error in allowing the claim to be struck out. But this is not altogether convincing either: claimants who prove grave breaches of duty in other areas of the law still have to prove causation without the benefit of rebuttable presumptions that they have suffered loss. Perhaps the best answer is that, if the defendant deprives the claimant of an action in circumstances where the prospects of success in the action cannot be known, then the court will be generous toward the claimant in assessing the value of the claim.[5]

1 (1722) 1 Str 505.
2 [2005] EWCA Civ 735; see [205] and [210] in the transcript, available on Lawtel: the report at [2005] PNLR 44 is only 1 page long. For a summary of the facts see the headnote of the first instance decision: [2004] PNLR 28.
3 Sc: with Simon Brown LJ's statements in *Mount* and *Sharif*.
4 Compare *Feakins v Burstow* [2005] EWHC QB 1931, [2006] PNLR 6, per Jack J at [80]: 'The reason for a level of generosity is simply that it is the defendant's negligence which has lost the claimant his opportunity.' If that is the reason, it is not clear why it applies in lost litigation cases but not in all other cases where solicitors lose clients opportunities.
5 See *Phillips & Co v Whatley* [2007] UKPC 28, [2007] PNLR 27, at [45]. Compare the discussion of *Fairchild v Glenhaven Funeral Services Ltd* [2002] UKHL 22, [2003] 1 AC 32, at paras 3.06 above.

(3) Nature of assessment of value of lost claim

12.42 In *Kitchen, Hanif v Middleweeks*[1] the claimant's counterclaim had been struck out for want of prosecution due his solicitor's negligence. The claimant had made an insurance claim arising from a fire and the insurers had contended that the claimant's partner had started the fire. Mance LJ, with whom Roch LJ agreed, held that in assessing the value of the claimant's lost counterclaim the trial judge should not seek to try out the original action, as if he or she had been the trial judge at a notional trial on the assumption that the counterclaim had not been struck out. He said that[2]:

'if the evidence or the law is so clear that the subsequent court can treat the prospects as overwhelming or negligible, then the claim against the negligent professional may be assessed at 100% or nil ... the judge's role here ... was to assess whether there were any, and if so what, significant prospects under the original counterclaim ... I consider that what [the judge] was doing was consistent with the task which he had set himself: working through the material before him with the single aim of coming to an ultimate conclusion as to the prospects of success on a trial in 1995. I think it is wrong to treat him as having assumed the role of deciding on the material before him what was the actual position regarding arson. Furthermore, if he had assumed that role, then I consider that he would, in the light of accepted principle and authority, have been wrong *in this case* to do so.' [Emphasis supplied]

Note the italicised words: Mance LJ was not saying that the approach set out in *Hanif* would necessarily be correct in every case. The reason for holding that the judge would have been wrong, on the facts of *Hanif*, to try the original action as if he were the notional original trial judge was that the material before the judge was much more limited than what a trial judge might have seen: there was no forensic evidence about causation of the fire, and much of the evidence which the judge did see was contained only in written witness statements without cross-examination, which might have put it in a different light. Further, the insurers might have made a settlement offer, which if accepted would have represented the value of the claim.[2]

1 [2000] Lloyd's Rep PN 920. See [15], [18] and [29]. Applied: *Sharpe v Addison* (above), *Dixon v Clement Jones* [2004] EWCA Civ 1005, [2005] PNLR 6, *Phillips & Co v Whatley* (above). It is open to question whether this approach was applied in *Hatswell v Goldbergs* [2001] EWCA Civ 2084, [2002] Lloyd's Rep PN 359, CA, but it appears that *Hanif* may not have been cited.
2 [18]–[21].

12.43 Some of the factors suggesting that the professional negligence judge should not try out the action will not apply in every case, but others, such as the possibility of settlement, probably will. The weight of authority quoted in fn 1 to para 12.42 suggests that generally speaking a professional negligence judge should not try out the original action or even come close to doing so. In *Sharif v Garrett*[1] Tucker J had struck out the original action for want of prosecution on the basis that it would in 1992 have been 'impossible to investigate' essential elements of the action. The Court of Appeal held that, in those circumstances, it would have been wrong for the judge trying the professional negligence action to act as if he were trying those same issues in 1999: 'the judge fell into the error of seeking to try the very issue which Tucker J had held, some seven years earlier, could not be the subject of a fair trial'.[2] Instead, applying *Mount* principle 4, the professional negligence judge had to[3]:

'put a value on the claim. This is not a science, but it is a task which lawyers are used to performing. The judge will obviously need to consider all the relevant material which was available up to the time when the original claim was struck out, including documents disclosed and witness statements exchanged by the other side. If he is asked to hear the evidence which the other side would have called, or expert evidence of the kind called in this case, he may agree to do so but I do not think he should feel bound to do so if he thinks he can otherwise make a fair evaluation. If he does hear such evidence, it would simply be for the purpose of enabling him to form a better broad view of the merits of the claim.'

1 [2001] EWCA Civ 1269, [2002] 1 WLR 3118.
2 Per Chadwick LJ at [36].
3 Per Tuckey LJ at [22].

12.44   Also in *Sharif*[1], however, Simon Brown LJ approved a passage from *Harrison v Bloom Camillin*[2], where the claimant's claim had been lost because their solicitor failed to serve the writ in time, in which Neuberger J indicated that there might be circumstances in which a court would be prepared to look at the prospects of success in considerable detail. This was because there was a considerable volume of evidence and argument available to the judge trying the professional negligence action, the delay since the notional trial was relatively short, and some of the delay had been the claimants' fault. On the other hand, Neuberger J said that[2]:

'... it would be wrong to be too ready to make firm findings as to what the court would have decided in the action on at least some of the issues which have been debated. First, it may be wrong in principle to do so because an issue might well be arguable either way even if I have a view on it[3]. Secondly, the oral and documentary evidence available to me is, I am satisfied, less than would have been available in the action. On witnesses, I did not hear from some witnesses whom I believe would have been called in the action. Also, a further 2½ years, while not substantial, is a significant period during which memories can be expected to weaken. Some of the documentation which would have been available in the action but was not available to me could be crucial.'

It is submitted that this passage reflects the correct approach. The court will not re-try the issue, but the extent to which it will consider the issues in detail, as opposed to with a broad brush, will depend on the extent to which the evidence which it has is the same as the evidence which would have been available at a notional trial which would have occurred if there had been no breach of duty.

1 [2001] EWCA Civ 1269, [2002] 1 WLR 3118 at [43].
2 [2000] Lloyd's Rep PN 89 at 99.
3 See Rix LJ's observations to the same effect at [45] in *Dixon v Clement Jones* [2004] EWCA Civ 1005, [2005] PNLR 6: an issue may strike different judges in different ways.

12.45   In cases where the claimant succeeds in showing that he or she has lost something of real rather than negligible value, after deciding on the extent to which the assessment should come close to holding a trial within a trial, how should the judge make the assessment? In *Sharpe v Addison*[1], Chadwick LJ suggested that this required the consideration of two factors:

> 'First, in what sum would judgment have been given if the earlier proceedings had proceeded to trial? And, second, what discount, if any, should be applied to that sum in order to reflect the uncertainty (inherent in any litigation to a greater or lesser degree) that a claim which has a real prospect of success may nevertheless, in the event, fail?'

In *Browning v Brachers (Damages)*[2], Jonathan Parker LJ described the trial judge (Jack J)'s approach of assessing damages for the loss of a chance in claims against solicitors for lost litigation as ' an entirely legitimate approach, provided of course that in addressing each of the two stages due regard is had to the *Armory v Delamirie* presumption'. Jack J's approach was as follows[3]:

> 'Where the claimant's chances of success on liability at the notional trial are in dispute and what he might then have recovered by way of damages at the notional trial is also in dispute, in my judgment the first dispute is to be resolved by determining the chances of success by way of a percentage. The second dispute is to be resolved by determining the figure representing damages which it is most probable that the claimant would have recovered if he had succeeded on liability. By "most probable" I mean the figure more probable than any other figure. That figure is then reduced by the percentage to reflect the risk of failure on liability. That provides the best estimate, which the court can make, of what the claimant has lost through his solicitor's negligence. Where there are separate claims or cross-claims, it may be appropriate to carry out the exercise separately in respect of each.
>
> It cannot be right to approach the assessment of the chances of success on damages as opposed to liability in the same manner as the assessment of the chances of success on liability. Take as an example a claim for £1 million damages by way of loss of profits. It may become clear that the figure of £1 million is inflated and that the claimant had no chance of recovering that amount. On a percentage basis he would then recover nothing. He might have some chance of getting as much as £800,000, a good chance of getting £600,000 and some chance of getting as little as £400,000, all depending on what view the judge at the notional trial took of the facts and the application of the law to those facts. If it appears that the figure that is most probable is £600,000, then that is to be taken as the figure for damages.'

While it is clear that different approaches may be taken in different cases, it is submitted that this is a helpful way of dealing with cases where there are uncertainties as to both liability and quantum. In the example, if the most probable figure for damages was £600,000, and there was a 10% chance of success on liability, then presumably the total damages award would be 10% of £600,000, so £60,000. On the other hand, Jonathan Parker LJ did not say that this was the only legitimate approach to the assessment of damages. There might be cases in which it was appropriate to award damages for both (i) a 10% chance of being awarded £1m and (ii) a 50% chance of being awarded £100,000.

1 [2003] EWCA Civ 1189, [2004] PNLR 23 at [45].
2 [2005] EWCA Civ 735, at [212].
3 *Browning v Brachers* [2004] EWHC (QB) 16, [2004] PNLR 28, at [20]–[21].

(b) Underlying claim settled but solicitor's negligence caused settlement at undervalue

12.46 *Ogilvy & Mather Ltd v Rubinstein Callingham Polden & Gale*[1] was a claim in which the claimant alleged that the defendant solicitors' negligence meant that he had achieved a worse settlement than he would have done in the absence of negligence. Simon Brown LJ, author of the *Mount* principles, said this:

'... if courts too readily hold this sort of loss of chance claim established then a large number of professional indemnity claims must be expected to follow. It can often be said that a party's settlement prospects could and should have been improved and/or accelerated by their solicitor taking some step or another in the proceedings. The reasons why parties settle are many and various. It will seldom be possible to demonstrate any certainties in the matter. The scope for argument will be well-nigh limitless. If satellite litigation is to be kept in check claims like this should be treated with some circumspection.'

This would appear to suggest that, in this type of case, it may be harder for claimants to demonstrate that the defendant solicitor's negligence has caused them to lose anything of value.

1 20 July 1999, unreported, CA.

12.47 More recently, in *Somatra Ltd v Sinclair Roche & Temperley*[1], the underlying action was a complicated and well-documented shipping claim against insurers. Somatra's case was that, as a result of numerous breaches of duty on the part of its litigation solicitors, Sinclair Roche & Temperley ('SRT'), Somatra lost all confidence in SRT a matter of weeks before trial; although it had subsequently settled the litigation, Somatra sued SRT and contended that the settlement had been at a much lower level than it would have been if SRT had not breached its duty. At first instance, Morison J found that various breaches of duty which SRT owed Somatra as its litigation solicitors were proved. He therefore had to consider what loss SRT's breaches had caused Somatra. In doing so, he recorded a submission that *Somatra* was an unusual case in that, by the time Somatra decided to try to settle because of its loss of confidence in SRT[1]:

> ' "all the evidence had been exchanged, ... trial bundles had been agreed and when all discussions were taking place between leading counsel on both sides as to speeches, timings and order of witnesses."

> Thus, say Somatra, this is not a case where the court is faced with the usual high degree of speculation where a case has been struck out for want of prosecution ... "in the present case, the precise arguments in play between the parties and the evidence which would have been relied upon in support of them are all before the court in their final developed form. Very little speculation remains as to what the claim was or, more importantly, as to what would have occurred at trial." '

Morison J appears to have accepted this submission, because he concluded that, in the absence of breach of duty, the claim would have settled with a payment to Somatra of 75% of its total claim as opposed to the 66% which it in fact achieved. Other than the fleeting reference to the position in cases that had been struck out for want of prosecution in the passage quoted, he did not make further reference to the *Mount* line of authority, and presumably concluded that it was not relevant in a case such as *Somatra* where, first, the claimant had not lost any chance of trial or settlement as a result of the solicitor's negligence, and secondly he knew so much about what the evidence would have been at trial. Although the case went to appeal, the judgments in the Court of Appeal[2] contain no discussion of the *Mount* line of authority either, so presumably it was accepted by all that Morison J's approach to this part of the case was correct.[3] It is submitted that, if that was Morison J's approach, then following the analysis of the *Mount* line of authority above, it was correct: the *Mount* line of cases does not directly apply where the effect of the solicitor's negligence is not to cause the client to lose any hope of trial or settlement.[4]

1 [2002] EWHC 1627 (Comm). See [256].
2 [2003] EWCA Civ 1474, [2003] 2 Lloyd's Rep 855.
3 The authorities on loss of a chance were summarised in four propositions at [77], at p 870 col 1 of the report, but there is no reference to the principles in *Mount*.
4 See also *Griffin v Kingsmill* [2001] EWCA Civ 934, [2001] Lloyd's Rep PN 716. Negligent undersettlement of personal injury claim; no reference to *Mount* principles in determining what would have happened in the absence of negligence, though *Mount* does not appear to have been cited.

12.48   *Hickman v Blake Lapthorn*[1] was another under-settlement case. Mr Hickman had a personal injury claim arising out of a road traffic accident. The negligent driver had no insurance. Mr Hickman instructed the defendants to bring a claim, which they did against the Motor Insurers' Bureau ('MIB'). The claim was fixed for a trial of liability only. Just before the trial started, the MIB made a settlement offer. Counsel and solicitors advised that it be accepted, negligently because they ignored the possibility that Mr Hickman might never be able to work again. Mr Hickman sued his solicitors and counsel, and proved negligence and that he had lost something of real value, namely the chance of a better settlement. In assessing loss, Jack J referred to *Mount*, said that insofar as it was more difficult for Mr Hickman to establish his loss that difficulty should not count against him but rather against his lawyers because their negligence had caused the delay in the trial, and quoted Jonathan Parker's statement in *Browning v Brachers (Damages)*[2] that the claimant should be given a fair wind in assessing the value of what he had lost. On one view, however, this ignores the point that in *Mount* Simon Brown LJ's principles were said to apply to cases which had been struck out for want of prosecution, whereas Hickman was not such a case: Mr Hickman did have a settlement, but he contended that it was at too low a figure.

1   [2005] EWHC QB 2714, [2006] PNLR 20. See [62].
2   [2004] EWHC (QB) 16, [2004] PNLR 28.

12.49   The *Mount* line of authority appears to have been distinguished in *Somatra*, though only on the basis that in *Somatra* the judge trying the professional negligence action had almost as much information as if he had been trying the original action. This perhaps provides an explanation for the judge's approach in *Hickman*. In *Hickman*, the question of assessing loss arose only after negligence had been proved. By that stage, therefore, it had been shown that solicitors and counsel had negligently ignored the possibility that as a result of the accident Mr Hickman might never work again. The claim settled for £70,000 even though the defendant solicitors had told the Legal Aid Board that it was worth around £500,000. Before assessing loss, the trial judge had already concluded that solicitors and counsel had acted negligently in ignoring the question of compensation for future loss. One might therefore argue that, as to the part of Mr Hickman's claim relating to compensation on the ground that he might never work again, the effect of the negligence was to lose Mr Hickman any hope of compensation for it, so that, as to that part of his claim, the effect of the negligence was similar to allowing a claim to be struck out. If, for example, he had failed to serve expert evidence in relation to his chances of working again, and that part of his claim had been struck out, the effect on him might have been the same. Hence one might say that the case is analogous with the *Mount* line of authority. Further, part of the effect of the lawyers' negligence was that the case was settled at a relatively early stage; there was still scope for considerable uncertainty and speculation as to the final evidence on quantum; so there was uncertainty and this was probably the fault of the defendant lawyers, so there was a basis for concluding that such uncertainty should count against the defendants rather than the claimant. It is submitted, however, that these considerations will not necessarily be the same in every claim where it is alleged that lawyers undersettled a claimant's claim: see *Somatra*. It should not, therefore, be assumed that the *Mount* principles apply with full force to every such case. Claimants who have proved significant negligence on the part of defendants often find that in practice they have a fair wind on causation, but this has not been elevated into a principle of law that applies in all cases.

(c) *Underlying claim tried but solicitor's negligence caused claimant to achieve worse result*

12.50 A similar point may be made in relation to this third category of case. If the contentions suggested above are accepted, then, in a case where a claimant alleges that a solicitor's negligence has caused his or her case to be presented in a weaker way at trial than it should have been, it does not automatically follow that the *Mount* line of cases applies with full vigour. In *Channon v Lindley Johnstone*[1] the claimant alleged that his response to his former wife's claim for ancillary relief had been poorly presented before the district judge deciding the ancillary relief claim. The claimant sued his solicitors for negligence, alleging that if his case had been better presented he would have achieved a better result. The judgments in the Court of Appeal contain no mention of *Mount* or cases following it, indeed at one point Potter LJ stated that the judge trying the professional negligence action should have assessed an issue 'as if himself sitting at first instance and apprised of all the facts which should have been before the district judge'. With respect, it is thought that this runs contrary to the cases so far discussed, which do not appear to have been cited. Further, the court in *Channon* did not appear to give the claimant an especially fair wind in assessing his loss.

1 [2002] EWCA Civ 353, [2002] PNLR 343, CA. See esp [41], though also [45] and [48] for an *Allied Maples*-style discounting exercise.

12.51 On the other hand, in *Feakins v Burstow*[1] in earlier litigation F had sued IBAP. B was a solicitor who acted for F. IBAP brought a counterclaim against F. The court awarded IBAP summary judgment on the counterclaim. F sued B, contending that a defence to the counterclaim had been raised too late, as a result of which the judge had refused permission to rely on it. The trial judge in the professional negligence action was again Jack J. He said that save as to one point there was no dispute among counsel as to the applicable principles, and then referred to *Mount*[2] and *Browning v Brachers* (*Damages*).[3] The one point of dispute was as to whether the *Armory v Delamirie* principle should apply in a case where the solicitor had not advised that the claim had good prospects of success. Jack J held that it should: 'the reason for a level of generosity is simply that it is the defendant's negligence which has lost the claimant his opportunity.

I refer to the quotation from *Mount*'. The judge must therefore have accepted that *Mount* applied to a case which, unlike *Mount*, did not arise from negligence leading to the striking out of a claim. Perhaps his reasoning was similar to what was suggested in para 12.49: the solicitors' negligence led to a particular part of the claimant's claim being lost; the whole of that part of the claim was lost; hence it is as if that part of the claim had been struck out for procedural default such as want of prosecution; hence the claim is analogous to *Mount*. This approach would explain why the *Mount* line of cases was applied in *Feakins* but not in *Channon*.[4] It would suggest that *Mount* does apply if procedural default means that a claimant loses any opportunity to advance a whole head of loss at trial, but does not apply if the claimant's contention is simply that his or her case was not presented as well at trial as it could have been. More authority would be helpful in order to clarify whether this is the correct interpretation.

1 [2005] EWHC QB 1931, [2006] PNLR 6, at [78]–[80], [88]–[90].
2 [1998] PNLR 493.
3 [2004] EWHC (QB) 16, [2004] PNLR 28.
4 An alternative explanation might be that *Mount* was not cited in *Channon*.

2   Would claimant have proceeded with the action?

12.52   We turn now to consider more specific points on the application of the general principles. In a case where the effect of the negligence is to deprive the claimant of the whole claim, or a specific part of it, the first question will generally be: if there had been no breach of duty, would the claimant have proceeded either to trial or to a settlement?[1] The claimant must prove this, or recover nothing. It must be proved on the balance of probabilities.[2] It is open to the defendant to contend that the claimant would not have proceeded, on the ground that the claimant could not have funded the costs of the action. In relation to publicly-funded claimants, if the defendant can prove that the claimant obtained public funding only by dishonesty then the court will proceed on the assumption that there would have been no public funding. As is normal in relation to proving dishonesty, the court will require evidence showing a higher standard of probability than it would simply to prove negligence.[3] As mentioned above, in relation to the loss of civil litigation, two possibilities are likely to arise: either the case would have been fought to trial, or it would have settled. We now consider these two possibilities, and then the position in relation to criminal litigation. We have already considered the position of parties who have in fact settled but contend that in the absence of negligence they would have had a better settlement or parties who have in fact gone to trial but contend that in the absence of negligence they would have achieved a better result at trial.

1 *Harrison v Bloom Camillin* [2000] Lloyd's Rep PN 89, per Neuberger J at p 93 col 1.
2 [2000] Lloyd's Rep PN 89 at 100 col 1.
3 [2000] Lloyd's Rep PN 89 at 100–101.

3   Trial or settlement?

12.53   Assuming, in a civil case, that in the absence of negligence the claimant would have proceeded, the next question is whether the trial would have fought or settled. As discussed above, however, even if one assumes that the claim would have fought, the exercise of quantifying its value involves a discounting approach which, unless there is evidence specific to the individual case which suggests that it would have settled for unusual reasons, is similar to the exercise which lawyers on either side would be likely to carry out when assessing the value of the claim for settlement purposes. So in many cases the exercise of working out the figure at which the claim would have settled will be similar to working out its value on the assumption that it would have gone to trial.[1] Thus, for example in *Dixon v Clement-Jones*, Rix LJ considered first the value of the claim if it had gone to trial and then as a cross-check whether the claim would have been settled at 'real value'.[2]

1 *Harrison* [2000] Lloyd's Rep PN 89 at 95–96.
2 [2004] EWCA Civ 1005, [2005] PNLR 6 at [47].

12.54   Although settlements tend be calculated by reference to what the parties think the court would award at trial, there may be subjective factors, specific to the parties, which would have determined their attitudes to a settlement. There may, for instance, be reasons why one party would have been keen to be extricated from the litigation quickly but at a higher price. All will depend on the evidence. In *Dickinson* v *Jones Alexander & Co,*[1] a claim relating to ancillary relief proceedings, Douglas Brown J considered that it was very unlikely that the husband would have compromised the wife's claim, so he ignored the possibility of settlement and looked simply to what the court would have awarded at a hearing. On the other hand, in *McNamara v Martin Mears & Co,*[2] another claim relating to ancillary relief proceedings, Peter Pain J considered that the most likely outcome would have been that the husband *would* have settled, though at a figure which represented accurately the value of the claim. Thus he concentrated on what would have happened if the case had settled. But in *Griffin v Kingsmill*[3], which related to the under-settlement of a personal injury claim, Stuart-Smith LJ held that the amount at which the claim would have been settled should be reduced by 5% because the infant claimant's mother was particularly cautious and would have settled at a lower level than the claim was worth. Further, in *Brinn v Russell Jones & Walker*[4], where defendants failed to serve a claim form alleging libel within the period of its validity and the claim became statute-barred, the claimants would have reduced their settlement requirements because they would have realised that the original defendant had little money, so damages were reduced.

1 [1993] 2 FLR 521 (Douglas Brown J). See also *Cook v Swinfen* [1967] 1 WLR 457 (Lawton J).
2 (1982) 127 Sol Jo 69 (Peter Pain J), and see the transcript, pp 16–17.
3 [2001] EWCA Civ 934, [2001] Lloyd's Rep PN 716, at [105].
4 [2002] EWHC Civ 2727 (QB), [2003] Lloyd's Rep PN 70 (Gray J).

4   Civil cases: loss of a trial

(*a*) *Notional trial date*

12.55   The first question is when, if there had been no negligence, the trial would have taken place. Assessing this is likely to be more a matter of the trial judge's experience than the subject of much evidence[1], but note that the date selected may be of significance in relation the evidence that would have been available at trial.

1 In *Harrison* [2000] Lloyd's Rep PN 89, Neuberger J declined to apply average timings contained in the Woolf Report.

(*b*) *Evidence which would have been available at trial*

12.56   The court must consider what the evidence would have been at the notional trial. A party is not entitled to be awarded, in a professional negligence action for the loss of litigation, sums to which, had there been proper disclosure at the notional trial, he or she would never have been entitled.[1] Further, as previously discussed, to the extent that it is unclear what the evidence at trial would have been due to delay caused by the defendant solicitor, this is likely to be to the benefit of the claimant and the court will give the claimant the benefit of any doubt. A difficult problem arises, however, in relation to the case where it appears that, at the notional trial, the evidence would have been to one effect, for example that the claimant might never work again due to the accident caused by the original defendant, but that by the time of the professional negligence trial new evidence would have emerged, for example to the effect that the claimant would have been completely cured. Or the evidence may be to the opposite effect: at the notional trial, that the original accident had caused relatively little damage, but at the professional negligence trial to the effect that the claimant will never work again. The question is whether, in either case, the professional negligence judge should take account of the new evidence.

1 *Green v Collyer-Bristow* [1999] Lloyd's Rep PN 798, per Douglas Brown J at 813 col 1. The principle was there expressed to relate only to ancillary relief, which was in issue in the case, but it is thought that it should be of general application.

12.57   In principle, the correct answer must be that the professional negligence court is compensating the claimant for what he or she lost by losing out on having a trial. If, at the notional trial, there would have been no evidence at all as to the new condition, so that the notional trial judge could not have taken it into account, then in principle the professional negligence judge should ignore it. The claimant might have been over-compensated at the notional trial, but, but for the defendant's negligence, the claimant would indeed have been over-compensated, and so is entitled to received that over-compensation as damages for the loss of the original trial. This approach has been taken in Scotland.[1]

1 *Campbell (or Pearson) v Imray* [2004] PNLR 1.

12.58 The English courts have adopted a more pragmatic approach. It is undesirable that a claimant who has in fact recovered and is now healthy should be compensated as if unable to work for a lifetime, or indeed that a claimant who in fact will not work for a lifetime should be compensated only for a short illness. The courts have thus been keen to take account of evidence known about at the time of the professional negligence trial but which might not have been known of at the time of the original trial. In *Charles v Hugh James Jones & Jenkins*[1] Swinton Thomas LJ said:

> 'I would be prepared to accept that if some entirely new condition which can be attributed to the accident manifests itself for the first time after the notional trial date it may be that it has to be ignored. I would wish to reserve any final opinion in relation to that. However, in contrast, if a condition has manifested itself prior to the notional trial but the prognosis was somewhat uncertain at that trial date, in my judgment the judge is entitled to, and indeed should, take into account what has in fact occurred.'

On the facts, it was held that *Charles* fell into the latter category, so it was unnecessary to consider the former category in detail.

1 [2000] 1 WLR 1278, 1290G–H, CA. Robert Walker LJ agreed and Sir Richard Scott V-C reserved his position in the same way as Swinton Thomas LJ.

12.59 *Charles* was discussed in *Dudarec v Andrews*[1]. Again, the Court of Appeal did not have to deal with the extreme form of the problem. Commenting on *Charles*, Waller LJ said that it was:

> '... authority for the proposition that if the further evidence which becomes available should, if the solicitors had not been negligent, have been available at the trial to assist the claimant's case, it can be taken into account to the advantage of the claimant. Swinton Thomas LJ was also clearly of the view (although that view was obiter) that if the medical evidence at the original trial date would only have indicated a strong possibility as to something, and by the date of the negligence action the result was known, the known result should prevail. He was also of that view if the result was to limit the claimant's damages on the basis that the claimant in that way would recover what he had actually lost as opposed to obtaining a windfall. This is a view with which Robert Walker LJ seemed to agree, but it is less clear whether Sir Richard Scott V-C did.'

Sedley LJ distinguished between facts which were discoverable but unknown at the notional trial date and those which were at that stage both unknown and unknowable. He appeared to concede that facts which were unknowable at the time of the notional trial in the underlying action might have to be ignored in assessing damages for professional negligence, but considered that facts that were unknown but capable of being known could be taken into account, on the basis that they should have been known by the notional trial date. Smith LJ said that unless new evidence 'relates to some entirely new matter which could not possibly have been known about at the date of the notional trial, the facts as they have since turned out should be taken into account by the trial judge'.[2] Although it was not necessary to decide the point, it looks[3] as if she might have been prepared even for facts of that kind to be taken into account. It therefore appears that the court will generally be keen to take into account important new facts which emerge after the defendant's solicitor's negligence, and will if possible hold that a competent solicitor for either party should have obtained such evidence in time for the notional trial. This approach appears to be intended to lead to fair results rather than necessarily complying strictly with the principle underlying compensation in this type of case.

1 [2006] EWCA Civ 256, [2006] 1 WLR 3002. See [33], [57] and [64].
2 For a case where the court did ignore evidence of an entirely new condition which would not have been available at the notional trial, see *Jones v Hibbert Pownall & Newton* (26 March 2002, unreported), (McCombe J), at [37]–[38].
3 [64].

(c) State of law at notional trial date

12.60 In *Harrison*[1], Neuberger J considered how the court should deal with a pure point of law that might have arisen at the notional trial. He held that issues of law should be assessed on a loss of a chance basis, as with issues of fact, but that in general the court should be far more ready to determine that the claimant would have failed or succeeded on a point of law than on a point of fact or opinion. He assessed damages on the basis of the House of Lords' decision in *SAAMCo v York Montague*[2], even though at the notional trial date *SAAMCo* had not yet reached the House of Lords. This was on the basis that the House of Lords' decision was not intended to be a departure from the past, and that it was possible that if damages had not been assessed in accordance with the principles in *SAAMCo* then either party might have appealed and by the time of the notional appeal *SAAMCo* would have been decided in the House of Lords and applied. It appears that, as in the context of important new evidence, just considered, the professional negligence court may be keen to apply the law as it stands at the time of the professional negligence judgment even if this is different from the law as it stood at the time of the notional trial.[3]

1 [2000] Lloyd's Rep PN 89 at 98–99.

2 [1997] AC 191.
3 See also *Knight v Haynes Duffell, Kentish & Co* [2003] EWCA Civ 223, where it was held that the law was clear so that it was inappropriate to apply a discount for the chance that a judge would have misapplied it.

(d) Interaction of risks

12.61 The court may conclude that the chances of success as to different heads of loss are different, and may therefore apply different discounts to the different heads of damage.[1] A different problem arises where the claimant has to overcome two different hurdles in order to succeed. If the claimant has a 20% chance of overcoming the first and a 50% chance of overcoming the second, then one approach is simply to multiply the two chances in order to arrive at a 10% chance of overcoming both.[2] But this approach may be too simple if there is a common issue, such as the claimant's credibility, which may impact on both chances. This was the case in *Hanif v Middleweeks*.[3] The claimant and his partner Mr Sheikh operated a nightclub. It burned down and an insurance claim was made. The insurers sought a declaration that the claimant was not entitled to an indemnity under the policy. They relied on three separate points. Each of the three issues had a common factor, namely the credibility of the claimant. The claimant counterclaimed for an indemnity but the counterclaim was struck out due to the solicitors' negligence. The Court of Appeal held that it was wrong simply to multiply the claimant's chances of success on each of the three issues: if the claimant succeeded on the principal issue, he was more likely to succeed on the others. This accords with trial experience which suggests that, once a judge has decided one point against a party, the judge may form a sceptical view of that party and be inclined to decide other points against him or her too.[4]

1 [2000] Lloyd's Rep PN 89 at 96 col 2.
2 See e g *Harrison v Bloom Camillin (No 2)* [2000] Lloyd's Rep PN 404.
3 [2000] Lloyd's Rep PN 920, CA.
4 Evans 'Lies, Damned Lies, and the Loss of a Chance' [2006] PN 99.

(e) Litigation risk

12.62 In *Charles*[1], the Court of Appeal rejected an argument that in every case there is a risk of failure, so that in every case there should be a deduction from the value of the claim on account of the claimant's risk of losing. It accepted that such deductions could be made if there was evidence to support them on the specific facts of the case. For a case in which there was such evidence, see *Griffin v Kingsmill*.[2]

1 [2000] 1 WLR 1278, CA, at 1294–5.
2 [2001] EWCA Civ 934, [2001] Lloyd's Rep PN 716.

(*f*) *Nominal damages*

12.63 If the claim would have been hopeless, or, in Simon Brown LJ's words, if it would have had a negligible prospect of success, then only nominal damages will be awarded[1] and, as mentioned in the passage quoted from Lord Evershed above,[2] the claimant should not be awarded damages for the nuisance value of the claim. Similarly, if a case in fact settled but the claimant alleges that it should not have been settled and that, if it had fought, more would have been awarded at trial, there will be nominal damages if more would not have been awarded at trial.[3] Again, if solicitors negligently fail to advise a claimant as to the claimant's rights in the event of legal aid being withdrawn, the claimant will recover only nominal damages if, had there been no negligence, legal aid would not have been reinstated and, had it been reinstated, he or she would have had no real prospect of success at trial.[4] *Mount*[5] itself was a case where there was no real chance of success. *Hatswell v Goldbergs*[6] is a more recent example of this, albeit a striking one, since medical records were said to have destroyed the credibility of witnesses who gave oral evidence.

1 See, for example, *Buckley v National Union of General and Municipal Workers* [1967] 3 All ER 767 (Nield J).
2 Para 12.28.
3 *Green v Cunningham John & Co* (1995) 46 Con LR 62, CA.
4 *Casey v Hugh James Jones & Jenkins* [1999] Lloyd's Rep PN 115 (Thomas J).
5 [1998] PNLR 493, CA.
6 [2001] EWCA Civ 2084, [2002] Lloyd's Rep PN 359.

(*g*) *Strong cases*

12.64 One might think that even the strongest case is not free from risk, and so one would imagine that it would be a rare case in which the court would award the claimant the full sum that it considers he or she could have hoped to achieve, at best, at trial. But in *Dickinson v Jones Alexander & Co*,[1] Douglas Brown J rejected the notion of any discount, on the basis that the husband would not have settled, and that there was no, or only a negligible, risk of the wife obtaining anything less than the proper award. It is thought that this will be the right approach only where there can be very little doubt as to the correct amount of damages.

1 [1993] 2 FLR 521.

(*h*) *Intermediate cases*

12.65 It is doubtful whether, once the principles on which loss is to be assessed have been established, the citation of authority can help much, especially in relation to intermediate cases. Each case turns on its facts, so the assessment of the probabilities in any given case will depend on the facts of that case and not of others.[1] It would, however, appear to follow from the analysis of general principles above that if cases are to be valued essentially in terms of their settlement value then most cases that come close to trial of the professional negligence action will fall into this intermediate category, where there is something to be said for each side's arguments.

1 Some examples are: *Yardley v Coombes* (1963) 107 Sol Jo 575 (Edmund-Davies J) – employers' liability claim, chance assessed at one third; *Gregory v Tarlo* (1964) 108 Sol Jo 219 (McNair J) – employers' liability claim, chance assessed at 75%; *Malyon* v *Lawrance, Messer & Co* [1968] 2 Lloyd's Rep 539 (Brabin J) – road accident in West Germany, assessment of likely damages in German court, 50% reduction for likely contributory negligence finding; *Gascoine v Ian Sheridan & Co* [1994] 5 Med LR 437 (Mitchell J) – medical negligence claim, chance assessed at 60%.

(*i*) *Appeals*

12.66   In some cases the court has to make an assessment of the outcome of not one but two hypothetical further hearings. Thus, in *Corfield v DS Bosher & Co,*[1] the claimant's case was that the defendant's negligence had caused him to lose the opportunity to appeal from the award of an arbitrator to the Commercial Court; further, if the appeal had taken place, the Commercial Court would have remitted the matter back for hearing before a fresh arbitrator. Thus the court had to assess the likely outcome of both the appeal hearing and the hearing before the fresh arbitrator, and discount the claimant's claim for the risk of failure at both stages. While this may be complicated, it is of course similar to the exercise that lawyers have to undertake in advising clients of the likely outcome of an appeal which, if allowed, would lead to the case being remitted for a further hearing. This is difficult but not impossible.[2]

1 [1992] 1 EGLR 163 (Judge Crawford QC sitting as a deputy High Court judge).
2 Cf *Motor Crown Petroleum Ltd v SJ Berwin & Co* [2000] Lloyd's Rep PN 438, CA (loss of planning appeal).

(*j*) *Costs*

12.67   The courts seem generally to have ignored the incidence of costs in assessing damages for the loss of a trial.[1] The court should approach the matter in the same way as an advocate advising a client on the prospects of settling the case. If the claim was for a maximum award of £100,000, and there was a 90% chance of success, then there was a 10% chance that the claimant would have lost and had to pay the defendant's costs. Ignoring for the moment the element of costs which would not be recovered on assessment, if the claimant had won the £100,000 then he or she would have had his or her own costs paid by the defendant. If costs on both sides would have been £10,000 each, then what the claimant has lost is a 90% chance of winning £100,000 and having to pay no costs, but he or she has also escaped a 10% risk of winning nothing and having to pay both sides' costs (£20,000). The value of what the claimant has lost can be expressed as (90% x £100,000 = £90,000) – (10% x £20,000 = £2,000), giving a total of £88,000 rather than £90,000. Of course, if the prospect of winning £100,000 is only 50%, then the calculation is (50% x £100,000 = £50,000) – (50% x £20,000 = £10,000) = £40,000 rather than £50,000. But even this analysis may be too simple, if the likelihood is that the claimant would have recovered damages in a range between say £60,000 and £80,000, or if there might have been a payment into court which would have been rejected.

1 See Evans *Lawyers' Liabilities* (2nd edn, 2002) at 11–05, where the point is developed. There is some reference to costs in *Corfield v DS Bosher* & Co [1992] 1 EGLR 163 (see para 12.66, above), *McNamara v Martin Mears & Co* (1982) 127 Sol Jo 69 (see para 12.70, below) and *Port of Sheerness Ltd v Brachers* [1997] IRLR 214 (Buckley J), discussed at para 12.70, below.

12.68 Writing extra-judicially[1], Sir David Neuberger made the same point with reference to *Dixon v Clement Jones*.[2] He pointed out that, on the facts of the case, the risk of paying the other side's costs was likely to have wiped out the claimant's £60,000 in damages. Why, he asked, did the value of the costs risk not have to be deducted from the claimant's damages for the lost chance of winning at trial?

'The answer to this seems to be that one has to assess the valuation of the claim against the accountants as an asset lost as at the date of the negligence of the solicitors in that case. Carnwath LJ at 53 described Mrs Dixon as having lost something of value. In that connection, what she lost was not so much a 30% chance of a successful outcome of her claim against the accountants, but the ability to negotiate a payment from the accountants to buy off the litigation against them.'

This rationale would be consistent with the approach to valuing claims which we considered under the heading of general principles above.

1 Notes of lecture to the Professional Negligence Bar Association on 9 February 2005.
2 [2004] EWCA Civ 1005, [2005] PNLR 6.

(k) *Enforcement*

12.69 Where the claim is that, in the absence of negligence, the claimant would have had either a judgment or an agreement to pay from the other party to the lost litigation, it is necessary to consider (i) whether that party would in fact have been able to afford to pay, at the time when he or she would have been asked for the money, and (ii) whether it would have been necessary and possible to enforce the judgment, if the other party had been unwilling to pay.[1]

1 See pp 16–17 of the transcript of *McNamara v Martin Mears & Co* (1982) 127 Sol Jo 69, para 12.70, below.

5   Civil cases: losing a settlement or obtaining a worse settlement

12.70   We have already considered the general principles applicable to this type of case at para 12.46ff, above. By way of example, in *McNamara v Martin Mears & Co,*[1] Peter Pain J considered it most unlikely that, in the absence of negligence, the husband would have wished to go to court for a hearing in relation to ancillary relief. Instead, he would have made a shrewdly judged settlement offer. Thus the questions were when, and in what amount, it was likely that he would have made it. In the events that had happened, the husband had in fact made a much lower settlement offer. Damages thus comprised the difference between the amount of the settlement which was in fact offered, and that which would have been agreed in the absence of negligence, making deductions for the hazards of litigation and costs. Further, there was a deduction because, in the events that happened, the claimant had been paid earlier than she would have been if there had been no negligence. In *Port of Sheerness Ltd v Brachers,*[2] the defendants negligently advised that, if the claimant dismissed its dockers on the ground of redundancy, the only payments it would have to make would be redundancy payments. The negligence was in failing to mention the risk of unfair dismissal proceedings, which were then brought and settled for a further £10,000 per docker. Buckley J found that, if there had been no negligence, (i) the likelihood was that the claimant would have settled with the dockers for a lower sum; he assessed the value of the chance at £2,000 per docker; (ii) there was a 90% chance that proceedings would have been avoided, so the claimants were awarded 90% of the costs of those proceedings.

1 (1982) 127 Sol Jo 69 (Peter Pain J), and see the transcript; also discussed at para 12.54, above.
2 [1997] IRLR 214 (Buckley J).

12.71   In *Charles*[1], on the other hand, the original claim had been struck out. It was a road traffic accident case. Before the striking out, the claimant's solicitors had written to accept the defendant's insurers' offer of settlement for £20,000, if the money was paid within 21 days. It was not paid within 21 days so there was no binding settlement. In the professional negligence action, the defendant solicitors argued that, if the claim had not been struck out, it would have been settled for around £20,000. The Court of Appeal gave this short shrift. The solicitors had been negligent to advise accepting £20,000. The claim was in fact worth nearly £200,000. So the court ignored the possibility of settlement.

1 [2000] 1 WLR 1278, CA.

6 Criminal cases

12.72 In *Acton v Graham Pearce & Co*,[1] the claimant was himself a solicitor, who was charged with obtaining money from the Law Society by deception, on the basis that he had submitted green forms to the society for payment when he knew that they contained false information. The defendants represented him in the criminal proceedings. He instructed them that responsibility for operation of the scheme in his office had been delegated to an employee, S, and that S had been forced to leave her previous firm. He further suggested that memoranda written by S, on which the prosecution relied, were not authentic. The defendants negligently failed to submit the memoranda to an expert to check their authenticity, or to take statements from the partners of S's previous firm. The claimant was convicted. On appeal, the Court of Appeal admitted fresh evidence from both those sources, and quashed the conviction. Having held the defendants negligent, Chadwick J assessed the claim as one for damages for loss of the chances that, if the claimant had been properly represented, either the prosecution would have withdrawn the case, or he would have been acquitted at trial. He considered the various events which would have happened, and said:[2]

> 'The quantification of the value of a chance lost cannot be an exact science. The task is made more difficult when, as in the present case, the value of the chance lost depends on the evaluation of a sequence of chances; each of which contributes to the loss of a favourable outcome overall. I do not think that the task is assisted by over-refinement. The court must make the best estimate it can.'

He assessed the chances that, in the absence of negligence, the claimant would have escaped conviction at 50%.

1 [1997] 3 All ER 909 (Chadwick J).
2 [1997] 3 All ER 909 at 935.

D   RECOVERABLE DAMAGE

1   Mental distress and psychiatric illness

(a) *Mental distress*

12.73 The House of Lords reconsidered the law on the recovery of damages for mental distress in *Farley v Skinner*, which we consider below.[1] *Farley* involved a claim against surveyors. It is thought that, after *Farley*, the general rule will continue to be that damages for mental distress arising out of solicitors' breaches of duty are not recoverable. In some cases decided before *Farley*, however, it had been held that, exceptionally, such damages were recoverable against solicitors. These cases were not disapproved in *Farley* and appear to remain good law. On that basis, if solicitors negligently fail to enforce an injunction to prevent harassment, and the client is harassed further, they may be liable for this further mental distress,[2] or if their negligence causes the client wrongly to be convicted of a criminal offence, they may be liable for mental distress caused to the client who perceives himself, wrongly, to be seen as a criminal by his friends, family and acquaintances.[3] They may also be liable for mental distress if their negligence causes a client to be made bankrupt.[4] Further, if solicitors are aware that the client is suffering from an anxiety syndrome related to the litigation, and that the syndrome will probably terminate as soon as the litigation does, if their negligence causes the litigation to go on longer than necessary they may be liable for the increased period for which the anxiety syndrome is suffered.[5]

1 [2001] UKHL 49, [2002] AC 732. For the general rule as to solicitors' claims before *Farley* see *Hayes v Dodd* [1990] 2 All ER 815, CA.
2 *Heywood v Wellers* [1976] QB 446, CA.
3 *McLeish v Amoo-Gottfried & Co* (1993) 10 PN 102 (Scott Baker J).
4 *Rey v Graham and Oldham* [2000] BPIR 354 (McKinnon J).
5 *Malyon v Lawrance, Messer & Co* [1968] 2 Lloyd's Rep 539 (Brabin J).

12.74 In *Farley*, the House of Lords held that the test of whether damages were recoverable for a claimant's annoyance caused by a breach of contract was whether a major or important object of the contract was to provide 'pleasure, relaxation, or peace of mind'[1] or something akin thereto such as freedom from molestation.[2] Subsequently, in *Channon v Lindley Johnstone*[3] the Court of Appeal held that a solicitor's retainer to conduct ancillary relief proceedings did not amount to a contract that fell into this category, so that the claimant was not entitled to damages for inconvenience, distress or disappointment. In *Hamilton-Jones v David & Snape*[4], Neuberger J suggested that in cases in which the solicitor's retainer related to a purely business transaction, such as *Hayes v Dodd*[5], damages would generally not be recoverable for mental distress. He considered that *Channon* should be seen in the same light, because although the context was a matrimonial dispute the negligence in question related to financial issues, namely the quantum of ancillary relief. He contrasted the facts of *Hamilton-Jones* itself: there, the claimant retained the solicitors because she was concerned that her Tunisian husband, from whom she was separated, might take her children to Tunisia. Due to the solicitors' negligence the husband was able to take the children to Tunisia for good; the claimant was unable to persuade the Tunisian courts to order their return to her. The question was whether the claimant was entitled to damages for mental distress occasioned by the loss of the company of the children. Neuberger J held that she was[6]:

> '... a significant reason for the claimant instructing the defendants was with a view to ensuring, so far as possible, that the claimant retained custody of her children for her own pleasure and peace of mind.'

1 Per Lord Steyn at [24].
2 See per Neuberger J in *Hamilton-Jones v David Snape* [2003] EWHC 3147 (Ch), [2004] 1 WLR 924, at [61].
3 [2002] EWCA Civ 353, [2002] Lloyd's Rep PN 342 esp at [56].
4 [64].
5 [1990] 2 All ER 815, CA.
6 [61]. There was no claim for psychiatric illness as it was statute-barred.

(b) Psychiatric illness

12.75   In *McLoughlin v Jones*[1], the claimant's case was that due to the defendant solicitors' negligence he had been wrongly convicted of a criminal offence. He claimed that as a result he had suffered psychiatric illness and that the defendants should compensate him for this. After a detailed review of the authorities, the Court of Appeal held that it was arguable that the defendant solicitors owed the claimant a duty to protect him from suffering psychiatric illness if he were wrongly convicted. The matter was remitted for trial. The trial judge found that the claimant's case as to causation of the psychiatric illness was not proved, so she dismissed the claim.[2] Her comments as to foreseeability of psychiatric loss were therefore obiter, and she did not consider the issue in any detail. She considered the Court of Appeal's review of the authorities but was not satisfied that some degree of psychiatric illness was reasonably foreseeable on the facts. The claimant was a former boxer and Grenadier Guardsman. He was a robust and active builder at the time of his arrest. He had a happy marriage and a stable and supportive family, and an income and assets that should have provided for his family during imprisonment. The charges were not particularly serious. The judge concluded that to award compensation for psychiatric injury would: [3]

> 'be tantamount to saying that there is a real risk of anyone in the claimant's position facing a trial on relatively serious charges suffering psychiatric injury if wrongly imprisoned as a result of their solicitor's negligence'.

She rejected that contention. Plainly, on different facts the result might have been different.

1 [2001] EWCA Civ 1743, [2002] QB 1312.
2 *McLoughlin v Jones, Espley,& Wish, trading as Grovers* [2005] EWHC 1741 (QB), Hallett J.
3 [120].

2   Costs and CRU certificates

12.76   Where claimants claim as damages costs that they have incurred in other proceedings, the appropriate method of assessment is to ask how much the claimant would have been awarded on an assessment on the standard basis: the claimant is not entitled to recover more in the subsequent professional negligence action than he or she would have recovered in the other litigation.[1] In a personal injury claim, if the claimant has lost the chance of being awarded damages that would have been the subject of a deduction of amounts stated in a certificate from the Compensation Recovery Unit, the claimant's damages award in the later professional negligence action should be in the net amount which he or she would have recovered after any CRU deduction. This is because, in the absence of negligence, the claimant would have received only the net sum. If the net sum is awarded as professional negligence damages it will provide the correct amount of compensation, because the professional negligence damages will not be the subject of a CRU deduction.[2]

1 *Redbus LMDS Ltd v Jeffrey Green & Russell* [2006] EWHC 2938 Ch, [2006] PNLR 12.
2 *Garrett v Wilson Davies & Co*, CA, 2 October 1998, unreported.

E MITIGATION

12.77 If the effect of a solicitor's negligence is that the claimant loses the opportunity to bring or defend the claim at all, then it will not be possible for the negligent solicitor to contend that the claimant should have mitigated his or her loss by bringing alternative proceedings. There may, however, be cases where such a contention is arguable. We dealt with mitigation in the sense of bringing alternative proceedings in chapter 3.[1]

1 See para 3.62ff, above.

Part 3

Procedure

Chapter 13

Costs orders against solicitors

A   THREE BASES FOR ORDER

13.01   In addition to the risk of being sued for negligence or breach of contract by their own clients, solicitors face the possibility of orders that they pay the costs of proceedings personally. The principal jurisdiction under which the courts may make such orders in civil proceedings is the wasted costs jurisdiction, pursuant to Supreme Court Act 1981, s 51(6). Most of the discussion in this chapter relates to civil proceedings, but provisions relating to criminal proceedings are dealt with at the end of the relevant sections.

13.02   Before examining the rules as to wasted costs in detail, the court's other powers to make costs orders against solicitors should be mentioned. In *Tolstoy-Miloslavsky v Aldington*,[1] Rose LJ said that there were only three categories of case that could give rise to an order for costs against a solicitor. The first was pursuant to the wasted costs jurisdiction. The others were:

'… (ii) if it is otherwise a breach of duty to the court such as, even before the Judicature Acts, could found an order, e g if he acts, even unwittingly, without authority or in breach of an undertaking; (iii) if he acts outside the role of a solicitor, e g in a private capacity or as a true third party funder for someone else.'

This was approved by Lord Woolf MR in *Hodgson v Imperial Tobacco Ltd*[2], where he also made clear that the court should consider making an order under the second head only after it had decided whether to make a wasted costs order. Following Lord Woolf's approach, in this chapter we first deal with wasted costs orders, and only then look at Rose LJ's second and third categories of order.

1 [1996] 1 WLR 736 at 745H–746A, CA.
2 [1998] 1 WLR 1056 at 1066H, CA

B   WASTED COSTS ORDERS

13.03   Wasted costs orders provide a means whereby solicitors and barristers may be ordered to compensate either their own client, or a party to litigation other than the client for whom they act[1], for costs incurred by that party as a result of acts done or omitted by the solicitors or barristers in their conduct of the litigation. 'Wasted costs' are defined in Supreme Court Act 1981, s 51(7), the text of which appears below in para 13.05. The Court of Appeal gave detailed guidance as to most aspects of the subject in *Ridehalgh v Horsefield*[2] ('*Ridehalgh*'). In *Medcalf v Mardell*[3] Lord Bingham, delivering a speech that commanded majority support, endorsed what had been said in *Ridehalgh* subject only to the House of Lords' decision in *Hall v Simons*[4], and as to further guidance on the effect of legal professional privilege which we consider below.

1 *Medcalf v Mardell* [2002] UKHL 27, [2003] 1 AC 120.
2 [1994] Ch 205.
3 [2002] UKHL 27, [2003] 1 AC 120 at [13].
4 As to the abolition of advocates' immunity: see para 12.02ff, above.

13.04 Making an application for a wasted costs order is not straightforward. Two principal points arise: first, the court will grant such an order only in plain cases, which are capable of being dealt with quickly and in summary fashion,[1] and secondly, in cases where a party seeks a wasted costs order against another party's lawyers it is necessary to consider carefully the impact of legal professional privilege[2]. Jackson J, who had appeared as counsel in *Ridehalgh*, referred to these problems in *Lady Archer v Williams*:[3]

> 'Despite the best efforts of judges ... the true nature of the wasted costs jurisdiction is still insufficiently appreciated. This is a procedure for dealing with relatively straightforward claims which are capable of summary disposal at a proportionate cost. It is not a vehicle for mounting a complex professional negligence action in circumstances where much of the relevant evidence is obscured from the court's view.'

Or, as His Honour Michael Cook put it, 'anyone thinking of applying for a wasted costs order should think twice.'[4] These and other potential procedural pitfalls are discussed below at para 13.10ff, where we also consider cases in which applicants have successfully surmounted them. After that we deal with the substantive rules as to the circumstances in which the court will make an order. But first we look at the scope of the jurisdiction.

1 See para 13.10ff, below.
2 See para 13.16ff, below.
3 [2003] EWHC 3048 (QB), at [63].
4 *Cook on Costs 2007* at [33.7].

1   Scope

13.05 The statutory provision granting jurisdiction to make a wasted costs order is Supreme Court Act 1981, s 51 of which the relevant parts state:

'51(1) Subject to the provisions of this or any other enactment and to rules of court, the costs of and incidental to all proceedings in–

(a)   the civil division of the Court of Appeal;

(b)   the High Court; and

(c)   any county court,

shall be in the discretion of the court ...

(6) In any proceedings mentioned in subsection (1), the court may disallow or (as the case may be) order the legal or other representative concerned to meet, the whole of any wasted costs or such part of them as may be determined in accordance with the rules of court.

(7) In subsection (6), "wasted costs" means any costs incurred by a party–

(a)   as a result of any improper, unreasonable or negligent act or omission on the part of any legal representative or any employee of such a representative; or

(b)   which, in the light of any such act or omission occurring after they were incurred, the court considers it unreasonable to expect that party to pay ...

(13) In this section "legal or other representative", in relation to a party to proceedings, means any person exercising a right of audience or right to conduct litigation on his behalf.'

Section 52(2A) extends the application of these provisions to civil proceedings in the Crown Court.

13.06   Difficulties have arisen in relation to the meaning of 'legal or other representative' pursuant to s 51(13). If a lawyer does not count as a 'legal or other representative' for this purpose then there is no jurisdiction to make a wasted costs order against the lawyer, so the definition matters. In *Byrne v Sefton Health Authority*[1] the claimant instructed solicitors called Dooley in September 1989 to bring a claim in respect of an injury that had occurred in May 1989. The solicitors obtained legal aid but failed to issue proceedings within the limitation period. Eventually another firm of solicitors was instructed and issued proceedings against the defendant health authority. Those proceedings were struck out on limitation grounds. The health authority sought a wasted costs order against the first firm of solicitors, Dooley. One ground for rejecting the wasted costs application might have been that it was the other firm of solicitors, those who had issued the proceedings, rather than Dooley that had caused the health authority's wasted costs. But the Court of Appeal did not rely on that argument in rejecting the wasted costs application. Instead, it interpreted s 51(13) (of the Supreme Court Act 1981) by reference to s 119(1) of the Courts and Legal Services Act 1990. The reason for doing this was that it was the 1990 Act which had, by amendment, introduced the statutory wasted costs jurisdiction by reforming s 51 of the Supreme Court Act 1981. On that basis, a party could be a 'legal or other representative' for the purposes of making a wasted costs order only if that party had issued proceedings in court or performed functions ancillary to the issue of proceedings. The Court of Appeal held that Dooley had not taken such steps, so that there was no jurisdiction to award wasted costs against it.

1 [2001] EWCA Civ 1904, [2002] 1 WLR 775, at [28]–[29].

13.07 Subsequently, however, in *Medcalf v Mardell*[1], Lord Bingham, giving the majority speech, rejected the submission that s 51(13) of the Supreme Court Act 1981 was to be interpreted by reference to definitions imported into the 1981 Act and contained in s 119(1) of the Courts and Legal Services Act 1990. This suggests that the reasoning of *Byrne* on this point should no longer be followed. But Lord Bingham approved the result in *Byrne*.[2] The result of *Byrne* was that there was no jurisdiction to make a wasted costs order against Dooley because Dooley had not acted in the litigation which ultimately ensued. If the reasoning in *Byrne* is rejected but the result accepted, what is the rationale for accepting the result? Lord Bingham said that s 51(13)[3]:

'was intended ... simply to make plain that no liability could attach to any practitioner not involved in the litigation giving rise to the claim.'

Lord Bingham did not explain why he approved of the result in *Byrne*, but presumably it was because, on his interpretation of s 51(13), s 51(13) does not apply in cases where the solicitor whose conduct is challenged was not at any stage involved in the conduct of the litigation in which the costs were said to have been wasted. On this view, where a solicitor acts unreasonably, improperly or negligently and thereby causes costs to be wasted, if the solicitor ceases to act before proceedings have been issued then the court has no jurisdiction to make a wasted costs order against the solicitor. If this is the rule, it is open to the objection that solicitors could escape liability for wasted costs simply by suggesting that their retainer be terminated before proceedings are issued and other solicitors be instructed to issue the proceedings and conduct the litigation thereafter.[4] The reason for this apparent anomaly may be the court's desire, evident in *Medcalf*, to reduce the scope of wasted costs applications.

1 [2002] UKHL 27, [2003] 1 AC 120 at [20].
2 See [2003] 1 AC at 134B. See also *Lady Archer v Williams* [2003] EWHC 3048 (QB), per Jackson J at [57].

3 [2003] 1 AC at 133H–134A.
4 See *Radford & Co v Charles* [2003] EWHC 3180 (Ch), [2004] PNLR 25, per Neuberger J at [47].

13.08 If, however, solicitors waste costs before proceedings are issued, but proceedings subsequently are issued and the same solicitors conduct the litigation *after the issue of proceedings*, then the court has jurisdiction to make a wasted costs order even in relation to the conduct of those solicitors *before* issue of the proceedings. This follows from the Court of Appeal's decision in *Wagstaff v Colls (Wasted Costs Order)*[1]. Ward LJ accepted that there was no litigation in existence when the impugned conduct occurred, but distinguished *Byrne* on the basis that: '… the solicitors were never exercising the right to conduct litigation. The respondents were here.'[2] Hence it appears that the crucial question, in relation to the conduct of solicitors before proceedings are issued which waste costs, is whether the guilty solicitors conduct the litigation after the issue of proceedings: if not, there is no jurisdiction to make a wasted costs order; if so, there is jurisdiction.

1 [2003] EWCA Civ 469, [2003] PNLR 29.
2 [74].

13.09 In the later case of *Radford & Co v Charles*[1], Neuberger J suggested that the difference of principle between the two cases was that:

'… in *Byrne*, the solicitors were negligent, but not in breach of any duty to the court, whereas in *Wagstaff* the solicitors had arguably acted improperly, in breach of duty to the court. It is fair to say, however, that on one reading of the judgments in the two cases, the difference is that in *Byrne* the solicitors did not act in the subsequent litigation, whereas they did so in *Wagstaff*.'

The argument in *Charles*, however, proceeded on the basis that no wasted costs order could be made unless the lawyer was in breach of a duty owed to the court. It appears, however, that that interpretation of the law has now been rejected by the Court of Appeal[2]. That being the case, it is thought that the remaining distinction between the cases, as stated in para 13.08, must be applied, in spite of the possible anomaly referred to in para 13.07.

1 [2003] EWHC 3180 (Ch), [2004] PNLR 25 at [55]–[56].
2 See para 13.32, below.

2 Procedure

(a) A simple procedure

13.10 The first point is that the wasted costs jurisdiction is intended to be a reasonably simple and summary form of procedure, to be used only in clear cases, where the issues can be dealt with relatively quickly and without the need for lengthy pleadings or hearings lasting weeks. The general principles of the procedure were set out by Sir Thomas Bingham MR delivering the judgment of the court in *Ridehalgh,* in a passage which merits quoting in full:[1]

'The procedure to be followed in determining applications for wasted costs must be laid down by courts so as to meet the requirements of the individual case before them. The overriding requirements are that any procedure must be fair and that it must be as simple and summary as fairness permits. Fairness requires that any respondent lawyer should be very clearly told what he is said to have done wrong and what is claimed. But the requirement of simplicity and summariness means that elaborate pleadings should in general be avoided. No formal process of discovery will be appropriate. We cannot imagine circumstances in which the applicant should be permitted to interrogate the respondent lawyer, or vice versa. Hearings should be measured in hours, not in days or weeks. Judges must not reject a weapon which Parliament has intended to be used for the protection of those injured by the unjustifiable conduct of the other side's lawyers, but they must be astute to control what threatens to become a new and costly form of satellite litigation.'

In *Warren v Warren,*[2] Lord Woolf MR with whom the other judges agreed, quoted this passage, emphasised the concluding words, and added that, in *Warren,* it would have been better if the application had never been made. Similarly, in *Wall v Lefever*[3], the other judges agreed with Lord Woolf, who said:

'… in relation to a decision of a judge of first instance who has heard the evidence and seen the witnesses, and who had come to the conclusion that a wasted costs order should be refused, great caution should be exercised before launching on an appeal. The wasted costs jurisdiction is salutary as long as it is not allowed to be a vehicle which generates substantial additional costs to the parties. It should not be used to create subordinate or satellite litigation, which is as expensive and as complex as the original litigation. It must be used as a remedy in cases where the need for a wasted costs order is reasonably obvious. It is a summary remedy which is to be used in circumstances where there is a clear picture which indicates that a professional adviser has been negligent etc. If a judge has come to the conclusion that the case is not one which falls within that category, then an appeal will only be justified if there is some point of principle involved which indicates that the judge's approach was wholly wrong.'[4]

This approach is now reflected in para 53.5 of the Part 48 Practice Direction, which provides that:

'the court will give directions about the procedure that will be
followed in each case in order to ensure that the issues are dealt with
in a way that is fair and as simple and summary as the circumstances
permit.'

1 [1994] Ch 205, CA, at 238G–239A.
2 [1997] QB 488, CA, at 494–5.
3 [1998] 1 FCR 605, CA, at 614a–d.
4 Parts of this passage were cited with approval by Simon Brown LJ in *Fletamentos Maritimos SA v
  Effjohn International BV* [2003] Lloyd's Rep PN 26, CA, at 28 col.1. Further, in *Tolstoy-
  Miloslavsky v Aldington* [1996] 1 WLR 736, CA, Roch LJ said at 747H that the jurisdiction
  should be exercised only in a clear case. See also *Turner Page Music Ltd v Torres Design
  Associates Ltd* (1998) Times, 3 August, CA.

13.11 In *Medcalf v Mardell*,[1] Lord Bingham cited a passage from the Privy
Council's decision in *Harley v McDonald*.[2] Although *Harley* related to a New
Zealand costs jurisdiction, it appears that Lord Bingham, with whom the
majority agreed, considered it equally applicable to the wasted costs jurisdiction in England and Wales:

'As a general rule allegations of breach of duty relating to the
conduct of the case by a barrister or solicitor with a view to the
making of a costs order should be confined strictly to questions
which are apt for summary disposal by the court. Failures to appear,
conduct which leads to an otherwise avoidable step in the proceedings or the prolongation of a hearing by gross repetition or extreme
slowness in the presentation of evidence or argument are typical
examples. The factual basis for the exercise of the jurisdiction in
such circumstances is likely to be found in facts which are within
judicial knowledge because the relevant events took place in court or
are facts that can easily be verified. Wasting the time of the court or
an abuse of its processes which results in excessive or unnecessary
cost to litigants can thus be dealt with summarily on agreed facts or
after a brief inquiry if the facts are not all agreed.

Save in the clearest case, applications against the lawyers acting for
an opposing party are unlikely to be apt for summary determination,
since any hearing to investigate the conduct of a complex action is
itself likely to be expensive and time-consuming. The desirability of
compensating litigating parties who have been put to unnecessary
expense by the unjustified conduct of their opponents' lawyers is,
without doubt, an important public interest, but it is, as the Court of
Appeal pointed out in *Ridehalgh v Horsefield*, at p 226, only one of
the public interests which have to be considered.'

The second paragraph quoted does not, of course, apply to applications by
parties against their own lawyers, but most of the reported cases relate to

applications against opposing parties' lawyers, where the passage does apply. In spite of this statement, there are some cases in which wasted costs orders have subsequently been made, which we consider below. They do not all fall into the categories identified in *Harley*, so it seems that there are circumstances in which wasted costs orders may be made outside those categories. But, in light of this guidance, applying for an order in cases which fall outside the recognised categories may well be risky.

1 [2002] UKHL 27, [2003] 1 AC 120, at [24].
2 [2001] UKPC 18, [2001] 2 AC 678.

13.12 A clear example of allegations not suitable for the summary procedure of the wasted costs jurisdiction is *Re Freudiana Holdings Ltd*[1] The applicant's points of claim seeking the wasted costs order were 40 pages long; there were 35 pages of points of defence on behalf of counsel and 40 on behalf of the solicitors, followed by 20 pages of points of reply. The respondents' costs of defending the wasted costs application were of the order of £400,000. Skeleton arguments in the Court of Appeal amounted to 100 pages. The Court of Appeal upheld the trial judge's decision to discharge his earlier order, which had required the respondents to show cause why they should not pay wasted costs. It was quite clear that the case was wholly inappropriate for a summary procedure, and would essentially involving re-trying the original action, as well as considering the knowledge of the lawyers who had acted in it. From the point of view of those seeking to apply for wasted costs orders, the importance of the case is as follows. The court considered that the application had been made unsuitable for a wasted costs order by the conduct of the lawyers applying for it: if they had kept their allegations brief, and alleged simply negligence rather than 'knowing participation in an attempt deliberately to mislead the court and to pervert the course of justice' then it might well have been possible to deal with the matter under the wasted costs jurisdiction.[2] But, once such serious allegations had been made against solicitors and counsel, it was inevitable that they would seek rigorously to defend them, thus increasing the length of the pleadings and issues. Thus the message of *Freudiana* for those seeking wasted costs orders is to keep the allegations short, and avoid extravagant allegations of bad faith on the part of the lawyers.

1 (1995) Times, 4 December, CA.
2 See Millett LJ's judgment.

13.13 On the other hand, it will be in the interest of those defending such applications to emphasise, in part 1 of the two-stage procedure,[1] the extent to which a further hearing will be long and cumbersome, dealing with many issues, and ultimately unlikely to produce a clear conclusion. In addition, under the CPR applicants must bear in mind the principle of proportionality.[2] Figures from the Bar Mutual Indemnity Fund suggest that the cost of defending a wasted costs application is often more than the sum in issue.[3] Proportionality was a strong factor in persuading the court not to allow the wasted costs application to proceed in *Chief Constable of North Yorkshire v Audsley*.[4] But *Audsley* was distinguished in *B v B*[5], a family law case where the issue was relatively straightforward. Wall J said that the respondent barrister's argument that the costs of investigating the matter would be disproportionate was:

'... unattractive and self-serving. The reality is that, on the facts of this case, the costs involved in an unmeritorious *defence* of the application for a wasted costs order greatly exceed the amount at stake. But that begs the question of the merits of the application. It cannot be right for a respondent to seek to prevent an otherwise wholly meritorious application for wasted costs proceeding merely because the costs incurred in defending it will be substantial.'

While each case must turn on its facts, it is thought that this scepticism about arguments from those responding to wasted costs applications which rely purely on the cost of defending the application is justified.

1 As to which, see para 13.24, below.
2 *Re Merc Property Ltd* (1999) Times, 19 May, (Lindsay J).
3 See Evans *Lawyers' Liabilities* (2nd edn, 2002) 131.
4 [2000] Lloyd's Rep PN 675, (Keene J).
5 [2001] 1 FLR 843 (Wall J), at [35].

13.14 The wasted costs jurisdiction is unlikely to be appropriate in cases that call for detailed investigations of fact, or in which allegations of dishonesty on the part of lawyers are made.[1] In *B v Pendelbury*,[2] the allegations made in support of the wasted costs order were inextricably bound up with questions of fraud and impropriety; Turner J held that in those circumstances it would be wrong to allow the wasted costs application to proceed to the second stage[3], since it could not succeed. In *Re Hallewell Bunyard,*[4] Neill LJ's prima facie view was that there had been serious negligence on the part of the solicitor, but he considered that a wasted costs order should not be made, because it was a matter that required further examination, and, in particular, interrogation of the solicitor. As this was not possible on a wasted costs application, it was not possible to conclude that the case was sufficiently clear to make a wasted costs order. On the other hand, in *Wagstaff v Colls (Wasted Costs) Order*[5] Ward LJ, with whom the other members of the Court of Appeal agreed, approved the proposition that 'it cannot be right that a legal representative can escape the consequences of the wasted costs jurisdiction by the mere fact that the litigation in which his conduct is challenged is complex.'

1 *Manzanilla Ltd v Corton Property and Investments Ltd* [1997] 3 FCR 389, CA.
2 [2002] EWHC 1404 (QB), [2002] Lloyd's Rep PN 575 (Turner J).
3 As to the stages of a wasted costs application, see para 13.24, below.
4 (5 June 1996, unreported), CA.
5 [2003] EWCA Civ 469, [2003] PNLR 29, at [59], quoting from the judgment of Peter Gibson LJ in *Medcalf v Mardell* [2001] Lloyd's Rep PN 146, 159.

(*b*) *Appeal against refusal to make order*

13.15 The effect of the second passage quoted in para 13.10, above, is that the Court of Appeal is keen to discourage appeals against judges' refusals to make wasted costs orders. This was underlined by the order which the Court of Appeal made in *Wall v Lefever:* the appellant had to pay the costs of the appeal taxed on the indemnity basis. Lord Woolf MR said that:[1]

'… this is an area where this court is very unlikely to interfere with a decision, made in the exercise of the discretion of the judge below, unless a very strong case indeed is made out.'

Following those indications, parties who fail to obtain wasted costs orders from the judge will wish to appeal to the Court of Appeal only in very strong cases. The Court of Appeal distinguished *Wall* in *Wagstaff v Colls* (*Wasted Costs Order*)[2], but on the basis that in *Wagstaff* the judge below had declined to make a wasted costs order for reasons related to jurisdiction. Appeals will be slightly less risky in cases where it is said that the judge wrongly *made* a wasted costs order: in those cases, the appellant will be able to rely on Lord Woolf's indication that such orders should be made only in clear cases and after summary proceedings. In *Medcalf v Mardell*[3], the original wasted costs order had been made in the Court of Appeal; there was no suggestion in the speeches in the House of Lords that the House should be slow to interfere with the Court of Appeal's decision.

1 [1998] 1 FCR 605 at 617f, CA. See also *Fryer v Royal Institution of Chartered Surveyors* [2000] Lloyd's Rep PN 534 at [39]–[40], and *Persaud v Persaud* [2003] EWCA Civ 394, [2003] PNLR 26, at [41].
2 [2003] EWCA Civ 469, [2003] PNLR 29, esp at [63].
3 [2002] UKHL 27, [2003] 1 AC 20.

(*c*) *The impact of legal professional privilege*

13.16 In cases where a party (A) applied for a wasted costs order against another party (B)'s lawyers, it was thought in *Ridehalgh* that, if B did not waive privilege, this might place B's lawyers in a very difficult position in responding to the wasted costs application. This was because B's privilege was absolute, and it was not open to B's lawyers to waive the privilege if B did not consent; indeed it was B's lawyers' duty to uphold B's privilege unless B waived it or the court ordered otherwise.[1] When the CPR were introduced, CPR 48.7(3) was intended to deal with this problem. It provided that, for the purposes of a wasted costs application:

'… the court may direct that privileged documents are to be disclosed to the court and, if the court so directs, to the other party to the application for an order.'

In *General Mediterranean Holdings S.A. v Patel*[2], however, Toulson J held that this sub-rule was ultra vires. As a result it was revoked. It has not been replaced.

1 *R v Derby Magistrates' Court, ex p B* [1996] AC 487, HL.
2 [2000] 1 WLR 272.

13.17 In that context, in *Medcalf v Mardell*[1] Lord Bingham cited with approval the passage from *Ridehalgh*[2] dealing with the impact of legal professional privilege:

'Where an applicant seeks a wasted costs order against the lawyers on the other side, legal professional privilege may be relevant both as between the applicant and his lawyers and as between the respondent lawyers and their client. In either case it is the client's privilege, which he alone can waive.

The first of these situations can cause little difficulty. If the applicant's privileged communications are germane to an issue in the application, to show what he would or would not have done had the other side not acted in the manner complained of, he can waive his privilege; if he declines to do so adverse inferences can be drawn.

The respondent lawyers are in a different position. The privilege is not theirs to waive. In the usual case where a waiver would not benefit their client they will be slow to advise the client to waive his privilege, and they may well feel bound to advise that the client should take independent advice before doing so. The client may be unwilling to do that, and may be unwilling to waive if he does. So the respondent lawyers may find themselves at a grave disadvantage in defending their conduct of proceedings, unable to reveal what advice and warnings they gave, what instructions they received. In some cases this potential source of injustice may be mitigated by reference to the taxing master, where different rules apply, but only in a small minority of cases can this procedure be appropriate. Judges who are invited to make or contemplate making a wasted costs order must make full allowance for the inability of respondent lawyers to tell the whole story. Where there is room for doubt, the respondent lawyers are entitled to the benefit of it. It is again only when, with all allowances made, a lawyer's conduct of proceedings is quite plainly unjustifiable that it can be appropriate to make a wasted costs order.'

So the other party's lawyers were entitled to the benefit of any doubt if the other party did not waive privilege. In *Medcalf*, however, Lord Bingham, delivering a speech with which the majority agreed, felt that that passage from *Ridehalgh* must be read with 'extreme care', and

'... should be strengthened by emphasising two matters in particular. First, in a situation in which the practitioner is of necessity precluded (in the absence of a waiver by the client) from giving his account of the instructions he received and the material before him at the time of settling the impugned document, the court must be very slow to conclude that a practitioner could have had no sufficient material. Speculation is one thing, the drawing of inferences sufficiently strong to support orders potentially very damaging to the practitioner concerned is another. The point was well put by Mr George Laurence QC sitting as a deputy High Court judge in *Drums and Packaging Ltd v Freeman* (unreported) 6 August 1999 when he said, at para 43:

> 'As it happens, privilege having been waived, the whole story has been told. I cannot help wondering whether I would have arrived at the same conclusion had privilege not been waived. It would not have been particularly easy, in that event, to make the necessary full allowance for the firm's inability to tell the whole story. On the facts known to D3 at the time it launched this application, D3 might very well have concluded that the firm would not be able to avoid a wasted costs order, even on the 'every allowance' basis recommended by Sir Thomas Bingham MR.'

Only rarely will the court be able to make 'full allowance' for the inability of the practitioner to tell the whole story or to conclude that there is no room for doubt in a situation in which, of necessity, the court is deprived of access to the full facts on which, in the ordinary way, any sound judicial decision must be based. The second qualification is no less important. The court should not make an order against a practitioner precluded by legal professional privilege from advancing his full answer to the complaint made against him without satisfying itself that it is in all the circumstances fair to do so. This reflects the old rule, applicable in civil and criminal proceedings alike, that a party should not be condemned without an adequate opportunity to be heard. Even if the court were able properly to be sure that the practitioner could have no answer to the substantive complaint, it could not fairly make an order unless satisfied that nothing could be said to influence the exercise of its discretion. Only exceptionally could these exacting conditions be satisfied. Where a wasted costs order is sought against a practitioner precluded by legal professional privilege from giving his full answer to the application, the court should not make an order unless, proceeding with extreme care, it is (a) satisfied that there is nothing the practitioner could say, if unconstrained, to resist the order and (b) that it is in all the circumstances fair to make the order.'[3]

1 [2002] UKHL 27, [2003] 1 AC 20 at [23].

2 [1994] Ch 205 at 237.
3 *Medcalf* [2002] UKHL 27, [2003] 1 AC 20 at [23]. See para 13.67, below for discussion of the
requirement that it is fair in all the circumstances to make the order.

13.18 In light of this, it might be thought that, in cases where A seeks a wasted costs order against B's lawyers, and B declines to waive his or her privilege, the effect of the passage just quoted would be to make it extremely difficult for A to obtain a wasted costs order against B's lawyers. There have certainly been cases since *Medcalf* where this problem has proved an insuperable barrier for the applicant: see for example *Lady Archer v Williams*[1], in which the respondent paid for the other party to have independent legal advice on whether to waive privilege, *Daly v Hubner*[2] and *Dempsey v Johnstone*.[3]

1 [2003] EWHC 3048 (QB), (Jackson J), esp [48], [53].
2 [2002] Lloyd's Rep PN 461 (Etherton J).
3 [2003] EWCA Civ 1134, [2004] PNLR 2.

13.19 In *B v B*[1], however, counsel had acted on an appeal that was incapable of success and which the judge considered to be an abuse of process. Counsel's client had not waived privilege. The judge pointed out that the client was publicly funded. The judge appears to have ruled out the possibility that counsel might have advised strongly against the appeal, but been forced by the client to make it. This was because, if that had occurred, it would have been counsel's duty to advise the Legal Services Commission that the client was behaving unreasonably, but there was no evidence that the Commission had been advised about the appeal. A wasted costs order was made. It would appear, however, that if the client had been privately funded then this line of reasoning would not have been available. Further, it is open to question whether Wall J's reasoning is correct in light of the authorities on the relevance of public funding summarised at para 13.61, below.

1 [2001] 1 FLR 843 at [42]–[46].

13.20 Further, in *Morris v Roberts (Inspector of Taxes)*[1], Lightman J said that if privilege was not waived in a case where a party sought wasted costs from the other party's lawyers:

'… a court should not make a wasted costs order unless satisfied that there is nothing the practitioner could say, if unconstrained, to resist the order. But privilege is not a trump card which will always preclude the making of a wasted costs order: *Medcalf v Mardell*, *supra*, at 146 per Lord Hobhouse. The acid test in all cases is whether the conduct of the solicitor permits of a reasonable explanation: see *Ridehalgh* at 232 and *B v B* [2001] FLR 482 at [22].'

He proceeded to make a wasted costs order even though it appears that privilege had not been waived. The application concerned the costs of an

671

appeal that the respondent solicitors had commenced but abandoned. Lightman J concluded that the solicitors must have known that the appeal was hopeless and that it was prosecuted for reasons unconnected with success on the appeal. It was the last of a series of acts and omissions on the part of the solicitors and their clients that was 'designed to evade or delay' liability to pay tax. Further, the solicitors knew that the clients would not pay any costs or penalties ordered to be paid to the other party, the Inland Revenue. So:

> 'At the very least as competent solicitors they should have been aware that the appeal was an abuse of process brought for an illegitimate collateral purpose and that their own actions were calculated to further and did further the inadmissible objectives which their clients were pursuing.'

Although a wasted costs order was made in *Morris*, it is thought that this was not inconsistent with the passages quoted above from *Medcalf*: in light of the judge's findings, *Morris* was an exceptional case. To conclude, if privilege is not waived then applications against another party's lawyers may well fail, but it may still be possible to succeed if there is a very strong case against the lawyers.

1 [2005] EWHC 1040 (Ch), [2005] PNLR 41; the quotations are from [53] and [59].

(d) Procedural rules

13.21 An application for a wasted costs order must be made pursuant to CPR Part 48.7, which provides:

> '48.7(1) This rule applies where the court is considering whether to make an order under section 51(6) of the Supreme Court Act 1981 (court's power to disallow or (as the case may be) order a legal representative to meet "wasted costs" in cases to which this section applies).
>
> (2) The court must give the legal representative a reasonable opportunity to attend a hearing to give reasons why it should not make such an order.
>
> (3) [Revoked].
>
> (4) When the court makes a wasted costs order, it must -
>
> (a)   specify the amount to be disallowed or paid; or
>
> (b)   direct a costs judge or a district judge to decide the amount of costs to be disallowed or paid.

(5) The court may direct that notice must be given to the legal representative's client, in such manner as the court may direct–

(a) of any proceedings under this rule; or

(b) of any order made under it against his legal representative.

(6) Before making a wasted costs order, the court may direct a costs judge or a district judge to inquire into the matter and report to the court.

(7) The court may refer the question of wasted costs to a costs judge or a district judge, instead of making a wasted costs order.'

13.22   The requirement of a fair hearing is expanded upon in the Part 48 Practice Direction.[1] Further, the need for any order made to specify the amount of money to be paid or disallowed (Part 48.7(4)) was introduced by the CPR, and reflects the general approach of those rules in favour of the immediate assessment of the amount of costs, though the court may instead refer the whole matter to a costs judge or a district judge (Part 48.7(7)). Thirdly, there is power to order that notice be given to the lawyer's client (Part 48.7(5)).[2]

1 See para 13.23, below.
2 See also Part 44.2.

(e) Part 48 Practice Direction

13.23   More rules on the procedure to be followed appear in the Part 48 Practice Direction, the relevant parts of which provide:

'53.1 Rule 48.7 deals with wasted costs orders against legal representatives. Such orders can be made at any stage in the proceedings up to and including the proceedings relating to the detailed assessment of costs. In general, applications for wasted costs orders are best left until after the end of the trial.

53.2 The court may make a wasted costs order against a legal representative on its own initiative.

53.3 A party may apply for a wasted costs order–

(1)   by filing an application notice in accordance with Part 23; or

(2) by making an application orally in the course of any hearing.

53.4 It is appropriate for the court to make a wasted costs order against a legal representative only if–

(1)   the legal representative has acted improperly, unreasonably or negligently,

(2)   his conduct has caused a party to incur unnecessary costs, and

(3)   it is just in all the circumstances to order him to compensate that party for the whole or part of those costs.

53.5 The court will give directions about the procedure that will be followed in each case in order to ensure that the issues are dealt with in a way which is fair and as simple and summary as the circumstances permit.

53.6 As a general rule the court will consider whether to make a wasted costs order in two stages:

(1)   in the first stage, the court must be satisfied–

(a)   that it has before it evidence or other material which, if unanswered, would be likely to lead to a wasted costs order being made; and

(b)   the wasted costs proceedings are justified notwithstanding the likely costs involved.

(2)   At the second stage (even if the court is satisfied under (1)) the court will consider, after giving the legal representative an opportunity to give reasons why the court should not make a wasted costs order, whether it is appropriate to make a wasted costs order in accordance with paragraph 53.4 above.

53.7 On an application for a wasted costs order under Part 23 the court may proceed to the second stage described in paragraph 53.6 without first adjourning the hearing if it is satisfied that the legal representative has already had a reasonable opportunity to give reasons why the court should not make a wasted costs order. In other cases the court will adjourn the hearing before proceeding to the second stage.

53.8 On an application for a wasted costs order under Part 23 the application notice and any evidence in support must identify-

(1)   What the legal representative is alleged to have done or failed to do; and

(2)   the costs he may be ordered to pay or which are sought against him.

53.9 A wasted costs order is an order-

(1)   that the legal representative pay a specified sum in respect of costs to a party; or

(2)   for the costs relating to a specified sum or items of work to be disallowed.

53.10 Attention is drawn to rule 44.3A(1) and (2) which respectively prevent the court from assessing any additional liability until the conclusion of the proceedings (or the part of the proceedings) to which the funding arrangement relates, and set out the orders the court may make at the conclusion of the proceedings.'

(f) *Stages of the application*

13.24   Paragraph 53.7 of the Practice Direction is a recent introduction, presumably intended to simplify the procedure in some cases. *B v B*[1] concerned the costs of an appeal on an interlocutory matter; Wall J considered that he had complied with the first stage of the Practice Direction by his judgment on the appeal. On the other hand in *Regent Leisuretime Ltd v Skerrett*[2], Lloyd LJ said that:

'... although an oral application in the course of the hearing is possible pursuant to paragraph 53, that is only likely to be sensible if the scope of the application to the costs said to have been wasted is narrow and clear; for example, if an adjournment is necessary because of a solicitor's or counsel's conduct, as regards the costs thrown away by the adjournment.'

At the first stage, the court considers essentially whether there is a case to answer, and whether the application is justified bearing in mind the costs involved.[3] By this stage the applicant will presumably have complied with para 53.8 of the Practice Direction, so that the respondent will know the allegations made and the quantum of costs claimed. If the applicant wins the first stage, the application proceeds to the second stage of the court's procedure, as provided for in para 53.6(2). At the first stage, the making of an order that the application proceed to the final stage:

'... is not something to be done automatically or without careful appraisal of the relevant circumstances. The costs of the inquiry as compared with the costs claimed will always be one relevant consideration. This is a discretion, like any other, to be exercised judicially, but judges may not infrequently decide that further proceedings are not likely to be justified.'[4]

675

13.25 *Costs orders against solicitors*

As to the final stage, the court is not bound to make an order even if improper, unreasonable or negligent conduct, and causation, are made out (see Practice Direction para 53.4(3)):

> 'but in that situation it would of course have to give sustainable reasons for exercising its discretion against making the order.'[5]

1 [2001] 1 FLR 843 (Wall J).
2 [2006] EWCA Civ 1036, at [36].
3 The court will have proportionality in mind at this stage; see paras 13.10–13.14, above.
4 *Ridehalgh* [1994] Ch 205 at 239B–C.
5 *Ridehalgh* [1994] Ch 205 at 239E–F. See also the second passage from *Medcalf* quoted at para 13.17, above.

(g) *Timing and judge*

13.25 Generally speaking applications for wasted costs orders are best made at the end of the trial.[1] There is even jurisdiction to make an order after the order dealing with other aspects of the claim has been drawn up, if good reasons are shown.[2] An example of an exceptional case in which it was appropriate, before the end of the trial, to make a similar order, against the Legal Aid Board rather than lawyers, for the costs of an adjournment, was *Kelly v South Manchester Health Authority*.[3] The court was apprised of all relevant material at the interlocutory stage and so it was appropriate to make the order then. Further, in the family case of *B v B*[4] it was appropriate to make a wasted costs order before trial because neither of the lawyers involved was still instructed in the litigation and the issue involved would not alter or be affected by the outcome of the litigation. Unless there is a good reason, the application should be dealt with by the judge who dealt with the matter that gives rise to the wasted costs application[5]. Good reasons might include the death or retirement of the trial judge.[5] If a claim is the subject of a stay, it is not necessary to apply for the stay to be lifted before application is made for a wasted costs order.[6]

1 Para 53.1 of the Practice Direction, and compare *Ridehalgh* [1994] Ch 205 at 238B–D, approving *Filmlab Systems International Ltd v Pennington* [1995] 1 WLR 673 (Aldous J).
2 *Gray v Going Places Leisure Travel Ltd* [2005] EWCA Civ 189, [2005] PNLR 26.
3 [1981] 1 WLR 244.
4 [2001] 1 FLR 843 (Wall J).
5 *Re Merc Property Ltd* (1999) Times, 19 May (Lindsay J), *Gray v Going Places Leisure Travel Ltd* (above).
6 *Wagstaff v Colls* (*Wasted Costs Order*) [2003] EWCA Civ 469, [2003] PNLR 29.

(h) *Court initiating application*

13.26 The court has power to initiate an application (Practice Direction para 53.2), but should be slow to do so except in very clear cases, such as failure to appear, lateness, gross repetition or extreme slowness. The reason is that, if the application is lost, the court will not compensate the parties for the wasted costs of the application itself.[1] In *Re G (Minors) (Care Proceedings)*,[2] however, Wall J said that care proceedings were very expensive, each party was ultimately funded by the taxpayer, but costs orders between parties were rare. He added that:

> 'In these circumstances, in my judgment, and in clear contrast to commercial or other adversarial civil litigation it is the court which has to be the watchdog over the proper expenditure of public funds'.

It was therefore entirely appropriate that the court should initiate a wasted costs application. It did, and the order was made.

1 *Ridehalgh* [1994] Ch 205 at 238D–F. See also Evans *Lawyers' Liabilities* (2nd edn, 2002) at 7–03, as to possible human rights objections to judges acting as prosecutor, judge and jury in such cases, though compare the position as to contempt of court.
2 [2000] Fam 104, [2000] 2 WLR 1007 at 1014–5 (Wall J). See further para 13.53, below.

(i) *Applications by non-parties*

13.27 Wasted costs orders may be made only in favour of those who are parties to the litigation.[1] This led Sedley J to hold, in *R v Camden London Borough Council, ex p Martin*,[2] that there was no jurisdiction to make a wasted costs order in favour of the respondent to a without notice application for leave to move for judicial review: until leave was granted, the application was expressed to be 'ex parte', and so the respondent was not properly a party. But in the later case of *R v Immigration Appeal Tribunal, ex p Gulsen*,[3] Buxton J held that the court did have power to make such an order pursuant to its inherent jurisdiction. Further, in *Lubrizol Ltd v Tyndalls*,[4] Carnwath J held that *ex p Martin* did not apply in a case where the application for leave to move for judicial review included an application for an interlocutory injunction. In that case, it was established that it was appropriate for the respondent to appear at the oral hearing seeking the injunction, so that the respondent was a party, and there was jurisdiction to make a wasted costs order in its favour.

1 See the definition of wasted costs in Supreme Court Act 1981, s 51(7).
2 [1997] 1 WLR 359.
3 [1997] COD 430.
4 (8 April 1998, unreported).

(j) *Settlement*

13.28 Where the court has decided that there is material which, if unanswered, would lead to a wasted costs order, but the application is subsequently settled, the lawyers involved risk being deprived by the settlement of the opportunity to clear any blot from their reputations. *Manzanilla Ltd v Corton Property and Investments Ltd* was such a case. Lord Woolf MR said:[1]

> 'In such a case as this, the court should be prepared to allow a written statement to be placed before the court, so that it can be transmitted to the judiciary who were previously involved, without counsel or other lawyers having to attend, as long as it is first produced to the other parties and they raise no objection to it being submitted. The statement should be short and succinct and not one which goes into unnecessary detail. It would also be desirable that, wherever possible, the statement is agreed by the other parties. However, where no agreement is possible, the position of the other parties can be protected by their also being allowed to submit an equally short statement in response to that of the initiator of the procedure. There it must end because otherwise the costs which I would seek to avoid being incurred would be incurred in producing a multiplicity of lengthy written statements which are not going to assist the court.'

1 [1997] 3 FCR 389 at 391E–G, CA.

(k) *Interrelationship between wasted costs orders and orders for costs against LSC*

13.29 If the case is one in which a wasted costs order should be made, this will normally be a reason for not making an order that the Legal Services Commission pay the costs. But, except in the clearest of cases, a party who applies for costs from the Legal Services Commission is not obliged also to seek an order that other lawyers pay wasted costs. At most, a party seeking costs from the Legal Services Commission need only mention to the court that it is possible that a wasted costs order should be made; if this is done, the court may then choose to inform the Legal Services Commission that it may wish to object to being ordered to pay costs, on the basis that a wasted costs order should be made instead. If the Commission does this, then the court will have to consider the issue of a notice to show cause to the lawyers in question.[1]

1 *Re O (wasted costs order)* [1997] 1 FLR 465, CA. See Lord Woolf MR's judgment at 472A–D. This case concerned the Legal Aid Board but it is thought that similar principles should apply in the case of its successor the Legal Services Commission.

3   Basic requirements

13.30 The basic requirements for the making of an order are that it be shown that the lawyer has acted improperly, unreasonably or negligently, that this has caused costs to be wasted, and that it is just in all the circumstances that an order be made.[1] In the following sections, the first three requirements are considered individually; then there is consideration of various subsidiary issues which arise in relation to those three issues; next, the issue of causation is dealt with, and finally the overall justice of making an order.

1 Part 48 Practice Direction, para 53.4.

13.31   Although it is of some assistance to consider the concepts of improper, unreasonable and negligent conduct separately, nevertheless:[1]

> 'conduct which is unreasonable may also be improper, and conduct which is negligent will very frequently be (if it is not by definition) unreasonable. We do not think any sharp differentiation between these expressions is useful or necessary or intended.'

1 *Ridehalgh* [1994] Ch 205 at 233E.

No need to prove breach of duty to the court

13.32   Before dealing with the requirements for the making of a wasted costs order identified above, it is necessary to consider whether applicants must also prove that the respondent acted in breach of a duty owed to the court. This was conceded in *Persaud v Persaud*,[1] though Peter Gibson LJ considered that the concession had been rightly made. In *Dempsey v Johnstone*[2], however, Latham LJ doubted whether it was necessary to show a breach of a duty to the court, and Mance LJ considered that it was not. Although Neuberger J held in *Radford & Co v Charles*[3] that it was necessary to show a breach of duty to the court, it appears that *Dempsey* was not cited to him. In *Isaacs Partnership v Umm Al-Jawaby Oil Service Co Ltd*[4] Gross J cited *Dempsey* to reject the proposition that showing negligence on its own was insufficient for the making of a wasted costs order. Finally, in *Morris v Roberts (Inspector of Taxes)*[5], Lightman J said that: 'The stricter test laid down by Peter Gibson LJ in *Persaud v Persaud* ... was disapproved of in *Dempsey* and is no longer the law'. The position therefore appears to be that there is no requirement that an applicant prove not only that the respondent acted improperly, unreasonably or negligently, but also that he or she acted in breach of duty to the court. It is sufficient, as to what might be termed liability, to prove that the respondent acted improperly, unreasonably or negligently.

1 [2003] EWCA Civ 394, [2003] PNLR 26, at [18] and [22].
2 [2003] EWCA Civ 1134, [2004] PNLR 2, at [24] and [40]–[42].
3 [2003] EWHC 3180 (Ch), [2004] PNLR 25.
4 [2003] EWHC 2539 (QB), [2004] PNLR 9, at [25] proposition 4.
5 [2005] EWHC 1040 (Ch), [2005] PNLR 41, at [52]. See also *Hedrich v Standard Bank London Ltd* [2007] EWHC 1656 (QB), [2007] PNLR 31 (Field J).

4   Improper acts and omissions

13.33   Improper conduct was defined in *Ridehalgh*[1] as follows:

> 'The adjective covers, but is not confined to, conduct which would ordinarily be held to justify disbarment, striking off, suspension from practice or other serious professional penalty. It covers any significant breach of a substantial duty imposed by a relevant code of professional conduct. But it is not in our judgment limited to that. Conduct which would be regarded as improper according to the consensus of professional (including judicial) opinion can be fairly stigmatised as such whether or not it violates the letter of a professional code.'

1 [1994] Ch 205 at 232D–E.

13.34   Five points arise. First, it is likely that conduct that is improper will also be unreasonable, so that it is unlikely to be necessary to rely upon this category alone. Secondly, although the passage quoted in para 13.31 suggests an overlap between the three concepts of improper, unreasonable and negligent conduct, note that, in that passage, the overlaps suggested are:

(i)   improper conduct may overlap with unreasonable conduct, and

(ii)   negligent conduct may overlap with unreasonable conduct.

On the other hand the definition of unreasonable conduct, quoted at para 13.36, below, suggests that unreasonable conduct will not necessarily be negligent conduct. It is submitted that it is helpful to consider the cases as falling into two broad categories. The first category, improper/unreasonable conduct, is conduct that tends not to be careless, but rather deliberate or intentional use of legal procedures in a way that is considered unethical or bordering on the unethical. The second category, negligent conduct, is conduct that is careless or based on ignorance, as in the familiar tort of negligence. This division mirrors the familiar distinction between intentional wrongdoing and negligence.

13.35   Thirdly, the fate of the wasted costs application in *Re Freudiana Holdings Ltd*,[1] shows that it is generally undesirable for those applying for wasted costs orders to make extravagant allegations of impropriety against lawyers, except in the clearest circumstances. The more serious the allegation for the respondent lawyer, the more the lawyer is likely to wish to defend the matter vigorously, and the harder it may be for the court to reach the conclusion that the lawyer has plainly acted improperly. Fourthly, in *Fontaine v the Home Office*[2] it was held that solicitors who deliberately withheld from the other party's solicitors information that their client had been incarcerated and would be unable to attend trial, thus requiring an adjournment, had acted improperly and should be the subject of a wasted costs order. Fifthly, it is well established that it is not improper to act for a client merely because the client's case is doomed to fail.[3] Finally, as there is an overlap between improper and unreasonable conduct, the cases discussed in the next section deal also to some degree with improper conduct.

1 (1995) Times, 4 December, CA, see para 13.12, above.
2 (2 March 1999, unreported), CA.
3 *Chief Constable of North Yorkshire v Audsley* [2000] Lloyd's Rep PN 675, per Keene J at 682 col 1. See further para 13.38ff, below.

5 Unreasonable acts and omissions

13.36   Again, the key definition was given in *Ridehalgh*:[1]

' "Unreasonable" … aptly describes conduct which is vexatious, designed to harass the other side rather than advance the resolution of the case, and it makes no difference that the conduct is the product of excessive zeal and not improper motive. But conduct cannot be described as unreasonable simply because it leads in the event to an unsuccessful result or because other more cautious legal representatives would have acted differently. The acid test is whether the conduct permits of a reasonable explanation. If so, the course adopted may be regarded as optimistic and as reflecting on a practitioner's judgment, but it is not unreasonable.'

1 [1994] Ch 205 at 232E–G. See also *R (Latchman) v Secretary of State for the Home Department* [2004] EWHC 2795 (Admin): solicitors were aware over two months before a hearing that it was academic, but withdrew the claim only four days before the hearing. They had made a number of attempts to contact their client without success, and so had not acted unreasonably.

(a) Agreeing expert evidence

13.37   This definition has been considered in a number of subsequent cases. *Greenhoff v J Lyons & Co*[1] is a straightforward one. In a personal injury action concerning relatively low levels of damages, the medical experts were in agreement on all points except one. The claimant's solicitors refused to agree the evidence. Agreement would have avoided the need for the experts to come to court. The recorder held that the claimant's solicitors ought to have agreed the reports, subject to agreement that their client could raise in evidence the one point on which she disagreed with the defendants' expert. Their failure to do so did not admit of a reasonable explanation, so it was unreasonable. He ordered the claimant's solicitors to pay the costs of the doctors' attendance at court. The Court of Appeal accepted that this conclusion was open to the recorder, and declined to overturn his decision.

1   (30 June 1998, unreported), CA.

(*b*) *Abuse of process and hopeless cases*

13.38   In two remarkable cases, *Tolstoy-Miloslavsky v Aldington*[1] and *Fleta-mentos Maritimos SA v Effjohn International BV*,[2] the Court of Appeal found that lawyers' conduct was vexatious and amounted to an abuse of the process of the court. Before considering the facts of those cases, it is necessary to consider the distinction between merely advancing a hopeless case, which is not improper or unreasonable, and abusing the process of the court, which is:[3]

> 'A legal representative is not to be held to have acted improperly, unreasonably or negligently simply because he acts for a party who pursues a claim or a defence which is plainly doomed to fail … Barristers in independent practice are not permitted to pick and choose their clients … solicitors are not subject to an equivalent cab-rank rule, but many solicitors would and do respect the public policy underlying it by affording representation to the unpopular and unmeritorious. Legal representatives will, of course, whether barristers or solicitors, advise clients of the perceived weakness of their case and of the risk of failure. But clients are free to reject advice and insist that cases be litigated. It is rarely if ever safe for a court to assume that a hopeless case is being litigated on the advice of the lawyers involved …
>
> It is, however, one thing for a legal representative to present, on instructions, a case which he regards as bound to fail; it is quite another to lend his assistance to proceedings which are an abuse of the process of the court. Whether instructed or not, a legal representative is not entitled to use litigious procedures for purposes for which they were not intended, as by issuing or pursuing proceedings for reasons unconnected with success in the litigation or pursuing a case known to be dishonest, nor is he entitled to evade rules intended to safeguard the interests of justice, as by knowingly failing to make full disclosure on ex parte application or knowingly conniving at incomplete disclosure of documents. It is not entirely easy to distinguish between the hopeless case and the case which amounts to an abuse of process, but in practice it is not hard to say which is which and if there is doubt the legal representative is entitled to the benefit of it.'

1 [1996] 1 WLR 736, CA.
2 [2003] Lloyd's Rep PN 26, CA. The case was decided in 1997 and reported late.
3 *Ridehalgh* [1994] Ch 205 at 233–4.

13.39 A relatively simple example of abuse of process of this kind appears in *Re a Company* (*No 006798 of 1995*).[1] The question was whether the court should make a wasted costs order against a solicitor who had sworn an affidavit in support of the winding up of a company, at a time when he believed, contrary to what he swore in the affidavit, that the company was able to pay its debts. Chadwick J said:

'... a solicitor who, in swearing an affidavit in the short statutory form to support a winding up petition, asserts on oath a belief that a debt is owing and that the company is insolvent acts improperly if he does not have that belief; and acts unreasonably if there are no grounds upon which a competent solicitor could reach that view on the material available to him.'

The background of the case was that it appeared that the winding-up petition was bound to fail, and that the application was launched not in order to wind up the company, but rather for the collateral purpose of putting illegitimate commercial pressure on the company.[2]

1 [1996] 1 WLR 491 (Chadwick J). See esp 506E.
2 For a case relating to the compromise of an application to wind up a company, which the Court of Appeal considered fell on the other side of the line and did not involve unreasonable or improper behaviour, see *Philex plc v Golban* decided at the same time as *Ridehalgh*: [1994] Ch 205.

13.40 We have already considered the Court of Appeal's emphasis that wasted costs orders should be made only in plain cases. The facts of the *Tolstoy* and *Fletamentos* cases demonstrate the sort of circumstances which will be sufficiently exceptional to justify a wasted costs order on the basis of improper or unreasonable behaviour. In both cases, the court concluded that the solicitors' conduct had crossed the line from merely taking hopeless points into abuse of the process of the court. So remarkable are the facts of these cases that it is hard to convey their full import by way of summary, and ideally they should be read in full. In the first, Rose LJ summarised the circumstances that led him to conclude that there had been abuse of process by the solicitors acting for the claimant, Count Tolstoy.[1] In particular: this was the second and possibly the third occasion on which Count Tolstoy had sought to defeat Lord Aldington by litigation in relation to the same matters; Lord Aldington had been harassed by the various proceedings; the proceedings were prima facie an abuse as they were a collateral attack on the final decision of a court of competent jurisdiction; the new evidence on which Count Tolstoy relied was extremely weak; Count Tolstoy had not paid Lord Aldington the enormous costs of the first action, was bankrupt, and there was no prospect of him paying the costs of this action. In Ward LJ's view the key factors were that:

13.41 *Costs orders against solicitors*

(i)   'as hopeless cases go, this really was plumbing the depths';

(ii) given the background of the previous litigation and insolvency of Count Tolstoy, the litigation was vexatious as it 'heaped fraud and perjury upon the vicious calumny of the allegation of being a war criminal';

(iii) the action was instituted to harass Lord Aldington, and no reasonable solicitor could have considered otherwise.[2]

1 [1996] 1 WLR 747.
2 See [1996] 1 WLR 736 at 752C–E.

13.41   Similarly astonishing are the facts of *Fletamentos*. In this case it was significant that the allegedly wasted costs were the costs of an appeal to the Court of Appeal. Thus, the appellants had already had the opportunity to advance their arguments in court, before Morison J. The question was whether the decision to bring the appeal amounted to an abuse, and unreasonable behaviour. Simon Brown LJ analysed each proposed ground of appeal, and showed that each one was extraordinarily weak; some of them were 'absurd'[1]. In relation to the solicitors, Zaiwallas, he concluded[2]:

> 'I have the clearest impression that Zaiwallas saw their role essentially as one of assisting their clients at all costs to stave off the evil day of judgment, meanwhile taking all possible points in an attempt to disrupt the arbitral process and achieve, if possible, a more compliant Tribunal ... These, in short, were wrecking tactics, designed rather to obstruct than to further the fair disposal of this arbitration. This litigation permitted of no reasonable explanation. It failed the "acid test". It amounted to an abuse of process.'

Other relevant points were that it was likely that there would be difficulties for the other party in enforcing costs orders against Zaiwallas' client, and that this was an appeal from an interlocutory rather than a final decision, so that there was less need to appeal.

1 [2003] Lloyd's Rep PN 26 at 31 col 1.
2 At 36, col 1.

13.42   Morritt LJ too analysed each ground of appeal, and considered them all hopeless. He also inferred that the appeal had been instigated by the solicitor Mr Zaiwalla rather than his clients Marflet. Mr Zaiwalla was motivated in part by his personal feelings in relation to one of the arbitrators involved in the case. This was unreasonable conduct. Mr Zaiwalla had failed to disclose material matters on a without notice application for permission to appeal; this was improper. Morritt LJ added, obiter, that it was possible that it might amount to vexatious conduct to advance a point which, though not utterly hopeless, had some small chance of success, if the conduct in question was intended to harass the other party rather than advance the resolution of the case[1]. Waller LJ agreed, for reasons similar to those already set out.[2]

1   [2003] Lloyd's Rep PN 26 at 44, col 1.
2   See 44–45.

13.43   In *Dempsey v Johnstone*[1] Latham LJ, with whom Aldous LJ agreed, suggested that, in cases where the allegation was that the legal representative had pursued a hopeless case, the question to ask was 'whether no reasonably competent legal representative would have continued with the action'. It was possible that a lawyer might have pursued a hopeless case due to being ignorant of an authority that was fatal to the client's case; in that case the lawyer's conduct would be negligent. But generally the question was likely to be whether the legal representative had acted unreasonably, which was akin to establishing an abuse of process. In *Dempsey* a claim was struck out but privilege was not waived. In the absence of a waiver of privilege, the Court of Appeal found it impossible to say whether the solicitors whose conduct was impugned had acted negligently or unreasonably.[2]

1   [2003] EWCA Civ 1134, [204] PNLR 2, at [28].
2   See also two cases where the court refused to make wasted costs orders against solicitors whose clients turned out to have weak cases: *Gandesha v Nandra* [2002] Lloyd's Rep PN 558 (Jacob J) and *Marsh v Sofaer* [2006] EWHC 1217 (Ch), [2006] PNLR 634 (David Richards J).

13.44   Finally, in *Morris v Roberts (Inspector of Taxes)*[1], Lightman J stated that, in a case where it was alleged that a wasted costs order should be made against a solicitor on the ground that the solicitor had acted in a hopeless case:

'... it is relevant to consider the ability and/or the willingness of [the solicitor's] client to: (a) bear the costs consequences of those proceedings, and/or (b) give effect to previous orders made against him in connected litigation ... and the fact that there is some small prospect of success in proceedings or on an appeal does not preclude a finding that the proceedings are abusive and this is most particularly the case where the solicitor knows that his client "cannot or will not pay"...

Actual knowledge on the part of a legal representative that the litigation he is conducting is an abuse of process is sufficient to render a legal representative liable for costs.

But a legal representative will also be liable to a wasted costs order if, exercising the objective professional judgment of a reasonably competent solicitor, he ought reasonably to have appreciated that the litigation in which he was acting constituted an abuse of process ... The circumstances may be such as to impose a duty on solicitors to investigate with the greatest care their clients' motives for launching proceedings or an appeal ...

> It is no answer for a solicitor who has improperly, unreasonably or negligently lent himself to such an abuse to say that he was instructed to do so …'

We referred to the facts of *Morris* at para 13.20, above. It was another exceptional case in which the court was prepared to make a wasted costs order against the solicitor on the ground partly that the solicitor was conducting a hopeless case, even though privilege was not waived. In the absence of such exceptional circumstances, however, an order will not be made in this type of case.

1   [2005] EWHC 1040 (Ch), [2005] PNLR 41.

6   Negligent acts or omissions

13.45   In defining negligent conduct for these purposes, as before, the starting point is *Ridehalgh*:[1]

> '… we are clear that "negligent" should be understood in an untechnical way to denote failure to act with the competence reasonably to be expected of ordinary members of the profession.

> In adopting an untechnical approach to the meaning of negligence in this context, we would however wish firmly to discountenance any suggestion that an applicant for a wasted costs order under this head need prove anything less than he would have to prove in an action for negligence: "advice, acts or omissions in the course of their professional work which no member of the profession who was reasonably well-informed and competent would have given or done or omitted to do"; an error "such as no reasonably well-informed and competent member of that profession could have made": see *Saif Ali v Sydney Mitchell & Co* [1980] AC 198, 218 per Lord Diplock.'

Thus, although technicalities are to be eschewed, the test of negligence is broadly the familiar common law test, as it applies to professionals. As indicated above at para 13.32, it is thought that it is not necessary additionally to prove a breach of a duty owed to the court.

1   [1994] Ch 205 at 233.

(a) Non-negligent conduct

13.46   It is instructive to consider the Court of Appeal's application of the test on the facts of the individual cases dealt with as part of the consolidated appeals in *Ridehalgh*. On the facts of *Ridehalgh v Horsefield* itself, the court found that the solicitors, acting for a tenant in a possession action, had made a concession to the landlord that should not have been made because it was based upon a misunderstanding of the law. The concession made it easier for the landlord to obtain an order for possession. The court nevertheless held that the solicitors had not been negligent in failing to understand the law correctly. The law was complex. The solicitors consulted textbooks that did not give a clear answer. The county court judge did not intervene to correct the error. The solicitors were not to be treated by the standard to be applied to specialist counsel, nor could they reasonably expect to be paid for prolonged research.[1] At first sight it might seem a surprising conclusion that lawyers who failed to understand the law correctly might not have been negligent, but it is submitted that this approach, in relation to a complex area of law being interpreted by high street solicitors, is realistic rather than utopian.[2]

1 *Ridehalgh* [1994] Ch 205 at 242. See also paras 2.10 and 2.12, above.
2 See also *Warren v Warren* [1997] QB 488, CA. The Court of Appeal held that a solicitor had not acted unreasonably in issuing a witness summons against a district judge, even though the judge was not a compellable witness. It is clear from Lord Woolf MR's judgment that the law as to the compellability of the district judge was, before that judgment, unclear and disorganised.

13.47   The next individual case which the Court of Appeal considered in *Ridehaigh* was *Allen v Unigate Dairies Ltd*[1]. The claimant had claimed damages for noise-induced hearing loss which he alleged was caused by exposure to a decrater machine at his workplace. On the first day of trial, the claimant abandoned the claim as it was accepted that the workplace had not been dangerously noisy. The judge ordered the claimant's solicitors to pay the wasted costs, on the basis that they should have found this out earlier and had negligently failed to so. But the Court of Appeal held that the solicitors had not acted negligently. They had taken the claimant's instructions and relied upon advice from an expert and counsel, none of whom had adverted to the reason which ultimately led to the case being abandoned. The reason was that there was a solid wall between the claimant and the decrater. But there was nothing in the defence, the defendants' expert's report, or the defendants' solicitors' correspondence, to suggest the existence or relevance of this wall. Thus it was not negligent of the claimant's solicitors to have failed to find out about it.[2]

1 [1994] Ch 205 at 245.
2 See *Ridehalgh* [1994] Ch 205 at 245–6. See also *Gandesha v Nandra* [2002] Lloyd's Rep PN 558 (Jacob J): solicitors whose client lost a trial because her evidence was not believed had not acted negligently.

13.48   A similar case is *Wall v Lefever*.[1] In the course of cross-examination the claimant's expert made a concession that led to the claimant, on the advice of his solicitors and counsel, abandoning the claim. The defendants sought a wasted costs order against the claimant's lawyers, presumably on the basis that they ought to have detected this weakness in their case at an earlier stage. The trial judge rejected the application, because there was evidence that counsel and solicitors had prepared the case very carefully. Lord Woolf MR said that his reasons could not be faulted.[2]

1 [1998] 1 FCR 605, CA.
2 Ironically, in considering the effect of the expert's concession on the trial, Lord Woolf indicated that it had not meant that the claimant's case was bound to fail. But if the concession did not mean that the claimant's case was bound to fail, why was it that, as a result of it being made, the claimant did abandon his case, following the advice of his solicitors and counsel? This would suggest an alternative error on the part of solicitors and counsel, namely, abandoning the case when it was unnecessary to do so. The consequences of such alternative negligence were not explored in the judgment.

13.49   The court's approach in *Sampson v John Boddy Timber Ltd*[1] was perhaps more surprisingly lenient on the lawyer. Sir Thomas Bingham MR originally thought the conduct in question was negligent, but, as the other two judges disagreed, accepted that it was not a sufficiently plain case for the making of a wasted costs order. In a personal injury action, the defendant's insurers wrote that they were 'prepared to negotiate a settlement of the plaintiff's claim on a compromise basis'. The letter was not marked 'without prejudice'. No settlement was agreed. The defendants listed the letter in their list of documents. Shortly before trial, the claimant's barrister told the defendant's barrister that he proposed to read the letter to the judge. The defendant's barrister objected strongly, on the grounds that the letter was an offer to compromise that was inadmissible, and warned that, if the letter was read to the judge, he would ask that the trial be adjourned to be heard before a new judge. The claimant's barrister contended that the letter was admissible because it did not bear the words 'without prejudice'; the defendant's barrister made clear that he rejected that view. At trial, the claimant's barrister nevertheless read the letter to the judge. The defendant's barrister objected. After argument, the judge adjourned the trial on the ground that he should not have been read the letter; he rejected the argument that it was not privileged because it did not bear the words 'without prejudice'. The question was whether the claimant's barrister should pay the costs wasted by the adjournment. The Court of Appeal held that he should not. Although the letter was privileged, the contrary was fairly arguable, so that it was not negligent of the barrister to have argued it. This case shows how the rule that wasted costs orders should be made only in plain cases works in favour of legal representatives, even when the lawyer's conduct is said only to be negligent rather than improper. The same principles would presumably apply to a solicitor advocate appearing in court.

1 [1995] NLJR 851, (1995) Independent, 17 May, CA.

13.50   In *Turner Page Music v Torres Design Associates Ltd*,[1] the Court of Appeal held that solicitors who declined to reveal to the opposing party in litigation that their client's insurance cover was limited, or to advise their client to settle, were not negligent. Further, solicitors who are under great pressure to act quickly to seek accommodation for a client who has had to sleep outside the previous night may not be negligent in launching an application which, with careful consideration and hindsight, turns out to have been doomed to fail.[2] Solicitors who acted for a company that existed at the start of the retainer but later ceased to exist did not act negligently because, at the later stage, they were unaware of any facts putting them on enquiry as to the status of the company.[3] Solicitors who act on the advice of specialist counsel as to difficult procedural questions relating to the mental capacity of a testator may not be negligent even if they fail to act upon warnings from the court as to the inadequacy of the procedure followed.[4] Solicitors acting in a personal injury action who failed to show an expert a supplementary, and negative, report of a different expert did not act negligently.[5]

1 (1998) Times, 3 August, CA, and see the transcript.
2 *R v Westminster London Borough, ex p Geehan & Butler* [1995] COD 204, (Dyson J).
3 *Padhiar v Patel* [2001] Lloyd's Rep PN 328 at 334 col 2 (Hilary Heilbronn QC sitting as a deputy High Court judge).
4 *Sherman v Fitzhugh Gates* [2003] EWCA Civ 886, [2003] PNLR 39.
5 *Afzal v Chubb Guarding Services Ltd* [2002] EWHC 822 (QB), [2003] PNLR 33 (HHJ Bowsher QC).

(b) Negligent conduct

13.51 In *R v Horsham District Council, ex p Wenman*,[1] Brooke J was unable to make a wasted costs order because the principal errors had occurred before the wasted costs jurisdiction came into effect. He nevertheless indicated that, in judicial review proceedings, lawyers should not regard it as unnecessary to write a letter before action merely because they believed it inevitable that the proposed respondent would deny their clients' claim. Further, judicial review proceedings were wholly inappropriate for cases that bristled with factual disputes. Thirdly, it was wrong to fail to draw the attention of the judge, on the without notice application for leave, to alternative remedies and evidence which told against the applicant's[2] case. Though this case was decided before *Ridehalgh,* and these comments were obiter dicta, it nevertheless supplies helpful guidance. Further, in *Lowline (PSV) Ltd v Direct Aviation Ltd*[3], Rix J held that a solicitor who, in acting in relation to an application made without notice for an injunction, had failed to ensure that full and frank disclosure of all material facts was given had acted negligently and should be the subject of a wasted costs order.

1 [1995] 1 WLR 680 (Brooke J).
2 On the facts of *Wenman,* the solicitors had not acted negligently as they had relied on specialist junior counsel. See below for reliance on counsel.
3 (8 March 1999, unreported), Commercial Court.

13.52 Next, in *D Walter & Co Ltd v Neville Eckley & Co,*[1] a firm of solicitors was advising the claimant, who was the managing director of a company in compulsory liquidation, in an action against the company's liquidator. They instructed junior counsel who specialised in company law. The liquidator's solicitors pointed out to the claimant's solicitors that the action against the liquidator lay in the company, not the claimant, and sent them a copy of a case called *Re Embassy Art Products Ltd*,[2] which they said was relevant. The claimant's solicitors decided not to refer this to counsel, as they trusted their own judgment that the case was irrelevant. Sir Richard Scott V-C decided that the case was highly relevant, and that the solicitors had been negligent in failing to consider it properly. Further, in counsel's written opinion he had said that there were grounds for proceeding but that this must be re-considered if further evidence showed that the company's financial position was worse than thought. The solicitors subsequently received a letter showing that the financial position was much worse, but they failed to consider the effect of this on the application, with or without counsel. This too was negligent. A wasted costs order was made.

1 [1997] BCC 331 (Sir Richard Scott V-C).
2 [1988] 3 BCC 292.

13.53 One relevant factor in the *Fletamentos* case[1] was that the costs in question were the costs of an appeal. The appellant had already had one opportunity to argue his points, and for the most part they had been rejected in clear but careful terms by the judge at first instance. In *Re J (A Minor)*,[2] a barrister was held to have been negligent in advising an appeal where all the supposed grounds of appeal were matters of fact in relation to which the Court of Appeal would not interfere with the judge's findings. The solicitors narrowly escaped a wasted costs order, on the basis of their reliance on counsel's advice (see below). But family law solicitors and counsel acted negligently in agreeing that directions be made in order to allow an application to be heard fairly, while at the same time appealing a consequential order that the hearing date be adjourned in order to allow time for compliance with the agreed directions.[3] Further, the conduct of lawyers who in care proceedings failed to brief expert witnesses properly or to ensure that two expert witnesses had seen all relevant statements was both unreasonable and negligent within the meaning of Supreme Court Act 1981, s 51(7).[4]

1 At para 13.41ff, above.
2 (25 March 1997, unreported), CA.
3 *B v B* [2001] 1 FLR 843 (Wall J).
4 *Re G (Minors) (Care Proceedings: Wasted Costs)* [2000] Fam 104, [2000] 2 WLR 1007 (Wall J).

13.54 In principle it is irrelevant to the exercise of the wasted costs jurisdiction that a party's lawyers' fees are being paid by public funding: those acting for publicly funded clients should be no more at risk of wasted costs orders than those whose clients are privately funded.[1] But there are some regulations that apply only to those acting for publicly funded clients, breach of which may be relevant to the exercise of the jurisdiction. In *Re Stathams*,[2] the Court of Appeal held that a solicitor acted negligently when, in breach of his duty under the former civil legal aid regulations, he failed to serve notice of discharge of the legal aid certificate of the claimant, for whom he acted, on the defendants. The defendants were given the false impression that the claimant was legally aided with a full certificate and that, on the appeal in question, if they won they would have the right to claim costs from the Legal Aid Board. In fact he did not have legal aid, there was no prospect of the Board paying the costs, and the claimant himself had no money. If the defendants had known this, they could have applied for security for costs, which they did not do.

1 *Ridehalgh* [1994] Ch 205 at 234–5, referring to Legal Aid Act 1998, s 31(1), now replaced by Access to Justice Act 1999, s 22(1).
2 [1997] PIQR P464, CA.

13.55 In *Veasey v Millfeed & Co Ltd,*[1] the solicitors in question issued and served a writ in which they named the claimant as a partnership of father and son, when in fact the partnership had already been dissolved, and only the son had instructed the solicitors. The defendants knew that the son was legally aided so that costs would not be recoverable from him, but were given to believe that the father was a party, not in receipt of legal aid, so that he might be able to satisfy a costs order. In truth, the father was not a party and the only claimant was the legally aided son. Had the defendants known the truth they would have settled the case in the sum at which they ultimately settled it when they discovered the truth. The Court of Appeal held that the solicitors had acted negligently in serving proceedings that named the father as well as the son as the claimant, when the father was not a party. They were liable for the costs caused by the delay in settlement.

1 [1997] PNLR 100, CA.

13.56 The relevance of public funding arose again in *Shah v Singh.*[1] The claimant's solicitors applied for an adjournment of the trial, a few days before it was due to begin. The partner dealing with the matter sent a litigation clerk to make the application, but failed to ensure that the clerk emphasised to the court that legal aid for the trial had only recently been granted. The application was rejected and the claimant lost the trial, but, on appeal, a re-hearing was ordered. The Court of Appeal held that it had been negligent of the partner to fail to ensure that the court was told of the recent grant of legal aid; if it had been told, an adjournment would probably have been granted, and the costs of the appeal avoided. Thus the claimant's solicitors were ordered to pay the costs of the appeal.

1 [1996] 1 PNLR 83, CA.

13.57 Delay in the conduct of litigation may be so great as to amount to negligent conduct, though it may be hard to show that the delay has caused any loss of costs.[1] As to a solicitor's disclosure obligations:[2]

'Although it is no doubt best practice for a solicitor either to take possession of the client's files which have a potential bearing on the dispute or to visit the client and inspect such files, I do not think that a failure to take these steps, whatever the circumstances, means that the solicitor is in breach of duty to his client or to the court. A solicitor must carefully explain the obligation of disclosure to the client, but if the client tells him certain categories of documents have been lost he is entitled to accept these instructions unless there are matters which cast doubt on the instructions or in any event require further investigation.'

Negligence of solicitors for the purposes of a wasted costs order may also depend upon their use of counsel, which we consider next.

1 *Kilroy v Kilroy* [1997] PNLR 66, CA, *Padhiar v Patel* [2001] Lloyd's Rep PN 328 (Hilary Heilbronn QC sitting as a deputy High Court judge).
2 *Hedrich v Standard Bank London Ltd* [2007] EWHC 1656 (QB), [2007] PNLR 31 (Field J), at [34].

7 Reliance on counsel

13.58 In *Locke v Camberwell Health Authority,*[1] Taylor LJ stated principles relevant to solicitors' reliance upon counsel, which, together with their amplification in *Ridehalgh*, are quoted in chapter 2 to which reference should be made.[2] In *R v Luton Family Proceedings Court, ex p R,*[3] the Court of Appeal overturned a decision that a solicitor had not been entitled to rely upon the advice of specialist junior counsel in relation to judicial review. There was no evidence as to the extent of the solicitor's own expertise in judicial review, nor was counsel's advice obviously wrong.[4] It is thought, however, that it might have been different if there *had* been evidence that the solicitor was himself an expert in judicial review: that would have made it easier to show that he ought to have taken a different view or pointed out errors in counsel's approach.

1 [1991] 2 Med LR 249, CA. See also *Davy-Chiesman v Davy-Chiesman* [1984] Fam 48, CA, and para 2.11ff, above.
2 See para 2.11, above.
3 [1998] CLY 496, CA.
4 See also *Reaveley v Safeway Stores plc* [1998] PNLR 526, CA and *Afzal v Chubb Guarding Services Ltd* [2002] EWHC 822 (QB), [2003] PNLR 33 (HHJ Bowsher QC) (reasonable to rely on counsel's advice as to prospects of success in personal injury action); *R v A* [2000] PNLR 628, CA (reasonable to rely on criminal barrister's advice that custody time limit had expired); *Regent Leisuretime Ltd v Skerrett* [2006] EWCA Civ 1184, [2007] PNLR 9 (reasonable to rely on counsel's advice as to distinction between claims of company and of directors).

13.59 The solicitors in the slightly earlier case of *Re J (a minor)*[1] escaped by a much narrower margin. Ward LJ held that two barristers who advised appeal from a county court judge's decision as to a care order were both negligent. There was no evidence from the appellants' solicitors that they had applied their minds to counsel's advice on appeal at all. But they escaped a wasted costs order because counsel's advice was not glaringly wrong. Ward LJ said:

> 'It seems [the solicitor] relied blindly on counsel and abdicated his professional responsibility to give independent consideration to whether or not this was a proper appeal. Such a lamentable failure to exercise any judgment at all seems to me to be a negation of professional responsibility. Solicitors and counsel work as a team, and as a team, each has an equally valuable contribution to make. They are lawyers, each of them, and they should be judged as lawyers, not as outdoor clerks. It is, therefore, with considerable reluctance that I find myself grudgingly accepting the submission advanced on behalf of the solicitors that the advice of counsel, also adopted as it was by those advising the local authority, was not so glaringly without some superficial attraction that the solicitors should have rejected or questioned it. I say begrudge that conclusion because, implicit within it, is an acceptance that the level of competence by which the standard is fixed must be pretty low and such conclusion is, in fact, the antithesis of the regard I have for the solicitors' profession.'

There is in this passage the germ of an argument that the standard to be applied to solicitors who rely upon counsel should be raised.[2] Presumably those trained as solicitor advocates are already subject to a higher standard, as they hold themselves out has having skills in advocacy similar to those of barristers.

1 (25 March 1997, unreported), CA.
2 Compare the discussion of solicitors' liability for the conduct of litigation in chapter 12, and see also *Dace v Redland Aggregates Ltd* [1997] EGCS 123 (Blackburne J). Counsel's advice that there had been a reasonable prospect of success in asserting the existence of an agricultural tenancy was unreasonable and negligent, and the solicitor had not been entitled to rely on it blindly.

13.60 In the *Fletamentos* case,[1] however, it was no excuse for the solicitor that, on the eve of the doomed appeal, leading counsel had advised by telephone that the application had a fair chance of success. As observed above, the circumstances of that case were exceptional. The solicitor had already received advice from two different leading counsel specialising in commercial law to the effect that the appeal was hopeless. He did not formally brief the third leading counsel to advise on the prospects of success. Further, there was a catalogue of other bizarre features.

1 See para 13.41, above.

8 Relevance of public funding and conditional fee agreements

13.61 As long as legal representatives comply with public funding regulations, public funding makes no difference to the likelihood of a wasted costs order being granted, and such legal representatives should not allow their conduct to be tempered by fear that it might.[1] In particular, it is inappropriate for privately funded clients to apply for wasted costs orders against those who act for publicly funded clients, simply on the basis that costs cannot be obtained from the legally aided clients.[2] Further, in *Afzal v Chubb Guarding Services Ltd*[3] HHJ Bowsher stressed the following passage from *Ridehalgh*:

> ' "It is incumbent on courts to which applications for wasted costs orders are made to bear prominently in mind the peculiar vulnerability of legal representatives acting for assisted persons ... which recent experience abundantly confirms. It would subvert the benevolent purposes of this legislation if such representatives were subject to any unusual personal risk." '

1 *Ridehalgh* [1994] Ch 205 at 234–5. See now Access to Justice Act 1999, s 22(1).
2 See Otton LJ's observations in *Wall v Lefever* [1998] 1 FCR 605, CA at 615–6.
3 [2002] EWHC 822 (QB), [2003] PNLR 33 (HHJ Bowsher QC), at [31].

13.62 In cases where privilege is not waived, to what extent may the court infer that, because a client is publicly funded, the client's lawyers must have given positive advice as to the merits pursuant to the relevant regulations? In *Brown v Bennett (No 2)*[1], Neuberger J considered that it was unhelpful and even dangerous to try to guess what must have passed between a legally aided litigant's advisors and the Legal Aid Board in a case where the Board had taken no part in the application. It was not possible safely to deduce what advice the Board had received from the lawyers: it was possible to think of various scenarios in which legal aid might have been extended without such a lawyer's opinion stating that there was a more than 50% chance of success. In *Gandesha v Nandra*[2], however, Jacob J appears to have thought, obiter, that it was appropriate to undertake such an exercise. But a different approach was taken in *Fryer v RICS*, which was not cited in *Gandesha*. At first instance privilege had not been waived. The judge refused to infer that, because a party had the benefit of legal aid, counsel must have advised that he had more than a 50% chance of success at trial. The Court of Appeal held that this was a perfectly permissible approach.[3] By the time the case reached the Court of Appeal, privilege had been waived. It emerged that counsel had advised that the claim had a 50–60% chance of success.[4] The Court of Appeal held that the advice was not negligent. The general tenor of these authorities is to the effect that, where privilege is not waived, it is not appropriate or safe to infer from the existence of public funding that lawyers have given particularly positive advice[5]. That accords with Lord Bingham's statements in *Medcalf* as to the correct approach where privilege is not waived.

1 [2002] 1 WLR 713 (Neuberger J), at [67]–[68], and [89].
2 [2002] Lloyd's Rep PN 558 at 560–1.
3 [2000] Lloyd's Rep PN 534 at [49].
4 [2000] Lloyd's Rep PN 534 at [82]. A different approach, however, appears to have been taken in *B v B* [2001] 1 FLR 843 (Wall J).
5 To similar effect, see *Daly v Hubner* [2002] Lloyd's Rep PN 461 (Etherton J).

13.63 So far as wasted costs orders are concerned, in principle the existence or otherwise of a conditional fee agreement should make no difference to whether the court will make an order, assuming that the solicitors have complied with the applicable regulations. It may be argued that such lawyers are in no different position from lawyers who act for claimants who have legal aid certificates requiring no contribution from the client.[1] Such lawyers' position may, however, be material to applications for third party costs orders which we consider below at para 13.77.

1 Cf *Hodgson v Imperial Tobacco Ltd* [1998] 1 WLR 1056 esp at 1066A–C, CA.

9 Causation

13.64 The Court of Appeal stated in *Ridehalgh*[1] that:

'... the court has jurisdiction to make a wasted costs order only where the improper, unreasonable or negligent conduct complained of has caused a waste of costs and only to the extent of such wasted costs. Demonstration of a causal link is essential. Where the conduct is proved but no waste of costs is shown to have resulted, the case may be one to be referred to the appropriate disciplinary body or the legal aid authorities, but it is not one for the exercise of the wasted costs jurisdiction.'

In *Brown v Bennett* (*No 2*)[2], Neuberger J held that causation in wasted costs applications should be determined on the balance of probabilities, and rejected a submission that the loss of a chance approach should be applied.

1 [1994] Ch 205 at 237E–F.
2 [2002] 1 WLR 713, at [52]–[56].

13.65 As to the application of the test of causation, in *Sawrij v Lynx* (*Helping Abused Animals*) *Ltd*[1] the defendant had consistently been in default of its obligations with regard to disclosure. The claimant applied at trial for the defence to be struck out on that basis, and two days were spent dealing with the application, at the end of which it was rejected. The Court of Appeal nevertheless accepted that the trial judge had been entitled to find that the making of the application had been caused by the defendants' defaults in disclosure, so that a wasted costs order against the defendants' solicitors was justified in relation to those two days. It was not necessary for the claimants to show that they were prejudiced by the failure to give disclosure; all they had to show was that it was reasonable to have made the application.[2] On this approach, the test of causation may be relatively favourable to applicants. On the other hand, in *Kilroy v Kilroy*[3] the applicant was unable to show that lengthy delay by solicitors in the conduct of litigation had caused any specific costs to be wasted.

1 (21 February 1997, unreported), CA.
2 See Pill LJ's judgment at p 34 of the transcript.
3 [1997] PNLR 66, CA.

13.66 It will be recalled that Supreme Court Act 1981, s 56(7) provides:

'(7) In subsection (6), "wasted costs" means any costs incurred by a party–

(a) as a result of any improper, unreasonable or negligent act or omission on the part of any legal representative or any employee of such a representative; or

(b) which, in the light of any such act or omission occurring after they were incurred, the court considers it unreasonable to expect that party to pay.'

What is the ambit of para (b)? Imagine that I carefully spend a day preparing a trial and arrive at court the next day to present the trial. You, the barrister or solicitor instructed to appear for the opposite party, sleep in, miss the train, and the hearing has to be adjourned. You acted unreasonably or negligently, and this caused costs to be wasted, but your negligence occurred after I had done the work of preparing. It is submitted that it is this type of case at which para (b) is aimed.

10   Justice in all the circumstances

13.67 As mentioned above, in *Ridehalgh* Sir Thomas Bingham MR made clear that, if the applicant shows that improper, unreasonable or negligent conduct has caused costs to be wasted, though the court is not bound to make a wasted costs order, it will need to provide sustainable reasons if it decides not to do so. Lord Bingham reiterated the point in the second passage quoted above at para 13.17 from *Medcalf*. *R v Secretary of State for the Home Office, ex p Wong*[1] was such a case. The solicitor of an applicant for judicial review should have come off the record when legal aid was withdrawn, and should have notified the respondent of the withdrawal. But Schiemann J decided not to make an order because, if the solicitor had come off the record, then the point that ultimately caused the applicant to win might never have come to light, so that an injustice would have been done because he would have lost a case which he deserved to win. Similarly, in *Pelling v Bruce-Williams,*[2] solicitors had negligently failed to serve an affidavit in support of an application to commit the appellant to prison. But the committal application related only to the appellant's failure to serve an affidavit of means, and only £200 was at stake. The making of a wasted costs order was not proportionate to the scale of the matter, so no order was made.

1 [1995] COD 331 (Schiemann J).
2 (16 December 1998, unreported), CA.

11 Contribution and indemnity

13.68 *Fletamentos* also contains some obiter discussion of what should be done if more than one party was to blame for the wasted costs, for instance both solicitors and counsel. Simon Brown LJ considered that, if the court made an order against solicitors, it probably did not have power to go on and make a contribution order in their favour against counsel, if the aggrieved party to the proceedings had not sought an order from counsel.[1] Morritt LJ, on the other hand, thought that it might be possible to order one legal representative to indemnify another in respect of payments to the applicant. In his view, however, normally the court would assess the percentage of the wasted costs which each lawyer should pay to the applicant.[2] In *Gandesha v Nandra*[3], however, a wasted costs application was made only against solicitors. The solicitors referred to what Morritt LJ had said and submitted that counsel was partly to blame and that the correct approach was to identify the part of the wasted costs for which the solicitors alone were liable. Jacob J rejected this submission. If solicitors and counsel were both 100% to blame for the costs which had been wasted, then if the wasted costs application was made only against one lawyer, that lawyer had to pay 100% of the wasted costs even if the other lawyer was equally to blame. The absence of a mechanism for contribution in the Act was simply unfortunate for the lawyer receiving the application. The subtext here may be that in practice it is insurers rather than individual lawyers who are likely to have to bear the costs; generally the sums in issue will be relatively low, and the court may feel that insurers simply have to bear them. But it still seems unsatisfactory that there should be no mechanism for claiming contribution.

1 [2003] Lloyd's Rep PN 26 at 33 col 2 to 34 col 1.
2 [2003] Lloyd's Rep PN 26 at 43, col 2.
3 [2002] Lloyd's Rep PN 558 at 562, col 1.

12 Criminal law[1]

13.69 So far we have dealt only with provisions relating to civil proceedings. The Supreme Court Act 1981, s 56 does not relate to criminal proceedings. But those are governed by almost identical provisions, that were introduced at the same time, and appear in Prosecution of Offences Act 1985, s 19A and Costs in Criminal Cases (General) Regulations 1986, regs 3A–3D.[2] The wording of these provisions is very similar to the equivalent provisions in civil law, and the Court of Appeal in *Ridehalgh* expressed the hope that its decision there would be of guidance in criminal cases, while realising that it could not be authoritative. In *Re a Solicitor (wasted costs order)*,[3] the criminal division of the Court of Appeal had to consider the meaning of the words 'improper, unreasonable or negligent' which appeared in the criminal statute. Giving the judgment of the court, Beldam LJ referred to the definitions suggested in *Ridehalgh*, and effectively adopted them. The court held that no reasonably competent solicitor would have issued a witness summons for the recovery of documents unless there was more than a speculative basis for believing that they might be relevant to the case; as there was no such basis, a wasted costs order was made. In *R v Mintz*[4], the Court of Appeal held that the court should ask (i) whether there had been an improper, unreasonable or negligent act or omission, (ii) whether, as a result, costs had been incurred by a party, and (iii) if the answer to (i) and (ii) was yes, whether the court should exercise its jurisdiction to disallow or order the lawyer to meet the whole or any part of the relevant costs, and if so what specific sum was involved. The standard of proof is the civil one, on the balance of probabilities.[5] As in civil proceedings, proving causation is a necessary element of applying for a wasted costs order.[6]

1 See generally *Archbold 2007* at para 6–40.
2 SI 1986/1335, though subsequently amended. Regulation 3 also gives the court power to order that one party pay costs to another party, if the costs have been caused by the 'unnecessary or improper act or omission' of the first party.
3 [1996] 1 FLR 40, CA.
4 Times, 16 July 1999, CA. See also *Re a Barrister (wasted costs order) (No 1 of 1991)* [1993] QB 293, CA.
5 Cf *Re Madden* [2004] EWCA Crim 754, [2004] PNLR 37.
6 *Re Lakha & Booth* (6 November 1998, unreported), CA. Cf *R v Wood Green Crown Court, ex p DPP* [1993] 1 WLR 723, DC, a case relating to an order that another party pay the costs, rather than a wasted costs order.

13.70 Reported cases in relation to wasted costs orders in criminal proceedings tend to be short and to turn on specific aspects of criminal practice. In *R v Basra (wasted costs order)*,[1] a solicitor had applied for a witness summons when there was no proper basis to do so. The criminal division of the Court of Appeal upheld the making of a wasted costs order against the solicitor. But in *Neill v Crown Prosecution* Service[2] no order was granted because the solicitor had not acted improperly when he requested an old-style committal in circumstances where there was good reason to believe that the prosecution case might collapse at that stage. In *R v Madden*[3], defence counsel called a witness despite indications that his evidence would not favour the defence case. The witness's evidence was not helpful to the defence. The judge granted defence counsel's application for the jury to be discharged, but ordered defence counsel to pay the wasted costs. The Court of Appeal upheld the order. In *R v Duffy*[4], a trial was adjourned due to the late appearance of counsel. It emerged that this was due to a late change in the listing by the court. Counsel had not behaved improperly or unreasonably and so the Court of Appeal held that no wasted costs order should have been made.[5]

1 [1998] PNLR 535, CA.
2 [1997] COD 171, DC.
3 [2004] EWCA Crim 754, [2004] PNLR 37.
4 [2004] EWCA Crim 330, [2004] PNLR 36.
5 See also *R v Qadi* [2000] PNLR 137 (solicitor's clerk negligent in taking instructions within earshot of jury members); *R v A* [2000] PNLR 628 (solicitors not negligent to rely on counsel's advice as to custody time limits); *R (on the application of the Director of Public Prosecutions) v Cheshire Justices* [2002] EWHC 466 (Admin), [2002] PNLR 36 (prosecution solicitor negligent as had to ask for adjournment in order to obtain a legal authority).

C   INHERENT JURISDICTION OVER SOLICITORS

13.71   Before the introduction of wasted costs orders, the court had an inherent jurisdiction to make costs orders against solicitors. Lord Woolf MR considered the exercise of this jurisdiction, in civil cases, after the introduction of the power to make wasted costs orders, in *Hodgson v Imperial Tobacco Ltd*[1] He said that 'this limited jurisdiction is only going to be relevant in a very small minority of cases'. He added:

> 'Mr Brennan makes three submissions about this jurisdiction which are not controversial except in one respect. The first is that it is limited to orders against solicitors and does not extend to orders against counsel. The second is that it must be regarded as having been supplanted in circumstances falling within the statutory wasted costs jurisdiction; and the third is that it should not be exercised until after a consideration whether an order should be made under the wasted costs jurisdiction. The point which might be controversial is whether today the courts would take the view that the inherent jurisdiction is limited to orders against solicitors. This is not a point which we have considered and as it does not arise we express no opinion on it.'

1 See [1998] 1 WLR 1056 at 1066E–H, CA.

13.72   Thus it appears that the court will rarely make orders under this jurisdiction. In particular, if the facts justify a wasted costs order, then the court will not move on to consider an order under this jurisdiction. In most cases, if the court is not prepared to make a wasted costs order, it will not be appropriate to make an order under this jurisdiction. What are the exceptions? Two examples given by Rose LJ in the *Tolstoy* case[1] were acting without authority, or in breach of an undertaking. These are considered in chapter 5. In criminal cases, the court also has an inherent jurisdiction to order solicitors to pay the costs of proceedings, but the jurisdiction is exercisable only if there has been a serious dereliction of duty on the part of the solicitor; mere mistake, error of judgment or negligence will not suffice.[2] For this reason, it is likely that, in criminal cases as well as civil, the wasted costs jurisdiction will be used more frequently than the court's inherent jurisdiction.

1 *Tolstoy-Miloslavsky v Aldington* [1996] 1 WLR 736, CA.
2 *Holden & Co v Crown Prosecution Service* [1990] 2 QB 261, CA.

D   GENERAL JURISDICTION OVER COSTS

13.73   In *Aiden Shipping Co Ltd v Interbulk Ltd,*[1] the House of Lords established that the court has jurisdiction, pursuant to Supreme Court Act 1981, s 51(1) and (3), to make orders that non-parties pay the costs of proceedings. In a subsequent decision, the Court of Appeal indicated that it was likely that such an order would be made in circumstances where a non-party had maintained the action, in the sense of:[2]

> 'wanton and officious intermeddling with the disputes of others in [which] the meddler has no interest whatever, and where the assistance he renders to one or the other party is without justification or excuse.'

This raised the question of whether solicitors who acted for no fee might be liable for the other party's costs, pursuant to s 51(1) and (3). The ratio of the Court of Appeal's decision in *Tolstoy-Miloslavsky v Aldington*[3] is that there is no jurisdiction to award costs against solicitors, pursuant to s 51(1) and (3), merely because they act for no fee. The jurisdiction under s 51(1) and (3) could be exercised against a solicitor only 'if he acts outside the role of solicitor, e g in a private capacity or as a true third party funder for someone else'.[4]

1 [1986] AC 965.
2 *Murphy v Young & Co's Brewery plc* [1997] 1 WLR 1591, CA per Phillips LJ at 1601, referring to the test which Lord Mustill set out in *Giles v Thompson* [1994] 1 AC 142 at 164, HL. See also Balcombe LJ's guidelines in *Symphony Group plc v Hodgson* [1994] QB 179, CA.
3 [1996] 1 WLR 736.
4 *Tolstoy* [1996] 1 WLR 736 per Rose LJ at 746A. Ward LJ agreed: 751B. See also Roch LJ at 750D–F. The House of Lords dismissed a petition for leave to appeal: 752G. Further, Lord Woolf MR referred to the decision with approval in *Hodgson v Imperial Tobacco* [1998] 1 WLR 1056 at 1066H, CA.

13.74   The court in *Tolstoy* was not suggesting that a solicitor could never be the subject of an order pursuant to Supreme Court Act 1981, s 51(1) and (3). A solicitor could presumably be made the subject of such an order if he or she truly maintained another's action, in the sense of intermeddling set out above. For instance, solicitors might be liable in this way if they funded a third party's action in which they were not themselves instructed as solicitors, and in relation to which they had no connection and no reason for such support.[1] It will be recalled from the discussion above that, in *Tolstoy,* the court considered that the solicitors had engaged in considerable meddling and interference in the litigation, for their own personal reasons. Yet, even on those facts, the court did not consider that there was jurisdiction to make a costs order under s 51(1) and (3): instead, the appropriate course was to make a wasted costs order under s 51(6).

1 Further, see *Nordstern Allgemeine Versicherungs AG v Internav Ltd* [1999] 23 LS Gaz R 33, CA: an order was made against a solicitor, but he had not been instructed to act as a solicitor in the proceedings in question. In *Globe Equities Ltd v Globe Legal Services Ltd* [1999] BLR 232, CA the defendant company had been formed by solicitors to hold the lease of their offices; the solicitors were the guarantors under the lease; it was appropriate to order them to pay costs as they were 'the real defendants'.

13.75 In the earlier case *of Mainwaring v Goldtech,*[1] the Court of Appeal had been prepared to assume, for the sake of argument, that a solicitor might be liable for the other party's costs:

'... if he conducts the litigation in the knowledge that there is no real likelihood of his ever having his costs and expenses reimbursed by or on behalf of the client, save in the event of the litigation being successful.'

But this was not part of the ratio, because the court did not hear argument on it, and counsel for the solicitors was prepared to accept it for the purposes of the appeal. It must now be considered in light of the decision in *Tolstoy.* In particular, Rose LJ's judgment in that case emphasised that it was in the public interest, and perfectly proper, for solicitors and counsel to act without fee.[2] It is submitted that the passage quoted from *Mainwaring* was originally obiter and should now be treated as effectively having been overruled by the decision in *Tolstoy,* especially as *Mainwaring* was cited in argument in *Tolstoy.*[3]

1 (1991) Times, 19 February, CA.
2 [1996] 1 WLR 736 at 746B–D.
3 See [1996] 1 WLR 736 at 738C. Note also that Lord Woolf MR observed in *Hodgson v Imperial Tobacco Ltd* [1998] 1 WLR 1056 that the court's jurisdiction to make an order against solicitors under Supreme Court Act 1981, s 51(1) and (3) would be exercised only in 'a very small minority of cases': [1998] 1 WLR 1056 at 1066F.

13.76 The Privy Council took the matter further in *Dymocks Franchise Systems (NSW) Pty Ltd v Todd*[1], where Lord Brown of Eaton-under-Heywood, giving the judgment of the Board, set out the principles as follows:

'(1) Although costs orders against non-parties are to be regarded as "exceptional", exceptional in this context means no more than

701

outside the ordinary run of cases where parties pursue or defend claims for their own benefit and at their own expense. The ultimate question in any such "exceptional" case is whether in all the circumstances it is just to make the order. It must be recognised that this is inevitably to some extent a fact-specific jurisdiction and that there will often be a number of different considerations in play, some militating in favour of an order, some against.

(2) Generally speaking the discretion will not be exercised against "pure funders", described in para 40 of *Hamilton v Al Fayed (No 2)* [2003] QB 1175, 1194 as "those with no personal interest in the litigation, who do not stand to benefit from it, are not funding it as a matter of business, and in no way seek to control its course". In their case the court's usual approach is to give priority to the public interest in the funded party getting access to justice over that of the successful unfunded party recovering his costs and so not having to bear the expense of vindicating his rights.

(3) Where, however, the non-party not merely funds the proceedings but substantially also controls or at any rate is to benefit from them, justice will ordinarily require that, if the proceedings fail, he will pay the successful party's costs. The non-party in these cases is not so much facilitating access to justice by the party funded as himself gaining access to justice for his own purposes. He himself is "the real party" to the litigation ...Nor, indeed, is it necessary that the non-party be "the only real party" to the litigation in the sense explained in the *Knight* case, provided that he is "a real party in ... very important and critical respects"

1 [2004] UKPC 39, [2004] 1 WLR 2807, at [25].

13.77 In *Myatt v National Coal Board (No 2)*[1], the Court of Appeal considered the application of these principles to solicitors in cases where litigation is funded by a conditional fee agreement ('CFA') and the issue is as to the enforceability of the CFA. Lloyd LJ, with whom Sir Henry Brooke agreed, considered that the impact of the decision was limited to such cases.[2] The costs in question were the costs of an appeal in four test cases as to the enforceability of CFAs. At stake in the appeal for the four claimants was approximately £2,500 each; but for the solicitors who acted for the claimants on the appeal, Ollerenshaw, the sum at stake was over £200,000 in a total of 64 cases: if the CFAs were unenforceable, the solicitors would not be entitled to their profit costs. The claimants lost the appeal. The defendants were entitled to the costs of the appeal from the claimants, but the claimants had no insurance in relation to those costs. The defendants therefore sought an order for costs against the claimants' solicitors, Ollerenshaw. Dyson LJ held that the court had jurisdiction to make an order for costs under the Supreme Court Act 1981, s 51(3) against a solicitor 'where litigation is pursued by the client for the benefit or to a substantial degree for the benefit of the solicitor'. The main reason why the appeal had been launched was to protect Ollerenshaw's claim to their profit costs. Ollerenshaw was ordered to pay 50% of the defendants' costs of the appeal. Lloyd LJ pointed out that the claimants had no interest in the issue as to Ollerenshaw's profit costs: whatever the result of the appeal as to the profit costs, it would have made no difference to the claimants. It followed that, in relation to the profit costs, 'the appeal was brought for the solicitor's sake, not for that of the client'. Ollerenshaw had funded the appeal because it had supplied its own services for free and it had to be assumed that it had paid counsel. Lloyd LJ considered that the solicitors had:

> 'acted in respect of the appeal in a dual capacity; acting for their clients, certainly, and with a real interest of those clients to protect, but primarily acting for their own sake ... Ollerenshaw were a real party to the litigation at the stage of the appeal, albeit that the claimants were also.'

On that basis, which he considered would probably apply only in cases where the enforceability of a CFA was at stake, there was jurisdiction to make a third party costs order against Ollerenshaw even though Ollerenshaw had acted as solicitors in relation to the appeal. He agreed that Ollerenshaw should pay 50% of the defendant's costs of the appeal. It is therefore thought that the scope of this ground for holding that solicitors acting in litigation must pay costs pursuant to s 51(3) Supreme Court Act is limited in the way which Lloyd LJ identified.

1 [2007] EWCA Civ 1559, [2007] 1 WLR 1559.
2 See [23], [27] and [29].

13.78 By s 19B of the Prosecution of Offences Act 1985, the court has power to make a costs order against a third party in criminal cases if:[1]

> '(a) there has been serious misconduct (whether or not constituting a contempt of court) by the third party, and
>
> (b) the court considers it appropriate, having regard to that misconduct, to make a third party costs order against him.'

In *R v Ahmati*[2] the Court of Appeal held that such misconduct must require more serious conduct than contemplated under s 19A of the same Act in relation to wasted costs.[3] McCombe J said that misconduct in this context would include deliberate or negligent failure to attend to one's duties or falling below a proper standard in that regard. It was necessary to consider the responsibilities of the office of the respondent, the importance of the public objects which the respondent served, and the nature and extent of the departure from those responsibilities. A department of the Home Office had failed to respond to questions from the Court of Appeal on five separate occasions. The misconduct was serious and an order was made.

1 See also the Costs in Criminal Cases (General) Regulations 1986, regs 3E–3I as to the procedure.
2 [2006] EWCA Crim 1826, [2007] PNLR 3.
3 Considered at paras 13.69–13.70, above.

Chapter 14

Disclosure and privilege

A   PRE-ACTION DISCLOSURE

1   Introduction

14.01   Contractual or equitable rights to the production of documents or to inspect and copy them are less important than they used to be because of the professional negligence pre-action protocol (and the costs sanctions for non-compliance[1]) and also the court's power to make an order for pre-action disclosure under CPR Part 31.16 (considered below). Nevertheless, there may be circumstances in which a claimant cannot or does not wish to give notice of a claim or to make an application for pre-action disclosure (for instance where the request for disclosure is made as part of a storage or an auditing process). Moreover, there may be a costs advantage for clients or former clients to invoke their contractual or equitable rights either independently or in conjunction with an application under CPR Part 31.16. The general rule is that parties against whom such an application is made are entitled to their costs of the application and of complying with the order on the basis that they are entitled to require applicants to satisfy the court that they are entitled to disclosure.[2] This reasoning cannot apply, however, where the claimant has a contractual or equitable right to disclosure.[3] Moreover, these substantive rights are relevant to the scope of disclosure that a solicitor can be required to make either on an application for pre-action disclosure under Part 31.16 or on standard disclosure where the solicitor was acting under a joint or multiple retainer and may have a competing duty to assert privilege or confidence in a number of documents on the file on behalf of another client. Solicitors' duties of confidentiality and to assert privilege on behalf of their clients or former clients also affect their own ability to disclose their documents to third parties (most obviously to notify circumstances of a potential claim to their insurers or to disclose documents to the solicitors appointed by their insurers or to co-defendants such as barristers). For these reasons a client's substantive rights to disclosure or to prevent disclosure remain of relevance. Finally, in the following discussion of the rights of access to documents a distinction is drawn between rights of ownership and rights to inspect and copy documents because the principles that apply to these rights are not the same.

1   See para 14.4, below.

2 CPR Part 48.1(2) provides that the general rule is that the court will award the person against whom an order for pre-action disclosure is sought under CPR Part 31.16 both (a) the costs of the application and (b) the costs of complying with any order made on the application. In *Bermuda International Securities v KPMG* [2001] EWCA Civ 269, [2001] Lloyd's Rep PN 392 at [31]–[33] Rix LJ indicated that parties may be deprived of the costs of the application (although not of the disclosure exercise) where they resist unreasonably. In *SES Contracting Ltd v UK Coal plc* [2007] EWCA Civ 791 at [17] Moore-Bick LJ stated the principle as follows:

> 'CPR r 48.1 provides that, where a person makes an application for disclosure before proceedings, the general rule is that the court will award the person against whom the order is sought his costs of the application, but that the court may make a different order having regard to all the circumstances, including the extent to which it was reasonable for the person against whom the order was sought to oppose the application. Although a Respondent to an application may incur some costs merely in considering what response to make to an application of this kind, in most cases he will only incur substantial costs if he opposes it. By laying down a general rule that the Respondent will be awarded his costs, therefore, I think that the Rules implicitly recognise that it will not usually be unreasonable for him to require the Applicant to satisfy the court that he ought to be granted the relief which he seeks. The reason for that (if it be necessary to find one) lies, I think, in a recognition that a private person who is not a party to existing litigation which brings with it an obligation of disclosure is entitled to maintain the privacy of his papers unless sufficient grounds can be shown for overriding it and that it is for the person seeking to invade that privacy to justify doing so. At all events, the rule is clear in its terms and provides the point of departure for a judge dealing with the costs of an application of this kind.'

3 Compare *Equitas Ltd v Horace Holman & Co Ltd* [2007] EWHC 903 (Comm) (Andrew Smith J) at [95]:

> 'They were justified in bringing proceedings to enforce their entitlement, and I consider that prima facie in these circumstances they are entitled to be paid the costs of bringing the proceedings.'

2 Production and inspection of documents

(a) Ownership of a solicitor's file

14.02 The rights of a client to the production or inspection of documents are primarily based on the contract of retainer.[1] In practice, however, it is rare that a client care letter will deal in terms with rights of this kind.[2] In the absence of any contractual terms (and subject to any lien for unpaid fees), the primary right of clients or former clients is to require the solicitor to deliver up or hand over documents which belong to them. The client is the owner of all documents that were created or received by the solicitor whilst acting as the client's agent.[3] This category of documents will include all transactional documents[4] (and drafts of transactional documents[5]), correspondence passing between the solicitor and third parties and attendance notes of conversations between the solicitor and third parties whilst acting as the client's solicitor and agent. It does not, however, include the solicitor's working papers.[6] These documents belong to the solicitor and this category includes correspondence to and from the client[7] attendance notes of discussions with the client and drafts of letters and notes of other research. The court may order a solicitor to deliver up documents under its inherent supervisory jurisdiction.[8] Initially, there was some doubt whether the court could exercise the jurisdiction over solicitors outside the conduct of litigation but s 68 of the Solicitors Act 1974 expressly extends the court's power to do so.[9] An application for the production of documents should be made under CPR Part 8.[10]

1 It is, however, unnecessary to prove the existence of a contract. The right to documents considered in this paragraph and the duty to make documents that are not owned by the client available for inspection, which is considered in the next paragraph, arise out of the agency relationship between solicitor and client. Such a relationship may arise even though there is no contract: see para 5.1, above, and *Yasuda Fire & Marine Insurance Co of Europe Ltd v Orion Marine Insurance Underwriting Agency Ltd* [1995] QB 174 (Colman J) at 185D:

> 'Although in modern commercial transactions agencies are almost invariably founded upon a contract between principal and agent, there is no necessity for such a contract to exist. It is sufficient if there is consent by the principal to the exercise by the agent of authority and consent by the agent to his exercising such authority on behalf of the principal: see *Garnac Grain Co Inc v HMF Faure & Fairclough (Note)* [1968] AC 1130, 1137, *per* Lord Pearson.'

2 The Solicitors' Code of Conduct 2007 does not impose any professional obligations upon solicitors to keep or make available documents. Rule 5.01(g) imposes an obligation to make arrangements for the effective management for the safekeeping of documents and assets. Guidance notes 22 and 23 impose a minimum requirement that the solicitors should be able to identify the owner of assets and documents.

3 See *Leicestershire County Council v Michael Faraday & Partners Ltd* [1941] 2 KB 205, CA (architects) at 216 (Mackinnon LJ):

> 'If an agent brings into existence certain documents while in the employment of his principal, they are the principal's documents, and the principal can claim that the agent should hand them over.'

See also *Gomba Holdings UK Ltd v Minories Finance Ltd* [1988] 1 WLR 1231, CA (receivers) at 1233D-E (Fox LJ):

> 'The basis of the claim to ownership is that the receivers were, during the receiverships, the agents of the companies and were paid by the companies. It is said that, as between principal and agent, all documents concerning the principal's affairs which have been prepared or received by the agent belong to the principal and have to be delivered up on the termination of the agency. In general terms that is a correct statement of principle but it cannot be applied mechanically to the somewhat complex position of a receivership.'

In that case Fox LJ identified three categories of documents which are relevant to joint or multiple retainers (see below).

4 Guidance note 22 (above) states that:

> 'The terms "documents" and "assets" should be interpreted in a non-technical way to include, for example, client money, wills, deeds, investments and other property entrusted to the firm by clients and others.'

5 See *Ex p Horsfall* (1827) 7 B & C 528 cited with approval in *Gibbon v Pease* [1910] 1 KB 810, CA (architects) at 814 (Cozens-Hardy LJ):

> 'In that case, as in this, there was a contract for the performance of certain work. There were things which were necessary for the completion of the actual deed of conveyance,

which was what the parties bargained for, and though a custom was set up by the solicitor of a right on his part to retain drafts and copies of deeds and documents, the originals of which he was admittedly bound to deliver up, the Court decided that the client who had paid for them had a right to the possession of them.'

6 See *Leicestershire County Council v Michael Faraday & Partners Ltd* [1941] 2 KB 205, CA (above) at 216:

'These pieces of paper, as it seems to me, cannot be shown to be in any sense the property of the plaintiffs, any more, as I suggested to counsel for the plaintiffs during the argument, than his solicitor client or his lay client could assert that his notes of the careful and strenuous argument which he addressed to us here could be claimed to be delivered up by him when the case is over, either to the solicitor or to the lay client. They are documents which he has prepared for his own assistance in carrying out his expert work, but they are not documents brought into existence by an agent on behalf of his principal, and, therefore, documents which it can be said are the property of the principal.'

The decision was cited with approval by Jenkins LJ in *Chantry Martin Ltd v Martin* [1953] 2 QB 286, CA (accountants) at 292. *Chantry Martin* has also been applied in *Gomba Holdings UK Ltd v Minories Finance Ltd* [1988] 1 WLR 1231, CA at 1234G (Fox LJ) and in *Casson Beckman v Papi* [1991] BCLC 299, CA (accountants).

7 See *Re Wheatcroft* (1877) 6 Ch D 97 (Sir George Jessel MR).
8 For the supervisory jurisdiction see para 5.25, above.
9 Section 68(1) provides:

'The jurisdiction of the High Court to make orders for delivery by a solicitor of a bill of costs and for the delivery up of, or otherwise in relation to, any documents in his possession, custody or power, is hereby declared to extend to cases in which no business has been done by him in the High Court.'

10 For further procedural points on the court's supervisory jurisdiction see para 5.34, above.

(b) Access to a solicitor's file

14.03 A principal's right to disclosure from an agent is not limited, however, to those documents that belong to the principal. An agent also owes a duty to provide his or her principal with access to records of all transactions into which the agent has entered on behalf of the principal. In *Yasuda Fire & Marine Insurance Co of Europe Ltd v Orion Marine Insurance Underwriting Agency Ltd*[1] Colman J held that underwriting agents owed a duty to provide access to insurers to inspect and copy about 80,000 files that the agents had formerly managed on their behalf and that this duty survived the termination of the contract of agency. He stated:[2]

'That obligation to provide an accurate account in the fullest sense arises by reason of the fact that the agent has been entrusted with the authority to bind the principal to transactions with third parties and the principal is entitled to know what his personal contractual rights and duties are in relation to those third parties as well as what he is entitled to receive by way of payment from the agent. He is entitled to be provided with those records because they have been created for preserving information as to the very transactions which the agent was authorised by him to enter into. Being the participant in the transactions, the principal is entitled to the records of them.'

The most obvious and important category of documents generated by solicitors to which this principle applies are accounting records. The accounting records of a firm of solicitors clearly belong to the partners or limited partnership rather than the clients. But clients and former clients must be entitled to full access to the firm's accounting records.[3] There is no authority that a client may obtain access to other documents owned by a former solicitor (such as working papers) by deploying this principle. But it is suggested that a former client ought to be able to require the solicitor to produce the entire file (including the solicitor's own working papers) on this basis. A former client should be entitled to access to all of those documents which would enable his or her new solicitors to take over the conduct of the relevant transaction or if the transaction has been completed to put the new solicitors in a position in which they can advise the client fully about its effect. A similar test was applied by Colman J *Yasuda Fire & Marine Insurance Co of Europe Ltd v Orion Marine Insurance Underwriting Agency Ltd.*[4]

1 [1995] QB 174. The nature of the relief sought by the insurers is dealt with at 175H–176A–B and 192A. The decision was followed by Andrew Smith J in *Equitas Ltd v Horace Holman & Co Ltd* [2007] EWHC 903 (Comm) at [26]–[27].
2 [1995] QB 174 at 185D-E.
3 The Solicitors' Accounts Rules 1998 (last amended on 16 October 2007) do not contain an express obligation to permit a client to inspect or take copies of the solicitor's accounting records: see r 32 (which identifies the accounting records which must be kept for a client account). Compare this with r 33 (which imposes an obligation to hand over the original records of a client's own account, i e an account in the name of the client which a solicitor usually operates under a power of an attorney). However, it is considered that it is unnecessary to spell out an express obligation. In *Yasuda Fire & Marine Insurance Co of Europe Ltd v Orion Marine Insurance Underwriting Agency Ltd* Colman J rejected an argument that the duty to produce accounting records was excluded by the contractual terms. It is suggested that any term to this effect in a contract of retainer would almost certainly be unenforceable under UCTA or UCTCCR: see para 1.5, above.
4 [1995] QB 174 at 184H-185A:

'At any given time before the completion of these functions the defendants would be in possession of a body of essential information for the conclusion of the run-off of each contract. If at that point of time the defendants were to cease to administer the run-off and it became necessary for that function to be performed by the plaintiff, access to the information as to the contracts of insurance and reinsurance binding on the plaintiff then in the defendants' possession would be essential, not only to ascertain what sums if any were due as between the plaintiff and the defendants but also what the outstanding rights and liabilities were as between the plaintiff and those whom it had insured and reinsured and those by whom the plaintiff itself was reinsured.'

In *Equitas Ltd v Horace Holman & Co Ltd* [2007] EWHC 903 (Comm) at [28] Andrew Smith J rejected an argument based on *Chantry Martin Ltd v Martin* [1953] 2 QB 286, CA (para 14.2 n 6, above) that underwriting agents were not obliged to disclose accounting records on the basis that: '*Chantrey Martin* is about the position between professionals and their clients not the position between principals and agents'. However, he was not considering the extent to which a professional adviser may be obliged to disclose accounting records or other documents which are not owned by the client and this point was not considered in *Chantry Martin* either.

3   The protocol

14.04   The professional negligence pre-action protocol imposes a number of obligations to make disclosure upon a potential defendant:[1]

> '**B4.3** The parties should supply promptly at this stage [ie the investigation stage] and throughout, whatever relevant information or documentation is reasonably requested. (Please see Guidance Note C5.)
>
> **B5.2** The Letter of Response will normally be an open letter and should be a reasoned answer to the Claimant's allegations:…
>
> (f)   where additional documents are relied upon, copies should be provided.
>
> **C5.1** Paragraph B4.3 is intended to encourage the early exchange of relevant information, so that issues in the dispute can be clarified or resolved. It should not be used as a "fishing expedition" by either party. No party is obliged under paragraph B4.3 to disclose any document which a Court could not order them to disclose in the pre-action period.
>
> **C5.2** This protocol does not alter the parties' duties to disclose documents under any professional regulation or under general law.'

The obligation of a defendant under the protocol, therefore, does not extend beyond that which he or she would be required to disclose if an application for pre-action disclosure were made. However, if a defendant does not disclose documents (whether he or she could have been ordered to on an action for pre-action disclosure or not), there may be a costs sanction. If the defence differs materially from the letter of response and the defendant fails to disclose documents which upon which he or she later relies, the court may impose sanctions.[2]

---

1 See *Civil Procedure* (2007) Vol 1 at C1—007.
2 See the Practice Direction – Protocols, 2.1 (*Civil Procedure* (2007) Vol 1 at C1—002):

   'If, in the opinion of the court, non-compliance has led to the commencement of proceedings which might otherwise not have needed to be commenced, or has led to costs being incurred in the proceedings that might otherwise not have been incurred, the orders the court may make include: (1) an order that the party at fault pay the costs of the proceedings, or part of those costs, of the other party or parties; (2) an order that the party at fault pay those costs on an indemnity basis;…(4) if the party at fault is a defendant and an order for the payment of damages or some specified sum is subsequently made in favour of the claimant, an order awarding interest on such sum and in respect of such period as may be specified at a higher rate, not exceeding 10% above base rate (c f CPR, rule 36.21(2)), than the rate at which interest would otherwise have been awarded.'

4   CPR Part 31.16

14.05   The court has a specific power to order pre-action disclosure against a potential defendant. The power was originally introduced by s 31 of the Administration of Justice Act 1970[1] following the recommendation of the Wynn Committee and limited to personal injuries (e g to enable a patient to obtain access to the hospital's notes). In 1996 Lord Woolf recommended that the power should be generally available in all forms of litigation.[2] CPR Part 31.16 now provides:

'Disclosure before proceedings start

(1) This rule applies where an application is made to the court under any Act for disclosure before proceedings have started.

(2) The application must be supported by evidence.

(3) The court may make an order under this rule only where—

(a)   the respondent is likely to be a party to subsequent proceedings;

(b)   the applicant is also likely to be a party to those proceedings;

(c)   if proceedings had started, the respondent's duty by way of standard disclosure, set out in rule 31.6, would extend to the documents or classes of documents of which the applicant seeks disclosure; and

(d)   disclosure before proceedings have started is desirable in order to—

   (i)   dispose fairly of the anticipated proceedings;

   (ii)   assist the dispute to be resolved without proceedings; or

   (iii)   save costs.

(4) An order under this rule must—

(a)   specify the documents or the classes of documents which the respondent must disclose; and

(b) require him, when making disclosure, to specify any of those documents—

    (i) which are no longer in his control; or

    (ii) in respect of which he claims a right or duty to withhold inspection.

(5) Such an order may—

(a) require the respondent to indicate what has happened to any documents which are no longer in his control; and

(b) specify the time and place for disclosure and inspection.'

The leading case on the application of the rule is *Black v Sumitomo Corpn*.[3] In that case C alleged that D had manipulated the copper market following an investigation into the activities of one of its employees, H. He alleged that D was guilty of conspiracy to injure by unlawful means, namely breach of s 57 of the Financial Services Act and Arts 81 and 82 of the EC Treaty. In pre-action correspondence, C's solicitors had requested documents relating to a particular deal. This was allegedly a sham contract between D and a third party for the supply of 90,000 tonnes of copper which was to constitute the best evidence of D's continued manipulation of the copper market. The Court of Appeal reversed the judge's decision to order pre-action disclosure of three classes of documents and in the course of doing so provided detailed guidance about the exercise of the jurisdiction.[4] The court held that the conditions set out in CPR Part 31.16(2)(a)–(d) are jurisdictional and must be satisfied before the court may order pre-action disclosure. The standard to be satisfied under paras (a) and (b) is not the balance of probabilities. A claimant need only establish that he or she 'may well' be a party to proceedings (to distinguish them from non-parties such as witnesses). In order to satisfy (c) the issues must be sufficiently clear to enable the court to be satisfied that the defendant would be required to give standard disclosure of the relevant documents. Paragraph (d) involves a two stage approach: first, a jurisdictional element and, secondly, the exercise of discretion. The jurisdictional threshold is a low one and the claimant need only satisfy the court that there is a real prospect that an order for pre-action disclosure will have one or more of the consequences set out in para (d). In *Black v Sumitomo Corpn* Rix LJ gave the following guidance for the exercise of the discretion:[5]

'That discretion is not confined and will depend on all the facts of the case. Among the important considerations, however, as it seems to me, are the nature of the injury or loss complained of; the clarity and identification of the issues raised by the complaint; the nature of the documents requested; the relevance of any protocol or pre-action

inquiries; and the opportunity which the complainant has to make his
case without pre-action disclosure.'

1 See now s 33(2) of the Supreme Court Act 1981:

'On the application, in accordance with rules of court, of a person who appears to the
High Court to be likely to be a party to subsequent proceedings in that court, the High
Court shall, in such circumstances as may be specified in the rules, have power to order a
person who appears to the court to be likely to be a party to the proceedings and to be
likely to have or to have had in his possession, custody or power any documents which
are relevant to an issue arising or likely to arise out of that claim-(a) to disclose whether
those documents are in his possession, custody or power; and (b) to produce such of
those documents as are in his possession, custody or power to the Applicant ....'

2 See *Access to Justice: Final Report on the civil justice system in England and Wales*. This
recommendation was given effect to by Art 5(a) of the Civil Procedure (Modification of
Enactments) Order 1998, SI 1998/2940.
3 [2001] EWCA Civ 1819, [2002] 1 WLR 1562. For useful summaries of the test see also
Moresfield Ltd v Banners [2003] EWHC 1602 (Ch) (Lawrence Collins J) at [32]–[34] and *Hands
v Morrison Construction Services Ltd* [2006] EWHC 2018 (Michael Briggs QC) at [26]–[31].
Moresfield Ltd v Banners involved a potential claim by solicitors against accountants under
CPR Part 20 and pre-action disclosure is obviously available in these circumstances: see [62].
4 [2001] EWCA Civ 1819, [2002] 1 WLR 1562 at [70]–[82].
5 [2001] EWCA Civ 1819, [2002] 1 WLR 1562 at [88].

14.06 Applications for pre-action disclosure are case management decisions
which require the court to take a broad view of the merits.[1] But can potential
claimants who are unable to plead and prove their case on the evidence currently
available use the powers of the court under CPR 31.16 in order to discover
whether they do in fact have a good cause of action? In *Rose v Lynx Express Ltd*[2]
the Court of Appeal expressed the view that it was necessary for the applicant to
establish that he or she had a real prospect of success before the court would
order pre-action disclosure under CPR Part 31.16. *Black v Sumitomo Corpn* was
not cited but in *BSW Ltd v Balltec Ltd*[3] Patten J analysed both decisions and
concluded that the test applied in *Rose v Lynx Express Ltd* was both correct and
also consistent with *Black v Sumitomo Corpn*.[4] He added:[5]

'It is clear from the judgment in *Rose v Lynx Express Ltd* that the
requirement to show a properly arguable case was the same threshold
test which Peter Gibson LJ described in *ED&F Man Liquid Products Ltd*.[6] For a claim to be properly arguable in that sense, it must
have a sufficient factual basis to support it. An applicant has not
made out a good or properly arguable case for breach of copyright or
design right infringement if there is no credible evidence of primary
facts from which one may at least be able to infer that an act of
infringement is likely to have taken place. Put another way, an act of
infringement must at least be one of the possible inferences or
conclusions which can reasonably be drawn from the known facts as
disclosed by the evidence.'

1 See *Total E & P Soudan SA v Edmonds* [2007] EWCA Civ 50 at [29] (Tuckey LJ):

'Such applications are in the nature of case management decisions requiring the judge to take a "big picture" view of the application in question. This obviously involves the judge taking a broad view of the merits of the potential claim, but should not necessitate an investigation of legally complex and debateable potential defences or grounds for stay.'

2 [2004] EWCA Civ 447, [2004] 1 BCLC 455 at [4] (Peter Gibson LJ):

'In our view it will normally be sufficient to found an application under CPR 31.16(3) for the substantive claim pursued in the proceedings to be properly arguable and to have a real prospect of success, and it will normally be appropriate to approach the conditions in CPR 31.16(3) on that basis.'

3 [2006] EWHC 822 (Ch) at [15]–[27].
4 [2001] EWCA Civ 1819, [2002] 1 WLR 1562. Patten J placed particular reliance on the following passage from Rix LJ's judgment at [68]:

'What, however, these authorities on the unamended section in my judgment reveal, and usefully so, is as follows. First, that at any rate in its origin the power to grant pre-trial disclosure was not intended to assist only those who could already plead a cause of action to improve their pleadings, but also those who needed disclosure as a vital step in deciding whether to litigate at all or as a vital ingredient in the pleading of their case. Secondly, however, that (as what I would call a matter of discretion) it was highly relevant in those cases that the injury was clear and called for examination of the documents in question, the disclosure requested was narrowly focused and bore directly on the injury complained of and responsibility for it, and the documents would be decisive on the conduct or even the existence of the litigation. Thirdly, that on the question of discretion, it was material that a prospective claimant in need of legal aid might be unable even to commence proceedings without the help of pre-action disclosure.'

Compare *Mitsui & Co Ltd v Nexen Petroleum UK Ltd* [2005] EWHC 625 (Ch), [2005] 3 All ER 511 at [26] Lightman J:

'A purpose of pre-action disclosure is to assist those who need disclosure as a vital step in deciding whether to litigate at all or to provide a vital ingredient in the pleading of their case. The purpose must include enabling a party to sign the required statement of truth.'

5 [2001] EWCA Civ 1819, [2002] 1 WLR 1562 at [20].
6 [2003] EWCA Civ 472. In that case the court was considering the test under CPR Parts 13.3(1) and 24.2.

14.07 At first sight CPR Part 31.16(2)(c) also presents a difficulty.[1] It imposes as a threshold condition the requirement to satisfy the court that the respondent would be required to disclose all of the individual documents or classes of documents on standard disclosure. In the ordinary way it will be impossible to satisfy the court that every single document on a solicitor's file will satisfy these conditions. However, condition (c) can be met by expressly limiting the categories of documents sought to documents that would be disclosed on standard disclosure.[2] However, it may not be enough simply to limit the scope of the application to those documents which the respondent would be ordered to disclose on standard disclosure unless the respondent also identifies the potential issues by reference to draft particulars of claim. Unless the respondent has seen the issues properly formulated, he or she may be unable to determine what documents should be disclosed on standard disclosure and the applicant cannot thrust the burden on the respondent of doing so simply by using an express limitation of this kind.[3] It may also be possible for the applicant to make use of CPR Part 31.17 (disclosure against a person who is not a party) if the applicant is a party to an existing action. This may often be the case where the applicant is a defendant to an existing claim and wishes to join his or her former solicitors as a defendant to an additional claim under CPR Part 20.6. In *Moresfield Ltd v Banners*[4] Lawrence Collins J confirmed that the standard applied by the Court of Appeal in *Black v Sumitomo Corpn* to CPR Part 31.16(2)(a) and (b) also applies to the conditions set out in CPR Part 31.17(3) and would have ordered disclosure under CPR Part 31.17 if he had not done so under CPR Part 31.16. It is sufficient for the applicant to demonstrate that the documents when viewed as a class 'may well' support the applicant's case or adversely affect the case of another party.[5]

1 See *BSW Ltd v Balltec Ltd* [2006] EWHC 822 (Ch) (Patten J) at [76]:

'In one sense, sub-rule (c) is therefore at odds with the low threshold test set for sub-rules (a) and (b) because it does require the court to formulate the claim and seemingly to extract from the evidence the causes of action which appear to be viable. If the purpose of pre-action disclosure is to allow a party to see whether it has a cause of action and what it is, it is difficult in advance of the disclosure itself to determine what the limits of any standard disclosure should be.'

2 See *Hands v Morrison Construction Services Ltd* [2006] EWHC 2018 (Michael Briggs QC) at [26]:

'The hurdle in (c) is (on its face) a strict test but cases show that it may usually be surmounted by appropriate drafting, for instance, the inclusion of a limitation to standard disclosure only, or a precise formulation of the issue to which the documents must relate. Both of those drafting techniques have been included by amendment in the order which I am asked to make.'

3 See *Total E & P Soudan SA v Edmonds* [2007] EWCA Civ 50 at [36]–[39] (Tuckey LJ) and *Cheshire Building Society v Dunlop Haywards (DHL) Ltd* [2007] EWHC 403 (QB) (Tugendhat J) at [27]–[44].
4 [2003] EWHC 1602 at [70].
5 See [2003] EWHC 1602 at [34]:

'It is not necessary that the documents will support the applicant's case or adversely affect the case of another party. It is sufficient that they are likely to do so, in the sense (again) of "may well" (and not "more probable than not"). When applying that test it has to be accepted, and is not material, that some documents which may then appear likely to support the case of the applicant or adversely affect the case of one of the other parties will turn out, in the event, not to do so. In applying the test to individual documents, it is necessary to have in mind that each document has to be read in context; so that a document which, considered in isolation, might appear not to satisfy the test, may do so if viewed as one of a class. There is no objection to an order for disclosure of a class of document provided that the court is satisfied that all the documents in the class do meet the threshold condition. In particular, if the court is satisfied that all the documents in the class, viewed individually and as members of the class, do meet that condition – in the sense that there are no documents within the class which cannot be said to be "likely to support ... or adversely affect" – then it is immaterial that some of the documents in the class will turn out, in the event, not to support: *Three Rivers District Council v Bank of England (No* 4) [2002] EWCA Civ 1182, [2003] 1 WLR 210.'

14.08 Finally, it is not always easy to demonstrate in concrete terms that an order for pre-action disclosure is likely to have any of the three consequences set out in CPR Part 31.16(2)(d). However, the court is usually prepared to accept that early access to the relevant documents will assist the fair disposal of the proceedings. In In *XL London Market Ltd v Zenith Syndicate Management Ltd*[1] Langley J made an order for pre-action disclosure in litigation between the managing agents of various Lloyd's syndicates. In relation the test of fairness he stated this:

'In general, where the relevant information is held by the Respondent and not otherwise available to the Applicant, I think it is likely that if the first two tests are passed so will be the test of fairness. To determine if they have a claim and to formulate it, XL London and Brockbank need access to the second category of documents. I also think that disclosure will save costs. It will enable further investigation of the reserves to be focused rather than random. If a claim is made it can be expected to be presented with particularity.'

In a number of cases applications have been made against professionals. In *Bermuda International Securities Ltd v KPMG*[2] the Court of Appeal ordered pre-action disclosure of the working papers of a firm of accountants in relation to a potential negligent audit claim. In *Moresfield Ltd v Banners*[3] solicitors who were defendants to an existing claim applied for pre-action disclosure against a firm of accountants that had also advised the client. Lawrence Collins J ordered pre-action disclosure of the firm's files and rejected the argument that the documents would be irrelevant as a ground for opposing the application. In *Cheshire Building Society v Dunlop Haywards (DHL) Ltd*[4] Tugendhat J dismissed an application for pre-action disclosure by a lender against a firm of valuers. The application was, however, made in support of a case of fraud (rather than negligence), the categories of documents were wide and the valuers had already disclosed the file in protocol correspondence. Finally, in *Saleem v Allen*[5] pre-action disclosure was ordered against a firm of solicitors where there were potential claims to trace trust property.

1 [2004] EWHC 1182 (Comm) at [31] applied by Jackson J in *Birse Construction Ltd v HLC Engenharia e Gestão de Projectos SA* [2006] EWHC 1258 (TCC) at [22]. See also *Hands v Morrison Construction Services Ltd* [2006] EWHC 2018 (Michael Briggs QC) at [26]:

'The desideratum in r 31.16(3)(d)(1), that is the fair disposal of the proceedings, is addressed to the question whether early disclosure, rather than disclosure at the usual time, will add fairness. That may be achieved not merely to give an opportunity to plead an otherwise unpleadable case but where it enables the Statement of Case to be better focused so avoiding the cost, delay and disruption which may otherwise be caused by amendment after normal disclosure, for example, leading to further consequential amendments and a yet further round of disclosure.'

2 [2001] EWCA Civ 269, [2001] Lloyd's Rep PN 392.
3 [2003] EWHC 1602 at [61]–[71].
4 [2007] EWHC 403 (QB).
5 [2006] EWHC 3555 (Ch) (John Jarvis QC). See, in particular, [14] where the judge declined to make orders of the disclosure of privileged documents.

5   Joint and multiple retainers

(*a*) *Joint retainers*

14.09   It is a question of fact whether a solicitor is engaged under a joint retainer or multiple retainers.[1] In cases where the solicitor writes an engagement letter and submits bills to both clients, the question may be easily answered. In *Re Konigsberg*[2], however, which involved the sale of one property and the transfer and re-mortgage of another by a husband and wife the judge held that at various times the solicitor was acting under a single separate retainer from the husband and a joint retainer from both husband and wife. He rejected the 'broad view of this question' and refused to hold that 'throughout the bankrupt and Mrs Konigsberg were the joint clients of the solicitors'.[3] It should also be noted that the existence of a conflict of interest does not automatically bring the joint retainer to an end and that a client under a joint retainer ought to be entitled to disclosure of any other documents on the file until the retainer has been properly terminated although the existence of a conflict may prevent one client obtaining disclosure of confidential and privileged communications with the other (as discussed immediately below).[4]

1 The term 'multiple retainer' is used here to describe the situation in which the solicitor is instructed *separately* by two or more clients but the retainer involves the solicitor in carrying out the *same* task (or part of the same task) for all of them.
2 [1989] 1 WLR 1257 at 1262D–G. Peter Gibson J also stated:

'But the fact that Mrs Konigsberg provided the money used to pay the solicitors ... does not mean that throughout she was the client, either alone or jointly, of the solicitors. Advice can be given to A by a solicitor but subsequently paid for by B without B becoming at the time of the advice or thereafter the client of the solicitor in relation to that advice.'

In *The Sagheera* [1997] 1 Lloyd's Rep 160 (Rix J) it was common ground that solicitors were acting under a joint retainer from the owners of a casualty and their war risk insurers. See also *Burkle Holdings Ltd v Laing* [2006] EWHC 638 (TCC) (HHJ Toulmin QC) where there was no joint retainer from lender and borrower of a private loan made for investment purposes.
3 [1989] 1 WLR 1257 at 1266D–1267G.
4 See *Lloyds TSB Bank plc v Robert Irving & Burns* [2000] 2 All ER 826, CA (discussed immediately below) at [13] (Morritt LJ):

'Thus the choice is between the automatic discharge of the retainer at the point of deception and a limit on the waiver implied at the outset of a joint retainer so as to exclude communications made after an actual conflict of interest has emerged. In principle I prefer the latter. The concept of automatic discharge is inconsistent with the general rule for the discharge of contracts. This confers an option on the innocent party

> to accept the repudiation, undoubtedly constituted by the deception, so as to discharge him from further performance or to affirm the contract notwithstanding the other party's breach. I see no reason why the innocent client should be obliged by an automatic discharge to instruct a new solicitor if he does not wish to do so.'

14.10 Where a solicitor acts for two clients under a joint retainer, the documents falling within the categories discussed in para 14.2 will be jointly owned by them and both parties must be entitled to inspect and take copies of them although they may not be entitled to physical possession of them (as against each other). Both parties will also be entitled to inspect the documents discussed in para 14.3. Neither client can assert legal professional privilege as against the other in relation to confidential documents passing between the solicitor and themselves. As between themselves and any third party, however, each party can maintain a claim of privilege and the privilege can only be waived jointly. In *The Sagheera*[1] Rix J stated this:

> 'Parties who grant a joint retainer to solicitors of course retain no confidence as against one another: if they subsequently fall out and sue one another, they cannot claim privilege. But against all the rest of the world, they can maintain a claim to privilege for documents otherwise within the ambit of legal professional privilege; and because their privilege is a joint one, it can only be waived jointly, and not by one party alone.'

However, this statement is subject to one qualification. Where a conflict arises between the interests of two clients who have instructed a solicitor under a joint retainer, one client is no longer entitled to access to copies of confidential communications between the other client and the solicitor although the retainer is not automatically terminated. In *TSB Bank plc v Robert Irving & Burns*[2] where an actual conflict had arisen between insurer and insured the insured sought to restrain the insurer from relying on information communicated by the insured to the jointly instructed solicitor (and to strike out the relevant references in the statements of case). The Court of Appeal held that although the retainer had not been automatically terminated when the actual conflict arose the insurer was not entitled to see or rely on all of the documents which had come into existence during the joint retainer:[3]

> 'Accordingly I would hold that the waiver of privilege implicit in the joint retainer extends to (a) all communications made by the insured to the solicitors down to such time as an actual conflict of interest emerges, and (b) to all communications made by the insured to those solicitors after the notification by the solicitors to the insured of such conflict and the lapse of such further time as the insured reasonably requires to decide whether to instruct separate solicitors.'

This analysis – although not the outcome – has been challenged on the basis that there can be no privilege as between clients under a joint retainer and their jointly instructed solicitor.[4] But the outcome was clearly correct. Where an actual conflict arises between the interests of the two clients, the solicitor should cease to act for both parties immediately.[5] But if the endangered client chooses to continue the retainer or to impart confidential information to the solicitor whilst making up his or her mind what to do, the law should protect that confidence. If the solicitor continues to correspond or deal with third parties under the joint retainer during this period, both parties should in principle continue to have access to this material (which would not be confidential to either client). Finally, if both clients continue to instruct the solicitor and the solicitor can continue to act[6], *TSB Bank plc v Robert Irving & Burns* suggests that neither can assert privilege against the other.

1 [1997] 1 Lloyd's Rep 160 at 165–6.
2 [2000] 2 All ER 826, CA.
3 [2000] 2 All ER 826 at [17] (Morritt LJ).
4 See Hollander *Documentary Evidence* (8th edn, 2003) at 14—05. It appears to have been common ground that the correct way to analyse the rights of clients under a joint retainer was in terms of waiver (see [11]) but it is suggested that the proper analysis is in terms of contractual rights: see *Winterthur Swiss Insurance Co v AG (Manchester) Ltd* [2006] EWHC 839 (Comm) at [74] where Aikens J analysed *Lloyds TSB Bank plc v Robert Irving & Burns* and *Brown v Guardian Royal Exchange Assurance plc* [1994] 2 Lloyd's Rep 325 in these terms.
5 See the Solicitors' Code of Conduct 2007, r 4.03.
6 The Solicitors' Code of Conduct 2007, r 4.04(1) provides:

'You may act, or continue to act, in the circumstances otherwise prohibited by 4.03 above with the informed consent of both clients but only if:

(a) the client for whom you act or are proposing to act knows that your firm, or a member of your firm, holds, or might hold, material information (in circumstances described in 4.03) in relation to their matter which you cannot disclose;

(b) you have a reasonable belief that both clients understand the relevant issues after these have been brought to their attention;

(c) both clients have agreed to the conditions under which you will be acting or continuing to act; and

(d) it is reasonable in all the circumstances to do so.'

(b) Multiple retainers: ownership of a solicitor's file

14.11 The position is more complex where a solicitor acts for a number of parties under a multiple retainer. In cases of this kind documents on the solicitor's file are owned by the client on whose behalf the solicitor was acting when those documents were created or received or by the client to whom the solicitor was discharging his or her duties when the documents were created or received. To take a simple example, solicitors make preliminary enquiries on the purchase of land in discharge of their duties to the purchaser and the replies received in response to them belong to the purchaser rather than to any lender even though the solicitor may be acting for both at the same time. In *Gomba*

Holdings UK Ltd v Minories Finance Ltd[1] the Court of Appeal had to consider who owned documents held by administrative receivers. Fox LJ stated:[2]

> 'I agree with Hoffmann J that the ownership of the documents in the tripartite situation of a receivership depends on whether the documents were brought into being in discharge of the receiver's duties to the mortgagor or to the debenture holder or neither. The fact that a document relates to the mortgagor's affairs cannot be determinative. All sorts of documents may relate to the mortgagor's affairs but to which the mortgagor cannot possibly have any proprietary claim.'

The Court of Appeal held that there were three separate categories of documents which belonged to three different principals:[3]

> 'The receivers in the present case plainly had a duty to manage the affairs of the companies. All documents which were created or received in pursuance of that duty must be the property of the companies. That would include, for example, the ordinary correspondence sent and received by the companies in the conduct of their affairs. On the other hand (and this is the second group), the receivers had to advise and inform the debenture holders regarding the conduct of the receivership. Documents created for that purpose, while they can certainly be said to relate to the affairs of the companies, cannot be the property of the companies. They were not brought into being for the purpose of the companies' business or affairs and the fact that they were created by or on behalf of persons who are, technically, the agents of the companies cannot be sufficient to create ownership in the companies. Thirdly, there are documents prepared by, or on behalf of, the receivers not in pursuance of any duty to prepare them but simply to enable the receivers to prepare such documents or perform such duties as they were required to prepare or perform for the purposes of their professional duties to the debenture holders or the companies. Such papers are, I think, the property of the receivers.'

It is suggested that similar principles should apply to the ownership of documents on a solicitor's file whether the solicitor is acting for an administrative receiver or administrator or acting under any other kind of multiple retainer (e g for insurer and insured or borrower and lender or vendor and purchaser). Thus documents will fall into three categories: first, documents owned by client A (and which were created or received in discharge of the solicitor's duties to that client); secondly, documents owned by client B (and which were created or received in discharge of the solicitor's duties to that client); and, thirdly, documents owned by the solicitor. It is, however, no answer to an application for pre-action or specific disclosure that the solicitor is unable to identify or separate documents owned by the client from the documents belonging to another client or the solicitor's own documents and the solicitor must deliver up all of the relevant documents and take the consequences.[4]

1 [1988] 1 WLR 1231, CA.
2 [1988] 1 WLR 1231 at 1234B.
3 [1988] 1 WLR 1231 at 1234D–F.
4 See *Yasuda Fire & Marine Insurance Co of Europe Ltd v Orion Marine Insurance Underwriting Agency Ltd* [1995] QB 174 (Colman J) at 191H–192A:

> 'If they are to perform their obligations to provide inspection of all such records as are relevant, but object to disclosure of that which is irrelevant, it is for them to find some means either of concealing the irrelevant (see *Gerard v Penswick* (1818) 1 Swan 533, 36 ER 494), or of extracting that which is relevant from the mass of their material. If such means cannot be devised with sufficient expedition, the plaintiffs will have to see the irrelevant material in so far as it is inseparable from the relevant. The computer database is, in my view, part of the records and, subject to what I have said about concealment of irrelevant material, ought to be made available for inspection. It is not open to the defendants to rely on the inseparability of irrelevant material as a basis for declining to permit inspection, extraction and copying of relevant material.'

See also *Equitas Ltd v Horace Holman & Co Ltd* [2007] EWHC 903 (Comm) (Andrew Smith J) at [27]:

> 'If, as they apparently do, Horace Holman keep their records so that those relating to Equitas are inextricable from records relating to other principals, that does not excuse Horace Holman from providing Equitas with copies of the records relating to their affairs when Equitas call for them.'

(c) *Multiple retainers: access to a solicitor's file*

14.12 Although the question whether a client is entitled to inspect and copy any documents held by a solicitor under a multiple retainer will largely be dictated by whether the solicitor was acting in discharge of a duty to the client when it was created, there may be other categories of documents which that client is entitled to see. For instance, there will be documents owned by the solicitor which the client will be entitled to see even if the solicitor is acting under separate retainers from two different clients.[1] If, however, documents are brought into existence whilst the solicitor is acting exclusively for client A, client B is only entitled to see them with the express or implied consent or authority of client A. Where client A has given express consent, there can be no dispute about client B's access to the documents (even where the relevant documents are confidential or privileged).[2] Moreover, in certain circumstances it may also be possible for consent to be implied. In *Mortgage Express Ltd v Bowerman*[3] Millett LJ stated:

> 'A solicitor who acts both for a purchaser and a mortgage lender faces a potential conflict of duty. A solicitor who acts for more than one party to a transaction owes a duty of confidentiality to each

client, but the existence of this duty does not affect his duty to act in the best interests of the other client. All information supplied by a client to his solicitor is confidential and may be disclosed only with the consent, express or implied, of his client. There is, therefore, an obvious potentiality for conflict between the solicitor's duty of confidentiality to the buyer and his duty to act in the best interests of the mortgage lender. No such conflict, however, arose in the present case. It is the duty of a solicitor acting for a purchaser to investigate the vendor's title on his behalf and to deduce it to the mortgagee's solicitor. He has the implied authority to communicate all documents of title to the mortgagee's solicitors.'

It is suggested that the expression 'documents of title' is being used here in the extended sense of all documents copies of which the solicitor could have been expected to receive if he or she had been deducing title for the mortgagee. In the case of a standard conveyancing transaction this will include the replies to preliminary inquiries in the example given above, documents of title, searches and correspondence with third parties, e g the vendor's or landlord's solicitors, where that correspondence is material to the mortgagee's retainer.

1 An obvious example is accounting records. Rule 32(6) of the Solicitors Accounts Rules 1998 imposes an obligation on solicitors to keep separate ledgers for borrower and lender. Each would therefore be entitled to see their own ledger but not the ledger of the other.

2 For an example see *Brown v Guardian Royal Exchange Assurance plc* [1994] 2 Lloyd's Rep 324, CA discussed by Aikens J in *Winterthur Swiss Assurance Co v AG (Manchester) Ltd* [2006] EWHC 839 (Comm) at [74]:

'... there was an express term in the contract for a solicitor's professional indemnity insurance that where solicitors or other expert advisers were employed in relation to a claim against the insured, then *"the Insurers ... may require the solicitors' reports to be submitted directly to them"*. The Court of Appeal held that this term in the insurance was crucial. It meant that if solicitors were appointed to deal with a claim against the insured solicitor, then the insurers were entitled to see communications from both the insured and third parties to and from solicitors employed in relation to a claim against the insured, provided that the communications concerned the subject matter of the claim against the insured. (Ibid at 327 per Hoffmann LJ; at 330 per Neill LJ.) It seems to follow that the person who has the right to exercise privilege must be entitled to agree with a third party to give that person access to privileged communications. The agreement might be general or for specified purposes. That will depend on the correct construction of the agreement. (Ibid at 329 per Hoffmann LJ; at 330 per Neill LJ.)'

3 [1996] 2 All ER 836 at 844j–845b. See also *Bristol and West Building Society v Mothew* [1998] Ch 1 at 20D–G. The duties of confidentiality owed to both parties and the consequences of a conflict are considered in detail in chapter 6, at 6.32ff.

14.13 Any implied consent is likely to be limited, however. Client A is not entitled to see or take copies of confidential or privileged communications passing between the solicitor and client B.[1] In *Nationwide Building Society v Various Solicitors (No 3)*[2] the judge held that a borrower was entitled to maintain privilege in all confidential communications to or from his or her solicitor even though the solicitor had been authorised to reveal certain information to the lender for the purpose of carrying out the solicitor's duty to the lender to report on title. He said this:[3]

> 'He [counsel for the defendants] submitted that the question is essentially one of what authority the borrower is impliedly giving to his solicitor in respect of the information in question. The authority, he submitted, is merely to pass on to the Nationwide the information. It does not extend to divulging the confidential communication – for example, a letter – in which the information is passed to the solicitor.
>
> In my judgment, [counsel for the defendants] is correct. The fact that the borrower authorises his solicitor to divulge to the Nationwide, or its solicitor, information which he has passed to his solicitor in the course of confidential communications does not mean that the communication in question ceases to be privileged. The fact that the solicitor also happens, with the borrower's consent, to be acting for the Nationwide can make no difference. As the quoted passages from the judgments of Millett LJ in the *Bowerman* and *Mothew* cases make clear, a solicitor who acts for both borrower and lender in a transaction owes separate duties of confidence to each client. The question in each case is whether the communication in question is confidential; and, if it is, what information contained in the communication the borrower has authorised the solicitor to disclose to the lender?
>
> The reason why, in the *Bowerman* case, the solicitor has the borrower's implied consent to communicate the documents of title to the lender and to hold them, as solicitors for the lender, and not just as solicitors for the borrower, was because deducing title involves showing the person to whom title is to be deduced the very documents of title themselves. The position is different where the implied consent concerns only the provision of information.'

In each case, therefore, the appropriate test is to consider which documents (as opposed to information) the solicitor would have received if both clients had been separately represented and he or she had been acting exclusively for one rather than the other.[4] It follows that apart from their own documents and any accounting records or working papers of the solicitor which they are entitled to inspect on the principles set out above, each client is only entitled to disclosure of documents which would have been received by the solicitor if he or she had been acting exclusively for that client. Each client will not be entitled to disclosure of any confidential and privileged documents created in the course of the separate retainer. Finally, this ought to be the position whether or not the client chooses to rely on contractual or equitable rights of ownership or inspection or to make an application for pre-action disclosure under CPR Part 31.16.[5]

1   For further discussion of what documents fall within this category see para 14.22, below.
2   [1999] PNLR 52 (Blackburne J).
3   [1999] PNLR 52 at 71G–72D.
4   The Solicitors' Code of Conduct 2007 is not particularly helpful in identifying those documents which a solicitor has the implied authority of a borrower to disclose. Guidance note 9(c) to r 4 states:

> 'Where a lender asks for a conveyancing file and you have kept a joint file for both borrower and lender clients, you cannot, without the consent of the borrower, send the whole file to the lender, unless the lender can show to your satisfaction that there is a prima facie case of fraud. If the client does not consent, you should send only those parts of the file which relate to work done for the lender.'

However, the CML Handbook, section 5, Part I provides a useful guide to the documents which the solicitor would have the implied authority to disclose. Section 5.1.2 also reflects what we would consider to be implicit, namely, that the solicitor has no implied authority to report information or provide documents to the lender where an actual conflict has arisen:

> 'If any matter comes to your attention which you should reasonably expect us to consider important in deciding whether or not to lend to the borrower (such as whether the borrower has given misleading information to us or the information which you might reasonably expect to have been given to us is no longer true) and you are unable to disclose that information to us because of a conflict of interest, you must cease to act for us and return our instructions stating that you consider a conflict of interest has arisen.'

5   It is theoretically possible that there might be a further category of documents (i e those documents which are confidential to client A and which the solicitor would not have received or seen when acting for client B but which do not attract legal professional privilege). There is no authority that the duty of confidentiality is any answer to an application under CPR Part 31.16. But it is suggested that the fact that the solicitor owed a duty of confidentiality to a third party would be a strong reason for refusing to order disclosure of these documents (depending on their relevance).

(*d*) *Joint or common interest privilege*

14.14   Finally, there may be circumstances in which third parties are entitled to disclosure of the solicitor's entire file including any privileged documents either at the pre-action disclosure stage or on standard disclosure on the basis that they shared a joint or common interest with the client. In *Winterthur Swiss Insurance Co v AG (Manchester) Ltd*[1] claims were brought by insurers against panel solicitors who had acted for personal injury claimants under conditional fee agreements funded by after the event insurance placed by The Accident Group or 'TAG'. The insurers brought claims for negligence in the conduct of the claims on the basis that they were subrogated to the rights of the individual clients. They applied for disclosure of the individual claims files and the panel solicitors resisted this application on the grounds that they were privileged. Aikens J held that the insurers could use the principle of joint or common interest privilege as a 'sword' to support a claim for disclosure of privileged documents and not just as a 'shield' to resist disclosure of privileged documents. He stated the principle in the following terms:[2]

> 'These cases demonstrate that where a communication is produced by or at the instance of one party for the purposes of obtaining legal advice or to assist in the conduct of litigation, then a second party that has a common interest in the subject matter of the communication or the litigation can assert a right of privilege over that communication as against a third party. The basis for the right to assert this "common interest privilege" must be the common interest in the confidentiality of the communication. The cases I have referred to concerned applications for production of communications to a third party, which was resisted. They assume that the communications concerned will be covered by one or other sub-type of legal professional privilege in the hands of the party that caused the communication to be produced in the first place. That type of situation, where a second party resists the application of a third party for production of communications, has been called "using common interest privilege as a shield". However, it is not this use of common interest privilege that arises in the present applications. The submission of [counsel for the claimants] is that NIG (and Winterthur) can rely on "common interest privilege as a sword". The principle is that if party B has a sufficiently common interest in communications that are held by party A, then party B can obtain disclosure of those communications from party A even though, as against third parties, the communications would be privileged from production by virtue of legal professional privilege.'[3]

The categories of joint interest which will give rise to a right to disclosure of privileged documents are not closed.[4] But the obvious examples are where a shareholder or beneficiary asserts a claim against a solicitor. If there was a joint retainer under which the solicitor acted for both a shareholder and a company or for both trustees and beneficiaries, the principles set out above in relation to joint retainers will apply. But shareholders and beneficiaries may also be entitled to access to confidential or privileged documents under the principle of joint or common interest privilege even if the solicitor was not acting for them but acting exclusively for the company or the trustees.[5] The same principle applies to liquidators or trustees in bankruptcy.[6]

1 [2006] EWHC 839 (Comm).
2 [2006] EWHC 839 at [78] and [79].
3 Aikens J accepted this proposition and the principal authorities which he cited in support of it were *Cia Barca de Panama SA v George Wimpey & Co Ltd* [1980] 1 Lloyd's Rep 598, CA, *Commercial Union Assurance Co plc v Mander* [1996] 2 Lloyd's Rep 640 (Moore-Bick J) and *Svenska Handelsbanken v Sun Alliance and London Insurance plc* [1995] 2 Lloyd's Rep 84 (Rix J) at 88.

4 See [2006] EWHC 839 at [80]:

> 'The cases have refused to be prescriptive about the circumstances in which the two parties will have a sufficient "common interest" in the particular communications concerned. The issue has to be decided on the facts of the individual case.'

5 For the joint interest privilege of shareholder and company see *CAS (Nominees) Ltd v Nottingham Forest plc* [2001] 1 All ER 954 (Evans Lombe J) at [19] and *Arrow Trading & Investments v Edwardian Group Ltd* [2004] EWHC 1319 (Ch) at [24] (Blackburne J):

> 'It is well established by authority that a shareholder in the company is entitled to disclosure of all documents obtained by the company in the course of the company's administration, including advice by solicitors to the company about its affairs, but not where the advice relates to hostile proceedings between the company and its shareholders ...... The essential distinction is between advice to the company in connection with the administration of its affairs on behalf of all of its shareholders, and advice to the company in defence of an action, actual, threatened or in contemplation, by a shareholder against the company.'

For the joint interest of beneficiary and trustee see *Re Londonderry's ST* [1965] Ch 918, CA at 938 (Salmon LJ). (Note, however, that the position of beneficiaries is complicated by the discretionary nature of the court's power to order disclosure: see *Schmidt v Rosewood Trust Ltd* [2003] UKPC 26, [2003] 2 AC 709 at [51].) The principle also applies to insurer and insured: see *Guinness Peat Properties Ltd v Fitzroy Robinson Partnership* [1987] 1 WLR 1027, CA; and to insurer and re-insuer: see *Svenska Handelsbanken v Sun Alliance and London Insurance* [1995] 2 Lloyd's Rep 84 (Rix J) and *Commercial Union v Mander* [1996] 2 Lloyd's Rep 640 (Moore-Bick J).

6 *Re Konigsberg* [1989] 1 WLR 1257 (Peter Gibson J) where the wife sought to prevent the trustee from relying on the evidence of a solicitor (who had acted for both her and her bankrupt husband). The principle also applies to successors in title both to land and other assets. For instance, a purchaser of property is entitled to disclosure of privileged communications in relation to the property transferred: see *Crescent Farm (Sidcup) Sports Ltd v Sterling Offices Ltd* [1972] Ch 553 (Goff J) and *Surface Technology plc v Young* [2002] FSR 387 (Pumfrey J). However, it is suggested that the category of privileged documents which may be obtained by a purchaser of property is relatively limited.

6 Solicitors' rights of disclosure

(a) When does the client waive privilege?

14.15 In principle, the duty of confidentiality owed by a solicitor to a client or former client is absolute.[1] Where the relevant documents also attract legal professional privilege, the privilege is the client's to waive – and not the solicitor's – and the privilege is again absolute[2] (subject to very limited exceptions[3]). Moreover, the solicitor owes a duty to assert privilege and defend any application for disclosure even if the client has no continuing interest in doing so and has given no instructions to the solicitor.[4] It follows, therefore, that a solicitor may only disclose confidential or privileged communications to third parties such as insurers or panel solicitors appointed by insurers to act for the solicitor where the former client has waived privilege. Waiver of privilege is considered in detail in paras 14.30–14.39 and the discussion about the scope of waiver is also relevant to the extent to which the solicitor is released from the duty of confidentiality by any pre-action waiver (and, in particular, whether there has been a waiver of privilege in relation to other files or transactions). But there is no authority that addresses the date at which any implied waiver of privilege becomes effective.[5] It is suggested that unless the issue is governed by an express contractual term in the client care letter, the earliest point at which a waiver can be said to have taken place is the service of notice of claim under the professional negligence pre-action protocol.[6] It is difficult to see any justification for the principle that a solicitor may disclose the contents of his or her file to third parties (including insurers) where the client has not given notice of a claim.[7] For instance, if a solicitor advises a client to take independent advice on the grounds that the client may have a potential claim against him or her, it is suggested that the solicitor is not entitled to disclose confidential information or privileged communications to his insurers in notifying the circumstances of the claim unless the client gives notice of a claim under the protocol. The right to disclose this information must, therefore, be the subject of express agreement with the client (or any new solicitors).[8]

1 See para 6.12, above. For discussion of the relationship between confidentiality and privilege see paras 6.2 and 6.3, above.

2 In *Daniels Corpn International Pty Ltd v Australian Competition and Consumer Commission* [2002] HCA 49, (2002) 213 CLR 543 at [9] (Gleeson CJ, Gaudron, Gummow and Hayne JJ), the High Court of Australia treated legal professional privilege as a substantive right:

'It is now settled that legal professional privilege is a rule of substantive law which may be availed by a person to resist the giving of information or the production of documents which would reveal communications between a client and his or her lawyer made for the dominant purpose of giving or obtaining legal services or the provision of legal services including representation in legal proceedings.'

In *Three Rivers DC v Bank of England (No 6)* [2004] UKHL 48, [2005] 1 AC 610 at [25] and [26] Lord Scott rejected this analysis but confirmed the absolute nature of privilege:

'Second, if a communication or document qualifies for legal professional privilege, the privilege is absolute. It cannot be overridden by some supposedly greater public interest. It can be waived by the person, the client, entitled to it and it can be overridden by statute ...... Certainly in this country legal professional privilege, if it is attracted by a particular communication between lawyer and client or attaches to a particular document, cannot be set aside on the ground that some other higher public interest requires that to be done. Third, legal advice privilege gives the person entitled to it the right to decline to disclose or to allow to be disclosed the confidential communication or document in question. There has been some debate as to whether this right is a procedural right or a substantive right. In my respectful opinion the debate is sterile. Legal advice privilege is both. It may be used in legal proceedings to justify the refusal to answer certain questions or to produce for inspection certain documents. Its characterisation as procedural or substantive neither adds to nor detracts from its features.'

3 The principal exception (as indicated in the above passage) is that legal professional privilege may be overridden by statute: see *R (on the application of Morgan Grenfell & Co Ltd) v Special Comr of Income Tax* [2002] UKHL 21, [2003] 1 AC 563. The Solicitors' Code of Conduct 2007, r 4.01 reflects this position: see guidance notes 10–20.

4 See *Nationwide BS v Various Solicitors (No 3)* [1999] PNLR 52 (Blackburne J) at 69B–C:

'I take the view that whether or not the client has any recognisable interest in continuing to assert privilege in the confidential communications, the privilege is absolute in nature and the lawyer's mouth is "shut for ever". I further agree with Mr Davidson that it follows from this that it is the lawyer's duty to claim the privilege on behalf of the client, or former client, whose privilege it is, at any rate where it is at least arguable that the privilege exists.'

The point was noted by Aikens J in *Winterthur Swiss Insurance Co v AG (Manchester) Ltd* [2006] EWHC 839 (Comm) at [24] although he did not express a view on whether it was correct.

5 The difficulty with the formulation of the principle of implied waiver by Lord Phillips MR in *Paragon Finance plc v Freshfields* [1999] 1 WLR 1183 at 188D–F (see para 14.33, below) is that its justification is based on a voluntary decision to expose the relationship between the solicitor and the client to public scrutiny in court proceedings. This would tend to suggest that any waiver take place when proceedings are taken and a claim form is formally issued and served on the solicitors. However, compare the formulation of the principle in *NRG Holding NV v Bacon & Woodrow* [1995] 1 All ER 976 at 986c–f (see para 14.31, below) where Colman J spoke of the client 'asserting that the solicitor has acted in breach of duty'.

6 See B1. Preliminary Notice:

'B1.1 As soon as the Claimant decides there is a reasonable chance that he will bring a claim against a professional, the Claimant is encouraged to notify the professional in writing. B1.2 This letter should contain the following information:

(a) the identity of the Claimant and any other parties

(b) a brief outline of the Claimant's grievance against the professional

(c) if possible, a general indication of the financial value of the potential claim.

B1.3 This letter should be addressed to the professional and should ask the professional to inform his professional indemnity insurers, if any, immediately.'

The protocol appears to assume that this will amount to a waiver of privilege. C3.1 states:

'There are a growing number of methods by which disputes can be resolved without the need for litigation, e g internal complaints procedures, the Surveyors and Valuers Arbitration Scheme, and so on. The Preliminary Notice procedure of the protocol (see paragraph B1) is designed to enable both parties to take stock at an early stage and to decide before work starts on preparing a Letter of Claim whether the grievance should be referred to one of these other dispute resolution procedures.'

7 In *Hakendorff v Countess of Rosenborg* [2004] EWHC 2821 (QB) Tugenhadt J held that a solicitor was entitled to rely on privileged documents in a claim against her former client for the recovery of fees and an application for a freezing injunction. The judge gave a number of reasons for reaching this conclusion. But one of them was that the principle of implied waiver extended to claims of this kind. He said this (at [82]):

'If I were wrong about that, and if I had to resolve the question of principle, I would also decide that in favour of the Solicitor. If, as happened in this case, a former client acts so as to entitle the Solicitor to relief under s 69, or gives the Solicitor grounds for applying for a Freezing Order, while challenging a bill in whole or in part, it seems to me that there may well be a situation analogous to that in *Paragon Finance*. In other words the former client cannot put the former solicitor in that position, and at the same time deny the solicitor the use of materials relevant to the action, which the law plainly permits the solicitor to take.'

It is suggested that this is very doubtful authority for the proposition that a solicitor may deploy confidential or privileged documents in advance of notice of a claim.

8 It is suggested that consent to disclosure should be sought as a matter of course when the solicitor advises the client to seek independent advice. A provision to this effect could be contained in a client care letter (i e that the client consents to the solicitor disclosing information to insurers or panel solicitors in the event of a conflict of interest). But it is suggested that any wording to be effective will need to be very wide and could erode the primary duty of confidentiality too far to be legally effective under the UCTRR: see para 1.5, above.

(b) What is the scope of the waiver?

14.16 Equally problematic is the question whether any pre-action waiver is limited or complete (i e whether the client has waived confidentiality in the documents for limited or for all purposes) and whether the solicitor can disclose documents to other potential parties such as accountants and barristers. The general principle is that a client may waive privilege for a limited purpose[1] and although the client will probably be taken to have waived privilege for all purposes by issuing proceedings,[2] the question whether the pre-action waiver is limited turns on whether the permitted disclosure is 'attended by a degree of confidentiality' which means that 'there was no waiver vis-à-vis the outside world'.[3] Where there is express agreement that the waiver is limited, the court will give effect to it.[4] Where there is no express agreement, it is suggested that any pre-action waiver will be limited to a solicitor's insurers and any solicitors instructed by the solicitor or insurers unless express terms are agreed for disclosure to third parties. The critical point is that a waiver of privilege is implied because it is necessary to enable solicitors to defend themselves[5] and that no waiver should be implied beyond what is necessary to give effect to that purpose. If this is correct, any implied pre-action waiver is limited to enabling solicitors to defend themselves by notifying their insurers and obtaining representation and not to assisting third parties (such as potential co-defendants).

1 See *B v Auckland District Law Society* [2003] UKPC 38, [2003] 2 AC 736 at [66]–[71] (Lord Millett). For further discussion see Thanki, *Law of Privilege* (2006) at 5.19–5.24 and Passmore *Privilege* (2nd edn, 2006) at 7.031–7.097.
2 See para 14.34, below.
3 For an example of waiver by agreement in relation to a claim against solicitors see *UCB v Thomason* [2004] EWHC 882 (Ch). In that case a claim form had actually been issued but David Richards J gave effect to a confidentiality agreement which covered the service of particulars of claim. For further discussion of waiver on agreed terms see Passmore *Privilege* (2nd edn, 2006) at 7.050–7.073.
4 See *USP Strategies plc v London General Holdings Ltd* [2004] EWHC 373 (Ch) (Mann J) at [21] citing *Gotha City v Sotheby's* [1998] 1 WLR 114:

> 'This means that the subsistence or otherwise of privilege, where advice is communicated to a third party, turns on the extent to which there is a waiver of privilege on that occasion. *Gotha City* demonstrates that it is not inevitable that there is a waiver in those circumstances. In that case it was held that the receipt of the advice by Sotheby's was attended by a degree of confidentiality which meant that, while there was waiver as between the owner and Sotheby's, there was no waiver vis-à-v is the outside world.'

In that case there was a confidentiality agreement between the client and the third party which was found to govern the privileged communications.
5 See paras 14.30–14.33, below.

(c) Who can waive?

14.17   One added difficulty which is much more likely to arise at the pre-action disclosure stage is presented where a potential claim is notified by one of two parties for whom the solicitor acted under a joint retainer or a third party who was not the client but closely connected with the client. The obvious examples are where a shareholder or beneficiary asserts a claim against a solicitor but not the company or the trustees. As discussed above, if there was a joint retainer under which the solicitor acted for both a shareholder and a company or for both trustees and beneficiaries, neither client can assert privilege against each other. But equally neither client can waive privilege without the consent of the other.[1] Again, although shareholders and beneficiaries may be entitled to access to confidential or privileged documents under the principle of joint interest privilege even if the solicitor was not acting for them but acting exclusively for the company or the trustees[2] the same principle must apply to any waiver.[3] A shareholder or beneficiary cannot waive the privilege of the company or the trustees. The position may be different, however, where the claimant is an assignee of the benefit of the claim. In *Winterthur Swiss Insurance Co v AG (Manchester) Ltd*[4] Aikens J held that the assignment of a claim which included wording which imposed an obligation on the assignor of a claim 'to do all such things as may be necessary or required by the Company for the purpose of enforcing any rights and remedies' entitled the assignee to waive privilege. Executors may waive privilege although it is unclear how far this right is available to any other successors in title.[5] Finally, if the solicitor mistakenly hands over the entire file to one client at the expense of another or to a third party or permits copies to be made, the solicitor cannot recover the documents without the authority of the client whose privilege it is whatever liability the solicitor may incur for breach of confidence.[6] This is not because there has been a waiver of privilege or confidentiality but because only the client and not the solicitor has a right of action to recover them.

---

1   See the passage from the judgment of Rix J in *The Sagheera* [1997] 1 Lloyd's Rep 160 at 165–6 quoted in para 14.10, above.

2   See the passage from the judgment of Aikens J in *Winterthur Swiss Insurance Co v AG (Manchester) Ltd* [2006] EWHC 839 (Comm) at [78]–[79] quoted in para 14.14, above.

3   For an example in which the court restrained debenture holders from using documents which had been handed to them by receivers see *GE Capital Commercial Finance Ltd v Sutton* [2004] EWCA Civ 315, [2004] BCLC 662. The claim to privilege was asserted by a shareholder against whom the debenture holder had brought a claim under a guarantee and Chadwick LJ accepted that he would have been entitled to restrain the use of privileged documents if he made out a case for joint interest privilege (or common interest privilege as it was described): see [58]. However, the primary basis of the decision was that the company had not lost its privilege (because the receivers had not acted within their powers): see [43].

4   [2006] EWHC 839 (Comm) at [136]:

   'In my view, that wording gives NIG the right to require the TAG Claimant to waive any privilege that it may have in documents if that is necessary or required by NIG for the purpose of enforcing claims against third parties if it is entitled to bring such claims upon paying an indemnity under the policy.'

5 See *Re Molloy* [1997] 2 Cr App Rep 283 where the Court of Appeal held that personal representatives may waive privilege. There is no clear authority that any other successor-in-title may waive privilege although in *Re Molloy* the Court of Appeal placed reliance on *Re Konigsberg* [1989] 3 All ER 289 where Peter Gibson J held that a trustee in bankruptcy stepped into the shoes of the bankrupt. See also *Winterthur Swiss Insurance Co v AG (Manchester) Ltd* [2006] EWHC 839 (Comm) (Aikens J) at [130]:

> 'In my view, an assignee is in a similar position to a successor in title with regard to the incidence of legal professional privilege. It is well established that a successor in title succeeds to and is entitled to assert any legal professional privilege that was available to its predecessor in title.'

It must be possible for liquidators and trustees in bankruptcy to waive privilege without the consent of the bankrupt or company where any claim against solicitors is vested in them. The position seems less clear where the predecessor in title may retain an interest in maintaining confidentiality. It does not follow, for instance, that a successor in title could waive privilege in counsel's advice obtained by the vendor for the purpose of making a good title to the property without the vendor's consent.

6 *Nationwide v Various Solicitors (No 2)* (1998) Times, 1 May (Blackburne J).

B   STANDARD DISCLOSURE

1   Introduction

14.18   CPR Part 31.6 sets out the duty of standard disclosure.[1] The duty of disclosure is a continuing duty[2] although the burden is on a party who seeks disclosure of relevant documents which are not adverse to either party's case to make an application for specific disclosure.[3] It usually presents no difficulty to satisfy these requirements and identify the material documents in a claim of negligence or breach of duty against a solicitor. In many cases the solicitor's file will provide the only relevant documents. In other cases where the claimant is an institution, each party will have a file and the forensic inquiry will be limited to an analysis of the two files. The most difficult disclosure issues in solicitors' claims usually arise where the defendant has acted for the claimant on other transactions or for a third party whose conduct is central to the claim. The issues that most commonly arise are, first, whether the conduct of other transactions is sufficiently relevant to the issue between the parties to justify disclosure; secondly, the extent to which the documents relevant to the transaction in question or other transactions are privileged; thirdly, whether the claimant may rely on the fraud exception to obtain an order for production of privileged documents; and, fourthly, whether the claimant may be taken to have waived privilege in relation to other transactions in which the defendant or other solicitors acted on his or her behalf. The Civil Procedure Rules also limit the duty of a party to make disclosure to those documents located by a reasonable search.[4] But even before the Civil Procedure Rules came into force, the court was reluctant to permit a roving search of a defendant solicitor's files.[5]

1 'Standard disclosure requires a party to disclose only – (a) the documents on which he relies; and (b) the documents which – (i) adversely affect his own case; (ii) adversely affect another party's case; or (iii) support another party's case; and (c) the documents which he is required to disclose by a relevant practice direction.'
2 CPR Part 31.11.
3 The notes to CPR Part 31.6 expressly state that the duty of standard disclosure extends to (1) a party's own documents (i e the documents upon which he or she relies) and (2) adverse documents. They also state that it does not extend to (3) 'relevant documents' (defined as "documents which are relevant to the issues in the proceedings but do not fall within categories (1) and (2)' i e documents which merely tell the story or background) or (4) train of inquiry documents. This does not mean that a party cannot be required to disclose documents which fall within categories (3) and (4). But it does mean that a party has no duty to disclose them on standard disclosure. This, therefore, places the onus on the opposing party to make an application for specific disclosure under CPR Part 31.12 and to make out a case for it before the court.
4 It will be clear from the disclosure statement in the defendant's list whether he or she considers other transactions relevant: see CPR 31.10(6). However, if they are likely to provide evidence of similar facts, they would not, it is suggested, fall within categories (1) or (2). If the number of files in question is small and can be easily located, the proportionality test will be satisfied and it will be reasonable for the defendant to conduct a search for them: see CPR Part 31.7. But if the number of files in question is very large, it may not be proportionate to carry out a search. For these reasons it is important to identify the extent of the search and whether files relating to other transactions have been excluded (and, if so, why).
5 See *Portman Building Society v Royal Insurance plc* [1998] PNLR 672, CA at 675C–D referring to the 'potentially poisonous effect of an over-literal application of the *Peruvian Guano* test'.

2 Relevance of other transactions

14.19 In civil cases the court will not order disclosure of documents which go solely to credit and more often than not evidence of what occurred on other occasions goes purely to the credibility of the evidence of one or other of the parties about the facts in issue. If one party's behaviour on another occasion was wholly inconsistent with the account which he or she now gives, this earlier behaviour will cast doubt on his or her credibility. The policy of the law is to limit the forensic inquiry to evidence which is logically probative of the facts in issue and, unless the evidence is compelling, to exclude more prejudicial material. In *Thorpe v Chief Constable of Greater Manchester Police*[1] the court refused to order disclosure of documents relating to earlier convictions or disciplinary findings against two police officers who were the subject of a claim for damages for assault and false imprisonment. It was held that evidence of this kind would be likely to be directed solely to cross-examination as to credit.

1 [1989] 1 WLR 665, CA.

14.20 On the other hand evidence of other, similar, transactions will be admitted in civil cases, as in criminal cases, if that evidence does not go solely to credit but is probative of the facts in issue. In *O'Brien v Chief Constable of South Wales Police*[1] Lord Phillips laid down a simple test for admissibility and a wider discretion in deciding whether to admit similar fact evidence. Similar fact evidence is admissible if it is potentially probative of a fact in issue. However, at the second stage the court should consider a range of factors in deciding whether to admit such evidence:

'I would simply apply the test of relevance as the test of admissibility of similar fact evidence in a civil suit. Such evidence is admissible if it is potentially probative of an issue in the action.[2] This is not to say that the policy considerations that have given rise to the complex rules of criminal evidence that are now to be found in ss 100 to 106 of the 2003 Act have no part to play in the conduct of civil litigation. They are policy considerations which the judge who has the management of the litigation will wish to keep well in mind. CPR 1.2 requires the court to give effect to the overriding objective of dealing with cases justly. This includes dealing with the case in a way which is proportionate to what is involved in the case, and in a manner which is expeditious and fair. CPR 1.4 requires the court actively to manage the case in order to further the overriding objective. CPR 32.1 gives the court the power to control the evidence. This power expressly enables the court to exclude evidence that would otherwise be admissible and to limit cross-examination ...Evidence of impropriety which reflects adversely on the character of a party may risk causing prejudice that is disproportionate to its relevance, particularly where the trial is taking place before a jury. In such a case the judge will be astute to see that the probative cogency of the evidence justifies this risk of prejudice in the interests of a fair trial. Equally, when considering whether to admit evidence, or permit cross-examination, on matters that are collateral to the central issues, the judge will have regard to the need for proportionality and expedition. He will consider whether the evidence in question is likely to be relatively uncontroversial, or whether its admission is likely to create side issues which will unbalance the trial and make it harder to see the wood from the trees.'[3]

There is no rule or principle that claimants who wish to rely on evidence of other transactions as similar fact evidence should plead those facts in their statements of case. But it is obviously in their interests to do so and any application for disclosure of files is likely to stand a greater prospect of success if this exercise has been undertaken and the court can test the relevance of the similar facts by reference to the claimant's pleaded case.[4] Likewise, if the claimant has pleaded similar facts, the defendant should consider whether to challenge this at the earliest opportunity. The court has a discretion to exclude similar fact evidence at an interim stage and in plain and obvious cases the relevant parts of the statement of case can be struck out pursuant to CPR Part 3.4(2) or the inherent jurisdiction. In *JP Morgan Chase Bank and others v Springwell Navigation Corn*[5] the Court of Appeal struck out allegations of similar fact on the basis that the transaction which was the subject matter of the litigation was well documented and that the similar facts were likely to be heavily disputed.[6] In contrast, in *Silversafe Ltd v Hood*[7] the judge permitted the claimant to amend to rely on a number of other instances of alleged VAT fraud on the basis that the test in *O'Brien* was arguably satisfied. The same principles should also apply to defendants who wish to rely on similar fact evidence subject to one qualification. If the similar fact evidence on which a solicitor wishes to rely is his or her conduct of other transactions on behalf of the claimant, the solicitor will not be able to plead or rely on this evidence unless the court is satisfied that there has been an express or implied waiver of privilege. If the claimant refuses to provide an express waiver, the defendant must apply to the court for specific disclosure under CPR Part 31.12 before pleading the similar facts.

1 [2005] UKHL 26, [2005] 2 AC 536 at [53]–[55]. Compare the traditional test applied by Lord Denning MR in *Mood Music Publishing Co Ltd v De Wolfe Publishing Ltd* [1976] Ch 119 at 127 and see *Phipson on Evidence* (16th edn, 2005) at 22—07.
2 It is unnecessary to establish that similar fact evidence is logically probative of a fact in issue without recourse to other evidence. Similar fact evidence is logically probative of a fact in issue if, when taken with that evidence, it renders the fact in issue more likely: see *JP Morgan Chase Bank v Springwell Navigation Corpn* [2005] EWCA Civ 1602 at [70]–[73] (Brooke LJ).
3 See also Lord Bingham at [6]:

> 'While the argument against admitting evidence found to be legally admissible will necessarily depend on the particular case, some objections are likely to recur. First, it is likely to be said that admission of the evidence will distort the trial and distract the attention of the decision-maker by focusing attention on issues collateral to the issue to be decided. This is an argument which has long exercised the courts …and it is often a potent argument, particularly where trial is by jury. Secondly, and again particularly when the trial is by jury, it will be necessary to weigh the potential probative value of the evidence against its potential for causing unfair prejudice: unless the former is judged to outweigh the latter by a considerable margin, the evidence is likely to be excluded. Thirdly, stress will be laid on the burden which admission would lay on the resisting party: the burden in time, cost and personnel resources, very considerable in a case such as this, of giving disclosure; the lengthening of the trial, with the increased cost and stress inevitably involved; the potential prejudice to witnesses called upon to recall matters long closed, or thought to be closed; the loss of documentation; the fading of recollections.'

4 See, for instance, *Cheshire Building Society v Dunlop Haywards (DHL) Ltd* [2007] EWHC 403 (QB) (Tugenhadt J) where the failure to plead the relevant allegations appears to have been decisive. The application was one for pre-action disclosure and it also involved allegations of fraud.
5 [2005] EWCA Civ 1602 at [76]–[82] (Brooke LJ).
6 See, in particular, [79]:

> 'But in our case the transaction under investigation, whichever of the disputed forms it took, was an orthodox and not in any way unusual commercial transaction, supported by a wealth of documentary record. What is likely to be added by similar fact evidence is thus much less obvious.'

See also [81]:

'All this threatens either to overburden the trial or, if steps are taken that are directed simply to avoiding that burden, to deprive Chase of effective scrutiny of the case put against it. Neither outcome is acceptable. There is in the end an unavoidable choice to be made between trying one case – the present one – and trying three.'

7 [2006] EWHC 1849 (Ch) (Peter Smith J) at [37]:

'Equally in my view it would not be appropriate to strike out the similar fact evidence at this stage. The question of its probative value is really a matter for the trial judge. It is always dangerous to make a pre-emptive decision as to the admissibility or probative value of any evidence in advance of trial when the full picture is not presented. For my part however the evidence arguably satisfies the test set out in *O'Brien v Chief Constable of South Wales* [2005] UKHL 26, [2005] 2 AC 534. It arguably has a probative value and I do not believe that reliance on the similar fact evidence is disproportionately oppressive and will lengthen the trial. I should stress that I do not rule out a fresh application by the Defendants when the full picture is known. By that I mean that any application in respect of these matters ought to take place after the Claimants have provided disclosure, Tattershall has provided disclosure and the overall structure of the Claims is re-evaluated in the light of all material then available.'

For a similar case before the introduction of the CPR see *Bradford & Bingley Building Society v Boyce Evans Shepherd* [1998] PNLR 250 (Neuberger J) at 255F–256A (upheld on this point by the Court of Appeal (6 July 1998, unreported)). In that case a lender claimed to be the victim of a number of mortgage frauds the judge permitted it to amend its pleadings to allege fraud in reliance on a second, copycat, transaction.

14.21   Evidence of other transactions may also relate to other claims brought by the claimant against the defendant. In *Maes Finance Ltd v Leftleys*[1], a lender's claim against solicitors, the judge gave leave for a number of actions against the defendants involving allegations of negligence and breach of fiduciary duty in relation to a number of transactions to be tried together on the grounds that the evidence in each action would be relevant evidence in the other claims. Evidence of other transactions may also be directly relevant to questions of causation and reliance even if there is no striking similarity. In *Lillicrap v Nalder & Son*[2] the defendant admitted negligence for failing to advise his clients of the existence of a right of way over land which they later purchased but argued that they would have proceeded with the transaction if properly advised anyway. The court held that evidence of their conduct in six other transactions in which the defendants had acted for them was directly relevant to the defendants' defence. Dillon LJ stated:[3]

'I do not regard this as a strict case of similar fact evidence. It is merely a question of trying the issue in civil proceedings of whether, on the balance of probabilities, the plaintiffs would or would not have resiled from the transaction, or taken some other course other than they did, if they had been properly advised about the rights of way, the presence of one and the absence of another.'

The court did, however, reserve the right of the trial judge to exclude the evidence on grounds of prejudice in the exercise of his discretion. At the interim stage, however, the defendants were entitled to plead the transactions and obtain disclosure of the relevant documents. The critical point here is that evidence of other transactions may not only be relevant to the hypothetical question whether the client would have withdrawn from the transaction if properly advised but also be the most cogent evidence by which the court can assess the answer. Even so, the court will not admit evidence of all other transactions. In *Lillicrap v Nalder & Son* the six transactions had all taken place prior to the transaction which was the subject matter of the claim. In *Nyckeln Finance Ltd v Edward Symmons & Partners*[4] by contrast the court ordered disclosure of one transaction which had taken place prior to the transaction in question on the ground that it was relevant to reliance and contributory negligence but refused to order disclosure of a number of transactions which post-dated the transaction which was in issue in the action. They threw no light on the state of mind of the client's officers at the relevant time.

1 [1998] PNLR 193 (Jacob J). Upheld on appeal (1998) Times, 13 November, CA.
2 [1993] 1 WLR 94, CA. Dillon LJ delivered the lead judgment in both this case and *Thorpe*.
3 [1993] 1 WLR 94 at 100F–H.
4 [1996] PNLR 245, CA.

3   Legal advice privilege

14.22   In most cases involving claims against solicitors no issues of privilege will arise over the contents of a solicitor's file because the assertion of the claim will involve a waiver by the client of both legal professional privilege and the solicitor's duty of confidentiality in relation to the relevant transaction. The assessment of what documents on the file are privileged from production usually arises, therefore, in cases where a third party brings a claim against a solicitor or in lenders' claims where the solicitor has acted under a multiple retainer or where an application for third party disclosure is made against the solicitor under CPR Part 31.17. The question of which documents are privileged may arise on standard disclosure or it may arise at the pre-action disclosure stage and in Part A we discussed the principles on which a claimant may be able to obtain pre-action disclosure of solicitors' files in the context of single, joint and multiple retainers and the rights of the solicitor to disclose them to third parties at that stage. In this section we consider which parts of the file are privileged from production. A detailed discussion of the recent developments in the law of legal professional privilege is outside the scope of this book. However, what can be attempted is a brief discussion of the principles which should be applied in determining which documents are privileged on a transaction file (which is likely to form the subject matter of a solicitor's claim). The traditional view is that almost all communications passing between a solicitor and his or her client are privileged. In *Balabel v Air-India*[1] disclosure was sought of all communications between the defendant and its solicitors (apart from those seeking or giving legal advice), drafts and working papers, attendance notes and memoranda of the defendant's solicitors and internal communications of the defendant. The Court of Appeal refused to order disclosure of any of these categories of documents. Taylor LJ gave the following guidance about the scope of the privilege:[2]

'[T]he test is whether the communication or other document was made confidentially for the purpose of legal advice. Those purposes have to be construed broadly. Privilege obviously attaches to a document conveying legal advice from solicitor to client and to a specific request from the client for such advice. But it does not follow that all other communications between them lack privilege. In most solicitor and client relationships, especially where a transaction involves protracted dealings, advice may be required or appropriate on matters great or small at various stages. There will be a continuum of communication and meetings between the solicitor and client. The negotiations for a lease such as occurred in the present case are only one example. Where information is passed by the solicitor or client to the other as part of the continuum aimed at keeping both informed so that advice may be sought and given as required, privilege will attach. A letter from the client may end with such words as "please advise me what I should do." But, even if it does not, there will usually be implied in the relationship an overall expectation that the solicitor will at each stage, whether asked specifically or not, tender appropriate advice. Moreover, legal advice is not confined to telling the client the law; it must include advice as to what should prudently and sensibly be done in the relevant legal context.

It may be that applying this test to any series of communications might isolate occasional letters or notes which could not be said to enjoy privilege. But to be disclosable such documents must be not only privilege-free but also material and relevant. Usually a letter which does no more than acknowledge receipt of a document or suggest a date for a meeting will be irrelevant or non-disclosable. In effect, therefore, the "purpose of legal advice test" will result in most communications between solicitor and client in, for example, a conveyancing transaction being exempt from disclosure, either because they are privileged or because they are immaterial or irrelevant.'

In practical terms, therefore, *Balabel* was treated as providing a rule of thumb that apart from certain well settled categories of document a party was not required to disclose any communications between solicitor and client (either because they were part of the 'continuum' of communications or because they were unlikely to be of any relevance at all if they were not).The dicta of Taylor LJ were directly applied in *Nationwide v Various Solicitors (No* 3)[3] in which the judge stated:

'I take the decision of the Court of Appeal in that case to mean that in an ordinary conveyancing transaction communications passing between the solicitor instructed in the matter and the client, being confidential communications made in connection with the matter, will be privileged if, although advice is not specifically sought or given in relation to any particular communication, the communication is made with the view, albeit unspoken, to legal advice being given if appropriate; or, as Peter Gibson J tersely put it in *Re Konigsberg* (*a bankrupt*) [1989] 1 WLR 1257, 1263:

> "Privilege attaches where information is passed by the solicitor or client to the other in the course of keeping each other informed so that advice may be sought and given as required." '

Applying this test the judge found that the following classes of document were privileged as part of the 'continuum' of communications: (a) letters passing between solicitor and client (although the letters from the client contained no express request for advice and all but one of the letters from the solicitor contained no formal advice); (b) letters passing between the client's agent and the client sent to the solicitor by the client for his information; and (c) completion statements and their earlier drafts.

1 [1988] Ch 317.
2 [1988] Ch 317 at 330D–331A.
3 [1999] PNLR 52 (Blackburne J).

14.23 Both *Balabel* and *Nationwide* involved conveyancing files. *N R G Holding NV v Bacon & Woodrow*[1] provides a good example of the scope of legal advice privilege outside the conveyancing context. The claim concerned due diligence work done by the defendant actuaries and accountants for NRG in relation to a number of insurance companies. In the course of the action a bill was disclosed containing a description of the work undertaken by NRG's solicitors. It was conceded that there was no privilege in documents written or copied by the solicitors to NRG's other advisers (including the defendants), notes of meetings with the non-legal team (save to the extent that those notes contained advice in addition to what was said at the meeting) or notes of meetings with the vendors (save to the extent that they contained the views of the solicitors on what had passed).[2] But the accountants also sought production of the legal advice given by the solicitors and NRG's foreign lawyers on two grounds: first, that the advice was commercial and not legal and, secondly, because it was not confidential or privileged. The judge rejected both submissions. He said this:[3]

'As Taylor LJ observed, a solicitor's professional duty or function is frequently not exclusively related to the giving of advice on matters of law or, in the context of this kind of case, on drafting or

construction of documents. It not infrequently relates to the commercial wisdom of entering into a given transaction in relation to which
legal advice is also sought.'

He also rejected[4] the second submission on the ground that it was implicit in
the retainer of the solicitors that they had the authority to disclose the legal
advice which they had given to their client to the other advisers in the team to
the extent that they thought necessary. But this did not mean that they owed
no duty of confidentiality to their client. Far less did it mean that there was no
duty of confidentiality in relation to the advice which the solicitors had given
to the client and which had not been disclosed to the rest of the team.

1 [1995] 1 All ER 976 (Colman J).
2 [1995] 1 All ER 976 at 981h–j.
3 [1995] 1 All ER 976 at 983j.
4 [1995] 1 All ER 976 at 984b–f.

14.24   The decision of the Court of Appeal in *Balabel* proceeded on the basis
that a wide view should be taken of what is considered to be legal advice in the
context of a standard conveyancing transaction.[1] In *Three Rivers DC v Bank of
England (No 6)*[2] this view was not directly challenged. However, the claimants
sought to argue that legal advice privilege should be limited to those cases in
which the purpose of the lawyer–client relationship was obtaining advice and
assistance in relation to the client's legal rights and obligations (as was the case
in *Balabel*).[3] The House of Lords rejected this argument.[4] In the course of their
speeches the members of the House expressed the view that provided that there
was a relevant 'legal context' legal advice privilege should extend to all
communications between solicitor and client relating to the relevant transaction. Lord Carswell (with whom the other members agreed[5]) stated this:[6]

> 'I agree with the view expressed by Colman J in *Nederlandse
> Reassurantie Groep Holding NV v Bacon & Woodrow (a firm)*
> [1995] 1 All ER 976 at 982 that the statement of the law in *Balabel v
> Air India* does not disturb or modify the principle affirmed in *Minter
> v Priest*, that all communications between a solicitor and his client
> relating to a transaction in which the solicitor has been instructed for
> the purpose of obtaining legal advice will be privileged, notwith-
> standing that they do not contain advice on matters of law or
> construction, provided that they are directly related to the perform-
> ance by the solicitor of his professional duty as legal adviser of his
> client.'

In the normal case, therefore, the practical guidance given in the authorities
before *Three Rivers (No 6)* in relation to the contents of a solicitor's
transaction file should continue to be followed. On the other hand, *Three
Rivers (No 6)* leaves a number of issues unresolved and, in particular, what

lawyer–client relationship will not attract legal advice privilege[7], whether legal advice privilege is limited to lawyer–client communications[8] and, if so, whether there is a dominant purpose test for legal advice privilege.[9] However, these issues are unlikely to arise in claims against solicitors other than in exceptional cases where the claim arises out of a retainer which does not involve drafting or advice on documents or representation in litigation.

1 See, for example, *R v Manchester Crown Court, ex p Rogers* [1999] 1 WLR 832, CA at 839C–D (Lord Bingham of Cornhill MR):

'It is in my judgment important to remind oneself of the well-established purpose of legal professional privilege, which is to enable a client to make full disclosure to his legal adviser for the purposes of seeking legal advice without apprehension that anything said by him in seeking advice or to him in giving it may thereafter be subject to disclosure against his will. It is certainly true that in cases such as *Balabel v Air-India* [1988] Ch 317 the court has discountenanced a narrow or nit-picking approach to documents and has ruled out an approach which takes a record of a communication sentence by sentence and extends the cloak of privilege to one and withholds it from another.'

2 [2004] UKHL 48, [2005] 1 AC 610.
3 See [2004] UKHL 48, [2005] 1 AC 610 at [35] (Lord Scott).
4 See [2004] UKHL 48, [2005] 1 AC 610 at [37] and [38] (Lord Scott), [60] (Lord Rodger), [61] (Baroness Hale) [112] (Lord Brown).
5 See [2004] UKHL 48, [2005] 1 AC 610 at [45] (Lord Scott) [49] (Lord Rodger), [61] (Baroness Hale) and [119] (Lord Brown).
6 [2004] UKHL 48, [2005] 1 AC 610 at [111]. Baroness Hale also stated at [62]:

'I understand that we all indorse the approach of the Court of Appeal in *Balabel v Air-India* and in particular the observation of Taylor LJ ([1988] Ch 317 at 330), that "legal advice is not confined to telling the client the law; it must include advice as to what should prudently and sensibly be done in the relevant legal context".'

7 One context is where a solicitor occupies the much wider role of a traditional 'man of business' attending business meetings or taking business decisions. At [38] (Lord Scott) stated:

'If a solicitor becomes the client's "man of business" and some solicitors do, responsible for advising the client on all matters of business, including investment policy, finance policy and other business matters, the advice may lack a relevant legal context. There is, in my opinion, no way of avoiding difficulty in deciding in marginal cases whether the seeking of advice from or the giving of advice by lawyers does or does not take place in a relevant legal context so as to attract legal advice privilege. In cases of doubt the judge called upon to make the decision should ask whether the advice relates to the rights, liabilities, obligations or remedies of the client either under private law or under public law. If it does not, then, in my opinion, legal advice privilege would not apply. If it does so relate then, in my opinion, the judge should ask himself whether the communication falls within the policy underlying the justification for legal advice privilege in our law. Is the occasion on which the communication takes place and is the purpose for which it takes place such as to make it reasonable to expect the privilege to apply? The criterion must, in my opinion, be an objective one.'

See also Baroness Hale at [62]. For another example see *USA v Philip Morris Inc* [2004] EWCA Civ 330 at [80]:

'While it would be wrong for this court, not being apprised of the detail, to express any views on any particular disputed item, there is obvious force in the general thrust of Mr MacLean's submission that advice or assistance in collecting and collating, listing, spring-cleaning, storing, transporting and warehousing documents does not amount to legal advice concerning BATCo's legal rights and obligations and is not the sort of assistance that requires any knowledge of the law.'

8 This depends to a large extent on the correctness of *Three Rivers DC v Bank of England (No 5)* [2003] EWCA Civ 474, [2003] QB 1556. The House of Lords declined to express a view on the correctness of the decision in *Three Rivers (No 6)*: see [46]–[48] (Lord Scott) and [118] (Lord Carswell). The decision is the subject of detailed criticism in Thanki *The Law of Privilege* 2.136 to 2.168. In some Commonwealth jurisdictions legal advice privilege has been extended to other communications: see *Pratt Holdings Pty Ltd v Commissioner of Taxation* (2004) 136 FCR 357, 207 ALR 217 and *Skandinaviska Enskilda Banken AB v Asia Pacific Breweries (Singapore) Pte Ltd* [2007] SGCA 9.
9 For instance, if there is a dominant purpose test a complaint about the lawyer would not attract legal professional privilege even if part of the continuum of communications: compare *C v C* [2002] Fam 42, CA. Again, this issue was not addressed in *Three Rivers (No 6)* although the question whether the court should apply a 'dominant purpose' test is likely to be much more significant if it is accepted that legal advice privilege extends beyond lawyer–client communications. In some Commonwealth jurisdictions a 'dominant purpose' test has been accepted as correct: see *General Manager, WorkCover Authority of NSW v Law Society of NSW* [2006] NSWCA 84. This issue is also considered in detail in Thanki *The Law of Privilege* 2.169–2.176.

14.25 It follows, therefore, that communications between solicitor and client should be treated as privileged unless either they were not created in a legal context at all or they do not 'involve a communication of information on which legal advice may be sought or given as appropriate'[1]. This principle applies to all correspondence and attendance notes. It also applies to completion statements and drafts of completion statements.[2] Time records are not privileged, however, whether recorded on a computerised billing system or in attendance notes.[3] Nor are client account ledgers.[4] Moreover, the solicitor can also be required to identify the client.[5] Particular problems arise with bills or feenotes which are analogous to accounting entries but may include privileged material as part of the narrative. In those circumstances, it is suggested that the appropriate course is to redact the privileged parts of the document (which may include the entire narrative).[6] Difficulties are also created where the solicitor is instructed by the client to give advice to third parties (such as accountants or valuers). In cases of this kind privilege will not be lost because the advice has been given to a third party if it was intended to be kept confidential.[7] Moreover, where the third party is an agent (such as a valuer carrying out a valuation of a property to whom the solicitor has given advice on title) the advice ought to be privileged. However, where the third party is not an agent but an independent third party taking advice in order to carry out an independent function (such as an auditor taking advice from the company's solicitors in order to assess whether provisions for claims or unpaid debts are acceptable), it is difficult to see how the client can claim legal professional privilege for the advice (although the third party may be able to do so themselves).[8] Copies of documents provided by the client or by third parties and held on the solicitor's file also present difficult problems. Original documents (or original copies) in the hands of the client do not, of course, attract legal professional privilege. However, a client may send copies to his or her solicitors and the question whether those copies are privileged can often be critical in a solicitor's claim where the client is not available and neither party has access to the original documents. Copies of documents supplied directly by the client may be privileged although there is some uncertainty about the basis on which privilege may be claimed.[9] Documents supplied by third parties may also be privileged under the rule in *The Palermo*.[10] Finally, where there is real doubt about whether a document is privileged, CPR Part 31.19 provides a procedure for enabling the court to determine this issue. CPR Part 31.19(3) provides that a person who wishes to claim that he has a right or duty to withhold inspection of a document or part of a document must state in writing (a) that he has such a right or duty and (b) the grounds on which he claims that right or duty.[11] CPR Part 31.19(5) also provides that a party may apply to court to the court to decide whether a claim under CPR Part 31.19(3) should be upheld. In *Atos Consulting Ltd v Avis plc*[12] Ramsey J gave the following guidance on how such applications should be dealt with:

'I accept and adopt the principle that looking at the documents should be a matter of last resort.[13] In my judgment the appropriate course to be adopted in an application under r 31.19(5) where the right being relied on is privilege or irrelevance, is for the court to proceed by way of stages as follows: (1) The court has to consider the evidence produced on the application. (2) If the court is satisfied that the right to withhold inspection of a document is established by the evidence and there are no sufficient grounds for challenging the correctness of that asserted right, the court will uphold the right. (3) If the court is not satisfied that the right to withhold inspection is established because, for instance, the evidence does not establish a legal right to withhold inspection then the court will order inspection of the documents. (4) If sufficient grounds are shown for challenging the correctness of the asserted right then the court may order further evidence to be produced on oath or, if there is no other appropriate method of properly deciding whether the right to withhold inspection should be upheld, it may decide to inspect the documents. (5) If it decides to inspect then having inspected the documents it may invite representations.'

1 *Nationwide v Various Solicitors (No* 3) [1999] PNLR 52 (Blackburne J) at 64D–E. Thanki *Law of Privilege* (2006) suggests that client care letters and conditional fee agreements do not attract legal advice privilege on the grounds that they do not relate to the performance of the retainer: see 2.132. This view seems difficult to justify although see *Dickinson v Rushmer* (unreported, 21 December 2001) at [33] (referred to by Thanki) which provides some limited authority for this proposition. However, in *Giambrone v JMC Holiday Ltd* [2002] EWHC 495 (QB) Nelson J treated this case as an example of waiver by disclosing documents to the court: see [29].

2 *Nationwide v Various Solicitors (No* 3) (above) at 64B–C and 64G–65A.

3 See *R v Manchester Crown Court, ex p Rogers* [1999] 1 WLR 832, CA at 839E-F (Lord Bingham of Cornhill MR):

'The record of time on an attendance note, on a time sheet or fee record is not in my judgment in any sense a communication. It records nothing which passes between the solicitor and the client and it has nothing to do with obtaining legal advice. It is the same sort of record as might arise if a call were made on a dentist or a bank manager. A record of an appointment made does involve a communication between the client and the solicitor's office but is not in my judgment, without more, to be regarded as made in connection with legal advice.'

4 *Nationwide v Various Solicitors (No 3)* (above) at 76B-D:

'Such entries are not created for the purpose of giving legal advice to the client, whether the borrower/purchaser or the Nationwide as lender, and are ordinarily not communicated to the clients. They are an internal record maintained, in part at any rate, in discharge of the solicitors' obligations under the solicitors' account rules.'

5 *R (on the application of Howe) v South Durham Magistrates' Court* [2004] EWHC 362 (Admin), DC at [20] (David Clarke J):

'The permissible questions do not in my judgment infringe legal professional privilege. They are questions solely as to the identity of the person disqualified from driving in 2000 and as to the identification of this claimant as being the same person. It is expressly recognised by the prosecution that they cannot go further into territory covered by legal professional privilege ....The admissible question will be whether, when Mr Wager first saw the claimant in connection with this prosecution, he knew him, he remembered him.'

6 See Thanki *Law of Privilege* (2006) at 2.128–2.129.
7 See para 14.16, n 4, above.
8 See *Pratt Holdings Pty Ltd v Comr of Taxation* (2004) 136 FCR 357, 207 ALR 217 where the Full Federal Court of Australia held that a briefing paper prepared by accountants for the client for the dominant purpose of taking advice was privileged. Even if the dominant purpose test is adopted, letters to auditors and other advice of this kind will not attract legal professional privilege unless the auditors themselves can be treated as the client. For the difficult question about who should be treated as the client see *Three Rivers District Council v Governor and Company of the Bank of England (No 5)* [2003] EWCA Civ 474, [2003] QB 1556 at [31]. But if, in principle, the auditors give the instructions there appears to be no reason why they should not be able to claim legal professional privilege for any advice given by the solicitors.
9 Copies of documents supplied by the client may be privileged under the rule in *Lyell v Kennedy (No 3)* (1884) 27 Ch D 1, CA (i e that they may tend to betray the trend of legal advice). There are conflicting decisions on whether privilege can be claimed on any other basis. In *Nationwide v Various Solicitors (No 3)* (above) at 64E, for instance, Blackburne J accepted that a copy of a letter from an estate agent to the solicitor was privileged on the basis that it formed part of the continuum:

'The first document, a copy of the letter from Cluttons to Mr Costa, setting out the terms of Mr Costa's offer, is claimed to be privileged because it was passed by Mr Costa to TC with a view to informing TC of the terms of the transaction on which they were being asked to act for Mr Costa and therefore to advise as appropriate. On that basis, in my judgment, the communication is privileged.'

For a more detailed consideration of this point with concrete examples (after the court had inspected the file) see *Barnes v Comr of Taxation* [2007] FCAFC 88 at [7] where the Full Court of the Federal Court of Australia accepted that copies of documents on a solicitor's file were privileged if the dominant purpose test was satisfied:

'As to the first ground of appeal, it is settled legal principle that the relevant time at which a claim for privilege is to be determined is the time when the document came into existence. The relevant question is whether the document came into existence for the dominant purpose of seeking legal advice or assistance. If the document satisfies that description, then it is privileged from production. The same question also applies in relation to copies of documents where the test is whether the copy itself came into existence for the dominant purpose of obtaining legal advice or assistance.'

Compare this, however, with *USP Strategies plc v London General Holdings Ltd* [2004] EWHC 373 (Ch) (Mann J) at [48]:

'(a) Any copy of the CAA which was created with a view to its being submitted to solicitors for advice does not, despite its purpose, attract privilege. That this is clearly the case appears from *Dubai Bank Ltd v Galadari* [1990] Ch 1980. This principle was recently applied and approved in *Sumitomo Corpn v Credit Lyonnais Rouse Ltd* [2002] 1 WLR 479. Any such copy ought therefore to be disclosed and produced. (b) Any version produced by the solicitor in draft for the purpose of carrying out his function of giving legal advice to a client would, in my view, be privileged. Such drafts, until communicated, are not communications, but it is quite apparent from para 29 of the judgment of Longmore LJ in the *Three Rivers* case that that judge considered that solicitors' drafts are privileged – "all documents passing between the BIU and Freshfield are privileged *as, indeed, are Freshfields' own drafts and memoranda.*" (my emphasis). (c) Drafts passed back to the clients, on the assumption that they were part and parcel of legal advice, are again privileged.'

10 (1883) 9PD 6, CA. The rule also applies to translations: see *Sumitomo Corpn v Credit Lyonnais Rouse Ltd* [2002] 1 WLR 479, CA (which contains a modern summary of the rule). Both this rule and the rule in *Lyell v Kennedy (No 3)* (above) are treated as exceptional and anomalous and privilege should only be claimed, therefore, if it can properly be justified: see Thanki *Law of Privilege* (2006) at 4.07–4.22.
11 The statement may be made in a party's list of documents: see CPR Part 31.19(4). But if it is to be made in the list it is essential that a full statement of the grounds of privilege must be set out.
12 [2007] EWHC 323 (TCC) at [37].
13 Following the decision of Neuberger J in *Bank Austria v Price Waterhouse* (16 April 1997, unreported): see [36].

4   The crime or fraud exception

14.26 It is also well established that the client may not continue to assert privilege in relation to documents which were brought into existence for the purpose of furthering a criminal or fraudulent purpose.[1] In *Kuwait Airways Corpn v Iraqi Airways Corpn (No 6)*[2] Longmore LJ stated the principle in the following terms:

'[L]egal professional privilege (at least of the legal advice kind) does not attach to communications between lawyer and client if the purpose of the client in seeking advice is to further or facilitate crime or fraud. This exception was authoritatively laid down by the Court for Crown Cases Reserved in *R v Cox and Railton* and is known as "the fraud exception".'[3]

No exhaustive definition of the conduct to which the exception applies has yet been attempted. In *Ventouris v Mountain*[4] Sir Thomas Bingham MR used the term 'iniquity' and this term was adopted in *Barclays Bank plc v Eustice*[5] where the court ordered the defendant to produce privileged documents relating to a transaction in fraud of creditors within s 423 of the Insolvency Act 1986.[6]

1 Again, this is an issue which usually arises in the context of multiple retainers. In lenders claims, for instance, it is reasonably common for a lender to assert that the solicitor owed a duty to report fraudulent conduct by the borrower (or conduct which might have led a reasonably competent solicitor to suspect fraud) or to cease to act. In those circumstances, the lender is also likely to apply for disclosure of the entire file on the basis that privilege has been lost.
2 [2005] EWCA Civ 286, [2005] 1 WLR 2734 at [14].
3 The leading criminal authority is *R v Cox and Railton* (1884) 14 QBD 153, CA and the leading civil authority in this context is *O'Rourke v Darbishire* [1920] AC 581.
4 [1991] 1 WLR 607 at 611E. In *Gamlen Chemical Co (UK) Ltd v Rochem Ltd* (CA, 7 December 1979, unreported) Goff LJ gave the following guidance about the exception in civil cases:

> 'For servants during their employment and in breach of their contractual duty of fidelity to their master to engage in a scheme, secretly using the master's time and money, to take the master's customers and employees and make profit from them in a competing business built up to receive themselves on leaving the master's service, I would have thought that commercial men and lawyers alike would say that that is fraud.'

However, he also stated:

> 'The court must in every case, of course, be satisfied that what is prima facie proved really is dishonest, and not merely disreputable or a failure to maintain good ethical standards and must bear in mind that legal professional privilege is a very necessary thing and is not lightly to be overthrown, but on the other hand, the interests of victims of fraud must not be overlooked. Each case depends on its own facts.'

Both passages are cited by Colman J in the *David Agmashenebeli* (20 November 2000).
5 [1995] 1 WLR 1238, CA at 1248H–1250D.
6 It should be noted that in dishonesty cases the Law Society has the power to override privilege in disciplinary proceedings and to compel the disclosure of privileged documents: see *Parry-Jones v The Law Society* [1969] 1 Ch 1 and *Simms v The Law Society* [2005] EWHC 408 (Admin) at [36]–[53]. The Law Society has now delegated this power to the Solicitors Regulation Authority.

(a) *Legal advice privilege*

14.27 The claimant may seek production of the privileged material on the grounds that the original transaction of which he or she complains was fraudulent or tainted by iniquity. In *Birmingham Midshires Mortgage Services Ltd v Ansell*[1] the judge held that the exception did not apply where a borrower misled a lender about the purpose for which he required a remortgage. Blackburne J refused to follow *Ansell* in *Nationwide v Various Solicitors (No 3)*[2] and held that:

> 'Deceiving a person into lending money in circumstances where, if no deception had been practised, no loan might well have been forthcoming is, in my respectful view, at least as iniquitous as entering into a transaction for the purpose of putting one's assets

beyond the reach of one's creditors or otherwise prejudicing the interests of those creditors. The fact that the motive was to relieve financial pressure does not seem to me to matter.'

Furthermore the judge held that in order to invoke the exception it is not necessary for the applicant to satisfy the court that the solicitor was a party to the crime or iniquity in the sense that he was engaged to assist his client to further that purpose or knew that his involvement would be of such assistance.[3] Indeed in *Barclays Bank plc v Eustice*[4] the Court of Appeal accepted that the exception might be invoked even if the client and solicitor shared the view that the scheme designed to put assets out of the reach of creditors was lawful.

1 (6 November 1997, unreported) (Jonathan Parker J).
2 [1999] PNLR 52 at 73G. The two cases can be distinguished on the basis that the solicitor in *Ansell* was not involved in assisting the borrower to commit a fraud. Jonathan Parker J refused the application on the following basis:

'In my judgment, the instant case does not bring the iniquity principle into play. The re-financing of the borrowers' outstanding liabilities in order to relieve the financial pressure under which they and their companies were operating, if that is what they were indeed engaged upon, was not in itself a "guilty purpose"....Rather, what happened here, if the plaintiffs are proved right, was that the borrowers deceived the plaintiffs as to the purpose of the loans and as to the size of their income. But there is no evidence that the defendants were asked to advise in relation to the completion of the application forms or the so-called self-certification clause. The solicitors were retained to undertake certain specific conveyancing transactions involving the re-financing and sale of a number of properties and the granting of first charges to secure the two loans made by the plaintiffs. On the facts as they appear at this stage in the proceedings the borrowers were not seeking advice from the defendants "for the purposes of carrying out a fraud".'

3 [1999] PNLR 52 at 74A. In *R v Central Criminal Court, ex p Francis & Francis* [1989] 1 AC 346 the House of Lords held that privilege was lost in a criminal case where a firm of solicitors was used to purchase properties with the proceeds of crime. In *Kuwait Airways Corpn v Iraqi Airways Corpn (No 6)* [2005] EWCA Civ 286, [2005] 1 WLR 2734 at [25] Longmore LJ stated:

'[T]he House of Lords in *R (on the application of Francis) v Central Criminal Court [1989] AC 346* held, in accordance with the common law, that the criminal purpose did not have to be in the mind of the holder (typically a solicitor) but could be in the mind of a third party (typically the solicitor's client).'

4 [1995] 1 WLR 1238, CA at 1252C–D.

14.28 In *Eustice*[1] the Court of Appeal left open the question whether it was necessary for the applicant to establish a prima facie case of iniquity or a strong prima facie case. In *Nationwide Building Society v Various Solicitors* the judge, whilst recognising that there may be little difference between them, adopted[2] the view expressed by Viscount Finlay in *O'Rourke v Darbishire*[3] where he said this:

'It is not enough to allege fraud. If the communications to the solicitor were for the purpose of obtaining professional advice there must be, in order to get rid of the privilege, not merely an allegation that they were made for the purpose of getting advice for the commission of a fraud but there must be something to give colour to the charge. The statement must be made in clear and definitive terms and there must further be some prima facie evidence it has some foundation in fact.'

Solicitors are often placed in a difficult position when applications for disclosure of documents are made against them on the grounds that the exception applies and the documents were brought into existence to further or facilitate the crime or fraud of the client. There is no clear authority that a solicitor is permitted to disclose documents voluntarily and without a court order especially where the applicant cannot demonstrate more than a prima facie case, or even a strong prima facie case, which the client might dispute if he or she were willing or available to give instructions. It is suggested that the proper course, therefore, is for the solicitor to indicate that he or she is prepared to disclose the documents under CPR Part 31.17 subject to a court order and will not contest the application (except for the purposes of correcting any factual inaccuracies in the evidence). Even if the solicitor is a party to proceedings, it is difficult to justify the solicitor actively defending the application (unless the application is clearly misconceived and the evidence of fraud is very weak indeed). Moreover, if a solicitor chooses to contest an application for disclosure, there is a risk of an adverse costs order.[4]

1 [1995] 1 WLR 1238 at 1241H. The passage from Longmore LJ's judgment in *Kuwait Airways Corpn v Iraqi Airways Corpn (No 6)* quoted in para 14.29, below, also suggest that a prima facie case is sufficient where the allegation of fraud is not one of the issues in the action.
2 [1999] PNLR 52 at 74D–E.
3 [1920] AC 581 at 606.
4 See, for instance, *Re Murjani* [1996] 1 WLR 1498 which was an application to set aside an order for the oral examination of a bankrupt's solicitors under s 366 of the Insolvency Act 1986 on the basis that the solicitors were not prepared to disclose privileged information. The application failed and Lightman J ordered them to pay the costs. He stated (at 1511G):

'The two applications by the solicitors were not in the nature of holding the ring between the trustee and the clients, but partisan hostile litigation against the trustee which (save perhaps for occasioning marginal improvements in the drafting of the orders to meet the exigencies of this case) has wholly failed.'

(b) Litigation privilege

14.29 One of the parties may also allege that privilege has been lost for documents which would otherwise attract litigation privilege by relying on the fraud exception. For instance, one party may allege that the way in which evidence has been gathered involves fraud or iniquity. In *Dubai Aluminium Co Ltd v Al Alawi*[1] there was a strong prima facie case that Dubal, the claimant, had obtained details of the defendant's bank, credit card and telephone accounts from inquiry agents who had made 'pretext calls' impersonating the defendant. These calls involved both fraudulent misrepresentations and criminal offences under the Data Protection Act 1984 and Swiss banking legislation. The defendant sought disclosure of the reports and other documents relating to the investigation. The judge held that criminal or fraudulent conduct undertaken for the purposes of litigation is no different from advising on, or setting up, a fraudulent or criminal transaction and ordered disclosure.[2] In *Kuwait Airways Corpn v Iraqi Airways Corpn (No 6)* an application was made for disclosure of the legal advice which the defendant had received during an earlier action in which false and perjured evidence had been given on its behalf. It was argued that the fraud exception applied only to legal advice privilege and that *Dubai Aluminium Co Ltd v Al Alawi* had been wrongly decided. The Court of Appeal rejected this argument and ordered disclosure. Longmore LJ stated this:[3]

> 'I would therefore summarise the position thus: (1) the fraud exception can apply where there is a claim to litigation privilege as much as where there is a claim to legal advice privilege; (2) nevertheless it can only be used in cases in which the issue of fraud is one of the issues in the action where there is a strong (I would myself use the words "very strong") prima facie case of fraud as there was in *Dubai Aluminium v Al-Alawi* and there was not in *Chandler v Church*[4]; (3) where the issue of fraud is not one of the issues in the action, a prima facie case of fraud may be enough as in *Hallinan*[5].'

1 [1999] 1 WLR 1964 (Rix J).
2 [1999] 1 WLR 1964 at 1970A–B:

> 'Ultimately, it seems to me that criminal or fraudulent conduct undertaken for the purposes of litigation falls on the same side of the line as advising on or setting up criminal or fraudulent transactions yet to be undertaken, as distinct from the entirely legitimate professional business of advising and assisting clients on their past conduct, however iniquitous.'

He did not, however, consider that searching dustbins and copying material found in them amounted to criminal or fraudulent conduct for the purposes of the rule: see 1968B.
3 [2005] EWCA Civ 286, [2005] 1 WLR 2734 at [42].
4 *Chandler v Church* (1987) 177 NLJ 451 (Hoffmann J) where it was accepted in principle that litigation privilege could be lost by the conduct of the proceedings themselves although disclosure was refused.
5 *R (on the application of Hallinan Blackburn Gittings & Nott (a firm)) v Crown Court at Middlesex Guildhall* [2004] EWHC 2726 (Admin), [2005] 1 WLR 766, DC where there was a conspiracy to pervert the course of justice. Rose LJ stated at 771E (in a passage quoted by Longmore LJ at [28]):

> 'Where ... there is evidence of specific agreement to pervert the course of justice, which is free-standing and independent, in the sense that it does not require any judgment to be reached in relation to the issues to be tried, the court may well be in a position to evaluate whether what has occurred falls within or outwith the protection of legal professional privilege as explained in *R v Cox and Railton* (1884) 14 QBD 153.'

5   Implied waiver of privilege

(a) *The defendant's files*

14.30   In order to pursue a claim against a former solicitor, it is always necessary for the client to waive privilege in relation to the defendant's file for the transaction which is the subject matter of the claim. Otherwise it would be impossible for the claimant to establish that the defendant gave the wrong advice or failed to give advice with skill and care.[1] When, however, the defendant seeks to obtain disclosure of documents that demonstrate how the client behaved on other occasions, for example when the claimant received legal advice from the defendant in relation to similar transactions or when he or she received independent advice from another solicitor in relation to litigation with third parties, the client may assert privilege in those documents despite their relevance to the proceedings. In principle a client who commences proceedings against his or her former solicitor will be found to have waived privilege in the defendant's own files to the extent that it is necessary to enable the court to adjudicate on the claim fully and fairly. In *Lillicrap v Nalder & Son*[2] the Court of Appeal held that there had been an implied waiver of privilege in relation to six other transactions. Dillon LJ stated:

> 'Thus, the client has the right to insist on his professional legal privilege and it is for him to choose whether or not to waive it. But it is accepted that the waiver may be implied and that there is an implied waiver when the client brings proceedings against the solicitor. Mr Bennett suggests that the waiver is only in respect of documents and information concerned with the particular retainer. This may, in general, prima facie, be so but it is not difficult to envisage scenarios where it is apparent that the waiver must have a wider scope. For my part, I accept May J's formulation of the scope of waiver. He said in his judgment:
>
> > "I return to what I regard as the heart of the matter–waiver. A client who sues his solicitor invites the court to adjudicate the dispute and thereby in my judgment waives privilege and confidence to the extent that it is necessary to enable the court to do so fully and fairly and in accordance with the law of evidence. I suspect that at the fringes each case will depend on its own facts. Normally the waiver will extend to facts and documents material to the cause of action upon which the plaintiff sues and to the defendant's proper defence to that cause of action. The bringing of a claim for negligence in relation to a particular retainer will normally be a waiver of privilege and confidence for facts and documents relating to that retainer, but not without more for those relating to other discrete retainers."

I agree with that. The waiver can only extend to matters which are relevant to an issue in the proceedings and, privilege apart, admissible in evidence. There is no waiver for a roving search into anything else in which the solicitor or any other solicitor may have happened to have acted for the clients. But the waiver must go far enough, not merely to entitle the plaintiff to establish his cause of action, but to enable the defendant to establish a defence to the cause of action if he has one. Thus, it would extend to matters under earlier retainers, as in the hypothetical example I had given[3] which established that the experience of the client was, to the knowledge of the solicitor, such that the solicitor was not in breach of the duty as alleged.'

1 The more difficult issue which is explored in para 14.15, above, is when the waiver can be said to be effective.
2 [1993] 1 WLR 94 at 98B and 99A–E, CA.
3 [1993] 1 WLR 94 at 98C–H.

14.31 The claimant will not, however, be taken to have waived privilege simply by bringing proceedings against other parties or advisers in relation to a particular transaction. It is only by bringing proceedings against his or her former solicitors that the claimant will be held to have waived privilege. In *NRG Holding NV v Bacon & Woodrow*[1] the defendants sought to argue that the claimant had waived privilege over advice given by its legal advisers in relation to a share purchase by taking proceedings against its other advisers, who were accountants and actuaries. Colman J, after citing *Lillicrap v Nalder*, said this:

'The true analysis of what the courts are doing in such cases of so-called waiver of privilege is, in my judgment, to prevent the unfairness which would arise if the plaintiff were entitled to exclude from the court's consideration evidence relevant to a defence by relying upon the privilege arising from the solicitor's duty of confidence. The client is thus precluded from both asserting that the solicitor has acted in breach of duty and thereby caused the client loss and, to make good the claim, opening up the confidential relationship between them and at the same time seeking to enforce against that same solicitor a duty of confidence arising from their professional relationship in circumstances where such enforcement would deprive the solicitor of the means of defending the claim. It is fundamental to this principle that the confidence which privilege would otherwise protect arises by reason of the same professional relationship between the parties to the litigation. The underlying unfairness which the principle seeks to avoid arises because the claim is asserted and the professional relationship opened for investigation against the very party whose duty of confidence is the basis of the privilege. It is against the unfairness of both opening the relationship by asserting the claim and seeking to enforce the duty of confidence owed by the defendant that the principle is directed.'

He held that by commencing proceedings against the non-legal advisers the claimant had not waived privilege in relation to confidential legal advice.

1 [1995] 1 All ER 976 at 986c–f.

(b) The files of other solicitors

14.32   Although the views expressed by Colman J suggested that the principle was confined to dealings between the claimant and the defendant, both *Lillicrap v Nalder* and *N R G v Bacon & Woodrow* left open for decision the question whether a client who sues one solicitor would be taken to have waived privilege in relation to advice which he or she had received from another firm of solicitors. A number of conflicting first instance decisions then followed.[1]

1 See *Kershaw v Whelan* [1996] 1 WLR 358 (Ebsworth J) (in which disclosure of the files of other solicitors was ordered); *Banque Bruxelles Lambert SA v Simmons & Simmons* (24 November 1995, unreported) (Blackburne J), transcript, p 40 (where the implied waiver was held to extend only to 'communications between the client and the solicitor whom he is suing'); *Hayes v Dowding* [1996] PNLR 578 (Jonathan Parker J) at 589C–F (where disclosure of a solicitor's file was ordered even though the claim was not against a firm of solicitors but against parties to a compromise agreement); and *Burdge & Burdge v John Hodge & Co* (11 March 1996, unreported) (Longmore J) (where it was held that the implied waiver did not extend to privileged documents in the hands of another solicitor instructed after the act of negligence which was the subject matter of the action).

14.33   This conflict of authority was resolved by the decision of the Court of Appeal in *Paragon Finance plc v Freshfields*.[1] In that case the claimants, a group of mortgage lenders, syndicated their mortgage books by selling the loans to special purpose vehicles and issuing a series of loan notes to investors. Sun Alliance and Eagle Star guaranteed the loans on terms that the lenders met certain lending criteria which were then specified in the mortgage guarantee policies. When the insurers refused to indemnify the lenders against heavy losses sustained by the claimants for failure to comply with these criteria, the claimants sued the insurance companies. This litigation was compromised and the lenders then commenced proceedings against the defendants who had advised them on the terms of the policies. The defendants sought production of the communications between the lenders and their new solicitors and counsel in the actions against the insurers. It was common ground that these documents were relevant to the proceedings but the Court of Appeal refused to order disclosure. Lord Bingham MR who delivered the judgment of the court made this important statement of principle:[2]

'When a client sues a solicitor who has formerly acted for him, complaining that the solicitor has acted negligently, he invites the court to adjudicate on questions directly arising from the confidential relationship which formerly subsisted between them. Since court proceedings are public, the client brings that formerly confidential relationship into the public domain. He thereby waives any right to claim the protection of legal professional privilege in relation to any communications between them so far as necessary for the just determination of his claim; or, putting the same proposition in different terms, he releases the solicitor to that extent from the obligation of confidence by which he was formerly bound. This is an implication of law, the rationale of which is plain. A party cannot deliberately subject a relationship to public scrutiny and at the same time seek to preserve its confidentiality. He cannot pick and choose, disclosing such incidents of the relationship as strengthen his claim for damages and concealing from forensic scrutiny such incidents as weaken it. He cannot attack his former solicitor and deny the solicitor use of materials relevant to his defence. But, since the implied waiver applies to communications between client and solicitor, it will cover no communications to which the solicitor is not privy and so will disclose nothing of which he is not already aware.

Thus, on the present facts, by bringing these proceedings the plaintiffs impliedly waived any claim to legal professional privilege in relation to confidential communications between them and Freshfields concerning the transaction briefly described above, up to the moment when Freshfields ceased to act. That is not in issue. The question is whether the plaintiffs have also impliedly waived any claim to legal professional privilege in relation to confidential communications between them and Slaughter and May relating to the pursuit and settlement of claims arising from those transactions. Approaching this question as one of pure principle, we conclude that they have not. The plaintiffs have not sued Slaughter and May. They have not invited the court to adjudicate on any question arising from their confidential relationship with Slaughter and May, and so have not brought that confidential relationship into the public domain. They have done nothing to release Slaughter and May from the obligation of confidence by which they are bound. They have chosen to subject their relationship with Freshfields to public scrutiny, but not their relationship with Slaughter and May. They are not seeking to pick and choose among the confidential communications passing between themselves and Slaughter and May: none of them is (so far) in the forensic arena. It is open to Freshfields, by way of defence, to rely on any communication passing between themselves and the plaintiffs; to hold that the plaintiffs have impliedly waived privilege in relation to confidential communications between themselves and Slaughter and May would be, not to enable Freshfields to rely on communications of which they are already aware, but to disclose to them communications of which they have no knowledge.'

The court restricted the application of *Lillicrap v Nalder* to former transactions handled by the defendant, approved both *N R G v Bacon & Woodrow* and *BBL v Simmons & Simmons*, disapproved Ebsworth J's reasoning in *Kershaw v Whelan* and overruled *Hayes v Dowding*.

1 [1999] 1 WLR 1183.
2 [1999] 1 WLR 1183 at 1188D–1189C.

(c) The 'putting in issue' exception

14.34 It still remains unclear, following *Paragon*, whether the doctrine of implied waiver can ever extend beyond a case where the solicitor in question is also the defendant. In *Paragon* itself the files in question were relevant to the defendant's case of contributory negligence and failure to mitigate and it was, therefore, unnecessary for the court to consider a case where the claimant has put in issue the legal advice which he or she has received but the adviser is not the defendant. It is clear that the principle of implied waiver extends only to cases in which the claimant has brought the legal relationship into the public domain. However, the difficulty is to identify the limits of that principle. If it is limited to cases in which the lawyer–client relationship is the subject of the action and the client only releases the lawyer from his or her obligation of confidentiality so that he or she can defend themselves, the doctrine is very narrow indeed. For instance, it would be impossible for a defendant against whom a claim of presumed undue influence has been made to rebut the presumption by relying on the legal advice which a claimant had received unless the claimant was prepared to waive privilege.[1] On the other hand, if it extends to all cases where the claimant has 'put in issue' the advice that he or she received either expressly or by implication the doctrine will be of wide application.[2] The judgment of the Privy Council in *B v Auckland District Law Society*[3] contains powerful support for the proposition that the narrower view of implied waiver is correct and that it is limited to a case in which the claimant bring proceedings against his or her former solicitors. Lord Millett stated this:[4]

> 'Some principles are well established and were confirmed by Lord Taylor of Gosforth CJ in *R v Derby Magistrates' Court, ex p B [1996] AC 487* at 503. First, the privilege remains after the occasion for it has passed: unless waived "once privileged, always privileged". Secondly, the privilege is the same whether the documents are sought for the purpose of civil or criminal proceedings and whether by the prosecution or the defence. Thirdly, the refusal of the claimant to waive his privilege for any reason or none cannot be questioned or investigated by the court. Fourthly, save in cases where the privileged communication is itself the means of carrying out a fraud, the privilege is absolute. Once the privilege is established, the lawyer's

mouth is "shut for ever" (see *Wilson v Rastall* (1792) 4 Term Rep 753 at 759, 100 ER 1283 at 1287 per Buller J).'

In *Shannon v Shannon*[5] the Court of Appeal of New Zealand considered *B v Auckland District Law Society* to be direct authority for the proposition that there was no 'putting in issue' exception to legal professional privilege and that the introduction of such an exception could only be made by Parliament. Two further issues also remain: first, whether by commencing proceedings against one of the lawyers who has represented him and impliedly waiving privilege, a client should also be taken to have waived privilege against any others (and this arises where a claimant chooses to sue a barrister rather than a solicitor); and, secondly, whether by waiving privilege in one action the client should be taken to have waived privilege for all purposes. The passages in Lord Bingham's judgment in *Paragon* with its references to 'the public domain' and 'public scrutiny' suggests that the answer to both questions is yes and the recent amendments to CPR Part 5 (which were brought into force on 2 October 2006) reinforce this conclusion.[6] It is suggested therefore that an implied waiver will usually take place for all purposes at the latest when the defendants file an acknowledgement of service.[7] It is also suggested that the position is the same for claims which were made prior to 2 October 2006.[8]

1 Consider the famous case of *Inche Noriah v Shaik Allie Bin Omar* [1929] AC 127 and see the discussion of this issue by Allsop J in *DSE (Holdings) Pty Limited v Intertan Inc* [2003] FCA 384 at [46] and [47].
2 In *Ramac Holdings Ltd v Brachers* [2002] EWHC 1605 (Ch) HHJ Seymour QC declined to rule on this issue although he suggested that it ought to be the subject of further argument at which the client whose privilege it was should be represented: see [7].
3 [2003] UKPC 38, [2003] 2 AC 736.
4 [44]. See also *Three Rivers DC v Bank of England* (*No 6*) [2004] UKHL 48, [2005] 1 AC 610 at [25] (Lord Scott):

   'Second, if a communication or document qualifies for legal professional privilege, the privilege is absolute. It cannot be overridden by some supposedly greater public interest. It can be waived by the person, the client, entitled to it and it can be overridden by statute (c f *R (on the application of Morgan Grenfell & Co Ltd) v Special Comr of Income Tax* [2002] UKHL 21, [2003] 1 AC 563), but it is otherwise absolute. There is no balancing exercise that has to be carried out (see *B v Auckland District Law Society* [2003] UKPC 38 at [46]–[54], [2003] 2 AC 736).'

5 [2005] NZCA 91 at [36]–[49] (Glazebrook J). See, in particular, [38]:

   'We agree with Potter J that the Privy Council decision in *B v Auckland District Law Society* is inconsistent with the broad form of the "putting in issue" exception argued for by Ms Duffy, where mere relevance to an issue is enough to destroy privilege.'

6 CPR Part 5.4C(1) (which was introduced by the Civil Procedure (Amendment) Rules 2006, SI 2006/1689) provides:

   'The general rule is that a person who is not a party to proceedings may obtain from the court records a copy of— (a) a statement of case, but not any documents filed with or attached to the statement of case, or intended by the party whose statement it is to be served with it; (b) a judgment or order given or made in public (whether made at a hearing or without a hearing).'

Rule 5.4C(2) also enables a non-party to obtain copies of documents filed with a statement of case (with the court's permission).

7 CPR Part 5.4C(3) provides:

'A non-party may obtain a copy of a statement of case or judgment or order under paragraph (1) only if—

(a) where there is one defendant, the defendant has filed an acknowledgment of service or a defence;

(b) where there is more than one defendant, either—

    (i) all the defendants have filed an acknowledgment of service or a defence;

    (ii) at least one defendant has filed an acknowledgment of service or a defence, and the court gives permission;

(c) the claim has been listed for a hearing; or

(d) judgment has been entered in the claim.'

A party may make an application to restrict access to statements of case: see CPR Part 5.4C(4). But unless the claimant makes such an application in relation to the claim form or particulars of claim, it is suggested that the implied waiver in commencing proceedings will be unlimited and that it will take effect when a non-party can obtain access to those documents.

8 Prior to 2 October 2006 CPR Part 5.4 formerly provided that a non-party could inspect a claim form but not the particulars of claim without permission. However, given that the claimant had no control over whether permission would be given, it is suggested that any claimant who waived privilege by commencing proceedings prior to that date waived privilege for all purposes. This is consistent with the decision of Richards J in *UCB v Thomason* [2004] EWHC 882 (Ch) at [7] and [8]. In that case disclosure of separate proceedings brought by the defendants against their former solicitors was refused because they had not filed the particulars of claim (which were subject to a standstill agreement). See, however, *National Westminster Bank plc v Brice Droogleever & Co* [2003] EWHC 1821 (Ch) (Lindsay J) at [130] (original emphasis):

'I do not doubt that if the Fee Proceedings had been fought further Mr Brice would have been able to use otherwise confidential solicitor-and-client material *in those proceedings*. The reason would have been that without such an implied waiver justice would not have been capable of being done *in that suit*. But it would be quite disproportionate to achievement of that end to enlarge that limited form of implied waiver in such a way as to free Mr Brice to use the otherwise confidential material wherever he might choose, including in these proceedings.'

In that case, a firm of solicitors brought proceedings to recover their fees from a former client. The claim was settled but in later proceedings the solicitors sought to argue that by defending those proceedings the client had waived privilege and confidentiality in the relationship. It is suggested that the facts of this case were unusual because the waiver relied on was not the issue of proceedings but filing a defence.

(d) *Reliance on legal advice*

14.35 Where the issue is whether the claimant received and acted upon the legal advice of the defendant, he or she will normally be taken to have waived privilege. Closely related to the question whether the claimant did in fact rely on the legal advice which he or she received is the question whether he or she would have relied on the advice which he now alleges he should have been given. As stated above, in *Lillicrap v Nalder & Son*[1] the Court of Appeal held that privilege had been waived in relation to six earlier transactions because they were directly relevant to the question whether the plaintiffs would have avoided the loss if advised in the way which they should have been.

1 [1993] 1 WLR 94, CA.

(e) *Limitation defences*

14.36 Where the claimant's claim is barred by a primary limitation period, he or she may need to rely on Limitation Act 1980, s 14A or s 32. In *Kershaw v Whelan*[1] the defendant pleaded that the claimant's claim was statute-barred both in contract and tort. In reply the claimant relied on Limitation Act 1980, s 32 and alleged that he did not and could not with due diligence have discovered the facts upon which his claim was based before April 1985 because they had been deliberately concealed from him by the defendant. It was held that this plea involved an implied waiver of the privilege in legal advice relating to the concealment and discovery of his claim.[2] In *Paragon* the Court of Appeal left open the question whether the case had been wrongly decided although they disapproved the reasoning of the judge.[3] If the analysis of *Paragon* set out in para 14.34 is correct, the decision cannot stand and no order for disclosure should have been made. By commencing proceedings the claimant was not bringing his relationship with his subsequent solicitors into the public domain and there was no reference to the advice which he had received in the claimant's statement of case which would have amounted to an express waiver of privilege.[4] If, however, there is a 'putting in issue' exception (contrary to the view expressed above), the decision was the right one. By asserting in his reply that he could not have discovered the facts on which his claim was based, the claimant put in issue the knowledge of his former solicitors and the advice which he received. That said, in order to prove their case at trial, claimants who rely on either s14A or s 32 will have to establish when they first received advice about the claim and may also have to reveal the terms of that advice.[5] This will normally require a conscious decision to waive privilege. The extent to which any of these actions involves a waiver of privilege in individual documents or a course of correspondence will depend on normal principles and a decision whether to waive privilege is best taken as soon as the defendant raises a valid limitation defence.[6]

1 [1996] 1 WLR 358 (Ebsworth J).
2 It appears that Ebsworth J ordered disclosure not only of the litigation files of the claimant's former solicitors but also of his current solicitors: see the headnote at 359B–D. However, this is not entirely clear: see the form of the summons and order at 360D–F and 370H–371A.
3 [1999] 1 WLR 1183 at 1192B–1193B.

4 It is doubtful whether a reference to the legal advice which the claimant had received would have amounted to an express waiver: see *Fulham Leisure Holdings Ltd v Nicholson Graham & Jones* [2006] EWHC 158 (Ch) (Mann J).

5 See *Fulham Leisure Holdings Ltd v Nicholson Graham & Jones* [2006] EWHC 2017 (Ch) (Mann J) at [307] set out in para 14.37, below. The decision referred to in n 4 (above) is an earlier interlocutory decision in the same case.

6 Despite the different wording of s 33 of the Limitation Act 1980 and the decision in *Jones v GD Searle & Co* [1979] 1 WLR 101 the position appears to be the same for claims for personal injury and death: see Thanki *The Law of Privilege* (2006) 5.88. A claimant will not be taken to have waived privilege but may be unable to prove his or her case without doing so.

(f) Damages

14.37   A similar problem arises for a party who claims as damages the costs of abortive litigation or other legal costs. In *Burdge & Burdge v John Hodge & Co*[1] the claimants claimed as damages the costs of litigation on which they had embarked to extricate themselves from the consequences of the defendant's negligence. These proceedings ultimately proved fruitless. Consistently with *Paragon*, the judge held that the files of the solicitors who had handled the proceedings were relevant but privileged. He added, however, that although there was no implied waiver, it was likely that the claimants would be obliged to consent to waive privilege if they wished to prove a causal connection between the negligence and the costs. In *Fulham Leisure Holdings Ltd v Nicholson Graham & Jones*[2] the claimant claimed the costs of taking legal advice. The claimant chose not to waive privilege and although the claimant recovered some of the fees the balance of the claim failed. Mann J stated this:[3]

> 'The Claimants have chosen to be coy about what counsel was being asked to do. It appears on the authorities that making a claim for the fees does not waive privilege (see *Paragon Finance plc v Freshfields* [1999] 1 WLR 1183) but that does not mean that the Claimant can get away with some inadequate level of evidence if it chooses to make that claim. The Claimant has a choice. If it wishes to claim the legal fees, it must adduce a sufficient level of evidence to prove its claim and demonstrate that the fees are properly recoverable as damages. If that involves a waiver of privilege then so be it. If it chooses to limit its disclosure in the interests of preserving its privilege (which is clearly what has happened here) then it runs the risk of not having proved its case. That is the position in this case. In fact, not only is there inadequate evidence of various matters, there are also certain limited positive matters which cast doubt on some of the claim …… I do not think it is appropriate for me to indulge in guesswork in relation to these fees.'

1 (11 March 1996, unreported) (Longmore J).
2 [2006] EWHC 2017 (Ch).
3 [307].

(g) Settlements and compromises

14.38   In *Biggin & Co Ltd v Permanite Ltd*[1] it was held that a claimant who sought to recover as damages the amount which he had paid to compromise a claim had to satisfy the court that the settlement was a reasonable one. In a number of cases[2] disclosure of legal advice has also been sought on the grounds that by relying on a compromise with a third party and asserting that it is reasonable a party has waived privilege in relation to the legal advice which he received. We consider that *Paragon* has resolved this issue too. Even if the legal advice is relevant to the reasonableness of the claimant's conduct, he or she cannot be ordered to disclose it. The claimant is free to choose whether to waive privilege and introduce evidence of the legal advice which he or she received or to rely on the terms of the settlement and open correspondence by themselves.[3]

1 [1951] 2 KB 314, CA, a sale of goods case.
2 *Oceanic Finance Co Ltd v Norton Rose* (26 March 1997, unreported) (Moore-Bick J), *The Society of Lloyds v Kitson Environmental Services Ltd* (1994) 67 BLR 102 (HHJ Havery QC, ORB) and *DSL Group Ltd v Unisys International Services Ltd* (1994) 67 BLR 117 (HHJ Hicks QC, ORB).
3 In both *Oceanic Finance* and *DSL* (see n 2), it was held that the advice was not relevant because the test of reasonableness was an objective one. In *Oceanic Finance* Moore-Bick J distinguished the decision in *Muller v Linsley & Mortimer* [1996] 1 PNLR 74, CA, in which Hoffmann LJ adopted a subjective test in ordering disclosure of without prejudice communications. In *Paragon* [1999] 1 WLR 1183 at 1191F Lord Bingham indicated that no real principle could be derived from the case.

Appendix

Law Society's Warning on Property Fraud*

LAW SOCIETY'S 'GREEN CARD' WARNING ON PROPERTY FRAUD (FEBRUARY 1999)

Could you be involved or implicated?

Could you be unwittingly assisting in a fraud? The general assumption is that if there has been a property fraud a solicitor must have been involved. Solicitors should therefore be vigilant to protect both their clients and themselves. Steps can be taken to minimise the risk of being involved or implicated in a fraud (see below).

Could you spot a property fraud?

The signs to watch for include the following (but this list is not exhaustive):

Fraudulent buyer or fictitious solicitors – especially if the buyer is introduced to your practice by a third party (for example a broker or estate agent) who is not well known to you. Beware of clients whom you never meet and solicitors not known to you.

Unusual instructions – for example a solicitor being instructed by the seller to remit the net proceeds of sale to anyone other than the seller.

Misrepresentation of the purchase price – ensure that the true cash price actually to be paid is stated as the consideration in the contract and transfer and is identical to the price shown in the mortgage instructions and in the report on title to the lender.

A deposit or any part of purchase price paid direct – a deposit or the difference between the mortgage advance and the price, paid direct, or said to be paid direct, to the seller.

* The following text has been reproduced by kind permission of The Law Society.

Incomplete contract documentation – contract documents not fully completed by the seller's representative, i e dates missing or the identity of the parties not fully described or financial details not fully stated.

Changes in the purchase price – adjustments to the purchase price, particularly in high percentage mortgage cases, or allowances off the purchase price, for example, for works to be carried out.

Unusual transactions – transactions which do not follow their normal course or the usual pattern of events:

(a)   client with current mortgage on two or more properties

(b)   client using alias

(c)   client buying several properties from same person or two or more persons using same solicitor

(d)   client reselling property at a substantial profit, for which no explanation has been provided.

What steps can I take to minimise the risk of fraud?

Be vigilant: if you have any doubts about a transaction, consider whether any of the following steps could be taken to minimise the risk of fraud:

Verify the identity and bona fides of your client and solicitors' firms you do not know – meet the clients where possible and get to know them a little. Check that the solicitor's firm and office address appear in the Directory of Solicitors and Barristers or contact the Law Society's Regulation and Information Services (tel: 0870 606 2555).

Question unusual instructions – if you receive unusual instructions from your client discuss them with your client fully.

Discuss with your client any aspects of the transaction which worry you – if, for example, you have any suspicion that your client may have submitted a false mortgage application or references, or if the lender's valuation exceeds the actual price paid, discuss this with your client. If you believe that the client intends to proceed with a fraudulent application, you must refuse to continue to act for the buyer and the lender.

Check that the true price is shown in all documentation – check that the actual price paid is stated in the contract, transfer and mortgage instructions. Where you are also acting for a lender, tell your client that you will have to cease acting unless the client permits you to report to the lender all allowances and incentives. See also the guidance printed in [1990] Gazette, 12 December, 16 [see Annex 25F, p 500 in the Guide].

Do not witness pre-signed documentation – no document should be witnessed by a solicitor or his or her staff unless the person signing does so in the presence of the witness. If the document is pre-signed, ensure that it is re-signed in the presence of a witness.

Verify signatures – consider whether signatures on all documents connected with a transaction should be examined and compared with signatures on any other available documentation.

Make a company search – where a private company is the seller, or the seller has purchased from a private company in the recent past, and you suspect that the sale may not be on proper arm's length terms, you should make a search in the Companies Register to ascertain the names and addresses of the officers and shareholders, which can then be compared with the names of those connected with the transaction and the seller and buyer.

Remember that, even where investigations result in a solicitor ceasing to act for a client, the solicitor will still owe a duty of confidentiality which would prevent the solicitor passing on information to the lender. It is only where the solicitor is satisfied that there is a strong prima facie case that the client was using the solicitor to further a fraud or other criminal purpose that the duty of confidentiality would not apply.

Any failure to observe these signs and to take the appropriate steps may be used in court as evidence against you if you and your client are prosecuted, or if you are sued for negligence.

Further guidance can be obtained from the Law Society's Practice Advice Service (tel: 0870 606 2522).

March 1991, revised January 1996, updated February 1999

LAW SOCIETY'S WARNING: PROPERTY FRAUD 2 (MARCH 2005)

This card has been updated to take account of knowledge gained from criminal prosecutions and suggestions from the profession.

Could you be involved or implicated?

Could you be unwittingly assisting in a fraud? The general assumption is that if there has been a property fraud a solicitor must have been involved. Solicitors should therefore be vigilant to protect both their clients and themselves. Steps can be taken to minimise the risk of being involved or implicated in a fraud (see below).

Could you spot a property fraud?

The signs to watch for include the following (but this list is not exhaustive):

- **Fraudulent buyer or fictitious solicitors** – especially if the buyer is introduced to your practice by a third party (for example a broker or estate agent) who is not well known to you. Beware of clients whom you never meet and solicitors not known to you.

- **Unusual instructions** – for example a solicitor being instructed by the seller to remit the net proceeds of sale to anyone other than the seller.

- **Misrepresentation of the purchase price** – ensure that the true cash price actually to be paid is stated as the consideration in the contract and transfer and is identical to the price shown in the mortgage instructions and in the report on title to the lender.

- **A deposit or any part of purchase price paid direct** – a deposit, or the difference between the mortgage advance and the price, paid direct, or said to be paid direct, to the seller.

- **Incomplete contract documentation** – contract documents not fully completed by the seller's representative, i e dates missing or the identity of the parties not fully described or financial details not fully stated.

- **Changes in the purchase price** – adjustments to the purchase price, particularly in high percentage mortgage cases, or allowances off the purchase price, for example, for works to be carried out.

- **Unusual transactions** – transactions which do not follow their normal course or the usual pattern of events:
  - client with current mortgage on two or more properties
  - client using alias
  - client buying several properties from same person or two or more persons using same solicitor

- client reselling property at a substantial profit, for which no explanation has been provided.

What steps can I take to minimise the risk of fraud?

Be vigilant. If you have any doubts about a transaction, consider whether any of the following steps could be taken to minimise the risk of fraud:

- **Verify the identity and bona fides of your client and solicitors' firms you do not know** – meet the clients where possible and get to know them a little. Check that the solicitor's firm and office address appear in the *Directory of Solicitors and Barristers* or contact the Law Society's Information Services (Tel:0870 606 2555).

- **Question unusual instructions** – if you receive unusual instructions from your client discuss them with your client fully.

- **Discuss with your client any aspects of the transaction which worry you** – if, for example, you have any suspicion that your client may have submitted a false mortgage application or references, or if the lender's valuation exceeds the actual price paid, discuss with your client. If you believe that the client intends to proceed with a fraudulent application, you must refuse to continue to act for the buyer and the lender.

- **Check that the true price is shown in all documentation** – check that the actual price paid is stated in the contract, transfer and mortgage instructions. Where you are also acting for a lender, tell your client that you will have to cease acting unless the client permits you to report to the lender all allowances and incentives.

- **Do not witness pre-signed documentation** – no document should be witnessed by a solicitor or his or her staff unless the person signing does so in the presence of the witness. If the document is pre-signed ensure that it is pre-signed in the presence of a witness.

- **Verify signatures** – consider whether signatures on all documents connected with a transaction should be examined and compared with signatures on any other available documentation.

- **Make a company search** – where a private company is the seller, or the seller has purchased from a private company in the recent past, and you suspect that the sale may not be on proper arm's length terms, you should make a search in the Companies Register to ascertain the names and addresses of the officers and shareholders, which can then be compared with the names of those connected with the transaction and the seller and buyer.

Remember that, even where investigations result in a solicitor ceasing to act for a client, the solicitor will still owe a duty of confidentiality which would prevent the solicitor from passing on information to the lender. It is only where the solicitor is satisfied that there is a strong *prima facie* case that the client was using the solicitor to further a fraud or other criminal purpose that the duty of confidentiality would not apply.

763

Any failure to observe these signs and to take the appropriate steps may be used in court as evidence against you if you and your client are prosecuted, or if you are sued for negligence.

Further guidance can be obtained from the Law Society's Practice Advice Service (Tel: 0870 606 2522)

SOLICITORS' CODE OF CONDUCT 2007, RR 3.16–3.22

3.16 Acting for lender and borrower in conveyancing transactions

(1) 3.16 to 3.22 cover the grant of a mortgage of land and are intended to avoid conflicts of interests. 'Mortgage' includes a remortgage. Both commercial and residential conveyancing transactions are covered. 'You' is defined in 23.01, but is to be construed in 3.16 to 3.22 as including an associated firm (see rule 24 (interpretation) for the meaning of 'associated firms').

(2) You must not act for both lender and borrower on the grant of a mortgage of land:

(a)   if a conflict of interests exists or arises;

(b)   on the grant of an individual mortgage of land at arm's length;

(c)   if, in the case of a standard mortgage of property to be used as the borrower's private residence only, the lender's mortgage instructions extend beyond the limitations contained in 3.19 and 3.21, or do not permit the use of the certificate of title required by 3.20; or

(d)   if, in the case of any other standard mortgage, the lender's mortgage instructions extend beyond the limitations contained in 3.19 and 3.21.

3.17 Standard and individual mortgages

(1) A mortgage is a 'standard mortgage' where:

(a)   it is provided in the normal course of the lender's activities;

(b)   a significant part of the lender's activities consists of lending; and

(c)   the mortgage is on standard terms.

An 'individual mortgage' is any other mortgage.

(2) A mortgage will not be on standard terms if material terms in any of the documents relating to the mortgage transaction are negotiated between the lender's and borrower's lawyers or licensed conveyancers contemporaneously with effecting the mortgage. In commercial transactions, the element of negotiation will often relate to the facility letter or facility agreement rather than the mortgage deed itself.

(3) Provided there has been no contemporaneous negotiation of material terms between the parties' lawyers or licensed conveyancers, a mortgage will be on standard terms where the lender uses a prescribed form of mortgage deed. Minor variations, such as the usual clause limiting the liability of trustee mortgagors, are not regarded as material and do not alter the nature of these terms as standard.

(4) In addition to its normal standard terms, a lender may have a different set or sets of standard terms applicable to specialised types of borrower, such as registered social landlords. Provided these terms are applied by the lender to all equivalent specialist borrowers or have been agreed between the lender and a specialist borrower as applicable to all transactions between them, they will constitute standard terms for the purposes of 3.16 to 3.22.

(5) The lender and the borrower must be separately represented on the grant of an individual mortgage at arm's length (see 3.16(2)(b)). 3.16 to 3.22 are not then applicable.

(6) You may act for both lender and borrower in a standard mortgage (see 3.16(2)(c) to (d)), provided:

(a)   there is no conflict of interests;

(b)   the mortgage instructions do not go beyond the limits set out in 3.19; and

(c)   in the case of a property to be used solely as the borrower's private residence, the approved certificate of title set out in the annex to rule 3 is used.

(7) The limitations of 3.19 also apply to a standard mortgage where the lender and the borrower are separately represented (see 3.22(1) which includes certificates of title). However, 3.22(2) allows the borrower's lawyer or licensed conveyancer, in a transaction where the property is not to be used solely as the borrower's private residence, to give a certificate of title in any form recognised by the Board of the Solicitors Regulation Authority. You also remain free to give any other form of certificate which complies with this rule.

(8) There may be cases where the lapse of time between the mortgage offer and completion (for example, when new properties are added) results in use of an earlier edition of a recognised certificate. That is acceptable.

3.18 Notification of certain circumstances to lender

(1) If you wish to act for both lender and borrower on the grant of a standard mortgage of land, you must first inform the lender in writing of the circumstances if:

(a)   the prospective borrower is:

    (i)   a principal in the firm (or a member if the firm is an LLP, or owner or director if the firm is a company), or a member of their immediate family;

    (ii)   a principal in an associated firm (or a member if the firm is an LLP, or owner or director if the firm is a company), or a member of their immediate family; and/or

    (iii)   the solicitor or REL conducting or supervising the transaction, or a member of their immediate family; or

(b)   you propose to act for seller, buyer and lender in the same transaction.

(2) 'Immediate family' means spouse, children, parents, brothers and sisters.

3.19 Types of instruction which may be accepted

If acting for both lender and borrower in a standard mortgage, you and the individual solicitor or REL conducting or supervising the transaction may only accept or act upon instructions from the lender which are limited to the following matters:

(a)

    (i)   taking reasonable steps to check the identity of the borrower (and anyone else required to sign the mortgage deed or other document connected with the mortgage) by reference to a document or documents, such as a passport, precisely specified in writing by the lender;

    (ii)   following the guidance given by the Law Society or the Solicitors Regulation Authority on property fraud and on money laundering;

    (iii)   checking that the seller's conveyancers (if unknown to you) appear in a current legal directory or hold practising certificates issued by their professional body; and

    (iv)   in the case of a lender with no branch office within reasonable proximity of the borrower, carrying out the money laundering checks precisely specified in writing by the lender;

(b)   making appropriate searches relating to the property in public registers (for example, local searches, commons registration searches, mining searches), and reporting any results specified by the lender or which you consider may adversely affect the lender; or effecting search insurance;

(c)   making enquiries on legal matters relating to the property reasonably specified by the lender, and reporting the replies;

(d)   reporting the purchase price stated in the transfer and on how the borrower says that the purchase money (other than the mortgage advance) is to be provided; and reporting if you will not have control over the payment of all the purchase money (other than a deposit paid to an estate agent or a reservation fee paid to a builder or developer);

(e)   reporting if the seller or the borrower (if the property is already owned by the borrower) has not owned or been the registered owner of the property for at least six months;

(f)   if the lender does not arrange insurance, confirming receipt of satisfactory evidence that the buildings insurance is in place for at least the sum required by the lender and covers the risks specified by the lender; giving notice to the insurer of the lender's interest and requesting confirmation that the insurer will notify the lender if the policy is not renewed or is cancelled; and supplying particulars of the insurance and the last premium receipt to the lender;

(g)   investigating title to the property and appurtenant rights; reporting any defects revealed, advising on the need for any consequential statutory declarations or indemnity insurance, and approving and effecting indemnity cover if required by the lender; and reporting if you are aware of any rights needed for the use or enjoyment of the property over other land;

(h)   reporting on any financial charges (for example, improvement or repair grants or Housing Act discounts) secured on the property revealed by your searches and enquiries which will affect the property after completion of the mortgage;

(i)   in the case of a leasehold property:

   (i) confirming that the lease contains the terms stipulated by the lender and does not include any terms specified by the lender as unacceptable;

   (ii) obtaining a suitable deed of variation or indemnity insurance if the terms of the lease are unsatisfactory;

   (iii) enquiring of the seller or the borrower (if the property is already owned by the borrower) as to any known breaches of covenant by the landlord or any superior landlord and reporting any such breaches to the lender;

(iv) reporting if you become aware of the landlord's absence or insolvency;

(v) making a company search and checking the last three years' published accounts of any management company with responsibilities under the lease;

(vi) if the borrower is required to be a shareholder in the management company, obtaining the share certificate, a blank stock transfer form signed by the borrower and a copy of the memorandum and articles of association;

(vii) obtaining any necessary consent to or prior approval of the assignment and mortgage;

(viii) obtaining a clear receipt for the last payment of rent and service charge; and

(ix) serving notice of the assignment and mortgage on the landlord;

(j) in the case of a commonhold unit:

(i) confirming receipt of satisfactory evidence that common parts insurance is in place for at least the sum required by the lender and covers the risks specified by the lender;

(ii) confirming that the commonhold community statement contains the terms specified by the lender and does not include any restrictions on occupation or use specified by the lender as unacceptable;

(iii) enquiring of the seller (or the borrower if the property is already owned by the borrower) and the commonhold association as to any known breaches of the commonhold community statement by the commonhold association or any unit-holder, and reporting any such breaches to the lender;

(iv) making a company search to verify that the commonhold association is in existence and remains registered, and that there is no registered indication that it is to be wound up;

(v) obtaining the last three years' published accounts of the commonhold association and reporting any apparent problems with the association to the lender;

(vi) obtaining a commonhold unit information certificate; and

(vii) serving notice of the transfer and mortgage of the commonhold unit on the commonhold association;

(k) if the property is subject to a letting, checking that the type of letting and its terms comply with the lender's requirements;

(l) making appropriate pre-completion searches, including a bankruptcy search against the borrower, any other person in whom the legal estate is vested and any guarantor;

(m) receiving, releasing and transmitting the mortgage advance, including asking for any final inspection needed and dealing with any retentions and cashbacks;

(n) procuring execution of the mortgage deed and form of guarantee as appropriate by the persons whose identities have been checked in accordance with any requirements of the lender under (a) above as those of the borrower, any other person in whom the legal estate is vested and any guarantor; obtaining their signatures to the forms of undertaking required by the lender in relation to the use, occupation or physical state of the property; and complying with the lender's requirements if any document is to be executed under a power of attorney;

(o) asking the borrower for confirmation that the information about occupants given in the mortgage instructions or offer is correct; obtaining consents in the form required by the lender from existing or prospective occupiers of the property aged 17 or over specified by the lender, or of whom you are aware;

(p) advising the borrower on the terms of any document required by the lender to be signed by the borrower;

(q) advising any other person required to sign any document on the terms of that document or, if there is a conflict of interests between that person and the borrower or the lender, advising that person on the need for separate legal advice and arranging for them to see an independent conveyancer;

(r) obtaining the legal transfer of the property to the mortgagor;

(s) procuring the redemption of:

    (i) existing mortgages on property the subject of any associated sale of which you are aware; and

    (ii) any other mortgages secured against a property located in England or Wales made by an identified lender where an identified account number or numbers or a property address has been given by the lender;

(t) ensuring the redemption or postponement of existing mortgages on the property, and registering the mortgage with the priority required by the lender;

(u) making administrative arrangements in relation to any collateral security, such as an endowment policy, or in relation to any collateral warranty or guarantee relating to the physical condition of the property, such as NHBC documentation;

(v)   registering the transfer and mortgage;

(w)   giving legal advice on any matters reported on under 3.19, suggesting courses of action open to the lender, and complying with the lender's instructions on the action to be taken;

(x)   disclosing any relationship specified by the lender between you and the borrower;

(y)   storing safely the title deeds and documents pending registration and delivery to or as directed by the lender; and

(z)   retaining the information contained in your conveyancing file for at least six years from the date of the mortgage.

3.20 Using the approved certificate of title

In addition, if acting for both lender and borrower in a standard mortgage of property to be used as the borrower's private residence only:

(a)   you must use the certificate of title set out in the annex to rule 3 (below) ('the approved certificate'); and

(b)   unless the lender has certified that its mortgage instructions are subject to the limitations contained in 3.19 above and 3.21 below, you must notify the lender on receipt of instructions that the approved certificate will be used, and that your duties to the lender are limited to the matters contained in the approved certificate.

3.21 Terms of rule to prevail

The terms of 3.16 to 3.20 above will prevail in the event of any ambiguity in the lender's instructions, or discrepancy between the instructions and 3.19 or the approved certificate.

3.22 Anti-avoidance

(1) Subject to (2) below, if acting only for the borrower in a standard mortgage of property you must not accept or act upon any requirements by way of undertaking, warranty, guarantee or otherwise of the lender, the lender's solicitor or other agent which extend beyond the limitations contained in 3.19.

(2) Provided the property is not to be used solely as the borrower's private residence, (1) above does not prevent you from giving any form of certificate of

title recognised from time to time by the Board of the Solicitors Regulation Authority (a 'recognised certificate'). Additions or amendments which arise from the individual transaction may be made to the text of a recognised certificate but, to the extent to which they create an increased or additional obligation, must not extend beyond the limitations contained in 3.19.

APPROVED FORM OF CERTIFICATE OF TITLE

Certificate of title

> TO: (Lender) Lender's Reference or Account No: The Borrower: Property: Title Number: Mortgage Advance: Price stated in transfer: Completion Date: Conveyancer's Name & Address: Conveyancer's Reference: Conveyancer's bank, sort code and account number: Date of instructions:

WE THE CONVEYANCERS NAMED ABOVE CERTIFY as follows:

(1) If so instructed, we have checked the identity of the Borrower (and anyone else required to sign the mortgage deed or other document connected with the mortgage) by reference to the document or documents precisely specified in writing by you.

(2) Except as otherwise disclosed to you in writing:

 (i) we have investigated the title to the Property, we are not aware of any other financial charges secured on the Property which will affect the Property after completion of the mortgage and, upon completion of the mortgage, both you and the mortgagor (whose identity has been checked in accordance with paragraph (1) above) will have a good and marketable title to the Property and to appurtenant rights free from prior mortgages or charges and from onerous encumbrances which title will be registered with absolute title;

 (ii) we have compared the extent of the Property shown on any plan provided by you against relevant plans in the title deeds and/or the description of the Property in any valuation which you have supplied to us, and in our opinion there are no material discrepancies;

 (iii) the assumptions stated by the valuer about the title (its tenure, easements, boundaries and restrictions on use) in any valuation which you have supplied to us are correct;

 (iv) if the Property is leasehold the terms of the lease accord with your instructions, including any requirements you have for covenants by the

771

Landlord and/or a management company and/or by a deed of mutual covenant for the insurance, repair and maintenance of the structure, exterior and common parts of any building of which the Property forms part, and we have or will obtain on or before completion a clear receipt for the last payment of rent and service charge;

(v) if the Property is a commonhold unit, the commonhold community statement contains the terms specified by you and does not include any restrictions on occupation or use specified by you as unacceptable, and we have or will obtain on or before completion a commonhold unit information certificate;

(vi) we have received satisfactory evidence that the buildings insurance is in place, or will be on completion, for the sum and in the terms required by you;

(vii) if the Property is to be purchased by the Borrower:

(a) the contract for sale provides for vacant possession on completion;

(b) the seller has owned or been the registered owner of the Property for not less than six months; and

(c) we are not acting on behalf of the seller;

(viii) we are in possession of:

(a) either a local search or local search insurance; and

(b) such other searches or search insurance as are appropriate to the Property, the mortgagor and any guarantor, in each case in accordance with your instructions;

(ix) nothing has been revealed by our searches and enquiries which would prevent the Property being used by any occupant for residential purposes; and

(x) neither any principal nor any other solicitor or registered European lawyer in the firm giving this certificate nor any spouse, child, parent, brother or sister of such a person is interested in the Property (whether alone or jointly with any other) as mortgagor.

WE:

(a) undertake, prior to use of the mortgage advance, to obtain in the form required by you the execution of a mortgage and a guarantee as appropriate by the persons whose identities have been checked in accordance with paragraph (1) above as those of the Borrower, any other person in whom the legal estate is vested and any guarantor; and, if required by you:

(i) to obtain their signatures to the forms of undertaking required by you in relation to the use, occupation or physical state of the Property;

    (ii)   to ask the Borrower for confirmation that the information about occupants given in your mortgage instructions or offer is correct; and

    (iii)   to obtain consents in the form required by you from any existing or prospective occupier(s) aged 17 or over of the Property specified by you or of whom we are aware;

(b)   have made or will make such Bankruptcy, Land Registry or Land Charges Searches as may be necessary to justify certificate no. (2)(i) above;

(c)   will within the period of protection afforded by the searches referred to in paragraph (b) above:

    (i)   complete the mortgage;

    (ii)   arrange for the issue of a stamp duty land tax certificate if appropriate;

    (iii)   deliver to the Land Registry the documents necessary to register the mortgage in your favour and any relevant prior dealings; and

    (iv)   effect any other registrations necessary to protect your interests as mortgagee;

(d)   will despatch to you such deeds and documents relating to the Property as you require with a list of them in the form prescribed by you within ten working days of receipt by us of the title information document from the Land Registry;

(e)   will not part with the mortgage advance (and will return it to you if required) if it shall come to our notice prior to completion that the Property will at completion be occupied in whole or in part otherwise than in accordance with your instructions;

(f)   will not accept instructions, except with your consent in writing, to prepare any lease or tenancy agreement relating to the Property or any part of it prior to despatch of the title information document to you;

(g)   will not use the mortgage advance until satisfied that, prior to or contemporaneously with the transfer of the Property to the mortgagor, there will be discharged:

    (i)   any existing mortgage on property the subject of an associated sale of which we are aware; and

    (ii)   any other mortgages made by a lender identified by you secured against a property located in England or Wales where you have given either an account number or numbers or a property address;

(h) will notify you in writing if any matter comes to our attention before completion which would render the certificate given above untrue or inaccurate and, in those circumstances, will defer completion pending your authority to proceed and will return the mortgage advance to you if required; and

(i) confirm that we have complied, or will comply, with your instructions in all other respects to the extent that they do not extend beyond the limitations contained in the Solicitors' Code of Conduct 2007, 3.19 (Conflict of interests – types of instruction which may be accepted).

OUR duties to you are limited to the matters set out in this certificate and we accept no further liability or responsibility whatsoever. The payment by you to us (by whatever means) of the mortgage advance or any part of it constitutes acceptance of this limitation and any assignment to you by the Borrower of any rights of action against us to which the Borrower may be entitled shall take effect subject to this limitation.

Signature box

SIGNED on behalf of THE CONVEYANCERS:

NAME of Authorised Signatory:

QUALIFICATION of Authorised Signatory:

DATE of Signature:

Index